THE FOUNDER

THE FOUNDER

Cecil Rhodes
and the
Pursuit of Power

ROBERT I. ROTBERG

WITH THE COLLABORATION OF
MILES F. SHORE

New York   Oxford
Oxford University Press
1988

Oxford University Press

Oxford   New York   Toronto
Delhi   Bombay   Calcutta   Madras   Karachi
Petaling Jaya   Singapore   Hong Kong   Tokyo
Nairobi   Dar es Salaam   Cape Town
Melbourne   Auckland

and associated companies in
Berlin   Ibadan

Published by Oxford University Press, Inc.,
200 Madison Avenue, New York, New York 10016

Oxford is a registered trademark of Oxford University Press

Library of Congress Cataloging-in-Publication Data
Rotberg, Robert I.
The founder: Cecil Rhodes and the pursuit of power / Robert I. Rotberg.
p. cm. Bibliography: p.   Includes index.
ISBN 0-19-504968-3
1. Rhodes, Cecil, 1853–1902.   2. Statesmen—Africa, Southern—Biography.
3. Capitalists and financiers—Africa, Southern—Biography.
I. Title.
DT776.R4R66   1988
968.04'092'4—dc19   88-5960 CIP

2 4 6 8 9 7 5 3 1

Printed in the United States of America
on acid-free paper

For
my parents

"The Grandest Opportunities"
A Preface

THE AGENDA WAS defined a decade ago: "A biography [of Rhodes] adequate for historians of Africa or of imperialism and a biography in its own right has yet to be written." A wise critic, Jeffrey Butler desired a study which would bring together "Rhodes the businessman and Rhodes the politician, Rhodes the creator and ruler of Rhodesia and Rhodes the Cape politician; Rhodes the South African and Rhodes the actor in English politics and money markets; and perhaps above all, Rhodes the formulator of 'native policy.'" The major unfinished business for biographers, he suggested, lay in producing a portrait that was "psychologically convincing," giving appropriate weight "to the favorable and unfavorable aspects of his personality and conduct." Cornelis W. de Kiewiet, who masterfully synthesized the history of South Africa, had earlier written that Rhodes was "not one man, but several men who blended their dissimilar and incongruous traits into a firm and successful union. The biographer [had not appeared who could] do justice to the contradictions of the loftiness to which he could rise and the baseness to which he could stoop." Why and how Rhodes proved so creative and effective in all his multifarious pursuits are key questions, and the driving ones of this new biography.[1]

Rudyard Kipling warned, however, that "Rhodes's personality would be a very difficult thing to translate to a man who did not know him well. . . ." That may be why Anthony Sampson, one of the ablest of recent writers, believes that "the character of Rhodes—with his combination of shrewdness and adolescence, romanticism and ruthlessness, imagination and vulgarity—has eluded all his biographers." For the same reason Geoffrey Wheatcroft, concluding his study of *The Randlords*, felt that "a satisfactory life of Rhodes is still to seek." For him, and doubtless for many others, "the looming gap between [Rhodes'] deeds and his unfathomable personality remains."[2]

Part of the problem is that Rhodes wrote no revealing letters to his loved ones. If his own speeches were the only guide, he would emerge omniscient and prescient, with the rough edges sanded round and smooth. He copied favorite sayings from classical authorities, but a man—particularly Rhodes—is more than the sum of appealing aphorisms. His commonplace books and jotting notebooks help a little, but nowhere are there recorded intimacies. Neville Pickering, in whom Rhodes may have confided, died young and inexperienced. Sir Leander Starr Jameson and Sir Charles Metcalfe lived on after Rhodes and were talkative, but they loyally "protected" Rhodes' memory. Like so many of Rhodes' less central contemporaries, Jameson and Metcalfe helped embroider a past that had been reworked systematically by Rhodes himself.

Rhodes' psyche is not the sole puzzle, however, for after many years of thinking about, researching, and preparing to write a long-planned interpretive biography of the Founder, I realized that Rhodes' was unlike any of the lives I had earlier examined or written about. In half or two-thirds of a normal lifetime, Rhodes had accomplished far more than most of the empire builders, corporate tycoons, and political giants of the nineteenth century. He had made a fortune, carved out countries, and governed an old colony and two new ones. He was not merely an important overseas figure in the heady last decades of Victorian aggrandizement, but a major actor in Europe as well. It is no accident that his name lives on through the gift of his scholarships. Nor is it surprising that his memory still occasions bitter controversy. Rhodes was great and good, despite his flaws, say his supporters (as they did in his lifetime). Rhodes was despicable and exceptionally evil—a true rogue—say his detractors. (One of the last, more muddleheaded than most, many years ago even argued that writing a biography of Rhodes was wrong. We should not write about bad men!)

Was Rhodes essentially good? Was he a true benefactor who, despite defects of method, not only meant well but also contributed—as he intended—to the betterment of mankind in Africa? Or, as critics have suggested, was he predominantly a devious power-monger who wanted riches and glory for himself, and deliberately destroyed other individuals, other cultures, and more promising initiatives as he cut his wide way through Africa? Choosing between or reconciling these two views, put only mildly here, is what a biography of Rhodes ultimately should be about. But to compile a balance sheet, and to draw an overall conclusion, turns out to have been too simple a charge.

What I discovered, and what the reader will also discover, is that Rhodes cannot be encompassed or revealed in one dimension. Rhodes achieved as much as he did because his energy and vision were greater than those of his contemporaries. He was involved on a daily basis in more initiatives, more schemes, and more dreams than most of us can juggle (or even encompass) in weeks, if not months. His pursuits were myriad, interactive, tangled, little recorded, and of a high and important order. In a word which cannot fully convey the sense of what Rhodes did and thought, his life was complex. He thought about many endeavors simultaneously, and carried within himself and in his head at all times the germs and the details of projects small and large which were by turns practical and improbable, ideal and sordid, and generous and ruthless. It is less that Rhodes' personality was enigmatic than that it was magnificently multifaceted. He *was* larger than life, and the favor and enmity that his name still evokes are appropriate responses.

For all those reasons, it became clear that the Founder required a wholly new, complete biography which would incorporate a detailed examination of Rhodes' personality. In order to comprehend Rhodes, everything that he touched, influenced, meddled with, created, and destroyed had to be understood. A new biography had to examine his philosophy, his life style, his sexual preferences, his relations with others, and his compassion or lack of compassion. It had to measure his impact on his age, on the country of his birth and on his several adopted countries, and on such epochal events as the consolidation of diamond mining, the extraction of gold, the start of the Anglo-Boer War, and, implicitly, today's bitterly divided South Africa. It had to articulate why a man of crowned glory involved himself so unnecessarily in an exercise as destructive and treacherous as the Jameson Raid. Why did the same man who went unprotected into the Matopos mountains to make peace with the warring Ndebele also behave with callous contempt toward the political rights of Africans in the Cape Colony? Jane Waterston, a missionary doctor, prayed that he might be "delivered from being one of those to whom the grandest opportunities have been given by Providence & who flung them away." She believed that he could have success "in every right way"—that he could be the conqueror of Rhodesia as well as "the great chief that ruled the many thousands of natives wisely & well."[3] Since Rhodes himself always believed that he could be the man whom Waterston wanted, indeed that he *was* that man, where, if anywhere, did he go wrong?

It is impossible to understand who and what Rhodes was without an exploration of the motivations of his life as they interacted with the events in which he was so engaged. Historical scholarship had to be joined with psychological theory and clinical experience to provide a rounded picture of a figure as multihued as Rhodes. *The Founder* thus reflects an intensive, long-term association between the principal author, a historian and political analyst of Africa, and his collaborator, a professor of psychiatry, practicing psychoanalytic clinician, and public administrator. I wrote the biography and am responsible for most of the prose as well as the historical, political, and economic research on which it draws. Shore, following upon his own research on Rhodes, leadership, and organizations, is primarily responsible for the biography's psychological insights, for focusing this book's conception of Rhodes' character and his psychological development, and for much of the medical interpretation. He joined with me in improving succeeding versions of the text. The blending of two disciplines, two approaches to data, and two different styles of work, enhanced what has become *The Founder*.

Biography is explanation and appreciation. Biography should also place the subject in his own era and focus him in the richest possible historical setting. Otherwise his own performance and the reasons for his actions may only imperfectly be understood. This biography attempts to add a further dimension. Without being reductionistic, it includes a psychodynamic interpretation whenever doing so assists an understanding of Rhodes the man and his motives.

The role of psychological theory and clinical reasoning is an issue whenever biographers attempt to capture and analyze human motivation. Our collaboration uses multiple frameworks, including the neurobiological, to understand Rhodes' behavior. It draws, when appropriate, on the insights of classical psychoanalysis, on self-psychology, and on major longitudinal studies of psychological development. It also borrows ideas from the still underdeveloped discipline of group psychology; especially useful have been studies focusing on leadership and organizational behavior.

There can be no biography without attention to human motivation, and a history of human interactions which avoids the psychological dimension is inconceivable. Yet this is not a psychobiography. Psychobiographers have tended to ignore history and to explain events purely on the basis of psychological factors. Biographers and historians, in many cases conversant with psychological theory but not with its nuanced application to real humans, have too often made unsubstantiated interpretive leaps. We try to avoid them. This book uses psychological theory explicitly, even chastely, and draws directly upon Shore's extensive clinical experience and understanding.

The secret of clinical practice is the employment of theory and training in the understanding of individuals. Theory serves the clinical encounter; the clinical encounter does not serve as a confirmation of theory. Clinicians apply to their patients the theoretical formulation which brings together and deepens their understanding of the particular person. Psychotherapy is several different kinds of intervention. At times its purpose is to unravel defenses in order to expose conflicts which have their roots in unacceptable wishes. At other times and for other patients, the primary purpose is the strengthening of defenses—the expunging from consciousness of the wishes which a patient cannot tolerate without psychological dissolution. With Rhodes as with a living patient Shore and I have sought to establish an empathic bond. Without a patient to confirm our empathic accuracy, however, we have looked for authentication in Rhodes' family and love relationships, and in his subsequent behavior. An advantage of biography is that we can know and can build upon the events that occur later as well as earlier in life.

As Butler instructs us, "to write a convincing biography of Rhodes, placing him properly in the context of his time and exploring the full range of his impact, will demand acute insight and great skill. He should not be sentimentalized, nor denigrated for the wrong reasons. Disapprobation, whatever its origins, should not stand in the way of accuracy, or plausibility."[4] Indeed: as a friend who is himself a Rhodes Scholar and part of the Founder's legacy cautioned, it is important to be dispassionate about a person for whom there are strong passions. "I do hope," said the friend, "that you won't vilify the

Founder." Nor sanctify him either. Rather, my Rhodes is intended to be the Founder himself, warts and all.

I set out Rhodes' life in detail. The detail comes from collections of the correspondence of his contemporaries, friends and enemies alike, and from the reminiscences, published and unpublished, of those, famous and little celebrated, who knew him well or in passing. Although *The Founder* also builds upon the accomplishments of previous biographers, it carefully subjects their received doctrine and their oft-repeated anecdotes to modern historical and psychological scrutiny. Contemporary newspaper accounts help understand the man and his deeds. So do the lengthy debates in which he participated in the Cape Colony's House of Assembly. Over and over again I seek to set out Rhodes' view of events. Sometimes his gloss is only self-serving. Often it is revealing. Always it is valuable, for even his own indulgent recounting of actions or motives assists our dissection of his inner life. Moreover, although Rhodes kept no diaries, he wrote far more letters than has generally been appreciated. His telegrams, both coded and clear, are numerous and vital. So is the bulk of his incoming correspondence, and his comments on it.

The Library of Rhodes House, Oxford, contains the central treasure trove of Rhodes materials and memorabilia. Assembled by successive librarians and by the care of the Rhodes Trust, it is the incomparable collection without which no biographer could proceed. Important for this study, too, are, among others, the archives of N. M. Rothschild and Sons in the City; the papers of Lord and Lady Milner in the New Bodleian Library, Oxford; the papers of Lord Rosebery in the National Library of Scotland; and the papers of Lord Loch in the Scottish Record Office.

The National Archives of Zimbabwe contains British South Africa Company official papers and the correspondence of at least fifty individuals who played a significant part in Rhodes' life. In South Africa the critical collections are in the South African archives, especially the Pretoria and Cape Town deposits; the South African Library in Cape Town (the Merriman, Innes, Hofmeyr, Schreiner, and de Villiers papers, among others of note); the J. W. Jagger Library of the University of Cape Town (the central deposit of Olive Schreiner papers and of the C. J. Sibbett collection of photographs); the Cullen Library of the University of Witwatersrand; and the Cory Library of Rhodes University. In Kimberley there are the private manuscript and photographic archives of De Beers Consolidated Ltd. and of the Alexander McGregor Memorial Museum. The Barlow Rand archives in Johannesburg are not yet fully accessible, but they contain important items pertaining to Rhodes and his early days on the Rand. The rich and indispensable private collection of Rhodes materials of Harry Oppenheimer is now housed in his sumptuous Brenthurst Library in Johannesburg. Much smaller caches of significant items are still in private hands and in the archives of such industries as Tongaat Ltd. in Natal. The Sterling Library of Yale University holds the papers gathered by Howell Wright of Cleveland, Ohio, to celebrate Rhodes while many of his contemporaries were still alive. Together this combination of sources is very rich; a fuller range of sources will be noted in the references for each chapter. What I am conscious of lacking, however, is the private correspondence of several of Rhodes' co-conspirators; Alfred Beit, James Rochfort Maguire, Charles D. Rudd, Jameson, and Metcalfe. Maguire, Rudd, and Jameson destroyed all incriminating evidence. So may have the others, although occasional items have survived.

No book of this length, the product of at least eighteen years of exploration and research, and about six years of detailed writing, can escape an assembly of important, meaningful debts. They are a pleasure to record.

Nearly all the contemporaries of Rhodes had died by the time I began my research in 1971. Fortunately, Georgia Rhodes, the Founder's niece, was alive then. She received me graciously in Hildersham Hall and kindly shared her many memories of Ernest Rhodes, her father, and of his views of his famous brother.

Harry Oppenheimer, as intrigued as I have been by Rhodes and his friends, has long gathered letters, telegrams, diaries, memorabilia, and books about the Founder. He generously gave me access to his personal library, and also enabled me to examine the archives of the De Beers Co. Ltd. both before and after they were professionally organized. His encouragement and interest since the early 1970s, and that of Julian Ogilvie Thompson, now chairman of De Beers, contributed immeasurably to my full understanding of Rhodes' life.

Marcelle Weiner, of the Brenthurst Library, has generously given her help from the days when she and I read through great parcels of yellowed telegrams to the modern era of climate-controlled, superbly appointed facilities. She and the Library merit warm thanks for permission to quote from those letters and other items indicated as being held by the Library.

When I first began seeking little-used or then undiscovered Rhodes materials, I met the late A. P. (Paddy) Cartwright, sometime editor of the *Rand Daily Mail* and prolific writer on the men who created Johannesburg's wealth. He helped me to explore the largely unsorted bundles of correspondence then in the basement of the headquarters of the Barlow Rand Ltd. There I found letters to and from Rhodes, Alfred Beit, Hermann Eckstein, and other Randlords. Since those items—if they still exist in the modern, professionally run archives of the successor Barlow Rand Corporation—have not yet been fully opened, my notes cite "Rand Mines" as the location of those original finds.

On my first prospecting trip in 1972, I also met Richard Liversidge, the renowned natural historian and director of the McGregor Museum. Liversidge's remarkable institution held the then little explored papers of Sir Frederic Philipson Stow, one of Rhodes' key colleagues. The writings of George Beet and other Kimberley pioneers, and important figures such as Colonel Robert Kekewich, were also in the Museum. Much of the foundation for this biography would have been impossible without the great goodwill and assistance of Cartwright and Liversidge.

Others also went out of their way to make my research visits productive and enjoyable. Anna M. Cunningham, at the Cullen Library, University of the Witwatersrand, and Leonie Twentyman Jones and Etanie Eberhard of the J. W. Jagger Library, University of Cape Town, guided me through their important collections. So did Moonyean Buys of the De Beers archives, J. M. Berning of the Cory Library, Rhodes University, and A. M. Lewin Robinson and the staff of the South African Library, Cape Town. Moore Crossey, knowledgeable curator of the African collection at the Sterling Library, Yale University, helped provide me with information and critical Cape Colony Hansards when I needed them most. Barry Avery kindly facilitated my visits to the four mines of Kimberley, and accompanied me to Barkly West. Judy Hoare, grandniece of Neville Pickering, provided Shore with anecdotes about Rhodes and his associates. Wendy Pickstone, granddaughter of Harry Pickstone, guided Shore and later me through the annals of fruit growing. Muriel Macey of the Kimberley Library led Shore through the collection of newspapers from the city's earliest days. Phillida Simons generously introduced me to the unpublished memoirs of her forebears: John Blades Currey and Harry Latham Currey. (The first has now appeared in published form.) She also facilitated a valuable investigation of the Rhodes materials in the Syfret Trust corporate archive in Cape Town and has been a friend and guide throughout the final period of research on this book.

T. W. Baxter and other archivists of Rhodesia were assiduous in collecting the letters and diaries of the pioneers and other followers of Rhodes. The aggregate is imposing and important, and I am grateful to them (for the early 1970s) and to Veronica Kamba and the staff of the National Archives of Zimbabwe for access to and help with the various papers in Harare which help round out important aspects of Rhodes' life.

Baxter, individually, made another lasting contribution to scholarship. After he left the Archives he assembled all of the letters known to him from Rhodes to others, transcribed and typed them, and bound the whole in a valuable, unpublished, 600-page book. Later he gave me a master copy. Entitled "Yrs., C. J. Rhodes," his compendium has proven a critical guide to original archival and private resources. Copies of the Baxter book are now in the Brenthurst Library, the Rhodes House Library, and the Sterling Library of Yale University.

June Williams reorganized the Rhodes papers in Rhodes House, Oxford, indexed them, and produced the invaluable and efficient guides to the great array of documentation there. (It also includes microfilms of holdings elsewhere.) Those of us who work on Rhodes and his times are all enormously indebted to her industry and perspicacity.

The Library of Rhodes House has been presided over in my time by three kind and thoughtful leaders, each of whom took or has taken a great and beneficent interest in the writing of the Founder's biography. Louis Frewer was the first and F. E. Leese the second. I gratefully acknowledge their unstinting help. Alan S. Bell is the third; he and Allan Lodge made important and lasting contributions to my work and this book.

When I began my search for the letters and papers of associates of Rhodes in the early 1970s, I received steady and careful help from Felicity Ranger of the Royal Commission on Historical Manuscripts. Martin Gilbert, of the Churchill Papers, Churchill College, Cambridge; Donald H. Simpson, Librarian of the Royal Commonwealth Society; Alan Rudd, son of Charles D. Rudd (who spoke to Shore); Phyllis Lewsen, of the University of the Witwatersrand; Kafungulua Mubitana, of the National Museums of Zambia; Charles J. Sawyer, the London rare book seller; Deryck M. Schreuder, of the University of Sydney; Joseph O. Baylen, of Georgia State University; Sir Alfred Beit, nephew of Alfred Beit; H. H. Grenfell; Robert Vicat Turrell; Arthur M. Keppel-Jones, of Queens University; and M. A. Welch, of the University of Nottingham Library, were responsive in the 1970s and since to detailed inquiries. I thank them all.

The archives of N. M. Rothschild and Sons Ltd. are now professionally organized and run and in recent years have been open to a range of scholars. It was a privilege to have been permitted to do research in the Rothschild archives before they were fully accessible. I gratefully acknowledge the help of Simone Mace, the archivist, and the Rothschild Archive London for permission to quote from those letters which are indicated as being located there (marked RAL in the notes).

In the text, citations to these and other documentary holdings are collected at the ends of paragraphs or groups of paragraphs. Throughout, I attempt to provide the fullest possible source descriptions, but doing so has not been possible in a small minority of the cases. Also, because my research extended over so many years, several archives have since been reorganized or renumbered. That fact will explain the occasional inconsistency in the form or depth of detail of references to Rhodes House Library manuscripts, to items in the Zimbabwe archives, and to files held by De Beers, Rand Mines, and the McGregor Museum.

Many kind persons have searched (and sometimes found) materials of value for this biography. I am grateful to Lord Gifford for the sight of letters from his grandfather, who served with Rhodes, and to those who helped me to locate the remaining nineteenth-century records of the Tanganyika Concessions Ltd. in the recesses of the City. Michael Young of Consolidated Gold Fields Ltd. provided me with prints of that firm's splendid portraits of the Founder and Charles D. Rudd. Tini Vorster guided me through Groote Schuur, and Harry H. White assisted on two subsequent visits. Judith M. Hawarden helped locate Rhodes' first farm, among other valuable sites. Jennifer E. Lavelle found crucial photographs and rescued missing microfilms.

Writing a biography of someone so all-encompassing and complex—even cunning—as Rhodes, and doing it in a manner that is detailed, depends not only on the support of friends and acquaintances, and the goodwill of archivists, librarians, and patrons, but also on the advice and suggestions of those with more specialized knowledge than myself. I want what I write to reflect reality, and to place Rhodes firmly and fairly in his historical, geographical, and industrial context. The criticism of others has helped me do so, although none of my mentors and friends need be held responsible for any failings which remain.

John S. Galbraith examined a very large part of this book in early and middle typescript. Jeffrey Butler, John W. Cell, John Flint, Stephanie D. Jones, Dennis Krikler, Robert Kubicek, Russell Martin, Colin Newbury, Richard Rive, Edward Selig, and Harrison M. Wright were thorough in their critiques and helpful in their comments on one or more chapters. Rhodes' image and this book have profited from their painstaking care and interest, and their suggestions, cautions, and corrections. Harry Levinson, George Vaillant, and Paul Myerson shared their knowledge of individual and organizational psychology with Shore. Richard Wolfe found excellent descriptions of Victorian medical practice. Walter Abelman, Antonio Gotto, and Eleanor Shore puzzled over Rhodes' health and helped me separate probability from fancy.

The chapter on the Jameson Raid (19) also benefited from a detailed dissection of its origins by students in my modern African history course at M.I.T. in 1987. Earlier, too, students in my course on imperialism devised a set of helpful timelines for the Founder's life. Harald A. T. Reiche, my kind colleague at M.I.T., unstintingly turned Rhodes' faulty and tortured Greek and Latin into English.

A legion of other friends sustained this biography through its long period of gestation. Helen and Moise Suzman let me visit Blue Haze over and over again, and were endlessly supportive. Kate and Neil Jowell, Alex and Jenny Boraine, and Libby and Tony Ardington were equally generous with their hospitality and support. Oenone and Denis Acheson shared their splendid London home, and joined me in one investigation of Bishop's Stortford.

Some of the research and writing on which this biography is based was supported first by a fellowship awarded by the John Simon Guggenheim Memorial Foundation, and then by a collaborative research grant (#RO-20302-82) from the Research Division of the National Endowment for the Humanities. I thank the Guggenheim Foundation, and Shore and I are grateful to the Endowment, and in particular to the wisdom of John Williams, then of its Research Division. A timely grant from the Provost's Fund of M.I.T. enabled me to travel, to purchase microfilms, to make photocopies, and to afford the lengthy help of one of several research assistants.

During the life of this biography my labor was blessed by several diligent and devoted associates. The results of their very valued help are reflected, however indirectly, on every page. Nancy Seasholes provided the core analysis of bibliographical materials. Later, Alison Hannah, Bonnie Chandler, Jennifer Hance, Thomas Hartley, Russell Landers, Martha Mbatha, Jeanie Park, Susanna Shore, and Laura C. Highstone, an asiduous and enthusiastic detective, found arcane references that eluded others, discerned missing links, and all, cheerfully, helped me complete this volume.

In the computer age a book even of this size can be written and rewritten many times without either the authors or their assistants losing heart. Every key-stroke, all millions of them, has been given lavish attention and much more by Pamela W. Smith, great teacher, technical writer, and enthusiastic compositor, by Laura L. Moser, adaptable and skilled, and by Andrea Gordon. Prunella Fiddian-Green completed the whole and added to it her own special flair and expertise. They *know* how grateful I am. Rhoda Fischer administered us all with great skill and diplomacy. Catherine Doheney, toward the end, helped me blend a new professional life with the conclusion of this pleasurable and exciting task. Rhodes, despite his personal predispositions, would have understood how much each contributed to the uncovering and analysis of his short and powerful life.

The members of my family were there in the beginning, when I rode off to the archives in Rhodes House, and have helped sustain the process of research in Africa and Europe, and of writing and revision in Lexington, Mass., and atop Boulder Hill in Madison, N.H. They have read and helped improve the prose, too. But, most of all, they have been there, in season and out, through the decades of Rhodes' life, and mine.

February 1988   —R.I.R.

Contents

List of Maps

List of Illustrations

Following pages 266 and 458

THE FOUNDER

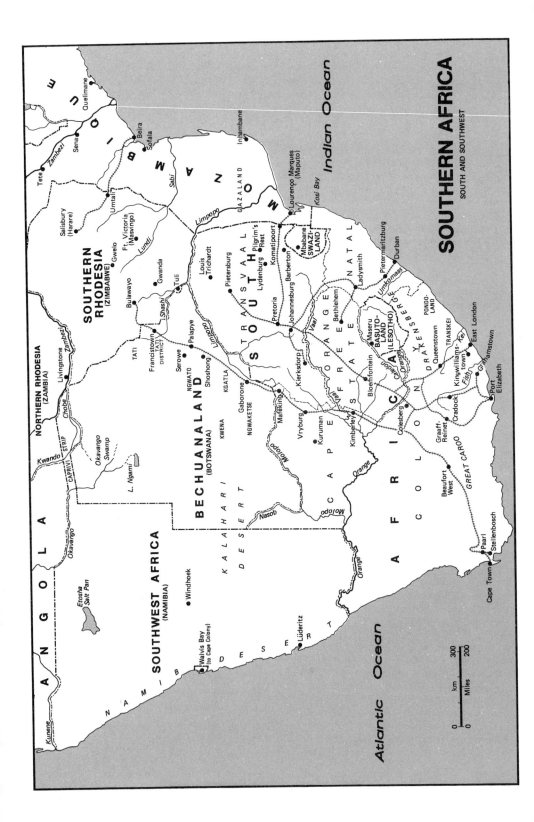

SOUTHERN AFRICA
SOUTH AND SOUTHWEST

Indian Ocean

Atlantic Ocean

ANGOLA

NORTHERN RHODESIA (ZAMBIA)

SOUTHERN RHODESIA (ZIMBABWE)

SOUTHWEST AFRICA (NAMIBIA)

BECHUANALAND (BOTSWANA)

SOUTH AFRICA

CAPE COLONY

TRANSVAAL

ORANGE FREE STATE

NATAL

BASUTOLAND (LESOTHO)

SWAZILAND

TRANSKEI

PONDOLAND

GAZALAND

KALAHARI DESERT

NAMIB DESERT

GREAT CAROO

DRAKENSBERG

Quelimane
Sena
Tete
Beira
Sofala
Inhambane
Zambezi
Salisbury (Harare)
Umtali
Ft. Victoria (Masvingo)
Gwelo
Bulawayo
Gwanda
Tuli
Shashi
Lundi
Sabi
Limpopo
Louis Trichardt
Pietersburg
Pilgrim's Rest
Lydenburg
Komatipoort
Barberton
Mbabane
Lourenço Marques (Maputo)
Kosi Bay
Pretoria
Johannesburg
Pietermaritzburg
Durban
Ladysmith
Bethlehem
Umkomaas
Maseru
Klerksdorp
Vaal
Vryburg
Bloemfontein
Kimberley
Kuruman
Mafeking
Colesberg
Queenstown
Kingwilliams-town
East London
Grahamstown
Port Elizabeth
Cradock
Graaff-Reinet
Beaufort West
Paarl
Stellenbosch
Cape Town
Lüderitz
Walvis Bay (to Cape Colony)
Windhoek
Etosha Salt Pan
L. Ngami
Okavango Swamp
CAPRIVI STRIP
Kwando
Chobe
Livingstone
Okavango
Kunene
Francistown
TATI DISTRICT
Serowe
Palapye
Shoshong
Gaborone
NGWATO
KWENA
NGWAKETSE
KGATLA
Molopo
Nosob
Orange
Fish R.
Kei
Tsomo
Kwa

km 0 300
Miles 0 200

MOZAMBIQUE

"Like the Sun on a Granite Hill"
The Man and the Mystery

B LOATED, GRAY, PREMATURELY AGED—that is the way Cecil John Rhodes usually appears. He is the brooding colossus, the wise empire builder, the clever entrepreneur, the majestic, all-powerful figure of later photographs and posthumous mythologizing. Saturnine, he looks imperial, even Roman, his steely eyes conveying strength, resolution, and confidence. Below a massive head, photographs show a Rhodes of ample girth, in a close-fitting, tightly buttoned jacket. His bronze likenesses portray the same figure of prosperity, albeit in baggy britches. He is *the Founder*—of international diamond industry, of Rhodesia, and of the Scholarships; *the Premier*—of the Cape; *the Lawgiver*— of the Glen Grey act, of the Rhodesias; *the World Statesman*—the confidant of Queen Victoria and Kaiser Wilhelm, the colleague of Lord Salisbury, Lord Rosebery, and other British political leaders; and *the Visionary*—the giant genius who dreamed of reuniting the English-speaking worlds, linking the Cape to Cairo by rail and telegraph, and propagating a heady gospel of decent deeds, of noble ends absolving questionable means, and of the compelling pull of purposeful magnets of destiny.

But this is not the only Rhodes. Long before he was a world figure he had been a mere small-scale miner. Tall, thin, thoughtful, occasionally garrulous, Rhodes as a youth was regarded as resourceful, if not wholly scrupulous. The miner became the entrepreneur, and the successful capitalist became the amalgamator, the political leader, and an imperial visionary capable of arousing enormous outpourings both of affection and of vituperation. Always, however, the human side of Rhodes was eclipsed by the vastness of his reach—the sheer grandeur of his undertakings and, indeed, his accomplishments. Rhodes was both far more and much less than he seemed, and both more complicated and less mysterious than he has often been portrayed.

In 1890, when he was becoming a celebrated international figure, Rhodes "could not be described," wrote one of his secretaries, "as stout, but seemed to be possessed of a vigorous and robust constitution. He was careless about his dress. . . ." He generally wore an ordinary tweed suit, often the same one day after day, and a peculiarly shaped brown bowler hat. "His carriage when walking was not very erect, and his style of dress did not command a second look from the casual observer . . . although when one looked into his clear, searching blue eyes, one could not help detecting there character, determination and intelligence."[1]

Another secretary described Rhodes as "a tall and powerful-looking man, just under six feet in height, but longer in the back than in the legs. He had piercing light steel-blue eyes and a wealth of curly locks which had turned grey in early life. In after-years he put on fat rapidly, and his face became florid and puffy. . . ." He was left-handed, with a badly misshapen little finger on his right hand. "He always wore . . . a soft squashy felt [hat], the crown of which he would bend into a cup shape—a style favoured by the Boer farmers. . . . He nearly always wore ties of a similar pattern—a sailor-bow of blue with white spots—and he invariably wore buttoned boots."

"When talking at table, he had a habit of leaning forward on his elbows, now and again passing his hand over his face with a lightning rub, and then he would, in making a reply, sit bolt upright and throw his head back with a smile, putting his cigarette down on the table-cloth.

"He would often walk up and down in pyjamas and then would rub his hands up and down his ribs, and at other times when dressed he would stick his hands down inside his trousers. . . .

"When interested or amused, he would give a sort of preliminary whine . . . and on occasion his voice would go off into a sort of falsetto, especially if he were angry or excited.

"In walking he took a quick short step; his toes turned in, and he seemed almost to tread upon his own feet. His hands he carried either thrust into his jacket pockets or one hand in his pocket and the other with closed fingers sharply swinging."[2]

An influential British editor met him in 1892. "Size was the first external impression you received of Cecil Rhodes. In whatever company you met him he seemed the biggest man present. Yet, though tall and broadly built, his stature was not really phenomenal; but there was something in his leonine head, and the massive, loose pose, which raised him to heroic proportions."[3]

Rhodes, declared Judge Laurence, his contemporary, "was a man, with some curious foibles and limitations, not too scrupulous about methods, but endowed . . . with an imagination which was at once practical and vivid, and in truth by no means devoid of [a] touch of spirituality. . . .

"One rather shuns the hackneyed word 'magnetic,'" continued Laurence, "but he certainly possessed an exceptional will-power and a peculiar skill in using the topics and arguments which most effectively appealed to his immediate interlocutor or audience. He was thus enabled, by a combination of force and knowledge of character, to exercise a singular ascendancy over all sorts and conditions of men—illustrious personages and powerful capitalists, politicians and men of business, country farmers, working men and native chiefs—who came within the ambit of his influence."

"A belief in Cecil Rhodes became a substitute for religion," the journalist Low decided. Rhodes appealed to the idealistic side of important men. Observers felt that they "were in the presence of a man dominated by an inspiring faith, and an ambition in which there was nothing narrow or merely selfish." Low, who had been a critic of the British South Africa Company and of Rhodes' methods in Rhodesia, called him a talker "of more compelling potency than almost anyone."

Rhodes described himself as an adventurer, and Lord Rosebery reproved Rhodes for using swashbuckling methods more suited to the reign of Queen Elizabeth I than to the circumspect era of Queen Victoria. Nevertheless, Laurence asserted, Rhodes was attractive and interesting less because he was a buccaneer than because he was "a man of original ideas, with his mind bent on something beyond the mere getting and spending which limits the ambition and lays waste the powers of the average man. . . . His manners were essentially those of an English gentleman."

Rhodes had a tenacious, retentive memory. It helped him order his innumerable activities, and must have made it easier for him to keep them compartmentalized and intelligible. He was especially interested in antiquities and history, particularly of the Roman empire, but as for literature, "he cared but little; he did not appreciate it as an art." He spoke only English, having "no grip of any language but his own."

Rhodes "generally got what he wanted," somehow or in some way. He always knew what he wanted. Though he pondered, he rarely vacillated—possibly only over the Jameson Raid. Even when young, in Kimberley, he took clear positions, and worked toward definable objectives. Rhodes had an "inflexible will," reported a secretary, and dominated the De Beers company board "to a ridiculous extent."

One of Rhodes' invaluable gifts was that of "being able to command sleep . . . whenever he felt inclined. Often, when out shooting, he would take a nap under a bush, with a stone for a pillow. On one occasion a dinner-party was given in his honour. The hour arrived, and the other guests; after waiting for him for some time in vain, it was concluded that he must have forgotten his engagement. After dinner some of the party went into another room, where they found him asleep in an arm-chair. He had walked in unannounced, rather before the time, and, finding no one in the drawing room, sat down and promptly fallen asleep, heedless of the convivial board and flowing bowl."

Rhodes could be patient, "when it was worth his while." In the Cape House of Assembly this good quality often was severely strained, especially when he had to endure long sittings as prime minister. There were harangues on tedious subjects, "often delivered in a language [Dutch] which he imperfectly understood, but [he remained] ever on the alert, if trouble arose, to pour oil on the ruffled surface and suggest something in the nature of a . . . 'reasonable compromise.' His object was very simple—to conciliate the Dutch in questions of parochial politics, and so secure their support in the matters in which . . . he was deeply interested."

"Some of Mr. Rhodes' ideas may have been crude and his theories economically unsound," Laurence concluded. "He was in some respects a visionary, and for the doctrinaire he had scant esteem. But of the visions which he saw, and the dreams he dreamt, much . . . [became] concrete. Few . . . are the men, since history began, who, in so short a period, have left so deep an imprint on the annals of their time."[4]

Unlike so many others who wrote about Rhodes shortly after his death, or even after decades of reflection, Laurence was neither overwhelmed by nor determined to undermine his subject. His account hints at the breadth and complexity of Rhodes' character, presenting a polychromatic rather than the usual monochromatic portrait. But he does not pretend to resolve all of the tensions and contradictions inherent in Rhodes' life; he leaves for the assessment of later epochs a fuller explanation of a man who, with few conventional gifts, did more than anyone in his or earlier or later generations to rearrange his own surroundings and destiny according to self-determined, single-minded, personal preferences. Exactly how he did so is the critical mystery.

Solving it requires setting Rhodes firmly into the historical and social context in which he lived and labored. Yet it takes an exercise of biographical will to avoid observing Rhodes solely through a modern lens. Lord Rosebery, who saw him in heroic terms, thought that Rhodes lived too late. But Rhodes flourished in the political, economic, and social climate of preindustrial South Africa; he took advantage of his surroundings, and made greatness of his opportunities. No assessment of Rhodes and his works can possibly be divorced from its time and place. He molded South Africa and was molded by it. He drew inspiration from Britain and significant strains of British thought. Reflections and rationalizations about the eschatology of empire were an essential component of the intellectual fabric of his day, influenced him, and were fashioned and refashioned to and for his own needs. Without Pax Britannica, without the explorations of David Livingstone, without the new Germany's victory over France in 1871, without the growing world prominence of the United States, and absent advances in mining technology which contributed to the new discoveries of diamonds and gold and then to their successful exploitation in South Africa, there might well have been no Rhodesia, no diamond monopoly, no Jameson Raid, and thus a different, conceivably diminished trajectory for the jarring cosmic entity that was Rhodes.

Rhodes made the most of his times, his family background, and his modest (but hardly deprived) beginnings in England and in South Africa. He confounded the initial assessments of contemporaries in Africa and at Oxford. He triumphed over a host of entrepreneurial, parliamentary, and imperial obstacles of considerable magnitude. Neither obviously born to succeed nor possessed of easily and early recognizable talents, his startling achievements cannot either be dismissed as bumbling luck or attributed simply to a clever Machiavellian streak which accorded well with the tenor of the times. Rhodes made his own breaks. He persuaded his economic, social, political, and intellectual betters to follow his lead, do his bidding, and subordinate their own inclinations to his visions and directions. Never acting alone, but always in the vanguard, Rhodes more than any single man transformed South Africa, southern Africa, and much of the British empire. He accomplished both more and less than he dreamed and realized, and in many more areas than has usually been appreciated.

Of Rhodes' forty-eight years, more than half were spent in Africa. During that brief period, indeed in the space of a mere decade from 1885 to 1895, Rhodes acquired two countries, Southern Rhodesia (Zimbabwe) and Northern Rhodesia (Zambia), that bore his own name. He gave British protection to Botswana and Malawi, almost took Mozambique from the Portuguese and Shaba (Zaire) from King Léopold of the Belgians, kept Lesotho independent, and prevented Paul Kruger's Afrikaner-dominated Transvaal from expanding far beyond its traditional borders. Simultaneously, Rhodes gained control of 90 percent of the world's diamonds and of rich gold mines as well. Involved closely in politics in the Cape Colony for fifteen years, he became its prime minister for nearly six, governing it and sponsoring invidious racial legislation. He also worried over and ruled his eponymous interior colonies, pushed rails and telegraph wires north, fought off African monarchs and white entrepreneurial competitors, and sponsored local armies. All the while he pursued the mundane together with the magnificent, running a complicated, multifarious personal empire held together entirely by the dominating, clear-sighted vision of a remarkable, controversial personality. Moreover, Rhodes had broad-ranging interests beyond money-making and conquest: in better education, in scientific fruit farming, in raising high quality Angora goats and karakul sheep, in irrigation, and in technical improvements to the mining industry.

Rhodes was a man of many parts, a man who could think of himself as a person apart, as a solitary springbok cut off from the herd. He assumed that everyone else had a price and could be bought. He could charm kings, queens, indigenous potentates, and endless ordinary mortals and still be remembered by many as damnable, despicable, and evil. Furthermore, he would plummet in his own lifetime from Napoleonic to discredited stature as a result of an absurd covert attempt to detach the gold mines of the Transvaal from their Afrikaner overlords.

Rhodes inspired his contemporaries, moved as they were by his strong will, commanding sense of purpose, and vast capacity for clothing defined objectives in the raiments of lofty idealism. Likewise his accomplishments and sense of overarching design have excited essayists and biographers, compelling even the most chaste of their species to write wondrously of a subject whose very achievements accord so well with the reach of his goals, and whose imaginative bequest extends those aims, living on as a perpetual dream renewed by each generation of scholars who bear his name and seek to do greatness throughout the English-speaking world.

"Rhodes was more Roman than any Englishman had ever been: realistic, tragic, and unmusical; a judge of men, a republican and a diplomat; unerotic, irreligious, educated; a romanticist of distinction, a genius as colonizer, an imperialist to the point of madness."[5] So believed Ludwig, whose panegyric compared Rhodes to Leonardo, Bismarck, Voltaire, and others.

The first of the biographers, writing when Rhodes was still alive, called him "a business man of supreme ability, a financier without superior—indeed, without a rival." Not one to immerse himself in "money-getting," "he cared for the possession of wealth only as a means to an end." From the first "Cecil Rhodes was . . . an exception. He never cared for money for itself, to hoard it, or to spend it in luxury or ostentation." He wanted it in order to realize a dominant idea. "The paramount idea in his mind, the expansion of our Empire and its supremacy in South Africa, was . . . [his] . . . great passion . . . what a supreme friendship is to [some men]. An enlightened patriotism has gradually become the one paramount sentiment of the great South African's life. . . ."[6]

Basil Williams, the Beit Professor of Imperial History at Oxford, produced the first systematic biography in 1921. "It frankly sets forth," he said of his own interpretation, ". . . the belief that [Rhodes] was, with all his grievous faults, a great man, and that at the root of his imperialism were qualities that have done good service to mankind. His character was cast in a large mould, with enormous defects corresponding with his eminent virtues." Yet he was moved by a "spirit of devotion to what [was] best for England and the world. As to his creed of imperialism, a worthy spirit will be engendered if we look, not to the blatant and exaggerated manifestations of national arrogance it contained, but to its deep sense of public duty, the tenacity of purpose it implied, and above all to the underlying sympathy and desire for cooperation even with opponents, without which it was meaningless."[7]

A contemporary who was with Rhodes in Rhodesia acknowledged flaws, but celebrated an unquestioned greatness and nobility: "Since the days of the Caesars the destinies of the world have been controlled and moved by men of strong character," McDonald began a summing-up. Rhodes resembled Oliver Cromwell in having one object, to the furtherance of which "everything else was subjected." "On the threshold of his life Rhodes dreamed, and he lived to mould a continent to the form of those dreams." The width and immensity of his dreams "were limitless and reached out into the far distant future. They were not bounded, as are the schemes of ordinary men, by the span of their creator's lives, but extended forward and moved onward down the further avenues of human progress." Considering his record dispassionately, "we must stand amazed at what he achieved in the short period that was available to him."[8]

The modern official biography asserts that there should be "no disputing the magnitude of his personality and its impact on the world. He was greatly hated and greatly loved. . . . Indifference toward Rhodes was an impossibility. And it was also in character that both the hatred and the love should be on a grand scale, for everything about Rhodes, every action and reaction, was magnified many times beyond natural size." "Those who hated him most were those who knew him least, and those who most admired and loved him were those who knew him best." Rhodes wanted power, but the "power to do good: to promote the good of his fellowmen and his native country."[9]

Two modern historians call him a "craggy genius," and grudgingly credit him with significant accomplishments among a welter of contradictions. Rhodes knew how "to put big business to work in politics and politics to work for big business—without putting off the shining armour of idealism. He thought big without thinking twice, and yet carried out schemes much larger than his words. A financier with no time for balance sheets but with time for dreams, awkwardly inarticulate, but excelling as a politician, passing as an Afrikaner in South Africa, an imperialist in London, his passionate belief in himself and in the destiny of South Africa left him innocent of inconsistency."[10]

Chesterton, by contrast, dripped scorn. "What was wrong with Rhodes was not that, like Cromwell . . . , he made huge mistakes, nor even that he committed great crimes. It was that he committed these crimes . . . in order to spread certain ideas. . . . Cromwell stood for Calvinism . . . but Rhodes had no principles whatever to give to the world. He had only a hasty but elaborate machinery for spreading the principles that he hadn't got. What he called his ideals were the dregs of Darwinism which had already grown not only stagnant, but poisonous." Chesterton turned even more sarcastic. To have " 'figured out that God meant as much of the planet to be Anglo-Saxon as possible' " was babyish. "But it was exactly because he had no ideas to spread that he invoked slaughter, violated justice, and ruined republics to spread them." Chesterton wanted Rhodes to have diffused the best Western ideal— of individual liberty. But Rhodes could not, because "he did not believe in it."[11]

There have been other biographers and scholars whose interpretations of Rhodes' life and actions have been as wholly critical as Chesterton's. But each has acknowledged the great force of Rhodes' character. Even as an agent of the devil, Rhodes operated on a grand scale. His critics credit him with an uncanny, even unprincipled ability to move men, and to manipulate commoners and royalty, whites and blacks, statesmen and felons—all with equal and consummate ease. Like Cromwell, his magnetic properties attracted persons as diverse as Olive Schreiner, the South African novelist, feminist, and early communard; General Charles George Gordon, of China and the Sudan; Lord Rothschild, the banker; General William Booth, of the Salvation Army; and Barney Barnato, the rough-hewn mining speculator.

Rhodes was boyish, sentimental, and shy; cynical, ruthless, impatient, and vindictive. He was as full of wiles as of money; dreamy, he certainly was, but also intensely practical. From the very beginnings of his acquaintance with Africa, as a young, inexperienced, and not yet wealthy cotton grower and diamond digger, it was easy for Rhodes to gain the cooperation of peers and superiors, and to forge the lasting entrepreneurial links upon which he later based his fortune.

Rhodes' progress was rapid. Arriving in Africa at seventeen, he grew cotton in a remote valley in Natal for a year. Calculating his chances carefully, he trekked to the new diamond fields at Kimberley, worked claims, teamed up with older men engaged in additional money-making activities, and shrewdly amassed a small but not staggering financial stake by the time he was twenty-three. Two years before he had gained entrance to the University of Oxford; for eight years he spent some terms in Oxford, where he was by no means a dedicated student, and others in Kimberley, finally receiving a degree in 1881. By that year he was a major diamond digger, but a dozen or more Kimberley men were wealthier and more powerful. Also in 1881, Rhodes was elected to the Cape parliament. In 1882 he intervened in the affairs of Basutoland. In 1883–84 he was instrumental in preventing British Bechuanaland (now the northeastern Cape Province) from falling into the hands of the Transvaal, and in creating the Protectorate of Bechuanaland (now Botswana). He was also busily expanding his diamond activities and, in 1886, he joined the rush to capture a part of the newly discovered gold reef near Johannesburg. In 1888 and 1889 he finally outwitted other men of fortune and put the Kimberley diamond mines under his own unquestioned control. Rhodes was catapulted from being a man of some wealth and some influence in South Africa into a person of unquestioned world power and significance. He was thirty-five.

Supported by dominance in diamonds and income from gold, Rhodes obtained a charter in 1889 for a company which, in 1890, became his vehicle for an invasion of the territories beyond the Limpopo River—subsequently Southern Rhodesia. Although his attempts to acquire central Mozambique and southern Zaire failed, Rhodes gained Northern Rhodesia, built railways and telegraphs to both colonies, and ruled them as personal fiefs throughout the remainder of his life. In Southern Rhodesia he and his legions also fomented and fought a successful war in 1893 against the powerful Ndebele and, three years later, overcame a determined and prolonged violent resistance by the Ndebele and the majority of Shona. He was a conqueror and a colonial monarch.

Throughout the first five years of the 1890s, Rhodes the capitalist and buccaneer exercised vast political power as premier of the Cape Colony. Less than a decade after entering parliament as an English twenty-eight-year-old, Rhodes ran it in alliance with Dutch farmers. He sponsored legislation favorable to their interests, and determinedly deprived Africans (who possessed the vote) of electoral power by altering franchise qualifications downward. He did much more to shape the Cape and South Africa politically—indeed, he was a dynamo in this, as in all other realms. Yet, at the very height of his power locally, and of his influence throughout the empire and in Britain, Rhodes sponsored the Jameson Raid, an ill-planned, amateurish filibustering expedition against the Transvaal. His fall from grace was shattering. Even so, his consummate, patient abilities as a negotiator successfully ended the Ndebele phase of the massive rebellion of 1896 and earned him renewed praise and affection. He attempted a political comeback in 1898 which was narrowly unsuccessful, and, again in 1899, when the outbreak of the Anglo-Boer war cut across all political ambition.

Within three years Rhodes was dead, remembered for his colossal accomplishments and, as he had designed, celebrated for his vision. The scholarships that carry his name perpetuate the romantic and heroic side of his nature, and yet are based on an entrepreneurial assertiveness that was just as central to his complex personality.

Rhodes wanted to cheat posterity, and has done so. Whether derided or praised, he remains an object of calumny, obsequy, and inquiry. As Iwan-Müller, a prominent British journalist, commented soon after Rhodes' death, Rhodes was "a great man, and a very great man, and . . . as such he must be tried by the standards we apply to his equals in the court of history."[12] His accomplishments must be scrutinized, his goals explored, and his suspect means placed before the light of both contemporary and modern practice. His ethical stance, never fully accepted in his lifetime, must be examined. So must an attempt be made to capture the essence of the great and mysterious man's motivational force. What drove him so relentlessly? What mesmerized others, for mesmerize them he did? How precisely did one so young and so seemingly unprepossessing lead all manner of South Africans and Britons? To earlier generations Rhodes was a man whose great good outweighed his cardinal faults. More modern generations judge Rhodes—or at least the legend of Rhodes—guilty of gross plunderings and heinous crimes against humanity. Seeking a resolution to the riddle of Rhodes' life demands a thorough reanalysis of both his deeds and his qualities.

Today it is as difficult to picture Rhodes simply as a Caesar, a Cromwell, or even a Clive as it is to define him as a mere machinator and manipulator, a crass, jumped-up speculator and mendacious imperialist. Yet his talents and abilities were not of the kind that manifest themselves either in precocity or in unusual notoriety. Judged solely on the basis of intrinsic intellect and academically displayed accomplishment, Rhodes rose far above the expectations of his peers. Had financial, political, and imperial greatness not been his, Rhodes might have lived without occasioning much remark, remembered for his grandiose ideas, for a dreamy quality which oddly contrasted with a relentless pursuit of practical detail, for a persistent prolixity of speech and writing that hid an inability to articulate his programs and visions simply, and for a squeaky voice which cracked into falsetto under pressure and seemed highly unusual in a robust, tall man. (Rhodes' voice "was peculiar. It was uneven and apparently under no control. Sometimes," said Low, "it would descend abruptly, but as a rule when he was moved it reached the upper part of the register in odd, jerky transitions. But if it had been full of music and resonance it could have had no more effect on the listener. . . .") "Readiness, quickness, an amazing argumentative plausibility, were his: illustrations and suggestions were touched off with a rough, happy humour of phrase and metaphor . . . if you sometimes thought you had planted a solid shot into his defences, he turned and overwhelmed you with a sweeping Maxim-fire of generalisation."[13]

That Rhodes had a contemplative side, and that many remembered him Rodin-like, chin on palm, elbow on knee, staring into space for long moments, might have been forgotten if the serious youth had not emerged from the diamond fields as a young man of big ambitions and enormous powers of persuasion. "Naturally of rather sluggish temperament, he had the great gift, rare in these days of hurry and pressure, of steadily thinking things out. In the early days," said Laurence, "he used often to sit for hours on the margin of the De Beers Mine, apparently idling, but really reflecting and getting his ideas into shape. He thus acquired the power of anticipating objections, and convincing others of the practicability of projects which, if advocated by anybody else, would have seemed chimerical. He had not only matured them in his own mind, but realized the best method of investing them with the appearance of simple matters of business or dictates of practical policy."[14]

Rhodes' name might have been lost if he, alone of the diggers of gems—hustlers all on a rough frontier—had not managed to pyramid a smallish stake into a progressively larger one and finally into a position of dominance. But his abundant wealth came later and more slowly than that of others. So did his political prominence, which was unprecedented, and based more on sheer magnetism than on oratorical brilliance or, at first, largesse and patronage. Rhodes was an outsider, dependent always on beneficial alliances artfully nurtured and arranged, on short run tactical advantages as well as long-run strategic planning, and on an alert mind that was best at reading character, not balance sheets. In explaining Rhodes' success, as well as attempting to understand his aspirations, the search is for those ingredients in his personality and intellect which caused others—men and women of every station—to believe in him, in his ideas, and in themselves.

If a boyish, moody, high-voiced diamond trader can be said to have had the gift of greatness, Rhodes had it, but at the core of that greatness was no sharp quantitative intellect, no surpassing commercial calculator, nor any unusual example of staunch integrity that stood out, as the son of a vicar might, on the rambunctious, shifty edge of Africa. Instead, his life came to use and define that gift of greatness for the realization of stupendous aspirations. Rhodes exuded a charisma which exceeded surface charm; it was developed to a high art after the first few years in Africa and was the nucleus around which Rhodes' many other, more pedestrian, talents flourished amid unlikely surroundings and within the least promising of physical contexts.

The sum of the man is more than the square of his works, more than the personality revealed by his own scrawled hand or repetitive speech, more than that glimpsed and recorded by his friends and enemies, and always less than the ideal or complete portrait. Yet, because fair measure of a man as energetic, determined, and action-oriented as Rhodes is by definition difficult, few have ventured more than saccharine estimates of his complex character. Moreover, Rhodes rarely revealed his motives. Worse, when occasionally he did hint at inner thoughts, and allude (especially in his latter years) to his own accomplishments, it is wise to suspect a reshaping or recasting of events to please posterity. With antennae well tuned to his present and future reception by others, he feared no inconsistency of act or thought, and was keenly, even morbidly, persuaded of his own mighty power to bend man's fate to his design. That he did so is a tribute to the era and the environment, and equally to the genetic endowment and talent for success that this one individual brought to the opportunity-filled ground of South Africa.

"A Very Bright Little Boy"
Life in the Vicarage

"A MAN WHO HAS BEEN the indisputable favorite of his mother keeps for life the feeling of a conqueror, that confidence of success that often induces real success."[1] If Freud is right, Rhodes' zest for life and sure sense of mastery drew on his mother's love, on the unusual quality of her nurturance, and on the positive manner in which her smiles of approval and affirmation fostered his own sense of omnipotence. She may have contributed little to the substance of his visions, but everything, it is possible to conjecture, to that vast sense of self and flair for persuasion (its offspring), which the many who were pulled toward him experienced as magnetism. We appreciate that power as the heart of Rhodes' charisma.

Out of a vast brood of nine closely spaced children (two others died young), Mrs. Louisa Peacock Rhodes loved Cecil John, her fourth son and sixth child, in a manner which was special. "He was his mother's boy, her favourite," reported Rickett, a family servant. Alone of the boys she always called him "my darling," said a nanny. Rhodes himself addressed his mother endearingly in letters and always remembered her with tenderness, affection, and a tinge of awe. Certainly he never loved another woman, being bound to her in sure ways while she lived, and in less evident but equally enduring ways after her death in 1873, when he was twenty.

Louisa Peacock, one of two daughters of Anthony Taylor Peacock, a wealthy Lincolnshire banker, was comparatively mature at twenty-eight when she became the second wife of Francis William Rhodes, then thirty-seven, on 22 October 1844. The Peacock family was one of the most prominent and best-placed in southern Lincolnshire. Anthony Peacock, Louisa's grandfather, was a large landowner who, with William Farnworth Handley and others, founded the Sleaford and Newark bank in 1792, sponsored the construction of the Sleaford Navigation, or canal, and was one of three commissioners appointed to administer the Lincolnshire enclosure acts in the 1790s. His son, Anthony Taylor Peacock, married well, and became a member of parliament in the 1850s, when his daughter was giving birth to Cecil and his siblings. Although married in St. Nicholas' church, Brighton, Louisa had lived with her family in the isolated but charming fen village of South Kyme, six miles from Sleaford. Its main claim to fame was the ruins of a thirteenth-century castle keep nearly eighty feet high.

"A plump, kindly capable woman with a cheerful, loud voice, a prettily-regular face & dark hair," Louisa Peacock was described as a woman whom everyone extolled. She may have been fearfully stout, especially alongside her thin, tall husband, and was referred to tactfully as "strongly-built," but her heart was warm and her spirit generous. For those who provided reminiscences about her, she had been a woman of equable temperament. One called her "very sweet, absolutely the lady." Rickett never saw her "out of her temper once."

She was the center of parish life: "Everybody loved her," reported the sexton. She tended the sick, and was also known for her immense energy, her industry, and for being a very early riser—earlier even than her maids. Most of all, however, she was regarded as an accomplished, motherly woman who was devoted to, "wrapt up in," and easy with her children. In dealing with her boys she "never took their mirth unkindly nor ever dealt out a harsh word where she could find excuse for a smile." Even when she was ill "she liked the door of her bedroom to stand open that the young voices might float in unchecked from the playroom just across the passage." The boys often ran wild, but she always "had a kind word" for them and, as a result, much more control over them than their father.[2]

Mrs. Rhodes was the core of a close ménage. "Of an evening she gathered all about her in the drawing-room & it was there that lessons were prepared, while she moved about among them, helping each in turn, for she was herself well-read & of a clear understanding." It was Mrs. Rhodes who accepted the adolescent playfulness of her boys, often protecting them from the wrath of her upright husband. She was the one who was linked most affirmatively to Cecil, possibly because he was more reserved than his brothers, perhaps because he was more bookish, more somber, and more moody, or most likely because she and he were bonded more tightly—for reasons that will become clear—than the others in the household. Mothers can never be equally engaged in the lives of each of their progeny. Cecil received more than his share of her sunny approbation and fair nurturance, and responded more meaningfully than the others to the encouraging signals that she sent to him and with which she greeted the world.

A mother's "gleam in the eye"—her capacity for empathy—is crucial in establishing a child's sense of self-worth. Recent psychoanalytic thinking about the development of personality stresses the importance of empathic rapport between mother and child as the foundation of healthy growth. As psychological development proceeds through adolescence, this healthy narcissism is transformed into the values by which a person lives—the ego ideal or the set of goals toward which a person strives and through which a sense of self-worth is reinforced. If a person falls short, there is shame. Moreover, since no relationship can be empathically perfect, a child also learns about the imperfection of the world in this earliest crucial relationship. Yet, experiencing a lack of perfection is tolerable only if that experience is buffered by a framework of love.[3] From all accounts, Mrs. Rhodes was unusually skillful in establishing supportive relations. Well-liked by contemporaries and servants, she provided an ample measure of love for her children, especially Cecil. It was that special love which was the foundation of his invincible self-confidence—an affirmative sense of self which was both a spur to accomplishment and a resilient buffer against the ravages of failure. To his credit and discredit, Rhodes throughout his lifetime was remarkably free of both guilt and shame.

Rhodes' nurse, who worked for the family for eight years beginning when Cecil was five, was asked whether he ever "got into hot water." "Times over," she replied. "One morning his mother havin' scolded him as he was getting up, Master Cecil runs away, jumps out of window in nothing but his nightshirt, and gets away on to the leads and down by a trellis work—he was like a climbin' cat—and us all after him on an April day, with the ground soakin' over the 'sparagis beds; but Cecil was light-footed. Then he got on the portico of the back door, and from it on to the wall by the high road puttin' them on quite cool, with Rush, the gardener, swearin' dreadful at the 'sparagis beds."

Another time the same nurse made some jam and put the pots to cool "as high as ever she could." When she returned the pots were empty. " 'Cecil' " she asked gravely, " 'did you eat that jam?' " " 'Yes,' " he replied, " '. . . I am sorry it's gone. . . . It was very good. Make some more,' " he said, "superior, and goes off whistlin'." She asked Mrs. Rhodes what should be done with "a boy like that?" " 'Let him alone. . . .' " she said, " '. . . as long as he speaks the truth.' " "But how he reached them shelves is a mystery," the nurse concluded.

Cecil "had many moods of abstraction." When serious he was "impossible to move to mirth." "He was never like an ordinary child," remembered his nurse. Very quiet, he only laughed "when he liked." When vexed he would hide in a dark corner under the staircase, not speaking for hours. He sometimes fled to the family summer house with a book, poring over it "by the hour together, resenting imperiously any attempted interruption." He was prone to "strange fits of moodiness . . . some vague uneasiness of spirit whose source he was never able to communicate, unaware himself of [whether] it was . . . melancholy [or] horror that seized him." Occasionally the young Rhodes rocked "himself to & fro & [kept] up a low crooning which was almost a moan, a crooning that never shaped itself into articulate words." At such times Mrs. Rhodes would go to her special son and "with her arms about him would beg him to explain the reason of his disquiet." But he never told her, locking himself then as later in a private, possibly solipsistic world. There were similar moments when he curled up under the dining room table, remaining there, invisible behind an overflowing tablecloth, despite the frantic searchings of servants. He sat underneath, dinnerless, through many a meal of his young years, "hugging his knees."[4]

The precise ages of the Cecil remembered by these anecdotes are never specified. Yet it is possible to guess that these episodes were from Rhodes' fifth and sixth years, when his mother was again pregnant, with Elmhirst.

Rhodes in later life rarely referred to the intimate details of his childhood. There are few recollections of his own, and his surprisingly colorful early letters to his mother from Africa dwell little on their happy times together at home. Rhodes once told a contemporary that his mother "got through an amazing amount of work: she must have had the gift of organisation, for she was never flustered and seemed always to have ample time to listen to all our many and, to us, vastly important affairs."[5] Doubtless he was thus trying to explain his own gift for detail and capacity for administration. Without realizing it, he was also revealing a source of that gift, his mother's validation of the importance of Rhodes' childhood activities. She listened and approved, providing the agreeable attention which was an enduring psychological affirmation of support. She was his most important person, and his internal audience. For the rest of his life she was the one to whom he brought his important affairs for confirmation. While she lived he reached for her affirmation through letters and in person; after her death he sought to please her in a variety of subtle ways. Thus his mother's attention to simple childhood matters influenced deeply what Rhodes was and would become.

Rhodes always welcomed audiences; despite his introspection as a child he eagerly sought to share his ideas and fantasies, gather eager disciples around him at particularly crucial turning points in young adulthood, and engender a sense of fellowship—the bonding of a band of brothers. (All his life Rhodes half-regarded himself as a boy. Like modern executives, his ambitious and empire-shaping activities were, for him, a kind of play.[6]) This last aspect of his personality, although reproducing the experience of siblinghood which remained central to his human relations and grand ideas, also recapitulated the joyful sharing which had been so central to his early years with his mother.

Although Louisa Rhodes was a mother to her boys, and was possibly even more of a mother than the times and most boys of Cecil's middle-class background could have expected, Francis William Rhodes more fully fits the forbidding, mid-Victorian stereotype of a critical, unapproachable father. Born in 1807, he prepared at Harrow School for Trinity College, Cambridge, and then was ordained a minister of the Church of England. He was the first and last in a long line of Rhodeses to enter the church or, indeed, any of the noble professions.

Cecil Rhodes' paternal ancestors, going back at least five generations, had been successful yeomen and traders who took diligent advantage of the available commercial opportunities of their eras, and did so consistently despite civil war, international conflict, recessions and depressions, and periods of domestic social upheaval. Although the surname Rhodes is of Scandinavian origin and refers to the process of clearing or reclaiming land, the earliest English Rhodes who can be identified was from Whitmore in Staffordshire in 1601. In 1660, James Rhodes of Staffordshire married Mary Christian. Thomas, their second son, lived near Stockport in Cheshire. There William, Thomas' eldest son, was baptized in 1689. He became a well-to-do grazier and yeoman farmer, and then moved to London in 1720. He purchased and farmed property which may have stretched in today's London from Mecklenburgh and Brunswick Squares (close by the modern University of London) into what became Regent's Park. William resided in St. Pancras. His 300–acre dairy farm lay on the east side of what is now Gray's Inn Road near the later St. Pancras and King's Cross railway stations. At that time William's farm was surrounded by rolling pastures and open fields; the growing edge of London was to the south. William milked his cows and sold dairy produce to the nearby urban dwellers. When a road was laid between Paddington and Islington, he purchased new acres to the north, amassed additional wealth and personal stature and, by 1733, had been elected a borough overseer of the poor. He was later to become a churchwarden. Thomas, William's son, farmed, ran several businesses with his father, was economically at least partially independent at eighteen, and an elected official (also an overseer of the poor) by twenty-five.

Samuel was born to Thomas in 1737. He was Cecil Rhodes' great-grandfather. In what was becoming a family tradition, Samuel worked the land and joined the enterprises of his father and grandfather, associating with them in business for nearly twenty years before William died in 1769. Under Samuel the family diversified beyond dairy farming into brick and tile making. They stripped the soils of their own fields and the ash dumps near Islington Green, then surveyed the now barren farmlands and laid them out as lots to meet a mid-eighteenth-century demand for construction sites and tenements. As late as 1901, Cecil Rhodes and his siblings received rents from nearly 1600 properties of the family estate in Dalston, Islington, which Samuel bought before his death in 1794.

Thomas, Samuel, and William, the three sons of Samuel who were born between the Seven Years' and American revolutionary wars, all retained their clannish knack of prospering during adversity. Thomas, who lived ninety-three years from 1763 to 1856, owned a full one-ninth of St. Pancras at the turn of the century. His fields of hay stretched from Tottenham Wood to Hornsey and his sheep and cows grazed from Alexandra Park to Muswell Hill. He made bricks and tiles, added land in Hampstead to his estate, created the manor of Dalston, and was a churchwarden. In the 1830s he paid more than £600 in tithes annually. Samuel, the second brother, was a major dairy farmer near what is now the Angel, in north London, and also owned pasture in St. John's Wood. William, the youngest brother (1774–1842), was in business with Thomas and Samuel, but he lived in Shoreditch, across the borough border from Hackney, and then resided in Hackney from the beginning of the nineteenth century. In 1802 he sold his share of Dalston to his brothers (Cecil was later to buy it back from their heirs for sentimental reasons) and became a land speculator. Although he married Margaret Cooper at about the same time, he continued to live for a substantial period with his mother and his several sisters. He grew richer from the bricks and tiles which he and his brothers sold to refugees from the Napoleonic wars who were settling in and near London. He helped to build and capitalize the Regent's Park Canal. Sometime during this period he moved north with his family, including Francis William (Cecil's father), William Arthur, and six daughters, to Leyton Grange, on the London fringe of Essex. But William for legal reasons leased his lands and estates there, never owning property outright nor baptizing his children in the parish.

William was rich, but after 1834, when an eleven-year court case in chancery was decided against him by a jury, his circumstances were reduced and his reputation sullied. He was adjudged to have fraudulently obtained a lease over the Peter de Beauvoir estate in Hackney, but a suspicion remains that William may have been misled by solicitors. One result of this harrowing experience was Francis William's deep distrust of the law and of litigation.[7] During the trial Cecil's father was in his late adolescence and, like most adolescents, quick to sense and react to shame. The scars of this period contributed to Francis William's decision to turn his back on the commercial pursuits of five generations of Rhodeses and to enter holy orders. Yet he became a priest who worked for the material as well as the spiritual good of his parish, testimony that his escape from the world of affairs was more surface than substance. His was an example to his own fourth son, who, although denying his father's formal faith, drove himself and his enterprises on behalf of a quasi-religious belief in modern imperium.

In 1833, with the expectation of a reduced but still ample annual income of £2,666 from his father's property, Francis William married. His first wife was nineteen-year-old Elizabeth Sophia Manet, of Hampstead, who was of Swiss extraction. Together, in the next year, they made a home in Brentwood, Essex, where Rhodes' father had accepted a position as curate of the then little parish. In 1835 Elizabeth Sophia gave birth to Elizabeth, but died herself. For the next fourteen years, while bringing up his daughter alone, Rhodes' father established a reputation as "the good Mr. Rhodes." Tall, angular, and "loosely made," with a "fine intellectual head," he is remembered for the chapel which he constructed at his own expense in the neighboring hamlet of South Weald. Its vicar, for whom he provided the new building, was also precentor of St. Paul's Cathedral in the City and an alternate patron of the living of Bishop's Stortford in the farthest reaches of Hertfordshire. In 1849 Francis William succeeded to that living, presumably through the favor of the precentor. Was this a foreshadowing of Cecil's ability to find every man's price—to "square" his opponents?

The place on the Stort that Evelyn called a "pretty watered town" had prospered mightily during the eighty years before Rhodes' birth. Thanks to the pioneering decision to open the Stort to seaborne commercial traffic by constructing fifteen locks and turning the river into a narrow canal in 1769, the town had become London's principal supplier of malt. (Its canal was connected to the Thames via the Lea.) Barges carried coal upstream to Bishop's Stortford. Using this fuel, and gathering ample supplies of barley from the rich farming districts of surrounding Hertfordshire and Essex, the industrial entrepreneurs of the town made malt so that the brewers of London could provide porter and stout to thirsty urban drinkers. Until well into the twentieth century, visitors to the town were immediately struck by the rich, coffee-like aroma from the hundreds of kilns in which the malt was roasted. Bishop's Stortford also brewed its own beer, and boasted a brickworks, a foundry, lime kilns, a coach and sacking factory, and a weekly cattle and horse market. By 1828, when the imposing Corn Exchange was constructed a few hundred feet downhill from St. Michael's Church to house halls and sales facilities, Bishop's Stortford was a thriving market center of about 3400 persons.

Bishop's Stortford, so named because William the Conqueror had given manorial rights to the Roman station at the Stort's ford to Maurice, Bishop of London, was "large, and well-built," according to Defoe, even before it became important as a malting center. From the 1730s, and particularly after 1744, it was well situated to profit from the construction of the Essex and Hertfordshire turnpike, connecting the town to London. The fastest coaches reached Bishop's Stortford in four hours. Their passengers ate and slept in one or another of the town's renowned inns, and then proceeded northward to Cambridge, to the races at Newmarket, or on to Norwich, then among England's largest cities.

By Rhodes' time, however, a further transportation revolution had begun to change the character of Bishop's Stortford. The Northern and Eastern Counties Railway had reached the town from London in 1842 and gone on to Cambridge. The inns thereafter relied for patrons only on those weary of steam journeys, and were less full than before. But farmers still supplied the kilns, even if the town gradually lost its comparative advantage in the malt business.

In 1861 nearly 5400 people lived in Bishop's Stortford. In addition to the Anglican parish, with its main church and two smaller ones constructed by the vicar, there was a Congregational church, Methodist and Baptist chapels, a Congregational primary school, a nationally sponsored Church of England school for the poor, and a workhouse. Towering over all—the principal landmark of the town aside from the mound of a Roman fort—was the great flint parish church dedicated to St. Michael and constructed on the site of Norman and Saxon churches in the reign of Richard III (1483–1485). An edifice of great dignity with a very plain interior, it boasted an 85-foot-long nave, a 40-foot chancel, two chapels, white-washed walls, and north and south porches. There were pews for about 800 parishioners. Its embattled western tower, topped by four pinnacles and an 182-foot spire, and pretentiously added to in brick in the late nineteenth century, now contains an eighteenth-century clock and a ring of ten bells. Nevertheless, its outward splendor was never matched in Rhodes' time by any interior display, all the costly plate, vest-ments, ornaments, and paintings which had once graced the church having been sold or destroyed.[8]

The Rhodeses who moved twenty miles north from Brentwood to Bishop's Stortford included the parents; Elizabeth, Cecil's stepsister, then fourteen; Herbert, the firstborn of Francis William and Louisa, who was four; Edith Caroline, whose character in later years was said most closely to resemble Cecil's, then two; and Louisa Sophia Margaret, who was one. Moving with the Rhodes establishment was a retinue of servants: a head nurse, a parlor maid, and several housemaids. In Bishop's Stortford this core staff was further augmented by the employment of an undernurse, several houseboys, and a cook.

At first the clan lived in the ample brick vicarage adjacent to the steepled church, but in 1850 Francis William moved his family into Thorleybourne, a cramped, unimposing, three-story semi-detached Georgian house nestled near a major malt kiln on the far southern outskirts of the quiet country town. It was set among towering trees and flowering shrubs close to the Stort. Here Mrs. Rhodes gave birth to Basil, who lived eleven days; to Francis William (Frank), born 1851; and to Ernest Frederick, Louisa Rhodes' only child who ever married, born in 1852. After Cecil was born at 7:30 p.m. on July 5, 1853, Mrs. Rhodes bore Frederick (1854), who died after five weeks; Elmhirst (1858); Arthur Montague (1859); and Bernard Maitland (1861). Elizabeth meanwhile left the crowded family about 1855 to marry Thomas William Rhodes, the son of the vicar's first cousin and the vicar's sister.

The spacing of these many births shows that after Cecil's birth and Frederick's early death, Mrs. Rhodes for the first time had a long period with but a single baby in her care. For four years she could enjoy her youngest son without the physical burden and danger of pregnancy or the distracting demands of another newborn. For the same period, Cecil enjoyed his mother's affectionate gifts without interruption. They were more than ordinarily bountiful years, for she had known few other sizable intervals between pregnancies; Cecil was the baby longer, and he had a mother to himself longer, than any of his siblings. The young Cecil, too, must have contributed an unusual quality of alert responsiveness to the relationship. The bright energy which was his response to life was manifested early; it would especially have enthralled his mother.

This idyll of shared delight ended abruptly with Elmhirst's arrival when Cecil was four and a half. This event would have been profoundly disturbing for Cecil, coinciding as it did with a period in life when boys normally long intensely for their mothers. Elmhirst's birth also signaled to Cecil that his beloved mother and his ambivalently regarded father had a special intimacy. Boys of this age, faced with such a double betrayal, naturally seek to resolve their hurt by a further identification with their fathers. This process ordinarily is facilitated by a father who makes himself available as a model of manhood. But Francis William was middle-aged, preoccupied, and too resentful of his gang of boys to offer Cecil a constructive, masculine escape

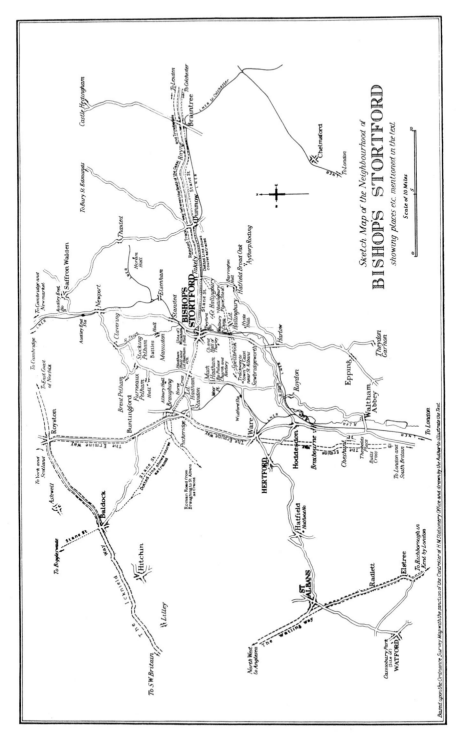

Sketch Map of the Neighbourhood of

BISHOPS STORTFORD

showing places etc. mentioned in the text

Scale of 10 Miles

Based upon the Ordnance Survey Map with the sanction of the Controller of H M Stationery Office and drawn by the Author to illustrate the Text.

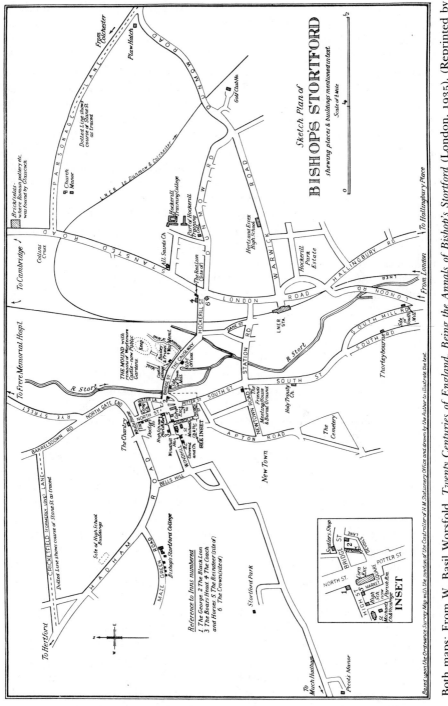

Both maps: From W. Basil Worsfold, *Twenty Centuries of England, Being the Annals of Bishop's Stortford* (London, 1935). (Reprinted by permission of Harvard College Library)

23

from the distress of Elmhirst's birth. It is likely that Cecil's disappointment with his father, already kindled by the vicar's aloofness and impatience, was reinforced when Elmhirst arrived. The bitterness and resentment which was rooted in this event would recur throughout Rhodes' life. It would curdle his relations with powerful figures, usually older men, who stood in the way of his dreams, especially the dream of a reunited family of English-speaking nations. The fact that Rhodes developed no compelling heterosexual interests is probably also related to his anger at his mother for abandoning their closeness as well as his failure to identify positively with his father or to deal in any other constructive way with the unmitigated loss of his first love.

Moreover, Rhodes was a middle child. Studies of genius and leadership conclude that first-born and only children are overrepresented among the ranks of high achievers, that revolutionaries tend to be later-born, and that successful political figures come from the ranks of middle children. Although first and only children receive disproportionate amounts of stimulation and attention from their parents and tend to be oriented toward achievement, middle children learn political and interpersonal skills in dealing with parents and older and younger siblings. In Rhodes' case, he was surrounded by a horde of family rivals, and had to outwit them or win them round. But he was also a special child for nearly five years, and thus received the kind of nurturance from his mother which is usually the fortune of eldest children only.[9] Did this unusual configuration contribute to his success as an achievement-oriented politician?

In this tight-knit but active and sometimes overwhelming household, Frank was known as Louisa's boy, and Cecil, perhaps in compensation for his mother's pregnancies, sought out Edith. The older sisters thus looked after their younger siblings, but a nanny was hired specifically to care for the final two. Mrs. Rhodes was, throughout, the center of the household, with the vicar being its presiding, but usually rather removed eminence. An austere man, Francis William stood "a little apart in his family, interfering but seldom in the daily discipline save when his ire was roused by some particularly aggravating boyish escapade." As patriarch, Francis William was "the final arbiter only in the worst misdemeanours & on those occasions he favoured the cane." He regulated the household, "insisting on rigid punctuality [and] consulting with the cook over the menus. . . ."[10]

Studious and large-minded, Francis William came to opinions in a decided manner, held them tenaciously, "but was not inclined to force them upon others, not even upon the very poor." Moreover, "he believed fully what he preached and preached only what he believed." He was known and admired for sermons of brevity (not Cecil's way), always exactly ten minutes long. In the home, too, "subterfuge & insincerity were unknown." He was energetic, being particularly concerned to improve his parish. Harrington recalled him as "pushing and persevering. He would take an idea which seemed almost impossible at the time and push it through till it was accomplished." He was also impulsive, jumping readily to conclusions. But the man who seemed rigid at home was willing, with a generosity of spirit not then common in the Church, to treat Anglican communicants and dissenters equally. To both he was "open-handed," with the same practical generosity and personal ease that marked Cecil's later relationships with his political and financial opponents, as well as his supporters.[11]

The vicar (like Cecil later in the century) strongly affirmed the value of education. Although Bishop's Stortford had boasted a high school in the eighteenth century, and there is a record of an educational establishment in the town as early as 1579, by the mid-nineteenth century Bishop's Stortford lacked any facility for the instruction of its elite sons beyond the elementary years. Within a year of his arrival, Francis William had successfully petitioned the Court of Chancery to give him control over the income of the parish's charity, school, and library estates. Those funds were used to support a new school. As its headmaster he installed Dr. Godfrey Goodman, the curate of St. Michael's. He also took his own growing family out of the roomy vicarage and gave it to the school as a residence for boarders and for Goodman. Under Goodman the school flourished, for the headmaster was known as a good organizer (though a teacher of but modest ability). As many as 150 pupils may have attended the school shortly after Cecil's day. The vicar also raised £20,000 to start a Diocesan Training College for Schoolmistresses in a gothic-style red brick building in nearby Hockerill, and in 1860 found the funds for additional premises for the high school, for a master's residence, and for a chapel.

The vicar, something of an oddity, was remarkable, it was later said, "for the unconventional attire in which he walked about the town." But his kindness to the poor and the weak was undisputed. As a minister to the sick, in lieu of modern medicine, he prescribed a specific cure of his own. Wearing his customary plaster of camphor and lard on his own chest, the vicar would "go to see some sick person and presently would say 'I know what will do you good' and undone would come his vest and he would hand over his own plaster and go home for another for himself." Secretly, he would give the sick bottles of wine, and shillings.[12]

But to his high-spirited sons the mature Francis William could seem irritable and impatient. When Cecil was born his father was forty-six, and when all the babies had been born, Francis William was fifty-four. Thus the only father whom Cecil knew was a reserved, largely uncommunicative figure whose energies and concerns were focused on his own activities as vicar, and certainly not on his fourth son. As father, he communicated a sense of impatience and exasperation to his children; it was thus left to his much more accessible, younger, more eagerly involved wife to provide parental understanding, kindness, and the empathic responsiveness which is vital for a child's development. That the vicar's positive influence on the children was less than his wife's is not to say that he had no effect on their upbringing and subsequent character. Painful experiences with parents may be as influential as soothing ones; negative role models can powerfully shape behavior. Francis

William's irascibility and his forcefulness were imprinted upon his children, not least upon Cecil, so that glimpses of the vicar in action recall some of the salient characteristics of his famous son.

Cecil ruefully attributed his own sense of realism to his father's acerbic examination of many of his youthful plans and fancies. "My father," he told McDonald, "frequently, and I am now sure wisely, demolished many of my dreams as fantastical, but when I had rebuilt them on more practical lines he was ready to listen again. He never failed to put his finger on the weak spots, and his criticisms soon taught me to consider a question from every possible point of view."[13] If it truly were from Francis William that the adolescent Cecil learned how to examine all of the possible angles, consider the different positions from which his plans could be opposed, prepare counter-arguments, and persevere despite opposition, then he was taught well and his father, usually dismissed as of little influence on the development of the great imperialist, can be seen as a positive and powerfully formative factor in Cecil's life.

Explicit evidence of Cecil's deepest feelings about and relations with his father is scarce. Although Cecil, Herbert, and Frank on several occasions reminded themselves of their father's dislike of the law, and would have known and acknowledged the standards of behavior which he had established for them as well as for himself, the complete impress of the older, busy, and preoccupied cleric on the development of any of his children—even the eldest—is now impossible to infer. Cecil sought to gain his father's approval, indeed, his father's attention. In letters home from Natal as a teenager, and then from the Kimberley diamond diggings, Cecil implicitly, if indirectly, courted his father's eye. In his determination to enter the University of Oxford despite a deficient secondary education, and in his initial efforts to seek a profession (albeit the bar), Cecil unconsciously cast himself across his father's path. Like his father he sought secular triumphs in the service of spiritual uplift. But it was with his mother, not his father, that the young man communed from the depths of South Africa. Indeed, when Cecil left England for Africa at age sixteen, the vicar failed entirely to say goodbye to his son. "I was so sorry," Cecil told his mother, "I did not see my father to say goodbye to and shake hands with but," he continued lamely, "I daresay we shall someday meet again."[14]

Following his mother's death, Cecil wrote occasionally to his "dear father," and in no antagonistic or stilted manner. Yet his letters became less and less frequent in the early 1870s, and in the three or four years just before his father's death, Rhodes passed messages to him via Ernest or Frank. (No letters from Francis William to Cecil have survived, but neither are there any of the numerous ones which must have been mailed to Rhodes by his mother.[15]) Shortly after Mrs. Rhodes died the vicar moved back into the vicarage, but he retired in 1876, on or near his sixty-ninth birthday, and moved to a cottage on the English south coast. Cecil, still grieving for his mother and not having resolved his resentment of his father, visited Francis William there only twice, despite being at Oxford almost continuously during this period.

Although Rhodes never complained about an unhappy childhood, and probably cannot be said objectively to have experienced a painful or even an unpleasant first sixteen years, he doubtless yearned for much firmer ties to his father than were ever realized. Warm and thoroughly affectionate as his mother certainly was, she would have been able to satisfy the young Cecil's developmental needs only in incomplete ways after early adolescence. Cecil and his brothers lacked a father who provided positive reinforcement for their activities. The vicar's eccentricities, his comparative age, his preoccupations, his emotional distance, and his sanctimonious rectitude must have limited his ability to guide and nurture his sons—or at least Cecil—during crucial phases of their development. The vicar's limitations were telling during the teenage years, when juvenile fantasies are transformed by male example into intellectual and manual skills and character traits—the raw materials of the initial psychological commitments to work and the love objects of late adolescence. Yet for Cecil to have missed the course of ordinary development in this way may have enhanced a potential for and certainly a striving toward greatness.

During Cecil's school years the band of brothers substituted in important ways for the absent masculine influence of his father. It is precisely the commitment to male adulthood which makes it possible for young men to pass beyond their youthful preoccupations. Lacking it, Rhodes repeatedly sought the support of a gang or band. Subsequently, in his personal relationships, he always gravitated to friends and lovers with whom he could stay young. That Rhodes remained a pre-adolescent in so many significant respects, and that those pre-adolescent characteristics shaped his strivings for greatness, is clear. In the grandiosity of his vision, the commanding quality of his ideas, and the assertiveness with which he pursued his goals we glimpse the certainty and self-confidence which was nurtured in the warmth of his mother's approval. That his extraordinary powers of persuasion were undeterred by a rambling prolixity and a voice that quavered at the higher ranges—that he was magnetic despite or because of limitations of intellect and character—is likewise explicable as an adult measure of his mother's unconditional delight in his ideas. So, too, can his impatience with the barriers to progress thrown up by world leaders and by circumstance, and his relentless desire to shape events in accord with his own wishes, be traced, marvelously elaborated, to the resentment against a father who bested him while denying him. Rhodes doubtless sought to possess that father and his power in order to distribute it himself. Employing the artistic economy of successful adaptation, he devised a sizable repertoire of ways and means: he cajoled, wore opponents down by repetitious sermonizing, dazzled them with his dreams, and shrewdly assessed their desires for cash or favor. If all else failed, like the perennial boy, he could deceive, for his mother always forgave and protected her mischievous sons.

In 1877, a year before his father's death, Rhodes committed to paper his considered views of the world and his own role as its shaper. In the "Confession of Faith," an ambitious, rambling *apologia pro sua vita,* Rhodes blames the fragmentation of Her Majesty's empire and the unfortunate scattering of young Britons—who would otherwise be united as a band of brothers striving for the betterment of mankind—on "two or three ignorant pig-headed statesmen. . . ." For them he had "murderous" feelings. Those murderous feelings, likely reminders of his relations with his father, were a major source of his drive to build and achieve. Such a pattern is consistent with modern studies of the entrepreneurial personality. They identify a burning desire to outdo a disappointing father as a key to entrepreneurial success. According to Levinson, "there is a smoldering anger that fuels the son's rivalry with the father. That anger shows up in the entrepreneur's dogged intensity to succeed, holding on, no matter what, coming back from failure to try again and again."[16]

Whether, given the mores of the era, the size of the family, the place of the young within Victorian establishments, the vast generational gap between the sixth born and the head of the household, and the era's accustomed reliance on servants, Cecil should have felt or was objectively neglected by his father, his own young life was lived apart—except at meals and at services—from his father's direct intervention. The children were "not much with their parents. They were out most of the day or in the top rooms. The little boys came down to lunch only. The family assembled in the drawing room before dinner but after dinner dispersed, the two girls would go to their rooms and Cecil would accompany them. . . ."[17]

The young Cecil, a "placid" baby who was brought up "by hand," that is, not breast-fed, was variously described as a "delicate, golden-haired little fellow," as a good-looking lad with fair hair and "a nice and agreeable way of speaking," and as "full-faced, very pale, always very delicate, having at times special foods." A late report describes him as "pigeon-toed and left-handed." The clerk of the church called him "always delicate" and "never *particularly* religious." A servant remembered him as puny and sickly, "as white as a sheet." But to a nanny who knew Cecil only in the last year or two before he left for Africa, the future adventurer and buccaneer was "very tall and very thin . . . never . . . ill" and of a complexion at age fifteen which was "neither dark nor fair." His hair was light brown.

The same nanny remembered that Cecil was fond of playing soldiers. With a houseboy he would barricade the top landing in Thorleybourne, marshal the younger children as troops, "and then when the maids came to do their work it was a job to get passed." He liked cold baths. "He took it very cold." The servants would hear him shout out in the bathroom, " 'one, two,' and then came a splash." According to Rickett, Cecil was inseparable from his slightly older brother Ernest. He was also very changeable. "At times he would be only too glad to get away from them all with a book. He always had a book under his arm, and would sit for hours in the arbour reading." At other times "he had a quick temper and let you know it. You always knew by his face." He was "powerful when roused." But at other times "he was most gentle and a child could lead him." He played croquet in preference to cricket. He was full of moods, sulky, but "never a fighter."[18]

Many of the childhood acquaintances agree with this general description, and all remember him as mischievous. He dressed up as a ghost in a white sheet and frightened parishioners when they came to church. One Saturday Ernest and Cecil were returning from school. There were mud heaps all along the path, and the two deliberately waded through them "to see who would make the bigger footmarks." When picnicking along the river nearby they portaged around the locks to avoid paying the tolls. The boys had a great game of making fire balloons of tissue paper soaked in methylated spirits and sending them, flaming, across the hedgerows. Cecil was fond of gunpowder— a good beginning for someone later to establish an explosives industry in Africa. "He would fill bottles with it, fuse them, and bury them in the ground," on one occasion nearly exploding the vicar. Cecil even obtained small cannon "and let them off with gunpowder and they used to fly all over the place." Although they refrained from touching their father's prized peaches, Cecil and the troop of young Rhodeses demolished the ripening cherries, and, climbing into the apple orchard, "you should [have seen] the apples fly." Despite these accounts, the nanny who knew Cecil in late adolescence asserted that he was "not at all wild." She said that "he was above that sort of thing. He was never the least rude to the servants always quite the gentleman."[19]

Cecil's sisters were tomboys, jumping instead of climbing over gates, and never carrying umbrellas or sunshades. Louisa "was small, dark, quiet rather prim and old maidish." Edith, by contrast, was "fair," "a strapping robust girl, much livelier than Louie." Edith, mannish of face and build, "had literary aspirations & as she grew up was apt to spend her nights with pen & paper in the production of novels rather daring in tone & expression, for [a] characteristic of this uncommon family, was its downrightness of speech which took its origin in a very fine scorn of what was hypocritical."[20]

Frank was the quietest of the boys when young. He often would "go off behind the bushes and kneel down and pray," but Herbert, the eldest and the bully of the family, would then "haul him if he found him and pummel him saying 'I'll prey you.'" Herbert also exploited Rickett on numerous occasions, having to be restrained more than once by the gentle remonstrations of Mrs. Rhodes. Herbert would slap Rickett "across the nose and forehead with his gloves until [Rickett] had such headaches he could hardly hold his head up." Then Herbert would "clap him under the chin to make him hold up his head." Herbert was feckless, too, and a worry, by all reports, to his parents even before he became an adventurer in Africa. Yet Herbert was a success at Winchester School, particularly at cricket.[21]

The fullest contemporary appreciation of the young Herbert is derived from the anonymous Rhodes-Livingstone Museum Fragments. "Of all that family," it asserts, "Herbert seemed the most promising of fame. Brilliant of mind, daring to recklessness, generous to a fault, of a dominating personality, he had all the traits of a born leader of men, save one." For, according to his mother, Herbert had "every sort of sense [but] common-sense." Herbert dived into the Stort off a mill-wheel while it revolved. "It was Herbert who on pony-back chas'd the village children right into their school house; it was Herbert who ranged his younger brothers in a row, each armed with a stick, & led them in a soldier's charge through & through their father's rows of peas, & brooked no breach of his authority." Nothing irritated the vicar more. Although "eager to lead, [Herbert] was unable to obey even himself." Herbert's temperament was "passionate . . . amenable to no restraint even from its own judgement." He was untamable, and resentful of his father's arbitrary character.[22]

Frank, invariably described as "beloved of women," and, to a lesser extent, Cecil were very close to Sophia, Louisa Peacock Rhodes' maiden sister. She lived alone in the manor house at Sleaford, a train ride away in Lincolnshire, and had the same ample, ready disposition as their mother. Indeed, Frank was "practically adopted" by Aunt Sophy, his godmother, and spent many vacations at the manor or with her in the Channel Islands. Together her abodes comprised a liberal environment that stood in contrast to the stricter routine of Thorleybourne. There Cecil learned to ride, if never with a good seat, and also began a long friendship with Robert Yerburgh, the son of the Rector of Sleaford. Yerburgh subsequently remembered that when the two young men cantered together through the countryside, Yerburgh would look at all of the young ladies whom they passed. Rhodes, by contrast, would have all eyes for the manner in which the farms of the neighborhood were being cultivated. As Mrs. Newman, the nanny, reported, Cecil "didn't look at women even as a boy, always shy of them."[23]

Frank was educated at Eton, partially with Aunt Sophy's help. After five happy years there, Frank was remembered as a boy with rather long hair who was "blest with remarkable cheeriness and good nature, who played a very plucky game at football." He was better known as a first-class cricketer, playing at Lords in 1869 and 1870. "He was a steady, but not particularly attractive bat, his wonderful keenness being the feature of his game. He always seemed to be in form, while his activity and energy in the field made him an invaluable longstop." One of his Eton contemporaries said that he was very popular—"keen, amusing, and sympathetic, always full of that tremendous *joie de vivre* which marked his whole life."[24]

Ernest, "red-haired, plain-featured," and "always behind [Cecil] in learning," followed Frank into the army, being sent to Woolwich to become a Royal Engineer. Ernest was Cecil's chief companion. "Together they went up the school . . . ranged the country-side, the younger [Cecil] in front, the elder following." Despite his "slower wits," Ernest laid down the law and "had a large repertory of opinions always on tap until Cecil's quietly satirical 'There speaks the Professor' would check their flow."[25]

Arthur was invariably reported as physically weak. He was thought to have had a consumptive constitution, and at times to have been too ill to walk about unaided. (But, thanks to Cecil, Arthur later farmed in South Africa.)

In addition to Sleaford, the Rhodes' children, especially the two girls, had access to a nearby second home in the 1860s, after William Arthur Rhodes, the vicar's brother, rented a manor house less than a mile from Thorley-bourne. Twyford House, a small late-Stuart mansion hard by a lock on the Stort, was a pleasant magnet to which all of the Rhodeses were often drawn to visit their two cousins. It was, said Cecil, his "favourite place." It was there that Cecil, doubting the truth of a gardener's explanation of the ways of bees, "cut a hole in the top of one of the straw hives," later saying "I only wanted to see how they worked; I don't see how they can do anything when there are such a lot of them in such a little space."[26]

Like Herbert, Frank, and Ernest before him, Cecil went to Goodman's high school in 1862, when he was nine. Daily for seven years he trudged uphill nearly a mile from the family's squat home along South Street and then past the Corn Exchange to reach St. Michael's Church and the nearby high school on Windhill. Classes began after breakfast, lunch at home was at one p.m., and then the boys returned to school and to the playing fields until five p.m., when they had tea at home. After tea there were formal class preparations with the boarders at Goodman's house, half a mile up Hadham Road.

Many years later, when the young Cecil had become prime minister of the Cape Colony, he used the rosy-hued memories of his school years to make salient points about anti-African legislation. Rhodes claimed that he had been "much more of a slave than any . . . natives." He had been "in a state of slavery for nine mortal years of his life, and it was compulsory slavery too. He underwent intellectual hard labour for six years at school and three years at college. During the period he was at school he had to work for five hours during the day and to prepare work for the next day for three hours in the evening. While at college he was compounded in the evenings and not allowed out after nine o'clock." At the close of those remarks one of Rhodes' astute opponents asked: "And you never went [out] I suppose?"[27]

"He studied with . . . vigour," is one report of a contemporary, "quickly passing his elder brother, & though he was never a bookworm he displayed a great facility for all those subjects in which taste & imagination play a part," perhaps foreshadowing the scope and configuration of his later talents. Although called "long-headed Cecil" by his brothers for his introspection and love of books, Cecil was nevertheless not deeply immersed in his studies. He was not a scholar. Conscientious about doing his school work, he was more thorough than imaginative. History and geography were his strongest subjects, although he also did well in religious knowledge (winning a third-class prize in 1864 and a fifth class prize in 1868), French (which he later spoke only poorly), and the classics. He was competitive, taking prizes in classics in the school of eighty-seven boys (sixty-seven of whom were boarders), and—astoundingly, given his later reputation—winning a silver medal for elocution. He achieved a prize in mathematics, never a strong point. At fourteen he took first class honors in the Cambridge Junior Examination, mostly in classics. In the next year he took a classics prize for first-class honors in the Cambridge Local Examinations. Cecil played cricket at thirteen for the school, although he otherwise was hardly distinguished for his love of or skill at sports.[28]

One of Rhodes' teachers at the high school remembered him from 1863 as "a very bright little boy" who "shewed signs of superior intelligence." He did not care for "maths" (arithmetic), and, said the teacher, "I cannot say he shewed any particular aptitude for these studies." A contemporary at school reported that Rhodes had been very good at classics but was generally "in such a hurry that his thoughts seemed to come quicker than his words." He disliked being outperformed academically in class, and became very angry if he were thus bested. Described as "openhearted, candid, plucky and very gushing, in which he took after his mother," he was also said to be untidy, gentlemanly, certainly not coarse, and rather "girlish in his way of talking, the result of being brought up at home and not associating with the boys of the school." Hardly strong physically, Rhodes appeared pale and thin. He was remembered by another schoolboy as pleasant and amiable, a combination of words rarely used about the great man at many later points in his life, except possibly when out on the veld with his young men or presiding over the high table of Groote Schuur.[29]

That the vicar refused to send Cecil on to a public school may reflect the young man's impatience as much as his father's decision to be frugal. Or there may have been serious questions about Cecil's stamina. Was Cecil considered too infirm to withstand the rigors of Eton or Winchester, and yet hardy enough subsequently to be packed off to Africa? Or was it that Francis William Rhodes was unimpressed by the real talents of his sixth born? After leaving the high school, it was intended that Cecil's education should be continued by his father, in the vicar's study. This might have provided Cecil's father with an opportunity to judge the boy's real worth, with decisions to follow, or it may have been a sop arranged for an ambitious youngster who possessed a passion for knowledge which was called "insatiable" and who knew that additional schooling was the key to any decent success. There is the further strong possibility that the vicar, who wanted all of his sons to follow him into holy orders—to become "the seven angels of the seven churches," saw his best—even his only—opportunity in Cecil. Although the children were required to attend services at St. Michael's and the boys to teach regularly in the Sunday school, Herbert and Frank were away from home early, and much of this duty fell to Cecil.[30] He was confirmed in March 1867 by the Bishop of Rochester. Yet, whatever the reason, Cecil studied little with his father, and was soon looking toward Africa.

The young Rhodes did not openly reject the church, but—in a spirit of indirect and tentative rebellion—wondered if his life's work might prove more satisfying and rewarding at the bar. Restless Herbert was still at home on the eve of a departure for Africa, and Frank and Ernest were not yet committed to the military. But none was inspired by the prospects of a clerical calling. Nor was Cecil impressed by the profession of soldiering. Shortly after his fifteenth birthday, he weighed his own options gravely. Responding to the direct and indirect aspirations of his father as well as a strong letter from his beloved Aunt Sophy, Cecil agreed that "a clergyman's life is the nicest." But it was not necessarily what he wanted. "Above everything," he confessed to her in a "strictly private" letter, he wanted to be a barrister. It was, he agreed, "a very precarious profession." Nevertheless, he refused to deny, for "it would be hypocrisy to say otherwise," that he remained attracted to the bar. "Next to that" was the church. In either case, a university education was essential. "Because I have fully determined to be one of these two," he told his aunt, "and a college education is necessary for both," he would "try most earnestly to go to college."

Rhodes was courteous but firm in explaining why he continued to hold to a position which accorded poorly with his aunt's expectations and prejudices but which was neatly poised between his father's wishes and his own search for autonomy. "I am afraid you will not like me for saying this," he wrote, "but it is no use for me to pretend to you that I have since your last letter changed in my course of life, or feelings, or inclinations, for it would not be the truth. I think that as a barrister a man may be just as good a Christian as in any other profession."[31]

It is easier to understand why Cecil failed to prepare for and then to enter one of the great British universities than it is precisely to pinpoint why Herbert chose growing cotton in distant Natal over other overseas options. Once Herbert had established himself there, however, sending Cecil out to join him was a clear choice. If few in the family were persuaded that the law constituted a worthy career for a Rhodes, if they believed that he was "too delicate for a military career [and] too sensitive, too finely-strung, for the rough-&-tumble of a public life," then they may have wanted him to gain experience on the African frontier—to find himself. Despite the school prizes that Cecil had won, the vicar may also have had qualms about the thoroughness of his preparation in Greek and Latin. Further, reported Michell, "his father recognised that he was unfitted for a routine life in England. . . ."[32]

Sons of the sturdy Victorian middle class went overseas. They went to America and India. They were beginning to go out to Africa. Herbert was twenty-three in April 1868, when he arrived in Natal. How he had occupied himself after leaving Winchester is unclear. But by twenty-three he must have been under personal and family pressure to find direction for himself and begin earning in a serious manner. In view of his character, it is hardly surprising that Herbert chose to try Africa. He presumably had heard that a new Natal Land and Colonisation Society was enticing prospective farmers from England with generous purchase terms for land. Cotton was a promising colonial crop in the immediate aftermath of the U.S. Civil War, the prospects for Natal were doubtless painted in vivid colors, and a new life in a distant land would obviously have attracted someone possessing Herbert's self-confidence, rash bravado, and distaste for the settled, humdrum life in a country town like Bishop's Stortford.

It is usually asserted that Cecil followed Herbert to Africa because the future imperialist "fell ill." He was supposed to have been consumptive, to have been afflicted by tuberculosis, a common Victorian complaint. Or, if not truly tubercular, at least he had weak lungs. After all, he had for long been frail, even "physically bankrupt." At least those are the standard—even hoary—interpretations. Yet they are modern myths; Rhodes becomes more and more tubercular the closer to the present his biographers write. A turn-of-the-century biographer reflected contemporary reality with reasonable versimilitude: "His health, though not really bad, was never of the strongest. . . ." But then, with unsupported assertions which may have begun the subsequent misinterpretations, Hensman declared that Rhodes studied too hard, caught a severe chill, and developed "a serious affection of the lungs which left him very weak for some time."[33] To cure his consumption, his father or the family physician supposedly sent Rhodes to seek a better climate in Africa and thus—so it has usually been said—began the great saga.

In fact, although Rhodes himself much later occasionally bemoaned his own presumed weakness in the lungs, he never exhibited symptoms of consumption or tuberculosis. Nor did his autopsy show tubercular lesions. It is dangerous even to assume that the cardiovascular disease which eventually killed him, and from which he may have suffered in his early Kimberley days, had manifested itself as early as sixteen. According to the son of Rhodes' family physician, Cecil received a letter from Herbert suggesting that Cecil join him in Natal. Herbert apparently "breathe[d] the most sanguine hopes of the success of the cotton culture. . . ." Indeed, there is new fragmentary evidence that Herbert had expected Cecil to follow him to Africa as early as 1868.[34] Herbert's overture appealed to Cecil, and seemed to be an opportunity to postpone answers to his own questions about a profession and his ambiguity about whether he could gain entrance to one of the colleges of the Universities of Oxford or Cambridge.

But the question of his delicate nature—of his health—remained. The vicar sent his sixth born to Dr. John Edward Morris, their local physician, for advice. Morris at some point told his own son that "the young man was in such a nervous and anxious state when he arrived . . . that he could not make a satisfactory examination. . . ." Morris advised Rhodes to "take a walk over the Windhill fields nearby to quiet him down. This he did and returned in about twenty minutes time in a much calmer state of mind. . . ." Morris was then able to examine Rhodes. "My father," said the younger Morris, also a physician, "was able to tell him that there was no reason to think that the climate of South Africa would be harmful to him in any way and that on the contrary [it] should prove beneficial and strongly advised him to accept the offer and join his brother over there."[35]

This version is consistent with Rhodes' own memory. Unable to sleep and "aflame with excitement," he "went down from his room to find a map of South Africa which he studied till morning, "by which time . . . Africa possessed my bones." It is also consistent with Rhodes' casual references to his own health in his first letters home. They were cheerful. "I . . . never felt better in my life."[36] His letters betray no fear of mortal danger, indeed, no anxiety whatsoever. Within a few years Rhodes would develop realistic premonitions of abbreviated life, and would talk about compensating for it by accomplishing his ambitions with a celerity greater than normal. Yet the Rhodes who sailed for Africa in 1870 was no sickly, contorted being, rushing away from family and future in order to preserve what was left of his precarious health. No one thought so. Father and son simply seized the earliest sensible suggestion. Aunt Sophy staked him to £2,000, a tidy sum, and doubtless hinted that more could be forthcoming. Nor would grasping the available opportunity necessarily foreclose Rhodes' university option. That would remain open; so would the law, the church, and other possibilities. By sailing to Africa, Rhodes gambled, albeit with his usual caution, for adventure and riches. He was not driven out of England because of his health. Rhodes emigrated to Africa for the same reason that so many other younger sons left Britain's shores: to seek their fortunes.

"I Am in Charge Here"
The Cotton Fields, a Testing

CECIL RHODES landed in Africa clear-headed, bright-eyed, enthusiastic, and with a characteristic confidence in his own resources. Although he was barely seventeen, and had never been far from the comfortable and nurturing surroundings of Bishop's Stortford, even a seventy-two-day, non-stop voyage aboard the tiny 322-ton bark *Eudora* had done little to limit his appetite for adventure or weaken his growing ability to make the most of whatever opportunities came his way. If outwardly composed, Rhodes was neither cocksure nor brash. Contemporaries noted his studious air, quiet maturity, and easy manners. He was tall and still thin, with high cheekbones, wavy brown hair, bright blue eyes, and a careful and striking gaze. For one so young, he clearly could put strangers at their ease. He was a "quick study," and had a nimble mind. Mature judgment he may have lacked, but creative ideas and schemes came easily to him, and, fortunately, he had the physical energy to match his zest for all things new, unusual, and challenging.

Durban was still raw and ramshackle when the *Eudora* reached the then treacherous bar outside its harbor on the afternoon of 1 September 1870. The town's buildings were mostly of galvanized iron; the streets were of sand. A new light railway was being laid two miles from the landing stage into the town. Sugar was being exported from the countryside, but this gathering place of English immigrants and Zulu laborers was still without proper port facilities or any of the commercial and resort pretensions which it would later assume. Pietermaritzburg, in the drier hills fifty-four miles northwest of Durban's open roadstead, was the embryo colony's capital and the center of the colony of Natal's nascent cultural and intellectual life. There the legislative council had been sitting yearly since 1856 under the eye of a lieutenant governor subordinate to the governor of the Cape Colony. Battles were still to come against the Zulu for paramountcy in the northern portions of this seaward outpost of Britain. So were attempts to attract immigrants and discover an economic underpinning for future growth. This was not an easy task in a largely hot, humid land without the minerals that were being unearthed in South Africa's more fortunate interior and, recently, in Australia.

At the time of Rhodes' landing in Durban, there existed three other areas which would eventually become part of South Africa. The Cape Colony, British since 1795, was then bounded on the north by the Orange River, and on the east by the Kei River, its total area approximately the size of Texas. The Orange Free State, established by Dutch-speaking trekkers in 1854, was an independent republic based on the grassy savannah west of the Caledon River, north of the Orange River, and south of the Vaal River. Its borders had never been fully demarcated, and there were areas almost immediately to be in dispute with the Cape Colony, which lay on its southwesternmost bounds. Across the Vaal, stretching to the Limpopo River, was the Transvaal, another Dutch-dominated and in this case theocratically based, autocratically run, republic.

Much of the area beyond the Kei River (later the Transkei), and the Sotho-populated mountain fastness between Natal and the Orange Free State, was effectively still independent and unannexed. Across the Orange River, the semi-desert lands populated by Tswana speakers were also essentially independent, as were the Nama- and Herero-controlled semi-desert grazing areas farther west, in what is now Namibia. North of Zululand, Portugal had historical claims and a limited official presence. Elsewhere in southern Africa, the white man's writ, both British and local Dutch, nominally ran everywhere. But even within Natal, the Zulu paid it comparatively little attention, and there were parts of the northern Transvaal, as well as the Transkei, Basutoland (later Lesotho), and Bechuanaland (later Botswana), where the writ was acknowledged but ignored. Across the Limpopo, the Ndebele and the Shona, their clients, were still completely free of white suzerainty. Beyond, although David Livingstone was still searching for the source of the Nile River amid the Bangweulu Swamps and the headwaters of the mighty Congo (Zaire) River, the heroic age of Africa's third discovery by Europe was slowly drawing to a close. The scramble for Africa, and its partition, was a decade away. Although there were extensive French efforts to extend their sphere up the Senegal River toward the Niger River, and Britain was obtaining coastal points of occupation in Nigeria and transforming forts into a zone of control along the Gold Coast (Ghana), the powers of Europe were elsewhere only beginning to position themselves strategically along the shoulders of the continent.

Victorian Britain was ascendant world-wide. Canada was about to gain its autonomy, soon to be followed by several of the Australian states. While Rhodes was at sea, Germany, only recently united, had invaded France. Confederates were battling carpetbaggers in the American South. John D. Rockefeller was constructing the mighty Standard Oil Company, having succeeded by one questionable method after another to create an almost impregnable cartel. President Ulysses S. Grant wanted to annex the Dominican Republic. At home in Britain, Prime Minister William Ewart Gladstone led a reform-minded Liberal government.

But the biggest news in Durban in 1870 was diamonds. As soon as he had landed, Rhodes learned that they were the rage of white South Africa, and, within days, the wistful youth would be introduced to a prominent early discoverer of the alluvial marvels. But first he had to arrange a new life in unfamiliar surroundings. Rhodes had never worked with his hands, and, like many South African pioneers of that era, knew nothing about cotton. Nor could he have known anything of mining or diamonds. Destined originally to use his limited high school classical education in some genteel profession, Rhodes was both young and untrained in what might be called the frontier arts. The vicar's serious son, pleased to have spread his books about a single cabin on the *Eudora,* and to have saved his pennies by refraining from extra purchases of bottled beer during the long voyage, thus began, as soon as he had arrived in Africa, to devote his mind to pursuits which were distinctly foreign to his upbringing.

Rhodes' first lengthy, artful letters to his mother, his sisters, and his aunt betray no anxieties about his immediate or long-term future. They express no alarm at the strangeness of his new surroundings, nor do they convey any sense of being overwhelmed by the prospect of making his own way in the unfamiliar world. At first there is only youthful interest, wonder, and a zest for new experiences. Perhaps it was his innate resourcefulness, a Victorian refusal to indicate his true feelings, or long experience with his brother's character and habits, but Rhodes seemed unconcerned that Herbert was neither at the quayside to meet him, upcountry in Pietermaritzburg, nor even in Natal. Herbert was 500 miles away at the Vaal River diamond fields when the seventeen-year-old first set foot in Africa in 1870.

Africa "looked very grand"; a thick brush grew right down to the sea, and the hills rose one above the other right from the shore; "the bluff on which the lighthouse is stands right out and can be seen a great way off." But, after being taken across a sand bar in lighters, the town looked "very rum." "The Kaffirs rather shock your modesty. They many of them have nothing on, excepting a band round the middle. They are fine-looking men, and carry themselves very erect. They all take snuff, and carry their snuff-boxes in a hole, bored through their ears. They also pay great attention to their hair and carry porcupine quills in it, with which they dress it. You often see them sitting down in groups, dressing each other's hairs, and picking the fleas out. The most disagreeable thing about them is their smell. I don't think anything equals the smell of a party of Kaffir women on a hot day if you pass on the lee side of them."[1]

Herbert Rhodes had at least sent a letter giving his whereabouts, enclosing £20, and providing instructions on how Cecil could find his cotton farm in the distant Umkomaas valley. Somerville, one of Herbert's neighbors in the valley, had, unbidden, taken the trouble to ride the 110 miles from the Umkomaas to greet Cecil in his brother's stead and to make him welcome. There was an invitation, too, from Dr. Peter Cormack Sutherland, the surveyor-general of Natal, whose responsibility it was to welcome new settlers to the colony. Sutherland had qualified in medicine at Aberdeen University, practiced briefly,

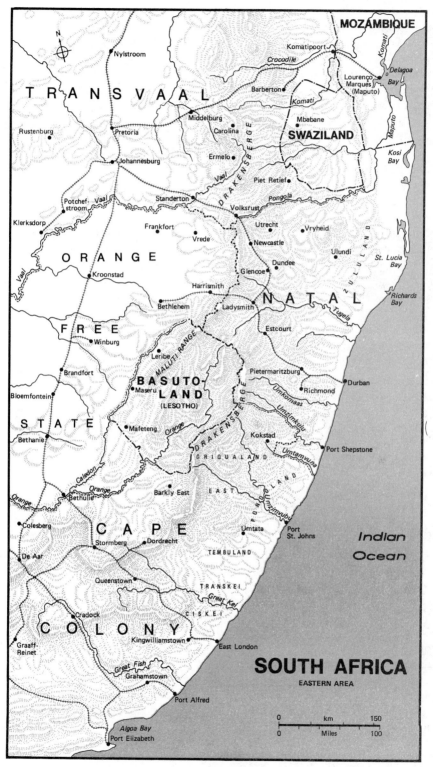

MOZAMBIQUE

Nylstroom

T R A N S V A A L

Komatipoort

Crocodile

Lourenço
Marques
(Maputo)

Delagoa
Bay

Rustenburg

Pretoria

Middelburg

Carolina

Barberton

Komati

Mbabane

SWAZILAND

Kosi
Bay

Johannesburg

Ermelo

Vaal

Piet Retief

Potchef-
stroom

Vaal

Standerton

Volksrust

Pongola

Klerksdorp

Frankfort

Vrede

Utrecht

Vryheid

Z U L U L A N D

O R A N G E

Vrede

Newcastle

Ulundi

St. Lucia
Bay

Vaal

Kroonstad

Glencoe

Dundee

Harrismith

N A T A L

Richards
Bay

Bethlehem

Ladysmith

Tugela

F R E E

Winburg

Estcourt

Leribe

MALUTI RANGE

Brandfort

BASUTO-
LAND

Maseru

Pietermaritzburg

Umkomaas

Durban

Bloemfontein

(LESOTHO)

Richmond

S T A T E

Mafeteng

Orange

Kokstad

Port Shepstone

Bethanie

Caledon

DRAKENSBERGE

G R I Q U A L A N D

Umtamvuna

Orange

Bethulie

Barkly East

E A S T

L A N D

Colesberg

C A P E

Umtata

Port
St. Johns

Indian

Ocean

De Aar

Stormberg

Dordrecht

T E M B U L A N D

Queenstown

T R A N S K E I

Cradock

Great Kei

C I S K E I

C O L O N Y

Kingwilliamstown

East London

SOUTH AFRICA

EASTERN AREA

Graaff-
Reinet

Great Fish

Grahamstown

Port Alfred

Algoa Bay
Port Elizabeth

| 0 | km | 150 |
| 0 | Miles | 100 |

and had then joined two whaling expeditions to the Davis Strait west of Greenland and the search in the Arctic for Sir John Franklin. He wrote a spirited two-volume account of his trials, and then went out to Natal.[2] After three nights in the comfortable Royal Hotel, Rhodes traveled by coach and four to Sutherland's home, covering the arduous miles from the sea into the Drakensberg foothills in nine hours, with five changes of horse.

Rhodes was quick to compare the countryside to the Sussex Downs. The country consisted of "high hills, and deep valleys, and sometimes you will see no trees at all." "What strikes you here most," he went on to say, "is how very little cultivated the land is. You may go for miles and only see one or two patches of cultivated land. This is especially the case up country. . . ." He had seen none of the snakes that were to be his main phobia in Africa, but he informed his mother, in that firm, insistent way he had about him, that there were "a great many curiosities of all kinds out here, and I intend to make a collection."[3]

The climate agreed with him. "One always feels light-hearted," he wrote. Possibly in order to reassure his distant mother, he blithely told her that he had been well since leaving England, having never felt better in his life. Hardly again did he write, even in such a limited way, about his health, probably because, until he suffered his first "heart attack" in 1872, it was of no further concern to him or his family. Before 1872, there is no evidence from Africa that Rhodes was in delicate health, or, because of any supposed infirmities, that he refrained from working hard, riding hard, and being in every way vigorous.

Cotton was Rhodes' first venture. Although cotton was planted in Natal as early as 1840, the first bales to reach Liverpool arrived in 1850. But capital, labor, and experience were short; exports had virtually ceased by 1860. The outbreak of the American Civil War, with its consequent shortages of cotton, revived a British market for colonial cotton. It was the final edge of this wave of interest on which first Herbert, and then Cecil, sailed to Natal.

Herbert and many other immigrants had been persuaded to seek government grants or buy land on which to grow cotton from the Natal Land and Colonisation Society, a British concern.[4] The climate of Natal was thought to be similar to that of the American South, although the rainfall pattern was very different, and much less certain. Valleys like that of the Umkomaas had untouched alluvial soils which were wrongly presumed to be as rich, and as easily worked, as the black loams of the American South. Nevertheless, the bottomlands of the Umkomaas indeed provided the best growing areas in Natal for cotton; and Herbert had acquired very promising acreage. Because of the American Civil War and the Lancashire textile boom, the price of cotton rose appreciably in the early 1860s. The prognosis for cotton prices throughout the 1860s was based on the false notion that the United States would not soon be in a position to export quantities of cotton, and the equally false but connected premise of limited supply and steady demand. But when Rhodes arrived in Africa the returns on cotton, although he could not have known it, were already beginning to slide precipitously downward from the ten pence a pound which good "New Orleans" varieties had fetched in Liverpool in 1866. The once promising Cotton Plantation Company of Natal went bankrupt in 1870.

Herbert had planted twenty acres of cotton in the 1869–70 season, but his seeds were a non-American variety, and Herbert, hardly an experienced farmer, had spaced his rows too close together. The cotton tangled and twisted and worms destroyed the bolls. The summer rains which fall in Natal from November to March had been poor, so the growing plants had also suffered from a partial drought. He grossed only £32. Yet Cecil Rhodes could not have permitted these depressing facts to cloud his hopes for his own and his brother's fortunes. After all, Sutherland, Major David Erskine, the Colonial Secretary of Natal, and other officials all assured him that cotton would absolutely provide for the embryo colony. They "quite believe[d]" in cotton, Rhodes told his mother.

Like so many other white agricultural experiments in Africa, the British attempt to make Natal pay was plagued by ignorance and self-deception. There was an insufficient awareness of even the most rudimentary transportation and marketing prospects; and the dreams of promoters rather than the calculations of crafty cultivators, coupled with a refusal to benefit from the knowledge of Africans, characterized the initial British attempts to make Natal a success.

"It is not all gold that glitters," Rhodes wrote home. He promised to stick to cotton, do nothing rash, and resist the great temptation of diamonds, at least until Herbert returned. This initial ascetic determination must have troubled him, however, for everyone was talking wildly and grandly of the "acknowledged fact that these diamond fields are the richest and the best that have ever been known." During his first days in Pietermaritzburg with the Sutherlands, Rhodes dined several times with Captain Loftus Rolleston, who had recently returned from the Vaal River diggings with an unusually large diamond. To hear him and to see his diamonds made Rhodes' "mouth water." The diamonds were being found in "unheard-of numbers," and Rolleston told him how an African had traded a diamond for a roll of tobacco; it was soon sold for £800. Herbert had apparently found a few small ones. One diamond merchant alone was spending £6,000 a week buying diamonds. Four hundred men were starting for the Vaal area from Durban; already thousands crowded the diggings, and, Rhodes reported, people said that soon the capital of southern Africa would be built (metaphorically, he was correct) on diamonds.[5]

South Africa's first diamond had been recognized in early 1867, when Schalk van Niekerk, a Dutch farmer, visited the De Kalk farm downstream from Hopetown along the Orange River. Erasmus Jacobs, a son of the farmer occupying the land, had probably found this foundation stone of South Africa's mineral wealth late the previous year along the banks of the river. He and his brothers and sisters casually played five-stones, or jacks, with it. Their mother gave it to van Niekerk who, wondering whether it could be a diamond, showed it to traders and others at the edge of the Cape Colony. Eliciting different assessments of its value, the bright stone made its way from trader to official and then to the official mineralogist of the Colony, who pronounced it real, and worth £500. It weighed 22 carats.

Van Niekerk neither rushed back to De Kalk nor prospected elsewhere. However, he developed a local reputation as a buyer of bright stones. In March 1869, a Griqua (Coloured) farm employee brought van Niekerk a large bauble that he had found a few months before somewhere along the Orange River in the vicinity of De Kalk. Van Niekerk promptly traded 500 sheep, ten oxen, and a horse for the bright object. It was an eighty-three-carat diamond, later called the Star of Africa, which van Niekerk sold for £11,000, and which Lord Dudley subsequently purchased in Britain for £25,000.[6]

By mid-1869, diamonds, although none so big as the Star of Africa, were being found by Africans and farmers along the Orange and Vaal Rivers, and near the confluence of the Harts River and the Vaal. In September or October 1869, too, Dutch-speaking farmers were finding diamonds twenty miles south of the Vaal River in the natural basins or pans which held the wash of the surrounding low ridges. Dutoitspan was one, on the Dorstfontein Farm in what was later to become the city of Kimberley. Bultfontein and Vooruitzigt (owned by the De Beer brothers) were two adjacent farms, the three together totaling about fifty-eight square miles. In late 1869, diamonds were also discovered eighty miles farther southeast, on the Jagersfontein farm near Fauriesmith. The finds in these land diggings did not immediately distract prospectors away from the rivers. In the unusually dry conditions of 1869, the farms lacked water sufficient for both human consumption and the washing of the diamondiferous earths. Although the boulder-strewn river gravels were much harder to work and sieve than the friable soils of the farms, water at least was at hand in the rivers and, during these initial months, the rewards of the alluvial areas appeared greater.

The prospectors could not then have known about the vast differences in potential of the river and the dry diggings. Few in South Africa would have guessed how differently the two diamond areas had been laid down, nor understood the processes which permitted the lands at last to lay bare their mineral secrets. The diamondiferous river gravels were the residue of erosive forces which had carried sheets of the uppermost layers of Africa seaward for millions of years. The diamonds in the dry diggings were fragments of compressed carbon bound with soils of iron oxide in material of igneous origin called kimberlite pipes and found only as the fillings in the necks—or pipes—of extinct volcanoes. The world's pipe which has been exploited most deeply, to 3,520 feet, is in Kimberley, but diamonds and kimberlite pipes do exist at greater depths. The pipe with the broadest surface of any yet discovered also lies in South Africa, near Pretoria. It covers eighty acres.

The upper surface of a kimberlite pipe crumbles easily and has a distinctive yellowish cast when it is exposed to the atmosphere. This was the yellow earth that excited the dry diggers in the 1870s. But, at first, the tops of the pipes were mostly obscured by trees and scrub bush, and none of the prospectors could really have known what riches lay beneath. Chance played a crucial role in determining South Africa's wealth and Rhodes' destiny.

Major alluvial finds were being made late in 1869 along an eighty-mile section of the Vaal from Hebron to the Harts River junction. It was soon crowded with prospectors and speculators. They roamed along the river, and dug deeply and with effort into the heavy gravels of the dry river banks, and sometimes into the beds of the rivers. They sorted the soil and sand with crude screens, finding erratic and incidental stones that had been carried downstream from the mountains above. By the end of the year, 10,000 diggers had jammed these alluvial grounds. Pniel (Hay), on the south bank, and Klipdrift (Barkly West), on the north side of the Vaal, became sizable settlements. Joseph B. Robinson and John X. Merriman, critical figures in late nineteenth-century South African commerce and politics, were among the early prospectors. So was a military party led by Captain Rolleston. One of its members was Herbert Rhodes.

The river diggings produced random results, made a few fortunes, and—as Cecil Rhodes was to comment to his mother—disappointed many. But even these sporadic finds whetted the appetite of fortune hunters in an otherwise staid, agricultural colony where cattle had earlier been the primary object of frontier avarice. Diamonds, like gold in California in 1849 and in Colorado in 1869, were a sparkling attraction. The possibility of easy money excited those already settled in South Africa and attracted thousands of new immigrants. Diamonds were a magnet for those who were prepared to live by their energy and their wits.

When Cecil Rhodes arrived in Africa, the search for diamonds, still concentrated along the rivers, was being redirected toward the surrounding plains. There had been a flurry of activity in and around Dutoitspan in early 1870, but the major rush of the dry diggings was still to come. The fever of diamond wealth had spread widely, but would not become an epidemic until the next year, when whites in their thousands began to live in tents all over the kopje and similar nearby outcrops. South Africa was about to be transformed by its geological gifts. Rhodes was in at the beginning, and had that combination of long-range vision and immediate practicality which permitted him to seize the opportunities presented by his place and time, and to make of their curious chemistry a much more complicated and grander synthesis.

Given the tales of hitherto unsuspected riches with which he was immediately pressed, it would have been unnatural if the young Rhodes had not begun fantasizing about riches for himself. Mrs. Sutherland had found the boy "very quiet and a great reader."[7] Certainly, the sober young Englishman who had stepped off the *Eudora* and had made his way to Pietermaritzburg appeared to others as a dreamer. But his daydreams, although they had their serious side, were easily stimulated by more romantic notions of great wealth from diamonds. Since he was too young and immature to have developed firm thoughts about his manhood, a family, and settling down in some standard way, essential aspects of Rhodes' character remained unformed. When Herbert and others agreed that a wife would bring order and assistance to their joint life in the Umkomaas valley, and suggested that Cecil, being the youngest, should marry, he "did not seem to see it."[8] There were rumors that Rhodes was subsequently engaged to Margaret Ballantyne, one of the daughters of the only large family in the district, but the brief mention of her father by Rhodes is slighting.[9]

Rhodes may have continued dreaming of a university education, and of life as a professional, probably a barrister. But these would have been dreams with utilitarian motives. For the moment, he was content to have "land of your own, horses of your own, and shooting when you like and a lot of black niggers to do what you like with, apart from the fact of making money."[10] The ease with which he could express such satisfaction was probably increased by the knowledge that his parents and Aunt Sophy were backing him and would continue for at least a year to support his sally into Africa. They could afford it, so Rhodes in those first years never had to worry about making money quickly, or about surviving while seeking some respectable (or less than respectable) source of local income.

Prospects of a carefree, money-making life were in Rhodes' mind after riding for the first time the forty-four miles to Herbert's farm. The way led from Pietermaritzburg to the even sleepier new town of Richmond and then another twenty miles across the undulating valleys and steep hills that led finally to the dried-up and autumnal Umkomaas River. The Umkomaas, winding in and out like a snake between the mountains, was described by a contemporary as quiet and silvery in appearance from a distance, but "the most treacherous and powerful river in the colony, having a fall every half-mile."[11]

Herbert's land was along an alluvial "flat" that stretched as much as a mile from the river along the valley floor to abruptly steep hills. In a loaded ox-drawn wagon it was reached only by a trying ascent (difficult today even in a modern automobile) of a line of hills, followed by a long, precipitous descent to the valley floor. Rhodes described the journey into the Umkomaas valley without any drama. A contemporary visitor, however, found the descent, at an angle of nearly 45 degrees, worrying. "Down—lower down—we go, the horses picking their way step by step, until we find it desirable to dismount and lead them; ever the rough road. Mounting again, we descend for a mile and a half, and come to the roughest part of the road, where the descent is literally as rough as the steps of the Monument. Such a getting down stairs for wagons and oxen (or cart) we never did see; and . . . none but plucky fellows would think of making their fortunes with such a hard road to travel."[12]

"There is no doubt this is one of the most beautiful valleys in the colony." It was covered, when Rhodes first espied it, with thick brush and small trees.[13] The hills rose for hundreds of feet all around. Two neighbors in the valley had a park-like terrain filled with mimosa trees; they and the several other single men and two families up and down the valley of the Umkomaas were also attempting to grow cotton. There was abundant vacant land, too, on some of which Rhodes soon had his eye, and an Anglican mission station. On the "top," as the plateau above the valley was called, there were other settlers trying to grow maize and raise cattle, in the more traditional African fashion. (Hail would have destroyed cotton there.) After a month, much of which was spent traveling with Sutherland in central Natal, visiting settlers and missionaries, staying in Zulu homesteads, and generally becoming acclimated, Rhodes clearly began to feel at home. Certainly, his letters give that impression, as does his own willingness to observe, comment, and pronounce upon his surroundings, his companions, and his own and his brother's prospects.

Few of his biographers have described Rhodes' admittedly boyish, but fresh and unaffected, even easygoing, reactions to the first Africans he encountered in the Natal hills. These initial impressions must have influenced the later entrepreneur, imperialist, and politician; they show an interest, if (for the time and circumstances) no particular affection or disdain. Proffered sour milk, or "twali"—Zulu beer—in the villages, he drank with delight. He ate what he was given and was now hardly squeamish about Zulu living arrangements despite the closeness of the air, and (considering how fastidious he became) the many bodies with whom he would have had to share the tight space. "A Kaffir hut is just like a beehive . . . [with] one little hole as entrance, which you crawl in at, and once in you see all the Kaffirs sitting on their haunches round the fire, which is lighted in the middle of the place. There is no chimney, and the entrance hole is wonderfully small, so that the smoke sometimes is rather overpowering, and you have to bolt for the entrance hole to get a little fresh air. Another objection . . . is the fleas and insects. All night long you are scratch, scratch, scratch, and then besides you keep feeling the larger ones running up and down your body." "But a Kaffir hut," he concluded, "is decidedly better than sleeping in the veldt." (Rhodes later expressed opposite views.) As far as Rhodes could tell, the Kaffirs had "no religion at all. The only religion to them is their . . . girls. They are a very amorous race . . . always talking or thinking of their women." [14]

Herbert returned to Natal in early October, having found a few diamonds worth £5 or £10. Quickly agreeing to become partners, with equal shares in the land and the expected profits, the two brothers began the arduous task of clearing and stumping forty acres to add to the existing twenty, and to ready the ground for planting at a cost of about £300. "We are hard at work," Rhodes rightly said. That is, "you don't work yourself, but are obliged to be constantly looking after the Kaffirs." With characteristic expansiveness, he expected it to be the largest cotton plantation yet established in Natal.

Along with other young white men, some of whom were relatives or friends seeking their own destinies, the brothers Rhodes lived in a small, round, wattle-and-daub thatched hut which Herbert had built the previous year. The furniture consisted of two beds, two chairs, and a table. Thanks to an African cook, who was soon succeeded by a "coolie," they ate well: chicken, antelope, goat, or suckling pig; homemade bread; tea, coffee, and a port-like wine. From the start, Rhodes' new life was comfortable, interesting, diverse—he caught and plucked birds for a knowledgeable friend, rode along rutted roads to Richmond to watch cricket or receive the mail, went all the way to Pietermaritzburg for dinners and other social events, spent Sundays at church, and was busy helping to manage the small plantation and devising the various ways in which cotton would make the Rhodes name and fortune.

A typical day during that first planting season consisted of rising with the sun at 5:30, rousing the workers, hoeing with them until 9 a.m., and then breakfasting on porridge and milk, meat, bread, and butter. Herbert supervised the laboring force from 10 a.m. until 1 p.m. Dinner followed, and then both brothers went out into the fields with their Zulu employees until 6 p.m., when they had tea. Cecil always bathed after breakfast. Sunday was the only day on which the brothers emerged from the valley, discarding their everyday shirts and trousers, "with more holes than patches," and pulling on "respectable clothes," greasing their boots, and riding four miles to the Anglican mission for Sunday services. Two or three times during the summer season, Herbert stole away to Pietermaritzburg to a ball, for a day of horse racing, or for a week of cricket.

"I like Natal very much," Cecil told his sisters during that first season. But he did not care to contemplate spending a lifetime there. He had begun to think seriously of diamonds, having ambitions greater than farming. Anyway, he doubted that cotton would ever provide more than a modest living. It had yet to be proved "trumps."[15] The Liverpool price had dropped below 6 pence a pound, and Rhodes was worried that it would continue to fall. He may also have wondered about his brother, who, despite their differences in age, was as mercurial as Cecil was steady, and lacked a feel for the soil (as did Cecil and so many of the other young would-be farmers).

By Christmas, after abundant rain, the cotton in the Umkomaas valley looked promising. The two Rhodes brothers had planted American seeds that Cecil had brought out from England (frost having killed the ratoon, or basal, growth from the previous year), and they had sown them in rows an appropriate seven feet apart. Grasshoppers, which could destroy the young cotton, were less numerous than in past years. In late January, the cotton was budding and flowering perfectly, and the world price was rising slightly.

For Cecil, cotton was a demanding crop, requiring planters to persevere, to "stick to it entirely."[16] Labor was a further problem, and Rhodes' analysis, if not profound, drew upon the kind of received wisdom which was to influence his own thinking for many years to come, not least of all when he later became prime minister of the Cape Colony: "For though there are any amount of Kaffirs out here, they are such independent fellows that the greater part of them won't work. Their daily food is mealie [maize] porridge. They grow their own mealies, and the only thing they must have money for is their hut tax, which is very light."[17] Rhodes called them independent, not "lazy."

But in these early days, amidst the cotton in a remote valley isolated from the main questions of labor supply and demand, the Rhodes brothers fared well. They paid wages similar to those common in the neighborhood and were apparently no harder on their men than were most employers in the valley. So their cotton was weeded and tended, and only its eventual harvesting could prove a problem.

According to an anonymous visitor who inspected the Umkomaas valley plantings in about March 1871, the brothers Rhodes had "planted mealies about every eighty feet, to attract the grub from the cotton." The brothers had also plowed rather than hoed between the cotton rows, and that new, less expensive technique appeared to pen up the soil to a greater depth, and improve the overall appearance of the bushes, then about four feet high. Their plants were "bolling well, . . . very large, and promise[d] a good crop."[18]

Baboons were a menace. They came every day, Rhodes wrote vividly, and "strip the cobs off, and very quickly clean row after row. If you try to get near them, they go, being very keen of scent, and they always have a baboon posted as sentinel. . . . If they are scattered, they very quickly form into a rank with the elders in the rear, and into the bush they go. We followed them up the other day, but it was a regular wild goose chase, and they soon got back into their holes in the rocks." They were "extraordinarily 'cute.' You will see them leaving your field, with a nice big cob in one hand, and three or four more tucked under their arms, and going along on their three legs, and in all their actions, they strike you as being so like human beings."[19]

Rhodes also did not count on abrupt climatic changes, one of which produced a storm full of hail. It blew the roof off the newly finished, sun-dried brick cotton house, and destroyed a number of cotton bushes and much of the maize plants, but the vast bulk of cotton survived, and continued to thrive. Maize was becoming so inexpensive that Rhodes fussed little about losses caused by the storm and the unremitting desecration by baboons.

What may have concerned him more was the sudden departure of Herbert. That there are no hints of displeasure in his letters doubtless reflects his lack of illusion about Herbert's character. As he wrote to his mother, describing Herbert's carelessness: "You see he has not altered since he left home." In late March 1871, having never devoted full attention to cotton, Herbert returned to the diamond diggings. The cotton was about to be harvested, a particularly delicate and critical operation for an elder brother to entrust to a novice. It involved the sole supervision of a process which was certain to last for at least six weeks, followed by ginning, which neither brother had ever done before, and the selling of the product—no longer an easy undertaking since differentials between local, coastal, and European prices would determine whether the cotton experiment was advantageous compared to diamonds. Tyro though Rhodes might have been, he doubtless had thought out every step during the long hours he supervised his field hands.

A simple explanation for Rhodes' equanimity about his brother's departure may be found in his own desire to try diamonds, too. Once Herbert was there, and successful, Cecil also could leave cotton behind. He acknowledged that his mother might think Herbert's abandonment of cotton foolish, but Rhodes would see that the cotton was picked properly, and, anyway, diamonds were sounding better and better. "It would have been really throwing a chance away, if one of us had not gone up." Then, of equal significance, was Rhodes' own desire to run the estate. Herbert was a chancer; Cecil could well have thought that he could do better. A born leader who would have ranked high on any modern assessment of a capacity to organize and direct the course of events, Rhodes could hardly resist an opportunity to orchestrate the workings of the farm, and concern himself, if at first in a minor way, in the affairs of the colony. "I am left in charge here," he proudly told his mother, "and have about 30 Kaffirs to manage, and feel quite a big man, with so many black attendants."[20]

Rhodes developed an affection for his regular laborers as a group and a set of perceptions of Africans as workers which were formative and, insofar as they were incorporated into his own view of himself as a white entrepreneur in an Africa of two nations, of lasting significance. Although his planter peers believed that Africans were "the laziest race under the sun" with few wants except the minimal hut tax, he soon discovered that his own labor force responded directly and indirectly to incentives and disincentives which would be well understood almost everywhere. After supervising the crucial picking of his cotton, which occupied Rhodes and his workers almost daily in the southern hemisphere's autumn of 1871, he made a rule: "never refuse to lend him money." (Rhodes described a form of debt peonage.) "You see," he told his mother and again and again repeated the same homily, "it gets your name up amongst them, and when they want to go to work, they are artful fellows for weighing in their minds the different advantages of the white masters, and of course it is a great inducement if they know that they are always sure of work, or money advanced by the master, because they sometimes come [and here Rhodes intuitively understood the ability of Africans to calibrate their own opportunity costs] from 20 or 30 miles distant, for work." If refused, Africans would not come again.

Rhodes also believed (as did Herbert) in the honesty of Africans. Justifying his lending small sums to Africans with no obvious usurious intent, Rhodes said that "Kaffirs are really safer than the Bank of England."[21] In this early episode, Rhodes showed the precursor of his extraordinary capacity to empathize and identify with his associates—whether friends or foes, and especially men. His unusual capacity to sense the similarity between himself and others was the basis of his important later alliance with the political representatives of the Dutch-speaking farmers. This tendency to include rather than exclude was a major component of Rhodes' charisma. It added immeasurably to his capacity to deal with—to "square"—opponents and work around barriers to success.

For some leaders the power to influence is derived from a group need for a sense of certainty, one of the defining characteristics of charisma. But in Rhodes' case, his charisma emanated from and was sustained by his own persistent commitment to a private agenda. Psychologically, it was related more to creative than to political urges. Indeed, unlike the messiahs described by Kohut who drew their charismatic abilities from capacities for empathy that were stunted by the traumatic interruption of intense relationships with early, deeply significant, self-objects, usually their mothers, Rhodes' empathic capacities were enhanced. Such stunting of the capacity to respond to others is linked in Kohut's messianic figures to a sense of utter conviction of the legitimacy of their own wishes and relative absence of a sense of guilt. It is this absolute moral righteousness that is so charismatically attractive to others. Rhodes' charismatic abilities, in contrast, were enlarged by a prolonged, intensely close tie to his mother. The traumatic rupture of their idyll by the birth of Elmhirst, although causing a sense of loss, a desire for restitution, and the reduced feelings of guilt which were characteristic of Rhodes' adult character, occurred developmentally late—when he was well into the oedipal phase of development. Thus his keen response to others—that acute empathic sense which was so central to his later success—could flow uninterruptedly from his early and sustained special relationship with a mother whose own empathic gifts were critical and persuasive.[22]

Rhodes could innovate, too. He persuaded women and children to pick, finding them better, that is, swifter, pickers of cotton than men. Did he also reckon to minimize expenses by paying women 3 pence for thirty pounds, presumably less than he paid the men? That is not clear, but, since he thought that his "permanent" labor force could probably pick 150 acres, not just 60, and since his notion was to employ too many in his first year in order to have sufficient for his second and subsequent years, his most salient trait during that initial sojourn in Africa was hardly parsimony. That he was conscious, even unusually watchful, of his finances is also evident from the care with which he calculated and justified each of his expenses in letter after long letter to his mother. He worked out the presumed exact cost of stumping, planting, and picking. There were apologies for buying two carts instead of one (Herbert took the smaller one to the diamond fields). He reminded his mother how much basic staples and other provisions cost in distant Natal. At one point, he asked her to send out articles of clothing so that it would be unnecessary to pay the exorbitant local charges for trousers, shirts, hats, and other basic necessities. For a teenager with limited prior experience, Rhodes had an instinctive urge to count and sum up, to rationalize most actions, to be didactic (and, at this stage, verbose), and to please his mother (and others) in ways in which his much more independent and brash elder brother could not.

For Rhodes, the beginning of his African adventure both in objective and in psychological reality was a collaboration between an adolescent and his mother. His letters home, considerably more numerous than would have been required, stand in marked contrast to anything else he ever wrote. They were composed with care. They conveyed a vitality which served to draw his mother actively into his own cotton-growing life. Kohut, attacking the notion that creativity is a solitary achievement, asserts that truly creative individuals choose companions or alter egos with whom they can share their bursts of genius and from whom they draw reassurance and hence new energy for further productivity.[23] Rhodes had both his mother's and his aunt's support as he created a new life.

In his brother's absence, Rhodes was a whirlwind of activity. With his workers, he brought in the cotton from late March to early May 1871. The work force came after breakfast, picked the fluffy white bolls all day, carried the filled baskets to him for weighing, and were paid by the pound. Only infrequent and late seasonal rains halted the harvest and slowed the race against cold weather. At the same time, he directed a smaller crew harvesting a few experimental acres of Virigina tobacco that the brothers had put down as a likely source of added profit. He looked after another set of laborers who were stumping and clearing acres for the next season's planting. He learned how to inoculate cattle to prevent his herd of oxen from dying of lung sickness. He went to Richmond and brought back loads of mealies for his labor force. That is all they eat, he explained to his mother, imagining her there. "I know you would laugh to see our Kaffirs . . . sitting on their haunches round their pots, and digging their big wooden spoons into the meal, and then ramming the spoon, meal and all right into their mouths, and they keep on doing it until the pot is empty."[24]

James Cole, Rhodes' white assistant, was in charge of the extended construction of a new house sixty feet wide, with a verandah and several large rooms. It was being made of sun-dried brick, the usual intermediate material between wattle-and-daub and kiln-dried brick, and was a clear investment in the long-term culture of the cotton estate. Rhodes, with his customary diversity of concern and talent, took a vigorous interest in this, as in so many other building projects: a stable; the drying platform which he built for the cotton harvest; and the house in which the cotton would be ginned, baled, and stored until it could be sold.

He also put himself in charge of the "awful work" of making sure that the new living quarters were roofed properly. Women traditionally brought thatch for a roof in large bundles. Rhodes had to count every small bundle for fear of being cheated. "Sometimes you might see a string of about 30 or 40 women and girls, all bringing grass on their heads, with no clothing at all, except perhaps a dirty handkerchief tied round the waist, or else a handsome bead arrangement, which they are very clever at making. They come up to the hut, chuck the grass off their heads, and they require you to come out, and count, and of course there is something that does not quite satisfy them, and they set up a clatter of tongues that would surprise you. They all talk at the same time, and require you to understand them, which is rather a difficult matter." "Some of the girls," he went on with interest and understanding, "are very nice-looking, but as soon as they are married, the men make them do all the work; their skin shrivels up, their forms get bent, and they look old women before they are 30."[25]

By mid-April, Rhodes was ginning cotton (separating the fiber from the boll), a task the one-time schoolboy could not have imagined doing a year before. He had brought out a small British hand-rolling gin. But it was very slow, if less harsh on the cotton fibers than the much faster saw gin which was in general use in Natal. As far as it is possible to discern, Rhodes and his fellow farmers knew very little about treating the cotton once it was harvested. ". . . Few in Natal . . . could claim to understand the factors which went to make for good cotton production." (Rhodes complained bitterly to his mother about the lack of information in much of the British literature that he had carried with him to Africa. But there was a book written by a Louisianan which was proving helpful. He asked his mother to help him find out how the Americans ginned their cotton.) Using a neighbor's saw gin, Rhodes eventually baled fifty fifty-pound bales of a quality similar to "Middling Orleans." It fetched 5 pence a pound locally, and might have reached the 7½ pence a pound level if it had been shipped home to Manchester. He expected to realize about £64 from his crop, for a net profit of about £2.10 an acre.

He showed four bales of regularly processed cotton at a show in Pietermaritzburg, without much success. But he claims to have almost won a prize— it was "highly commended"—for the special cotton that he had processed himself on his own small McCarthy hand gin, with its toy-like handles. Unfortunately, he managed to prepare less than a single bale, too little in quantity for the judges to have given him the £5 award.[26]

Cotton promised a steady income. Rhodes knew that his brother would "let the farm go" in favor of diamonds, but at least until the 1871 crop of cotton was sold, Rhodes still assumed that he himself should not risk all on the chance of finding glittering stones. He was not then, nor ever later, much of a gambler. The sense of the interior dialogue that he committed to paper in 1871 corresponds well with the import of his letters to Charles Dunell Rudd, Alfred Beit, and his other financial partners during the later 1870s, the 1880s, and even into the heady 1890s. His brothers Herbert and Frank were both flamboyant risk takers. He, like his slightly older brother Ernest, was steady, even cautious. In 1871, as much later, he kept and covered his options.

Throughout the first half of 1871, even when harvesting cotton was uppermost in his mind, Rhodes calculated the advantages of obtaining this or that parcel of land in his own name. He kept his eye on land adjacent to his brother's flat, looked at others in distant valleys and farther down the Umkomaas, and at one point coveted an area which had been cleared by a local chief. It was not in a zone which was reserved for Africans, so the chief could be ousted and "the fruit of his labours turned to a white man's advantage." Rhodes did not know whether to do so was "right," but it was "legal."[27]

Finally, he decided to lease and later purchase land from the Colonisation Society which abutted that granted to his brother in the Umkomaas valley. The lease to 120 acres of the so-called Spitzkop Farm was intended to run for seven years. Thirty acres were plowable, the other ninety rough and unfit for cultivation. On these thirty acres, Rhodes would plant cotton from American seeds. The thirty, added to his brother's ninety, and the purchase of a neighbor's twenty, would give them a total of 140 acres, which he expected would prove an economic proposition. The first fifty acres with cotton at 5 pence a pound would pay for the farm, Rhodes assumed, the next thirty would cover one's own expenses, and the third fifty would be clear profit. He had the laborers and the knack of keeping them. With four of his neighbors, he would invest in a steam-powered gin, sharing the cost and the ease of production. Transport would be a problem, for roads were rough and carts were unreliable and kept upsetting when traveling out of the steep valley filled with cotton. But he was content with the life, and may fully have intended to try farming at least for a few more years. He certainly wrote grandly of his plan to plow more and more acres in the spring of the South African year. Yet farming was lonely, and dependent on climatic changes and the vagaries of the international market. He could do it. He could see himself doing it. But the excitement and the real opportunities were farther inland, where men were digging frantically for diamonds.

"You cannot understand what an awful enticement the diamonds are. Any day you may put up an immense fortune, any day you may find a diamond that will astonish the world. Many fellows have found small fortunes just as they were giving up in despair. . . ." A Dutchman had arrived, found a diamond worth £14,000, and departed, all in one pleasant day's work. Positively, Rhodes had heard it asserted that nine-tenths of those who arrived in the fields were fortunate. The finds were increasing, and Herbert had found three good stones during his first ten days. In June, Cecil had a plan: he would continue ginning and baling and selling the cotton, and generally behave in a prudent manner. But as soon as he obtained cash sufficient to pay all of the farm's bills and clear about £50, he would take it and five African laborers to Herbert, leave it and them there and return to the Umkomaas valley in time to plant the cotton in October, at the beginning of the growing season.[28]

By mid-July, however, Rhodes had not budged. Herbert implored him to bring as many laborers as possible to the diamond fields, but Cecil did not consider himself ready to incur the heavy extra expense of traveling across the Drakensberg Mountains and the rolling plains of the Orange Free State at the height of the dry season. Traveling depended upon oxen, and oxen depended on grass. In mid-winter, there was no grass, and oxen were reported to be dying regularly on the main road to the diamond fields. Traveling could take months, and the transport contractors charged high prices for whites and Africans, and refused to guarantee arrivals, even after a few months. So Rhodes abandoned any ideas of doing Herbert's bidding and going to him by a regular route.

But he refused to give diamonds up altogether. Another, much quicker, way of going to the diamond fields was on horseback, by a largely uninhabited and little-known route directly across the mountains. There were few houses along this route and it was inherently risky, but much less expensive, much faster, and much simpler. Rhodes was a simplifier. In this case, he would go, look around, and return—perhaps with a few diamonds—in time to plant cotton.

Rhodes rode out of the Umkomaas valley in October 1871. Why he waited until the very start of the planting season, why he disregarded his own tactical advice to himself to start earlier, and what he did between July and October is uncertain. Many of his biographers have overlooked these questions, the later ones repeating the confident assertions of their predecessors that he went out on horseback, early in October, carrying tins of biscuits, tea, sugar, a "wonderful box of lozenges . . . which my father sent me," a pick, two shovels, several volumes of the classics (including his prized copy of Plutarch's *Lives,* which he lost en route), and a Greek lexicon, together with a cart pulled by four oxen.[29]

But the reports of biographers are a conflation of what Rhodes wrote to his mother in July and the uncertainly authenticated, frequently repeated statements that may conceivably have been based on hearsay or on Rhodes' own offhand remarks to someone like Lewis Michell, his banker and early biographer. The only slightly less circumstantial account of Rhodes' departure and trek, but not of the long delay, is contained in McDonald's biography: "It was never an easy matter to get Rhodes to talk of any part of his life that was past—he lived entirely in the present and the future—and scarcely anything is known of his long trek to Colesberg, but I gathered from him during a rambling ride one day that his pony died and that afterwards he always walked ahead of his cart, which covered about fourteen miles a day—Sundays were, however, rest days. Most of the trekking was done in the late afternoon and again in the very early morning so that the oxen could feed during the day when they would be observed if they strayed."

The 400 miles from the Umkomaas to the diamonds fields at the slow pace of oxen obviously took well over a month, giving Rhodes almost unbounded opportunities to muse on cotton and diamonds, but also, looking ahead, on his own place in the great expanse of the rapidly developing continent. Of the books that Rhodes chose to take with him to the diamond fields, the *Meditations* of Marcus Aurelius would have been pre-eminent. Perhaps Plutarch, too. (More certain are the books that he left behind, in the keeping of Cole, now farming and trading on his own, nearby. They included many of his schoolboy prizes: Henry Nelson Coleridge's 1846 *Introduction to the Study of the Greek Classical Poets;* an interlinear translation of Homer's *Iliad* and *Odyssey;* a pocket classic copy of Homer's *Odyssey* in Greek; Virgil's *Aeneid,* in Latin; the New Testament, in English (his confirmation present from the Bishop of Rochester); Thomas Wilson's *Instruction on the Lord's Supper;* I. Todhunter's 1864 *Plane Trigonometry;* and W.J. Conybeare and J.S. Howson's *The Life and Epistles of the Duke of Wellington.)*[30]

When Rhodes left the Umkomaas valley, he also carried with him the experiences of a ripe first year in Africa. He had mastered any concern about his health, overcome the strangeness of Africa, and had learned to work successfully with older whites and peoples of different color and culture. He had found a focus for his energies. He knew that he could live and prosper on his own. At an age when most Victorians of his class were apprenticing themselves to careers or entering upon professions, Rhodes was learning the basic lessons of entrepreneurship in a distant colony. He was working with his hands, but also using his head and exploring, in however protean a manner, his capacity for leadership.

A first year in a strange land is always instructive, especially for a young man of great promise who is at work on his transition to adulthood. Hitherto, this pre-diamond interlude has been slighted, thus misunderstanding the true significance of Rhodes' later assertion that, since he could grow cotton when others said that it would be impossible, he could do anything. The antidote to adolescence is real achievement; both the destructive acting-out of disturbed youngsters and the ceaseless activity of healthy adolescents tests the growing individual's ability to survive and thrive. Through this process a person gains a sense of mastery which forms one of the focuses of adult identity. Thus it is hardly surprising that Rhodes was less discomfited than pleased when Herbert left cotton for diamonds. It threw him on his own resources. His were the hard decisions to make. His ingenuity and resolve were tested; so was his father's belief that his fourth son would succeed best away from a routine professional life in Britain. Without the self-reliance that often comes from any frontier farming experience, it is likely that Rhodes' independence would have grown more slowly, and that he might not have been ready for diamonds, for the rough life of Colesberg kopje (later De Beers' New Rush), or for the many opportunities to make his way among miners and magnates, English and Dutch, and Africans and Coloureds.

These real experiences—his failures and frustrations as well as his successes—strengthened his confidence in himself and eased the transition into late adolescence. As with most youngsters of extraordinary capacity, however, Rhodes' commitment to work and to love remained open for much longer. It would be another dozen years before he would devise and commit himself to a program for his life's work. His choices of whom to love, too, would follow an unusual path leading, at last, back to the products of his own mind and his own dreams. But his sense of strength and his confidence in his own judgment and abilities had taken a major leap forward. Rhodes had come to the Umkomaas a youth; he left a young adult, ready for larger things.

Rhodes never again felt cotton fall between his fingers (although much later he sponsored other agricultural experiments on a large scale); indeed, infestations of bollworm ended serious cotton cultivation everywhere in up-country Natal after 1871. He never again saw the silvery Umkomaas River thread through the red dolerite hills of central Natal. Nor did he live to regret his decision to flee the farming life that had so nurtured his first months in a strange continent.

4

"Digging, Sifting, and Sorting from Morning till Night"
Scraping Together the First Riches

"IMAGINE a small round hill, at its very highest part only about 30 feet above the level of the surrounding country about 180 yards broad and 220 long, all round it a mass of white tents, and then beyond them a flat level country for miles and miles, with here and there a gentle rise."[1] That, Cecil Rhodes informed his mother with roseate pen, was the setting for the richest diamond mine that "the world ever produced." It was Colesberg kopje, later De Beers' New Rush, and was set in an "immense plain" along with the three other nearby dry-land diamond properties that had been proved in 1871. Together, their bounty catapulted South Africa into the industrial age.

From one or two properties and then from all of the mines, Rhodes slowly gained immense wealth. The mines were the basis of Rhodes' fortune, the fount of his imperialistic drive, the resource that fueled his political ambition, and the locus for many years of most manifestations of his talent, gift, or genius—however it is finally judged. Moreover, its tents and small houses were his primary homes in the 1870s and 1880s before he occupied a position of prominence in Cape politics and international imperialism. The young Rhodes grew astute and acquisitive, and his ambition unfolded and flourished in these spartan, even rough, surroundings.

The immense plain held little scenic allure for the casual visitor. "Our first peep at the famous Du Toits pan . . . ," wrote a contemporary of Cecil Rhodes, "was certainly unsatisfactory; little was to be seen but dense masses of fine dust ascending heavenward. Slowly onward rolled our waggon. . . . We were now all agog with interest and excitement as the scene before us gradually unfolded, and one's heart began to beat faster as the Diamond City of the Plains became more and more distinct. The strange, vague landscape of tents widened and grew whiter and clearer. It now became apparent that the dusty pall observed from afar was occasioned by the continual sifting and sorting of the precious soil by thousands of busy diggers and their vast army of native helpers. The novelty of the panorama became intensified as our waggon at last entered this great human bee-hive, and wended its way in and out among the canvas shelters dotted promiscuously here, there and everywhere, creaking and groaning through deep sand and ruts, or staggering over mighty mounds of debris. The few wooden tenements, scattered about at rare intervals, had been fashioned out of packing-cases, and the owners thereof considered themselves the aristocrats of Diggerdom.

"Still moving forward, one found the mass of tents becoming denser and more bewildering in its chaotic array. Water was then very scarce, and the many unwashed faces that peeped out curiously as we passed seemed to match the colour of the dusty canvas abodes. Hordes of dogs and semi-nude Kafirs were everywhere, and handy Scotch carts drawn by teams of oxen, mules or horses, were noisily bumping their way along the labyrinthine roadways."[2]

Colesberg kôpje had become the centerpiece of the dry diggings only a few months before Rhodes' arrival. In late July 1871, while Rhodes gathered in the cotton, ginned it laboriously, and cautiously wondered whether he should join Herbert's quest for diamonds, a group of men from the town of Colesberg found the top of the geological pipe or fissure which later became the New Rush mine. It was located on a small hill on the Vooruitzigt farm, about a mile from the first diggings, "Old Rush," at the site of the De Beers brothers' farmhouse.

An African employed by Fleetwood Rawstorne to herd cattle noticed the first small diamond and inaugurated what became a stampede of whites to peg claims. Within two days at the end of July and the beginning of August, nearly 1,000 were marked out. By October, 5,000 miners were working the 600 to 700 claims (the remainder having been abandoned), many of which had been divided into halves, quarters, eighths, and so on. By December, about 7,000 whites and blacks were digging and sifting vigorously as deeply as seventy feet, and possibly to ninety feet in a single case. Still, the diamonds continued to be found in abundance. "No field," wrote a contemporary, "has yielded diamonds in greater quantities. . . . Already thousands of gems have been unearthed; and . . . many individual diggers have found . . . hundreds of diamonds . . . [and] the richness of some claims is almost beyond belief."[3] No other dry digging had produced so well, not even Dutoitspan in its earlier glory.

"What a busy scene of life presented itself to you!" a contemporary wrote of New Rush. "There were hundreds of diggers, in every kind of garb. . . . There were faces of every conceivable cast and colour of the human race . . . the Kaffir, the Englishman, the Hottentot, and the Dutchman, the Fingo and the German, the Yankee and the Swede, the Frenchman and the Turk, the Norwegian and the natives, the Russian and the Greek—in fact a smattering of people from every nation on the face of the earth—digging, sifting, and sorting from morning till night, day after day, month after month, until they have obtained what they consider sufficient. . . ."[4]

New Rush and Old Rush were nearly three miles away from the Dutoit-span and Bultfontein mines, which were themselves separated from each other by less than a mile at the southern end of what later became the city of Kimberley. (New Rush was to be called the Kimberley mine—"the big hole"—and Old Rush the De Beers mine.) The richest yielding earths of New Rush were soon found to lie at the foot of the kopje, not on the hill itself. Because of the nature and configuration of volcanic pipes, there was a magic circle within which the real wealth of each mine was to be collected. Fortunately, the claims of the Rhodes brothers were from the very beginning within that charmed center of diamondiferous abundance.

What they could not then do was to buy up other claims or operate, at least in terms of the mining of diamonds, as individual entrepreneurs. The dry diggings until late 1871 were in a governmental no-man's land over which the authority of the Cape Colony, the Orange Free State, and the Transvaal Republic had not formally been imposed. Absent a recognized sovereignty, the diggers themselves had decided to limit individuals or groups to two claims each, but to permit the subdivision of claims and to specify that claims had to be worked each day. They had agreed to set aside portions of claims for haulage roads, but had wisely refrained from attempting to order the non-mining lives of the chaotic collection of fortune hunters, traders, hangers-on, and companions that crowded the alternatively mud-filled and dusty wagon paths of the raw tent-and-shanty settlements.

Although the allure of alluvial diamonds had swiftly attracted the attention of the rulers of the Transvaal, the Orange Free State, and the Cape Colony, and had even led to the establishment of a short-lived Diggers Republic at Klipdrift (later Barkly West), it was the promise of much greater and continued wealth from the dry diggings, and especially from the Colesberg kopje, that forced these internecine colonial rivalries to a conclusion and brought a defined form of administration, if not a settled government, to the area. From about the turn of the nineteenth century, its unpromising and often drought-ridden soil had been farmed and grazed by Griqua, an ethnically mixed people descended from much of the human material of early South Africa: Boer frontiersmen; remnants of Khoisan hunters, gatherers, and pastoralists; escaped slaves from the Cape; free blacks from the same domain; and Africans somehow detached from their own communities. Like the Afrikanders (later Nama) of Namibia, they were in a genetic sense the only true South Africans. Divided into captaincies, for decades they occupied a fragile ecological and mercantile niche on an expanding frontier between the missionary and farming settlements of the Cape Colony and the outposts of the trekking Boers of the Transvaal and the Orange Free State. Before diamonds were discovered, the Griqua had become Christians and had, along with the Dutch republics, been granted underlying title to the collection of farms on which diamonds were later found.

A family of Griqua, descended from Chief Waterboer, ruled this portion of Griqualand, its jurisdiction having been largely, but not fully, recognized

by the Dutch governments. Nevertheless, there were a number of border disputes, none of which seemed of critical consequence until avarice was unleashed. Control over the Vaal river diggings, boldly grabbed by the Transvaal and answered by the local proclamation of a republic, was further confused
by the unexpected find of diamonds twenty miles away at Dutoitspan. The
English-speaking diggers, many of the earliest of whom were Australian, asked
the Cape Colony, the strongest power in southern Africa, to provide a government. The British officials at the Cape sent a representative, too, initially
to assume control of the diggers' republic. The Free State then dispatched a
wise Swedish surveyor as its own representative with delegated powers. By the
time of the discovery of Colesberg kopje's wealth in mid-1871, the Free State
delegate was collecting a portion of the Vooruitzigt license fees and presiding
over elected diggers' committees at each of the four sections of the dry diamond fields. Together, they made and enforced the early regulations.[5]

Free State influence alarmed, just as the clear prospect of diamond wealth
excited, Britons at the Cape. Sir Richard Southey, the Cape's long-installed
colonial secretary, or second-ranking official, was a visceral imperialist. Sir
Henry Barkly, the governor and new high commissioner, also favored annexation. Otherwise, and here Barkly had the same kind of concern on which
Rhodes was subsequently to focus, the Free State would become wealthier
than the Cape and refuse to enter into a South African confederation. Prospects of ultimate unification, in other words, would be lost and the economy
of the Cape (and thus its ability to support itself) undermined.

After arbitration in late 1871 had defined the northern and western limits of Chief Waterboer's territory (as against the claims of the Transvaal), Barkly
went ahead and annexed what continued to be called Griqualand West, a
community then comprising about 20,000 whites, 30,000 blacks, and a few
thousand Griqua. Rhodes was among these 50,000 new settlers, but if he were
then aware of the flimsy nature of Britain's claims to the diamonds, the extent
to which Barkly—the man on the spot—had exceeded instructions from London, or the damage which this display of imperial power could inflict on a
Boer-British rapprochement in South Africa, no evidence survives. Nor do
Rhodes' comments about the nature of British rule, the refusal of the Cape
parliament in 1872 to vote funds for the annexation (because of its Dutch
constituency), and the subsequent irregular rule of the diamond fields by three
commissioners dispatched from the Cape by Barkly on dubious authority.

Cecil Rhodes arrived at the diamond fields in his nineteenth year. According to the later reminiscences of a close friend, "he was then an untidy
boy but always very interesting. I used to see a great deal of him and I always
found him very original."[6] Another contemporary later described Rhodes as
"long and loose-limbed, with blue eyes, ruddy complexion, and light-curly
hair." Herbert, by contrast, was tall, lean, and "hatchet-faced." Although "sparely
built his strength was considerable, and he was a splended boxer."[7]

Another digger remembered Cecil Rhodes as a teenager, "tall of stature,
over 6 feet with rather a well-knit frame and with none of that burliness of

figure which manifested itself in his maturer days. He had eyes of a most interesting nature, beaming with intelligence. . . . He had a full rounded face, a well-made chin with a stiff upper lip. He had a peculiarity of holding his left shoulder a little lower than his right, a feature that usually betokens a man who is kept close to his deck although I do not believe this was the case with Mr. Rhodes. In walking, the length of his stride was gigantic and would be the despair of any drill instructor. In planting his feet down he did so fairly and squarely and his footprints would not be difficult to trace by a spoor finder. He had light brown wavy hair, parted on the left side. In disposition he seemed to be extremely reserved, though in reality he was not so, but certainly one had to know him first in order to get over this impression. To me he never showed any signs of lung trouble. . . ."[8]

This untidy, original, bright-eyed youth, earlier described as "dreamy" but clearly more than the sum of all his disparate parts, naturally wanted his mother to appreciate exactly of what his working life (if not his inner life) consisted. A long, detailed description, written as 1872 opened, was also intended to please his favorite human being and the one to whom he was then primarily attached. As well, she was his main financial supporter. Unless other letters home failed to survive, he had—unusually—not written since July because he had been so "busy" with diamonds. It was his first report from New Rush.

"I should like you to have a peep at the Kopje from my tent door. . . . It is like an immense number of ant-heaps covered with black ants, as thick as can be, the latter represented by human beings; when you understand there are about 600 claims on the Kopje, and each claim is generally split into 4, and on each bit there are about 6 blacks and whites working, it gives a total of about ten thousand working every day on a piece of ground 18 yards by 220. The way the place is worked is rather interesting. Take your garden for instance, and peg the whole off into squares or claims of 31 by 31 feet and then the question is how to take all the earth out and sort and sieve it." This was the obvious central problem of mining the upper reaches of the funnel-like kimberlite pipe, and one to which Rhodes time and again turned his mind. At the moment of his arrival, however, the Orange Free State authorities had decreed a set of fourteen east-west and north-south parallel roadways over the top of the increasingly deep hole for the removal and haulage away from each claim of the diamondiferous earth and associated waste debris. "All through this Kopje," Rhodes explained, "roads have been left to carry the stuff off in carts [he enclosed a sketch] . . . that is, of every claim of 31 ft 7 ft 6 inches are not allowed to be worked, but is left for a road."

The process of finding diamonds was very similar to, if less physically demanding than, the method used by the alluvial prospectors. "To begin with, the ground is first picked [broken up with a pick], then the lumps smashed up, and you put the stuff through a very coarse wire sieving, this lets the fine stuff pass through and keeps all the stones which are thrown on one side; it is then hoisted out of the claim [by buckets on a primitive pulley mechanism], and either carried [by Africans] or carted [by mules] to the sorting table, where it is first put through fine wire sieving which sieves all the lime-dust away. What remains is put on the sorting-table, and then one sorts away with a small scrapper [scraper] spreading the stuff out on the table with one scoop and taken off with the next. The diamonds are found in all ways. The big ones generally in the hole by the caffre, or else in the sieving, and the small ones on the table."[9]

An American entrepreneur, prospector, inventor, and rifle salesman left a description which jibes closely with that furnished by Rhodes. Claims, he wrote, were worked by two white men and four Africans. "It takes four natives all their time to dig and sift out enough dirt to keep the two white men sorting. The negroes dig out the soil (there are no large stones like at the river), and laying it in a basin that they cut in the claim, pound it with a heavy sledge, to break up as many lumps as they can; they then shovel it into a coarse hand-screen, the wires of which are about one inch apart, and shake it through, throwing all the lumps aside to be carted away, then shoveling the balance into an oblong sieve, three feet long by two feet wide, the . . . holes being one-eighth of an inch in size. After shaking the fine stuff through this last sieve, all that remains in it is emptied on a common board table, where the sorters are; each sorter has a table-knife shaped instrument in his right hand, and from the pile he scrapes about a handful, spreads it out with one sweep, and tells in an instant [for they glitter brightly] if there are any diamonds or not; if there are none, he throws it off, and repeats this all day. It is not hard work, but rather monotonous."[10]

Chapman, a careful observer, was there at the same time and provides an even more detailed description of the process. "Diamond-finding at the New Rush," he wrote, ". . .is not much unlike fishing for trout . . . you may sit for hours or days hoping for a catch or a find, and to get a ghost of one; but you may all of a sudden light upon a good haul . . . and you are continually in expectation of 'a little piece of good.'

"The above-mentioned diggings are all being worked in an oval space, enclosed all round by a trap-dyke, the diameter of which is about 1,200 feet . . . while the side, or shorter workings, are about 800 feet in length; it is on these workings that the claims of thirty feet square are marked out. . . .

"Along the sides of [the] roadways there are crooked stumps of trees fixed as firmly into the ground as possible, and the end parts made to overhang the claims, so that the buckets or baskets of the sorting stuff are hoisted up and do not rub against the sides of the claims. . . .

"The first dig with the pick falls and penetrates a dullish, red kind of soil, the layer of which is from three inches to three feet in depth or thickness. This layer . . . is all put through a sieve . . . the stuff that has passed through the sieve is pounded up into fine half-sandy like stuff, and spread out in flat heaps to dry, and when quite dry, this also put on to the sorting-table, and very minutely examined in precisely the same way."[11]

Rhodes was sorting, categorizing, and then generalizing about diamonds and diamond mining on the basis of what he had assimilated during his first six or eight weeks at the dry diggings. "It will puzzle you," he told his mother and reflected what must have been his own, untutored thoughts, "why one does not find the diamonds all over the place. People always have the idea before they get here that diamonds are picked up in any part. You might search the country round for years and not find one. They are only found on these Kopjes, and along the river, where they very likely have been carried by water. There are reefs all round these diamond mines—inside which the diamonds are found. The reef is the usual soil of the country round red sand, just at the top, and then a black and white stony shale below."

Inside the reef, the crumbly soil at the upper reaches of the pipe contained the earliest diamonds discovered. Rhodes compared the composition of this friable, easily worked, reddish-yellow earth to Stilton cheese. But neither he nor his contemporaries then guessed that the yellow earth would give out, and that under the Stilton-like earth there would be solid blue rock, later to be broken only with heavy picks in the same way a spooner of Stilton would have to shift to a sturdy knife to cut a chunk of farmhouse cheddar.

"At the present moment," Rhodes wrote home, "the Kopje has a great circle of mounds all round the outside, consisting of the stuff that has been taken out and sorted through. Inside the roads are the only grounds that remain of the original level. On each side of every road there is now a continuous chasm from top to bottom of the Kopje, varying in depth from 30 to 60 feet. They have been able to find no bottom yet, and keep on finding steadily even at 70 feet." To the astonishment of those who had dug the nearby rivers for diamonds or prospected, with even fair success, elsewhere in the world, the diamondiferous earths of the Colesberg kopje ran deep. New Rush was no shallow pit like every other diamond digging that had ever been found. Even Dutoitspan and Bultfontein had stopped yielding rich returns; yet both Old Rush and New Rush were reaching unheard of depths by the time that Rhodes took the time to tell his mother of his amazing good fortune.

Colesberg kopje was the ultimate prize, an average of £50,000 worth of diamonds having been recovered each week since August. "You will understand how enormously rich it is," Rhodes explained, "when I say that a good claim would certainly average a diamond to every load of stuff that was sorted—a load being about 50 buckets. Some day," he said with no particular prescience, "I expect to see the Kopje one big basin where once before there was a large hill."

There were obvious problems with an arrangement where 10,000 miners and their employees and 600 or so mules and carts jostled for space along a limited set of narrow roadways cluttered with hoisting rigs and piles of earth and buckets. Rhodes explained: "There are constantly mules, carts, and all going head over heals [sic] into the mines below as there are no rails or anything on either side of the roads, nothing but one great broad chasm below. Here and there where the roads have fallen in, bridges have been put, and they are now the safest parts of the Kopje. The question now of course is, how are the roads to be worked[?] Every claim holder has an interest in them, as a portion of every man's claim is in the road, and one has no idea of leaving ground every load of which stands fair chance of holding a diamond."

How to foster cooperation between claim holders and the amalgamation of the claims were questions of common concern in the New Rush area. Since he described the problem to his mother, Rhodes doubtless thought about solutions, but at this early stage and, indeed, for many years, he advanced none and was in no financial position to buy multiple claims (nor was it then legal to hold more than two). Interrupting his own exploitation of diamonds for constructive activities on a broad scale was also still in the distance.

After a mere six or eight weeks, Rhodes was regularly finding the equivalent of thirty carats a week. His average gross return was £100 per week, the best profits coming from his own quarter-claim, purchased presumably with the remainder of the capital supplied to him in 1870 by his mother and his aunt. Another quarter, owned by Herbert C. Beecher and worked by the Rhodes brothers, also yielded well. One of Herbert Rhodes' two full claims (it helped to have been present for the original "rush") was also rich. Together the Rhodes brothers also had control of Chadwick's half-claim.

Cecil Rhodes gave his mother a glorious, wholly positive report of his new fortune. True, one long letter indicated that not all diamonds were valuable, and that yellow, glassy stones were dangerous to keep, "having a nasty habit of suddenly splitting all over."[12] He admitted to no creature hardships. Yet water for drinking and cooking, and for washing diamonds, was difficult to obtain, much of it then being hauled fifty miles from the Vaal River. At New Rush, a bucket of water cost from nine pence to a shilling. In summer, and throughout the many dry months of the year, because of the pitiless dust, thirst was a torture. In October 1872, a British digger started working a part claim at New Rush. "There was a strong wind blowing; as usual the whole camp was enveloped in clouds of stifling, penetrating white and red dust; the heat was excessive, and it was very thirsty work. The enormous profits made by hotels and canteens, and the increase in drunkenness, are not to be wondered at. . . ."[13]

Liquor took the place of water, and so-called canteens were erected on the perimeter of the mines. Filled with customers, they added to the noise and turmoil that afflicted the diggings, day and night. Donkeys brayed, mules snorted, cattle lowed, dogs snarled, and chickens clucked. The shouting of the cart-drivers competed, as did the noise of the mines themselves. There was camp fever and dysentery, a vast armada of flies, and a celebrated infestation of fleas. The required physical labor was hard, for whites as well as for Africans, and there was constant danger from crumbling roadways, falling claim walls, and fire in the tented city. Supplies were hauled from Cape Town or Port Elizabeth at vast expense, only hard spirits being readily available. For the men, there were few women. Life for the white as well as the black diggers was hardly idyllic, and for this and a number of obvious reasons, their mobility in the early years was high.

In addition to the many discomforts, the level of exertion was more than that usually encountered by most whites in South Africa. "Men," wrote a contemporary publication, "who have been habituated all their lives to sedentary occupation coming to the Fields and digging in the heat of the day in midsummer naturally experience the effects of such exposure. . . . They have a large share of privations and discomforts, and these naturally produce disease and sometimes death." It is no wonder that the local press was crowded with advertisements for doctors, druggists, and other healers. But the death rate compared favorably with Cape Town, and Rhodes never seemed to worry about falling prey to epidemic disease.

Rhodes ignored the discomfort because the returns were so generous and the future so full of promise. Or he may simply have wanted to spare his mother concern. For either reason, in none of his letters from Kimberley did he ever allude to the presumed privations of mining camp life. John Xavier Merriman, older, and more cultured, and perhaps also more sensitive and refined, told John Blades Currey, the future second-in-command of Griqualand West, that the diamond fields were "an awful place." He called them "a sort of canvas London, for no one seems to know their next-door neighbors." Since women were scarce, "a shipment of these would command extreme rates, in fact it is the most virtuous place in the world. The things which pay best are carts, which run from the New Rush to Dutoitspan every minute. . . . As for the [new] government, that is of course in evil repute. . . .

"Nothing is more common than to see the canteens adorned with a row of dead-drunk corpses at ten a.m. Policemen there are none, and they [the drinkers] never appear in the streets unless three parts gone. . . ."[14]

Shortly after Cecil arrived from Natal to supervise their family venture, by the end of November 1871, Herbert left for home via the Umkomaas valley. He planted no more cotton, and may merely have collected their belongings and dismissed the remaining laborers. Cecil later continued to pay rent to the Colonisation Society, but the prospect of cotton was a trifle compared to diamonds. With Herbert gone, Cecil once again could demonstrate control and maturity. His long letter to his mother is boyish, but confident and controlled. If he felt alone or out of place, and worried about his brother's desertion, there is no hint. Indeed, whatever Cecil's dreams may have been and would be, his few letters, the accounts of contemporaries, and his actions all delineate a young person seized by the happy prospect of unimagined wealth moving confidently into young adulthood, propelled by a growing awareness of his own capacities. Not that he thought in these early months of millions; tens of thousands were within his reach, and with such sums his own university and professional years, and a better life for his family, doubtless seemed at last possible. If an abiding fantasy of adolescence is to generate by real accomplishment the parental admiration and appreciation that every child needs, being the only son to do so would have had a magical appeal. The senior brothers were flashier but unsteady. Cecil, the fourth son to have lived to maturity, had, in addition to ordinary incentives to achieve, those which might have originated within and been engendered by his special place in the family constellation.

"I daresay you think I am keen about money?" Rhodes asked Norman Garstin in 1872 or 1873. "I assure you I wouldn't greatly care if I lost all I have to-morrow, it's the game I like."[15] Perhaps. But Rhodes played the game, if that is what he considered it to be, with a seriousness of purpose that echoed his attitude to childhood competition. Frank and Herbert, his elder brothers, one day found Cecil "down in the claim, measuring his ground with his lawyer and in a tremendous rage with another man in the next claim to him, who has encroached on his ground. . . . I know the Father will be horrified at the idea of Cecil going to law."[16]

The other contemporary accounts that survive also support the conclusion that Cecil was a meticulous, purposeful, young entrepreneur who was compulsive about details. Ambitious financially despite his protestations to Garstin, he was careful, possibly even (as he later complained) overcautious. Certainly, amid the tough bilious crowd of roustabouts, chancers, gamblers, burly prospectors, and unscrupulous diamond buyers, Rhodes stood out. "Fair, blue-eyed, and with somewhat aquiline features, wearing flannels of the school playing field, somewhat shrunken with strenuous rather than effectual washings, that still left the colour of the red veldt dust. . . ," he cut a remarkable, even unworldly, figure that belied his essential resourcefulness.[17]

Merriman, twelve years older than Cecil and already a promising, principled politician in Cape Town, shared a tent with Rhodes in early 1872 and praised his business abilities "to the skies." Unfortunately, Merriman may or may not have been a good judge. A patrician figure, he loathed the rough camp life of the diamond fields, was either too impatient or too fastidious to focus on the tedious aspects of making money, and, despite many interesting investments in the same mines to which Rhodes devoted his formative years, never made a fortune. Yet Merriman may also have appreciated those qualities in Cecil which he himself lacked. Certainly, there is no question but that Rhodes' maturity was impressive to Merriman, as well as to the other young men of the period. Cecil's brother Frank resented the fact that everyone at New Rush thought Cecil the senior of the two. Whatever the imperfection of his dress—the fresh and neat Merriman also commented on Rhodes' sloppiness—Rhodes radiated a sense of competence which compelled the young hopefuls of tent city to pay him respect and to welcome (and not merely tolerate) his moody, alternately abstracted and shrilly talkative, repetitive, staccato-style interjections.[18] These two oddly coupled strains—a boyish unworldliness and a seriousness which was beyond his years—betrayed much about his character and persisted throughout his life. Years later, as a world figure and personification of the British empire, he would say, "I am a boy! Of course I shall never grow old."

Whatever Rhodes' innate commercial or financial acumen, or however much his economic success flowed from inborn or developed qualities of dogged persistence, a prime gift impossible to overestimate was the skill with which he chose and motivated his business partners. He picked well, as indeed he had a flair for judging people in general. Doubtless a set of distinct individuals can be credited with major contributions to each of Rhodes' victories, as well as to his one signal failure. Several were greater intellects, sharper financiers, and shrewder entrepreneurs. Yet to ask how much they were responsible for his success or he for theirs is to misunderstand the nature of collaboration. Every partnership was symbiotic. Rhodes was full of his own ideas and free with the ideas of others. Although he could expound his own thoughts enthusiastically and at great length, he was also a careful listener, adept at drawing others out. Either manipulatively or by the power of his vision and the impress of his entire personality—his charisma and his charm—Rhodes appealed to and forged fruitful bonds with others of talent. His gifts advantaged them as well as himself and, at the very least, and however base or noble his motives, transformed southern Africa and the history of late nineteenth-century imperialism.

Among the fortune hunters at the diamond fields in the early 1870s, the acumen of Charles Dunell Rudd was especially respected. Certainly, Rudd had experience, both in the affairs of South Africa and in diamonds, and claimed the kind of origins and background with which Rhodes preferred to associate. Born in Norfolk nearly nine years before Rhodes, Rudd was the third son and fourth child of a wealthy shipbuilder who had prospered in his own grandfather's industry and then expanded it. Rudd went to Harrow, where he achieved a number of athletic distinctions, failed—despite prominent coaching—to gain a scholarship to Balliol College, Oxford, and instead went up to Trinity College, Cambridge. There, in 1862–1865, he was a champion rackets player and a crack distance runner. But, according to his own unsubstantiated account, overtraining for the mile run destroyed his health and, without ever taking a degree, he sought to recuperate by traveling to South Africa.[19]

As it did for so many others, South Africa easily provided the necessary cure. After six months in Cape Town and Port Elizabeth, Rudd spent another six months hunting game in northern Zululand with John Dunn, a white trader, gun runner, and Zulu chief, and Edouard Mohr, a German entomologist. Surviving a severe attack of malaria in the region between the Delagoa and St. Lucia bays, Rudd was carried by Zulu porters to what has become Maputo, and placed on a ship bound for Mauritius. He went on to Sri Lanka (then Ceylon), suffered again from malaria, returned to Natal, and made his way overland through the Orange Free State and the Transvaal to Cape Town and home in 1867. Later that year, after learning of the discovery of diamonds near the Orange River, Rudd, backed by his brother Thomas, a successful merchant in London, returned to Cape Town, began a trading business, married, and, after the Vaal River diggings were rushed in 1870, went to Pniel and Klipdrift to prospect for diamonds and purchase the finds of others.

For about a year, success eluded him. Lacking capital, he "lived under atrocious conditions, often subsisting on mealie meal and game flesh for weeks at a stretch." He lived in a ragged tent and over and over staggered 300 yards from his claim to wash and sieve his heavy loads of gravel with the waters of the river. Then described as tall, erect, slender, "having fine dark eyes, a wispy mustache, and thick fair hair, with a well-trimmed black beard," and characteristically dressed in moleskin trousers, flannel shirt, and an untidy hat, Rudd was among the many unlucky ones.[20] He found few diamonds and also succumbed to typhoid. He had to go back to Cape Town to recover both his health and his financial stability. With new backing, he tried his hand with somewhat better results first along the Vaal River and then, after the dry land discoveries of 1871, at Old and New Rush. As an importer of supplies for the diggers, as a seller of insurance, and as a diamond buyer, Rudd began to recoup his earlier losses as more and more stones were found in the two De Beers mines. However, the theft in 1872 of an important parcel of diamonds for which he was responsible proved a major setback. The repayment of creditors took several years.

It was about this time, in late 1871 or early 1872, that Rudd and Rhodes first met. Considering the critical impact of each on the careers and destinies of the other, and the presumably decisive influence of Rudd on the younger Rhodes during the early years when Rhodes was still a seeker of fortune and a stripling among the local men of commerce, it is unfortunate that Rudd's own account of their meeting was vague and, in some particulars, wildly inaccurate. Rhodes himself never shed any direct light on the beginnings of their friendship. Earlier biographers and other writers say that the two were accidentally thrown together because their claims were nearby or adjacent. Rudd, buying into the New Rush mine after Rhodes, may have suddenly found himself next to an introspective youth of some appeal. Equally, Rhodes may have sought out the older Rudd even if their claims were not necessarily contiguous. Or William Alderson, an Australian, may be credited with the suggestion that Rudd and Rhodes (and Alderson) should work together. One chronologically doubtful suggestion is that Rudd met Rhodes in the Umkomaas valley in early 1871 while Rudd was trying his hand at the merchant business in Pietermaritzburg. At any rate, by February or March 1872, Rhodes had joined his energy and vision to Rudd's hard-won, cautious practicality, and to his mercantile connections in Cape Town and London.

Both would have reduced their working costs and supervisory time by digging claims, hauling soil, and sorting and selling in common. Both would have thus been able to expand their available options, and to concentrate on other commercial ventures while continuing to gamble on diamonds. (One of the advertisements in an early Kimberley directory read: "C.D. Rudd, Wholesale Wine, Spirits, and Cigar Merchant . . . Agent for the Phoenix, North British and Mercantile Fire Insurance Companies."[21]) Rhodes and Rudd were not the first at New Rush to become partners and rationalize their employment of capital, but theirs was one of the few early joint ventures to endure and later develop into a significant enterprise.

Without Rhodes, Rudd would have been unable to expand his rope and machinery business (which merged with a rival and eventually became the largest in South Africa), or to tend his insurance agency. Without Rudd, Rhodes would have been unable to leave the mines to spend terms at Oxford, and eventually to serve in parliament. Together they exerted a synergistic force greater than the mere sum of their efforts. Rhodes had ideas, enthusiasm, drive, and persistence. Rudd was steady and sure, a reliable executor of their money-making schemes and, much later, a cautious steward of their growing wealth. Rhodes is often presumed to be the architect of their grand design, but the foundation stones may well have been put into place by Rudd.

It was the recognition of another's talents, and his own innate ability to nurture, sustain, and grow with such colleagues that was one of Rhodes' special gifts. Whether or not Rhodes was "tutored" by Rudd and others, or the other way round, is now impossible to ascertain. However, even those of his associates who differed considerably from him in temperament and talent gave to and received from him in mutual enrichment.[22]

That Rhodes was a versatile and persistent collaborator is clear and hardly surprising in view of his place in the family constellation. Rhodes relied first on Rudd's judgment. His mistakes helped Rhodes to know what to avoid, and his caution freed Rhodes to be more daring. Later Rhodes used the geological and engineering expertise of Francis Oats. Alfred Beit brought financial acumen, steady thinking, and access to German and English financiers. The mining experience of Gardner Williams and later John Hays Hammond played a part. Rhodes' genius lay not only in choosing associates of talent; it lay as well in his capacity to sustain these relationships over many years through good times and bad. His genius rested further on a capacity to inspire loyalty by being loyal, and by accepting the failings of others. The sheer power of his vision and the clarity with which he articulated it gave associates the sense that they were participating in great events with a man of growing and, eventually, of great stature.

Diamond digging and careful sorting were the mainstays of their mutual endeavor. Rudd once told McDonald of the "very hard manual work he and Rhodes had to undertake. . . ." When labor was scarce, they "carried the 'pay dirt' in bags, boxes or buckets to the sorting tables," Rhodes one day breaking the finger that was forever after a source of embarrassment.[23] But sizable fortunes could not have been made from a mere mining partnership or a handful of claims. After mid-1872, as local laws gradually changed, and prices slumped, Rhodes and Rudd together bought whatever they could, even sections of claims, particularly in Baxter's Gully, a part of Old Rush. Rudd later said that Rhodes constantly opined that the time would come when the "small man" would be compelled to quit the diamond game.[24] The mines could not be worked profitably forever without major concessions to efficiency, if for no other reason than the varying depths to which individuals were bound to work the over 400 claims in each mine. Some claims were dug deeper faster, others were suspended, and the roadways therefore traversed a small-scale alpine universe.

Obvious to Rudd and Rhodes, and to others, was the utility of expanding the claims that could be worked by each partnership. This obvious conclusion became more central to their thinking after diamond prices collapsed in 1874 (coinciding with the world depression in agricultural prices) and water flooded the deeper parts of the main mines. After 1874, when each owner could legally control as many as ten claims, Rudd and Rhodes invested their proceeds in yet more of Baxter's Gully. They continued to buy claims through 1880, when they formed De Beers Mining Ltd., and then on a grander scale to 1887, when they gained effective control of the entire mine. Why Rhodes as early as 1872 switched his focus from the rich loams of New Rush to the lower yielding Old Rush has never been clear. Does an explanation lie in the fact that claims at Old Rush were less expensive, or did Rhodes have an intuitive understanding of the value of the deeper ground, or pipe? Old Rush was less expensive to work, and less prone to reef falls. It also produced larger stones than New Rush. Or was Rhodes impressed with Old Rush's reputation as a more aristocratic camp than New Rush? "Many gentlemen blessed with wives and families have encamped here, and made themselves comparatively comfortable," a contemporary wrote, "and the English element predominates pleasingly over the Dutch or Boer."[25]

What is more obvious is that neither Rudd nor Rhodes was sufficiently liquid financially throughout the 1870s to take advantage of every opportunity. In 1876, they could have gained sole proprietorship of De Beers' mine for a mere £6,000, instead of the £1,600,000 that it cost in 1887. They had sunk their capital into the diamond-bearing ground, and banks would lend no more. They had also put their funds into several other kinds of money-making, but somewhat speculative, ventures that diverted their energies from diamonds and provided them merely with short-term profits.

Rudd remembered ordering an ice-making machine from Britain. Eventually, it was hauled to the diamond fields by mule wagon, but this investment paid well only during the hot months of the next summer, probably 1873–74. The machine churned out ice which Rhodes and Rudd sold to the miners so that liquid refreshments could be kept cold. It was not used, as far as can be ascertained, to chill food or accommodations, but it was essential to the making of ice cream.

Francis Robert (Matabele) Thompson, seven years younger than Rudd and a South African by birth, thought that the first attempt at money-making by Rhodes and Rudd involved selling ice cream. "You are to imagine the great Cecil Rhodes standing behind a white cotton blanket, slung across a tent, turning a handle of a bucket ice-cream machine, and passing the finished article to Rudd to sell from a packing-case at one of the corners of the Diamond Market. The ice-cream was retailed at sixpence a wine-glass full, with an extra sixpence for a slab of cake."[26]

Whether or not ice-making and ice-cream making were part of the same or separate operations, Rudd remembered selling the imported machine at the end of the first successful summer season for £1,500. It was his first substantial return, and he (and Rhodes) promptly purchased more of Baxter's

Gully. Did Rudd remember incorrectly, or did Rhodes and Rudd buy another machine and continue to manufacture ice in the hot months? Not giving up a profitable venture would have been more in Rhodes' character. There is a distinct reference to an ice-making machine in a letter that Rhodes wrote to Rudd in 1876.[27] Or did Rudd and all previous authorities date the coming of the ice-making business to 1871 or 1872 when the years 1875 or 1876 might be more accurate?

In 1873, Rhodes put some of his own earnings into railway shares in Durban. He asked Sutherland, whom he could not have seen for at least two years, to buy them for him since interest rates were much higher in South Africa than in Britain. He was specific, too, wanting shares in the railway that ran about two miles from the town to Durban Point, not those of the new railways that were opening up the interior of Natal. But less than £200 was involved—or a dozen shares at slightly less than £15 each. The care with which Rhodes arranged this particular investment, and his several rather detailed letters about it, was characteristic. Even so, it was not long before Rhodes asked Sutherland to sell the same shares: "I have a bill to meet. . . ." If there were a balance, he asked—in a typical burst of quiet charity—that it go to a man with consumption and without friends whom Rhodes had befriended aboard ship in early 1874, when he himself was on his way back to Africa from Oxford.[28]

When Rhodes returned from his first term at Oxford (see the next chapter) at the beginning of 1874, miners and traders were beginning to leave the fields in the wake of falling diamond prices and a series of natural calamities. The Vienna Bourse had collapsed in 1873, Egypt was bankrupt, and Russia and Turkey made financiers nervous by going to war. In Kimberley, roadways and claims were collapsing, and unusually heavy rains in February had inundated the mines. In late May, Rhodes told Sutherland that New Rush was "full of water no money coming in from ground all going out." The previous year's drought had already made transport by ox-cart from the railhead, and thus goods from the Cape and Port Elizabeth, much more expensive than before. Combined, these disasters severely reduced returns from diamonds. Life on the fields appeared precarious. By the end of the year, fewer than 8,000 whites and 10,000 blacks remained.[29]

The board that governed the mine property decided to pump out De Beers and asked for bids. Rhodes, Rudd, and Alderson, an engineer, possibly with advice from Oats, secured this contract, and one for the Dutoitspan mine.[30] They were clearing the water as late as 1877, demonstrating Rhodes' ability to seize any and all opportunities to profit from changing circumstances. The saga of the pumping tenders also illustrates two facets of Rhodes' developing character: first, even tied to Rudd, he employed a variety of sharp practices, including bidding without owning machinery; second, despite the shoddy nature of the bids, and, in one case, an allegation of sabotage and bribery which was aired in a court of inquiry and vigorously denied, Rhodes often—but not invariably—delivered what he had promised. By one daring, imaginative—

conceivably even fraudulent—expedient after another, he kept his fortunes buoyant.

There was the celebrated occasion in 1874, when he won the pumping contract and then had to find a suitable engine. Not one could be found in Kimberley, many having failed to survive the rigors of the overland journey from Cape Town. But Rhodes knew that an Afrikaans-speaking farmer was pumping water intermittently in Victoria West, about eight days away from Kimberley by cart. Rhodes trekked there and tried, with at first but little success, to buy the 7500-pound engine. Finally Rhodes prevailed, but only after camping for days on the farmer's doorstep, wearing him down with persistence, cajoling him with charm, "bluffing" him, and ultimately agreeing to pay the enormous sum of £1,000. "Every man," Rhodes claimed to have learned, "had his price."[31]

Another time, Rhodes persuaded Rudd to satisfy an existing contract rather than risk new bids. "Anything in my opinion is better than fresh tenders." He explained to Rudd that their rival would win a further competition. It was up to them to hold off the mine owners for three weeks until the pump and sufficient piping arrived (which would happen before rain fell and the mine flooded again). Otherwise, their opponent would drive them out of the business entirely. "For in fact he knows all your cards and has his own concealed and taking his position when driven in a corner it would pay him to sell for less than his machinery cost." "These are my sentiments," Rhodes told Rudd. "You may take them for what they are worth."[32]

On an occasion possibly connected with this one, his pumps had been slow in arriving from the coast. The members of the De Beers Mining Board were anxious, perturbed, and understandably impatient. A friend who went to the meeting with Rhodes reported that he had "never forgotten the way in which he [Rhodes], still quite a youth, handled that body of angry men and gained his point, an extension of time."[33] Any investigation of Rhodes' career invariably celebrates similar incidents in which Rhodes successfully delayed for advantage, and used his powers of persuasion effectively. On this occasion, doubtless it was his dogged refusal to be rebuffed and his tenacious sense of conviction, more than his rational arguments, which wore down the aggrieved and disarmed the antagonistic.

The pumping team of Rhodes, Rudd, and Alderson was initially compelled to use inadequate, asthmatic machinery to raise water out of the mines. From the Cape they purchased old agricultural engines and centrifugal pumps. But on the immense plain of the dry diggings, there were few trees and no coal. Rhodes himself scoured the countryside early every dawn, meeting the Boer and Thlaping wood merchants as they lumbered toward town in order to secure his own supplies before others. When Alderson was away, Rhodes and Rudd took turns attending the steam engines that drove the pumps deep down in the pits until one evening when Rhodes, in a fit of absence of mind, neglected to supply the boiler with water, causing an explosion that neither he nor his friends ever forgot.

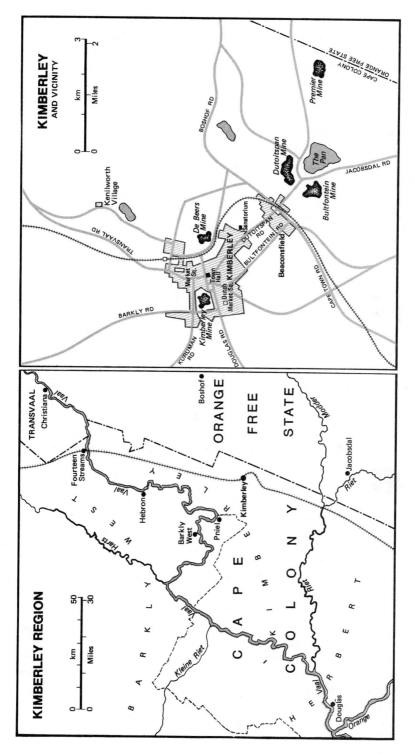

KIMBERLEY AND VICINITY

Premier Mine

Dutoitspan Mine

The Pan

Bultfontein Mine

De Beers Mine

Sanatorium

Kenilworth Village

KIMBERLEY

Market Sq.

Town Hall

Dutch Market Sq.

Kimberley Mine

Beaconsfield

BOSHOF RD

JACOBSDAL RD

TRANSVAAL RD

DUTOITSPAN RD

BULTFONTEIN RD

CAPE TOWN RD

KURUMAN RD

DOUGLAS RD

BARKLY RD

CAPE COLONY

ORANGE FREE STATE

km
Miles

KIMBERLEY REGION

TRANSVAAL

Christiana

Vaal

Fourteen Streams

Hebron

Barkly West

Pniel

Kimberley

Boshof

ORANGE FREE STATE

Jacobsdal

Riet

Vaal

Harts

BARKLY WEST

KIMBERLEY

CAPE COLONY

HERBERT

Kleine Riet

Vaal

Riet

Douglas

Orange

Modder

km
Miles

71

These and other difficulties prevented Rhodes' team from clearing the De Beers mine completely of water. Rhodes blamed the weakness of his pumps. But he managed to remove all of the water from Dutoitspan by mid-winter, 1875. Two further contracts with both mines followed, the first worth £400 a month, and the second £500. As he told his brother, the new contracts put his "money matters . . . all right again."

Earlier, although he was "financially worth a good deal of money," he had been "very hard up for the ready." Indeed, he had been obliged to draw on his father's account. "I am ashamed myself that I drew," he wrote, "but I was very hard pushed." Because his father had always promised him funds for a university education, Rhodes had not expected his father to mind. Thanks to the pumping arrangements, and, presumably, continued earnings from diamonds, the crisis had passed and Rhodes anticipated "being worth a considerable sum of money" by the end of 1876. "Please thank our Father for his kindness and tell him I shall have no need to bother him again."[34]

The Rhodes-Rudd partnership was still pumping water and making ice through 1876 and possibly 1877, when Rhodes was at Oxford. Rhodes was also adapting existing engines to the particular requirements of the deep mines during his first weeks in England. With newly found technical knowledge, he negotiated with mechanical suppliers and demanded special attachments to ease their efforts in Kimberley. He copied a rival by ordering a particular model of a ten-horsepower engine capable of continuous operation. He requested a winding drum with a custom-made clutch gear, and, in detail, specified the kinds of pumps which would work in places like Baxter's Gully. "The engine," he wrote to one supplier, "should be constructed so as to be able to travel over 600 miles of very bad roads on its own wheels with movable fire box and capable of burning wood, refuse and inferior fuel, a supply of any parts liable to breakage such as gauge glasses necessary."[35]

The specifications are less important in understanding Rhodes' life than the manner in which Rhodes lavished attention on the intricacies of every aspect of his pursuits, at this stage, later, and always. He trusted Rudd, for example, but left little to chance. Because of these traits, because he seized opportunities so well, because of luck, or because he could muster resources of personality as well as intellect, Rhodes was sufficiently well off in the mid-1870s to be able to afford to go up to Oxford (and leave Rudd in charge of their enterprise), and to invest heavily in property in England. From his own scattered references to his expenditures at Oxford, and the costs of sea passages to and from Africa, Rhodes' style of life required at least £10,000 a year, and he was probably earning more than that sum from diamonds, pumps (netting £3,528 a year in 1878), and ice. The basis of a fortune had been laid. At twenty-three, he had demonstrated the Midas touch. But doing so may not have been enough for Rhodes' ambition. The achievement of early riches joined with some powerful individual capacity and spurred him toward new goals and to the kinds of searching self-examinations that are characteristic of the late adolescence and early adulthood of persons destined to live out a higher and accelerating trajectory than their fellows.

"I cannot help feeling I was made for better things," Cecil wrote to Frank in a rare and revealingly introspective mood in 1875. "Really what is life worth at my present mode of existence with no object, no aim?" He had a proven ability to make money, yet from his letters of this period (but from almost no other evidence), Rhodes' ambitions and strivings were propelling him toward challenges more complex than he had hitherto experienced. They went far beyond what would have been expected of the ordinary youthful opportunist and dreamer turned successful entrepreneur.

The eulogistic biographers follow John Verschoyle, the first of their kind, in raising Rhodes' success at money to a loftier plane. "Money-getting tends to become mere money-grubbing," Verschoyle wrote for the Victorians, "and is the dry rot of anything great and magnanimous in a man. But Cecil Rhodes was from the first an exception. He never cared for money itself. . . . His wants remained perfectly simple. . . . At first he cared for money-making because he enjoyed the excitement of success, as a marksman enjoys bringing down a difficult shot, or a fox-hunter enjoys taking a stiff fence."

Although phrased as an elegant rationalization, Verschoyle's description of Rhodes' attitude depicts a familiar sequence of adolescent psychological development. Real success is the antidote to adolescent self-doubt and fears of relinquishing emotional dependence on parents. It is that success mixed with some measure of failure which hones realistic expectations and develops the confidence on which further maturation can be based. The final integration of character takes place under the organizing power of unresolved hurts from earlier childhood. As shall emerge, Rhodes' "one dominant idea," expressed at the age of twenty-four in his "Confession of Faith," bristled with implications of old injuries. Thus, as Verschoyle supposes, "gradually his financial schemes all centered round and were undertaken to advance his one dominant idea," but not the simple one of imperialism.

There is another kernel of truth in this advertisement which was later embellished upon by the fullest of the subsequent biographers—by Michell, by Williams, and by Lockhart and Woodhouse. It concerns Rhodes' ostentatious lack of ostentation and, even more relevant, his pleasure in the chase. Doubtless for Rhodes, the making of money was more exciting than the spending of it. It provided proof of personal value, stature in the sight of others, and the coin of self-esteem. But there is no hard support at this early stage for the belief that Rhodes focused on the amassing of funds in order to achieve a distant goal. Certainly he fantasized, but in 1875, aged twenty-two, Rhodes was far less worldly and less confident than he was to become. Unexpectedly worth tens of thousands of pounds sterling, he still intended to return to Britain in the next year to "strain every nerve to become a barrister."

Being a barrister would admit him into better circles and give him a broader stage on which to test his abilities. At least those were among the motives which drove Rhodes at this point in his life. Thus, the gaining of wealth was not a complete end in itself, albeit it had enabled him to qualify for a profession which might please his father (despite his father's negative opinion of "the law"), and exalt the memory of his mother.[36]

Even if Rhodes were never to become a barrister, and were merely to fulfill his earlier ambition to obtain a degree at Oxford, he had been brooding more and more deeply and bitterly about his life and his prospects. Not only had a friend recently died "by inches" but Rhodes had been severely affected by the process and the loss. "Poor Thompson died about a month ago," he wrote. "His last week I went over and stopped with him and helped Carr to sit up with him. . . . They told him one week before he had no chance, so he had a week's dying, which is not a pleasant thing, either for lookers-on or sufferer. He was religious, but awfully plucky, and made his jokes to the very last. One's belief in anything to come gets very weak out here when as you know every mortal is an atheist, or next door to it."[37]

This death, and Rhodes' proximity to it, only reinforced his own early premonitions of mortality. These fears were to grow markedly in later years. Understandably blaming his shortness of breath and chest pains on his lungs rather than on his heart, he felt that they were ". . .to be a sort of skeleton in the cupboard ever ready to pounce down and clear me off. . . ."

Rhodes had been compelled to confront his essential vulnerability in 1872, when he was living alone and supervising both his own and his brother's claims. Early in that year, he was prostrated by a "heart attack," and nursed back to health by Merriman, John Blades Currey, the portly local colonial secretary (Southey's first assistant), and Mary, Currey's wife. At a public banquet years later, Rhodes said that the Curreys were "mother and father to me when I was a sickly and penniless lad without a home and never a thought of having money."[38]

The nature of the attack is not known. Described secondhand as mild, and as a result of "over work," it certainly shook Rhodes severely. After recovering, the nineteen-year-old drew up his first will, leaving all of his worldly goods not to his brothers or to his father, nor to the Curreys, but to the British Secretary of State for the Colonies—to be used for the extension of the empire. This was the genesis of Rhodes' later "Confession of Faith," the forerunner of his many subsequent and increasingly elaborate wills, and the nucleus of the final manifestation of purpose which became, through his legacy, the Rhodes Scholarship program. In its embryonic form, the first will translated Rhodes' fantasies into a kind of reality, but without more than a vague and pious, bald affirmation of patriotism that any of the colonial secretaries of the 1870s might have found both perplexing and tiresome. Yet, the longer Rhodes lived, the more he returned to this theme in ever increasingly elaborate forms.

Although none of his contemporaries viewed him as a snobbish Little Englander and he was at ease with Afrikaners, even the very young Rhodes wanted somehow to help strengthen the empire—to provide its presumed benefits to more and more of the world's benighted regions and peoples. Note that Rhodes never proposed that his inheritance be employed to improve the quality of the empire's trusteeship. Nor did he leave his estate to Queen Victoria, as did so many filiopietists of the era. His romance, as hardheaded as it may have appeared, was primarily with a boyhood dream—which never left him—that right-thinking, English-speaking young men, separated from one another by the ineptness of politicians, should unite in the common endeavor of spreading a new Roman civic spirit (he had read and digested Gibbon) to recivilize the earth. In this first will, however protean, there is a glimmer of the moral imperative (later much derided and thoroughly suspect) which stimulated the reflective side of Rhodes. This was the Rhodes that in 1872, in 1874, in 1875, in 1877, and continuously thereafter was preoccupied with destination (and perhaps with predestination)—what his contribution to mankind was to be and by what accomplishments (not by what grace) he would be remembered.[39]

Herbert Rhodes returned to the diamond fields with Frank in May 1872. After a few weeks, driven as much by his own curiosity about the finding of gold in the northern Transvaal as by anxiety over Cecil's health, Herbert decided a journey northward was in order. Leaving Rudd and Frank in charge of their claims, and borrowing a wagon from young William Scully, Herbert took the still shaky Cecil on what proved to be a leisurely trek through the other South Africa. With Cecil riding ahead of the wagon, they followed the missionary road from Vryburg to Mafeking, and then turned northeastward, probably passing through Rustenburg and Pretoria (of which there is no mention), and then on to Marabastad, south of the modern Pietersburg and toward the farthest reaches of the Afrikaner Republic. There the promise of gold in quartz reefs was fading, and most of the miners of Marabastad had begun to move on to Lydenburg, to the southeast, where prospectors had unearthed a new—but later equally chimerical—zone of promising quartz. The Rhodes brothers were only a year or so early; alluvial gold was discovered beyond Lydenburg toward the Portuguese border in 1874. On the Blyde River, near Pilgrim's Rest, rich gold was panned by English-speaking prospectors for a brief few years in the 1870s.

The Rhodes brothers turned southward again at Marabastad, making their slow way back via Middleburg to the diamond fields. Michell says that they spent seven or eight months on the road whereas Williams and McDonald state that the return occupied only a few months. Scully, possibly the most reliable witness, since his wagon was used, says that the trip took four months.[40] There is no direct word about the peregrination from any of the Rhodes brothers themselves, but it is inherently unlikely that Cecil would have wanted to have been absent from Kimberley for more than a few months, or that even an arduous journey by ox-wagon would have taken that long. There was time, however, for Cecil to purchase a 3,000–acre farm near Roodepoort in the Transvaal; he shortly afterward described it as being of "no earthly good and only sunk money."[41]

The eulogistic biographers also credit this journey with having imbued Rhodes with an intangible, ineffable love of Africa and simple Dutch- and Afrikaans-speaking farmers, and with first turning his mind dramatically toward the possibilities of "the north," of the trans-Limpopan regions beyond Marabastad. "On this earliest journey," one wrote, ". . . the spell of Africa was laid on Rhodes, shaping him in these days of his youth, just as in the time to come he moulded Africa to the form of his dreams." Another reported that during the trek "the great love he bore to the country, the people and even the animals of South Africa became rooted in his being. It is a love that breathes in every speech. . . ."[42]

Spell or no spell, until Rhodes went up to Oxford, briefly in 1873 and then for two full terms in 1876, three in 1877, and two in 1878, he focused primarily on the coining of cash from diamonds, ice, and pumps. During this period he forged a variety of friendly and reasonably intimate bonds with a number of the more interesting young English-speaking fortune-hunters on the mining fields. Initially, he lived in a large, imposing tent with Herbert and Frank, and "messed"—his own word for boarding—with a collection of these elite frontiersmen, most of whom had pitched their own tents or halted their wagons near a feeding marquee in the so-called West End of Kimberley. The West End was one of the poorer, multiracial sections of the town. The men with whom the Rhodes brothers ate and shared during 1872 and 1873 included Rudd, Beecher (from the Natal days), George Paton (an older, universally trusted and respected sometime sheep rancher and miner in Australia, gold prospector in California, farmer in the Cape Colony, and successful diamond finder along the Vaal River and in Kimberley), H.C. Seppings Wright (later an artist for the *Illustrated London News*), William Charles Scully (then a lad but later a recognized South African poet, novelist, magistrate, and raconteur), Dr. Thorne, Hugh McLeod, Tommy Townsend, Archibald Campbell (who later fought for the Ottoman empire against the Czar's army), Reginald Fairlie (the painter), Jacob Barry (later Sir Jacob and the Judge President of the Eastern Districts court of the Cape Colony), Garstin (a well-known turn-of-the-century artist in Paris, Florence, and Newlyn, Cornwall), and, off and on, Merriman.

In 1873, after Herbert left Kimberley for good, Scully tented with Frank and Cecil. After Cecil returned from his first term at Oxford, in 1874 and 1875 he lived with Robert Dundas Graham, with whom Rudd and Rhodes later became mining partners, and messed with Garstin, Captain John Carr, A. Carr, Gordon James Halkett (a barrister), and Sidney Godolphin Alexander Shippard (the attorney general of Griqualand West and later Sir Sidney and the first administrator of Bechuanaland).

Most of these intermingled sets of men married and had children. The Rhodes brothers remained bachelors, but Herbert was known as a racy playboy and Frank was described as "gay and debonair . . . perfectly at home in any company; a boy who loved his life, and was a friend of all the world. It has been said of him, in his later days, that he was one of the few men equally loved by men and women alike. . . ." From Kimberley, Frank wrote home that it was "quite a mistake to suppose that there are no nice girls out here."

Scully, admittedly commenting long after Rhodes had become celebrated, and a decade after his death, remembered the great person as "a man in mind and body," while he himself was still an ignorant, opinionated boy. Rhodes was "even then somewhat intolerant in discussion." "I can very clearly picture Cecil Rhodes in one of his characteristic attitudes," Scully continued. "After dinner it was his wont to lean forward with both elbows on the table and his mouth slightly open. He had a habit, when thinking, of rubbing his chin gently with his forefinger. Very often he would sit in the attitude described for a very long time, without joining in whatever conversation happened to be going on. His manner and expression suggested that his thoughts were far away, but occasionally some interjection would indicate that, to a certain extent, he was keeping in touch with the current topic. Indeed, it often seemed to me that the larger part of his brain was dealing with something of which no one else had cognizance."

Garstin subsequently searched deep into his memory for the Rhodes of the early 1870s. "I seem to see a fair young man, frequently sunk in deep thoughts, his hands buried in his trouser pockets, his legs crossed and possibly twisted together, quite oblivious of the talk around him; then without a word he would get up and go out with some set purpose in his mind which he was at no pains to communicate. . . . He was a compound of moody silence and impulsive action. He was hot and even violent at times, but in working towards his ends he laid his plans with care and circumspection. . . . The duality of his nature, the contemplative and the executive, had a curious counterpart in his voice, which broke, when he was excited, into a sort of falsetto, unusual in a man of his make; his laugh also had this falsetto note."

Generally, his contemporaries regarded Rhodes as "somewhat eccentric and a dreamer, though admitted to be a far-sighted man of business with a head for finance." At New Rush he sat on an upturned bucket and supervised his laborers, "his eyes on a book, or his mind deep in thought. . . ."

Louis Cohen, who arrived in Kimberley to purchase diamonds about the same time as Cecil Rhodes, would not have been permitted in the mess because of his ancestry, but he, too, recalled Rhodes. The young Rhodes was silent and self-contained. Many times Cohen saw him, "dressed in white flannels, leaning moodily with hands in his pockets against a street wall. He hardly ever had a companion, seemingly took no interest in anything but his own thoughts, and I do not believe if a flock of the most adorable women passed through the street he would go across the road to see them." Cohen admired Rhodes, but "for the fair sex he cared nothing." Yet—a lonely man—Rhodes was "fond of a glass or two," and could, when "jolly with the bottle, talk like a Mirabeau."[43]

In 1874, about the time of his twenty-first birthday, the Curreys apparently persuaded the young Rhodes to sleep in a place of his own. He duly constructed a single room of corrugated iron near the Currey dwelling. "But," remembered Currey, Rhodes' hut was "hardly habitable in winter at our elevation of over four thousand feet . . . ; and one evening when a violent snow storm set in he rushed into our little sitting room and, getting almost into the fireplace, announced his intention of staying there till the weather was over. And so he did, having his dinner brought to him and a shakedown made up in front of the fire. He was subject," continued Currey, "at this time to bleeding from one lung and my wife thought he wanted more care than he was disposed to take of himself."[44]

Late the previous year he had been sent back to Kimberley from Oxford with but six months to live. Before the end of his initial term at Oxford in 1873, he had allegedly caught a chill while rowing and had been hustled out to Africa by Dr. Morell Mackenzie, at that time a London chest and throat specialist and, later, one of Britain's best known laryngologists. Yet, shortly after departing, on December 15, 1873, Rhodes had felt so well that he had been tempted to leave his steamship, the *Asiatic*, when it landed outbound at Plymouth. Then for nearly two weeks he was ill again aboard the ship, recovering by the time he landed at Cape Town. Nevertheless, so fearful had he been of the fourteen days alone in a wagon from the Cape to Kimberley (as New Rush and the other mines were being called after Lord Kimberley, the then British colonial secretary), that he had engaged a steward from the boat to look after him along the road as the steward had done aboard ship. At the halfway mark he wrote home, admitting to his father that he still suffered "at times from my lungs, but nothing at all like I used to." In this same letter he admits to having "got quite over that feeling of depression I used to have."[45]

The depression was hardly unrelated to the intermittently disruptive state of his health. But a more likely cause was the death of his beloved mother. She had been ill at least from before Rhodes' return from Africa in mid-1873. "She looks so very thin in the face," Rhodes had commented to his aunt, "but Mr. Cribb [the doctor] says she is going on as well as she can and she does not suffer now as she did, though she must have had a most severe attack from all accounts. They prayed for her in church." Whether it was her heart, or another vital organ, which had been assaulted, is not now known. She died from a "stoppage" in the first week of November 1873. Rhodes apparently felt the loss acutely. It presumably fed his melancholy, which may have been reflected in the curious subsequent report that Rhodes had broken down during a concert at the Albert Hall en route to Africa. Burying his face in his hands, he had suddenly sobbed uncontrollably. A Mrs. Bennett tried to calm him, and recalled how he had apologized afterward. The next day he was sailing for Africa, the doctors having told him that only a sea voyage would save his life. His heart was heavy with grief.[46]

His mother's illness, and not the desire to go up to Oxford as has always been assumed, may conceivably have been the real reason for Rhodes' decision to return home with Frank in 1873. Frank was destined for the Royal Dragoons, a cavalry regiment into which he had been commissioned. But Rhodes could easily have remained in Kimberley another few months, if entering Oxford in the autumn impelled him to go. Moreover, there is no particular reason why he chose to attend Oxford in 1873, and little evidence that he had asked to be admitted to Oxford before he actually arrived there. A letter to his aunt exists, too, in which Rhodes belatedly and profusely thanked her for letting him stay with her at the manor in Sleaford. "You can understand it made this difference that I did not go back to the Cape."[47]

Instead, with his mother still in danger, and needing to remain in Britain, he hurriedly asked for admission to Oxford. This is a new, if only circumstantially substantiated, hypothesis which conforms to what little we know about Rhodes' character: in this case he drew upon his ability to adapt to changing opportunities. Rhodes always struggled to turn seeming adversity to good fortune. Going up to Oxford was but another example of that trait. In addition to revising how we view the planned as well as the unplanned nature of Rhodes' accomplishments, this interpretation emphasizes how thoroughly upset Rhodes must have been when his mother's death propelled him rapidly back to Africa.

Rhodes grieved in 1874. But his contemporaries more often recalled Rhodes the dreamer; Rhodes the moody, emotional, lonely thinker.[48] Rhodes the often silent but suddenly voluble, arousing, even persuasive talker; Rhodes the schemer, especially in the 1870s on the variety of legitimate ways in which he and Rudd could make money. Rhodes the man of detail, of determination, of grit, of tenacity, of patience. Rhodes as a man of temper. Rhodes the intolerant, repetitive, dogmatic, verbal bully. These seem to be among the attributes of the early character of the man, at least as seen through the eyes of those of his closest associates who wrote or spoke about the Founder's formative years in South Africa. He had a magic that captivated unlikely persons like Rudd and Merriman, Garstin and Scully, and, from 1875, Alfred Beit, a German-born diamond merchant with an impeccable judgment of precious stones and a wise and careful approach to matters of low and high finance.

Merriman was much more established, for example, than Rhodes, as well as more intellectually adept and better read. Even so, Merriman was captivated by Rhodes' "quality of largeness, simplicity, and even intuitive penetration." Rhodes had charm, too, and appeared ingenuous. A relatively unsuccessful speculator in diamonds and in other property and commercial ventures, Merriman was more interested in politics; he claims to have been the first to steer Rhodes toward a political career—"the only intellectual occupation in South Africa."[49] He also asserted advanced views about Africans.

Merriman, the son of a strong-minded Anglican Bishop of Grahamstown, was exercised in the years from 1872 to 1875, when he and Rhodes were particularly close, by the various ways in which the miners mistreated their African labor. But little of Merriman's humanitarian fervor was transferred to Rhodes. Although Southey's administration of Griqualand West had removed restraints that prohibited Africans from holding claims, mobs of miners believed in the older law and enforced their own informal prohibitions, attacked and bullied unwilling or recalcitrant black laborers, harshly established their own color line, and administered a wild frontier justice to Africans and the poorer whites. In 1874, there was a canteen, or bar, for every forty persons. Each served cheap Cape Smoke (brandy) to Africans, as well as better drinks to whites, around the clock. There was incessant gambling, including high-stake games of faro organized by wandering Americans.

Southey's government was badly run and penurious, being held on a typically tight string by a reluctant and antagonistic British Colonial Office (and the British Treasury). It made money from the high import fees on guns and therefore permitted, even encouraged, the heavy traffic in rifles and ammunition which passed through Griqualand West toward the interior. Southey also welcomed the trade, unsettling to whites as it might be to place 18,000 guns a year in African hands, because British merchants profited from it, and because the free sale of guns in and around the diamond fields helped to attract abundant migratory labor from the east and north.

Southey was an autocrat and Currey, his deputy, was peremptory in his dealings with the population of the mining camps. They were unpopular even though Southey was a philosophical populist who favored diggers—small, independent workers—over companies and tried to limit the power of the landed proprietors (the owners of the original farms on which the mines were now situated). An imperialist before Rhodes, he opposed the pretensions of the Afrikaner republics and sought to increase the scope and borders of his diminutive crown colony. He tried to improve conditions in the camps and to bring order as well as better amenities to Kimberley.

But Southey alienated those who might have been his supporters within the Colony and in Whitehall. The times, too, hardly lent themselves to the kind of economically expansive, gently pro-African, anti-capitalistic policy that Southey espoused. At a time of straitened circumstances due to world-wide recession, falling diamond prices, flooded mines, and rapid local depopulation, Southey tripled taxes. The cost of goods from the Cape simultaneously sky-rocketed as a result of duties placed by the old Colony on its already expensive exports to its new neighbor. Speculation was rife (to Rhodes' presumed advantage); interest rates soared. Foreclosures were common. Then the Vooruitzigt proprietors raised claim rents exorbitantly, and the miners, in 1875, slipped from discontent to unrest and then to riotous assembly.

The diamond economy was beginning to recover in 1875. Nevertheless, Southey could do little that seemed right to the diggers. By this time, they had blamed all of their woes, real and imagined, on the administration of the colony. They were incensed about prices and taxes, about Southey's attempts to curb what they regarded as their freedom to drink, carouse, jump claims, and behave independently in every way. Alfred Aylward, editor of the *Diamond Field,* one of Kimberley's newspapers, was a leading rabble rouser, brilliant orator, inflammatory publicist, and fiery Fenian with a clear personal agenda. Many supported him, particularly those miners who saw their ruin in Southey's paternalistic attitudes toward African labor and African claimholders. The miners universally blamed Africans for the contamination of illicit diamond buying—the smuggling of gems from the diggings and the sorting tables directly to unscrupulous, mostly white, dealers. American miners had added their own attitudes to home-grown South African ones: racial prejudice was rife despite or because of Southey's own, largely futile, attempts to impose the liberal standards of the western Cape on the canvas city of the plains. "The only point on which the malcontents join issue is niggers being allowed to hold claims," Paton told Merriman. "If the Government were to put down that nest of thieves . . . and stop issuing licenses to colonial niggers, and to all blacks but natives of Griqualand—they don't go in for it—everybody would be contented."[50]

Aylward formed a Committee of Public Safety in early 1874, and he and his allies established the Kimberley Defence League and Protection Association (usually called the Diggers' Protective Association) in November of the same year. By March 1875, a few hundred rebels had begun drilling with smuggled weapons. Southey issued a proclamation warning the citizens of the town against taking illegal oaths or assembling in arms. In April, a canteen keeper was arrested for supplying rifles illegally to Aylward. His conviction in a local magistrate's court proved the obvious spark of rebellion. A militant digger unfurled the black flag of unrest above a whim atop a pile of debris called Mount Ararat. But his attempt to duplicate the short-lived riverine Diggers Republic of 1870 proved even briefer and less successful than that earlier revolt.

The actions of a careful magistrate and judicious police work calmed the diggers, most of whom cheered Aylward at Mount Ararat and then resumed their sieving and sorting. In May, while the little colony remained tense, the wealthiest miners and proprietors, led by Joseph Benjamin Robinson, later Rhodes' most vigorous rival, sought to mediate between the administration and the diggers, and to encourage the members of the Association to lay down their arms. But it was the arrival in late June of troops from the Cape which finally ended the incipient rebellion. Southey was relieved of his office in August, and the Griqualand West experiment, thanks to the agitation of the diggers as well as the maladroitness of Southey and Currey, ended with the victory of capital over labor, and white over black, and the arrival of a semblance of order (curtailed were grog shops, brothels, illicit diamond buying, claim jumping, and gun-running).

Of particular relevance to Rhodes, with Southey went an administrative preference for diamond mining by a vast number of individuals on their own innumerable holdings. Oats, the provincial engineer, and many others felt strongly that the prosperity of the mines could continue only if consolidation prevailed.[51] After the replacement of Southey by Major William Owen Lanyon in 1876, more stringent imperial control was exercised until responsibility for the deficit-ridden territory could be thrust boldly upon the Cape Colony. In 1877, when Rhodes was at Oxford, a reluctant but continually pressured Cape legislature finally passed the necessary enabling legislation; but the transfer took place only in 1880, after the British government's policy of confederating all of South Africa (and thus ending wars and minimizing imperial expenses) had foundered on the lasting rock of Afrikaner republicanism.

Unlike Merriman, Rhodes was little concerned during these years about the rights of Africans, the morality or lack of morality of their behavior and treatment, the grievances of the diggers, the licentiousness and general atmosphere of the mining camps, and questions of governance and order. He was much more focused on the practical everyday concerns of his livelihood. Admittedly, the abstracted and dreamy appearance that impressed most of his friends may have hidden a spirit brooding over these issues. But it is more likely that his bouts of thought simply reflected manifestations of a profound absorption in his own concerns. He mused about how he was going to complete his education at Oxford, and contemplated a career as a barrister. "I have a tremendous desire to get home to college," he told Frank in 1875.[52]

Comparing him at such an early age to the older and aesthetic Merriman may be unfair, for the son of the bishop was already an ambitious politician who had made a name for himself. Rhodes, not yet fully adult—with no firm choice of career, no decision on whom to love, and unsure about what would give meaning to his life—was more than a minor figure on the diamond fields, but certainly not a leading light. Within the Cape Colony generally, he remained largely unknown. Between the ages of twenty and twenty-three he could hardly have been expected to be as politically sophisticated as he was to become. Even so, he alone, or he and Merriman together, are credited in 1873 with helping Southey draft a proclamation which, for a time, closed the gambling places of Griqualand West.[53] Otherwise, there is no evidence that he was more than casually interested in the riotous events of Southey's administration.

When Aylward planted the black flag of revolt, Rhodes was busy manning the pumps at Dutoitspan. He hustled back to the center of Kimberley and joined the pro-order moderates who were loosely allied to the government and to Robinson. For nearly three months, until the troops from the Cape arrived, Rhodes was among those who guarded the jail and the government offices, interposing themselves between the rioters and Southey. "It was frightful nonsense," Rhodes contended. "It was a most ridiculous sight to see them drilling and parading and the Government looking on quite helpless. One could not help sympathizing on certain questions with them."[54]

Rhodes was hardly then attracted by anti-British Fenians, by the stump oratory of crafty polemicists, by virulent antagonism to Africans, or by the logic of a rising, even if he noted a sympathy with some, alas, unnoted questions. Morever, he was close to Currey, and doubtless admired Southey's imperialistic fervor if not his methods of administration. Throughout his life, Rhodes sought favor among local governing and administrative elites. He gravitated toward the powerful (if not necessarily the parvenu or the nouveau riche) and knew that his own ambitions, growing and maturing as they continued to do, could be achieved only with the assistance (providing he had the "ready") of those who controlled decision-making. He placed himself advantageously. Conceivably, it could be said that he maneuvered himself so as to maximize the number of his available, presumably beneficial, options. Whether he daydreamed more about the future of the universe (the impression that the legion of hagiographers hoped to impart), or about how he could elevate his own ultimate position in that universe, may be less salient than the fact that, without being overtly political in Merriman's manner, he was an intuitive calculator capable of judging others and, therefore, in a more lasting sense, of proving himself able to advance his ends by two crucial political gifts— mobilizing and exciting his contemporaries.

Rhodes may have sent himself to Oxford initially in order to fulfill an unmet yearning to prove himself the equal of his father and the best of his brothers. Or, in one who carried the classics across the veld and thumbed through them, noting aphorisms and making a commonplace book of the most ennobling of those pithy conclusions, there may have been a genuine thirst for greater knowledge. When Rhodes returned to Oxford in the mid-1870s, however, he was also going there to accomplish that quintessential aim of so many other British and American undergraduates: Rhodes wanted to make contact with the cream of the English ruling class. There would be men at the colleges and in the clubs who could help him achieve his goals. At Oxford, he would be among the best and the brightest, and certainly would mingle with those who were bound to influence the destinies of Britain and South Africa for decades to come.

In 1876, when Rhodes went back to Oxford from Kimberley, he knew prosperity. He might have been worth as much as £40,000, a substantial sum anywhere in the empire. He could afford the fees and the fares, had the funds with which to speculate on property in England, and could rely upon Rudd to keep their joint investments strong in South Africa.

◄ 5 ►

"I Think You Will Do"
A Band of Brothers amid
the Dreaming Spires

A s RHODES BELIEVED in the integrity and esteem of England, so he revered
Oxford, its classical, aesthetic, mannered core. The university had long
been the lodestar of his aspirations for himself. The embodiment of boyhood
dreams, it was a place of redemption. The failure to be educated in a public
(non-state) school could, in the Britain of the 1870s, at least partially be erased
by matriculation at Oxford. As a little-heralded colonial he could achieve an
acceptance, however belated, among the best and the brightest. Going up to
Oxford would remake the recent past. It could also position an ambitious
young man more favorably, the better to use his new wealth and achievement
in an outpost of empire creatively and broadly.

Rhodes had emerged from adolescence among sharp but rough men of
the frontier. If he were already at least musing about a future which would
incorporate but also transcend South Africa, then a close study of and association with the British ruling class was essential. Where better than Oxford
could he so examine and participate in the ways of those on whom the realization of his plans would someday depend? At a simpler level, where else
could he make fruitful contacts? Where else could he learn how to employ his
funds to best effect, either for his own or some larger entity's apotheosis?

Rhodes was hardly the typical Oxford undergraduate of his time. Nor
did his experience at Oxford provide the kind of ideal model which later
generations of earnest scholars from the colonies would have wanted to em-
ulate. Yet for Rhodes, the fundamental impact of Oxford was more than the
clubs he joined, the friends he made, and the many intellectual and social
opportunities that he disdained. Instead, he silently accomplished an important advance in his personal growth. He constructed a plan of life.

In view of Rhodes' later grandiosity and the turn of his own thought
toward global issues, it would be natural to connect his eventual prominence

with his time at Oxford. Rhodes himself emphasized the importance of an Oxford education to his own and other great lives. The creation of his scholarships implied that he was strongly influenced by his Oxford years. It is thus hardly surprising that all of his biographers follow the first of their kind in assigning to Oxford a major contributing role in the formation of Rhodes' genius.

Since he had always wanted to study there, and since life at Oxford in the twentieth century revolves around learning and ideas, every biographer asserts that Rhodes went up to Oxford to refine his mind. Even the best and most modern of the biographers reports that Rhodes sought in Oxford the meaning and purpose of life, and that he found it there.[1] Others are more sweeping in their claims or grandiloquent in their prose. Several, even the better ones, turn Rhodes at Oxford into a disciple of John Ruskin, aesthete and proto-communard. Another suggests that he could have met Oscar Wilde, for they were members of the same club. A third and fourth indicate that Rhodes at Oxford was studious, amazingly so for an already successful entrepreneur who simultaneously busied himself with the details of pumping and mining machines, with the selling of diamonds, and with property investment in Britain. Like so much concerning the early Rhodes, however, hard evidence for these several propositions is lacking. Considering that the university kept records, dons were trained to recall, and undergraduates might be expected to remember early impressions, the lack of data about Rhodes at Oxford sufficient to support the myths is, at least, suggestive.

It has always been assumed that Rhodes, anxious to end his colonial exile, would have tried to enter Oxford before 1873 if only his financial situation had been sufficiently stable. Perhaps. But his father had, it seems, long before set aside funds for Cecil's education. Those sums could have been drawn upon for Oxford, as they were for other pursuits, briefly, in 1875 in Kimberley. Anyway, Rhodes lacked means less than security. It is reasonable to think that the leaving of his business affairs, even in the hands of Rudd, might have troubled Rhodes before 1873, or again in 1874 and 1875. Indeed, it was the need to construct a firm financial foundation in Kimberley that kept him there, but not against his will or because of his inability—before 1873—to afford the fees and the passage to Britain.

If his mother had not ailed in 1873, he might not have realized his dream of Oxford until later, if ever. If he had to return home for the first time because she were seriously ill, only to realize upon his arrival that her death was not necessarily imminent, then knocking on the doors of Oxford would for him have combined duty with dream. If attending Oxford came about in this unexpected manner, as an opportunity to be grasped, a number of puzzles become more explicable: his behavior and accomplishments there, the brevity of his initial stay, and—particularly—the absence of any application from afar by him to the colleges of his choice, as well as any prior correspondence with friends or relatives about Oxford.[2]

Although Rhodes arrived in England in August 1873, he apparently sought admission to Oxford only in late September or early October. He went first to University College, then as now an intellectually distinguished foundation. Its master was Dr. G.G. Bradley, a learned divine. Why Rhodes chose University College is obscure, but the likeliest reason is that Robert Armstrong Yerburgh, a childhood friend from Sleaford, had matriculated there and knew its dons. (Yerburgh went up to University College in 1873 and later moved to St. Albans, a small, elite college, from which he took his B.A. in 1877.)

Rhodes also had an introduction to Bradley and expected it would help gain him admission. Many years later Yerburgh wrote that Rhodes, at a disadvantage because of his lack of a public school education, sat an entrance examination in Latin prose and failed. Several of the biographies aver that he merely wanted to read for a pass or ordinary degree (permitted in Oxford from 1874) and that University College was accepting men for honors only. But University was not then an honors college only, and there were men in residence taking pass degrees. More critically, before World War I, 90 percent of all men accepted into Univ., as it is known, were from public (private) schools, and only 5 percent each from grammar and other, lesser, private schools. Of the public schools, Eton and Charterhouse each supplied 10 percent of all Univ. undergraduates. Whatever Rhodes' Latin prose results, Bradley would naturally have regarded Rhodes as poor Univ. material: he lacked a public school or even an acceptable grammar school education. He was raw, older, and tainted by the frontier. According to a modern Univ. account, "candidates would just turn up on the College doorstep, have an interview with the Master and be immediately accepted or rejected."[3] For one reason or another, Bradley rejected Rhodes and, supposedly, sent him to Oriel.

Oriel, Bradley said, was "less particular" about degrees. But Oriel, down the High Street from University, could not have been unknown to Rhodes. Sidney Shippard, his friend and messmate from Kimberley, was an Oriel man. So was Henry Caesar Hawkins, a friend from the early days in Natal and the nephew of Edward Hawkins, then (as he had been since 1828) the provost of Oriel. When approached by Rhodes, could Provost Hawkins possibly have "stared down at his table in hostile silence" and then said, "All Colleges send me their failures"? Another version indicates that Hawkins read Rhodes' letter of introduction, said "Pff" twice, "very contemptuously," and then declared: "So the Master of University sends me his leavings." Rhodes protested vigorously. Finally Hawkins told the young diamond digger: "I think you will do." Whatever Hawkins said, and whatever he may have thought of Rhodes, the young entrepreneur was duly admitted as a student of Oriel on 13 October 1873. Term had begun; Rhodes entered late and, as a contemporary later explained, he therefore had to live in lodgings rather than in college.[4]

Rhodes resided around the corner from Oriel on the High Street and read initially for Responsions. In those days this preliminary examination of classical knowledge (Latin and Greek grammar, Latin prose composition, arithmetic, and geometry or algebra) could be taken after a candidate for admission had actually been admitted to a college; in subsequent decades it became an entrance test. Presumably studying hard, especially after failing at Univ., and, despite the impact of his mother's death in November, Rhodes succeeded in passing Responsions in early December. According to an Oriel man who was in his second year in 1873 and was still sentient in 1953, his only memory of Rhodes during that first term was the fact that Rhodes went down once and only once to the river, and there the man who was to become the Rev. J.S.M. Walker had the "(unperceived) honour of coaching him."[5]

Was this the time, if Rhodes really only rowed once on the Isis, when he caught a chill and had to go back to Africa? Or is the "chill" a part of the skillfully embroidered biographical myth of Rhodes at Oxford? The "chill," as an explanation for Rhodes' return to Africa in late 1873, after but one Oxford term, originates with Hensman in 1901 and Williams in 1921 and has been taken on faith by all subsequent biographers. But Hensman followed A.G. Butler, and Williams confirmed the theory of the chill from J.H. Hall, a junior fellow at Oriel during Rhodes' time. Hall told Williams only: "At the end of his first term symptoms of chest weakness shewed themselves. Some say owing to his exertions on the River in rather inclement weather and he went off to the Cape to recruit."[6] Williams clearly embroidered Hall's account, and linked it to the received (but here discredited) notion that Rhodes was tubercular when he first went to Africa. From this time, if not before, there was doubtless a confusion in Rhodes' mind, as well as in the minds of those (such as the Curreys) who were close to him, about the pains in his chest and the breathlessness of which he was at times conscious. It was Rhodes' heart, not his lungs, which was at fault.

A few modern writers suggest that Rhodes may have been forced back to Africa in 1873 by a shortage of funds. It is supposed that he ran out of money and was compelled to return to Kimberley to make more before he could continue in Oxford. But there is nothing to support such a supposition. His mother's death would have meant at least a small legacy for Rhodes, and if he could afford a sea passage to Africa as well as the investment of about £1,800 on property in London, he presumably could have scraped together enough of "the ready" to continue at Oriel.

Rhodes went back to Africa in late 1873 because of two events: his mother's death and the grief and depression that it caused, and the fact that he had passed Responsions and was thus sure of a continuing place at Oriel. He could afford to take time off. Grief, almost certainly, possibly a "flu" (the chill which he may or may not ever have caught), and not financial stringency moved Rhodes to flee England for Africa. His letters to his father from this period reflect bereavement and depression as much as a concern for his own physical well-being.

An Oxford degree required nine terms in residence. Rhodes completed one in 1873, returned for a second in April 1876, and, despite the fact that he was "feeling my lungs rather" and that it was "frightfully damp," he was "very anxious to remain," as "he was . . . regularly back in the old groove."[7] Stay he did, his doctor apparently deciding that his health would not deteriorate. After spending the long summer vacation of 1876 in Sleaford, "reading hard," he returned promptly to Oriel for the normal three seven-week-long terms (including the dank winter ones) of 1876/77 and 1877/78. Still lacking a ninth term and immersed in the developing financial reorganization of the De Beers mine, Rhodes deferred taking his degree until the autumn term of 1881. Thus he indulged (if that is the correct verb) in the undergraduate life of Oxford essentially for two years, from 1876 to 1878. These were the only years of his adult life when he could shed a daily preoccupation with tasks, schemes, and money-making. This is not to suggest that Rhodes at Oxford ever divorced himself from such pursuits, or neglected Kimberley. Rather, for two years he broke the self-made mold and enjoyed the luxury of thought, conversation, and—if he had desired it—unparalleled opportunities for intellectual enrichment.

"Oxford was perfectly to his taste, in the opportunities it offered him of serious reading and of sharpening his wits in long disputations, the means by which he cleared his mind on any subject that might be interesting to him. The freedom of life and the discipline of scholarship appealed to him; and he found a society and a way of thought he had never encountered [before]."[8] This is the romantic view, polished from biographer to biographer and appreciated by those who themselves were Oxford men. But only Rhodes' subsequent fame, and his undoubted genius for imperial and financial pyramiding, supports such a rosy report of the years at Oriel.

A close examination of the admittedly sparse Oxford record gives greater credence to the account of the one person who might have been expected to have known something about the ways in which Rhodes used his days and his mind at Oxford. The Rev. Arthur Gray Butler was the dean at Oriel from 1875 to 1895. Previously headmaster at Haileybury College and a successful scholar and athlete, he was remembered as Rhodes' chief friend as well as his instructor and college advisor. Butler wrote that Rhodes' "career at Oxford was uneventful. He belonged to a set of men like himself, not caring for distinctions in the schools and not working for them, but of refined tastes, dining and living for the most part together, and doubtless discussing passing events in life and politics with interest and ability. Such a set is not very common at Oxford, living as it does a good deal apart from both games and work; but it does exist, and somehow includes men of much intellectual power which bears fruit later."[9]

As before at Kimberley and later at both Kimberley and Groote Schuur, Rhodes surrounded himself with a band of brothers. It was to them he was bonded, even if, despite his age, he was less central to these men of Oxford than to his peers in Africa. It was from the set of men to whom Butler refers that Rhodes took his cues; he seems not to have lived among the intellects, the aesthetes, or the adventuring imperialists. His friends were not aristocracy either, but pretentious gentry, at least one being particularly pleased when he married well and secured a safe Tory parliamentary seat. As a collection, these were men exhibiting comfortable ambitions, expressing confined and conforming interests in matters of the mind, and taking no particular pleasure in answering larger questions about man's fate, man's purpose, or man's social responsibilities.

No one ever accused Rhodes of following an academically oriented furrow at Oxford. But it is also difficult to discover exactly what Rhodes did at Oxford other than talk and play. He harangued his contemporaries and joined, even led, clubs that were prestigious but frivolous. He never attended debates at the Union, even those on imperial subjects; he never advanced in discourse beyond the verities of his autodidactic youth, and the notion that he was intellectually influenced by the humanitarian outpourings of Ruskin depends on a circumstantial scrap of neo-Ruskinian prose found among Rhodes' papers after his death.[10] It is clear that he attended lectures and tutorials rarely, and occasionally incurred the displeasure of Butler and the other dons at Oriel. Once, when Butler complained to Rhodes about his failure to attend the college lectures that were prescribed for pass degree candidates, he apparently replied: "I promise you I shall manage it. Leave me alone and I shall pass through."

When he deigned to attend these lectures, Rhodes apparently proved easily distracted and also distracting. Characteristically, he carried diamonds in a little box in his waistcoat pocket. Once, an exact contemporary reported, "when he condescended to attend a lecture, which proved uninteresting to him, he pulled out his box and showed the gems to his friends, and then it was upset, and diamonds were scattered on the floor, and the lecturer looked up and asking what was the cause of the disturbance received the reply, 'It is only Rhodes and his diamonds.'" It was also reported that Rhodes did not "read hard during his Oxford life, and was more than once remonstrated with for non-attendance at lectures." He is said to have replied: "I shall pass, which is all I wish to do!"[11] Whether for similar breaches of protocol or other offenses, Rhodes had what he himself called "tremendous skirmishes" with Oriel dons. On one occasion early in his first term back at Oxford in 1876 he was nearly caught (it is not clear how) going off to Epsom for the races. "But I still do not think I will be sent down," he wrote to Rudd.[12]

Rhodes was not so much of a hell-raiser as Richard Francis Burton, an earlier Oxford swashbuckler who was, in fact, sent down. Several of Rhodes' Oxford contemporaries indeed remembered him as being rather staid. Nevertheless, both the objective facts and the subjective recollections of those who knew him in the 1870s imply that Rhodes took little advantage of Oxford's mind-forming and character-building opportunities. If he had not subsequently become a great man, his Oxford career would have passed into oblivion. Or he would have been dismissed as a playboy.

At Oxford the slim, 147-pound young mining magnate's main distinction was the fact that he became master of the Drag Hunt in 1876. Yerburgh preceded him in this honor and passed it to him or inveigled him to accept it. It is said that the appointment was quaint: Rhodes, who possessed a "rolling slouchy walk," "rode with a loose rein and had an eminently unsafe seat in the saddle." Can one imagine Rhodes yelling "tally-ho" and leading younger men to the chase? Nevertheless, he even drove his Oxford neighbors to distraction by seeking proficiency on the hunting horn. Lord Desborough succeeded Rhodes as drag master and complained that Rhodes had made him purchase four "inferior dogs."[13]

Rhodes played polo. He belonged to the Bullingdon and Vincent's clubs, Oxford's smartest. Both accepted only men of wealth, dandies, and bon vivants. The Bullingdon was composed of "cheerful young gentlemen who were wont to wear gray bowlers and on festive evenings to parade the High Street with horsewhips and hunting cries." After Oxford, Rhodes, proud of possessing the Bullingdon uniform, always wore it "on occasions when something was required in the way of fancy dress." Oscar Wilde was a member of Bullingdon's in the late 1870s. So was James Rochfort Maguire, who remembered Rhodes as "popular" among the boys and men who attended the banquets put on by both institutions. Another contemporary and self-described "close friend" remembered that Rhodes "hunted the drag . . . was a 'good fellow' to everybody, and a most popular member of all the clubs." Presumably Yerburgh introduced him to or inducted him into one or both, for in the 1870s Rhodes lived in lodgings with Yerburgh and men from University and Christ Church colleges. Francis Newton, who was up at University from 1876 to 1879, remembered Yerburgh and Rhodes as a most unlikely-looking pair: "Yerburgh beautifully dressed and rather precious, Rhodes every inch the roughdigger."[14] Yerburgh later became a Tory member of Parliament from Chester from 1886 to 1906 and from 1910 to 1916. Newton became private secretary to the governor of the Cape Colony.

Whether one or both of these contemporaries was a Freemason is not known. In June 1877, however, Rhodes paid £5.10 and became a life member of the Oxford University Apollo Chapter of the Masonic Order. At a banquet marking his induction, the story goes, he became angry at some criticism and, not untypically, shocked the assembled brethren of the Order by babbling away about the mystic cult secrets of the 33 Degree Rite into which he had been admitted. But was the joining of the Masons a serious venture for Rhodes? He derided the devotion by a large body of men "to what at times appear the most ridiculous and absurd rites without an object and without an end." Should it then be concluded that this was another manifestation, as membership in the Bullingdon and Vincent's clubs would have been, of Rhodes' desire constantly to be among a band of brothers? Was this simply an obvious way to seek easy acceptance among the kind of men to whom he was attracted then, and for his schemes afterwards? Certainly the often quoted "Have you ever thought how it is that Oxford men figure so largely in all departments of public life? The Oxford system in its most finished form *looks* very unpractical, yet, wherever you turn your eye—except in sciences—an Oxford man is at the top of the tree" can be read as extolling the virtues of the university or, in the context of the Bullingdon and Vincent's sodalities, as praise more for the men themselves and for their combined spirit—the "mystic mantle of greatness" with which Flint cloaks Rhodes' appreciation of Oxford.[15] At another level the Masonic interlude presumably helped shape Rhodes' "Confession of Faith," the later wills, and the protean thinking which led ultimately to the scholarships.

Where Rhodes left a mark on his Oxford contemporaries he left it because of his displays of diamonds, his dogs and the drag, his rough clothes and unrefined and direct approach, and—considering the general view of Rhodes later—his surprising garrulousness. Lord Desborough said that Rhodes was "continually talking," but the talk was not "particularly good." "He was always talking," reported Maguire. Rhodes insisted upon talking about his reading, especially "some passage from Plato." Incessantly, he would badger his friends for their opinions.

Metcalfe was not at first terribly impressed by Rhodes, for he expressed such "low views of human nature, due no doubt to the crowd he consorted with in South Africa." Another contemporary did not at first "take to him." He was unyielding and he trod on me, but I gradually got to understand him, and we became fast friends." A college acquaintance who was afterwards a British cabinet minister remembered Rhodes as a "quiet good fellow with what I should call the instincts of an Englishman, but I do not recollect that there was any indication of the great strength of character and genius for empire-building, which made him so remarkable a man afterwards." After praising Rhodes' clubbableness, a "close friend" noted that Rhodes' "leading characteristic" at Oxford was a "cynical detachment" from the ordinary ideas of the youth of his day. He had not been "moulded into uniformity" by a public school. Most of all, he remained a mystery to his colleagues, "himself uncertain and doubting as to his future, but with this great claim to greatness—viz., that the ordinary ideas of ordinary men, with the means to pursue them, had no interest or fascination for him."

An Oriel man who had matriculated at the same time as Rhodes recalled that "few of his contemporaries ever imagined that he would attain to such colossal greatness as he later achieved. We did not conceive that this delicate and somewhat lackadaisical young man should ever play the most striking part in the history of modern British imperial development." Another Oriel man, later ordained, wrote that Rhodes' greatness was unperceived. "I think we all liked Rhodes because he was natural and unaffected; but he was reserved about his own private affairs, and I can recollect . . . a certain coldness of speech and manner which betokened an unconventional attitude towards things in general and towards the university in particular. . . ." Barnes-Lawrence also remembered that Rhodes' knowledge of classical literature was "only elementary"; he struggled "manfully" with Latin and Greek. Rhodes, according to this friend, took little part in college sports. "He could handle an oar, and . . . he was active limbed and well-proportioned," but there also was a "delicacy of constitution which prohibited him from taking part in any violent exercises; and he did not present then that massive appearance to which we are accustomed to-day. . . ." It is striking that both Oriel contemporaries remembered him as "delicate," a Victorian usage which has since ceased to be as directly descriptive of someone in marginal health as it was then.[16]

Yerburgh had known Rhodes since both were young. The Rev. Richard Yerburgh, Robert's father and the rector of Sleaford, had wanted to marry Louisa Peacock, Rhodes' mother. Rhodes had spent holidays in Sleaford and visited his favorite aunt whenever he could, not least before going up to Oxford in 1873. For the years in the later 1870s when the two old friends were together, part of the time in an old timbered house in Oriel Lane overlooking the Univ. garden, and then in King Edward Street nearby, Rhodes was "full of go and spirit and very gallant." Yerburgh did not consider him talkative. Rhodes was opposed to writing as a vocation for Yerburgh because it "wasn't man's work"; Rhodes—as he did throughout his life—denounced such pursuits as "mere loafing." "Every man," Rhodes told Yerburgh, "should have active work to do in life."

Already at Oxford, Rhodes expressed his opposition to marriage, either for himself or for others. He seemed to believe strongly, Yerburgh recalled, that marriage interfered with "work." (Later Rhodes wrote from Oxford to a friend in Kimberley: "I hope you won't get married. I hate people getting married, they simply become machines and have no ideas beyond their respective spouses, and offspring."[17]) Nevertheless, again according to Yerburgh, Rhodes during this period was attracted to a Miss Evett of Watney Park, near Oxford. (Unfortunately, nothing else is known about her, and this is a sole mention by Rhodes' contemporaries; he never alluded to a female friend from his Oxford days.) Despite the depiction by a few others that Rhodes at Oxford was aloof and distant and despite the aura that he later carried of being similarly cold, Yerburgh, who fondly remembered the youthful Rhodes as "jolly" and "up to things," also reported that at Oxford Rhodes spent time sorting out the lives of others. He "took enormous pains for friends . . . disentangling unhealthy alliances" and so on.[18]

How did Rhodes spend his Oxford days? What did he do during the comparatively lengthy holidays which separated the autumn, winter, and spring terms from each other? During one, at least, he had intended to "read hard." During another he hunted. During others, and during term time, he bought property, purchased equipment in Britain for shipment to the Cape, tried vigorously to keep up with the affairs of his partnership in Kimberley, and took dinners at the Inner Temple in London in order to begin to qualify for the bar. Otherwise, and he said that he liked the life, Rhodes rode, talked, spilled diamonds, cavorted with his classy friends, went to the races, and—the predominant impression—sampled but a cloistered part of the great offerings of Oxford.[19]

Is this a Whiggish rewriting of the past—a holding up of Rhodes to subsequent standards? It seems not, for Oxford in the 1870s was undergoing a vigorous intellectual renaissance. After sleepy, ecclesiastical decades, a Germanic-like rigor had begun to march across the Channel and to embolden the classicists of the university. English history was being written systematically for the first time. Constitutional history was being codified, and serious study was everywhere discussed. The notion that Oxford dons should do research as well as teaching was becoming respectable, if still a question for strident debate. Scientific subjects were being introduced. Most of all, the composition of the student body was changing, and a reasonable percentage of graduates were entering professions or joining the civil service. Formerly they had come almost exclusively from manses and had returned to them.

In the university, as in the Commons and the country, a fervor for imperialism was apparent. In 1874 the liberal government of Prime Minister Gladstone, with its stress on fiscal rectitude and on frugality overseas, was replaced by a Tory government led by the much more romantic, jingoist, and expansionist Benjamin Disraeli. David Livingstone had died deep in the heart of Africa in 1873, unleashing an outpouring of sentiment that mixed imperialist opportunism with a world power's responsibilities for trusteeship. Disraeli's government annexed Fiji, gained greater influence than before in Malaya, and acquired the Khedive's shares in the Suez Canal, thus stimulating conflict between Britain and France. Britain acquired Cyprus and looked covetously at nearby Egypt. Meanwhile, in 1877, Queen Victoria was proclaimed Empress of India. Much closer to Rhodes' interests, if not to his inspiration, in the same year Disraeli authorized the annexation of the Transvaal, and the notion that there should be a confederated South Africa under British control became a dream to be realized. Many of these and other imperial possibilities waxed and waned more as a result of local than metropolitan considerations, but by the time that their overall realization was dimmed by Gladstone's defeat of Disraeli in 1880, Rhodes was back in Africa, expounding and defining his own imperial ambitions.

Even if Rhodes' imperialphilia had its roots in Bishop's Stortford, with reinforcement in Kimberley, he could hardly have been unaware and uninfluenced by the sentiments that extolled expansion as a virtue and trusteeship as its ultimate glorification. Ever observant and calculating, Rhodes would have felt the strength of the positive currents then pulsating through the mother country and its premier university. A suspect source even reports that, taunted by friends weary of his constant talk about the empire, Rhodes in 1877 or 1878 wrote a long letter to Disraeli, then in his early seventies, giving advice on how best the empire could be ruled. No answer was received, and Rhodes never talked of emulating Disraeli. Nor did he ever consciously acknowledge deriving his dream of a line of British possessions "from Cape to Cairo" from the writings of Gladstone, whose views on the partition of Africa were hardly consonant with those of the later Rhodes. Gladstone argued against the annexation of Egypt, but others grasped the nettle of his negativism and envisaged a positive extension of empire: Britain's first site in Egypt, Gladstone said, "be it by larceny or be it by emption, will be the almost certain egg of a North African Empire, that will grow and grow . . . till we finally join hands across the Equator with Natal and Cape Town, to say nothing of the Transvaal and the Orange River on the south. . . ." Sir Edwin Arnold, editor of the *Daily Telegraph*, focused these unintended aspirations for a line of British possessions from the Mediterranean to the Indian Ocean into the catch phrase "from the Cape to Cairo," and Lord Salisbury and then Rhodes later echoed it and made the slogan their own.[20]

Most of the biographers eschew the influence of Disraeli, Gladstone, and their era on Rhodes and attempt, elegantly, to demonstrate the extent to which Ruskin's ideas must, a fortiori, have exerted a profound influence on the dreamy, impressionistic young Rhodes. Undated, among the papers in Oxford, Williams found the following signed holograph: "You have many instincts, religion, love, money-making, ambition, art and creation, which from a human point of view I think the best, but if you differ from me, think it over and work with all your soul for that instinct you deem best." He, and those writers who followed, have assumed, despite the lack of discernible links, that those words echoed Ruskin's, and, since the whole university thronged to Ruskin's lectures (he preached a gospel of "beauty and public service to an age wearied of ugliness and commercial self-interest"), that Rhodes must have been there as well. But Ruskin's famous inaugural lecture was in 1870, long before Rhodes reached Oxford. The lecture was printed, and widely distributed, but did Rhodes ever read it?

"One of those who influenced him most," wrote Lockhart and Woodhouse, was Ruskin, whose inaugural lecture set out a destiny for Britain which was "the highest ever set before a nation to be accepted or refused." Britain, said Ruskin, still had "the firmness to govern, and the grace to obey. . . . Will you, youths of England, make your country again a royal throne of kings; a sceptred isle, for all the world a source of light, a centre of peace; mistress of learning and of the Arts; faithful guardian of great memories in the midst of irreverent and ephemeral visions; faithful servant of time-tried principles? . . ." This is what England must "either do, or perish: she must found colonies as fast and as far as she is able . . . seizing every piece of fruitful waste ground she can set her foot on, and there teaching these her colonists that . . . their first aim is to be to advance the power of England by land and sea. . . . All that I ask of you is to have a fixed purpose of some kind for your country and yourselves; no matter how restricted, so that it be fixed and unselfish."

Ruskin went on in a vein that Rhodes, if he ever read the inaugural address, would have appreciated: "I know that stout hearts are in you, to answer acknowledged need; but it is the fatallest form of error in English youths to hide their hardihood till it fades for lack of sunshine, and to act in disdain of purpose, till all purpose is vain."

Ruskin led an army of young men to swampy ground north of Oxford. There he and they, armed with picks and shovels, attempted to construct a necessary road to Hinksey. The road itself was never finished, and the labor of many for two months resulted in a roadway that was mostly crooked and humped. Nevertheless, by this effort Ruskin successfully imbued many of the young of Oxford with his own fervent belief in the dignity of manual labor, especially on behalf of England. Even Alfred (later Lord) Milner, no mere acolyte, joined hands and helped to break the ground between Oxford and Hinksey. Yet, as Newbury so cogently argues, there is absolutely no evidence—not even the note found by Williams—that Rhodes was ever affected by Ruskin's popularity and the cult which helped spread his message of light, right, and duty.[21] Rhodes supervised laborers in Africa and might not have been attracted to a pious project of manual effort in the Oxford marshes. He could not have helped being aware of Ruskin, but so much that was central to Oxford seems to have interested him little. Not responding to Ruskin's influence should be considered another in the catalogue of Rhodes' omissions (or wise allocations of time), not his accomplishments.

Whatever course of study Rhodes pursued in his own, idiosyncratic fashion, however much he was or was not shaped by Oxford and the ideas of the 1870s, it is known that he continued to read and argue about the meaning of the great books to which he had always been partial. Aristotle's *Ethics,* Plato's *Republic,* Marcus Aurelius' *Meditations,* Plutarch's *Lives,* and Thucydides' *History* were still his own set pieces. Before Oxford, too, and more so then, he read and reread Edward Gibbon's *The Decline and Fall of the Roman Empire.* From it, as from Ruskin, he could have imbibed a heady, mystical brew justifying and extolling the fervor of imperialism which was already turning British heads. Britain was Rome's successor in world leadership. Destiny decreed its role, and Oxonians were to be its servants. If it is fair and accurate to insert these ideas into the complexity that was Rhodes, it is certainly much less likely that he was interested in the ideas for their own sake than he was for their practical application. For Rhodes, like other charismatic leaders, was always a simplifier and an applier; as he grew older he honed and crafted a unique view of the universe which was less affected by doubt than by a handful of commonplace, received, rather unremarkable concepts about man and his purpose.

In other hands these ideas might have led nowhere. It was his passion, bolstered by earnest, relentless repetition, that transformed these concepts into a creed which swept others up into his service. Massaged by Rhodes' powerful fingers, the ideas thus provided the sinews of achievement and the raw material of greatness. For him England was both mighty and right. It was obligated to extend its grasp (as Ruskin wanted and Gibbon had adumbrated) to make the world a better, purer place. Having discovered in himself a talent to coin money, whether by a happy coincidence of fortune and genius or of fortune alone, Rhodes could lend that ability to a mother country in whose eyes he would have wanted to gain favor and for whom the good works would matter and thus give him, and his own self, real meaning.

Oxford might have put the stamp of approval on such thoughts. It probably also inspired some of them, or at least gave them newly raised importance and, in conversation with his friends, further support and conceptual underpinning. Moreover, the impact of Oxford, like any other undergraduate experience, need not have been felt at the time, or all at once. Only gradually might Rhodes have understood its full contribution to the development of his own life. At the time, as he so often implied later, it was a place to make important contacts, to come to know representatives of the ruling class, and to gain the cachet that he felt he lacked. Until his father died in 1878, perhaps he also needed to pass through Oxford in order to gain merit in those critical eyes.

He never thought of Oxford as a place for narrow professional advancement. "I think I shall end in being jack of all trades, and a master of none," he wrote in 1877. So, together with Yerburgh, it was to the law that he turned, in 1876 beginning the curious process of paying fees and eating the required dinners at the Inner Temple. "I can get through in two years from now and have determined to do it," he told Rudd.[22] He then drew on his partner for £50, the price of entrance to the Temple. That payment entitled Rhodes to attend the public lectures of the Temple, and there to learn about the law, but no evidence remains to demonstrate that Rhodes (like so many of his peers) ever sought any actual instruction in the law. Rather, he wanted the security that would come from having a profession. Before being admitted to the bar through the Temple he would have to pass an examination, and before being permitted to sit the examination he had to eat the requisite dinners in the Temple in order to demonstrate that he had in fact attended the lectures to which few went.

Rhodes claimed that he wanted a profession in order to become a better speculator. With a secure vocation on which to fall back, he could be less cautious, have more pluck, and thus, or so he said, pyramid his fortune. "On calmly reviewing last year," he wrote to Rudd from Oriel in 1876, "I find we lost £3,000 owing to my having no profession. I lacked pluck on three occasions through fearing that one might lose and I had nothing to fall back on in the shape of a profession." He referred specifically to the abandoning of several claims at Dutoitspan and letting Robert Dundas Graham and E. Grey, Jr., purchase a part of the Rhodes-Rudd claims at the De Beers mine. "If I had not funked collapse," Rhodes confessed, none of those failures would have been necessary. "You will find me a most perfect speculator if I have two years and obtain a profession. I am slightly too cautious now." Much later in the same letter Rhodes reiterated: "By all means spare me for two years. You will find I shall be twice as good a speculator with a profession at my back."[23]

Whether or not this was but an excuse invented for Rudd, traditionally regarded as the more cautious of the two entrepreneurs, or a means of enhancing his personal prestige in the eyes of friends at Oxford and men like Merriman in South Africa, Rhodes still sought to become an adult. To prepare for the bar also expressed a quiet rebellion against his father. In psychological terms, reading for the law was artfully overdetermined.

Rhodes took but a mild interest in the bar. "My law experiences, up to the present time," he wrote in 1877, "consist of eating dinners and the theatre." He ate dinners and paid the necessary fees in 1876 and 1877. In 1880 he was still intending to "pass at the Bar."[24] But he did not return to the Inner Temple in 1881, and sometime after returning to Africa and after his father's death in 1878 he probably stopped paying the necessary stipends, his name being withdrawn from the register of the Temple in 1888. It was restored in 1891, presumably when Rhodes, then prime minister of the Cape Colony, remitted funds sufficient to pay the arrears. But there is no record that Rhodes ever sat any examinations of the Council of Legal Education.

Property in Britain was another hedge against the uncertainty of diamonds as well as a profit-making vehicle in its own right. At the end of 1873 Rhodes paid £6,200 for ten newly built brick houses three minutes from the West Hampstead railway station. He paid out £1,800 in cash, mortgaging £4,400 at 4 percent a year. Rents on the houses brought him an income of about £600 a year. By 1876 the ten houses were valued at £7,000, and Rhodes proposed either to realize his £800 profit (so that he could pay legal bills and loans from his lawyer or lawyers) or to sell a half share in the properties to Rudd. "This property of mine is so prettily situated and from all accounts is likely to increase in value, but of course if you accepted we would count from the last valuation." Rudd was either more cautious even than Rhodes or simply failed to want fancy houses in Hampstead; according to his son, Rudd did not in this instance go halves with his partner.[25]

Possibly Rudd's confidence in any investments had been sapped by an analysis of the future of diamonds that Rhodes presented in the remainder of a long letter from Oriel during his first months back at Oxford in 1876. He intended it to be cheerful and upbeat. "You will be in thick of bad times now," he warned Rudd, "but do not funk. The application of machinery to diamonds," he prophesied, "will lick depreciation in prices. England will recover gradually [from its panic over riots in Salonika, fears of war in Turkey, and resultant foreign bond losses]." "Diamonds," he observed, "are worn as much and more than ever. Only this year people are so poor that half London is unlet. There is simply no Season." And a few paragraphs farther on, he repeated himself. "If bad times have got you in a mess, do not funk. They are temporary. Diamonds in themselves are more liked than ever, all the swells now wear them in preference to anything but the people hit in foreign loans have been as you can understand selling their houses and diamonds, dropping their carriages and horses in town." Rhodes had faith in their mutual future.

"Considering everything," Rhodes concluded, "it is better to knock along with what we have got." He was referring specifically to the ice-making machinery, even though the earlier part of the same letter described the ordering of an elaborate ten-horsepower engine with winding gear, costing £485, and the prospective purchase of new steam pumps costing about £75 each. Nevertheless, he recommended minimal amounts of new machinery. "I say knock along as you can, be fined [by the mine board] for it and in the next contract make them cut connections."

His overall advice to Rudd on the future of their diamond properties was equally cautious. "Do not plunge," he wrote, "for much more at the Fields. We have a sufficient block at De Beers to make a fortune if diamonds last and have enough property in Kimberley. If we make more money I would sooner say lend it or go in for a nest egg here at home. . . ."[26] What could be less buccaneering than the modest entrepreneurial initiative of Rhodes at Oxford in the spring of 1876?

From the time he left home in 1870, Rhodes had explored the opportunities available to him, unconsciously seeking a set of activities to which he could commit himself and which would define him as an adult. He had traveled alone, literally to one of the ends of the earth. He had succeeded in an entirely new endeavor, growing cotton. He had established himself firmly, if provisionally, on the diamond fields. He had speculated successfully in diamond claims and land and had purchased and operated ice-making and pumping machinery. All the while he had kept open the possibility of returning to England to become a member of the legal profession. Yet by the time he sailed to Britain in 1876 to commence the main leg of his Oxford sojourn, he was still only twenty-two. He was ahead of himself, with an unusual breadth of adult experiences, yet by lacking serious commitment to a career he remained fully a late adolescent.

On the basis of studies of normal men, Levinson has identified the period from seventeen to twenty-two as Early Adult Transition, the stage of development in which there are two tasks: first, to move out of the pre-adult world by questioning and then separating from family relationships; and, second, tentatively to make and explore an initial adult identity. The next stage, Entering the Adult World, extends from about twenty-two to twenty-eight. In it young men establish a preliminary adult home base from which to test "a variety of initial choices regarding occupation, love relationships (usually including marriage and family), peer relationships, values and life style." Levinson notes the need "to *explore* the possibilities for adult living: to keep his options open, avoid strong commitments and maximize the alternatives. This task is reflected in a sense of adventure and wonderment, a wish to seek out all the treasures of the new world he is entering." Levinson contrasts a second task of this stage, *"to create a stable life structure:* become more responsible and 'make something of . . . life.' "[27]

Rhodes, enrolled for his second term at Oxford in 1876, may not have been prodigiously intellectual. But he was surely a prodigy of psychological development. He had, without faltering, begun to struggle at twenty-two with the developmental tasks of persons eight to ten years older. Or was he simply out of phase with himself? Was he both ahead and behind? Although precociously mature, had he retained hidden pockets of immaturity?

Rhodes was in no pathological way scarred by his precipitous entrance into adult activity. On the contrary, his experience at the diamond fields served to prolong a psychologically useful uncertainty. By precluding closure it kept possibilities open. As he entered Oxford, Rhodes may have needed to catch up with his lost youth. He required time to consolidate his sense of himself unhindered by direct involvement with the solemn responsibilities which he had left behind in Kimberley.

Rhodes' superficial, seeming aimlessness at Oxford can be seen as more than the dalliance of an intellectual lightweight, a South African parvenu seeking prestige for himself and advantageous contacts with which to further his career. His years there constituted a moratorium, a period of personal consolidation away from the serious calculations of the diamond fields. It allowed the unfolding of a significant psychological process.

According to Levinson, a major task to be accomplished in this early phase of adulthood is the formation of a "Dream." Levinson views it as a transitional phenomenon placed at the boundary between the present reality of a pre-adult world and what might be in the adult world. The "Dream" pulls together a vision to guide young men toward what they wish to become. For some it is a vague conception toward which they work more or less successfully.

These important psychological realities, and Rhodes' activities at Oxford, whatever their separate importance, were brought into focus by his introduction to and induction into the fraternity of Freemasons. At least it was sufficiently evocative in personal terms to occasion the commitment to paper of Rhodes' premier and forever most detailed statement of philosophy and belief. This was his "Dream." It matters that this uncharacteristic outpouring was the germ of his various subsequent wills and, ultimately, the Rhodes Scholarship scheme. But it matters more that his remarkable "Confession of Faith," written on June 2, 1877, articulates in a juvenile fashion both the principles and the coherent life agenda which had come to seem vital to Rhodes. They had been shaped by his first full year at Oxford—when the rationale of the universe may have begun to seem clear—but more so by the spirit of the classical authors and Gibbon.

William Winwood Reade, the then-obscure British Darwinian, influenced Rhodes' search for understanding. An unsuccessful novelist, Reade visited West Africa twice in the 1860s, the second time while Rhodes was in Natal, and published *The Martyrdom of Man* in 1872. Begun as an attempt to revise England's accepted and critical view of the contribution of Africans to human civilization, *The Martyrdom* became a universal history of mankind, with long sections on Rhodes' favorite mysteries: ancient Egypt, Rome, Carthage, Arab Islam, and early Christianity. *The Martyrdom* consisted of the kind of late nineteenth-century pseudo-science that appealed to Rhodes. It was larded with philosophically impressive arguments about the true "meaning" of man based on the post-Hegelian as well as neo-Darwinian notion that man's suffering on earth (his martyrdom) was essential (and quasi-divinely inspired) in the achievement of progress. Man was perfectable, but only by toil. He could not be saved, nor would his rewards be heavenly, for Reade was a pre-Tillichean gnostic who believed in God's existence but, at the same time, not in deism and certainly not in the accessibility of an anthropomorphic Christian God.

The rewards of man were in continuing and improving the human race. "To develop to the utmost our genius and our love, that is the only true religion," wrote Reade.

Reade was Rhodes' Ayn Rand or Antoine de Saint Exupéry. Or perhaps his Jules Verne, too, for Reade prophesied a locomotive force more powerful than steam, the manufacture of flesh and flour chemically, travel through space, and the discovery by science of a destructive force which would be so horrible as to end all wars. Rhodes read Reade only shortly after its publication and later said that it was a "creepy book." He also said, mysteriously, that it had "made me what I am."[28]

It is from Reade, Gibbon, Aristotle, and Marcus Aurelius, from the rough days at Kimberley, perhaps from the Umkomaas experiences, even from Bishop's Stortford, and somehow from a part of Oxford—and from the rushing imperial tide of Disraeli's Britain—that Rhodes drew inspiration. The Confession begins with an oft-quoted Aristotelian sentence that has become the hallmark of Rhodes' thought: "It often strikes a man to inquire what is the chief good in life; to one the thought comes that it is a happy marriage, to another great wealth, and as each seizes on his idea, for that he more or less works for the rest of his existence." For Rhodes the same process of thinking led to an answer: "The wish came to render myself useful to my country," that is, England. Most important, there were too few Britons. Rhodes referred not to birth limitations but to the fact that too little of the globe was British territory. "If we had retained America there would . . . be millions more of English living." Since "we are the finest race in the world and that the more of the world we inhabit the better it is for the human race," Anglo-Saxon influence could vastly improve those parts of the world "at present inhabited by the most despicable specimens of human beings." Wars would end, too.

"The idea gleaming and dancing before ones eyes like a will-of-the-wisp at last frames itself into a plan. Why should we not form a secret society with but one object the furtherance of the British Empire and the bringing of the whole uncivilized world under British rule. . . ." Particularly worthy, he reiterated, would be the recovery of the United States, where corruption and misgovernment had caused disgrace. Without the "low class Irish and German emigrants" it would have been a finer country. He blamed the loss of America on a few "pig-headed" statesmen of the eighteenth century.

"Africa," he went on in the Ruskinian manner, "is still lying ready for us it is our duty to take it." More territory would mean numerically more of the "most honourable race the world possesses." To forward such a scheme, Rhodes recommended a society working in secret for such an object. Justifying a secret society, he praised the efficacy, if not the results, of the Jesuit order, and condemned the mediocrity of the membership of the House of Commons. He asserted that there were many men currently unutilized, and equal in stature to the great statesmen of the previous century, who would enlist their talents in a cause as great as the one he was proposing. He wanted a "Church for the extension of the British Empire." It would be "a society which should have its members in every part of the British Empire working with one object and one idea. . . ." Tried and tested, those men who qualified for entrance into the society should be elected, bound by oath to serve, and supported financially.

Rhodes waxed nearly biographical. "Take one more case of the younger son with high thoughts, high aspirations, endowed by nature with all the faculties to make a great man, and with the sole wish in life to serve his Country but he lacks two things the means and the opportunity, ever troubled by a sort of inward deity urging him on to high and noble deeds, he is compelled to pass his time in some occupation which furnishes him with mere existence, he lives unhappily and dies miserably." The Society should find such men and use them.

Rhodes also advocated filling colonial legislatures with persons capable of advocating and promoting closer union with the mother country and the crushing of any colonial disloyalty to England. His proposed society should (precisely foreshadowing his own later activities) purchase portions of the press "for the press rules the mind of the people."

The conclusion of the Confession is simple: "For fear that death might cut me off before time . . . I leave all my worldly goods in trust . . . to try to form such a Society with such an object." He entrusted Shippard, then attorney general of Griqualand West, and whoever was Colonial Secretary when he died, with this all-encompassing task.[29]

The writing of the Confession stimulated no other immediate outburst of creativity, and was followed by no other written expressions of idealism. It remained largely unknown to his contemporaries at Oxford. However, Rhodes carried it to Kimberley in July and August, and had it copied, adding the final, informal paragraph disposing of his property. Along the way, in particular, in a Scotch cart between Port Elizabeth and the diamond fields, he had a lengthy discussion with Captain (later General Sir) Charles Warren about man's place in the universe—particularly whether or not station and accomplishment were predestined. Rhodes, of course, believed in the efficacy of achievement. As a disciple of Reade, Rhodes knew that man and man's accomplishments made a difference that was hardly trivial. Warren, who was subsequently to quarrel bitterly with Rhodes, recalled that despite their heated disagreement over this question as well as the Thirty-Nine Articles of the Anglican creed, and despite (or because of) the juvenile quality of the sentiments of the Confession, he found Rhodes one of the most fascinating men he had ever met. "It was impossible not to recognize that he had every prospect of a brilliant career in life."[30]

About a month after this discussion, in September 1877, Rhodes turned the last part of the Confession into the second of his formal wills. Shippard and the secretary of state for the colonies (then Lord Carnarvon) were appointed executors of his entire estate. They were instructed to establish a secret society, "the true aim and object whereof shall be the extension of British rule throughout the world, the perfecting of a system of emigration from the United Kingdom and colonization by British subjects of all lands wherein the means of livelihood are pragmatic by energy, labour, and enterprise, and especially the occupation by British settlers of the entire Continent of Africa, the Holy Land, the valley of the Euphrates, the Islands of Cyprus and Candia [Crete], the whole of South America, the islands of the Pacific . . . the whole of the Malay Archipelago, the seaboard of China and Japan. . . ." The United States was to be recovered and made an "integral part" of the Empire. A system of colonial representation in the British Parliament was to be inaugurated which would "weld together the disjointed members of the Empire" and thus create a power so great that wars (in the manner of Reade) would be rendered impossible. The trust was also designed, rather vaguely, to "promote the best interests of humanity."[31]

The extensive fantasies of the Confession, stimulated at least in part by the mystical links among Freemasons and Rhodes' own, Ruskinlike diagnosis of the ills of the world and mankind (with their roots in his own life story), were here embodied in a formal document drawn with legal assistance and seen by at least a lawyer and a copyist. As befits a dream, it far exceeded what was readily pragmatic by the exercise of his talents and resources. Instead, it served a developmental purpose by existing on the border between what was pragmatic and what might only be desired. It could express the farthest reaches of Rhodes' potential place in life, the height of his ambitions, and the largest scope of his concerns, without limiting him during the exploratory phase. The will set out a program, however general, for the conquest of the world by a secret society. Clearly, his means were not then adequate for the task. Shippard and Carnarvon were unlikely to be equal to his task either.

The Confession was a dream which served as a distant goal. It organized his actions and supplied coherence and meaning to the next phase of his growth. Reality testing could come later. Moreover, Rhodes was of serious intent, even if the practicalities of the confessional scheme were not then developed. The frequency and determination with which in subsequent years he commended it to persons he thought like-minded is indicative that the Confession and the will of the same year were never jettisoned from a central position in his ideological universe. In psychological terms, they represented his ego ideal.

The impetus to draw up another will, rather than leaving the Confession in its original form, might well have stemmed from a "heart attack" that Rhodes allegedly suffered in August 1877. It so "shook his nerves that his friends once found him in his room, blue with fright, his door barricaded with a chest of drawers and other furniture; he insisted that he had seen a ghost."[32]

Soon, too, he revealed his cherished ideas even to strangers. Joseph Millerd Orpen, a surveyor and sheep farmer, had been a landdrost, or magistrate, in the Orange Free State, and a member of its first Volksraad. Later he became a member of the Cape's legislative assembly and the magistrate in charge of Griqualand East. Subsequently, while engaged on a survey of the Hay district, he met Rhodes. On a visit to Kimberley which he dates to May 1877 (but Rhodes was then in Oxford), Orpen's elder brother took him to meet "a nice young Englishman." Rhodes' quarters were "a very small two roomed corrugated iron house with a wooden floor . . . iron walls and roof. In one room were a deal table and three chairs and in the other, opening out of it two stretchers and two chairs for himself and his chum." In the evening they all dined—Rhodes; Joseph Orpen; Francis Henry Orpen, the local surveyor-general; John Padden; and H.J. Feltham, manager of the local branch of the Cape of Good Hope Bank. Rhodes sat at the head of the table. After dinner he said: "Gentlemen I have asked you to dine . . . because I want to tell you what I want to do with the remainder of my life. I think if a man when he is young determined to devote his life to one worthy object and persists in that he can do a good deal during that life even if it is to be a short one as I know that my life will be but he can do still more if he has a few like minded friends as I believe you to be who will just lend him a helping hand when they are able to do so. The object of which I intend to devote my life is the defence and the extension of the British Empire. I think that object a worthy one because the British Empire stands for the protection of all the inhabitants of a country in life, liberty, property, fair play and happiness and it is the greatest platform the world has ever seen for these purposes and for human enjoyment. Everything is now going on happily around us. The Transvaal is much happier [since annexation] and much better off than it was and is quietly settled under government. The Free State is perfectly friendly and can join us when and if it likes. It is mainly the extension of the empire northward that we have to watch and work for in South Africa."

Joseph Orpen agreed, saying that he was "delighted to hear from him of his excellent intentions." The British government was "fundamentally the best." And the most economical. It was also a government particularly positive regarding Africans, Orpen having had experience in establishing the government of the Transkeian Territories. Francis Orpen went on to say that since all of those dining were of one mind, they should form themselves into a little committee. Whenever each wrote to another "earnestly about the principals and points" of Rhodes' ideas, they were to add before their names "the symbol of a five on the dice—the pyramid of brothers."[33]

By the time that Rhodes returned from Africa in the autumn of 1877, he was more secure in his wealth, possibly more confirmed in the philosophical positions which he had staked out in the Confession, in his will, and in his conversation with Warren, and no less disengaged than before from the academic pursuits of most of Oxford. Having reached some satisfactory psychological closure, his club life, hunts, theatre, and eating of law dinners continued and his air of "cynical detachment" presumably grew more apparent. At least until his father died on 25 February 1878, Rhodes' days at Oxford followed their usual intellectually and socially desultory course.

The Rev. Francis William Rhodes had retired from Bishop's Stortford to Hastings, Sussex, in 1876. There is no evidence that Cecil visited his father while at Oxford more than twice, and it is improbable that he spent any of the between-term holidays there. As one biographer notes, the senior Rhodes' death was for Cecil but a "minor bereavement."[34] Nevertheless, from about the time of his father's death Rhodes appears (the indications are all tenuous and external) to have had less and less interest in the Inner Temple and, for what little difference it may have made, in Oxford. Moreover, after the long vacation of 1878 he did not immediately return to Oxford, for all intents and purposes abandoning his quest for a degree until the brief and fulfilling return in 1881.

The lack of externally expressed emotion about his father's death, as well as his seemingly matter-of-fact but actually acute reaction to his elder brother Herbert's macabre demise in 1879, need not imply an unfeeling or self-centered reaction to such losses. There was always a defensive quality to Rhodes' relations with his father. Rhodes, although neither cold nor unresponsive in his relationships, usually guarded his deeper feelings. The untimely death of his mother and the manner in which he ultimately managed to survive her passing may have made the drama of first his father and then his brother's deaths easier to disguise.

Herbert was known for his great strength, his capacity for making friends of whites and untutored Africans alike, his athletic prowess, and a disposition which can easily be called roving. Cecil was fond of Herbert, following him to Natal and Kimberley, and then accompanying him on the long trek to Marabastad. But their temperaments were vastly different. Herbert was hardly content with diamonds, in late 1872 abandoning both Cecil and the possibility of a fortune there for the promise of gold in the interior. For the next three years he prospected for gold at Pilgrim's Rest, a miner's town in the eastern Transvaal, and settled down to the extent that the motley crowd of chancers and freebooters of nearby Lydenburg elected him to represent their area in the Transvaal Volksraad, or legislature, in 1874. Herbert Rhodes was also known as the proprietor of the "Spotted Dog," a notorious saloon in Pilgrim's Rest. The town may have been named for Herbert Rhodes' own band of twelve brothers, whom he called "pilgrims."

At one point, too, Herbert attempted to run guns from Delagoa Bay (Maputo) to the Pedi chief Sekhukhune; it was the failure of this initiative that propelled Herbert northward. In 1876, together with three Australians, he sought gold in the Zambezi River region and found alluvial sources in the sands of the Mazoe River, southeast of Tete in what is now Mozambique (and north of the white settlements in Zimbabwe that were later founded by Cecil). He returned to Natal briefly and visited Zanzibar. Then, in 1877, he joined James Frederic Elton, sometime explorer and South African labor recruiter and then British consul in Mozambique town, on a journey of imperial inspection up the Zambezi toward the northern end of Lake Nyasa (Malawi).

Like Livingstone before him, Elton was seeking an easy road from the southern Tanzanian coast to Lake Malawi, a task which Joseph Thomson continued. Herbert hunted elephant and gathered ivory wherever they went; together they also examined an agricultural experiment on the Zambezi devoted to the growing of opium. Elton wanted to see Britain annex the Nyasa regions; Herbert was more interested in gold, trade, and commercial opportunity. After he buried Elton in late 1877 en route to Zanzibar, Herbert returned to the western shores of Lake Nyasa and continued looking everywhere for gold. But all he found were traces of coal near Mount Waller. In late 1879, along the Shire River in southern Malawi, he continued to look for gold, to hunt, to talk to white planters about sugar, cotton, and coffee, and to visit African leaders. At the time of his death he was at the village of a Kololo chief; a demijohn of rum exploded accidentally or was set alight by African thieves. Herbert Rhodes died at thirty-four.

Herbert Rhodes' dramatic demise was communicated to Cecil by Frederick Courtenay Selous, the hunter, after the two brothers had long been out of contact. According to Lady Alexander, Cecil believed Herbert "very good company." His death was "a mystery, whether killed and then burned or burned accidentally." McDonald, who knew Cecil Rhodes well in Rhodesia, reported that Cecil felt Herbert's death "keenly, for Herbert and he had been greatly attached to each other, and from his elder brother he always said he had learned a lot." His only known written reaction was contained in a letter to his aunt about bills. It betrayed emotion: "What a sad affair Herbert's death is! I send you the paper with the account of it." He continued with an indirect and thus convincing evidence of his own depression. "I cannot write you any more news simply my life being that of a diamond miner there is dull monotony about it." Eventually, twenty years after Herbert's death, Cecil had a marble monument to his brother placed on the left bank of the Shire River, but incised with an incorrect year of death. Even if Cecil were as "deeply moved" by his brother's death as is commonly averred, this by turns emotional and brooding young magnate grieved in ways which were private and, in this instance as well as that of his father's death, out of the public eye.

It is also suggested that Herbert's wanderings and his untimely death directed Cecil to territories beyond the Limpopo and Zambezi rivers. Perhaps. Le Sueur, one of Rhodes' later secretaries, claimed that Cecil often credited Herbert with directing his sights northward—imbuing him with "his great ideas of acquiring the hinterland of the southern colonies for the British Empire."[35] But the Confession, the dinner gathering, and the formative if not necessarily informative experiences at Oxford all predated Herbert's end. It is impossible to discover what Cecil said to Selous, or what Cecil then turned and said about Herbert's death to his closest confidants in Kimberley. It is easier to believe that Herbert's death directed Cecil's curiosity to the Nyasa regions than that Cecil advanced his larger imperial ideas because of the example and death of Herbert. Whatever that influence, Rhodes turned his attention there only in the 1890s, as a naturally occurring, inexorable, and inevitable part of his gradually unfolding responsibility for trans-Zambezia.[36]

By the time of his brother's death, Rhodes had been back in Kimberley for at least eighteen months, without an Oxford degree or legal qualifications. With Rudd and Beit he was buying claims, focusing more and more on gems instead of ice, ice cream, and pumping, and gradually gathering the economic power which could make reality of his dream and would soon lead to the formation of De Beers, Ltd., control of that mine, and, subsequently, a tight-fisted monopoly encompassing all of the diamond fields. Possibly two years at Oxford had made his economic instincts bolder. His success as a young jack-of-all-trades was becoming evident. For these reasons, Rhodes stayed away from Oxford from April 1878 to October 1881. (Rhodes' faithful Aunt Sophy, as instructed periodically from Kimberley, kept his name on the college books by paying term fees and battels.)

When Rhodes returned to England for his final university term in 1881 he was both a successful entrepreneur and a newly elected member of the parliament of the Cape Colony. For seven weeks he read hard, at length "by dogged effort" passing the examinations for an ordinary B.A. On December 17, he also became an M.A. of the university; since more than seven years had elapsed since his original matriculation at Oriel he could, in effect, pur-chase the second degree to accompany the first. At the same time he "com-pounded for his dues," thus keeping his name on the books of Oriel and Oxford for life.[37]

Rhodes had no significant impact on the Oxford of the 1870s. Nor would it have been plausibly expected that an older, rugged colonial who kept terms episodically and largely consorted with men who found him unusual but not inspiring could have had much discernible influence as an individual in a college of 135 or a university of 2600. Lord Milner, Lord Asquith, and Wilde were all up in the 1870s and cut a wide swath even if Rhodes never knew them. Milner was president of the Union in 1875 and took first class honors, as did Asquith and Wilde. Rhodes stepped into college infrequently and con-fined his university exertions to the selected confines of the hunt and the clubs. "Rhodes did not strike either his college authorities or his contempo-raries," recalled a fellow of Oriel, "as a man of any great mark or as a man who was likely to have a very distinguished career."[38] Thus, it was only after his death that Rhodes, by his gifts to Oriel and through the splendid benefac-tions of his final will, made a perceptible mark on the university which he ultimately claimed as his own.

The legion of loyal biographers, working backwards from his will and taking at face value his own later evaluations of the Oxford experience, widely credit the nine terms there with a transformative influence on Rhodes the man, Rhodes the imperialist, and Rhodes the visionary. "For him," a recent biography gilds, "Oxford was not merely a matter of the terms he kept or the friends he made or the books he there found time to read. In Oxford fantasy and fact met, a conjunction that seldom happens in the life of any man. He had dreamed of a city hardly of this world, and found it much what he had imagined." Toward the end of his life Rhodes told Lady Grey that "no thinker . . . could escape [Oxford's] compelling influences, her wonderful charm." There are more accurate assessments of Oxford's meaning: in the early 1880s he exclaimed to Edward Arthur Maund that he loved Oxford and lived for it, but he also said—less ethereally—that it was "a good mill for turning out

Englishmen of a stamp fitted to either govern or develop the still unknown and measureless possibilities of Africa." In 1892 he instructed an assistant in Kimberley to show visitors from England around the mines. "They are from my old university," he wrote, "and I feel sure you will take extreme pleasure in knowing them. . . . They represent the cultivated thought and feeling of Oxford."[39]

This utilitarian response is the better key to a real understanding of the full range of Oxford's direct contribution to the making of Rhodes the man, the thinker, and the entrepreneur. Consciously, he went up to Oxford for veneer and, equally, in order to make useful friends. He wanted the security of a profession, too. Thanks to Rudd, however, who kept their joint enterprises functioning during the critical years of 1876, 1877, and 1878, the need of qualifications in Britain began to appear less urgent. Rhodes served time at Oxford. He took little advantage of its intellectual resources, hardly became more learned, was content as few were with a pass degree (and never later rued his failure to try for an honors qualification), and was—as the remainder of this book will show—influenced much more obviously in the development and realization of his grand design by the formative experiences of the years before Oxford and those afterward than by any particular intellectual germ which can even remotely be traced back to the great university. As Dicey later appraised Rhodes' time there, "Oxford has a peculiar art of putting a stamp of her own upon her pupils, but of this stamp in Rhodes I, personally, could never discover any trace whatever." However lavish the praise which Rhodes later heaped upon its dreaming spires, the Oxford of humanism and learning was not really essential to his ideas or his economic or imperial accomplishments.[40] Rhodes himself once told Merriman during a parliamentary exchange that the men who were successful at Oxford were, with rare exceptions, not those who subsequently "commanded . . . respect or admiration."[41] Rhodes paused and consolidated at Oxford. He brooded, constructed, and dreamt, and dreamt some more. Without this moratorium, Rhodes might never have honed his own sense of purpose or realized the immensity of his own inner conviction and strength.

6

"The Richest Community in the World"
Pursuing Position and Fortune

WHEN RHODES left Oxford in 1878 he intended to stay only six months in Kimberley. Two years later he was still there, still planning to return soon to Oxford, take his degree, and finish reading for the bar. Instead, Rhodes remained on the diamond fields until late 1881 when, studying hard, he passed his examination for the B.A., abandoned all immediate thoughts of the law, and as rapidly as was then possible, sailed south to resume his role as a successful financier and embryonic politician.

During those few years, when Rhodes was detained in South Africa by maneuvers on the mines and escapades of frontier war, a number of new, critical, and astute personal and financial relationships were established in Kimberley, and schemes for the extension of the economic power of Rudd and Rhodes (and their new partners) were confirmed and advanced. The foundations of Rhodes' own fortune, and the fortunes of many of his associates, were decisively, if still inconclusively and somewhat haphazardly, laid. The majority of biographers assert, following the earliest of their ilk, that Rhodes, having penned the "Confession of Faith" and begun to think, Ruskin-like, about painting the map of Africa British Red, sought riches primarily in order to further his grandiose ambitions. They argue, in the manner of Hensman, that "having found a definite object in life to which to devote himself, Rhodes . . . [saw] that it was of no use to attempt the erection of the . . . edifice before . . . [possessing] sufficient wealth to enable him to accomplish his purpose. . . ."[1]

Life is more than narrative. Nor is it always possible to discern motivation from an ex post facto array of events. Alas, motivation, particularly for the young, is rarely derived so simply; frequently ambivalent at its core, it stumbles over misunderstandings and hesitates because of old anxieties. It collides with the possible and must delay, detour, and defer. Although developmental periods of adults can be identified with considerable precision, individual lives display great diversity and fragmentation at the level of concrete events.[2] In establishing any calling, there are significant false starts and abandonments.

Rhodes' career in the years immediately following the enunciation of his Confession rarely followed a linear, deterministic course. Visionary he certainly was, but the translation of big ideas into purposefulness was never exact, and clearly less so in those hectic, comparatively tentative days. That he may much later have grandly told his mates that money was but the servant of power, and that wealth merely enabled him to carry out his (and their) dreams, cannot be doubted. But no close examination of the young Rhodes supports the notion that a fully fashioned grand design was being elaborated upon as early as the late 1870s. Rather, a much simpler explanation will do: when Rhodes came back to Kimberley at the beginning of Oxford's Trinity Term, 1878, he found his opportunities buoyed by a rising tide of world prosperity, by the growing complexity of digging the deeper reaches and blue ground of the main mines, and by instability (and consequent labor problems) on the Cape's eastern frontier, in the Transvaal, and in Zululand. A clear head, an awareness of how the many local parts composed a greater whole, an entrepreneurial initiative, the ability to make synergistic use of the assets of newly developed colleagues, and the sheer pleasure in simultaneously making money and gaining power and prestige better explain why, if not how, Rhodes stayed in Kimberley and promoted a series of acquisitions which soon provided him with a large measure of the town's diamonds.

Each step led to the next, and that is the manner in which Rhodes, allied firmly with Rudd, proceeded. He was not so much patient as reactive. The dreamer still dreamed the big dreams, but at this stage his economic actions on the mines betray no great sweeps, no striking strategic coups, and no imperious magic. Rather, Rhodes was, as before, persistent, careful of details, alert, and immensely capable of moving men and making the utmost of individuals. He was still aged little more than twenty-five, known only in narrow circles in Kimberley, and was not, before about 1880 (when he was twenty-seven), nearly so prominent as many of his partners and several of the men, like Joseph B. Robinson, who were to become his major competitors.

Although Rhodes never seemed to notice, Kimberley was as unlike Oxford as any colonial town could be. In 1877, it was the second largest urban agglomeration in South Africa, after Cape Town. Among a population of 18,000 in greater Kimberley, about 8,000 were white, two-fifths of whom were women. Of adult males, two-thirds were black or Coloured. They all lived in conditions Trollope, who visited briefly, described as "distasteful . . . in the extreme." He commented on the torrid heat (a steady temperature of nearly 100 degrees Fahrenheit in the shade) and the fetid atmosphere of dust and flies—"dust so thick that the sufferer fears to remove it lest the raising of it may aggravate the evil, and of flies so numerous that one hardly dares to slaughter them by ordinary means lest their dead bodies should be noisome." Trollope's complaint—"when a gust of wind would bring the dust in a cloud hiding everything, a cloud so thick that it would seem that the solid surface of the earth had risen diluted into the air, and when flies had rendered occupation altogether impossible"—stimulated jovial invitations to come back in a December or February when the dust and flies were truly bothersome.

"In all Kimberley and its surroundings there was nothing pretty," Trollope reported. There were no trees within five miles of the town nor blades of grass within twenty. Everything was brown. Within the town all of the buildings were of "hideous" corrugated iron. Moreover, "the meat was bad, the butter uneatable, vegetables a rarity . . . milk and potatoes were luxuries." Trollope wondered how anyone could possibly endure, much less live so meanly, even for diamonds. "An uglier place," he said of the town's famed square, "I do not know how to imagine."

Yet Trollope was pleased to describe the Kimberley mine as one of the "most remarkable spots on the face of the earth." About nine acres in extent, "the largest and most complete hole ever made by human agency" was then 230 feet deep, oblong, light brown (from iron) near the top and down the sides, and the remainder, and the working surfaces, blue. Around the edge there were high raised boxes used to hold the earth as it was brought up out of the mine by whims (horse-drawn aerial tramways hauling buckets), half barrels, or large iron cylinders. One firm had sunk a shaft to avoid employing aerial means, another had constructed an ordinary inclined plane into the mine. In 1877 there were about 408 full working claims subdivided into a total of 514. Nearly 4,000 Africans used picks and shovels in the mine itself, being paid about ten shillings a week, plus food. "Perhaps the most interesting sight at the mine is the escaping of the men from their labour at six o'clock. Then, at the sound of some welcomed gong, they begin to swarm up the sides close at each other's heels apparently altogether indifferent as to whether there be a path or no. They come as flies come up a wall, only capering as flies never caper,—and shouting as they come."[3]

In Trollope's time (Rhodes returned five months later), the Kimberley mines were little recovered from the economic recession that had encouraged revolt and the first serious steps toward amalgamation. In 1878, reaching the blue ground, firmer and more difficult to excavate than the arid yellow soil of the upper part of the mines, did not appear to mean the end of Kimberley's prosperity. Everywhere in the world before, mining bonanzas had been temporary wonders; when the blue ground was reached in the mid-1870s and digging and sorting proved more laborious and at first less rewarding, the confidence of hardscrabble miners deteriorated along with the external financial climate. Ground water seepage as well as flooding during the rainy season continued to be a hazard. Graver problems followed the disintegration of the encasing reef of decomposed basalt and shale. Exposed to air and moisture in the deepening, open pit, the unstable walls of the mine crumbled rapidly. Cutting straight downward without the provision of terraces or stable slopes (more prevalent at the Kimberley than the De Beers mine), also proved imprudent, causing serious slippage. Lone claim holders could hardly bear the cost of removing the dangerous reef. Expensive machinery became more and more necessary; mining by a single white prospector and two or three black pick-and-shovel operators on a part-claim proved less and less efficient. Most of all, because the blue ground had to be weathered for long periods before it could be broken and the diamonds discerned, and because more laborers were required, the single digger lacked the kind of assured financing which larger combines could command. In terms of efficiency, sustained cooperation was preferable to energy or initiative alone. "Unluckily for the advance of diamond mining and the fortune of many struggling claim-holders," wrote a contemporary authority, "this irresistible conclusion was not made clear to the mass of miners until it was demonstrated after long years of costly fumbling in the diamond-bearing funnels."[4]

Rhodes may have "clearly" seen the opportunities presented by this transition as early as 1874 or 1875.[5] He may further have wanted restrictions relaxed on the number of claims capable of being controlled by a single proprietor or company. But there is no evidence that he ever agitated for such changes, wrote to Rudd or others about a thoroughgoing reconstruction of the diamond industry, or appreciated the full significance of the structural alterations until they were well under way in the late 1870s. Success, particularly in entrepreneurial affairs, may rest on factors other than individual innovation and the singular creative breakthrough. Rhodes' achievement rested in part on the instinct for collaboration of a middle child with an adoring mother and a band of older brothers. It was an instinct which happened to fit well with the technical requirements of diamond mining at a particular phase of its history in Kimberley. The result was that rather than leap, he drifted, partly unwittingly, toward the modus operandi that would ensure success. Others saw that collaboration and consolidation were imperatives. Rhodes may have been better than they were at realizing such objectives. After Southey scrapped the two-claim limit on holdings in 1874, and capped companies and individuals at ten claims, Rhodes and Rudd (in partnership with Grey and Graham) bought as much as they could of Baxter's Gully in De Beers mine.

Further expansion and control was blocked, however, until 1876, when a British commissioner investigated the financial position of Griqualand West and recommended that, to cut its own costs severely, the British government ought to abolish all ordinances that hindered mining operations. Companies should be free to acquire and consolidate multiple claims, to amalgamate, and to expand to the extent that market forces would permit. Indeed, the commissioner even contemplated the development of a monopoly which could control the supply of diamonds to the world market and, in Kimberley, police illicit diamond buying, thefts, and other security matters in lieu of an expensive colonial-sponsored operation. He envisaged a new regime in which only whites would be permitted by law to hold claims or wash diamondiferous earths; Africans would be restricted to unskilled labor occupations. He wanted limitations placed on saloons, and an end to gun sales and wide open brothel keeping. The reduced responsibilities of the new government of the colony would be financed not by Whitehall but by taxes raised from the companies, which would expand oligopolistically.

The Colonial Office and its local administrator in mid-1876 accordingly eliminated all bars to the entrepreneurial employment of capital, to enlargements of scale, and to the consolidation of different holdings deep in the emerging big holes. Rhodes, Rudd, and Graham took advantage of this shift to continue buying in Baxter's Gully, a rich area threatened by an overhanging reef of barren ground. Across the reef, George W. Compton gained control of Poor Man's Gully, broke through the reef toward the Baxter properties, and was soon persuaded to merge by Frederic S. Philipson Stow and Robert English, both of whom were in hot competition with Rhodes, Rudd, et al. for claims in the Baxter area. During Rhodes' time at Oxford, Rudd and Graham must have done most of the buying and most of the jockeying for prominence in the ten-acre De Beers mine; when they began the properties were more numerous (622 claims in all), less expensive, and more cheaply worked than those in the richer Kimberley mine.

At the Kimberley mine, amalgamation and consolidation were being pursued during the late 1870s even more aggressively than at De Beers. The Francis Baring Gould company (soon the Central Company) was in the vanguard. So was Robinson's own concern (later the Standard Company). Also powerful and growing was a company which had been launched by Jules Porges, a Dutch-based jeweler. It was represented in Kimberley by Julius Karl Wernher, a handsome, commanding, young German merchant. Wernher and Porges merged its claims in 1880 with those of the Kimberley Mining Company, controlled by Isaac and Barnet Lewis and Samuel Marks, and others, to form the Compagnie Française des Mines de Diamants du Cap du Bon Esperance, the so-called French company. There were also the holdings of Barnett Isaacs (Barney Barnato) and his brother, the claims of Woolf and Solly Joel, and others of lesser rank.

Rhodes' return to Kimberley coincided with an upswing in confidence about diamonds and the long-term richness of the blue ground. Nevertheless, the reef was slipping faster than it could be hauled away, and much of Kimberley mine (less of De Beers) was being covered by fallen reef. Haulage and drainage were proving much more costly than expected, and as promising as the crater appeared, the more difficult it seemed to the faint-hearted that steady riches were to be won from its depths. Rhodes, remarkably confident for a twenty-five-year-old, refused to be timorous.

Despite those latter-day skeptics who assume that Rudd's role in the speculation of this period must have overshadowed that of Rhodes, the very fact that Rhodes remained at Kimberley for three years longer than planned testifies to his undeniable role in making Rhodes, Rudd, et al. a formidable force in the emerging company-dominated world of Kimberley. Rudd was like a reassuring older brother whose restraint and loyal support gave Rhodes the confidence to speculate, but Rhodes had many of the ideas and the savvy.

Thompson, Rudd's friend, recalls that both men realized (as so many others did not) that if the mines were craters, the unyielding and at first unproductive blue ground must continue to hold diamonds. The blue, initially thought to be bedrock, and then waste ground, was finally appreciated to be a form of compressed blue mud which slowly pulverized upon months of exposure to the air. Given such a positive analysis of prospects for diamonds (which would be proved only a few years later), Rhodes, taking a calculated risk that was critical to his fortune, persuaded Rudd that buying claims cheaply from less sanguine holders, or from banks which had foreclosed on defaulters, made good sense. Their capital came from profits on their pumping and ice businesses, as well as from continued earnings on their own diamonds.

First Rhodes had to overcome Rudd's innate caution (he then had two small children) and Mrs. Rudd's opposition. In the process Rhodes doubtless refined his own schemes as he had been compelled to do by his father. The partners started with £4,000, added the capital of Grey and Graham, forged ahead during 1874 and 1875, and then did so decisively in the period after 1876. By 1878 they owned forty claims, worth £9,000. Rudd was the senior working partner in this period and, obviously when Rhodes was at Oxford, bore the brunt of the responsibility and the burden of the actual supervision of their assets in Kimberley. A good collaborator whose instincts complemented Rhodes' own, he curbed but also provided an anchor to Rhodes' financial and visionary flights of fancy.[6]

Rhodes' correspondence betrays nothing but equality between the two. During the late 1870s and from 1881 on, however, Rhodes' career trajectory began to accelerate rapidly. He began to emerge as an initiator, even as a leader. He was in a greater hurry than Rudd, and had ambitions for their joint pursuits as well as for himself in other capacities. Moreover, Rudd, cautious and astute, never put all of his economic bread into Rhodes' basket. His other ventures remained important and profitable: the wire-rope business, his insurance agency, the sale of cigars and spirits, and so on. In 1879 in the local *Independent* appeared two standard advertisements for C.D. Rudd: one selling "Bottled ale and stout, Bottled Cider, Champagne, Claret, Sherries"; the other (bearing the same address on Natal Street) selling "Oilmans Stores, Corrugated Iron, Sheet, bar, and angle iron, Sheet and bar Steel, Pine Boards etc."[7]

Of the founders of modern Kimberley, Robinson stands out as a stubborn, single-minded capitalist who demanded sole control of each of his enterprises. Rhodes, starting with fewer means, and being many degrees less wealthy in the 1870s than Robinson, Baring Gould, Stow, Barnato, and Porges— to name but a few rivals—necessarily, as well as characteristically, preferred a wholly different approach. From the early links with Rudd, Rhodes naturally saw advantages in joining his energies and ambition to those of others. Thus it was during the critical months leading up to the formation of the De Beers Company that Rhodes, probably less accidentally than the usual anecdotes imply, met Alfred Beit.

Late one night Rhodes was passing Beit's office and found him still working. "Do you never take a rest?" he asked Beit. The latter replied, "Not often," and when Rhodes continued the conversation by asking Beit, "Well, what's your game?," Beit supposedly replied that he intended to control the diamond output of Kimberley before he was too much older. "That's funny," was Rhodes' response. "I have made up my own mind to do the same." And, keeping absolutely in character, Rhodes proposed not to compete (as Robinson or Barnato might have done). Instead, he is said to have told Beit: "We had better join hands."[8]

A few months older than Rhodes, Beit was born into the sophisticated German-Jewish family of a once-prosperous Hamburg merchant. Because his father was in ill-health during much of Alfred's early years, and because his mother determinedly exercised a greater and greater sway over the family during those particularly difficult times, Alfred (like Rhodes) always cherished an unusually close bond with his mother. Young Alfred was educated in a private school, where he was hardly the brightest of pupils. He was uninterested in pursuits athletic, and only upon coming to Kimberley, where horses were a necessity, did he learn to ride.

Since neither his family fortunes nor his success at school justified a university education, the young Beit was apprenticed to a diamond-broking firm in Amsterdam. This proved a turning point, even though both Beit and his firm regarded his capabilities as only average. When he was twenty-two, he left Amsterdam for Messrs. David Lippert & Co., a trading house of Hamburg. Lippert was a cousin. Beit was sent shortly to Lippert's branch in Port Elizabeth. "Within two years after his arrival," reports his biographer, "this environment had converted the boy of mediocre talents . . . into a man of impetuous unremitting energy and enterprise, whose solutions of financial problems and of business intricacies were so almost spontaneous, and so invariably correct, that they could only be ascribed as due to the working of a form of genius."[9]

Whether it was environment, opportunity, or new-found maturity, the later-blooming Beit soon showed a financial acumen, an uncommon grasp of the diamond business, and personal traits which ultimately endeared him to Kimberley's capitalist fraternity. During 1875, Lippert & Co. sent him there, 400 miles from Port Elizabeth, to buy diamonds for the firm. His reputation as a sharp-eyed broker developed slowly, but by the time that Rhodes made his acquaintance, Beit was established as an independent buyer. He was still a man of comparatively modest means. Even so, his judgment of the value of diamonds was more and more widely recognized as superior to any competitor's. Before this period, the buying and selling of uncut stones in Kimberley was done more by chance than by skill. Values fixed there, during the first sales (or "sights") were not always confirmed in Antwerp, Amsterdam, and London. Trained carefully in Europe, and developing a growing confidence, Beit's ability to assess values accurately made his name and consolidated the fortunes of those who sold their finds through him.

"When I reached Kimberley," Beit told Frank Harris, "I found that very few people knew anything about diamonds; they bought and sold at haphazard, and a great many of them really believed that the Cape diamonds were of a very inferior quality. Of course, I saw at once that some of the Cape stones were as good as any in the world; and I saw, too, that the buyers protected themselves against their own ignorance by offering for them one-tenth part of what each stone was worth in Europe."[10] Beit eventually employed his knowledge of the European markets to invest in diamonds on his own account. He also bought land, erected a dozen iron shanties, and rented them for handsome prices.

Rhodes was attracted by Beit's skill and standing, possibly by his potential connections to the financial world of Dutch, German, and Jewish Europe, and certainly by the expertise which such a person could bring to Rhodes' growing ambitions to encompass the diamonds of Kimberley. Rhodes may have been equally attracted to Beit's learning and his acquaintance with the sophisticated central European culture of which Rhodes was only gradually becoming aware. After all, in the late 1870s in Kimberley there were only a few men with such interests and pretensions. Moreover, Beit had simple tastes (like Rhodes), was known for his gentle demeanor, his probity, his generosity of spirit and giving, his charm, his ease of friendship, his lack of interest in women (he never married), and a retiring manner that bordered on shyness. He loved to gamble, and win, but never enjoyed playing cards (preferring the role of banker), drinking, or the usual pursuits of Kimberley after dark. Fastidious, conscious of detail, and careful, he complemented Rhodes in many ways. "At bottom," reported Harris, "Beit was a sentimentalist. . . . This was the fine side of the man, the side through which Rhodes used him, the side which, by contrast with his love of money, showed the breadth and height of his humanity. Of all the millionaires I had chanced to meet, Beit was the best."

In person, however, Harris did not consider Beit—then in his prime—as remarkable. He was short and plump, with a head seemingly too large for a little body. But, said Harris, the head was "excellently well-shaped, the forehead very broad, and high-domed to reverence and idealism, like a poet's; and the rest of the face was not so good; the nose fairly large, but slightly beaked . . . a good rudder; the chin rather weak than strong—no great courage or resolution anywhere." Beit's brown eyes were prominent, "the glance at once thoughtful and keen; the mouth coarse and ill-cut, the lower lip particularly heavy. It reminded me of Rhodes's face; but Rhodes's mouth was coarser and more cruel than Beit's; his nose, too, larger and more beaked; his chin and jaw much more massive—altogether a stronger face, though not so intellectually alert."[11]

One particular quality which may have endeared Beit to Rhodes was an apparent disdain for the actual accumulation of capital, while doing so well. What moved Beit most, Rhodes later declared, "was to be rich enough to give his mother £1,000 a year." Upon the occasion of Beit's first return from South Africa he took his mother for a drive, inquired whether she liked the carriage, the horses, and the coachman, and then gave them all to her. "Mother," he said, "when I was a boy I always hoped that one day I should have enough money to give you a carriage and a pair of horses, and now my dream has come true. . . ."[12] Rhodes' mother died before he could do the same.

As sympathetically as Rhodes and Beit regarded each other, they began to work closely together only in the mid-1880s, after Beit had left Lippert and started representing the diamond buying firm of Jules Porges & Co. Even so, given their mutual interests and the joy with which each always remembered their first conversations, it is reasonable to assume that Beit may have encouraged Rhodes to enlarge the scale of his mining enterprise, or at least provided financial advice. By 1879, Rudd, Rhodes, and Graham (Grey had been absorbed) had merged with Runchman, Leigh Hoskyns, and W. Puzey. Subsequently they joined forces with H.W. Henderson Dunsmore and Graham Alderson. In competition for the best ground in De Beers were the firms of Stow, English, and Compton; the Elma Company, owned by Thomas Shiels and others; James Ferguson's Victoria Company; and the United Diamond Mining Company. The better to deal with the technical problems of mining, as well as to gain some control over supply, and therefore prices, Rhodes was instrumental in merging the first three of the above firms into the De Beers Mining Company. It owned ninety claims, with a value of £175,369.

This, the centerpiece and major contributor to Rhodes' fortunes, imperial adventures, and benefactions, was established as a joint-stock company on 1 April 1880, with a nominal capital of £200,000. Alderson held 631 shares; Rudd, Graham, and Rhodes 280 each; Dunsmore 209; and three others 54, 53, and 25. Only 100 were offered to the public. Graham became chairman, and Rhodes secretary, positions conceivably representing Rhodes' desire to keep a close watch on the finances of his fledgling enterprise. In 1878, Stow, the leading commercial attorney in Kimberley, had begun to buy claims in De Beers mine with English, and in 1879, with Compton. In February 1881, Stow, English, and Compton exchanged shares with De Beers, effectively merging their forces and together gaining an unassailable hold on the mine. The new De Beers was capitalized at £665,550. Stow held 16,000 shares, Alderson 11,000, English 6,000, Rhodes 5,000, Graham 4,000, and Rudd 3,000.

Stow's subsequent account of this amalgamation is one-sided, written as it was after a long friendship with Rhodes had soured because of what Stow was convinced was Rhodes' bad faith. Nevertheless, Stow stated, with at least some accuracy, that the second merger had been forced on Rhodes and De Beers because Stow et al. held rich claims, and the best position strategically, cutting off any amalgamation east and west across the mine. When Rhodes realized the strength of Stow's position, "and that no further combination of ownerships of an advantageous nature was possible he approached [Stow] and made overtures which eventuated in our accepting a portion of his firm's holdings as of sufficient value to justify an amalgamation. . . ." After the merger, Stow went on to explain, "a great intimacy between Rhodes and myself sprang up which continued unbroken for many years."[13]

This second merger brought into being yet another "band of brothers."

From 1881 the principals in the enlarged company met each morning in a little shack near the mine to arrange their operations and report progress. For several years they were interested primarily in purchasing existing claims and expanding their area of control. By 1883 they had bought out all but six other companies and three individuals. By 1885 they owned 360 claims, and only three companies and two individuals remained outside. But they also hired a manager and combined their experience and skills in the service of more economical mining. Working together proved advantageous, particularly since many of their claims were threatened by a floating reef: "when the reef fell they could concentrate upon it all their tackle, and all their boys, and clear the ground so as to have a good spell of the blue ground before another fall came down."[14]

Rhodes was more confident than others of the continued viability of Kimberley. "There is every chance," he wrote to Merriman, "of our prosperity lasting; the old fear of the mines working out is rapidly fading, for instance the Kimberley mine, which is now 300 feet deep, has a shaft in its centre 180 feet below that level and no signs of change, diamonds being found out of the stuff coming out at the bottom of it. . . ." The Dutoitspan mine, once derelict, was also proving a cornucopia of diamond wealth. "What I want to impress on you," Rhodes wrote, "is the fact that this is now the richest community in the world for its size and that it shows every sign of permanency."[15]

Once De Beers was formed, its shares rose rapidly during a speculative boom. Kimberley, Rhodes wrote in 1881 to Rudd (who was in England), "is full of money." But Rhodes, careful in these early years of costs, worried that Edward Jones, the new manager of De Beers, was spending too freely. Although he had training and experience in Cornwall and Wales, and although Jones was someone of whom Rhodes pronounced himself personally fond, there were possible excesses. Jones was a "swell engineer" and employed a number of whites to assist his operations, spared no expense, and, reported Rhodes, "makes the money fly." He was spending about £6,000 a month. "I do not complain of him but still it is the old story these swell men will not work cheaply and you cannot make them. Jones . . . piles up the white men and expenses frightfully. . . ." Later in the same letter Rhodes repeated: "The expenses are simply damnable."

Rhodes neither contemplated nor hinted to Rudd that Jones should go. He was in fact looking beyond the working of their mine properties to further speculation. He particularly implored Rudd to obtain information from the Colonial Institute in London, and other sources, about the legal standing of abandoned diggings. "Please attend to this," he told Rudd, "you know exactly what I require Book on Mining rules in Australia and New Zealand would also apply as to lease of abandoned diggings it was done I know there."[16] At this stage, too, Rhodes and Rudd were jointly involved as shareholders in Kimberley's first water supply company, and Rhodes—although certain that he and Rudd had been shabbily treated by a switch of concessions—had no intention of selling his holdings, even to realize a profit. Rhodes additionally sat on the boards of six other diamond companies, including one of questionable quality, and had stakes in the tramway, laundry, coal, and other commercial areas. He was a director of the local stock exchange and made good profits there. But he was never a listed diamond buyer. Rhodes made most of his early money honestly, but some was made as a result of shady dealings in shares; he floated at least one company shell.

Despite his emerging position as a mining amalgamator and leading commercial promoter of the town, and despite a reasonable estimate that Rhodes and Rudd in 1880 could each have been worth as much as £50,000, Rhodes was often without liquid funds. One of his first acts as secretary of De Beers was to draw an advance on salary for himself. The amount was £5. In 1881 he had to sell some De Beers shares prematurely to raise "the ready." He had been dependent, too, on Aunt Sophy and his brother Frank for the payment of bills (especially to tailors) in Britain. Apologizing profusely to his aunt in early 1880, he remitted more than £400 in order to expunge a range of debts and to repay Frank £100. In explaining his tardiness, he alluded very casually to the final stages of the critical consolidation of the De Beers mine, a project upon which his future depended, and with the success of which he was intimately absorbed. "I own I am to blame," he admitted, "but every mail almost I intended leaving and the whole of our mines here are going into large home companies and negociations still drag on and yet I do not like to go until I have settled, and thought tailors and bootmakers might very well wait."

In the next paragraph, despite the prosperity which he was forecasting, the political shifts which were about to transfer the diamond fields into the Cape Colony, the end of the frontier wars, and the intricate financial arrangements which he and his associates were concluding, Rhodes, who was also feeling the effects of Herbert's death, could give his aunt little news "simply because my life being that of a diamond miner there is but a dull monotony about it . . . really this country is without change and is merely a Dead Sea plain." Probably in response to an entreaty from his aunt, he waxed sentimental, personal, and very curious in his turn of phrase: "I would like very much to see you again. You can quite understand that excepting just at times one completely forgets about home and home ideas. . . . The only way I can fully make you understand it is by saying that I am in the same sort of point to you in this remote corner of the earth as you will be to myself if you get to heaven, just I mean total oblivion on your part as to earthly matters."[17]

Rhodes was rarely unaware of his own precarious mortality, and Herbert's death had made him much more concerned. For him the word "oblivion" was not a casual association. Conceivably, this off-hand comment to his aunt was simply another indication that Rhodes had contemplated grand plans of universal importance, and greatly feared being denied their accomplishment. Or, more simply, he had no wish to be cut down on the brink of financial and personal success. As a speculator in diamond properties, and as a producer of gems, he and his colleagues were becoming more powerful and potentially very prosperous. As a longtime resident of the young town of

Kimberley, Rhodes was becoming better known and more widely respected. To have been knocked to oblivion would have ended Rhodes' quest for standing and control in a South African, an imperial, and an intensely personal sense. From his late twenties, if not before, Rhodes was always closer to death in his own mind than others of his age.

Rhodes had glimpsed armed combat. "The only thing I can say," he told his aunt, "is that I have escaped being shot." [18] Specifically he was referring to his own participation in a punitive expedition against Africans who had attacked the outlying reaches of the small colony. Armed with rifles, Rhodes and other volunteers in early 1879 swelled the ranks of the crack Diamond Fields Horse regiment, commanded by Colonel Charles Warren (Rhodes' recent acquaintance), and saw action against dissident Korana at Saltpan, near Christiana, on the Vaal River. Brave as Rhodes may have been, and as critical as this engagement might have seemed to him, another prominent local resident described the affray as "much ado about nothing." The only shot fired, Matthews said, was by accident. [19]

Earlier, in 1877, the Horse had been mobilized under Warren to help the Cape Colony. Its 120 Kimberley volunteers rushed to the eastern marches of the Cape to assist British and Cape forces in overcoming a serious attack by Xhosa-speaking militants from both sides of the Kei River. The soldiers of the Horse saw action in Pondoland, 500 miles from Kimberley, and, after five months in the field, were summoned back home to cope with two other violent protests by hungry Africans. First, in January 1878, north of the Orange River, the Tswana-speaking Thlaping rose against whites who were carting away their precious firewood and attempting to take their land. The Horse relieved the besieged mission village of Kuruman. Second, in April 1878, the regiment put down a Griqua insurgency in and around Griquatown. Like so many other conflicts between black and white, land was at issue. "So gross was the injustice sustained by these people in the land court," a former deputy governor told the Cape parliament, "that had I been a Griqua, I too would have rebelled." [20]

It is unfortunate that little is known about Rhodes' role in these wars—or about precisely how and why Rhodes became so involved in events which would have disturbed his steady focus on diamonds and ancillary, profit-making activities. It is clear, however, that he took at least several trips "to the border" in connection with the northern war, and possibly also with the war against the Transkeian Gcaleka and their allies.

Rhodes reported in 1880 that Griqualand West, and the entire diamond industry, had endured two unsettled years because of these "Kaffir Wars." In addition to skirmishes in his own vicinity, Rhodes alluded to a particularly costly combat which had begun in 1877 on the borders of the Transkei. The eastern Cape frontier, peaceful for twenty-five years, began to be troubled from about 1876, when a cruel drought started to take its toll. Like so many other peoples who depended on precious rain during the few months of summer, the Xhosa-speaking Gcaleka were devoid of other resources. Lung sickness affected their cattle, too, and as the presence of powerful whites prevented them from migrating to more promising locales, the Gcaleka and the other subdued peoples of South Africa tried by stealth or war to restore their fortunes. The harvests of 1877 and 1878 were total failures. Whether the Gcaleka were provoked or were obstinate and truculent, as the colonists averred at the time, they fought the collaborationist Mfengu, and, as a result, a white Cape police force attacked the Gcaleka in late 1877 and forced them to retreat well back into the Transkei. Their old lands were to be confiscated.[21] But, after being humbled, the Gcaleka soon regrouped and forced their way across the Kei into the anxious Cape Colony. There they made common cause with their close kin, the Ngqika, who lived in the Colony near Kingwilliamstown. The Ngqika may well have feared a pre-emptive strike by whites. Thembu, also living in the Colony, joined the hostilities against the whites. Yet once two regiments arrived from Britain to join the defensive efforts of a Cape detachment and the Diamond Fields Horse, which had hastened from Griqualand West, this last Cape frontier war was brought quickly to an end.

But there were other wars, too, which would have impinged upon Rhodes' consciousness. In 1878 Pondo and Griqua fought whites for control of Griqualand East, in what is now the northern Transkei and southern Natal. Sekhukhune's Pedi (northern Sotho) in the eastern Transvaal near Herbert Rhodes' Pilgrim's Rest, who had also endured drought, attempted during the same period to reclaim a measure of independence from Boer and Briton. Early in 1878 they tried to overrun white settlements east of the Lulu mountains; British troop reinforcements found the Pedi resistance formidable and overcame it only by a war of attrition which lasted until late 1879. Of greater significance for South Africa and the onward march of imperialism, even if of less immediate relevance to the diamond fields, was the final crushing defeat of the great Zulu kingdom. At the beginning of 1879 Zulu legions overwhelmed 800 British troops at Isandhlwana in the same way that Ethiopia was to humble Italian invaders at 'Adwa in 1898. But the Ethiopians made good their independence; not so the Zulu. Six months after their initial defeat the British returned, conquered the Zulu at Ulundi, and annexed the kingdom to Natal.

It was in the context of these wars and their victories for whites, as well as an emerging consensus among whites about the ways in which the labor needs of South Africa could be met most efficiently, that Rhodes, now twenty-seven, began to enter upon his political maturity. Given the gist of his Confession and his conversations with men like the Orpens, Rhodes' consciousness as a protean political doer certainly would have been influenced further by the failure, in these same years, of a vigorous attempt to unite South Africa. His views were less well formed than those of Merriman, however, who brooded about the future and wondered whether South Africa was really destined to become an outpost of Europe. "I think much of the future of our Native races," Merriman wrote to his mother. "It looks dark at present and will do so as long as we persist in regarding them as enemies and in imagining that this place is ever going to be a great European Colony—and shutting our eyes to the manifest future which I see before us, of being the great controlling power over the black races in the southern half of the continent."[22]

But this kind of thinking, rare enough even in Cape Town, was largely absent, even on the clerical and missionary circuit, throughout South Africa. More common in the late 1870s, especially where thousands of unskilled workers were in demand, was the belief that the time had come for whites to ensure the steady and dependable exploitation of African labor by almost any reasonable means. Tapping the reservoirs of African human energy in the British colonies and dependencies, as well as in greater South Africa, became a single-minded goal of locally based officials as well as settlers and their political representatives. At the magisterial level, representatives of the colonial system believed that it was their duty to force Africans to migrate toward the towns and mines of the Cape, Natal, and Griqualand West. Otherwise, in times of recurrent famine, there would be no income flowing into the rural areas, and taxes could not be paid. Many, including missionaries, sincerely believed that Africans would become civilized only if they learned the virtues of work. Trollope, visiting Kimberley in 1877, waxed positively saccharine: "Who can doubt but that work is the great civilizer of the world—work and the growing desire for those good things which work only will bring?" The winning of diamonds from the earth by Africans permitted such a civilizing influence to be expanded. "I have not myself seen the model Christian perfected; but when I have looked down into the Kimberley mine and seen three or four thousand of them at work . . . I have felt that I was looking at three or four thousand growing Christians."[23]

Further rationalizations abounded: Africans were indolent because they were tribal. They could not be introduced successfully to Christianity and civilization without the erosion of indigenous habits and pursuits, which would come when tribal Africans were in the wage service of whites. Africans were simple and natural. Therefore they would surely benefit from direct and enduring contact with whites. It followed that they ought to be squeezed "out of their unimproved simplicity into the fruitful contact with European civilization that was found at railway construction works and diamond diggings." The notion that Africans had simple wants was a further excuse for paying them little, or taxing them out of all proportion to their wealth. The Cape legislature in 1881 officially wanted "in the interests of the Agriculturalists and other Employers of Labour in this Colony, as well as in the interests of the Native Tribes upon and beyond our Borders, to encourage in every practical way such Natives to engage in Agricultural and other Labour." To use de Kiewiet's words, "the unintentional collusion between the genuine humanitarian desire to improve the condition of the natives and the selfish motive of exploitation" became institutionalized in South Africa during, and with causal connection to, the shift at Kimberley from the era of the digger to the epoch of entrepreneurial oligopolistic-seeking capitalism.[24]

Rhodes the diamond miner needed no romantic idealizations to justify his employment of black labor. Kimberley's prosperity depended upon a steady flow of migrants willing to work in its gaping craters. Even so, as a disciple of Gibbon, Marcus Aurelius, and even Reade, it would have made no sense to Rhodes to eschew the employment of Africans or the spread of British rule by conquest or other means over peoples like the Gcaleka. Likewise, he may not have been anti-Boer, in 1880 or later, for Rhodes generally tried to avoid making enemies, but he was very seriously pro-British. He believed sincerely in the benefits of Pax Victoriana, and certainly would have welcomed Britain's annexation of the Transvaal in 1877 as much as he would have deprecated—and drawn lessons from—Britain's failure to make that annexation a cornerstone of a South African empire.

The fourth Earl of Carnarvon was Disraeli's Secretary of the State for the Colonies from 1874 to 1878. Earlier, holding the same office from 1866 to 1867, he had sponsored the British North America Act, which effected the confederation of Canada. Beginning in 1875, Carnarvon promoted the idea of a similar union of the South African colonies, republics, and unannexed "native" territories.

The South African Republic (the Transvaal) had fallen on hard financial times and was essentially bankrupt. Griqualand West was expensive to administer, as was Natal. Policies toward Africans (especially with regard to gun selling and defending against their collective military threat) were not congruent in the region, and many asserted that the development of the whole, to the benefit of all, even Africans, could best be achieved by a British-sponsored union. Carnarvon's treasury mandarins were seeking economy as well as efficiency, but Carnarvon (and Disraeli) were equally persuaded that the spread of British imperium was a positive good, particularly in unsettled areas which abutted critical sea routes (in this case to India). A conference called by Carnarvon in 1876 proved inconclusive, so, at the end of that year, his civil servants drafted a Permissive Federation Bill (modelled on the North America Act) which was intended to be adopted, but never was, by the colonial and republican legislative bodies. He also approved the peremptory annexation of the Transvaal as a supposed step to federation.

Accompanied by a small police force, Sir Theophilus Shepstone, formerly chief native commissioner of Natal, entered the Transvaal from Natal early in 1877. His instructions were to assume control, with or without popular consent. This he did, in April, somewhat to the relief of the insolvent government in Pretoria, but certainly without its support and with the clear opposition of the Volksraad, or assembly. The Volksraad had refused to vote new taxes; Africans were threatening the Republic from several directions, and the recent recession had made the farmers of the comparatively isolated land less confident about their future. But Shepstone had neither the funds nor the skill with which to administer the Transvaal or overcome Pretoria's suspicion of British intentions. Nor could Sir Bartle Frere, the new high commissioner and putative governor-general, develop any broad constituency in southern Africa for Carnarvon's policies.

With the replacement of Carnarvon by Sir Michael Hicks Beach in 1878, the imperial momentum slowed. It braked further after the military disaster at Isandhlwana, and then met a growing, if at first passive, resistance among the Boers of the Transvaal. Meanwhile, Gladstone and the Liberals, no friends of imperial extension, returned to power in Britain. Finally, Boers tested British strength at the end of 1880 and early in 1881, winning three skirmishes, including a critical one at Majuba. Later in the year the two sides signed the Convention of Pretoria, which restored independence to the Transvaal but prohibited the settlement of Boers beyond its then existing borders. A British Resident, with limited powers, was placed in Pretoria, and the Transvaal and Britain concluded an agreement over the Transvaal's debt and British financial aid. Reserved to the Crown, and called suzerainty, were continuing imperial rights over the Transvaal's foreign affairs and its dealing with Africans. The Transvaal had endured the trial of an imperial confederation; from the viewpoint of Kimberley and the Cape, the Transvaal, now stronger than before, remained a major obstacle to territorial expansion and the free flow of migratory labor.

Out of the collapse of confederation, the imperial government salvaged only one important initiative. In 1880 the Cape Colony legislature finally agreed to incorporate Griqualand West; under confederation it would have remained a separate province. But the terms of the merger were at first sufficiently in dispute for Rhodes to lobby his old friend Merriman, a member of several Cape cabinets and most recently minister of Crown lands. Rhodes urged Merriman to look with favor upon any proposals to give more than the promised four representatives in the Cape Assembly to Kimberley and its environs, and also—for obvious reasons—to support the proposed extension of the railway from Beaufort West, halfway to Cape Town.

"We are evidently to be at last annexed," Rhodes wrote. "I hope if there is any chance of increased representation for this place you will not oppose it." Rhodes knew that Merriman disliked railways built for the sake of patronage—"that wretched system of making a railway to every village in the country for the sake of the political support of its members"—yet Kimberley's wealth and promise merited a direct line. "If you will take a word of advice from an old acquaintance, do during this session," Rhodes remonstrated, "show a consideration for this Province . . . namely, an increased representation and railway extension here, both of which are fairly due. . . ." Doing so, Rhodes enticed, would "not be regretted by you afterwards."[25]

Griqualand West was officially folded into the Cape Colony in October 1880. Despite Rhodes' letter to Merriman, its representation remained four, two from the electoral division of Kimberley, and two from the essentially rural constituency of Barkly West. The first parliamentary election was scheduled for March 1881. Although Rhodes was still a mere twenty-seven, and had never entered political contests in Griqualand West, his fame was beginning to spread beyond his special coterie of intimates, sometimes called the twelve apostles, and the corporate band with whom he was associated in business. It is not known whether Rhodes joined Joseph B. Robinson and other worthies in 1879 in opposing annexation to the Cape and in forming the Constitutional Reform League as an expression of opposition to Cape domination and probable neglect. (Robinson and others wanted greater home rule for Griqualand West, and the inclusion within their own colony of African lands to the north.) Nor is it known whether Rhodes supported Robinson's successful candidacy for mayor in 1879. But it is clear that he worked closely with Robinson as a member of an official committee to build and organize Kimberley's first public library. In early 1881, too, Rhodes, who decided to stand for Barkly West, was among those prominent men who promoted Robinson's candidacy for one of the Kimberley seats, and helped overcome Robinson's reluctance to stand. After many entreaties over a number of weeks, Robinson finally agreed to become one of three candidates. The voters backed him too, at least over George Bottomley, a temperance figure, but Dr. Josiah W. Matthews, a popular, caustically liberal physician who had been vice president of the Griqualand West legislative council, topped the poll. "The unlimited expenditure of money by the one, and the pertinacious sectarian adherents of the other [Bottomley], proved a formidable opposition, but the all-round support given the 'red, white and blue' enabled me," wrote Matthews, "a second time to become the senior member for Kimberley."[26]

Rhodes also had an easy time. "I am pretty safe," he wrote to Rudd on 1 February 1881.[27] That may have been the understatement of his political career, for, at no time thereafter did Rhodes, who in 1881 shared the Barkly West double seat with Francis Orpen, stand for election without opposition. Even so, Rhodes represented Barkly in season and out until the day he died.

Many writers have found it puzzling that Rhodes should have cast his political lot across the Vaal, with a handful of remaining river diggers and a small number of Afrikaans-speaking farmers—the main voters of this vast and rawest of parliamentary divisions. In 1877 Trollope described Barkly as "half-deserted," with but a score of houses and a small hotel. A modern authority suggests that Rhodes may have been attracted to Barkly and its farming vote by some "atavistic urge," for Rhodes was fond of saying that his ancestors were "keepers of cows."[28] But there is no deep mystery: Rhodes was not one to take too many chances. To have tangled with Robinson or Matthews would have risked defeat and reputation. True, he was a Kimberley man, and diamonds were his consummate interest, but being elected from Barkly would do. The needs of the mining industry, and his own ambitions, if any, for more than diamonds could just as easily be furthered from any seat in the Assembly. Conceivably, too, Rhodes may have thought that the largely unlettered farmers would have been more impressed by his university education than would the rougher crowd that eventually voted for Matthews. Whatever led Rhodes to seek a seat in Barkly, the choice was canny.[29]

More important in some ways is the larger decision. Why did Rhodes, hitherto little interested in politics, decide to leave the stewardship of his mining company for distant Cape Town? None of his partners, least of all, Rudd, would have encouraged such political ambitions.[30] Rhodes was not then nor later terribly interested in the give and take of political life. He never enjoyed campaigning or the finer points of debate. Clearly he had particular goals in mind, whether or not they were fully imperial and programmatic. Flint suggests that since Rhodes had imperial ambitions, and in 1881 lacked the wealth-based power that he would later wield, he appreciated that his ultimate goals could be achieved only with the political support of greater South Africa, particularly that of the Cape Colony. A parliamentary seat was thus a clear means to a series of ends.[31]

Such is a plausible conclusion. But it credits Rhodes with a prescience and a knack for long-range planning that he had not then begun to display. Rhodes was a tactician, always, and a grand strategist only later (when he could tug at many levers of power). To suppose that Rhodes in 1881 could think his way forward, and know how each step would lead to the next, is to misrepresent his abilities and his genius, as well as the means by which persons with a higher curve of accomplishment realize their potential for achievement. It is more in keeping with the development of the man to suggest that for Rhodes there were parochial needs which could best be advanced by parliamentary preferment. In order for both his company and his town to prosper, Kimberley needed to be connected to the sea by rail. There were questions of taxation and of tariffs which would intimately affect his own fortunes as a mining proprietor. Other young men might have been content to wait their turn, but the high-potential individual "at 25 years of age can be seen to be able to detach himself from the concrete; that is how he achieves his initiative and imaginativeness. The great industrial innovators were never bound down to a perceptual relationship with the concrete, even when employed as youths in starting positions as manual workers or clerks."[32]

If the concerns of Kimberley were foremost in his mind, Rhodes also would have viewed parliament as a place in which his name and influence could spread. If that spread occurred, and if he prospered, then a seat in parliament might assist in the realization of his greater fantasies. Rhodes was inherently reactive. He brooded and he schemed, but most often took pawns before approaching the bishops and rooks.

Rhodes was doubtless further encouraged by others to seek a parliamentary seat. Dr. Leander Starr Jameson may have urged him to represent the area, and Merriman claims to have had an influence. Merriman and Rhodes rode together in the mornings during the early days of Kimberley. "He used to talk," Merriman wrote much later, "not about ordinary sort of subjects but of the future of the country and things rather out of usual talking [for a] boy." Later, when Rhodes traveled through Cape Town on his way to and from Oxford, he stayed with Merriman. "He was a curious fellow and some times had fits of religion rather morbid in fact," said Merriman. On at least one occasion, Merriman persuaded Rhodes that "the most intellectual occupation for a man to take up in S. Africa was to go into Parliament. He was imbued with that and when we annexed the Diamond Fields he came down with the first lot of members. . . ."[33]

Jameson was Rhodes' alter ego. As surgeon and friend, but mostly as true intimate, he exerted a life-long influence on Rhodes. Their acquaintance began in 1878, shortly after Jameson arrived to share the established medical practice of Dr. James Perrott Prince, an American. (Prince had written to University College, London, asking for a partner.) Robert William, Jameson's father, was a Scottish lawyer and a member of the prestigious legal corporation known as the Writers to the Signet. But Robert also was well known as a Radical free-thinker who preferred to involve himself controversially in local politics and to write epic poetry and plays, at least one of which was performed on the Edinburgh stage. Whether because of his suspect views or because he preferred to practice his literary rather than his legal gifts, Robert Jameson prospered little financially. By the time that Leander Starr was born, on 9 February 1853, in Edinburgh, the eleventh and final child, his father was focusing more on affairs of the pen than of the law, and was leading the large assemblage of Jamesons into the kind of distinguished impecuniousness that was also present in Beit's early life. Jameson's mother, Christian Pringle, the daughter of a major general, was another of those women of character: "A strong sense of duty was the best part of her inheritance," says the official biographer, "and corrected, as far as possible, the effects of her husband's rashness." Leander Starr, the last of so many, must have been a favorite, and, like Rhodes and Beit to their own mothers, was close to this central figure of the Jameson clan.

Robert Jameson's distaste for or growing lack of success at the law led him, in 1854, to assume the editorship of the Wigtownshire *Free Press,* based in Stranraer, on the Scottish border with England. Leander Starr lived there until he was seven, when Robert went south to edit two papers published in Sudbury, Suffolk, coincidentally twenty-five miles northeast of Bishop's Stortford. After less than two years, the family moved permanently to London, to Chelsea and Kensington. Robert wrote for the many weekly reviews of the capital, and Leander Starr, who had been named for an American, went to school privately in Hammersmith. Robert Jameson died in 1878, when both Leander Starr and Rhodes were fifteen. Later, with an elder brother paying his fees, he entered University College, London, and there received B.S. and M.D. degrees. He obtained his clinical training at the nearby University College Hospital, successively achieving stature and preferment within its walls. He qualified for membership in the Royal College of Surgeons and, so his contemporaries believed, had a brilliant future before him as a significant London surgeon.

Unexpectedly, Jameson gave it up for a general practice in a remote colonial mining town. Why? Possibly, his biographer suggests, because there was "an overpowering restlessness in his Northern blood." Or perhaps because an elder brother already in South Africa sent home a large diamond. Was it avarice or adventure that propelled Jameson to Kimberley? Or did Kimberley in the 1870s have a reputation which would have attracted a young man who was anxious to avoid the entanglements of courtship and marriage?

At twenty-five, when he sailed to South Africa, Jameson was short, slim, boyish, with a manner both brusque and winning. Like Herbert Rhodes, he exhibited a "joyous almost reckless zest for life and carelessness of self and selfish interest."[34] In Kimberley, he soon achieved a medical and personal following, being widely known for his skill and charm, as well as for his love of poker and gambling. In 1879 he was appointed one of the first three consultant medical officers of the town. "Hardly a more popular notability resided on the Diamond Fields," wrote Cohen, "than clever, wellfashioned Dr. Jameson—especially with the ladies. No matter what happened to be the trouble with matron, maid, or widow, a visit from the dexterous Doctor would always set things right." Even so, Jameson was not the marrying kind, "never," as he himself wrote, "having felt the least inclined in that way."[35]

By the time that he had purchased Prince's share of their lucrative practice in 1881 (much of it caring for African employees of the mines) and become an established fixture in town, Jameson and Rhodes were close acquaintances. "From the day of my arrival at Kimberley, when I fell in with him," Jameson later recalled with a touch of hyperbole, "we drew closely together, and quickly became great friends. . . . We were young men together then, and naturally saw a great deal of each other. We shared a quiet little bachelor establishment together, walked and rode out together, shared our meals, exchanged our views on men and things, and discussed his big schemes, which even then filled me with admiration. I soon admitted to myself that for sheer natural power I had never met a man to come near Cecil Rhodes. . . ."[36] Jameson may be dating the day of their taking up residence together a few years prematurely, for Rhodes in the late 1870s was eating ("messing") with Shippard, Graham, and a host of others, still known as the Twelve Apostles. But the remembered attachment cannot be faulted.

Rhodes was strongly attracted to other men, and lived with at least one in preference to Jameson, but from 1878 or a few years later, Rhodes and Jameson were unusually intimate; only Metcalfe spent as much time with Rhodes. Jameson recalled that Rhodes by the early 1880s was thinking out everything for himself independently, and was growing in self-confidence. Jameson would have encouraged Rhodes to seek a parliamentary seat and would have helped him, if need be, to deter potential opposition. Jameson's support, and his infectious sparkle, may have added to Rhodes' unique ability to seize the main chance and turn it (and almost everything) to his own advantage.

In 1881, Rhodes, the successful amalgamator, the advocate of railways and of the rationalization of diamond mining, entered the lower house of the parliament of the Colony of the Cape of Good Hope. Ten months later, after completing his degree at Oxford, Rhodes returned to South Africa to make money from diamonds, to advance his political career, and to develop and then enlarge upon an array of projects which together, after a time, constituted Rhodes' personal imperial imperative.

7

"I Don't Have Many Principles"
Forging Political and
Personal Alliances

WHEN RHODES took his seat in the Cape of Good Hope House of Assembly in early April 1881, Gordon Sprigg was prime minister at the head of a cabinet of seven others. Parliament itself comprised seventy-two members, was riven with antagonistic personalities, and divided bitterly in a variety of unpredictable ways on issues as fundamental as the treatment of Africans and white farmers, taxes and tariffs, the building of railways, and how best and with what degree of commitment a young, hesitant colony should engage itself in the ongoing struggle for hegemony in southern Africa.

Sprigg was only the Cape Colony's second leader since the whites had won responsible government from the Crown in 1872. He had served since 1878, and had largely pursued an aggressive policy toward Africans on the frontiers of the Cape. Encouraged and emboldened by Sir Bartle Frere, the Cape had acted as a sub-imperialist agency, annexing Fingoland (Mfenguland) in the eastern Cape and Griqualand East in the Transkei. Its magistrates controlled the remainder of the territories beyond the Kei, and were responsible in Basutoland (Lesotho). Griqualand West, with its diamond fields, had been brought into the Colony. But as successfully as the Anglo-Cape alliance had mastered Xhosa-speaking Africans and the Thlaping to the north, the Sotho were still in rebellion in 1881.

Even more ominous, when Rhodes entered parliament the devastating defeat of Britain by Afrikaners at Majuba was only six weeks old. The attempt to extend imperial rule to the Transvaal by annexation in the name of confederation had thus failed, and failed signally. The Transvaal and the Orange Free State were destined in at least the short term to remain independent of any overall southern African coordination. The Cape had once again to look more to its own, unique interests. Moreover, Majuba had signified a British refusal to be strong and to interfere, which Gladstone's resumption of the British premiership had cemented. Rhodes entered upon his political career at a time when federation was dead, if not buried, when Britain was perceived widely as a power infirm and dilatory, and when antagonism between speakers of Dutch and English—because of both the taking of the Transvaal and Britain's failure to keep it—was growing in importance politically.

Cape Town itself was less isolated than before. Steamships were beginning to rush their way from Europe, taking only three weeks. Railways were radiating out of the Cape to Beaufort West and on to Hopetown, Colesberg, and Aliwal North. Within the capital itself there were electric lights, and fresh water from the first reservoir. A breakwater had been constructed to shelter large vessels, and a graving dock had been built to repair them. In the Colony there was new money: from troops and contractors engaged in and supplying the frontier wars; from diamonds; from the produce of the prolific Cape farms. There was a boom which followed a period of inflation elsewhere in the world, and work was resumed on the actual houses of parliament, the construction of which was begun in 1875 and was to be completed a decade later.

This was the setting for Rhodes' introduction to political life. Even if he had not subsequently monopolized diamonds, occupied the lands of the Shona and the Ndebele across the Limpopo River, and bestowed the munificent scholarships which bear his name, Rhodes would still have achieved local recognition and at least modest biographical attention for his influential, if quirky and unexpected parliamentary career. He had a surprising and lasting impact on the political development of the Cape, as well as on larger events and the spread of imperialism. From the first, too, Rhodes, although twenty-nine and doubtlessly callow, exerted his will on men his senior in both age and experience. They were, for the place at least, urbane and skilled in the maneuvers of politics. The House was formal and mannered, as befitted a colonial outpost of the empire. It had a code and a pattern to which Rhodes, despite Oxford, was loath to conform. What he accomplished in a place largely foreign to his nature, using methods which were much more stilted than those to which he was accustomed, he achieved despite a cranky, idiosyncratic assertion of independence, and despite a variety of personal traits which endeared him to few. The experience in the House was a true test of Rhodes' magnetism—of that special will and genius which explain his many successful assertions of personal conviction and persistent leadership.

Rhodes' entrance into the House, and his behavior and first speeches there, hardly pleased its older members. One friend predicted that he would be a "parliamentary failure." Refusing to don formal apparel, Rhodes created an early spectacle by dressing "without the least consideration for fashion." He himself said later that he was "still in Oxford tweeds, and I think I can legislate as well in them as in sable clothing." Equally offensive and defiant of the authority of substantial men such as his father, Rhodes began his career by referring to other members by their names instead of their constituencies, and was rebuked by the Speaker. His "free and easy manners" bothered those of his fellow representatives who were accustomed to the sedate ways of the chamber.

An unnamed reporter or other observer recorded that Rhodes in those early days presented "a good upstanding appearance, being somewhere about six feet in his shoes. He ha[d] a good physique, [was] a muscular-looking man, well-shaped in every way, ha[d] a pleasant intelligent face, and [was] a very good type of a well-bred English gentleman. He . . . [was] always unaffected and unpretending; he [was] an exceedingly nervous speaker, there [was] a twitching about his hands, and he ha[d] a somewhat ungainly way of turning his body about. . . . . He [was] in a continued state of restlessness, whether sitting in his seat or standing on his legs. He [was] never still from the time he enter[ed] the House until he [left] it."[1]

Thomas Fuller, then one of the leaders of the parliamentary opposition, remembered him in 1881 as a "tall, broad-shouldered man, with face and figure of somewhat loose formation. His hair was auburn, carelessly flung over his forehead, his eyes of bluish grey, dreamy but kindly. But the mouth—aye, that was 'the unruly member' of his face. With deep lines following the curve of the moustache, it had a determined, masterful, and sometimes scornful expression. Men cannot, of course, think or feel with their mouths, but the thoughts and feeling of Cecil Rhodes soon found their way to that part of his face. At its best it expressed determined purpose—at its worst, well, I have seen storms of passion gather about it and twist it into unlovely shapes."

Few members of the House of Assembly so combined a brash personal insouciance with the forceful expression of independent views on important issues. Hardly anyone else delivered those opinions in rambling, egocentric phrases, and in a voice that every now and again broke into falsetto. For one so young his speech was "bluff and untutored in style with no graces of oratory." "He doesn't make a speech at all," was one report. "He gets up and has a sort of confidential chat. . . . His abrupt, jerky style, it may be added, has made him the terror of shorthand reporters, who find some difficulty in following his alternate halts and very quick dashes of speech." Rhodes was "not a rhetorician in any sense," reported Fuller. "His speeches had no introduction and no peroration. He went straight to the point, dealing with the subject under discussion with an easy, masterful confidence. He was not a hard hitter in debate, but rather a persuader—reasoning and pleading in a conversational way as one more anxious to convince an opponent than to expose his weaknesses." Now and then he was sarcastic, but he did not try to score points in debate. Instinctively empathetic, even in parliamentary debate, his method was to speak in a conversational tone, employing language less than terse and sentences hardly epigrammatic. "His style," said Fuller, "like his manner and the movements of his body, was leisurely and easy, and somewhat lumbering. 'To be fair with you' was a common phrase of his, as if he wished to give full weight to an opponent's argument, and go with him as far as he could." When attacked personally, no matter how bitterly, he would employ his empathic talents and "endeavour to conciliate and turn away wrath rather than resent it." He asked adversaries to "come and dine and we will talk it over." This characteristic, Fuller assures us, was a matter of method, not cowardice. It was better to reason issues out rather than fight. Nevertheless, continued Fuller, his speeches displayed "strength of will and purpose. The disposition to compromise was on the surface," and did not disturb the achievement of his underlying aims.

When he spoke, Rhodes had little gesture. "He often kept his hands behind him, or thrust one forward towards the person or persons he was especially addressing, or passed it over his brow in a pausing way. When he considered his argument especially convincing, he would conclude his speech by flopping down on the seat with an expressive jerk, as much to say, 'Answer that if you can!' " Others remembered his gestures, which were thought to be boyish and "uncouth," and odd affectations like his "trick of sitting on his hand and laughing boisterously when amused." He openly expressed impatience with the speeches of the other members of the House. And he fidgeted, which must have driven his colleagues to distraction.[2]

Yet the members of the assembly came to listen attentively to what Rhodes had to say. "In some subtle way" he loomed above them all. Was it his refreshing candor which appealed? Was it his logic, difficult though it might have been to follow amid the tangents and the repetitions of his oratory? Or did the fact that he was one of the new rich from the diamond fields gain attention and even respect despite his mannerisms and lack of traditional forensic talent? Rhodes himself would have asserted that it was the sheer weight and common sense of his advocacy which gained him an early following. Like the vicar, he "spoke from his toes," believing passionately in whatever he was arguing. Further, Rhodes articulated positions on the issues of the day which transcended petty loyalties and were designed to advance the best and broadest interests of the whole Cape. He would have denied being a sectionalist; many contemporaries extolled his imperial foresight and bold attention to geopolitical realities. From the very first, said Rhodes years later, he had been influenced by the humiliation of Majuba, and had determined to overcome the destructive vacillations of "the Home Government."[3]

There is certainly a measure of truth in positive answers to the questions just posed. There is support for the depiction of Rhodes as a political visionary, but the weight of evidence from his early parliamentary career suggests that Rhodes was careful to serve his constituency, to work ceaselessly on those who would at least not oppose what he thought desirable for Kimberley and later for the Cape, Britain, and southern Africa. Thus Rhodes befriended Jan Hofmeyr, the leader of the Dutch in the assembly. Hence, too, the young man of ideas, with a characteristic attention to outcomes and influence, cynically and stealthily purchased a controlling interest in the *Cape Argus,* the main newspaper in the Cape, the better to report his speeches in full, the better to blunt or at least answer any criticism, and the better to control the reactions of the public to the debates of parliament.

In 1881, Rhodes, in great secrecy and through an intermediary, gave Francis Dormer £6,000 in two installments to effect the *Argus'* transfer. It was owned by Saul Solomon, the doughty Cape liberal and longtime senior member of parliament. Dormer had been his editor for many years. Before the bargain was struck, Rhodes and Dormer had a lengthy discussion. Rhodes agreed that Dormer should "steer a middle course so far as native policy was concerned." Rhodes, like later white South African leaders, believed that African questions received much more attention in the press than they deserved. Now that diamonds were being mined at Kimberley and the rails were being advanced northward, there was no question but that whites, not Africans, would "be the predominant factor in South Africa." The central question was whether English-speaking or Dutch-speaking South Africans would control the future of the interior.

Rhodes at first favored a pro-English policy, Dormer one more even-handed. Finally Rhodes, after pacing up and down the room in which they were talking, said that he did not dislike Dutchmen. But if they tried to trample on the English, then Rhodes would not be found wanting. "I don't pretend to have many fixed principles; but I do believe in doing to others as we would be done by, and I am sure that vengeance is no policy for a nation [the English] such as ours." Thus, reported Dormer years later, "the bargain was concluded, with firmly fixed resolves on my part; but not, I fear, without certain mental reservations on the part of my young and eager friend."[4]

Hofmeyr was a target obvious to someone as skilled in the arts of conciliation and personal maneuvering as Rhodes. For Hofmeyr controlled the largest single, obedient bloc of votes in the House. Rhodes understood intuitively how the retrocession of the Transvaal might, paradoxically, have unnerved Hofmeyr and his prosperous Dutch-speaking supporters. Rhodes would also not have wanted to antagonize his own Dutch constituents in Barkly West. Rhodes thus worked assiduously from 1881 until the Jameson Raid to cultivate Hofmeyr and his men. Hofmeyer was eight years older than Rhodes, roughly the same gap as between Herbert and Cecil, and Rudd and Cecil. This distance was comfortable, allowing for frankness within the protective mantle of mentoring. Rhodes later characterized Hofmeyr as "without doubt" the "most capable politician in South Africa."

Hofmeyr, the editor of *De Zuid Afrikaan,* the main Dutch newspaper in the Cape, was also the spokesman for the western Cape winegrowers. In 1878 he had formed the Boeren Beschermings Vereeniging (Farmers' Protection Society) in order to oppose an excise tax which Sprigg, from the eastern Cape, was determined to put on wine. The next year Hofmeyr won a seat in parliament from Stellenbosch. Meanwhile, elsewhere in the western Cape, a movement had already begun to reassert and reaffirm the prerogatives of the up-country Boers, many of whom preferred to speak Afrikaans, a South African simplification of Dutch. This movement was in large part a reaction to responsible government, to Lord Carnarvon's attempt to unite South Africa under the British flag, to the English-dominated wealth of the diamond fields, and to the increasing fear that Afrikaners were fast losing real power in their own country. In 1879, the Rev. Stephanus Jacobus du Toit, one of the chief advocates of a pro-Boer, abusively anti-British policy in the rich farming town of Paarl, established the Afrikaner Bond as the overt political manifestation of this ethnic solidarity. The Bond was avowedly nationalistic, boosted Afrikaans, and proclaimed "Africa for the Afrikaners."

The Bond began in part as a vehicle for the promotion of the narrow interests of farmers who were less established and rather more rural in their outlook than those who supported Hofmeyr. By the end of 1880 the Bond could list only fourteen branches in the Cape Colony, but the Boer uprising in the Transvaal encouraged a rising tide of sentiment for the Bond everywhere in South Africa. These developments naturally worried Hofmeyr, who saw his own appeal to Dutch and Afrikaans-speaking farmers being eroded by the radical, virulently anti-African, disruptive, xenophobic, impractical, and illusory notions of the Bond and its intemperate leaders. For these reasons Hofmeyr was compelled to advocate the greater use of Dutch (not Afrikaans) in the official and educational life in the Colony. He also had to make the other aims of the Bond his own, and to seek some form of accommodation between the two rival bodies. This Hofmeyr finally accomplished in 1883, folding the Farmers' Protection Society into the Bond, and adroitly emerging as its unquestioned leader.[5]

Like Hofmeyr, Rhodes developed a set of short- and long-term aims which he determined to pursue by political means in and out of parliament. His early rapprochement with Hofmeyr—because the Dutch were "the coming race in South Africa"—his assiduous courting of him and them thereafter, and his attempt to lead the Griqualand delegates and barter their votes in order to advance his own causes served from the first to place Rhodes in a position where he could gradually gain a significant strategic hold on the loyalties of the House. Rhodes groped initially for ways in which to accomplish his goals, but soon had a good hold of the likely means, if not necessarily the knowledge of the particular issues, by or through which he would promote his own interests and visions.

Shortly after entering parliament in 1881, Rhodes allied himself with Hofmeyr, and several dissident English-speaking members, in order to oppose and then help dislodge Sprigg's faltering ministry. Rhodes could not have picked the occasion, but he turned a debate on the administration of Basutoland and the Transkei, which commenced four days after he had taken his seat, to excellent advantage. In 1869 Britain had annexed Basutoland at the request of King Moshweshwe, the aging amalgamator of the modern version of a Southern Sotho monarchy. The Orange Free State had recently won a war against Moshweshwe's legions, and the kingdom's complete dismemberment would have been assured. But Britain wanted its local colonies to administer such inescapable imperial responsibilities and, with almost indecent haste, in 1871 transferred Basutoland to the Cape Colony.

With their traditional crop lands lost to the Free State, the Sotho went out to work—on Free State farms, on the railways, and, not least, as laborers on the diamond fields. There they purchased guns, and gradually rearmed the Sotho nation. At first the Cape administered Basutoland through an astute Agent who refrained from challenging the powers of Moshweshwe's heir and his several princely rivals. By the late 1870s, when the renewed frontier wars of the eastern Cape, the conflict with the Zulu, and the recalcitrance of the Pedi had alarmed the government of the Cape, Frere and Sprigg decided that the time had come to disarm all Africans within or near the jurisdiction of the Colony. The Cape parliament accordingly passed the Peace Preservation bill, which gave the governor the authority to order colonial Africans to lay down their arms.

The Sotho gasped. One chief in the southern section of the kingdom immediately defied a magistrate's order in another matter, and led a bitter battle against Cape order throughout much of 1879 before being subdued in his mountain fastness.[6] Before this chief had been humbled, Sprigg, with more bravado than sense, had announced to a great gathering of Sotho that they were nevertheless to be disarmed, that their hut tax payments were to be increased, and that whites were to be allowed to settle in the district where the chief had rebelled. The conditions of the Peace Preservation Act were formally applied to the whole of Basutoland in April 1880; war broke out in September and soon spread southward and eastward to East Griqualand and the Transkei. The white Cape volunteers and conscripts were a mixed bag, being poorly trained and armed, and they fought without any imperial military assistance (particularly after the Boers rose in the Transvaal). By April 1881, when Rhodes entered parliament, order had been re-established in East Griqualand and the Transkei, but the Sotho were still successfully employing guerrilla tactics in the mountainous reaches of their country.

Rhodes was not alone in condemning Sprigg for making a mess of Basutoland. Francis Orpen emphasized how illogical it was to insist on total disarmament at a time of widespread tension. Merriman decried Sprigg's wild inconsistencies. Thomas Scanlen and others felt that Sprigg had been less than candid with the House. Twelve days after entering the House, in his maiden speech, Rhodes made his own criticism evident; a few days later he again opposed Sprigg. "It was the speech of one who *will* speak his mind out fully," remarked one of the reporters present. "But the frankness of his nature may expose him to the designs of the wily." Rhodes hewed to the line that "we sold them the guns; they bought them out of hard-earned wages, and it *is* hard lines to make them give them up again." This pro-African, but also pro-commercial stance, might have been expected from one conscious, since his days in Natal, of the difficulty of attracting and retaining capable African labor. Joseph Robinson stridently took the opposite view, but Matthews, Orpen, and Rhodes believed, as Rhodes' election manifesto had suggested, that the disarming of the Sotho could well make the diamond fields dangerously less attractive to those who had been among the most industrious and reliable of their mining work force.

If this approach to the problem of Basutoland need not be considered novel, Rhodes' advocacy of the transfer of both Basutoland and the Transkei to the Crown was heretical and ahead of its time. He saw early and clearly that if Britain would but control Basutoland, the Cape would "lose the natives as their enemies but regain them as customers." Rhodes likened disarming the Sotho to the "greased cartridges in the Indian mutiny." He believed that the Cape lacked the even-handedness and public backing to administer African territories well. The Colony was in no financial or political position to deal with African problems so removed from its predominant, parochial interests. The Cape, he reminded his colleagues, could claim a (white) population no greater than that of a "third-rate English city spread over a great country."

"It is not as if white colonists could be settled in those territories," Rhodes continued. "The policy of the Imperial Government would not allow that. The Parliament would never allow Basutoland to be confiscated; no colonist could go there; the land would simply be peopled with the native races. How could this weak colony retain those territories?" The Cape lacked the necessary resources, and, thus, for him the metropole had an inescapable duty to shoulder the burden of "native governance."[7]

If it would be misleading to view Rhodes' approach to the Basuto question without considering the industrial and parliamentary context in which he acted, it is more balanced to appreciate the varied objectives that Rhodes was then attempting to achieve through his call for common sense and transfer of authority. In addition to his role as a representative of the mining interests of Kimberley, he was slowly nurturing ideas about Hofmeyr and the Dutch connection. He had another very short-term, but highly valued goal: to bring rails rapidly across the intervening miles from the Cape to the diamond fields. The Barkly and Kimberley members were few, but their votes were capable of being decisive in a narrowly divided assembly. So, despite Rhodes' own caustic and already public views on the folly of Sprigg's Sotho policy, he voted along with the other members from Griqualand West to support Sprigg against Scanlen's motion of censure. As long as Sprigg, the railway builder, continued to promise progress in driving steel toward Kimberley, Rhodes would remain with him, despite Basutoland. The crucial vote backing Sprigg was 37 to 34. Yet, ten days after voting one way, Rhodes persuaded Matthews and Francis Orpen to change sides, and thus to bring the Sprigg government tumbling down. Rhodes had suddenly decided, to Robinson's discomfort, and possibly because of suggestions from Merriman and Hofmeyr, that Sprigg was "too weak" to push the rails forward with sufficient speed. Rhodes, aware of the political importance of the votes from the new districts, also desired to demonstrate his power a second time. As a result of what was an unexpected and important little coup, Scanlen, from Cradock in the eastern Cape, became prime minister at the head of a new cabinet which included Merriman as minister of railways and Hofmeyr as a reluctant, token, Dutch-speaking member without portfolio. Of Rhodes, partially responsible for the abrupt shift in leadership, Solomon, parliament's senior liberal member, said: "Watch that man. He is the future man of South Africa and possibly of the world."[8]

Rhodes intervened in the debates of the House only twice more in the session, which lasted through June 1881. Once he spoke controversially in favor of extending the boundaries of Griqualand West. On the next occasion, he took a major role in defeating an attempt to permit the use, optionally, of the Dutch language in the House of Assembly. He sensed no great desire in the country for such a change (but did so a year later, when Hofmeyr moved a similar motion, and the House passed it).

After parliament had adjourned, Rhodes returned to Kimberley and, along with Matthews and Robinson, was fêted by his erstwhile constituents at a banquet presided over by the mayor. Their speeches after dinner were meant to give the local people a direct report on the proceedings of the session. Matthews' was, for him, matter-of-fact and anodyne. But Robinson created a storm by accusing Rhodes and Matthews of reneging on their pre-election pledges by voting against Sprigg. "The attitude of Rhodes," reported an attorney who attended the dinner, "was far from popular . . . [and] when he rose . . . to make his speech, he met with rather a disconcerting reception. . . ." Indeed, Rhodes was "received with cries of 'rat' and mingled cheers and hisses." This was Rhodes' second public attempt to justify himself, and the first on a question of political expediency. Ultimately his long-winded, forceful explanation—hinging on the railway that they all wanted—turned the persons at the dinner in his favor. He derided Robinson, denied having "ratted" on the electors, "and reasoned out his position and justified his conduct with so much force and spirit," recalled the attorney, "that he quite carried the audience with him, and sat down amid repeated cheers."[9]

Rhodes failed to carry Robinson, however, a man he never again could square. Furthermore, when Robinson was involved in yet another of many libel cases against the Kimberley press, this time versus the *Diamond News*, Rhodes—on the eve of his departure for a final term at Oxford—gave damaging evidence against him. It is not clear what the evidence was about or whether Rhodes was motivated by anything other than serving the ends of justice, but if Robinson remembered Rhodes' support earlier in the year, and if he could forgive Rhodes' vote for Scanlen, he could not forgive or forget testimony which helped hold him up to ridicule. (Yet Robinson technically won his case.) This was an animosity—and Rhodes disliked having foes—which was to complicate Rhodes' later amalgamation of the diamond mines and his pursuit of fortune on the Witwatersrand.

Even so, in parliament, and in support of the mining industry, this new friction could not immediately prevent Rhodes from working together with Robinson. In August 1881 Robinson and others established the Diamond Mining Protection Society in Kimberley to seek stiff legislative curbs on illicit diamond dealings. Illicit diamond buyers (IDBs, as they were known) purchased gems which were stolen and smuggled out of the still unfenced mines or various sorting operations. Their activities caused a general flattening of the prices of all Kimberley diamonds, and encouraged even more crime than usual on and around the fields. "Unless you take a firm stand and show that you are determined to cope with this evil," Robinson told the 150 representatives of firms and individual claim holders in the several mines of Griqualand West, "your mines will be closed. The mining industry will be swept away altogether."

Scanlen's government referred questions like these concerning the future of diamond mining to a special committee chaired by Merriman and including Robinson and Rhodes. One of Kimberley's newspapers regarded Rhodes' appointment to the committee as dangerous, for Merriman was excessively liberal and was suspected of being "soft" on whites and Africans who dealt in purloined diamonds; so long as Merriman was chairman, Rhodes would "follow him as a blind man follows a dog."[10] These fears may have been merited, but Rhodes went off to Oxford two weeks after the committee was constituted, and returned at the end of the year to find that Robinson and the Society had prepared a tough draft, and that Merriman had accepted it.

The Diamond Trade bill put the burden of proof of legitimacy on the person possessing uncut stones, specifically sanctioned extensive body searches without warrants, permitted "trapping" suspects by employing Africans in systematic, often provocative, scam operations, and authorized the continuation of a special diamond court in Kimberley. Since 1880 that court had been comprised of three persons who were not necessarily magistrates. They judged evidence by the standards of the frontier and, on occasion, gave to hearsay and circumstance the weight of fact. "The Illicit Diamond Court of Griqualand West," accused a former attorney general in parliament, was "a blot on the judicial system of the country." Others joined this attack on the proposed bill by James Weston Leonard, but Robinson and Rhodes tried to defend its many questionable aspects with equal verve.

It is claimed that Rhodes was particularly shrill and assertive in his support of the proposed legislation in 1882, having earlier, in 1881, failed to bring about a full amalgamation of the De Beers mine because he had not personally been regarded with confidence, or as having sufficient stature, by the remainder of the mining community. Thus, he championed Robinson's bill in order to curry favor with his rival and with others for whom the prosperity of diamonds was central.[11] But Rhodes would have been expected to support such legislation in any event. He was just as much a foe of IDBs as Robinson, and in 1882 Rhodes still operated in parliament as a constituency representative. Some traditional biographers to the contrary, he had not yet begun to devote himself only to imperial issues. Moreover, Robinson was absent from parliament (pursuing yet another libel claim in Kimberley) during critical phases of the debate. So it fell to Rhodes to defend the bill from personal experience. He also chaired a select committee of the House which met for a few weeks to consider the matter.

Rhodes answered Leonard, in the words of the official report: "As regard the system of trapping, [Rhodes] admitted that if one was to argue generally that was a system which no-one could approve of. But the circumstances were very exceptional and it was only the great necessities of the community that impelled the sanction of the system. He would like anyone to show him any method or means whereby this crime could be checked except by this exceptional and obnoxious system."[12] Later, eliciting little surprise, the report of his Select Committee agreed that illicit diamond buying was indeed a formidable threat to the industry and that near-draconian legislation would be appropriate. Ends justified means.

The Diamond Trade Act that emerged from parliament (and which applied only to Griqualand West) embodied most of Robinson's original provisions: suspects were guilty until proven innocent, policemen could search without warrants, mail and packages could be opened on suspicion, only licensed persons could export or import diamonds, diamond cutters were to be registered, special permits were necessary before diamond debris could be washed and sieved, accessories to diamond crimes could be charged as principals, and penalties were raised to fifteen years imprisonment or £1,000 on each count. In a compromise, the special court was retained, but one member henceforth had to be a qualified judge. Rhodes fought to keep an additional provision in the bill—flogging as a punishment for anyone handling stolen diamonds. But this was too much for parliament, and flogging was removed from the provisions of the act after Matthews and Solomon argued that such an extreme infliction was inappropriate for crimes against property. "I was so far successful," Matthews crowed, "that such brutal ideas were expunged from the act."[13]

The newspaper that had feared Rhodes' appointment to the original committee was unstinting in its praise. Rhodes, said the *Independent,* spoke soundly. It regretted that "his efforts to perfect the Bill were to a great extent counteracted by the sensational and somewhat imaginative stories of Dr. Mat[t]hews, notably on the flogging question. . . ." Rhodes believed "in his baby the Diamond Trade Act," at least at the time and through the mid-1880s. Then, both because he came to recognize how inappropriate it appeared to Britons and because it had failed to stamp out the illegal diamond trade, in subsequent years he (and his biographers) conveniently ignored his forceful role in the passage of legislation which Lord Randolph Churchill, among others, condemned as reprehensible, although "in thorough conformity with South African sentiment." So in conformity to local sentiment was the act in Kimberley that Matthews was hounded out of his parliamentary seat, and Rhodes was that much more revered for his espousal of severe "law and order" ideas. He was also much praised in Kimberley, in 1883, for seeking legislation to prohibit the sale of spirits to Africans within five miles of any mine. This attempt to amend the colony's liquor licensing laws failed by nine votes, but the *Independent* extolled his efforts "in the cause of morality and the general well-being of the community."[14]

Rhodes' outspokenness during the debates that buried the Sprigg ministry, as well as his determination to serve the labor needs and other interests of the mining industry, in 1882 involved him further, and significantly so, in the affairs of Basutoland. However, the government headed by Scanlen, which he had helped bring to power, was as saddled as Sprigg's had been with the consequences of the bitter internecine Sotho rivalries which Cape policy had fostered in the decade after Moshweshwe. Sir Hercules Robinson, high commissioner for South Africa and governor of the Cape, had successfully brought about a cease-fire between the Sotho chiefs and the Cape in April 1881. The award which resulted from his efforts of arbitration confirmed disarmament, but returned guns to the Sotho in exchange for a token yearly registration fee. Those Sotho who had refrained from rebelling were to be compensated; those who had opposed the Cape were to pay a fine in cattle. If they paid fines their lands would not be confiscated and they would receive a full amnesty for actions perpetrated against the Cape during the period of rebellion. In other words, the Peace Preservation Act was a dead letter. The Sotho had triumphed, but were still, in victory, divided. Lacking the political will or the military muscle, the government of the colony would have enormous difficulty in ruling decisively amid conditions of disequilibrium. The Cape was faced, between 1881 and 1883, with a southern Sotho nation which had largely disintegrated. What remained was "a raging crowd, upon some of the ringleaders of which an award was forced."[15]

One set of chiefs was loyal to the Cape, and cooperative. The successful rebels remained recalcitrant, seeking to strengthen their hard-won independence both from the Cape and from any Sotho rivals. Although there were influential members of the Cape parliament who proposed to give the "native territories" beyond the Kei and Orange Rivers (thus, Transkei and Basutoland) back to Britain, the home government at this point wanted no further non-self-supporting areas to administer, and the Cape was compelled to seek a lasting peace in Basutoland through implementation of the award. But it was clear that adherence to the provisions of the award could be obtained only by careful negotiation; the colony was deeply in debt and tired of war, and Britain would not help. Throughout the second half of 1881, Jacobus Sauer, Scanlen's inexperienced secretary for native affairs, and Joseph M. Orpen, the acting agent in Basutoland, therefore struggled with limited coercive powers to dampen the spirit of resistance, especially in the most stubborn of the chiefly strongholds. So unsatisfactory were these proceedings that, in early 1882, Scanlen considered partitioning Basutoland into territory controlled in the south by Sotho of loyal tendencies, and in the north by rebels. Britain refused to approve such a step. Nor could it contemplate "so grave a step as the withdrawal of all civilised government," which was another solution widely advocated in Cape Town.[16]

The muddled events and the incapacity of the Cape to restore its authority led in March 1882 to the cancellation of the award and, in effect, to the widespread acknowledgement that the two-year-old attempt to pacify the Sotho had failed. Moreover, those who had submitted to the authority of the Cape, and had suffered at least £130,000 worth of losses, now could not look to the award for compensation, but to some new arrangement. Scanlen's ministry therefore appointed a Compensation Commission consisting of Rhodes, Abraham Auret, and Jacobus Burger (assisted by Colonel Charles Griffith, a recent Agent), which set to work in August 1882 to evaluate the claims of the loyal Sotho. Furthermore, in the hope of solving its overriding problem—that of the future of Basutoland—by the working of some form of cabalistic magic, the sedate legislators of the Cape also proceeded to enlist the services of Major General Charles George Gordon.

Gordon, former governor-general and chief suppressor of slavery in the Sudan, and the hero of the imperial Chinese subjugation of the Taiping rebels, was between missions of glory and excitement. He was the most famous of the many illustrious Victorian guerrilla fighters. Equally, Gordon was popularly thought to have some unnatural affinity with so-called backward peoples. Because of his own streak of mysticism, or because of other, mysterious qualities, it was alleged that this slight, opinionated soldier could exercise an influence over non-Europeans which was nothing short of hypnotic. He "knew that he possessed what some described as a mesmeric power over primitive peoples and he himself called the faculty of getting into their skins." [17] In 1880, Gordon had refused to assume command of the colonial forces at the Cape. In 1881, about the time that Rhodes was entering parliament, Gordon had learned of the troubles in Basutoland and offered his services to terminate the Cape's war and to administer the territory. But Sprigg had rejected the suggestion. After another year of confusion and trauma, not to mention expense, it was hardly surprising that Merriman and others finally prevailed upon Scanlen to seek assistance from an upright, God-fearing, self-confessed miracle worker who sought divine guidance from the randomly revealed revelations of Scripture.

The white politicians of the Cape hardly knew what to do with Gordon once he arrived. Without even visiting Basutoland, he quickly prepared memoranda containing detailed solutions to the crisis. Against further war, and instinctively on the side of a people wronged, Gordon proposed a kind of indirect rule, with the Sotho achieving self-government under a Sotho council guided by a Cape-appointed Resident with comparatively limited powers. This was hardly a policy which appealed to Scanlen or Merriman. In any event, Gordon had also been recruited as commander of the Colony's army, and he spent much of the Cape winter of 1882 in Kingwilliamstown and the Transkei, reorganizing its troops along imperial lines. Only in late August did he reach Basutoland to attempt, in one grand gathering of the fractious Sotho chiefs, to achieve overall synthesis and reconciliation.

Rhodes' Commission arrived in Basutoland at about the same time. Among its tasks was the valuing of property which loyal Sotho had lost to the rebels during the Gun War. For example, Rhodes put a price on 2,000 trees belonging to one Sotho who could not return home. (Basutoland supplied wood to the diamond mines.) With regard to larger issues, he advised Scanlen that the position in Maseru was, to understate the case, "strained." Writing as a supporter, Rhodes appreciated that "abandonment or fighting are out of the question with your Ministry the former, and with the colony the latter. There is at present nothing left but present course, namely a gradual attempt to restore order by moral influences. I cannot say I am hopeful but I own it is the only present course to pursue. The only other alternative not now but for parliament if matters do not improve will be a suzerainty. That is an advising resident with a border police."

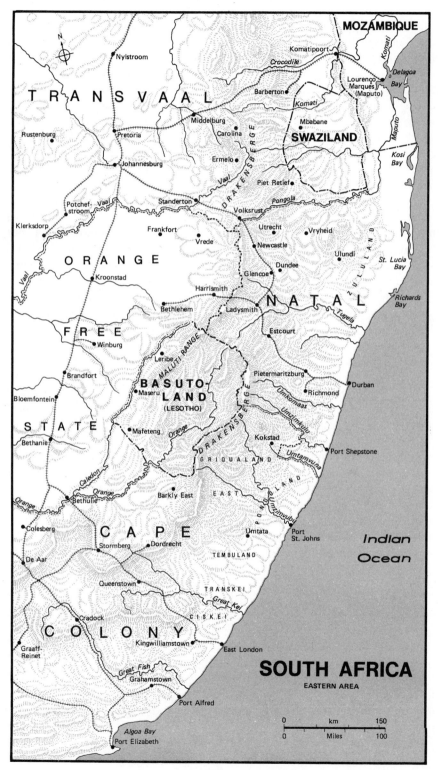

MOZAMBIQUE

T R A N S V A A L

Nylstroom

Komatipoort

Crocodile

Barberton

Lourenço
Marques
(Maputo)

Delagoa
Bay

Komati

Rustenburg

Pretoria

Middelburg

Carolina

Mbabane

SWAZILAND

Johannesburg

Ermelo

Piet Retief

Vaal

Kosi
Bay

Potchef-
stroom

Vaal

Standerton

Volksrust

Pongola

O R A N G E

Klerksdorp

Frankfort

Vrede

Utrecht

Newcastle

Vryheid

Ulundi

*St. Lucia
Bay*

Kroonstad

Glencoe

Dundee

N A T A L

*Richards
Bay*

Harrismith

Bethlehem

Ladysmith

Tugela

F R E E

Winburg

MALUTI RANGE

Estcourt

Leribe

Brandfort

BASUTO-
LAND

Maseru

Pietermaritzburg

Richmond

Umkomaas

Durban

Bloemfontein

(LESOTHO)

Orange

Umzimkulu

S T A T E

Mafeteng

Kokstad

Port Shepstone

Bethanie

Caledon

GRIQUALAND

Umtamvuna

Orange

Bethulie

Barkly East

E A S T

Orange

Colesberg

C A P E

Umtata

Port
St. Johns

Indian

De Aar

Stormberg

Dordrecht

TEMBULAND

Ocean

Queenstown

TRANSKEI

Great Kei

Cradock

C O L O N Y

CISKEI

Graaff-
Reinet

Kingwilliamstown

East London

SOUTH AFRICA

Great Fish

Grahamstown

EASTERN AREA

Port Alfred

Algoa Bay
Port Elizabeth

| 0 | | km | | 150 |
| 0 | | Miles | | 100 |

Rhodes had apparently come to that same conclusion before conferring with Gordon. Rhodes seemed to think that Masopha, a prominent dissident chief, would agree to suzerainty, or home rule, and would let his followers pay their hut taxes if that were the result. But such a course of action was, Rhodes admitted, "humiliating." As a last resort, it was a policy only for "extremes." "But at the same time," he advised his prime minister, "you must not shut your eyes to the fact that the present policy not only may fail but has a fair chance at failure." Although coercion had not worked, the Cape was attempting to restore the authority of white magistrates by moral persuasion only, and the chiefs understood perfectly well, as Rhodes sagely suggested, that to accept a resumption of magisterial rule would mean their end. There was but thin hope. "At the present moment you are without civil authority in this country. I am hopeful that the continued drunkenness and violence of the chiefs," wrote the practical politician, "may in time alienate the people but the feudal tie is strong and the people cannot at present forget that the boldness of their chiefs saved their guns and they think their lands, and they utterly mistrust us."

Rhodes understood the absolute core of the problem. "With such factors against you, though I do not despair I think you should be prepared for an alternative. . . ." Rhodes suggested gently that Scanlen appoint a commission to advise on the future of Basutoland. He thought that it could be comprised of men like Gordon, Solomon, and, although he never said so directly, himself. Rhodes ended his letter in a manner characteristically solicitous and repetitious, reiterating a central idea: "You must understand I do not advocate a suzerainty but merely feel that if present course fails as there is a strong possibility you ought to prepare for some other scheme." [18]

Rhodes' appreciation of the main lines of Sotho politics was as sure and as sensible as any of the other major white participants. In this realm, as before, he demonstrated an easy ability to absorb new ideas and see the outlines even of complicated imbroglios well removed from his main sphere of operations on the diamond fields. At the time that he wrote to Scanlen he also knew, instinctively, that Gordon should not go to see Masopha alone. Masopha should instead be summoned to meet with Gordon. He surmised that Gordon would defeat the search for peace in the territory if he continued to act as if he were a delegate of Queen Victoria, and not, in fact, an advisor to Sauer.

Rhodes could not have predicted the precise denouement as it unfolded, but in late September Gordon went alone to Masopha's fortress at Thaba Bosiu near Maseru in order to persuade the wily chief to trust and cooperate with what would be a new, favorable, white-applied dispensation. Joseph Orpen, the Agent, had a long acquaintance with the Sotho. He strongly advised Sauer against such a visit. It will "ruin everything," said Orpen. "Besides that, Gordon is quite uncontrollable; he will say exactly what comes uppermost at the time and not what you may wish him to say. . . . He seems quite mad sometimes."

Gordon hoped that a display of compassion, mysticism, and symbolism would convert Masopha; Sauer and Paramount Chief Letsie were, however, leading an all-out assault on the fortress. Neither approach succeeded, for Masopha successfully stalled Gordon, and with Gordon in the way Sauer stayed his martial hand. Then the summer rains broke early and sent some of the Sotho soldiers back to their fields. Finally, to cap Masopha's victory and, in effect, destroy the last of the Cape's moral and political claim to Basutoland, Gordon resigned, claiming treachery and despicable interference, a claim with which Rhodes appears to have agreed. As Merriman later blamed himself, "a brilliant genius like Gordon, full of impulses often noble but singularly bewildering [to folk like us], was quite unsuited for the service of a colony where the deeds of its rulers are subject to Parliamentary criticism. In a sense he was too good for his work. . . ."[19]

Before this debacle had played itself out, and while Rhodes, twenty years Gordon's junior, was primarily engrossed in the mundane adjudication of claim and counterclaim, he met Gordon in an encampment of little clay-walled thatched houses in Magistrate Alexander C. Bailie's headquarters in Thlotsi Heights, near Leribe. The Compensation Commission was sitting there, and Sauer and Joseph Orpen were preparing for a major gathering with chiefs Jonathan and Joel.

This is a biographical set piece not unlike the famous meeting of David Livingstone and Henry Morton Stanley in 1871. There came a sudden conjunction of two meteors, perhaps in the little hut that Gordon had been allocated under the shadow of the northern mountains of what, much later, was to become Lesotho. Or, to give a romantic interpretation to this encounter: Rhodes and Gordon, lonely men of misogynist impulse, both being "absorbed in [their] gigantic dreams," were delighted to find each other. Like Gordon, Rhodes "was in some ways as simple as a child. He possessed too a shrewdness, piercing like Gordon's, yet vastly more practical since it was not perpetually in conflict with a theocentric impulse. The two talked long together," wrote Lord Elton, "and each conceived for the other a fascinated respect which he never forgot." They were attracted to each other; each was self-confident, forceful, and capable of immense charm. Gordon, moreover, was "transparently simple and sincere." Then, too, he was "good-looking . . . with a remarkable forehead, both broad and high."

Rhodes and Gordon went on long walks together during what must have been a period of no more than a week when they were together north of Maseru. On several occasions, reports Rhodes' earliest biographer from first-hand information, Gordon vigorously chided Rhodes for having such independent opinions. "You always contradict me," said Gordon. "I never met such a man for his own opinion. You think your views are always right and everyone else wrong." On another occasion he accused Rhodes of being a narcissist—"the sort of man who never approves of anything unless you have had the organising of it yourself." Yet Rhodes was relentless, successfully urging Gordon to cease stealing the limelight from Sauer, his official superior.

"You ought to explain to the Basutos," said Rhodes the Cape politician, "the truth that [Sauer] is somebody and you are nobody."

Because Rhodes was so assertive, or because Gordon was drawn in special ways to someone so young and distinctive, he one day pleaded with the youthful magnate and politician to abandon Kimberley and Cape Town and remain with him in Basutoland. "Stay with me," he implored. "We can work together." Rhodes refused, for several reasons, and Gordon pressed his suit again. When he had failed to sway Rhodes, he said that there were "very few men in the world to whom I would make such an offer. Very few men, I can tell you; but, of course, you *will* have your own way."[20]

Rhodes also refused another entreaty in 1884, when Gordon was on his way to try to wreak a special magic on the Mahdi. But Rhodes retained a warm affection for Gordon, and, like so many others, mourned his death at Khartoum in 1885. A year later, in conversation with Edward Arthur Maund, a member of General Warren's staff in Bechuanaland and a special correspondent of *The Times*, Rhodes admitted that Gordon had exercised a strange influence on him. Gordon "united spiritual ideas or sentiment with tremendous activity and had such a belief in his own way of doing things as to amount to obstinacy. He was a good listener but self-willed." "We got on well," Maund quotes Rhodes as saying, "for we both believed in moral suasion rather than force in dealing with native chiefs." At the time, Maund perceptively noted that Rhodes was depicting himself rather than the Gordon whom Maund had known. Rhodes, thought Maund, "had failed to fathom the inner man and his peculiar individuality." Rhodes was evidently fascinated by Gordon's romantic nature, but "he seemed unable to realize the restless energy and force of character in the quiet unassuming man who claimed no merit for himself and abhorred publicity." Rhodes and Gordon, Maund reflected, had little in common since Gordon was unbending and Rhodes capable of compromise. Moreover, in 1882 Rhodes was still a self-styled agnostic while Gordon, who hated politics, considered himself motivated by the "spark of the God head."[21]

There was one curious affinity which Rhodes and Gordon may have realized. In 1881 Gordon wrote a letter to a young member of Parliament proposing a kind of secret community of men for the betterment of society. His suggestion had no impact until after his death, when William Thomas Stead, the editor of the *Pall Mall Gazette*, and others tried to carry on Gordon's idea that there should be a group of ombudsmen in Britain modeled on the so-called College of Censors in China.[22]

Whatever Gordon's impact on Rhodes, and of Rhodes on Gordon, Masopha and Gordon had in their separate ways demonstrated the very weakness and impossibility of Cape rule. The question that perplexed the parliament of the Cape in 1883 was how to extricate itself with the greatest dignity and the least damage. The opposition, led by Thomas Upington, advocated total unconditional abandonment. Merriman and Rhodes, opposed by Hofmeyr, favored a return of all responsibility to the mother country. "I do not know what policy Scanlen may propound," Rhodes wrote to Merriman, in disillusionment with both his prime minister and Sauer, "[but] no doubt it will not be formed until the votes have been gauged. . . ." He pronounced himself in favor of "an appeal for joint action with the Home Government with an alternative of abandonment if refused. . . ."[23] But at first Scanlen and Sauer persuaded the assembly to permit the Sotho to rule themselves (along the lines that Rhodes and Gordon had proposed) if, and only if, the Sotho accepted such a shift.

When the Sotho chiefs rejected any form of home rule under Cape control, the government of the Cape pleaded with London for de-annexation. Merriman, its representative, even tried to shed colonial responsibility for the Transkei, presciently suggesting that together Basutoland and the Transkei would comprise a homogeneous and self-supporting territory with a sea coast, and if ruled together by Britain, that their separation from the Cape would prove of incalculable advantage to the future of South Africa.

Rhodes' views were strong, expressed in prolix fashion, and rather confusing. However, in the crucial debate in the House he labeled the Sotho an "uncivilised race" with whom nothing could be done "until we show them that we are masters." He went on to say that although the Cape was not then capable of war, "we must not let the matter run on, that is, do nothing, and at the same time we must remember that there is a volcano in Basutoland. We have tried every scheme of settlement, and every scheme has failed; we cannot fight, and we must not abandon. Abandonment is not re-transfer to the Imperial Government. It would mean anarchy." He further worried that the interests of the Orange Free State had to be taken into account, since anxious Africans might make war against the Afrikaners of that republic.

Rhodes deviated from the question of de-annexation, which was under discussion, to give his own views of the future of South Africa. "I believe," he said, "in a United States of South Africa, but as a portion of the British Empire. I believe that confederated states in a colony under responsible government would each be practically an independent republic, but I think we should also have all the privileges of the tie with the Empire." He disagreed with Hofmeyr, who favored a similar grouping, but under its own flag.

Finally, at the end of this long speech, Rhodes summed up his position. The Cape's Basuto crisis was now at a crossroads: "One path leads to peace and prosperity in this country, by the removal of native difficulties, leaving us free for the development of the country; the other path leads to ruin and disaster." Rhodes was shedding problems, that is, Africans, and gaining customers, time, and funds for expansion elsewhere.[24]

Lord Derby, the British colonial secretary, persuaded Gladstone grudgingly to accept most of Merriman's (and Rhodes') formula, but balked at the responsibility for the Transkei as well. He conditioned the resumption of imperial responsibility on the agreement of the Sotho chiefs and a regular Cape contribution to the costs of governing the territory. The Cape parliament reluctantly approved Merriman's de-annexation, nearly all of the Sotho chiefs affirmed the shift, and, as Rhodes had suggested as early as 1881 and again in 1882, the Cape returned Basutoland to Britain in 1884.

Merriman's attempt to give away the Transkei, as well as Basutoland, may have been influenced as much by Rhodes' strong views as by his own appreciation of how badly the Cape had compromised itself beyond the eastern frontier. The latest irritant had been an Afrikaner trek into Thembuland, a part of the Transkei confiscated by the Cape as a result of the 1879 hostilities and never demarcated. In 1882, without waiting for official permission, 250 whites of Dutch descent entered "into the heritage of the Heathen," and were soon rivaling landless Thembu for fertile sections of the available territory. In 1883, Merriman prohibited trespassing and summoned white troops from the Cape to police Tembuland. Disturbances were prevented by this timely show of force, and the trekkers slowly returned to the Cape borderlands from whence they had come. Rhodes, who had privately advocated that very action and had predicted the favorable result, was quick to congratulate Merriman. "The only bit of advice I did tender you last session was shew firmness and move the troops if necessary or else you better give up all ideas of government. You have shewn firmness and this bugbear has collapsed."[25]

While these negotiations were continuing, Rhodes' Commission, his other connection with Basutoland, had continued its investigations throughout the remainder of 1882, spent the early part of 1883 debating its conclusions, and finally reported to parliament in May. Rhodes agreed with the other two members that moderate compensation should be paid to Africans who had forfeited their property during the Gun War. But he opposed, interestingly enough, the recommendation of the other two parliamentary members that two white traders should also be reimbursed for losses. His objection was based on precedent and financial prudence: "if once the principle of the liability of the Government for the losses of its subjects owing to rebellion is recognized, it would expose the Colony to an obligation that it has neither the means nor the power to fulfill." Moreover, Rhodes believed that the two merchants suffered from the "known risk" assumed by anyone brave or foolish enough to trade on or across the unsettled frontiers of the Colony. There was no favorable precedent, and Britain, for example, had not compensated its subjects who had been severely disturbed by the Indian Mutiny.

In his prosecution of this relatively minor matter, Rhodes showed characteristic patience and persistence. The Commission's report, and his minority opinion on the two traders, testify to the conscientious manner in which Rhodes conducted himself throughout its time-consuming proceedings. Given his growing lack of confidence in Scanlen's approach to the larger problem, and the comparative press of the financial issues of Kimberley, this attention to the activities of the Commission was unusual. However, he was its chairman, and may have wanted to show Scanlen and Merriman how well he could discharge what was virtually his first official political leadership task of more than ephemeral significance.

What makes Rhodes' careful completion of his tedious Basuto task the more surprising is that he had, probably for the first time, fallen desperately in love. To have refused Gordon was thus easy, but to have remained away from Kimberley for three out of every four weeks over a period of nearly five months would have remained trying, if not disconcerting. Exactly when Rhodes was initially consumed by passion is uncertain, but on 27 October 1882, when he was in the midst of Commission hearings at Thlotsi Heights, but had rushed back (a three-day ride) briefly to Kimberley, Rhodes drafted his third will: "I, C.J. Rhodes, being of sound mind, leave my worldly wealth to N.E. Pickering." The next day, presumably having second or further thoughts, Rhodes handed Pickering a letter, together with the sealed will: "Open the enclosed after my death," it read. "There is an old will of mine with Graham, whose conditions are very curious, and can only be carried out by a trustworthy person, and I consider you one." Rhodes added: "You fully understand you are to use interest of money as you like during your life."

Rhodes may have met Neville Ernest Pickering as early as 1880, when Pickering was employed by a Port Elizabeth firm which had property interests in Kimberley. Nor is it precisely certain when in 1881 Rhodes hired Pickering as the secretary, or chief clerk, of the growing De Beers Mining Company. It would have been after Rhodes, Rudd, et al. merged with Stow, English, Compton, et al. in March. Someone like Stow may have insisted that the new firm employ a full-time office person to relieve the peripatetic Rhodes, who was soon to be spending so much of his time in Cape Town. Pickering may or may not have been an efficient and obedient adjutant (Dormer did not regard him as especially intelligent[26]), minding the minutiae of business while Rhodes became a politician, tussled with Robinson, took his degree at Oxford, and then, upon returning to South Africa, became almost immediately embroiled in the affairs of Basutoland. Pickering was twenty-three, four years younger than Rhodes.

From 1882, Rhodes and Pickering "shared the same office and the same dwelling-house, worked together, played together, rode together, shot together." Pickering became Rhodes' "bosom friend" and "confidant of all his dreams." Pickering was a decade younger than Rhodes—"a frank, sunny-tempered" Englishman. He was described as gregarious, popular (not least with the young ladies of Kimberley)—in many compelling ways everything that Rhodes was not. Hardly driven, much more happy-go-lucky, less ambitious, and with a limited sense of his own destiny, Pickering (like Rhodes' subsequent young men, secretaries, and valets) would have been valued for his happy disposition, his irreverence, his capacity for the hearing and the keeping of enormous confidences and grandiose dreams, and for the supply of whatever personal comfort and solace the maturing Rhodes might have required. Perhaps, too, as he moved farther out onto the stage of adulthood, Rhodes saw in Pickering a link to the boyishness which he never totally abandoned. In their sharing, mutual appreciation, and validation Rhodes also re-created some version of the close relationship to his mother which had meant so much to him earlier.

Pickering, remembered a contemporary, had a "complete understanding of the processes of Rhodes' mind." Graham Bower, the imperial secretary in Cape Town during the 1880s and 1890s, characterized Rhodes' relationship with Pickering as an "absolutely lover-like friendship." Sir William and Lady Solomon reported that Rhodes cared little for people in general, but was "most devoted" to Pickering.[27]

Certainly Rhodes' devotion is amply supported by the impulsive rewriting of his will, and the entrusting to Pickering not only of mere money but of the sole responsibility for carrying out Rhodes' rendezvous with destiny. Never before or after did Rhodes entrust his grand design to a single, private person. That he did so, having at last found his true soul mate, and not merely an intelligent executor, is evident. It was also unlike Rhodes to be so spontaneous in matters of such import; but with his young men Rhodes frequently acted impetuously, and in a state of sometimes enduring bliss.

Pickering and Rhodes lived happily together from 1882 to 1886 in a small, sparsely furnished cottage where wooden chairs, bare tables, iron bedsteads, and horsehair mattresses were the only comforts. Rhodes, it is said, hardly even bothered with a proper pillow. He continued dressing in a shapeless sports coat and baggy white flannel trousers, and often wore tennis shoes. Even with Pickering, and despite what by now was ample wealth, Rhodes continued to live simply, shun ostentation in clothing or other ways, and follow a regimen in Kimberley which was only occasionally social. A Coloured cook/valet looked after them both, although Rhodes and Pickering may have continued to take their main meals in Rhodes' old mess.[28]

Pickering brought a whole new dimension to Rhodes' life, and, as is often the case with "hidden" collaborators, may have helped generate the enormous explosion of creative energy which was evident during the period when Rhodes was twenty-nine to thirty-three.[29] By Rhodes' thirtieth birthday, in 1883, he had taken an Oxford degree, begun the process of amalgamating the diamond mines, started making his mark in politics, achieved an impact (which may have seemed much more important to him) on Cape policies regarding Africans and African states, and succeeded in gaining newfound esteem both in Kimberley and in the Cape. This was the period of a quantum leap in Rhodes' corporate, political (even imperial), and personal ambitions. He jumped from the status of a young man of no more than parochial relevance to a magnate with interesting ideas and some political force. Although his impress on the Cape by 1883 should not be exaggerated, it is equally important not to ignore the general confirmation of his own abilities and influence that came from contacts with the likes of Sprigg, Scanlen, Merriman, Solomon, Gordon, and others, not least Pickering. These relationships as well as his growing success and widening influence must have provided a sense that his dreams could be realized. Rhodes was rounding a critical corner with speed, and was about to accelerate out of the curve and down a long and vigorous straightaway of accomplishment. At thirty he was poised to look north, to make more of diamonds, and even of gold, and to contemplate the transformation of some of his fantasies into worldly victories. He had also achieved what he doubtless believed would be an enduring relationship of love which could give added structure and meaning to his life.

8

"Annex Land, Not Natives"
Forestalling Bismarck and Kruger— An Imperial Prologue

S LOWLY UNROLLING a map of Africa, and with deliberate movements laying it flat on a deal table in his small corrugated iron cottage in Kimberley, Rhodes would place his large hand athwart the African territories beyond the Transvaal and up to Uganda. "All this to be painted red; that is my dream," he would say expansively. Again and again he would belabor his friends with the same speech. Sometimes he would add details or embellishments, the grace notes of a true imperial visionary. And his colleagues, whether the Twelve Apostles or Neville Pickering, would presumably nod, or murmur "Hear, hear!"

Such is the accepted lore. Earlier assessments have commonly implied that Rhodes began thinking about the road to the north in the 1870s, probably after coming down from his major period at Oxford. Before he entered parliament, it is assumed, his vision was clear, frequently enunciated, and awaited only the means or an occasion capable of facilitating its transformation into reality. Rhodes is said to have perceived grandiosely, idealistically, and imperialistically (at a time when service to imperialism was regarded in many English quarters as a virtuous calling) that beyond the Transvaal's northern borders lay Britain's manifest destiny in Africa, and that he had been chosen to be its instrument. It is thus supposed that his first moves to secure a road to the north in the 1880s were but a part of a canny inching forward along a path toward a glorious destination previously established by Rhodes but only revealed in private.

Perhaps. But neither his public utterances nor his private writings ever hint at so much. It is easier to argue parsimoniously: Rhodes reacted. He seized opportunities. Like a sculptor, he brought his work to light, bit by bit, adapting his vision to the deeper structure of the raw material as it was revealed in the act of creation. He had general ideas about Britain's future and about his own fantasied role in achieving something splendid for the mother

149

country. These ideas were often expansive and impressive. In retrospect they are more easily construed as a programmatic prescription than in fact they were.

This distinction, which is significant for an appreciation of the man as well as the mover and doer, is not academic. Rhodes possessed a sure touch for reordering the past to suit the present. He developed justifications and explanations after the fact which were intended to imbue events with an inexorable logic as well as with the broad, statesmanlike sweep of prescience that they may never have had. Thus a re-examination of Rhodes' progress northward supports a more modest interpretation than has usually been offered. It makes Rhodes' activities more rather than less comprehensible.

Treating Rhodes more as a man than as a myth demeans neither his motives nor his ultimate contribution. Rhodes wanted to protect Kimberley's commercial and labor hinterland, and also harbored loftier passions. The Confession is the basic statement: "I contend that we are the finest race in the world and that the more of the world we inhabit the better it is for the human race. . . . Every acre added to our territory means in the future birth to some more of the English race." Many years afterward Rhodes recalled that he had read the history of other countries. "I saw that expansion was everything, and that, the world's surface being limited, the great object should be to take as much of it as we could."

Jameson remembered that Rhodes, as early as 1878, had "formed the idea of doing a great work for the over-crowded British public at home, by opening up fresh markets for their manufactures." This was a notion which had much older roots, going back at least to the founding of the Africa Association in the late eighteenth century. It was also common to Europeans who had been thinking about and rationalizing what was shortly to be called the scramble for Africa. Sidney Shippard remembered a conversation early in the same year when he was walking with Rhodes in the Christ Church meadows in Oxford. "We discussed and sketched out the whole plan of British advance in South and Central Africa," Shippard crowed, but without indicating whether the details of the plan bore any real resemblance to the eventual shape of Rhodes' activities. Jameson also remembered that Rhodes had been "deeply impressed with a belief in the ultimate destiny of the Anglo-Saxon race." This had been the revelation of the Confession. Rhodes, reported Jameson, "dwelt repeatedly on the fact that their great want was new territory fit for the overflow population to settle in permanently, and thus provide markets for the wares of the old country—the workshop of the world."[1]

Rhodes was espousing the notions of *lebensraum* and mercantilism which were then, if expressed a little more eloquently, in common currency. He thus urged the Cape parliament to "annex land, not natives." Further, having seen Carnarvon's policy fail, Rhodes was still in favor of a United South Africa, under British dominion, and not—as Hofmeyr wanted—as an independent republic. These were all factors which certainly helped to focus Rhodes' approach on the north, and would have shaped his tactics. But painting Africa British red came after, not before he appreciated the importance to Kimberley of the road north. Additionally, internal evidence indicates, narrowly, that Rhodes was far less aware than he might have been of the emotional tide of imperialism which had already been launched toward the shores of the Third World. From the Cape it might have appeared obscure, but Rhodes seems to have been motivated only after the event by the likelihood that Africa would soon be dismembered and that he and Britain should both grab a share. Dormer, then the editor of the *Argus,* dates the beginning of Rhodes' great dream of imperial expansion to 1884.[2]

In the early 1880s, Rhodes was motivated not by gold, not by the promise of the regions beyond the Limpopo, not by the Cape-to-Cairo road, not yet by German and Portuguese encroachments, and probably not by any narrow hope of personal fame or gain. Hobson, the anti-imperialist Manchester economist, was wrong about his motives, too.[3] Instead, Rhodes feared that the Transvaal would block any expansion of the Cape Colony to the north, that its growth would limit the prosperity of the Colony in which he was becoming one of the richest proprietors, and in which and for which he could do so much—and become powerful—if only there were "scope." Shedding Basutoland and the Transkei made sense, providing Britain assumed control, because those were costly territories to administer. But the indigenous inhabitants along the northern route were few, and the Cape could, by moving there, limit the rivalry of the Transvaal and the economic mischief which, after Majuba, the Transvaal was already inflicting on the still-poor Colony. The trade with the interior along this traditional path was significant and of growing value. Moreover, labor to Cape farms, and fuel wood and labor to the mines, traversed the same corridor.

Rhodes was more and more confident of his gifts, and wanted to exercise them on as broad a canvas as possible. It is also possible to explain his first moves northward simply by his constant desire both for tidiness and logic. He was adept at appreciating and making the most of the opportunities that presented themselves. Even without an overarching vision, a man with Rhodes' quick, intuitive appreciation of how one parry led to the next thrust would have found himself contemplating the open spaces of the north. He would then easily have developed a philosophy which could explain it all for posterity.

David Livingstone, whose travels originated from Kuruman, northwest of Kimberley and not far from the borders of Griqualand West, was conscious of the need to keep open the missionary and trade route to the north. At the time of his epic trans-continental journey, he demanded the exercise of British power as the only way to safeguard "the English route to the North." Ignoring "the rights of English residents," he explained, "and the interests of English commerce was certainly most Un-English policy."[4] His successors kept up a similar verbal pressure, never permitting the vital strategic importance of the road to be forgotten. Thus it was the missionaries, long before Rhodes, who asserted a humanitarian interest in the corridor northward which was specifically anti-Boer, imperialist, and expansionist.

From Kimberley the road passed through Kuruman, the headquarters of the London Missionary Society in the country of the Thlaping (a southern Tswana group), toward Mafeking, or went via Taung to Mafeking, and then across the Molopo River toward Molepolole, Shoshong, and Serowe, the colonial capital of the Ngwato, before traversing the empty lands en route to Pandamatenga and the Chobe and Zambezi rivers. To the west of this line were the waterless reaches of the Kalahari desert, no place for ponderously moving wagons pulled by thirsty oxen. To the east were the fertile highlands on the outer reaches of the Transvaal from which the Tswana had been pushed within recent memory, first by the Ndebele and other Zulu-speaking Africans, and then by the white trek-Boers who had helped found a South African Republic beyond the Vaal River. Lying between the Kalahari and the Transvaal was the "corridor," a narrow stretch of moderately elevated, and thus comparatively temperate, terrain which received modest amounts of rain and in which springs and perennial rivers were common. Its soil was sufficiently rich to permit staple crops and fodder for oxen to be grown. This narrow belt of territory was an obvious corridor to the north which, if retained in indigenous or at least non-Afrikaner hands, permitted merchants and missionaries to continue their accustomed journeys to and beyond the Zambezi.

The peoples from Kimberley and Kuruman north to the Zambezi, including many still within the western bounds of the Transvaal, belonged ethnically to a great Setswana-speaking confederacy. (Their descendants live in modern Botswana and adjacent South Africa.) In the south, at the beginning of the missionary road, were Thlaping; moving north there were two groups of Rolong, the Rratlou and the Tshidi; then there were Kwena and Kgafela-Kgatla; across the Molopo River (the southern border of modern Botswana) there were more Kgatla, Ngwaketse, Kwena, Kgatleng and then the dominant Ngwato. In or near the Thlaping and Rolong areas, Coloured and Khoikhoi groups who had gathered arms and fled the Cape Colony had established their own refuges. They were farming the land in a similar manner to the Tswana. There were longstanding rivalries among the Tswana, especially those in the south, for control over water and land. So, too, was there competition between the Tswana-speaking herdsmen and agriculturalists and the Coloured and Khoikhoi settlements. South of the Molopo River all of these chiefdoms and satrapies were weak; each turned for support and patronage to the much stronger white states, seeking assistance in their own local disputes.

Access to the corridor—Rhodes called it Africa's "Suez Canal"—lay through the wedge-shaped region south of the Molopo and west of the Vaal. Fractious and volatile conditions there had given rise to innumerable frontier skirmishes as well as petty internecine wars during the 1870s. These conflicts were alleviated after 1878, when British troops and police intervened. The police remained in the area for three years, but despite local missionary and administrative recommendations that the troubled wedge be proclaimed British, they were withdrawn in 1881 in conjunction with the collapse of Carnarvon's unification schemes and the restoration of autonomy to the Transvaal. The borders of the restored Republic, as defined by the Pretoria Convention between Britain and the Transvaal, excluded these long-disputed lands.

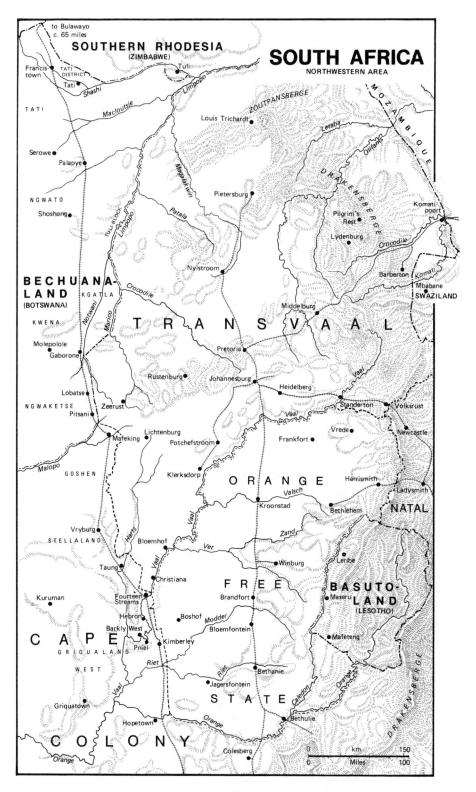

SOUTHERN RHODESIA
(ZIMBABWE)

SOUTH AFRICA
NORTHWESTERN AREA

to Bulawayo
c. 65 miles

Francis-
town
TATI
DISTRICT
Tati   Shashi
Macloutsie
Limpopo
Tuli
Louis Trichardt
ZOUTPANSBERGE
Leraba
Olifants
DRAKENSBERGE
MOZAMBIQUE

T A T I
Serowe
Palapye

N G W A T O
Shoshong
TULI BLOCK
Limpopo
Maqhakwin
Patala
Pietersburg
Pilgrim's
Rest
Lydenburg
Crocodile
Komati-
poort

BECHUANA-
LAND
(BOTSWANA)
KGATLA
Crocodile
Nylstroom
Barberton
Komati
Mbabane
SWAZILAND

KWENA
Notwani
Marico
T R A N S V A A L
Middelburg

Molepolole
Gaborone
Rustenburg
Pretoria
Johannesburg
Heidelberg
Vaal
Standerton
Volksrust

Lobatse
N G W A K E T S E
Zeerust
Vaal
Vrede
Newcastle
Pitsani
Lichtenburg
Potchefstroom
Frankfort

Mafeking
Malopo
G O S H E N
Klerksdorp
O R A N G E
Harrismith
Valsch
Ladysmith
NATAL

Vryburg
S T E L L A L A N D
Harts
Bloemhof
Vet
Kroonstad
Bethlehem

Zand
Winburg
Leribe
BASUTO-
LAND
(LESOTHO)

Taung
Christiana
F R E E
Brandfort
Maseru

Kuruman
Fourteen
Streams
Hebron
Boshof
Modder
Bloemfontein
Mafeteng

Barkly West
Pniel
Kimberley
C A P E
G R I Q U A L A N D
W E S T
Riet
Vaal
Riet
Bethanie
Drakensberge

Jagersfontein
S T A T E
Caledon
Orange

Griquatown
Bethulie

Hopetown
Orange
C O L O N Y
Orange
Colesberg

0   km   150
0   Miles   100

The terms of that document specifically prohibited meddling in the wedge by Transvaalers. But many of the Tswana and Coloured groups straddled both sides of the western border of the Transvaal; a section of Thlaping territory had been included by mistake in Griqualand West, and thus constituted a tiny portion of the Cape Colony. A zone of weakness and contention abutting two strong ones, the wedge was certain to attract avaricious attention from whites who knew it to be one of the last areas of cheap land in South Africa.

In 1881, as the British withdrew, the Thlaping under Chief Mankurwane were being attacked by Korana, a Coloured/Khoikhoi community led by David Mosweu of Maamusa. One hundred miles farther north, Chief Montshiwa of the Tshidi branch of the Rolong was locked in a contest for primacy with Chief Moswete of the Rratlou section of the Rolong. Mankurwane and Montshiwa had sided with Britain against the Transvaal; Mosweu and Moswete were creatures largely of Afrikaans-speaking adventurers from the Transvaal. Filibusterers, freebooters, and farmers, whites from both the Colony and the Republic were enlisted as mercenaries by all sides, and sought and claimed substantial rewards in the form of cattle and extensive grazing lands. By mid-1882, thanks to the concerted help of 120 well-armed Afrikaners headed by Nicholas Claudius Gey van Pittius, Moswete's men had overwhelmed those of Montshiwa and pushed them back against the Molopo River. In the south, Mosweu and 600 Afrikaner frontiersmen led by Gerrit Jacobus van Niekerk overcame Mankurwane's resistance during the balance of 1882. As a result, those Afrikaners who had fought for the victors staked out 6000-acre farms in two separate domains. One in the south came to be called Stellaland, with its headquarters in Vryburg. Another, in the north, centered around Rooigrond, near Mafeking, and was named Goshen.

Rhodes, hardly alone of the leaders of Kimberley, was aware of these crucial shifts of power immediately beyond the borders of Griqualand West. Twice in May 1882 he drew the attention of the House to these ominous developments. Not least because of continuing problems with Basutoland, Rhodes' colleagues were slow to notice, or to take his worries seriously. However, Rhodes managed to persuade Hercules Robinson, the high commissioner, that the petty republics of Stellaland and Goshen blocked the only potentially feasible British-controlled rail route northward to the Zambezi. But when Robinson, seized of the strategic significance of the problem, in turn tried several times to elicit action from Gladstone's colonial office, all he received was a wringing of hands. The Liberal government was then seeking to limit its African exposure and thus reduce expenditures. "A most miserable page in South African history," scrawled an official, "but as we shall not attempt to coerce the Boers, [Montshiwa and Mankurwane] must face starvation as best they can."

Despite the active agitation in London against this Colonial Office attitude by the impassioned Rev. John Mackenzie, the British government remained unmoved. (Mackenzie was on home leave in 1882–83 from his mission station at Kuruman and was being advised and encouraged by Robinson.) Lord Kimberley, the colonial secretary, opined that annexation, the only real remedy, "would be worse than the disease."[5] Rhodes, for his part, despaired of receiving timely help from Britain against the Transvaal, and understood that the only way the Cape could possibly hope to maintain its northern flank free of Afrikaner encumbrance, keep its trade flowing, and sustain the possibility of a rail route, was to make the problem of the petty republics an issue central to the debates of the Cape Colony.

Rhodes had limited, parochial, largely sub-imperial aims in mind when he sought support for firm action by the Cape in Stellaland and Goshen— what Mackenzie called an "abode of anarchy, filibustering, and outrage."[6] In 1883 Rhodes persuaded Scanlen to appoint a commission to examine the boundaries of Griqualand West, on the Cape side of which some of Mankurwane's territory was thought to be included. This was but a pretext. Rhodes, as one of the commissioners, arrived in Taung, Mankurwane's village, in late May 1883. Quickly he arranged a cession from the chief and his councillors to the Cape of all of the chief's putative principality. The "Boers appear to be leaving him alone just now and he has still a good deal of territory left," Rhodes reported to Scanlen. "Its cession, of course, gives you power to deal with [white] Stellaland . . . I feel confident the question could be settled without firing a single shot, and your trade lines kept open. The alternative is absorption by the Transvaal and stoppage of all Colonial trade with the interior."

By 2 June, Rhodes was back in Barkly West after a visit to Vryburg. He told Scanlen by wire that he had been very well received. Even the headmen, Rhodes made plain, say that they "cannot stand alone, but must be annexed to Cape Colony or Transvaal." He thought that the majority favored the Cape, "and all would be with proper management, especially if they could be told soon that the Imperial Government will not allow of extension of Transvaal boundary." Rhodes was particularly worried that emissaries of the Transvaal, one of whom was in Vryburg at the time of his visit, would succeed in making Stellaland part of the larger republic.

"The annexation of [Mankurwane's] country and Stellaland," Rhodes cabled Scanlen, "is the only solution of the Transvaal question." He repeated his plea: "If Transvaal get them [Stellaland and environs] and Goschen we are shut out from interior trade, and our railway to Kimberley comparatively useless. . . ." The Transvaal might also gain control over any route via Kuruman. Delay, he implored, would be fatal. "Transvaal has helped Stellaland with money and arms and is now waiting for permission from home to annex it." Yet "the Boer section admit Cape title worth more than Transvaal one, but if no movement is made by us they will join the Transvaal. . . ."

"You must act at once," urged young Rhodes. First, he said, ask Merriman (who was in London, negotiating the Basutoland retrocession) to persuade Lord Derby to block any moves by the Transvaal into the disputed area. Second, "have the courage to take it for the Colony." Rhodes promised Scanlen the Kimberley vote. Anyway, he said, "if you have to go out, is it not better to go out on what is real policy?" Or so thought Rhodes, who was being typically blustery and single-minded. But Scanlen had to consider a Colony still smarting over the costs of the fiasco in Basutoland, not to mention its continuing responsibilities for the Transkei. Furthermore, his hold on the assembly was precarious, and he knew that Merriman desired the home government, not the Colony, to take control in what was being called Bechuanaland. Hofmeyr, and the Afrikaner bloc in the House, wanted neither imperial intervention nor Cape interference. As far as Hofmeyr was concerned, tiny Afrikaner republics capable of being absorbed by the Transvaal would be a reasonable outcome.

When Scanlen's telegraphic temporization clattered up the open line from the Cape to Barkly West, Rhodes instructed his own harassed operator to send another reiteration: "Don't part with one inch of territory to Transvaal. They are bouncing." Part with the interior road that runs along the western edge of the Transvaal "and you are driven into the desert." Again, "if you part with the road you part with everything." He warned Scanlen of the potentially "complete annihilation under their [the Transvaal's] protective system of your interior trade." "While you have been asleep," he berated, the Transvaal has never failed to keep an ambassador in Vryburg. Then he suggested pressure that Scanlen could employ, if he wished: "my Commission will report that you have illegally taken a large portion of Mankoroane's territory, and unless you act . . . you will have to pay heavy compensation. Any questions?"

Scanlen sought evidence that the white freebooters wanted British rule. Rhodes replied that he could persuade them to petition, but that they were afraid of annoying the Transvaal unless they were confident that the Cape would act. He patiently explained that the whites in Vryburg believed that their farms would be worth more if they were placed within the Cape rather than within the Transvaal. Scanlen also wanted evidence that the trade which would be captured by the Transvaal (and its railway to Delagoa Bay, the modern Maputo), and thus lost to the Cape rail system and the harbor at Cape Town, was considerable. Rhodes replied that three firms in Kimberley estimated that their trade alone was worth about £120,000 in 1882—a comparatively large sum for the Cape—and that they would lose it all if Stellaland and Goshen were surrounded by the tariff wall of the Transvaal. A letter of early June to Rhodes from one of his clandestine English-surnamed contacts in Vryburg also reported a rumor that Stellaland contained gold, but Rhodes apparently gave it little credence.[7]

Rhodes was thwarted. Despite Scanlen's mild interest, Merriman judged that the moment was not ripe, and never raised the question of Bechuanaland with Lord Derby. Even after Merriman arrived home in July, Rhodes failed to enlist his support for annexation. The time was inopportune, given the need to conclude the question of Basutoland, and Merriman also believed that Rhodes' method of resolving the question was unfair and injurious to Mankurwane, who would lose both his land and his status. Rhodes was annoyed.

"I really do not know your policy I long gave it up in despair. After spending a good deal of my time . . . in assisting an idea I came down . . . and heard you blackguard it and repudiate almost everything you had written me on question . . . When I think how I wasted time and my own money in Stella-land and [Mankurwane's] territory whilst thinking you had a policy in matter and then came down to receive buckets of cold water and a final repudiation . . . I would say I shall be in no hurry for any fresh departure."[8]

Rhodes, always hostile to disloyalty or lack of support by real or surrogate fathers or brothers, misjudged Merriman's political caution for antagonism. Merriman was very much alive to the political and ethnic realities of Bechuan-aland, and was concerned with the impact on all of South Africa of the inter-vention of white adventurers in African affairs. "We do not wish to counte-nance the law of the stronger as the law of South Africa . . .," he told the House. "The existence of a community such as Stellaland is a standing men-ace to the good government and peace and order of every state in South Africa."[9] Yet, notwithstanding Rhodes' frantic negotiations and the worries of Merriman, Scanlen, and others, van Niekerk officially proclaimed Stellaland an independent republic on 6 August 1883. About the same time, in an un-dated document, van Pittius did likewise in Goshen. For most of the previous months of 1883, however, both "republics" had been parceling out land and otherwise acting as if they had an independent status.

Rhodes persisted, being unwilling as usual to be denied an objective on which he had set his sights. Despite Scanlen, Merriman, and Hofmeyr's known political reservations, Rhodes rose out of a fevered bed and, in August 1883, tried to reason with and then to persuade the House. He moved an amend-ment to a relatively innocuous resolution which would have committed the Colony to send an official representative to assist Chief Mankurwane. Speak-ing at excessive length and without notes in support of his amendment, Rhodes' words reflected his motives for expansion northward at this early stage. They also demonstrated his reliance in public (as well as in private) on logical, care-fully marshaled evidence, direct speech, and forceful repetition—rather than wit or entertaining artifice. In this case his audience was composed not only of fellow members of parliament but also of Afrikaners and their English-speaking allies (the Country party), both essentially hostile; the Scanlen min-istry, worried but hesitant; and the press, with which a jingoistic approach might find favor.

"I look upon this Bechuanaland territory as the Suez Canal of the trade of this country, the key of its road to the interior," Rhodes began. The issue was more important than the disposal of Basutoland and Transkei, for both of those territories would always remain, but Bechuanaland could be lost to the Transvaal and set serious limits to the future of the Cape. "The House will have to wake up to what is to be its future policy." The central questions at their simplest were: will the Cape Colony "be confined to its present bor-ders"? Will it "become the dominant state in South Africa"? Will it be able "to spread its civilisation over the interior"?

Rhodes was articulating a basic concern of his own: that South Africa should be united, but British. He acknowledged that Hofmeyr also had aspirations for the union of South Africa, "but I regard this question first in its consequences to the interests of the Cape Colony." He told the House that the Suez corridor led to a land beyond the Transvaal, later to be called Rhodesia, which had great prospects. Thus Bechuanaland was the key both to the interior and the little-known reaches beyond. "I solemnly warn this House that if it departs from the control of the interior, we shall fall from the position of the paramount state in south Africa, which is our right in every scheme of federal union in the future, to that of a minor state."

"What we now want," Rhodes urged his colleagues in a memorable phrase, "is to annex land, not natives." He made it clear that he was "no negrophilist, and I hold to the distinct view that we must extend our civilisation beyond our present borders." He said he had no scruples about dealing with the whites of Stellaland who had usurped Mankurwane's land. "The natives are bound gradually to come under the control of the Europeans. I feel," and here he echoed the Confession, as well as Ruskin, "that it is the duty of this colony, when, as it were, her younger and more fiery sons go out and take land, to follow in their steps with civilised government." Furthermore, the railways of the Cape were not built to lie unused. They were constructed to secure the trade of the interior. "I respect the Transvaal," he said for the benefit of Hofmeyr's followers, "but as politicians we have to look to our position as the future paramount state in South Africa. . . ." He feared a prohibitive Transvaal tariff, which would lead to the abandonment of the rail network and the Cape's consequent inability to pay for the huge debt which had been contracted on the assumption that the Cape would gradually develop.

These were persuasive, largely economic, arguments, and Rhodes perceived the issues behind them clearly. He understood the lines of the struggle for paramountcy in South Africa, knew that a united South Africa was the region's unquestioned destiny, and realized that the decision on whether South Africa would be English- or Dutch-dominated would be made by the accumulation of many small advantages. Others in the House doubtless also glimpsed the contours of the same answer. But their approaches were more gradual, circumspect, and less impelled by a sense both of personal destiny and of personal doom. Rhodes later accused Cape politics of being "very localised." The "mist of the Table Mountain covered all."[10] Because Rhodes was a little ahead of his time, but probably more because his own recognition of urgency and sight of clear goals was well in advance of what the House could then contemplate politically, Rhodes' amendment was defeated decisively.

For a successful resolution of the problem of Bechuanaland's petty republics, Rhodes had to scheme further politically and imperially. Fortunately, Hercules Robinson appreciated precisely what was involved. "I suppose it will end in our having to recognize these ruffianly freebooters," the high commissioner told Merriman. "If we had only to deal with the Colony and the freebooters and the Natives, I should not hesitate . . . but how about the Transvaal?" He saw two alternatives, annexation by either the Cape or the Transvaal.

"Bad as both courses are, the first is the least bad for the natives." He continued: "The more I think of the thing, the more difficult do I find it to discover any way out of the mess which is free from objection and discredit, and so I am with reluctance coming round to the idea of Colonial annexation [Rhodes' idea] as the least disadvantageous course now open to us." Later Robinson thought that the best settlement would be to retain the then present boundaries and impose a joint Transvaal-Cape-British protectorate over Bechuanaland.[11]

Such sentiments were anathema to Gladstone and Lord Derby, Robinson's superior at home. Neither wanted to assume responsibility, spend money, or exert force under any circumstances, yet Britain could hardly abandon Bechuanaland to its main local rival. Moreover, in the British parliament there was a forceful pro-African and pro-missionary group which had responded to the choleric Mackenzie's many articulate and well-received public attacks on the new Afrikaner republics. Although they were soon to become bitter antagonists, in 1883 and early 1884 Rhodes and Mackenzie were unwitting accomplices, the one seeking to preserve a trade route and a crucial corridor to the north, the other attempting to ensure a comparatively tolerant, progressive environment for his African charges and converts.

A deputation from the Transvaal, led by President Paul Kruger, arrived in London in late 1883 to seek a rewriting of the invidious Pretoria Convention. Simultaneously, Scanlen, then in London, was advising Lord Derby that the Cape would contribute financially to some form of joint control in the disputed wedge of Bechuanaland. Robinson was in London to inform Lord Derby of the seriousness of these frontier issues and to suggest which initiatives would and would not prove successful.[12] As a result, the London Convention of late February 1884 that modified the terms of the Transvaal's home rule specifically excluded the road to the north, and most of Stellaland and Goshen, from the newly described borders of the Transvaal. Britain wrote off some of what the impoverished state owed, agreed to style it the South African Republic, and scotched the notion of imperial suzerainty. In turn, the Transvaal agreed to respect its new boundaries, to prevent encroachments by its erstwhile subjects, and to conclude no treaties with African chiefs outside of the Transvaal without British sanction. The Liberal government, despite troubles in Ireland and Egypt, and mollified by the thought that neither war nor substantial imperial funds would be required, also agreed to "protect", that is, to become responsible for, the troubled lands from the Molopo River south to Griqualand West. This was a particularly fateful conclusion, for it squared exactly with the intent of Rhodes' failed takeover amendment of 1883, and enabled him to become involved further in the arrangement of Bechuanaland's future.

It is usually suggested that Rhodes was an imperialist, in the ordinary sense that he wanted to paint the map of Africa British red, extinguish African rights to land and riches, and settle Britons everywhere in the occupied areas. Another set of writers asserts that he sought not the spread of imperial but the advance of Cape authority to the exclusion of the Crown. This second body of opinion portrays Rhodes as a fiendish, narrowly focused colonialist who sought the territories to the north as the nucleus of a united, English-speaking, but not necessarily British South Africa. Both generalizations cannot, logically, be true. Yet both are partly correct, and helpful in conveying an understanding of Rhodes' real role in the extension of British rule in southern Africa during the age of African partition. As will be seen, Rhodes acted out of insight and conviction—out of a pellucid grasp of the untold damage which could be done to his dreams of and for southern Africa—but not according to the carefully plotted dictates of some master scenario. Rhodes was an opportunist with Kimberley-focused economic interests and a consummate solver of problems. "No obstacle was insurmountable; no arrangement too difficult to conceive."

In the case of the road to the north, and Bechuanaland, by 1884 Rhodes had specific objectives to accomplish. Whether they would be achieved best by imperial or colonial means mattered less than simply achieving them. Rhodes was not anti-Afrikaner, anti-African, or anti-imperial. He desperately sought to keep the road northward free of interference from the Transvaal and Germany. However that goal could most expeditiously be attained, he was for it, and his own actions and the direction of British and Cape policy regarding Bechuanaland were increasingly influenced by such expedient, firmly focused, thinking. As in other parts of Africa, the direction and pace of the imperial thrust northward from the Cape resulted from initiatives taken by an assertive, ambitious man on the spot. As in Nigeria, on the Gold Coast, and in East Africa, imperial advance was accomplished piecemeal, and in reactive response to the actions of others—in this case the Transvaal and Germany.

By the time of the signing of the London Convention, Rhodes and Robinson were constructing joint answers to the difficult questions of Bechuanaland. Rhodes' influence on Robinson's thinking may have already begun to be important; within a few months there was no doubt that they were working together for common goals. Yet, on the eve of the signing of the Convention, Robinson had recommended a manner of administering the new protectorate which Rhodes (and Merriman) would surely have argued against. He suggested to Lord Derby that Mackenzie be asked to sort out Stellaland and Goshen. But Mackenzie's agenda was not exactly Robinson's: "I am . . . more interested in the initiation of a Native Policy in South Africa by the English Government which would pacify the country, lead to union and establish our own rule there . . . I hope to live to see a practically united South Africa, and England relieved of her present irritating responsibilities in that part of the world," said Mackenzie. As Sir Robert Herbert, Derby's principal civil servant, noted, Mackenzie was highly qualified but, he said, "I cannot feel quite satisfied that either the High Commissioner or H.M. Government would be able to control him. And there is reason to suppose that he might desire to press forward more rapidly and more thoroughly than H.M. Government [or

Rhodes, for that matter] would approve his scheme . . . for organising native territories." [13]

Indeed there was. Mackenzie wanted a true exercise of trusteeship, on behalf of his wards. That method might prove very expensive, whereas the Colonial Office wanted a cheap, non-assertive exercise in damage limitation which could ultimately be assumed by the Cape. Moreover, Mackenzie, a Congregational missionary and a humanitarian imperialist, had widely publicized his deep antagonism to settler South Africa. Thus his appointment in 1884 as deputy commissioner of Bechuanaland was greeted with dismay by Hofmeyr and others. Merriman knew it to be a serious political error. Rhodes was publicly silent. And Robinson, confronted with the hostility of the Cape parliament and that of Graham Bower, his own assistant, began to have second thoughts. These worries deepened when the Cape parliament refused to back Scanlen's offer to help pay for the administration of the protectorate, and when Mackenzie almost immediately exceeded the spirit of his instructions.

The Colonial Office intended Mackenzie to restore order, construct a rudimentary administration, prevent further harassment by whites of Chiefs Mankurwane and Montshiwa, neutralize sympathy among whites and Africans for the Transvaal, and seek a means of regularizing the claims to farms that were at the core of the existence of Stellaland and Goshen. These tasks Mackenzie briskly undertook in April 1884. Assisted by a British officer and ten locally recruited policemen, he proceeded to persuade the Tswana chiefs to acknowledge his authority. He took control of Stellaland by expediently making van Niekerk a temporary assistant commissioner. But he shortly riled the whites there, and in Goshen, by running up the Union Jack and asserting that all the land claimed by whites belonged to the Crown. Naturally there were howls of opposition in the petty republics of Stellaland and Goshen, and threats of violence in the more turbulent northern one. There were many appeals to Rhodes, who had maintained good contacts in Vryburg and who, along with Bower, was in any event attempting to undermine Mackenzie's approach.

By this time, too, the Cape parliament had begun to favor Bechuanaland's annexation by the Colony. Hofmeyr had realized that almost anything was better than imperial rule with Mackenzie in the cockpit. Mackenzie had pursued the personal agenda about which he had warned Robinson and the Colonial Office. But he had gone too far, tactlessly and unsuccessfully. As the high commissioner cabled in horror, "You are not authorized to hoist the British flag as that implies sovereignty and Bechuanaland is just a protectorate." On the same day Robinson further remonstrated that "nothing would justify you in . . . involving us in a conflict between two parties. The consequences would be disastrous throughout South Africa."

The concluding sentences of the second cable brought Mackenzie's brief imperial adventure abruptly to an end. "Come down here at once," Robinson demanded. "I have asked Mr. Rhodes to proceed from Kimberley to Vryburg and he is authorized to act as Deputy Commissioner. . . . He is in full possession of my views as I talked over the position with him before he left Cape Town." (One of the extraordinary sidelights of Rhodes' role in Mackenzie's fiasco was that Rhodes, using Bower as an intermediary, subsequently offered to help Mackenzie buy a newspaper in Grahamstown, presumably as a way of turning a potential enemy into a client, and also out of a sense of fairness. Bower said that Rhodes wanted Mackenzie, now jobless, to "get something.")[14]

Rhodes, originally an independent member from the mining districts who had helped unseat Sprigg and had been outspoken on Basutoland, had, for a man not yet thirty, remarkably rapidly achieved a position of prominence in Cape political life. "What information have we respecting Mr. Rhodes?" the Colonial Office asked on learning of the appointment. Another member of the staff replied that he was sensible although inexperienced and untrained in administrative work. However, the collective opinion in Whitehall was that he would "do very well as a stop gap." Robinson was this time appointing wisely, for Rhodes was no longer a political tyro despite his own expressions of despair.

"Politics to me are perfectly hopeless," he had complained to Merriman in late 1883. "I shall stand again and believe I shall be returned [which was the case, easily, in early 1884] but I have not much heart in matter. The remote object of taking a berth for which [mediocre] men . . . are equally qualified I must say is not a very high aim in life and if when attained you have to exhibit the sorry spectacle of continually denying what you think is the right thing I must say again it is not good enough."[15] Nevertheless, in March 1884, when Mackenzie was making his way north toward Stellaland and Goshen, Rhodes accepted the position of treasurer-general in Scanlen's cabinet, and began to prepare a budget.

Merriman was enormously pleased that Rhodes had joined the cabinet. To the Cape's agent in London he described him as "a man . . . of the greatest talent and originality, and I look on him as by far the rising man in South Africa. . . . He is a man of much wealth, made up here. . . . Not much of a correspondent but with a surprisingly good head, especially for figures, and great industry." Merriman's wife, who also knew the rising star, was of another mind. "I am in such a fluster of rage that I can scarcely write calmly." That Rhodes had become treasurer, "Well! All I can say—the fate of the Ministry is sealed, and I give you three weeks after Parliament meets. I am *thoroughly* disgusted. The idea of appointing a man as Treasurer who can't manage his own money affairs, and one who has never had the smallest insight into business and above all a man who we all know to be not quite steady—is *this* the man to be given a seat in the Cabinet?" She continued, ". . .for the sake of the country I can only hope you may be turned out soon. . . . Why did you ever offer it to him?"[16]

Agnes Merriman was but a trifle ungenerous. Six weeks after becoming treasurer, Rhodes was again a member of the backbenches, as the Scanlen government collapsed over questions concerning the proposed retrocession of the Transkei, the German encroachment in Southwest Africa, the Mackenzie mission in Bechuanaland, and the growing power of the Bond's alliance with Sir Thomas Upington and the Country party. Rhodes never completed a budget, which would have been an interesting test. Scanlen ultimately accepted defeat over the minor matter of whether the bug that transmitted phylloxera, the deadly vineyard plague, could, as the Afrikaner grape growers wrongly assumed, live in potato seedlings. Scanlen's government had recently lifted an embargo on all plants except vine cuttings. Thus Scanlen, and Rhodes, fell from power—as Rhodes and Merriman so wittily explained—ostensibly because of faulty knowledge about a pest. "I retired on a 'bug,'" reported Rhodes, "whose nasty leg entirely covered the Transkeian map." "I write amid the crash of empires," Merriman told John Blades Currey. "The government is in full retreat amid, I venture to say, the ridicule of the Colony. What impelled Scanlen to join his fortunes to that ill-fated bug I know not. . . . I write sorely as I feel very sore, for . . . Rhodes would have made a great success with his budget." Merriman also praised Rhodes' "steady work" and "excellent head".[17]

Rhodes' talents as a public financier were wasted, except for a long and devastating commentary on his successor's initial effort at presenting a budget similar in many ways to his own, but which included new taxes which Rhodes criticized as likely to drive trade away from the Colony toward Natal. "One naturally feels a hardship when one's clothes are stolen," Rhodes wryly told the House. "But there is a greater hardship when one sees the thief walking about in those clothes; and the hardship is greatest when one sees the thief walking about with the clothes on in the wrong way."[18] But for all of Rhodes' attention to the details of customs duties and taxes, the loss of the ministry, and with it the chance to make his mark as a young cabinet member, may have been less important to him than the fact that Upington's government (with Hofmeyr as its real power) put a severe brake on rail development in the northern sector of the Colony. The main line reached Kimberley only in 1885, and was held there until 1890, when a new government extended it northward.

Progress in Bechuanaland was paradoxically easier, for the new Cape government, much of the old, and the high commissioner and his staff were now all in favor of whatever was the opposite of Mackenzie's much abused intent. There arose a political swell in favor of annexation of Stellaland and Goshen to the Cape, and Rhodes was fully prepared to ride its crest. Indeed, Mackenzie's attempt to assert an imperial sway that hardly anyone wanted made Rhodes' own response more popular. Rhodes spoke forcefully in parliament in July in favor of Upington's motion to consider extending the Cape borders to the Molopo and Vaal rivers. Repeating what he had said, unheeded, the year before, he urged parliament to prevent the Transvaal from acquiring the whole of the interior: "Bechuanaland is the neck of the bottle and commands the route to the Zambesi. We must secure it, unless we are prepared to see the whole of the North pass out of our hands." Rhodes, recalled an official of the chamber, spoke with "great power and conviction." "I do not want to part with the key of the interior, leaving us settled just on this small peninsula. I want the Cape Colony to be able to deal with the question of confederation as the dominant state of South Africa."[19] Hofmeyr would have expressed himself in a different manner, but Rhodes was addressing a pliant parliament. Upington's motion passed easily, without a division.

It was as a result of a portion of this address to the Cape parliament, as well as some of his subsequent activities, that Rhodes developed an undeserved reputation among some influential sections of the British political public for being an ungrateful, disloyal colonial legislator whose activities had better be watched carefully. In an opportunistic attempt to curry a little favor with the Bond, the better to support his and Robinson's campaign for Bechuanaland and to separate himself from Mackenzie, Rhodes warned his colleagues that, should the Cape not annex, then the home government would "interfere" and there would be a repeat of those "unfortunate occurrences which they had had in connection with the Transvaal. . . . We must not have the Imperial factor in Bechuanaland."[20] In the Cape these words were greeted with little astonishment, for most of the other members of the assembly knew for what and where Rhodes stood, and were not carried away by what was clearly a sentence or two of well-phrased hyperbole. Throughout, Rhodes' own approach was practical, not ideological. As he subsequently told Merriman, Bechuanaland had either to "remain under an Imperial Protectorate or else be annexed to the Cape Colony. . . . Any other plan will simply hand the interior over to the Transvaal."[21]

Rhodes' form of parliamentary words consequently strengthened his hand when, in the capacity of deputy commissioner, he too attempted to bring Stellaland and Goshen to account. On the way there, Rhodes and Matabele Thompson, his newly appointed secretary and interpreter, stopped at Thompson's farm on the northern border of Griqualand West. Thompson spoke Setswana and knew the leading chiefs of the region. At the farm Rhodes walked into the sitting room and "taking a kit-bag swept into it as many of [Mrs. Thompson's] books as he could find." This was Rhodes' manner; he abhorred passivity, and could enthusiastically substitute mental for physical activity. "Something to do," he explained to the startled Mrs. Thompson, "if I am faced with a weary and boring wait in the veld." But Rhodes' reputation had preceded him, and Mrs. Thompson feared either that she would never see her books again, or that they would be returned mutilated. Even this early in his life Rhodes had a habit of "reading a few chapters and then, if the book pleased him, of tearing off the part he had finished and handing it on," said Thompson, "while he read the rest. He said this would make the book more interesting." Two people could "share the pleasure of the story, and the discussions would be more intelligent." As Thompson commented, "It was the action of a future millionaire, but hardly good for my wife's little library."[22]

Stellaland and Goshen were again immersed in conflict between whites and Africans, with the more serious raids and affrays occurring in Goshen.

Stellaland was less tense, and Rhodes managed to calm and settle van Niekerk and his followers, some of whom were English-speaking and from the Cape. One of the main opponents of a submission to British rule, however, was Adriaan de la Rey, a strongly built Afrikaner from the Transvaal. Rhodes needed his acquiescence, and one morning tried to tackle de la Rey at breakfast. He strolled over to his tent, where hospitality was compelled to take the place of hostility. De la Rey was frying chops over an open fire. He said nothing, and Rhodes sat down opposite him in silence. At last de la Rey looked up from the frying pan. "Blood must flow," he said. Rhodes was cool. "Well," he said, "give me my breakfast, and we will talk about blood afterwards."[23] Later, with Thompson's assistance, Rhodes promised to recognize the titles which the Stellalanders claimed for their farms if, in exchange, they would accept the overrule of Britain. Rhodes insisted "upon the practical recognition of Her Majesty's Protectorate." He also assured the white farmers and freebooters in Stellaland that they would soon become citizens of the Cape, and not be subject to an unsympathetic overseas mistress.

Rhodes' method was to deliver peace to Mankurwane and his Tswana followers, but to do so by giving much of the chief's patrimony to those whites who had already taken his lands as booty. He justified this disregard of African expectations, indeed rights, by suggesting to Merriman that "the occupation of Stellaland had gone too far to have been disturbed, and if there is anyone to blame we must lay that blame at the doors of the British Government for their prolonged delay."[24]

Stellaland was easy to square, for Rhodes was dealing with a situation where the whites were of mixed background, more powerful than their African opponents, more numerous, wealthier, and more independent of Transvaal support. Goshen was much more volatile. There the whites were fewer, almost exclusively Afrikaners from the Transvaal, and constituted—according to Rhodes—a class of Boer which "never thinks of consequences and therefore is liable to do acts contrary to all reasons."[25] They also specialized, to a degree, in cattle rustling from across the Molopo River, as well as against Montshiwa. Furthermore, Rhodes quickly learned that Kruger's government was encouraging the Goshenites to maintain a staunchly anti-British posture, provisions of the recently signed London Convention notwithstanding.

Rhodes' own mission to Goshen was precarious. Fearful of traveling there through the protectorate over which he had theoretical authority, but where he would be at some physical risk, he and Thompson approached Rooigrond, its tiny capital (which he described as no more than a rude collection of mud huts), via the Transvaal, and never crossed the border into Goshen. There a British subject had recently been killed and another official been imprisoned. Rhodes ordered the Goshenites to come to account, but they ignored him. On the night of Rhodes' arrival in the (Transvaal) outskirts of Rooigrond, van Pittius and 500 of his men even attacked Montshiwa's village of Mafeking, "firing upon the unfortunate inhabitants, wholly regardless of the fact that they had been taken under the protection of Her Majesty the Queen." Rhodes explained that the Goshenites reckoned that should Montshiwa be killed and his town destroyed before Rhodes could possibly intervene, "a great point would have been gained in subsequent negotiations."[26]

That was the plan. The Goshenites presented Rhodes with demands for a recognition of their de facto local sovereignty. Without coercive instruments and bereft of bargaining tools, Rhodes rejected the proposals, warned them sternly, and hustled back to Stellaland to report and regroup. Taking advantage of Rhodes' ejection, Kruger decided a week later, in September 1884, to annex Goshen. The Rev. Stephanus du Toit, formerly of Paarl and the Bond, who had been advising Kruger and then the men of Goshen, on 3 October 1884 ran up the flag of the South African Republic in Rooigrond. This was the final provocation. Not only were Afrikaner ambitions challenging those of Rhodes and the Cape; the Transvaal's expansionist aims were endangering imperial hegemony across a dimension which was new in the scale of its challenge.

Rhodes had been more clairvoyant than he could have known in alerting the Cape public and, through Robinson, the British government, to the critical connection of Bechuanaland to the wider European scramble for Africa. Germany, to Britain's profound surprise, had suddenly taken a threatening interest in the coast of western Africa north of the Cape Colony. Because the latitude of the Transvaal on the eastern side of the missionary road approximated that of Germany's new focus and because both entities were hostile to British paramountcy globally and locally, Cape Town and London in 1884 suddenly feared that Chancellor Otto von Bismarck's newly aggressive nation could act in concert with Kruger's equally thrustful Transvaal in excluding Britain from the interior.

No longer could a British government contemplate keeping its imperial options in southern Africa (or elsewhere, for that matter) open indefinitely without the outlay of considerable effort and expense. The simple days, or the illusion of simple days, were gone. This is not to gainsay the generalization that the struggle for control of South Africa began before 1884 and grew out of the "politics of local contest and partition," but Bismarck's separate agenda raised the stakes considerably, transformed the nature and the context of the arguments, and made Britain much more responsive than ever before to the importance of its imperial position in southern Africa. Germany's intervention contributed to a new—not a declining—willingness to license entangling extensions of empire by proxy.[27] Although Rhodes was hardly responsible for the injection of Germany into the southern African region, he and his allies in Cape Town and London could and did employ the adventitious timing of Bismarck's own maneuverings to accelerate a northern (Bechuanaland) movement that, hitherto, had obtained little support and gained limited momentum.

Merchants from the Dutch-ruled Cape traded in the eighteenth century along the largely inhospitable southwest African coast of what is now Namibia. After Britain assumed control of the Cape, and for much of the nineteenth century, a desultory commerce continued, and twelve of the small off-shore islands were exploited for their deposits of guano. The interior from the Orange River, in the south, was penetrated as far north as the territory of the Herero, and in a few rare instances as far as the Kunene River and Cape Frio. Explorers, hunters, traders, and missionaries ventured into this region from the Cape. But the involvement of the Cape in any official manner was inconsequential until 1861, when it began to take possession of the guano isles. Their official annexation took place in 1866. A Cape Town fishing company was active, too, but only in 1878 did Britain actually exert a claim to any mainland part of the region. In that year a naval officer annexed Walvis Bay, about 374 adjoining square miles, and the offshore guano islands, holdings which were officially incorporated into the Cape Colony in 1884. Meanwhile, in 1876, the Cape had shown an official interest in the interior by appointing a commissioner extraordinary for Namaland and Damaraland, the southern two-thirds of the territory. Additional magistrates were briefly stationed among the Herero, as well. But both Britain and the Cape, assuming that the region lay within their spheres of influence, also acted casually with regard to the area, and were little motivated by considerations of strategy and commerce until a rival claimant appeared.

F. Adolf E. Lüderitz, the head of a German merchant house (specializing in tobacco) from the old Hanseatic port of Bremen, had once attempted to establish a trading enclave in Mexico, but had failed to obtain support from Bismarck. In early 1883, Heinrich Vogelsang, on behalf of Lüderitz, was attracted to Angra Pequena, a small harbor north of the Orange River and south of Walvis Bay. German missionaries had labored in its vicinity for several decades, and a few German traders had followed in the 1870s. Introduced by the missionaries to the local chief, Vogelsang traded £100 worth of gold and sixty rifles for a cession of the port and the surrounding 215 square miles, nearly all of which were desiccated and barren. There—"a long way from everywhere"—he need have bothered no one in South Africa. British officials initially regarded Vogelsang's actions as unremarkable. Angra Pequena had no known economic value, and the Cape had never demonstrated a desire for it or for control over the indigenous inhabitants of this sparsely settled section of southern Africa's thirstland.

Angra Pequena need not have figured at all in the diplomatic maneuvers which culminated in the partition of Africa. But Bismarck, at first opposed to colonies in general and against yet another attempt by Lüderitz to involve imperial Germany, was encouraged, even infuriated, by British and Cape ineptness. He thus transformed a private assertion of an ordinary commercial claim into one of the first salvos in the Anglo-German battle for pre-eminence in the world. The German traders wanted to be protected by the mother country. Bismarck asked Britain to assume this role; Gladstone's government said that although the area was within the British sphere, Britain had no official rights and would not protect the German merchant community. By August, alerted by the Cape Town fishing firm, Merriman and others became concerned about the German intentions, but during the balance of 1883 the British government assumed that Bismarck would not act in any harmfully definitive manner, and the government at the Cape tried to avoid bearing the financial burden of administering the coast and instead urged the mother country to bring southwest Africa into the empire. Since Scanlen was in London for much of this period, Rhodes was reduced to showing his concern by badgering Merriman, who was already alarmed, but had been unable to persuade his distant prime minister to move decisively.[28] At the end of the year, Scanlen and Merriman finally prodded Britain to proclaim a South African Monroe Doctrine.

It is important to ask why Rhodes did not do more. In every other territorial controversy in which the Cape became embroiled during the late 1870s and 1880s, Rhodes spoke his mind and, whenever he was able, attempted to bend the forces of decision to his will. By contrast, as much as he was acutely aware of the dangerous consequences that would follow from the planting of Germany's flag in Southwest Africa, he did not become directly involved in the Namibian crisis. The conclusion of the crisis came at an awkward time, for Scanlen's government was being ousted just at the moment when it could have attempted to intercede in Angra Pequena. Moreover, Rhodes was more directly focused on his problems in Kimberley and his ambitions to the north. But the better explanation is that Rhodes, with his fixation on trade routes and therefore on the far interior, underestimated the potential of what became Namibia. It did not appear to be rich in minerals, a place for white settlers, or a natural outlet for expansion by and from the Cape. Rhodes was much more interested in the growth of white dominions, not mere dominion and not mere grazing land—which is all (aside from guano) that Namibia appeared to promise.

Lord Derby and his advisors at the colonial office in London were not looking for trouble. Indeed, they were more worried that German traders and their rivals from the Cape might together provoke an unfortunate international conflict than they were that Bismarck would oppose Britain. Yet Bismarck's personal impatience, his sure hand for the diplomatic maneuver which would discomfit a European rival, his clever if gradual awareness of southwest Africa's value in the competition for choice portions of the continent, and a public agitation at home in favor of the Angra Pequena merchants, persuaded him to declare an official "interest" in the area and then, at the end of April 1884, to give formal protection to this commercial possession. It was Germany's first bid for an African colony.

Britain still underestimated German intentions, and responded lamely. Throughout the early 1880s, British policy consisted of a determined effort to "avoid all action until events had accumulated to a point where action was inescapable." There was a new regime in the Cape, however. Scanlen's outgoing ministry had hesitated interminably—"I do not want to touch any further annexations if it can possibly be avoided," Scanlen had said, for "a large expanse of territory is a source of weakness and humiliation"—until Rhodes joined it and, with Merriman, promoted definite action.[29] Their own awareness of events was overtaken by the collapse of the Scanlen government, but as the mantle of urgency passed to Upington, the new prime minister, it was taken up assertively. He declared movement unavoidable and sought to take control for the Cape of the coast of southwest Africa as far as Walvis Bay. In July an amendment, proposed by Merriman and passed unanimously, extended this putative Cape annexation to Cape Frio and the Portuguese (Angolan) border.

Britain reported this new boldness to Bismarck and assumed that such an announcement would presage the beginning of the end to a tiresome business—the Capetonians would do what was needed, and the imperial government would have little to worry about. But, as early as April, Bismarck was no longer willing to be fobbed off, least of all by the Cape. By June, this point was clear to the British cabinet, even though the Cape parliament was outraged, and made threatening noises. By the end of August 1884, when Rhodes was squaring Stellaland and being rebuffed in Goshen, Germany impatiently annexed Angra Pequena (soon to be called Lüderitzbucht) and, responding to further moves by the Cape, extended its original borders to encompass all of the land from the Orange River for 600 miles to the ill-defined northern frontier of a region claimed by Portugal.

The new German colony stretched along the Atlantic coast. How far it extended inland, however, was suddenly an issue of extreme importance to all the imperial players. As Rhodes, Merriman, Upington, British publicists, ranking British civil servants, even British politicians, and such interested parties as President Kruger quickly appreciated, an eastward extension of the new German colony and a westward extension of the Transvaal to a mutual meeting place on the map of Africa could forever block Britain's route to the north. Commercial possibilities might be lost, and, not least, long-held political and economic aspirations for a British-dominated united South Africa would be forfeited.

Rebuffed on the west coast of southern Africa, Britain could hardly let itself be humbled a second time, and by but a minor power in the interior. The effective creation of a German colony within Britain's nominal sphere made the raising of the Transvaal's flag in Goshen unthinkable and untenable. Moreover, these contentions of empire were troubling Britain throughout the continent: French and British interests were questing for hegemony along the Niger River, and the Germans were active in nearby Kamerun and Togo; British and German explorers were racing against each other for prominence in eastern Africa, and Britain's position in Egypt and the Sudan was at risk. Locally, the Transvaal Afrikaners were flexing their muscles in Zululand, again in contravention of the London agreement, and there were great fears in Whitehall and Cape Town that Bismarck was seeking a toehold in the northeastern corner (Zululand) of the same vulnerable Indian Ocean region.

Even at this late moment in the jockeying for imperial position, the British government remained reluctant to become directly embroiled in a counterthrust against the Transvaal. There was an official awareness that the Transvaal must be contained, but London still wanted to shield itself financially, as well as administratively, behind the Cape. There the high commissioner, working closely with Rhodes, was doing his best both to push the British cabinet and to provide evidence of simmering discontent among all sections of the Cape public. Rhodes spoke strongly in late September 1884, demanding the dispatch of an imperial force to oust the Boers from Goshen. With Robinson and Bower's encouragement, a public meeting about the same time pressed the same case and led to the establishment of a local pressure group called the Empire League. But these colonial agitations, even when combined with public pressure in Britain, may have mattered less than a sharp War Office critique which suggested that British paramountcy in the interior was essential for the security of Cape Town.

By October, the British cabinet had accepted the notion that Bechuanaland was vital to British as well as Cape strategic concerns. It steeled itself to be decisive—"I wish I could resist the conclusion that we must interfere by force . . . but I see no other way out of that miserable business," worried Lord Kimberley. Whitehall finally permitted Robinson to tell Kruger that his annexation of Goshen was unacceptable. Protests from Upington and Hofmeyr delayed any forceful reiteration of this policy, as did an attempt at direct arbitration in Goshen by Upington and Sprigg, which Merriman termed lunatic.[30] Britain finally persuaded itself that a show of force was essential for regional as well as particular reasons, and dispatched a massive 4,000-man military expedition. It was commanded by Major-General Sir Charles Warren, whom Rhodes had earlier known and claimed to have recommended, as had Robinson. His task was to support right by might. Warren was also styled special commissioner, and had broad political responsibilities.

Rhodes, and also Robinson, were unwilling to leave the success of the expedition to chance. At a meeting in Cape Town on his way inland, Warren was persuaded by Robinson to take Rhodes along, again as deputy commissioner. In the same interview, Robinson obtained Warren's support for the concord by which Rhodes had successfully pacified the Stellalanders in September. Warren initially appeared pliable, and Rhodes may have felt confident of a quick and relatively favorable conclusion to the problems of southern Bechuanaland. From his viewpoint it consisted merely of how best to oust the Goshenites.

Rhodes' aims at this juncture have been described as anti-imperial and pro-colonial: that is, of seeking to advance a narrow, sectarian cause, and of being motivated by a desire to conciliate the Bond. He is also accused of being hostile to the interests of Africans. Certainly he was conscious of the Bond, and may have harbored the political ambitions of which a few of his colleagues were then jealous. He was always prepared to effect those compromises—in this case among whites—which would have ensured peace regardless of African rights. But, most of all, Rhodes wanted to see the job done, and southern Bechuanaland secured in a way which would never be endangered by shifts in official British sentiment. Rhodes wanted to be certain that control over this area could not be wrested away, and the road to the north some day blocked. He also saw immense regional political advantages for the Cape in adding or protecting sparsely inhabited indigenous domains (the annexing of land, not natives).

Rhodes and Robinson ultimately obtained what was at best a partial victory. Warren, they discovered, was not easily controlled. Because of a friendship with Mackenzie dating from the general's tour in Kuruman in the late 1870s, and because of Mackenzie's vision and experience, Warren insisted on attaching the humanitarian to his staff, and making him a second deputy commissioner. Robinson and Rhodes were appalled, but Warren, a fervid teetotaler, whose belief in his own rectitude was almost as impassioned as that of Gordon, credited Mackenzie with "far-sighted sagacity." (Fuller, who knew them all well and later took Rhodes' side, called Warren "cranky . . . upright, but crotchety." So did Harry Currey, Rhodes' aide-de-camp, who called Warren "difficult.")

Warren, both impetuous and obstinate, was motivated by an appreciation of Cape and settler avarice. He wanted to preserve as much land and autonomy as he could for the Tswana. It would be useless, he told Robinson, "to turn the freebooters out of Goshen if the Cape politicians are to be allowed to put them back again." Warren and Mackenzie had the same aims in mind, Warren describing Mackenzie as an "apostle of peace," a "good, sterling, honest man" who was capable of rendering the kind of assistance of which no other man in South Africa was capable. He had the qualities which, Warren later implied, Rhodes lacked.[31]

With Mackenzie and Rhodes, Warren met President Kruger in January 1885 at Fourteen Streams, on the Vaal River border. Warren was unable to persuade Kruger to accept the fact of British sovereignty in Bechuanaland. Rhodes later said that he had been impressed by the bearing and single-mindedness of Kruger, the untutored, stiff-necked, and very stubborn sixty-year old, self-styled prophet. What these natural antagonists and later wrestlers for the body and soul of South Africa said to one another, and how they interacted, is not known in any detail. Kruger is alleged to have regarded the young man hovering in Warren's background as someone who would cause Kruger "trouble" if he did not "leave politics alone and turn to something else." Kruger compared Rhodes to a race-horse: "Well, the race-horse is swifter than the ox, but the ox can draw the greater loads. We shall see."[32]

After the meeting at Fourteen Streams, which Rhodes believed that Warren had mishandled, there was growing friction between the two former friends. The personal antipathy was new, perhaps derived from Warren's jealous rivalry with Robinson, perhaps fanned by Mackenzie's criticisms of Rhodes' moral character, perhaps exacerbated because Rhodes had earlier established procedures and alliances which he hardly wished to see undone. Or perhaps Rhodes' manner and bearing offended, for the young industrialist and politician in 1885 wore "a big slouch bush hat, the shabbiest and most ragged of coats, and a very dirty pair of white flannel trousers, with old tennis shoes as his footgear."[33]

At Warren's request, Rhodes had earlier been sent to restore order to Stellaland. Rhodes; Henry Latham (Harry) Currey, the son of John Blades Currey, who was acting as Rhodes' temporary secretary and aide-de-camp; and two Coloured servants comprised the party as it moved in a wagon drawn by mules from the railhead near Kimberley to Vryburg in late December 1884. "We drove in the cool hours of the morning and evening," Currey remembered, "getting out of the wagon to shoot partridges and koorhaan [a South African flightless bird] of which there was an abundance. . . ." On arrival in Vryburg, Rhodes hired a small corrugated iron hut, labeled it Government House, and proceeded to control Stellaland. "Government House" was so small, Ralph Williams (Warren's civil intelligence officer and subsequently Resident Commissioner of Bechuanaland) later recalled, "that in the day we had to put the mattresses outside to make room for the table, and at night the table outside to make room for the mattresses." Currey also slept there; Rhodes, as was his habit, slept in the wagon.

"The first thing we did," remembered Currey, "was to go in search of a pool in which we could bathe. When we found one we put a few natives on to enlarge it and to swim in it morning and evening was a great relaxation after listening to all the [motley crowd of ruffians] who claimed rights in the area in dispute." A second task set by Rhodes was that Currey should order whiskey and supplies of Guinness stout, from Kimberley, for themselves, but also for the entertainment of the local people.

When Warren finally arrived in Vryburg from Fourteen Streams, he and Rhodes dined together regularly, along with Currey and the senior officers of the Sixth Inniskilling Dragoons, who were the elite of Warren's expeditionary force. One of those officers was the man who later became Field Marshall Sir Henry H. Allenby. In 1884 he was a young subaltern who on at least one evening shared a single shakedown (blanket roll) with Rhodes. In the middle of the night Allenby woke up feeling chilled and found that Rhodes in his sleep had pushed him out from under the blankets. "Allenby resumed half-possession, but in an hour or two he again awoke to find that the same thing had happened, only this time Rhodes had firmly wrapped the two blankets round his own person, and was happily snoring." Being the junior of the two, Allenby gave up the unequal struggle. He believed that Rhodes did not deprive him purposely, but "acted according to his unconscious will to get all he could."[34]

On the political front, since Warren abhorred liquor and Rhodes and the other officers liked a drop, there was disagreement from the start. Warren also quarreled with Rhodes over—of all things—the proper way to run the diamond industry. One evening he also chose to arrest van Niekerk—whom Currey described as a "timid vacillating creature the last man in the world you would think to be the leader of a gang of hardy Trek Boers"—while van Niekerk was dining with Rhodes.[35]

Whatever their personal differences in Vryburg, overriding all matters of style and taste was a fundamental clash of principle. This was no cleavage in the abstract. Warren preferred imperial rule and Rhodes wanted local rule. But the cause of the bitter rupture was a basic disagreement over whether the rights and authority of indigenous Africans should be subordinate to settler claims, as Rhodes had already decided, or whether the Thlaping and the Rolong should be restored to their previous paramount positions. As Warren later summarized his own stand, upon arriving in Stellaland he discovered that the agreements that Rhodes had concluded were "fictitious." Rhodes had canceled Mackenzie's earlier arrangements because Mackenzie had been too sympathetic to Africans. Rhodes thought that "the settlement had in fact gone too far to be disturbed," since many of the original freebooters had sold their claims to real farmers, but Warren believed otherwise. "I quite agree . . . a conciliatory policy is advantageous," Warren told a London audience, "but if this means giving everything to the robber and marauder . . . and destroying and extirpating the native races, it must be condemned."[36] The differences between himself and Rhodes were precisely put.

When it became clear in February that Warren was determined to undo all of Rhodes' careful compromises in Stellaland, was reneging on his promises to Robinson and Rhodes, and was even prepared to declare martial law and prosecute the white leader of Stellaland, Rhodes exploded. "The course you have pursued since your arrival in Stellaland has been most prejudicial to the peace not only of this district but of the whole of South Africa," he told Warren. "By your action," he remonstrated, "it was only too apparent that you did not admit the right of the people of Stellaland to have their own government." He acknowledged that it was a "crude" administration, but because the original agreement had been made between himself as a representative of the Queen, and subsequently ratified by the colonial secretary, he urged that it be "carried out to the very letter." Otherwise, "Her Majesty's word is given and broken as occasion requires."[37] In fact, it was Rhodes' word that was important. He had come to terms with the situation and saw his Stellaland model as one which could be used elsewhere in the interior, even in Goshen, to advance white interests.

Rhodes resigned (the only time he ever did so before the Jameson Raid), telling Robinson in a long, angry official communique that he could take no part in a program which "bids fair to leave us with all our difficulties in Bechuanaland unremoved, and a people on our borders animated by feelings wholly opposed to the sentiments of friendship which it had been my consistent purpose to promote." The people to whom Rhodes referred were white, however, and included no more than 600 families in both Stellaland and Goshen, but he was also looking beyond Bechuanaland to the question of how an English-dominated white South Africa would ultimately be created. He envisaged a coming together based on common interests. There also was a more immediate object—keeping the trade route for the Cape Colony. Rhodes told the House that he had fought to retain that path for the commerce and labor of the Cape, and sought to make it British, "at the risk of my political position and personal relationship with all sections of the country."[38]

Ultimately, it was. Warren proceeded from Vryburg, where he had reversed Rhodes' policy and overawed the Stellalanders by force, to Goshen, where van Pittius and his followers prudently retired into the Transvaal. There was no bloodshed, and by the end of February, Warren had restored order to southern Bechuanaland. Meanwhile, there was action in Whitehall. Reacting to threatening moves inland by the Germans and to the deliberations of a conference of world powers at Berlin, which was then setting rules for the subsequent partition of Africa, a British Order in Council of late January had extended the jurisdiction of the Crown westward. It put under imperial control the disputed borders with the Transvaal to the twentieth meridian (today's border between Namibia and Botswana) and northward to the twenty-second parallel (including the southern half of today's Botswana). This protectorate was welcomed by the leading chiefs north of the Molopo River, especially by Chief Kgama of the Ngwato. Indeed, he feared the Transvaal as much as did Rhodes and, noting that the twenty-second parallel cut his kingdom in half, requested an extension of the protected area to the banks of the Zambezi River.

Britain hardly wanted so much, at this stage, and refused. So, too, thanks to the fervent opposition of Rhodes and Robinson, the Colonial Office rejected an elaborate plan submitted by Warren, based on a memorandum by Mackenzie and drafted by George Baden-Powell, which would have turned the entire area south of the twenty-second line of latitude into a full-fledged Crown Colony completely divorced from the Cape and dependent upon local sources of revenue, including the sale of land to thousands of white farmers. Prompted by Rhodes and Bower, Robinson raised vociferous and repeated objections of cost, of practicality, and so on. If Warren were backed, Robinson warned, Britain could hardly hope for support from the Cape. Additionally, all three men had come so to dislike Warren and Mackenzie that their opposition, and that of other influential figures in Cape political life, was assured.[39]

Rhodes—setting out a theme which he would echo until death—attacked Warren's proposals because they contained a provision that only persons of English descent should be allowed to obtain land. "I think all would recognise that I am an Englishman," Rhodes declared, "and one of my strongest feelings is loyalty to my own country. . . ." Yet Rhodes was prepared to raise his voice "in most solemn protest" against the exclusion of colonists of Dutch descent, "and it is the duty," he continued, "of every English man in the House to record his solemn protest against it. . . . The introduction of race distinctions must result in bringing calamity on this country, and if such a policy is pursued it will endanger the whole of our social relationships with colonists of Dutch descent, and endanger the supremacy of Her Majesty in this country." What Robinson had recognized and Rhodes praised was the realization that in southern Africa the "supremacy of British interests" could never rest upon a "system which is founded on injustice or distinctions of race."

Indeed, Rhodes was merely restating imperial policy of some standing. "The whole policy," Grant Duff told parliament in 1881, "which the present Government or any other Government must maintain in South Africa [was] the absolute necessity of preventing the development of race-hatred between men of British and Dutch descent." Warren's proposals would never have resulted, Rhodes later informed a British audience, "in that union of races which, after all, is the only true basis of commercial and political prosperity." Further, it was "only through a course of firmness and impartiality that we can hope to see the day when the separate States of South Africa will be a united Empire under the English flag."[40] This was the nub of Rhodes' plural (but purely white) vision in the mid-1880s.

It is important to note that all of this diplomatic activity regarding the lands north of the Molopo River focused Rhodes for the first time publicly on what was to become Rhodesia (Zimbabwe). He also began to display a strategic knowledge of the area, probably as a result of long conversations with Edward Maund, of Warren's entourage, and young Ralph Williams. Until then Rhodes knew little of the lands beyond the Cape. "He had no real sketch of 'Rhodesia' in his head," remembered Williams. It was while living together in Vryburg, awaiting Warren's arrival in 1885, that "Rhodes' scheme for expansion to the north was hatched." At least that is Williams' plausible report. "He knew nothing of the country and I knew a great deal. We talked it over morning, noon, and night, from every point of view." But, wrote Williams, Rhodes was not then thinking of the lands of Lobengula, of Lewanika, or of the territories that he conquered in the 1890s. Rather, aware of German efforts in the same direction, "it was to the lake country of Tanganyika and the lakes to the north of it which Rhodes then wished for, and his primary object was to keep the road thither open." Williams goes on to report: "I have that in his own handwriting."

Rhodes supported Lord Derby's refusal to annex Bechuanaland beyond the twenty-second parallel for the sensitive reason that much of what Kgama wanted to cede was in fact ruled by the warlike Ndebele—"the most powerful tribe between our settlements and the Zambesi." Yet, Rhodes explained, even if Kgama could not legitimately give away that territory, it was important that it be secured for the Crown. "Otherwise," Rhodes said, "we may find ourselves burdened with the permanent responsibility of a poor tract of country shut in on every side by States with hostile tariffs, and yet unable, through the responsibilities we have undertaken, to retire from the situation." The Cape would not want Bechuanaland if Germany or the Transvaal, or perhaps Portugal, controlled the region north of the twenty-second degree of latitude.

"It would be advisable at once," Rhodes urged with a logic that foreshadowed his activities a few years later, "to enter into such arrangements with the Chief of the Matabele [Ndebele] as would preserve the only road that is left to us." Trade there was potentially great. So, too, beyond the Ndebele, were the "capabilities" of Mashonaland. "It has been frequently traversed by reliable explorers and is known to have pastoral resources and mineral wealth such as do not exist in any portion of Africa, south of the Zambesi." Its climate was good, its elevation high, it was free of malaria, and there were reputed to be numerous quartz reefs, he suggested before the existence of the great Witwatersrand deposits were known, "with exceedingly rich auriferous indications," a fact—Rhodes had been reading and listening—which was supported by the "old Portuguese records."

Rhodes' rhapsody continued. North of the Zambezi River lay the "great Lake system, with its vast population [in northern Zambia], and its almost unlimited market for the consumption of our [i.e., British] manufactures." A railway, he lured, could reach this region in easy stages from Kimberley, and would be easier and more preferable than any route to the interior via the Congo River system. Rhodes therefore advocated the inauguration of communications with the chief of the Ndebele and the extension of the new Bechuanaland Protectorate onward to the Zambezi. Bechuanaland, he rightly said, was suitable for cattle ranching but not for large-scale British emigration. "Its real value is as the link which may join our settlements [in the Cape] to the richer districts beyond."[41] In 1885 that clearly became one of Rhodes' prime objects.

The Colonial Office, having solved the immediate problem of southern Bechuanaland and successfully separated the Transvaal from German Südwest Afrika, wanted to devolve as much further responsibility and initiative as possible upon its junior partner in the Cape. It sought the Cape's cooperation, not its antagonism, and, prompted always by Robinson, fell quickly into line with Rhodes. This approach was as much that of Lord Salisbury's Conservative government, after June 1885, as it was that of the preceding administration of Gladstone. But when the Cape agreed to accept responsibility for southern Bechuanaland, it offered to do so only if it could control all future settlement and development, and if Britain paid for a portion of the envisaged expense. (Rhodes, blamed by some for such terms, was not in a position to influence the Upington government; he would not have been so crude.) Hercules Robinson termed the Cape's offer "impudent."[42]

Backing as usual into conquest, Britain finally decided in August 1885, to transform the wedge of dispute south of the Molopo River into the Crown Colony of British Bechuanaland, to continue with a bare-bones protectorate north of the river, and to recall Warren. Sidney Shippard, former attorney general of Griqualand West and the trustee of Rhodes' second will, and now a judge of the Eastern Districts Court in the Cape Colony, was appointed administrator of the new colony and deputy commissioner of the Protectorate. Most important, since Britain still hoped in the future to shunt all of its responsibilities to the Cape, Shippard was made responsible in both capacities to Robinson, and was told to run British Bechuanaland in a manner consonant with the policies of the Cape Colony. His headquarters, by some final irony, was established in Vryburg. Thus Stellaland—a polity that had long existed because of Rhodes' willingness to strike a deal with a mixed bag of claim jumpers and squatters—and Goshen—an entity into which life had been breathed by Kruger—passed into history.

Rhodes had certainly secured the first section of the road to the north. Indeed, thanks to the timely intervention of the Germans, that route, and a limit to encroachments from the Transvaal, had been set much deeper into the interior than Rhodes had ever contemplated. The dry lands of the Namib had been lost forever, but the creation of British Bechuanaland and the Bechuanaland Protectorate, as well as an arousal of the Cape and the mother country to the dangers of Afrikaner and German expansionism, were reasonable recompense. These developments facilitated Rhodes' later territorial acquisitions. Yet it would be a profound mistake to view his role in this first chapter of the Bechuanaland story as thoroughly deterministic. He exerted a personal will, and was more consistently active than others in urging his political colleagues in the Cape to focus upon the strategic relevance of the missionary corridor. His influence over Hercules Robinson was also considerable, although Robinson was still a man of some independence and force. Robinson had been a politician in Britain, and keenly gauged the political realities of the Cape. In the final settlement of the Bechuanaland issue, and at most critical points along the way, his impact on London was important. Rhodes thus exerted influence on British policy through Robinson (and Bower), even if the extent of that influence can only be hinted at and not measured completely.

This influence, and what Rhodes had done or not done to obtain it, were nevertheless a source of deep suspicion in many Cape quarters, not least among the ranks of his old supporters and friends. Eddie Mackenzie, the missionary's son, was a Kimberley physician who attended Rhodes in Vryburg when he suffered episodes of fever in late 1884 and early 1885. He wrote that Rhodes was "fearfully rich" and "his character [was] very difficult to get at. He [was] very willing to act straight, but if he [were] benefitted in another way he does not at all object to making the crooked straight." Many others naturally deprecated the young Rhodes' unseemly public row with Warren, the esteemed soldier, for verbal battles between prominent persons left all sides besmudged. But there were also deep suspicions that over Stellaland and Goshen Rhodes had betrayed his principles, or at least the principles of equality and tolerance which Merriman, John Blades Currey, and others close to Rhodes had mistakenly presumed that Rhodes shared.

Merriman had returned from London in late 1884 and, almost immediately, had expressed his disquiet to Currey, who was in Kimberley. "I trust you to keep Cecil Rhodes up to the mark; his wretched compromise with the Stellalanders was a bitter pill to swallow and surprised all those who looked on him as a strong Imperialist, but it is no use crying over spilt milk." A few weeks later, after Rhodes had tried to explain why and how he was compromising in favor of whites, Merriman wrote to his wife: "I cannot make out Rhodes' proceedings. He seems to be making a terrible mess of matters. . . . I disapprove most strongly but cannot say so owing to friendship. Politics are very disheartening, all the men one seems to lean upon and trust give way."

A few days later Merriman telegraphed and then wrote to Currey. Rhodes' recent "proceedings under the Stellaland flag seem to me perfectly incomprehensible. Of course they are real jam to the Afrikaner party. Does he mean to serve Baal or what? He will end by shipwrecking his own reputation." Merriman was worried that Rhodes had put himself in a false position as Warren's deputy, but when Rhodes telegraphed to Merriman that he had broken with Warren, Merriman responded by wire that "conflict just now" would have a disastrous effect. After Rhodes warned Merriman not to credit anything Warren said, and promised, uncharacteristically, that he would fight Warren "to the bitter end," Merriman moaned to Currey. "What a dreadful mess this quarrel of Rhodes and Warren is." Rhodes was playing into the Bond's hands, Merriman worried. "I am very grieved about Rhodes."

When Merriman and Rhodes finally came together again in Kimberley (in March), Rhodes gave Merriman "a grand blowing-up for not being more cordial in espousing his side of the question." Merriman kept his temper, but Rhodes was "very sore, and finding no-one here to sympathize with him makes him much worse. Really politics are terrible things for breaking friendship. . . ." Rhodes' approach, reported Merriman, was "so warped that he has got to take a sort of pleasure in any failure or mistake of Warren. . . ." Rhodes began making slashing attacks on Warren in the *Argus*, which pleased the Bond, but annoyed Merriman and Currey, both of whom told Rhodes so. "Currey will have it," Merriman told his wife ominously, "that Rhodes is playing for the premiership" with the assistance of the Bond.

In April, John Blades Currey reported that his suspicions had become certainties. "I am very loath to believe any evil of a fellow whom I like so well," Merriman replied, "but really his conduct lately has been almost as inexplicable as that of Hercules [Robinson] himself. Of all men in public life, Rhodes has the least object in running crooked: he has ample means of his own—office would be to him merely the means . . . to the end of public life in England—he can afford to try and make a reputation. . . . Yet, according to you, he is prepared to sacrifice everything for the purpose of intriguing with the ignorant and anti-English section of the community."

Rhodes and Merriman came together again, but the old trust and intimacy had gone. Rhodes was anxious to win Hofmeyr's support, was competing with Merriman in the diamond amalgamation battles (see Chapter 9), and gradually came to realize how thoroughly he had vexed both Merriman and Currey. It was easier for Rhodes to remain on excellent terms with someone like Fuller, a new acquaintance from parliament. Fuller unpardonably (from Rhodes' view) organized a vast and very warm reception for Warren when the general withdrew home via Cape Town. "He wired down to Cape Town that I was 'burning incense to Warren, and that he would never speak to me again,'" wrote Fuller. But a little while later, when Rhodes himself came down from Kimberley, he invited Fuller to "'help him consume a salmon'" which had been sent to Rhodes on ice from Europe. "Over the salmon and the wine and the politics of the future, Sir Charles . . . [was] forgotten—in fact . . . never mentioned," burbled Fuller.[43] Rhodes had created another acolyte, a role neither Merriman nor the elder Currey—both mentors—were ever prepared to play.

Despite his many critics, and his enormous controversy with Warren, Rhodes by late 1885 had secured the route to the north, accomplished the annexation of British Bechuanaland and the protection of Bechuanaland proper, and become one of the outstanding politicians in South Africa. Even if he were in some circles distrusted, his prescience, his striking persistence, his growing wealth, and his genius—most of the time—for compromise and conciliation had made him a person of obvious consequence. Merriman and John Blades Currey wondered whether he would seek a seat in the British parliament, but Rhodes was steadfast in his determination to be a force in the smaller political pond rather than a voice in the imperial assembly. In the end, he transcended both, and depended upon support from neither. Yet in 1885, at thirty-two, he could at least congratulate himself on hard won significant achievements in the struggle for control over southern Africa. They were obtained at a time when he was also concentrating on the financial expansion of his holdings in Kimberley, and investing much of himself in his burgeoning personal relationship with Pickering.

Rhodes was restless, too. In 1883 he had informed Merriman that he was looking forward to the time when he might "stroll around the world for a couple of years." In 1885, his brother Ernest learned that Rhodes had told one of their sisters that a "stroll around the world" was still his ambition.[44] Whatever that image meant to him, he was never to see the world (aside from trips to Europe and Egypt), or to indulge in any kind of prolonged leisure. For Rhodes there was always too much to do. He had so early and so young been involved in so many momentous and formative decisions that even Rhodes might not have realized that they were but grist for those bigger and more world-shaking developments in the accomplishment of which his steadying hand would soon be directly noticeable.

·◄ 9 ►·

"If Only We Have the Pluck"
Seeking Dominion over Diamonds and Gold

R HODES DEALT seriously in diamonds throughout the 1870s, but he also made ice, pumped water, shuttled to and from Oxford, and accepted a more mature role only when he was about twenty-eight, in 1881. Then he abandoned the pursuit of a profession in Britain, gave up the law, embraced colonial politics, and—definitively and imaginatively—tied his financial destinies to diamonds. After creating De Beers Mining Ltd. with Stow and others, and becoming one of the significant men of money on the mines, he busily carved out a place for himself in Cape Town, and—piece by piece—secured for himself, the Colony, and the Crown a sphere of influence which extended well beyond the confines of Kimberley.

Active in Basutoland and Bechuanaland, and more and more imperial in his ambitions, Rhodes could not and did not neglect the basis of his fortune. Nor was he any less assertive in his financial adventures during the 1880s than he was in extending his territorial reach northward. As busy as he was with the affairs of Stellaland and Goshen, or as occupied as he was in Basutoland or Cape Town, Rhodes' focus never strayed far from diamonds, and the opportunities for further aggrandizement and economic growth that his stake in De Beers represented.

Rhodes was a man of a few fundamental and powerful ideas. Two shaped his thinking about the diamond industry and motivated him year in and year out. He was one of the few who never lost his faith in the rewards of the Kimberley pipes. Each time a portion of the mining community decided that the fields were reaching the end of their useful life, Rhodes assured himself that there would be diamonds yet. He stayed with the blue earth and had confidence when reefs fell or the world price of diamonds faltered. He persisted stubbornly, even doggedly, as the sons of determined fathers do, and prospered after each period of local or international recession. Second, Rhodes was guided throughout these early decades by a notion of scale. Boyle, a perceptive visitor from Britain, came to similar conclusions, and proposed similar remedies, after examining the economic underpinnings of the Kimberley mining operations as early as 1872. "I do not believe that the supply of diamonds is falling off," he began, "therefore prices will not rise seriously, if they keep their level. Even now, it does not pay one man in five to dig. . . . This pick-and-shovel business is a mistake. Diamonds are not a proper subject for exemplifying the theories of Political Economy. You cannot drown the market with an article only appertaining to the highest luxury . . . without swift and sudden catastrophe. These things require the most delicate manipulation . . . they need a hand to hold them back or loose them as occasion asks. . . ."

Boyle's analysis prefigured Rhodes' own. "By royal monopoly alone, or by means of great and powerful companies, can jewel digging be made a thriving industry. Into the hands of a company," Boyle prophesied, "all these public fields must fall, and, thus used, they may benefit the country for generations to come. . . . When that time arrives there will be. . .news of a rising market. . . ."[1] Great diamond pipes could most efficiently and profitably be exploited by single companies, pooling and organizing the resources of many entrepreneurs.

Others, following Boyle, had the same vision, but Rhodes was single-minded in Kimberley about pursuing it, patiently and opportunistically. At an early stage he also grasped, as did others, the importance of controlling as much of the world's productive capacity of diamonds as possible. The introduction of dynamite in 1880 made the working of larger claims more cost-effective. But until joint-stock companies were permitted to secure mineral claims in 1880, no fundamental alterations in the corporate structure of diamond mining was feasible. Even so, Rhodes already suspected in the 1870s that the main market of the time—the vanity or romantic market—was inelastic in terms of demand. Only so many diamonds could be sold each year because only so many men married each year, population growth in the developed world being—he thought—essentially static. Thus, only control over the production and the distribution of diamonds could avoid the cyclical boom and bust which affected the supply of diamonds and all other raw materials. He wavered from these conclusions in the mid-1880s, but most of the time he knew that controlling the De Beers mine was a step basic to the control of all the South African sources of diamonds and to the efficient, oligopolistic, measured, and steady release of diamonds onto the world market.

Whether or not Rhodes understood all of the steps in this chain of elementary economic logic as early as the 1870s, and how all were interrelated, he pursued the goal of increased scale from 1880 and achieved the first quantum jump in 1881. Then, employing a variety of questionable financial and personal tactics, he set his sights on attaining the next quantum leap—the amalgamation of the rival firms on the De Beers mine. Rhodes had long-term goals, too, but he usually advanced objective by objective. His assault on the multiple ownerships of the mine which he and his partners had been quarrying since 1875 continued assiduously, if in fits and starts, from the accomplishment of the first major consolidation in 1881.

Many others of local prominence, and visitors and observers such as Boyle, understood as well as Rhodes that only when the surviving private claims were extinguished and the companies merged would the diamond industry prove rewarding, possibly even continue to exist at all. Yet Rhodes was unusually relentless, far-seeing, and skillful in his pursuit of that objective. After helping found De Beers Mining Ltd., and thus greatly increasing the leverage of his own and Rudd's capital, he entered the Cape parliament, made an early mark there, and finished a final term at Oxford. While overseas he brooded about how to put his mining capital to even better use. He devised a scheme to bring all of the four Kimberley mines—De Beers, Kimberley, Dutoitspan, and Bultfontein—together through one grand, encompassing merger. According to Stow, at the very end of 1881, when both were in Britain, Rhodes presented him with an elaborate program for joining the principal diamond-producing centers. "I see it now!" Stow wrote many years later. "Folio after folio of intricate figures and calculations for arriving at a basis of valuation of the many conflicting interests. The labour bestowed upon the elaboration of this project must have been prodigious." But Stow received it skeptically. "A cursory glance sufficed to convince that it was inherently faulty and impracticable. But what had more influence upon and determined me at the outset to vote its rejection was the conviction that the interests of our own Company would be served best by consolidating the various holdings in the De Beers Mine in the first instance." Moreover, "the agents it was proposed to employ to conduct the financial arrangements did not inspire sufficient confidence. Neither their repute nor ability to carry the venture to a successful issue was re-assuring."[2]

Next, Rhodes sought to influence a prominent French financier in the tidier project of unifying the De Beers mine alone. Exactly what his plan was, and how it related to the voluminous figures that he tried out on Stow is not known, but it is clear from a reading of the local press in Kimberley that Rhodes' efforts were neither derided nor opposed by opinion makers. Yet, because economic conditions were not yet suitable, because Rhodes' financial inducements were too weak, or because Rhodes lacked sufficient "weight" and respectability—which he himself may have concluded at the time—this straightforward attempt to buy out the other companies on the mine failed. A few of the recalcitrant firms backed off at the last moment, seeking higher payments for their sections of the mine. "Owing to the silly selfishness of one or two outside and unimportant companies," wrote the editor of the local *Independent,* "the scheme for the amalgamation of the De Beers Mine seems to hang fire. . . . If the promoters will accept our advice they will leave the contumacious outsiders where they are at present—in the cold—or, the reef."[3] Rhodes and his colleagues could do nothing else, and for the next five years the question of efficiency and control had to be pursued in a more piecemeal fashion than Rhodes—fresh from Oxford—would have desired.

"I do not despair of the place," Rhodes wrote in 1883 amid a wave of bankruptcies and suicides among the miners of Kimberley, "as the wealth in diamonds, if regulated must eventually become a source of profit to the holders instead of as at present being chucked away for the benefit of home consumers." Without revealing or, possibly, even yet knowing that post-tax profits would remain reasonable, he gave Merriman a basic economic lesson: "The yield is as good as ever but at present rates leaves no margin. Bad as things are fancy S. Africa without . . . this £300,000 per month of diamond export worked so unprofitably that the results are all distributed in the country in return for labour, fuel, food etc. and nothing is left to be remitted to home shareholders or shared by bankrupt colonial ones."[4]

What Rhodes meant by "regulated," which contrasts with his eventual view, was that the miners should have agreed among themselves not to offer their diamonds on the world market for less than the cost of production. Prices should be fixed as close to the source as possible, by mutual consultation. But he did not believe at this stage in attempts artificially to restrict output. Joseph Robinson, by contrast, thought that the best answer to the low prices caused by overproduction was a common agreement to curtail individual and company mining by setting quotas. In any event, in 1883, no common cause was to be made voluntarily among the still numerous producers. Because the diamond market had taken a turn downward, competition was keen, trust was lacking, and there was no body or group to enforce a program of regulation. Rhodes doubtless appreciated, again, that a cartel could be created only if one or a few firms could discipline both sides of the market.

Possibly, if Rhodes had focused fully on Kimberley instead of politics and imperialism, the amalgamation of the mines would have been accomplished with greater speed. But Stow and others possessing financial acumen were even more active during this period than Rhodes in seeking to purchase or merge their firm with other, weaker companies on the De Beers mine. They had modest successes, too, between 1882 and 1884, but Rhodes' ambitions remained unrealized until a combination of accumulated natural calamity, the acceptance of innovative mining techniques, and the acquisition of new capital permitted Rhodes and his partners to enlarge the scale of their operations once again.

Beginning in 1882, the two richer diamond holes began to suffer severe falls of reef. Undermined by the diggings themselves, millions of cubic feet of rock collapsed into the De Beers and Kimberley properties. These falls buried about half the claims in both mines, and compelled the mining boards and some of the richer and unfortunate companies to try to dig out the massive debris and start again to win diamonds. But doing so was beyond the capacity, the patience, and the capital of the unconsolidated firms and the boards, the most important of which went bankrupt. A viable, if expensive, alternative in 1884 was to sink shafts and thus bypass the debris. But tunneling implied cooperation among rivals, for from the sides of a mine many of the buried properties could be reached only by traversing the claims of competitors.

As in the 1870s, this need to alter or improve upon existing mining methods coincided with a period of increased costs and depressed world prices for diamonds, and consequent shortages of liquid capital. Robinson, for example, owned a series of companies on the Kimberley and Dutoitspan mines which ceased paying dividends during the early 1880s and left him, not uniquely, on the verge of insolvency. Newbury suggests that Rhodes was strapped for cash, too, during this difficult era, and survived financially only by relying on his family, especially his brother Ernest.[5] But this could be an exaggeration based on an incomplete cache of family letters; even so, Rhodes in 1885 had a disposable income of more than £20,000 and perhaps as much as the usually attributed £50,000 a year. Rhodes had wealth, but would not have been among the richest magnates in South Africa; his fortune—not all from diamonds— was hardly in the same class as that of Barnett Isaacs (Barney Barnato), who owned a sizable portion of the Kimberley mine and earned about £200,000 in the same year.

Barnato had come to South Africa in 1873 from the Whitechapel slum in the East End of London. A year older than Rhodes, he had left school at thirteen and, together with an older brother and several nephews (two of whom preceded him to South Africa) had sought shillings as an itinerant street salesman, barman, entertainer, and also by using his fists. Chunky, spunky, short, and always in rumpled clothes, the cocky young Jewish Cockney arrived in Kimberley with forty boxes of suspect cigars, a few pounds in cash, and great ambitions. "He was a strongly built young fellow," reported a close contemporary, "wore a pair of spectacles on his uninviting dust-stained face, and had the ugliest snub nose you could imagine, but as good a pair of large grey blue eyes as ever flashed through a pair of glasses."[6] At first the state of the local industry and his own meager talents made it difficult for Barnato to prosper as a diamond buyer. He boxed, and performed to popular acclaim on the local stage. Barnato also helped his brother manage one of the local hotels and, toward the end of the 1870s, was elected to the town council. He and his brother also amassed capital sufficient to begin buying and working claims on the Kimberley mine.

This was the beginning of a legendary Kimberley fortune. Although many of Barnato's contemporaries wondered if his rise had been helped by illicit dealing, by the early 1880s Barnato had parlayed his first few claims into a number of solid companies. His financial acumen was acclaimed and widely celebrated. Surviving a serious shakeout in 1884 by digging underground and accumulating additional holdings, after 1885 Barnato was securely one of the wealthiest, and certainly among the most colorful, entrepreneurs on the diamond fields.

During the early 1880s, Kimberley's commercial confidence and financial stability had been badly compromised by the crumbling nature of the reefs, the likelihood of additional and continuing falls, and the rise in production costs that followed. The purloining of diamonds by illicit diamond buyers (which the legislation that Rhodes promoted in 1882–83 had been intended to curb) and the fickle quality of gem sales compounded the problem. One

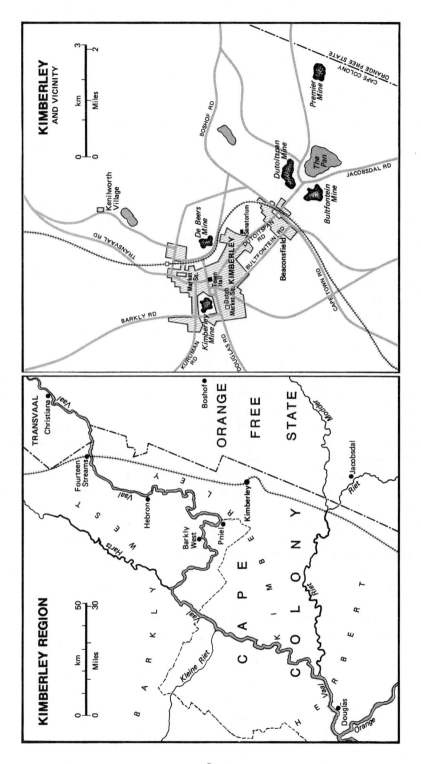

185

who was young and observant during this period remembered the many problems: "Owing to the multiplicity of companies and owners working alongside of each other on the bottom and sides of the vast [Kimberley] hole, all sorts of difficulties arose between them. Means of access, rights of way, limits of boundaries, and falls of reef were among the chief causes of trouble. The Mining Board . . . had become a regular bear garden, where the disputes became so violent that one of its members . . . always attended the Board meetings accompanied by a hefty pick handle wherewith to enforce his arguments. The worst trouble the mines had to contend with was the constant falls of 'reef,' as the rock forming the surface rim of the mine was wrongly called. . . . The constant fall of reef rock caused many accidents and violent deaths. . . . It became evident that the system of open mining had reached its end. . . ." Moreover, two epidemics of smallpox, in 1882 and 1883–84, frightened both labor and capital, added to costs, and heightened the overall atmosphere of anxiety throughout Griqualand West.

In 1882 smallpox had infected the Cape Town area and threatened to spread northeastward to Kimberley. Rhodes was active in establishing and helping to pay for a quarantine camp thirty miles south along the main road from the Cape. There, at a crucial crossing point on the Modder River, travelers were intercepted, examined, vaccinated, fumigated through exposure to burning sulfur, and, if necessary, quarantined at the insistence of Johannes (Hans) Sauer, a tough, newly qualified physician.

Sauer became acquainted with Rhodes, and with the consuming mystery of Rhodes' magnetism, only in 1883. "Even with the little knowledge I had of him I felt that he had a remarkable power of attraction for his fellow-men, so that one became fond of him without exactly knowing why. I often used to pass him in the streets of Kimberley," continued Sauer. "He always appeared to be reflecting deeply on something or other, and had the habit, when his thoughts were puzzling him, of vigorously rubbing his nose, the dominant impression one had of him being that he was always thinking of something both serious and important."[7]

Sauer's camp saved Kimberley from smallpox in late 1882 and early 1883, but near the end of 1883 the dread disease arrived again, this time from the north. Laborers from Delagoa Bay (modern Mozambique) were accused of having carried it to the largest labor area south of the Suez Canal. Sauer was summoned back from the Transvaal to take charge, but on the eve of his return a massive attempt to cover up the contagion was perpetrated by Jameson, Matthews, F. Rutherfoord Harris, and two other prominent physicians of the town. At the behest of at least some of the mining owners and other local businessmen (neither Rhodes nor Stow seems to have been implicated, despite Jameson's central involvement), this cabal of physicians attempted to deny that the pox was in fact the dreaded smallpox. They and their backers understandably feared a wholesale desertion of the mines by their African work force. (But the Africans stayed, long being aware, according to Sauer, of smallpox and the effect and virtue of vaccination.)

Edmond Sinclair Stevenson was summoned from Cape Town to Kimberley by Jameson to decide whether the epidemic was smallpox. "If it was smallpox," recalled Stevenson, "a quarantine would be called, the result being that the comparatively large population, mostly niggers and others, would be thrown out of work. . . ." Stevenson continued proudly: "Needless to say we pronounced it chicken-pox, otherwise it might have led to serious trouble."[8] Jameson, a well-trained surgeon, could have had no doubts about the correct diagnosis. That he, and Harris, tried to avoid the obvious conclusion speaks to their fundamental lack of integrity.

Jameson and the other physicians opposed Sauer's efforts to obtain prompt notification of all cases and the vaccination of those who had been in contact with the cases. So difficult was the situation that Sauer had to prevail upon his brother, a prominent member of the Cape parliament, and other members of that body (but not Rhodes) to urge the passage of a Public Health Act which, several months later, made notification compulsory and strengthened Sauer's hand measurably. He showed that the contagion of smallpox had infected all of the mine housing areas and the local hospital. Ultimately 700 died (of whom 51 were whites) and about 2300 others (400 of whom were white), were infected before wholesale vaccinations and quarantine-like measures finally eradicated the disease early in 1885. It is important, too, that during this same period Kimberley was infested with syphilis. A "formidable" problem, syphilis was second to smallpox in its deadliness, and almost impossible to eradicate.

During these troubled times Rhodes was hardly alone in viewing the merger of mining companies, and the ultimate rationalization of the industry, as Kimberley's only salvation. The Rothschild merchant banking firm of London made inquiries in 1882, but its attempt to amalgamate Dutoitspan in 1883 was frustrated by the impossibility of reconciling the many competing claims and hopes. Joseph Robinson was active then and later, but he reported to Merriman that "it seem[ed] impossible to carry out the measure no matter what efforts are put forth. . . ."[9] Robinson encouraged Merriman to consult with the Standard Bank, South Africa's largest, with headquarters in Cape Town, and to seek a role as an arbitrator or facilitator. This he did in 1885, failing in his efforts to consolidate first Dutoitspan and then Kimberley. Merriman was also active, during 1885 and 1886, in assisting the amalgamationist plans of Charles Roulina, who owned a large share in Dutoitspan, and of Charles J. Posno, the London-based head of a diamond firm with large holdings in the Bultfontein and Dutoitspan mines and investments in the Amsterdam cutting industry.

What Roulina and Posno envisaged was the merger of all South African diamond companies into a new London-based Unified Diamond Mines, Ltd. Merriman returned to Kimberley at the very beginning of 1886 to advance this plan. By this time the 3600 claims into which the four mines of Griqualand West had originally been divided were owned by ninety-eight companies and individuals. Nineteen controlled the Kimberley mine, ten De Beers, thirty-two Bultfontein, and thirty-seven Dutoitspan. The railway had just reached the dusty metropolis, and an upswing in the cycle of boom and bust had begun to encourage everyone again. Posno had formed a syndicate to purchase as many mining properties as possible. He was backed by £600,000 from two French banks.

Merriman was optimistic, for Posno was prepared to offer about £19 each for shares worth only about £5 locally. But there were unexpected obstacles: Robinson, on whose support Merriman had counted, had no remaining resources. Francis Baring Gould's Central Company was hostile. The small companies and single claimholders sought some form of government-sponsored buy-out. The local shopkeepers were also anxious, fearing that a Kimberley amalgamated would be a Kimberley deserted. A public meeting denounced the plan. Furthermore, Rhodes was not at first pleased. Merriman explained that his old friend was "as queer as ever, so suspicious." He was "inclined to oppose the scheme because it did not emanate from him." However, reported Merriman, "He is quite aware of its importance and the value of it to him personally." [10]

Merriman dickered with the magnates of the mines. For several weeks he despaired. Then, apparently as a result of a number of long conversations between Merriman and Rhodes, and presumably much brooding by the latter, Rhodes, who had become the chairman of De Beers, on 20 January 1886 decided to favor Posno and Merriman's plan—if appropriate terms could be arranged. What persuaded Rhodes to favor a plan which could have robbed him of a secure base of power, not to mention long-term, if still uncertain, financial rewards? Was Rhodes losing faith in diamonds, or in Kimberley? The company had done well between 1884 and 1886. Was he despairing of his own ability to create the same kind of cartel? Had he, of all men, grown weary of the cyclical chase up and down the summit of prosperity? Perhaps so, if momentarily, for a week later Merriman told his wife that he had talked at length with Rhodes. "He wants me to secure enough from this to go home and join him in the British parliament to form a colonial party. He is quite hot on this."

Joined by Stow, Rhodes apparently worked with Merriman throughout the final weeks of January 1886 to persuade the other nine De Beers mine owners to sell out to Unified. At first they were unmoved. "The jealousy of each other is so indescribable," wrote Merriman, "that there is no length to which it will not carry them." [11] But by the end of the month Merriman, who was inexperienced in these matters, confidently cabled Posno that he and Rhodes had managed to bring about the virtual amalgamation of the De Beers mine. He expected next to be able to obtain a similar kind of agreement with the Central Company, the leading syndicate on the Kimberley mine. If so, he anticipated a successful consolidation there as well.

Rhodes, whatever he confided to Merriman, and no matter how thoroughly he seemed to be supporting the Unified effort, abruptly and single-handedly scuttled it. At the beginning of the second week of February he issued a prospectus for an amalgamation of his own. A few days later the local newspapers carried a large advertisement inviting the main companies on the mines to exchange shares with each other at a commonly accepted level of value. All the mines would thus be owned jointly, and consolidation could be achieved with deceptive simplicity and without much wrangling. It must be presumed that Rhodes, as the originator of this deft scheme, expected to emerge as the leader of the powerful, mutually owned concern. Or perhaps, knowing the opposition of his own directors, he never anticipated that such an ingenuous scheme would prevail, but instead suspected that it would sabotage Merriman's at a moment when that one seemed about to win the day and thus deprive Rhodes of power and control.

Rhodes' announcement never so much as hinted that he had earlier agreed to cast his lot with the Unified plan. "Rhodes," wrote Merriman sententiously, "is the same in business and politics, tricky unstable and headstrong. Never able to take a line and follow it! It is a serious defect in his character and unless he mends it will destroy his usefulness and mar what may be a fine career. I have felt both in politics and now in business the effect of this curious fashion of lukewarm agreement. Actually as an opponent he would do far less harm than he does as a sort of half-and-half friend. I am all the more sorry because I like him personally so much."

Merriman was resigned to his defeat, but he grew more bitter a week later when he learned from John Blades Currey, their mutual friend, that Rhodes had told Currey and others that Rhodes had never intended his own and his board's scheme to succeed. He was opposed to outsiders—presumably anyone other than himself—interfering in the consolidation of the mines. "Putting two and two together we came to the conclusion that he was hanging on just to raise the price of De Beers' shares and to further some private plans of his own. . . ." Whether or not Currey and Merriman correctly analyzed Rhodes' motives, they lamented his behavior. "If Rhodes had run straight the thing would have gone through but he is as unstable in business as he is in politics—and one can only take him as one finds him, make the best of his good qualities and regret his bad." [12] In fact, amalgamating the De Beers mine first was better for his company. Rhodes would be vindicated.

By unstable, Merriman did not mean devious and manipulative, but with the benefit of hindsight it is evident that those adjectives are descriptive: Rhodes had brooded further, rejecting the romantic notion of entering the British parliament. "I tell you candidly I have not the slightest idea of quitting S. Africa for any other country," Rhodes declared in 1888. "Here I can do something but were I to go to England as a politician I should be lost in obscurity." [13] He had calculated the clear disadvantage of Merriman's scheme to himself in terms of power and prominence, probably persuaded Stow and the other directors to agree, and then prepared his counterstroke secretly. (Rhodes could still commit the company to little without the consent of his fellow directors.) Always anxious to avoid unnecessary personal conflict, he would not have warned Merriman before issuing his own prospectus. And he would never have apologized or explained. Thus what he told Currey was, more than likely, at best a partial reason for his seemingly abrupt double-crossing of an old friend. For Rhodes there was much more at stake than loyalty. After all, had he lost out to Merriman, the pyramid of diamonds and politics which he was attempting to erect, and upon which all else would soon depend, would have been knocked asunder.

Hans Sauer says that, before Merriman's effort, Rhodes had made up his mind that amalgamation was essential. "I often saw him seated on the edge of the De Beers' mine, gazing intently down into its depths, absorbed in his reflections. Later," Sauer recalled, ". . . I asked him what he was thinking about. . . . 'I was calculating the amount of blue ground in sight and the power that this blue ground would confer on the man who obtained control of it all,' was his answer."[14]

"Power" and "control" were central organizing principles for Rhodes as he entered the period of his life typically characterized by concerns over generativity. In Rhodes' case those concerns were related primarily to the achievement of his dreams—of great accomplishments in the name of empire. Having realized that marriage was not for him, Rhodes lived to achieve significance and meaning not through the generation of children but through more grandiose but less personal offspring—wealth, power, and influence. Rhodes kept moving successfully toward his goal despite numerous deflections, detours, and delays. In part that may be why modern critics overlook and dismiss his capabilities so easily. Although his internal compass pointed steadily in a direction of progress, he often appeared to be engaged in trivial pursuits.

In his thirty-third year, financial rewards were no less a preoccupation and a measure of self-worth and successful endeavor than they had been a decade before. To ensure a steady growth in his own and his company's assets, in order to prevent threats to the wealth of his own diamond position, and immersed as he was in an industry known for the volatility of both supply and demand in an era marked by the celebrated consolidations and corporate coups of John D. Rockefeller, Andrew Carnegie, John Pierpont Morgan, and Cornelius Vanderbilt, Rhodes naturally would have been intrigued by the gains to be achieved by amalgamation. But, much more than his fellow entrepreneurs, Rhodes was alive to South Africa's expanding horizons. If only incompletely developed, Rhodes had plans for the north and for the enlargement of his own political role in the Cape. They would be furthered if he dominated diamonds. Rumors of significant gold discoveries in the Transvaal would also have quickened his quest for hegemony in Kimberley. Until he created a monopoly, Rhodes knew that he and his dreams would be imperiled by the vagaries of the market and the speculative connivings of his competitors.

Rhodes presented his anti-Unified proposals to the stockholders of De Beers at a special meeting in April 1886. He criticized the "attempt to carry the whole four mines home," that is, to Posno and Britain. His own method would retain local ownership, he said, and no sale of any mine could occur "to an English Syndicate without our consent." Realistically, he pointed out the obvious—that if the Kimberley mine came under single ownership, and was not "working with us," it could pose "a very serious danger to our Company."[15] The stockholders voted a fund to establish a London share transfer office. They also authorized Rhodes to effect a broader consolidation even though, as Merriman had understood in February, only by securing a complete hold on the De Beers mine could he proceed in any secure fashion to rationalize the industry. Stow further recalled that Rhodes' broad-gauged amalgamation scheme had been "ridiculed" by the owners of claims in the other mines, and by those who still held separate stakes in the De Beers ground.[16]

Rhodes was then insufficiently powerful, insufficiently wealthy, and insufficiently popular to override Kimberley's multiplicity of separate entrepreneurial interests and aversions. Even if others might theoretically agree—and many did—that amalgamation was good for diamonds and good for Kimberley, and would be good for them, none wished to concede control to Rhodes. Yet Merriman's attack and Rhodes' counterattack had escalated the competition for Kimberley's destiny to a new and challenging plateau. The blocking of their schemes commenced an intense race for commanding positions in the two big mines. Rhodes and his fellow directors focused on De Beers, which remained very profitable, while the other mines and companies suffered from falling prices and rising costs.

In 1883, De Beers Mining Company, with Rhodes at the helm and Rudd and Stow manning the engines, had acquired four firms with claims to substantial sections of their mine. In the next year it bought out the Baxter's Gully, London & South African, and Independent concerns. In 1885 the Eagle and Australian Gully Block claims were folded into De Beers. After the April 1886 meeting of De Beers' board, Rhodes focused his attentions on the Elma and United companies, with Beit's help soon obtaining a commanding stake and then complete control over their shares. Elma cost £105,000, half in shares and half in the blue ground from which diamonds were won.

Of the five remaining distinct operations on the mine, the Victoria Company was the strongest. First Rhodes had to isolate Victoria by taking the Gem and Oriental firms, especially the latter. Rhodes outlined his tactics: "We are inclined to take [Oriental] on a basis of £6,000 a claim . . . so as to confine the Victoria on that side." Cynically, Rhodes did not think that De Beers could yet "afford to quarrel" with Francis Oats, the principal owner of Victoria, since Rhodes' syndicate "was driving through the Victoria claims to prove those of the 'Gem' Co., & until that work is completed we must maintain friendly relations with him."[17]

Rhodes' motives were obvious. If Victoria had acquired Oriental it might have become strong enough to resist Rhodes' raid. And the great amalgamator was determined to overcome, go around, or undermine any opposition to his final, energetic, finely timed plan to consolidate the smallest mine on the fields (in terms of acreage and third of four in the number of claims). Fortunately, to his own resources Rhodes could add those of Beit, with whom he had an intensely personal working arrangement which proved the rock on which Rhodes' economic pyramiding in the late 1880s was balanced. Together, at De Beers' behest, they bought controlling shares in Gem and Oriental throughout 1886, and were able to join both, under De Beers' aegis, in early 1887. Beit also made an enormous personal fortune by buying and selling shares in these companies for himself.

The assault on Victoria began about the middle of 1886. Rhodes estimated that shares in that company might be worth as much as £18 each, but it was heavily in debt. He urged Stow, then in London, to buy any he could for about £12. "I quite see that amalgamation at the present moment is hopeless—we must wait for them to come to us, but a chance might occur to you at home to pounce on a large parcel of shares, & if so, I say 'do it.' "[18]

Even before the battle for Victoria and thus for the De Beers mine could be fully joined, Rhodes was distracted by reports of an immense new find of gold in the Transvaal, and then by a searing personal tragedy involving Neville Pickering. Biographical assertions to the contrary, Rhodes was neither reluctant nor uncommonly slow to appreciate the significance of the new discoveries. But he was cautious and so was Rudd. Like so many other South Africans, several times before they had both been excited and disappointed by the promise of gold. Straightforward quartz reefs were known in the Transvaal from 1853, and after 1874 more than £1 million had been made, if arduously, from alluvial sources along the Blyde River near Lydenburg and Pilgrim's Rest. Herbert Rhodes had cast his lot with Pilgrim's Rest, and had then trekked even farther north. In 1884 a spectacularly rich quartz vein was unearthed near what became Barberton, also in the eastern Transvaal, and for a time the Sheba mine there was the most profitable in the world.

The area was rushed; companies were floated; investors in Britain and South Africa tumbled over themselves to buy shares. There was a boom, and then a collapse, for the Barberton field contained only pockets of good gold. Thousands lost their savings, and, on the eve of the greatest discovery of all, the bloom of South African gold faded. Avarice had been replaced by prudence. Rhodes and Rudd do not appear to have lost much, if anything, at Barberton, but, like so many others, they had learned what they thought was the appropriate lesson: diamonds were a comparatively safe investment, and gold was chancy, particularly since so little was known about its geology in southern Africa.

Rhodes and Rudd were certainly amateurs as far as gold was concerned. Hans Sauer, who had visited Pilgrim's Rest and had experienced the boom and bust of Barberton, led Rhodes and Rudd in late July or early August 1886 to a barren area forty miles south of Pretoria and sixty miles northeast of Potchefstroom. There, in a district called the Witwatersrand (Ridge of White Waters), prospectors a few months before had found a gold-bearing reef that ran thirty miles from west to east. Ultimately the field of gold was proven to be by far the largest in the world, covering an area of the Transvaal and the Orange Free State 170 miles long and 100 miles wide.

Mining experts were for some time divided over whether the Rand would prove a paying proposition over the long term. Its gold was found not in the customary quartz reefs, as it had been at Barberton and Pilgrim's Rest, but mixed in a compressed waterborne gravel conglomerate of sedimentary origin that was called banket, after a sweet Dutch dessert made of a combination of almonds, other nuts, and cloves, pressed and covered with sugar. The conglomerate layers were often thin and compressed between very much thicker layers of a sandy quartzite. Not all of the conglomerates contained gold. Some instant authorities said that it was geologically impossible for conglomerate reefs to persist beyond a depth of 200 feet. Others worried that the unoxidized sulfide ores within which the gold was bound could not be treated without prohibitive expense. It was all new, and both greatly promising and greatly risky.

During that first visit to the Rand, Rhodes and Rudd vexed Sauer, who later complained that Rhodes had forfeited millions by refusing to fund all of Sauer's hunches. Certainly the methods which they all employed for testing the reef were primitive and unreliable, but they were the only ones then known. They scraped away at surface outcrops and used panning techniques to verify what they had found. But their methods were haphazard. During this early foray north, Rhodes and Rudd, and even Sauer, missed much that later turned out to be rich, and purchased land on which the reef was absent, or of too low a grade to be exploited. A year later it was apparent how mistaken their judgment had been, especially when compared to the extraordinary luck or acumen of Robinson, Beit, and other speculators.

Part of the problem of this first attempt to find payable gold, and a partial explanation of Sauer's intense frustrations, was the extraordinary physical and psychological difference between gold and diamonds. Both Rudd and Rhodes were overwhelmed by the different scale of gold, and the need to crush tons and tons of rock and gravel in order to obtain payable ounces. Sauer reports that after he failed to induce Rhodes to purchase a block of claims on the main reef, Rhodes faltered: "It is all very well; but I cannot see or calculate the power in your claims." Sauer asked Rhodes to explain such a cryptic remark. "When I am in Kimberley," Rhodes said, "and have nothing much to do, I often go and sit on the edge of the De Beers mine, and I look at the blue diamondiferous ground, reaching from the surface, a thousand feet down the open workings of the mine, and I reckon up the value of the diamonds in the 'blue' and the power conferred by them. In fact every foot of blue ground means so much power. This I cannot do with your gold reefs." [19] Nevertheless, Sauer persuaded Rhodes that the Rand was for real, and was big, and Rhodes both bankrolled him and traveled away from diamonds long enough to see for himself. He personally signed checks on the spot. (Rhodes may also have once tried simply to buy the entire Rand, but his resources and available time were inadequate.)

There were those who were desperate and others who loved to gamble. They wanted to believe in the Rand, and became rich. But Rudd was notoriously skeptical of Sauer's finds and timid to boot, and Rhodes was still as methodical as he was in the early diamond days. For example, he insisted on devoting one whole evening to rehearsing Sauer on the course of the next day's negotiation with an Afrikaans-speaking farm owner. "He constructed the essentials and details of the deal in much the same way as French criminal authorities reconstruct the details of a murder drama," remembered Sauer.[20] Even so, it was an urgent summons from Kimberley, and not wholly his fastidiousness, that aborted Rhodes' first inspection of the gold prospects. As a result, he obtained a smaller stake in the new discoveries than might otherwise have been anticipated and gave up further fortune for love.

Pickering's health was questionable. The young secretary for whom Rhodes had developed an intense affection in 1882, and with whom he had lived ever since in a small house in Kimberley, tumbled from a horse into a thornbush in 1884. Pickering was only bruised, but thorns had pierced his legs below the knees. They were difficult to extract. He developed a chronic infection, probably osteomyelitis, that caused Pickering to hobble on crutches and, it is said, never fully to recover. Jameson attended the ailing man and Rhodes nursed his sole heir devotedly whenever Pickering relapsed. It is also evident that for reasonably long periods Pickering was well enough to continue working for De Beers and for Rhodes. In early 1886, for example, Merriman responded favorably to recent news that the young person he fondly called "Pickling" was feeling better and on the mend. To Merriman he was "a remarkably pleasant and promising fellow with everything before him."

When news of gold reached Kimberley in 1886, Pickering had only recently returned from a visit to his family in Port Elizabeth. Rhodes was aware of the precarious nature of Pickering's health, and doubtless worried about him when prospecting for gold with Rudd and Sauer. Yet, according to FitzPatrick, Sauer's brother-in-law, "even those who knew Rhodes well would not have believed it possible that he could feel so deeply and be so tragically affected."

Certainly a message, probably from Jameson, that Pickering had taken a turn for the worse and was near death took Rhodes' mind off gold, as gold had temporarily displaced his focus on diamonds. Rhodes had been on the Rand less than a month and there still was much to do. To Sauer's surprise the summons from Kimberley proved electric. "I'm off," Rhodes told the protesting Sauer. But there were no seats on the evening coach. "Buy a seat from someone who has already booked," he ordered. Or "get a special coach— anything." A place was finally found for Rhodes on the mail bags atop the coach. He rode for fifteen hours over 300 jolting, dusty miles to be at Pickering's side. And there, while Pickering drifted, he stayed "careless of anything but the wants and comforts of his friend." FitzPatrick remembered that Rhodes would attend to nothing. "Without irritation or impatience, but with utter indifference, he declined to see anyone on the urgent and important matters of business that always needed attention."

The end came early in the morning of 16 October. Pickering was but twenty-nine. He asked his brother William to summon Jameson, but the physician could do nothing. Pickering whispered to Rhodes: "You have been father, mother, brother, and sister to me," and then died in his arms. At the funeral in Kimberley "a great concourse of miners and diamond-buyers of the Fields gathered round the grave." Barnato blubbered and Rhodes, "alternating hysterically between laughter and tears, said in his high falsetto, 'Ah, Barney, he will never sell you another parcel of diamonds!'"

A few days later FitzPatrick came unexpectedly upon Rhodes and Willie Pickering. In a back room of the De Beers' offices they were huddled over a bare table. On the table were a gold watch and chain in a rough pile. It was being pushed back and forth between the two men, both of whom were crying. "All I heard," FitzPatrick reported, was " 'No, you are his brother,' and 'No, you are his greatest friend.'"[21]

These snapshots of Rhodes, bereft, say a good deal. They reveal him in the throes of deeply felt grief—ample evidence of the emotional depth and genuineness of his love for Pickering. They provide touching proof that not all of his relationships were manipulative, and that he could be as passionate about those whom he loved as he was about his dreams and ideas.

Despite his evident grief, Rhodes quickly resumed the threads of his uncommonly active life. Possibly to help him do so, he abandoned the house he had shared with Pickering and moved into Jameson's sparsely furnished, little, single story, iron-roofed bungalow across and down the street from the Kimberley Club. Rhodes and Jameson had two untidy bedrooms and a sitting room that was reported to resemble that of "an undergraduate at college."[22] They ate at the Club, and at least for a few years before the conquest of Rhodesia, and then the Raid, separated them, Rhodes and Jameson shared these and other simple accommodations.

Rhodes also plunged decisively back into the battle for diamonds and the search for payable gold. By December, Rhodes (for De Beers), allied to Beit and Porges, had busily and secretly amassed a vast number of shares in the Victoria company. "The only way we could deal with them," Rhodes explained, "was by obtaining such a large interest in the Company that they must look upon us as one of themselves." Moreover, by buying on the London market and not in Kimberley, Rhodes believed that "it would excite no remark."[23] They purchased steadily throughout the southern summer months, their raiding tactics proving easy against the poorly defended Victoria. But as active as Rhodes had to be in marshaling his financial forces against Victoria and the other remaining holdouts on the De Beers mine, he was just as excited by the Rand.

Rhodes was torn between the need to supervise the final integration of the mine on which his own basic fortune must rest, and his anxiety not to be denied further riches from gold or a chance to fix a position of power there, too. "I shall be glad to hear when you are returning," he wrote anxiously to Rudd at the end of 1886. "As between gold and diamonds there is much to attend to and I feel I ought not to be leaving De Beers but I am required in

Transvaal." Rhodes wanted Victoria settled (which was still to take a few months) so that he could devote his whole attention to "gold speculations in which I truly believe," said the convert, "a large return lies."[24]

Rudd was then in London establishing the Gold Fields of South Africa, Ltd., for himself, Rhodes, and Harry Stratford Caldecott, a lawyer and Rudd's brother-in-law. It was to be the vehicle of their second fortune, but it took months—much longer than Rhodes anticipated—to be floated. Taking Harry Currey with him as a secretary—"He is quicker and can write a good letter"—in place of John Grimmer, who had in turn substituted for Pickering, Rhodes returned to the Rand before Christmas 1886.[25] At a place called Ferreira Camp, after Colonel Ignatius Ferreira, who had been among the early claimants, they bunked in a small hotel along a street that Currey described as being filled with a string of "reed shanties," drinkers, and continuous fistfights.[26] Later they moved to a farmhouse at Rietfontein, closer to the reef.

From both bases Rhodes continued to investigate, to buy, and to reject properties in what he thought was a rational but in reality was a muddled and uninstructed manner. Rhodes was still being advised by Sauer; Edward Jones, his manager from De Beers; and Gardner Williams, an experienced mining engineer from the United States who was surveying the area for Rothschild but was soon to work for Rhodes. The main problem was that Williams thought that the broad reefs would be too expensive to work and that the thin reefs would peter out. Jones was optimistic but ill-informed, and Sauer was betting on mere hunches.

Rhodes was also hobbled by a shortage of cash. At least he was unwilling to risk too much of his own. Thus he pressed Rudd by letter and cable for news and action, and also for the capital—initially £100,000—which Rhodes needed from investors in London. His faith in gold and his desire to take advantage of all available opportunities were both growing dramatically, but without evidence stronger than the fact that his rivals were also investing heavily. (At this point there was hardly any machinery on the Rand with which to crush the gold bearing ores and do any definitive tests.) Robinson and Porges were buying wildly (and well), and so was Beit.

"I can get a great many good things and very much cheaper than others . . . but am cramped for funds and as I do not know what you are doing I am not inclined to go deeper on my private account," Rhodes wrote anxiously to Rudd from Pretoria in January 1887. "If you get your syndicate formed telegraph me a credit as I am daily missing really good things for lack of money." At the end of the month Rhodes even confessed that he was planning to establish a residence at Rietfontein. "I am . . . getting my furniture up from Kimberley," he said, without indicating how little that implied (a bed, perhaps, and a desk and chair). He told Rudd in February that they could make very good use of £100,000 worth of new shareholder funds. By this time he proudly owned a mile and a half of what was called the main reef (but which turned out to be worth little), and had taken a portion of what he mistakenly thought was the even richer Botha's reef. "Your business," he instructed Rudd, is "to get as much money as you can," order a large amount of "stamps" and other mining machinery, "draw a Trust Deed with very wide powers"—for Rhodes already knew that he wanted to use the rewards of gold in the north—and "obtain us a good remuneration or else the Company is not worth working for."

Rhodes was impatient. "The people you are arranging with must remember that in dealing with us they are dealing with no ordinary representatives, that we have the whole thing at our fingers end, that if the Company once goes through I shall feel in honour bound for the future to take nothing on my own private account, that personally I am not crippled for funds to the extent of say £20,000 and therefore two things are essential [if they were to reward everyone well]." Those two requirements were that he receive an amount to invest which was much more than £20,000, and that he be given an "adequate" share of the whole—"otherwise it would be better," Rhodes threatened, "for me to confine my investments to my own money on which I should receive the entire profit."[27]

Rhodes really wanted as much leverage as he could get. He wanted it to enhance his entrepreneurial position within the minerals market and within South Africa. He was obliged, by the inner logic of financial competition, furthermore, to move aggressively against his erstwhile colleagues, associates, and rivals for a stake on the potentially rich Rand. This was less a personal imperative than an institutional necessity. Averse to high-risk ventures, and intuitively (and historically) distrustful of gold, he nonetheless was compelled as much by the activities of the men who locally were his peers as by mining developers to acquire auriferous properties of a kind that he had never seen before. He was driven less by naked greed than by his growing position in the overall industry, by the economic expectations of his associates (even Rudd), and by his desire to control diamonds. Moreover, he had become ambitious imperially. Without ranking the motives, by 1887, if not late 1886, Rhodes was thinking more and more seriously about the north. His territorial aspirations, still as yet sketched only broadly, further fueled his acquisitive activities on the Rand. For the north as well as for his other schemes, Rhodes required large amounts of capital capable of generating still more (through gold and diamonds). He sought such an investment pool, and proposed to employ it with as few constraints and as little supervision as possible.

Rudd, heeding Rhodes' many letters and telegrams, finally provided him with abundant capital and a corporate umbrella under which he could pursue his trail of gold and his other financial and imperial fantasies. Moreover, Rudd and Rhodes were consciously tapping into a vein of overseas capital distinct from that employed by their main competitors; the new company was backed by the broad resources of the City, not just public or private merchant banking houses on the Continent or in South Africa. Even though it was unusual for a South African mining firm to be floated in London (most were incorporated in South Africa), and even though British investors were skittish about gold after Barberton, Rudd registered The Gold Fields of South Africa Ltd.

in early February 1887. Its authorized capital of £250,000 could be used legally to acquire, develop, or explore for any kind of mineral anywhere. Control of the company resided in Rudd and Rhodes, the managing directors, and five others: Thomas Rudd, Charles Rudd's elder brother and a director of the Joint Stock Bank of London, who became chairman; Leigh Hoskyns, formerly a Crown prosecutor and magistrate in Griqualand West and an old friend of both Rudd and Rhodes; a British stockbroker; a former civil servant in India; and a businessman with interests in South Africa. Practically, this was a board which would (and did) follow the dictates of the resident managers—Rhodes and Rudd.

The first £100,000 of the firm's authorized capital was subscribed in Britain by mid-March. The remainder was obtained there in August and October, and in South Africa. The promoters of other South African prospecting companies typically asked for 75 percent of the capital and shares subscribed as their entrepreneurial reward. Rudd and Rhodes easily raised their first £100,000 by taking only the equivalent of 10 percent each in shares as their equity. They also refrained from allotting themselves salaries or remuneration as managing directors. They promised to give the company all properties which they then owned and not to prospect on their own. However, if the Gold Fields Ltd. prospered, then they reserved to themselves together a full one-third of any profits.

From Rudd and Rhodes' point of view they were gambling with their own opportunity costs, and with the capital which both had already invested, but the stakes for each were diminished by the continuing promise of the Rand and by Rhodes' own faith in his ability to enhance the value of their shares through an adroit manipulation of the market. The investors, for their part, were gambling on what Thomas and Charles Rudd could both tell the City of Rhodes' genuine success in diamonds. The reputations of Charles Rudd and Rhodes attracted investors. So did Thomas Rudd's position. Many of the public shares were taken through or by the brokerage houses of the City, by Thomas Rudd's bank, by Scottish merchants, and by London diamond dealers.

Yet at no time before mid-1887 could Charles Rudd describe in any more than vague detail the actual properties which Rhodes had or was acquiring. No list was put before the first general meeting of the stockholders of Gold Fields in March. Indeed, Charles Rudd said that because of the great competition in the Transvaal he could divulge almost nothing (he also had little precise knowledge about what Rhodes had obtained). He admitted that the Gold Fields was a "personal" company and that the directors other than himself and Rhodes were largely ignorant of the Transvaal and its prospects. Yet the share offering was oversubscribed, and, at this stage, no one objected or raised questions. Rhodes had obtained the cash and free hand that he had wanted.[28]

This promising financial start in gold paralleled Rhodes' assiduous pursuit of diamonds. With Beit's help, Rhodes and his partners in late 1886 and early 1887 had gained control of the sections of the De Beers mine owned by Gem and Oriental. In November 1886 they had for the first time also established a strong position in the smaller Dutoitspan mine by purchasing the West End company. There were other major owners of that mine, and Rhodes as yet had no stakes in the Kimberley or Bultfontein mines. But De Beers would be his entirely if he found a means to end Oats' ownership of the strategically placed and comparatively profitable Victoria Company. Beginning in 1886 and continuing throughout the first three months of 1887, Stow and Beit (who was then working both for himself and for Porges) bought Victoria's shares separately and secretly in London.

If Rhodes had attempted to buy into Victoria alone his efforts would probably have been discovered, and been thwarted by Oats or others determined to prevent the amalgamation of De Beers. But associates of Beit and Porges were able gradually to amass shares of Victoria without the links to Rhodes being suspected. Although Beit and Rhodes were firm friends, they had only recently been allied financially in any significant ventures. Indeed, Porges and Rhodes were competitors, and Beit was regarded until this point more as a diamond dealer than a financier. Thus the coup de main which ended Victoria's independent existence, and which cost a total of £57,000 (Stow and Beit paid about £20 per share for the bulk of the shares of Victoria, about £8 more than Rhodes had earlier valued them) marked the open acknowledgment of the Rhodes-Beit financial partnership.

By April 1887 Rhodes informed Oats that De Beers controlled the majority of Victoria's shares and that amalgamation was necessary. By early May, Rhodes and De Beers had accomplished the task that others had long thought too daunting: one of the two major diamond mines in the world was under the control of a single company. He could at last rationalize the way in which all of its blue ground could best be exploited. He wanted to be able to "place the diamond mining industry in the position it ought to occupy, that is, not at the mercy of the buyers, but the buyers under the control of the producers. . . ."[29] But, buoyed by the comparative ease of his recent efforts and by the overall accentuation of the pace of consolidation on the diamond fields, as well as his burgeoning prospects in gold; he could hardly pause to contemplate or absorb his signal victory. It was not in his nature to rest content, particularly when the swells of success were running strongly in his direction. Nor could he, for the amalgamation of De Beers stimulated the kind of fierce competition from which no one with ambitions of monopoly could afford to withdraw. Likewise, Rhodes' new prominence propelled others forward both defensively and offensively. From his beachhead in De Beers, Rhodes was bound to mount an assault on Kimberley, and also on the two less rich mines. Likewise, those who were prominent in the ownership of Kimberley were intent upon amalgamating that mine and, using what would then be their superior economic leverage, taking De Beers from Rhodes.

Even after his amalgamation of the De Beers mine, Rhodes was vulnerable. He and his colleagues owned no part of Kimberley. Indeed Barnato had only a few months before emerged as a consolidator conceivably even more powerful than Rhodes. Having in 1884 initially decided to liquidate the Barnato Mining Company, which then owned a portion of the Kimberley mine, but a portion where the claims had been buried by a reef fall, Barnato late in that year re-evaluated the prospects of diamonds in general and that key digging in particular. He merged his property with the British Company, and began excavating for gems beneath the rubble. In deciding to sink shafts Barnato was following the lead of Robinson's Standard Company. By mid-1885, after the Merriman-Posno-Rhodes attempt to amalgamate the mines from above, Barnato was sufficiently strong to begin attacking Robinson's hold on the Standard, then the largest single concern on the Kimberley mine. Barnato, or persons in his employ, managed clandestinely to spread rumors that the Standard's underground workings were dangerous and would soon collapse. A bank with significant holdings in the Standard sold vigorously; Barnato bought cheaply. By late 1886 Barnato's grip on the Standard was firm. In March 1887 the Barnato and Standard companies were merged into the new Standard Company. Barnato now owned 40 percent of the Kimberley mine, which as a whole was a good 20 percent richer than De Beers.

The frantic race—it was nothing less than a mad scramble—for control over the world's premier diamond properties was abruptly joined. Rhodes was thirty-four, Barnato thirty-five. Both were born British, the one of English, the other of Jewish stock, the first originally of the less than moneyed middle class, the latter up from the slums. Both were clearly accomplished financiers; Barnato was the better gambler than Rhodes and had amassed much more wealth more quickly. His stake in gold was already impressive, too. Rhodes told associates that he feared the "cunning little Jew."[30] But Rhodes had broader ambitions, a determined vision that went beyond mere business (Barnato's horizon), and a patina of sophistication which Barnato lacked. Moreover, if Barnato initially controlled the richer properties and had readier access to capital, Rhodes had Beit and Stow, and could draw upon a wide range of financial and commercial associates and acquaintances.

Rhodes appreciated that even the conclusive strength of his new control of De Beers would prove a weakness if he could not enter the competition for Kimberley soon, and with a sizable stake. In May 1887, Rhodes therefore attempted to buy any claims on the Kimberley mine which would permit his own consortium to oppose Barnato's continued rush toward consolidation. He attempted to acquire the so-called Hall claims, which were owned by the Cape of Good Hope bank. Those claims stretched into the center of the mine, between the big eastern and western blocks, owned respectively by the Standard and the Central companies. Also between Standard and Central were the medium-sized holdings of the French company; they cut through the mine from south to north.

Sir Donald Currie, the canny investor and British owner of the Castle steamship line, purchased the bank's Hall holdings for £120,000 in cash before Rhodes could make a respectable bid. Currie, called the Scotch Fox by

Rhodes, had sailed to Cape Town in October to place his tender before the bank on behalf of a syndicate that presumably also had designs on the whole Kimberley mine. Rhodes, flush with success but also desperate not to lose any edge in the new and more demanding competition with Barnato, was determined to persuade Currie to re-sell his shares to De Beers. Preoccupied by a reconvened parliament and the affairs of gold, Rhodes dispatched two associates to cajole Currie aboard ship as they all sailed to London in February 1888. According to the usual story of these negotiations, the "Scotch Fox" was tempted to turn a quick profit. But, upon docking in Lisbon he discovered that the market price of the shares was higher than the amount offered by Rhodes. He blamed Rhodes' "young thieves" unfairly for what could have been a financial loss and what looked like a scam.[31] Currie's rejection of Rhodes' terms in Lisbon nevertheless proved costly. By the time his ship had docked at Plymouth, Rhodes, informed from Lisbon about the failed negotiations, had sold sufficient Hall shares to depress the value of Currie's holdings. Even so, and despite the impression given in all of the published accounts of this first attempt by Rhodes to obtain a position on the Kimberley mine, Currie held his shares for a few more months and refused, even then, to sell them to Rhodes.

Barnato was the dominant figure. After outwitting Robinson, Barnato and one of his nephews had rushed off to London, there to woo the main owners of Baring Gould's Central Company. The Central, formed in 1881 by pooling a dozen significant sets of claims, was as rich in assets and promise as the Standard. It was reputed to be better managed. Nevertheless, Barnato was able to persuade Baring Gould and the other principals in the Central to join forces with him, doubtless in order to create a new mining unit strong enough to withstand, if not overpower, Rhodes and De Beers. Although Baring Gould remained influential, Barnato and his family held the controlling interest in the new Kimberley Central Company that was established in early July 1887. A month later Barnato's new, larger company grew further, swallowing up six smaller entities, including the one owned by Currie. Still outstanding were the significant holdings of the French company, its underground shafts accessible only by tunneling under land belonging to the Central.

Rhodes had waited until the parliamentary session of 1887 was drawing to a close to move decisively. By then, on the very eve of the Standard-Central merger, he was well behind Barnato's group in the race to control the Kimberley mine. Victory may have seemed distant, even unattainable. In May, however, he had installed Gardner Williams as the general manager of De Beers, replacing Jones (who was sent to the Transvaal). Williams, forty-five, was an American who had obtained his basic education at the College of California (later the University of California, Berkeley), and had then been trained as a mining engineer in Germany. He had been active in the salt industry in lower California, prospected for gold and silver in Nevada, worked in the United States mint in San Francisco, opened up a silver mine in Nevada, managed another in Utah, and run a gold mine in California. In 1884 he went to

South Africa to investigate gold prospects in Barberton for a British exploration company. In 1885, after visiting the Witwatersrand, he met Rhodes in Kimberley. It was later that year, while together on a voyage to Britain, that Rhodes and Williams became close. They spent hours discussing Rhodes' intention to amalgamate the diamond mines and then gain control over the lands north of the Transvaal. (Williams thought it odd that Rhodes was uninterested in devising a method to continue extracting diamonds from mines no longer capable of being worked easily from the surface.)

At the time, Williams never expected to come back to Africa. After Lord Rothschild, the British financier, and Edmund G. de Crano and Hamilton Smith, two American consulting mining engineers, formed the Exploration Company in London in 1886, however, Williams returned on their behalf to evaluate the new gold finds as well as prospects for diamonds. (The Exploration Company was a limited investment fund specializing in overseas mining properties.) Rhodes and Williams talked incessantly, on the Witwatersrand and in Kimberley. "My success in the amalgamation of the diamond mines," Rhodes told Williams, "will make everything else easy for me in the future, but I must have a qualified mining engineer." Later, probably in January and before Rhodes had fully formulated an offer, Williams recalled that Rhodes had listened with "delight" to Williams' outline of how Rhodes' mines could supply all the diamond markets of the world.[32]

Williams was as orthodox and well-trained a mining engineer as South Africa had seen. Yet he was spectacularly wrong about the riches of the Witwatersrand, and advised Rhodes—as everyone realized much later—erroneously. Nevertheless, he was worth his salary in Kimberley, where he put the diamond mines on a solid footing, sinking dangerous shafts and separating diamonds from overburden in a modern manner. That was to be his great contribution to South Africa and to Rhodes' fortunes in the long term. In the short term, however, his most positive attribute was his acquaintance with and stature in the eyes of de Crano, Smith, and—most of all—Nathaniel M. Rothschild. These were the associations which Rhodes required if the larger amalgamation of the diamond fields were to become a reality. When he employed Williams, Rhodes was looking ahead, arraying whatever pieces he might conceivably need for a victorious assault on the remaining mines.

The French company represented the one possible obstacle in Barnato's path. Because its claims bifurcated those of the old Standard and Central, the Barnato union of July would remain financial, and not physical, until Barnato and his allies could purchase control. Only by doing likewise could Rhodes derail Barnato's runaway ambitions and begin to give substance to his own pretensions as an amalgamator. The French company had been established in 1875 by Porges, who still held the largest body of shares. His agents in Kimberley were Beit and Julius Wernher, Beit's new partner. Thus Beit was privy to information helpful to Rhodes, and could guarantee access to Porges. Yet, although Rhodes had this inside track, only money could truly speak. If Porges were to be folded into another's combine, he would do so prudently, selling out beneficially to the top bidder.

In order to make major purchases of shares in the French company, Rhodes required a massive injection of funds. Only then could he buy every available share at once, and overcome Barnato. This reasoning prompted a long report from Williams to de Crano in May; it was destined for Rothschild. Even before Rothschild could react to the Rhodes-Williams request for funds to purchase the French company and to amalgamate all of the mines, Rhodes summoned Williams and boarded a steamer for London. Barnato was on the verge of joining Standard and Central; Rhodes had to act immediately or forever forfeit his program of rationalization in the diamond industry. He needed more than £1 million.

In London Rhodes and Williams were soon talking to Rothschild. The merchant banking house of N.M. Rothschild & Sons was the wealthiest in Europe. In 1847 it had helped raise £8 million to assist the British government in relieving the Irish famine. In 1854 it had floated a £15 million loan that had permitted Britain to fight the Crimean war. In 1875 Rothschild's father had provided £4 million to back Prime Minister Benjamin Disraeli's instant purchase of the Suez Canal from the ruler of Egypt. Because Carl Meyer, one of Rothschild's advisors, prompted by de Crano, had been favorably impressed by the arguments in Williams' report, Lord Rothschild was disposed to be helpful. And de Crano had already undertaken several useful visits to Paris, where he had commended Rhodes' plan to the directors of the French company. Beit had also urged it on Porges. But the key decisionmaker was Rothschild—aristocratic, haughty, fiercely conservative, and capable of being unbearably rude—whom Rhodes was determined to impress. It was an interview crucial to more pursuits than the amalgamation of the diamond mines, and a challenge to which Rhodes' charm and magnetism, as well as the fitness of his proposals, were ultimately equal.

Toward the close of their first session in the City at the end of July, Rothschild said: "Well, Mr Rhodes, you go to Paris and see what you can do . . . and in the meantime I will see if I can raise the £1,000,000 which you desire." Then, a moment later, he told de Crano to tell Rhodes more definitively that if Rhodes could buy the French company, Rothschild would find the £1 million. Newbury suggests that Rothschild's firm appraised more than Rhodes' charm. Rothschild could have backed Barnato, Baring Gould, and the Central Company instead of De Beers. Yet he and his firm were impressed by De Beers' technical competence, its comparative freedom from debt, and its ability to respond flexibly (the great contribution of Rhodes and Beit) to new opportunities. Most of all, Rothschild may have been influenced by Rhodes' ability to protect the prospective diamond monopoly politically—through connections made in Cape Town. Baring Gould, after all, was an investor in tramways, and Barnato had come up from the slums. Once Rhodes and De Beers had passed the crucial tests, Rothschild's financing (he demanded an enormous fee, by one calculation £250,000 on £750,000 advanced) provided the critical difference between successful monopolization and mere mining proficiency.[33]

In Paris two days after the crucial interview with Rothschild, Rhodes, de

Crano, and Ludwig Lippert, a diamond broker who worked for Rothschild, soon concluded a deal with the French company. For £1,400,000 its directors would sell out, pending the formalities of an approval by a meeting of the shareholders in Kimberley in October. Rhodes often boasted of the ease with which he had squared the French company and checked Barnato in a mere twenty-four hours. But the ground had ably been prepared by Beit and de Crano. Indeed, without Beit's ability to secure the backing of separate, additional syndicates of French and German financiers, even the suppport of the great house of Rothschild might not have been enough. The £1,400,000 purchase price was secured by a £750,000 loan from Rothschild, and by the issuance to the French and Germans of 50,000 shares of De Beers, each worth £15. Any profit made as the value of De Beers rose was to be shared between De Beers and the syndicates, including Rothschild. Since the shares soon rose £7 each, everyone profited handsomely, in an atmosphere of little risk.

The weeks after the French purchase and before a special meeting in Kimberley were hectic and tense, and marked by much purchasing activity by the house of Rothschild and by Stow. Ratification should have been assured, but Barnato held a fifth of the shares of the French company. He further believed that his own resources were far more ample than Rhodes', whose wealth was anything but liquid. Barnato declared a willingness to pay the directors of the French company £1,700,000, topping Rhodes' tender by a handsome £300,000. He put this offer before the shareholders in Kimberley in late September, castigating both Rhodes and the directors who were prepared to sell out. In the manner of a modern opponent of a hostile takeover bid, Barnato called the directors ignorant of the real values of the French claims, decried the gains which the directors would make at the expense of the small shareholders, and promised to fight the sale in the courts.

Rhodes had not then arrived back in Kimberley to defend himself and counter Barnato's arguments. Porges could probably have prevailed in the courts, but litigation would take time and Rothschild implored Rhodes to avoid a prolonged public brawl. Rhodes first tried common sense. Supposedly he told Barnato and his associates, "You can go and offer £300,000 more than we do for the French, but we will offer another £300,000 on that; you can go on and bid for the benefit of the French shareholders *ad infinitum,* because . . . we shall have it in the end."[34] But Barnato felt financially secure, and probably knew how weak Rhodes remained, even with the not-yet-fully-tested support of Rothschild. Rhodes had to back down.

Rhodes returned to Cape Town from London by the end of September 1887. Within a month he had come to an understanding with Barnato and Baring Gould—"a weak man" who will "go with the tide"—which was expected to effect the peaceful amalgamation of De Beers and Kimberley, as well as the takeover by the new joint endeavor of Bultfontein and Dutoitspan. Barnato, reported Rhodes, had pledged to "go to the end" with him. He was also confident that Beit had "burnt his boats" with Porges and "would sooner quarrel with his home firm than sell me and he is working heartily for same object." The details of the understanding were spelled out at great length and in all their inordinate complexity in letters and cables to Stow, together with appropriate provisions for contingencies: "You must always remember if a panic comes I shall amalgamate at once with Central even if I sacrifice in order to restore confidence so that we are playing with certainties."

After consulting with Beit, and possibly with Rothschild, in October 1887 Rhodes sold the French company back to the Central Company for about £1,375,000 in cash and shares. The Kimberley mine was now controlled by a single, Barnato-dominated concern. But Rhodes and his team also owned a significant stake in it, as well as all of De Beers.

"We must have the four mines," Rhodes warned Stow, "and I will allow no foreign vulture to step in at the end and form a separate mine on the Stock Exchange apart from us to get a flotation on our name. . . ."[35] Yet the actual merging of the two rich mines, and then the swallowing up of the poorer ones, was much more complicated and involved than Rhodes had expected. It also took much longer than the nine months which he had anticipated. The Central Company had been giving its shareholders as much as 36 percent a year on their investments. De Beers's dividends were only 16 percent, and the French company had been paying nothing. The agreement between Barnato and Rhodes for the sale and disposition of the French company, which was ratified on 1 November at a shareholders' meeting, did give Rhodes an important, conceivably conclusive stake in Kimberley Central, but by then there was much more unity of purpose on the part of the principal diamond magnates than has hitherto been appreciated by biographers. Rhodes had certainly appealed to their self-interest, and presumably had held out the long-term allure of industrial rationalization and shared power. But there had been no agreement on the proportionate value of their separate stakes. Which was the wealthier mine? As Stow nagged at Rhodes: "Of course the control of sales is the most important point of all, but what about output? Does that remain the same as for the last six months or are the Companies mentioned in your cable at liberty to work and produce any quantity diamonds?"[36] Indeed, with the merger of the holdings of the French and Central companies, the Kimberley mine was fused, and Barnato could at last work it more economically as a whole.

This new advantage encouraged Barnato, Baring Gould, and others to value their mine even higher than before; the cost of producing diamonds would henceforth be reduced and profits increased. By early 1888 the directors of the Central Company were becoming what Stow called maddeningly "impracticable." That is, they were flooding the market with diamonds, hoping to demonstrate Kimberley's superiority over De Beers. But both sides could only suffer. Rothschild and other backers might lose heart, and the still unconsummated overall merger might be deferred or destroyed—all at a time when Rhodes was also nervous about losing the edge in the north, in Matabeleland.

It was in an atmosphere of growing anxiety that Rhodes, Beit, and the

De Beers board late in December 1887 (not in February 1888 as most accounts state) decided to act more assertively. As Stow put it, "finding that the Central Directors were as obdurate as ever and that his and their ideas of the relative values of the two mines differed so widely and fearing that an attempt would be made to take the Kimberley Mine to London for the purpose of floating it *separately* as a public Company and knowing that the position of the mine was daily improving so far as the working facilities were concerned," Rhodes (for De Beers) resolved to buy as much of Central as he needed to gain control, and to bring Barnato to heel.[37] Moreover, Rhodes knew that Kimberley was in a position to increase its output substantially. Once its directors found themselves favorably placed it would become more and more difficult to arrange terms acceptable to De Beers. Concerted action was imperative.

Beit and Rhodes huddled together one morning in Kimberley. At least so Rhodes later asserted. The only way of ridding themselves of Barnato, of gaining total control of diamonds, and of rationalizing the industry once and for all, they decided, was by buying shares in Kimberley Central sufficient to provide control. It would take millions. Rhodes recalled that they together agreed "if we only have the pluck to undertake it we must succeed." Then Rhodes wondered where the money would come from. "But Mr. Beit only said, 'Oh! we will get the money if we only can buy the shares.' "[38] The money came, even if Rhodes were reluctant to admit it, from Europe, especially from the continent. Beit, personally hostile to Barnato, was instrumental, contributing £250,000 of his own funds and calling vigorously upon Porges and other entrepreneurs in Paris. Both Rothschild houses, in London and Paris, added their powerful resources.

Barnato had pushed diamond prices down. At the same time the bidding war which Rhodes had started escalated the price of shares from £14 to £49. Rhodes needed the reserves of his supporters, nerves of steel, and the steady hand of Beit. Without those trumps, he might quickly have been bankrupted. Additionally, a key contribution to Rhodes' ultimate triumph was the greed of Barnato's coterie. When the value of their shares skyrocketed, they sold. But Beit's team held, being persuaded of the long-term value of their endeavor.

There were tense times in the Rhodes camp, nonetheless, and moments of near panic. One came when Rhodes heard that Rothschild or some other major supporter was about to waver, taking profits and releasing thousands of shares onto the market, where Barnato would buy them. The rumor proved false, but before its veracity could be checked, Rhodes and Beit went to the Kimberley Club for their customary morning drink. Demanding blank promissory notes from the barman, according to a suspect but friendly account, Rhodes "went over to a writing table, signed them in blank, folded them rather clumsily, and came back offering them to Beit." Since Beit had "staked everything on the success of this in backing" Rhodes, and since Rhodes did not "know how it [would] end now that these people [had] gone back on us,"

Rhodes wanted Beit to take the forms, signed in blank. "Whatever I have got is yours to back you if you need it," Rhodes promised. Over Beit's protests, Rhodes ended the episode by "crumpling the notes up and stuffing them into Beit's coat pocket and walking off." (Beit put them in the bottom of an old despatch box, forgot them, and found them again a few years later, when they were destroyed.)[39]

The final battle, momentous and consequential as it was, lasted but a few weeks. By the very end of February 1888, when Rhodes and Beit met Stow in a hotel in Cape Town, Barnato had capitulated. As Rhodes explained to Stow, when Barnato appreciated that Rhodes and Beit had cornered nearly three-fifths of the Central shares—or £1 million worth to Barnato's £750,000—he agreed to talk. After innumerable meetings, Rhodes persuaded Barnato to cease their mutually ruinous econocide and, instead, to join forces. Rhodes' magnetism had again squared a rival, this time when the intrinsic stakes were colossal.

In the existing accounts of this dramatic end to the expensive competition for control over diamonds, Barnato finally agreed to be bought out because of social more than financial ambitions. Born poor and still regarded even in Kimberley and certainly in London as disreputable, Barnato yearned—so the books say—for rewards of status. He was capable of being fobbed off by the kinds of ephemeral baubles which Rhodes was sufficiently patronizing to bestow. Barnato wanted to be a member of the Kimberley Club, where he had always been refused. He also desired to be elected to parliament, which Rhodes could ensure. There is a tale, too, that Barnato was tickled to be able to show someone like Rhodes a full bucket of diamonds, and this relatively low-level largesse on Rhodes' part helped bring Barnato round.

But Barnato was never a fool. The embroideries of contemporaries and the fancies of generations of other writers should not bemuse a more modern audience.[40] It is true that Rhodes did introduce Barnato into the Club, but it already had a few, if admittedly a very few, Jewish members. Rhodes helped to consummate Barnato's subsequent elevation to parliament in the elections of 1888. But these were friendly, even generous gestures to a bested rival more than payoffs. Rhodes disliked conflict that lingered, and would have wanted to assuage Barnato's residual ill-feelings. Moreover, Rhodes doubtless respected Barnato's acumen, and wanted him on his side in the inner councils of what soon became the premier monopoly of its kind in the world, controlling 90 percent of all diamond production. Most of all, Barnato was impressed with wealth more than power; Rhodes would have had to promise him a reasonable reward that could never be removed or eroded. True, Barnato was compelled to see reason, but when he did Rhodes was ingenious enough to support that new rationality in a financially generous manner. Indeed, Rhodes may have had no other realistic option. Later Barnato wrote to Rhodes that he hoped that he had been of "some assistance" to him. He said that he had never really opposed his plans.

Rhodes and Beit had come to Cape Town to persuade Stow, the other large shareholder, to accept Barnato's terms. The new firm was to be run by "life governors" entitled to a quarter of all profits beyond the first 30 percent (which would go to ordinary dividend recipients). The life governors, a position largely unknown to British and South African finance, would also control the operations of the concern, and be able to operate in nearly all respects as if there were no other shareholders. Stow could appreciate the advantages to De Beers—three of the five life governors, Rhodes, Beit, and Stow, would dominate the firm. Barnato and, possibly, Baring Gould, would be the other two. (Rudd was never a potential life governor.) But Stow detested Barnato, whose personality, station, and background were offensive. "His antecedents were freely discussed," Stow wrote later, "and our opinions differed but little as to them. I urged the expediency of keeping him where he was, without our circle. . . ." But Rhodes said that Barnato had insisted on being appointed a life governor and "would not yield that point for any consideration."[41]

Although Barnato could well have insisted upon that arrangement, the life governorships were among Rhodes' several pathbreaking adaptations from the ideas of others or practices elsewhere. The life governorships were created as much to serve his affinity for a tightly committed band of brothers and his determination to realize present and future dreams as they were to maximize personal profits. The purpose of the life governorships, according to Rhodes, was "to have men with a large stake who would devote their lives to working for the Company and conserving and advancing its interests." As he told Stow, "I feel with a Company that will be worth as much as the balance of Africa you must have four or five men to whom you make it worth their while to devote a great portion of their time to it, otherwise it will be terribly mismanaged and I should not care to retain my fortune in it. It [De Beers under the new trust deed] is the best thing in the world but its interests will require most careful watching and human nature is such that you cannot expect people in the future to work as we have in the past simply for the honour. . . ."[42]

Back in Kimberley, after stewing for a week and consulting with his friends about the propriety of allowing Barnato, with all his shares, into the inner circle, Stow reluctantly pocketed his pride and prejudices and, on 7 March 1888, walked across the road to give the good news to Rhodes and Beit. A moment later Beit told Barnato, who was waiting thirty paces away. (Barnato said that he was conscious of having been an obstacle in the way of an easy settlement of their battle over shares.) It was thus agreed that the life governorship scheme was acceptable and that a new De Beers Consolidated Mining Company Ltd. would be formed. (Rhodes had earlier wanted to call it the De Beers and South African Diamond Mines Ltd.) Every ten of Barnato's shares in the Central Company were to be acquired by the new company in exchange for fourteen of the old De Beers.

But before any new firm could come into existence, a set of regulations for its governance—a trust deed—had to be devised. To do so the four principals again had to haggle. Stow had a number of reservations, most of which concerned his fear that Rhodes, Beit, or Barnato might act privately with regard to new diamond properties to the detriment of De Beers. He was still suspicious of Barnato personally and of Beit as a dealer or jobber. (He also viewed Rhodes as having "little regard for the truth.") But it was Barnato who caused the lengthier delay. For almost a week he withheld his signature. Rhodes had demanded a trust deed which permitted the broadest and most imaginative use of De Beers' resources. To this potentially imprudent employment of the firm's wealth Barnato and his nephews naturally objected.

With a treaty between Lobengula, chief of the Ndebele (Matabele) only weeks old, Rhodes was even more anxious that the best resources of the diamond fields should be used to support his plans for the north. There was a final confrontation between Rhodes and Barnato that began well before lunch one day and dragged on and on, with many a drink, until just before sunrise the next morning. Rhodes outlasted his rival, as naturally he would when his dreams were at risk. Barnato, worn down by Rhodes' relentlessly reiterated arguments, was exhausted when he uttered his famous submission. "Some people," he murmured, "have a fancy for one thing, some for another. You want the means to go north, if possible, so I suppose we must give it you." Later he excused his weakness by an allusion to Rhodes' oft-credited magnetism: "When you have been with him half an hour you not only agree with him, but come to believe you have always held his opinion. No one else in the world could have induced me to go into this partnership. But Rhodes had an extraordinary ascendancy over men: he tied me up, as he ties up everybody. It is his way. You can't resist him; you must be with him."[43] Barnato spoke not only of Rhodes' powers of persuasion but also of his refusal to be diverted—to his endless repetitions and his unending appeals to reason, to avarice, or to whatever would succeed.

What Barnato had conceded was a broadly drawn trust deed that permitted the De Beers Consolidated to acquire any asset of any kind by any means. It could own mines, water rights, houses, farms—anything. It could trade in precious stones, all manner of minerals, and any kind of machinery, patents, inventions, and products in Africa or elsewhere. It could construct and operate canals, railways, gasworks, reservoirs, factories, and so on. It could engage in banking. It could even acquire "tracts of country" in Africa or anywhere, together with rights transferred to it by indigenous rulers, and expend moneys for the pacification and administration of such estates.

No individual raised objections to these extravagant provisions or to the existence of the life governorships when Rhodes put the plans for De Beers Consolidated before the shareholders of the older De Beers company at the end of March. There were a number of unresolved issues—the actual consolidation of the properties was still months away, for Barnato controlled but did not own Kimberley Central. Bultfontein and Dutoitspan had not been brought into the web, and the outstanding owners of those two mines would have to be bought out during the remainder of 1888 and 1889. But the biggest obstacle was the objections of the Kimberley Central shareholders; they were angry at Barnato for rewarding himself handsomely and leaving them out in the cold.

Rothschild had serious qualms, too, as did the British financial community, and a flurry of anxious cables flew back and forth in April and May between Rothschild and Rhodes and Stow and Rhodes. In London, Stow meanwhile consulted Rothschild or Meyer nearly every day about the munificent manner in which the life governors were to be rewarded with the bulk of the anticipated profits. Rhodes subsequently compromised, but not about the very existence of the life governorships. He diminished them slightly in the scale of their rewards and diluted some of their other powers. Ultimately Barnato was allocated nearly 7,000 shares and Rhodes, Beit, and Stow more than 4,000 shares in the Consolidated concern. Between them it was agreed that they would receive a fourth of all annual profits in excess of £1,440,000, a distribution which began in 1896 with an amount of £120,000 and ended five years later with £316,000. Then the firm commuted the rights of the life governors, giving them and their descendants shares at the time valued at £3 million.

It was a suit by disgruntled shareholders in the Cape Supreme Court in August 1888, however, which delayed the consummation of the De Beers-Central consolidation even more drastically than did the negotiations over the emoluments of the life governors. During it Justice Smith interrupted the arguments of plaintiff's counsel to say that "it would be far shorter to tell us what the company may not do" than to keep reading its multifarious objectives. Rhodes had drawn a trust deed easily subject to objection. James Rose Innes, the counsel, told the court that De Beers could "do anything and everything, my lord." They were not "confined to Africa," and they were even "authorised to take steps for the good government of any territory." However, as the court held, the trust deed of Kimberley Central permitted a merger only with a similar company; i.e. one having goals confined to mining diamonds. De Beers Consolidated was clearly something else, and a simple unification was impermissible. But Chief Justice Sir Henry de Villiers, who wrote the opinion, provided a legal loophole. The merger would not be prevented if the shareholders were paid fully in cash.[44]

"The minority have beaten me on the interdict," Rhodes wrote to Rothschild. "I can assure you I did everything to carry out the amalgamation but on a technical point of law," he excused himself, "they won." To Stow he wrote, "We practically cannot amalgamate with the Kimberley mine and can only get them by sale. . . . I can only say I have done all I could, it just shews the difficulties attendant on the absorption of a number of private interests." He was unwilling simply to admit that he and the directors of both the De Beers and Central companies had tried to circumvent the minority shareholders and had been thwarted. Moreover, his attention had been diverted at the last moment by a critical fire in the De Beers mine; 24 whites and 178 Africans (a third of the work force) were killed as a result of De Beers' negligence. The firm lost two or three months' production. (Stow, a lawyer, replied that the twist of legal events could have been more tangled. "I did not at all relish the dormant Volcano we have been sitting on for the past six months. When I come to think what one or two small shareholders might have done it makes my blood turn cold. If the Central opposition had only been properly led we should have cut a sorry figure in a court of law.")[45]

What to do? His own fortune, as well as a portion of some of the fortunes of Beit, Barnato, Stow, and Rothschild, were bound up in the contemplated merger. There was only one option. Rhodes advocated increasing the financial inducement that De Beers Consolidated was using to tempt the outstanding holders of Central shares to exchange their various situations in Central for those in the new firm. It would cost about £1.5 million more, he estimated. "The whole case," he appealed to Rothschild, "depends on whether you have any confidence and trust in yourself. Perhaps someone else can do it better. I really do not know. You know my objects and the whole case is a question of trust I know with you behind me I can do all I have said. If however you think differently I have nothing to say." Rhodes rolled the dice brazenly. In further explanation, Rhodes intended to "go on gradually opting until there is hardly any left and then make a sale to close the matter, but it will take time . . . I do not want to embarrass our position by a further cash payment."[46]

With Rothschild's firm backing and, it appears, careful guidance, Rhodes assiduously took in more and more shares on better terms until, at the end of October 1888, it was clear that he controlled a preponderant majority of the total. A massive fall of reef in the Kimberley mine also eased the process. Further, the owners of the other two mines were becoming more reasonable, and Rhodes was waiting for the costs of purchasing them to decrease. "If we chose to wait for the reef to fall, we should get them for half, and they are now about 400 feet deep. . . . You can see that they have reached a depth," he told Rothschild, "at which the reef is bound soon to fall, that with their low yield they can neither haul out the reef nor work underground at a profit, and therefore they must arrange settling."[47] Indeed, although it took a few more months to conclude the conquest of the Central Company, by the end of January 1889 Rhodes and Barnato put it into liquidation. De Beers Consolidated subsequently "purchased" all of its assets, tendering a single check for £5,338,650 to conclude the deal.

The outstanding portions of the Dutoitspan and Bultfontein mines were folded into De Beers later in 1889, but not without a number of careful tactical maneuvers. The city of Kimberley had worried that the resulting broad amalgamation of the diamond industry would cause widespread unemployment. By one measure, about a quarter of the white working force did, in fact, immediately become redundant. Precise figures are unavailable, but at least the same proportion of Africans, and perhaps up to 50 percent, initially must also have been thrown out of work. Then Rhodes added to unemployment by dismissing nearly 1,000 more. He was hardly popular. Indeed, two days afterward a twilight procession of white and Coloured unemployed marched from the Dutoitspan to the Kimberley mine pushing a cart containing an effigy of Rhodes. Outside the headquarters of the new Company they burned the effigy, saying: "We . . . now commit to the flames the last mortal remains of Cecil John Rhodes, Amalgamator General, Diamond King and Monarch of De Beers. . . . Thank God! And in doing so let us not forget to give three cheers for a traitor to his adopted country, panderer to the selfish greed of a few purse-proud speculators, and a public pest. May the Lord perish him. Amen!"[48] As one way of absorbing the white unemployed, Rhodes may have invented the white settlement of Rhodesia (Zimbabwe), which began in 1890 with an armed trek from Kimberley through and beyond the territory of the Ndebele. But by then there also were ample opportunities for mining employment on the Witwatersrand.

Another result of the final merger of the mines, and the actual operation of all four as a single operation under Williams' management, was the inauguration of the life governorships. Baring Gould had been promised the fifth one, to be elected by the first four. But in August and again in October 1888 Baring Gould had actively attempted to dissuade the remaining Central shareholders from exchanging their rights in that company for parts of the new Consolidated. This infuriated Rhodes and Beit and surely also annoyed Barnato. As a result, Rhodes and Barnato, and presumably Beit as well, decided in February 1889 to deny Baring Gould the previously promised position of wealth and influence. "Barnato refuses to accept Gould," Rhodes wrote to Stow. "He says he shuffled up to the last and that it is now one of the conditions of last agreement." Certainly, continued Rhodes, "we cannot force Barnato," perhaps assuming Stow's acquiescence. But Stow believed that denying Baring Gould, however questionable his behavior had been in 1888, constituted a serious breach of faith. Among other issues, it led a few years later to Stow's tragic rupture with Rhodes, and to a steady stream of slurs on Rhodes' character. To the end of his long life Stow always assumed that Rhodes had engineered a classic, dastardly double-cross out of sheer greed. (In the late 1890s, after Barnato's suicide, one of Barnato's nephews confirmed or implied what Stow had long suspected, that Rhodes had instigated Barnato's refusal to accept Baring Gould. Rhodes denied this story, and tried unavailingly to clear the air. There was "no truth whatever in the statement that Barnato's refusal to appoint Baring Gould was suggested and encouraged by me," he tried to tell Stow.[49])

In 1889, a watershed year in so many other ways as well (see Chapter 10), Rhodes had by brilliant, if ruthless, tactical pincer movements and the exercise of enormous charisma strikingly established himself as Africa's leading entrepreneur. Backed solidly by Rothschild and ably abetted by Beit and Rudd, his company held unquestioned control of diamonds. Of his broader dreams for De Beers, he believed that there was "every chance of making it another East India Company." Soon, even sooner than they had realized, it would hold a complete monopoly of diamonds, and, he predicted, make about £2 million a year. Industrial capital dominated labor in Kimberley.

Rhodes' investments in gold, however, had proven less successful. Although he held "a good deal," he had experienced "bad luck" and had "missed the best part." Because of worries about De Beers, he had been unable to reside continuously on the Witwatersrand, and "returned too late to buy into the richer parts."[50] This explanation obscured the fact that Rhodes had husbanded his capital more than his competitors, and had feared plunging too deeply into unproven prospects. He had been too cautious. He had also followed poor advice. The outcrops of gold on which he had spent thousands did yield gold, but not in the quantities soon being won from the far richer claims of Robinson; Beit, Hermann Eckstein, and James B. Taylor (all working for Porges); and Barnato. Robinson was exceptionally fortunate, winning five to ten ounces of gold from each ton of ore. Rhodes and Rudd were able to secure less than an ounce from each ton, barely a respectable return in an era when the price of gold was still fixed.

Rhodes nevertheless made money initially for the shareholders of Gold Fields (and for himself) by floating subsidiary mining companies and selling digging rights held by Gold Fields to these new concerns. He also leased claims on lands owned by Gold Fields (and the other companies) to other prospectors. Yet, instead of using such profits and capital otherwise lying idle to better the position of the firm on the Rand—he could have purchased in the better areas—Rhodes and Rudd invested primarily in diamonds, that is, in De Beers. Rhodes simply felt that what they were being offered elsewhere on the reef was too expensive, and too speculative. Further, when it was clear that the first £100,000 invested in gold was giving a poor return (by the standards of Kimberley), Rhodes took shelter. Nevertheless, he permitted, indeed demanded, that Gold Fields invest heavily in the very speculative shares of his new British South Africa Company, which intended to find and exploit great gold reserves across the Limpopo River. When the British holders of Gold Fields' shares mutinied, disdaining expensive purchases of the new company and urging that holdings in De Beers also be sold, Rhodes became choleric. The shareholders had behaved "disgracefully," he told Rudd. "I am thinking of resigning but shall await your decision. I always said you made a mistake giving them up the [British South African Company] concession and I must add I think I ought to have been consulted. . . . I have no intention of working for these fellows for the balance of my life. A more ungrateful crew I have never come across. I do not think I shall attend the yearly meeting. . . . The one point you forgot was though you obtained the concession, I may have to spend my life in developing it and you have handed me over to a crowd I will not work for."[51]

Soon there was more worrying news. In the early months of 1889 those who dug for gold along the Witwatersrand realized that the ore body was changing. As their shafts struck more deeply than before, the gold-bearing rocks became contaminated with pyrites. Until this point the miners had been able to crush their ore with stamp mills and then to extract gold by passing the result over copper plates coated with mercury. To separate gold from the surrounding sulfides they had to use expensive chlorines. The low-grade producers, like Rhodes, were doomed.

By the end of 1889 Gold Fields had sold most of its Rand holdings and was out of gold. It no longer controlled even one company. Instead it was heavily into diamonds. Rudd put the best complexion on these events when he reported to the shareholders in 1890, but he was more hopeful than confident. "Witwatersrandt after a year or two is, in my opinion, going to be the biggest gold-field in the world. . . . [It is] the business of Mr. Rhodes and [myself] to represent the investor and not the speculator, who is the curse of the mining companies. And I myself believe that, although the shares of Gold Fields . . . are now £3.10s. while this time last year they were at £7, the intrinsic value of the shares is infinitely superior now. . . ."[52]

The disappointment of gold contrasted sharply with Rhodes' vast success in diamonds. In 1889, he was also extending his reach beyond the Limpopo, where "someone has to get the country and I think we should have the best chance," he told Rothschild.[53] Rhodes intended to bring within his personal domain what would become three provinces of the Crown—three outposts of empire and the germs of three independent republics. At thirty-six, poised on the brink of these new exploits and of political dominance in the Cape, Rhodes—visionary, entrepreneur, and buccaneer—with his diamond wealth and his political connections, almost overnight had become the most powerful man in Africa and, potentially, one of the most creative persons in Queen Victoria's vast empire.

"We Are to Be Lords over Them"
Fashioning a Distinctive Destiny as the Solitary Springbok

R HODES HAD DEVOTED much of his immense energy during the second half of the 1880s to the creation of a diamond monopoly. During this period, when he was also investing actively in gold properties, he continued to participate vigorously in the parliamentary and party politics of Cape Town. As consumed as he may have been with the high finance of mining amalgamation, he was equally assiduous in expanding his political base and reputation.

There was a third passion during these years. By the middle of the decade, Rhodes had become determined to push the Cape and, if possible, Britain, beyond Stellaland, Goshen, and Bechuanaland through Matabeleland to the Zambezi. Indeed, the drive north—the seeking out of an interior destiny—was intimately intertwined in Rhodes' mind and actions with his other two prominent lines of endeavor. Yet diamonds were not accumulated simply to finance a northern vision. Nor were political chips acquired and positions established solely in order to steer his northern aspirations toward reality. Rhodes' motives were more complicated, and so were the times. Each object had its own reality, but their trajectories intersected. As crucial and all-encompassing as were Rhodes' negotiations with Rothschild, Barnato, Beit, and Stow as he gained more and more economic power, so he devoted days and weeks to the parallel pursuit of political power, and—more fitfully until his hands were finally forced—to the acquisition of potential imperial advantage. During these few years Rhodes was still in his early thirties, a period when most men, feet firmly set on the lower rungs of an occupational or professional ladder, have much to learn. Rhodes was also settling in, but his feet were planted far higher, and on a steeper ladder, than most. In these middle years of enormous creative thrust, careful positioning, and artful compromise, he was successfully playing the game of much older men.[1] His reach for both tactical and strategic personal advantage was broad and fulfilling.

Even before the discovery of the gold of the Witwatersrand, Rhodes had a healthy respect for the ambitions of the Transvaal, and for President Kruger. His experiences in Stellaland and Goshen had convinced him that only determined moves by the Cape (and Britain, if its leaders could be prodded to take timely action) would check a Transvaal that was as anxious to relieve its own isolation as Rhodes was to contain it. Links from the Transvaal with the Germans north of the twenty-second parallel (northern Botswana) were still a threat. "Our work [in] the interim," Rhodes wrote to Shippard in early 1886, is "to see we do not get shut in by the Germans cutting across our path."[2] In the face of British weakness and inattention in Natal, the Transvaal was also moving toward Amatongaland, establishing the New Republic in northwestern Zululand—it was to annex that Republic in 1887. Portugal was fragile internationally, and could also fall prey to the Transvaal. Its harbor at Delagoa Bay (Maputo) was ideally placed to receive the exports of the Transvaal and to deprive the Cape of new interior commerce. There were the trans-Limpopo regions, too—the gateway to the distant Central African lakes.

Rhodes focused on the trans-Limpopo regions with increasing persistence during the 1880s, especially after the gold finds in the Transvaal suggested that Matabeleland might also be rich in minerals. But it was not mere avarice which impelled Rhodes to apply the visionary impulses which had characterized the "Confession of Faith" (1877), to follow up his discussions with Ralph Williams in Stellaland and his letters to Merriman, and to act upon the broad trust deed of De Beers Consolidated. Rhodes had begun to associate his own proposed contribution to humanity with the spread of the empire and the extension of English culture and values. He therefore identified with the Cape Colony, knowing that there could be no firmer political and economic base for a private citizen like himself who nourished grand, even audacious notions about the national acquisition of distant, interior lands half a continent away.

Just as Rhodes looked north on many accounts, and just as he desired the control of diamonds for its own sake as well as for the wider uses that such wealth would permit, so Rhodes from the mid-1880s onward adroitly maneuvered himself so as to enhance his personal power within the circumscribed world of Cape party politics. He undoubtedly did so in part to strengthen Kimberley's economic position and to secure the short- and long-run prosperity of his mines. But there is little doubt that he also did so in order to advance the practical outlines of his imperial and territorially expansive aims.

The support of the Bond—the Dutch burghers and farmers in the Cape—was essential. But it is incorrect to suggest that Rhodes shifted ground politically in the 1880s solely in order to accomplish his dreams of northern glory. As before, as almost always, Rhodes was a tactician and an incrementalist. He had ideas and visions, but those ideas were options, and Rhodes always toyed simultaneously with several desirable objectives. Thus—just as the motives of any great, complicated, and energetic personality may be simplified only with the loss of veracity and nuance—what Rhodes accomplished or sought to accomplish in addition to his creations of commerce should be seen as intrinsic, and not ancillary, components of the whole. Too often overshadowed in biography by the dream of diamonds and gold, his other strivings during this crucial period are as important as his entrepreneurial victories in understanding the man and his deeds.

There is a further consideration. In 1885–86, in Cape Town and London, if not in Kimberley, Rhodes' reputation had been sullied by his verbal battles with Warren and Mackenzie. Official circles in London wondered if Rhodes were not dangerously pro-Dutch. After all, in Stellaland he had favored restoring land titles to Afrikaners and not to African traditionalists. Bondsmen in the Cape, on the other hand, knew him to be hostile to Kruger and to the aims of the Boers of the interior, and thus to be anti-Dutch. Although Rhodes protested in 1885 to Lord Harris, undersecretary in the colonial office (and about to become undersecretary of state for India) that he was not pro-Dutch in his sympathies and that none of his actions over Stellaland or Bechuanaland should be construed as other than efforts to "retain the interior and shut the Transvaal in," ultimately on behalf of Britain, he soon set about establishing solid credentials with the Bond.[3]

From 1886 Rhodes more and more espoused views which he had earlier disdained. He did so from newfound personal conviction, a capitalistic desire to avoid taxation on diamonds, naked political expediency, and a conscious desire to bridge the ethnic gap between Dutch and English voters. Although a member of a party opposed to the Bond and its coalitions with Sprigg's coterie, he voted regularly with the Bond and, on several occasions, spoke enthusiastically and at length in favor of drastic alterations in the political, economic, and social fabric of Cape life. These alterations were vigorously opposed by his closest friends and political colleagues.

The Bond, still led firmly by Hofmeyr, was a party capable of commanding pluralities, but not majorities, in the Cape House of Assembly. Fearful of being outmaneuvered by representatives of English-speaking commerce and others loyal to Britain, the Bond had become a significant political force in the Cape. Its members farmed; the Bond sought protection for agricultural products against imports from Europe. As the Transvaal could hardly compete with Cape wine and brandy, or with its citrus or wheat, the Bond tried to persuade the Transvaal and the Orange Free State to lower tariff bars against the Cape. Before 1886 its members preferred that rails be extended within the farming districts and not necessarily beyond Kimberley, into the interior. The Bond thus had an economic program which made sense to its members, if not to others of a broader view.

Bondsmen in the 1880s also took positions which were antithetical to Africans. Naked prejudice may have influenced a growing anti-African agitation during this period. Bond branches systematically refused to admit even Coloured members. More telling was the fact that only with the assistance of enfranchised Africans could English-speakers outvote those for whom Dutch or Afrikaans was the mother tongue. The *Port Elizabeth Telegraph* had put the position plainly in 1881: "If the Africander Bond is to be well beaten it will have to be done by the assistance of the black vote. . . . The Dutch in the colony are to the English as two to one, and . . . if they combine they can outvote us, and inflict upon us all the absurdities of their national and economic prejudices." South Africa's first African newspaper consistently attacked the Bond, too. John Tengo Jabavu, the founder and editor of *Imvo Zabantusundu,* explained that African votes had been used "discreetly in the best interests of the country and of civilization, and . . . have steadily and consistently been employed to strengthen the English or the party of right and justice in the House."[4]

At a time when Rhodes was actively courting the Bond, the Bond was becoming more and more openly hostile to Africans, to the incorporation of new African voters, and, more generally, to a process of growth and development which could be termed modernization. As forward-looking, progressive, and far-seeing as Rhodes was, he soon found himself yoked to a political ox-cart which was by and large distrustful of new ideas and of a visionary's dreams of a united, greatly expanded South Africa. The Bond was burdened by the baggage of parochialism and narrow self-interest. Yet Rhodes was to ride the ox-cart to fame and to power. The oxen came to do his bidding.

During the early part of the parliamentary session of 1886, Hofmeyr, supported by the shaggy-browed Sprigg and his cabinet, moved to amend the act that regulated primary and secondary education for whites in the colony. He and the Bond, responding to a cascade of emotion among rural members of the several Dutch Reformed churches, wanted to return religious instruction to state schools. Because an existing law prohibited religious teaching during ordinary hours, Christian teaching before school was the customary practice. Yet Hofmeyr and his followers believed state schools irreligious and godless if their regular hours could not be infused with the Gospel. Indeed, his people had more and more abandoned the state system in favor of voluntary schools because of the absence in the former of regular religious teaching.

Rhodes favored the change, as did the majority of those who cast votes. He did so because he wanted to strengthen a state system of education, not because of any feelings for religion. If state schooling were undermined by the growth of voluntary schools, then the opportunity of "killing . . . race differences" through education would be lost.[5] By "race differences" Rhodes meant the animosities between English and Dutch—South Africa's dominant warring tribes. He felt deeply about the need to conciliate the two, but he also used this early opportunity of a cause championed by Hofmeyr to express solidarity with Dutch demands.

A few weeks later Rhodes sided with Hofmeyr on the Sabbatarian issue of whether the government railways should run passenger trains on Sundays. The government had recently prohibited the sale of liquor in hotels and bars in Kimberley, and A.B. de Villiers, the maker of the motion, was incensed that special trains still ran on Sundays between Kimberley and Modder River

Junction. As a result "people left Kimberley and went to Modderfontein to spend their day in debauchery, drinking, gambling, dancing, etc. . . . directly against the Ten Commandments." A Christian government should not allow such practices. Moreover, because the government "did not do what it ought to do . . . the colony was visited by such plagues as the phylloxera, failures of the crops, etc."

Thomas Fuller called the motion unnecessary, asserting that there was less Sunday traffic in the Cape than in any other country in the world. "Why not go further and propose that all the cart wheels should cease running on Sunday?" he asked. Moses Cornwall said that it was only on Sundays that the people of Kimberley had an opportunity to breathe fresh air. He himself lived near the railway station and affirmed that he had never seen drunkenness on the Sunday trains. For Rhodes, however, the Sunday trains from Kimberley were "a public scandal." He wanted those trains stopped.[6] The motion, however, narrowly failed to pass.

Rhodes became a sudden protectionist, too, joining Hofmeyr in attempting to repeal a tax on locally produced brandy that had been imposed in 1884. Speaking at length in the debates immediately after Hofmeyr, he lamely said that the excise was unfair, for it "pressed on the producer." Merriman called the debate most dreary and lamentable, the whole being enlivened only when Rhodes—"bouncing on the resilient cushion"—shot interruptions at Upington. Upington, an immaculately dressed man who parted his hair down the middle, half-heartedly defended the tax. Rhodes, said the lanky-jawed Merriman, "got fearfully mauled in the attempt." "I am more than sorry," continued Merriman, "for the part played by Rhodes, who seems to have pleased no-one and who is too open and undisguised in his assault on the 'cocoanuts.'"

Merriman saw Rhodes as exposed to ridicule, first because of the Sunday trains vote and then because of the one for brandy. "The people he wants to conciliate laugh at him while they use him. . . . What a curious farce it is that Rhodes, who took a leading part in starting the Empire League, should now be courting the advances of the Afrikaner Bond. . . ." Later, after Rhodes had unequivocally joined the protectionists, Merriman turned choleric. "The idea of Rhodes, who used to quote manuals of political economy with all the zeal of a lad fresh from the Oxford schools," he wrote to Currey, "taking his stand on the platform of . . . protection whose sole *raison d'etre* is extreme anti-British feeling!" However, the excise repeal passed, if narrowly, and without official government or opposition votes. Rhodes was publicly thanked by Hofmeyr. In a speech in Paarl, the center of Cape farming interests, Hofmeyr reminded his listeners that "the separation between English and Dutch-speaking Africanders had not yet been cleared away. That must surely be the great aim of all. . . . The men who contributed to this were benefactors."[7]

It was in search of such praise, and even more so in order to enhance his appeal to the Bond, that Rhodes followed Hofmeyr in seeking to limit the compulsory dipping of sheep to control the scab pest. He and others were aware that the Colony's wool exports could grow only when the scab insect was contained. Throughout the world this had been done by forcing stock-men to disinfect their sheep and goats on a regular basis. Insects respected no borders, and it thus made little sense in the absence of elaborate fencing to proclaim some districts closed and some not. But because of the hostility of the Dutch farmers, parliament passed an act which restricted dipping to a few districts only.

Rhodes introduced a motion of his own to impose taxes on huts in Afri-can locations and on state-owned lands. He wanted the revenues thus raised to be devoted to road building. After all, he explained, Africans at present contributed nothing to divisional roads, which was unfair to white farmers. "The great desire," he told the House, "was to remove the friction between the farmers and the natives. . . ."[8] Although Merriman, Jacobus Sauer, and others opposed this bill, and several members suggested that its enactment would upset Africans, it easily passed.

There was a long, bitter debate in the House on a bill to limit the period in which African mining workers could be confined to the new compounds that had been established in 1885 in Kimberley supposedly to inhibit the se-creting and smuggling of diamonds, but also to control and discipline labor. Rhodes passionately defended harsh limitations on the mobility of mine work-ers. He said that his object was to prevent the theft of gems and to deprive shady traders of their supplies. (He also used African convict labor, and built a special compound for them at De Beers in the late 1880s.) Merriman, usu-ally the last to favor such deprivations of liberty, also supported the com-pound system wholeheartedly. If parliament wished to "see natives ad-vanced," he said, "they must do everything they could to foster the compound system." Illicit diamond buying was the greater evil.

Matthews, a local physician and parliamentarian, was pleasantly surprised by the quality of the Central Company's compound in 1885. "I . . . found a large yard some 150 yards square inclosed partly by buildings and the re-mainder by sheets of iron ten feet high. Within this inclosure were sleeping-rooms for 500 Kafirs, a magnificent kitchen and pantry, large baths, guard-room, dispensary and sick-ward, store and mess-rooms. . . ." Ten years later Bryce was also positive about Kimberley's two compounds, "the most striking sight at Kimberley, and one unique in the world." He said that they were huge enclosures, unroofed, but "covered with a wire netting to prevent any-thing from being thrown out of them over the walls, and with a subterranean entrance to the adjoining mine." Rhodes' mines were often worked on three eight-hour shifts, so his 2600 African employees were underground for eight hours and then confined to the compounds for the remainder of the day or night. "Round the interior of the wall," Bryce described, "there are built sheds or huts, in which the natives live and sleep. . . . A hospital is also provided . . . as well as a school. . . . No spirits are sold. . . . Every entrance is strictly guarded, and no visitors, white or native, are permitted, all supplies being obtained from the store within. . . ."[9]

Where Rhodes parted company with Merriman, Rudd, and his other usual friends, and disagreeably so, was over a proposal to moderate the sanctity of the compounds in Kimberley. African laborers were confined there for two or three months, the usual length of their contracts. Matthews, a contemporary observer, said that the system simply prevented "a company's boys . . . [from] being allowed to wander about the town at their own sweet will, to feed at Kafir eating-houses (which are too frequently the favorite resorts of black I.D.B. runners, and whose proprietors are not invariably above reproach), and to drink at low canteens or smuggling dens. . . ." Within the compounds they were kept from "deleterious and adulterated liquor." But the system roused opposition from owners of canteens and stores, "the I.D.B. gentry," and others.

The mining companies obviously installed their own stores in the compounds for the confined employees. This "truck" system had been forbidden in Britain because of the easy abuse of workers through such tied sales, and the South African opposition to the compound system in 1886 was spearheaded by representatives of Kimberley's petty commerce. Without directly attempting to abolish the compound system, they sought to subvert it by prohibiting the sale of any goods within the compounds. If their bill had passed, the companies would obviously have had to open their gates at least once a week.

To Merriman's disgust, Rhodes, always prepared to compromise the smaller principle for the larger gain (in this case broad support), agreed to convert the company shops into stores controlled both by the Cape Colony and the companies, with the city of Kimberley gaining any profits. Merriman called this notion unworkable and "ridiculous." Yet Rhodes apparently wanted to gain friends and also to prove that he did not want wealth derived from the selling of cheap goods to Africans. In the process, however, he lost his temper and, Merriman reported, became very disagreeable—especially when the measure went down to defeat despite the backing of the Bond and of Upington.[10]

Merriman had earlier complained about Rhodes' penchant for apostasy. After all, in Merriman's eyes they were still old and deep friends despite what Rhodes had done to him over the amalgamation of the diamond mines. They rode together in the mornings. During the parliamentary sessions of the mid-1880s, they even spent occasional quiet weekends together (and with Mrs. Merriman, the J.W. Sauers, and the Inneses) at Muizenberg on False Bay. Walks across the pristine, empty sands were varied by expeditions to the boulder-studded coast beyond Simonstown. Rather than fishing, for they were "fishers of men," the vacationing politicians talked politics. Rhodes, recalled Innes, was "enormously impressed by the potentialities" of the Bond as a new political machine. The Dutch farmer, he thought, would always "get the better of the English shopkeeper, for he was a born politician." Moreover, for Rhodes "the Bond was the only coherent parliamentary party whose support once gained could be implicitly relied upon"—a shrewd analysis. "I did not realize then," Innes remarked, "how vitally" Rhodes' tilt toward the Bond "was to affect the fortunes of the rest of us." For Rhodes the "key of Cape politics" hung in the headquarters of the Bond.[11] Clearly his actions in 1886 demonstrated a grasping for that key.

Merriman was not at first prepared to give up entirely on Rhodes. He "*is* a good fellow, and that makes his occasional lapses the more painful to his friends . . . but his instincts," Merriman still hoped, were "of the right sort. He may do much good out here if he would manfully throw in his lot with the honest and intelligent party. . . . I doubt not but in time Rhodes will find out that labouring for Dutchmen *qua* Dutchmen, and pandering to their prejudices, is only sowing the wind. When once a party forms itself on national lines, on race lines, any alien who assists it is only welcomed as a tool and will be rewarded with ingratitude." Merriman wanted Rhodes to oppose the Bond because it worked "on purely Afrikaner lines."[12]

But Rhodes *was* prepared to pander to the Bond, even to its prejudices. His plans were much more important than the regard of his peers and friends. Unlike Merriman, he had great ends which to him justified any trifling means, even principles in parliament. He also worried little about ingratitude in the usual sense, seeking as he did the indirect support of the Bond for his amalgamationist designs and his far-reaching aims, as well as for himself as a trusted wielder of power.

The Bond's hostility to Africans as voters was clear to all politically active persons in the Cape. The Colony's constitutional ordinance of 1853 had given the vote to all male adult British subjects who owned property worth at least £25 a year or who received £50 worth of income a year (or £25 plus room and board.) By the 1880s neither were terribly tough tests, although slightly increasing the required thresholds would have excluded some whites along with many Africans. In any event, the Bond was initially reluctant to risk the certain loss of African support by proposing blatantly racial restrictions of the franchise. Yet it was undeniable that in a few constituencies, especially in the eastern Cape, liberal opponents had won seats thanks to the African vote. These political considerations became more urgent after 1885, when the Cape incorporated the Transkei, with about 80,000 potential new African voters and about 2,000 new white voters. Of the total population of the Cape— 1,250,000 Africans and 250,000 whites—males of voting age numbered about 200,000 and 50,000, respectively. But only a small proportion of Africans in the Colony had already been enfranchised.

The Bond congress of early 1886 urged higher qualifications and a literacy test for voters, and sought additionally to limit new Transkeian voters to those who could demonstrate "substance." The Bondsmen also demanded that rights of usufruct under communal tenure be eliminated as a property qualification under the franchise tests. Upington, in alliance with the Bond, thus proposed in parliament in 1886 that the Transkei be a single constituency, with two members, one to be elected by whites with 1853 qualifications and those (presumably few) Africans who owned land worth £100 under individual tenure. The other seat would be filled by election from a new Native Elective Council (the forerunner of the United Transkeian Territories General Council, or Bunga), in turn composed of delegates elected by all male Africans who paid a hut tax.

In the debate in the House, Upington explained that "natives were not fit to exercise the franchise the same as others entrusted with that privilege." Sir Jacobus de Wet, the secretary for native affairs, agreed. Africans, he said with feeling and an awareness of some current practices, "were simply the tools of the white man, and were brought up to the poll like so many sheep. They did not ask for representation, but the Government were giving it to them under certain provisions of voting."

Merriman and several others vehemently opposed anything that smacked of a differential franchise. Doing so, he said, would create "in the native mind a feeling that they were altogether apart from us." Merriman told Currey that the bill was clearly intended to disfranchise "the whole coloured race," and was an "earnest of what is to be done in the Colony." Africans were entitled to vote, Hofmeyr explained, but it was important that the prospective African voters in the Transkei not swamp white voters. He favored the bill as a temporary measure, but over the long term believed that the right to cast a ballot in the Cape should be based both on material worth, with greater wealth conferring multiple votes, and on the successful completion of secondary school. For Rhodes, who had begun to favor stricter qualifications for voters, the bill still had too many defects, prominent among which was a distinction "laid down on the basis of colour." He wished franchise qualifications to be based on simple literacy. Until the Africans of the Transkei could pass such a test—"until they were fit to have representation"—he recommended that they be ruled "under a personal government": that is, under their own indigenous chiefs subordinate to a resident commissioner. Ultimately, the critics of the 1886 legislation prevailed, and—as Rhodes had hoped—Upington withdrew his bill.[13]

Whether as a conciliator or as a schemer and manipulator, but certainly not as an ideological convert, Rhodes knew that he could ride to power and influence on the backs of the Bond only if he were as solicitous of the economic needs of Dutch farmers as he would want to be of the needs of the diamond mining industry. He also chose to balance his ambitions for extraterritorial hegemony and a free hand against Kruger with a significant shift away from traditional Cape liberalism (and the views of the likes of Merriman, Sauer, and Innes).

The franchise was a central issue. It divided white voters into two camps. Rhodes ignored it during the parliamentary debates of 1886 but, shortly thereafter, began to demonstrate to the Dutch that Hofmeyr's new confidence in the sound judgment of the young English magnate was well placed. At a luncheon in Paarl, Rhodes spoke strongly in favor of protecting Cape-produced grain and wine "so that when the farmer puts his plough into the soil he can see a chance of reaping a profitable harvest." With equal fervor he indicated that voting qualifications should be raised. But how was it to be done "without creating any ill feeling?" he asked rhetorically.[14]

Rhodes' opportunity to advance his own answers came in 1887, when the Cape departed from its traditional color-blind franchise. Sprigg was again prime minister, this time with Bond support. He devised a sly measure which would prevent anyone living in either the Colony or the Transkei with even a portion of his qualifying property in communal tenure to be eligible for the vote. His object was to diminish greatly the impact of new Transkeian black voters on the political fortunes of the Cape, less than 1 percent of African males being estimated as capable of qualifying under the proposed rule. In the rest of the Colony the new regulations would also limit the black vote in the Ciskei, where there was much intermingling of individual and communal tenure. Whites, even poor whites, would be unaffected.

Sprigg and many Bondsmen wanted to "cleanse and purify" the Cape register of voters and to prevent whites from being overwhelmed by the "blanket" vote—the vote of the presumably uncivilized and unwashed from the Transkei and other areas. Although introduced as the Parliamentary Voters' Registration bill, Jabavu immediately termed it the "natives' disrepresentative bill." For Merriman the bill was a "miserable sham." He, Sauer, and Innes opposed it "on the ground of truth" and on "the ground of liberty, for," Merriman said, "we have no right to take away the rights that have been conferred upon the Natives." He opposed it further on the "ground of justice," for he wanted to see equal justice meted out to all." Finally, he opposed it "on the ground of expediency, for if there is any one thing likely to damage the country it is the stirring up of a bitter feeling amongst the Natives. . . ."[15]

Although Innes agreed with Sprigg (and Rhodes) that "purely tribal tenure" did not entitle Africans to the franchise, and regarded the new bill as a "clever move" on the part of the government, he opposed it vigorously, and on many fronts. He knew that the magistrates who would be empowered to define tribal tenure at the local level would readily strike Africans off the rolls; yet many Africans would have constructed decent houses. Others would have grazing rights on commonly held lands, but would also own farming plots individually. "The practical result will be that nine-tenths of the native votes will disappear." To a fellow parliamentarian he explained that the bill would entirely do away with the African vote. "I doubt whether any man who does not wish to see the political influence of this country in the hands of an extreme and retrogressive political party would welcome the abolition of the native voters." To Jabavu and the Rev. Pambani Jeremiah Mzimba, the first ordained African minister of the Free Church of Scotland, he pledged an all-out campaign against what he called "one of the most iniquitous and unjust measures which has ever been before Parliament."[16] He urged Jabavu and Mzimba to circulate petitions (which Innes drafted) among the Mfengu in the Ciskei and Border districts.

Rhodes was in parliamentary opposition, along with Merriman, Sauer,

Innes, and Rudd. But he voted with Sprigg and the Bond. In the course of a long speech in the House, he enunciated what for him was a wholly new policy. Admitting that he was "out of touch on this question" with his usual colleagues, he asked if the bill were right or wrong. He was compelled to agree in one respect with its critics. It was "a perfect farce" to call the new parliamentary registration bill a mere interpretation of the constitutional ordinance. Nevertheless, it was the "basis upon which we shall have to govern the country, if the country is to be governed as it should be."

Should the "native population" vote or not? In the past, Rhodes said, the Cape had let too many Africans vote. Now, he continued, was the time to change. The "native question" divided the country, that is, divided English from Dutch. For his own part he was now persuaded that the government of the colony had to "govern the natives as a subject race." Some Africans should retain the vote, but not those living under communal tenure. "I came down here as the most rabid Jingo," Rhodes admitted, being an imperialist to the core. But now he had to deal with the fuller South African question. There were five times as many Africans as whites; if they were to exercise their franchise Africans would be in a majority. But Natal had effectively disfranchised Africans as well as Chinese and Indian immigrants—why should the Cape not do the same? Giving Maoris the vote in New Zealand, Rhodes declared, had proved a failure. "There are those who wish to endow the native at once with the privileges it has taken the European eighteen hundred years to acquire."

Rhodes maintained that limiting the Cape franchise to Africans with substantial property would not be unjust. Is it right that "men in a state of pure barbarism should have the franchise and vote? The natives do not want it." They had only to spend £25 and build a house, and then they would be able to vote and become an ordinary citizen of the country. "There had to be class legislation," he declared. "There must be Pass Laws." "We have got to treat natives, where they are in a state of barbarism, in a different way to ourselves. We are to be lords over them." Rhodes continued in his usual repetitive fashion, driving the message home: "The native is to be treated as a child and denied the franchise." Moreover, in further alliance with the Bond, Rhodes said that if he could not keep his position in parliament "as an Englishman on the European vote, I wish to be cleared out, for I am not going to the native vote for support." He returned to a central premise: The critical question was the cleavage between Dutch and English, and the African vote was the cause of the antagonism. Therefore, he did not want "the real interests of the natives" to be complicated by the question of the franchise.

There could be no united South Africa, Rhodes spoke correctly and prophetically, without a solution to the African question. So long as the Cape allowed Africans to vote in number, the other South African territories would shun any proposed unions. Because of the ultimate problem of joining disparate white-run lands, and the possibility that Britain might shift territories like Bechuanaland into the Cape, Rhodes said that his fellow parliamentarians should adopt a system of despotism, on Indian lines, to deal with the "barbarians of South Africa." It was his duty and desire, he said, to awaken in the House an interest in politics greater than can be felt in the local municipalities. He would vote for the bill: "Whatever source it comes from, whatever motives had dictated it, and whatever recantations it represents, it still is a good Bill; it meets the desires of the country, and it extends justice to the natives. . . ."[17] Rhodes made very evident that the greater end justified the means, and no amount of cant, hypocrisy, principle-shading, or ethical legerdemain would make him cringe—or reconsider.

He wanted to stand on the side of the Dutch, and to consolidate his collegiality with the one coherent party in Cape politics. Psychologically there was his usual need for fusion. He abhorred conflict, and usually sought to bridge cleavages between persons, if not ideologies. But, even before he focused fully on imperialist expansion to the north, there were demonstrable motives for his new alliance which flowed from a longstanding economic and political concern for the future of South Africa. Because he always explored the larger implications of otherwise petty and mundane tariff and railway policies, and because he was ambitious for the Colony as well as for Kimberley and himself, Rhodes during 1886 and 1887 (after the discovery of the Rand) coupled his attention to the Dutch to a renewed advocacy of practical proposals for knitting the component parts of South Africa into a whole.

Rhodes wanted the rails to Kimberley to be extended through the Orange Free State to the heart of the Transvaal in order to strengthen the commercial interdependence of the three territories and to wean Kruger and his compatriots away, if at all possible, from a competing rail line running from Delagoa Bay to the Witwatersrand. Such an extension would help Kimberley, even—he admitted reluctantly—if it might hinder the commercial growth of Port Elizabeth. In order to reassure the merchants of that city and his fellow parliamentarians, Rhodes suggested several shipping scenarios and alternative cargo formulas which could enhance rather than destroy the prosperity of Port Elizabeth and other eastern Cape towns that feared the loss of traffic and revenue if the rail line were extended into the neighboring provinces.

Rhodes also understood and drew up mental plans for coping with the existing reluctance of both the Free State and the Transvaal to forge rail links with the Cape. There was the issue of internal tariffs, Rhodes naturally promoting free trade—a customs union—between the three territories and Natal despite his new stance as a protectionist versus Europe. In the case of South Africa, particularly given the new markets on the Rand and his ultimate goal of political union, he remembered the political economy manuals of Oxford and hewed closely to his original dreams and principles. He still hoped to convert the Bond and, ultimately, with the help of Kruger's obstinacy and cantankerousness, did so.

Rhodes made his positions on these interrelated and critical issues perfectly clear in 1886 in a much-overlooked intervention during a parliamentary debate on border custom duties. The long-planned railway from Delagoa Bay was again moving forward. Fuller had correctly warned that if it were constructed the Cape would be unable to compete effectively for the exports of the Transvaal. Scanlen had already alluded optimistically to the general desire for union on the part of whites in the Cape and in the three other South African entities. "If the Delagoa Bay Railway were carried out," Rhodes said, "the union of South Africa would be indefinitely deferred. . . ." A competing line could yet be constructed from Kimberley to Pretoria if the government were prompt. The issue which divided the Transvaal and the Cape, he acknowledged, was serious: the Transvaal was unwilling to forgo duties on traffic over its territory. Rhodes was prepared to compromise, an anathema to most of his colleagues and to farmers: "If we laid down the principle that these neighbouring States could not share in our Customs duties, and threw a wet blanket over the question of internal duties . . . ," there would never be a railway, and no union. These questions, he suggested, "should be met in a broad and not in a petty spirit, with the idea that we were the predominating State in South Africa."[18] Conceptually his plan was simple, but ahead of its time; Rhodes would remit a portion of the duties paid by importers at the ports of the Cape to the interior republics and would make whatever other concessions were needed to persuade the Free State and the Transvaal to link hands with the Cape.

A year later, with the Delagoa Railway underway and the Transvaal having refused to treat realistically with the Free State over tariffs, Rhodes urged the government of the Cape to agree to give the Free State a reasonable share of its customs duties so as to facilitate the building of a line at least from Kimberley to Bloemfontein and, if possible, on to the Vaal Drifts, opposite the Witwatersrand. Given the posture of the Transvaal, the present was "a golden opportunity which may not soon recur," for the Free State was tired of being isolated. Acknowledging that the Bond was still unpersuaded of the importance of subordinating present economic advantage to future gain, he "put it to the Bond members that they ought, above all things, to regard South Africa as a whole. . . ."[19]

The Cape Bond had indeed begun to alter its views on the virtues of union, the discoveries of gold in the Transvaal having encouraged such a shift. But the leaders of the Bond still vacillated over railways. Wanting to accommodate Kruger, they were prepared to halt extensions beyond Kimberley if he would cease building the line from Delagoa Bay and negotiate an internal customs agreement. Even Rhodes temporized as late as 1888, hoping still that the long recalcitrant Kruger could be cajoled into cooperating. As Merriman (who had interviewed him in 1887) had predicted, however, Kruger persisted in playing his own independent, resolute game, snarling the progress of railway building northward from the Cape, dividing his rivals, and playing the Cape off against the Free State.

By 1889 the Cape and the Free State had finally entered into a customs union (Natal remained aloof), and the Cape was extending its Port Elizabeth rail line from Colesberg to the Free State border, and thence to Bloemfontein. The Delagoa Bay line, stalled for most of a year near the international border between Portuguese East Africa and the Transvaal, was again under construction toward Komatipoort. At the same time, largely due to Kruger's intransigence but also because of Rhodes' renewed interest in the north (and his failure to make much of gold), he at last decided that Kruger could neither be turned nor squared. Even Hofmeyr and the Bond turned assertively against the thundering president. Rhodes abandoned his expedient approach of conciliation and reverted to the old cry of constraint. If the rails could not be sent to Pretoria they would go to Mafeking, skirt the Transvaal's western farming areas—theoretically draining their trade as it crossed Bechuanaland—and proceed onward to Matabeleland and the Zambezi. This route worried Kruger, but it suited Britain's concern for Bechuanaland. Focused as Rhodes became in 1889 primarily on Chief Lobengula's hinterland, the new direction began to seem infinitely preferable to the old.

Rhodes had emerged from the scrum of burghers, traders, farmers, frontiersmen, miners, promoters, and chancers as the Cape's leading young personality, economic and political actor, and energetic force. He had breached the citadels of colonial power as he had cornered diamonds—cleverly, doggedly, and with rounded, if adaptable objectives. His dynamism matched a determination which critics could later call ruthlessness, and his manner of ingratiating himself with Hofmeyr and the Bond was labeled shifty, even traitorous. Certainly he was flexible in his principles and determined somehow to accomplish his big idea. But in the late 1880s Rhodes was unquestionably central to every issue of importance to the people of the Cape and—less obviously—to South Africa.

Not only did he dominate the Cape's only important industry, largest employer of labor, and largest source of foreign exchange earnings, but, still in his mid-thirties, and presumably boosted in esteem by his economic prominence, Rhodes had become a persuasive and influential member of the House of Assembly. Hofmeyr and other Bondsmen trusted him, and looked to him as an English speaker and industrialist who, despite his heritage, would cooperate with the Dutch. Rhodes had tugged the Cape into Bechuanaland, had promoted a forward-looking railway policy, and was in the vanguard of those initially attempting to work with and then to oppose and circumvent Kruger. Indeed, Rhodes was largely responsible for the policy of containment which characterized the Cape's as well as his own stance toward Kruger's Transvaal from 1889. Rhodes was unquestionably a magnetic doer whose ability to move individuals, companies, and even states was widely accepted if not necessarily admired. Rhodes had swiftly become a man of consequence in a society that was still small, but riven with many complicated personal and group cleavages.

That Rhodes deployed his new riches for ends of power as well as wealth, that he managed unconscionably to manipulate individuals of all stations and make them into converts rather than enemies, and that he was uncommonly ambitious was assumed. But for what was he ambitious? He himself, his cohorts extolling him after his death, and nearly all of the biographers, following the lead of the man and his acolytes and extrapolating backwards from the final will, ascribe the assertiveness of this period, his entente with Hofmeyr, and his maneuverings everywhere to his drive to accomplish the grand dream of imperial extension. It is said that he wanted wealth and power to realize Britain's destiny and his own burning desire to civilize and Anglicize inner Africa. He sought to be the instrument of ideals deemed lofty by at least a generation of late nineteenth-century, post-Livingstonian Victorians.

There is some truth to these claims. But Rhodes' life and aims never followed a simple direction. Those who observed him closely in a contemporary setting, moreover, saw disjunctures and discontinuities as much as a single, bold pattern. As early as 1885 Merriman suspected that Rhodes was angling for supreme political power in the Cape—the premiership—for its own sake. He also suspected (and openly voiced his thoughts) that Rhodes wanted a seat in the British parliament.[20] Others were concerned, too, particularly after the youthful magnate intervened audaciously in British politics.

In 1887 Rhodes sailed back to Africa from England after financial negotiations with Lord Rothschild and Jules Porges. Aboard the R.M.S. *Garth Castle* was John Gordon Swift MacNeill, a fund raiser for Charles Stuart Parnell's Irish parliamentary party and the holder of an Irish seat in the House of Commons. MacNeill's seat was one of eighty-five controlled by Parnell (of a total in the House of 670). This bloc was employed as a disciplined phalanx of considerable size to press the cause of home rule for Ireland, Britain's closest "colony." A year before, Gladstone's Liberal government had in fact failed narrowly to convey home rule to Ireland, and simultaneously to eliminate Irish representation in the British parliament. Parnell had strongly supported Gladstone's initiative, but the possibility that a future, successful bill would forever prevent representatives of overseas parliaments from sitting in the mother parliament and integrating the empire alarmed Rhodes.

Rhodes believed in a kind of imperial federation, with the distant colonies contributing to the cost of empire and helping to govern it. Although never spelled out in policy or manifesto, he desired no interference in the domestic, only in the imperial questions of Westminster. Likewise, he expected that any imperial parliament would avoid interfering in the internal affairs of the individual colonies. Rhodes feared the separatist tendencies which the passage of a home rule act (similar to the one that failed) would foster.

Aboard the *Garth Castle*, MacNeill, who had never heard of Rhodes before, soon made his acquaintance. Indeed, they met abruptly. "He was trying to get his sea legs," MacNeill recalled quaintly, "by endeavouring, while the ship lurched, to walk along a single plank in the deck. I was engaged in a similar recreation, and as we were going in opposite directions on the same plank we met—with some force." They talked at dinner, and discovered they had many mutual friends from Oxford. They also talked in Rhodes' cabin, which MacNeill reported was filled with books, including Olive Schreiner's *Story of an African Farm,* which had appeared four years before. MacNeill said that Rhodes was astonished that such a book could have been written by young girl from the *veld.*

Rhodes read quietly in his cabin, only occasionally taking part in the ship's games. He preferred, said MacNeill, to keep himself aloof from fellow passengers, particularly on a fifteen-day voyage. Rhodes explained: "It takes four or five days to form an acquaintanceship, then four or five days more for a friendship; and then the voyage is too long, for in a few days more the acquaintanceship and friendship stop, and then there comes the row—I have seen several rows and I want to keep clear of them."[21]

Rhodes persuaded MacNeill, who had intended to air his lungs on the voyage and sail swiftly home again, to speak about Ireland in Cape Town, Kimberley, and Port Elizabeth. It was on the train to Kimberley that Rhodes offered to give the Irish party £10,000 if, against its known inclinations, it would seek a form of home rule that included the retention of Irish seats at Westminster.

MacNeill claimed that Rhodes gave him a letter along these lines, which MacNeill conveyed to Parnell in Wicklow in October 1887. Parnell dictated a favorable reply over MacNeill's signature, but no response was received from Rhodes. In mid-1888, however, Rhodes was again in London. MacNeill arranged that they should dine with him in the House of Commons.

An opportunity for Rhodes to assert his federationist point of view, and to attempt (in this case abortively) to influence the shape of British politics, had thus arrived. Parnell and MacNeill wanted Rhodes' funds, but Rhodes demanded a significant shift in Irish political theory and tactics. Parnell believed as a matter of politics and principle that a self-governing Ireland should not also be represented in Westminster. If it were, however, he could not agree to reduce its (admittedly overrepresentative) number of 103 seats to anything like the thirty-four that Rhodes was ingeniously suggesting as a proper reflection of Ireland's contribution to the imperial treasury. For Parnell it was all or none. For Rhodes the question was of realizing an ideal by a compromise that squared the different political realities of Ireland and Britain.

During their three memorable meetings in London in June 1888, Rhodes bargained hard for at least one principle of great importance to his vision of the possible future. After telling Parnell, according to Rhodes' later explanation, that his interest in Ireland was imperial—that Irish home rule would lead to imperial home rule, but only if the retention of Irish parliamentarians set a precedent—he went on to demand a clause—"a little clause"—giving any colony that contributed to imperial defense a proportional right of representation at Westminster.[22] This new notion Parnell easily accepted, but he balked at any reduction in his parliamentary numbers until home rule, including control over the Irish police and judiciary, had been secured. Given the disagreement about how many seats should be retained and the fact that home rule was by no means assured (and would not come in his own time) Parnell was ultimately persuaded to concede Rhodes' principle that the Irish should keep a position in parliament. As Parnell pointed out, it was more Gladstone's issue anyway.

Rhodes found Parnell stiff, but not difficult, for £10,000 was at stake—a sizable contribution to any party. They agreed to exchange letters, with Rhodes' one being amended in draft by Parnell before it was put into final form and dispatched. Rhodes' views on the Irish question were naturally influenced by his experience in and designs for the Cape. "If the Irish are to be conciliated," he wrote with a prescience that would please twentieth-century readers, ". . . they should be trusted, and trusted entirely. Otherwise the application of popular institutions to Ireland must be deemed impracticable. . . . My experience in the Cape Colony leads me to believe that even the Ulster question is one which [will] soon settle itself. Since the Colonial Office has allowed questions at the Cape to be settled by the Cape Parliament, not only has the attachment to the Imperial tie been immensely strengthened, but the Dutch, who form the majority of the population, have shown a greatly increased consideration for the sentiments of the English members of the community." He added frankly that his paramount interest was the "commencement of changes which [would] eventually mould and weld together all parts of the British Empire." Rhodes admitted making the Irish question a "stalking-horse" for imperial federation, but, in exchange for £10,000, he nevertheless asked for "hearty support" for a home rule bill to his own liking.

Parnell's circumspect reply gave Rhodes the necessary assurances without committing himself or his party to any specific line of action.[23] He would not pronounce himself in favor of the Imperial Federation idea, nor did he even promise to reject home rule proposals that might counter Rhodes' principles. He implied a concurrence of views about ideal results, stood back, and readily took Rhodes' money. Parnell "was the hardest man, but one, to convince whom I ever met," Rhodes later told a group of parliamentary friends from Britain. "He trusted no one. I tell you that man suspected his own shadow. He was unhappy and saw little good in the world, but . . . after a prolonged talk I got him into agreement with me, but I did not care for him—there was too much of the gimlet in him: he was not quite human."[24]

The agreement between Parnell and Rhodes soon became public, and the text of their letters known. Thus there is every reason to suspect that for £10,000 Rhodes wanted more than Parnell's adhesion to an abstraction. By mid-1888 Rhodes was already actively engaged in preparations for the acquisition of Matabeleland. Parnell's eighty-five votes in Westminster were relevant. Rhodes would not have wanted their opposition to any maneuvers (and the charter had not yet taken full shape in his mind) which Rhodes would use to secure the distant territory. When the British South Africa Company charter was granted in 1889, Parnell and his party were uncharacteristically silent, circumstantial but important evidence of Rhodes' ministrations.

Rhodes was using Parnell to deflect potential opposition over some as yet undeveloped policy regarding the northward expansion. He was also serious in seeking to remove obstacles to the realization of his larger dream of imperial and psychological integration, incorporation, and unity. But what he was not doing, despite the fears of his erstwhile friends, was buying his own way into Westminster.

Merriman had learned of Rhodes' dabbling in Irish waters immediately after MacNeill's visit to South Africa. "What is Rhodes about!" he asked Currey. "What is his object in identifying himself with the set of Irish miscreants who are trying to ruin England and break up the Empire? Does he want a seat from Parnell . . .?" To his wife, Merriman sounded a familiar refrain: "As for Rhodes, my heart grieves to see a man with so many fine qualities sink into a mere money grubber. He makes a mistake if he thinks the *mere* possession of money gives any power in a democracy, and by his more than erratic career he has lost confidence all round. . . ."[25]

Others took up the refrain, for Rhodes' involvement with Parnell was perplexing to the politicians and even to the voters of the Cape. In his own constituency, where Rhodes was a kind of a demigod, the rural voters may have demanded an explanation for this and other potentially aberrant behavior. A candidate for re-election to the Assembly, he put himself before the farmers and shopkeepers of Barkly West in September 1888. He spoke at inordinate length about his life and his plans. "There have been many things invented respecting my career," he said. "I have been told that my object is to obtain a seat in the English Parliament; but of course I give no heed to these rumours—there is no truth in them. It is my intention," he made plain, "to remain attached to Cape politics, for I take a great interest in them; and I tell you candidly I have not the slightest idea of quitting South Africa for any other country." His mind was clear and his program vast. He spoke with utter candor: "Here I can do something; but were I to go to England as a politician, I should be lost in obscurity."

About the contribution to Parnell, £5,000 of which had already been delivered in the form of fifty £100 notes, and the other £5,000 pledged but not yet transferred, Rhodes indicated that his gift was hardly a way of buying a parliamentary seat. "I have the presumption to say that I believe I could at any time obtain a seat in the English Parliament without paying . . . Parnell; . . . and that if I ever stood for the English Parliament, I should not stand for an Irish constituency." He also vehemently denied that he desired to become premier of the Cape.[26]

Rhodes may also have grandly wanted, as he once said, to "solve" the Irish question—that is, to establish a united self-governing Ireland, as a willing partner in the empire, living in harmony with Britain. This was a noble and worthy objective, but perhaps not one entirely susceptible to individual initiative. As in other areas, Rhodes' ideas may have been in advance of the times. Yet there was never a full test, aside from the lack of Irish opposition to the charter, of the power of his gift. By the time a home rule bill was again proposed, in 1893, Parnell had died, his party had split, and the notion of an imperial federation was passé everywhere except in Rhodes' mind. Moreover, if Parnell had ever received the second £5,000, he had retained it for personal and not party use. Perhaps Rhodes' generosity had given pleasure primarily to Mrs. Katherine Wood O'Shea, Parnell's lover.[27] Yet Rhodes found support for his northern policies among the Irish members of parliament. And they had opened their ranks to Rochfort Maguire, Rhodes' confidant, giving him a safe seat in the British House.

Another byproduct was a curious and little-noticed further dealing between Rhodes and Parnell. During early 1891, when Rhodes was visiting London, Parnell called every evening about 6 p.m. at the Westminster Palace Hotel. He was then fighting for his political life, and needed money. He waited patiently each night with Rhodes' secretary until Rhodes became free. One evening he told Rhodes that he would lose the searing battle; when Rhodes asked him why, Parnell said that the priests were against him. "Rhodes, walking up and down the room, as he was wont, suddenly turned and asked, 'Can't we square the Pope?' "[28]

In addition to satisfying or at least mollifying his detractors, Rhodes used the 1888 Assembly elections in the Cape to cement his relations with Barnato and to back industry against workers. Whether or not he had secured Barnato's agreement to the elaborate De Beers' trust deed by pledging support for a seat for his wealthy rival in the House—among the noble and the elect—it positively pleased Rhodes' puckish sense of noblesse oblige, as well as some rarely seen but not inconsiderable desire to flaunt his new power, to help Barnato campaign for—some would have said purchase—one of the four Kimberley seats. Certainly, amid the heckling and rowdiness of his opponents, and the slashing attacks of Merriman, Barnato cut a figure of flamboyant, manic kitsch. Obtaining a coach from Cape Town, he decorated it in gilt, installed monogrammed "B"s on all the panels, and paraded about behind four matched grey horses, a trumpeter, two cockaded footmen, and six outriders dressed in gold braid, lace, and jockey caps. The candidate wore a silver-grey morning coat with scarlet silk facings and a grey topper and handed out cigars with his name on them. "I confess that I would sooner go to hell alone than arm in arm with Barney Barnato," Merriman had declared, but he soon found himself together with the self-made promoter in parliament, for which disgrace Merriman blamed Rhodes.[29] In November 1888, Barnato easily topped the poll (followed by three other "Company" men) in Kimberley. He entered the House of Assembly in rakish style.

Rhodes had been so preoccupied during the hectic months of 1888 with diamonds, gold, and raising capital; his dreams of empire and imperial advance; Matabeleland; Kruger; railway building; a customs union; and his dealings with Parnell that only in mid-1888 did he manage to cope with an outstanding preoccupation, and one which must have been nagging him for nearly nine months. Rhodes had been without a satisfactory will since Pickering's death had deprived him of a designated heir. In June 1888, after treating with Parnell, and perhaps impelled by some renewed intimation of mortality, Rhodes made another will, his fourth. Sitting in De Beers' London office, and using De Beers' headed notepaper, he left equally "among my brothers and sisters" 2,000 shares in De Beers. The balance of his property he gave to Lord Rothschild.

The will was odd in several respects. First, Rhodes was then worth about

£1 million, even if he could hardly have realized that amount quickly and his annual earned income would not have yielded much more than a fraction of that amount. Two thousand De Beers shares represented but a minor part of his wealth, and throughout the 1880s—before writing this fourth will—he had assiduously assisted his younger brothers in their assorted commercial ventures, and had helped Ernest, his steadiest brother, improve upon the family fortunes for all. He was soon to purchase Dalston, the Rhodes' family seat in Islington, London, for sentimental as well as investment purposes. (In late October 1888, he persuaded William Rhodes, scion of another branch of the family, to part with Dalston, which had been a section of his own grandfather's estate and in which Rhodes and his brothers already had a partial stake.) But to provide so little for his family and to give the enormous sum that remained to Lord Rothschild, who hardly needed additional capital, was a curious enterprise capable of being explained only by Rhodes' determination to survive himself by an embodiment of his dreams.

In a letter to Lord Rothschild which accompanied the will, and in the sentiments of which Rothschild acquiesced, Rhodes instructed his imperious social better to use the funds released by Rhodes' death to establish a society of the elect for the good of the empire. "In considering question suggested take Constitution Jesuits if obtainable and insert English Empire for Roman Catholic Religion," he directed Rothschild cryptically. In other words, Rothschild was to procure a copy of the constitution of the Society of Jesus and then to make the necessary insertions which would transform it into a charter for the accomplishment of Rhodes' dreams.[30]

Rhodes could not have known the details of the constitution of the Society of Jesus. Indeed, the "constitution" was no single document from which a basic schema could be cribbed. The Jesuit order was inspired by the meditations of Ignatius Loyola of 1522, advanced by his admittedly limited vows at Montmartre in 1534, and developed significantly in the Institute of 1539, as approved by a Papal Bull in 1540. Not until a decade later, however, did St. Ignatius complete the drafting of the first of the constitutions of the Society. The Jesuits themselves accepted these terms only in 1558, after St. Ignatius' death, and it is to those final documents that Rhodes might have referred. They are a set of rules for members of the Society and include provisions both philosophical and trivial.

The first part of the constitution discusses how candidates to the order are to be admitted; the second deals with dismissals; the third, with the novitiate; the fourth (and the longest) explains how "scholastics"—scholars accepted as candidates—shall be prepared for an active life of service. The fifth section specifies vows; the sixth, the spiritual life of Jesuits; the seventh outlines missions that the Jesuits could undertake for the Pope and the Society's occupations of mercy. The eighth part gives instructions on preserving union between members, though they may be scattered across the globe. This section specifies the manner in which the General Congregation of the Society shall rule, and who shall be elected to it. Part nine outlines the powers and qualities of the head of the order, and the tenth indicates ways in which the Society shall be strengthened and preserved.[31] Rhodes would have wanted to have employed some of the emphases in the eighth, and also of the seventh section, but it is difficult to believe that he ever knew what they actually contained, and how different Ignatius Loyola's society was in organization from the one that he adumbrated in his "Confession of Faith" and several wills. Rhodes must have been inspired more by his sense of the Society's power, and its far-flung activity, than from any real acquaintance with Jesuits (despite the accessibility of the order's English headquarters in central London) or their history.

Yet the grandiosity of the intent, as well as the simplicity of the method, must have impressed even one so cynical as Rothschild. By presuming to reduce complicated, even revolutionary, propositions to their bare essentials, Rhodes may have enhanced his reputation as a visionary. To read his spare instructions today, even knowing their confused intellectual antecedents in Freemasonry, Reade's *Martyrdom,* and Gladstonian liberalism, is to sense the ruminations and even fantasies of a madcap bumbler more than the outpourings of a shrewd mobilizer of ambition, avarice, and idealism. (Rhodes was also fascinated by a novel of Boston manners and intrigue that he read about this same time. It chronicles the rise of a scrupulous Yankee politician who knows that "the men who succeed are the men of one idea" who refuse to let anything divert them from "the main object of their lives." They were to live like Jesuits, without ties, until that main object was achieved. Equally important, an Anglo-American secret society was involved in assisting the rise of the good politician. Rhodes thus commented on F. Marion Crawford's *An American Politician,* but where and why he read this particular one of Crawford's thirty-two popular novels, is obscure. It had appeared in 1884.)

The utter simplifications of a seer, oblivious to obstacles, are not difficult to reconcile with Rhodes' actions in polar opposite—as a promoter and buccaneer of utter practicality, as a punctilious financier obsessive of detail, and as the prolix, incessantly repetitive generator of political and economic positions. Far-seeing vision, to be successful, must be accompanied by attention to practical detail, political know-how, and reasonably good personal relationships. One aspect of Rhodes' greatness lies in the breadth of his genius—the sweep from grand design to minutiae.

It is impossible to ignore, dismiss, or deride Rhodes' visionary impulses as inconsequential. Judged by modern intellectual criteria, they do poorly. But judged according to their efficacy and influence, his dreams were extraordinary. Infected with Rhodes' own passionate conviction and untiring oratory, they excited other men to work for his goals. Men (and sometimes women) were seized with the nobility of what he intended. His dreams may appear to modern readers as commonplace and megalomaniacal. Yet even in today's cynical, technologically sophisticated age, outlandish ideas about health, religion, and the functioning of the mind, properly packaged for a susceptible audience, prove mightily influential. In an era of Social Darwinism and pater-

nal imperialism, Rhodes' sweeping, chauvinistic program of expansion inspired a broad range of intimates and acquaintances to believe that the acquisition of chattels, goods, and territories could serve lofty, broad, and redeeming
purposes. Rhodes was capable of calculating at several levels, of working with
a variety of methods for a myriad of short, medium, and long-term goals, and
of charming or otherwise overcoming most human and material obstacles.

The wellsprings of Rhodes' own view of himself during the late 1880s are
deep and murky. Modern biographers who are concerned to separate received myth from reality and true motive from convenient rationalization must
infer answers from the subject's speeches, infrequent writings, his actions and
reactions, and the comments and responses of others.

Simple explanations for the behavior of complicated, multifaceted personalities are to be distrusted. But, now and again in an examination of Rhodes,
a glimmer of some central light is refracted through the prism of previous
obscurity. The Confession and the wills are important, as are many of his
rambling reflections to constituents and friends. In the late 1880s a sense of
his inner self—of internal coherence amid accusations of traitorous behavior—was revealed at the end of the long, pro-Bond speech in parliament in
favor of limiting the African franchise. Rhodes' own words speak to more
than a defiance of convention and expectation. Possessed by a vision which by
the use of poetic imagery he may genuinely have believed transcended mere
expediency, Rhodes placed himself amid the ranks of those great men of the
past who served humanity by espousing unpopular views or seeking impossible goals well in advance of their compatriots.

"I have been styled a free lance . . . ," he told the House, "but I have
the satisfaction of knowing that in the disorganised state of this [place], I can
come down session after session with an object and an idea. To express it
more clearly, it is as if I were a little sailing-boat on Table Bay, and knew
exactly what port I am aiming for. . . . I know exactly what I am after. I
have got my interest in this country, I have my mining speculations, I have
my interest in its future, and coupled with all this, I am a member of the
House. Every year I can come down here and work at my problem.

"It took me fifteen years to get a mine," he continued, "but I got it. Though
my boat may be slow in the race, I know exactly what I am starting for. There
are honourable members opposite who have racing-boats, but I dare to challenge them, and to say that they do not know what ports they are sailing for;
and though they may be manned with a smarter crew, what with their backing
and filling, I am not sure they will not scuttle and go to the bottom. I have an
object, and I can wait to carry it out," Rhodes said with meaning and great
feeling. Although separated from his usual friends on the question of franchise, he said that he was fighting for his principles.

Rhodes explained himself. "It has been my lot in this life to travel through
many regions of this country, and it has been my fortune to see a solitary
springbok separated from the herd. I have often pitied his feelings and wondered how he works out the day; but I have a sort of idea that the time comes

when he returns to his old associates, and perhaps the temporary dissociation will have strengthened the original ties."[32]

Rhodes could wait and devise a way to carry out his objects. He disliked being separated from any band of brothers, but there sometimes were higher objects. If necessary, he would wander as a solitary springbok, but unlike the antelope which, when thrust out of the herd, is usually on his own, Rhodes suspected that his own isolation from the mainstream would be temporary only. For he had a star to steer his sole ship by, and a destination (really several destinations) that he was determined to reach by one or multiple navigational means.

"Giving a Man the Whole of Australia"
Employing the Sinews of War
in the North

LOBENGULA BECAME king of the Ndebele (Matabele) six months before Rhodes landed in Africa to grow cotton. In 1870 their paths were distant; neither they nor anyone else could have imagined that within a quarter-century the slim white youth with the abstracted air would grow rich and ruthless, destroy the imposing king's power, take his kingdom, and be the instrument of his death. Even if Ndebele clairvoyants guessed as early as 1870 that their conquest state would before long collide with the expanding white empire in Africa, they could not have supposed that a fortune based on the accumulation of diamonds and gold, when combined with and fed by grandiose personal visions, would result so rapidly in its and their undoing. Nor was Rhodes, as much as he contemplated and conjectured about the north, consumed by desire for Ndebeleland, or even terribly interested in its specific character and aware of Lobengula's existence, before the mid-1880s. Until then Rhodes was establishing himself and his fortune and molding his adult personality.

Before the mid-1880s he lacked the confidence and the means with which to extend his reach to the farthest limits of his imperial, territorial, power-seeking dreams. Moreover, in the 1870s the European scramble for Africa was still tentative, if discernible and real. A decade later, after the conclusion of the Congress of Berlin in 1885, the occupation of Africa was on every national agenda, the Germans had injected themselves as a third, worrisome, alien factor in contention for southern Africa, and Rhodes had utilized his manipulative skills for sub-imperial objectives in Stellaland, Goshen, and Bechuanaland. The Rhodes factor was a crucial added component among the rush of events that were to overwhelm Lobengula and the Ndebele. Moreover, his personal intervention in and acceleration of what was to become the conquest of Central Africa was planned and pursued during those very few years when Rhodes, with a burst of sustained creativity, was also amalgamating diamonds, gaining gold, preparing for political supremacy, and recovering from the loss of a great personal love and transferring his affections to a second, long-term companion.

Rhodes was a formidable figure in southern Africa in the late 1880s. So was Lobengula. As the quasi-authoritarian head of a tightly centralized, strategically stratified state that a few decades before had established itself through military prowess as the dominant indigenous polity between the Limpopo and Zambezi Rivers, and sometimes north of the Zambezi as well, Lobengula was Central Africa's premier chief. Mzilikazi, his father, had been a feared and despotic warrior leader who, as the head of the Khumalo, a minor Nguni-speaking clan, had helped Shaka create and consolidate the great kingdom of the Zulu after 1818. A few years later, after quarreling with Shaka over the spoils from one or more raids, Mzilikazi took his comparatively limited company of warriors across the Drakensberg Mountains onto the high plains of what became the Transvaal. Amassing cattle, women, and tribute from sanguinary warfare against the militarily weak Tswana and the northern Sotho or Pedi, Mzilikazi's legions reigned supreme near what is now Pretoria until Coloured cattle raiders and Afrikaner trekkers began to contest the Ndebele for hegemony on the highveld after 1829. The Ndebele, with their innovative assegais, or short stabbing spears, their irruptive, non-traditional military tactics and formations, and their martial confidence, easily overwhelmed the agriculturalists, who were accustomed to defending their homes with throwing spears and less sustained combat. But they found themselves disadvantaged when faced first by the guns of the Korana and Griqua, freebooters of mixed background from south of the Vaal River, and then by Boers. These more modernized men also attacked on horseback, which added to Ndebele vulnerability. There were renewed clashes with the Zulu in the 1830s, too. Yet the Ndebele devastated Tswana-controlled areas that now comprise the Transvaal-Botswana borderlands, having moved their center of operations there in the early 1830s before skirmishing with the first trekking parties of Boers.

The paramountcy of the Ndebele in the Transvaal came to an end in 1837, as a result of a week-long battle with Henrik Potgieter and 300 Afrikaners. These better-armed foreigners compelled the Ndebele, as they in turn had earlier compelled the Tswana, to leave the fertile plains for lower-lying lands on the edge of the Kalahari desert. There most of the Tswana settled. But Mzilikazi's people, coming after them and propelled by the realities of white interference, undertook their own long march. Mzilikazi led the warriors west as far as Lake Ngami and then northeast, to the Zambezi River, before rejoining the bulk of his people (who had traversed the northern Transvaal and then crossed the Limpopo River with their cattle) at a settlement on the pasturelands near modern Bulawayo. Sometime about 1838 the Ndebele established a new, permanent capital at nearby Gbulawayo.

Although the densely populated core of the kingdom then and later included the forty towns of the warrior regiments into which Mzilikazi had divided his realm, and the whole was contained within a cramped forty-mile radius from Gbulawayo, the writ of the Ndebele ran throughout nearly all of modern Zimbabwe, much of northern Botswana, and up and across the Zambezi to encompass much of western Zambia west and south of the Kafue River. The Tswana and nearly all of the different Shona groups were subjugated during the 1830s and 1840s, and paid tribute thereafter. The humbling of the Lozi and Ila in Zambia came later and was frequently episodic; the Tonga of Zambia were vulnerable and always feared the wrath of the onrushing Ndebele.

If the Ndebele nation began small, no more than a few hundred warriors having broken away from the Zulu with Mzilikazi, the addition of refugees from the Mfecane (the Zulu diaspora), others dissatisfied with Shaka, captives, and concubines soon swelled its size. During the long march the Ndebele probably numbered a few thousand. After establishing itself in what is now southwestern Zimbabwe, it included more than 10,000 individuals. By the 1880s forty regiments staffed an army of 15,000 to 20,000, and the total population of the predatory entity was more than 100,000.

Capable of growing by plunder and incorporation, the Ndebele fashioned a strong state where regionalism, separatism, and subversion were contained by the promotion of kingship as a unifying social, religious, economic, and political principle. Nevertheless, the king, certainly in Lobengula's time, lived more by his wits and political sagacity than by the sheer force of autocracy. Decisions were his to make, and judicial-like judgments his to render, but the induna (or advisors and councillors) met with him and offered opinions. Cattle collected in raids were the king's by right, but they were in practice his primarily to distribute in the form of patronage. After Mzilikazi's death in 1868, and a brief internal war of succession, the leading induna chose a reluctant Lobengula, then a young and sheltered son of the first chief, as the king's successor.[1]

Lobengula's was a troubled, if powerful and important, inheritance. No indigenous state between the Limpopo and Lake Victoria was as feared—by whites and blacks alike—for its military prowess or as respected for its administrative efficiency and overall cohesion. The Ndebele in the 1880s were regionally dominant among Africans, albeit the increasing availability of rifles in the hands of their erstwhile subject peoples was beginning to limit the range of the kingdom's unquestioned hegemony. But the major cause for concern among the Ndebele, and especially Lobengula and the leading induna, was the marshaling of white power on the southern borders of the kingdom. Mzilikazi had confronted white avarice, and wisely turned away. Yet other whites, if not the land-hungry trekkers, followed. Missionaries came and began to preach the gospel. Elephant hunters, ivory buyers, traders of trinkets and piece goods, and adventurers crowded Gbulawayo. Labor recruiters also arrived, and from 1876 a few Ndebele traveled to Kimberley and other mining areas to labor for whites. Prospectors came, too, for there were rumors of gold and other precious minerals.

Mzilikazi welcomed visits from Robert Moffat, the doyen of southern African missionaries from 1829. He later permitted John Smith Moffat, the first Moffat's son, to open a station of the Congregationalist London Missionary Society at Inyati in 1859. But Mzilikazi, and later Lobengula, curtailed the freedom and access of these first missionaries and their successors; unlike Kgama, paramount chief of the Ngwato Tswana, the Ndebele kings eschewed outright cooperation and were loath to encourage the wholesale Christianization of their country. As a result, the church accomplished little before the era of Rhodes; instead, the missionaries worked quietly but effectively for the overthrow of what they regarded as a brutal indigenous tyranny.

The despoilers of elephants, and those who killed for sport, were permitted to operate in the kingdom from 1853. Later the Ndebele kings gathered ivory and ostrich feathers and traded for themselves, but neither Lobengula nor his father used their commodity monopolies systematically to enrich themselves or their kingdom, or as barter for vast supplies of guns. A small knot of white traders began to live more or less permanently around Lobengula's capital in the 1880s, but they were all dependent upon the king's whim and avarice, and on their ability to purchase protection with bribes, until Rhodes focused his energies on their situation.

Over all of these early intruders, Lobengula exerted a firm control throughout the 1870s and 1880s. As he checked the more headstrong and antagonistic of his xenophobic warriors, so he restrained the cupidity of the whites. He chose not to exclude them entirely, however, for, like the foreigners in Theodorus' Ethiopia, they could be used. They introduced the inventions, notions, and customs of the West to the Ndebele. The availability of guns, blankets, tools, and the gospel ended the kingdom's isolation and self-sufficiency. The presence of these diverse whites also provided Lobengula with a window on the activities of the white nations and peoples to the south.

Lobengula doubtless knew that the whites who lived with him and spoke his language, and those who visited for profit or curiosity, were but the leading edge of white expansion. How it would or could be contained, channeled, or thwarted were concerns which perplexed, disturbed, and ultimately convulsed the kingdom. But, Rhodes or not, there was no escape from the press of whites. Rhodes determined whom and how, and to a minor extent when, but not why. That was answered by geographical location—by Ndebeleland's proximity to the goldfields of the Transvaal—by the thrust of the Germans and the pretensions of the Portuguese, by the failure of Sir Bartle Frere and Lord Carnarvon to confederate or otherwise unify South Africa, and by the inexorable spread in the 1880s and 1890s of white capital and white conquest from one end of Africa to the other. That Rhodes was the instrument of this concatenation of circumstance, as well as its molder and shaper, is clear. Moreover, the fact that Rhodes gained Ndebeleland and the adjacent country of the Shona for a chartered company as well as the Crown, and most of all for himself, determined the peculiar nature and lasting bitterness of Lobengula's demise and indigenous central Africa's incorporation into the Empire.

Rhodes was not the first to covet Lobengula's domain. After Carl Mauch

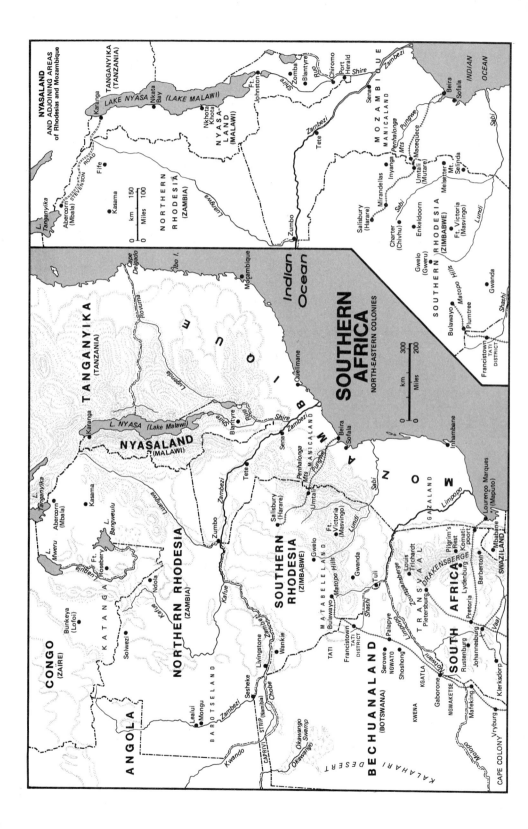

NYASALAND
AND ADJOINING AREAS
of Rhodesias and Mozambique

TANGANYIKA
(TANZANIA)

Karanga
LAKE NYASA (LAKE MALAWI)
Nkata Bay

Nkhota Khota

NYASA-
LAND
(MALAWI)

Ft.
Johnston
Zomba
Blantyre
Chiromo
Port Herald
Ft. Herald
L. Shire
Chiromo
RUO
Shire

Zambezi
Senac
MOZAMBIQUE
Beira
Sofala
INDIAN OCEAN

Fife
STEVENSON ROAD

Abercorn
(Mbala)
L. Tanganyika

Kasama

NORTHERN RHODESIA
(ZAMBIA)

km 150 100
Miles

Luangwa

Tete
Zambezi

Zumbo

MANICALAND
Penhalonga
Mts
Pungwe
Macequece
Umtali
(Mutare)
Inyanga
Mirandellas
Melsetter
Mt.
Selinda

MOZAMBIQUE

Salisbury
(Harare)

Charter
(Chivhu)
Enkeldoorn
Ft. Victoria
(Masvingo)

Gwelo
(Gweru)

SOUTHERN RHODESIA (ZIMBABWE)

Sabi

Lundi

SOUTHERN RHODESIA

Matopo Hills
Bulawayo
Plumtree
Gwanda
Shashi

Francistown
TATI
DISTRICT

SOUTHERN AFRICA
NORTH-EASTERN COLONIES

Indian Ocean

Cape Delgado
Ibo I.

Mopambique

TANGANYIKA
(TANZANIA)

Rovuma

Lugenda

L. NYASA (Lake Malawi)
Karanga

NYASALAND
(MALAWI)

Blantyre
Ruo
Shire
Senac
Zambezi
Beira
Sofala

Quelimane

Tete
Penhalonga
Mts MANICALAND
Pungwe
Umtali

MOZAMBIQUE

Inhambane

km 300 200
Miles

L. Tanganyika

Abercorn
(Mbala)

Kasama

L. Mweru
Ft. Roseberry

Luangwa

Zumbo

Zambezi

Salisbury
(Harare)

Ft. Victoria
(Masvingo)

Lundi

Sabi

GAZALAND

Lourenço Marques
(Maputo)

Bunkeya
(Lofoi)

KATANGA

Solwezi
Ndola

L.
Bangweulu

NORTHERN RHODESIA
(ZAMBIA)

Kafue

Kafue

Gwelo

SOUTHERN RHODESIA
(ZIMBABWE)

MATABELELAND
Bulawayo
Matopo Hills
Gwanda
Tuli
Shashi

TRANSVAAL
Zoutpansberg
Louis
Trichardt
Pietersburg

DRAKENSBERG
Pilgrim's
Rest
Lydenburg
Komati-
poort

Mbabane

SWAZILAND

CONGO
(ZAIRE)

L.
Mweru

Eden

ANGOLA

Lealui
Mongu

BAROTSELAND

Livingstone
Wankie
Sesheke

Zambezi

CAPRIVI
STRIP (Namibia)

Chobe
Kwando

Okavango
Swamp

Okavango

KALAHARI DESERT

BECHUANALAND
(BOTSWANA)

Serowe
NGWATO
Shoshong
Palapye

TATI
Francistown
TATI
DISTRICT

Limpopo

KWENA
Gaborone
KGATLA
NGWAKETSE
Mafeking

Vryburg

CAPE COLONY

SOUTH AFRICA
Pretoria
Rustenburg
Johannesburg
Klerksdorp

Barberton

Vaal

Limpopo

and Henry Hartley traveled there in the late 1860s, and came back calling it the true land of the biblical Ophir—so rich were the territories of the Ndebele and Shona imagined to be in payable gold—a rabble of prospectors clamored for permission from Lobengula to dig and explore. Even after steady disappointment, relieved only in the 1880s by marginal successes in the Tati district south of Ndebeleland, the promise of Ophir continued to entice the mining community of the south.

There were diplomatic overtures, too. In 1878 Frere, high commissioner in South Africa, attempted to establish friendly relations with Lobengula. But his primary emissary died when returning from the king's country. Before Rhodes, the main approaches by whites were from Portugal and the Transvaal. Although Portugal traded with the great Shona empire of Mwanamutapa in the seventeenth and eighteenth centuries, by the 1870s its presence in the region was limited to small outposts along the Zambezi River, and a few rundown prazos, or plantations, in the lowveld that drained into the Zambezi. Yet, on historical grounds, the Portuguese felt entitled to claim all of the Limpopo-Zambezi hinterlands as a portion of a vast swath of territory from the Atlantic to the Indian Ocean. The case for the Transvaal was as easy to make: as the number of whites increased and their cattle and sheep sought new pastures, the Boers would naturally want to cross the confining Limpopo and settle among and later displace the Shona and their Ndebele overlords. The Germans had a potential interest, too, but of equal importance after 1885 was the new British protectorate over much of Bechuanaland. The fact that its northern boundary at first was the twenty-second parallel (to avoid arguing with the Ndebele), created a further incentive for Rhodes and new worries for Lobengula.

By the mid-1880s, Rhodes was only one—and the least overt and least fully committed—of the many Ophir-attracted Britons and Boers who were seeking ways to importune Lobengula and his induna and insert themselves or their patrons into the presumed Ndebele honey pot. As yet Rhodes' plans for the north, however, remained vague and unfocused. In 1877 he had promised to render himself useful to England by furthering the British Empire and by bringing "the whole uncivilized world under British rule. . . ." Africa, he declared, was "lying ready for us." It was his and Britain's "duty to take it." A few months later, in the second of his formal wills, Rhodes instructed his executors to establish a secret society, the objects of which were to be the extension of British rule and the occupation by British settlers "of the entire continent of Africa." When the young Rhodes gathered a group of friends and acquaintances around a rough dinner table in Kimberley and told the startled assembly of his life's plan, he warned them that it was "mainly the extension of the Empire northward that we have to watch and work for in South Africa." In the next year, while walking with Sidney Shippard in the Christ Church meadows in Oxford, he "sketched out the whole plan of British advance in South and Central Africa." Jameson also dated the origin of Rhodes' focus on Central Africa to 1878.[2]

But there is no good contemporary evidence that Rhodes turned his attention to the trans-Limpopo region, or tried to inform himself about the Ndebele or the Shona, before the mid-1880s. Only after the designs of the Transvaal and the unexpected arrival of the Germans concentrated his concerns did the unfolding of events point him decisively northwards. Furthermore, dreamer though he was, Rhodes was also influenced in the direction of his thinking by the ideas and suggestions of others. That he intuitively understood as early as the 1870s that the natural outlet for British and Cape Colony expansion would follow the missionary road through the lands of the Tswana to the Zambezi is evident; that he had devised a mental map of this expansion, or that he had defined particular objectives in his own mind, is unlikely and hardly in keeping with his character and method of operation. Only the onrush of conflicting interests which ultimately quieted the tempest in Stellaland and Goshen, and led to the protection of southern Bechuanaland, turned Rhodes in the precise direction of the lands which later carried his name.

Not until 1885, when Rhodes had battled General Warren to a standstill and, with the important assistance of Hercules Robinson, had contrived to keep open the "Suez Canal" to the north, did his ambitions specifically encompass the Ndebele and Shona territories. Only after lengthy conversations with Ralph Williams and Edward Maund did he begin to appreciate how much of an obstacle Lobengula could be to the realization of his evolving designs for a central African dominion.

Both Williams and Maund were attached to Warren's expeditionary force, and Maund was also writing reports for *The Times*. In Vryburg, while Rhodes and the others awaited Warren's arrival, they had ample opportunity to talk. Rhodes made a lasting impact on both men, Williams rapidly becoming a convert, although Maund, for a few years at least, resisted Rhodes' charm and magnetism. "When I first met Rhodes," recalled Maund many years later, "he lived in a tin shanty of corrugated iron about 18 feet by 10 feet. . . . I expected to meet an austere middle-aged don-like man. Instead I was met by a big loose jointed fellow in shirtsleeves well curled up looking for all the world like a young farmer with a pleasant sun-burnt face and inquisitive blue eyes, and yet with a bit of a grim look about the mouth, as he rather snapped out: 'Well what do you want?' "

Lieutenant Maund was in uniform, and hesitated to enter Rhodes' hovel. It was the "acme of discomfort and untidyness." There were papers strewn on a desk and many empty soda-water bottles on the floor in the opposite corner. Maund saw no Cape brandy or gin, but doubtless there were bottles under Rhodes' bed, for, when he offered Maund a chair, he also blurted out: "Have a drink." He was full of invective until Maund hinted that he, like Rhodes, was a Mason. That changed Rhodes' manner. "He became thoughtful and calm and friendly." After learning that Maund had even visited Rhodes' own Masonic lodge in Oxford from his in Cambridge, Rhodes "left the desk, grasped [Maund's] hand and with a face wreathed in smiles said, 'splendid.' "[3]

Williams claimed that Rhodes' attention was directed toward the area of modern Zimbabwe because of what he perceived to be threats from Germany as well as the Transvaal. There was the new colony of Südwest Afrika, and Rhodes was also worried by the renewed explorations of Emil Holub, a German-speaking Bohemian who had demonstrated an uncanny interest in trans-Zambezia. Rhodes may have suspected—wrongly—that Holub was in German pay, when in reality he was a self-motivated ethnographer and traveler.

Williams suggested that Rhodes, like Holub in some ways, was originally more interested in the far interior—in the lake regions of Tanzania and Uganda—and became obsessed with Lobengula's realm only as a necessary early prelude to a broader and more audacious assault on Africa as a whole. In mid-1885, Rhodes was "not fully alive to the resources of Matabeleland and Mashonaland." Yet he knew that those regions were healthier than the "fever-stricken" country of northern Botswana, and understood that a railway might be built along the high and healthy ridge which traversed the Limpopo-Zambezi regions. The railway, he wrote to Williams, would tap the trade of the great lakes of inner Africa from the south (Sir William Mackinnon had not yet planned the rail line from Mombasa to Lake Victoria) and would also bar Germans from crossing the consequent British spine of Africa and linking their Southwest and East African colonies. "As you are aware," he reminded Williams, "this is the object of all my endeavours." Rhodes fully recognized that "the best chance of tapping the lake system of central Africa" was through the Cape Colony. The extension of British influence "worked in accordance with the sentiment of . . . [Britain]" could not be achieved, he said, without the help of the "much despised Cape politicians."[4]

When Rhodes, Williams, and Maund talked in Vryburg none of the three had yet crossed the Limpopo. But Williams and Maund knew more about the area, from their conversations with others, than did Rhodes. They told him of the supposed gold of Ndebeleland and of Lobengula's vast influence over the peoples who lived between the two great rivers. Fortunately, too, a few months after the meeting with Rhodes, Warren dispatched Maund to convey official British greetings to, and to discern the true state of Lobengula's king-dom. Upon his return, Maund claimed to have found abundant evidence of gold, confirming the earlier tales. He had heard about ancient diggings, and assumed that they were hints of a modern bonanza. Maund also told Warren that Lobengula could probably be persuaded to accept British protection in lieu of a new Boer invasion. If not, Maund thought that the Ndebele could be subdued without too much difficulty. A mere 1500 mounted men with modern weapons could, Maund said, oust the predominantly spear-wielding Ndebele. (Maund estimated that the Ndebele possessed only 600 to 800 old-fashioned breech-loading rifles and carbines and 6,000 to 7,000 rounds of ammunition.)

This was the opinion, too, of Major Samuel H. Edwards, who led Maund's expedition as an emissary of Shippard. Edwards' task was to inform Loben-gula of the annexation of Bechuanaland and to observe. Edwards agreed that the military strength of the Ndebele was diminishing and, therefore, that Lobengula's bargaining position had depreciated. Edwards and Maund may have arrived at a time when Ndebele war prowess was temporarily at an ebb; nevertheless, Edwards' report helped to persuade Shippard and, along with Maund's views, Rhodes that the kingdom of the Ndebele was tottering on weak if not broken legs. Maund also glowed with praise for the country. He "knew of no country better adapted for European colonization." It had wood, water, gold, and iron in abundance.[5]

Rhodes' earliest clear statement of his ambitions for what was to become Rhodesia appeared in *The Times* in late 1885. It drew on Maund's report of his visit, the gist of which was conveyed by Maund to Rhodes in London in late October 1885. Rhodes called the Ndebele the most powerful tribe between the Cape and the Zambezi, and urged Britain to make arrangements with Lobengula to preserve the road to his kingdom and beyond. Rhodes asserted that Ndebeleland possessed ample trade opportunities, pastoral resources, and vast mineral wealth, and that the climate was good and free of malaria. He advocated the opening of relations with Lobengula and the extension of the brand new Bechuanaland Protectorate to the Zambezi, that is, through and beyond the territory controlled by the Ndebele.[6] How Britain should accomplish such a vast acquisition was hardly suggested; Rhodes doubtless was writing more as a dreamer than an architect grasping a refined blueprint.

Rhodes soon returned from Britain, and from this time—early 1886—the question of Ndebeleland was never far from his thoughts. "The only thing we have now to work for," he wrote Shippard in January, "is that the Germans shall not take Matabeleland." Explaining that the Tories would remain in power for at least a few years, and that there would be no anti-colonial resurgence of Liberal power, their own work remained "with the interim to see we do not get shut in by the Germans cutting cross our path."[7]

In fact, the independence of Ndebeleland was menaced more by other British gold seekers, Portuguese diplomatic draftsmen, and the canny calculations of President Kruger's Transvaal, than by the Germans. Throughout the balance of 1886 and the first half of 1887, the attention of Rhodes, nearly all the other prominent Cape entrepreneurs, the burghers of the Cape and the Transvaal, and the bourses of the world were focused on the Witwatersrand, where the globe's most extensive seams of gold were being found. It followed, particularly since Mauch, Hartley, the artist Thomas Baines, Maund, and innumerable other visitors had already extolled the auriferoid quartz reefs of the trans-Limpopo region, that Lobengula sat astride equally rich lands. "On my next visit to the King," Lieutenant (later Sir) Frank Johnson recalled a visit in early 1887, "I found about fifty women dancing before him, so we squatted for three hours pending His Majesty's condescension to notice us. . . . I gave some of the presents I had brought for him. . . . He protested that there was no gold in his country. 'How do you know there is gold here?' " he asked. Maurice Heany, Johnson's partner in prospecting, explained that Baines had said that there was gold. "Further, there was gold in the Transvaal, Swazieland and the Tati; it followed by the laws of Nature that there must be gold in the Mashona country." "The King," reported Johnson, ". . . did not grasp the point of our geological arguments."

Johnson, a youth of twenty-one who had already served with General Warren and in the Bechuanaland Border Police, and had become general manager of the Bechuanaland Exploration Co., Ltd., reported that Lobengula "was an enormous but majestic figure of a man, with his waxed head-ring and a plume of crane's feathers. Naked apart from some skins hanging from his waist, he yet maintained a regal appearance." Looking "every inch a king," Lobengula "had a fondness for food and drink." He consumed "enormous meals of half-cooked meat, washed down with plenty of Kafir beer." John Cooper-Chadwick, a British soldier and traveler who lived near the king during the period, described Lobengula as "over six feet in height, but . . . so enormously fat that it makes him look smaller, though his proud bearing and stately walk give him all the appearance of a savage king. His features are coarse, and exhibit great cunning and cruelty; but when he smiles the expression completely changes, and makes his face appear pleasant and good-tempered."

As far as Johnson could tell, Lobengula in 1887 "possessed a native shrewdness and abilities of no common order. He had a force of character and was a good judge of his fellow men." Lobengula confessed that he failed to understand "this digging for gold." There was no place in his heartland where whites could dig for gold. But he promised to look for such a place, and regretted that Johnson and Heany (and so many others) had "come so far for nothing." According to Johnson, the king wanted to give him a concession to search for gold—rival concession hunters led by a German called Schultz, and Joseph Garbett Wood, William Cecil Francis, and Edward Chapman from Grahamstown having lost patience and returned the way they had come or gone hunting—but his induna were bitterly opposed. They argued rightly that if one white were allowed in, Ndebeleland would soon be overrun.

By mid-July 1887, Johnson, Heany, and Harry Borrow had waited for two months on the king's pleasure, and tactfully sought his permission. Finally, Johnson offered Lobengula £100 to prospect and £200 a year in the future. "You are troublesome people," the king replied, "for when I say there is no gold in my country you do not believe me. . . . How can you find gold in rivers? Gold is found in stones. You speak good words now, but after this there will be trouble." Finally, after endless meetings with his induna, Lobengula relented a little, permitting Johnson to look for gold along the Mazoe River, north of Harare. Two months later Johnson indeed struck gold in the Mazoe, "finding gold in every panful taken from the river." Traveling 300 miles along the Mazoe and its tributaries, Johnson found 124 traces of alluvial gold, all exploitable.[8] These confirmations of the older tales, when retailed in Kimberley and the Cape, added to the luster of Lobengula's land. So would Johnson's tales of the king's rapacity have fed legends of his tyranny and magnified his presumed importance.

Even before Johnson's return to Bechuanaland and the Cape, Shippard spoke grandly and persuasively of the country beyond the Limpopo. The whole of the land that lay north of the Bechuanaland Protectorate as far as the Zambezi and east as far as the Portuguese holdings was fabulously fertile and rich in gold. The future of greater South Africa would depend on the possession of these dominions, and Delagoa Bay—a "future San Francisco"—could be its port. "The Power that can acquire that territory . . . will hold the key of the wealth and commerce of South and Central Africa," he said. "The whole would support itself, and thus hardly cost the British Treasury a penny. And what would happen to the Ndebele? Their warlike members would be compelled to emigrate beyond the Zambezi, and their former domain as well as their former subjects would be the better for such a change."[9]

Shippard, speaking for the northernmost salient of the empire in southern Africa, was not alone. The leaders of the Transvaal agreed that the key to the north was the acquisition of the lands of the Ndebele. Hemmed in to the west as they were by the protocols of the London Convention, which also curtailed their expansion to the east, they could only look north. Once the discovery of gold south of Pretoria had begun to ease the republic's precarious financial position, its leaders could also contemplate adventures that were both speculative and diplomatically bold. Thus Kruger initiated or approved an overture to Lobengula which, coming unexpectedly, was designed to anticipate and frustrate any similar moves by the Cape or Britain.

Pieter Johannes Grobler, an experienced trader in horses and other commodities, who knew the interior, was Kruger's instrument. Mzilikazi and the Transvaal had concluded a treaty of commerce and friendship in 1853, and Lobengula had been reminded by the Transvaal in 1882 that the Afrikaners and Ndebele were brothers.

At the end of July 1887, Lobengula and four induna affixed their names to a seven-part agreement (drafted by Kruger personally) which bound the Transvaal and the Ndebele to "perpetual peace and friendship." It acknowledged Lobengula as an independent chief and declared him to be "an ally of the South African Republic." Lobengula promised to assist the Republic with troops whenever called upon, to extradite offenders to the Republic, to permit Transvaalers holding passes from their government to hunt or trade in his country, and to accept a resident consul with powers to try offenders from the Republic. Grobler gave Lobengula £140 in cash, as well as a rifle and some ammunition, and Lobengula sent ivory to Kruger with Grobler. The treaty implied that Lobengula was a vassal of the Republic; at least that was a common interpretation, especially during those many months when Grobler's accomplishment was known in Kimberley and Cape Town more by word of mouth than by document. Grobler's treaty could also be construed as an offensive and defensive alliance. Certainly it was meant to be and had the effect of being an obstacle to the pretensions of others in this desirable northern region.

It mattered little to Rhodes, then or later, that the Grobler treaty was suspect—that the induna who signed it had odd-sounding names and unusual signatures and that on the white side the only signatories were Grobler and his brother. The document lacked the customary affirmations by two independent white witnesses. Lobengula may simply have given his consent under the impression that Grobler was asking him to sign a copy of an old friendship agreement, for the king could neither read nor write. A subsequent critic concluded that Lobengula could not have known to what he was committing his kingdom—especially clauses putting the Ndebele fighting forces at the disposal of Boer commandants and giving extra-territorial rights to a foreign consul.[10] This is a correct analysis, however the treaty was obtained, or if it were obtained, but Rhodes could not afford to test it or argue about its authenticity. The Grobler mission started a flow of adrenalin.

Rhodes took Grobler's accomplishment very seriously, especially after receiving a secret and urgent message of alarm from Ralph Williams in mid-December 1887. By that time Williams had become Her Majesty's Agent, or consul, in Pretoria. His duties were to observe the doings of the Afrikaners, to remind them of their obligations under the London Convention and, unofficially, to serve as Rhodes' as well as Hercules Robinson's eyes and ears. Williams was playing cricket one afternoon under the summer sun when a note from a merchant in the capital city summoned him urgently from the pitch. Williams strolled into the private office behind the merchant's store, closed the door, and asked: "What is it?" The merchant told Williams to look out the window. "Do you see that man out there loading his wagon? That man is . . . Grobler. He is starting to-morrow . . . to try and revive an old half-promise alleged by the Boers to have been made many years ago to General [P.J.] Joubert, to the effect that if any rights were in future granted to any white man over Matabele territory, they should be granted to the Boers and not to the English. If that mission succeeds there is an end of British expansion to the north."[11]

Grobler was off again to Gbulawayo to become the Transvaal's first emissary to the Ndebele. Had he taken up such a post, it could well have curtailed British expansion across the Limpopo.[12] Fortunately for Rhodes, John Smith Moffat had just arrived in Gbulawayo as Shippard's emissary. After leaving mission service in 1884 to become assistant commissioner for Bechuanaland, Moffat helped Shippard establish the new administration of the British protectorate. Fluent in Setswana and conversant with Sindebele, a language he had spoken during boyhood, Moffat was well known to the king and his induna. In an atmosphere of heightening interest in Lobengula's dominion, Shippard—possibly having heard rumors of Grobler, and possibly because of his and Rhodes' sense that the situation was fluid—dispatched Moffat to Gbulawayo to discuss the boundary between the countries of Kgama and Lobengula, which included the disputed Tati district. Moffat's visit also followed the dispatch of a letter from Shippard in which Shippard warned Lobengula to grant no concessions for prospecting, grazing, or other purposes to non-Britons without consulting Moffat.

Moffat talked at length with Lobengula. "I think he wants to be left alone," Moffat reported to Shippard. The king vociferously denied having placed himself under the protection of the Transvaal. A few weeks later, Moffat indicated that Lobengula had been "so worried with importunities during the last 12 months . . . that he turns away from any approach [such as a treaty], . . . and no wonder." Yet Williams' report (as well as one probably from Alois Nellmapius and Beit) had galvanized Rhodes, and he in turn had pressed the situation's urgency on Robinson, the high commissioner.

Fortunately for Rhodes, the message from Williams found him in Kimberley. Summoning Shippard from his headquarters in Vryburg, and learning that Robinson was then on a ceremonial visit to Grahamstown to help celebrate the Queen's jubilee, together they raced there as quickly as the conveyances of the day could carry them. Sympathetic to Rhodes' cries of alarm, Robinson also knew how suspiciously Lord Salisbury's government viewed new commitments and entanglements, even in so locally important a sphere as Ndebeleland. He was also aware that Lord Salisbury and the civil servants who ran the Colonial and Foreign offices would have a very different perception than he would of the strategic value of Lobengula's country. The metropolitan officials had a global, Eurocentric sense of the game. Rhodes, however, was playing for high stakes on a regional board where he, alone of the many competitors, was possessed both of a keen sense of the diverse tactical realities and of the means to influence the ultimate contest.

Robinson may not have easily been persuaded, for he was loyal to Whitehall. But, like so many nineteenth-century men-on-the-spot, his long service in the Cape, his alliance with Rhodes as the most far-seeing and successful of the new magnates of South Africa, and his own belief, which he shared with Rhodes, that Ndebeleland should and was destined to become British, predisposed him to accept a compromise which was less than the establishment of the protectorate that Rhodes wanted and more than the total non-involvement that London would probably have wished. This was imperialism on the march. On the day after Christmas, 1887, Robinson authorized Shippard to instruct Moffat to persuade Lobengula to sign a treaty acknowledging Britain's predominant influence in the countries of the Ndebele and the Shona.[13]

Telegraph lines had not then been constructed beyond Vryburg. Rhodes and Shippard thus had to send these new instructions by a mounted messenger who rode the 700 miles with such alacrity that they reached Moffat by the end of January. Rhodes also added a further option. John Larkin Fry spoke Zulu and worked for the De Beers Company in Kimberley. Once Moffat had arranged an accord of amity with Lobengula, Fry's task was to press the monarch for a general mining concession. Unfortunately, Fry was already deathly ill with a cancerous condition in his jaw, and had to halt his journey to Gbulawayo, returning to Kimberley, where he died. But Moffat was a sturdy and persuasive accomplice.

No white could have been more trusted by Lobengula than Moffat. He "pressed very earnestly upon [Lobengula] the importance of giving us some such assurance as we are asking of him, pointing out the advisability of it from every point of view. I went further in this way," he said, "than I might have done possibly had I been acting simply on my own judgement. . . ."[14] But Rhodes and Shippard wanted some documentation capable of countering the Grobler agreement. The missionaries, bereft of converts and beholden to a harried king and his capricious-acting court, were also anxious to alter their position of weakness. Moffat may also have suspected that the independence of Ndebeleland was coming to an end, by one means or another, and that its heir ought to be British rather than Boer.

With surprising alacrity, Moffat persuaded Lobengula in mid-February to acknowledge that the trans-Limpopo region was within Britain's sphere of influence. By the provision of the Moffat treaty, Lobengula agreed to refrain "from entering into any correspondence or treaty with any foreign State or Power to sell, alienate, or cede, or permit or countenance any sale, alienation or cession of the whole or any part of the said Amandabele country . . . without the previous knowledge and sanction of Her Majesty's High Commissioner for South Africa."[15] This was a simple affirmation of Lobengula's sovereignty and of his desire to be left alone. Moffat may have persuaded him that it would free him from the importunities of the Boers and others, and secure rather than limit his power. And so it did, but only in the short term. Certainly it committed Britain to little, and for that reason the Secretary of State for the Colonies permitted Robinson to accept the modest result, an assertion of influence without responsibility.

For Rhodes, Moffat's successful intervention was a critical achievement. It bought time at a crucial juncture when Rhodes was otherwise fully absorbed in the final process of amalgamating the diamond mines of Kimberley and in fashioning a broad trust deed to permit additional exploitations of the far interior. He had also obtained an open-ended arrangement with the Gold Fields' shareholders. "I am very glad you were so successful with Lobengula," Rhodes congratulated Shippard. "At any rate now no one else can step in." That was the main result. Rhodes also advised Shippard not to try to "move the Matabele over the [Zambezi] river." It was much better that the Ndebele should remain where they were as a buffer. Otherwise, wrote Rhodes wisely, "the whole country would be jumped from the Transvaal Republic."[16]

Rhodes moved to fill the resulting vacuum with no more than deliberate speed. Although most narratives rush headlong from the Moffat treaty to the Rudd concession, there was a six-month hiatus in Rhodes' assault on the north. The distance between Kimberley and Gbulawayo was great, and communications correspondingly slow. The better explanations for the delay are twofold: Rhodes was neither certain about the next step nor persuaded of its allcompelling urgency. Moreover, from February to August and September 1888, and even well into 1889, Rhodes was preoccupied by the postlude to Barnato's acquiescence. The amalgamation of the diamond mines, as already discussed, was achieved not by one or two all-night sittings but by a year-long campaign to buy out shareholders, outwit competitors, and withstand legal actions, and by the assiduous manipulation of the markets for company shares as well as diamonds. Rhodes negotiated all the while with Rothschild, too, whose concerns were many and onerous. Further, for at least a few months he thought that Fry would succeed in obtaining a mining concession, and after him, as another stopgap, Rhodes sent Ivon Fry, his son.

The ante was raised, and Rhodes was pushed—reluctantly—to greater creativity by the actions of others. News of the signing of the Moffat treaty intensified the already heightened interest of other British and colonial promoters, anxious as many were to profit from the continuing promise of the southern African minerals boom. Johnson and Heany, rebuffed by Lobengula, had obtained a mining concession from Kgama to 400 square miles of Ngwato territory. This prospecting grant Johnson and his sponsors sold to Francis I. Ricarde-Seaver, representing the Caisse des Mines of Paris, and Ricarde-Seaver promptly transferred these rights to George Cawston and Lord Gifford's Bechuanaland Exploration Company. Gifford won a Victoria Cross during the Ashanti War of 1873–74 and had served as colonial secretary in the imperial outposts of Western Australia and Gibraltar. He had fought with General Sir Garnet Wolseley in the campaign against the Zulu in Natal and had earlier attempted to gain prospecting privileges from Lobengula. Cawston, a shadowy London stockbroker, share-jobber, social climber, and cartographer, brought Gifford and Ricarde-Seaver together; along with other City brokers, including Mosenthal & Sons (who had a branch in Port Elizabeth) and Baron Henry de Rothschild, they registered the Bechuanaland Company in April 1888. When Cawston and Gifford learned of the Moffat treaty, they also incorporated an entity called the Exploring Company to extend their Bechuanaland operations into Ndebeleland and Shonaland. Its objects were the location and exploitation of gold and the construction of a railway from the Cape through Kgama's country toward the Zambezi.

Sir Charles Metcalfe, an engineer, was the force behind the ancillary railway part of the plan. Known to Rhodes from Oxford, Metcalfe was then linked genuinely with Cawston and Gifford, and had become an earnest advocate of the rail extension beyond Kimberley that Rhodes had separately, but only very recently, begun to believe necessary. Metcalfe dreamed of a trunk line from the Cape into the interior and, afterwards, of rails from the Cape to Cairo.

For Rhodes, the best defensive strategy was to mount an offensive. During his brief visit to Britain in June 1888 to discuss his diamond monopoly with Nathaniel Rothschild, Rhodes learned that Cawston and Gifford were moving rapidly to realize the aims of their two companies. In London, they had the ear of Lord Knutsford, the British colonial secretary, and others of influence. They had also employed Maund, who was trading on his supposed warm relationship with Lobengula, to go back to Gbulawayo in search of a solid prospecting and mining grant. Preparing quickly, and doubtless aware (as were Gifford and Cawston) of other entrepreneurial rivals, Maund reached Cape Town at the end of June and Kimberley in July. Metcalfe and John

Blue, another engineer, arrived in Cape Town shortly afterwards, and soon proceeded upcountry.

Their movements, the uncertainty surrounding the likely attitude of the British government, the titled and other influential connections of the Gifford-Cawston group, and a sense of accelerating momentum, all impelled Rhodes to prepare not one but several counterthrusts in order to protect his own newly aroused awareness of what was or could be at stake. Once again, Rhodes was reacting, keeping options open, utilizing and adapting the ideas and innovations of others, and turning events to his own advantage. He clearly was not acting over Lobengula's domain in accord with a grand tactical design that had been conceived long before.

Sir Hercules Robinson, governor and high commissioner, was a key factor in any defensive alliance. Already Robinson had come to regard Rhodes as the most far-seeing, resourceful, and resolute of the businessmen and politicians with whom Robinson, as the Queen's representative, had long been in touch. For Robinson, Rhodes was virtually unique in being a leader in both spheres as well as being personally magnetic. It is possible that Robinson was guided in his actions and opinions by the expectation of being rewarded handsomely by Rhodes; conceivably, Rhodes may have even dropped welcome hints or given Robinson substantial direct gifts. Certainly Robinson later benefited substantially by his connections with Rhodes, but Rhodes was always generous to those who furthered his plans, and, knowing how in accord Rhodes and Robinson had been for so long, it is unnecessary to taint the motives for Robinson's helpful cooperation in 1888–89 by assuming a mercenary incentive. They had already been working together closely; they believed in the same vision (at least, Rhodes had persuaded Robinson to share his own entrancing dream of the southern African future), and Robinson would, after eight years in Cape Town, have become more colonial than metropolitan in his sympathies and perspective. Thus, primed by Rhodes or not, it is hardly surprising that Robinson greeted Maund noncommittally, even coolly, in late June, and, beneath a cloak of impartiality, hedged when Metcalfe approached him a few weeks later. Rhodes' plans, Robinson told them both, also had to be considered. Robinson expressly sent Moffat back to Gbulawayo in July "to prevent Lo Bengula from making any more promises or concessions of any kind except such as may hereafter be expressly sanctioned by the High Commissioner."[17]

Sir Sidney Shippard was another important ally. Long a believer in Rhodes' aspirations, long a confidant, and a onetime sole executor of Rhodes' will, no other British official could have been better placed to further the diamond magnate's approach to Ndebeleland. Shippard was responsible for Bechuanaland to Robinson, through whom he reported, and with whom he and Rhodes had already cooperated to achieve the Moffat treaty. Although the Ngwato may have called Shippard *Marana-make,* the father of lies, he cut a striking figure as the Queen's deputy commissioner, and his word carried weight in Downing Street as well as with significant figures like Lobengula.

Backed by Robinson and Shippard, Rhodes in mid-1888 could compete on at least equal terms with other British competitors, no matter how advantaged the latter might have been through connections in the City and at the court. It is true that Rhodes was still little known in Britain. Lord Salisbury, the prime minister, later labeled him "rather a pro-Boer M.P. in South Africa, I fancy," and the responsible civil servants in the colonial and foreign offices were little better informed.[18] Cawston and Gifford were better acquainted with such circles, but Rhodes had achieved the cooperation and confidence of Nathaniel Rothschild, and was beginning to cultivate Rothschild's close relations.

Rhodes possessed a further advantage which even he may not have appreciated fully. Copying Cawston, or taking hints from Lord Knutsford and Sir Robert Herbert, a principal secretary in the colonial office, Rhodes understood that the British government would be partial to a company which proposed to pay the expenses of administering as well as exploiting the mineral riches of any new country like the one belonging to Lobengula. Three years before, Rhodes had rejected such a proposal by Merriman. Now, however, Salisbury and his Treasury were anxious to spend as little as possible on the occupation of Africa. "The Home Government will stand no expense," Rhodes explained to Shippard.[19] It favored the extension of empire by means of a chartered company, an expedient successfully employed to control India and to open up the Canadian West.

Chartered companies had been reintroduced by Gladstone's government when it empowered the British North Borneo Company to govern that Asian possession. In 1886, George Goldie employed this precedent to persuade Gladstone to charter the Royal Niger Company as Britain's official commercial and administrative agency in what was to become Nigeria. Backed by Britain, he was able to prevent French and German claims to the regions around the Niger and its tributaries from ousting his own. Two years later, a mere few months before Cawston, Gifford, and Rhodes all left London knowing that their sights were set on Lobengula's domain, Salisbury had decided to promote Britain's interests in East Africa, which was being contested primarily against the Germans, by giving Mackinnon's Imperial British East Africa Company an official license to manage the sphere north of Kilimanjaro and east of Lake Victoria on behalf of and for the Crown.

Imperialism on the cheap had always been the British way. In the 1880s, with so many overseas responsibilities, so many new demands, and so much caution and indecision on the part of the Treasury mandarins, encouraging private enterprise to extend the empire (for the Foreign and Colonial offices to thus outmaneuver the Treasury) made excellent sense to almost everyone in Downing Street and Whitehall. Even if less well known in London than Gifford and Cawston, Rhodes possessed financial resources of a dimension that they lacked. Moreover, Whitehall reasoned, a chartered company could be saddled with the costs of Bechuanaland, and also with the far greater developmental charges of any railway. Let Rhodes do it! may have been a quiet cry in various corridors of power in London after the young entrepreneur's visit there in 1888. Even so, Whitehall had not yet chosen definitively between Rhodes and Gifford/Cawston.

Rhodes did not underestimate his main obstacle. "I am still working out my old idea," he wrote to Shippard, "and seen Home Government about Charter for Matabeleland. They appeared favorable but unfortunately I had no concession to work on." Rhodes believed, possibly correctly, that Salisbury's government would give a charter or back him only after a tangible grant of mining and other rights had been secured from Lobengula. It is important, given subsequent controversies, that Rhodes' letter to Shippard implies that he knew a concession could not be limited to the exploitation of the minerals. "I am aware that you can do nothing in matter," he continued, "but I am going to have another try [the older Fry having failed], as what I am afraid of is that Lo Bengulu may give away his whole country to bogus companies who will do nothing for the Government and what is left of that country will not be worth our De Beers Co while to make any offer to pay expenses of good government. It is an awful pity that Fry was so ill he could not stop and he has got no concession which I could use as a ground for making an offer to H.M. Government." That was an essential point—the making of an offer to Salisbury which the prime minister could accept.

Rhodes continued: "I am sending now young Fry to try but he is a mere boy. I know Moffat cannot in any way directly support me but you can tell him all my ideas and see if my Company is not able to obtain one, that Lo Bengulu does not give away his territory in mining concessions to a lot of adventurers who will do nothing but simply tie the country up." Anything but that.

Rhodes was candid: "I got my trust deed through with all its increased powers, and only hope I may be able to use them. If you can give me any help," he implored, "without in any way committing yourself do so." Since Lord Salisbury's government would remain chary of spending money on overseas ventures, it was essential that the chartered company should control real resources. "If country is given to others De Beers will have nothing to obtain in return for offer to pay expenses of Government." Rhodes said that he would soon send another agent. Meanwhile young Fry, as he was "on the spot," would act for Rhodes. "I have told him to make another try when Moffat arrives who is taking a parcel for us to Fry for Lo Bengula containing big present though he [Moffat] is in no way aware of the objects."[20]

Shippard urged his friend to do the job himself, doubtless arguing that Rhodes' persuasive abilities, when bolstered by Shippard's authority and Moffat's family connections, would turn the head of Lobengula and gain favor in his court. Shippard, like Robinson and Moffat, believed in Rhodes, his aims, his ambitions, and in the mutual destiny in which each had a stake. Maund was making his way overland, too, so there was little time to be lost.

Rhodes explained, however, that he could not leave Kimberley just yet. The folding of the De Beers and Kimberley mines into the De Beers Consolidated Diamond Mining Company was still in process. He estimated that it would take a month. Then, he declared grandly and optimistically, he would be "free to join you in the interior for as short or long a period as you like." Rhodes further reassured his old accomplice: "You are perfectly right in your remarks as to the point that in assisting me you are doing your best for H.M. Government. I propose to deal with whole question of good government and the expense thereof. Your danger is in the repetition of [the concession which Kgama had granted to several British companies] . . . and you may wake up to the responsibility of the government of a country as big as Europe, and all your means of revenue signed away." Rhodes further cautioned: "You know you cannot expect much revenue from pastoral sources and if all the minerals are given away before you adopt the responsibility of the territory I would ask where would you get your revenue for good government. My plan," he outlined grandly, "is to give the chief whatever he desires and also offer H.M. Government the whole expense of good government. If we get Matabeleland we [Rhodes and the cabal of 1877] shall get the balance of Africa. I do not stop in my ideas at Zambezi and I am willing to work with you for it." Fortunately, although Kruger might contest the interior, Rhodes believed that the Bond was now behind him.

"My only fear," Rhodes admitted, "is that I shall be too late with Lo Bengula as of course if his whole country is given away to adventurers it is of no use stepping in for my company to assist in the Government of a shell. You will see this as clearly as I do—Do not think I am delaying but I must get things right here before I start [north] otherwise I would be called back and my whole success in the interior depends on my getting my trust deed right here in order to have the sinews of war for our plans." Those sinews of war, Rhodes explained in a second letter, were the £20 million that came with the diamond monopoly, the broad trust deed, and, he could have mentioned, the funds available through Gold Fields.[21]

"I am awfully restless that I cannot get away to run my hobby in Matabeleland," Rhodes told Francis J. Newton, about the same time.[22] Newton had been Robinson's private secretary, was now colonial secretary, or the deputy administrator, of Bechuanaland, and was an old chum of Rhodes' from the 1870s in Oxford. For "hobby," read dream of a band of brothers ordered along Jesuit lines for the extension of the empire and the spread of good government as well as the glorification of Rhodes. "Hobby" also justified Rhodes' by-then successful lust for fortune, power, and growing fame.

Instead of doing the main deed himself, Rhodes was busy squaring his various rivals; by early September he regarded Maund as his only possible competitor. He had also arranged a powerful proxy for himself. To impress, charm, cajole, and negotiate with Lobengula and the induna, to overawe Maund and others, and, afterwards, to eliminate second-guessing in London, Rhodes in mid-August had dispatched a powerful team of friends from Kimberley through the Protectorate to Gbulawayo. In command of this mission was his own wealthy business partner and alter ego, Charles Rudd. Frank Thompson, who could speak Setswana and both knew and feared Africans from a harrowing childhood in the rural Cape Colony, accompanied him. So did Rochfort Maguire, a lawyer who had been a brilliant undergraduate at Merton College, Oxford, where Rhodes knew him.

On the basis of his "double first" degree in his final examinations, Maguire had been elected to All Souls, that Oxford college which has only research fellows and no students. He had served as private secretary to Graham Bower, Robinson's deputy. Slight, neat, witty, charming, and cultured, he may have fascinated Rhodes. But would a man who was described as the caricature of an "effete snob" and a "spoiled child of fortune" have impressed the Ndebele?[23] Presumably Rhodes had other of Maguire's attributes in mind when he persuaded the debonair man of affairs to join Rudd, the wealthy capitalist, and Thompson, the rough-hewn frontiersman, on this special, vital, errand which could serve or, if it failed, certainly frustrate the realization of Rhodes' dreams.

Rudd, although a longtime associate of Rhodes and someone who had no overwhelming economic need to help, doubtless undertook the mission only after being subjected to the full onslaught of Rhodes' magnetism. Rudd, a principal in Gold Fields, owned little of De Beers, and the thought in 1888 was that De Beers would control and exploit any concession. This was the plan shortly before the High Court decided against Rhodes and the trust deed and compelled Rhodes, Beit, and Barnato to buy out Baring Gould and others who opposed the final merger of the Kimberley mines.

Rudd was an odd choice in another sense, for he apparently was not privy to Rhodes' grand scheme. "I am quite aware you cannot act freely with him," Rhodes told Shippard, "but in case he lays the ground work the objects are the same as though he does not know our big ideas, he will try and obtain what he desires for our Companies whose trust deeds I shall use for the objects I have in view."[24] Indeed, Rhodes may purposefully have kept Rudd ignorant of his trans-Zambezian and all-African vision. He wanted Rudd to obtain a concession which could be used to secure a charter which, in turn, subsequently could be employed to acquire further territory. Possibly it was best if Rudd knew only a part of the plan. Thompson certainly knew only a part, too, and was the one of the three most dependent on Rhodes' largesse.

Maguire's inclusion has puzzled writers, not only because of his metropolitanism. Many have argued that Maguire was included so that the resulting concession could be phrased in proper legal language, and thus be unassailable. They have suggested that he accompanied the others to add a touch of culture and class with which to impress Lobengula and the rival concession hunters. Maguire was probably aware of Rhodes' vision, and he could have been persuaded to go into the interior on the strength of Rhodes' big idea and to assist its furtherance. For Rhodes, another, stronger, point in Maguire's favor was his entrée into British society. Maguire was friendly with the Rothschilds and others; before long he married Julia Peel, daughter of the Speaker of the House of Commons. To cover later contingencies, Rhodes needed Maguire, and needed him in Gbulawayo. He was Rhodes' counter to Gifford and everything which Gifford and Cawston represented and Rhodes lacked. Since Maguire shortly afterwards obtained a safe parliamentary seat from Parnell, his willingness to journey to destinations distasteful becomes explicable.

Rhodes sought the prize of Lobengula's kingdom. But by dispatching Rudd and company he was hardly emboldened by the likelihood that he and they would easily realize their objectives. Rothschild, as executor of his latest will, was clearly knowledgeable about all of Rhodes' grand dreams for Africa and beyond. It was to a firm supporter, but not the usual acolyte, that Rhodes thus wrote about prospects in the north. Even so, he was less ebullient than to others, probably because the amalgamation of the mines had not proceeded as smoothly as he had earlier suggested it might. Rhodes told Rothschild—ironically, on the eve of a success about which he could not have known anything for another month—that the Rudd mission was not particularly promising. "Still," he wrote, "someone has to get the country, and I think we should have the best chance." Rhodes revealed at least some of his operational motives: "I have always been afraid of the difficulty of dealing with the Matabele king. He is the only block to Central Africa, as, once we have his territory, the rest is easy," Rhodes stressed, "as the rest is simply a village system with separate headmen, all independent of each other. . . . I have faith in the country, and Africa is on the move. I think it is a second Cinderella."[25]

The Rudd party left Kimberley for Vryburg and the north on 15 August 1888. Maund had preceded them. But Moffat was ahead of both. He reached Gbulawayo from Shoshong in late August, finding Lobengula worried by the fawning crowd of concession-hunters. "There is a distinct tendency to draw in, and to concede less and less to Europeans," he reported. Shortly thereafter, this additional crucial contributor to Rhodes' eventual success indicated that he had "put the chief in possession of the views and wishes of the Government respecting the grant of concessions," although not too strongly for fear of appearing to dictate. "He will in all probability be unconsciously influenced by what I have said to adopt the course we desire."[26] In such understatement lay the foundations of Rhodesia. The ultimate concession to Rudd, on which Rhodes' northern pyramid was based, owed everything to such partiality from Moffat, acting for himself, for his missionary friends, and for his superiors.

Moffat would not have needed further encouragement from Newton: "You know yourself what an enthusiast Rhodes is in the matter of the extension of British influence northwards," Newton commended. "In this case he is doubly enthusiastic, viz. politically and financially." Newton had talked with him in Kimberley and Cape Town. "He is . . . prepared to do everything that Lo Bengula and those around him may wish, if the king will trust him and make an *extensive* concession. What he does not care for," Newton reminded Moffat reasonably, "is to be merely one of a number of concessionaires. . . . I confess I should like to see a thorough imperialist and good man of business at the same time, as he undoubtedly is, get a good footing in that country. Much more can be done by private enterprise than by the lukewarm advances of the Colonial Office at home." This was the ethos of British imperialism. Many years later, Newton confessed that he and his contemporaries "admired Rhodes and put him on a pedestal." He and they "would have done anything for him."[27]

The Rudd party arrived in Gbulawayo in late September 1888. Immediately they went to greet Lobengula, who came out of his buck kraal (or private sanctum within the village)—Rudd described it as "the most dirty miserable affair"—to meet these whites whom he had been expecting. "He came out . . . and we then rose, took off our hats and saluted him as Kumalo (Royal Chief), and shook hands with him." The king climbed up on his wagon and sat on the driving box while Rudd and his compatriots squatted below. Rudd explained through an interpreter who he and his friends were and what they represented. He said that they had come on a friendly visit and begged the king to accept a present of £100. A few days later Thompson explained in Setswana what they wanted. Lobengula, said Thompson, "listened attentively and showed considerable intelligence." Thompson explained that he and his friends were not Boers, were not seeking land, "but only asked the right to dig the gold of the country." Further, Thompson "told him that all eyes were turned to his dominions, which [Thompson] likened to a dish of milk that was attracting flies."

"The King," declared Rudd, "is just what I expected to find him—a very fine man, only very fat, but with a beautiful skin and well proportioned. He was perfectly naked except [for a skin apron suspended from the hips on a girdle] and ring on his hair. He has some sixty wives or queens, some of whom we saw, and also slave wives as well. . . . The King has a curious face; he looks partly worried, partly good natured and partly cruel; he has a very pleasant smile." Later, he "went back into the wagon . . . and lay down with his head and arms on the front of the box of the wagon, and a great mass of meat—like the pieces they give lions at the zoo . . . was put before him, and some kind of bread. He told the slave boy who brought the meat to turn it over, and then he began to tear pieces off with a kind of stick. Altogether very much like a wild beast."[28]

Maund was still on the road, three weeks behind Rudd, having lost a month (to the fury of his sponsors) by seeking new concessions from the Ngwato and engaging in a filibustering expedition for Kgama. But Gbulawayo was nevertheless crowded with a motley collection of would-be syndicate creators, hunters, traders, prospectors, and other hopefuls. Ivon Fry was there. So were George A. ("Elephant") Phillips and C.D. Tainton, two prominent traders, and Samuel Edward ("Far Interior") Edwards, manager of the Tati Gold Mining Company, Lobengula's representative in that confused and contested district, and a sometime merchant. Edward R. Renny-Tailyour and Frank Boyle, representing Beit's estranged cousin Edouard Lippert, had recently arrived from Swaziland to seek prospecting permission. (Renny-Tailyour was soon to side with Maund.) Other would-be concessionaires were Francis and Chapman from the Grahamstown syndicate.

Charles D. Helm and David Carnegie, missionaries of the London Society, were nearby. Moffat was also in residence, and prepared to assist Rudd with precision and discretion. It would be advantageous, he soon told Lobengula, for the Ndebele to work with but one powerful company. Rather than dispersing the kingdom's privileges among many weak entities, joining hands with a big concern would "simplify matters for him." As Rudd gently confided to his diary, "Moffat took the chance of putting in a good word for us."[29]

Moffat counseled the king to do nothing until Shippard paid what amounted to a state visit. Although ostensibly a flag-waving ceremonial opportunity for discussions between the monarch of the interior and the Queen's "impartial" representative, Shippard's journey was calculated to advance the interests which he and Rhodes shared in common—whatever the Colonial Office may have wanted. His arrival in mid-October was an event. "A bald, pot-bellied little fellow with Dundreary whiskers," Shippard still managed to cut an imposing figure in a tightly buttoned black frock coat, gray kid gloves, and patent leather boots. He carried a malacca cane with a silver knob, and had the spanking symbol of his knighthood pinned prominently to his chest. Atop all was a white solar topee, necessary in theory to protect him from the sun's penetrating rays during this, the hottest time of the central African year. Moreover, he was accompanied by Major Sir Hamilton John Goold-Adams and sixteen policemen.

There is no record of Shippard's words with Lobengula in October, while Rudd and Maund and the others cooled their heels elsewhere in Gbulawayo, but circumstantial evidence suggests that his talk could not have been unhelpful to Rudd's immediate quest. Shippard frightened Lobengula with the prospect that land-hungry Boers would soon be overrunning his kingdom from the Transvaal. He also appears to have assured the monarch that Rudd's party represented a group with substantial resources, solid backing, and the support of the Queen. (Curiously, bearing out the supposition that Rudd remained unaware that Shippard was a strong supporter of Rhodes' visions, the coming of Shippard was hardly welcomed by Rudd, who feared it might "delay" the concession.) Maguire was persuaded that the visit "did a great deal of good removing much misunderstanding which was steadily growing worse." Shippard's sympathies were clearly opposed to the continued independence of the Ndebele. "I must confess that it would offer me sincere and lasting satisfaction if I could see the Matabele . . . cut down by our rifles and machine guns like a cornfield by a reaping machine. . . . The cup of their iniquities must surely be full or nearly full now."[30]

Rhodes had meanwhile been sending long messages to Rudd. He warned him of Maund, who represented those "guinea pigs at home" with their notion that a great interior concern should possess all minerals and build a railway to the Zambezi. "I quite agree with them," Rhodes said, "but the Interior

Company must be De Beers & Gold Fields. . . ." Later he reminded Rudd that their only serious opponent was Maund. "If you find him a dangerous antagonist," characteristically suggested Rhodes, "take him over personally." Or if "he represents the Bechuanaland [Company] . . . join hands and give their Company a share as . . . 'there is room for all' but only in case he is dangerous." Better yet, "buy him personally unless he is bound to [the Company]." Since their aims were "very large including a Charter and the whole interior . . . we must beat them or join hands as you deem fit."

In terms of positive advice, Rhodes wanted Rudd to find a means of slyly persuading Lobengula that they would be working for the monarch and his kingdom. Since Lobengula would not understand how companies operated, "my advice," Rhodes wrote, "is to take concession to work for him with large share of profits in your name. . . . you can apportion it afterwards. Go on lines of becoming his Gold Commissioner and working for him." He shrewdly suggested that Rudd should "offer a steamboat on Zambezi to King same as [Henry Morton] Stanley put on the Upper Congo." Additionally, Rudd was urged to "Stick to Home Rule and Matabeleland for the Matabele I am sure it is the ticket."

Fortunately, Newton had assured Rhodes that Moffat was thoroughly with them. He said nothing about Shippard or Helm, who was to do the translating and was later accused of benefiting Rudd with his nuances. Rhodes did ask Rudd to square Tainton, but said nothing about Edwards, and worried little about the others. Most of all, Rudd was not to retreat from Ndebeleland. "You must not leave a vacuum." Later he repeated the order not to let the group return empty-handed. "Leave Thompson and Maguire if necessary or wait until I can join. Nature abhors a vacuum and if we get anything we must always have someone resident or else they [the other whites] will intrigue and upset us"—which was soon to be the case.[31]

Rudd was, in fact, anxious to return to the Witwatersrand, and to a pursuit—coining money through mining ventures—about which he knew more. But the king naturally kept his party waiting throughout October. Until Shippard had come and gone the king listened only half-heartedly to Rudd's entreaties. It was for the Queen's representative to tell him that Rudd indeed came on behalf of Rhodes *and* the Queen. Yet Rudd naturally fretted: partially to move the proceedings along and partially because Rudd indeed did have other business. He told the king that he was very anxious to get away. "The King replied that we had surely not understood him: that he would send [for us] when he was ready to talk business." At the end of the third week of October, shortly after Shippard had arrived, Rudd again told the king that he truly had to leave, and that Lobengula should say "whether he would do business with us or not." The king said "he had told us to wait; I said that my affairs down below were all going wrong in my absence; he replied that his affairs were all going wrong up here. I said that we should both be in better circumstances if he did business with us; he laughed. . ." and promised a subsequent talk.

Three days later, on the eve of Shippard's departure, Lobengula finally examined Rudd's version of the concession. (Rudd, not Maguire, did most of the drafting.) "We had a talk for an hour or more over some of the clauses." And Rudd made known his intentions definitely to leave at the end of that week, but, as he bemoaned to his diary, "there seems to be no way of pushing the King on." At noon on 30 October, after Rudd's various leave-taking bluffs had failed, Lobengula summoned him urgently. The king had been talking at length with the induna. Several of the induna had tried to persuade Rudd to take a concession to the Tati district, but Rudd held out for all of Shona country, up to the Zambezi. Finally, Thompson and Lotshe, a leading induna who later lost his life for so convincingly advising Lobengula to give Rudd what he wanted, went together to see the king. After fifteen minutes, Thompson said that Rudd should bring the concession at once, for the king was ready to sign.[32]

"We seated ourselves in a semicircle," reported Thompson, "with the king in the centre. The Concession was placed before him, and he took the pen in his hand to affix his mark, which was his signature." And so the great leader of the warlike Ndebele put his mark to a controversial document which, whether he understood the consequences or not, was the piece of paper which Rhodes parlayed into the conquests of his kingdom and all of the lands that were to become Rhodesia. Central Africa was to be British. "This is the epoch of our lives," Maguire, unsmiling, yawned to Thompson at the time.[33]

The Rudd Concession begins with a promise on Rhodes' behalf to pay Lobengula £100 in British currency every month and to provide 1,000 Martini Henry breech-loading rifles, together with 100,000 rounds of suitable ammunition. The first 500 of the rifles and 40,000 of the cartridges were to be delivered with reasonable dispatch, the remainder to be conveyed "so soon as the . . . grantees shall have commenced to work mining machinery" within Lobengula's domain. Rudd also promised to place an armed steamboat on the Zambezi (or, if Lobengula wanted it instead, £500). In exchange, the king assigned Rudd and company "the complete and exclusive charge over all metals and minerals situated and contained in my Kingdoms Principalities and dominions together with full power to do all things that they may deem necessary to win and procure the same and to hold collect and enjoy the profits and revenue . . . from . . . metals and minerals." Lobengula also gave Rudd and his partners authority to exclude all others seeking land or prospecting privileges from his kingdom.[34]

Lobengula wanted the guns and ammunition—"the only things really worth having"—to strengthen his own weakening hand among the Ndebele warrior age groups. He may have fancied a ship on the Zambezi. Ample British currency could purchase more guns, horses, and satisfy his and his supporters' consumer wants. But Lobengula could hardly have understood completely what the concession would permit Rhodes and Britain to claim. Nor need Lobengula have fully appreciated the legal language of the concessions. Thus it is plausible, as others have suggested, to suppose that Lobengula finally granted the concession because of misleading verbal assurances about its limitations. Shippard, Moffat, and others had at least hinted that Lobengula's best protection from the swarm of concessionaires, Afrikaner avarice, and the onrush of the scramble for Africa would be an alliance with a powerful man like Rhodes. These considerations would have weighed heavily upon a monarch like Lobengula, fearful as he was of the fast pace of externally orchestrated political change. But even more important were the hints or ambiguities which permitted Lobengula to believe, and to tell his induna, that only very small matters had been conceded. "A great deal of course passed at the *indaba* [the talk with Lobengula and the private meeting with Lotshe and Thompson] that I cannot put down," said Rudd, "the most noteworthy being that Thompson and I, after they showed weakness, explained fully to them their own position and pointed out how they must be driven out of their country if they did not get friends and arms in to help them. . . ."

Clearly there were additional understandings. Helm, who interpreted during the final two days, later said that Rudd and Thompson had promised not to bring more than ten whites to work the mines of Lobengula's territory. They also agreed not to dig near towns and—as Rhodes had urged—promised to "be as his people." Lobengula may further have been assured, although the authority is largely circumstantial, that he was giving away rights for the whites to dig in one hole, or in one place, only. At any rate, that was the king's view. The critical conversations may have been between Thompson, Lotshe, and Lobengula, but Thompson's autobiography is mostly silent on that brief encounter. However, Thompson told Lobengula that his group meant "to do what was right." He "who gives a man an assegai," Thompson told the king, does not expect "to be attacked by him afterwards." That, reported Thompson, was his answer to the Ndebele fear that the concession would only open the door to "white aggression."

Helm's support could have been essential to the success of all of these conversations, particularly the intimate ones. It is clear that Helm understood that he could receive a substantial subsidy from Rudd for the missionary endeavor of his society; but it is doubtful whether that expectation of indirect reward influenced the interpreter's tongue or his reassurances to Lobengula. Helm was already predisposed to the order and presumed stability which Rudd and Rhodes would bring to the vineyard in which he and the other missionaries had so gallantly and fruitlessly labored for so long.[35]

Whatever Lobengula thought that he was doing, and however little or much Rudd believed that he had accomplished by enduring the long weeks in unpleasant surroundings and the headlong rush across the Bechuana desert that almost cost Rudd his life and Rhodes the signed concession, the king had been cajoled, bribed, bullied, and possibly even blackmailed to give permission for a claque of whites to enter his hitherto closed and fearsome kingdom. They may have been meant to poke into a few crevices only, and to disturb the tenor of Ndebele life but a little. Nevertheless, Lobengula was at last succumbing, as soon enough most of his fellow chiefs would do, to an imperialism which—the great king may well have sensed—could hardly be forestalled indefinitely. Letting a diamond magnate's nose into the kingdom's threatened tent may have seemed a reasonable gamble, especially in exchange for guns—the wherewithal with which to withstand any invaders.

On the other side, Rhodes was jubilant. "Our concession is so gigantic," Rhodes crowed in a very uncharacteristic way, "it is like giving a man the whole of Australia. . . . ." He quickly offered Nathaniel Rothschild a share in this bonanza and envisaged a further fortune being made. It hardly mattered how complete or authentic the concession might ultimately be considered or whether or not it had been obtained by "means that were essentially fraudulent." For the moment it was constituted and could be read by the Colonial Office as providing a clear and significant transfer of rights well within Lobengula's gift to Rhodes and his associates—not to Maund, nor to the others. The "full power to do all things . . . necessary" was, for Rhodes' scheme, the crucial clause. Clearly, Rudd could never have asked Lobengula outright for a transfer of sovereignty. Nor did Rhodes necessarily want so much. What he had desired, and what he correctly thought that Rudd had obtained, were rights which went beyond those required merely to dig for minerals, and which approximated a role for whites which would not trouble Ndebele "home rule" directly—at least not immediately. Rudd, however limited his appreciation of Rhodes' far-flung vision of an imperialized Africa, had earlier agreed that they both wanted a concession to the whole of Lobengula's country. And Rudd had insisted upon that scope in talks with the induna. "Rhodes and I have come to the conclusion," Rudd revealed to John Blades Currey before leaving for Gbulawayo, "that our best chance of a big thing is to try to make some terms with Lobengula for a concession of the whole of his country."[36]

Rhodes initially believed that he might have "technical" problems perfecting the concession, or that Lobengula might give additional, confusing, and cross-cutting concessions to others. Furthermore, Rhodes, a man of detail as well as dreams, worried that earlier concessions (verbal or written) might now be resuscitated or revamped, and thus muddy the clarity of his own arrangements. The key practical question was the matter of guns, for the concession could be challenged if Rhodes did not soon deliver what Rudd had promised. Moreover, as the concession said and the oral hints implied, as far as the Ndebele were concerned, Rhodes (Ulodzi to the Ndebele) could neither prospect nor even pretend to realize the concession until the guns that Lobengula desired were visible.

The first hitch, of which Rhodes was certainly aware, was that Cape Colony law and an international treaty undertaking prohibited the sale or gift of firearms to Africans living outside the Colony. Anyone who removed or transported guns or ammunition across state boundaries could be fined or imprisoned. Furthermore, the Colony had already gone to war to disarm the Sotho, ignominious failure though that earlier initiative of Sprigg may have been. Rhodes, persuaded after talking to Rudd that guns had alone clinched the contract with Lobengula, was not about to let such fine legal and diplomatic obstacles block the bargain. As Rhodes explained months later, the merits of the case were that "Lo Bengulu would not have given a concession unless he received what he desired. His concession has led to the Charter which will result in Civilising the interior."

Robinson and Lord Knutsford had to be persuaded by misleading information from Rhodes and Shippard about the inability of the Ndebele to set their gun sights correctly before they were prepared (even if Knutsford's juniors were not) to ignore the inconvenient matter of the weapons. Rhodes argued then, as he rationalized later, that the Ndebele guns were less "dangerous than assegais. The result of our presence in Matabeleland . . . is that there has been no slaughter of the Mashonas."[37] Shippard even had the effrontery to argue that arming the Ndebele was humanitarian. They would use the guns in place of their potent assegai, but because—as savages—they would be unable to fire their Martini Henrys with any consistency they would, perforce, become less rather than more of a threat to their neighbors!

This was nonsense, but Shippard and others were reacting both to the anxieties of their British superiors as well as to attacks on the scheme by individuals whose humanitarian credentials could hardly be challenged. There was no ignoring the Rt. Rev. George Wyndham Hamilton Knight-Bruce, the young Anglican Bishop of Bloemfontein, who visited Lobengula's domain during the period of Rudd's residence and who, after learning about the concession, denounced it in a well-reported speech in Vryburg. "I consider that giving one firearm to any of the Matabele—and everyone must know that it would be used to assist in the murder of hapless innocents—would be an act which, if not in this world, certainly in the next, a man would be sorry for indeed. Such a piece of devilry and brutality as a consignment of rifles to the Matabele cannot be surpassed." But, within eight days of the report of the bishop's speech, Rhodes assured Rudd that they need fear the bishop no longer: "Without telling you a long story I will simply say I believe he will be our cordial supporter in future. I am sorry for his . . . speech . . . but he has repented . . . ," Rhodes chortled. How Rhodes converted the bishop is not known (by promising a generous contribution to his mission endeavor?) but Rhodes chided Rudd for having "rubbed him up the wrong way." Else Rudd, too, could have converted the bishop on the Limpopo, Rhodes said.[38]

Having dealt with or diverted humanitarian and diplomatic obstacles, Rhodes had to purchase a vast quantity of guns—that caused no particular problem—and then spirit them through the Cape Colony and Bechuanaland—which he did by arranging to move them legally as far as Kimberley, and then under cover of De Beers (an unintended prelude to the much more consequential clandestine doings that contributed to the Jameson Raid) smuggled them in three consignments out of the Cape with approval from the administrator of Bechuanaland, who happened to be Shippard. Rhodes' participation in this movement of matériel was essential. It was one of several reasons why, although Rudd and Thompson implored him to cement the contract with Lobengula in person, he never budged northward.

Among the intriguing sidelights of this period is the fact that Rhodes intended to convey the arms himself, and to cap Rudd's concession with a personal reaffirmation of his own. Thompson and Maguire had remained behind, chafing all the while, and Rhodes also intended to reinforce their presence by inserting his own. Rhodes' letters to Rudd indicate that the two missions were intertwined, but the main intent was political: "I shall not approach Lo Bengulu without the guns . . . [and] cannot leave here without seeing safe departure of guns," he told his colleague in mid-December. He had "no intention of leaving without [the guns] and making a fool of myself with Lo Bengulu by finding out they have been stopped in the Colony or Bechuanaland." Rhodes also wanted Rudd to float a new issue of Gold Fields shares quickly, because the concession would require capital to develop it. "Delay is most dangerous, either a reaction in gold, or some difficulty as to concession either in getting up guns or by row breaking out or repudiation." At the end of the year he was, he said, "slightly nervous as to getting guns through but will do my best." Two weeks later he reported that the governor [Sir Hercules Robinson] had been "a little funky after that brutal assault by the bishop. . . ." Rhodes still had to look after a shipment of guns up from the Cape; the first would be going off—he promised—the very next day. And then he would follow with the second.

In the event, Rhodes sent two shipments of 250 rifles in January and another of the same size in February, all to be given to Lobengula by Jameson, Rhodes' confidant, assisted by Dr. Frederick Rutherfoord Harris, another Kimberley physician, and George Musson, a trader who lived in Shoshong. Rhodes and Jameson worried that Kgama would try to seize the guns, but, as Jameson reported, the Ngwato chief—"a wonderful man . . . unusually respected by both white and black"—gave and would give "no trouble." Rudd explained: "We have been very anxious about the guns . . . S[hippard] has behaved like a brick and sent them thro Bechuanaland and . . . will send for K[gama] personally and make matters right with him."[39]

Harris, although often criticized and derided by his contemporaries, was destined to become Rhodes' close confidant, henchman, and hatchetman, and to play a critical role during the Jameson Raid. Born in 1856 of a family well-connected in the Indian Civil Service, Harris studied at Leatherhead Grammar School and the University of Edinburgh, where he qualified as a physician. He came to Kimberley in 1882, and sided with Jameson in the local smallpox war. When he became acquainted with Rhodes is uncertain, but they probably knew each other from 1882 or 1883. Harris had a financial setback in 1886 or 1887, and abandoned medicine for Rhodes' employ in 1889, when he went with Jameson to Gbulawayo. He never married.

By mid-February 1889, given his concerns with concessionary rivals and with his still-uncompleted amalgamation of the mines, Rhodes had not budged from Kimberley. Was he reluctant to endure the hazards of a long and uncomfortable trip, and the questionable food and accommodation of Gbulawayo? Probably not, for Rhodes enjoyed the veld, and never shirked rough

The Family, c. 1873, in Sleaford or Bishop's Stortford. Francis William Rhodes is at the upper left, and Louisa Rhodes is sitting below him. Cecil Rhodes is sitting on the ground in front of Aunt Sophia Peacock. Edith Rhodes is in the center. Her sister Louisa is probably to her right. There are two servants in aprons. The younger brothers are hard to identify, as is the woman behind Sophia. *(Sibbett Collection, Jagger Library, University of Cape Town)*

The Diamond Diggings, c. 1872. Standing: John Edward Dick Lauder, Norman Garstin, Hugh McLeod, Guybone Atherstone. Sitting: Herbert Rhodes, Frank Rhodes, Cecil Rhodes, R. A. Nesbitt. *(Gold Fields Collection, London)*

Robert Coryndon, Cecil Rhodes, and Johnny Grimmer, 1897, in London. *(Sibbett Collection)*

Opposite

Top left. Louisa Rhodes, Cecil's mother, shortly before her death in 1873. *(Sibbett Collection and Zimbabwe archives)*

Top right. Neville Pickering, c. 1882. *(De Beers archives)*

Bottom. Cecil Rhodes, aged 24, at Oriel College. *(Gold Fields Collection)*

KIMBERLEY·MINE·1874·

Kimberley Mine, 1874. *(Gold Fields Collection)*

Kimberley Mine, 1875, showing elaborate pulley system for conveying ore from the different claims. Horsedrawn whims provided the power for the pulleys. *(De Beers archives)*

Kimberley Mine, c. 1880, showing different levels of excavation, and an inclined shaft. *(De Beers archives)*

Kimberley Mine, 1875: Workers at the end of a shift. *(Gold Fields Collection)*

De Beers Mine, 1891. *(De Beers archives)*

Opposite. The Scanlen Cabinet, 1884: John Merriman, Jacobus Sauer, James Leonard, Rhodes, Thomas Scanlen. *(Sibbett Collection)*

The Pioneer Column, 1890: Leander Starr Jameson, F. Rutherfoord Harris, Frederick Selous, Archibald Colquhoun. The Africans in the photograph are said to be servants. *(Sibbett Collection)*

Rhodes on the veld, c. 1897. *(Gold Fields Collection)*

Opposite. Planning the conquest of trans-Zambezia, 1890. Sitting: James Rochfort Maguire, Henry Hamilton Johnston, Rhodes, Archibald R. Colquhoun. Standing: James Grant, John Moir, Joseph Thomson. *(Sibbett Collection)*

Lewis Michell, c. 1902.
(De Beers archives)

Francis Oats, c. 1896.
(De Beers archives)

Barney Barnato, c. 1890. *(De Beers archives)*

Carl Meyer, c. 1900.
(De Beers boardroom)

Col. Robert G. Kekewich, c. 1900.
(De Beers archives)

Alfred Beit, c. 1902. *(Sibbett Collection)*

Sir Hercules Robinson, c. 1895.
(De Beers boardroom)

Frederic Philipson Stow, c. 1890.
(De Beers boardroom)

Rhodes, c. 1894. *(De Beers archives)*

Rhodes in Port Elizabeth, c. 1896. *(Sibbett Collection)*

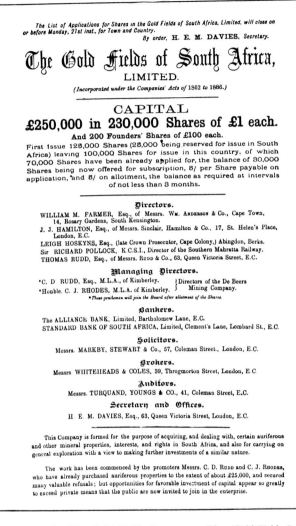

The Gold Fields of South Africa,

LIMITED.

(Incorporated under the Companies' Acts of 1862 to 1886.)

CAPITAL

£250,000 in 230,000 Shares of £1 each.

And 200 Founders' Shares of £100 each.

First Issue 128,000 Shares (28,000 being reserved for issue in South Africa) leaving 100,000 Shares for issue in this country, of which 70,000 Shares have been already applied for, the balance of 30,000 Shares being now offered for subscription, 5/ per Share payable on application, and 5/ on allotment, the balance as required at intervals of not less than 3 months.

Directors.

WILLIAM M. FARMER, Esq., of Messrs. WM. ANDERSON & Co., Cape Town, 14, Rosary Gardens, South Kensington.

J. J. HAMILTON, Esq., of Messrs. Sinclair, Hamilton & Co., 17, St. Helen's Place, London, E.C.

LEIGH HOSKYNS, Esq., (late Crown Prosecutor, Cape Colony,) Abingdon, Berks.

Sir RICHARD POLLOCK, K.C.S.I., Director of the Southern Mahratta Railway.

THOMAS RUDD, Esq., of Messrs. RUDD & Co., 63, Queen Victoria Street, E.C.

Managing Directors.

*C. D RUDD, Esq., M.L.A., of Kimberley. } Directors of the De Beers

*Honble. C. J. RHODES, M.L.A. of Kimberley. }   Mining Company.

* *These gentlemen will join the Board after allotment of the Shares.*

Bankers.

The ALLIANCE BANK, Limited, Bartholomew Lane, E.C.

STANDARD BANK OF SOUTH AFRICA, Limited, Clement's Lane, Lombard St., E.C.

Solicitors.

Messrs. MARKBY, STEWART & Co., 57, Coleman Street., London, E.C.

Brokers.

Messrs. WHITEHEADS & COLES, 39, Throgmorton Street, London, E.C.

Auditors.

Messrs. TURQUAND, YOUNGS & CO., 41, Coleman Street, E.C.

Secretary and Offices.

H. E. M. DAVIES, Esq., 63, Queen Victoria Street, London, E.C.

This Company is formed for the purpose of acquiring, and dealing with, certain auriferous and other mineral properties, interests, and rights in South Africa, and also for carrying on general exploration with a view to making further investments of a similar nature.

The work has been commenced by the promoters Messrs. C. D. RUDD and C. J. RHODES, who have already purchased auriferous properties to the extent of about £25,000, and secured many valuable refusals; but opportunities for favorable investment of capital appear so greatly to exceed private means that the public are now invited to join in the enterprise.

Prospectus for The Gold Fields Company, 1887. *(Gold Fields Collection)*

Opposite

Top. The first stamp battery on the Witwatersrand. *(Gold Fields Collection)*

Bottom. Rhodes, c. 1887, after a sketch by the Marchioness of Granby, later the Duchess of Rutland. *(Sibbett Collection)*

Rhodes, c. 1890. (*Sibbett Collection*)

country assignments. Yet Rhodes legitimately could have feared being detained for weeks if not months by Lobengula. As he was moved in mid-February to explain to Thompson—something he rarely did to a subordinate—"You must not think that I am avoiding coming up but I saw clearly if I left the guns would never have got through so with great difficulty I have managed to get them through the Colony and Bechuanaland." He indicated that he might have to go home—to England—and, he said, "as soon as I feel our base perfectly clear I shall come up but it is no use carting myself at once to Gbulawayo and then finding the guns stopped and the Home Government dead against our Concession." He continued: "If I had left when desired not a single gun would have ever got through."

Thompson was threatening to leave Lobengula. "That was a time," said Thompson later, "I wouldn't go through again to be a millionaire twice over." "It would be fatal if you left now," implored Rhodes, who also offered Thompson the princely sum of £2,000 a year (and a house for his wife, whom Rhodes would send up.) Thompson was distressed and fearful. So Rhodes responded with his most persuasive appeal: "Do you believe you could have a grander chance in the world if the thing succeeds? (Your share alone will make you a millionaire besides all the kudos of carrying through such a work.)" Rhodes was contemplating a long-term residence for Thompson, possibly of two to three years' duration. "But what a prize you have in view," Rhodes declared.[40]

Rhodes was on his own sure ground when it came to calming bishops. How, he must have thought, doing so would have pleased his father, the late and long-neglected vicar! By 1888–89, Rhodes was also a master of providing incentives and profits for colleagues, associates, competitors, and—in the instance of the concession—clearing the underbrush of suspected obstacles. Earlier he had bought off Henry Clay Moore, an American who vaguely claimed a prior agreement from Lobengula. In the aftermath of the Rudd concession he learned that Thomas Leask, James Fairbairn, George Arthur Phillips, and George Westbeech in 1884 had received a grant of mineral rights from Lobengula for the area between the Gwelo and Hunyani Rivers, in what is now central Zimbabwe. In mid-1888, before Rudd arrived, Lobengula had also given Fairbairn and Leask a further concession to his "entire dominions." "I quite see," Rhodes told Rudd, "that worthless as Fairbairn's concession is, it logically destroys yours." So Rhodes and Rudd persuaded Leask and Fairbairn to sell in February. Subsequently he managed to settle financially with Fry and Edwards, with William Filmer Usher, another trader, and then with Tainton. All ended up being aligned with Rhodes in one or more favorable capacities, but they were somehow not fully "squared" immediately, several working against Rhodes in 1889.

At the end of 1888, Alfred W. Haggard, a brother of Henry Rider Haggard, the well-known author, and John Fellowes Wallop, second son of Lord Portsmouth, representing the Austral Africa Exploration Company, were turned back from Ndebeleland by a war party of Ndebele commanded or assisted by

Maguire. Rhodes feared a "literary campaign against us" and thus proposed to Rudd that they give the two men and their company a few shares and an eventual "show." (Rider Haggard later backed Rhodes against his brother.) As Rhodes summed up the position to Rudd in 1889, "the mistake was that after you left [we] did not settle with the few whites having concessions." Rhodes' final plan of all plans was to encourage everyone from Fairbairn to Edwards and Tainton to press Lobengula for concessions to sections of the country "in case big one fails." More options would be covered. Rhodes explained to Rudd: "Try in each case allowing them to please King so as not to invalidate." As Rudd told Currey, "You will quite grasp Rhodes' idea of as many small specific concessions as possible, to consolidate the main *abstract* one."[41]

For a surprisingly long time—a matter of nine weeks—Rhodes remained largely unaware of the most immediate and most dangerous attacks on the concession. Maund and Renny-Tailyour, left empty-handed in Gbulawayo—in January Rhodes wondered whether he and Rudd should give "Maund's crowd something"—were agitating against what they knew about the breadth and reach of the Rudd Concession. Lobengula denied giving his country away. But many of the more powerful induna suspected that the nation had been betrayed by the doings of the king. Lobengula was therefore compelled to try to undo the Rudd Concession. A message to the press in South Africa was sent off in early 1889. In February, what Rhodes called a "flaring notice" appeared in the *Bechuanaland News* denying that a concession of any kind had been granted to Rudd, Maguire, and Thompson, and suspending all further action "pending an investigation to be made" by Lobengula in his own country.

In late November, Lobengula, in another defensive maneuver, had also dispatched two prominent induna to London. He asked Maund to convey and accompany them. Their most important message was that the Rudd Concession was invalid. Maund, fearful of being detained or sidetracked, spent only moments in Shoshong on his journey southward, and detoured through the Transvaal rather than through British Bechuanaland and the northern Cape. But he arrived in Kimberley toward the end of January being, as Rhodes told Rothschild, "very annoyed at our success."

Rhodes did not know of the message being carried by the induna, and Rhodes claimed at the time that Maund suggested that he and Rhodes should unite. Rhodes said that he temporized until he could follow Maund to London and discuss terms with Cawston and Gifford. But Maund's version was that Rhodes, again in character, offered great inducements if Maund would jettison his own backers and join hands (as had Leask and Fairbairn) with Rudd and Rhodes.

Maund's memory was that Jameson summoned Maund from the Kimberley Club to see Rhodes. "I found Rhodes lying on his bed (a favourite thinking and scheming place of his) and Jameson sitting on the edge of the bed in a small room . . . just close to the club. . . . Rhodes asked quite a lot of questions about the route I had followed . . . through the Transvaal." He asked if Maund had seen Kruger. He told him that the concession was signed and a certainty. Rhodes then threatened to block the passage of Maund and the induna entirely, preventing them from traveling to London. Indeed, when the party, with Johann Colenbrander (a colleague of Renny-Tailyour from Natal and a frontiersman) accompanying it as an interpreter, reached Cape Town, Robinson at first was exceedingly difficult. He attempted to discredit and, if necessary, disbar the mission from traveling home. But shortly afterwards, Robinson was restrained when Rhodes, in a new mood, arrived in Cape Town. Having meanwhile received an offer of amalgamation from Cawston and Gifford, Rhodes was prepared to see Maund continue on his way and to assume that he and Maund's principals could come to terms. Treating with a rival was always more satisfying to Rhodes than naked competition. As Rhodes wrote to Maguire and Thompson after arriving in London in April, "We have settled with Maund at the request of H.M. Government so as to have no opposition in interior. . . ."[42]

Even as Rhodes sailed to Britain to contain, curtail, and overcome growing opposition to his vast concession, there was a growing disquiet in the interior. Though his induna had not yet reported on their visit or on the mood of Britain, and Lobengula would have no word of their doings for months, the king had become more and more persuaded by other induna, by resident traders, and by the news that filtered out of South Africa that the extent and meaning of the Rudd Concession had been grossly misrepresented. Lobengula may have sensed fraud, and felt himself betrayed, without knowing or needing to know precisely in what way or to what extent the trick had been perpetrated.

When Jameson, Harris, and Musson conveyed the consignment of guns and cartridges to his kingdom, they and the shipment were refused entrance. Maguire prevailed upon the king to let the symbolic affirmations of the concession into Ndebeleland. But Lobengula declined to accept them, look at them, or permit any of his men to touch them. Instead they were placed in Maguire's camp, stacked one atop the other in their tin-lined cases, under canvas. And there they sat. Jameson claimed to have made a good impression during his ten days in Gbulawayo, which was subsequently to prove valuable to Rhodes. But Lobengula's refusal to receive payment in guns (he had, however, regularly received his monthly stipends in sterling), indicated a hostile attitude toward Rhodes and the supposed grant of rights. Maguire abandoned his post, fearing the king's growing displeasure, and fled south with Jameson.

Lobengula made his hesitations known more directly a few weeks after Jameson had departed. In a letter drafted by Fairbairn according to Lobengula's instructions, the king informed Queen Victoria that he had never intended to sign away mineral rights. He and his induna withdrew their recognition of the document, and he repudiated the interpretations which Rudd and Rhodes were placing upon its words. This letter arrived in London in mid-June.

Meanwhile, Lobengula, Maund, or the dissident induna in Gbulawayo—whoever had conceived the masterstroke of sending two representatives to Britain to plead the Ndebele case directly—were making an effective case against the implications of the concession in London. The impact of the induna, imposing in their unfamiliar Western attire, their bearing, and the mystery which they imparted, combined to give them an instant appeal to London society. Curiosities, they were brought before the Queen. They saw bullion deposits and a military display. The Aborigines Protection Society feted them. Everyone concerned with imperium, for and against, wanted to hear what they had to say. More important, when they placed Lobengula's questions about the real nature of British designs in Central Africa before Lord Knutsford at the Colonial Office, he authorized a famous reply in the Queen's name which could only have heightened anxiety levels in Gbulawayo. Using language popularized by Rider Haggard and believed appropriate for illiterate potentates in far-off lands, the Queen said that she had been pleased to receive the king's messengers. "They say that Lo Bengula is much troubled by white men who come into his country and ask to dig gold. . . . The Queen wishes Lo Bengula not to grant hastily concessions of land or leave to dig. . . . It is not wise to put too much power into the hands of the men who come first, and to exclude other deserving men. A King gives a stranger an ox, not his whole herd of cattle, otherwise what would other strangers arriving have to eat?"[43]

Two weeks before, in the House of Commons, Joseph Chamberlain, a Liberal Unionist, complained (on behalf of the South Africa Committee) about the harm that could be caused to the Ndebele, to southern Africa, and to Britain by the Rudd Concession and any monopoly which Rhodes would control. Baron Henry de Worms, the parliamentary under-secretary at the Colonial Office, assured Chamberlain that the government disapproved of the part of the Concession which transferred arms and ammunition. Furthermore, in a rebuke to private imperialism, he flatly said that the Colonial Office would urge Lobengula to grant future concessions only after careful consideration, and to give no individual special prerogatives. Thus the Queen's letter, which John Bramston or Sir Robert Herbert wrote and Knutsford approved, was no aberration. Nine months before, however, Cawston and Gifford had been advised by Knutsford to seek a concession in the trans-Limpopo region, and in January Knutsford had encouraged Cawston and Gifford to join hands with Rhodes. These are contradictions which are explicable only by assuming that the Colonial Office was opposed primarily to action which would involve the reluctant Tories in imperial advance. During the weeks when Rhodes was on the high seas, the Colonial Office could not have been contemplating more than the weakest of backing for Rhodes. Indeed, it was about to remove Robinson because of his affinity for Rhodes, and was worried politically about Liberal and humanitarian reaction.

Shortly after he arrived in London, Rhodes anxiously cross-examined Maund about the contents of the Queen's letter to Lobengula. The usual story, based on a recollection of Maund, is that Rhodes was told about the damaging

phrases in that communication, sent Maund to Knutsford to have them removed, and failed because Knutsford would not alter a letter from the Queen.
Rhodes then instructed Maund to toss the letter overboard on his return. But
Maund refused, in part because the Aborigines Society had wisely sent a similar missive to Lobengula by another route, and also had the forethought to
have a copy mailed to the *Bechuanaland News* in Mafeking. Be "wary and firm
in resisting proposals that will not bring good to you and your people," the
Society told Lobengula.

This oft-repeated tale is a legend. As Rhodes told Cawston in late September (repeated in early October), he had only just learned about the contents of the dangerous letter and about the communication from the Society.
"If it was not so serious it would really be laughable to think that our own
servant should be devoting his brains at our expense to destroy all our plans.
You remember," he said, "how he lied in that room of mine [in London in
March] and said there was no such message in the Queen's letter. If he told
the truth we could then have remedied the evil but he deliberately denied
there being any such expression." (Maund had in fact told Lord Gifford, not
Rhodes, about the offending sentence. Gifford asked to have it eliminated,
and Maund saw Knutsford unavailingly. When Maund many years later compiled his reminiscences, his memory simply confused Gifford and Rhodes.)
On the dangers that might follow the letter from the Queen—and, even with
the charter in his grasp, Rhodes was still anxious about its reception across
the Limpopo—Rhodes told Cawston that it was "not the wretched gold I care
so much about but how can we be expected to gradually gain the confidence
of the chief when his own messengers have been told by the Queen to warn
the king against us. . . ."

Rhodes worked hard in the spring and summer of 1889 with no knowledge of the letters. But he was aware of how antagonistic the South Africa
Committee and the Colonial Office had been before he arrived as the new
man in town. Indeed, his tactics might have been different had he not assumed, from March, that the induna had returned home with a polite but
noncommittal response. As he would have feared, too, when the Queen's
warning reached Gbulawayo in August (Maund having deliberately slowed
the group's return), the Ndebele reacted predictably. "If the Queen hears that
I have given away the whole country," Lobengula wrote to London, "it is not
so. . . . I thank the Queen for the word which my messengers gave me by
mouth, that the Queen says I am not to let anyone dig for gold in my country
except to dig for me as my servants. . . ."[44] Conceivably this response might
even then have sidetracked the charter momentum which had been built up
in London; however, thanks probably to Rhodes' accomplices in high places
in southern Africa, the letter of August took much longer than usual to arrive
in London. It appeared in the Colonial Office only in late October, as the
royal charter was being inscribed.

London had lionized Lobengula's messengers. In their wake, John Mackenzie, Rhodes' missionary antagonist, had activated the seven-year-old South

Africa Committee, chaired by Chamberlain and including among its members a coterie of influential and titled men of affairs. Among them were Sir Thomas Fowell Buxton, head of the Aborigines Protection Society; Albert Grey; Evelyn Ashley, former parliamentary under-secretary for the colonies; R. Wardlaw Thompson, secretary of the London Missionary Society; John Walton, of the Wesleyan Methodist Missionary Society; the Earl of Fife; William Thomas Stead, editor of the *Pall Mall Gazette;* and many others of liberal prominence.

The Committee lobbied strenuously for a paternalist, truly imperial (that is, British-controlled and not Cape-controlled or -funded) takeover of central Africa to thwart the Germans and the Portuguese, oppose Rhodes, and safeguard the interests of Africans. Mackenzie and his committee were early advocates of the notion that only late-Victorian Britain was fit to be a trustee for Africa and Africans—to take upon itself the white man's burden and the noble civilizing mission of David Livingstone. Allied to the Committee, but more broadly humanitarian in its advocacy, was the Aborigines Society. The modern embodiment of anti-slaving sentiment and British liberalism at its most assertive, the Society had friends in parliament and the press, and a position in circles of influence which could hardly be ignored.

When Rhodes reached London at the beginning of that packed spring of 1889, he was little known—Knutsford confused him with Graham Bower, Robinson's deputy at the Cape—and possessed primarily wiles, charm, liquid capital, and the promise of future riches. All such attributes, not least the last, were essential if a youthful diamond magnate from Kimberley were to induce the Crown and British imperialism to serve his ambitions. Yet he could not immediately have known how crucial to his own realization of those ambitions would be the alarmingly parallel ambitions of the Tories in power. They made Rhodes' magnetism and money serve the detailed, short-term objectives of a British foreign policy which had thus far addressed itself only very lamely to the opportunities presented to a world power by the ongoing partition of Africa. As Lord Salisbury, British prime minister and foreign minister, had recently replied to those who demanded the extension of British hegemony to Nyasaland (Malawi): "It is not our duty to do it. We should be risking tremendous sacrifices for a very doubtful gain. . . . We must leave the dispersal of this terrible army of wickedness [African recalcitrance] to the gradual advancement of civilisation and Christianity."[45]

Yet events were moving in Rhodes' favor: the accelerating scramble for Africa which had made Germany and even Portugal a threat to British and African interests in the interior, and the rapid occupation of the Congo Independent State by King Léopold of Belgium, worried Britons, especially their political leaders. Moreover, although he need not have been aware of it, Rhodes' aims were in large part also those of unimpeachable African-oriented institutions like the Church of Scotland and the Free Church of Scotland, both Presbyterian missionary societies in Nyasaland being threatened by Portuguese territorial pretensions and indigenous Muslim slavers. The London Missionary Society also wished to be backed officially in the distant reaches of Bechuanaland and in the country of the Ndebele.

Rhodes' timing was thus fortunate; Lord Salisbury was a practical man who played diplomatic chess cautiously, painstakingly, and usually one precise move at a time. As prime minister and foreign minister he carried the woes of governance on his own solid shoulders; Lord Goschen, his treasury minister, was institutionally even more parsimonious than Salisbury. He had recently banned all additions to staff and increases in expenditure. There were those—like the South Africa Committee and the Scottish missionaries (who had many Scottish MPs at their political disposal)—who wanted Salisbury to extend British influence over southern Africa. Others pressed him year after year to spend more British money on Bechuanaland, on telegraph lines, and on a railway with which to develop it and bring the benefits of commerce and civilization to Africans and white promoters. For Salisbury, Rhodes, Cawston, Gifford, and their other principals represented an opportunity which could be grasped and shaped only by a grand international statesman who combined expediency with expediency. For Rhodes and Salisbury to be brought together in the spring of 1889 was the acme of synergistic serendipity. Unbeknownst to each other, and personally unacquainted, each capitalized on the ambitions and cynicism of the other. As a biographer of Salisbury properly concluded, "there cannot be many instances of two men so naturally uncongenial to one another jointly contributing on so large a scale to the same ambitious enterprise. . . . Lord Salisbury acquiesced in his scheming. . . ."[46]

Their meshing of aspiration was not foreseen, foreordained, or historically inevitable. Nor, for once, was the entente which developed based on Rhodes' magnetism or charm entirely. (It was indirect: Rhodes swayed others capable of intervening with Salisbury and Knutsford.) Indeed, Rhodes arrived in London in late March 1889, unsure whether or how his objects could or would be achieved. He was uncertain whether the Rudd Concession would be upheld—not because of Lobengula's objections, and not primarily because of competing concessions, but because it conveyed limited mineral rights only and gave a Cape-based mining man a significant stake in what had been regarded as an imperial sphere.[47] Earlier, in acknowledging the opposition to the concession in Britain, Rhodes had asked Rothschild to help turn it and to "check" Maund if he tried to make mischief at the Colonial Office. (He had offered the great banker a large share, gratis, in what Rhodes believed would eventually "prove a great thing.") Until arriving in Britain he could not be sure whether Cawston and Gifford, Maund's backers, would actively agitate against him and the concession or whether, as he hoped and as word from them to Cape Town had hinted, they would agree to strike what Rhodes quaintly called "an arrangement." The Portuguese might prove a problem, as they had protested against the Rudd Concession. "But they [were] an effete nation and will," he correctly predicted, "be limited to paper protests." The stakes, as he reminded Rothschild, were truly high: "As to gold all my reports only verify previous statements—the gold bearing reefs are simply endless and on the Mazoe there is rich alluvial."[48]

The stakes were also high for Rhodes personally. He had invested his ambitions in a northern adventure at a time when lesser but more prudent thirty-five-year-olds might have nurtured their new riches, focused on the recently revealed but not yet matured bonanza of Witwatersrand, or at least husbanded their accumulating capital for adventures less far-flung, chancy, and audacious. Moreover, Rhodes' new initiative was inherently expensive. It was an attempt to conquer, administer, and exploit not only the trans-Limpopo region subject to Lobengula, but trans-Zambezia, the copperlands of Shaba (Katanga), and—because of Salisbury—the borderlands of Lake Malawi. Moreover, Rhodes was not by nature a high-stakes gambler. Usually he proceeded cautiously, not by tortoise-like moves but with a cat-like preparation before intermediate or seemingly grand jumps. Generous to persons, he never expended his limited liquidity frivolously. Nor, for the central African adventure, were he or his colleagues initially disposed to fund their gamble with real as opposed to paper funds; Zimbabwe was occupied and administered with moneys obtained by pyramiding shares backed by promises rather than assets. De Beers and Gold Fields had solid stakes, but the famous trust deeds were licenses for stock speculations. Rhodes did not at first intend to perfect the Rudd Concession and the Charter that followed by employing hard-earned profits from diamonds or gold. Yet even if he remained more hesitant financially over the charter than is usually assumed, failure in London in 1889 would have undermined Rhodes' sense of self and his potential, modified the trajectory of his flight, and confined his ambitions to more directly entrepreneurial pursuits within South Africa.

Rhodes does not appear to have known or guessed the vast extent to which the realization of most of his dreams—not just permission to move forward in central Africa—depended upon success or failure in London. This was hardly because of timidity or lack of self-esteem; rather, Rhodes respected the many obstacles in his way, appreciated (as he always did) how much of an outsider he continued to appear to the British establishment, and probably understood how little he knew about the inner workings of Whitehall and British politics. When he arrived in London he knew that he would be able to move forward only in concert with others, like Cawston and Gifford, that many jealous men of influence would have to be squared, and that some mechanism like a chartered company would prove to be the successful instrument of his acquisition. Rhodes, after all, had always been alert to the signals of others. He solved problems rather than took positions. Thus, Rhodes stepped off the ship that brought him home to England in 1889 with a confidence in his ability to adapt and prosper—with an insouciance born of experience—that matched that of the youth who stepped off the *Eudora* in 1870 onto the shores of Africa. At this second epochal watershed, however, Rhodes possessed resources, contacts, and a record of success. He need not rely entirely—only largely—on his wits.

Rhodes' family was unknown. He himself—despite his connections to Rothschild and his prominence in the Cape and his wealth—was still an object of some mystery and suspicion. Salisbury was suspicious of his sympathies, and others, like Chamberlain, knew of Rhodes primarily because of his loan to Parnell. To be a leader in the provinces of the empire was no certain recipe of success. To be sure, Rhodes had advantages: money and the promise of more, the ability to make others rich by giving them stakes in his enterprises, support from Hercules Robinson, the backing of Maguire and others with ties to the establishment, and Rothschild's influence. He had the Concession, too. Most of all, he had presence, determination, a vision, a superb salesman's sixth sense that enabled him to calculate true advantage (for himself and for others), and no rigid notions about how best to achieve his long-held but recently focused ambitions for himself as an empire builder and extender. Rhodes was on the edge either of realizing or forever renouncing his long-cherished fantasies.

When Salisbury and others came to judge Rhodes and Rhodes' mettle in April and May 1889, he and his ideas passed muster. Rothschild may have told his friends that Rhodes was really a little Englander at heart. Rothschild may even have quoted Rhodes on the subject of southern Africa: "With the development of the gold in the Transvaal, we shall gradually get a United S. Africa under the English flag."[49] Others, like Mackenzie and his friends, thought that Rhodes could only succeed by chicanery and bribery: "If Rhodes gets his charter," a friend of Mackenzie decided, "it will have a very questionable aroma attached to the getting thereof—one will smell a rat in high places."[50] But there was both more and less to the getting than met the eye. The more was financial: through a series of striking financial maneuvers that were revealed only years later, Rhodes converted the Concession into a formidable instrument of potential riches. The less was the surprising extent to which Rhodes' appearance on the British political horizon served Salisbury and the predominant Tory desire to achieve African, world, and imperial hegemony on the cheap.

Cawston and Gifford had earlier been told by Knutsford and his principal officials at the Colonial Office (notably Herbert and Bramston) that Her Majesty's government preferred an amalgamation of Rhodes' Cape interests and those of the British backers of Cawston and Gifford rather than any painful arbitration between the two. (The Colonial Office had primary responsibility for Africa south of the Limpopo, the Foreign Office for the northern territories and relations with other international powers.) There had been hints that the employment of a royal charter formula would be welcomed in Whitehall; Rhodes' financial resources were essential if the potential problems of the woefully undercapitalized Imperial British East Africa and Royal Niger companies were to be avoided. Furthermore, Metcalfe's railway and the costs of Bechuanaland could be absorbed only, thought Salisbury and the officials, if the profits of the diamond mines were harnessed to such imperial endeavor. Salisbury and Knutsford (certainly not Goschen) may have seen Rhodes as the salvor of a myriad of their difficulties. The record implies less: they wanted Rhodes' help first with but a few of these difficult problems. Only as the spring wore on, and as Rhodes proved an astounding social as well as political success, did he and his millions comprise the solution to all, or nearly all, of London's expensive chores and putative responsibilities in southern Africa. The imperial initiative was arrived at piecemeal, with no overarching strategy.

It is difficult to pinpoint the precise pivot of governmental opinion, but a convincing case can be made that the opposition to the Concession and, by extension, to Rhodes and the Charter, that was enunciated by the Colonial Office in early March had largely been removed by mid-April as a result of the arguments contained in a timely dispatch from Robinson at the Cape. His insights persuaded Herbert that the Colonial Office's constant worries about the costs of administering Bechuanaland could be removed by favoring rather than opposing Rhodes. Equally important, competition for Lobengula's domain would embroil Britain, prove financially draining, and could possibly result in the intervention of the Transvaal. Robinson urged Herbert to avoid such a result by promoting a charter for Rhodes. A charter, Robinson hinted, Herbert developed, and Knutsford later extolled, could (at least in theory) give Her Majesty's government a means of controlling the activities of a promoter like Rhodes in the interior. The alternative was a joint stock company, responsible to no government, and a likely source of trouble for Britain in distant parts.[51]

Rhodes had been in England barely more than a fortnight when Cawston and Gifford were encouraged by the Colonial Office to join hands with Rhodes and develop a charter proposal. By mid-May Knutsford (prodded by Herbert) had agreed in principle to recommend the granting of such an instrument, and Salisbury was officially informed of the initiative only then. By mid-June the Foreign Office (and thus Salisbury) were agreed; even so, the charter was granted officially only in October. Details had to be fixed, opposition to the charter from parliamentarians and humanitarians diverted, and public opinion manipulated. In each of these pursuits Salisbury found a ready and consummately accomplished ally in Rhodes. For the young amalgamator, conquering London was easier and much more exhilarating than wooing the Cape Assembly, outwitting Barnato and Baring Gould, besting Warren, and (through subordinates) rushing Lobengula. The imperial tides were with him, buoying him along with a rush toward fortunate shores which could hardly have been anticipated a mere few years before.

Rhodes knew that the amalgamators could achieve nothing without presenting a united front. Immediately after landing in Britain, he therefore began fashioning financial arrangements with the Cawston-Gifford syndicate, although at first he disliked Cawston. As early as 28 March, Rhodes offered a quarter-share in the Rudd Concession to the Exploring Company. Maund vividly recalled the hectic meetings that took place in late March between Rhodes, Beit, Cawston, Gifford, and Maund and his brother. Rhodes and Beit dominated those sessions, "the former by his personality, the latter by his shrewd grasp of detail." Maund saw Rhodes "in a totally different light to the brusque Rhodes I had met [earlier in Africa]. In London he was the man of affairs, moderate, affable, jolly, considerate of the opinions of others. He took the broad views and left to Beit the details. No haggling, just careful consideration followed by minor adjustments." To Maund personally "he was now as cordial and cheery as he had been violent and threatening." Rhodes, "when he spoke of his ideas . . . electrified us with his fervour." England, he said, must carve up Africa as a "duty to civilization."[52]

Seven weeks later, after endless bargaining and scheming, a carefully calculated plan that displays the hallmarks of Rhodes and Beit was accepted by the contending parties. Gold Fields, which had funded the Rudd, Maguire, and Thompson mission and hence "owned" the Concession, and the Exploring Company, with its more tendentious claims, conveyed their assets and goodwill to a newly minted shell called the Central Search Association, Ltd. Together with the Concession, they also sold to the Association all other past and future claims to minerals in the domains of Lobengula and adjacent territories. The Association's capital was a nominal £120,000, £92,000 of which was paid back out to its creators: Gold Fields received £25,000; Exploring Company, £22,500; Rhodes, £9,750; Rudd, £9,000; Beit, £8,250; and Rhodes, Rudd, and Beit together, another £9,000. Rhodes also saw that Rothschild received £3,000, and gave Maguire the same amount. He also feared the Haggards and their Austral Africa Company sufficiently to give it £2,400. The remaining 27,600 shares were to be sold at par by the original parties. Shortly afterwards, Jameson was given £1,000 worth of shares and Robinson (who might be said to have deserved more) 250 £1 shares. The controlling directors of Central Search were Rhodes, Rudd, Gifford, Cawston, Beit, John Oakley Maund (Edward Arthur Maund's brother), and Thomas Rudd. Some of the same persons, headed by Rhodes and not Cawston, also ran a new Exploring Company, which replaced the existing one in May.

Both this last company and the Association existed solely to transform the comparatively intangible asset of the Rudd Concession into something more tangible and profitable. Moreover, ingeniously, although the Foreign and Colonial offices and the investing public were led to believe that any company charter for central Africa would be based on and "own" the Rudd Concession, very few Britons ever knew that the resulting chartered company was a mere licensee of the closely held and Rhodes-dominated Central Search Association.[53] What mattered most was that by this clever mechanism Rhodes could cement alliances and promise to make allies and competitors wealthy while retaining a tidy portion of such profits for himself, Rudd, and Beit. He thus avoided committing his main, hard-won, and still challengeable asset to any body over which the investing public might have an influence. (A year later, after the Charter had been secured and Rhodesia settled, Central Search became the United Concessions Company. Of its inflated capital of £4 million, Thomas Rudd and H.D. Boyle owned 339,200 shares together; the Exploring Company, 293,700; Rhodes, 132,000; Beit, 112,400; Rhodes, Rudd, and Beit together, 90,000; Charles Rudd, 66,800; Austral Africa, 80,000; Matabele Thompson—long promised a sizable reward—49,770; Maguire, 49,000; and

Rothschild, 39,200. Jameson and Henry Clay Moore each had 10,000, and Robinson 2,500.)[54]

There were minor but noisy claimants who Rhodes was prepared to square: the Ochs brothers, who had succeeded to verbal promises made to Thomas Baines; the Grahamstown syndicate; and Sir John Swinburne, a member of parliament with a dated and vague claim to the Tati district. Some were paid outright, some received shares in the chartered company, some rights to search for gold, and so on. Rhodes proved his usual expedient self, ably assisted by Beit. In another direction, and for very different reasons, Rhodes and Cawston were encouraged by Salisbury to aid the African Lakes Company. Founded in 1878 under a similar name by well-meaning evangelical philanthropists to assist Presbyterian missionaries in the development of Nyasaland, in 1889 it was an essentially insolvent, poorly managed, asset-poor enterprise locked in a draining struggle with Muslims for control of Lake Malawi and its environs. Salisbury was being pressured to act forcibly by Scottish MPs, by the heads of Oxford colleges, by earls and dukes aroused by the missionaries, and by the press.

Nyasaland, as yet a contested portion of a British sphere and not a protectorate or a colony, was also prey to Portugal. No matter how "effete," Portugal controlled the Shire River's outlet to the Zambezi River and the Zambezi's Indian Ocean port at Quelimane. Salisbury desired a vigorous African Lakes Company to help stabilize the Lake Malawi region and oppose the Portuguese. In May, Knutsford suggested to Salisbury that the proposed charter could serve the "public interest" if it were required to include in its sphere of operations those territories north of the Zambezi and west of Lake Malawi which contained missionaries crying out for protection against the Portuguese and slavers.

One of the leading champions of British intervention was Alexander Livingstone Bruce, a Scottish businessman who had married Livingstone's daughter Agnes, was related to Lord Balfour of Burleigh, and was well acquainted with Albert Grey. Rhodes had met Bruce in Johannesburg in 1888, and had been impressed by the man's connections, if not the man. Bruce was also a director of Mackinnon's East Africa Company. In 1888 Rhodes had "pointed out to [Bruce that they] ought to try and join; that is, [Bruce's] Company should work down through Tanganyika to the Zambesi to join [Rhodes'] development from the South, getting in between the Germans and the Congo State." Rhodes reassured Rothschild that he had not, of course, told Bruce his "visionary dreams," but Bruce had "eagerly caught the idea and [would] work at it."[55] In 1889, Bruce favored merging the Lakes Company with the proposed chartered company. Together with Balfour and Grey, he was impressed by Rhodes' promised contributions to the administration of the lakes regions and his support for the missionaries and an end to traffic in slaves and liquor. The Foreign Office was also impressed, indebted, and grateful, even if other members of the Lakes Company board, especially the brothers John and Fred Moir, delayed any actual merger until long after the charter had been granted.

The politics of a charter also required that Rhodes, a stripling with a colonial rather than a metropolitan record, and Cawston, a City man, enlist support among and recruit for their board directors of sufficient social and political standing to impress parliamentarians and investors. To be asked thus to provide a front might have galled a less self-assured and supple man than Rhodes. He, however, welcomed the instruction, knowing it to be prudent advice of a kind that he was always prepared to give his own subordinates. Balfour, sometime lord-in-waiting to the Queen and soon to become a parliamentary undersecretary at the Board of Trade, Sir Donald Currie (of the shipboard affair with the French company), and Mackinnon all refused Rhodes' entreaties (which were delivered by a trusted intermediary), although Balfour was tempted. Finally, Rhodes persuaded the Duke of Abercorn, a wealthy northern Irish peer with vast estates in Donegal and Scotland, to chair the company. The Earl of Fife, shortly to become the son-in-law of the Prince of Wales, and to be elevated to a dukedom, agreed to be vice chairman. He was a banker and an influential member of the Liberal party as well as a member of the South Africa Committee. Abercorn had served in parliament for twenty years. Nevertheless, neither added more than cosmetics to the company. Neither had hitherto been associated with or interested in Africa. Both were appropriate as nominees for Rhodes; both would remain passive and obedient surrogates for him throughout the early years of Company life. They merely wanted to be assured of the opportunity, which both enjoyed, to make substantial profits by buying and selling Company stock.

The real catch, and the third public member, was Grey. (The other directors were Rhodes, Beit, Gifford, and Cawston.) Long associated with Africa and southern Africa, heir to the earldom of his uncle, who had been a colonial secretary, Grey was a serious personage. Moreover, a member of the South Africa Committee and a close associate of Mackenzie, he was known for his integrity. "The Paladin of his generation," with a proud record of public service, he called the Empire his country and England his home. During the talks over the future of the Lakes Company, or in additional contexts, Grey came under Rhodes' splendid spell. He later said—even after the Jameson Raid— that Rhodes had, above all other men, impressed him by "the bigness of his mind and the tenderness of his heart." Perhaps Jameson, who later derided Grey as "a nice old lady, but not a genius, who does not like committing himself to any opinion," thus explained why, but there is no doubt that, in seeking the grant of a royal charter, Rhodes and Salisbury could not have asked for a more significant and loyal ally.[56]

Rhodes ingratiated himself and his charter during London's late spring and early summer. He offered Lord Robert Cecil, Salisbury's son, the sinecure of becoming standing counsel for the proposed chartered company. Cecil accepted. J. Scott Keltie, geographer and journalist, was employed to write articles favorable to the charter and to place them in *The Times* and other publications. The Rev. John Verschoyle, deputy editor of the influential *Fortnightly Review* and a subsequent biographer and compiler of Rhodes' speeches, was paid well to remain loyal. Sir Charles Dilke, the Radical M.P. who wrote on imperial matters for that *Review,* obtained shares in the company at par. So did a host of politicians in London and persons of prominence (some of whom were doubtless also politicians) at the Cape. Many of those who were favored with shares at a nominal £1 each made enormous profits when they sold all or part of their gifts. Rhodes was no amateur when it came to currying favor.

Of Rhodes' more significant, idealistic rather than materialistic conquests, an unlikely trio was, like Grey, of considerable long-term as well as immediate importance. The first of the trio was Flora Shaw, colonial correspondent for *The Times,* and a unique early professional woman. She came under Rhodes' spell sometime in the spring or summer of 1889.[57] Earlier, in May, Verschoyle invited Henry Hamilton (later Sir Harry) Johnston to dine in Marylebone with Walter Pater, the aesthete and author of authoritative exaltations of the Renaissance; Frank Harris, nominal editor of the *Fortnightly Review,* bon vivant, and gossip; and "an extraordinary fellow over from South Africa, Cecil Rhodes." Johnston, a diminutive, jaunty, unmarried man who had earlier used British guns to compel Nigerian merchant-kings like Ja Ja of Opopo to accept British hegemony, had recently been appointed British consul at Mozambique. Salisbury had employed him as a special emissary to Lisbon and had, in 1888, encouraged him to write boldly, if anonymously, in *The Times* that Africa "must inevitably be exploited by the white races. . . ." Johnston advocated an end to Britain's "magnificent inactivity" in colonizing Africa. He urged the linking of Britain's possessions in southern Africa with her sphere in East Africa and the Egyptian Sudan "by a continuous band of British dominion"—the germ of the Cape-to-Cairo rallying cry.

Johnston described Verschoyle, a bachelor who also was curate of an Anglican church in the Marylebone district of London, as a strange character: "young, rather good-looking, very blond and gray-eyed, Ulster, [and] of such broad theology that all the strait Christian doctrines seemed to have slipped through the meshes of his mind." Harris remembered Verschoyle as "a line battle-ship cut down to a frigate" with a chest fifty inches around and "prodigiously strong." "He was handsome, too, with a high forehead, good features and long, golden mustache." Johnston realized that Verschoyle had no more "faith" than he himself had. Yet he "worked desperately hard as an Imperialist and a kind of liberal conservative." His rooms were untidy. In them he gave at a moment's notice "large dinners or small and cosy ones . . . to politicians and leaders of movements."

Johnston took to Rhodes. They talked deeply over oysters and soup until midnight. Then Verschoyle sent them off by cab to Rhodes' suite at the Westminster Palace Hotel, where they schemed until dawn. "We settled as we thought the immediate line of action in South and Central Africa," recalled Johnson. "I jotted down on paper the heads of the scheme I was to propose to Lord Salisbury. . . ." Rhodes gave Johnston £2,000 for treaty-making expeditions across trans-Zambezia toward Katanga, and—at a time when the Treasury was being particularly tight-fisted—promised more—£10,000 a year—for the occupation and administration of Johnston's allotted dominions as well as "Central Africa between the Zambesi and the White Nile." Johnston much later acknowledged that Rhodes had personally "been the direct means of saving for the British Empire all the territories stretching between the north of the Transvaal and the basin of the Congo, in addition to having given a valuable impetus to the growing idea among the British people that we should not abandon our control over Egypt, but that we should rather seek to open up a continuous chain of Empire from Cape to Cairo."

Johnston explained breathlessly to Salisbury on the afternoon after his meeting with Rhodes that they together wanted to use the chartered company to extend British influence to Lake Tanganyika and possibly all the way to Uganda. Rhodes' munificence and Salisbury's acquiescence made it possible, all of a sudden, for Johnston to sail in May to Mozambique, and then to proceed up the Zambezi and the Shire to commence the process of occupying and pacifying what today is Malawi. It is also evident that Johnston saw in Rhodes much more than a patron; Johnston imagined Rhodes a soul mate, an inspiring imperialist with broad British dreams. Rhodes, however, merely welcomed Johnston's enthusiasm, especially because of his ties to Salisbury, and was prepared to use it for his own ends. Johnston thought that he had helped to shape and influence Rhodes' thinking, and so he doubtless had. But Rhodes was then and afterwards looking beyond Johnston to the charter and to the flanks of a central Africa that Johnston might well protect.[58]

A month before the meeting with Johnston, when Rhodes was fresh from Africa and still learning to judge the contours of British imperial politics, he asked to see Stead of the *Pall Mall Gazette*. A weekly, the *Gazette* anticipated yellow journalism. Stead was a sensationalist, a crusader, and a didact in an era when newspapers were written circumspectly for the elite. Stead had used the *Gazette* to promote "the Imperialism of responsibility as opposed to Jingoism. . . ." Much to Rhodes' presumed delight, he had even written an article in the *Gazette* advocating Anglo-American reunion. Stead believed, and wrote passionately about, closer union between the mother country and the colonies. He wanted to make the colonies jointly liable with Britain for the defense of empire. As Stead reported, Rhodes, "brooding in intellectual solitude in the midst of the diamond diggers," found in the *Gazette* "the crude ideas which he had embodied in his first will." Rhodes apparently told Stead that his own ideas had been molded and modified by the *Gazette*. In 1885, when Stead published a series of articles on prostitution—"The Maiden Tribute"—and went to jail for his pains, Rhodes realized that the *Gazette* was being directed by a man prepared to do more than write piously. Rhodes, given his deep, continuing attachment to his mother, may also have been attracted by a defense of virginity—of the chasteness of women. Whatever the motive force, Rhodes tried to pay homage to Stead by visiting him in prison, but was turned away. Rhodes also—most uncharacteristically—attended a meeting in Exeter Hall (the home of humanitarian protest) called to protest Stead's imprisonment.

It was with an unaccustomed degree of fervor and hero worship that

Rhodes sought out Stead in 1889. Yet Rhodes had visited Britain in 1888 and earlier without trying to find Stead. In 1889 Rhodes sought control over central Africa; Stead was a prominent member of the South Africa Committee. He was a close confidant of Mackenzie, and had battled with Mackenzie against the Rhodes-inspired takeover of Bechuanaland. He also edited an influential publication. Naturally, as Rhodes arranged to meet Verschoyle, Dilke, Shaw, and others who could influence the opinions of those in power, so he began his assault on London by visiting the quintessential imperial dreamer. Yet Stead accepted an invitation to lunch only reluctantly, since everything that he had heard about Rhodes from Mackenzie and others gave him pause. "To say that I was astonished by what he said to me is to say little," Stead reported. "I had expected nothing—was indeed rather bored at the idea . . . but no sooner had Sir Charles Mills [agent general of the Cape and their host] left the room than [sic] Mr. Rhodes fixed my attention by pouring out the long-dammed-up flood of his ideas."

That afternoon Stead wrote hurriedly to his wife: "Mr. Rhodes is my man!" After three hours of intense conversation, Stead declared that Rhodes was full of "gorgeous" ideas of "federation, expansion, and consolidation of Empire." Rhodes also gave Stead £2,000 to settle a libel judgment and promised £20,000 immediately and more later to promote their mutual ideas through the *Gazette* or in other publications. Stead said that Rhodes told him "some things he ha[d] told to no other man—save Lord Rothschild," which was an embellishment, and spoke loftily about "underpinning the Empire by a Society which would be to the Empire what the Society of Jesus was to the Papacy." Rhodes urged Stead to read the novel that expressed these ideas so remarkably: Crawford's *The American Politician*.

Stead described Rhodes as not personally very prepossessing, but full of ideas. "He believes more in wealth and endowments than I do. He is not religious in the ordinary sense, but has a deeply religious conception of his duty to the world, and thinks he can best serve it by working for England." Stead asserted, probably correctly, that Rhodes took to him. Before they parted that afternoon, confirmed in letters of that week and later, the two had "struck up a firm friendship," Stead, with his boundless optimism, believing that almost alone he had "the key to the real Rhodes."[59] Stead, the third of the trio, was to become more than a mere acolyte; he was made a trustee of the will and the big idea. He corresponded feverishly during the 1890s with Rhodes and turned the *Review of Reviews,* which Stead founded with Rhodes' money shortly after their encounter in 1889, into a supporter of Rhodes' dreams for Africa and the world. Converting Stead also helped, as did the winning of Grey and others, to destroy Mackenzie's coalition. Even Chamberlain conceded that Rhodes was not so bad as he had been painted.

In these several, rather familiar, ways, Rhodes proceeded assiduously, in keeping with a closely knit personal agenda, to articulate a grand design for imperial Britain in a manner and with a determination and an assurance which was riveting and commanding. His program was vast, even grandiose, but in the late 1880s it was not wholly beyond the imagination of a heady post-Darwinian age when men and women were accomplishing intellectual and physical deeds which far exceeded the expectations even of their fathers and mothers. The earnest young entrepreneur, politician, and promoter captivated, impressed, interested, and delighted those who believed in boundless progress and the fruits of spectacular energy. His open checkbook strengthened his arguments.

Rhodes was at his most dynamic. Trolling endlessly for supporters down the gilded streets of the West End and into the more skeptical City, and sometimes venturing beyond to the country estates of his social betters, Rhodes was successful in confirming the Concession, for no one examined it carefully or subjected its limitations and absence of administrative permission to serious scrutiny. So also was he successful, in time, not only in obtaining a chartered license for the exploitation and subjection of central Africa but also in extending its and his ambit beyond any of his earlier expectations. Thanks to the meeting with Johnston, the discussions with Bruce and Balfour, the support of Grey, and Salisbury's preoccupations, the ultimate parameters of the chartered company, and thus of Rhodes' dominion, encompassed central Africa to the edges of the great interior lakes on which Rhodes had much earlier set his sights.

Nevertheless, the road to victory was not entirely open. Just as the charter seemed assured—Knutsford backed it and Salisbury seemed favorably disposed; Abercorn, Fife, and Grey were lending credibility; parliamentary and other opposition had largely been neutralized; and the press was beginning to swing behind the scheme—Lobengula's written repudiation arrived in the Colonial Office. It was the middle of June. Maguire, in London, was again pressed into service by Rhodes. Writing to the Colonial Office, he cast aspersions on the bona fide character of a letter which had not been witnessed by an independently minded missionary. Corresponding apprehensively at the same time to Thompson, still in Gbulawayo, he asked urgently for indications, evidence—anything—that would show that the king had been misled.

Robinson, recalled from South Africa over Rhodes' objections, had by this time also arrived in London, where his influence with the Colonial Office on behalf of Rhodes and the Cape-based imperial factor proved surprisingly strong. Knutsford had earlier objected to his close ties to Rhodes and Rudd, and Knutsford and Salisbury may also have regarded him as a liability because of his intemperate attacks on such parliamentary opponents of the Rudd Concession as the Speaker of the House of Commons. Robinson had spoken out strongly against those who believed in the permanent relevance of an imperial as distinct from a locally based British hegemonic influence in southern Africa. Chamberlain had complained about Robinson, and Salisbury told Chamberlain in June that the Cabinet was unanimous in barring Robinson's continued tenure in South Africa. Robinson accordingly was replaced by Sir Henry Brougham Loch, at a time, ironically, when the policies which Robinson and Rhodes had long germinated were about to burst into full flower.

Nevertheless, Rhodes, commenting at the beginning of June, when he had overcome opposition to the Concession and the proposed charter with greater ease than he could have hoped, professed not to be troubled by the loss of Robinson's support at the Cape. "Do not be alarmed," he told Shippard. "I am very sorry but the policy will not be altered. He asked them to give him a definite assurance of support and though they argued with him they were afraid to do this. They felt [probably correctly] it meant turning him into a dictator for South Africa for the next four years."[60]

Rhodes was initially uneasy about defraying the cost of administering Bechuanaland. He took a few weeks to be persuaded that his consortium would have to promise to construct a telegraph and railway through Bechuanaland from Kimberley toward the Zambezi, but by June he was ready to move forward on these and all of the other possible central African fronts. His impatience made him bold, for he even attempted to pay for and dispatch an official representative of the Crown to Gbulawayo well ahead of the actual granting, or even the consideration by the Queen in Council, of the plans for a charter. He tried to send £30,000 to the Colonial Office for such purposes, and presumably grew irritated at the way in which the officials there persisted in temporizing needlessly; his request, and subsequent ones, were rejected until the charter was finally approved.[61]

Yet Rhodes' effrontery hardly made him less popular or his proposals less welcome. By mid-June, despite Lobengula's letter, he had won the day. Salisbury's aspirations for central Africa and concern for the Portuguese and the Germans, and Rhodes' charm and financial largesse, had proved decisive. In no more salient way was this victory signaled than by the way in which Lobengula's renunciation was shrugged away officially, and Maguire and Robinson's tendentious explanations permitted to stand in its stead. And this by the very men who had warned Lobengula to watch his oxen, and trust no strangers bearing gifts!

Equally disarming was the failure of any of the officials in the Colonial and Foreign offices to do more than assume that the chartered company would in fact own the Rudd Concession. Had they inquired or pressed, they would have learned that an agreement between Central Search and the chartered company provided that the Company would bear all developmental expenses but would divide its profits with the Association. It took a change of government in 1892, and hard times in central Africa, for the truth to be revealed: the chartered company was but a shell, inside of which was another; if the chartered company collapsed there would be no assets to attach, and the British government would be faced with a scandal of South Sea proportions. In 1892, Sydney Olivier of the Colonial Office declared that the government had been misled. Sir Robert Herbert, who had been or allowed himself to be gulled, said that "no persons connected with Her Majesty's Government had any idea that such a scheme was in contemplation. . . . If it had been disclosed the charter would certainly have been refused."[62]

These and many other recriminations came later. In the spring and summer of 1889, all went well for Rhodes. He returned to the Cape from London in August, having done everything to assure the creation of the British South Africa Company, as it was finally labeled. The final details could be left to Cawston, and to Bourchier Hawksley, their solicitous solicitor. "My part is done," Rhodes told Maund, "the Charter is granted supporting Rudd Concession and granting us the interior. I am just waiting until I hear of its signature and to finish many small details. . . . We have the whole thing recognised by the Queen and even if eventually we had any difficulty with king the Home people would now always recognise us in possession of the minerals they quite understand that savage potentates frequently repudiate." He anticipated further moves to extend the new dominion: "I have claimed as to boundaries that they should recognise no claim of Portuguese west of a straight line drawn from Tete. . . . I do not see why Gaza country should go to Portuguese." A few weeks later he gave Maund additional assurances and instructions. Thanks to the Charter, he said, "whatever Lo Bengulu does now will not affect the fact that when there is a white occupation of the country our concession will come into force provided the English and not Boers get the country."[63]

The British South Africa Company received a royal charter on 29 October 1889, a year nearly to the day of the signing of the Rudd Concession. In the interim Rhodes had successfully, cynically, astutely, and with the unwitting assistance of impressionable if not equally cynical men of presumed rectitude in Whitehall, ballooned the Concession to the farthest reach of his own grandiosity. As Rhodes' letters to Maund foreshadowed, he transformed the Concession into a royal permit to conquer, occupy, administer, and absorb a vast hinterland which had not and would never welcome the vision of its future which Rhodes had, all in the rush of an English spring, now set in train. The territories of the Ndebele, the Shona, the Lozi, the Bemba, the Ngoni, and a host of others were ripe for the plucking; Rhodes was reaping the harvest of the scramble for Africa.

The charter of incorporation of the British South Africa Company defined its sphere of operations in an almost limitless manner: "the region of South Africa lying immediately to the north of British Bechuanaland, to the north and west of the South African Republic, and to the west of the Portuguese Dominions." There was no mention of the Germans, or the Congo State, or of any northern or western bounds. In effect, Rhodes had received the kind of hunting license which his predecessors in the East India Company would have appreciated. Moreover, the omission of any confining borders to the north and west, and the vagueness of the one to the east, was deliberate. Rhodes could acquire what he could acquire, and that was, in part, the purpose of the charter. The third clause of the charter empowered the Company (subject to the approval of the British government) to obtain lands and powers by grants or treaty from indigenous authorities anywhere in Africa. The British government could also countermand any dealings of the Company with foreign powers.

The Company was enjoined to remain "British in character and domicile." It was responsible for the preservation of peace and order in its domain "in such ways and manners as it shall consider necessary." It could raise a police force. It was to abolish the slave trade, limit the sale of liquor to Africans, refrain from interfering with indigenous religion "except so far as may be necessary in the interest of humanity. . . ." Local customs were to be respected. And nothing in the charter was to be deemed to authorize the Company to grant a monopoly of trade or commerce. Finally, the Queen in Council could revoke the charter.[64]

The omissions in the charter are in fact surprising: it conferred no specific powers of government or administration; those were to be obtained from local chiefs. The Company was not licensed specifically to mine, trade, grow cash crops, or pursue any of the other occupations that customarily justified the creation of such a special entity. In effect, the British South Africa Company, presumed holder of a limited mining concession, was intended to live by its wits (which doubtless suited Rhodes more than Cawston) and by gaining new concessions and the other legitimizing paper of Africa's partition by foreigners. Salisbury also intended Rhodes and his Company to fulfill the occupational requirements of the Treaty of Berlin of 1885; if not, central Africa could be claimed by another of the metropolitan powers. Rhodes was also expected to make money for a number of well-connected Britons while simultaneously relieving the exchequer of wearying expenditures on the extension of empire in southern Africa. It was a Faustian bargain.

Over Cawston's objections, Rhodes insisted that the Company be capitalized at £1 million in £1 shares. "After all," he told Cawston, "what is the expenditure of £1,000,000 if it means the possession of the whole of Matabeleland?" Moreover, "as I said before we have undertaken a big job and we know that we have the sinews of war even though we never use them." In this case the funds were actually subscribed, for Rhodes needed the infusion of capital to occupy and develop the new dominion. De Beers advanced more than £200,000; Gold Fields, nearly £100,000; the Exploring Company, £75,000; Rhodes, £45,000; Beit, £34,000 (and Rhodes and Beit together £11,000); Barnato, £30,000; Maguire, £18,000; Rudd, £18,000; Thompson, £12,000; and Rothschild, £10,000. Fewer thousands were assigned to Abercorn, Fife, Grey, Harris, Jameson, Cawston, Bruce, Maund, Robinson, and so on. Even Buxton received or purchased 500 shares. Approximately half of the authorized capital, in other words, was held by the principals, particularly by Rhodes, Beit, Rudd, and their associates. Moreover, the shares were held off the public market for two years, presumably in order to permit Rhodes to infiltrate an invading force into the land that was soon named after him—without any need to report to shareholders generally. He was also still worried about threats to the charter and the concession from Lobengula, and wished to handle any such complications without interference.

Rhodes had turned thirty-six in July. By October, his fantasies had been transformed into realizable ambitions. He expected to construct a telegraph line and a railway far into the interior. He had achieved financial suzerainty

over lands as distant as northern Malawi and the still-undefined borders of
the Congo State. He had been challenged to obtain treaties or other concessions over at least 700,000 square miles, or perhaps more. In the case of the
immediately adjacent Limpopo region, his filibustering attempts of 1888 had
been confirmed, enlarged, ennobled, and sanctioned. There was still much to
do. But Rhodes at least now had the kinds of funds at his disposal which he
knew these immense challenges would demand: "With a million behind me I
guarantee," he told Cawston, and promised himself and his subsequent judges,
"to give you Matabeleland."[65] And so he was shortly to do.

"The Power of One Man"
A Rush of Cynicism and Conspiracy—
The Acquisition of Rhodesia

R HODES—young, intense, newly famous, still comparatively slim although about to begin putting on weight in a way that would soon transform his appearance—now had to reach beyond opportunity to realization. After the signing of the Charter, his fantasies—vague, inchoate, and not necessarily practical—suddenly became challenges rather than hopes and longings. Indeed, the Charter gave him more scope and opportunity than even overvaulting ambitions had anticipated. Because Britain's official reaction to the scramble for Africa was hesitancy laced with acute parsimony, because Rhodes offered cash and was induced to add more, and because the very origins of the Charter and the British South Africa Company provided anything but checks on Rhodes' inititative and his lusts for land, minerals, power, and profit—because Salisbury wanted partition by proxy and additions to empire on the cheap, and Rhodes wanted mammon, glory, and a slice of prosperity—the peoples and lands south of the basin of the mighty Congo River and north of the Limpopo River were arbitrarily and indiscriminately placed within the orbit of a vicar's wealthy son who was about to become premier of the Cape Colony.

Rhodes had sought to check the Transvaal and gain a northern outlet for his Cape-fed aspirations; instead, the British government had given him the opportunity to chisel away at a great block of undressed imperial marble. To sculpt it to his satisfaction and modern Africa's glory was a life's task, particularly when Rhodes, the principal architect, was possessed as well of other absorbing internal obligations: the political future of the Cape, railways and telegraphs, the further aggrandizement of diamonds, the renewed mining of gold, and the struggle for hegemony (and unity) within South Africa.

The Charter was a permissive instrument. It gave approximate bounds to Rhodes' new endeavor; authorized the acquisition of additional conveyances of authority from Africans; and by implication transformed the Company, a commercial vehicle with no tangible assets, into an administering and policing engine. In other words, Salisbury created a sphere of influence; it was for Rhodes to give form and content to this grand, ambiguous outreach of empire. That he did so, creating two countries called Rhodesia, is a tribute to his abilities as a creative financier, his drive and organizational stamina, and his gift for generating enthusiasm for visionary objectives among frontiersmen and metropolitan officials alike. That he cynically defaced the block of marble, following a ruthless, colonial-oriented design, and left a legacy of bloodshed and conquest rather than peaceful Westernization and modernization, reflects the age, the motives and methods of the man, and a preoccupation with other endeavors and destinies as well as a fundamental shortage of capital. Rhodes had leveraged diamonds and gold; now he cast his net across the Limpopo.

Rhodes knew how ultimately insubstantial the Charter could become if challenged by indigenous or competing international powers. Rhodes' prime concerns during 1889, 1890, and 1891 hence were nine: (1) How to appease, cajole, overawe, or bludgeon Lobengula into accepting the Company's suzerainty over and eventually within his dominions. (2) How to settle and effectively to administer the presumably gold-rich parts of Lobengula's kingdom, especially the land of the subordinate Shona, before others, whether English-, Afrikaans-, or Portuguese-speaking, could likewise insert themselves. (3) How to ensure the Company (and thus Rhodes) the broadest and fullest geographical opportunities within the vague and as yet undefined limits of the Charter. Gaining concessions, treaties, and other acknowledgements of British/Company hegemony were crucial if other contending parties—the Portuguese, the Germans, the Belgians, and other British-backed concerns— were to be prevented from splitting off chunks of potentially precious stone from Rhodes' as yet only partially charted and explored land. (4) How to strengthen his Cape and as yet tenuous Transvaal mineral base by achieving direct control of all of the subterranean riches which were to be found within the far-flung and expanded reaches of the Company's sphere. Nothing could be left to chance; all known alluvial and surface indications of wealth, by this logic, had to be annexed. (5) How to give the putative Rhodesia access to the sea; Rhodes was always acutely aware of logistical and infrastructural considerations. To prevent Rhodesia from being land-locked, Rhodes looked eastward, to a shadowy region controlled only nominally by "effete" Portugal. (6) How to build a railway north from Kimberley toward the Zambezi at the least expense. (7) How to fling a telegraph line northward toward Cairo expeditiously and cheaply. (8) How to accomplish all of the foregoing on a veritable shoestring without, as Rhodes constantly grumbled, spending his own assets and forfeiting the golden, but separate, opportunity to amass enormous paper profits by manipulating the demand for shares in his main and allied companies. (9) How to do all of the above, bar the last, by proxy, through subordinates of questionable acumen, at a time in his hectic and pressed adulthood when his many schemes and plans taxed even Rhodes' own hard-developed genius for concentration and compartmentalization.

Rhodes had truly come into his own at a time and in a season when most men, then and now, did and do so. That his season was fuller and more demanding than even he could have envisaged was but a reflection of his special gifts. That he rolled triumphantly from victory to victory in the seven years from 1889 to 1895, overcame obstacles of a variety and a kind before which others would have balked, and simultaneously established stable entre-preneurial, political, and sub-imperial empires which were the envy of many, testifies to his awareness of his own unique qualities, and the ways in which they could best be employed within Rhodes' particular context and era. But as awesome and repetitive as were his victories, so (and often overlooked) were the defeats which he received in number and consequence. They pre-figured the eventual, devastating fall from grace which overtook him in 1896. Both victory and defeat reflected the workings of the same genius. Or, as some of his contemporaries later asked, did Rhodes' personality and methods alter noticeably after 1889, reflecting premature aging, increasing strain on his heart, and an immense self-satisfaction with his great gifts?

High on Rhodes' agenda for the north even before the Charter had been signed and the Company created, and then in a redoubled sense afterwards, were Harry Johnston's enlargement of Rhodes' overall sphere in Nyasaland; negotiations with Sir Gordon Sprigg's government at the Cape over the rail extension; and the acquisition of Barotseland, across the Zambezi River. He was worried about the ultimate disposition of the copper-rich Katanga; uncer-tain about the Transvaal's next moves across the Limpopo; and—most of all—understandably fearful that Lobengula would repudiate the Rudd Concession anew, otherwise invalidate the Charter, and upset all of his plans. Clearly this was no idle anxiety, for Rhodes knew how tenuous were his claims, and on what flimsy documentary evidence they rested.

Rhodes was no fool, and in these and other such endeavors he was blessed with the not uncommon ability to justify means by ends. Thus, although he ought rightly to be judged unscrupulous or worse in his dealings with Lob-engula and others over whom he successfully sought advantage by expedience and legerdemain, Rhodes also knew that no indigenous potentate (excepting Menelik) and few indigenous peoples could or would survive the onrushing juggernaut of Europe's scramble for Africa. One or another European entity would become central Africa's overlord. "If we do not occupy," Rhodes wrote home simply in 1889, "someone else will."[1] With no discernible feeling for the fate of Africans, but a keen desire to decide the fate of Africa, Rhodes brushed aside the inconvenient admonitions of humanitarians, and seemingly suffered no pangs of conscience over his part in the partition of Africa. In-deed, Rhodes believed that he was doing the Lord's work by extending the empire and ordering the destinies of endless varieties of heathen.

Lobengula's fears were not to be allayed in traditional ways, for he was rightly aware of his and his people's impending jeopardy. During August and

September 1889, after the Queen's problematical letter had finally arrived and Lobengula had replied: "If the Queen hears that I have given away the whole country, it is not so," the king's antagonism and that of his induna intensified. They were determined to repudiate all concessions, and to attempt to recoup their autonomy before it vanished forever. Thompson, still reluctantly in Gbulawayo as Rhodes' man, was more and more frequently subject to what Moffat called an Ndebele "onset." The Ndebele leaders abused him verbally. As Maund reported, Thompson had been "harassed by questions for hours by the Indunas. . . ." Next, in September, Lotshe, a very old and influential induna, rich in cattle, and friendly to the whites, was put to death along with many of his relatives, and his cattle confiscated. Lotshe had advised Lobengula to sign the Rudd Concession. Thompson, who had just told his wife that he was "getting desperate" and could not possibly "stand it" for too much longer, learned of Lotshe's fate, feared that the Ndebele would take him next, and—as Maund reported—"quite lost his head." Thompson fled in great haste southward to Shoshong and Mafeking.[2]

Rhodes had earlier implored Maund, ostensibly independent but actually in his employ, to "get the concession through." Rhodes fretted about the underlying weakness of his and the Company's position. Thus, when word arrived in Kimberley that Thompson had, to use Rhodes' words, "got jumpy," he persuaded Jameson once again to retrieve the position of the Company in Ndebeleland. According to both Rhodes (writing to Beit) and Jameson's biographer, Rhodes' roommate "volunteered" for the assignment. By the end of September, when Jameson was on his way north with Dennis Doyle (a transport rider), Major Thomas Maxwell, and the unfortunate Thompson, Rhodes instructed Maund to "talk quite freely with Jameson." He "knows everything," Rhodes said. "I have given him full powers and you must do your best to help him." Jameson had a copy of the not-yet-signed Charter, continued Rhodes. "It fully recognizes our concession and whatever Lo Bengulu does now will not affect that fact that when there is a white occupation of the country our concession will come into force. . . ." A month later, shortly after Jameson and his party would have arrived at Lobengula's capital, Rhodes reported that he was "perfectly confident as to getting Matabeleland but it will take 2½ years and I think my plan cannot fail." He did "not regard in the least what Lo Bengulu may do but at present it is just as well to keep him quiet."[3] In other words, Rhodes was rather less than more sanguine about the Concession and the various ways in which its validity could be assailed. The Concession, Rhodes believed, still required ratification. "If we lose the Concession," he told Thompson, "we have nothing for the Charter." Lobengula had not yet accepted the stacked guns and was not to do so for several years. His hostility to Rhodes and to gold seekers generally was apparent, as was the enmity of his induna. Jameson's job, as Rhodes' alter ego, was somehow to mollify, sweet-talk, and "square" the king.

"I should have accompanied Jameson," Rhodes confessed, but his own plate, he pleaded, was well and truly full. He enumerated: "1) Sir S. Shippard,

2) the police question to which I am contributing, 3) Home Board of Charter, 4) Extension of railway and relations with Sprigg, 5) Extension of telegraph Mafeking to Tati for which I am paying, 6) Amalgamation with Bechuana Co, 7) Negotiations with Paul Kruger to arrange as to his giving up all claim to North." Rhodes went on candidly and probably fairly: "If I were to isolate myself in the interior at this moment the whole of the base would go wrong."[4]

For the next six months Lobengula sought to talk face to face with Ulodzi, or Rhodes. "I will not be satisfied," Lobengula said over and over again, "unless I can see Rhodes himself." As Merriman commented sharply, "I see that Lobengula is anxious to see Rhodes, so I suppose he will have to go up and face the music. Pity he does not take Barnato with him and leave him there." But it was not to be. In Rhodes' stead, from his arrival in mid-October, Jameson repetitively, imploringly, put Rhodes' case before the king. Fortunately, as much as the great monarch detested Thompson, he tolerated, even enjoyed, Jameson. According to Jameson, who was hardly impartial, Thompson had "played the garden idiot from start to finish, and [was] universally hated from the king down. . . ." Jameson, a man of charm and wit, and little fear, joked with Lobengula, was at ease in the Ndebele court, and maintained good relations with all manner of induna as well as the whites who still sought the kings' favor. As contemptuous as Jameson was in private of the savages and "niggers"—notably the king—with whom he lived for months at a time, and as racist as Jameson was in his private estimation of African abilities and qualities, he served Rhodes' diplomatic needs admirably, even faultlessly. Jameson's manner and soothing words were important in carrying out his assignment of preventing a premature outbreak of hostilities between the Ndebele and the whites. In addition to his words, however, as a physician Jameson possessed the ability to alleviate excruciating pains in the king's joints. "Yesterday," Jameson explained on one occasion, Lobengula "had a relapse with most infernal pain—groaning with it, & it takes a lot to make him groan."[5] Lobengula had gout; Jameson carried a hypodermic needle and morphine, and used both to good effect.

Without medical skill, Jameson's mission to the Ndebele might have failed as ignominiously as had his first in April. For Rhodes wanted nothing less than a reaffirmation of the all but rejected Rudd Concession and permission from Lobengula to settle whites in the high, well-watered, allegedly mineral-rich northeastern country of the Shona. These were impossible requests, given Lobengula's weakened leadership and the agitated state of his capital. Indeed, they were never achieved, and Jameson wisely never tried to obtain an explicit agreement to such far-fetched hopes. Instead, Jameson tried to "bounce" the king—to persuade him to consent to the digging of but "one hole" in an obscure part of the kingdom, and to use that grant, or anything like it, as a ruse to justify the wholesale invasion that Rhodes had in mind. He felt such an influx of settlers was essential to forestall Boer interlopers, the Portuguese, and other concessionaires, and also to demonstrate the "effective occupation" which would breathe life into the Charter internationally and on the stock exchange. There were desultory meetings in November and December; Jameson found them tiresome. In mid-December he thought that he had obtained a "ratification of the original concession, at all events as near a ratification it is possible to get from a kafir."[6] By this time Lobengula had been officially informed of the Charter, and could not understand how the Queen could speak out of two mouths.

The talks went on. Lobengula clearly would not be squared. Jameson, by his own testimony, kept waving his arms in the general direction of the northeast, and Lobengula now and then nodded, but permission—as such—was withheld. Rhodes' men might go dig a hole in some corner in the south, Lobengula conceded, but that was all. Indeed, Lobengula told Frederick Courtenay Selous directly that he could never allow a number of white men to skirt Gbulawayo and plant themselves even in a distant section of his domain.[7] However, Jameson assured Rhodes otherwise, and Jameson's mostly manufactured accounts were used by Rhodes to gain widespread support and approval by the Colonial Office for his invasion of the lands of the Shona. Jameson's patient efforts certainly prepared the way for the Pioneer Column, as Rhodes' collection of filibusterers was known.

Jameson was the velvet glove. Meanwhile Rhodes had been readying a mailed fist. Although he told Beit that "getting Matabeleland" might take two and a half years, Rhodes was hardly prepared to wait that long. Sooner or later the Ndebele state would succumb to a white onslaught. Whenever it did so, Rhodes wanted the Company to be well placed and in firm command of the region's destiny. Moreover, Rhodes was convinced well before the end of 1889 that his aims and his impatience were compatible with the otherwise likely pace of change in the African interior. Now that a Charter had been granted and a Company established, the Ndebele were prime obstacles. "The plain fact remains that a savage chief with about 8000 warriors is not going to keep out the huge wave of white men now moving north," Rhodes said. As Jameson reported in early November, "I have spoken freely to Helm and Carnegie and they with Moffat are convinced that Rhodes is right in his decision that he will never be able to work peaceably alongside the natives and that the sooner the brush is over the better."[8] Rhodes did not expect to lose.

Rhodes judged geopolitically that "the occupation of Mashonaland" was "the key of the position."[9] With the support of the home board of the Company (to the authority of which he was still nominally subject), Rhodes first contemplated an arrival in force from the north, by steamer along the Zambezi River beyond Tete, and then a brisk march up the escarpment and across the high plateau to Mount Hampden, hard by the future site of Harare (Salisbury). Doing so would challenge Portugal's claims to the river route, a challenge Rhodes wished to make anyway and which the Foreign Office seemed to support. Rhodes ordered the construction of shallow draft gunboats. But then he talked to Selous, the hunter and explorer, who recently had found the middle Zambezi too low to take ships with 300 soldiers and heavy materiel very far, and who warned that the Portuguese would fight. Moreover, the terrain between the river and the highveld was infested both with tsetse fly and malaria. Who would carry the cannon and guns overland? Could soldiers survive?

Rhodes often followed a two-track policy, keeping multiple options open. Being pessimistic about Lobengula's ability ever to sanction a white occupation and about Jameson's ability to pacify the monarch, and having at first sought to avoid confronting or provoking the Ndebele war machine directly, Rhodes in late 1889 began thinking about the utility of an overland entrance into Shona country from Botswana, skirting the Ndebele stronghold, or possibly purposely seeking a confrontation with its war machine.

According to one plan, Rhodes would supply guns and white officers to 600 Ngwato cavalrymen, who would cherish an opportunity to even scores with the Ndebele. According to a second, a force of 500 whites, supported by a number of Ngwato, would mount a lightning attack on Lobengula, either killing or kidnapping the great chief, or holding him hostage in Gbulawayo in exchange for the surrender of the entire Ndebele kingdom. Whether the idea of this audacious assault originated with Rhodes or with Frank Johnson and Maurice Heany, those rough freebooters, the tyro imperialist apparently believed that he could sponsor such a brazen coup and emerge with his reputation unscathed. Presumably he and Johnson—thick-set, dark-eyed, with a deep, resonant voice, and only twenty-three—hoped to claim provocation; several missionaries were aware of the scheme and welcomed it. Or perhaps Rhodes thought that he could prevail upon official London to overlook or excuse what—in his own mind—was an inevitability. Might he have tried to justify means by manifest destiny, too, as he did after the Jameson Raid?

For Rhodes, crippling the Ndebele was a question of timing, not ethics. Johnson and Heany actually drew up a secret contract with Rhodes, who promised them £150,000 and a land grant of 50,000 morgen (about 110,000 acres) if they succeeded in usurping Lobengula. Rhodes would procure 1,800 rifles with short bayonets and 600,000 rounds of ammunition; Johnson would select the sharpshooting 500. Together—although Selous called an assault on Gbulawayo with a mere 500 whites laughable—these numbers (plus the Ngwato) were thought adequate for signal, brisk, victory deep in the interior. Johnson would manufacture an incident on the border of the territory disputed between Lobengula and Kgama, and would "by sudden assaults [carry] all the principal strongholds of the Matabele nation . . . break up the power of the Amandebele as to render their raids on surrounding tribes impossible . . . to reduce the country to such a condition as to enable the prospecting, mining, and commercial staff of the British South Africa Company to conduct their operations in peace and safety."[10]

Rhodes was usually more cautious. Yet in this attempt to force events, as later during the Jameson Raid, he allowed attractive, appealing promoters with grand promises and fancy pleadings to feed his wish to believe. He desired the deed done. He wanted to move on to the more exciting and more fulfilling stage of settlement and national development. He hardly desired to be stalled by a monarch for whom the future was already inscribed.

Putting the plan into effect would have been a political and personal disaster, even if it had succeeded by stealth or butchery. But, fortunately for Rhodes' reputation and ambitions, the full ramifications of the scheme were not widely known at the time, and it was aborted early.

Rhodes probably had second thoughts after meeting with Selous, who reached Kimberley on the day the contract may have been prepared. Nearly forty, Selous was over medium height, with a blonde, pointed beard, massive thighs, and clear blue eyes. His soft, musical voice and charming manners supposedly "ensured him a welcome everywhere."[11] Selous had not married, and he knew the interior, the Ndebele, and the Shona. For twenty-five years he had hunted and explored in the region that Rhodes now intended to conquer. Selous doubted that the Ndebele could be vanquished even by a well-equipped force, and promised that they would react (as they did in 1893 and 1896) by fighting a bitter guerrilla retreat. Rhodes reconsidered. Two weeks later word arrived from Jameson that Lobengula might indeed be squared. And Rhodes wavered further.

On the first day of 1890, Rhodes rejected the initial scheme of Johnson and Heany and readied another shaped by Selous' estimates of how Rhodes' objectives could be achieved without bloodshed. Under the new agreement, Johnson would take a peaceful party of whites from the south around and not through Ndebeleland proper, and then to the highveld near Mount Hampden. Selous would guide the group, and Rhodes would pay the recruits and offer the whites rewards of land, even though he and others well knew that the country was not yet theirs to distribute. (In a subsidiary arrangement, Rhodes gave Selous £2,000 from his own funds to stop him writing articles with his "able pen" about the supposed independence of the Shona from Lobengula. Doing so would have undermined Rhodes' attempt to prove the Charter by occupying a key portion of the Ndebele domain. A concession which Selous had obtained from Chief Mapondera was also folded into the Company.)

The views of Selous and Jameson were influential in altering Rhodes' mind as well as in shifting his thinking away from the Zambezi route. Rhodes also remained remarkably frugal throughout this and later periods of adventure and expansion. He never proceeded as if money were no object. Like Salisbury, he wanted conquest on the cheap, for he possessed assets more than ready cash. That Johnson had offered to organize the more peaceful expedition to the Shona country for a total out-of-pocket cost of under £100,000, impressed Rhodes. (The final cash outlay was about £89,000.) As Rhodes justified to Beit, who was in London, "the cost of the expedition to Mashonaland will be a trifling compared with the Zambesi Expedition. . . . The whole of Mashonaland is a high plateau and therefore healthy, and apparently the gold is situated there. . . . It must be very similar to Witwatersrandt. Our expenses this year with telegraph, 250 police, and occupation . . . may appear heavy, but it is far better to spend a big sum at once and obtain an occupation, than to go and dribble our money away, and you must remember that we could not have afforded to leave Mashonaland vacant for another year."

At a remarkable conference in Cape Town in mid-January, Rhodes and Selous easily persuaded Loch, as high commissioner and representative of the Colonial Office, Shippard, and Sir Frederick Carrington, commander of the Bechuanaland Border Police, to accept his latest plan. A 360-mile route from the Shashi River, skirting the Ndebele towns, was plotted. Rhodes explained that Tswana-speaking Africans would slowly make a smooth road for 100 wagons; that there would be several hundred white settlers (conveniently labeled miners), and that the whole assemblage would be protected (over Johnson's protests and to the horror of the missionaries in Gbulawayo) by a strong police force of 500 troops. Those troops, and the stationing of a contingent of the Bechuanaland Police under Carrington on the southern border of the Ndebele kingdom, would discourage any retaliation from Lobengula's side. Or so Rhodes thought. "If, however, they attack us . . . they carry no commissariat [and] would be a disorganized rabble. . . ."[12]

Rhodes reassured Beit after the meeting that the expedition would not come closer than 180 miles to Gbulawayo, and Selous (and Johnson) "feel sure they will not be interfered with." Moreover, "the Governor has given his support . . . and you can now abandon all idea of the Zambesi. From the class of men that are undertaking [the expedition] I feel sure of success. So far as we can gather from Lobengula's mind he will not interfere. . . . If successful this occupation will give the "Charter" a bona fide occupation of the best part of the territory." That is, "you will now be able to assure the Government," said Rhodes, "that we are doing something practical." Finally, in a comment on his earlier arrangement with Johnson to storm Lobengula's citadel, Rhodes suggested that the present plan was better than the one he had outlined in a private letter. "The advantage of this policy is that we shall occupy Mashonaland without coming into collision with Lobengula and our occupation will [also] settle [or so he hoped] the Portuguese difficulty south of the Zambesi." "I am not a sanguine man," he concluded, "but I think I can . . . [say] that the Expedition will be a success."[13]

Rhodes may have been sanguine. Certainly he was putting a risky venture in its best light. What is astonishing, however, is that neither he nor any of the senior representatives at the Cape Town meeting regarded Rhodes' proposed invasion as alarming. At home, however, British officialdom was amazed. Lord Knutsford and Sir Robert Herbert wondered with aroused understatement whether Lobengula might conceivably mistake the intentions of such a large party. The king might think that Rhodes sought land after all, and not just minerals. Certainly no supposed permission from Lobengula to work the Concession could justify, they said more forcefully, what clearly was an invasion of the Shona country. "The cat," said Edward Fairfield of the Foreign Office, "is being let out of Mr. Rhodes's bag, and proves a very ferocious animal indeed." Fairfield assumed that Rhodes' incursion was bound to involve Britain in war, and that he had to be stopped. The War Office was outraged at the idiocy involved in supposing a comparatively small white police force could withstand rampaging Ndebele hundreds of miles beyond secure lines of communication and reinforcement. Moffat, in Gbulawayo, was also horrified, for the Ndebele would certainly view the police as a menace, and compel a catastrophic collision. As Fairfield remarked, "the people in South Africa are getting out of hand." And so they were. In mid-February Knutsford finally put a stop to the embodiment of Rhodes' juvenile smash-and-grab fantasies. He cabled urgently to Loch: Her Majesty's Government could sanction no forward movement toward the country of the Shona until Lobengula approved.[14]

Jameson went north again to attempt afresh to obtain the king's unambiguous assent. From the beginning of the year he had emphasized the "peaceful tone" of the Ndebele country and deprecated the likelihood of an assertive response by the Ndebele unless they were provoked unreasonably. He wanted a "peaceable" occupation to be attempted first, "even if the warlike becomes inevitable in the end." Jameson's efforts were thus devoted to dampening bellicosity in Gbulawayo and Kimberley, and to strenuous, if always disingenuous, efforts to persuade Lobengula to give Rhodes' men the road.[15]

By the time Jameson reached Gbulawayo at the end of April 1890, on his fourth and final visit, the wagons of the Pioneer Column had begun to roll north from Kimberley. Lobengula knew that they were on their way, and spoke openly to Jameson about the possibility of war. A few days later, in May, the last time that they saw each other, a desperate Jameson tried to bully Lobengula into letting Rhodes' men enter the Shona country. Reminding the king of an earlier promise (or what Jameson had interpreted as a promise), that white miners could sweep northeastward around the Ndebele, Lobengula said, "I do not refuse, but let Rhodes come." As Jameson reported, "I have not got a refusal, but devilish little else." In the king's own words, said Jameson, he had not said "no." "Surely that in a kafir is as good a ratification of his former permission, and we are justified in going on with the expedition. . . ."[16] Perhaps. Jameson still hoped that Lobengula could restrain his war parties, but the continued calm for which he had talked so long and well had in no way been achieved. Whatever the Company's men would say, and Rhodes authorize be said, it was abundantly clear to Jameson, if not to Rhodes, that the king was neither bowing to the inevitable nor granting permission. He was temporizing, and the many Ndebele regiments were preparing for battle. Later, when the Column reached the borders of the kingdom, Lobengula ordered it to halt. "Had the king done any fault? Had any white men been killed or had the white man lost anything that he was looking for?"

Jameson's smooth talk and steady injections of morphine calmed the king—Moffat extolled Jameson's tact and skill—but could never deliver the road.[17] Yet the Column was nonetheless assembled and a full invasion mounted with the explicit permission of the British government. Once again the Foreign Office overruled the Colonial Office. Fortunately for Rhodes, the Transvaal, or at least residents of the Transvaal, had again been looking covetously across the Limpopo. The sweet lands beyond that river promised good grazing; alternatively, there were highlands in the eastern reaches of Lobengula's Shona domain over which his writ ran weakly, if at all. At the beginning of 1889, Louis P. Bowler, a British entrepreneur, claimed permission from a Shona chief to settle Afrikaner farmers. He circulated a prospectus and sought customers. Few took Bowler seriously, and President Kruger officially disapproved of the venture. More threatening was a grassroots migration of 1,500 to 2,000 Afrikaners from the sourveld of the Zoutspansberg. They were trekking for the same reason as had their forebears: to escape governmental control and the Britons who had entered the Transvaal to mine its gold. Even before Loch and Rhodes met President Kruger in mid-March to discuss the trek and other, more important issues (including the future of Swaziland and a customs union), Salisbury had instructed Knutsford to stop fussing, and to leave it to Loch to decide whether or not Rhodes could invade the country across the Limpopo.

A letter of special pleading from Rhodes to Herbert, reaching the Colonial and then the Foreign Office through personal and therefore irregular channels, may have proved influential: "I think the only difficulty we may have in the north is from Kruger," Rhodes wrote. "There is no doubt he does not like being surrounded and I believe he is at the bottom of the proposed trek of Boers from the Zoutspansberg. I think they mean mischief and . . . I think that Swazieland should be held as a guarantee of his good faith until we occupy Mashonaland. [President Kruger's Transvaal wanted to annex Swaziland and a belt of what today is northern Natal, to provide an outlet on the Indian Ocean.] . . . Lo Bengulu has given us permission to go in," Rhodes reported confidently on the strength of Jameson's mixed assurances, "so I hope we shall have no trouble from him and my only fear is from Kruger as I am afraid he is not to be trusted. . . . I want breathing time in order to occupy [Mashonaland] in front of the Boers. . . . The whole situation has been forced by the granting of the Charter—as long as no one has been willing to do anything the matter could rest. Both Boers and Portugal looked on the North as their preserve to be taken whenever they wished. The presence of a third party has forced the pace but it would make England ridicuous," he drove the argument home, "to have retired the Portuguese claims only to make room for a Boer occupation."[18]

Salisbury, like Rhodes, understood the march of events internationally, worried less than Knutsford about humanitarian pressures, and needed Rhodes' assistance over a variety of southern African issues as much as he distrusted the man and muttered at his methods. Salisbury, like Rhodes, was a cynic when it came to Africa. It was better for Britain, he decided, to have Rhodes in place between the Limpopo and the Zambezi to counter the Portuguese, possibly the Belgians, and certainly the Boers. Neither he nor Rhodes concerned themselves about indigenous rights; Knutsford and his civil servants wore their hearts on their sleeves. Salisbury's officials also worried about propriety and fair play. But in this instance Salisbury overruled them, using the Afrikaner treks as his rationalization.

Even with the support of the British government, Rhodes was not inclined to trifle with the Ndebele. He instructed Johnson to recruit his "pioneers" from influential, largely English-speaking families throughout the Cape Colony and the rest of South Africa. (Yet most were not from the better families; they were a true mixture of men, representing a cross-section of whites in the Colony.) If the Column were cut off, or attacked, the prominent fathers of the young pioneers would demand assistance, and the imperial factor would come to their aid.[19] Moreover, political support for his colony would flow from the involvement of the young blue bloods. For added safety, Rhodes and Johnson purchased machine guns and searchlights, salted horses, 2,000 oxen, 117 wagons, and vast quantities of food. The Pioneers themselves numbered 186, plus nineteen honest-to-goodness prospectors of the kind that Lobengula expected. More than 350 Ngwato laborers accompanied them, plus an assortment of African cooks, drivers, and artisans from the Colony. Jameson was in overall, but unannounced, charge. As Merriman observed from the sidelines, "There are enormous preparations going on and vast expenditure. Machine guns with sailors to work them. Electric search lights (to frighten the Ndebele)—all the paraphernalia of modern warfare. I regard the future with dread. . . . It is a remarkable instance of the power of one man, for the whole scheme is got up for the glorification of Rhodes."[20]

The expedition could have been halted in May or June, but Rhodes still worried about the Transvaal more than about Lobengula. In a letter to Loch that was remarkable for its candor, Rhodes reassured the anxious high commissioner that the invasion must go forward and that it would succeed. Temporizing would be wrong. "I feel if we do not move in this year [the Boers] will move in front of us so it only shows how necessary the Mashona expedition is, if we intend taking the country before the Boers get it." Jameson had recently seen Lobengula, who had "granted a good deal as to amount of men going in but in the end said 'I do not refuse to let them go in but Rhodes should come and see me.' Jameson thinks my seeing him would not be of any advantage but that it is surely his desire for procrastination and delay as of course he does not like the idea of a large European population in Mashonaland fearing," and rightly so, that "it may lead to the loss of his country."

Rhodes continued with understandable understatement: "I think [Lobengula] is getting nervous at the large numbers arriving on his Southern border. . . ." As to the possibility of a "collision," Loch's major anxiety, Rhodes argued that the size of the force and Lobengula "being sure through his spies of our strengths" provided the best precaution. Furthermore, Rhodes' men in Ndebele country believed that Lobengula was no fool, that he would "quietly acquiesce in the matter but naturally does not like it and on account of his people will not appear too willing and also has always hoped to continue the policy of procrastination and delay." Rhodes told Loch that they should move quickly. He was sending forward the balance of the horses "as fast as possible."[21]

The large and unwieldy column of supposed prospectors crossed the Shashi River into Ndebeleland on 1 July 1890. "I wish you to know," Loch lied to

Lobengula, "that these people come as your friends." The chief's reply, which reached Cape Town only long after it might have had any impact, was the more telling: "The Chief is troubled. He is being eaten up by Mr. Rhodes." [22] And so he was. During the nine weeks of July and August the ponderous column inched its way across the lowveld through a country of dense bush and ancient baobab trees. The going was slow, particularly across the sandy river beds and the occasional mighty river. But by 1 August the new road had reached the edge of the Shona plateau, and was soon to climb arduously through a jumble of hills to the highveld that the whites were sure was speckled with gold. Within a few days, too, the possibility of a Ndebele attack fast receded. If Lobengula had ever planned to unleash his warriors, the time had passed.

On 11 September the bulk of the settlers and soldiers reached the vicinity of Mount Hampden, found the Makabusi River with its flowing water and large pools, and decided that they had attained their destination. Lieutenant Colonel Edward Graham Pennefather climbed the kopje that became Harare's most notable feature, and looked east across an open, treeless belt of flat veld. "The new grass was springing and amongst it were little bushes with bright green leaves and yellow heads of flowers." Pennefather determined that Fort Salisbury, the capital of the new settlement, should be built there. He wrote grandly to Kimberley: "Site selected. . . . All well. Magnificent country. Natives pleased to see us. Everything satisfactory." [23] Thus the capital of Rhodes' private empire was established. Whether the Shona of the plateau were or were not pleased to see the whites need be no matter of dispute, for it was as yet unclear to the pioneers, to Rhodes, or to the Shona precisely what transformations to this trans-Limpopan fastness would follow the arrival of whites with the gleam of gold in their eyes and avarice for land in their blood.

When the pioneers were officially demobilized at the end of September, the Company's representatives promulgated a mining law so that the pioneers could peg out fifteen mining claims each. But Rhodes had also arranged that 50 percent of everything won from a successful prospecting venture (no matter who or what kind of company dug into the ground) belonged in perpetuity to the Company. "It practically means a system," Rhodes crowed to Abercorn, "by which we, as the Charter, shall get half the minerals of the country." [24] In addition, as the new settlers fanned out from Harare to find the large farms which each had been promised and for which Rhodes was required to pay no one, they happily took lands to which there could not for some time be title; the promising acres on the highveld did not yet belong to the Company or to Rhodes. Even Lobengula would have been hard pressed to convey title.

Lobengula had not dared attack, and Rhodes had assured that result both by massing men and arms and by repetitive requests for indigenous consent. Jameson, wittingly or not, had purchased precious time. But Rhodes' final plan also succeeded in large part because Lobengula was too canny to be provoked into a confrontation which would certainly, if not immediately, have led to his and his people's demise. The British were too strong, Rhodes too determined, and the Ndebele too isolated and too devoid of fundamental resources. In the end, the Ndebele's very paramountcy ensured their destruction, but that end was at least deferred temporarily. Humiliation was heaped high upon the once-proud kingdom, even though its autonomy remained intact for a few years more.

Rhodes' colonial experiment began in 1890 without the war for which he most uncharacteristically had spoiled. "Rhodes has a very lucky star," Merriman concluded. "The bloodless nature of the enterprise has surprised everyone."[25] Rhodes' men, allowed to "ride off" large farms and claim them as their own, were to spread his name and to make money for the Company by finding gold and other precious metals throughout the country of the Shona. They were to prosper, as were the Company and its promoters. By doing so, Rhodes may have expected to fulfill his earnest desire to extend Britain's dominions and to create his own kind of British colony as a model worthy of global emulation. Although the Company dealt at this stage with "pure barbarism," Rhodes in 1890 prophesied ultimate self-government for the new possession.[26] He meant it for whites, however, intending that the white country, when wealthy and populous, should join the Cape Colony, a white-run Botswana, and the Transvaal in some kind of federal union, thus fulfilling his earlier dreams of southern African unification.

"I do not think there was a happier man in the country. . . ," Rhodes congratulated himself when he learned that the pioneers had in fact pushed "through to Fort Salisbury." He had been unusually anxious during August and September, fearing that his men were in greater danger than he had anticipated. But at no time did he or they worry about whether the Shona would receive these whites well, and welcome a settlement which was to displace them from the lands of their fathers. Instead, Rhodes looked back to his own youth and his longings to be young: "If I could quit [being premier of the Cape Colony]," he told farmers at Paarl, "no man would be happier than myself, because I [could] then go and live with those young people, who are developing our new territories."[27]

But that truly was a dream. Rhodes had been propelled into the Cape premiership in July. Much as he genuinely, gleefully, wanted to escape an official tour with Loch of Bechuanaland and the Transvaal in October 1890 and rush up farther north to embrace the pioneers, there was still much to be accomplished with regard to rail and telegraph lines, not to mention the realization of his ambitions to bring Portuguese East Africa and trans-Zambezia within his expansive reach.

The construction of a railway north from Kimberley had been a condition of the granting of the Charter. In the aftermath of Rhodes' alliance with Hofmeyr and their mutual new antagonism to Kruger, a railway to open up the lands on the Transvaal's western flank had become necessary. It lessened the expenses of the British administration of Bechuanaland and made good imperial sense generally. Rhodes was not then thinking primarily of reducing the costs of his still to be won possession beyond the Limpopo. Indeed, the authorities in London and Rhodes and his colleagues at the Cape initially focused on an extension of the main South African rail route a mere 126 miles from Kimberley to Vryburg, the capital of British Bechuanaland (situated as it was well to the south of the modern border of Botswana).

Even before negotiating for a charter in London, Rhodes had purchased on De Beers' behalf a private right-of-way from Kimberley northward toward British Bechuanaland. In London he had given "a pledge to H.M. Government before obtaining the promise of the Charter" that he would drive the rails onward "if it lay in my power to do so." He further told Sir Gordon Sprigg, again prime minister of the Cape Colony, that "it was upon the strength of this pledge" that his application should favorably be regarded. Rhodes was now ready to begin laying the line, but he also wanted to cooperate as much as possible with Sprigg's government. The Cape had already expended funds on a cart road. "I feel that [there] is clearly a case for arrangement," Rhodes told Sprigg.

Sprigg thought so, too, for Rhodes' opening request and Sprigg's reply two days later were clearly orchestrated. (Merriman presumed that Rhodes had "bought" Hofmeyr.) On behalf of his government, Sprigg promised to help Rhodes to build the rails economically, and to purchase the entire line upon its completion. Meanwhile, after heavy negotiations by Beit, the British government, in exchange for the rail line, gave Rhodes' Company 6,000 square miles of Crown land in British Bechuanaland, together with mineral rights. Another 6,000 square miles and mining rights were promised if the line were subsequently extended to Mafeking. Rhodes and the Cape agreed that freight would be carried at rates prevailing in the Colony—even if doing so meant a commercial loss.

Rhodes told Beit that the land and mining rights would be the "profit" on the deal. Although the Cape government would ultimately own the railway, and probably pay for it, Rhodes instructed Beit not to let that be known in London. Instead, he was to tell the British government that the extended line would "not pay." Moreover, he told Beit, "get as much of Bechuanaland as you can. It is not to be despised. There is a belt along the German border which someday will surprise you."[28] What did Rhodes know?

That was the too-simple beginning, not the conclusion, of a set of complicated financial negotiations by which Rhodes sought to maximize the Company's advantage, and Sprigg and Colonel Frederick Schermbrucker, the commissioner of crown lands and public works, sought to do the same for the Cape. Rhodes was particularly anxious to avoid saddling the infant Company with major expenses and heavy calls on its borrowing capacity at a time when he intended to fund the filibustering expedition into the Shona country. Even though the Duke of Fife, as well as the Duke of Abercorn, were "unceasing" in their desires for progress on the railway, he also appreciated the London board's concern for the financial future of the fledgling entity. Although the controlling personality of the Company, he was not to be given sole and autonomous authority over its activities until May 1890. (He threatened to resign in April, and to let the London board run "the show" without him. "For goodness' sake," Harris urged Beit, "let them leave things to Rhodes until we have a bona fide occupation of Mashonaland."[29])

In early 1890 Rhodes was able to persuade Loch and Sprigg to give him a monopoly over any and all northern rail extensions from the Colony; especially after working so hard to amalgamate diamonds, he greatly feared competition. He had continued to worry about the impact of the Delagoa Bay rail line and the traffic it would siphon off from the Transvaal. He wanted the trade of the north to be funneled through the Cape. "It is everything for us," he explained to Beit, "to increase the trade and revenue of the Cape Colony as our diamond mines represent half the real value of the Cape Colony and if their revenue suffers we shall suffer." Without a right to determine the future of railways beyond Kimberley, Kruger, or Kruger and some subsequent government of the Cape, could place a junction at Mafeking and—Rhodes was persistent about such matters—"by rates ruinous to themselves" drag the trade through the Transvaal down to Delagoa Bay.

Additionally, Rhodes arranged for the Cape to pay for the actual construction of the line to Vryburg in exchange for a sizable proportion of the land given to the Company by the Crown. Rhodes would temporarily cover the monthly labor costs, but be reimbursed by the Cape. In 1891, the Cape would own the line as far as Vryburg. True, Rhodes would be obligated to continue the line to Mafeking, and pay for it himself, but the distance was only 97 miles, and by then Rhodes believed that he would find it easier to raise the needed loans. "I . . . preferred," Rhodes said, in a partial switch of his earlier argument, "to obtain a small land grant and let Sprigg build the Railway rather than be responsible for the whole construction of the Railway . . . to Mafeking however good the land grant might be."[30]

When Rhodes finally wrote a long letter, his first, to the controlling board of the British South Africa Company in late March, he explained all he had been doing since the Charter had been granted, and elaborately justified his failure to keep the Board fully informed about all of his intricate dealings on the many matters of interest to the board and the Company. In summing up a detailed, even candid, explanation of the finances of the rail expansion, he said, with that masterful understatement of which he was often capable: "I feel that the Home Board should consider the railway arrangement a most advantageous one. . . ."[31] Rhodes had managed to control a railway which he wanted and needed, which the Cape Colony would pay for and run, and to the costs of which the British government would contribute a huge block of land and subsoil rights that Rhodes, at least, believed valuable.

These important details out of the way, and a tense and tedious battle won with the Exploring Company over its rights in the final railway venture, the actual laying of the tracks was accomplished with unusual speed. (A telegraph line was also flung northward with equal alacrity.) By Christmas 1889, steel snaked out of Kimberley to the north. By October 1890 the line was sufficiently complete to Vryburg for Rhodes to open it ceremoniously. He, who had once battled to affiliate Stellaland (later Vryburg) to the Cape, and who, less than a decade before, had been excoriated because of his partiality for settlers and freebooters, had now brought the Stellalanders a rail connection to Cape Town. Rhodes was proud to be able to convey them such valuable ties. He promised to annex them to the Colony, too, when and if they wished it. By the end of 1890 the line was operational to Vryburg; within four years, at Sir Charles Metcalfe's insistence, the line had reached Mafeking, and even—to Rhodes' surprise—had begun to pay for itself. But for several years Rhodes would go no farther, protecting his monopoly and husbanding his expenses.

Mafeking, long central to Rhodes' grand economic and imperial design for the Cape Colony and the African interior, was the Ismailia of the Suez Canal of the interior. Yet it was too distant from Salisbury to serve the Shona settlement as an efficient rail head. About 1400 miles of thirstland, menaced for the final 300 by vengeful Ndebele, separated the two entrepôts. Rhodes had made those calculations early. When he obtained the Charter, and with it more far-ranging responsibilities and possibilities than he had initially anticipated, Rhodes' nimble mind grasped the importance to the Company of the lands that lay to the east of the Shona high plateau. Spurred perhaps more by Selous, who knew the area, than by the memory of his brother who had been blown up along the Shire River, Rhodes understood, as did Kruger, how an outlet to the sea would improve the commercial viability of his new entity. From the coast to Harare (Salisbury) by the shortest distance the miles are only 374. Rails and roads would be more easily laid if a single company or government could control the terrain. More critical, too, Rhodes did not want his creation to be surrounded or hemmed in; just as Kruger wanted Swaziland and Kosi Bay in Natal, so Rhodes wanted a window on the Indian Ocean.

There was but one problem; the Portuguese claimed the coast and actually administered some of it. They had influence and historical presence in sections of the interior, too. But Rhodes had entered a phase of grandiosity, unchecked aggrandizement, and cynical bullishness. True, he disdained the Portuguese, but it was not only his prejudices or his dislike of the Mediterranean peoples and their "accursed rule" that emboldened him to try to add much of Mozambique to the Company's sphere. He simply thought that he needed that terrain, he assumed that it (particularly Manicaland) was rich in gold, and he believed (and was nearly right) that Portugal could be bullied, bought, beaten, or swindled.

Toward the end of 1889, Rhodes asked Herbert whether the British government had ever recognized Portugal in the entire possession of the coastlands from Maputo to the Zambezi River. A "capital" port could be made at Pungwe Bay, the modern Beira, said Rhodes. Such a harbor would help make any new interior settlement more viable. "Once occupied," he reminded Herbert, "the outlet in the future for Mashonaland will undoubtedly be on the east coast [yet] as you are aware the occupation of the Portuguese even along the coast line is in most places merely a paper one and if this has not been recognized by international agreement," he cautioned, "I think it might be left open."[32] It is not known how Herbert replied to this private letter, but Rhodes' inquiry, and his gentle suggestion at the end, plus a letter on a similar subject to Maund, show that Rhodes was aware that the diplomatic interests of the British government would have to be considered. He was attempting to ascertain how strongly the Colonial Office, and perhaps the Foreign Office, felt about the Portuguese, and therefore to gauge how forcefully he should and could act.

There is a letter of this period from Cawston to Rhodes which may account for some of Rhodes' subsequent assertive insouciance—his brazen disregard of the otherwise clear diplomatic preferences of Britain. Abercorn and Salisbury had talked. Cawston told Rhodes that Salisbury had intimated to Abercorn that the Company should—despite public and official protests to the contrary—go forward steadily. Salisbury would help as he could. He would object to Portuguese encroachments on the Company sphere. " 'Diplomacy,' Salisbury said, 'shall not interfere with your projects,' " Cawston reported.[33] Conceivably, Abercorn misinterpreted Salisbury, and Cawston may have further dramatized what had been said. Nevertheless, Salisbury may have been attempting to strengthen his international and imperial negotiating hand by such an ambiguous and yet deniable encouragement of Rhodes' rough methods. If so, he succeeded admirably.

Lord Salisbury had no particular love of the Portuguese, and called their claims to large swaths of Africa "archaeological," but neither he nor the British government could dismiss the pretensions of the Portuguese altogether.[34] In the early 1880s, Portugal effectively administered only a comparatively few portions of the 1300-mile coastline from Cape Delgado in the north to Delagoa Bay in the south. The governor-general of Portuguese East Africa observed the enclaves of his crumbled empire from a little island, also called Mozambique, off the north-central coast of the territory and country that later assumed that name. His writ hardly ran on the coast immediately opposite. Ibo was another offshore island settlement, important in the sixteenth and seventeen centuries, but of limited value in the 1880s. At Quelimane, an Indian Ocean port slightly north of the tangled delta of the Zambezi River, there was a small garrison; another was at Inhambane, to the south, and a third at the still small harbor of Lourenço Marques (Maputo). Up the great Zambezi there were soldiers at Sena and at Tete. A few Portuguese of mixed descent owned and worked plantations, or prazos, in the hinterland.

This was not much, by way of a legitimizing display of control or interest, but it could hardly—much as Rhodes would have preferred—be waved aside. Moreover, stimulated in the mid-1880s by the results of the Berlin Conference (where Portugal lost its historic hold over the mouth of the Congo River), by the activities of Germany along the East African coast opposite Zanzibar, and by Rhodes' initial thrust northward into Bechuanaland, the Portuguese monarchy and its overseas officials attempted to prove their grip on the Mozambican interior. (By the terms of the Treaty of Berlin in 1885 their authority along the coast was hardly open to serious challenge.)

Inland, especially in the great central portion between the Limpopo and Sabi rivers, the successors to Soshangane, the first Shangaan chief, held sway over what was called Gazaland. In the aftermath of the Mfecane, or triumphs and dispersal of the Nguni-speaking peoples after the conquests of Shaka, Soshangane had established a conquest state to the east of the lands of the Ndebele. To the north across the Zambezi, there were other Nguni warlord states which had also resulted from the Mfecane: in the northeastern corner of what became Zambia, Mpeseni's Ngoni was the effective local power. At the northern end of the highland spine to the west of Lake Malawi, the Ngoni of Mwambera were dominant. Closer to the southern end of that lake were the Ngoni of Ciweri Ndhlovu. Along the Shire River itself, there was a small knot of Suto-speaking Kololo. They were descended from migrants who had fled the Mfecane and had been settled there by Livingstone.

Soshangane and Mzilikazi effectively divided and ruled the interior between the Limpopo and Zambezi rivers. Soshangane had reigned in the east without serious indigenous or Portuguese opposition until his death in 1858. Likewise, Mzila, Soshangane's son and ultimate successor, ruled and terrorized the eastern end of the Shona highlands from a capital near Mount Selinda on the present Zimbabwe/Mozambique border. His army of 30,000 was as relentless in its sphere as was Lobengula's to the west. When Mzila died in 1884, he was succeeded by Gungunyane, a monarch whose resourcefulness, and resources, were ultimately found wanting. In the late 1880s, however, he bent only an intermittent knee to the Portuguese.

Because it was high, presumably fertile, and had always been rumored to be rich in gold, one of the more attractive parts of Gungunyane's kingdom was Manicaland, an area ruled by the subordinate Shona chief Mtassa. In the early 1880s, Captain Joaquim Carlos Paiva de Andrade, an explorer and promoter, visited the area and later floated several British-backed but Portuguese-controlled companies which proposed to exploit the area's riches. By mid-decade Portugal had proclaimed the administrative district of Manicaland, with its capital at Macequece (Rhodes' Massi-Kessi) and its western border beyond Mount Hampden. Paiva traveled across much of northern Shonaland in the next few years, hoisting flags and staking territorial claims. Lieutenant Vitor Cordon, an officer dispatched for this purpose, worked his way south toward Shona country from Zumbo (which became another administrative district) on the middle Zambezi at its confluence with the Luangwa River. In 1889, Cordon gained pledges of friendship and fealty in a region which could have been either Portugal's Manicaland or Rhodes' Mashonaland.

A few months after Cordon and Paiva had traveled across the plateau on which Rhodes had his eye, and a mere week after the Charter itself was granted in London, Britain and Portugal came to blows over another part of Rhodes' new sphere. After Livingstone's death, the Scottish missions had planted stations in the highlands between the Shire River and Lake Malawi and along the shores of the great lake. The only practical entrance into this interior region was up the Zambezi and Shire rivers; Portugal clearly controlled Quelimane, the trans-shipment point for persons and goods, and for a time in the early 1880s operated a customs house at the confluence of the Shire and Ruo rivers, the acknowledged southern bounds of the informal British sphere. The missionaries clamored throughout the 1880s for British protection, but neither Gladstone nor Salisbury wanted to incur the obligations and expenses which would, whatever the missionaries and their parliamentary supporters said, inevitably follow. Yet, in early 1889, Salisbury also refused to approve a draft treaty with Portugal which would have resolved the local border questions; it had given the Portuguese the Shire highlands and the Scots had howled.

It was in an atmosphere of increasing tension between Britain and Portugal over this remote, otherwise irrelevant corner of Africa, that Salisbury had dispatched Johnston to oversee British interests and strengthen Britain's claims. Once Rhodes had agreed to fund Johnston's mission, and had provided Johnston with the financial and moral encouragement to pursue his own (and not necessarily the Foreign Office's) imperial instincts, a significant shift in the relative strengths of the two competing interests became possible. Rhodes was hardly enamored of missionaries, but he was ambitious for territory—for buffer zones if not always for areas of exploitation. Thus Johnston and Alfred Sharpe, his vice-consul and a former solicitor turned hunter, like Paiva and Cordon to the south, spent the African winter months of 1889 gathering the signatures of chiefs to previously printed treaty forms. These chiefs, in a vast region from the Ruo west to the Luangwa River and north toward Lake Tanganyika, were bound by the agreements not to cede territory or sovereignty to any other European power without the approval of the British government. The treaties testified to the existence of "peace" between a tribe and the Queen of England. The documents neither conferred nor promised protection. Nevertheless, they provided a paper foundation for any territorial claims which Salisbury (and Rhodes) might wish to assert in trans-Zambezia. As Johnston told Rhodes rather grandly in mid-October 1889, "I have secured the Shire R. and all Western Nyassa by treaty. I have sent agents inland to search the unknown country along the Loangwa down to the Zambesi. . . . I have utterly cut the ground under Serpa Pinto's feet, although he started three months before me and has a thousand armed men behind him. . . . You may consider my task here accomplished. If you loose [sic] Nyassa land now, it wont be for lack of treaties."[35]

The previous year the Portuguese had obtained similar pledges of loyalty from chiefs near the southeastern corner of Lake Malawi. An expedition under Major Alexandre Alberto da Rocha de Serpa Pinto, as Johnston told Rhodes, proceeded up the Zambezi and Shire rivers in mid-1889 to seek additional expressions of friendship and to exert a Portuguese presence. Its 731 soldiers and many civilians made it a formidable enterprise. But before Serpa Pinto and his entourage could cross the Ruo into "British" territory, another of Johnston's assistants formally declared it a British protected area. When Serpa Pinto persisted in breaching this river barrier, he triggered an international drama by turns serious and farcical.

Implored by Johnston, the Scots, and Rhodes to respond, Salisbury in December demanded that Portugal should pledge to interfere no more in Britain's Nyasa sphere, with its chartered area south of the Zambezi, or with any other region on which Britain was focused. Salisbury demanded that Portugal withdraw Serpa Pinto. A British flotilla polished its guns at Gibraltar. Plans were laid to invade Goa. The cables flew back and forth between Lisbon and London. Salisbury threatened to break off diplomatic relations. Nearly bankrupt, weakened by a tottering monarchy, and clearly an international weakling next to Victoria's John Bull, Portugal had little choice but to back down, humiliated, in mid-January 1890. Decisions later that year and in 1891 about the official borders between the British and Portuguese possessions in Africa reflected the resolution of this initial crisis as well as the behavior of Rhodes and his accomplices throughout the same years.

It was a season of diplomatic definition. The partition of Africa by Europe had proceeded apace. Salisbury now wanted to draw precise lines between the diverse claims and spheres so as to avoid potential clashes and encourage stable development. He feared the growing might of Germany, too, and wished to avoid any disagreements that could lead to conflict. Once borders were arranged with the Germans, Salisbury could turn back to Portugal, and to King Léopold II's private territorial estate. There was more at stake in Africa than the vast sphere that he had given to Rhodes: the Germans were energetic in the east as well as the west, becoming active contestants for the brisk uplands beyond Kilimanjaro to the central African lakes and the headwaters of the mighty Nile River in Uganda. Britain had concerned itself with Zanzibar and the East African coast because of Livingstone's legacy and its determination to end the slave trade. Furthermore, Zanzibar guarded the Indian Ocean flank of India, Britain's richest possession. Likewise, the Nile waters were important for Egypt, over which Britain had established its rule, and hence for the Suez Canal and India.

Rhodes wanted Salisbury to maintain the proposed Cape-to-Cairo connection whenever the prime minister committed Britain to boundary arrangements in Africa, and forcefully pushed a number of other primarily local territorial requirements upon the Foreign Office, both directly and via Abercorn. When negotiations with the Germans became serious in May and June 1890, Rhodes pressed the telegraph keys frantically. He indicated how crucial the Stevenson Road, the watershed corridor between Lakes Malawi and Tanganyika, would be to the territorial integrity and economic development of the Company's trans-Zambezian sphere. He grandly envisaged a monopoly for the Company over the trade of the eastern African interior and the lakes region—"all the trade of Central Africa would naturally go down the lake system to the Zambesi rather than be dragged across Africa by caravans to the German port opposite Zanzibar." Moreover, a safe road between Lakes

Malawi and Tanganyika would, he declared, shut off "any European power from coming across to the west coast." If the road were lost it would block the expansion of the Company as well as the realization of the first stage of his newly adopted Cape-to-Cairo dream.

Rhodes greatly feared that Abercorn and the board would let Britain "give in" to the Germans. They had immediate access to Salisbury and the Foreign Office, and it was from them—not Rhodes—that Salisbury had requested advice over the new borders. (Rhodes also warned Abercorn against giving Léopold any kind of corridor [which Léopold had requested] between the Congo State and Lake Malawi.) "The only thing I am strong upon," he said with exaggeration, "is that we do not give up the Stevenson Road to Germany. You have merely to look at the map and see that it is the whole question. It is all nonsense about giving up the territory and making arrangements for free trade with Germany. I feel sure," he rose to heights of persuasion, "that you and the other members of the Board did not join the Board for the sake of arranging the sale of candles and soap under the German flag." Rhodes said that he would have nothing to do with "pulling the chestnuts out of the fire" for the Germans. He also objected, for good measure, to "those paper arrangements at Berlin where the African map is marked out in red, green and blue blotches, and under which we always get the worst of it." [36] To sweeten the request, Rhodes decided to name a town at the southern end of Lake Tanganyika after Abercorn.

Abercorn described Salisbury as extraordinarily anxious to please the German government. "He must be watched," Abercorn told Cawston. Yet, in the final analysis, Salisbury granted Rhodes and the board everything that they needed to round out the Company's dominion. By giving Heligoland, an islet commanding the Elbe estuary, back to Germany, Britain gained Zanzibar, Kenya, including a disputed northeastern segment, and Uganda. Because Count Georg von Caprivi, Germany's foreign minister, wanted a port on the Zambezi for Südwest Afrika (no one bothered to tell Caprivi about the several prominent cataracts that barred navigation along that river), Salisbury gleefully recognized the odd appendage of modern Namibia that bears the Count's name. In exchange Germany dropped its claims to the Lake Ngami area of what became Botswana. The frontier between Togo and the Gold Coast (Ghana) was adjusted. Finally—an issue of sufficient importance to be mentioned by Salisbury in his messages to the Queen—Germany conceded the Stevenson Road, as Rhodes had wanted. However, either because Rhodes had not battled hard enough for the grand abstraction, preferring to prevent the possible loss of the connecting link between the lakes, or because Salisbury thought the notion silly, Salisbury fought little, if at all, for the Cape-to-Cairo line. "A curious idea," he called it. Of the strip of land between the Congo and German East Africa, which would have provided the crucial link between the spheres of the British South Africa Company and Uganda, Salisbury told parliament that he could "imagine no more uncomfortable . . . possession." [37]

Rhodes, who said nothing at the time about the loss of the Cape-to-Cairo route, was obviously pleased about the link between the southern lakes. He fared far less well a few months later, when Salisbury decided to treat with Portugal. Rhodes made his position plain in June. Now that Britain had settled with Germany (the treaty was announced in mid-June and signed at the beginning of July), Rhodes believed that it was "totally unnecessary" to "start marking off huge tracts of territory to such a Power as Portugal." "As to Portuguese everything will be right as long as we do not arbitrate. Their frontier is the coast fringe and nothing more. If Mashonaland is as rich as they say it is in the dim future the Portuguese will disappear from Africa," he told Herbert. To Abercorn, he declared that Britain should "not claim further definitions of boundaries." This was no perverse imperialist musing, but the considered thought of a buccaneer who had obvious designs on much of what might be allotted to Portugal. The balance of the territory of Africa south of the Zambezi was there to be divided between Britain and Portugal; the Portuguese might even agree for a "consideration," Rhodes suggested, "to retire entirely from the East Coast if we give them the West." There should be no hurry in coming to terms with the Portuguese, Rhodes repeated.[38]

Salisbury and the officials at the Foreign Office ignored Rhodes, however. They preferred to deal with Cawston, who represented the Company through his managing directorship of the Company in London. So long as the Nyasa missionary sphere was enshrined in the treaty, and Lobengula's domain and much (but not all) of trans-Zambezia kept free, Cawston seemed satisfied. He understood that the Manyika area—the Shona land east of Salisbury—might not be pried away from the Portuguese. As the treaty took final shape in August, much that Rhodes wanted and was preparing to secure was conceded to Portugal.

Some of the officials feared war with Portugal more than they feared Rhodes' ire. And Salisbury was not inclined to be bullied by a man whom one of Knutsford's underlings sarcastically suggested should be "Prime Minister and Foreign Secretary of Great Britain as well as Premier of S. Africa!"[39] They thought Rhodes both unreasonable and annoying.

There were additional bureaucratic considerations. The officials and cartographers who advised the principal negotiators preferred precision and neatness. Rivers suited them, and both the Zambezi River in the west and the Sabi River in the east became the dividing lines. Unhappily, by using the Zambezi as a boundary, half of Barotseland was lost. By using the Sabi, all of the eastern highlands of Zimbabwe were given to Portugal. The missionary zone and added territory to the south and west were ceded to Britain, and curious arrangements were proposed for the Zambezi to and beyond Zumbo. The Portuguese were compelled to agree to dispose of no territory south of the Zambezi without the permission of Britain. They promised to build a railway from the mouth of the Pungwe River (modern Beira) to Salisbury.

Rhodes was apoplectic. Although Johnston cabled him from London that he should accept the treaty's terms as "the best thing that can be done," because "unless this Portuguese difficulty is first settled, the Government will not do anything towards consolidating our influence and interests over Trans-Zambesian Africa. . . ." Rhodes remained adamant. He instructed the London board to abandon the agreement. He urged Cawston to tell the Foreign Office that "I strongly object to [the treaty] and hope they will take this opportunity to drop the whole matter."

Abercorn was unable to see how Rhodes thought the Company could dictate foreign policy to the prime minister, but Rhodes could hardly imagine being crossed by a government whose work he was doing, whose minions he was paying, and whose reputation he believed he was saving. Moreover, Rhodes was sure that he understood the geopolitical needs of southern Africa better than Salisbury. He knew what was best for the region, as well as what he wanted. It was not mere petulance at being crossed which made Rhodes such a pest to the Foreign Office and his own board. Yet only when he threatened to resign as managing director of the Company would Abercorn, who called him an autocrat, remonstrate with Salisbury: Rhodes was too important and too indispensable to empire, and now too significant at the Cape. Without him, Abercorn said, the Company and its shares were nothing.[40] Finally, in September, the board lost its unequal struggle with its founder and asked the Foreign Office to abandon the treaty.

Rhodes made Johnston the scapegoat for the damaging provisions of the treaty. This was unfair, but in September Rhodes was still flushed with anger and at the peak of his bitter campaign by cable against the Foreign Office. "I cannot congratulate you on your work in England," Rhodes sneered. "I trace your hand all through the . . . treaty. It is a disgraceful treaty and I will have nothing to do with it. You have given away the whole west including ½ the Barotse . . . and the whole of Manika and Gazaland and we have got nothing which we had not already got. I can only express my opinion that you ought to be thoroughly ashamed of your work," he scolded, "but in spite of your desertion [from the band of brothers, the vision, and so on] I shall go on fighting and I have not the slightest intention of giving way to the Portuguese."[41]

Nor had Salisbury much intention of giving in to Rhodes. Indeed, in September he let Abercorn know that he had "had enough of Rhodes."[42] As a last resort, Rhodes clearly was prepared—having already (in June) given such orders to Jameson and other pioneers—to take Manicaland and argue afterwards with the Foreign Office. Sir Philip Currie, of the Foreign Office, understood Rhodes' intentions well: "I am quite unable to understand Rhodes' policy," he wrote to Cawston, "unless he proposes to make war on Portugal, seize her territories, and occupy her ports. The arrangement we have . . . is a vast improvement on the present state of things, and the utmost possible without the use of force." The Company would not be permitted to attack a European power, and, anyway, Rhodes will "have his hands full dealing with Lobengula and other coloured potentates."[43]

The test of strength between the British government and Rhodes ultimately was deferred. As the Pioneer Column came to the end of its march and built Fort Salisbury, the Portuguese Cortes, or parliament, unwittingly did Rhodes' bidding. Living in a "fool's paradise," according to Salisbury, and objecting to the "no cession without permission" clause as an infringement on its sovereignty, the Cortes adjourned without ratifying the treaty. However, in November, to avoid the complications that Rhodes' forward policy was sure to bring, Britain and Portugal signed a modus vivendi that froze their territorial claims as of the negotiation of the proposed treaty. But Rhodes and his acolytes had already begun to take advantage of their reprieve. Before the main thrust into Shonaland had been consolidated, a section of the pioneers moved on impertinently to Manica and Gaza.

"I am now occupying Manika and I do not think even you and the Portuguese combined will turn me out," Rhodes told Johnston in September. To Herbert, he declared that if the Portuguese treaty had been devised in order to avoid a collision, too bad. "I cannot restrain my people." Although the Portuguese might now claim a "country in which they have not got a single subject . . . and . . . ask our people either to walk out or else accept their wretched rule . . . we shall do neither the one or the other." That was a threat, in line with Rhodes' bluster over the Anglo-Portuguese agreement. But Rhodes rarely bullied without cajoling. "I do hope you will try and help me," he asked Herbert, "as it must be annoying when an artist has a conception and has started painting a picture to have a kind friend in his absence continuing his work with the result of spoiling the whole idea."[44]

Such a homely, beguiling image—Rhodes as artist—must have occasioned smiles as well as renewed impatience in London. Had the officials known, as Currie had guessed, precisely with what pointed palette knives Rhodes had intended to carve up the Portuguese sphere, there would have been rueful smiles at best. Rhodes had earlier reasoned that if his subordinates could persuade Gungunyane and Mtassa to grant Rudd-like concessions to the Company, he could make a diplomatic case for their longstanding independence from the Portuguese and strengthen both his and their positions by defending the chiefs against any Portuguese counterattacks.

Archibald R. Colquhoun, a hard-drinking dandy, former public works official, and journalist with experience in Burma, to whom Rhodes had given administrative authority for Mashonaland; Selous; and a small phalanx of troopers and pioneers crossed the upper Odzi River north of the modern Mutare and climbed up to Mtassa's village at 5,200 feet on 13 September 1890. On the following midday Mtassa appeared, "attired in a naval cocked hat, a tunic (evidently of Portuguese origin but of ancient date . . .), a leopard skin slung over his back, the whole . . . being completed by a pair of trousers that had evidently passed through many hands, or rather covered many legs. . . ."[45] His Shona people were and always had been independent of Gungunyane's Shangaan, he averred. Portuguese guns had cowed his people, but he claimed never to have granted them territorial rights. Thus, presumbly because Mtassa preferred to hedge his allegiances, being unsure whether the arrival of Britons from the west meant a changing order in the eastern highlands, this chief of the Manyika Shona quickly assented to a treaty proferred by Colquhoun. For £100 worth of rifles, powder, and caps, and a promise to defend him against both Portuguese and Shangaan might, Mtassa grandly gave the Company on behalf of Queen Victoria exclusive rights to prospect and mine; permission to construct bridges, harbors, railways, tramways, canals, reservoirs, telephonic and telegraphic lines, and other "works and conveniences of general or public utility"; and agreed to enter into no other alliances with foreign nations or give any other concession of land without the permission of the Company.

The stage was set for opera buffo. When the Portuguese learned of the British incursion upon their territory, they mounted a military counterattack, arriving at Mtassa's village in November with sufficient force to compel a recantation of the chief's recent pledges to the Company. Fortunately, Colquhoun had posted a young trooper there; he raised the alarm in Mashonaland. Soon Captain Patrick W. Forbes ("a typical British bulldog" with "about as much sense"), formerly of the Inniskilling Dragoons, and sixteen soldiers arrived from Salisbury. But the Portuguese, with superiority in armed numbers, took little notice of Forbes, rejecting his several peremptory notices of eviction. In mid-November, they converged on Mtassa and publicly proclaimed the area Portuguese. Mtassa agreed. Meanwhile, the reinforcements for which Forbes had been waiting finally arrived under the leadership of Lieutenant the Hon. (later Sir) Eustace Fiennes. On the afternoon of 15 November, Forbes and Fiennes surprised and overwhelmed the seventy Portuguese, took as prisoners Paiva and Manuel António da Sousa (Gouveia), a Goanese warlord, and sent them under guard to Salisbury and thence to Cape Town. Major Arthur Glyn Leonard, who met Paiva during the progression of the prisoners to the Cape, described him as "a gentleman, and a very nice fellow. . . . He is very swarthy and slight, and, in appearance, not unlike a dark-skinned dancing-master." Indignant at having been captured by "mere filibusters," he had become an "insensate fury." Gouveia, on the other hand, was dressed in a "striped sleeping-suit" and appeared to be "a retiring, mild-mannered old half-caste gentleman." Leonard said that from Gouveia's looks one could not imagine that he was a "notorious slave-dealer and villain."[46]

Unfortunately, the modus vivendi had been concluded in Lisbon and London on the previous day, and Portugal's citizenry were understandably aroused when they learned of the lightning, nasty raid on Mtassa, the subsequent taking by Forbes of the Portuguese outpost of Macequece (which the Company kept until April), and the kidnapping of Paiva and Sousa. Forbes compounded the horror by proceeding royally to the sea, en route gaining grants from African chiefs for a Company railroad.

With his grasping hand strengthened by Forbes' bold move in Manica, Rhodes could—despite the modus vivendi and the imprecations of London—begin to wrest the Mozambican coast, or at least the section of it closest to Mashonaland, from the Portuguese. Already, in early October, Dr. Aurel Schulz, a physician, this time from Natal, had made his way by sea and overland to

Gungunyane's new capital near the mouth of the Sabi River and, after bargaining hard, received a concession of mineral rights and construction privileges in the form of a treaty of alliance between the Shangaan nation and Queen Victoria. Gungunyane insisted upon roughly the same emoluments as Lobengula: £500, 1,000 rifles, and 20,000 rounds of ammunition. But there was a small problem. Gungunyane signed nothing. The agreement was an oral one, later committed to writing by Schulz; the chief had cannily promised to ratify the treaty in writing only when cash and the instruments of war had been received.[47]

Gungunyane's writ could be asserted to have run traditionally from the Sabi to the Zambezi, or at least to the Pungwe. (He had, after all, recently transferred his capital and 50,000 people from the Chamanimani mountains 150 miles to the sea without interference from either Portuguese or Africans.) Consequently, Rhodes could use the Schulz concession, and Forbes' various paper and military deeds, to take as much as he needed of the coast around the Pungwe mouth and perhaps as far south as the outlet of the Sabi. The cost of shipping goods overland from Kimberley to Salisbury was estimated to be at least four times what it was to send them by sea to the Pungwe and then up-country to Salisbury on a new railway. Indeed, when the rains came to the new white settlements in December and January and the road from the south became impassable and the pioneers began to run short of supplies and succumb to malaria, Rhodes quickened his concern for an easier, durable, Company-controlled route into the new possession. Nothing that had occurred since August persuaded him that he could rely on the cooperation of the British or Portuguese governments, or on the friendly assistance of the Portuguese who controlled Mozambique.

By Christmas 1890, Lisbon and London were becoming aware of the Mtassa imbroglio and the occupation of Macequece. Rhodes had received word of the Gungunyane concession, and Jameson (who had earlier gone overland from the Shona country and then rowed to the mouth of the Pungwe in a collapsible boat) had returned to Mashonaland to take Colquhoun's position as the administrator. Jameson called it a "swagger 'billet' " and probably knew that Rhodes had dismissed Colquhoun because of his penchant for paying more attention to instructions from London than to those from Kimberley.[48]

Rhodes understood perfectly well that the Foreign Office expected his associates to avoid harassing the Portuguese in accord with the terms of the modus vivendi. Nevertheless, Rhodes initially tossed off such constraints. "As long as armed Portuguese slaves raising Portuguese flag everywhere within the sphere of our [Mtassa] Concession it is impossible to withdraw the police force."[49] Two weeks before, Rhodes had ordered Forbes and soldiers from Fort Victoria simply to occupy Beira and the line of march between that nascent port and Salisbury. He had contemplated sending a second pioneer expedition into Manicaland so as to end all speculation about its future. Salisbury, for his part, simultaneously was assuring the Portuguese ambassador that the Company could only have invaded Macequece in error, and was bound to withdraw. Messages were hurriedly sent to the Cape, and Loch instructed Rhodes' office in Kimberley to remove its detachment from the salient, which was deemed Portuguese.

Even if communications between the metropolitan center and the distant periphery had been rapid, it is doubtful if Rhodes would or could have slowed his rush to the sea. Certainly he refused to withdraw into Rhodesia (Zimbabwe) proper, as the London board wished. But he consented to visit Britain with Loch in January 1891 to see if he and the board could—as Salisbury hoped—purchase a controlling interest in a Portuguese-dominated and British-financed entity which held mining rights from Beira to Macequece.

Beit sailed to Madeira to meet Rhodes, signifying the importance of the issue and the potentially intricate financing that could be involved. "We landed at Plymouth," recalled Rhodes' private secretary, "and arrived in London at one o'clock in the morning of a bitterly cold winter's day. On the platform at that grim hour to meet Mr. Rhodes was the Duke of Abercorn . . . who accompanied us to the Westminster Palace Hotel . . . where we very gladly sat down to a hot meal." Abercorn, possibly because of the hour, was not terribly interested in the growth and development of the company's territories. At least that was the impression Currey received, "because when His Grace should have been paying closest attention to Mr. Rhodes he turned to me and said 'We have had a capital black-cock season this year . . . !' and Mr. Rhodes' face was a study."

From then on the visit was more hectic. Lord Rothschild was announced in the morning, "and it is no very great exaggeration to say that from that moment until we left London three weeks later there was a progression of visitors . . . of all kinds and sorts. Society folk, politicians, financiers, newspapermen . . . followed one another in an unceasing flow while every postal delivery brought shoals of invitations and requests of all kinds."

Rhodes dined with the Queen at Windsor Castle, and was adored or at least sought out constantly. It was fortunate, reported Mills, that Rhodes took "being lionized with becoming modesty and patience, and never [lost] one of his innumerable chances of pushing forward his policy and South African interests." Rhodes' own reaction to his social success and fame was largely indifference. "Oh yes," he told Merriman, "they have made a Buffalo Bill of me for 30 days." Yet Rhodes' round of activities became so rushed that he even had to stop the ship on which he was due to sail in order to dine with Lord Salisbury on his last evening. The Union Steamship Company said that it could not delay the ship's departure from Southampton, but it could hold her at anchor out in the water until Rhodes arrived. At 2:30 a.m. Rhodes boarded his special train and was on the ship by breakfast, thus solving the mystery which had been puzzling his fellow-passengers.[50]

The more serious accomplishments of the short visit were few. Rhodes and Loch took the opportunity to discuss the proposed terms of a revised Anglo-Portuguese convention with Salisbury and his officials. Those talks may have helped mold the final accord; with regard to the takeover of the Mozambique Company, however, Lisbon refused to sanction any such deal, and Rhodes sailed away empty-handed. Nevertheless, he had achieved a first-hand appreciation of Foreign Office thinking and of the further ways in which its principals would continue to strew barriers across Rhodes' buccaneering path.

He also made his fifth will. Currey remembered that just before Rhodes began to dress for one or another special dinner, he summoned him to witness his will. Currey reminded Rhodes that two witnesses were necessary; the floor waiter was summoned. Different from the first four, this will made the eldest of his living brothers the executor, gave Dalston to Frank, and then to Ernest and the rest of the men in the Rhodes family, with the ladies last. Rhodes directed his trustees to produce £5,000 a year from his estate and to divide it equally among his brothers and sisters of whole blood. The remainder of his income was to be reserved for his big idea. The trustees were to devote themselves to its realization, with Rhodes' funds. Rothschild remained a trustee. The big surprise was that Rhodes named Stead as a second trustee. In Stead, Rhodes now and for many years reposed enormous confidence. Alone of his many associates, Rhodes felt that Stead really shared his vision of how Britain's destiny was dependent upon his big idea.

According to Stead, Rhodes from this time was willing to realize his dream of a unified English-speaking people (called a "race" by both Rhodes and Stead) by the absorption of the British empire into the United States. Hitherto he had recoiled from the idea. But, as a last resort, he succumbed to Stead's persuasion and agreed that it was an acceptable goal. Rhodes also explained to Stead that if he were to die the bulk of his fortune was Rothschild's to dispose. "But," Stead quotes him as saying, "the thought torments me sometimes . . . that if I die all my money will pass into the hands of a man who, however well-disposed, is absolutely incapable of understanding my ideas. I have endeavoured to explain them to him, but I could see from the look on his face that it made no impression . . . and that I was simply wasting my time." Rhodes hence added Stead's name and proposed to leave a letter to Rothschild with his will authorizing Stead to expend the funds "in the assured conviction that [Stead] would employ every penny of his millions in promoting the ideas to which [Rhodes and Stead] had both dedicated [their] lives." Rhodes did so despite Stead's understandable worry that Rothschild would be "considerably amazed" to be linked with someone like Stead. Stead wanted Rhodes to talk to Rothschild about it, but Rhodes refused, wishing as always to avoid unnecessary conflict. Should there be any "ructions," said Rhodes, "I shall be gone then."[51]

In mid-February, while Rhodes was in England, the *Countess of Carnarvon*, a tiny, tatty coastal steamer of 100 tons, steamed up the Limpopo River. Act II of the comic opera was underway. The Portuguese, hearing of the Schulz concession, had sent their own men to reaffirm Gungunyane's presumed subordinate status. Schulz, in turn, called for help and for the payments that had been promised. It was the Lobengula problem, in miniature. Thus Jameson, Doyle, and Dunbar Moodie set out from Salisbury, and Harris (with Rhodes' agreement) dispatched the *Carnarvon,* loaded with guns and ammunition. The little steamer would have to run its cargo under the very noses of the Portuguese, however, but almost nothing was too audacious for Rutherfoord Harris. The *Carnarvon,* in fact, slipped into the estuary of the Limpopo and offloaded its clandestine goods without any hindrance. In keeping with the farcical qualities of the day, a Portuguese official simply demanded a customs fee, and let the guns go on to the Shangaan chief.

Gungunyane was impressed. Shortly after this missed opportunity for a successful Portuguese intervention in the evolving Gungunyane saga, a bedraggled Jameson and friends arrived after slogging 700 miles for several weeks across sodden country to which the Shangaan legions had only recently laid waste. Jameson somehow persuaded Gungunyane that the ability of his Company to deliver a quantity of arms meant that Britain was more powerful than Portugal. Gungunyane confirmed the earlier concession in writing, agreeing to accept an alliance with Queen Victoria. Or did he? The Portuguese officials who were present at the signing claimed that Gungunyane had told Jameson that he was a Portuguese subject, and that the chief had only affixed his mark to Jameson's document after its contents had been misrepresented.

Nevertheless, Jameson rushed to Kimberley. Marching eighty miles to the Limpopo, he found the *Carnarvon,* which had steamed to Durban and back, waiting for him. Jameson and the others comfortably settled themselves on board, but then a bigger Portuguese gunboat appeared. Soon the *Carnarvon,* the administrator, and the other Britons were placed under arrest. Jameson complained of being taken to Lourenço Marques "in the hold, with all the filthy Portuguese and niggers. . . ."[52] But he was soon released, albeit the hapless *Carnarvon* was detained for months until Rhodes guaranteed to pay a fine.

The initiatives of Schulz, Jameson, and Harris were to no avail. Even the seizure of the *Carnarvon,* which might otherwise have aroused British jingioism to renewed heights, counted for little. No matter how Rhodes ranted and raved, with Loch as an ally, and with Verschoyle and Stead pumping the bellows of imperialism at home, Salisbury was adamant. The Queen wanted the Portuguese throne to survive. For reasons connected with Salisbury's intricate appreciation of the prevailing balance of power in Europe, the prime minister wanted to retain Portugal as a colonial suzerain of some significance in Africa.

Certainly it was not the moment to reduce the influence of Portugal along the African coasts; Germany might create new difficulties for Britain. The requirements of international law may further have remained a charge on the prime minister's conscience. At least that is what he told the House of Lords. Doubtless, too, Rhodes' personality had become an endless source of grief. Salisbury doubted his loyalty to the empire, and neither the prime minister nor his juniors trusted the full veracity of the communications which they received from the Kimberley offices of the Company, and even from Rhodes and Loch themselves. In early 1891, when the rivalry for Gungunyane's favor

had come to a head, Salisbury and his officials refused to ratify the Schulz/
Jameson concession and reminded the Company that its Charter limited the
Company to a region lying to the west of the Portuguese dominions. Moreover, Britain had always affirmed Portugal's right to its coast. "No high phi-
lanthropic, progressive or humanitarian considerations," Salisbury concluded
a speech to the Lords, "would justify us in disregarding the plain rule of
right."[53]

Rhodes had other intentions. Sometime in late February, after he and
Loch had returned to South Africa, the premier of the Cape Colony, in his
capacity as chief of the British South Africa Company, decided to force a
passage up the Pungwe River and start building a cart road and then a tramway toward the interior. If the Portuguese barred his way, his subordinates
would provoke an international incident, and thus, he planned, the British
government would be compelled to back the Company on patriotic grounds.
Although the Colonial Office, hearing of these plans, tried to halt any expedition, its cable arrived after the ships had sailed from Durban.

In command of the advance party of the larger expedition was brusque
Captain Sir John Willoughby, an estate-owning graduate of Eton College and
the University of Cambridge. He was accompanied by thirteen whites and
ninety-one Africans—a roadmaking party—tons of equipment, and a stage
coach. At Beira, Willoughby confessed the ostensible object of his mission—to
settle down near Sofala and start building a road through, at the very least,
disputed territory. He was ordered not to steam upriver, did so, and shots
were flung across his bow by a Portuguese gunboat. Willoughby claimed an
insult to the British flag and peaceful British subjects; Rhodes had his provocative proof that Portugal had closed the Pungwe. Exactly as Rhodes had supposed, Salisbury rose to the occasion, sent British gunboats steaming toward
Beira from Zanzibar and Lourenço Marques, and demanded that Portugal
permit the free passage of Britons up the river.

This, the Beira outrage, stiffened Salisbury's hand in the negotiations which
had again begun between Britain and Portugal. Although Rhodes did not
immediately relieve his transportation problem to Mashonaland, nor strengthen
any claims to the Mozambican coast, his long-term position in the interior was
buttressed. True, in the imperial tidying that followed this consternation, the
Company was finally compelled to abandon Macequece, but only after a major
skirmish in which a small group of Britons repulsed a larger detachment of
Portuguese, with serious loss of life. Rhodes was very pleased when his forty-
seven men defeated the Portuguese "mob" and killed "twenty of them it was
a very good performance. . . ." Shortly afterwards, however, Major Herbert
Langton Sapte, Loch's military secretary, arrived from Cape Town by sea and
the path from Beira. He conveyed the high commissioner's direct orders for
a prompt withdrawal of the Company. "But why didn't you put Sapte in irons
and say he was drunk?" Rhodes asked.[54]

The Anglo-Portuguese convention of 1891 settled Rhodes' audacious, irrepressible, and unscrupulous attempts to grab Portuguese East Africa as he

had taken Ndebeleland and Shonaland. Because of the Beira outrage as well as Rhodes' incessant scheming, it took far less away from Rhodes than had the convention of 1890. The western delimitation of Barotseland was moved considerably toward the Atlantic, the outer bounds of the Lozi kingdom. In Shona country, the dividing line was moved eastward from the Sabi River to a line of longitude that ran along the highest slopes of the mountains. Mtassa's Manyikaland became entirely British, although Macequece remained just over the border in Mozambique. Northern Gaza was given to the Company, although its lower-lying lands, and the entire coast, were confirmed in Portuguese hands. Portugal was compensated by the transfer of an enlarged wedge of territory along the middle Zambezi to Zumbo. Passage along the Zambezi, Pungwe, Sabi, and other rivers through Portuguese territory was declared free, with import and export fees limited to 3 percent of value. Portugal also promised, as it had before, to construct a railway speedily (it took seven years) from Beira to the Company's sphere.[55]

Rhodes should have welcomed the conclusion of such a helpful agreement. But he knew how difficult it would be to reinforce his colony across territory controlled by Portugal. Thus he deplored the failure of the treaty to recognize Gungunyane's independence, and even tried to upset its ratification by sending two of Gungunyane's induna and Doyle (not Maund) to London to see the Queen. When the treaty became official, and after Rhodes had in fact experienced practical difficulties in using the Beira route, he penned a long, bitter letter to Salisbury that illuminated Rhodes' petulance and his new refusal to accept being thwarted. It also displayed a quintessential lack of sophistication which, throughout the year, had tried the patience of those in Whitehall whose agenda had been so very different. "It is no use . . . complaining of your treatment of oneself, after the fight at Massi-kessi," Rhodes complained, "when I could have taken the coast, and by this time had a tramway constructed through the fly, if you had only let me have a free hand; that is past history. But I think I can at least ask you to have your Treaty fulfilled. I cannot feed the people of Mashonaland by the overland route and I cannot feed them from Beira with 90 miles of [tsetse] fly, which kills all the oxen. I must have a railway or tramway. . . ." He then summed up what he had done for the Chartered sphere. "Considering the difficulties of taking a new country, I do not think we have done badly. We have stopped the Boer Trek, we have kept the Matabele quiet, and hammered the Portuguese, and should have had a tramway from the coast already if you had not given in to the Portuguese."[56]

13

"A Man Might Be Proud"
Assaults Across the Zambezi

SECURING THE COUNTRY of the Manyika was among Rhodes' more critical accomplishments. Had he not been so assertive and Forbes so forceful, the Company (and Zimbabwe) might have lost that high and pleasant area to the Portuguese. Likewise, had the upper Zambezi River become an international boundary, as had been originally proposed, the Lozi nation would have straddled the Angolan-Zambian border, and Rhodes' empire, as well as the successor national state, would have been smaller and more vulnerable. Although Rhodes in the late 1880s and early 1890s was less concerned with the total shape of trans-Zambezia than he was with rounding out his personal dominion south of the Zambezi, he welcomed oversight of vast lands which probably held minerals or would serve as gateways to those parts of Africa which were rich in precious stones, gold, or copper. The acquisition of trans-Zambezia also protected the flanks of his Shona settlement and the Nyasa sphere over which Johnston held sway. Then, too, Rhodes always welcomed the addition of territory. "Land," he told Beit, "is the only thing in the world apart from the precious metals which always has a certain value. . . ."[1] Even so, Rhodes' immediate involvement with the region across the Zambezi began before the Charter was his to exploit.

The Lozi were the premier people north of the river. Although they feared Ndebele marauders and had acknowledged Lobengula's superior power, they themselves had imposed their own regional hegemony over a vast area between the Kwando River on the west and the Kafue River on the east, and from the Chobe and Zambezi rivers in the south to the headwaters of the Zambezi and the Congo watershed in the north. Before about 1830, the Luyana, or Lozi (Barotse), occupied the flood plain of the upper Zambezi and gained superiority over the surrounding non-Luyana. From 1833 to 1835, however, the Kololo, a Sotho-speaking warrior group which had fled Lesotho

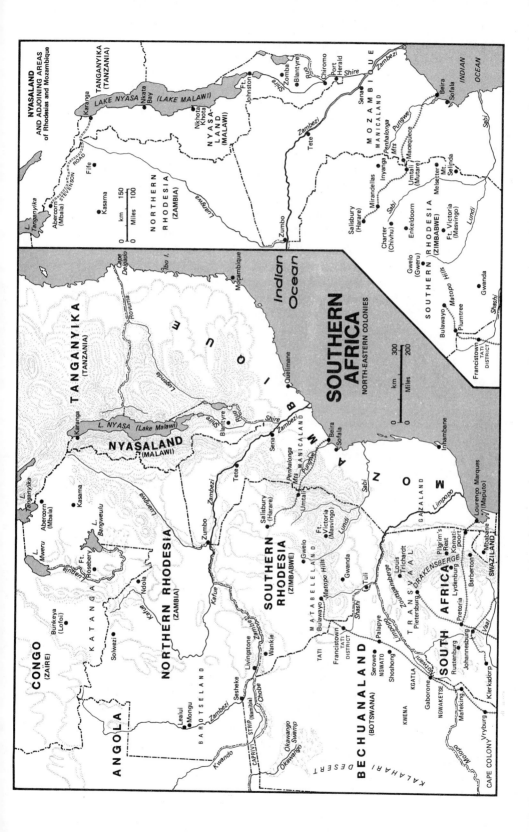

NYASALAND AND ADJOINING AREAS
of Rhodesias and Mozambique

TANGANYIKA (TANZANIA)

Karonga

Lake Nyasa (LAKE MALAWI)

Nkata Bay

Nkhota Khota

NYASA-
LAND
(MALAWI)

Ft. Johnston

Zomba

Blantyre

Chiromo

Port Herald

Shire

Shire

Senga

M O Z A M B I Q U E

Zambezi

Beira

Sofala

INDIAN

OCEAN

Aberrom (Mbala) STEVENSON ROAD

L. Tanganyika

Fife

Tete

Zumbo

NORTHERN RHODESIA (ZAMBIA)

km 150
Miles 100
0

Kasama

Zambezi

Salisbury (Harare)

Mirandellas

Charter (Chivhu)

Enkeldoorn

Gwelo (Gweru)

Inyanga

Penhalonga

Mts

Pungwe

Macequece

Umtali (Mutare)

Mt. Selinda

Melsetter

Ft. Victoria (Masvingo)

Lundi

MANICALAND

S O U T H E R N   R H O D E S I A
(ZIMBABWE)

Matopo Hills

Bulawayo

Plumtree

Gwanda

Shashi

Francistown
TATI DISTRICT

CONGO (ZAIRE)

Bunkeya (Lofoi)

Solwezi

KATANGA

Ndola

L. Mweru

L. Tanganyika

Aberrom (Mbala)

Kasama

Luapula

L. Bangweulu

Ft. Rosebery

ANGOLA

Lealui

Mongu

B A R O T S E L A N D

Sesheke

Livingstone

Zambezi

Kafue

Kafue

NORTHERN RHODESIA (ZAMBIA)

Zumbo

Karonga

L. NYASA (Lake Malawi)

NYASALAND (MALAWI)

Tete

Shire

Shire

Blantyre

Senga

Mopambique

Cape Delgado

Ibo I.

Rovuma

Lugenda

TANGANYIKA (TANZANIA)

Luangwa

Indian Ocean

Quelimane

M O Z A M B I Q U E

Beira

Sofala

SOUTHERN AFRICA
NORTH-EASTERN COLONIES

km 300
Miles 200
0

Salisbury (Harare)

Penhalonga

Umtali

Mts MANICALAND

Pungwe

Gwelo

Ft. Victoria (Masvingo)

SOUTHERN RHODESIA (ZIMBABWE)

Matopo Hills

Bulawayo

Gwanda

Shashi

Tuli

Sabi

Lundi

GAZALAND

Inhambane

Lourenço Marques (Maputo)

Limpopo

CAPRIVI STRIP (Namibia)

Chobe

Kwando

Okawango Swamp

Okawango

K A L A H A R I   D E S E R T

BECHUANALAND (BOTSWANA)

Serowe
NGWATO

Shoshong

Palapye

Francistown
TATI DISTRICT

TATI

MATABELELAND

Limpopo

KWENA

Gaborone

KGATLA

NGWAKETSE

Mafeking

Vryburg

CAPE COLONY

Klerksdorp

Johannesburg

Rustenburg

Pretoria

T R A N S V A A L

Lydenburg

Pietersburg

Louis Trichardt

Zoutpansberge

DRAKENSBERGE

Pilgrim's Rest

Barberton

Komatipoort

Mbabane

SWAZILAND

SOUTH AFRICA

Vaal

Limpopo

and Shaka's Zulu during or as a result of the Mfecane, plundered their way northward through Botswana, around Mzilikazi's Ndebele, to the Zambezi. Under Sebitwane, their forceful leader, they pre-empted land among the Tonga and Toka who grazed cattle north of the Zambezi. But then they moved westward to the more fertile Zambezi floodplain or Bulozi. In the 1840s, Sebitwane's warriors defeated the soldiers of Mubukwanu, the Lozi chief, and Sebitwane and the Kololo assumed the prerogatives of their defeated subjects, married their women, and imposed Sikololo as the language of the state's ruling class.

David Livingstone admired Sebitwane, who ruled harshly and successfully along the Zambezi. His son Sekeletu, and Mbolulu, who soon succeeded Sikeletu, lost the confidence of their supporters and subjects. In 1863–64, the Lozi revolted, ousting the Kololo, who fled into what is now northern Botswana. Sipopa became litunga, or king, of the restored Lozi monarchy and increased the reach and scale of the restored state. During his reign, and the reigns of Mwanawina and Lubosi (Lewanika), the Lozi fashioned a strong, agriculturally based state; the waters of the mighty river annually replenished their garden mounds and refreshed the grazing lands of their cattle. When the first whites arrived in Bulozi to trade and preach the gospel, the kingdom was the focus of commerce and statecraft across half of what is now Zambia, and a portion of eastern Angola.

In 1878 and 1879, François Coillard, a French-speaking evangelical Protestant, his Scottish-born wife, and others from Paris Missionary Society stations in Basutoland attempted to plant a new religious outpost among the Lozi. From 1882 to 1884, Frederick Stanley Arnot, a Scottish member of the fundamentalist Plymouth Brethren, lived near Lealui, Lewanika's capital. In 1885, Coillard returned for good, establishing several stations in the Lozi valley immediately after Lewanika's rule, interrupted by a year-long civil war, had been re-established. From that year, the Lozi were troubled more by external events, especially the growing threat of a white incursion from the south, than by internal convulsion. Coillard, who gradually won the grudging respect of the Lewanika and his principal induna, played a pivotal role in shaping the Lozi response to this new danger, and in focusing Rhodes' eyes in the direction of Lozi country (Barotseland).[2]

Lewanika wished to entrench his own rule among the Lozi and also to avail himself of the physical support and new resources which, rumor had it, could be secured if he allied his kingdom to a white nation. In 1888 he talked to Coillard and the English-speaking traders who visited his capital and sent one or more messages to Kgama, chief of the Ngwato. Lord Gifford of the Bechuanaland Exploration Company, with an agent in Shoshong, Kgama's capital, learned of Lewanika's interest in possible links to Britain in September 1888. Gifford so informed the Foreign Office, which was then and for another year largely concentrating on the Limpopo hinterland and basically unconcerned about a land so remote and unlikely to lie within any future British sphere.

In early 1889, a letter from Coillard to Shippard alerted the South African arm of the Colonial Office, and Rhodes, that Lewanika wanted to establish ties to Her Majesty's government. About that time Lewanika again asked Kgama if Britain were a helpful and friendly associate and, if so, how an arrangement with Britain might be sought. Nor was he deflected from this quest by the cautious quality of Kgama's reply: "Concerning the word you ask me about the government of the English," Kgama informed Lewanika, "I can only say it is a thing for each chief to do for himself. I rejoice in it, but I cannot advise you, you are a Chief and must do for yourself what you desire." He went on: "I have the People of the great Queen with me and I am glad to have them. I live in peace with them, and I have no fear of the Matabele or the Boers any longer attacking me, that is the thing which I know. . . . If you wish to speak with the great government and if you wish to see some great man from the Queen's government then if you ask me I will let the Government know and a man will be sent to speak with you and hear your words."[3]

After being at first reluctant to encourage Lewanika's overture to the representatives of the Queen, Coillard became a convert. By then his and his colleagues' efforts to Christianize the Lozi had met with little success. "Our work is a difficult one," said Coillard, "and really I think sometimes that our difficulties increase as we go on. We have little encouragement. . . . There are no signs of conversion. . . ."[4] Like Arnot before him, and missionaries everywhere in the early phases of their African tenure, Coillard was discouraged. Moreover, Coillard viewed Lewanika as a weak, vacillating, vexatious monarch. Coillard thus became an advocate of a strong connection to Britain, especially some form of alien rule which would impose discipline and order on the people among whom he was making little headway. This was a common sentiment among missionaries. Coillard's invitation to Shippard even dangled the prospect of a land ripe for European agricultural development, which the transhumant nature of the upper Zambezi, with its required yearly migrations into and out of the central flood plain, had always precluded. That Coillard wanted settlers might have been calculated to appeal to someone like Rhodes, but minerals were of greater significance, and of their presence Coillard wrote nothing.

Lewanika and Coillard's overtures, and Gifford's awareness, insured the inclusion of Barotseland within the sphere of the Charter and of the Company. Rhodes guessed that there could be minerals there; Lewanika's domain provided egress to the copper-rich lode of Katanga and possibly even to the Nyasa area. He and Johnston both agreed at that memorable overnight meeting in May 1889 to include Lewanika's kingdom in the trans-Zambezian adjunct to the company's main prospect in the south. As Rhodes wrote Grey in mid-1889, Lewanika's request should not be refused by Britain, and the Company should offer to relieve the Foreign Office of all expenses (but Rhodes only envisaged paying Lewanika £100 a year). He would attempt to obtain a monopoly of minerals there. Grey should try to persuade the Foreign Office to assign the most extensive possible area to Lewanika, and then Rhodes and the Company would hold it for exploitation after the Ndebele question had been resolved. "My plan is to secure all territory before it is gone," he added.[5]

Rhodes had intended to bank the Lozi land—to keep Portuguese, Germans, and others out—but the intervention of a minor concessionaire, and Rhodes' sudden realization that Léopold was marching toward Katanga, accelerated the rush of Rhodes' sub-imperial interest. The unexpected element, a chance byproduct of the scramble, was Henry Ware. In June 1889, Ware, an itinerant trader with little capital of his own, persuaded Lewanika to give him a mining concession over the lands of the subsidiary Toka in exchange for £200 and a 4 percent levy on anything dug out of the ground. Lewanika wanted "trade and civilization," or so he said. The Toka were an insignificant people who lived north of the Victoria Falls and west of the Kafue River. Although their territory may have belonged to the Lozi, the Ndebele raided it whenever they wished. Thus Lewanika was risking little by allowing whites to mine in such an outlying part of his kingdom. Coillard, who witnessed the transaction and kept a copy of the concession, urged such a grant on the Lozi court on behalf of the missionaries, since he was more and more anxious to cement good connections with the south.

Ware, however, had no intention of working his grant; he sold it in Kimberley for £500, and his successors in turn offered it to Rhodes. But what they demanded in Company shares disgusted Rhodes. He decided to have nothing to do with "that crowd" until they altered "their tone," nevertheless finally squaring them in December at a favorable rate—£9,000 and 10,000 shares in the Company. He had "got Barotse," he told Herbert. By then, however, he had also dispatched a representative to Lewanika to seek a fuller, definitive concession and to end all ambiguity. "I have sent a man in to get a royalty over their heads," he told Beit with characteristic aplomb. In the same breath, however, he also professed a mild disinterest in the outcome. "The country is remote and I believe unhealthy but still would . . . complete . . . our area. . . . It does not matter very much."[6]

This lack of enthusiasm for the Lozi country was new, possibly because Rhodes was better and more correctly informed about its potential than he had been when he had written to Grey, but probably also because, in the African summer of 1889–90, Rhodes had much more consuming concerns: the organization of the raid on Shona country, the railway extension, and the confrontation on the Shire, to say nothing of Cape politics and gold and diamond dealings (which will be discussed in subsequent chapters).

Frank Elliott Lochner was Rhodes' man. A former member of the Bechuanaland Border Police, he was dispatched by Rhodes in September 1889 and reached Shoshong in November. There, thanks to Shippard, who sent a message to Lewanika implying that the Company was an arm of Her Majesty's government, and to the Rev. James D. Hepburn, the local London Missionary Society representative and a strong believer in imperial extension, Lochner obtained three important letters. They introduced him to Lewanika and Coillard, and gave his expedition a legitimacy and significance which both impressed the court in Lealui and exceeded strict reality. A letter from Kgama to Lewanika warned the Lozi against Ware—"a self-seeker"—and advised Lewanika to listen to Lochner. Doing so, Kgama suggested, would make the Lozi as prosperous as the Ngwato. To strengthen these sentiments, Kgama sent men with Lochner bearing gifts. Another letter was from Hepburn to Coillard. It stretched the facts: Lochner, said Hepburn, had "full power to offer Lewanika protection against the Matabele. . . . One of the great objects before the Chartered Co. is to combine commerce with philanthropy. . . ."[7] The third letter was from Rhodes to Coillard.

Philanthropy was not precisely what Rhodes had in mind for the Lozi, as his own private asides make clear. Nor did Lochner, an uncouth man of obstinate manner and choleric temper, travel for eleemosynary purposes. The arduous journey to Lealui during the wet season sorely tried him; he arrived there only at the end of March. Then he sat, drying out while the chief and his induna considered granting him an audience. Lewanika, remarked Coillard, hardly seemed "anxious to face the question of the so-called protectorate, for many chiefs were "on the warpath." "I have no chiefs here," said Lewanika. "With whom . . . can I sit in council? If you press me so much now, how can I discuss questions of such importance alone? Do not be impatient and do not worry, messenger of the great Queen. It is the regular thing for an ambassador always to be kept waiting. . . ."[8] There was new opposition, too, over the Ware concession, several chiefs claiming that Lewanika had sold the country. A few white traders worried about the loss of their own livelihoods if the Company came, and were arousing antagonism. But the second thoughts and new fears of the Ndebele may also have been communicated to the Lozi, and the overall threat that Rhodes and his company posed had become more, if not definitively, apparent. At least to the Lozi.

Coillard, however, now wanted the Company, and thus, even at one remove, the Queen's government. He wanted efficient transport links, helpful to his missionaries and their work. He wanted to modernize and Westernize the Lozi nation, the better to evangelize successfully. He was also beguiled, personally, by the offer contained in Rhodes' letter. Coillard, like Moffat, should be the Company's agent in Lealui at a handsome stipend, said Rhodes. "I cannot serve two masters," Coillard replied. "But if without any official title I can be to your Company of any service as a medium of communication and until you get the proper man, I willingly place myself at your disposal."[9]

Without Coillard's strong assistance (as well as his demand that the Company offer Lewanika a sizable annuity), Lochner might well have disappointed Rhodes. "Coillard," Lochner reported, "is doing everything in his power for the success of my mission." Later, he added to his praise, "I am sure that the Company owes as much if not more to Coillard than to myself. . . . He is heart and soul with the Company. . . ." Coillard was motivated by his desire to make wish the father of deed. Yet Lochner may well have fed those dreams, and spun not uncommon, and not necessarily unrealistic, tales of Rhodes' powers and aims. After all, to his supporters Rhodes was all, and could and did move obstacles in accord with a far-reaching vision. Thus it may be less surprising than it seems that Coillard hoped Rhodes and Rhodes' concession would herald a new dawn. "A break in the darkness of our horizon seems to be the Chartered . . . Company. . . . We should at least have the advantage of regular Postal communication & our transport would also become easier if not cheaper. Here they expect to push the railway through to Cairo!"

Even so, the proposed treaty was suspect; even the presents from Rhodes that Lochner had distributed with "hitherto unknown liberality" were a source of suspicion. "You would be surprised to hear of all the intrigues that have been going on," Coillard wrote home. More to the point, Lewanika was a monarch with much less power internally than Lobengula. He sat precariously on a hard-won throne, and could sign nothing without a broad-ranging consensus among the chiefs of the land. Particularly difficult to please were the chiefs of the Sesheke district, who had only recently been incorporated into the Lozi state.[10] Coillard had to work hard.

Lochner's patience and Coillard's persistent advocacy were finally rewarded in late June, at a time when the Pioneer Column was moving out of Bechuanaland toward the Shona country. The litunga finally fashioned broad support. On behalf of the Lozi, Lewanika signed a concession which gave Rhodes rights over all of northwestern Zambia more presumptive than those construed to be implicit in the Rudd Concession.

The Company received an exclusive monopoly to find and mine precious metals in the whole of Barotseland. The Company agreed annually to pay Lewanika £2,000, the princely sum upon which Coillard had insisted. It promised to defend Lewanika and his people from attack. The Company (to please Coillard) agreed to assist the efforts of Christian missions, help build schools, foster trade, arrange a postal and telegraph service, and dispatch a British representative to reside in Lealui. The Company promised not to send settlers into Lozi country without permission of Lewanika. Annexed to the pre-printed document of concession was a compendium of Lozi assertions of vast, exaggerated, territorial suzerainty. The more extensive the kingdom the better for Rhodes, Lochner, Coillard, and the Lozi. As Lochner reported home after the concession finally was signed, "Country very much larger than was supposed . . . cannot be less than 225,000 square miles." Lochner's telegram, which Harris quickly communicated to Loch, also said that Lewanika had accepted a protectorate of the Chartered Company and that "they understand the right of the Company to govern people and country through the King and Chiefs."[11]

There were problems with the concession. Territorially it infringed on the German sphere which had, a few weeks before, been allotted by Salisbury's treaty. But the major problem was that both Lewanika and Coillard soon believed themselves duped. Lewanika asserted that he had signed the concession only because Lochner bullied him. Lewanika repudiated the concession, saying that he wanted "to be under the Protectorate of the Queen,

& not at the mercy of a Gold Mining Company," only to have Loch, Rhodes' accomplice from the best motives, assure him rather disingenuously that he was. But to the end of his days Lewanika protested against the concession and the implication, never intended, that he had signed away his territorial rights. Moreover, both Lewanika and Coillard expected evidence of material progress—if not a railway to the heart of Bulozi, then the postal and telegraphic ties that had been promised. At the very least, they desired a British resident advisor.[12] Not until 1895 did Forbes, of the expeditions against Mtassa and Macequece, arrive as a token representative with few funds and less support. Indeed, the era that Lewanika and Coillard had keenly anticipated began only in 1897, when the Company was no longer directly involved in administering areas across the Zambezi.

What neither Coillard nor Lewanika, nor even Lochner, could have anticipated, nor altered, was Rhodes' and therefore the Company's profound disinterest in this part of trans-Zambezia. Once the mineral prospects were realized to be poor and the terrain and climate likewise, Rhodes naturally preferred to spend the Company's hard-won funds in more immediately productive places. Lewanika's powerlessness was patent, for it was only obvious long after the fact that Rhodes had merely acquired an option over Barotseland to hold German and Portuguese territorial ambitions at bay, and (in case it possessed greater promise than he had thought) to prevent others from taking it. Thus Rhodes was much more active in defending and extending the Lozi boundaries than he was in promoting development there. The definitive Anglo-Portuguese treaty of 1891 included all of Barotseland within the Company's sphere, but left its western limits to be defined in 1905 by the King of Italy, who crafted a compromise.

Coillard unintentionally provided a cautious contemporary reflection on the actions, later regretted, which subjugated the Lozi to Rhodes and Britain. "The British South Africa Co. have succeeded in getting the whole country as a concession. . . . I expect it will prove a mixture of good and bad. But I am more and more firmly convinced that it was the only chance the natives had to escape destruction. . . . The Barotsi . . . are always plotting against each other. . . . If the Co. can give the country some sense of security it will be a blessing hitherto unknown. But we shall have to see whether their dealings correspond with their promises."[13]

Rhodes, who habitually gathered miscellaneous information from travelers, hunters, and prospectors and stored it away for future use when needed, had originally imagined Barotseland to be a stopping place on the way to Katanga, where the presence of precious metals was better authenticated. Africans had carried lumps of raw copper to both coasts for a century or more; Portuguese, German, and British explorers had seen outcrops. Rhodes had therefore instructed Lochner to grab Barotseland and then continue on to Katanga, where he should attempt to make similar arrangements (and use additional versions of the pre-printed concession forms) with the local chiefs and warlords. It mattered little to Rhodes in this cynical phase of his life that

Katanga had probably been assigned to Léopold's Congo. Indeed, while attending the anti-slavery conference in Brussels in early 1890, Cawston discovered that the copper areas of Katanga, particularly the section ruled by Msiri, had been acknowledged to be Léopold's. In a "secret" and "very private" letter he corrected Rhodes' cherished belief that Katanga could still be acquired legitimately. Nevertheless, he thought that they together might find a way to thwart Léopold. Perhaps there were loopholes in Léopold's claims. If not, he continued, "I gather here that the king is getting rather tired of the £80,000 a year which he has to spend [on the conquest of the Congo]. My idea is to buy from him the right to Garenganze [Msiri's Katanga] . . . or if not rent it from him on a percentage of profits [basis]."[14]

Msiri had gained power in Katanga about ten years before. The grandson of a minor chief from what became northwestern Tanzania, and the son of a man who had carried ivory and copper and hauled slaves from Katanga to the East African coast, Msiri assumed control of the family ivory and slave "business" at mid-century, conducted a number of successful expeditions, and emerged as a local warlord. With troops that he recruited and armed, Msiri conquered several minor chiefs and then, in 1862, usurped the power of the leading Tumba and Sanga rulers on whose behalf he had originally become involved in local wars. Arranging marriages between his own Nyamwezi followers and women of the leading families in the area, he consolidated his hold over central Katanga. He allied himself with the Luba ruling house to the north, and then hastened the ultimate disintegration of the Lunda empire of Mwata Yamvo by taking sides in its internal quarrels. By 1871 he ruled a wide area from the headwaters of the Zambezi River in the west to the banks of the Luapula River in the east. He traded with the Portuguese and Arabs of both coasts, exchanging copper, ivory, salt, and slaves for cloth, guns, and powder. In 1879, Msiri crowned himself mwami or king of Garenganze, establishing a new capital at Bunkeya on the Lofoi River. At its height in the 1880s, Msiri's state was approximately the size of Great Britain. Arnot, who had moved north from Barotseland, described Msiri as "an old-looking man, with a pleasant-smooth face, and a short beard, quite white." When Arnot visited Bunkeya he saw human skulls "all round his yard. . . ." "The sensation," said Arnot, "creeps over one of being in a monster's den."[15]

When it was clear to Rhodes that Lochner was mired in the physical and metaphysical swamps of Barotseland, he wired Cawston to send Joseph Thomson. Only thirty-two, Thomson had already established a reputation as a swift, energetic explorer who could lead major expeditions into the African interior and emerge triumphant without undue expense or bloodshed. Cutting his spurs at twenty-one, when he tramped nearly 3,000 miles from Zanzibar to Lakes Malawi and Tanganyika and into eastern Zaire, and then gaining fame by an epic trek across Masailand to Lake Victoria and Mounts Elgon and Kenya, Thomson had obtained important treaties in West Africa for the Royal Niger Company, and traversed the Atlas Mountains of Morocco. Thomson, Cawston told Beit, was "one of the best African Explorers free and

I believe that Rhodes was very pleased with him." [16] (Rhodes had met Thomson in London during his visit a few weeks before.) Moreover, Thomson wanted a mere £100 a month, whereas others demanded ten times that amount. By May Thomson was in Kimberley to receive instructions from Rhodes.

Thomson was astonished to find himself only one of a bevy of men summoned to discuss and lay the groundwork for the acquisition of trans-Zambezia. As a contemporary photograph indicates so well, Rhodes had surrounded himself with Maguire; Colquhoun; John Moir, manager of the African Lakes Company; Johnston, down from Nyasaland; and James A. Grant, the son of Colonel James Augustus Grant, the well-known explorer of the Nile River region. In Kimberley, Rhodes told Thomson to "get Msiri's." He instructed him to annex Garenganze and then to obtain an analogous understanding with Mwata Yamvo. Afterwards he was to travel to Barotseland to assist or take over from Lochner. If the precise orders were committed to paper, they have not been found. More than likely, Rhodes elaborated upon his needs and hopes, then waved his hand in the general direction of distant Katanga, and told Thomson that he was on his own. Johnston urged Thomson to travel to Katanga via Bechuanaland, and Rhodes may have seconded that suggestion, but Cawston had told Thomson to be secretive and surreptitious. "Thomson is a terribly obstinate man as I dare say you know," Johnston complained. "He would not take any advice as to the route he would follow nor would he listen any more to Rhodes. We gave up advising him because he is after all such a wily and successful traveller that he is pretty sure of [overcoming] all difficulties if left to himself." [17]

Thomson's mission was kept quiet, at least in London, because its prime object was dramatically controversial. The Company was then deeply involved in discussions with Léopold over the extent of his African fief and its borders with the British sphere. In such circumstances, Cawston cautioned Rhodes, an assault on Garenganze could only demonstrate a great lack of good faith. Moreover, Sir Percy Anderson, at the Foreign Office, had recently assured Cawston that Msiri's kingdom was regarded in Whitehall as part of the Congo. Clearly Cawston, who shared Rhodes' avarice for territory, but appreciated the tactlessness of crossing Lord Salisbury, wavered. As Johnston told Rhodes, for whom he was acting in London, "I have been trying very, very hard to get Garenganze . . . the King of the Belgians is sending out an expedition to collar it & I want the Government to say 'hands off.' But they will not unless you show more signs of life. Cawston is too limp." Johnston also prepared a map with Msiri's domain circled in British red. It carried a legend that the area was "British" because Rhodes had dispatched an expedition in that direction. As Johnston told one of the senior officials of the Foreign Office, in confidence, Rhodes had "set his heart on getting [Msiri's]." [18]

Like so much over which Johnston enthused, that statement was too strong. Yet there is no doubt that Rhodes still had Garenganze in his sights during mid-1890, despite the opposition of Britain and despite an agreement that had been concluded in May 1890 between the Company and Léopold. According to its terms, Msiri's kingdom lay within the Congo. Yet Rhodes had determined upon a plan of action which the London board of the Company never tried to curb and which its members may individually have wished success. Rhodes clearly hoped, even assumed, and certainly rationalized that Léopold was too weak and too poor to keep Katanga and retain its undoubted riches for himself. Thus, Rhodes and the Company were compelled to seek concessions which they could themselves work or use as bargaining counters. It mattered little to him and his sense of morality that he and his treaty-making missions were transgressing international arrangements. If challenged, and if he had thought about the indigenous inhabitants of Katanga, he might have said that they would be better off under his and British than under Belgian or any other rule. He certainly argued that the partition of Africa remained incomplete in the interior, and that such uncertainty and incompleteness was reason enough. His opinion of the Belgians and the French, furthermore, was almost as prejudicial as his contempt for the Portuguese.

Rhodes set out his thoughts and plans in a long letter to the Duke of Abercorn: "I do not think that even the wealth of the King of the Belgians will be able to carry through his scheme," Rhodes argued, "and I doubt whether Belgium will give him the support he desires. No one can conceive the enormous difficulties he has to face. He has an enormous tract of country but I believe the most worthless in Africa. It is a huge alluvial basin in the centre of the tropics with a climate totally impossible for an European constitution to stand. As far as we can gather he has no minerals [outside of Katanga] and I do not think can ever hope to pay for his administration out of the ivory and cocoa-nuts which, apparently, are his only exports. . . . When he exhausts his present funds [he will] attempt to get his country to take it over and failing this it will undoubtedly be sold to the French." Rhodes had a good look into the future. "We shall then be faced with having to deal with the French people who are a most exciteable nation and sure to get into complications with us. . . ."

The natural outlet of the gold and copper which would be found in Msiri's domain was to the south, through Rhodes' territory. Therefore Rhodes asserted (he was too sure to speculate) that Léopold would before long offer Garenganze to the Company. "If we have the minerals and practically the Customs dues of Msiri's it is not difficult to foresee that Msiri's kingdom will fall to us." Rhodes added, ingenuously if not outrageously, "You must also remember that so far as our Government is concerned we have not recognised Msiri's Kingdom as part of the Congo State. . . . Not even Germany has done this. It is only an arrangement with France. I believe that we have held that the definition of the Interior of Africa still remains to be settled."[19] In his mind, certainly, it still did.

Rhodes was using Thomson, accompanied by the younger Grant, and Sharpe (as well as Lochner) to secure the lands across the Zambezi that had been allotted to the Company, and for which Rhodes was paying, but which were not yet officially transferred. The copper of Garenganze was the prize, but the territory between the Zambezi and the Congo watershed was also essential if Portugal and other foreign powers were to be thwarted and the presumed minerals of the area to be brought within Rhodes' unchallenged grasp. Rhodes thus had a strategic objective, but he was too busy with other territorial and political acquisitions, and with his duties as the Cape's premier, to involve himself closely in the detailed tactical considerations. Katanga and northern Zambezia were never goals as all engrossing as Manica, Gaza, and Beira.

Thomson and Grant worked hard for Rhodes, but their journey was hazardous and dogged by misfortune. From Blantyre, Nyasaland's new commercial and mission center, they walked to Lake Malawi, sailed up its western shore, and set out from Nkhota Kota westward to the Luangwa River, Lake Bangweulu, and Garenganze. Sharpe continued along the lake to Karonga, there to commence a more northerly approach to Msiri. Since neither Sharpe nor Thomson could understand why both men were being sent to the same destination, they decided—amicably—to take different routes. "If one should fail," Sharpe told Rhodes, "the other might not."[20]

From late August 1890, Thomson, Grant, and company tramped westward through what was to become Malawi and Zambia. Thomson concluded the first of many treaties with a Bisa chief along the banks of the Luangwa and then began climbing up out of the valley onto an elevated plateau. Soon, however, Thomson learned that his porters carried the dread signs of smallpox. Leaving a trail of disease in its wake, Thomson's caravan continued toward Bangweulu. Porters died; villages shut their gates. Forcing his way to the Luapula River, 200 miles from Bunkeya, Thomson realized that he, too, was desperately ill. Thomson had cystitis, a painful inflammation of the bladder, perhaps caused by schistosomes. It robbed travel of its few remaining joys and made Thomson fear for his life.

In these parlous circumstances it is probably understandable that Thomson made so little of his opportunities for geographical and geological discovery. A trained geologist, he passed within about fifty miles of the great Zambian and Zairese copper deposits without searching for outcrops. Deferring a dash to Msiri's capital, he wandered through what is now called the Zambian Copperbelt, and returned to Nkhota Kota early in January—"just in time," Thomson wrote, "to keep my soul and body from parting company."[21] He had covered 1200 miles at a cost to the Company of £3,000, and was seriously ill.

Rhodes was interested in what Thomson had and had not accomplished. Thomson believed that he had acquired inalienable rights for Rhodes to the Kafue-Luangwa plateau—in fact to a large portion of the future northeastern Zambia. He had concluded no fewer than thirteen treaties with chiefs who were, Thomson claimed, representative leaders of their people. Thomson argued that he had obtained the X's of men and women who were in a proper position to dispose of large areas of valuable territory. By marking preprinted treaty forms, they had signified a willingness to enter into a mutually beneficial formal relationship with himself, Rhodes, the Company, and Queen Victoria. Indeed, as far as Thomson and Rhodes were concerned, the signed and witnessed documents legally secured the Company's role as a mining, commercial, and administrative entity in trans-Zambezia.

Even by the loose standards of African treaty-making, however, these documents left much to be desired. Their wording was vague and absurd. Men who knew how to hoe the ground and fight with spears were asked to sign pieces of paper and acknowledge a system of property about which they knew nothing. Nor were the domains of each chief properly delimited. Most of all, neither Thomson nor his companions could speak the local languages. And even if they did communicate, chiefs could not traditionally have signed away their land or sub-soil rights. Some might not have been chiefs at all. Even the Company later agreed that its rights had been "founded upon a very large number of contracts made with personages whose existences [in 1904] are somewhat mythical. . . ." Anderson, at the Foreign Office, decided that Thomson's treaties contained "engagements which it was beyond the powers of the Company to contract on behalf of Her Majesty's Government, and which Her Majesty's Government are not . . . [in 1894] prepared to accept." Nevertheless, at the time, and until the independence of Zambia, Thomson's dubious treaties were used to justify the annexation of northeastern Rhodesia by the Company and the rights of the Company to the later discovered copper deposits of that country. Johnston sanctified the treaties, and Rhodes subsequently begged the Foreign Office to accept the treaties "for what they [were] worth."[22]

Thomson had failed to enter Msiri's kingdom. Nor had he gathered information of much strategic or economic value to Rhodes. Sharpe, who attained Bunkeya with ease and talked with Msiri several times, accomplished little more. No matter how earnestly Sharpe pleaded and argued, Msiri had adamantly refused to sign a treaty of friendship or give away his mineral rights. Early in 1891, therefore, with the Portuguese East African coast and highlands still disputed, and Shona country and most of Barotseland secure, the copper of Katanga continued to entice Rhodes, as it did Léopold. Rhodes as yet refused to acknowledge that Msiri's kingdom lay within the Congo. So, in May, Rhodes sent Thomson two imperious telegrams: "Await further instructions," they said. In July, Rhodes was direct: "I want you to get M'siri's, I mean Katanga. The King of the Belgians has already floated a company for it, presumably because he does not possess it. . . . You must go and get the Katanga. If you are too seedy send Sharpe with Grant." This was Rhodes at his assertive best.

Although Thomson was still gravely ill, he ignored the advice of his missionary doctor, recruited eighty porters, and readied himself for a trek along Sharpe's route to Garenganze. The letter from Rhodes, Thomson wrote ecstatically, had rung in his "ears like the bugle call to an old cavalry horse." Thomson would have to be carried the entire way in a litter, but he was nevertheless determined to go. "There was nothing for it but to risk it myself"—to do it for Rhodes.[23] At the last moment, however, a telegram from Kimberley freed Thomson from the almost sure prospect of leaving his bones in Africa. The Foreign Office had demanded that Rhodes stop competing with Léopold. The British government wanted no new border difficulties. Yet Msiri's denouement still had much to do with Rhodes indirectly. In late 1891 an expedition sponsored by Léopold, and spurred on by rumors of Thomson's supposed activities, reached Bunkeya, murdered Msiri, and swiftly attached his kingdom to the Congo.

Yet even if Thomson or Sharpe had managed to persuade Msiri, no mere unsophisticated African chief, to part with his patrimony, the Foreign Office (Lord Salisbury may have behaved with less consistency) determinedly wanted no disagreements with Léopold or the Belgians. It was therefore perverse as well as persistent for Rhodes, even at the crest of his sub-imperial wave, and exultant with personal power and fulfillment, to have tried. As Salisbury told the Queen, "The Company as a whole are quite inclined to behave fairly, but Mr. Cecil Rhodes is rather difficult to keep in order."[24] The Company and Rhodes might have obtained a concession and then operated it on behalf of or sold it to Léopold. So the diplomatic obstacles were not the only ones. But they were the major ones. Moreover, as aggressive as Rhodes may have seemed to London and Brussels, latter-day critics are largely correct to suggest that he committed only a portion of his energies, and then never unequivocally, to the Katanga quest. Rhodes and the Company probed, pushed, and prodded to see what could be obtained, so as to miss no opportunities. But in comparison with the major operations south of the Zambezi, a unified, fully prepared, and carefully marshaled attack on the sovereignity of Katanga was never mounted. The explanations are at hand: Bunkeya was as far from Kimberley as Moscow from London, and very distant in an age of rudimentary communications. Rhodes later claimed that Léopold was too tough. "I thought I was clever," he told Sir Robert Williams of the Tanganyika Railway, "but I was no match for Léopold."[25] But it was less Léopold's toughness than the availability of other, easier, and more tangible prizes—and the unexpected double failure of Thomson and Sharpe—that prevented Rhodes from adding Katanga to his collection of African fiefs, and a scrap with Léopold to his many imperial adventures.

By mid-1891, the combined initiative of Rhodes and Salisbury had rounded out the sphere of the British South Africa Company, and settled—as Johnston and Rhodes had so boyishly hoped two years before—the colonial destiny of peoples and places from Lake Tanganyika in middle Africa to the countries of the Shangaan and the Ndebele in the south. British accords with Germany and then with Portugal, and the Company's understanding with the Congo Independent State, had provided formal bounds to the lands that were soon to be called Rhodesia and Nyasaland. Within that grand, internationally recognized perimeter were local divisions and administrative arrangements that largely followed the contours of Rhodes' purse. The guiding instrument, subsequently formalized between the Company and the Foreign Office, was a plan privately sketched by Rhodes in 1890 and bargained out by Johnston and Rhodes in a face-to-face meeting in London in February 1891.[26] Since Rhodes' money and ambition still ruled and would for several more years dictate overall imperial policy in an area of little strategic interest to the Foreign Office or to Britain, his willingness to provide annual cash flows avoided any serious unpleasantness between the Foreign Office and the Treasury, although Johnston always required more funds than even Rhodes could provide.

Rhodes committed the summary of his understanding with Johnston to paper, and Johnston carried it to the Foreign Office for approval. In a very few words it sketched a division of territory and the rudiments of an administrative program. In order to please the missionary societies, Rhodes said that his idea of "the best settlement over the Zambesi" was that "Nyasaland should be marked out as small as possible," which it was, and managed by Johnston "for the Imperial Government." Rhodes thought that the balance of the territories "should be placed under the Charter and managed as far as political administration by [Johnston] also for the Charter and that [he] should give [Johnston] £10,000 per annum. . . ." Commercial expenditures would be extra, "and by us," and Johnston "should not mix in it. . . ." In a postscript Rhodes made it clear that within the Chartered territory, Johnston was to report "on everything" to the Foreign Office as well as to the Company.[27]

Flowing from this agreement between two imperially minded Victorians, one of whom had the necessary wherewithal, a mass of land the size of Spain, France, and the Low Countries, and containing nearly a hundred separate, hardly consulted, peoples speaking seventy languages, was transferred from a kind of post-partition limbo into the hands of a Company and a commissioner acting under the aegis of Queen Victoria. The Nyasaland Districts— modern Malawi—became a protectorate in May, and Rhodes was given authority over the separate "local jurisdiction" beyond the Zambezi in July. In London the underlying legitimacy for this bold passage of control was derived from the consent which was presumed to have been given by Litunga Lewanika and the smattering and scattering of chiefs from whom Thomson, Sharpe, and Johnston had collected individual treaties. But the main force behind this enormous enlargement of Rhodes' theater of operations flowed from the absence of objections from any neighboring European powers, and the final deflecting of his assault on Katanga. Nevertheless, because Rhodes had long felt that he had "quite enough to do south of the Zambesi," and because he believed that "taking the keys of the country, and establishing trading stations rather than starting immediately on expensive government of the territory" would be sufficient (for it had no minerals which could balance expenditures with revenues), he was content to run trans-Zambezia under the supervision of the Foreign Office. Until 1894, "Her Majesty's Commissioner and Consul General for the Territories under British Influence to the North of the Zambesi," as Johnston was styled, held day-to-day authority, while Rhodes' £10,000 supported the pacification expenses of a police force of assorted Africans, Sikhs, and Britons which operated in Nyasaland and, occasionally, beyond its borders.[28]

Once having prevented other powers from taking it, and having lost Katanga, Rhodes' involvement with and concern for trans-Zambezia during the early 1890s was insignificant. He and the British South Africa Company had arranged to absorb the African Lakes Company—that ramshackle operation—although the ultimate dissolution of the smaller concern and its replacement by a Rhodes-controlled African Lakes Trading Corporation took place only in 1893. (Rhodes was amused enough by the Scots who were refusing to let go of the African Lakes Company to tell Johnston that their steamers on Lake Malawi could remain. "Let the Scotch people continue to run them and make their profits out of each other, it will amuse them and not hurt us but give them no power and we shall instruct them to put their steamers at your disposal when required."[29])

Other than giving Johnston his head, and applauding his subjugation of recalcitrant chiefs and slavers in Nyasaland proper, Rhodes made no important moves before the mid-1890s to open up trans-Zambezia. In 1891 Johnston detailed a subordinate to establish a governmental presence near Lake Mweru, in order to forestall Belgian encroachments across their common Luapula River border, but the British missionaries who were active elsewhere in northeastern Zambezia had to wait until 1894 before receiving the political backing of the Company. Likewise, Lewanika was left alone and all of his large domain ignored, except by missionaries. Johnston bemoaned Rhodes' lack of vigorous involvement, and took it personally. He concluded that Rhodes' attention was easily captured by new projects, and that he was weary of Central Africa. What Johnston never fully appreciated, however, was that Mashonaland—the old project—was and would be Rhodes' compelling commitment outside of South Africa.

There, no one had yet found the mother lode. The pioneers, and speculators in South Africa and Britain, continued to believe that there must be gold—quartz reefs would surely yield precious ounces even if alluvial and other surface indications were scarce. (Nevertheless, if located, such reefs could only be worked with expensive machinery hauled from South Africa or Britain.) More than 7,000 claims were pegged within the first six months; several dozen syndicates were floated locally and in London to work such claims; and promoters quickly made sizable paper profits while those ordinary investors who purchased and held were effectively defrauded.

As Lord Randolph Churchill, who visited the new settlements in the late African winter of 1891, reported, "Many months, probably a year or two, must elapse before any certainty can be arrived at as to whether Mashonaland is a gold-producing country or not. Even if it turns out to be a country possessing gold deposits, the payable character . . . depends entirely upon whether cheap and easy access . . . can be gained." Churchill was skeptical, deprecating as he did both the prospecting that had already been attempted and the agricultural and overall attractiveness of the colony. It contained no "fine country," he declared. Certainly Rhodesia was "no promised land."[30]

With hardly any immediate sources of revenue, Rhodes' great pioneering adventure rapidly consumed the Company's subscribed capital. As Rhodes mused to Stead, "I quite appreciate the enormous difficulties of opening up a new country but still if providence will furnish a few paying gold reefs I think it will be all right." After all, "gold hastens development."[31] Kimberley was 800 miles away, and the summer rains of 1890–91 made the terrain impassable and the rushing rivers of that route unfordable. Opening a road from the Indian Ocean proved impossible for diplomatic as well as natural reasons; the dreaded tsetse fly doomed the first attempts to bring freight by wagon from Beira. Oxen and unsalted horses soon succumbed to trypanosomiasis.

The 650 Company police, employed to safeguard the new settlement against Ndebele atttack, and also to contest the neighboring Portuguese sphere, cost £300 a year each, or a total of £195,000. Transport expenses, and the stocks of relief food that Rhodes hurried to Salisbury throughout early 1891, added to the Company's burden and financial anxiety. "After tremendous efforts," Rhodes reminded Lord Salisbury, "I have thrown into the country about 500 waggon loads of food and with good fortune may just be able to save the population [of 2,000 whites] from starving during the next summer when all transport is closed down. . . ."[32] Within a year Rhodes had spent £700,000 on his fancy. Finally, pressed by the Company, by the De Beers and Gold Fields' boards, and by Beit, he ordered economy. Toward the end of 1891, police numbers were slashed to 100, and a force of local volunteers was raised in its stead. Administrative and transportation expenditures were likewise cut, and Rhodes thereafter struggled to maintain romantic notions of an interior dominion within a framework of parsimony. Admittedly, Rhodes anyway lacked the authority from Lobengula to govern Mashonaland, but that technical defect was hardly a practical hindrance during the three years before war made it obsolete.

Rhodes and his colony had been afflicted from its origins with an even greater long-term problem. The Company's subsoil rights were recognized, at least by Britain, but it had no rights to the land, and therefore could not convey title and accept fees and rents from the early farmers. Edouard Lippert, a cousin of Beit's whose person and whose methods neither Beit nor Rhodes could abide, had meanwhile sought to undermine the Rudd Concession and obtain opposing grants of his own through Renny-Tailyour, the Company's constant antagonist. In April 1891, Renny-Tailyour claimed that Lobengula had granted him and Lippert rights to give away land, establish banks, and even coin money in the Company's area. Although his document had not been authenticated independently, Rhodes at first decided, contrary to what has usually been written, that it was "absolutely essential" that the Company should acquire it. The new concession, he perceived, was "the one thing needful to give the Company the fullest jurisdiction in Lo Bengulu's territory." Rhodes was immediately prepared to pay Lippert any reasonable sum, but Lippert wanted an extortionate amount in cash and shares, so Rhodes, despite urgent cables from Francis J. Dormer in Johannesburg, where Lippert was then based, decided to resist what he considered outright blackmail. He argued that the Lippert arrangement had no legal standing since the Rudd Concession bound Lobengula to give away no land without Rudd's consent.

Rhodes and Loch turned their backs on Lippert, and together denounced Renny-Tailyour's grant. Loch even issued a proclamation which declared invalid all concessions concluded without his sanction. He arrested Renny-Tailyour in northern Bechuanaland over Lobengula's protest. But this concerted antagonism toward Lippert and his accomplishment soon gave way to expediency. Whatever the lack of merit of the new concession, Beit counseled Rhodes to settle. Lippert's paper might conceivably be validated by the British courts. Rhodes thus returned to his very first posture. Renny-Tailyour's breakthrough with Lobengula could be employed to improve his own position. After all, Lobengula had at last granted rights in land. A compromise was forged with Lippert: if he and Renny-Tailyour obtained a reiterated land grant from Lobengula which the Colonial Office could ratify, then the Company promised to give Lippert and his syndicate seventy-five square miles of Ndebeleland, together with mineral rights. (Of course Rhodes as yet could exert no claim of his own in the country of the Ndebele.) Rhodes further agreed to give Lippert cash and substantial shares of both the United Concessions and British South Africa companies.

The cynical deed was soon done. Loch warned Moffat not to change his public and official attitude toward Lippert and Renny-Tailyour too abruptly, but nevertheless to assist them in what were altered circumstances. Moffat did as he was bid, at the same time telling Rhodes that deceiving Lobengula in this way was "detestable, whether viewed in the light of policy or morality. . . . When Lobengula finds it all out . . . what faith will he have in you?" In November 1891, Lobengula gave Lippert the sole right to allocate farms and townships within the sphere of operations of the Company in exchange for £1,000 and £500 a year. Moffat, who certified the result, called it a "palpable immorality," and so it was.[33] But, as the Colonial Office noted and Rhodes and Loch knew, the Lippert concession powerfully added to the Company's prerogatives and removed a crucial impediment to the Company's administration of and its ability to raise revenue in Mashonaland. What was important was that by assuming Lippert's supposed powers, Rhodes obtained the right to confer land on Lobengula's behalf. It mattered little that in 1918 the judicial committee of the Privy Council, Britain's highest tribunal, found the whole transaction illegal. By then Rhodesia had long since become a reality, indeed a thriving quasi-dominion, and the principal winning and losing parties, Rhodes and Lobengula, were both dead and Lobengula's kingdom thoroughly dismembered.

By 1891 Rhodes, only thirty-eight, had chiseled out a territorial monument to the fantasies of his early adulthood. As a colony, Mashonaland's future was precarious, and required the attention and capital which Rhodes, otherwise more than fully committed, could hardly give. Across the Zambezi there were peoples and places the potential of which might best be exploited by Johnston, if at all, and be retained until they were ready for the grasp of the master's hand. Yet, although the promise of the interior looked questionable, problematic, and capable of absorbing bags of money made from gold, diamonds, and gullible investors, Rhodes doubtless felt proud and fulfilled. He had undeniably fenced off the Transvaal Boers, prevented both the Portuguese and the Germans from connecting their coastal principalities, and persuaded Britain to take on those responsibilities (with his cash) which he and other imperialists in their minds had assigned to the Queen. That his methods had been dubious, that he had been more aggressive and less conciliatory than usual, and that his conquests were entirely without African sanction, mattered little to him, and probably only a trifle more to most of his contemporaries. Rhodes' conquests were judged harshly (and understood as the land grabs they were) by but a comparative handful of critics in South Africa and Britain. Since his own motives were more for power than riches, and were as much cosmic as crass, his conscience would not have been stained by what he had managed to achieve. Privately, however, he might have berated himself for losing Gaza, Katanga, and the thin, red right-of-way to Uganda.

For him and others, the magnitude of his individual accomplishment came to be expressed in the simplest of terms. By mid-1891, Mashonaland was starting to be called Rhodesia. A weekly newspaper, originally called *The Mashonaland Herald and Zambesian Times,* began publishing in late October as *The Rhodesia Herald.* Two months before, Rhodes had told Stead with evident pride that "they are calling the new country Rhodesia, that is from the Transvaal to the south end of Tanganyika. The other name is Zambesia." Indeed, the title had been introduced as early as 1890, when a "special correspondent" trekking with Rhodes and Loch through Bechuanaland had reported in the weekly edition of the *Cape Argus* that the territory across the Limpopo would be called "Rhodesland." Later that same year Jameson said Zambezia would in fact be called "Rhodesia." But not until 1895 was the name in steady use. Nor was it an official title before 1897. Yet for Rhodes there was symmetry between fantasy and reality. "Well, you know," he told a friend, "to have a bit of country named after one is one of the things a man might be proud of."[34]

14

"To Preserve the Landed Classes"
Ends and Means, the First Premiership

R HODES BECAME prime minister of the Cape of Good Hope Colony in mid-July 1890. He was then attempting to manipulate the world market in diamonds and to retrieve his fortunes in gold. In the north, his pioneers had crossed into Ndebeleland and were slowly making a road through the lowveld around Lobengula's immediate dominions. It was an anxious time for Rhodes personally, and for the fledgling Company. But Frank Elliott Lochner had just obtained a concession over Barotseland, and Joseph Thomson and Alfred Sharpe had been dispatched to "get M'siri's, I mean Katanga." Harry Johnston was gaining supremacy over Nyasaland; Charles Metcalfe was extending rails from Kimberley to Vryburg; and the recent Anglo-German boundary convention had added the vital watershed between Lakes Malawi and Tanganyika to the sphere of the Company. For Rhodes to have wanted the premiership, with its trying administrative as well as legislative responsibilities, and then to have accepted it, testifies either to his power-seeking gluttony or to a realization of the manifold uses to which that office and the political leadership of the Cape could be put. Or both.

The House of Assembly in the Cape still had seventy-six members. Thirty-seven, the only significant plurality, owed allegiance to Jan Hendrik Hofmeyr and the Afrikaner Bond, but the square-shouldered Hofmeyr had consistently refused to head and form a government. Thus, after Sir Thomas Upington's premiership, Sir Gordon Sprigg once again led the Cape. Rhodes, as has been shown in earlier chapters and contrary to what has usually been asserted, played a major role in the House through 1888; he took official leave during 1889, when parliament met during the months when he was negotiating a royal charter and could hardly return from London. But he did not otherwise remove himself from the affairs of parliament, being kept aware of its deliberations by Barnato, Hofmeyr, and Harris.

As a man of local influence, wealth, political sagacity, and new international stature, Rhodes—with his ties to Hofmeyr—in early 1890 could almost certainly have engineered the downfall of Sprigg's ministry. But there is no evidence that Rhodes actively sought to replace Sprigg himself. Instead, he was among those several differently motivated parlimentary leaders who became more and more dissatisfied with Sprigg's methods as well as his policies. In order to bolster his own flagging credibility, Sprigg in 1889 had attempted to enlist as allies in his cabinet Hofmeyr and James Sivewright, a clever Scottish engineer, pioneering telegraph official in Britain and South Africa, and wealthy speculator who was a principal parliamentary figure in the Bond. But both refused. Sprigg's ambitious plan to construct new railways throughout the eastern Cape, and thus gain crucial votes from settlers, also foundered.

In 1890, Sprigg proposed a further rail-building spree of epochal proportions. To cost more than £7 million—an unprecedented sum for the Cape—to take years, and to absorb the scarce capital which the Cape could not claim, the scheme was blatantly political, even for a colonial legislature in a swashbuckling age. Debt service for the still modestly endowed Cape would have been astronomically high. Sprigg could not demonstrate that the new lines would pay for themselves. And there were competing interests. The merchants of Port Elizabeth were hardly anxious to see new lines and extensions penetrate their natural Orange Free State markets from East London. Rhodes and others could hardly see the logic of connecting the newly discovered coal fields at Indwe to East London rather than linking them to the main line and thereby serving the Cape's only serious industry in Kimberley. Many members of the Bond thought Sprigg's plan foolish. Rhodes, Jacobus W. Sauer, and John Xavier Merriman all called it wasteful folly. Ignatius Johannes van der Walt, a Bondsman from Colesberg, decried Sprigg's proposals as mad and astonishing. John Laing called them a "huge bribery bill," and Olè Anders Ohlsson, favoring railway construction in general, nevertheless said that Sprigg's scheme would "simply ruin the Colony." The government, he said, "had been trying to please everybody and had succeeded in pleasing nobody." James Rose Innes decared that the Colony wanted "progress, but not ruin." Sprigg's plan, wrote Merriman, "will dish Sprigg, but what a fool the man was when he had a surplus and a clear field. Idiot!"[1]

It was not the moment for such an ambitious, capital intensive program of construction. The Colony was already heavily in debt to the extent of about £26 million; the Johannesburg stock exchange had crashed; and throughout South Africa banks were failing. Rhodes was among the many members of parliament who, worried about the collapse of commercial confidence in South Africa, was appalled by Sprigg's scheme much more for fiscal and economic reasons than for those of personal or party ambition. Thus Rhodes, who had absented himself from the House throughout May and June 1890, rushed to Cape Town in July, when it became clear that Sprigg seriously intended to push his rail proposals through the House in a series of separate but linked votes. (Sprigg wanted all nine rail initiatives to be started simultaneously so that a subsequent government would be compelled to complete them all.) Rhodes and the majority in parliament negated each as it was put before the House, and Sprigg's ministry fell. Rhodes' motives were those of his fellows: bankruptcy of the Colony was bad for the health of all commerce as well as for De Beers and Kimberley. As a matter of economic prudence—for principle rather than the furthering of any narrow political hopes of his own— Rhodes lent his considerable support to Sauer, who was leading the liberal opposition to Sprigg in the House. In Sauer's words, Sprigg was clearly seeking "more to consolidate a party than to meet the interests and demands of the country."[2]

Sauer was prepared to become premier. He could count on the backing of Merriman and Innes, a Cape-born barrister of repute who was two years younger than himself, and the favor of the *Cape Times,* but he could secure no support from Hofmeyr and the Bond. Hofmeyr was up-country, in the Transvaal, having been sent there a few weeks before by Sir Henry B. Loch, the governor, to continue earlier negotiations with President Paul Kruger about a South African customs union, railway links with the Cape Colony, the future of Swaziland, and Afrikaner treks into Rhodesia. Hofmeyr's absence made Sauer's accession even more difficult than it might have been in more normal times.

In most similar parliamentary situations the party with the largest set of followers, in this case the Bond, would have assumed control of the government, particularly since its votes had been decisive in spelling Sprigg's defeat. But Hofmeyr had never wanted to hold office at the head of an "irresponsible majority," as he once told Rhodes. Instead, he preferred to back "men with good sound Africander views and independence of feeling who will not pin their faith to either opposition or ministry, but judge for themselves. . . ." Sauer, the head of a group opposed both to limiting the African vote and to protection for Dutch-speaking wine growers, could hardly expect to win Hofmeyr's enthusiastic backing. Sauer thus suggested that Loch should summon "one who might be able to combine in his government a wider representation of the several parties in the country," that is, to establish a coalition government bridging the interests of farmer and merchant, Dutch and English, and Bond conservative and Anglophile liberal.[3]

Privately and publicly Rhodes claimed that he had been "forced" to assume the premiership. "They want me to be premier but I have not the time," he wrote to Stow. "Being much occupied with the North," he told a Kimberley audience, "I had made up my mind not to attend Parliament, but I found there was a huge Railway Bill proposed, and I thought it was my duty to oppose it, as it would place too great a burden upon the revenue of this country." Kimberley had a large stake in the revenue of the Cape, and railways which could not pay their way would burden all. So Rhodes said that he "hurried down" to Cape Town, where "events hurried on faster than I expected, and before I knew where I was I saw it would be forced upon me to take the responsibility of the government of this country." Should someone already guiding the destinies of De Beers and the British South Africa Company assume a political mantle as well? "I concluded," Rhodes remembered, "that one position could be worked with the other, and each to the benefit of all. At any rate," he congratulated himself later in 1890, "I had the courage to undertake it, and I may say that up to the present I have not regretted it."

In addressing parliament he was not modest in justifying himself. "I think I may say that with the development of the interior devolving on me, and with the many other responsibilities I have, I would have been glad to be out of the position I now occupy, but it resolved itself into this, that if I had also declined to undertake the responsibilities Constitutional Government in this country would have been an admitted failure." To his predominantly English-speaking audience, he also justified his consultations with the Bond. "I think that if more pains were taken to explain matters to the members of the Bond party, many of the cobwebs would be swept away and a much better understanding would exist between the different parties."[4]

Rhodes stressed his courage. At a time when he had dared challenge and rechannel Britain's foreign policy regarding southern Africa and had successfully circumvented Lobengula's allegedly antagonistic impulses, he chose to acquire even more power—to continue stretching a potential which had been acknowledged only suddenly. Rhodes said that he had been "induced" to become prime minister because he had made up his mind that the Cape should "extend to the Zambesi. I felt that having completed the amalgamation of the diamond mines, and having perhaps an active imagination, unless I shared in the policy of the Cape Government and joined my interests with those of the Cape people, I should have to leave and go to the North."[5]

Rhodes' decision to assume the premiership should thus be seen as integral to and fueled by the enormous burst of energy which drove his seven-year period of generativity. Psychologically it reflected a fusion of raw ambition and the ideals which had been set out in the "Confession of Faith." That fusion, following Kohut, determines the adult configuration of normal productive narcissism which balances self-absorption with other-directedness and selfishness with altruism. The complexities of Rhodes' psychological makeup are particularly related to precisely that balance which, in him, was always uneasy. In seeking the premiership Rhodes was surely seeking power in order to realize his ideals and gratify his wish to be effective. Simultaneously, he sought political safeguards for his wealth and for his vast imperial vanity. When he declared that he had been *compelled* to become prime minister—that circumstance had decreed his fate (and sealed it, too, as it subsequently transpired)—he was expressing the immodest sentiments of one who had every reason in 1890 to think himself chosen, elect of God. Rhodes' creativity burst the very seams of his physique, and carried him and, as he then chose to think, English-speaking humanity to ever loftier heights. When Rhodes said that he was assuming a weighty responsibility, he meant that it was a responsibility before the universe, before the god or the destiny by whom or which fates were arranged.

Rhodes proclaimed governmental aims which, naturally, were loftier than any the governments of the Cape had hitherto known. "The Government's policy will be a South African policy," he told the audience in Kimberley. "What we mean is that we will do all in our power, whilst looking after the interests of the Cape Colony, to draw closer and closer the ties between us and the neighbouring states. . . . It is a matter of time to arrive at a settlement of the various questions which divide the States of South Africa. It may not come in our time, but I believe," he stated his creed, "that ultimately the different States will be united." He looked forward beyond a customs union of the states of South Africa to a union of the same territories. "I mean that we may attain to perfect free trade as to our own commodities, perfect and complete internal railway communication, and a general Customs Union, stretching from Delagoa Bay to Walfisch Bay. . . ." He believed that the Cape Colony would extend in his lifetime as far as the Zambezi. For Rhodes, such a union would be brought about under a British flag. "If I have to forfeit my flag, what have I left?"[6]

Rhodes could neither have taken nor have kept office without the Bond. Hesitant about how to use politics directly to serve his larger objects, he would have preferred for political as well as personal and economic reasons to have served under or with Hofmeyr, wielding power behind the scenes and compelling the Bond to take day-to-day responsibility for the administration of the Colony. But he was sufficiently astute politically to know that Sauer was right; if Hofmeyr refused, as he had since the early 1880s, to assume a public leadership role and to thrust the Bond forward, then no other than Rhodes could command both Dutch- and English-speaking support. Rhodes, abhorring a power vacuum, sought to avoid the national indecisiveness which would have flowed from the governance of the Colony in the early 1890s by a weak regime, especially one which at best could count upon only tepid support from the Bond. Thus Rhodes attempted to forge a coalition between the Bond and liberals which was to be unique for the Cape. "His government would be Afrikaans, his native policy his own, and any minister who did not go along would be expelled."[7] Moreover, whether or not he gave Hofmeyr an explicit veto power over the actions of Rhodes' government, there were private understandings, and on those matters which Hofmeyr considered crucial to the interests of the Dutch, Rhodes effectively deferred to the Bond. (Hofmeyr was known to Merriman and others as "the Mole." "You never see him at work but every now and then a little mound of earth . . . will testify to his activities.")

Rhodes was the only independent English-speaking member of the Cape Parliament who could have commanded the Bond's support. Rhodes had established himself since 1881 as much more than a Little Englander. An industrialist and a magnate he clearly was, and the Dutch-speaking farmers would have distrusted him on those grounds. He had also been suspect because of his antipathy to Kruger and opposition to the Transvaal. But Kruger had recently alienated Hofmeyr and the Bond because of his refusal to contemplate a customs union, or to deal openly and squarely over those issues with the Cape. Moreover, and probably of greatest import, Rhodes' advocacy of a curtailed African franchise, and his apparently sound views on what Bonds-men regarded as the threat of African numbers, significantly helped his cause. As Rhodes told a Congress of the Bond in 1891, "For nearly nine years I have voted and worked with your party, for the simple reason that I looked upon that party as representing the people of the country. I did so with no ultimate hope that one day you would hoist me into power, but simply feeling that that was the proper policy and the proper politics to pursue in the Cape Parliament."[8] What Merriman and others regarded as outrageous in Rhodes the Bond welcomed and admired. Then, too, Rhodes had distributed shares in the British South Africa Company to Hofmeyr and many other Bondsmen.

Upon receiving the call from Loch, Rhodes presented himself and his policies to a caucus of the Bond. Advised from afar by Hofmeyr, whose influence was important but not conclusive, the Bond promised Rhodes "fair play."[9] It backed him unanimously, indeed also agreeing to support Rhodes' rail plans and other northern (and Company) objectives in exchange for agricultural protection and a pro-white African policy. Hofmeyr was enthusiastic—he wired from Johannesburg—but would neither head nor join in such a government. Instead, Rhodes cemented this new alliance by appointing two Bondsmen to his cabinet: Sivewright, clever, ambitious, unscrupulous, and conservative in terms of the role of Africans; and Pieter H. Faure, a mild-mannered, pliable, solid member of the Bond. Sivewright became commissioner of crown lands and public works—in charge of railways—and Faure became secretary (or minister) of native affairs. (Rhodes would in effect command that department and be his own secretary.)

To complete this remarkable cabinet of all talents Rhodes turned to the liberals, or the progressives, as the knot of English-speaking men of influence and broader views were known. It is a testament to Rhodes' self-confidence and bravado that he believed that he could govern the Cape with the combined assistance of three high-minded liberals and two narrowly focused Bondsmen. To Sauer he gave the position of colonial (or home) secretary, and to Innes, who had never held office in previous Cape cabinets, the post of attorney general, or chief legal arbiter and government conscience. Merriman, efficient, energetic, and passionate—an old but mostly estranged friend with whom Rhodes was soon again taking morning rides along the flanks of Table Mountain—became treasurer and deputy prime minister. Sivewright and Merriman had not spoken to each other for years, and distrusted each other, but Rhodes induced them to conclude a truce for the greater glory of the Cape. As Merriman commented within a few months of joining the cabinet, Sauer, Innes, and himself had "a good many things to gulp down. I therefore hardly like to predict a very long life for our craft . . . [and] I cannot say that I feel either proud or pleased. . . ."[10]

Rhodes was to keep this unlikely, fissured, but powerful combination of egos and interests together for far longer than might have been supposed.

He did so by the force of his own personality, by casuistry, but also by being indispensable. Despite his many other preoccupations, the grievances of the progressive trio on that account, and their objections of principle to many of his legislative initiatives, even this group was subject to the force of Rhodes' magnetism and to the power of his leadership.

Innes distrusted Rhodes from the start, believing him both sharp and unfair. Innes, reported Merriman in 1891, was "very *antipatico* to Rhodes." "Rhodes's ways are not everyone's ways, and Innes does not find him easy to get on with." [11] Yet Innes was a proto-imperialist, favoring Rhodes' expansionist plans for the north. Before long the liberal triad was compromised in one or several ways, and Merriman let his abilities and drive be exploited. He took on additional portfolios and other ministerial responsibilities and organized the day-to-day running of the country for Rhodes. In exchange he received undoubted psychic satisfaction, but little public recognition, no preferment, and hardly any consultation over policy. Indeed, Sivewright was more influential than Merriman, and Hofmeyr was a regular and significant confidant, even schemer. Only Sauer, of the liberals, was ever consulted, but he was less astute than Innes or Merriman, and more easily lulled into complacency by the premier.

Rhodes' carefully crafted coalition was for a surprisingly long time to survive controversy and slide over a number of important political compromises. He skillfully constructed a legislative edifice that stood above the usual jealousies and local loyalties of the members of the House and built upon temporarily deferred enmities between the Bond and the progressives. All he offered to the House at the outset, however, was what he called "a purely South African policy." With regard to the budget and public expenditures, he promised "extreme caution." He asked the House for "fair hearing." [12]

This rather anodyne initiative received a complacent response in all but two quarters of the House. Rhodes first faced questions about the dubious way in which he had attempted to hold the prime ministership. The second, more fundamental, question of principle arose because Rhodes proposed both to govern the Cape and, simultaneously, to continue as managing director of the British South Africa Company—to be, as everyone realized, the absentee governor of the lands beyond the Limpopo that would be called Rhodesia. Rhodes' reactions to both vehement challenges reflected his political philosophy, governing style, and inbred contempt for the usual protocols of parliamentary life.

Within moments of Rhodes' assumption of power, Sprigg suggested that it was illegal. Upon becoming premier, Rhodes had left himself administratively unencumbered. He had assigned cabinet responsibilities to his five ministerial colleagues, but had made himself prime minister without portfolio. "I had hoped," said Rhodes after this arrangement had been questioned, "that I could have held office without portfolio . . . for I held the opinion that the office of Premier was of importance great enough to warrant that." Unfortunately, the constitution of the Cape Colony made no such provision. Sprigg and Upington, both former prime ministers, said that Rhodes was required to run a department. Sir James Tennant, the speaker of the House, and the governor agreed. In fact, the wording of the constitution was subject to interpretation, and Innes at the time and many years later believed that Rhodes had acted properly, a position that the chief justice upheld in late 1890. But in the days immediately following this presumptuous breach of protocol, if not law, Rhodes, profoundly ignorant of the Cape's constitution, was uncharacteristically nervous and rattled. In anticipation of an attack on his position he opened cabinet meeetings with a reference to himself and his colleagues as "hunted mice." When Merriman exclaimed, "The what?," Rhodes said that they were all "the hunted mice, they attack us before we have had time to look round, and we have to scuttle about and get under the benches."

Rhodes' reaction was to retreat, and then to engage in subterfuge. Rhodes became commissioner of crown lands and public works as well as premier. (Sivewright served without portfolio but actually ran both departments.) "Rhodes was casual enough," reported Innes, "to concur in the Speaker's view without reference to the legal member of the Administration."[13] The arrangement with Sivewright, calculated to leave Rhodes as free as possible to pursue his other interests, lasted for two months. Thereafter, following a second contradictory and ambiguous ruling by the speaker, and until the passage in 1893 of an act specifically permitting the Cape's prime minister to serve without portfolio, Rhodes' resumed position as premier without departmental charge was irregular, if never judged improper by the courts.

Rhodes was accused of being more than cavalier by Laing, a principled former cabinet minister from Fort Beaufort. "I have taken it upon myself," Laing told the House, ". . . to state publicly . . . and to prove conclusively that in consequence of the official position of [Rhodes] with the Chartered Company, it is not desirable he should be Prime Minister of this colony." Laing praised the Company and the extension of British influence into the northern interior—"no such event of political importance has taken place previously in South Africa." He extolled Rhodes' ability, foresight, and "wonderful organising faculty." But there was an obvious conflict of interest. It was thus wrong that Rhodes should hold both positions. The Company was an Imperial effort; the concerns of the Cape Colony were bound to prove secondary and the two could clash. To link the Cape so closely to the fortunes of the interior would distort the proper modernization and development of the Colony. At the particular level, too, Rhodes could sell Cape land to himself as head of the Company, or likewise transfer it for railways. It was "neither a politic nor a desirable thing that the representative of the Chartered Company should be Prime Minister of this colony," Thomas P. Theron agreed. "No one could serve two masters." The House should "watch him carefully." William H. Hockly thought that a dual position was "certainly against the spirit of the Constitution." The colonial idea, he said, was that a prime minister should "look after our Colonial interests first and last."

Rhodes rose to this direct challenge, knowing that he commanded a working majority in the House, but aware, too, that he could forfeit his hard and so recently won credibility either by a wavering or an insincere performance. The interests of the Cape and the Company could not clash, he asserted. "I have interfered in the interior because I wished the movement to the interior to be conducted as an expansion of the Cape Colony. I have interfered in the case of Bechuanaland, and the result is that that colony will in the end belong to the Cape Colony [which it did]. The case as it existed was that the Cape Colony had not resources such as would warrant it in itself developing the country to the north, but many of its people were most anxious to have some share in that movement." Rhodes was proud of "interfering," and meant the word and his activities which it described to convey positive attributes in an era which applauded bold actions. In later decades, however, such interference would be judged rapacious, and Rhodes be condemned by his own utterances.

Rhodes asked the House to judge whether his northern policy had harmed or benefited the Colony. He reminded its members that the employment of citizens of the Colony had been furthered, that Bechuanaland would soon be absorbed by the Cape, and that he had "worked with the idea that eventually the country right up to the Zambesi should also belong to the Cape. . . ." It was, Rhodes said, "the whole of [my] policy and object that the Cape Colony shall prosper, as through the prosperity of the Cape Colony the interests which I represent will also prosper." Not entirely disingenuous, this was a fair if less than full statement of Rhodes' intentions in 1890. Furthermore, he told the House, he believed (as he had since at least 1877) that because the Cape could not take on pioneering responsibilities in the interior, and, as he put it, "I had the good fortune to possess the wealth and the means to seize the interior, I did so, but I did it on behalf of South Africa. . . ." Expressing a wise strategic understanding of the scramble for southern Africa, Rhodes knew that losing any of the lands to the north would have weakened the Cape's role in accomplishing the consolidation of South Africa. But he intended to organize the northern interior as a part of an overall plan, indeed vision, for a unified southern Africa. His Company, therefore, was pursuing a South African, not an imperial policy. Although his contemporary critics were justifiably skeptical of such avowals, Rhodes was accurate in describing his activities in such a light. The prime minister promised to ask for no financial help from the Colony. Nor would he, after the ratification of the agreement which he and Sprigg had concluded a year before, ask for help of any kind with the northern railway. However, assured Rhodes, "if ever such a contingency should arise— which I cannot foresee—when the interests of the Chartered Company and this colony may clash, I will at once place myself in the hands of . . . the Governor" and resign.[14]

In fact, there was a fundamental if often ignored antagonism between the interests of the Colony economically and politically and those of an aggressive Company in the interior. When they shot to the surface, however, and Rhodes was indeed forced to resign, the cause was an even more basic clash between Rhodes as leader and statesman and Rhodes as swashbuckling conspirator.

These decisive events, and even most suspicions, were for the future. Rhodes, though he shunned direct ministerial duties and was even more active than before in pursuit of his private ends regarding Rhodesia, diamonds, gold, and territorial acquisitions, was an energetic prime minister. From 1890 he took charge of the House and concerned himself equally, and with seeming interest, in policy matters small as well as large. He responded to inquiries about particular bridges and water boring machinery. He worried about fencing railways, about the baths at Olifants River, about the sewers of Cape Town, about the purchase of a particular individual's house, about the Wynberg railway station, about provisions for the widow of a lunatic asylum patient, and so on. In other words, the ephemeral as well as enduring matters that concerned a nineteenth-century colonial legislature were not shirked by a premier who had other, weighty, matters on his mind and who, it was no secret, found the minutiae of parliamentary life uncompelling.

Yet Rhodes' true commitment to parliamentary pursuits became a source of concern to the members of his cabinet during the three months in early 1891 when the premier was in Britain. Merriman was alarmed by Rhodes' apparent total disinclination to attend to or even take notice of Cape business. Absorbed in his imperial and Company endeavors, he treated the premiership as a sideshow. While in London he replied to no letters from his cabinet ministers and apparently took no interest in the government of the Cape. Even upon his return from abroad, in late March, Rhodes paused not at all in Cape Town, but instead took the train straight up to Kimberley where the annual congress of the Bond was in session. "This is governing the Cape with a vengeance—everything, principles and everything else, being sacrificed to the Chartered Company," Merriman complained to his wife.[15]

On the eve of the second Cape parliamentary session, in April 1891, Merriman worried that Rhodes would prove an unsteady, mendacious leader partial to Afrikanerdom. Rhodes returned from London a heavy brooding man, having put on added weight. He had aged and looked older than his years. He seemed on the one hand more irritable than before, but on the other could still exude his old charm. Merriman and Rhodes cantered together again in the mornings along the slopes of Table Mountain; the premier, wrote Merriman, was "living like a gentleman." His head had not been turned, Merriman was pleased to note, by all the lionizing in London. In fact, for a few weeks Merriman regarded Rhodes as more at peace with himself than he had been for years. Even so, the persistent character of the clever Rhodes reemerged more and more. "He trusts no-one really and thinks everyone can be bought." Other than Jameson and Harry Currey, Merriman told the young Currey's father, "all his familiars are self-seekers and stuff him with adulation for their own purposes." They were a money-grubbing lot, too.[16]

Merriman need have had no qualms about Rhodes' willingness to lead the Cape with determination. From the beginning of his second session he took his prime ministerial responsibilties more seriously than has hitherto been appreciated. He was a working, not an ornamental or merely supervisory premier. He responded in parliament to the trivial as well as the great questions and personally guided the complicated and bitterly divisive franchise and ballot bill through the House, step by step, participating intensely in all stages of the bill's consideration. He followed and intervened—displaying an observant knowledge—in the floor discussions on even the most arcane or parochial subjects.

Still a speaker of no particular oratorial flash, Rhodes sought to persuade by the sheer force of his ideas. Nor did he debate, in the parliamentary sense. For him, a sense of accomplishment came not from the cut and thrust of clever words, but from didactic, expansive, and thoroughly repetitive articulation. When Rhodes expounded at length he chose subjects like the British South Africa Company, railway expansion, or the African franchise which were to him of transcendant importance. On those large issues of policy he set out his government's (really his own) position boldly. His words carried the implication that only narrow-minded fools could possibly disagree, or fail to understand and support the intrinsic logic of his message. Rhodes so dominated the House, and his colleagues, that few took offense at a manner which was as unusual as it was successful. Rhodes' personality and style had come to be accepted, or at least discounted, by most of the ordinary members of the House.

Rhodes was hardly a leader in the mold of his predecessors. More "political" than has usually been thought, he instinctively smoothed the reception of his government's program, and his own ideas, by the prior, private manipulation of members. He distributed shares in the British South Africa Company to Bondsmen and others, offered land in Rhodesia to them, and promised other favors. He gave jobs in Rhodesia, or preferment in the Cape, to outstanding critics. Others he eventually took into his second cabinet. On a day-to-day basis he busied himself with extra-parliamentary understandings—with the squaring of critics and opponents. No modern politician, certainly no one cut in the cloth of a Lyndon Johnson, would remark at Rhodes' methods; for the Cape in the 1890s, however, they were new in scale, and probably also in kind. Merriman's harsh critique may now be read as ironic compliment: under Rhodes, said his sometime friend, parliament became "demoralised by the practice of underhand agreement, lobbying and caucuses." [17]

What was also new, and decisively so, was Rhodes' close working relationship with Hofmeyr. They rode together often, and consulted almost daily in the prime minister's residence. Together they decided what should and could be accomplished, and how parliamentary obstacles were to be removed. "I know when I am dealing with your representatives," Rhodes told the Bond, "that I am dealing with the representatives of the people." After being attacked in the House for these contacts with Hofmeyr, Rhodes characteristically flaunted his association with the leader of the Bond. Colonel Frederick Schermbrucker had suggested that Rhodes was subject to dictation by Hofmeyr, as if that were wrong. Rhodes was prepared "to take the House into his secrets. He did consult the hon. member for Stellenbosch. He consulted him in the first place because he represented a large section of the people in this country, and in the second place, because he found his sound judgement was of enormous assistance to him." On a second occasion he declared that he consciously helped the Bond rather than opposing it. "Is not that the better way?" he asked disingenuously. "It pleases them and it pleases me." Or, in Merriman's words, quoting Rhodes, he was " 'humbugging' " the Bond just as the Bond believed it was " 'humbugging him.' "[18]

Employing his abundant charm and considerable magnetism, but other methods as well, Rhodes disarmed and blunted opposition. "He had a special gift for dealing with men," Innes remembered, "and the tact which he displayed in handling people of different types was remarkable." Yet he was also domineering, even offensive and hectoring to colleagues. But when men stood up to him and spoke plainly, Rhodes was usually accommodating. " 'Well have it your own way,' " he told Innes after his attorney general had exploded over Rhodes' impertinence. Rhodes preferred to settle disputes by talking them out among the brilliant blue hydrangeas in his garden at Groote Schuur. Innes wrote him letters of complaint. Rhodes told Innes to write no more letters, but to come up to the hydrangeas and "talk it out."

Rhodes, who during his early parliamentary career was described as having "a nervous temperament, and a vivid imagination," wished no surprises. With regard to the major issues which divided the groups in the House (there were as yet no real parties, aside from the Bond), he preferred to ascertain positions beforehand. He liked to cope with potential apostates, generalized disaffection, and other complaints as much as possible outside the confines of parliament.

Green compared Rhodes, always restless in parliament, to Sprigg, the consummate man of the House. Sprigg, "neat and prim as an old maid, sat . . . motionless like Patience, . . . never stirring a muscle or betraying the least sign of impatience." Rhodes, "the man of action," fidgeted constantly "like a schoolboy." "At times nervously massaging his neck with swift, spasmodic strokes, and at others bending down in a variety of queer unparliamentary postures while he surreptitiously devoured the afternoon paper, which contraband . . . he held beneath his desk so as not to attract the Speaker's eye."

Rhodes reigned supreme over parliament—in retrospect much too easily—for nearly all of his six years in office. His innate political skills—an acute sensitivity to the weaknesses and strengths of others coupled with an instinctive ability to manipulate—joined tactical qualities, thorough preparation, and a good sense of timing. Additionally, Rhodes was larger than life. As prime minister "he was a phenomenon, a man of great wealth, prepared to expend it in furtherance of a political ideal." His "immense prestige" implied "freedom in regard to details and method." As to both, Innes wrote rather drily that "those were matters for his own conscience, which was not a nonconformist conscience."[19]

F. Edmund Garrett, in early 1890 a young, impressionable special correspondent of the *Pall Mall Gazette* and later the editor of the *Cape Times,* was
entranced by the combination of animal energy and lofty spiritual idealism
which Rhodes exuded. Garrett appreciated how Rhodes used people. But
Garrett, a young acolyte, was also prepared to gild this unattractive alloy and
thus place Rhodes' character as a political being in its contemporary idiom. "I
have heard Mr Rhodes defined as a cynic whose one formula for success was
'Find the man's price.' If you read price in a large enough sense, I am not
disposed to dispute that, nor to deny that even when the price is of the most
sordid quality Mr Rhodes will often use the man for an end worthy of a better
instrument. But if he is a cynic, he is also an enthusiast, and he presses the
former's quality into the latter's service."[20]

Rhodes differed from previous prime ministers of the Cape in a second
profound way. Unlike Scanlen, Sprigg, and Upington, politicians of reactive,
largely parochial vision, Rhodes came to office with programmatic notions.
He had an objective which went beyond the amassing of power or the mere
protection of his interests in Kimberley and in the north. It is often suggested
that Rhodes joined forces with the Bond in the Cape in order to gain a free
hand elsewhere. He did so, but the reality is more encompassing and complicated. Rhodes assumed the premiership with an implicit, if not fully formed,
legislative outline which would indeed cement his alliance with the Bond and
provide him with the freedom to expand deeply into the interior. But he was
concerned with and gave at least equal if not greater priority to the development of a new, united South Africa. For him the Cape Colony was the fitting
cornerstone of a state or federation which would broaden the scope of British
dominion in Africa. Much of Rhodes' political energies were focused in the
early 1890s on making that protean dream a reality. Yet, in consummate irony,
his unquestioned and unparalleled success summoned failure and tragedy.

During his otherwise unremarkable, truncated first year, when Rhodes
was inexperienced and more tentative as a leader than he was to become, he
staked out a new, assertive role for the Cape in international relations and,
with no hesitancy, opposed Britain's failure to consult her colonies over diplomatic and other matters which affected them as much, if not more, than the
mother country. At the same time, he used a debate over the consequences
of the Anglo-German negotiation of their respective spheres in Africa to
enunciate a policy for South Africa as well as the Cape. Rhodes made it clear
that unity among the colonies and republics of southern Africa was his foremost aim. It would be forged, he said, by rail connections and a customs
union. That is why, he replied to a long lament by Upington, the loss of "the
west coast"—Südwest Afrika—had been such a blow. Nevertheless, he prudently opposed using the Cape's control over Walvis Bay, the German colony's main port, as an antagonistic stick with which to beat the Germans into
some kind of submission. True, Südwest Afrika could become a dangerous
smuggling area. True, too, "the map of Africa was being rearranged; the
whole of the [Namibian] territory was being parcelled out. . . ."

Even so, Rhodes recommended not reimposing Cape customs dues on

German imports through Walvis Bay. To do so would be poorly timed and "undignified." Rhodes wanted to strengthen, not weaken, the Cape's hold on its west coast port. "One day the German Empire would wake up and find that it was impossible to develop a colony on the West Coast," Rhodes suggested. Without Walvis Bay, Germany could do nothing; its colony would be "practically useless." Rhodes thus wanted to wait, patiently, until the whole of Südwest Afrika could revert both to the Cape and be an integral part of his own grand customs and rail union for southern Africa. "Some remote island, inhabited by barbarians," Rhodes sarcastically joined the very recent past of the Anglo-German Convention to the near future, "might be for disposal, and in that case [Rhodes] could only hope that the disposal might assist Cape Colonists in obtaining some reconsideration of the boundaries south of the Zambesi, because [Rhodes] felt strongly that if any proper South Africa union was possible south of the Zambesi, some reconsideration by the German Empire of its position on the West Coast was necessary."

Were Walvis Bay to fall into foreign hands, enormous harm would be done to the idea of union. Rhodes' statement was also meant as a warning to Britain. The Cape was the "dominant State" in the region. Its voice should be heard and its people consulted by Britain before the map of Africa was further redefined. Indeed, he preferred that the Cape should take the lead in any future negotiations over territory.[21] An amendment to that effect, in language proposed by Rhodes, was unanimously approved by the House, much to the annoyance of Lord Knutsford, the British colonial secretary.

Rhodes made his aspirations for the union of southern Africa from the Cape to the Zambezi (but not beyond) absolutely clear in early 1891, during a long speech to the Bond's annual congress. "If I had my wish," Rhodes harked back with some omnipotence to his "Confession of Faith," "I would abolish that system of independent States antagonistic to ourselves [the Cape] south of Zambesi. . . ." His "active ambition" was to bring about union by "working quietly, year after year, to bring South Africa into one system as to its railways, as to its customs, and as to its trade in the various products of the country." Rhodes instructed the Bond that, as was essential to the amalgamation of the diamond mines, where he had been through "fire," a "powerful rule to follow is that you must never abandon a position." The Cape must not abandon the northern territories of Bechuanaland and Rhodesia. "If your ambition . . . is a union of South Africa, then the Cape . . . must keep as many cards as it may possess." Rhodes envisaged the spread of self-government throughout the region, leading to union with the Cape. "The great actuating feeling of a white man," said Rhodes, "is that he must govern himself, and therefore I know that up to the Zambesi—for the climate will allow it—these northern territories must eventually be . . . self-governing. . . ." "Day by day the principle of self-government is growing and developing," Rhodes prophesied.[22] The United States was Rhodes' model. There the abolition of tariffs and the construction of railways had brought about a unified people—the fusion or closure that Rhodes sought for himself personally and for his adopted zone of endeavor as well.

Although Rhodes strongly preferred "land without natives," during these years of triumph he sought the union of territories south of the Zambezi, including Südwest Afrika, Rhodesia, Bechuanaland, the Dutch Republics, Natal, the Cape, and even the African protectorates (Basutoland and Swaziland). It was an endeavor no less practical than the amalgamation of diamonds or the taking of Mashonaland and trans-Zambezia. In his view, it would come about incrementally, by the trade ties that would flow from rail links, by the downing of tariff barriers, and by common educational institutions, in particular—he told the Bond in 1891—a teaching university where young men from all of the constituent territories could come to know one another and hence be infused with the spirit of union.

As he had as a backbencher, Rhodes as premier favored a fourfold, essentially commonsensical rail policy for the Cape. First, within the Colony itself he backed short spurs connecting productive white farming areas to main lines. Such lines would benefit the farmers (who voted) and open up new markets for importers or manufacturers in the cities or for producers in other parts of the country. Second, he attempted carefully and cautiously to strengthen the economic underpinnings of the old main line from Kimberley to the Cape. Third, he fought to preserve his freedom to set the pace of the northern extension to Mafeking and beyond. As his fourth and major priority, Rhodes sought assiduously, and as warily as he knew how, to extend the Port Elizabeth line to Bloemfontein and then to Johannnesburg and Pretoria. He had mixed political and economic motives: to further trade generally and bolster the health of the Cape ports and to strengthen the mutual interdependence of the Cape, the Free State, and the Transvaal and thus to encourage union. At the very beginning of his premiership Rhodes negotiated a rail route with the Free State from Colesberg to Bloemfontein and then on to the banks of the Vaal River. The key to this intermediate phase of a route to Johannesburg and Pretoria was the lowering of commercial barriers between the two neighboring states. The Free State finally saw the advantages of enduring transportation ties to the Cape as well as Natal and the possibility of beneficial imports and exports.

As negotiations were concluded with the Free State in late 1890 and early 1891, Rhodes worried again about competition from the Delagoa Bay railway, which by late 1889 had reached Komatipoort, on the Transvaal's border. There had been a pause before the construction of 340 miles of rails to Pretoria began again in May 1890. Rhodes wanted to win the rail race and thus accustom the Transvaal to the ease of shipping via Cape Town. (On Rothschild's initiative, he and Merriman also tried to buy or lease either the undercapitalized line from Delagoa Bay to the Transvaal border or, more dramatically, that harbor and its hinterland. Unhappily the Portuguese would not sell.) The fifty-one-mile stretch from the Vaal to Johannesburg was serviced in 1890–91 by a cart road only, and President Kruger was in no hurry to mortgage his sovereignty by cooperating with Rhodes.

Yet Kruger did need the other railway to the Mozambique coast. Thus Rhodes, using Sivewright as his emissary, was able to bring Kruger into his imperial net in late 1891, after the Transvaal's credit had collapsed and a precipitous fall in gold prices had depleted the funds available in Pretoria to complete the construction of the Transvaal's own railway from Johannesburg to the Mozambican border. Rhodes, kept informed of the depths of the Transvaal's liquidity crisis by Beit's agents in Johannesburg, agreed in effect to lend Kruger much of the sum required, providing that the Transvaal in turn laid a line toward the Vaal.[23] Although Sivewright and Rhodes were heavily criticized in the House for the loose manner in which the Cape had agreed to finance the Transvaal's rails, and though the much-hailed Sivewright agreement was in fact full of loopholes (especially its failure to retain control over rail charges by the Transvaal), in September 1892 Cape wagons rolled on steel rails all the way to Johannesburg.

The promotion of closer union by rail—an over-simplification of Rhodes' policy—was rebuffed by the Transvaal almost as soon as the last spike anchored the cross-Vaal extension. Kruger decided to protect his own farmers by raising Transvaal duties against Cape produce. So much for free trade. As Dr. Cornelis Pieter Smuts said during a heated debate in the Cape parliament, the Transvaal was treating the Cape with "contempt." The new duties ended a promising market for Cape produce. He and others called it a scandal.[24]

The Bond was aggressively angry, particularly since Free State produce entered the Transvaal free. As Merriman reported the Bond's fury, "where the breeches pocket comes in, brotherly love takes a back seat."[25] Nevertheless, Rhodes the statesman counseled calm in the hope—never realized—that he could patiently persuade Kruger to restore customs courtesy and reciprocity. The crucial battle with Kruger over this issue, and the larger one with him over autonomy and equity, took place later, during Rhodes' second ministry. It led to the Jameson Raid and, ultimately, to war. In 1892–93, however, the Bond was incensed at the Transvaal and solidly behind Rhodes.

As premier, Rhodes diligently promoted the cause of farming. He did so because of his alliance with the Afrikaner country party, because of his concern to disarm Bond antagonism to Kimberley and diamond profits, because of his understanding of how the prosperity of the Cape and its rail network (and his own federal policies) depended upon the export of cash crops, and—not necessarily least—because his own initial year in Natal had given Rhodes a surprising attachment to agriculture. A mining magnate he may have been, but Rhodes throughout the 1890s did more than any other public individual to introduce new ideas and methods into local agricultural practices. Rhodes was doubtless conscious of the hard facts: of the Colony's annual export earnings of approximately £9 million, cash crops contributed less than half, hardly £2.4 million. If diamonds were to slump or the mines fail, the Cape would have only a weak agricultural base from which to restore its fortunes. Moreover, the Colony imported wheat and flour worth about £500,000 a year. Butter and cheese imports cost another £100,000. Rhodes appreciated the urgent need to develop the Cape's agriculture. For him a growth in manufacturing represented no salvation. Indeed, what set Rhodes apart from other colonial premiers of his day was a profound disdain for the artificial support of infant industries and the placing of local enterprises behind high tariff walls.

Consciously modeling the Cape on California, Rhodes, with Merriman's strong assistance, attempted to expand the Colony's exports of fruit, thus founding what later became a thriving industry. Rhodes had himself already experimented with scientific fruit-growing in a small way; later he was to import American and British experts to advise the white growers of the Cape and, in the late 1890s, himself to sponsor a series of premier demonstration farms. Rhodes, always thinking expansively, even told the House that the Cape should establish fruit farms along the rail lines—"through the most fruitful districts of the Colony." More generally, the new fruit-oriented program had three prominent goals. First, better varieties should be planted and methods of cultivation improved. Second, a market in London should be arranged, and third, British importers should teach Cape farmers how to pack and transport their apples, pears, grapes, and so on for sale overseas.

Merriman believed that a fruit industry "properly worked . . . would transform the Western Province and do more to give an infusion of new blood than anything else. What we lack is some agricultural pursuit that will pay people of small money and that can be carried on in reasonable comfort." Hofmeyr was skeptical, being unpersuaded that "the English were a great fruit-consuming people."[26] But, after Rhodes created a new ministry of agriculture in 1892–93 and added its chores to Merriman's manifold other burdens, the new Cape initiatives proved overwhelmingly helpful to those white western Cape farmers who were prepared to adopt new ideas.

About a third of the members of the Cape parliament represented districts where the growing of grapes for wine was the primary industry. In the early 1890s phylloxera, an insect infestation which attacked the roots of Cape vines as it had ravaged the French countryside, was beginning to threaten the health of the colony's vineyards. In the vineyards, reported Rhodes, "a plague like the plagues of Egypt was spreading, threatening to sweep the Colony in time." He wanted whites to be given a bonus for the planting of American phylloxera-resistant root stocks. Merriman and Captain Charles Mills (the Cape's agent-general in London) arranged to have them imported, and through their collective efforts saved the Cape's oldest agricultural mainstay. Rhodes also sought the restoration of an ancient market for Cape wine in Britain. There Cape wines had lost their competitive edge in the years since the duty on nearby French wines had been reduced for political reasons.

Rhodes, a firm believer in free trade, audaciously wrote to the U.S. Senate to protest against the passage of raised tariff barriers by Washington. He corresponded with the premiers of Canada and New South Wales to promote an imperial customs union and later invested Cape funds in an Australian bond issue to back words with deeds. But when the interests of his own territory were at issue, "he thought it was time for the English government to do all it could to retain the friendly commercial feeling of all the various portions of the Empire." Rhodes wanted Britain to "extend some special consideration to Cape wines" and so lobbied the British government during his visits home throughout the early 1890s, but to no avail. He pleaded with Sir William Harcourt, the chancellor of the exchequer in early 1893, but received no more than an elaborate rejection; the French had to remain unprovoked. Even so, Merriman was acid about Cape prospects. "Our people are so hopelessly self-satisfied," he grumbled, "and they will not understand that people in England wouldn't buy their muck if it was duty free—and yet hitherto [the] government has signally failed to improve the staple." Only the South African market remained available, and a part of that, the gold fields—the Colony's best prospects for growth—had at least temporarily been shut by Kruger's protectionism.[27]

No agricultural issue was too small or too big. Rhodes backed the appropriation of funds to eradicate the prickly pear where it was impinging upon good grazing land, particularly near Grahamstown. He sponsored the importation of American ladybirds to control an insect infestation that seemed likely to destroy the Colony's orange groves. In this instance several members of the House thought that the Cape ladybird could control dorthesia (the pest in question) as effectively as ladybirds imported at vast expense from California. But Rhodes was adamant, having personally observed the superior abilities of the American variety on his own orange trees in Kimberley.

Rhodes sponsored a series of irrigation projects. "Step by step irrigation could be carried out," he assured the House, for "there were many fertile districts throughout South Africa which only wanted water." Horse breeding was also important. Rhodes said that he had the idea that "the Arab of the desert with the upcountry mare might produce a superior animal well adapted" to South Africa, and so he imported stallions from Arabia for experimental interbreeding.[28] Later he imported Angora goats from the Ottoman Empire to cross with local breeds and thus improve the quality of the Colony's mohair exports. But Rhodes deserved gratitude most of all from the Colony's white sheep farmers. He pressed the issue of scab eradication as he had in the 1880s, but waited until the consolidation of his power during his second term of office to push through the decisive legislation (over bitter Bond opposition) which saved the Cape's wool industry from destruction.

Rhodes reformed the Colony's banking system. In 1889 the boom in gold had become a dull thud as miners reached hard sulfide ores beneath the easily worked outcrops. New techniques were to be developed, but Transvaal and Cape banks faltered and failed; the Cape banks, even otherwise well-run ones— had speculated wildly in gold shares. So had the Barings Bank in London, which closed it doors. As banks throughout the Colony collapsed, financial panic followed. A Cape loan on the London market proved impossible to float, and the government of the Colony lived precariously on periodic sales of its own stocks. Only the Standard Bank of Cape Town had survived, thanks to prudent, cautious management. Taking advice from Lewis Michell, its manager, Rhodes and Merriman thereafter fashioned banking legislation which would prevent future collapses. The bank act of 1891 was a drastic departure from the loose, laissez-faire—almost casual—methods of the era. Based on Rhodes' intuition and Merriman's careful comparing of legislative models from Australia, Canada, and the United States (especially the National Bank Act of 1864), the Cape act was designed to provide security by compelling disclosure of bank balance sheets, governmental inspection of bank books, and investment in government borrowings. Moreover, the Colony established a national currency for the first time, and promised to honor all notes. Although introduced by the banks, Cape paper could henceforth be convertible into gold. It was backed by securities guaranteed by the government.

Some members of the House worried that Africans would not accept paper in place of silver or gold, but Merriman and Rhodes reassured their colleagues, regaling them with anecdotes about the receptivity of Africans to cardboard or tin surrogates for coin at Kimberley or in the Free State. After lengthy debate throughout 1891, Rhodes and Merriman prevailed; together they prevented amendments from weakening the regulatory provisions of the bill, and the anxieties of more old-fashioned bankers from prevailing. The result, wrote Michell two decades later, was that "banking institutions of the Colony have carried on their business with satisfaction both to their shareholders and to the public, recurrent crises have been avoided and confidence has never, in the most anxious times, been for a moment shaken."[29]

Rhodes never wavered in his espousal of a great South African university, based near Cape Town along the warm eastern side of Table Mountain. He dreamed of an Oxford-like teaching institution which would attract pupils from all of the white settlements south of the Zambezi, and arouse in those students an enthusiasm which would sustain closer union. The young white men who attended his university would, he proclaimed, "make the union of South Africa in the future. Nothing will overcome the associations and the aspirations they will form under the shadow of Table Mountain." "Rhodes' object," said Merriman, "is to try and create an educated class who by living together at a period of their life when impressions are readiest formed, may imbibe a South African *esprit de corps* of the best kind."

Victoria College in Stellenbosch was a largely Dutch institution. In Bloemfontein there was the Grey Institute. Diocesan College, near Cape Town, like Victoria and Grey, was essentially a secondary school. The oldest similar institution was South African College, in Cape Town, another secondary school. The University of Cape Town, modeled on the University of London, had been established in 1877. It sent South Africans to British universities and gave degrees at home by examination only. It could provide neither the fellowship nor the education by example which Rhodes, down from Oxford only a decade before, had learned to exalt. As Merriman explained to a financial contributor, Rhodes' university "will aim at giving the students not only mere instruction but what is far more wanted—discipline and moral training."[30]

"My ideas were formed . . . in Kimberley," Rhodes recalled, "but there is no place that can form, train, and cultivate the ideas of the young men of this country, no place better suited to such objects, than the suburbs of Cape

Town." As a Cape colonist, Rhodes wanted to make Cape Town "the centre of South Africa." But whether it was his domestic imperialism which was too much for the Bond, or whether they distrusted a single, thus English-language, cathedral of higher learning, or simply still distrusted Rhodes himself, the Bond would not back such a project. Although Rhodes promised to donate land for it near Rondebosch, and began the onerous task of collecting public subscriptions, he dropped the idea at the end of 1891.

Rhodes did not live to see the University of Cape Town flourish as it has in this century, much along the lines he espoused. However, Rhodes was able to found and then to realize the positive results of a school for miners that was established under his and Beit's aegis in Kimberley in 1894. In this instance Rhodes demanded, as he would, practical, vocational education. "I am entirely sick," he said, "of these theoretical things, which end in a flourish of trumpets."[31]

Despite the rebuff by the Bond to the idea of a university, Rhodes supported Hofmeyr's continued attempts to promote Dutch as a language equal to English. The immediate occasion in 1892 was a motion which requested parliamentary approval for the principle, recently recommended by a commission, that candidates for the Cape's school leaving examination be tested in Dutch as well as English. Hitherto they had been tested in English only, and the Dutch had naturally grieved. Rhodes, himself hardly fluent in Dutch, welcomed the proposal and described the "great disability" persons in South Africa would have if they knew only one of the languages. With his backing, this principle of language duality, new to South Africa, easily prevailed.[32] It foreshadowed Rhodes' new order, and the comity of whites against Africans which he was determined to promote.

From his first months as premier Rhodes fashioned a pro-Boer, anti-African policy of enforced separation which was more politically (and thus more power-) motivated than anything the English-speaking empire in southern Africa had yet seen. The policy issued from Rhodes (and Hofmeyr) less as a result of a preordained remaking of the Cape and southern Africa, or from innate prejudice, than as a response to the demographic, industrial, and interstate competitive realities of the region during the last decade of the nineteenth century. Africans were becoming settled, even competing agriculturally with whites. There was a growing, mission-educated, black middle class. The Cape segregated informally, and the existing property franchise limited black voting. But, compared with its neighbors, the Cape Colony was a liberal, tolerant outpost of Europe. In fact, the Bond thought it too liberal. So did Rhodes, who both needed the Bond's support and also believed that the Cape's liberal aura harmed medium-term prospects for a customs union, a federation, and so on.

Despite his early years in a vicarage and his association with Oxford, Rhodes had no innate feelings for the natural law, for the political culture of Britain, for the verities—what he called the sentiments—of men and women steeped in the post-Enlightenment tradition and values of fair play. He had no outstanding fear of public opinion. Rhodes as premier was, as was Rhodes the entrepreneur, expedient. Or, as he might have explained himself, the importance of his overall goals, significant as he considered them for South Africa, the empire, and mankind, certainly justified the employment even of unpopular means.

In characterizing his prime minister, Innes, everywhere acknowledged as an upright man of severe probity, suggested that all politicians must compromise, at least occasionally. The means that a politician may properly employ to influence his colleagues were "matters to be determined by each in the forum of conscience." Ordinary politicians found the determination simple, but "the man with big plans and great ambitions is apt to fall a victim to the doctrine that the end justifies the means. The more important his plans seem to himself, the more steadily," Innes' axiom continued, "does the significance of the methods dwindle by comparison to vanishing point. And then the goal alone fills his vision." Even so, Innes admitted that Rhodes was no simple character. Rather, he was a complex soul, "full of contradictory qualities whose divergencies were accentuated by the scale of his personality." Indeed, "his vision, his pertinacity, and the material resources at his command made him a mighty force—all the more powerful because concentrated on a single purpose."[33]

Rhodes made his approach to the "native question" evident during the initial session of premiership. Even before he had assumed office, a Bondsman had tabled an amendment to the Masters and Servants Act. The motion was designed to mandate the flogging of Africans by rural magistrates when and if farmers complained that their laborers had been disobedient. Fines or jailings would not deter disobedience or crime by farm employees. Africans feared the lash more than jail. Moreover, farmers lost the labor of their workers when they were imprisoned. The Cape, Isaac van der Vyver said in speaking for the bill, "was behind others because they had such bad servants." Furthermore, "servants always defied their masters . . . when the latter were in the greatest difficulties." Rhodes favored flogging. He was often to say that he considered "natives as children." Farmers labored under a number of great difficulties. In Natal and India magistrates could order a lashing. Why not in the Cape, where farmers needed relief from their burdens?

Others opposed such license. "It was a monstrous proposal," thought John E. Wood, "to impose by law corporal and criminal punishment for a very trivial offense." Children might be affected since the amendment contained no age restrictions. "The Bill . . . would have the effect of making servants perpetual slaves, liable to severe punishment for a slight neglect of duty." Alfred George Robertson called the bill a "disgrace." He "believed in treating servants with firmness, but as human beings, not slaves." He deplored the fact that the proposed amendment would compel magistrates to inflict a whipping in the case of an inability to pay a fine for minor offenses, like failing to clean a pair of boots. They were legislating not for good farmers but for bad ones. Merriman was opposed, too, but narrowly, and primarily because the passage of a flogging bill would cause a howl in Britain. Lewis A. Vintcent, from George, objected to the bill because it practically made the farmers, or masters, the judges of their own causes. The magistrates would have too little discretion. John Mackay argued that the bill would estrange Africans, who would not offer themselves as laborers. Henry William Pearson was ashamed that any members of the House would defend flogging, a most degrading pursuit.[34] When the amendment was eventually put to the vote, only twenty-three, including Rhodes, Faure, and Sivewright, voted for it. Thirty-five, including Innes, Merriman, and Sauer, cast negative votes, and the question of how farmers were to maintain discipline in the backwoods of the Cape was deferred until Rhodes was more firmly ensconced in his prime ministerial seat.

As Merriman wrote to Mills at the time, more reassuringly than he really believed, no sharp disagreements punctuated cabinet life. This peacefulness arose, he conjectured, because Rhodes was wholly devoted to "extra-Colonial questions." However, Merriman reminded himself and Mills, "we always have the black man with us." Indeed, on the eve of Rhodes' return from his extended British visit of early 1891, Merriman learned that his prime minister, from whom nothing had been heard directly, intended to reintroduce the flogging bill and push it through. "Possibly," Merriman told his wife, "this may be a way out of a very ignominious position [in general], and with honour too. . . ." He would have to resign. Or, Merriman supposed, Rhodes might count the cost "and not drive matters to extremes," which turned out to be the safer prediction for 1891.[35] The 1890 amendment was reintroduced in 1891, but ignored by Rhodes and discharged at its second reading.

As astute as Rhodes had been in refusing to become personally involved in the second round of parliamentary agitation for a sharp, symbolic, anti-African measure such as the attempt to legalize widespread lashing, he refrained primarily in order to keep the cabinet intact. He wished to focus his, theirs, and parliament's attention on an issue of far more importance for southern Africa. He had made the franchise problem his own in 1887, when he spoke harshly against giving the vote to Africans whose primary property was held communally. But he was less fearful of masses of African voters than he was mindful of the anxieties of the Bond and desirous of avoiding future conflict over African voting rights with the Transvaal and the Orange Free State, both of which explicitly denied the franchise to non-whites; and with Natal, where a very high property qualification all but excluded its large African population from participation in the political affairs of that colony. The Cape's liberal tradition—and the consequent absence of a common "native policy"—was an obstacle, or a presumed obstacle, to the drive toward federation.

In 1860 the Cape Colony included 180,000 whites and 314,000 Africans. By 1891 the white population had doubled, to 376,000. With the annexation of nearly 500,000 people in the Transkei, by the same year the total African population had nearly quadrupled, to 1,148,000. The annexation of Pondoland, clearly on the horizon, would add another 200,000 Africans. In the 1890 election, about 91,000 names had been on the rolls. The vast majority were white males. Yet Africans had also voted in greater numbers than ever before. In fact, they were reckoned to have had a decisive influence in seven of the Colony's thirty-seven constituencies, that is, on the election of twelve of the seventy-six members of the House.[36] The trends in voting alarmed the Bond.

The Cape franchise, despite the distinctions introduced by Sprigg, Rhodes, and others in 1887 to deflect increments in Africans' voting power, was still officially color-blind. The occupation of a house or the possession of other property worth at least £25, or annual wages of at least £50 (or only £25 if board and lodging were included), qualified adult men to vote. There were no literacy or educational tests. Furthermore, the progressive wing of the Cape House had, throughout the 1870s and 1880s, become an advocate of maintaining the access of Africans to the franchise. Enabling Africans to vote contributed to their political education, their general uplift, their Westernization, and their overall contentment. The fact that Africans could vote also minimized their ill-treatment at the hands of what still was a white settler ruling class.[37]

Although the 1887 alterations had sharply reduced the numbers of Africans who could vote—about 24,000, or 28 percent of all eligible Africans, were thus disfranchised—this check on black numbers was thought insufficiently permanent by the Bond. It wanted further reductions in the size of the African vote, especially in the English-speaking eastern districts where the Bond's appeal to voters was weak anyway and where there was a widespread suspicion that white hustlers "packed" Africans off to the polls. At its congress in Kimberley in 1891 the Bond approved specific proposals which Hofmeyr later put before parliament as the opening salvo in what was to be a prolonged multi-year attack on the Cape's constitutional underpinnings.

Rhodes, by careful preparation within the cabinet and many appeals to individual loyalties, was able in 1891 to orchestrate a prolonged hearing for Hofmeyr's innovative solutions and an agreement that a search for more generally appealing answers would continue in 1892. What Rhodes and Hofmeyr did so well in 1891, in preparation for the decisive debate of 1892 and the reconstruction of 1894, was to persuade even those of their opponents who were most wedded (and pledged) to the existing franchise—like Innes—to consider some modifications as inevitable. Initially a consciousness-raising and sensitivity-testing exercise in the House and in the Colony at large, the cause of the Bond was transformed by Rhodes into his own most important and most enduring issue.

By so fundamentally altering the context in which the Cape and South Africa observed the natural and inherent rights of Africans, Rhodes introduced a basic realignment of black-white power relations. The changes in attitude which he sponsored and orchestrated were, although mere subtle readjustments on paper, drastic in their reordering of the prevailing psychological climate. As well, they prepared Cape opinion to receive the results of the strange mutation of Rhodes' union which emerged from the ashes of bloody war. Rhodes' disregard of (antagonism toward is too strong) the human and political value of Africans foreshadowed, indeed, prepared the path for the segregationist attitudes and legislation that were so prevalent during the decades of actual union.

Hofmeyr, much more moderate and restrained than most of his followers, warned the House in 1891 that there was a widespread dissatisfaction in the country regarding the existing franchise regulations. The growth in the numbers of black voters and potential voters was alarming, and there was prospect of much more. The Cape might before too long (with Pondoland, Bechuanaland, and even Rhodesia) include five times as many Africans as whites. "The white population . . . would be utterly swamped." Moreover, Hofmeyr painted a vivid portrait of probable disaster: "Give the mass of the natives active leaders and organisers . . . give them individual tenure . . . maintain the franchise at its present low level . . . and Heaven only knew what was going to happen in the future." As far as prospects for a united South Africa were realistic, he doubted whether the other sections of South Africa would be prepared to sit side by side with black representatives from the Cape. The lack of a common franchise, he echoed Rhodes, would prove a cause of separation, not unity. Moreover, it was not yet too late to enact important changes. "The natives were not organised as yet. So far the natives were only feeling their way, and some hon. members would wake up when it was too late."

Hofmeyr's remedy was complex, and positive in its structure of rewards. It had been accepted beforehand by Rhodes and the cabinet; Rhodes had a discernible hand in its composition. Hofmeyr proposed no denial of the franchise to existing voters, although retroactive disbarments had been common in other imperial outposts. Instead, he wanted to give an additional vote to persons with higher than the basic income or property qualifications. His principal object, said Hofmeyr, was to set the threshold for the second vote so low that "decent [white] mechanics" could obtain it, but sufficiently high to put it out of the reach of "the ordinary aboriginal barbarian." Hofmeyr also advocated an educational test: those who had graduated from secondary school (presumably most whites) or who were members of the learned professions should have a second vote. Here Hofmeyr echoed the practice that existed in Oxford and Cambridge until 1948. Van der Walt, of the Bond, put the same case directly: Negrophilists had used "the native vote" to limit the representation of Afrikaners. "The blacks would get the upper hand completely if the franchise were not altered." Jurgens Hendrik Smith said, "The natives . . . increased like rabbits, because they were so well treated and protected. The barbarians should be subject to the civilised classes." [38]

Rhodes welcomed Hofmeyr's initiative. Presented in no final form, it would enable the feelings of the country to be consulted. Legislation so important should not, he advised, be rushed through the House. (Rhodes wished to discover the sentiments of the Colony before risking his own position and potential legitimacy.) Nothing in the world was immune from change; the present Cape franchise should not, he urged, be regarded as inviolate. There was a great danger that "half-educated barbarism" might in the near future interfere with the way the citizens of the Colony were represented. Yet Rhodes refused to advocate a color bar. Rather, he preferred a franchise qualified by educational attainments.[39]

The progressive members of the House greeted these proposals, and Rhodes' approach, with scorn. Laing decried the establishment of a "privileged plutocracy." "The system of making money the standard of worth and good citizenship was a dangerous and pernicious one, and utterly antagonistic to liberal and broad-minded sentiments." Giving extra rights to capitalists and landowners would mean revolution and disruption. Rather than offering extra votes to the educated, the Cape could give the University of Cape Town its own representative. Moreover, Laing reminded the House that Africans had exercised the franchise with "great discretion," and had in no way abused those privileges, "as the members who represented native divisions themselves proved." Arthur Douglass urged the prime minister to enunciate real principles and then stand by them "manfully". "If they wished to have a progressive colony, it would be well rather to lower than to raise the franchise." He wanted whites "to take the natives by the hand and help them out of barbarism and make them good and intelligent citizens." Taking away their vote thus made no sense. "The only way to build up Africa was by giving freedom to the people, not by suppressing and keeping down those who had shown themselves worthy of the franchise." Douglass concluded his intervention with the kind of rhetorical flourish to which Rhodes paid little heed: the government should "stiffen its backbone . . . and refuse to hold a candle to the devil."

Herbert Travers Tamplin feared that the passage of the proposed or similar legislation would ignite "a flame of . . . terrible discontent" within the country. He also noted the illogicality of penalizing "the coloured population" for having achieved progress and influence. He begged the House to "treat the native as one who was a responsible member of the community." Further, Tamplin suggested that "so long as the statesmen of [the Cape] conceded the natives the rights of free men and the privileges of the humblest British citizen, so long would the natives on their part conduct themselves in what was upon the whole a satisfactory and orderly manner." There should be no shift away from "fair play," he demanded. For John Frost the issue was "political slavery." If the franchise were restricted, "a bad feeling would be created; if a man were made to feel that he were but half a man he would become dissatisfied, and great danger would arise." Sprigg and Upington were also opposed, Merriman was mildly in favor—it would "minimize the Coolie and the barbarian," and Innes, who represented Victoria East, where Africans voted in great number, wanted to see whether a bill could be devised which would satisfy the Bond without destroying the principles of a color-blind franchise which he had promised to uphold. Sauer said that he would never back changes in the franchise which would separate voters by color. But he was not "wedded to abstract principles" and approached the question with an open and fair mind.

Rhodes offered the already-anticipated compromise, which Sauer later moved and the House voted overwhelmingly. Rhodes' ministry would contemplate the questions during the 1891–92 parliamentary recess, look at the latest census returns, take the pulse of the country informally, and prepare legislation which would elicit a consensus. In effect, Rhodes cleverly committed the House to at least some limitation of black voting.[40]

During much of the half-year before parliament could meet again and Rhodes could bring the debate over the franchise to a successful conclusion, there were a host of other issues which preoccupied the cabinet and the country: Sivewright was negotiating the rail extension to Johannesburg; Merriman spent two months in London in early 1892 seeking funds to keep the Colony and its railway ambitions afloat; Rhodes was out of action for a month over the new year after tumbling badly from his horse while riding with Merriman. He broke his collarbone, suffered a heavy concussion, and then contracted what was termed a severe case of influenza. Upon his return, Sauer was prepared to forge some kind of compromise over the franchise if only Innes, who threatened to resign, would become reconciled.

"If Innes goes, our position," said Sauer, "will be very difficult. You, he and I came together, and I don't like one going and the others remaining." Sivewright and Rhodes were pressing Sauer, and he in turn (with Merriman away) was worrying Innes. Innes accused Sauer, whom he and Merriman called "The Bumbler" after the appellation given to him by the *Cape Times,* of being "clay in the hands of the potter." Short, thick-set, untidy, genial, and informal, Sauer bumbled around the House "helping himself to pinches of snuff." Rhodes was the potter.[41] In turn, Sauer complained that Innes was standing alone in opposition to reasonable change.

"The more I think over this beastly franchise," Innes told Merriman, ". . . the more do I incline to the view that the proper and right thing for *me* to do, is to stand out and to refuse to put my hands to any change. . . . Really the Bond fellows are like the daughters of the horseleech, their constant cry is 'give,' 'give!' Unless we make a stand soon, we shall not know where consistently and logically to stop." In February Innes told Rhodes that he might have to leave the cabinet. "I am averse to any change at present," Innes explained to Rhodes. "I do not think it is necessary and I feel that the danger which so many say they see has no real existence. If I followed my own inclinations I should retire from the Cabinet. . . . But I am unwilling to place Merriman and Sauer in an awkward position, and I am also genuinely desirous that you should not be hampered in your work more than was absolutely necessary." Yet he was prepared to compromise, leaving his gentle character open to blandishments and artful giving proffered by Rhodes (with Hofmeyr in the wings). "Much against my inclinations I have agreed to a sloppy sort of compromise," he wrote to Merriman, "but my inmost soul abhors the whole thing." The Bumbler was "dying to settle." Being a minister was difficult, Innes sighed. "One lives in an atmosphere heavily charged with carbonic; there are so many things to be considered apart from one's own honest opinion, that the latter is sometimes perforce crushed into a back seat."

It is not known how many times Rhodes had taken to the hydrangeas with Innes. But, assisted by Sauer, Innes' innate decency and dislike of conflict led him—and thus the cabinet—to a legislative proposal which, though it differed substantially from Hofmeyr's, accomplished the same purpose with greater simplicity. The loss was significant, but there was one forward step—the secret ballot—for which Innes and the progressives could take credit.

Innes wisely recapitulated the six elements of their new agreement: Rhodes would not support any scheme of dual voting (the basis of Hofmeyr's stalking horse was discarded); would agree to a "rudimentary" educational test; accept no retrospective disfranchisement; accept the existing wages qualification; accept the inclusion of compulsory balloting; raise the occupational qualification level to no more than £75, and give Innes "perfect freedom of action" to speak and vote against the cabinet position. Rhodes further agreed to making the entire bill a package, and to refuse to accept any amendments which might weaken (or strengthen) the compromise. In order to buttress his position further before the parliamentary debate, Rhodes—to Innes and Merriman's disgust—elevated Upington, who was ill, to the Cape Supreme Court. "I do not at all subscribe to the Young Burgher's [Rhodes'] doctrine of buying off the Opposition," Merriman exclaimed.[42]

Discussion of the momentous Franchise and Ballot bill dominated the 1892 session of parliament. (Although Rhodes also recognized the need for a redistribution of seats, since constituencies in the Cape parliament were badly gerrymandered, he had enough to do in 1892 without adding another controversial issue to his government's agenda.) He offered the bill in his name and, as he had promised (and maneuvered?) Innes, as a measure on which the government would stand or fall. Introducing the proposed legislation to parliament, Rhodes emphasized its popular appeal to whites, carefully ignoring adverse African sentiment. During a speech that lasted a full hour, he reviewed the history of the franchise in Europe, the United States, and elsewhere in the empire. The Cape's qualifications were low; raising them would infringe upon no sacred principles. Moreover, the lesson of Jamaica (Rhodes alarmed parliament by reminding his colleagues that a revolt had occurred there after liberalizing voter's rights) showed "that extreme caution must be used in granting the franchise to coloured people." Even so, his own bill, Rhodes reiterated and his ministers solemnly affirmed, introduced no distinction based solely on color. Disfranchising no one then on the rolls, it nevertheless was intended to limit the prospective growth in voting numbers. Such restrictions—every member of the House understood—would primarily, even overwhelmingly, apply to Africans and, marginally, to Coloureds.

"What should a man be who exercised the franchise?" Rhodes asked his colleagues. Having himself contemplated the question long and hard, Rhodes confided that those who voted should be citizens of "some education" who were "possessed either of some slight means or one who has recognised the dignity of labour." Personally, Rhodes admitted, he favored the franchise requirements of Natal, which were so high that only a handful of Africans had qualified to vote. (Indeed, in 1891 Rhodes had secretly arranged a wholesale purge of Africans from the register in Kimberley.[43]) But proposing so radical a change was impolitic. Instead, among the eighty-three clauses of his bill were a set of innovations which flowed from Innes' compromise and the discarding of Hofmeyr's idea of a dual vote. New was a shift in the occupational threshold from £25 to £75 a year. (This tested the amount paid annually for a lease or in rent.) *Owners* of property worth only £6 a year also would be allowed to vote. A separate clause qualified (white) alluvial miners in Griqualand West who held diamond claims and lived in tents and spent less than £6 a year on their property but who were "educated men . . . of great intelligence who spent £300 or £400," said Rhodes, "in digging and mining" (and also voted in Rhodes' constituency). More radical was a literacy requirement: prospective voters had to be able to write their names, addresses, and occupations. Even more profound, especially for Rhodes himself, was the provision that Innes had insisted upon for voting by secret ballot. Hitherto citizens of the Cape had trooped to the polls and registered their preferences openly. Rhodes reported that he "objected to the ballot *in toto*, because he liked to know how a person voted." He had no "ulterior motive" in wanting to know who a person favored, but men should "vote openly" and not by stealth.[44]

Support for Rhodes came from several corners of the House. Sauer admitted that he had altered his own convictions. The changes were moderate and reasonable; his Dutch colleagues were more moderate and reasonable on this issue than he had expected, no longer "given to the extreme views that they wished to do away with the black man." Furthermore, everyone in the House would surely not contest the need to prevent "the blanket Kafir, who did not work himself but sent his wife out to work for him" from voting.

Innes admitted that the existing regulation "had worked very well . . . indeed wonderfully well, considering the conditions of the country." Yet this issue constituted a great threat to relations between Afrikaans- and English-speakers in the Cape. It was intolerable to Innes that "the native vote should be contended for on race lines between Europeans." He wanted to prevent "a race conflict in the Colony" between Afrikaners and the English, so compromise of principle was acceptable. Anyway, to require literacy was appropriate.

Although Merriman affirmed that it was hardly politic to exclude blacks from equal privileges with whites, and though there was a tendency in the Colony "to become browner"—the real problem was the uneducated Cape Town "coolie"—the educational test was a crucial reform. It would clip the wings of demagogues and publicans alike. Since only about 4 percent of African males on the frontier could write and possibly 11 percent in the settled parts of the colony, plus 26 percent among Coloureds, the important and discriminating thrust of the bill was the demand for literacy. An additional strong argument for the bill, thought Merriman loyally, was the fact that the present, moderate measure would forestall new agitation and the introducton of more drastic proposals.

Bondsmen were more direct. Pieter Jacobus du Toit welcomed the bill because its provisions would "exclude the ignorant natives who were not capable of properly using the franchise." It would prevent Africans from someday sitting in the House. Sivewright feared that an "overflooding [of] the native vote would be the practical disfranchisement of the European races." The "yellow man [was] also a very great danger." Johannes Petrus du Plessis said simply that the existing franchise was too low, for it put "many respectable white men on a level with coloured people who were little more than savages."[45] Hofmeyr wanted the bill to pass even if its provisions were different than the ones he had offered in 1891. So long as the "European element" could be protected "against barbarism" he was content. Of equal significance, the passage of the bill, he again echoed Rhodes, would improve "understanding between the two great European races, and . . . then they could talk of an United South Africa in its best sense."

The opposition to the bill, although vocal and virulent, mustered only twenty votes (against forty-five in favor) at the conclusion of its second reading. George Morrison Palmer reminded his colleagues that "poor, scabby South Africa" was the only country in the world which desired to raise the franchise. Douglass believed that altering the constitution in the manner proposed would simply open a door to further abridgments of black rights. He also criticized Rhodes for desiring to raise the dignity of labor while simultaneously proposing to deny the vote to men who earned less than £50 a year. "The Prime Minister," he said, "was easily led away by his immense wealth into thinking that men were vagrants if they had only just enough to keep themselves alive." Many upright men were the premier's equal but earned less than £50. If South Africa were to make progress—Douglass argued the fundamental liberal position—"it would pay . . . to give [honest laborers] the constitutional right to make their grievances heard." As plainly as possible, Hockly suggested that there was only one way to avoid lasting color conflict—to "treat the natives as equals, and gradually bring them up to the higher level." The new legislation, Captain Edward Yewd Brabant warned, "was calculated to cause widespread dissatisfaction and race feeling in the country." William Hay reminded the House that "native electors were as a rule a very respectable class." Yet the bill before the House would remove the vote from hard-working but poor farmers, and from underpaid African teachers.

Several members cried "shame," for notions that the bill made no distinctions of color was nonsense. They and others also pointed accusing fingers at the Bond, claiming that Rhodes' proposals were simply aimed at placating Afrikaners, who were prejudiced against Africans. Further, the Bond wanted those seats in the eastern districts which now returned English-speaking representatives. As Tamplin said, "An organisation prejudiced to the interests of the country had got the better of discreet guidance . . . and no one knew what the end would be." The prime minister had made an unholy bargain. The hands of his ministry were tied, their "withers wrung with agony by doing what they did not like to do, in order that a section of the people . . . might be pacified." What would come next? Thomas O'Reilly, the volatile and voluble member from Cape Town, called the bill a naked political arrangement. He labeled Innes and Sauer "white sepulchres," all "white and fair outside, but they must not break them open."[46]

When the clauses introducing a secret ballot were discussed at the committee stage, Rhodes again indicated his strong preferences for open voting. Otherwise, at Kimberley, the diamond industry would be ruined, "loafers" might be elected, and the African compounds would be thrown open, with free liquor and "robbery of diamonds" to follow. Yet, he backed his own compromise measure because its provisions (to which others objected) would come into force only after the next general election. "The people should be gradually accustomed to the ballot." In another context Rhodes, hardly a democrat or a populist, declared that the Prussian franchise pattern, which supported rule by an oligarchical elite, was best. "I wish to preserve the landed classes of the country," he said on yet a further occasion, "as a conservative element in connection with changes that are coming over the country . . . as a bulwark against the march of legislation . . . which is often hurried and mischievous." As Lord Grey of Falloden told his wife, Rhodes "is not exactly what you would call a liberal; he has a new version of 'one man, one vote' for South Africa, viz. that he, Rhodes, should have a vote, but nobody else should."[47]

In the end Rhodes accomplished the passage of the Franchise and Ballot Act with ease, the vote at the final reading of the bill being forty-seven to thirteen. He managed to deflect amendments from progressives who desired to mitigate the bases on which the government and the Bond had established their pact, out-talked those who wanted to redraw the boundaries of the existing constituencies, and was forced to lower his guard only over votes for convicts. Although a petition against the bill with more than 10,000 Coloured and Asian signatures was presented to the Queen, Rhodes also managed to avoid any interference (which was still legal) by the British authorities.

Equally, Rhodes kept his cabinet of all talents together. To his satisfaction and possible private amusement, Sauer, Merriman, and Innes danced like political puppets before the House, swallowing their principles and "trimming" publicly. As Innes later wrote, "The danger of a division on racial [i.e., Dutch-English] lines, which might result in a drastic measure, was very real. I hesitated long, but finally decided that if we could abate a demand which it was impossible to resist and could prevent any real injustice by so doing, it was the part of wise statesmanship to consent."[48]

The immediate consequences of the new act, however, were less than either side had feared. Only 3,000 Africans, Coloureds, and Asians were dropped, presumably because they moved from an old polling district to a new one and thus lost their rights as previous voters. Psychologically, however, Rhodes readied parliament and the Colony for more far-reaching measures. He also used the Franchise bill to strengthen his strong alliance with the Bond and with Hofmeyr personally, while maintaining ties with urban liberals and old friends until they could be sustained no longer and were expendable. Rhodes straddled and incorporated as long as he could, and then, with added political stature and almost unfettered power, stood astride the full legislature, accountable only (more or less) to the Bond. No more important initiative was eased so deftly through the House. It transformed South Africa and increased Rhodes' own belief in his omnipotence.

Rhodes also needed both Bond and liberal support for a much tougher challenge to his very legitimacy as the Cape's leader. Just as Sprigg and Laing had questioned the propriety of potential conflicts of interest in 1890, so in 1892 Sprigg returned to the attack. Although the British South Africa Company was constructing a railway north from Vryburg to Mafeking on behalf of the Cape, its completion was well overdue. For reasons connected with the Company's lack of capital, work on the line had in fact been suspended. The Company was in breach of its contract, as Sprigg (who had originally made the deal with Rhodes) well knew. Now their positions were reversed. At least Rhodes as premier should be pushing Rhodes the Company managing director hard, and demanding compliance with the letter and spirit of the contract. Aha! Sprigg had his quarry at bay. Lance extended, sabre at the ready, Sprigg sallied forth with a flourish of partisan trumpets.

Although, according to the original agreement of 1890 and a reaffirmation of 1891, Rhodes had "bound himself to complete the railway extension to Mafeking provided the Cape Government purchased the Kimberley-Vryburg section," which it had, construction had nevertheless ceased. Since then the Company had done nothing. "They had shamelessly neglected the solemn promises they had made to the . . . Government," Sprigg accused. After taking the rails to Vryburg the Company "began to shuffle." For a year the Company continued to "shuffle." Then the prime minister, occupying "two positions, which were incongruous, inconsistent, and . . . unconstitutional," promised the House to resume building immediately on either a standard 3'6" gauge or along a narrower 2'6" width. Rhodes, shouted Sprigg, had said that he was "ready at any moment to build." Nearly a year had passed. "Had he turned a single sod of the railway from Vryburg to Mafeking?" "Absolutely nothing. The solemn, deliberate promise of the managing director of the Chartered Company, the member for Barkly West, the Prime Minister of this colony, had been deliberately broken and without a vestige of excuse." Was the House "going to sit still after such a flagrant breach of contract?" Moreover, Sprigg understood that the Company was moving forward with a rail line from Beira to Salisbury (Harare), presumably in further breach of Rhodes' agreement with the Cape. (Indeed, that was among the salient reasons for the delay.) Since the Cape had paid £730,000 for the line to Vryburg, and was now being defrauded by the prime minister in his other capacity, would the Company refund that amount to the Colony? Obviously the interests of the Colony were "being sacrificed to the interests of the Chartered Company." For how much longer would Rhodes be permitted to "play fast and loose with the representatives of the people?" It was a good and fair question.

Rhodes initially responded to this emotional invective with deliberate circumlocution. He "recognised the responsibility of completing the railway, and there was no intention of evading that responsibility." As to the reason for the lack of completion, "there had been difficulties," but not financial ones. The Company had ample funds, he prevaricated. "He recognised that the obligation had to be fulfilled, and he intended to fulfill it. As to the exact time of fulfillment . . . financial troubles had been considerable in many parts of the world." Yet the "railway would be completed." Later, when Sprigg had transformed his inquiry into a full-fledged motion of censure, Rhodes rose to a much more considered, clever defense. Employing his most reassuring manner, but with a delivery, Innes recalled, which was "diffuse and jerky," Rhodes appeared candid, contrite, conciliatory, and firm. He refused to apologize for his dual role. Indeed, he emphasized how his control of the Company would assure the prosperity of the Cape, and had been designed to accomplish that objective. He brazenly contradicted Sprigg on two crucial points: first, the previous government of the Cape had come to the Company, not the other way around, and had proposed the arrangement now in dispute. Second, the agreement of 1890 had never specified a precise date by which the railway northward was to be finished. (Sprigg claimed that someone had deleted the word "forthwith" in the 1890 agreement.) Rhodes conceded lamely that after the rails had been driven to Vryburg in late 1890 it had "perhaps [been] his duty immediately to have proceeded with the line to Mafeking." But he had not done so because the "task of northern development had far exceeded what he had expected." Yet, as he reminded the House at great length, "he had done great work there." This, grandly and rather disingenuously, he described as "Colonial expansion through Imperial extension." It would benefit the Cape because the "whole of the work had been carried on with one idea; occupation from the south, assimilation of customs, free-trade with the Cape Colony, and the full and thorough knowledge that the ultimate destination of these people would be union with the Colony."

Rhodes painted an inspiring portrait of his ambitions. It elicited cheering from the House, and much good feeling. "The Cape should stretch from Cape Town to the Zambesi," he declared, "with one system of laws, one method of commerce, and one people." He had kept the Germans and the Transvaal out. "Although there were many things he regretted, . . . he did not regret his work in connection with the northern territory." For those reasons, at least, he would of course complete the task. He would fulfill his obligations. But he needed time. He requested the backing of the House. Its members, he appealed, "should look upon this question upon higher grounds than they had been wont to do, and that if the work had been done well, they should think twice before they gave their vote against him." (Toward the end of this long, conversational appeal, Rhodes suddenly deflected his critics and made the members of the House smile by telling them that the debate was happening on a "very suitable day. It happened to hit upon his birthday." But Rhodes misled. He was then thirty-nine years and two days old.)[49]

Whether Rhodes persuaded or merely succeeded in disarming parliament is uncertain. Sprigg's attack may have been too intemperate and too nakedly political to elicit more than passing support. It moved Schermbrucker to deliver a tirade, during the excitement of which he pounded his desk so vigorously that he broke a tumbler and slashed his wrist, but few others joined him. Hofmeyr, Sauer, Sivewright, and Merriman all rushed to Rhodes' side, Merriman pointing out that the House in other railway matters had allowed four and five years to elapse before pressing for the fulfillment of construction contracts. Innes gave a reasoned legal defense. Others suggested that the charge against Rhodes was just, but that he should nevertheless not be bullied. Finally Fuller and Sprigg wrangled loudly over whether or not members were being influenced by profits on Company shares. "No vote of confidence," remembered Innes, "ever ended in a more complete fiasco."[50] At its conclusion, Rhodes' approach had been stained, but not indelibly, Sprigg was compelled to withdraw his motion, and the great charge collapsed.

If Rhodes had been chastened by the attack, there were few indications. During the months following he altered no fundamental operating procedures, took no new care to separate his multiple and conflicting responsibilities, and gained strength from Sprigg's failure. Furthermore, the board of the Company finally, but only reluctantly and after Rhodes' personal intervention in October 1892, voted money for the final extension to Mafeking. Lord Ripon, Britain's colonial secretary, also gave Rhodes the financial, mineral, and land concessions that he wanted, plus direct subsidies. The rails themselves ultimately reached Mafeking in late 1894, and within an additional year, the excuse of an extension beyond Mafeking was used as a cover for the great subterfuge of 1895; Sprigg's initiative of 1892, and Rhodes' response to it, bears an important lineal relationship to that debacle.[51]

With consummate political skill, studied bravado, some sleight-of-hand, and the full force of his magnetic personality, Rhodes steadied his Janus-faced cabinet through the crises both of confidence concerning his multiple and conflicting interests and of conscience concerning the franchise. But it could not survive a further crisis—that of graft and morality. This new outrage of political opportunism weakened Rhodes' broader legitimacy as a leader, confirmed growing suspicions among South Africa's elite of his underlying ethical deficiencies, and demonstrated clearly to many how Rhodes the powerful behaved when even mildly cornered. The extent to which Rhodes was duplicitous may even have startled his friends, including those who had long before accepted that the great and powerful man had great and glaring flaws. As Mills commented as the Sivewright affair grew more ominous, "We have hitherto stood straight and uncorrupted before the world and it would be a sad calamity if that proud, though perhaps exceptional position of the Cape amongst her sister Colonies, were not maintained."[52] Rhodes himself was troubled less, however, for he had long before focused himself on the greater good, not the mere conventional means.

Rhodes liked Sivewright. He appreciated his efficiency, accepted his antagonistic attitude toward Africans, and counted him a clever, scheming ally. When Sivewright arranged Rhodes' favorite rail line to Johannesburg, Rhodes ordered Sivewright up a knighthood, and he became Sir James in mid-1892. Sivewright, too, was goal-oriented. But Sivewright was a crook, and Rhodes may unwisely have discounted that aspect of the jaunty Scotsman's character. When he came under definite suspicion in late 1892, it was discovered that he had seriously abused two earlier public works positions. As head of the Johannesburg Water Company he had, for a handsome profit, sold it water rights which he had earlier acquired for himself. Moreover, the consumers of Johannesburg had complained frequently of the quality and cost of the water which his pioneering concern had supplied. As manager of the Johannesburg Gas Company in 1890, he had signed a contract in exchange for a healthy bribe. It was alleged that a byproduct of the great railway negotiation was a side agreement for him secretly to share in a profitable contract for the cartage of goods between the Vaal and Johannesburg prior to the completion of the railway. Upon joining Rhodes' cabinet and becoming responsible for public construction and railways, he had distributed patronage lavishly to Bondsmen, and possibly accepted many a kickback. In 1891, when Innes was in Britain, Sivewright had attempted in a particularly underhanded way to reinstitute a magistrate who had earlier been discharged for harshness and severity toward African offenders. Only Innes' adamant attitude (when he discovered what had been attempted during his long absence) persuaded Rhodes to countermand Sivewright's excessive zeal.

The malfeasance in Sivewright's past only became relevant toward the end of 1892 when the *Cape Times* ran an exposé about the granting of a contract for the sale of meals and food on the entire railway system. The sale gave off a "very ancient and fish-like smell," said that newspaper. On the day before, Sivewright and Rhodes left Cape Town for a trip that would take them both (Merriman said that Sivewright "sticketh closer than a brother" to Rhodes) to Britain, the Continent, Egypt, and then back by the east-coast route.

Sivewright, the *Cape Times* revealed, had given James D. Logan a monopoly of food and beverage sales on all Cape trains and in all stations for eighteen years. Moreover, he had done so without taking competitive bids and without contacting the Colony's law department. Logan had risen from impoverished circumstances as a railway porter to wealth as the owner of a chain of stores along the Cape's main rail line. He owned a well-known resort hotel and already controlled some of the catering on the rail network. He and Sivewright were intimate friends.

"I was astonished the other day," Innes wrote to Rhodes, "to find . . . that Logan had been granted the monopoly of supplying refreshments at *all* stations upon the entire system for a term of years. Hardly believing the report," Innes continued, "I sent down to the Railway Department and they sent me up a copy of the contract. Anything more improper, in my opinion, it would be difficult to conceive." Among the documents that Innes had discovered, but which he and Merriman kept to themselves until they confronted Rhodes during the following April, was a letter from Logan requesting the desired terms, together with an explicit endorsement in Sivewright's hand.

(Sauer, however, told Rhodes of these details on 23 November 1892, which makes Rhodes' temporizing behavior even more venal than has long been suspected.) Logan was to pay a trifling amount, and "no tenders were called, though in the past tenders have always been called, even for the lease of a single refreshment-room." Innes declined to "share any responsibility for a job of this description." He disliked the need to write such a cheerless letter to Rhodes. However, Innes said, "I can't help it. I like fighting; but I do not like hanky-panky."[53]

Although Sivewright falsely claimed that he had never seen Logan's contract, Rhodes and Sivewright quickly agreed to a demand from the remaining cabinet members, and from Hofmeyr, that the monopoly be repudiated. "The contract must be cancelled," Rhodes telegraphed and wrote to Sauer on 19 and 25 November 1892. Aside from Logan's threat to sue the government for damages, that might have been the end of the nasty affair. Innes, at least, presumed that Sivewright would resign and spare his colleagues embarrassment. But he refused, a "sufficiently remarkable proceeding, and one which the pride of most of us would have made us," commented Innes, "hesitate to adopt." Even if he would not, Merriman, Sauer, and Innes assumed that Rhodes would dismiss him, thus relieving the cabinet of its sudden, unwelcome reputation as a "jobbing Ministry." Yet until Rhodes could return and decisions could be reached collectively, they did what was proper and contained themselves and their public responses. Considerately, they did not wish to force the premier's hand in any premature fashion. As Merriman explained to Currey, with Sauer and Innes he had come to the conclusion that "as honourable men we cannot continue to sit in the same Council Chamber [with Sivewright], and as soon as the Young Burgher comes out we shall put our reasons for thinking so before him." A month later Merriman told Mills that the cabinet was "waiting Rhodes's arrival for the inevitable row."[54] But Rhodes was playing a very different game, and playing it out of direct contact with his colleagues, with Sivewright often at his side. Throughout the northern winter months, when Rhodes was slowly making his way through Europe to Egypt, he studiously ignored their messages. "Surely," Rhodes cabled to Sauer in November, "you can manage without me" until January. To the governor, Rhodes cabled that he so wanted to see Egypt: "It is most probably my only opportunity."[55]

Merriman and Innes were readying their resignations, but hoping that Rhodes would keep the cabinet together by dismissing Sivewright. Rhodes, meanwhile, thought that he could retain Sauer, elevate Innes—"the Brutus of the conspiracy"—to the bench, and ship Merriman off to London as agent-general.[56] When he finally returned to Cape Town in March, with Sivewright following, Rhodes appeared "affability itself." He took the liberal trio's indictment of Sivewright quietly, but postponed action until the culprit himself should return. Although Merriman and Innes apparently thought that Rhodes would prove honorable, it is clear that Rhodes used this probably contrived hiatus— a matter of five weeks—to think through his options. He never intended to drop Sivewright, possibly because of the problems that doing so would occasion with the Bond, possibly because he liked Sivewright and Sivewright's style, and possibly because Sivewright knew sufficient to implicate Rhodes in some other unsavory business.

In late April Rhodes asked Innes for a full indictment. It was supplied on April 24. On the next day the liberal trio demanded that Rhodes procure an answer from Sivewright. Else they would resign. As Merriman and Rhodes were riding early the next morning, Rhodes casually told Merriman that Sivewright had provided a reasonable explanation of all the charges: the Logan matter was but an error in judgment and the Johannesburg accusation false. Merriman pulled the incriminating copy of the Logan contract out of his pocket. Rhodes then pretended to become angry at Sivewright, and sought to dissuade the liberal three from resigning. But he also deferred calling upon Sivewright to account for his actions for at least three days.

For a week longer Rhodes played a double or triple game. To Merriman and Innes he appeared morally outraged and in search of a resolution of the crisis. Yet his real desire was to preserve his own maneuverability. He needed to prevent their resignations. On April 30, Rhodes told Innes and Merriman that, since he could neither dismiss Sivewright nor continue to sit with him and " 'be besmirched with mud,' " he himself would resign and give the government back to Sprigg. Meanwhile he was plotting a different end game with Hofmeyr. Together they had decided to persuade Sir Henry de Villiers, the Colony's upright and stern chief justice, to leave the bench and become prime minister. Rhodes would remain as a minister without portfolio, and Hofmeyr would continue to help govern the country with Rhodes from behind the scenes. They reckoned that de Villiers would be content to take high level initiatives toward potential federation and leave the day-to-day governance of the country to them. Thus Rhodes began persuading de Villiers to take his own place on 27 or 28 April. By 29 April Rhodes smelled success. But in discussing who should be asked to sit in the cabinet, Rhodes carelessly showed the chief justice a list in Hofmeyr's hand. They were still talking, however, on the next day, 30 April, when Rhodes was pretending to follow a different line with Innes and Merriman. That evening de Villiers swallowed his pride, accepted Hofmeyr's list, and decided to take the premiership.

Rhodes and de Villiers were scheduled to meet on 1 May, a Monday. But Rhodes never again called on the chief justice. Apparently accidentally, Rhodes had met Sprigg on the steps of parliament. Nine months before Rhodes had contemplated moving Merriman out of the cabinet and giving Sprigg, his leading opponent, the treasury. "Rhodes thought that as he & I agreed upon so many great questions there would be no difficulty in our working together," remembered Sprigg. But Sauer was the obstacle, for Sprigg refused to work with someone he and others distrusted. Rhodes, always willing to square problems, asked Sprigg what he should then do with Sauer. Sprigg suggested sending him to Rhodesia, but Rhodes said that he wanted subordinates there upon whom he could "thoroughly rely." Because of the Logan scandal, Sprigg talked no more to Rhodes about joining the cabinet until their accidental rendezvous. At that meeting, Sprigg demanded a wholly new cabinet, not merely a remodeled one. Sprigg, always anxious for office despite his harsh criticisms the previous year of Rhodes, would bring Frost and Laing, the latter another strong critic of Rhodes, with him. Rhodes assented, and they had a deal which superseded that which was developing with de Villiers.[57]

Hofmeyr still had to be consulted. But he was away in Somerset West. So Rhodes spent "hours" on 2 May imploring Innes and Merriman to stay on. When he found that they were still intent on resigning, he "flounced out of the room in great temper"—supposedly to tender his own resignation. But it was all show. Rhodes that afternoon asked Sprigg if he could see him at 8 a.m. on the following day. Immediately after that talk, with no word to de Villiers or his liberal friends, Rhodes suddenly went to the governor, resigned, and accepted the governor's call to reconstitute a government. Faure remained as colonial secretary; Sprigg, who had recently denounced Rhodes' "ministry of discord," became treasurer general; Frost, secretary of native affairs; and Laing, commissioner of crown lands and public works. William P. Schreiner, a political neophyte, gifted advocate, and the younger brother of Olive Schreiner, the novelist, assumed the mantle of attorney general. "High honesty and a nice sense of honour, brilliant biting wit and moral courage, erudition and fearless criticism, [all] left Rhodes' cabinet," commented Vere Stent, a correspondent of the *Cape Times,* "and the door was open for sycophancy, opportunism and time-serving."[58]

Rhodes' first period as prime minister thus came to a self-boosting and ignominious end. He attempted to mollify the chief justice by intimating that he had of necessity had to do his best and "pull through" on his own—whatever that was supposed to mean. In the end, too, he even managed to protect Sivewright. Hofmeyr headed a parliamentary select investigation of the Logan contract. That committee, in turn, called the contract undesirable but ignored Sivewright's responsibility for its approval.[59]

Rhodes, in an adolescent fashion, tried to retain his ties to Merriman, too. He wanted and savored the victory, desired no break with friends, and also wished to keep abreast of what Merriman would say in opposition. Although he had made a better bed for himself, he wanted Merriman to continue riding with him. "I do not see why we should not have our morning rides. It is pretty wet and of course with shortening days they may be interrupted but I like to know your ideas. . . ."[60]

Merriman and Innes had been used. Rhodes had manipulated their indecisiveness. "The fact is," Merriman's wife confided to her diary, "that they ought to have sent their resignations in, as they all along intended to do, but got overruled by Mr. Rhodes." Sir Jacob Barry told Merriman that he should have resigned "the *moment* you found that Rhodes would not discard S. By not resigning, you gave R. the opportunity of *dishing* you and putting you in a false position." Barry also called attention to the dishonor of Sprigg and

Laing serving under Rhodes, having said that his dual positions were incompatible. "What does Mr. Rhodes say to having for his colleagues two men who have now repudiated those views?" For Merriman the result was indeed odd. "Elsewhere one would say that it was impossible, but here we are easy-going and people easily forget." Anyway, "the public conscience is seared with a hot iron."[61]

Rhodes had cauterized his own conscience, too, as his second period as prime minister so demonstrated. He dominated the new cabinet, dominated the country, and soon showed that the arrogant legislative course of his first term was but a precursor to that of his second. Merriman's mother assumed that Rhodes would be feeling "abashed," despising himself "for the line he has taken," but there is no indication that contrition or rigorous self-examination were ever discernible features of Rhodes' character. Had there been a de Villiers-Rhodes partnership, Innes suggests, there would have been no Raid.[62]

15

"I Must Have My Lions and Tigers"
Creating a Castle and Courting
the World

RHODES HAD CREATED a place for himself in the world. Its dimensions had already been affirmed by diamonds, gold, railways, interior territory to the north, and the bountiful reception he had received during the London season. The premiership of the Cape had expanded his public prominence and placed him in the center of concentric parliamentary, African, and imperial circles. Unlike so many men, he had succeeded in making his grandiose fantasies real and had laid the foundations for further triumphs.

"The feeling of a conqueror, that confidence of success," which Freud ascribes to a man's favored relationship with his mother, is usually put to the test by a man's mid-thirties. For many, especially the most self-absorbed and those whose dreams are far larger than their capabilities, the results are unhappy. Unmodified by the large and small vicissitudes of real life, their desires for special renown and extraordinary accomplishment are rebuffed. Stirred by the physical news that their youth is fleeting, by recurring evidence, even failures, that life is unforgiving, and by the passing calendar that the future is not forever, they come to know that the success to which they had felt entitled will remain elusive. The magnitude of their disappointment is measured by futile further attempts to achieve their dreams, by renewed fantasies, or by myriad forms of self-destruction.

For another group, the largest, the reports are mixed. Conditioned by the rough and tumble of human experience, most men are little surprised to learn that their time is limited and their horizons less than infinite. Cushioned by the warmth of their relationships, and less blinded by self-absorption, their interest in the application of their gifts propels them forward with fewer illusions to confront the second half of their lives.[1]

A very few, catapulted like Rhodes along a higher trajectory, discover in their mid-thirties that their youthful fantasies have been realized. For them the primrose path to the midpoint of their lives is marked by the kinds of successes which encourage further elaborations of their dreams and an expanding platform from which to thrust themselves into ever higher orbits. Everything that Rhodes had accomplished, from the amalgamation of the diamond mines through his added financial base in gold, and including the Rhodesian and Cape political experiences, confirmed his enriched sense of self.

In susceptible individuals, accomplishments of such a magnitude reinforce existing exuberant activity. In the Janusian manner of all useful personality traits, such activity affords protection against feelings of worthlessness and futility while simultaneously generating further victories. This was Rhodes' gift. More than many men, Rhodes hated passivity and relentlessly kept himself occupied and on the move. During his earlier years his world shifted with him; headquarters became wherever he happened to be. Aided by a loyal staff and the telegraph, he managed innumerable projects at the same time. He exulted in making things happen, especially if the results led to the achievement of greater goals.

The cascade of activities from 1888 to 1895, which began with the melding of the mines, was fueled by that first major triumph and each of the successes that followed. Those victories and the overwhelmingly upward slope of his personal projection permitted Rhodes to pass through the reassessment of his early midlife without pause. His vitality and swelling creativity were reaffirmed, his powers enhanced, and his capacities even more fully released.[2] By mid-1890 he had, almost overnight, entered the ranks of the most powerful dozen individuals in the English-speaking world. So doing neatly fitted his internal sense of closure and his confident, renewed pursuit of the goals set out in the "Confession of Faith"—that jumbled combination of youthful frustration against his own father and a longing to create a substitute fraternity of brothers. But his lifestyle, in harmony though it may have been with the pursuit of extreme entrepreneurialism on a rough frontier and with occasional forays as a back-bencher to Cape Town or as a promoter to London, hardly matched either his new status or the image of himself as a maturing man. Rhodes' myriad local and world responsibilities inevitably altered his carefree ways and led him to adopt at least a few of the trappings of adulthood.

Rhodes settled down more of psychological and social necessity than by preference. The requirements of politics and prominence demanded a fixed abode and a place in which to entertain, make deals, and orchestrate what was to remain a crucial, but only part-time occupation of colonial leadership. After he became premier, the managing director of the British South Africa Company, chief string puller for Rhodesia, railway manipulator, diamond magnate, and head gold digger needed something permanent. True, he preferred to be out on the veld, cascading telegraph messages from obscure sidings to subordinates across Africa and Europe, never quite abandoning his affinity (even in London and Paris) for the operating manner of a vagabond. The disciplined, fiercely concentrating mind of a supreme calculator could function in austere, inconvenient quarters. He asked for neither substantial nor ostentatious trappings of greatness, providing that there were problems to be solved, audiences (the mightier the better) to enthrall and excite, and reasonable access to attractive young male amanuenses, alcohol, and tobacco. Indeed, Rhodes, restless and reaching, was so much on the move that the great man at rest seemed to violate physical laws and contradict fundamental behavioral principles. Nevertheless, Rhodes intuitively understood how the assumption of the premiership, when coupled to his other titles, mandated a need not to slow down but to create a base for himself and his growing retinue of cronies, contacts, and acquaintances of influence. He needed a tangible representation of his newfound sense of place and prominence.

The acquisition of Groote Schuur in early 1891 marked a signal departure in Rhodes' way of life. Hitherto he had lived simply, in a rude hut near the Umkomaas River, amid the dusty hubbub of rambunctious Kimberley, in a wagon on trek, and in small hotels in Cape Town or its suburbs. Rhodes later boasted to parliament that he had lived for ten years in a house which cost £25 and had been "perfectly happy."[3] In these undistinguished surroundings he had taken his meals, no less casually than he had chosen his quarters. Never known for refined tastes, he particularly appreciated a "chop" or two while trekking. In Kimberley or Cape Town he dined—when he needed or wanted to dine—at his club or in assorted small hotels. As a neophyte prime minister he shared noisy rooms with Captain W.J. Penfold above a bank in Adderley Street, the city's main thoroughfare that runs downhill from parliament to the harbor. Penfold, harbor master and docks superintendent, is credited with ensuring that Rhodes, instinctively casual if left entirely to himself, made his social rounds in clothes which were sartorially suitable, if not smart. This last task fell to others—his secretaries or friends—when Rhodes traveled to London, where he usually occupied suites in one of two good hotels. Making sure that Rhodes was dressed appropriately kept his secretaries and valets permanently busy, especially as he grew older and more corpulent.

Although Rhodes owned Dalston, the family holding in Hackney (north of the City of London) after 1889, that estate had long before lost its manor house and never provided a home away from home. For him, it remained a source primarily of nostalgic investment. (Today it is a jumble of low- and high-rise council or public housing flats, one small, beige brick portion of which is named the Rhodes Estate.) Nevertheless, in his will of 1891, Rhodes styled himself "of Dalston in the Parish of St. John, Hackney."

Installed as premier in 1890 after rushing down to Cape Town from Kimberley, Rhodes had no time, and little inclination, to alter this gypsy-like pattern of life during the remainder of that year's legislative session. After returning to Kimberley, however, he decided that the business of politics required a house. "I find that my duties as Prime Minister will necessitate my being at Cape Town during the greater portion of the year," Rhodes informed Stow with a sense of practical urgency. He offered to lease Stow's unoccupied manor house in Wynberg, eight miles from Cape Town along the high eastern slopes of Table Mountain, and to maintain Stow's vast garden exactly as its owner desired. "Would you let me the house for twelve months . . . as I wish to take a house as soon as possible," he asked.[4] (He was also negotiating with three other owners, including Thomas Scanlen.) Either Stow wanted too much, or Rhodes learned that a more desirable, less distant, property was available. In early 1891 he arranged to lease Groote Schuur, then called The Grange, from the Jan van der Byl family for two years. He subsequently purchased the property's freehold for £200 in 1893, and lived there until his death.

Groote Schuur (the Great Granary) began its useful life in the eighteenth century as the residence of a Dutch East India Company's senior storekeeper. In the last years of the seventeenth century the Company had established three barns or store houses in De Rondedoorn Boschje, or Rondebosch (the Round Bush), across the Liesbeek River a few miles from the eastern edge of Cape Town. In these barns the Company kept its revenue-producing tithes and the wheat and wine with which it supplied its dependents in the nearby capital and the ships that called at the Cape amid their globe-girdling sails to distant Batavia. In 1791 the house and grounds passed into private hands; by the 1850s its early Cape Dutch fabric and lines had been altered and, after a fire in 1866, its traditional thatch was replaced by great slabs of blue slate. Nevertheless, it was considered grand enough as a neo-Georgian mansion to be occupied as a summer retreat by Governor Sir Henry Barkly in 1873–1876 and by Sir Hercules Robinson in the late 1880s. Although very few features of the original house remained by 1891, Rhodes doubtless was attracted to it as much because of its age and authenticity as he was by its favored location some way up the steep slope of Table Mountain, beneath the Devil's Peak extension.

The house faced the rising sun: "I know nothing more beautiful in the Cape landscape," said Fuller, "than the red glow in which it is bathed on a winter morning when the sun is searching the mists for the veiled rocks beyond." Groote Schuur's grandeur, its setting—"one of the most charming . . . that it is possible to find anywhere in the neighbourhood of Cape Town"— and the fact that governors had occupied it may also have appealed to Rhodes' growing sense of majesty.[5] Whether or not it invoked memories of Twyford House, his favorite haunt near Bishop's Stortford, it reinforced long-harbored but hitherto submerged fantasies of greatness. Rhodes was to make of Groote Schuur, and the 1500 adjoining acres along and on the mountain (soon acquired for £60,000), a formidable castle where the emperor and his great and small ideas had a free and glorious run. Groote Schuur was more than a habitation; it became an extension—a confirmation and a template—of Rhodes' mature personality in a time, admittedly, when wealth for him was of little object.

Realizing the fullness of Rhodes' aspirations for his first (and only) real dwelling place became possible after 1892, when a chance dinner meeting with Herbert Baker, a young, untried British architect who had come to the Cape to study the old houses and visit his brother, inspired Rhodes and inaugurated a fresh, creative, and synergistic partnership. At a dinner in the home of Louis Vintcent, a member of parliament and Merriman's brother-in-law, Baker claims to have "sat entranced," saying little or nothing, and leaving "discomforted at having proved myself so unable to make the most of [the] golden opportunity" of sitting opposite Rhodes. The premier, however, had noticed, and asked Agnes Merriman to tell him about "that silent young man." His looks or his manner must have made an impression. Rhodes was "fascinated." A few days later Rhodes asked Baker to help him restore Groote Schuur to its original style and character.

Baker, of a minor Kentish landowning family, "enjoyed from his youth an affinity with country life that inspired his devotion to traditional materials and workmanship." Educated in a small British public school, at the School of the Architectural Association, and at evening classes of the School of Design of the Royal Academy, where he was associated with the Arts and Crafts movement, Baker became a follower of Ruskin and William Morris. Morris, the author and social preacher, had founded the Society for the Protection of Ancient Buildings. Baker was also apprenticed to his uncle, an architect in London who restored churches. Baker believed in "rugged yet dignified simplicity," orderliness, and the "marriage of all the arts, with an emphasis not so much on novelty as quality of craftsmanship." After Rhodes' death, Baker explained that, as an architect, he opposed "conscious straining after invention or originality . . . . There must be good building and a frank acceptance of modern methods and materials. The controlling mind must heat and weld into his orderly conception . . . [the] subtlety and industry [of indigenous] . . . craftsmanship." The best buildings "have eminently the attributes of law, order, and government, to the extent, some might say, of dullness, the defect of these qualities." When he worked in India (and his public buildings in South Africa and Britain also show the same tendency) Baker sought through structure to "put the stamp of British sovereignty"—British classical architecture—on the structures of the raj.[6] Rhodes would have been attracted to the earliest manifestations of this post-Ruskinian approach, as well as to Baker's qualities as a horseman, to his aesthetic cast of mind, and to his determination to conceive solid, easily accessible buildings with the Roman echoes which pleased Rhodes' growing acceptance of his own personal imperial qualities.

Other than its quaintly twisted chimneys and many gables, when Baker took Groote Schuur in hand there was little external evidence of its seventeenth-century origins. A watercolor sketch, probably rather idealistic, existed of the original front of the house, but that was all. Moreover, in a disconcerting way, Rhodes refused to think through in any detail what he wanted from the massive project of architectural renewal. "I was surprised," said Baker, "that such a man, the chairman of great business corporations, should give me no details or defined instructions of what he wanted." After telling Baker in a few words of his "thoughts," he "trusted" the youthful but appealing artist to "do the rest." Rhodes had a host of visions, but could hardly bother himself with every precise plan, particularly since some schemes were invented to engage the talents of men to whom he was attracted, or with whom he wished to remain closely involved.

Yet Baker discovered that Rhodes had definite, if untutored and rather rustic tastes that were well ahead of his contemporaries. In the early 1890s, the painstaking handiwork of local artisans had largely been superseded—thanks to the transportation revolution which had followed the introduction of commercial steamships on the long haul from Britain to the Cape—with inexpensive goods and fittings ready-made in Europe. Rhodes wanted none of the new gimcracks; he abhorred imported iron fittings, hinges, handles, and so on. Preferring "the big and simple," the "barbaric," he wanted original, unpainted woods, whitewashed walls, and metalwork hammered of iron or cast in brass or bronze in the older manner. Sir Henry Lucy praised a wardrobe—"a massive structure in black oak, severely simple in design, a silver lock and silver hinges glistening on his dark surface."[7] Rhodes told Baker to replace painted deal planks with teak, to expose the old beams of rough wood, and to try to transform the whole edifice into a mansion adapted to the wet, cool winters and hot summers of the Cape peninsula.

Baker provided a new front for the rambling, run-down house, "restored" the rear portion, added a long stoep, or verandah, built a block for the kitchens and for Rhodes' staff, and then supplemented the whole with a wing containing a ground-floor billiard room and second-story bedroom for the master with a large bay window facing Devil's Peak. Before this final addition was completed in 1894, Rhodes had insisted upon sleeping in a little room at the back of an outbuilding attached to the main house, in what had been a part of the original slave quarters. Baker finally demolished the slave quarters to improve a view of Table Mountain, but also to help propel Rhodes into quarters that Baker and others believed more suitable for their hero and patron.

Visitors praised the reconstructed house. It was approached "by a long avenue of enormously high Scotch firs, which almost [met] aloft, and remind[ed] one of the nave of some mighty cathedral, such is the subdued effect produced by the sunlight even on the brightest summer day," wrote Lady Sarah Wilson (Randolph Churchill's sister) after a visit in 1895. "A slight rise in the road, a serpentine sweep, and the house itself comes into view, white, low, and rambling, with many gables and a thatched roof."

The house's most distinctive feature was the wide rear stoep, or covered verandah, with a floor of black and white checkered marble. It stretched the length of the building and was used as a "delightful lounge."[8] In fair weather it was the focus of activity; receptions, discourses, and frequent meetings of the famous and the important were held there under the massive stucco pillars which supported its canopy and "so strikingly" harmonized with the mountain views on which it opened. "I once saw as many as fifty people taking tea under this verandah," recalled Fuller. He described the view of the mountain from the stoep as one which, "singularly beautiful," possessed Rhodes "all the years of his life . . . particularly when the flowers were in bloom. On the right was a deep-cut ravine [which] . . . as it opened to the sunshine with a sweeping curve, was filled with hydrangeas of a rich blue tint, so that to the visitor looking from the stoep, the whole valley was filled with colour, softening into paler hues, and mingling with the mountain grasses as it reached higher ground."[9]

Inside the house Baker created a spacious, formidable hall, framed by massive, solid teak pillars, where Rhodes displayed artifacts of the African interior, including many formidable shooting trophies, African shields, spears, and guns (products of the conquest of the Ndebele). A dark drawing room and darker dining room with high beams and walls of somber but impressive teak set a stately tone. The main dining table was a slab of teak. Indeed, the entire house was remarkable for its use of teak, imported from Burma and the east as the early Dutch and Huguenots had done, but on a lavish scale new to the Cape. Most of the other rooms, smaller than might have been expected in so large a house, had, as Rhodes wished, walls and ceilings of plaster and whitewash. Although Baker tried to wallpaper several rooms in 1895, Rhodes insisted that the "horrid" stuff be removed.

His own bedroom was simply furnished. The bed, cramped, high, and austere, appears harshly uncomfortable to modern eyes. On the walls nearby were a portrait of Prussian Chancellor Otto von Bismarck and, later, a small photograph of Nyambezana, a Ndebele matriarch who, in 1896, helped bring Rhodes together with the chiefs against whom he was making war. He liked to invite visitors to see the bedroom because of its commanding view of Table Mountain. "So large was its window," remembered McDonald, "and so near the mountain that one felt when looking out that one was already treading one of the paths upon the steep hillside."[10]

Yet it was his bathroom, down a passageway from the main bedrooms, which conceivably bore the full stamp of the man and his feeling for himself. The walls and floor of this room were of green and white marble—cool and serene. Its centerpiece was a magnificent eight-foot long bath hollowed out of a solid block of granite and transported forty-five miles from Paarl. "What a bath! Always the horrid cold of the marble as one sat down, a bath full of hot water despite," reported Will Stuart. (Stuart, Olive Schreiner's young nephew, often played at Groote Schuur during the late 1890s.[11]) Like the complicated contraption that served as a traveling bath in his private railway car (now in the National Museum of Zimbabwe), the tub at Groote Schuur accommodated Rhodes' growing girth and declining mobility. As with the house itself, for Rhodes the grandeur of the bath echoed what he had read of the attachment of Roman emperors to their own baths as statements of status.

Rhodes' cleanliness was fundamental to his being. Although he dressed casually, his clothes were described as shabby, and he usually never cared much about his surroundings, he was obsessed with keeping his body clean. No matter the circumstances of his travel in the bush, Rhodes never failed to bathe and shave. "He loved to have his bath in the open," reported a secretary. "As soon as the waggons were halted . . . [his valet] spread a waterproof sheet behind the nearest tree, . . . [and] provide[d] a bucket of water. . . ." Rhodes bathed with a huge sponge "which he dipped into the bucket . . . and squeezed over his body." Fastidious as he was about his own cleanliness, he also commanded his companions to bathe after their exertions, and had a horror of them—even on the veld—appearing unshaven. "I always thought that it was most curious that he should be so particular about shaving," reported Jourdan. "He could shave himself even in a train traveling fifty miles an hour and swerving from side to side."

Although a heavy smoker, he hated the refuse of other smokers as he hated dirt and untidiness (or unpunctuality) of any kind. It irritated him intensely, so much so that he and Baker purchased a number of antique brass cuspidors (spittoons) which Dutch housewives had formerly placed on their red-tiled floors. "Rhodes," remembered Baker, "would often shame his guests by rising and transferring their messes to the spittoon." An employee in the headquarters of the Gold Fields Company, which Rudd controlled more directly than Rhodes, remembered that the great man was very fussy about the kemptness of others and of the company's offices, even though his own dress was hardly exemplary. "I had to clear the back of the Goldfields office every day of litter when Rhodes was about, and to run to the mines beforehand to warn the managers. . . ."[12] Even on trek Rhodes remained fastidious, refusing to camp unless the selected site was cleared of all unsightly debris. However tired he might be, he would always search for a virgin outspan.

Within the recesses of his reconstructed house Rhodes created one of the more unusual libraries in the Western world. There Rhodes did most of his work; it was in that room "that the details of many of his big schemes have been thought out and decided upon," reported his second biographer. "The most striking thing in the room," Hensman continued, was "a tattered old union-jack, a memento of some hardfought field . . . which hangs on the wall . . . facing the chair in which Rhodes usually sits." There was a Portuguese flag, too, captured by Forbes in Manicaland in 1891. The dominating features of the library, however, were the well-filled shelves of books and documents that ran three-quarters of the way up the walls. Rhodes collected old maps of Africa and books and journals about the exploration and history of his adopted continent. In 1892 he sent a member of the staff of the Cape parliament to Europe to purchase rare books and manuscripts on Africa for his own library. Central to his personal reading and abiding interests, however, were the classics of his youth—Seneca, Epictetus, Plutarch, Gibbon, and *The Meditations of Marcus Aurelius*. He carried a well-thumbed, personally marked-up copy of this last book with him everywhere, favoring such aphorisms as "Can any man think he exists for pleasure and not for action or exertion?" or "Go to the Ant, thou sluggard; consider her ways and be wise." For him the *Meditations* were the epitome of common sense.[13]

The 101 passages which Rhodes underlined in the *Meditations* betray a preoccupation with four ideas. They were his "guide in life," he told Cecilia Sauer (the wife of Hans). She had thoughtfully despatched a "choice" copy of the *Meditations* to Rhodes, thinking that his prized copy had been lost in a fire. A few months later, when they dined together in the Burlington Hotel in London, Rhodes returned the "choice" copy to his friend: "I don't want it— you see my own copy never leaves me," he explained. However, Rhodes had been deeply touched by her concern. " 'I want to show you that I appreciate the kind thought very much—yes! very much!' " he exclaimed in "the jerky awkward way he spoke when he was at all moved." Rhodes said that he would do for her what he had never done for anyone else in the world. He drew his own copy of the *Meditations* from his pocket and urged her to take it home and keep it for exactly three days. " 'It is my guide in life,' " he cautioned, " '. . .my most precious possession.' " " 'Don't lose it,' " he commanded. " 'Don't let it out of your possession, there are many people who would give a great deal to see it. Don't lend it to anyone—don't let anyone see it.' " Sauer did as she had been bid, but since Rhodes had indicated that he had " 'marked the passages which should rule [his] conduct. . . ,' " Sauer underlined those same maxims in her own copy, fortunately recovering it from a house in France after World War II.[14]

Each of the aphorisms which Rhodes marked reinforced his own view of himself, confirming that particular mixture of guile, naïveté, and self-deception which characterized so much of his adult behavior. More than a quarter of the underlined assertions deal with death—with death as an aspect of life. The end may come at any time, lifespans are short, and wealth, fame, and grandeur are extinguished with an individual's death. Those who die young are not appreciably less fortunate than those who live long. In either case it makes sense to live one's life as if death were imminent and, fatalistically, to accept whatever comes as the playing out of a natural order.

A second set of passages reflected Rhodes' desire that intellect should prevail over the emotion to which he was so susceptible. They also provide a moral framework for his empathic gifts. Reason was declared to be more important than passion. One should study one's own motives as well as the motives of others. Making moral judgments was hazardous unless one understood the other person's reasoning about right and wrong. Evil hurts the evildoer more than the victim.

Rhodes' life-long allegiance to grand designs and his belief in hard work directed his pen to a third set of passages. They affirm the need to do what was serious, not frivolous, and what was right, even if unpopular. Actions, directed Marcus Aurelius, should primarily be for the good of others or society. Just acts were their own reward. Finally, a fourth but linked group of underlined passages asserted that, although self-reliance was important, success in life involved working with others and being prepared to alter one's inner convictions if more powerful arguments were offered by one's friends or associates.

Rhodes was an omnivorous reader; but not necessarily with direction.

Instead of focused intellectual activity he displayed the versatility of interest which studies of leadership have found to be more highly predictive of eminence among leaders than standard measures of intelligence. He doted on William Makepeace Thackeray's *Vanity Fair* and on the historical works of Thomas Carlyle and Anthony Froude, scanned contemporary novels and classical treatises, and had an affinity for the mystical and cabalistic.

He read at night for a half-hour before falling asleep. According to Harry Currey, Rhodes' reading lacked any method. Before one sea voyage to Britain Rhodes asked Currey how many days they would be on board. "Twenty," said his secretary. Rhodes promptly walked into a bookshop and selected forty books at random. "One for the morning and one for the afternoon," Rhodes said. Jourdan remembered bringing fifty books along on other voyages. "Of course he could not read them all, but he loved to sit in his cabin and have them scattered on the floor round him. He liked dipping into one and then putting it down and taking up another, and so he went on until he found a volume that interested him. . . ."[15]

Although Rhodes' personal reading and interests were thus wide and eclectic, he returned again and again to Gibbon's *Decline and Fall of the Roman Empire*. Its account of the glories of Rome as well as its celebration of the virtues of celibacy for pre-medieval popes inspired his vision of his own and Britain's imperial destiny.[16] But, deprived as he had been of a classical education, he could not delve more deeply than Gibbon itself. Good English translations of the classical authorities cited in Gibbon being unavailable, and his own Latin and Greek being deficient, Rhodes could hardly satisfy a long-suffered curiosity easily. Complaining about this quandary during a visit to Britain in 1893, he was directed to the manager of Hatchard & Company, the prominent London firm of booksellers. One afternoon, reported Arthur Humphreys, Rhodes and Rochfort Maguire called on him in Charing Cross. Rhodes asked for translations of all of the original authorities used by Gibbon: they were to be in English and completely unabridged. Realizing the magnitude of this undertaking, Rhodes asked Humphreys to employ a body of scholars (eventually thirty) under a "parson-pedagogue" who would serve as general editor, as well as indexers, typists, and binders. The translators— "men, matrons, and maids"—for the most part toiled away in the British Museum reading room. They included ex-dons of good Oxbridge colleges, who had "drifted into matrimony," and others of talent. All were sworn to secrecy: their client, explained Hatchard, was "a millionaire who does not wish his name to appear." Before too long there were 200 volumes, all handsomely bound in square-sized morocco. They included the works of Aeschylus, Aristides, Catullus, Dio Cassius, Euripides, Horace, Martial, Menander, Nicolaus of Damascus, Plautus, Procopius, Quintus Curtius, Sabine, Statius, and Terence; a description of the wives of the twelve Caesars; studies of Islam; the works of Muslim geographers and a few medieval philosophers; and something called Erotic Epigrams. Many had never been consulted by Gibbon. Hatchard added a supplementary series of eighteen biographies of Roman emperors, possibly because Rhodes, believing that he physically resembled the Emperor Titus and that his thought processes were like those of the Emperor Hadrian, wished to learn about their lives. (Rhodes called a halt to this vast indulgence of compiled knowledge only in 1898, by which time more than £8,000 had been expended, and books—the works of fathers of the Church, among others—were arriving which he had not expressly ordered.) Lucy remembered him at Groote Schuur, seated after dinner on the stoep, "with the moon shining in a blue sky almost as brightly as the sun over London town," talking "by the hour about ancient Rome and its warrior emperors."

In Rhodes' library this expansive collection presented a remarkable appearance, contrasting as it did with the Founder's more orthodox assemblage of published books. Over all brooded an abstract soapstone figure of a bird that had been liberated from the ruins of Great Zimbabwe. (Five similar birds were carved of wood to embellish the teak bannister as it climbed the ample stairs from the ground floor hall to the upper floor's many bedrooms.) Elsewhere in the library, Rhodes kept a large collection of solid stone phalli, also from Zimbabwe. What these phalli meant to or for Rhodes can only remain a matter of speculation. Whether the similarly frank accounts in the unabridged typescripts of the ancients excited him, or whether he even read deeply in them, is obscure; only a few carry his characteristic underlinings.[17]

Rhodes, guided by Baker, gradually developed strong views about how Groote Schuur should be furnished. Although initially he was content to stuff Groote Schuur with antiques (fake and otherwise) shipped from Europe, he came to admire the plain and the old, particularly those heavy farmhouse pieces which had been fashioned from indigenous woods peculiar to southern Africa. They were Baker's ideal, but the search for local craftsmen to fashion fittings and furniture, shutters, and massive doors, and to replace the Welsh slate with local thatch, were as much a product of Rhodes' insistence as Baker's inspiration. Where Rhodes could buy no local older furniture, his new atelier of artisans fashioned them of local stinkwood, rosewood, and Zambezi teak. Baker reported that Rhodes was particularly pleased with a glass cabinet of black ebony, and chairs and benches made by Afrikaners on the far frontier. He purchased engraved Dutch glass, Chinese and Japanese porcelain—anything, in fact, which had been imported into the Cape by its original proprietors. Baker described Rhodes as less a collector and connoisseur than a man of slowly awakened knowledge and interest who "took pleasure" in "seeing that each piece had its own purpose and place in his house." Because they were the playthings of other men of wealth, and possibly because his aesthetic sensibilities were both original and idiosyncratic, he never purchased paintings other than one of Sir Joshua Reynolds' portraits of a young married woman, which was hung over the main fireplace in the dining room where Rhodes could see it from his place at the head of the table. It was a painting that he knew in reproduction from his childhood; when he acquired sufficient capital, he bought it and possessed memory as well as art. "Now I have my lady and I am happy," he said.[18]

Merriman and others of prominence in Cape political life, who derided Rhodes' emphasis on the traditional, thought that in so recreating and furnishing a domicile in accord with the Dutch and Huguenot heritage of the Cape (and, unwittingly, setting a national standard for subsequent generations) Rhodes was seeking through personal means as well as his public endeavors to curry favor and cement relations with the Bond. Merriman, among the more cultured men in the Cape, even suggested that Baker, instead of renovating the old granary, should construct a fine Tudor mansion for Rhodes.

Fitting Groote Schuur into so parochial a framework was unfair. Rhodes was historically minded, as his readings and the nature of his library exemplified. He admired Britain, but in his life work sought to transcend any tendencies which might be considered effete in English life or, indeed, in himself. Whether or not by himself he would have come to appreciate the simple lines of the Cape houses and furniture, under Baker's tutelage he promoted the authentic over the trendy, the solid over the ephemeral, and the indigenous over the imported.

Rhodes also had an instinctive feel for the broad, open, uplifting expanse of Africa. Entranced and spiritually ennobled by the omnipresent hulk of Table Mountain, as well as by views from its heights of the great arch of Table Bay to the north, with ships at anchor from Europe and Asia; of the distant Cape of Good Hope to the south, where the waters of the Atlantic and Indian oceans mix; and of the Cape flats, False Bay, and the snowcapped Hottentots Holland mountains into the glare of the sun in the eastern dawn, Rhodes impressed nearly all of his acquaintances with his love of the Cape's fairest majesty. A ledge, well above Groote Schuur, and now adorned with the original of George Frederic Watts' statue, *Physical Energy,* provided cherished views both of the Atlantic and Indian oceans. As well it was a special place where Rhodes could brood, commune with nature, and—if solitary—scheme, or—if with others—expound and elaborate. Here, remembered Fuller, Rhodes came to be "alone with the Alone." The mountain, which Rhodes loved with an "intensity," was where he found his church.[19]

In his own lifetime, no contemporary ever doubted or denied the depths of Rhodes' devotion to the mountain as an embodiment of nature. An instinctive conservationist and ecologist long before such views were fashionable in most of the empire, Rhodes in his prime echoed many of the sentiments about the elements and his surroundings that he shared with his mother when still young, writing to her from and about Natal. During the 1890s, at least, he thought of himself as a custodian who could use his new wealth to preserve and protect the Cape's and South Africa's natural heritage for future generations. Even within the confines of his own estate, indeed on the very steps of Groote Schuur, he welcomed passersby, picnickers, and others who his employees would have preferred to discourage. Rough with rivals, and ruthless in business, Rhodes displayed a warm, soft side. He looked always beyond his own lifetime, and accepted a responsibility to posterity in his dealings with and reverence for the natural as well as the traditional built environment.

From his first days in Groote Schuur, Rhodes sought to expose the house to the widest and boldest views, to bring Africa into it and to place it in Africa. He wanted to tame as well as respect the mountain which towered everywhere overhead: "I have bought all this," he told Baker after he had painstakingly acquired much of the land on the eastern flanks of the mountain, "but I don't possess it."[20] In order to add to the mountain's glory, to celebrate its tree-covered granite mass, and to strengthen his own claims, Rhodes attempted both to restore it to an earlier, undesecrated state and to make its beauty more accessible. He purchased the rights of several water companies in order to remove their unsightly reservoir from the mountain's summit, established paths and roads to open up its scenic vistas, planned the long highway which, nearly a century later, carries streams of automobiles from the city around and through the forests of its northeastern shoulders to the suburbs of Rondebosch and Constantia Nek. He planted rows of oak and pine, laid out vast grasslands and walks below the mountain and Groote Schuur, planted brilliantly hued salvia and pale blue plumbago beyond his stoep and let the wild pelargonia and arum lilies lie undisturbed. He placed great gates of teak and sneezewood (both impervious to termites) at the edges of his estate.

Beyond, toward the higher elevations of Devil's Peak, Rhodes created a paddock for antelopes, zebra, eland, wildebeeste, ostriches, and other African wildlife, and for kangaroos, wallabies, and emu imported from Australia. A few lions were caged, but for them and others he contemplated a much larger, grander enclosure where the kings and queens of the grasslands could roam near his own abode in semi-freedom. "I must have my lions and tigers roaming about in their natural state: I cannot have them cooped up in a little den," he told Menpes, identifying with their power and their need to be free and unfettered. But he wanted to view them from a marble platform modeled, as he once discussed with Baker, on the Roman Temple of Theseus. This was a project which never succeeded; nor did his attempt to introduce British rooks and songbirds to the Cape. Although the nightingales, chaffinches, thrushes, blackbirds, and rooks proved poor colonists, Rhodes is responsible for letting loose on the Cape a plague of starlings, those adaptable immigrants. There were later times when he envisaged a Roman-influenced memorial of stone on the mountain and a temple or "bath" of Roman inspiration for Kimberley. The first alone was achieved as, also after his death, the Oxford-like university that he had wanted was constructed above Groote Schuur in Rondebosch.

Not far from his own manor house, and realizable during his own life-time, were two other constructions—houses in the Dutch style on the foundations of much earlier ones. Rhodes conceived them, and Baker, instructed not to "be mean," oversaw their construction. The first, a modest Cape Dutch building in shining white and teak, with a thatched roof, became Welgelegen, the initial occupants of which were John Blades Currey and his wife, old friends from Kimberley. Rhodes told Baker that he could not "forget that in the early days of Kimberley, when I was friendless, Mrs. Currey always asked me to spend Christmas with them." The second reconstruction, a smaller cottage of vintage proportions, became the Woolsack, and the winter home in the late 1890s of Rudyard Kipling. It was built "for poets and artists, in order that the mountain might inspire them. . . ."[21]

For a bluff, unsentimental man of epoch-shaking interests, Rhodes cared passionately for his garden. "I love to dream there," he told an artist toward the end of his life. Rhodes talked grandly of "handling clumps and masses of colour. 'I must feel the colour,' he said." Indeed, Rhodes' horticultural philosophy was in keeping with his instructions to Baker about Groote Schuur and his affinity for the towering mountain. "You can't overdo the massing of flower in a garden," he said. "In South Africa everything must be done in masses." He had planned his garden to be in sympathy with Table Mountain, not with the suburban English ideal. The flowers in his garden were not grouped together in trim beds of careful contrast, but were instead "permitted to grow in semi-wildness in huge masses." There were clumps of scarlet and orange cannas, bougainvilleas, and fuchsias, and all around one end of the house a profusion of roses, "bewildering to the eye." Just as camphor and oak were his favorite trees, passionflowers with their unusual star-shaped flowers of greenish-white, blue, and deep purple were his favorite ornamentals. When an avenue of trellises was being planned for these vines at the Groote Schuur estate, a manager asked whether it should be fifty or one hundred yards long. "Make it a mile," was Rhodes' reply.[22]

Rhodes was beginning to create a historical and symbolic affirmation of his own creative being and an affirmative expression of an intuitive mid-life reassessment. Groote Schuur (the house, estate, and aesthetic statement) was the metaphor of a practical visionary, of a ruthless entrepreneur who possessed gentle aspirations to build structures for the pleasure of future generations and whose sense of himself was in contemplative harmony with and in control of a vigorously altering world. Yet the center of the physical edifice was destroyed in December 1896. A mysterious fire turned the thatched house into a blackened ruin; despite the zinc and asbestos that lined the roof, personal papers, some of the valuable furniture and furnishings, and some of his 2,000 books were destroyed.[23] Baker and others contemplated rebuilding the house on a position higher up the slope, with a command over distant views, "better" air, and more space. But Rhodes, who was in Rhodesia at the time and apparently took the news calmly, even matter-of-factly, decreed a thorough reconstruction (Baker's fullest) on the original site for reasons of sentiment and because of the existence of his extensive garden.

Earl Grey received the disquieting report of the fire from A.H. Holland, one of Rhodes' secretaries in the Cape. When Grey told Rhodes that there was bad news, Rhodes, who had earlier been warned by Bourchier F. Hawksley that Jameson was ill, cut him off. "Do not tell me Jameson is dead." When he heard that the news was only of Groote Schuur gutted, he said, "Thank goodness: Groote Schuur can be rebuilt, but Jameson could never be replaced." Subsequently he ordered Stevens to make his bedroom and billiard rooms habitable. Put up tents for the others, he said. "I mean to stay at my house and nowhere else. I am very pleased to hear so many of the old things have been saved."[24]

Every detail of the first reconstruction was repeated in the post-fire restoration. Baker added new flourishes, too. Rhodes was persuaded that thatch was too dangerous; British-made tiles (rather than slate or the corrugated iron which covered so many houses of the era) were the tasteful substitute. He also installed electric light rather than tallow candles or lanterns.

Before and after the fire, Rhodes deployed his house both as a retreat and base to which he could invite others and from which he could dispense lavish hospitality. His house, and certainly his grounds, were his alone most fully in the early morning. Indeed, if the weather were fair he would rise with the dawn and, after a cold bath, ride for miles around, about the mountain or down on the flats before breakfast—sometimes to the impatience of hungry guests such as Kipling. "I think Rhodes was happiest when he was on horseback," his valet recalled. "He used to put on a pair of his white duck trousers and a white shirt—usually open at the neck—jam a slouch hat on his big head, and he'd be off up the mountainside on his horse. He'd carry his switch at arm's length and ride with a long stirrup, his legs stuck straight out in front of him in the old South African way."[25]

If the weather were foul he sent for his secretary at daybreak and, pacing up and down the back stoep in his pajamas, would dictate letters and cables. Then he would go to his office in a Cape cart. If parliament were not sitting, he would return home after lunch to work or hold court, again on the back stoep. Sometimes he indulged in billiards or played whist; during the day he preferred to talk little, conserving his voluble side until dinner. At dinner there were nearly always a few, sometimes a dozen or more guests. He would sit at the long teak table absorbed in talk until ten. Suddenly, at that hour, he would "break off and steal away to bed."[26]

Le Sueur called Rhodes' method of dealing with his correspondence "extraordinary." In the 1890s his secretary (Le Sueur was one) opened everything that arrived, and on his own, answered about 90 percent without consulting Rhodes. The important 10 percent was shown to Rhodes, who would provide replies for a small proportion and make no comment on the remainder. Yet he would "by no means forget" about the ones that he had at first ignored. Weeks or months afterward he might ask for one of those letters. "His memory was marvelous. He seemed to carry a sort of ledger in his head & would criticize & correct pages of a/cs. without reference to any books."

When traveling to Rhodesia or elsewhere Rhodes would receive twenty or thirty messages at a telegraph station. He would read them two or three times and hand them back to his secretary before going to bed. "Next morning early [he would] start dictating replies . . . without again referring to the wires." He would not "miss a point."

Rhodes was not always methodical, however. "Now & then he would cram a telegram into his trouser or breast pocket & it would never be seen again." Or he would shove important, confidential documents into unlikely receptacles, like the vases in Groote Schuur, or under cushions there. Some remained in those hiding places "to the day of his death."[27]

Rhodes' moments of enjoying Groote Schuur in any kind of solitude were rare, for his business and political interests, as well as his practice of keeping an open house for local and overseas visitors, meant that Groote Schuur was rarely empty. Presumably that is the way Rhodes in his late thirties and early forties preferred to live. Dispensing largesse had its political purposes; so did bringing numerous parliamentary foes as well as friends home for lunch. But Rhodes, intolerant of inactivity, also appreciated being the center of constant bustle. In his home he could direct the conversation and the pace and quality of the unfolding tableau. Gathering around himself men and women of talent and importance he could, or not, as he chose, make himself the center of rapt attention and concern. Without counting the costs of food, running Groote Schuur the way Rhodes wanted it to be run cost about £4,000 a month.

"One did not know the real Rhodes," said Michell, "until one sat at his table and heard him discourse at large on the great political events and social questions of the day, or, at rarer intervals, on those profounder problems of the future, to which he bent a forward and far-seeing gaze." Fuller, one of his close colleagues in parliament, suggested that there was no more "interesting luncheon and dinner table in the whole Empire." At it visitors found themselves talking to hunters and surveyors from the interior; railway and telegraph builders; Roman Catholic and Protestant missionaries, including smooth Anglican bishops and rough Primitive Methodists; businessmen from the Rand and Kimberley; mining and agricultural experts from overseas; British soldiers and politicians; financiers from Europe; the political elite of the Cape; journalists from all over the world; and, in time, ladies of title or special attainment. "There was no stiffness, no formality," said Fuller. "Every guest was at his ease, and full of talk of hunting adventures, perils on the lakes . . . , [the] successes or discouragement in missionary work, and of the progress of the railways through the interior, while through it all ran that touch of romance which life and work in half-explored regions is sure to give."

In 1893 William Alexander, Archbishop of Armagh and Primate of all Ireland, arrived in Cape Town to marry his daughter Kathleen to George Bowen, one of Rhodes' pioneers. Alexander was well-connected; these ties resulted in an invitation to hold the wedding at Groote Schuur, and for the bride's family to stay with Rhodes there along with Rhodes' sister Edith, brother Ernest, and a cousin, who had all traveled out together on the *Dunnottar Castle*. The Governor and Lady Loch attended the wedding; Rhodes gave the bride away with "a gentle air," the archbishop recalled, trying to restrain all emotion, but there were tears in Rhodes' eyes. "One of the strange contradictions of [Rhodes'] nature," said Alexander, "was its intensely emotional side."

Rhodes, his contemporaries said, "was always the life of the gatherings. He was never more winning, never more mesmeric, than at the head of his own table. He never dominated the company, as some hosts do, with dogmatic opinions, but [as his mother might have done] drew information and ideas from his guests with happy tact and skill." For Lady Sarah Wilson, the magic was Rhodes' "singularly expressive voice, [his] (at times) persuasive manner, and, above all, the interesting things his big ideas gave him to say," and certainly not any eloquence, which kept both his guests at his table and his colleagues in parliament attentive.

To Baker, Rhodes had a natural gift for hospitality. "He would think out, as his method of talk was, those of his own thoughts most suited to each person in his company and, dismissing gossip and small talk, would lead conversation by plunging directly and frankly into deep issues. . . . He had the skill [like his mother] of making each person think his own subject and point of view of the greatest importance." In late 1895, for example, Charles Wellington Furse, an English artist hoping to paint Rhodes' portrait for Oriel College, attended a dinner in Cape Town a few weeks before the Jameson Raid. "Last night," he wrote, "I dined with Rhodes . . . Jameson, Sir Charles Metcalfe, and two others." Rhodes started the dinner "by saying things about English artists with the intention of drawing me—it resulted in a very amusing conversation—his method is to begin by being rude and if he frightens you, you are dished—if you keep your end up, however, and especially if you get him to the boundary, he soon thaws and become very genial." Groote Schuur thus attracted a continuous stream of distinguished men, nearly all of whom fell immediately under Rhodes' spell, and proceeded to "unburden themselves with a charming freedom which the atmosphere of the place seemed to favour."[28]

"It has been my lot during a long life to converse with some of the most distinguished talkers of the day," recalled Archbishop Alexander. "I must say that, in my opinion, Cecil Rhodes [in 1893] would have been hard to beat when he was quite at home with his company, and sure of understanding and sympathy. There was power of thought, originality of expression, and more humour than those who knew him slightly were ready to credit him with. There was also a most intense and shrinking sensitiveness, a key to his character not, I think often found." Lucy felt that Rhodes "had a heart as tender as a woman's." Baker, who knew Rhodes over a longer period, and in a variety of companies, was equally impressed with Rhodes the talker. But, just as often, Rhodes' remarks proved a cadenza of platitudes. He bored experienced guests with stories and thoughts endlessly reiterated. "I can confirm," said Baker, "that in some ways he retained some of the characteristics of a child," not least when he presided over his own table in his own mansion. Kipling reported that Rhodes' character was "child-like in its simplicity and with a feminine intuition."

This allusion to the child in Rhodes was echoed by Menpes, the painter. In the late 1890s Menpes assured Rhodes that he would never grow old. "Your mind is young, and you are young: you must always be a boy!" This was welcome music to Rhodes' ears. Rhodes repeated the thought over and over again in exultation, " 'I am a boy! I am a boy! Of course I shall never get old!' "[29]

Rhodes had a serious, brooding side. But, at least during the 1890s at Groote Schuur, he delighted in expressing his boyish, competitive self by playing parlor games of the mind, as well as bridge, billiards, and pool. Lady Alexander reported that he was also fond of palmistry and crystal gazing. Contemporary observers remarked on his juvenile pleasure for what they called absurd games that taxed remembrances of trivia. "Who is the cleverest man you ever met?" he would ask persons assembled around his table. During that part of the 1890s when A. Conan Doyle's Sherlock Holmes mysteries were all the rage, Rhodes was taken, too. With anyone he met Rhodes would "play a game about . . . what he was and what he had been doing."

At a country house in England he surrounded himself with titled ladies and gentlemen, and then asked them questions of abstruse fact; they took turns guessing the precise number of regiments in the British army or the number of ships in the Navy. At breakfast in Groote Schuur, Rhodes discovered that Archbishop Alexander had an unusually retentive memory for quotations. So Rhodes plied the prelate with snatches of poetry. Where, Rhodes inquired, does this line occur, or another line end? After several such breakfast encounters, Alexander was "astonished at his . . . apparently varied and accurate knowledge of poetry. . . ." One morning, when Alexander was stumped by an unusually tough quotation from Richard Graves, Rhodes, "laughing, produced from under the tablecloth a *Book of Familiar Quotations* whence he had been cribbing unseen. . . ."[30] Rhodes hated to lose.

Rhodes was playful, too, with his secretaries and his servants. He treated them all more as friends and intimates than as employees and was generous and usually understanding until that fateful moment when those few who followed women opted for marriage instead of comparative fame and fortune as bachelors in Rhodes' entourage. After Pickering and a hiatus came Harry Currey, who greatly disappointed Rhodes when he married; Charles van der Byl, who lasted but a few months; Harry Palk, an officer on a Union Castle ship who appealed to Rhodes in 1891, was later tutored by Stead, and served Rhodes briefly until he married and, in 1897, chose to return to his expectant wife;[31] Robert Coryndon, who also had a brief tenure and later became governor of Kenya; Philip Jourdan, a shy, prim, young civil servant in the Cape civil service who worshipped Rhodes and became his most efficient secretary during the 1890s; John S. Grimmer, an incompetent lout and rough playmate who Rhodes liked best of all; and Gordon Le Sueur, virile and brash, who was the last of the lot. For twenty years Antonio de la Cruz, a Mozambican of mixed descent, cooked for Rhodes and served as his valet. There were white butlers, too, but only at Groote Schuur or in London during the last decade of Rhodes' life.

Currey was Rhodes' secretary off and on for seven years, living in his house, having his power of attorney and being on what Currey called "the most intimate and confidential terms." It was a mutually rewarding relationship which unraveled rapidly when Currey announced his engagement to Ethelreda Fairbridge. Rhodes went "off the deep end" at the thought of losing Currey. At the wedding reception Rhodes made his feelings clear to the new Mrs. Currey: "I am very jealous of you," he said simply. Thereafter, Rhodes' attitude toward, and relations with, Currey were profoundly altered.

In 1890 Jourdan was employed in the Cape parliament. Rhodes "seemed to have a liking for young men, and, although I was only a youngster," recalled Jourdan, who was twenty, ". . . he always had a kind word for me on going into or coming from the House." They talked and Rhodes gave advice until Jourdan was transferred out of parliament and posted elsewhere in the Colony. He assumed that Rhodes had forgotten him. But in 1894 Rhodes summoned him back to Cape Town, and placed him first as a member of the new prime minister's office. There, in addition to his regular duties, he acted as Rhodes' personal secretary. In 1895, when Jourdan fell seriously ill with typhoid, Rhodes watched over him. Then, after the Jameson Raid and Rhodes' resignation, Jourdan was summoned to Rhodesia to become his official private secretary. Jourdan thrived in this role, and later as an administrator in the Rhodesian colony. Jourdan, who alone of the secretaries took shorthand and was therefore regarded with awe by the others, was described by a contemporary as being sedentary and delicate. Never—from his own testimony—did Jourdan waver in his admiration for Rhodes. "No father could have reposed greater confidence in his son than Mr. Rhodes placed in me," he said. "Nothing was hidden from me, and he expressed his opinions to me of persons and public questions of the day in the freest possible manner. I loved him for the faith which he had in me, and I served him as I cannot possibly serve another man again." (Jourdan married only after Rhodes' death.)

When Jourdan fell ill again in 1897 he recommended Gordon Le Sueur, then a twenty-two-year-old member of the Cape civil service, as his successor. Le Sueur was with Rhodes until the end, surviving many a "stand-up row." "After a stormy scene," remembered Le Sueur, Rhodes would seek him out, "especially if he felt that he had not been perfectly fair, and in an awkward manner want to know what one had been doing. . . ." Then Rhodes would offer money, like any anxious parent. He could not bear sulking, which Jourdan and Grimmer could feign particularly well. Overall, said Le Sueur, Rhodes treated him very well, with "kindness and consideration." "It was the absolute unquestioning confidence that Rhodes placed in the men whom he selected for the privilege of assisting him in his work that made one in turn unhesitatingly follow him with blind trust, yielding him service and confidently entrusting him with all one's affairs. . . ." When Rhodes was ill he asked his young men to hold his hand or place their hands on his fevered brow; at those times, said Le Sueur, "one's feeling was perhaps most stirred by him."

Grimmer was Rhodes' favorite. Grimmer came from Barkly West, where his father was a physician and an acquaintance of Rhodes', like the fathers of Currey and Coryndon. Jourdan and Alpheus Williams thought that Rhodes had taken a "fancy" to Grimmer when he was still "quite a lad," after watching him repeatedly mount a recalcitrant horse. Grimmer served in the British South Africa Company police from the early occupation of Rhodesia and in

the 1893 war against the Ndebele. Rhodes attached Grimmer to his own retinue in 1896, after he had been among the police who accompanied Rhodes
during a tour of Rhodesia in 1896. He took Grimmer and Coryndon with
him to London in 1897 for the inquiry into the Jameson Raid, and, thereafter, either as a secretary or as a companion, Grimmer was by Rhodes' side
until his death. In the former capacity Grimmer was neither efficient nor
more than barely literate, and his relations with his employer were often more
obstructive than helpful. But he clearly gave pleasure. Rhodes loved him, said
Alpheus Williams. Rhodes often said that Grimmer's "quiet demeanour" had
a restful and soothing effect. "Although Grimmer was undemonstrative and
phlegmatic," reported Le Sueur, "he was devoted to Rhodes and capable of
any sacrifice in his interests."

Grimmer looked on Rhodes "as a great baby, incapable of being left to
himself." Grimmer cared nothing for politics, nor to identify himself with
Rhodes' creations; he was just a sterling, big-hearted, loyal friend, deeply attached to 'the Old Man,' and inspired by the very highest motives. . . ." When
Rhodes was ill, it was Grimmer whom he preferred. In fact, said Le Sueur,
"he evinced more pleasure in Grimmer's companionship than any other." They
wore each other's clothes and shoes, remembered a magistrate who served in
Umtali. Grimmer even slept in Rhodes' bed, but when Rhodes was not at
home. When Grimmer fell ill, Rhodes tended him. A member of the Groote
Schuur staff recalled Grimmer becoming sick and Rhodes "sitting at his bedside for hours feeding him teaspoonfuls of champagne." Yet his teasing of
Grimmer had an aggressive quality which bordered on the sado-masochistic.
Rhodes enjoyed rousing Grimmer's temper and would "chuckle with glee"
when he succeeded. He liked to challenge Grimmer to shooting competitions
and, uncharacteristically for Rhodes, sometimes let Grimmer win, or at least
tie. "Rhodes used to say that Grimmer was the only man he was afraid of,
and it is equally certain that Grimmer was by no means afraid of him—in fact,
to see them together," said Le Sueur, "one might have come to the conclusion
that Rhodes was in charge of a keeper."

In 1898 Rhodes settled Grimmer on his 44,000-morgen farm at Inyanga
in Zimbabwe, but soon objected to Grimmer's lazy approach to agriculture
and to his expectation that Rhodes would continue to keep him in luxury
even though the farm was producing almost nothing. Grimmer protested petulantly. "If you still feel Mr. Rhodes [his standard form of address] that my
behavior during the time with you was ungrateful and unfeeling I must do
my duty. . . . I will leave and you will never be bothered by me again. On
the other hand you will find that I can stand by you as well as any other
human being and see you through as much. You will (if you have not already)
live to find I am not the callous unfeeling brute you think me." Grimmer
explained that he had not written before because at their last meeting Rhodes
had ridden off without even saying goodbye. "I have a heart and feeling and
naturally was cut by such treatment," he said. This quarrel was patched up,
but they continued to bicker, and like a pair of young lovers, in 1900 refused

for several days to talk. "Each," said Jourdan, "was too proud to make the first advances."[32]

Rhodes confined his deep personal relationships in adulthood to his secretaries, Jameson, Metcalfe, and a very few others. His entanglement with Olive Schreiner, although fleeting and episodic, was more freighted with emotion than most. For her there was an intensity about it which Rhodes, uniquely, tolerated. Rhodes' knowledge of Schreiner, two years his junior, began in 1887, when he at last read *The Story of an African Farm* and was struck by its force, passion, and progressive qualities. Not only was hers the first serious contribution to English literature by a born South African, but it also was a startling evocation of the vast space of the South African interior. Rhodes believed in the kind of idealistic striving toward perfection which was exemplified in *African Farm;* her characters were part of an indestructible universal life with which Rhodes had a pronounced affinity. Whether he was also taken by her agnosticism, her open feminism, and her acceptance of the importance (more than the mere normality) of sexuality and sexual unity is likely but not known. Conceivably, too, the character of Gregory Rose, an effeminate young man who achieves worth through his love of the young lady Lyndall (the novel's surrogate for its author), and his forays into transvestism, touched a responsive chord in Rhodes.

That the spirit of the mannish Olive Schreiner, who longed passionately for love in the 1880s and 1890s but failed to obtain it fully from innumerable male suitors, including Havelock Ellis, a psychologist and writer, and Karl Pearson, a mathematician, should also have appealed to Rhodes, may no longer seem strange. A Schreiner biographer believes that she was a latent homosexual with bisexual tendencies that were never resolved.[33] The informally educated daughter of a German missionary to South Africa and an English mother who forbade the use of Dutch or German in their isolated home on the Cape-Lesotho border, Schreiner had a childhood that she always remembered as bitter and dark. She was left with an overarching sense of individual sin, a desire for punishment, and other eddies of masochism which joined recurrent asthma in torturing her body and soul. Rhodes stirred something very large in her.

Schreiner returned home to South Africa in late 1889, after eight years in England. She was on the rebound from a disastrous love affair with Pearson, a bisexual don at the University of London. Although she had not yet met Rhodes, who was then in Kimberley, she had seen him in August and had liked him "so." In London she had heard enough from Stead and others to suppose him "a splendid man, the only man of genius we have in this Colony." A few weeks later she clearly hoped both to be introduced to Rhodes and to obtain some manner of financial backing from him: "I am going to meet Cecil Rhodes, the only great man and man of genius South Africa possesses," she told Ellis. "If he backs me up at all I shall be able to carry out my plan [to travel into the interior]. He likely will, as Will [her brother and the future prime minister of the Cape] tells me he has been for years a great lover of the *Story of an African Farm*." In April, after Schreiner had moved on account of her asthma to Matjesfontein on the dry upland edge of the Karoo, she complained to Ellis about how intolerably Philistine most South Africans were. "Fancy a whole nation of *lower* middle-class Philistines, without an aristocracy of blood or intellect or of muscular labourers to save them!" Only Sir Henry Loch, the governor, and Thomas Fuller, the politician, were exceptions. "I think [if] I lived fifty years in Africa I should never make one friend." Then she reiterated her earlier hopes. "There is one man I've heard of, Cecil Rhodes, . . . whom I think I should like if I could meet him. . . ."[34]

Matjesfontein was a desolate, isolated stop on the railway line from Cape Town to Kimberley; in an era before dining cars, passengers on the through trains took meals in the station café, and James Logan (of the Sivewright scandal) was shortly to construct a grandly imposing resort hotel there which, together with gardens, drew visitors even from Europe. In this far-off spot Schreiner began to work again—on essays on South Africa, on short stories, and on what she called her "monumental sex book." The last was about full sensual expression and the extent to which persons of a higher "state of evolution" rightfully compelled those of a lower state to abide by the upper group's sexual ideals. She recognized her loneliness, her wish to marry, her craving for love and sex, and her longing for a soulmate—for intellectual as well as physical stimulation. "There are times," she told Stead, "when one longs to rub one's brains up against another human's. There are plenty of women and children and niggers to love here, but sometimes one wants the other side of one's nature satisfied, that *thinks*." Much later she confided to Jessie Rose Innes that the "loneliness of woman's lives is very terrible. Our unused emotional & intellectual energy, lying unused often within us, that breaks out in force as though it would almost overpower us at times."[35] She was weary of women, and wanted a man of quality and substance.

Schreiner had already insinuated herself into the mainstream of serious Cape Town society. As Merriman reported, "Miss Olive Schreiner is now starring it. . . ." She knew the Inneses, the Sauers, and the Lochs; she also came to know Rhodes.[36] In July 1890 Schreiner told Stead that Rhodes was the only big man in the Colony, and that the only big thing was the Chartered Company. "I feel a curious and almost painfully intense interest in the man and his career." She was afraid that he would make a major mistake by accepting the premiership of the Cape.

Possibly Rhodes was the "typical dominating male for which part of her nature longed"; possibly she wanted him because he was the most important male and she considered herself the most important and interesting female in the Colony. In any event she was strongly and warmly attracted to him even before they met. Her husband, who knew her only later, felt almost certain they met face to face for the first time in late June when she was in Cape Town for a fortnight. She had certainly planned to do so. Whether or not they saw each other again before November, she wrote of a positive and mysterious feeling for Rhodes. She had never had the same feeling for anyone. "It's not love, it's not admiration . . . it's not that I think him noble or good . . . it's the deliberate feeling, 'That man belongs to me.' "

When Schreiner and Rhodes were much better acquainted and clearly on closer terms, she sent him an enigmatic note in pencil apologizing for sending him a letter, the precise contents of which are unspecified but clearly involved matters of the heart. "I have suffered the agony of a lost spirit about it ever since. Please forgive me, and don't mention it to me." A few nights before he had expressed sympathy for her work. "No one has ever done so in just the same way. I am very thankful to you for [it]. . . ." Then she spoke directly to her hero: "You have never felt the same sympathy with my work—that I have with yours. It is just as creative, only you have to realise your imaginations in things, which [are] more permanent." It is likely that no one else had ever spoken or written in this vein to Rhodes before.[37]

In late November Rhodes stopped at Matjesfontein to have dinner with her: Schreiner described him as having "masses of close curly hair," a "curious, far-off look," and a "huge, almost gross body." She found him a "man of genius as a sort of child," and felt appropriately tender toward him. In mid-December she and Rhodes traveled together to open the rail line extension to Bloemfontein. "He is even higher and nobler than I had expected," she wrote afterwards, "but our friends are so different [that] we could never become close friends. [Yet] he spoke to me more lovingly and sympathetically of *An African Farm* than anyone has ever done."[38] It was during this period, when Rhodes and Schreiner were seeing each other periodically, that he offered— as she had hoped—to send her and two ox-waggons at his expense through Rhodesia; but she refused, possibly because her writings would inevitably be influenced by the trip's sponsorship.

At some point in early 1891 she wrote to him on blue-lined paper from a hotel in the city, asking to talk about her work, and about three articles in particular. (They were a section of *Thoughts on South Africa,* published partially in mid-1891 and more fully only in 1896.) It would be a favor, but, she effaced herself, "you must not allow this to influence you if you are not inclined to come or feel the conventionalities of Cape Town life make it difficult for a man to visit a woman as he would another man. . . . You are the only man in South Africa I would ask to come and see me because I think you are large enough to take me impersonally."[39] Perhaps he came.

Rhodes gave Schreiner precedence at Groote Schuur over other ladies on several occasions in 1891, not least when Lord Randolph Churchill visited on his way up country. She and Rhodes more than once toured the Cape Peninsula together in a coach. When Swift MacNeill visited Groote Schuur in the same year she was there, and in conversation was "very delightful." She "seemed to speak on the spur of the moment, in style as perfect and as sparkling as that of her writings." MacNeill remembered that she greatly admired Rhodes, "of whom she spoke with enthusiasm as a great man in a difficult position, on which his genius and force of character shed lustre." "Any accident to him," Schreiner told Stead in September 1891, when Rhodes was traveling in Mashonaland, "would, I believe, mean the putting back of our South African development for fifty years. . . ." In November, relieved that Rhodes had returned safely, she reminded Stead that in no other country had so much depended upon the life of one man—a genius.

Shortly afterwards, Schreiner woke in the night and found herself "standing on the floor in the middle of [her] room, crying and wringing [her] hands." She, a spiritualist, was experiencing one of her nightmarish visions: "I'd dreamt that I saw Rhodes walking by with his old big felt hat on, drawn down very low on his head, and an overcoat on with the collar turned up and his head sunk very low between his shoulders. I ran up to him and stood before him. He did not speak a word, but he opened his overcoat and as he turned it back I saw his whole throat and chest covered with blood and his face ghastly pale like a dead person's; he said nothing. . . ."[40] Sometime later she learned that Rhodes had fallen off his horse and been badly bruised.

MacNeill was at Matjesfontein in September. After lunching, Rhodes and Schreiner went off for a walk on the veld, but Schreiner asked MacNeill not to link her name with Rhodes. Rumors were circulating in Cape Town that she desired to marry Rhodes. Stead and others wanted Rhodes to marry Schreiner, and Bramwell Booth later claimed that it was Schreiner's fault that they had not. As much as she may have originally liked the idea of a permanent union with Rhodes, Schreiner hated the publicity and the personal agony which romantic gossip would cause. Moreover, hers was always the more open ardor. Jameson even reported (it is not clear how he knew) that one day while walking together on Table Mountain, Schreiner "downright" proposed to Rhodes, who turned and fled.[41]

That Rhodes continued to see Schreiner despite the overtures which were so unfamiliar to him is the most remarkable part of the story. Although arguably not the extreme woman hater he was thought to be by some (and which he steadfastly denied to Queen Victoria and others), Rhodes was not at ease in the company of most women. It was only those who were more masculine in their intellect and forthrightness, or like the dowagers of the South African Dutch aristocracy of a certain reassuring age and position, with whom he felt at ease. Schreiner had a masculine demeanor; yet her passion, however disguised as an intellectual interest, had a feminine, covertly sexual thrust which could not have failed to touch Rhodes at least in some subliminal fashion. That he was willing to countenance her approaches even temporarily suggests an attraction which, uncharacteristically, would prove consistent with a need to reassess himself during his late thirties. The attraction may have been to her original intellect or her forthright and arresting personality. It may have even had a heterosexual tinge.

Schreiner herself thought that Rhodes did not love her, and might even have had an antipathy toward her. She was also aware that Rhodes uniformly disdained women. "I do not wonder at [it]," she told Stead. "If you knew Cape women you would not." On the other hand, however little it was, Rhodes spent more time conversing and arguing with her than he had ever done, or would ever do, with a woman other than his mother. Schreiner's husband later suggested that she was the greater intellect, a claim which it is very easy to believe. Certainly she was more worldly and opinionated than other women; she smoked incessantly in public, which ladies had not yet begun doing; and she discoursed at length on sex and politics. She also knew Britain and had a special feel for politics there which Rhodes might have welcomed. A female contemporary remembered Schreiner in those times as a "dominating presence" despite her very small height. She had "wonderful eyes" and a face that came "alight with intellect and power." She "staggered and dumbfounded" Adela Constance Villiers and finally woke in her "a force of feeling and a power to realise some phases of human nature which, but for her, would," Villiers thought, "always have remained dormant." She possessed a "vivid personality," a "wide mind," and a "large outlook over the whole range of humanity. . . ." Villiers, Loch's niece, viewed Schreiner as a "symbol, a seer, a teacher with her intellect afire for all that was great and beautiful and her heart aflame with love and pity for those who were despised." Merriman dismissed her as a "very clever woman who would be happier if she believed in what the rest of her sex believe." Rhodes may have seen less, but he was certainly entranced.[42]

Schreiner remembered that she and Rhodes were attracted because of their mutual love of life and energy. With regard to religion and similar matters, she and Rhodes were as one. But they also fought and argued bitterly. "As long as he and I talked of books and scenery we were very happy, but," she wrote about a towering hero whose feet had subsequently been found to be the grossest clay, "when he began on politics and social questions, I found out to my astonishment that he had been misrepresented to me. . . ." In England, Stead had extolled Rhodes; she had been told or had assumed that he shared her ideals, particularly that he desired to educate and develop downtrodden Africans as well as the poor and despised everywhere. "When we got on the Native Question," she told her mother, who always admired Rhodes, "we ended by having a big fight, and Rhodes getting very angry." Thereafter they never met, she claimed, "without a royal fight."

Schreiner condemned his vote in favor of what she and liberals called the "Every Man Wallop His Own Nigger Bill"—the Masters and Servants or strop bill. Rhodes' vote for this bill took place in 1890, before the time that they were first becoming acquainted. He was instrumental as premier in shelving a second consideration of the bill in 1891, however, at a time when she was writing a clever satire about the bill entitled "The Salvation of a Ministry," and subtitled "Children, How Hardly Shall a Politician Enter into the Kingdom of God?" In the satire, Merriman was admitted to Heaven despite his antiquated views of women, Sivewright for his rare moments of personal charity. About Innes there was no hesitation. Sauer was allowed to abide because of his opposition to the strop bill. Then Rhodes appeared at the door, billed as "Capitalist. Upholder of the Strop Bill." In the eyes of God he was damned and consigned to hell. But the devils of hell dragged him back. They had tried to pull him through the gates of hell but found him too wide. He stuck; he was too big for hell. "And C.R. walked up with his hands behind him and a smile on his face . . . and he sat down in the front seat before the throne, and folded his hands." He had entered heaven "through grace, not merit."[43]

Despite vast differences in their political and social sensitivities, Schreiner remained as passionate as before (if much less hopeful about altering his character or of a lasting, reciprocal relationship) during 1892. Even Rhodes' antagonism toward Africans, and his successful attempt to deprive a class of Africans of the franchise, at the time attracted no known venom from Schreiner. In 1892, she even admired Jameson. As late as mid-September 1892, after the lengthy debates on the African vote had been concluded and before the Logan case had broken, Rhodes called on Schreiner in Matjesfontein. She told her brother afterwards that Rhodes was "great and sincere himself," with "not a spot of hypocrisy." He "never calls his diplomacy principle." She saw Rhodes as the "sincerest human creature" she knew. "He sees things direct without any veil." Then, revealingly, she told Will that there was no other man in the world to whom (spiritually at least) she would show herself "nakedly." Nor was there any other man who could "show himself as nakedly to me."[44]

Schreiner was still attempting to save Rhodes from himself. Like some passions, hers was of reform. She tried to save him from his downward course. "I have gone out of the House of Parliament, when he was speaking," she reminded her mother, who doted on Rhodes, "and written a note . . . imploring him to abstain from damning his own soul. . . . With all his genius, with all his beautiful wonderful gifts, to see it going so!" She urged him to break with the kinds of men (the Rutherfoord Harrises and Sivewrights) by which he was perpetually surrounded, at which suggestion Rhodes apparently flew into a violent rage. *"Those* men my friends! They are not my *friends!* They are my tools, and when I have done with them I throw them away!" But she finally broke conclusively with Rhodes only in 1893, over the Logan case. "I saw," Schreiner wrote to her sister about the Logan contract, that Rhodes ". . . had deliberately *chosen* evil and that I could not save him." She continued: "The perception of what his character really was in its inmost depths was one of the most terrible revelations of my life."

Rhodes and Sivewright came to Matjesfontein. "We had a talk," recalled Schreiner, "and my disappointment at Rhodes' action [or inaction] was so great that when both he and Sivewright came forward to shake hands, I turned on my heel and went to my house." Rhodes later invited her to dinner, but she refused. He then persuaded Sauer to ask Schreiner why she was upset. She replied through Sauer that she would fight him on every political issue. Still Rhodes invited her to dinners, and she adamantly declined.

A few weeks before her marriage in 1894 to Samuel C. Cronwright (who became Cronwright-Schreiner), a farmer and editorialist for the *Midland News* of Cradock who had bitterly criticized Rhodes, she met Rhodes and her brother, now Rhodes' attorney general, in a hotel in Matjesfontein. She attacked them both over new anti-African legislation. Her brother went out and she was alone with Rhodes, who turned to her and, in a way she knew "so well cottoned up to me and said I must not think he agreed with Will, that his sympathies were all with me on the Native Question."

Olive Schreiner was naturally contemptuous of this attempt to square her. "I shall never forget looking at those two men's faces that day." Her brother, lacking imagination and creative insight, but "so good, so simple, so pure: Rhodes with all his gifts of genius and insight—and, below the fascinating surface the worms of falsehood and corruption creeping." She accused him of betraying all the men who trusted and loved him; she foresaw that he would thus betray her Will. "Rhodes wants no mental enlightenment," she wrote bitterly, it was "the man's *heart* that is corrupt." Africans, she saw, were to be "thrown as the sop to the Boer."

Schreiner wrote in much the same vein to her brother, the attorney general, well before the Jameson Raid, which finally unleashed all her venom and was her final disenchantment with what greatness could have been in Rhodes. She worried that rumors that Rhodes was drinking heavily, and had become a "physical wreck," might be true. "He might have all that was best and greatest in South Africa" on his side, she said in 1895. "We that would have loved him so, honoured him, followed him!—but he has chosen, not only to choose the worst men as his instruments, but to *act on men always through the lowest sides of their nature,* to lead them through narrow self-interest instead of animating them with large enthusiasms." "I sometimes wish I sent him the love letter I wrote him . . . [last January], but all my writing & talking never had the least effect on him before, why should it now?" Rhodes would have argued that he did inspire men, and only employed mean self-interest when lofty sentiment proved insufficient. Schreiner, however, had weighed his character and finally, even before the Raid, had found it sorely wanting. Rhodes was a man who had "looked steadily and carefully at both and chosen the lower!" To Schreiner he was "an almighty, might-have-been." "For the man himself I feel such awful pity. . . ."[45]

Two strong, visionary personalities, each with special incandescence, illumined each other and the South African darkness during the first years of the 1890s. When Rhodes was achieving unquestioned political mastery and Schreiner writing well and conquering at least some of her deep-seated conflicts, they shared a common belief in bold, brave, awesome achievements for the greater good. But they clashed irredeemably over the definition of that good, as well as over the means that should and could be employed. Two bright stars in complementary orbits, they rotated around each other and then, coming too close and discovering fundamental incompatabilities, spun away. For Schreiner, too, there was an infatuation which was at least unrequited, for as mannish as Schreiner may have appeared to women, she was ultimately too womanly for Rhodes. Additionally, he sought acolytes, not rivals and critics, and tried to win her mind as she attempted to subdue his heart. Of Rhodes' few attempts to reach out to another human of equal or greater intellect, class, and accomplishment, this liaison could have been transformative. As she said, it was a might-have-been. But his preferences, human, sexual, and ideological, led elsewhere. Indeed, it led before long down that road of purgatory that Schreiner had foreseen, and from which her mystical, prophetic self had sought to save him.

Throughout his adult life Rhodes consorted with men, and only occasionally with women. He was a confirmed bachelor, as were all but one of his six brothers. Recent research suggests that there is a significant familial composition to male homosexuality. It does so, however, without arguing that homosexuality runs in families for only genetic or birth-hormonal reasons. Overprotective mothers and detached fathers are still believed to play a part in gender orientation; some combination of environmental, cultural, and biological causes contributes to homosexuality.[46]

Rhodes always claimed that he had no time for women—that his life's work was all-consuming. But he was no mere misogynist: there is an obscure reference to a close relationship to a woman in Natal when Rhodes was very young, and one with a young lady in Cape Town. A radical parliamentarian swore that Rhodes kept a harem of Coloured women on his estate. A second-hand rumor that circulated in South Africa years after his death associated Rhodes in promiscuous behavior with Zulu maidens (from whom he is said to have contracted syphilis). Nonetheless, Rhodes as an adult was never linked even marginally with women other than Schreiner and Princess Radziwill (see Chapter 23). Schreiner received his praise, and although she herself fantasized a strong, romantic relationship, Rhodes admired her zestful spirit and the strength of her mind much more than he sought or enjoyed her as a woman. Toward the end of his life, too, when his fame and notoriety were assured, titled and well-connected women were welcome at Groote Schuur. Some asserted mental intimacy, but even such platonic claims are suspect. Put simply, Rhodes had no strong interest in women, feeling much more comfortable in the company of men.

When Rhodes finally could afford a secretary he employed a young man. Neville Pickering, to whom Rhodes was openly and strongly attached, was succeeded as secretary by other appealing young men. From early times there were male cooks and other male servants in Rhodes' primitive, cramped households. At Groote Schuur men were always in charge. From the middle years of his prosperity, at least, Rhodes always traveled with and was looked after by a valet, usually a younger man of no particular training to whom Rhodes had taken a fancy, sometimes aboard ship, sometimes in Kimberley. With the more enduring of the valets, Rhodes was easy and playfully free in ways which were otherwise rare. Only with these few young men, with his first secretary, with Jameson, with whom Rhodes for years shared a tin-roofed house in Kimberley, and with Sir Charles Metcalfe, could Rhodes ever behave as a boy among boys. On those rare occasions when Rhodes relaxed it was with a small, tight knot of boys and men who, with the exception of Jameson and Metcalfe, were not social equals or business or political partners. They constituted the frivolous or nakedly sensual, hidden side of greatness, majesty, and control.

The authorized biographers strained hard: "No doubt the weaknesses of Rhodes's character would have been less damaging if he had had a good wife. His nature craved and needed family life; but his restless energy, coupled perhaps with scruples about his precarious health, denied him the satisfaction of it except for transitory substitutes. Marriage would have softened the asperity, even brutality, of some of his dealings with other men. . . . His relations with women were peculiar, in no sinister sense of the term. Those who knew him best strenuously denied allegations of immorality. . . . They did not trouble to deny, because only a later and more vindictive generation chose to make the fashionable calumny of a lifelong bachelor, that he was a homosexual. It might seem hardly worth commenting on an accusation that was never made in Rhodes's lifetime, nor would it be if some of those who later wrote about him had not chosen to imply that there was something abnormal about his emotional friendships with other men." Even so, the same authors comment that "no woman's company could take the place" of the young men to whom he was unfailingly generous and from whom he was "inseparable."[47]

Frank Harris, that great Victorian voyeur, gossip, and cynic, reported that one of Rhodes' secretaries (presumably one active in the 1890s) had told him stories about Rhodes' "erotic tendencies" that were worthy of Oscar Wilde. But Harris never believed in them wholeheartedly. "Rhodes always seemed to [Harris] to be lacking in virility; political ideas engrossed his attention, when really good erotic tales scarcely induced him to listen. And in Cape Town, where he was well known, his reputation in this respect was never even assailed."[48]

True, as far as is known. Yet his secretaries later wrote, when it may have been more permissible, about Rhodes' fondness for young men. "As Prime Minister he was always busy," one wrote, "but he invariably called me into his office every afternoon to go through his private letters with him. I looked with the greatest pleasure to the half-hour or hour with him every afternoon. He was exceedingly kind and tender towards me. He made me draw up my chair quite close to him, and frequently placed his hand on my shoulder. He used to send for me even when he did not have any work for me. On these occasions he talked to me more as a friend than as my chief. He affected this free and easy style to make me feel at home with him."

The great man liked to interview the appealing young men who applied to him for employment, but rarely saw the women. He liked to examine the faces of these young men, believing himself a "great reader of character" who went by first impressions. If Rhodes warmed to the face—and he preferred those with piercing blue eyes like his own—he would find a position for the applicant. Some, including the baker's dozen he sent from Kimberley up to Rhodesia, were known to all as Rhodes' lambs. Rhodes, reported another secretary, "collected a sort of bodyguard of young men in whom he was interested, and who were chosen on account of various and varied qualifications."

Even the secretaries "were all much more companions than secretaries," said one, "in the ordinary sense of the word." Only one was able to take short-hand, for example. Another, Grimmer, was anything but subservient; Rhodes indulged his surliness and was sometimes even told by the youngster that he was "too busy" to take a letter.[49]

It is not difficult to share Roberts' conclusion: "No woman ever came closer to [Rhodes] than his mother." "The reason for Rhodes not marrying went deeper than his preoccupations. Not only did he not take a wife but it is highly unlikely that he ever took a woman." "Women did not attract him sexually." But if "his attitude towards women was austere, his emotions were very much in evidence in his relationships with young men." But not as peers: Rhodes was not involved with his "lambs" or his "angels" because of their resonance with his own entrepreneurial, political, imperial, or philosophical pursuits. These hearty young men (his first secretary aside) shared few of his thoughts, schemes, hopes, trials, or tribulations. "What existed between them and Rhodes was an almost adolescent relationship; banter, horseplay and practical jokes."

Metcalfe, a big, jolly bachelor, had an intriguingly special relationship with Rhodes about which too little is known. Metcalfe, the railway builder, has attracted no biography; his papers have not survived, and were probably de-stroyed. Yet, after an acquaintance at Oxford, during which period Metcalfe was distinctly not attracted to Rhodes, they met again in southern Africa in 1889. From about that time they traveled together frequently; during the later 1890s Rhodes and Metcalfe were inseparable. Metcalfe was "always with him" and "somewhat parasitical." Metcalfe was Rhodes' "best and most intimate friend," claimed Jourdan. "Theirs was indeed a friendship in the true sense of the word: a mutual respect and affection . . . deepened as the years went on. . . . Sir Charles probably knew his friend better than anybody." Jourdan observed that Metcalfe possessed "exceptional tact" and never bored or irri-tated Rhodes. " 'Metcalfe soothes me,' " said Rhodes. When Beit, Frank Rhodes, and others complained about Metcalfe, and urged Rhodes to be rid of him, Rhodes remained staunchly loyal. He said that he liked Metcalfe for inexpli-cable reasons, but like him he did—" 'the same way that Beit likes Sauer-kraut.' "[50]

It stretches credulity to suppose that Rhodes was comfortable with het-erosexuality. He betrayed intense emotions only with and about men. But Rhodes was never effeminate and nearly every one of his "lambs," valets, and other young men grew up into robust, macho specimens, many ultimately having wives and female lovers. Rhodes liked his men to act like men. And most, if not all, of his close relationships with young men were almost cer-tainly platonic, thus supporting Harris' notion that the absence of scandal was evidence of a physical circumspection, whatever his underlying desires. Yet Rhodes' attraction to these men, if not necessarily theirs to him, was homosex-ual. "Overt homosexuality would have horrified him," and so it probably might have in the latter decades of the Victorian era. Martin, who wrote about Ed-ward FitzGerald, suggests that Victorian men of a persuasion similar to Rhodes probably never "directly faced the emotions" that attractive boys provoked within them. If "our own day overemphasizes sexuality as the cause of behaviour and emotion," he says, ". . . many Victorians managed what seems to us the difficult balancing act of believing that love between men which had no overt physical consequences was therefore untouched by physical motivation." Nevertheless, there is at least the suspicion that Rhodes confronted his deepest feelings at least once or twice, if not more often. He was not wholly in control, nor always as serious as all but his young men found him. "It is not unknown for repressed homosexuals to divert their sexual inclinations into purely emotional channels."[51]

It was not Victorian homosexuality that was different from our society, but rather the prevailing social attitude toward repression (the unconscious exclusion of impulses from awareness) and suppression (the conscious exclusion of impulses from awareness). Our late twentieth-century society, spurred on by the misapplication of principles derived from the psychoanalytic consulting room, champions the awareness and, by implication, the expression of impulses. Having to some extent narrowed the distance between impulse, awareness, and action, we assume that in other periods those who had the tendency to act were as likely to have been aware of, and to have acted out, their tendencies as we are supposed to do. In fact, even in our society, repression and suppression are not entirely absent. They live in individual psychodynamics and defensive structures despite the blandishments of the media. And in late Victorian society, even more, it was possible to be unaware of homosexual leanings. It was even possible to act them out in the name of hygiene, or without being fully conscious of the emotional commitment or the issues of sexual identity involved. It is conceivable that Rhodes' strong emotional attachments to Pickering, Jameson, Grimmer, and the "lambs" could have been rationalized as mere manly attachments. Rhodes need not have faced their deeper implications.

Victorian homosexual activity is generally identified with Wilde and his notorious trial in 1895. But Wilde was only the most obvious representative of what has been called a Victorian homosexual subculture. Wilde was at Oxford with Rhodes and they were members of the same club, although there is no evidence that they knew one another. One of the patterns of that homosexual culture was that men of the upper classes had physical and emotional attachments to younger men, or to men of lower social class. Some of these affairs were passionate and prolonged. Thus FitzGerald had his East Anglian fisherman, and John Addington Symonds, like other upper-class men of the day, was fond of guardsmen who supplemented their limited incomes by making themselves sexually available for pay. It was this sort of physical involvement which was readily and discreetly available to Rhodes as an alternative to recognizing the full nature of his attachment to his male friends. His cook and valet, acquaintances among the cabin crews aboard ship to and from Britain, and African laborers were all potentially available to Rhodes for sexual purposes.[52]

A crucial question remains: What difference did it make that Rhodes was at least an emotional if not a practicing homosexual? Blake suggests that "the matter is of no importance," and asks his readers to "leave it at that." But Rhodes' homosexuality has for too long been swept under a biographical rug. Did his attachment to Jameson affect his judgment about Jameson's talents and character, most critically over the Raid? Did his emotions blind him to the consequences of his drive for power and hegemony? Was the curious pattern of playful, occasionally painful, dominance and submission in which he and the most faithful of his young male friends engaged themselves ultimately expressed in a more sinister fashion by his drive to dominate the world? Is it possible that his vaunted ambitions were fed by repressed feelings of inadequacy regarding his father's amply demonstrated heterosexual potency? Did his homosexual leanings give him automatic though unwitting entrée to an unacknowledged network of prominent homosexuals which furthered his purposes? Or is it simply, as he himself implied, that without the ties to family and children that would have resulted from marriage, he had extra time and energy to devote to his grandiose pursuits?

A reductionistic answer to any of these questions would be inconsistent with the complexity of reality, of Rhodes' character, and of the broad view of events which is the explanatory framework of this biography. Nevertheless, it is clear that Rhodes' homosexuality, which is indisputable on the basis of the available evidence, was a major component of his magnetism and his success.[53]

Despite his love of games, his pleasure in his secretaries, his soul struggle with Olive Schreiner, and his political and financial accomplishments in the early part of the decade, Rhodes aged rapidly from the mid-1890s. There was a somber, greying counterpoint to the swelling crescendo of his triumphs. In appearance he was visibly deteriorating faster than men of his early middle years usually do, reflecting or recapitulating those earlier interruptions of physical unease which, understandably, had so worried him and resulted in the penning of the initial will. In mid-1877 he had turned blue and been so overcome by acute anxiety that he had barricaded the door of his room. This episode of *angor animi,* an antique term for the feeling of impending death that accompanies some heart attacks, was followed a month later by a grandiose statement of destiny and an accompanying will. Love of Pickering and a desire to ingratiate himself with Lord Rothschild motivated the succeeding wills of 1882 and 1888, but an underlying fear of an innate physical fragility may also have contributed to these affirmations of a personal destiny.[54]

Yet, as far as can be determined, Rhodes enjoyed good health from 1877, when he was twenty-four, to the early 1890s, when he was turning forty. In 1890 he was not yet stout, and appeared vigorous and robust. A photograph from that year shows him heavier than before, but without gray hair. He looks self-satisfied. "He generally wore an ordinary tweed suit and a peculiarly-shaped brown bowler hat," reported Jourdan. Although "his carriage when walking was not very erect, and his style of dress did not command a second look . . . when one looked into his clear, searching blue eyes, one could [detect] . . . character, determination, and intelligence."

Over the next few years Rhodes came to look more and more massive, crag-like, even puffy. His blond hair became gray and then white. Eventually he moved more slowly. Admittedly, two accidents may have contributed to an increasing infirmity. In late 1891, Merriman, Currey, and Rhodes were cantering along the Cape flats. Either Rhodes' Irish mare inexplicably stumbled and threw her rider or Rhodes suffered some kind of cardiovascular disturbance and slipped from the saddle. Knocked unconscious, and bleeding profusely from a cut on the temple, Rhodes suffered a broken collarbone. He contracted what was called influenza but which could have been a respiratory condition related to a circulatory episode. Currey commandeered a spring cart to haul Rhodes back to Groote Schuur, but because Rhodes was so heavy it took three men (Merriman, Currey, and a local farmer) to put him into it.

Rhodes, a compulsive worker, was not really fit for activity for a month. Many years later Bower remembered that Rhodes "underwent a change after his fall & concussion. He was unconscious for a whole day."[55] Ten months later, while touring with Sivewright through Montague and the Swartberg Pass in the snow, their cart overturned on a mountain road; Rhodes was tossed out and badly bruised. In 1894 he fell from his horse near Kokstad. It was, said Rhodes, "a nasty fall." Then, in late 1895, he endured a long bout of influenza, combined with malaria. He is said to have had heart attacks or heart trouble both in 1895 and 1897. Rhodes was rarely free from worry about his physical endurance during the 1890s. As Williams, reporting on the early part of this period, concluded, "He used often to say that he would not live beyond forty-five, and that, within his few remaining years, he must accomplish all he still had left unfinished."[56]

Photographs, as well as the comments of visitors, affirm a hastened process of aging. In a photograph from 1893 Rhodes' hair is gray. He looks far older than forty. In 1896, a photograph shows Rhodes with blotchy skin and a congested-looking face, probably the result of the gradual ballooning of the great vessels in his chest. Within a few years they would contribute to his death.

Visitors were conscious of his growing girth. In the South African autumn of 1894 John Hays Hammond, an American mining engineer, was summoned to Cape Town. Rhodes "presented a striking figure," recalled Hammond. He was "typically Augustan . . . with his heavy forehead, his strong mouth, and square cleft chin. The impression of his origin was strengthened by the curly blond hair, always in confusion. His large gray-blue eyes could be cold as ice, but when he smiled, as he frequently did, they were no longer cold." As Rhodes aged, said Hammond, his slender frame filled out "until he seemed to tower rocklike over most of his companions. His hands were blunt and powerful, expressive of himself. He rarely moved them to gesticulate." In late 1895 a visiting artist described him as a "fat man with a fine carriage and bearing, a puffy face, good forehead, greyish hair and keen eyes." A few weeks later Lady Sarah Wilson stopped at Groote Schuur; more than a dozen years later she recalled Rhodes' tall figure, his white flannel trousers and tweed coat, and his habit of passing his hands through his hair when he talked or thought. "Shy and diffident with strangers," he seemed abrupt, but no one could fail "to be impressed with the expression of power, resolution, and kindness on [his] rugged countenance, and with the keen piercing glance of his blue eyes."

After the Jameson Raid, the world's censoriousness, and the deterioration of his heart had all taken their toll, it was Rhodes' bulk that impressed acquaintances along with what was still a formidable manner. "In appearance alone he filled the picture," said Bramwell Booth of the Salvation Army. In 1898 Rhodes "was a mountain of a man, over six feet high, broad and deep chested, and with the look of a Viking. One had the feeling that his enormous bulk was governed by a mind correspondingly large and powerful, and that his huge head and massive brow betokened a tremendous will. His whole presence spoke of personal force, of faith in ideas, and of iron self-reliance. He was a man in whom temperament as distinct from character, and character as distinct from training, and training as distinct from either of the others, all combined to make a rare example of what a man could be. . . . He was a man of profound melancholy. It enveloped him. . . . He was indeed a great soul dwelling in the shadows."

A year later, during the Anglo-Boer War, Menpes met Rhodes in Kimberley. "When you first see . . . Rhodes," he said, "you think 'What an enormous man!' He seems to tower above every one else; but, curiously enough, his stature is not over the average. It is the head that is so big,—like the head of some great lion—full of brain and capacity. He is all head—it seems to fill the room. The face is like the face of Nero on a coin—strong and determined, with a mouth like iron. In repose his expression is very severe; but when he is talking the lines of the face turn up and the eyes look down benignly upon you. One realised how those lines could tighten and the blue eyes become like burnished steel, and that at times he could be very formidable indeed." Rhodes cared not "two straws" about his personal appearance. Generally he wore a rough tweed coat "that seems to have been dragged on through sheer force with the buttons invariably hitched up to buttonholes that were never meant for them." Menpes also found him with a cobalt blue necktie and the habitual white flannel trousers.

Photographs taken of him within a few years of his death show a man of middle age who looked sixty-five. In one photograph taken with Alfred Beit, his "leonine" look and his posture, propping himself with his extended arms on the seat, strongly suggest the use of the accessory muscles of respiration to overcome serious difficulty in breathing.[57] The slim, handsome thirty-year-old had become a pasty-cheeked, ponderous figure who, though he habitually liked to wear his clothes loosely—he had a favorite ill-fitting suit of rough blue serge—could no longer easily fasten his jacket across his chest. Puffed and pained, Rhodes ballooned with facial edema and became, by 1900, a caricature of epic proportions.

Despite, or perhaps because of, his growing girth, a discomfort or dismay which was reflected both in melancholy and by comments to acquaintances and friends that he expected to die young—that there was so much to do and so little time—Rhodes consumed food, drink, and tobacco on a scale which seems colossal by late twentieth-century standards, but was not unique in Africa or Europe in the 1890s. Moreover, like any person of undeniable stature, Rhodes was the subject of gossip, conjecture, rumor, vilification, and calumny, just as he received the tributes of sycophants. Many of the tales spread about Rhodes during his heyday, and after, were doubtless designed to humanize— to make more believable—the man in Rhodes. Some may have been based on reality, too.

F. Edmund Garrett, editor of the *Cape Times* during Rhodes' premiership, was a Victorian apologist. Nevertheless, his is a description of Rhodes in the 1890s which implicitly poses, even if it fails definitively to answer, important questions about Rhodes' habits and personal proclivities. "I have heard him say things brutal or cynical," Garrett admitted, "—it was an ugly foible—but things gross, such as men even of exemplary life often affect in the licence of the smoking-room, never. He was no ascetic; he liked to eat and drink heartily what was put before him; but the character of a voluptuary is one for which he held and expressed the deepest contempt. He liked best the riding and camping life which he often led for months at a time, away on the veldt in Rhodesia. As for drinking habits of the kind and degree attributed to him by the most widely spread rumour of all, it would have been impossible, as a doctor once remarked, for a man with heart-mischief like Rhodes's in his later years to live at all with such excess—much more to live as strenuous a working life as his. The truth is that the life-work which was to Mr. Rhodes a devouring passion, if it left too little scope for some of the virtues, left even less for most of the vices."[58]

In 1893 Harry Johnston visited Rhodes at Groote Schuur. He appeared decidedly different from the man Johnston had met and admired in 1889 and 1890. "He had lost that look of keen masterfulness and healthy ability which had so stamped him [earlier]." Rhodes himself blamed the change on the nasty fall from his horse in late 1891. He had "felt a different man" since the fall. "His manner had become much more somber; he had long fits of sulky silence or dreamy taciturnity, alternating with rapid conversation so full of great propositions backed by monetary proposals, that one felt almost obliged to ask him to pause. . . ." Rhodes summoned Johnston one midnight for a talk. Johnston had retired, so he rushed there in a dressing gown hastily thrown over pyjamas. Rhodes was in evening dress and smoking. "In the case of much lesser men I should have concluded that he was partly inebriated or under the influence of a drug, but there was no adjacent evidence of champagne or whiskey, and although his speech was rapid and his proposals were magnificent his utterance was perfectly distinct."

Johnston stayed several days, although "not for the sake of the sumptuous hospitality and the really remarkable and interesting luncheons at which all sorts of special people appeared." Rhodes' moods were "variable." Some days they would drive out to an inn along the Cape peninsula, and lunch off cold sirloin of beef and "similar homely fare, Rhodes sulkily reproaching [Johnston] for [his] enormous appetite, and eating very little himself." Rhodes would smoke or nap while Johnston bathed in the sea or "botanized." Other times Rhodes would take Johnston into Cape Town, to lunch with the members of his cabinet, and permanent officials, "and occasionally look at me half-mockingly at the sight of my amazement at finding most of them drunk."

Johnston called the extent of inebriation in South Africa in the early 1890s simply "unbelievable." He described two of Rhodes' close cronies as thorough sots. Jameson, said Johnston, "drank far too much." Rutherfoord Harris, a "good-looking man with a pleasant manner," was at times "a furious inebriate." Even Rhodes, recalled Johnston, called him (presumably affectionately) a rogue. Merriman and Sprigg were exceptions to this catalogue of contemporary carousing, and so was Rhodes. Censorious though he was, Johnston never *saw* Rhodes the worse for drink. Yet because Rhodes appeared so different in manner, speech, and appearance from the earlier Rhodes, Johnston later wondered if Rhodes used drugs. Jameson, writing to Johnston after 1902, "admitted the possibility of this," presumably having dosed Rhodes with painkilling opiates. They lived, after all, in the era just prior to the enactment of laws to protect the public against drugs. Many proprietary medications were still loaded with opiates. Prominent physicians and public figures experimented dangerously with morphine derivatives and cocaine; their dangers were just beginning to be appreciated. Did Rhodes try drugs? No one except Johnston ever linked Rhodes to their use.

Food and drink were his overt vices. "He was a valiant trencherman," Le Sueur said of his patron, "--one might almost call him a gross feeder. On the veld he liked getting the joint in front of him and cutting off great hunks of meat; and at home at Groote Schuur he would get up and go to a side-table, carve for himself, and carry over to his plate on his fork, what he carved." No stranger to brandy, Rhodes drank a special champagne before lunch and dinner, and sometimes mixed it with stout at lunch. "His system required a stimulant. . . ." After dinner he habitually downed five or six glasses of Russian Kummel, a caraway-flavored liqueur. After lunch and dinner he lit one special Turkish cigarette after another.

So long as Rhodes lived and, increasingly after his death, eyewitnesses reported that he was and had been a heavy drinker. To have established that Rhodes had been overcome by the demon liquor would hardly alter today's view of his contribution to history, and it might even make late twentieth-century readers marvel that so much could have been accomplished despite the befuddlement of alcohol. But to have been a drinker, a wild carouser, or a person who indulged in pursuits or passions which defied polite society of the time would have demonstrated to contemporaries, at least, that Rhodes had feet of clay—that, despite his power and his greatness, his character was weak, even reprehensible. Those who focused on his ruthless, self-serving qualities could and can dismiss him more readily if his personality were stained, and his reputation thus more easily sullied.

Keir Hardie, the Labour member of parliament and radical opponent of Britain's bashing of the Boers, blackened imperialism by calling Rhodes a "confirmed drunkard—a dipsomaniac. . . ." When Rhodes came to Britain after the Raid, Hardie claimed, "he had to be constantly watched by his friends, so that he might be fit for the duties of the hour." Rhodes, he said, made merry in Kimberley. "Champagne flows copiously, and the special refrigerating plant keeps the nectar of the diamond gods deliciously cool."[59]

Others reported Rhodes' intake from first-hand knowledge. "He used to eat and drink," reported Rhodes' architect, ". . . with absent-minded carelessness, swallowing food as he 'swallowed continents.' . . . His only special likings . . . were for the wild asparagus that grew on the mountain and for marrow bones. When tired at dinner he might drink strange mixtures of stout and champagne. . . ." Rhodes was never ostentatious, requiring few imported luxuries beyond champagne, stout, and cigarettes, and coffee from Nyasaland. He is said to have preferred simple, heavy foods of the grilled chop and potato kind, but he fed often and with gusto from a lavish, groaning board, and always accompanied his meals with liquor.

"I traveled long distances with him in Rhodesia," wrote Lord Winchester, "and his usual drink was Colares," a Portuguese red wine from a district west of Lisbon on the Atlantic Ocean, diluted with water. "At home his favourite drink was black and tan [Guinness and bitter]." When Rhodes was engaged in combating the Ndebele rebellion he traveled everywhere with "a plentiful supply" of champagne and stout. Sir Charles Mills, the Cape's agent in London, reported that Rhodes in 1891 drank a whole bottle of chartreuse at a sitting. (Metcalfe reported that Rhodes ate and drank "plenteously.") In the middle of a major speech one morning in 1899 to the shareholders of the British South Africa Company, he paused to ask an attendant to "fetch . . . a glass of Apollinaris," the German sparkling water. "I always find I can speak better after that," he said. (The company that distributed Apollinaris henceforth advertised itself with a photograph of the Founder and his unprompted endorsement. Rhodes, it transpired, was a large shareholder in the company.)

Rhodes loved his food, and was not abashed at enjoying it openly. He won the heart of much of the public, and even of Henry M. Labouchere, his usual Radical critic, by lunching boldly before the parliamentary committee investigating the Jameson Raid. "I like his porter and sandwiches," Labouchere said. "Members arriving after one o'clock . . . in the South Africa Committee's room discovered Mr. Rhodes with his mouth full of ham-sandwich . . . ," wrote Sir Henry Lucy, a *Punch* columnist. "He was seated in the chair between the forked ends of the horseshoe table, at the upper end of which ranged fifteen of the ablest and cutest members of the House of Commons. He was in laager with rounds of sandwiches, over whose level heights rose what at first looked like a Martello tower, black with age and the smoke of battle. On nearer inspection it turned out to be only a tumbler of stout. But

Mr. Rhodes is a man of large ideas, and he carries them out in all the details of daily life. Thus when he asks for a glass of stout, he expects the refreshment to be trundled in a vessel of Rhodesian proportions." Rhodes simply took his lunch at his accustomed hour; the members of the committee assembled, watching around the horseshoe. Then, in between intervals of munching sandwiches and drinking stout, he lectured them on constitutional law, international relations, and the state of affairs which had preceded the Raid.

A man who served Rhodes closely for eight years in the 1890s recalled him as "a regular drinker," consuming chablis for lunch, whisky and soda before dinner, "two or three glasses of champagne with his dinner, and occasionally, if alone, stout and champagne, and two or three whiskies from dinner to bedtime." When he was excited in the evenings "he smoked to excess and suffered for it the next morning." But for seven of the same years Norris "put him to bed" and was prepared to affirm that Rhodes "was not once the worse for liquor." Frank Harris, who knew Rhodes from the late 1880s, in London, confirmed this general picture, and, anticipating moderns, nevertheless blamed too much food and drink for weakening the great man's heart.[60]

As extreme as this appetite now appears, Le Sueur's judgment is reasonable for the day: "Rhodes was no drunkard." The social drinking of the era, especially in South Africa, was by modern standards heavy, and Rhodes clearly was not abstemious through temperament or conviction. Moreover, he was never above employing conviviality and the comfort of mutual imbibing as one of an arsenal of negotiating weapons in commerce and politics. But Rhodes took no solace in alcohol or drugs, and there is little evidence—even from his early years in Kimberley—that Rhodes ever made the rounds of the infamous canteens of the town with his cohorts. Rhodes was a serious and ambitious man when young and an earnest and preoccupied magnate when older. His own thoughts were usually sufficient to make him heady.

Resolution of the conflicting reports about the effects of Rhodes' alcoholic consumption doubtless lie in modern studies of alcoholism, whose conclusions may have been intuitively understood by his contemporaries. A conservative calculation of Rhodes' average daily alcohol intake during his prime shows that he consumed about ten ounces of pure alcohol between noon and 10 p.m. This is the equivalent of a fifth of vodka per day, an amount that an inexperienced drinker would find overwhelming. Rhodes, however, was an experienced drinker who took most of his liquor with food, and functioned well. Studies of the intake of severe alcoholics indicate that habituation permits them to tolerate very large amounts of alcohol. Although not an alcoholic, Rhodes drank heavily without overtly betraying that consumption.

Rhodes rarely abstained from alcohol; its calories rather than any temporary loss of clarity may have damaged his ability to function over time, and certainly *could* have contributed to the weakening of that great muscle which circulated his blood. Moreover, modern controlled studies of the effects of alcohol on social drinkers have begun to show strikingly that the consumption of elevated quantities of alcohol (even amounts far less than Rhodes habitually drank) is associated strongly both with decreased cognitive functioning and with increasing symptoms of depression. This is not to imply that Rhodes should be classed as a depressive in the clinical sense; rather, alcohol could have contributed in the 1890s to reduced acuity and to recurrent bouts of depression-related impatience, grumpiness, and intransigence.[61]

Smoking a pack or more a day of cigarettes is now known to be a prime cause of hypertension; in Rhodes' day the extent of his own smoking was normal for a man, and believed harmless. It is now known, too, that heavy smoking may contribute to diseases of the heart muscle. Smoking, but heavy alcoholic consumption even more so, is associated with cardiomyopathy, a condition that results in heart failure in persons who may show no signs of alcoholism.[62] Rhodes exercised on horseback; otherwise he was essentially sedentary. Given the quantities of food and drink that he is known to have ingested, it is hardly a wonder that an already weakened heart was further imperiled by a wealthy man's ample, as well as stressed, lifestyle.

Rhodes never checked his personal as well as his corporate, political, or imperial appetite; yet as he grew corpulent, so he simultaneously sensed infirmity. He traversed his adult life after about thirty-eight accompanied by an abiding sense of intensifying physical inferiority and of transcendent, eventual mortality. He may never have linked overindulgence and failing health, as moderns do. Or, with an all-consuming faith in his own creative energies, and a strong aversion to signs of personal weakness, he may half-consciously have chosen to disregard the potential connection (then largely unsuspected by physicians) in order to follow his comet's compelling cosmic orbit.

An awareness of his own seeming mortality encouraged Rhodes in the 1890s more energetically than in the 1880s to pursue the objectives of his "Confession of Faith," and also to give more precise form to his special place in posterity. In 1889, when in Britain, he and Stead continued their lengthy conversations about how best to promote the ascendancy of the English race (meaning Anglo-Saxons and their dependents generally) so as to achieve justice, liberty, and peace in the world expeditiously. Rhodes' reasoning, according to Stead, was megalomaniacal: "If there be a God, and He cares anything about what I do, I think it is clear that He would like me to do what He is doing Himself. And He is manifestly fashioning the English-speaking race as the chosen instrument by which He will bring in a state of society based upon Justice, Liberty and Peace. He must obviously wish me to do what I can to give as much scope and power to that race as possible." What "He would like me to do," concluded Rhodes, was "to paint as much of the map of Africa British red as possible, and to do what I can elsewhere to promote the unity and extend the influence of the English-speaking race."[63]

Rhodes' only other extended linking of his own ambitions with those of Christ appears in an undated but early essay on "success and failure." It is consonant with the creed of the Confession and also foreshadows his expectations for Rhodes Scholars. "I contend that the success of any undertaking depends mainly on the total devotion of the human mind to it and the abandonment of all other ordinary pursuits and pleasures to it." Our Savior, wrote Rhodes, "was continually telling [his disciples] that for him everything must be abandoned. . . . He was starting an entirely new faith the success of which depended . . . on the character and lives of its first exponents. . . ." Rhodes, incidentally, defined success as the doing of something out of the general run, and thus the application of every individual faculty to the "one object in view." Successful men cared for no amusements or pleasures. Genius was not essential, but having a distinct "goal in view" to which all other interests were subordinated was the guiding principle.[64]

After 1891 Rhodes was even prepared to sacrifice monarchical rule if doing so would hasten a reunion of English speakers and the creation of a more perfect empire. He thus approved Stead's promotion of the Association of Helpers, a secret society allied to the *Review of Reviews*. The Association was designed to mobilize public-spirited Britons behind the greater empire which Rhodes and Stead both envisaged. It was at this time that Rhodes added Stead's name to that of Lord Rothschild as an executor of his fourth will.[65] In late 1892, in London, he drew up a fifth will, naming Bourchier F. Hawksley, a solicitor employed by the British South Africa Company in London, as a third executor. Rhodes both liked Hawksley and found him sympathetic to his big ideas. Moreover, Rhodes assumed that Stead would see that that scheme was carried out—that he was the custodian of the secret flame—that Stead would allocate sums accordingly, that Rothschild would be responsible for the administration of Rhodes' millions, and that Hawksley would deal with any legal problems that might arise. During his visit to London in 1891, Rhodes talked and later corresponded with Reginald D. Brett (subsequently Viscount Esher), an equerry of the queen, about a secret league of "the English race" based on the "snowball" form of subscription whereby each acolyte would be pledged to obtain two other backers and so on. "It could begin with you," said Brett to Rhodes, "and might roll up indefinitely!"[66] Brett was a well-connected, ingratiating homosexual and pederast.

In 1894 Stead attempted to persuade Rhodes to endow the Association of Helpers with an annual income of £5,000, but heavy financial responsibilities for Rhodesia made Rhodes reluctant to spend sums on other projects. "When we get the northern country settled," Rhodes promised, he would be ready to carry out their mutual schemes for the formation of libraries and lectureships, the acquisition of a newspaper to serve their cause, and "the despatch of emissaries on missions of propagandism throughout the Empire." Rhodes espoused racial unity, that is, the merging of different white interests, and believed in home rule for the colonies along the lines of the U.S. constitution, that is, as a federation of self-governing constitutent parts analogous to the modern British Commonwealth. "The Americans have solved the problem," he said, of how home rule could prove consistent with empire. By 1892 he had also begun to contemplate a scholarship program which would send colonial students to Oxford.

In 1894 and 1895 Rhodes made it clear to Stead that, however much he worried about a premature end, he still felt "full of vigour and life." He hardly expected that he would require anyone but himself to administer his money for "many years to come."[67] It was only after the Jameson Raid, and after his heart began to weaken palpably in the late 1890s, that he began seriously to perfect and stabilize his dreams.

"The Predatory Instincts of Our Race"
Making War in Rhodesia

R HODES FINALLY VISITED his newly fashioned colony in late 1891, after the
conclusion of his first full legislative session as premier. This inspection,
at a time when the Rhodesian experiment was established, but was still vulnerable to African attack and financially precarious, inaugurated an intensified, empirical involvement by Rhodes in the detailed affairs of his creation.
Much more than the mines, Stellaland and Goshen, his parliamentary accomplishments, or even the rebuilding of Groote Schuur, Rhodesia was his triumphant offspring.

In Rhodesia, Rhodes found an object of care and concern of the kind
that Erikson has identified as a mark of a man's sucessful navigation of the
early mid-life crisis of generativity. It gave Rhodes, unmarried and childless,
an outlet for that natural desire to be needed which most men satisfy in par-
enthood. What Erikson calls "the widening concern for what has been gener-
ated by love, necessity, or accident" which "potentially extends to whatever a
man generates and leaves behind, creates and produces. . . ," for Rhodes
became a preoccupation and passion.[1] Along with seeking a personal destiny
through the mechanism of his many wills, Rhodesia drew Rhodes out of himself, thus countering the self-absorption which inevitably is the chief vulnerability of those who are able to translate their dreams into concrete accomplishments. To nurture the young Rhodesia into adolescence was for him more
than the obvious imperial task. After all, the colony by no accident carried his
name; if Rhodes were to live on after death, that territorial extension of himself must prove a success.

Given the scale and complexity of Rhodes' varied endeavors, his association with this singular activity was more direct, personal, and intense than it
might ordinarily have been during the busy 1890s. It was his troubled child.
That he interrupted his pursuit of a diamond monopoly and of political ad-

vantage in the Cape to tour Rhodesia in 1891, that he installed Jameson, his closest intimate and alter ego, as administrator in his own stead, that he busied himself with the day-to-day arrangements of the colony, and that he personally made the decision to go to war against the Ndebele demonstrate how thoroughly, even overwhelmingly, his sense of self was tied to the fortunes of the land that he had seized between the Limpopo and Zambezi rivers. Rhodes' self-esteem was so intimately bound up with its internal well-being and external success that he reacted emotionally, as if it were a part of himself. To the extent that Rhodesia was imperiled, so was Rhodes.[2] Much later, after the Jameson Raid and the Ndebele and Shona insurrections, when Rhodes' reputation had been sullied, his connection to Rhodesia was to become stronger and more obvious. But even before the Raid, when none was so powerful and unchecked in Africa and the Empire as was he, Rhodes was tightly bonded to this extension of himself. He was emotionally at risk over all aspects of the young entity beyond the Limpopo.

It was a year since the pioneers had arrived in Mashonaland. Rhodes had worried about their passage around Ndebeleland and had wanted to be with them in their initial triumph. But their situation, his, and the young colony's was in innumerable ways even more parlous in late 1891 than in late 1890. Not only had no gold been found, but both the local settlers and visiting experts had begun to doubt even the hypothetical promise of future mineral wealth. The soils still appeared rich, but opening up farms had proved slow and difficult without seeds and equipment from the Cape. Most of all, the comparative handful of settlers who were still on hand to greet Rhodes in 1891 were disgruntled, even angry, at what they considered their neglect by the British South Africa Company.

Many believed that Rhodes and the Company had abandoned them. Cut off from the south during much of the first half of 1891 by heavy rains, and prevented from opening up the shorter route to Beira because of Portuguese antagonism and natural obstacles, they had endured shortages of food, supplies, and equipment. Maize meal, their staple food, rotted before it could be conveyed to them. Coffee, sugar, flour, pepper, and even peas became impossibly scarce. Quinine, essential to ward off malaria, soared in price from several shillings to £5 an ounce. Jam was £2 a pot. And whiskey, without which few whites in southern Africa could begin to endure either isolation or privation, reached £1 a bottle. They also learned to their displeasure that Rhodes and De Beers controlled the subsoil rights, that all mining successes would be shared with the Company, and that—in sum—their great individual dreams of easily won wealth were more mirage than reality.

Only persons who floated companies and gave half of their shares to the British South Africa Company could mine gold. But the gold could not be beaten from its quartz surround by hand. Machinery was necessary, and Rhodes and his subordinates had failed to import even one stamp battery to crush or mill the ore. On what basis, complained the pioneers, could the Company thus claim its 50 percent? On the first anniversary of the occupation of Mashonaland, the pioneers and their successors held a big protest meeting in Salisbury, and were repeatedly critical of the Company and its leaders. Rhodes therefore went north largely to dispel discord among whites, to reorganize Rhodesia's management, and to establish a personal foundation for his own distant oversight and boosterism on behalf of his troubled fiefdom.

The directors of the Company in London were also becoming edgy. These were nervous times in British and South African capital markets. Investments in the Transvaal and the Cape, and in gold, looked less secure than they had a year or two before. Rhodesia seemed much more problematic, particularly in light of local discontent, transport difficulties, and the swift, relentless way in which Rhodes and his subordinates had spent Company funds with little return. In less than a year to March 1891, the Rhodesian sponge had absorbed £580,000. Of the £932,075 that had been issued as shares in London, only £606,291 had been realized. Hardly any capital remained; the Company faced bankruptcy, being saved by short-term loans, probably from Rhodes and Beit, and also from De Beers.[3] Then, to make matters worse, the directors and the British public began to receive or at least to hear word of disappointing reports by visiting experts. Beit, for example, visited Rhodesia in August 1891. "I think I will not undertake anything here," Beit quietly told Lionel Phillips. "So far I have not seen anything that I think worth putting £100 into."[4] He was less impressed with its mineral potential than he was with its soils. More significantly, hard-headed man that he was, he pronounced the experiment a failure until Rhodesia's logistical isolation could be alleviated. Without a rail route from the Indian Ocean to Umtali (Mutare) and Salisbury (Harare), or until one could be constructed, the colony's development would be slow. Heavy machinery would be needed for the extraction and processing of gold from underground workings; there seemed little evidence of alluvial gold, or, for that matter, of any other metals which could be exploited easily and were of value. Salisbury was 1600 miles from Cape Town, and any supplies delivered by ox-wagon from Vryburg and Mafeking during the winter (when grass was short) cost about £70 a ton. During the summer, when the rains swelled the many rivers between Bechuanaland the Mashonaland, the ox-wagons were halted, got stuck, or overturned.

Lord Randolph Churchill, the *enfant terrible* of Tory politics and former chancellor of the exchequer, owned shares in the Company. With Rhodes' blessing, even connivance, he traveled to Rhodesia in 1891 with a large retinue and abundant supplies. Rhodes expected booming support for the Company from Churchill, and sent Beit to accompany and guide him during the central phase of a journey that included controversial and much-ballyhooed visits to Kimberley, Johannesburg, and Pretoria. But Churchill's increasingly prominent fits of melancholy and cantankerousness, early but definitive signs of the syphilitic dementia which was to claim his life in 1895, gave an incendiary quality to his perceptions of the true state of affairs. Churchill traveled through southern Africa in choler and distemper, leaving annoyance and disdain in his wake. Overseas his reports had an impact, too. The Kaiser called

Churchill's comments those of some "wild schoolboy."[5] Nevertheless, Churchill's twenty widely read columns in the *Daily Graphic* (London), which netted him the then splendid sum of 2000 guineas, were devastating to the image of Rhodesia and, in late 1891 and early 1892, to the price of Company shares. The shares halved in value as a result of Churchill's cutting remarks.

Major Arthur Glyn Leonard, a commander of the British South Africa Company police, was at Tuli when Churchill made his way into Rhodesia. Churchill had the "cute look of an intelligent fox terrier," said Leonard. Otherwise his face betrayed "insignificance." He talked "well and fluently," and was knowledgeable, but he hardly gave Leonard the impression that he was either a "particularly brilliant, or specially able, much less a great, man." He lacked physical or mental stamina. "He strikes me," said Leonard, "as being merely sharp and clever." "A man more eaten up by his own conceit I have never seen—a conceit that, in combination with a bad temper, accounts more than anything else, I should think, for the unstability of his character." Moreover, although Churchill was chronologically young, he appeared "as old as a badly-preserved man of over fifty." As a sign of his advancing infection, Churchill shook like "an old man."

Beit was there with Churchill. Leonard saw Beit as the "most unassuming and altogether unostentatious man of wealth, and as kindly, courteous, and quiet as it is possible to be. Very ordinary and meagre in his ideas, and very commonplace in his conversation, he is one of the last men that I should have picked out of a crowd as able and capable! . . . Beit must be either so deep or so shallow, that in one case it is impossible to get to the bottom of him, and in the other, although it is possible to look through, it is quite as impossible to see anything!"[6]

For Churchill the country between Fort Victoria (Masvingo) and Fort Charter (north of Chivhu) was "grievous either for man or for domestic beast." Profitable cultivation of the sandy soil was impossible and the climate capricious, either boiling hot or bitterly cold, with occasional thick fog. "Where, then," Churchill asked himself, was the "much-talked-of fine country of the Mashona? Where is the 'promised land'. . . ?" On the low veld, where the soil was fertile, malaria was endemic and tsetse-fly-borne sleeping sickness was prevalent. On the high veld, largely free from fly and fever, the soil, reported Churchill, was "barren and worthless." To but one kind of person, the sportsman or hunter, would the area be attractive, concluded Churchill.

Churchill finally reached Salisbury—the promised land—in mid-August, admittedly in the depths of the southern hemispheric winter, when at 5,000 feet the nights were still cold. Its 300 white settlers gave the little town a "thriving, rising, healthy appearance," and they seemed content and confident. Nevertheless, the "necessaries of life," said Churchill, "whether food or raiment, were luxuries at Fort Salisbury and costly in the extreme." Bread, beer, butter, and meat were all impossibly dear. Of gold, to provide income in order to offset the expenses of consumer imports, there were few traces. Where some shafts had been sunk for gold, there was water, and no pumps.

Moreover, Churchill correctly cautioned his readers, the payable character of any gold finds depended upon access to them easily and cheaply, and preferably by the east coast route, as yet hardly guaranteed. Indeed, as Rhodes was soon to discover, it existed only as a future promise.

As much as the Company and Rhodes' friends and many other visitors had gilded and were later to embellish the Company's propaganda, Churchill, his brain relieved of civility by the syphilitic spirochete, was brutally frank. Relying on the judgment of Henry Cleveland Perkins, an American gold-mining expert in Lord Rothschild's employ with whom he (and Beit) had been traveling, and who had inspected the Mazoe mines along with Beit, Churchill declared that Rhodesia's future could not be considered golden. "Neither the extent of the reefs, the quality of the ore, nor the general formation of the country, . . . could justify the formation of large London companies. . . ."[7] Yet Rhodes and Jameson's new strategy of growth was based, in lieu of minerals, on the development of large tracts of countryside by overseas and local syndicates, and the sharing of their profits with the Company.

Even before Beit and Churchill had reported, the directors in London had grown alarmed about the administration of Rhodesia. Rhodes instructed Jameson, who replaced Colquhoun as administrator in mid-1891, to reduce expenditures rapidly. One of the subsidiary purposes of Rhodes' visit later in the year was to confer with Jameson and to impress upon him and others the enormous need to economize, especially by reducing the heavy cost of the police. Toward the end of his travels in the territory with Jameson, Rhodes instructed him "with all despatch" to reduce the police numbers, dealing liberally with all of those who were made redundant. "The police should now gradually assume a civil form," he said, and the local population should be mobilized into a part-time citizen militia to defend the country against the possiblity of Ndebele attack.[8]

Jameson was a haphazard, impulsive, and ineffective administrator, but neither Rhodes nor others were to discover how loosely he ran the country until much later, and not conclusively until 1896, when William H. Milton replaced Jameson, reorganized the running of the Company's possession, and began to clean out what Fox called an "Augean stable of the past."[9] During the years before the war against the Ndebele, and then until the Raid, Rhodes probably only dimly perceived how badly Jameson served his own and his associates' ambitions for the interior land. So long as Jameson quickly reduced costs, stifled or assuaged the disaffection among the settlers, and found ways to produce at least some return, Rhodes was apparently content.

Anyway, it was Jameson's charm and charisma upon which Rhodes relied to satisfy the board and detractors inside and outside the new country. Several of the early pioneers reported, "with a certain rueful appreciation," how Jameson "cajoled and fooled them." " 'He flirted with men,' " reported one, " 'like a woman; he fooled us and then laughed at us.' " As Jameson's brother, hardly an impartial observer, wrote home, it was "really extraordinary [Jameson's] popularity here, especially as the Company with Rhodes and . . .

[F. Rutherfoord] Harris have come in for a good deal of criticism. . . . Many of the Company's laws and mining regulations are much disliked, but somehow or other [Jameson] has a way of talking them over and getting the malcontents to agree with him."[10] Moreover, Rhodes trusted Jameson as he trusted no other; Jameson's aura was clearly perceived through a sparkling, intensely personal prism. "I am more indebted to [Jameson]," said Rhodes, "than to any man in South Africa."[11] Both Rhodes and Rhodesia were to suffer much as a result of this artful misalliance.

Rhodes hardly traveled northward in 1891 solely to be with Jameson or to oversee his administrative activities. He could not normally have afforded three months away from Cape Town and Kimberley—especially being distant from a telegraph line—in any year, much less the frenetic years of the early 1890s, when he was at his zenith. But if his offspring, to the fortunes of which his self-esteem was tightly tied, was being threatened by Churchill's venom and local discontent, he simply had to go. Presumably he asked David Christaan de Waal to accompany him as de Waal and Matthys Marthinus Venter had done in 1890, when they had traveled to Tuli and back. This time, in order to enhance the new territory's image in the eyes of the Cape Afrikaners, Rhodes wanted de Waal to see Rhodesia proper. De Waal, like Venter a member of the Cape parliament, was particularly close to Hofmeyr and other leaders of the Bond. Hofmeyr was his brother-in-law. Moreover, de Waal, whose devotion to Rhodes was secure, was a fluent writer in Dutch. De Waal could be counted upon to praise Rhodes' projects lavishly.

De Waal claimed to have himself insisted upon taking the east coast route to avoid the long slow trek with oxen which Rhodes preferred. But Rhodes may also have wanted to see whether a road or a railway could be driven up the steep mountainsides from the Pungwe estuary to Umtali. Joining Rhodes and de Waal for this purpose, and as guide, was young Major Frank Johnson of the pioneers. Months before he had attempted to build a road and start a coach service for the Company from the Pungwe to Umtali, using capital supplied by Rhodes.

Together with Antonio de la Cruz, Rhodes' servant, this small party sailed from Port Elizabeth in mid-September, reaching Beira twelve days later. Along the way de Waal was greatly annoyed by "a host of blackbeetles" that crept up and down the iron walls of his stateroom and across his bed; he detested his "beetle infested" cabin. Rhodes, promptly consulted, was indifferent. "I cannot say I like [the beetles]," he said, "but, as I have had many a worse time than this in my life, I don't worry myself much about such minor discomforts." De Waal nevertheless remained distressed. "Oh, my good friend," the premier supposedly said, "take the world as it is!"

Johnson, however, found Rhodes much less relaxed. The hurried trip north reflected more than customary impatience. Seething internally at Churchill and vulnerable narcissistically since his prize creation was being challenged, Rhodes behaved with less than his usual studied control. Rarely thinskinned, Rhodes became furious when the captain of their coastal steamer refused an invitation to join the party for a drink, and livid when the Portuguese authorities prevented him from recruiting Africans as and when he wished and, adding insult, when they insisted on inspecting his personal baggage. "I'll take their [expletive] country from them!" he is said to have screamed. Much later, on the road from Umtali, Rhodes beat de Waal's African servant for alleged slackness, causing the unfortunate Shangaan to stumble among the horses, one of whom kicked him strongly in the stomach. "I had anything but a kind feeling towards the Premier, who had been the cause of the accident," commented de Waal.

On another occasion, when they were camping along the escarpment, Rhodes became visibly annoyed when Johnson insisted on making big fires all around their tiny tent, into which the three whites attempted to squeeze for the night. Johnson explained that the fires were necessary to keep marauding lions away. Rhodes, reported Johnson, indicated that if he wanted to see lions he would go to a zoo. "I will not be frightened," he declared. Later, in the bright of the moon, Rhodes got up and moved beyond the flames. Johnson heard a lion's roar, although probably from some distance. "Almost immediately," remembered Johnson, "I saw the strange spectacle of the Prime Minister . . . dashing back towards our tent . . . while the trousers of his pyjamas were hanging down well below his knees." "I would gladly pay ten pounds," wrote de Waal, "for a photo of our Premier as he looked when he entered the tent with his fallen pyjamas."[12]

Lions aside, the travelers found the 242 miles from the coast to Umtali unfit for easy or swift carriage of either hardy pioneers or their baggage. It was a test of Rhodes' personal mettle and physical stamina, as well as of his unaccustomed endurance of a long communication gap with the outside world. The first part of the journey was aboard a riverboat to a point sixty miles up the Pungwe. The broad road that Johnson had promised had been replaced in reality by a footpath so rugged that even their horses found it formidable. They were compelled to abandon their carts and to trudge on alone through tsetse-fly-infested country during the most torrid time of the year. Fortunately, Rhodes and Johnson were able to shoot what they called pheasants (probably guinea fowl or francolin), zebra, and buck, thus keeping the party in meat. Otherwise their slog up over the mountains was tortuous, tiring, and vexing—at least for de Waal; that Rhodes took the vicissitudes and disappointments of the trek with fortitude was less a sign of inner equanimity than an indication that the terrible physical demands of the journey were subordinate to the need to salvage all that Rhodesia meant to him. Ultimately, after passing through Macequece and over the Penhalonga Mountains, Rhodes and his group reached Umtali twenty days after leaving the shelter of the Pungwe River. Now he knew at first-hand how precariously his little colony was situated, and how isolated it would remain until permanent transportation links were forged from both the east and the south.

Jameson was at Umtali to meet Rhodes, and to guide him within a week across the remaining 174 miles of pleasant upland country to Salisbury. But first Rhodes insisted, certainly as a means of reinforcing his own notion of his place in the world at a time when his inner feelings were shaky, on visiting a little hospital recently established by two intrepid nurses from Britain. Rose Blennerhassett and Lucy Sleeman had made their way out to Africa from Cardiff and Southampton. After assisting in Durban and Johannesburg, they had traveled north by the east-coast route that Rhodes had so recently endured, and started to care for the sick of Umtali. "As we were leaving the hospital hut," they wrote of a Saturday in October, "Mr. Rhodes rode up alone. His appearance and Roman Emperor type of head are too well known to need description." They insisted that he should see their tiny clinic, although Rhodes said with characteristic empathy that if he himself were sick he would hate to be the object of such a visit. When he entered, the patients said nothing, simply stared "with all the powers of their eyes. . . ." "We discovered afterwards," said the nurses, "that they could not understand his not having finer clothes. I think they expected a more gorgeous apparition, a chain and ring man probably. . . ." Rhodes generously gave the nurses a check for £150—more than they had wanted. Rhodes' "generosity is proverbial," they said. "Everything about the man is big—faults, virtues, projects." They called him "the darling of Fortune," and wisely suggested that "that blind goddess does not often select her favourites from the Sunday School." The nurses were charmed by Rhodes' simple manner, and by his boyish enjoyment of a joke.[13]

As the small party trekked toward Salisbury, de Waal was so taken by the shape and presumed fertility of the land between Umtali and Marandellas that at one favorable spot he paused and claimed a vast expanse as the farm which had been promised to him by Rhodes. De Waal was impressed, too, by Marandellas, where the country was "exceedingly beautiful [and] the Kafirs . . . all in good condition; some of them are as fat as pigs. . . ." Rhodes' reactions are unknown, although Johnson remembered him as being "more and more excited . . . like a schoolboy. . . ." the closer they came to Salisbury. He was "obviously delighted to be in his own country." But, even as de Waal marveled at the little settlement on the high veld, Rhodes was depressed by the lack of substantial buildings, possibly having expected his action to have been centered upon some magnificent city instead of a few corrugated iron shacks and some wattle-and-daub huts along the Makabusi stream. Finally, Johnson showed Rhodes the foundations of the settlement's first synagogue. Then the founder brightened up: "My country's all right," he kept repeating. "If the Jews come, my country's all right," he exclaimed with a stereotypical faith in the sound commercial instincts of Jewish merchants.[14]

Already Salisbury was full of traders and speculators. Actual prospectors were few, and the original band of pioneers had largely been succeeded by others less imbued with Rhodes' ideals. The country was no longer short of food, but because the promised land was not delivering as fruitfully and abundantly as had been expected, and because the local residents correctly perceived that Rhodes and his cronies had no intention of relaxing their firm grip on the country's economic development, the town still simmered with discontent. One deputation of complainers arrived shortly after Rhodes' arrival, and found him in his bath, a water-filled sponge over his head. Rhodes spoke of the empire and posterity. The townsmen, led by a Scot, made it clear that they had come to Rhodesia for profit, not posterity. When he and his fellows persisted, Rhodes reminded them that every African village was stocked with maize, pumpkins, beans, and eggs. What more could they want? "No," he told them, "your agitation has not arisen from want of food, but from something else: it is want of *liquor* that displeases you!" Whether or not Rhodes managed to calm the troubled spirits of Salisbury, and whether or not he learned all he could about his own country, he tarried only four days there before heading south toward home.[15]

En route to the distant railhead, Rhodes, de Waal, Jameson, and their ox wagons traveled south past Charter and through the country which Churchill had condemned but which de Waal (and Selous) thought pretty, healthy, well-populated, and certainly suited to large-scale white settlement. They also saw ample evidence of gold: rock formations that looked to the eye as if they were auriferous; what seemed to be ancient workings; and new shafts from which prospectors were digging seven to nine ounces of gold per ton of overburden. When they reached Fort Victoria they found that the telegraph lines from Mafeking had arrived the day before, and that messages were waiting for Rhodes. He was thrilled to be back in command again of the Cape, his corporations, and his corner of the world.

Only that morning, wrote Churchill, the transcontinental telegraph line had been brought within two miles of Victoria's fort. Churchill rode out with Rhodes to find a peculiar and "very African" scene. "Amid waggons, oxen, mules, and horses, piles of telegraph poles, coils of wire, boxes of insulators, and odds and ends of baggage and provisions could be seen meandering a little green string communicating with the waggon, which it entered, the elevated wire being some yards off."[16] Inside the wagon sat the operator, pounding away at the keys to the empire.

In February 1892 the telegraph line arrived in Salisbury, carrying a prolonged conversation between Rhodes in Cape Town and Jameson. Subsequently, it was carried north on wooden, termite-endangered poles across the Zambezi into Nyasaland, and up to the Company-controlled southern shores of Lake Tanganyika. Rhodes intended these vital links with his possessions to be but the first stages of a transcontinental communication system between the Cape and Cairo. But it was a long time before Rhodes' successors were to realize his dream; the Germans controlled Tanganyika and for years resisted a line, no matter how thin, of British red across their territory. The Mahdi controlled the Sudan. And Uganda, the centerpiece of the great interior lake region, was embroiled in a series of local wars. Later in 1892, Rhodes would personally influence the course of Britain's policies toward Uganda, and not only to advance his telegraphic cause.

In 1891, before Rhodes continued his journey southward from Salisbury to Kimberley, he and de Waal detoured slightly to view and experience the imposing and mysterious ruins of Great Zimbabwe. "We were now confronted," de Waal wrote of his initial glimpse of its granite bulk, "by the massive ruins of the . . . temple, and the historical hill that rises close to it. A strange feeling ran through me as I stood there and cast my eyes upon the ruins; it was the same sensation I felt when I beheld the remains of ancient Rome, and, at a later date, those of Pompeii and Herculaneum."[17] Presumably—although de Waal does not say—those were Rhodes' sentiments as well, for it was evident throughout the remainder of his life that Rhodes had been awed by Zimbabwe (as he was often awed by those examples of human grandeur with which he identified), whether or not he fully shared the contemporary prevailing view that such an astounding edifice must have been constructed by whites, probably Phoenicians in Biblical times.

As Rhodes and de Waal saw, Zimbabwe was but the largest and most dramatic-looking of a host of similar, if smaller, stone edifices scattered throughout eastern and southern Africa. Zimbabwe, probably the capital and certainly the ritual center of an early African interior kingdom, was surrounded by a so-called acropolis—a massive defensive fortification on a lofty hill above the surrounding plain. It contained intricate passageways, numerous ruins, and betrayed abundant evidence of gold smelting. In the valley below these battlements was an elliptical great enclosure or temple, and the footings of many houses built of stone. The enclosure's outer perimeter, 800 feet around, 17 feet thick at its base, and 32 feet high, was constructed of 900,000 large, undressed granite blocks—about 200,000 cubic feet of stonework. Inside, there were more stone embankments and a peculiar, conical tower (called Phallus by de Waal) which dominated the valley's stillness. All of the high stonework in both the acropolis and the enclosure was fitted without mortar. The original workmen used wooden or stone lintels and also constructed an extensive drainage system. They carved attractive soapstone birds (crowned hornbills?), one of which Rhodes carried away or otherwise obtained, and traded extensively with the East African coast—or so the vast hoard of glass beads, Chinese porcelain, and copper coins that was discovered in the ruins would suggest.

Zimbabwe moved de Waal to prophecy and praise. "I am fully persuaded," he told his countrymen, "that the day will soon come when we shall see large cities round about Simbabe, and when the produce of that country will surpass that of any other country in Africa. Just as once the eye of Europe was turned to America, and a great migration thither followed, so it shall fall on Africa—and with the same result. . . . *Now* is the time to trek! Mashonaland is still open to all. . . ." The Shona inhabitants of the Zimbabwe region were "fine, strong and fat"—certainly prosperous.[18]

After leaving Jameson and others, Rhodes and de Waal trekked in a leisurely fashion southwestward along the route of the pioneers. They hunted often, after which Rhodes enjoyed long soaks in his elastic, fold-up bath. At nights he slept curled up in an armchair rather than in his usual hammock.

Rhodes preferred this seemingly uncomfortable position presumably because doing so permitted him to breathe more easily. If so, he may already have been suffering from the heart problem which was to prove the dark companion of his remaining years. Moreover, the creeping agonies of his heart were probably influenced by accumulated stress—the impotent fury with which he must have reacted to Churchill's treacherous columns, the slurs of the pioneers about their (and his) country, and the trials of the trek itself. All would have combined to add a measure of deep distress to physiological deterioration.

When Rhodes' party finally reached Tuli, on the border with Bechuanaland, it accelerated its pace, and rushed southward in a light wagon, changing oxen frequently. Pausing only for a conversation with Chief Kgama in Palapye, and several telegraphic talks with Cape Town (one of which was to arrange a meeting with James Sivewright prior to his rail negotiations in the Transvaal), and to shift to a mule-drawn coach in Notwani, Rhodes insisted on a rapid dash to Sir Sidney Shippard's house in Vryburg. The hurry may well have represented Rhodes' typically active way of denying anxiety, particularly his fears that all was not well with his heart. Whatever the reason, Rhodes and de Waal traversed 4,000 miles in three months, the final 625 miles from Tuli in seven days and six nights, a record for southern African travel by oxen and mule. "No one else had before completed that distance in so short a time with only draught animals," rued de Waal, "and, I may safely assert, no one ever will."

Within another day, toward the end of November, Rhodes was back in Kimberley, planning with Sivewright, ignoring his heart, and ready to resume his battle for Rhodesia and southern Africa's future. Indeed, one of Rhodes' first and most important acts was to send Maund home to give a positive report about Rhodesia's potential to the board—"to counteract the mistatements as to the prospects of Mashonaland." Maund had "untiring energy," Rhodes told Cawston. Earlier, Rhodes had instructed Jameson to give Maund 10,000 morgen (22,000 acres) of prime land in the new colony. "He goes home," Rhodes assured Jameson, "to fight our battles." [19]

By the end of 1892, those battles had been contained, if not fully won. In reviewing the progress of the Company for its shareholders, Rhodes could provide a sanguine report. Admittedly, he said, the early pioneers could not "pick up gold like gooseberries." They had to toil, and be patient, and consequently became depressed. The country had been condemned as barren and worthless, but after Jameson took charge and Rhodes paid his own visit, the situation improved markedly. "I found . . . a discontented population of about fifteen hundred people," Rhodes recalled. Since then, settlers had purchased building lots in the towns and he had provided a telegraph system for £90,000 which was sending all Company messages free and even making a profit. He was starting to build a railway from Beira. He assured the shareholders that both Mashonaland and Northern Zambezia were healthy. Moreover, Rhodesia was "mineralised throughout." He spoke of a vast gold-bearing country and promised "good returns" to those who had invested in him and his Company. As Rhodes had written privately to Stow after his trip, "I like the country much. It will . . . carry a white population. There appears to be gold everywhere. . . ."

Possibly to cement the Company's position with financiers at home, but also because Rhodes regularly warmed to sympathetic audiences and liked to share his fondest dreams with potential followers, he indicated that when his new territory had "filled with white people" he would insist upon self-government—the assimilation of Mashonaland to the Cape Colony and other autonomous parts of southern Africa. "When the day arrives there [should] be no difficulty in the change from government by a charter to government by the people of the country." Again, "people" meant whites; Rhodes and his contemporaries largely ignored any claims that the indigenous inhabitants of the territory might assert. The interior of Africa, Rhodes and others believed during the heyday of imperialism, was theirs to conquer and, implicitly, theirs to improve.

Rhodes further addressed the financial concerns of his shareholders. When he traveled to Rhodesia, its administration was costing £250,000 a year, largely funds spent on a permanent police force. Jameson said that he could run the country on a mere £3,000 a month, which De Beers lent. Jameson did so by reducing police numbers from 700 to 40, and the overall annual outlay to about £30,000, even less than his first estimate. Moreover, in order to defend the country, Jameson enlisted a force of volunteers, paying each man £4 a year. Rhodes considered the 500 men of this militia, and especially the 300 who could be mounted quickly on horses, "amply sufficient to defend the country from attack." Where that attack would come from, he asked rhetorically, one could hardly guess. The Transvaal and Portugal were no longer threats. Even the Ndebele constituted no danger. "We are on the most friendly terms with Lobengula. . . . I have not the least fear of any trouble in the future from Lobengula," he declared in late 1892.[20]

The shareholders were misled, hardly inadvertently, for Rhodes' optimism was calculated to divert the gullible and faithful. As Olive Schreiner remarked in another context, Rhodes was "morally dangerous" because he gained his ends by "wriggling, wriggling, wriggling."[21] Rhodes knew the real state of the territory: he knew that whites remained unhappy—that 1892 had been punctuated by persistent white protest against the half-share that the Company claimed of all syndications, that whites continued to grumble about shortages and high prices, and that many had lost faith in the mineral bonanza.

James Johnston, an acerbic Scottish missionary physician who had served in Jamaica, reached Salisbury in mid-1892 and found "stagnation in every line of business . . . [and] bankruptcy . . . the order of the day." "Every other night indignation meetings are held," and cablegrams of protest dashed off to Britain. The cruelest deception of all, he said, had been the encouragement of farmers and families to come to Rhodesia and settle on the high veld. "No one looking out on the dreary wastes we have traversed," said Johnston, ". . . could hope to earn even a bare living from the arid soil." A Company official invited Johnston to examine the town's vegetable market. "A jackass could have carried away all the garden produce displayed without being over-loaded," he reported. "That there is gold in the country there can be no ques-tion," Johnston argued. But it was there only for those who were willing to "risk their lives in an insalubrious clime." Rhodesia was "but another 'South Sea bubble.' "[22]

Africans were also discontented. Rhodes knew that there had been skir-mishes between Shona and whites, and a few brushes with the Ndebele, but he may genuinely have been entirely ignorant of the depth and seriousness of the growing antagonism between settler and Shona and settler and Nde-bele. Even more critical, Jameson probably never hinted (even if he knew) how relations between black and white were deteriorating, and what conse-quences the rule of vigilantes on a sparsely settled, raw frontier could have for the fragile colony. Rhodes himself was hardly anxious in 1892 to precipi-tate a war which would prove costly in Africa and unpopular at home. He knew few of the details of how Jameson and a handful of whites were abusing the Shona and provoking the Ndebele, and hardly supposed that the massive economies which he and the board had decreed would soon push the country toward war. At this time Rhodes cared too little for the welfare of Africans to appreciate where Jameson's administrative methods could well lead.

Settlers took the law into their own hands. The British government had carefully instructed the Company to limit its jurisdiction and application of law to whites, leaving Africans almost entirely alone. Yet when Jameson's gov-ernment and those whites for whom he was responsible were effectively shorn of military protection, they acted as if only their own boldness could possibly make secure what, objectively, was a situation of utter precariousness. Jame-son appointed four magistrates from among the ranks of the most powerful settlers, and largely let them administer their vast districts on behalf of their own kind. They, like so many early colonials, had little regard for Africans and tolerated—as one might expect—the worst kind of abuses by whites.[23]

Everywhere there were men who, because of the absence of any real civil authority, were deputed to exercise that authority as field cornets on the South African model. (In event of hostilities, armed farmers and prospectors under their field cornets could be mobilized as a defensive militia.) They, or whites enrolled on the spot to act, or whites simply possessed only of approval after the fact, could discipline Africans, coerce their labor, punish presumed male-factors, burn villages suspected of harboring defectors or miscreants, seize cattle and goats, interfere (for payment or other advantage) in intra-African quarrels, and generally assume the role of conquering lords. Such activities occurred during a period when in Lobengula's and British eyes they were still interlopers subject (at least until the signing of the second Lippert protocol) to an overarching indigenous suzerainty.

Throughout 1892 and early 1893 Jameson authorized vigorous police patrols which were consciously designed to demonstrate the might (the superior arms and training) of whites despite their pronounced numerical inferiority. Few as they were, bold assertions of right and vigor by whites may have been as clever as it was a natural and successful tactic. When a white trader was killed early in the year under circumstances that were never completely explained, a patrol burned villages in the vicinity and, upon its return, punished an unrelated village—simply because there had been complaints by whites. They killed and wounded a number of its inhabitants.

As far as Jameson was concerned, these applications of a frontier code of pseudo-law were justified because the local Shona had been "impertinent and threatening." Rhodes was pleased that Jameson had been "maintaining the dignity of the law." On a subsequent occasion when a white merchant alleged that his trading goods had been stolen by men from a particular village subordinate to Chief Mangwende, and that he had been abused physically by Africans, a patrol under Captain Charles Frederick Lendy was directed by Jameson to take "summary" action. Off to the offending village it dragged a seven-pound cannon and a Maxim machine gun, in addition to the usual rifles. With the Maxim firing rapidly and the seven pounder blasting into Mangwende's flimsy huts, the carnage was severe: twenty-three Africans died and forty-seven cattle were seized. "I am sure a very wholesome lesson has been given to all the chiefs of the district," reported Lendy.

Yet both the high commissioner's office in Cape Town and Lord Knutsford, the colonial secretary in London, were horrified when they learned of this outrageous, utterly disproportionate retribution. Lord Abercorn, chairman of the Company, remonstrated mildly to Rhodes. Jameson, in charge and on the spot, explained that such fastidiousness was fine for the board but impossible for whites who could only survive if they showed their strength.[24]

Morality and legality aside, the representative of the Company who was stationed near Lobengula in Gbulawayo sounded the most certain alarm. After an incident of reprisal similar to those connected with the two white traders, he told Rhodes' secretary that Jameson had been wrong to "mix himself up" in a dispute between two Shona chiefs in the Fort Victoria area. "Small matters like this will bring on difficulties and cause us both endless trouble and lengthy palavers."[25] Nevertheless, the small matters grew larger and more frequent. Jameson attempted to prevent Ndebele raiding parties from collecting tribute from their Shona vassals and, as Shona chiefs on the edge of Ndebeleland began to appreciate that Jameson's whites might well intervene on their behalf, the potential for open clashes became real. Jameson even tried to insist that Lobengula should ask the Company to collect tribute on his behalf from recalcitrant Shona chiefs; Rhodes grasped at any evidence of this kind that Lobengula's writ had ceased to run in Mashonaland. By September 1892 the Company told Lobengula that he ought to keep his raiding parties away from the Victoria district; it was becoming too thickly populated with whites.

Jameson sought no excuse for war. Likewise the great monarch wisely restrained his people and desired no confrontation with the Company. His induna were under instruction to molest no whites, indeed to be patient under all circumstances providing that his own ascendance over the Shona was not undermined. A few whites who tried to prospect in Ndebele territory were harried, but that is all.

During the first half of 1893 neither the Ndebele nor the Company prepared for war. Jameson's position was still too weak and easily compromised; Lobengula feared white firepower. True, Lobengula expected an attack and some of his warriors spoiled for combat. In March 1893 he sent a detachment to defend his northern border and, the next month, another to defend his southern marches. True, too, Africans persisted in cutting the Company's telegraph wire, presumably because the accessible copper wire made excellent jewelry and was certain acknowledgement of a family's wealth.

However innocent the cause, Jameson could hardly take the loss of his communication links complacently; Rhodes for one would vent his wrath. Yet, after sending an officer to Lobengula to complain, Jameson discovered that Shona, not Ndebele, had in fact been responsible. On a second occasion, in May 1893, when wires may or may not have been cut, whites used the supposed theft as an excuse to take cattle from Shona as compensation. However, the cattle were Lobengula's. He demanded them back, explaining that only his patience had held his followers in check. "Why should you seize my cattle—did I cut your wires?" he asked Jameson by cable. "You accuse my people when probably the damage was done by some of your own . . . men." Moreover, "[my people] begged and prayed . . . to allow them to go and fetch the cattle, but I would not allow it and prefer settling . . . matters amicably."[26] Jameson promised to return Lobengula's cattle.

There were powerful reasons why the Company, and the whites in Mashonaland, should have wanted war in 1893. The isolated colony was still struggling. Most of the small-time traders and prospectors, any who were farming, and even some of the more amply backed syndicators had as yet discovered no bonanza. Their prospects looked no better in 1893 than they had during the dark, disgruntled days of 1891 or 1892. By eliminating the threat of Ndebele reprisals against the Shona, there would be more security of investment. Psychologically, the settlers could sink their new roots deeper into the promised land. There was a growing stream of labor into Victoria, Hartley, and Salisbury from Ndebeleland; conquest would preserve ready access to this pool of labor on which mining and agriculture depended. Costs of transport would be reduced if the long road northeastward could cut directly across Ndebele territory. Most of all, many assumed that an easier prosperity could be achieved by overwhelming the Ndebele and taking their cattle and, especially their land. Surely the great, glorious reefs of rich gold on which Rhodesia's entire existence had been predicated must be discovered somewhere north of the Limpopo. If not in the country of the Shona, then certainly in the lands controlled by the Ndebele.

Rhodes' territorial creation had been concocted of rumor and supposition, settled and funded by reckless speculation, and sustained by obfuscation, legerdemain, and hyperbole. Crushing the Ndebele was an inevitable further step in the inexorable march of imperialism across Africa. The immediate causality of any challenge and the precise timing of the attack by whites on the Ndebele was determined, however, less by large historical forces than by a set of very localized, unpredictable events, the rapidly altering perceptions of power by each of the contending parties, and profound shifts in the personal tactics of Jameson, Rhodes, and Lobengula.

Overwhelming the Ndebele would not necessarily prove easy. From the perspective of the later 1890s, after a successful war, it was simple to have translated white greed into vigorous white action. But the whites were few, the number of horses available for cavalry attacks were even fewer, the ranks of the white police had been decimated, and the Ndebele could mass angry spearmen in their thousands and numerous gunners to battle any white challenge. The Ndebele were still regarded as formidable fighters. (Despite Lendy's encounter, Hiram Maxim's new machine gun had not yet fully proved its efficacy against masses of African warriors.) Moreover, from a financial standpoint Rhodes could not afford a long war. The British government had no stomach for any kind of conflict which might involve its own troops and, thus, heavy costs. Citizens in the Cape were as yet little concerned about the Ndebele. No one inside or outside the colony harbored grievances against the Ndebele sufficient to serve as more than a transparent pretext for war.

Lobengula, tricked or outsmarted by Rhodes, and in many ways humiliated by the establishment of Rhodesia in the country of the Shona, had behaved impeccably. He had restrained the hotheads among his induna who had wished to teach the whites a lesson. Over and over again he had avoided conflict and curbed his war parties. He had refrained from maintaining a tight hold over the Shona, whom he still regarded as his subjects and serfs. He had turned the other cheek, away from white provocation. Knowing that sooner or later whites would try to take his country, he had attempted to reduce or contain potential sources of conflict. He had readily agreed to an informal border between white and Ndebele spheres, and apologized on those occasions when his men mistakenly crossed the line to chase or levy tribute on Shona. But Lobengula was under steady pressure from within. Many of his induna believed him too passive and insufficiently challenging to whites. He was accused of allowing the Shona to shelter under the white man's tent— of not pursuing the true interests of the Ndebele nation with sufficient vigor. Given these tactical disagreements, given the growing boldness of the whites and the complementary impatience of the Ndebele, given what Colenbrander had warned were unnecessary and worrisome challenges to the indigenous regime, and given what appeared to be a stagnancy—a lack of urgent development in Rhodesia—it is neither surprising that the local whites began to spoil for a fight nor that Africans, unwittingly, soon provided opportunities for an escalation of hostilities.

"When they knocked me in the eye the 2nd day I was there I [resolved]

. . . that when the bell really rang for their disappearance . . . that I wd. be there to help them leave." Harris, always pugnacious, expressed the bellicose sentiments of those who had dealt with or been victims of the Ndebele. And he was well placed, as Rhodes' British South Africa Company secretary in Cape Town, and Rhodes' channel of communication to the north, to influence the pace of events. But even Harris (he meant well, Jameson commented, but was "really a muddling ass—on the surface a genius but under the crust as thick as they are made") in early 1892 believed that it would be at least two years before the clash would come. Or maybe it never would, the Ndebele possibly being able to "accommodate themselves to their environment" as the Swazis had done.[27]

The whites of Victoria were the most fully exposed of the settlers. They were naturally jittery, suspicious, and antagonistic. They harbored real and imagined grievances against the Ndebele. Their chief protector, as the head of the tiny police detachment stationed in Victoria, was the notorious Lendy, never one to shy away from a good brawl or an opportunity to bash blacks in general or Ndebele in particular. Jameson barely kept Lendy in check at the best of times. Yet in June 1893, when Lendy and his men confronted a Ndebele tribute collecting party on the outskirts of Fort Victoria, he and they satisfied themselves that Lobengula merely wanted cattle from the Shona; it was a dispute between Africans that was not intended to involve whites. Lendy refrained from interfering. Nor was he troubled when he learned that this small raiding group could well be followed by larger ones, all directed at teaching the cheeky Shona a further lesson.

Jameson was pleased with Lendy's report, and assured Rhodes that calm and mutual restraint were still the order of the trans-Limpopan day. Rhodes, in response, expressed himself satisfied by Lobengula's appropriately peaceful regard for whites. But Lobengula should be told, Rhodes instructed, that although he could continue to punish his own subjects as he saw fit (in accord with British policy), his war parties must not cross the informal border with the colony. He should reach and punish his subjects only through the Company. In this manner, Rhodes reasoned, the authority of the Company over the Shona would be strengthened and its ability to be the sole guarantor of law and order in the colony demonstrated in a conclusive fashion.[28]

Rhodes was not, as some have suggested, shifting suddenly from a pacific to a war-mongering policy. True, he was supremely confident in the Cape, having recently reshaped his cabinet after the Logan scandal and strengthened his already strong hand politically. His imperial standing had never been higher. His South African mines were producing diamonds in abundance and some gold. In every sphere, even within himself, Rhodes' omnipotence had been recognized or was being acknowledged. It makes good sense to suggest that Lobengula was but another obstacle to topple—that Rhodes accepted few bounds to his newly formed personal dominion and that the early winter of 1893 would have proved an appropriate moment for Rhodes to have pushed Jameson toward conflict as a result of broad strategic rather than narrower, parochial considerations. Yet there is little evidence that Rhodes wanted war (although Jameson may have believed otherwise), or that he had lost faith in squaring people and potentates. A true middle child, outright confrontation was not usually his way.

Ndebele attempts to impose themselves on Shona near Victoria continued, however, as Lendy had been informed. Early in July 1893 a massive force of several thousand warriors set out to teach recalcitrant Shona a lesson they would hardly forget. Lobengula was punctilious and proper in warning Moffat, Jameson, Lendy, and whites everywhere that his war party or impi was on African business only. My impi, Lobengula told Lendy, "will probably come across some white men, who are asked to understand that it has nothing whatever to do with them. They are likewise asked not to oppose the impi in its progress. Also, if the people who have committed the offence have taken refuge among the white men they are asked to give them up for punishment."[29] Yet the messages, telegraphed as they were intended to be, reached Lendy and Jameson only after the impi had descended upon the nervous residents of Victoria and, indeed, had begun slaughtering Shona along the streets, behind the church, and near the hospital within the little settlement. Soon, however, they were gone from the town to cow and cripple Shona in villages throughout the surrounding district. The number of dead and wounded are subject to dispute; not at issue is the impact of the Ndebele irruption on the availability of labor and on the collective white psyche.

Jameson nevertheless reacted calmly. Although "the Victoria people naturally have got the jumps," he told Harris in Cape Town, reports about the Ndebele incursion were exaggerated. He told Lendy to repulse the impi, but without a collision. "From a financial point of view," Jameson reminded Lendy, war ". . . would throw the country back till God knows when." To Lobengula, Jameson was also restrained. The great chief could continue to punish the Shona in his own way, but he could not send impi across the border, must recall any impi at once, and must return to their owners any cattle taken in the recent raid.

Rhodes, presumably guided by Jameson, also refused to be provoked. Because of the letters and cables from Lobengula, Rhodes suggested that the chief was still determined "not to come into collision with the white men." Loch, telegraphing Lobengula from Cape Town, was much more bombastic: "These acts," he said, ". . . cannot be permitted to continue. . . . I wish to control the anger of the white people, but when aroused in just indignation I shall find it difficult to restrain them. . . . You must withdraw your impi." If not, Lobengula's impi would be scattered "like chaff is blown before the wind. . . . Be warned in time."[30] Lobengula's reply to Jameson was a humble apology.

Jameson rode 188 miles from Salisbury to investigate. A companion on the journey reported that the administrator, even after hearing more details of the Victoria incident, was "most loath to take offensive measures." After attaining the little town, Jameson grew no more belligerent. However, he appreciated that the killing of Shona was having a disastrous effect on the availability of labor. The raid itself was simply a large one, he cabled south. But, more seriously, "every native has deserted from mines and farms . . . [and] unless some shooting is done I think it will be difficult to get labour even after [the raiders] have all gone."[31] He contemplated a need to "drive the Matabele out" to restore confidence among the Shona. Still, Jameson knew that as much as some of the induna wanted to fight, Lobengula himself had peaceful intentions. Jameson also appears, contrary to what many have concluded, to have been little swayed by the pressure of local and Salisbury whites, baying now as never before for Ndebele blood. He thought that their agitation would pass. Yet Jameson had ordered Lendy and a relatively tiny contingent of mounted whites to repulse one section of the impi. They had done so easily, with no loss of white life. That the superior firepower and élan of the whites could in fact rout a much larger Ndebele force was the critical, determining experience.

Jameson—at once Rhodes' "necessity and his curse"—thus urged Rhodes to "consider the advisability of completing the thing." It "could be done pretty cheaply. . . ." Opening up Matabeleland "would give us a tremendous lift in shares and everything else," Jameson continued. "The fact of its being shut up give it an immense value here and outside." Rhodes' initial response was to understand that it might be necessary "in the interests of the Mashonas, women and children, to drive the Matabele away." He concurred, but he instructed Jameson, "If you do strike, strike hard." On the evening of 18 July Rhodes and Jameson monopolized the telegraph lines, conversing by dots and dashes and the clack and clatter of the early sending and receiving equipment. It appears—no precise record survives—that this exchange of views was crucial to shaping Rhodes' receptivity to a war, and in hastening preparations within Rhodesia and elsewhere for such hostilities. Bullied by Jameson—"you have got to tell me that you have got the money"—Rhodes may well have reluctantly promised the £50,000 that he later pledged from selling his own shares. Over the telegraph lines, however, he also tested Jameson: How could a handful of whites win a war against the much more numerous Ndebele?

"Read Luke XIV.31," came the imperious command from the front benches of parliament. Rhodes, although not well read biblically or accustomed to quoting Scripture, had a point to make. Jameson quickly scanned that passage—"Or what king, going to make war against another king, sitteth not down first, and consulteth whether he be able with ten thousand to meet him that cometh against him with twenty thousand"—and, influenced by Lendy's recent action against a part of the impi, replied that he had read Luke, and that it was "all right."[32]

Rhodes or Jameson? Or both? Or circumstance? Rhodes would not have wanted war. But Jameson would never have plotted war without at least Rhodes' tacit approval. In this unwitting preliminary to the Jameson Raid, Jameson encouraged Rhodes to take a fatal decision, lulled Rhodes' usual caution into comparative complacency, and—this time—was proven correct in his assessment of the conquest's ease and its limited consequences in terms of adverse British opinion. It is not that Rhodes would have had moral qualms about destroying Ndebele power or taking black lives. Nor would he have supposed that a struggle could have been avoided indefinitely. Thus, when Jameson decided that the time had come, Rhodes trusted Jameson's gambler's instinct rather than his own usually more painstaking method.

Rhodes' consent was more a bowing to the inevitable rather than a well-conceptualized determination to go to war. In August, Rhodes reported that Lobengula had forced "this question on us." He told the London board that he would "much rather it had been postponed for a year. . . ." The "it" was not the decision to go to war but the assent that Rhodes had given to massive preparations which would almost certainly lead to war, but still might not. Indeed, as late as August Rhodes even contemplated employing 500 armed Zulu to guard the borders of Ndebeleland and prevent clashes between Lobengula's impi and Shona working in the mines of the nascent Rhodesia.[33]

Deeply in debt, without important income, and with a zero if not a negative cash flow, the Company's future (and Rhodes' continued control and administration of his colony) was in serious jeopardy during the precise period when Rhodes was making faltering decisions to move toward war. That a bitter conflict would drain the Company's finances beyond compensation (the British government would never pay) was clear. That Rhodes engineered or let Jameson arrange a war primarily in order to boost the Company's prospects is less clear, even though the ease with which the war was won, and the enthusiasm with which that victory was achieved, permitted Rhodes to advance the Company's interests. He could reorganize the Company, raise substantial new sums from his own enterprises (De Beers, Gold Fields, and the Exploring Company) and refloat an African ship that had seemed stuck in the mire of investor dissatisfaction. (Yet the shares of the British South Africa Company had fallen steadily in 1893, and the occupation of Ndebeleland did little to increase their value.) Thus, as much as Rhodes took advantage of the war to rescue the Company financially, doing so was neither Rhodes' sole nor even his primary motive in agreeing to fight.[34] When his offspring was troubled, he was personally uneasy. He had been backed into war; it had to come sometime, and the need to assuage white colonialist dissatisfaction (and avarice), as well as shrewd calculations about Ndebele weakness, propelled him into acquiescence.

Even the British government accepted the inevitability of a martial clash. Fed with rumor and partial truths by Loch, who sought both to cleanse the interior of a cruel and unreformable monarch and to take Ndebeleland under the Crown's aegis rather than let it fall to Rhodes, the Colonial Office under Lord Ripon agreed halfheartedly to and certainly never seriously impeded the momentum of war. In late August, Ripon warned Loch that he would prohibit aggressive actions by the Company and any menacing of Lobengula. He would not permit the Company to implicate the British government in its quarrels with Lobengula. But the Company could certainly defend its own interests and its occupation of Mashonaland. (*The Economist* termed Ripon's instructions "absurd.") Furthermore, Ripon and his officials permitted Loch to begin moving the Bechuanaland Border Police toward the southern borders of Ndebele country, and otherwise preparing that Protectorate for hostilities. Ripon's only requirements were that he and Loch should be seen to "have done all we could to maintain peace," while acquiescing in the preparations for an invasion, and that no part of the conquest should cost the imperial exchequer or his own ministry a farthing. "This war is their war," Ripon told Loch, "and . . . the Company must not look to us for any financial aid."[35]

Rhodes' war against the Ndebele was purely parochial in its origin and in the satisfaction that it gave. It expanded the imperial perimeter, but it occurred for distinctly sub-imperial reasons. There was no imperial imperative. For Jameson and Loch, and then for Rhodes, however, there was a Company imperative—for gold, if any were to be found; for the rescuing of his nearly exhausted financial enterprise; for the colonialists, who wanted new opportunities and a little revenge; and for land. Rhodes could always be talked into territory.

Loch was a problem for Jameson, but primarily because he wanted it to be his war, not the Company's. In late July, Jameson warned Maund that cables to Loch about the coming conflict had to be phrased carefully and be thoroughly incomplete. Although Jameson believed that he had an understanding with both Rhodes and Loch that the whites in the interior should "settle the affair" themselves, the High Commissioner considered him dangerously cocksure. Loch, Jameson complained, would not let him "do anything," and "the military swells" in Cape Town were "preaching . . . disaster from my plans." But, he said, "one must cut one's coat according to the cloth—we can't lose this year or our show is burst for some time to come."[36]

Once Jameson had tempted whites with the booty of war, there was no turning back. The method of paying soldiers according to their successes sharply limited financial risk to the Company, and eased the task of recruiting volunteers. Jameson would provide recruits with horses—Jameson bought mounts throughout August and September wherever he could procure them—and, if victorious, each invader would receive 3,000 morgen of land in Ndebeleland. Each was promised fifteen underground and five alluvial gold claims. Moreover, the enormous herds of Ndebele cattle, as tangible a prize as the lands on which they fed, would be divided between the Company and the mercenaries. With such a prospective division of the spoils—"nothing less than a contract for robbery under arms"—Jameson had no shortage of enthusiastic volunteers.[37] His cause was theirs, and was immensely popular among the outmanned but supremely confident pioneers, adventurers, freebooters, and quondam settlers who comprised Rhodesia's white male population in mid-1893.

The Ndebele war was thrust upon Lobengula. Without allies, and effectively abandoned by the British government, the Ndebele were powerless to prevent the slide toward disaster. Only an abject surrender of rights and territory could have avoided annihilation once Jameson concluded that the Company and its settlers could win a war, retrieve its faltering fortunes, and also appease the white pioneers on whom the colony so uniquely depended. But fearful as Lobengula doubtless was, and as persuaded as he must have been that massing impis would prove no match for white might, his induna would never have permitted a supine response to a mendacious and scattered enemy. After Lendy had chased an Ndebele war party from Victoria in July, and taken their cattle, Lobengula grew genuinely angry. "I thought you came to dig gold," he wrote to Harris, "but it seems that you have come not only to dig gold but to rob me of my people and country as well. Remember that you are like a child playing with edged tools." He wrote more intemperately to Loch, but certainly still wanted peace at almost any price. He cabled querulously to Moffat: "I want to know from you. . . . What great wrong have I done? . . . Tell me." He pleaded with Queen Victoria, and declared his and his impis' innocence to her and to Loch. Whites who resided in or near Gbulawayo knew that the king sought no confrontation.[38]

Lobengula finally attempted to stave off an attack by sending a peace mission to Queen Victoria. But the High Commissioner, Rhodes, and Jameson were all so deeply complicit by the end of September, when the induna vainly tried to save their kingdom, that Loch prevented the delegates from traveling beyond Cape Town. By then, too, at the beginning of the inland territory's hottest season, the white attackers had mobilized their volunteer army and recruited a collection of Boer mercenaries. Loch had massed the Bechuanaland Police and a large force of Kgama's Tswana on Lobengula's southern border, and Jameson and Rhodes had skillfully planted a trail of deceit to cover their own provocations of the Ndebele and induce a gullible British public to believe that bloodthirsty Ndebele wardogs had threatened and would continue to menace the colony.

Ultimately, in the opening days of October, Jameson told Loch that an impi of enormous size had started for Shona country, crossed the informal border, and even passed north of Victoria. Loch, not knowing that the impi's existence and size were figments of Jameson's imagination, authorized the administrator to secure the Company's position. On 5 October, after hearing further reports of supposed Ndebele aggression, the High Commissioner told Jameson, in effect, that he (and Rhodes) could go to war. As Lobengula, who had started to flee, wrote to Loch, "Every day I hear from you reports which are nothing but lies. . . . What Impi of mine have your people seen and where do they come from? I know nothing of them."[39]

Rhodes' role in deciding precisely when to go to war was not great, but he had hardly held himself aloof from the decision to find a pretext and then to make war on the Ndebele. As Leonard remarked, "As for the Matabele, [Rhodes] will make short shrift of them if he gets the chance, or, if they do not give it to him, he and Jameson between them will make it, as sure as eggs are eggs!"[40] Rhodes argued, probably ingenuously, that it would cost the

Company less in the long run to eliminate Lobengula's power at once than to defend the Shona and the colony continuously against marauding impi. By September neither Loch nor other close observers in the Cape Colony had any illusions about the inevitability of a clash. Since August, whites had been spoiling for a fight. Jameson had delayed solely in order to buy sufficient horses. Rhodes had slowed the pace of events while he tested the temper of London and examined the options available for financing hostilities. But, by September, neither Rhodes nor Jameson would have countenanced any outcome other than a test of martial strength. Moreover, they had to attack before the yearly rains began in November.

When war was clearly at hand, Rhodes went north. On 18 September 1893, after adjourning the Cape's Legislative Assembly session, he rushed off to Rhodesia by the east-coast route. At Jameson's request, Hans Sauer met him (and Charles Metcalfe, Gordon Le Sueur, and Cruz) on the road between Beira and Macequece. George Pauling, at Rhodes' behest, had already constructed a toy railway of two-foot gauge nearly seventy-five miles across malarial, tsetse-fly-infested territory inland from a point fifty miles from the coast along the Pungwe River. Rhodes rode on the new rails and then, in greater comfort and much more swiftly than in 1891, he and his party followed a serviceable wagon road up the escarpment into Mashonaland proper. They hustled through Umtali, Rhodes being unexpectedly anxious to avoid the inhabitants of the town. They continued rushing toward Salisbury on horseback, followed by a wagon pulled by mules. Halfway between Marandellas and Salisbury, Rhodes suddenly asked Sauer to "ride forward and choose a good camping-place some three or four miles either to the right or left of the road and in a well-wooded locality." Earlier Rhodes had been in a great hurry, now he wanted to dawdle in private. "We remained in this camp day after day, and the longer we remained," wrote Sauer, "the more I wondered." "All Rhodes' hurry seemed to have vanished; he was in good fettle and seemed happy." The little group saw no one and spent its time hunting. No whites farmed in the vicinity; it was improbable that any would stumble onto the camp. Yet one morning a mounted policeman from Salisbury found them without difficulty (presumably by prearrangement) and handed messages to Rhodes. Quickly Rhodes demanded that they break camp and make haste for Salisbury. Jameson had started for Gbulawayo, and the war was on.

Rhodes had hidden himself in the bush until Jameson was beyond telegraphic recall. Fearing not so much a cable from Loch, but a cable from Ripon through Loch, Rhodes had made himself inaccessible during those days when provocation was about to be declared and a white attack launched. Indeed, Loch had telegraphed frantically for news of the premier's arrival in Salisbury, perhaps to slow down preparations for the final blow, perhaps to seek reassurance that Rhodes and Jameson would surely win. Yet only when it was far too late, on the evening of October 9, could the harried and obedient telegraph operator in Salisbury finally inform Cape Town that he had espied "Mr. Rhodes approaching over the brow of the hill." Rhodes dashed into town and spent almost the whole of his first daylight hours on the telegraph, communicating with Cape Town. A few days later he presided over the first gold crushing at the Salisbury Reef Mine, fifteen miles from the capital, where a stamp battery had recently been erected, and gave an extemporaneous, inflammatory, jingoistic speech antagonistic to the Ndebele.[41] After a few more days in Salisbury, Rhodes suddenly left for the southern front, and his second private war.

The Ndebele were easily conquered. Lobengula only realized that his kingdom had been attacked five days after two columns of white troops, one from Salisbury and another from Victoria, had joined together and crossed into Ndebeleland proper. They numbered 650 volunteers and 155 Cape and Tswana drivers and cooks, and 900 Shona extras. (A third contingent—Loch's combined white and Tswana legion from the south—had massed in Tuli and begun marching toward Tati, but were too slow to reach Gbulawayo before the men of the Company.) Moreover, Lobengula had given no new provocation and still presumed (as Loch had always professed) that the representatives of the white queen would warn him before they attacked. Moffat suggested that Loch had "taken leave of his senses. I suppose," he continued, "the war party has just overpowered his better convictions—or else he has been. . . . I am sorry for ourselves—that we can demean ourselves to act so dishonestly."

Even after learning that a great detachment of armed whites was approaching, Lobengula stayed the fighting hand of his induna for too long. The Ndebele army had recently been weakened by a rampaging epidemic of smallpox; half of the remaining soldiers never had the opportunity or received orders to defend their nation. Most of all, though the Ndebele had numbers, the whites had a new and hitherto untested technological superiority. As Belloc rhymed so poignantly, " 'Whatever happens we have got/ The Maxim Gun, and they have not.' "[42]

Hiram Maxim, a Maine-born inventor who lived in Paterson, New Jersey, designed electrical lighting systems before Thomas Alva Edison did, fashioned countless other practical and impractical gadgets, and in 1885 constructed the world's first serious machine gun. The rapid fire gun invented in 1861 by Richard Jordan Gatling, another American, had to be cranked by hand. Maxim's weapon of destruction could be fired continuously simply by steady pressure on the trigger. Maxim had managed to combine the processes of cocking, firing, ejection of spent shells, and reloading in one smooth movement. His contribution to improved firepower was a spring-loaded bolt action that could store up the recoil energy released by a shot and employ that same energy to prepare the gun for its next one. It was also necessary to keep the gun's breech tightly closed until each bullet was sent on its way. Otherwise the expended cartridge would be ejected too soon and the gun's barrel would burst. A toggle mechanism based on the articulation of the human leg was Maxim's answer.

Maxim's method revolutionized warfare. He impressed Europe before the

United States, and settled in Britain largely because the royal family and the British army embraced his invention earliest. The gun had hardly become standard issue by 1893, but Captain Frederick Lugard had used Maxims to pacify Buganda in 1892, and Leonard saw one on the border of Rhodesia in 1891. Rhodes either learned of the efficacy of machine guns from his military contacts or read about Maxim's demonstrations in England. However knowledge was in this case diffused, at the battle of Bonko (Shangani), fifty-five miles from Gbulawayo, on October 25, 1893—the first confrontation of the Ndebele war and the first major skirmish between Ndebele and whites since the late 1830s—Jameson's men had five Maxim guns as well as three other, clumsier, rapid-fire guns, two cannon, and 200 rifles. Thanks to the devastating effectiveness of the Maxims' concentrated firepower, wave after wave of advancing Ndebele with slower, older Martini Henry rifles were conclusively repulsed. Moreover, according to Hubert Hervey, a young British secretary in the colony's law department who had enlisted as a trooper, "the Matabele firing was very inaccurate and poor, and did hardly any damage." Rhodes, relaying a report of the battle to Sprigg, gleefully said that "the shooting must have been excellent. . . . It proves the [white] men were not only brave, but cool, and did not lose their heads, though surrounded with the hordes."

But at the battle of Egodade (Bembezi), a mere twenty miles from Gbulawayo, about 6,000 Africans attacked the white column and its followers on 1 November. "We had just finished luncheon," wrote Hervey, "when the alarm sounded and we saw niggers advancing out of the bush in considerable numbers, in skirmishing order. This attack included some of their best regiments, and was a more determined one than at Shangani; but they were utterly unable to withstand the fire from the Maxims and the Gardner guns, and from the rifles, and only a few of them had the courage to come anywhere near the laager."

Bishop Knight Bruce was there too. "It was a nasty ten minutes," he wrote of the power of the Maxims, "especially as the Matabele shooting with the rifles was much better than it had been, and they came on with wonderful courage to within eighty yards of the waggons. . . . It all made one realize what those terrible machine guns mean. It must have required extraordinary courage to have come up the hill against the fire." Again thanks to the Maxims, sheltered between wagons in a basic defensive circle, 800 Ndebele were killed, and only three whites lost their lives. As Hervey concluded, "They were completely beaten off, and their best regiment smashed." Whites had demonstrated an unquestioned technological superiority that compensated for their tiny numbers. Withering, repeated firing—a Ndebele prisoner compared it to a hailstorm— had decisively destroyed the Ndebele resistance. Even so, the correspondent of *The Times* praised the Ndebele for their conspicuous bravery, pluck, and gallantry. "As showing their tenacity . . . I may mention that many were found 3000 yards away from the spot where they had received their death-wound."[43]

Bulawayo fell on 4 November, when Jameson's combined force marched into the deserted town. Lobengula had fled to the north, along with much of what was left of the Ndebele army. "Perhaps it is just as well," Rhodes said pragmatically of the king's escape. Near the confluence of the Shangani River with the Zambezi River, the great king poisoned himself. As Moffat later commented, Lobengula was a noble king and in his way a gentleman. But he was "foully sinned against by Jameson and his gang."[44] The resistance of the Ndebele ended, to be resumed again in a few years—at the earliest available opportunity. Whether or not the Ndebele were crushed militarily by Jameson's small force or, as some modern historians assert, that their army stood down in a tactical retreat only, Ndebeleland was now under Rhodes' sway, whatever other arrangement Loch had planned.

Rhodes knew that Loch, and possibly Ripon, would try to claim the Ndebele conquest as his own. Fortunately, as Gbulawayo fell, Loch's legion was still struggling north from Tati. The high commissioner had forfeited the immediate race for sub-imperial hegemony, but Rhodes was equally determined that he should lose all subsequent competitions, too. "When you take Bulawayo," Rhodes had earlier ordered Jameson, ". . . retain management for the Company." As Jameson's men were pursuing Lobengula, Rhodes instructed that the king must never be handed over to the imperial police. To Harris, Rhodes explained that they "must watch [the English people] closely for we know the predatory instincts of our race. Their present position," he cabled with feeling, "is entirely due to plunder and when not plundering a foreigner sooner than do nothing they plunder each other."[45]

Loch desperately wanted to see Rhodes so that they could discuss final arrangements for the administration of the conquered territory. But Rhodes with equal passion wanted to avoid Loch's clutches for at least another few weeks. Jameson required time to consolidate his grip over the Ndebele and to begin organizing an effective apparatus of control. Rhodes first traveled from Victoria to Tuli and then to Palapye. There he paused long enough to have a prolonged and critical telegraphic conversation with Barnato regarding the sale of £700,000 worth of diamonds. He also talked in the same manner to Loch. Informing the high commissioner disingenuously that he needed detailed information from Jameson, and that they would arrange to meet in Tati, Rhodes doubled back to the north. He rode to Tuli and, skirting Tati, headed for Jameson's tent in what was emerging as the white man's Bulawayo. "Well, I'm damned!" exclaimed Jameson when Rhodes suddenly appeared on 4 December. "Where the devil have you come from?"[46]

Escorted by Major Raleigh Grey, twenty white soldiers of the Cape Mounted Rifles, Metcalfe, and Cruz, Rhodes entered the conquered city on horseback, but hardly like a proper centurion. He sat, said Stent, on "his horse loosely, riding, like all Colonials, by balance rather than by grip. His clothes were rough, his hat soft and drawn tight over his forehead; his face heavy, mobile, deep lined, thoughtful, and still a little absent in expression." Behind were the troopers, their "rain rusty scabbards clinking against the flanks of their tired horses." They were excited by the honor, said Stent, of escorting the new master to the capital of the dominion which he had just added to the empire. Yet the new master presented a less than imposing appearance. "His gestures were awkward, his hat was nondescript. . . . He spoke in jerky sentences [to the whites of Bulawayo], clasping and unclasping his hands, nervously folding his arms and diving deep again into his pockets."[47]

"I have to thank you for all the excellent work you have done," Rhodes told the volunteers who had assaulted the Ndebele stronghold. "You have been able," he said proudly, "to conquer Matabeleland." Although the Company had not wished to "interfere," he claimed, "interference was forced upon us." Rhodes rewrote history as was his usual wont: at Victoria, Shona were murdered. Whites could not "stand their servants being slaughtered under their eyes." Although offensive actions could only be undertaken with the approval of the British government, once that sanction had been obtained the work of ten thousand men was done by a mere 900 whites and for a total expense of what ultimately became £113,000. Throughout the preparations for the invasion, Rhodes made it clear that all he had wanted "was to be left alone by people in the Colony, in South Africa, and also in England, to carry out the work which in Mashonaland was considered necessary."

"You would have thought the English would have been satisfied," Rhodes went on. Yet the conquerors had instead been called "freebooting marauders, bloodthirsty murderers," and so on. "I am as loyal an Englishman as any one can be, but I cannot help saying that it is such conduct that alienates colonists from the mother-country. We ask for nothing, for neither men nor money, and still a certain portion vilify us. In the same spirit," he made his usual observation, "it was that the mother-country lost America." He told his men that they were the conquerors of Rhodesia; hence Ndebeleland should be settled "in a fair way, and not be left entirely to negrophilists at Exeter Hall" (the base of the British Aborigines Protection Society). He reminded his listeners that they could remember one central fact with pleasure: they had "effected the destruction of ruthless barbarism . . . and established a further extension of the British Empire, and done this practically by their own unaided efforts."

Now that the Ndebele were crushed, Rhodes focused on the development of the country. They had only come to fight, he agreed with the men, because they had known that their properties in Shonaland were worthless until the Ndebele had been ousted. "Nine hundred of you have created another state in South Africa, large in extent, with every possibility of being proportionately valuable, and . . . you have put an end to savage rule south of the Zambesi." He pledged his personal support: "The future will have many obligations, but there is one thing that presses me the most, and that is that I must use my brains in getting fresh capital here for railways and public works to found a state south of the Zambesi, which I hope will be one of the largest, and at the same time one of the richest, in South Africa."[48]

Rhodes warned Britain not to trouble his realm. Knowing that Loch wanted to administer it, and that Ripon and others might succumb to pressures from pro-African circles in Britain, Rhodes promised that "if the Imperial Government interfered the consequences would be very unpleasant indeed!"[49] Indeed they might, as the local wags said, be most unpleasant—but mostly for the Company and the men who were now seeking to carve up the conquered territory to their satisfaction.

The battle for Rhodesia was next to be contested in the south. Immediately after his morale-lifting, solidarity-creating speech to the victorious volunteers, after gathering firsthand information (and ammunition) for his coming negotiation with Loch, and after helping Jameson and others lay out the pretentiously wide streets of the new town, Rhodes rode toward Cape Town. There, on 3 January 1894, he received a hero's welcome. Presented with an official address on behalf of the proud city and its citizens, Rhodes replied that he still feared that Loch and London would seek to usurp his new possession, removing it not only from the Company but also from the successful and thus especially deserving colonists. As Harris cabled Jameson about the continuing danger: "Rhodes says, remain at Bulawayo until we wire you all danger is over."[50]

In Cape Town the premier first reminded his friends that the conquest of Ndebeleland and Rhodesia had come about because he had possessed "an idea." Twelve years ago, he said, "I thought it would be a good idea to work in season and out of season to obtain the unknown interior as a reversion to the colony." It has come out "all right." In the process he had learned one important lesson: "If you have an idea, and it is a good idea, if you will only stick to it, you will come out all right." Somewhat gilding that lesson as far as his subsequent actions had been concerned, Rhodes reminded the citizens of his adopted city that he "knew that Africa was the last uncivilised portion of the empire of the world, and that it must be civilised." He had an idea and, fortunately for him, had the funds with which to support his propositions. Rhodes admitted that his had been a dual responsibility. It was his allotted task to direct Rhodesia from afar while sitting daily and hourly in Parliament. "You will share with me," he said, "the feeling, the strain in dealing with some local questions of the country, and yet having at the same time . . . the statement that these people in the north would no longer stand the position. . . ." Moreover, the conquest of the Ndebele had a particular relevance to the Cape Colony. The defeat of the mighty people of the interior would be noted by their own 1.2 million Africans. "The destruction of Lobengula . . . is going to render it a perfectly easy thing for us to deal with the Pondos, and other native tribes." In terms of the future, Rhodes reminded his listeners that he still anticipated that someday the Cape would extend to the Zambezi or beyond. There would be a united southern Africa, under the Crown. That was his biggest idea.

One immediate obstacle remained. The imperial factor had to be persuaded or bullied to leave his regime alone. "If it should unfortunately happen that the settlements to be effected with the Imperial Government . . . may not meet the just expectations of those who had shed their life's blood for us, I shall earnestly and resolutely fight the battle on behalf of the people of this country and of . . . England, whose children shared the dangers of the campaign." He would "fight it on constitutional grounds."[51]

Julia Merriman, the politician's doughty and determined mother, was shocked and startled by Rhodes' speech. "My diagnosis," she told her daughter-in-law, "is that the man must have had a good deal of champagne to [have] enable[d] him to speak in such a strain." What Rhodes said reminded her of Nebuchadnezzar. "Will Rhodes go out of his mind too?" she asked. What a "vainglorious outpouring from beginning to end," she said. The speech had been patronizing to the Crown, and she thought that his comparison of the invasion of Ndebele country to the expeditions of Hernando Cortés and Francisco Pizarro was "overstrained." Since Spain had lost its power afterwards, she trusted that the results of Rhodes' invasion would "prove far different." Overall, she concluded that Rhodes was "a clever, deep-scheming man."[52]

Rhodes battled hard to realize the fullest extent of his unsullied vision for the new dominion. Although Ripon and Loch had together agreed in October that Lobengula should surrender to the Imperial government, not to Rhodes or Jameson, and that subsequent arrangements would be made by the high commissioner, again not by Rhodes or the Company, no formal surrender or transfer of sovereignty ever occurred. More important, the ease with which the Company overcame Ndebele opposition, never materially drawing upon Imperial resources, weakened Ripon's position significantly. Ripon had little stomach for a confrontation with Rhodes. "I have a personal liking for Rhodes," Ripon confessed. "His boldness & resource attract me; & if he quarrels with me it will be his fault not mine." Ripon's cabinet colleagues feared the cost of direct administration; better to let Rhodes do it, as the Company charter had intended. Some also believed, with Ripon's officials, that any attempt on the part of the British government to take Ndebeleland away from Rhodes, at the height of his popularity in the Cape, would cause a dangerous breach with South African white public opinion.

Prompted by a cable from Rhodes, Sprigg and the Cape cabinet had implied as much in a memorandum to Loch. To Rhodes, Sprigg, the acting premier, had given private reassurance: "I hope you will fully understand that I consider the interests of the Company and of the Colony identical in regard to the settlement to be made." To do otherwise than submit to Rhodes would, Fairfield said, "probably lose us South Africa."[53] Thus, by the time that Rhodes returned to the Cape Colony, no one in authority in Britain was attempting to deprive the Company of its conquest. However, there were bound to be detailed discussions, from January to May 1894, about what ways Rhodes' free hand would be checked by imperial concerns for African rights and broader imperial notions about how conquered territories in Africa were to be governed. Those prerogatives and licenses for which Rhodes struggled in 1894 were indicative of his attitude toward and the disposition he envisaged for the indigenous inhabitants not only of Rhodesia, but of southern Africa more broadly.

The battle for power in Ndebeleland and, by extension, in Shonaland, pitted Rhodes against Loch, Ripon, the officials in the Colonial Office, and a committee of the cabinet. The Company, after all, was a collection of private persons. It could only exercise administrative rights by leave of either an indigenous ruler or the conquering power. With a suspicion honed by ego-bruising battles with the vicar long before in Bishop's Stortford, Rhodes feared that Britain could undeservedly thwart his grand plans. The Colonial Office naturally wished to legitimize Rhodes' conquest and give it a scrupulous veneer internationally. The Colonial Office wanted a complicated, elaborate governmental apparatus so as to provide checks on the Company. Rhodes, however, wanted both more and less. As always, he wanted to go his own way, untrammeled by officious oversight. The result of these twin pressures was, as might have been expected, a compromise both of intent and of legalisms.

Rhodesia would be run by an administrator, assisted by a council composed of the territory's presiding judge and the heads of the colony's executive departments. The administrator, the chief judge, and the councillors would be appointed—as Rhodes had demanded and Loch had opposed—by the board of the Company (i.e., by Rhodes), subject to the approval of the colonial secretary. The board could also reverse any of the actions of the administrator. The directors of the Company were permitted to legislate for their territory with a scope and a freedom that was unprecedented. The administrator could make regulations, although the approval of the high commissioner would technically be necessary. The Company's police were forbidden to operate beyond the borders of Rhodesia (a clause that Rhodes opposed) without London's express permission, but in 1894 no one, perhaps not even Rhodes, believed such an occasion would ever arise. Otherwise, the British government was prepared in practice to give Rhodes nearly all the power, bar a few lofty-sounding but vague safeguards for Africans, that he needed to run a private commercial state within the queen's empire.

The Colonial Office wished the Order-in-Council which it was preparing to include a ban on legislation discriminatory against Africans. Rhodes hardly wished his hands tied. Ultimately the two sides agreed that Rhodes could have his way except with regard to the supply of arms and liquor, questions of taxation, and anything else on which the high commissioner might wish to legislate. In other words, Africans had less real protection than Exeter Hall might have wished and the Colonial Office intended. This conclusion was immediately true, too, with regard to land, the white alienation of which helped exacerbate the conditions which led to the Ndebele resumption of hostilities in 1896. Rhodes cannily understood that he might have to provide for African reserves in 1894, but by carefully wording the Order he avoided having to give substantial land in the future to any increased population of Africans. A Land Commission appointed by the colonial secretary and the Company would allocate acreage to Africans, but where African-occupied lands were needed for towns, mines, railways, public works, and so on, they could be appropriated. Crucially, Rhodes managed to restrict the allocation clause to

Ndebeleland proper, leaving Shonaland to be occupied by whites without restriction. Yet he did not object, as he shortly did in the case of the Cape Colony (where the support of the Bond was at stake), to the purchasing by Africans of land outside their reserves. "If any of them show intelligence or capacity to acquire property of their own, they certainly should not be debarred from doing so," he said. "But then I think they should be treated as ordinary citizens."[54]

During the months when Rhodes was seeking official sanction for an allocation of Ndebele resources along lines that would distinctly favor the Company, he also gave orders to Jameson to behave as the conqueror he was and to parcel out Ndebele lands and cattle without waiting for permission from London. Military rule of the occupied region began at once, for Jameson and Rhodes had promises to fulfill. Yet the Colonial Office had humanitarian interests to appease. Thus, although the Order-in-Council provided for a Land Commission which was intended to allocate sufficient land and cattle for the defeated Ndebele, while simultaneously retaining vast acreages and numerous heads of cattle for the Company and its soldiers, most of the Ndebele land and cattle was appropriated before the Order had been promulgated.

Comparatively quickly the defeated Ndebele were shunted onto outlying, badly watered, unsuitable lands and condemned to the kind of penury which would make revolt imperative. Whites occupied the whole of the rich terrain around Bulawayo. As in the highlands of Kenya during the early years of this century, Africans suddenly found themselves dispossessed, subject to white landlords (because few moved readily into the reserves) and reduced in every imaginable status, income, and attribute. "Land," Viscount Milner later reported, "was alienated in the most reckless manner . . ." and "a lot of unfit people were allowed to exercise power . . . with regard to the natives."[55]

The Company also acquired all Ndebele cattle, the nation's wealth, for it was the one liquid asset with which Jameson could pay his social as well as his real debts. This was the "loot" which had made the tidy little war worthwhile for the winners, and was to make the peace unusually burdensome for the defeated. Moreover, rinderpest soon attacked the few cattle remaining in indigenous hands, thus compounding the misery to which Rhodes and Jameson had condemned the Africans, and for which Rhodes showed little interest or concern until his own bubble of personal manifest destiny burst ignominiously in the last days of 1895.

The proclamation of the Matabeleland Order-in-Council of 18 July 1894 fettered Rhodes with juridical niceties that meant little in practice, and would have meant hardly anything at all if he and Jameson had not, eighteen months later, displayed how they had been infected by the ego-inflating lessons of the Ndebele war. Lobengula and his induna had been outwitted and defeated by bold, cheap strategies, preponderant firepower, enormous self-confidence, insouciant forays, and the blazing of a broad trail of deceit. Not the forces of London nor the strength of imperial potentates had as yet blocked the accomplishment of Rhodes' grand dream—his "big idea," his territorial megalomania. Before he had turned forty-one, the sense of his own power had again been validated and expanded into a feeling of invincibility which would soon precipitate his downfall. Thanks to Jameson's sense of timing and risk and his own ability to assemble sufficient resources and to marshal lofty and powerful arguments, Rhodes could now consolidate his control over all of the conquered area between the Limpopo and Zambezi rivers. While simultaneously continuing to govern the Cape Colony and to corner diamonds, he could quietly advance his ambitions for a united South Africa and an extension of a personal influence beyond the Zambezi toward Uganda. Rhodes had reason to be pleased with himself in 1893 and 1894.

◄ 17 ►

"A Dominant Race Among a Native Race" The Second Premiership

R HODES DEVOTED his second premiership to the "native question." As secretary of native affairs as well as prime minister of the Cape, he transformed his own idealized vision of white-black relations, his own notions of the proper position of Africans in the future of the region, his own prejudices, and his own understanding of what the political traffic would bear into legislative directives which were broadly significant and far-reaching. Each of the major bills which shaped the place of Africans within the Colony during the 1893, 1894, and 1895 sessions formed an integral part of a grand design which Rhodes had adumbrated during the debates on the Registration Act of 1887, the Masters and Servants bill of 1890, and the Ballot and Franchise Act of 1892. His was the guiding hand, cognizant always of the anxieties of the Afrikaner Bond and mindful, but less so, of his standing and reputation within the Empire.

In his second term as leader of parliament Rhodes was more overbearing, but also more relaxed and more confident than before. His cabinet of Sprigg, Laing, Frost, Faure, and Schreiner (with Henry Hubert Juta replacing Schreiner as attorney general during most of 1894) was more pliant and less captious than the first ministry of all talents. Indeed, surrounded in the second term by men whom he could easily dominate and who were less troubled by principle than were Merriman, Innes, and Sauer, Rhodes boldly broke with the parliamentary traditions of the Cape and, with the adroitness of an experienced middle sibling, began agreeing upon and orchestrating governmental business before much of it even reached the House of Assembly. He convened caucuses of his Bond/English-speaking independent alliance well before the Cape realized that it had parties in the British sense.

Caucuses were an innovative departure from the past, and their existence infuriated the liberal opposition. As Merriman remarked, "If they were going to settle things in the lobby and the caucuses, they destroyed all sense of Parliamentary government. Why were measures brought into the House so crudely? Simply because there had been some underhand agreement. If there was anything that had tended to demoralise this Parliament from what they could recollect it years ago, it was this practice of underhand agreement, lobbying, and caucuses." Merriman said that "he preferred to stand up and take his fighting in the House; the Premier preferred to take it in the lobby."[1]

A healthy debate on contentious measures had hitherto characterized the proceedings of the House; during Rhodes' second term detailed discussions were more and more pre-empted by the private considerations of the caucus, where Rhodes could reign supreme out of earshot of the public and the press. Thus it was primarily the parliamentary opposition, led by Innes, Merriman, and Sauer, which spoke out against legislation affecting Africans. Rhodes had already overcome or hushed dissent within the ranks of his own supporters. Moreover, he had continued his earlier practice of consorting with Hofmeyr, and thus had already ensured himself of an understanding with the Bond. It held the largest single bloc of seats in the House and, as far as Rhodes was concerned, could have its way on legislation affecting Africans, agriculture, and protective tariffs. The English-speaking independents, many of whom had recently opposed Rhodes and followed Sprigg, now largely supported his initiatives or kept quiet during the debates.

Rhodes' chief critics from 1893 through 1895 were, as might have been expected, Merriman, Sauer, and Innes. They were joined on crucial issues by John Charles Molteno, who represented Tembuland and owed his seat to a large Xhosa vote; William Hay, from the equally African-oriented constituency of Victoria East; and Charles William Hutton, from Fort Beaufort. For each of these men, and most of all for Merriman, Rhodes reserved doses of sarcasm, a newfound ability to generate bursts of real humor, and, ultimately, disdain. Yet he also exhibited a capability, on more than one critical occasion, of compromising with those with whom he now differed so profoundly. As a man and as a politician, Rhodes always preferred to blunt criticism rather than to confront it. During his second term he was sufficiently strong politically to parry or, if necessary, ignore the opposition of his former cabinet colleagues. He had an able and experienced deputy in Sprigg, who managed the routine business of the prime ministership, remained loyal and largely uncritical (Sprigg's own views on Africans paralleled Rhodes'), and dealt with the nettlesome budget as treasurer-general. Until 1895, Rhodes also relied upon Hofmeyr's strong support. Moreover, Rhodes was forty in 1893, at the apex of his power and in the process of realizing his vast potential along a broadly creative front. As the second premiership unfolded Rhodes also conquered the Ndebele, successfully surrounded the Transvaal, tried to intervene in Egypt, the Sudan, and Uganda, extended railways and telegraph lines to the north, and added to his unquestioned control of diamonds and his sizable stake in gold. Just as he thoroughly dominated the affairs of southern Africa and the Cape on the imperial periphery, so he also exercised a profound influence on the British government in the empire's center.

In local political terms Rhodes demonstrated the strength of his position

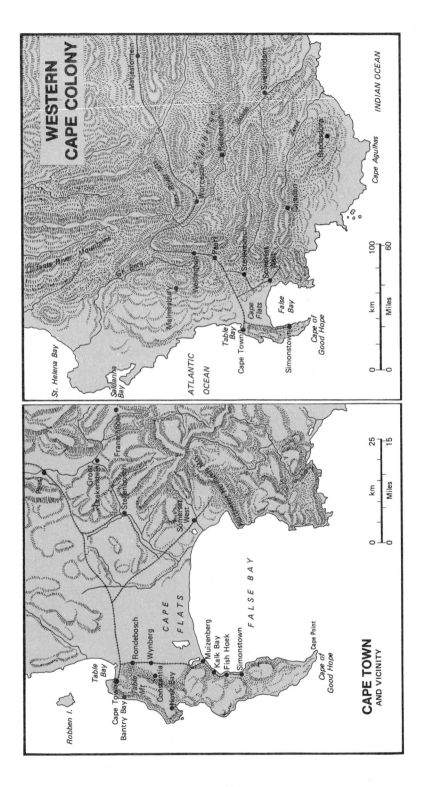

WESTERN CAPE COLONY

St. Helena Bay

Olifants River Mountains

Saldanha Bay

ATLANTIC OCEAN

Malmesbury

Wellington

Paarl

Stellenbosch

Cape Town

Table Bay

Simonstown

Cape of Good Hope

False Bay

Cape Flats

Somerset West

Worcester

Robertson

Ceres

Swellendam

Caledon

Cape Agulhas

INDIAN OCEAN

km 0 100

Miles 0 60

CAPE TOWN
AND VICINITY

Robben I.

Table Bay

Cape Town
Bantry Bay

Table Mt

Constantia

Hout Bay

Rondebosch

Wynberg

CAPE FLATS

Muizenberg

Kalk Bay

Fish Hoek

Simonstown

Cape of Good Hope

Cape Point

FALSE BAY

Paarl

Groot Drakenstein

Franschhoek

Stellenbosch

Somerset West

km 0 25

Miles 0 15

452

by winning an outstanding victory in the general elections of 1894. The force of his personality obviously contributed, for Rhodes was the "biggest" man in the Cape and in southern Africa. So did his willingness to make arrangements with the Bond and other smaller groups and to spend lavishly on behalf of favored candidates, especially in the eastern districts of the Colony. In Kimberley he arranged for George Paton to step down in favor of Daniel Johannes Haarhoff, a Bondsman who could be relied upon to be a friend of De Beers. Haarhoff was a better prospect for De Beers' and Rhodes' needs than another member of the Bond who was a critic of the Company and was likely to be nominated by the Afrikaners in the city. "Mr. Paton," Rhodes said later, "withdrew out of consideration for the difficult position in which I was placed." In Kimberley, too, he directed his associates to persuade Africans who worked for De Beers, lived in its compounds, and could write their names to register to vote. He instructed William Craven to "get on as many as you can. . . . Think out the educated man in the compound who can read and write the others are doing it." The opposition was registering "coolies and malays"; "you must object to Indians signing in their own language it is illegal. . . ."[2]

Rhodes was assiduous in the care with which he took over such parish details. More broadly, and in order to influence the contests beyond Kimberley, Rhodes defrayed the campaign expenses of numerous candidates (Schreiner, exceptionally, insisted on paying his own way). To others he distributed shares, as before, in his Rhodesian enterprise, extended his influence over much of the South African English press (not so as to inspire articles, he once said, but so as to ensure that the press "took care" over facts), and sought ingenious ways of placating or subverting his parliamentary opponents.[3] For example, in order to ensure the support—especially of his northern policies—of Thomas P. Theron, a prominent Bondsman, Rhodes promised to make him chairman of the committees in parliament, an important position that had been held by Sir Thomas Scanlen, the former prime minister, and which Scanlen still coveted. When the House reassembled in May 1894, Rhodes arranged that Theron should receive more votes than Scanlen. In turn, Rhodes gave Scanlen a good position in Rhodesia.

Rhodes overwhelmed his opposition because it was fractured and disconcerted. And it battled along lines that were already anachronistic. There were regional associations of farmers, some loosely tied to Rhodes and others to the opposition, but the election was not fought, as it would surely have been a decade later, between parties. Before the 1894 contest, Edgar H. Walton, the astute editor of the *Eastern Province Herald* (of Port Elizabeth), urged Merriman to organize his cohorts as a party and to fight Rhodes from strength, but Merriman, Innes, and Sauer were too distrustful of each other, too committed to a dying era of parliamentary personalism, and too compromised (and both attracted and repelled) by Rhodes to adopt Walton's tactics as their own.

"The political harvest was ready for reaping, and is being allowed to rot, overripe," wrote Walton, "and the result is that there is every prospect of another five years of something rather worse . . . than we have experienced before. I believe," he chided Merriman, "the people were perfectly ready to approve your action in leaving the late Ministry, and had you put your party flag out then, there would have been no lack of followers." However, Merriman, Innes, and Sauer had put out no flag, and there was no party, no organization, and no policy, object, or intention. "All we in the country can do, is to ask the people to send down representatives to support the Opposition. [But] . . . people won't sign blank cheques of that kind."[4] There were smaller parties and associations appealing for votes in the provincial centers, but Rhodes, as the leader of the government, could promise each more than could the opposition. Even so, Walton suggested that energetic steps could and should be taken. After all, Rhodes was still across the Limpopo, conquering the Ndebele, and the election would not be held until late January 1894.

By then Rhodes had returned home a hero, and his own speeches in Cape Town and later in Kimberley, Barkly West, and Klipdam stressed the competence and progressivism of his ministry and his policies. He also promised action on the question of Pondoland, where Africans not yet incorporated into either the Cape or Natal were fighting each other. Rhodes and W.P. Schreiner topped the poll in Barkly West, Merriman was returned in Namaqualand without opposition, and Thomas Fuller, Ludwig Wiener, John L.M. Brown, and Henry Beard—the "ticket of four"—won in Cape Town. Liberals were ousted in Aliwal North and Somerset East. Overall, Rhodes and his associates won fifty-eight of the seventy-six seats. A full forty of Rhodes' supporters were Bondsmen, however, over whom Rhodes could exercise but an indirect influence.

The precise size of Rhodes' and the opposition parties in 1894–95 remains debatable. As Innes wrote at the time, "I never count a man an Opposition man unless he is so out-and-out, and of that class I reckon we have not more than sixteen at the outside," though twenty-seven voted for Scanlen against Theron. "In addition," said Innes, there was a "small fringe of eight or ten more who on a great many if not most questions . . . would take the Opposition side, but who, if it came to a crisis, would not . . . vote . . . against Rhodes" on a vote of no-confidence.[5]

Within Rhodes' camp were the members of the new Moderate party, who followed Fuller and numbered about sixteen. Many had been Progressives before, but, like the opposition, which generally coalesced behind Sauer, the English-speaking Cape knew personalism much more than party politics until the beginning of the next century. So long as he retained the confidence of the Bond, Rhodes could thus pass the legislation he preferred, and could continue to act with a free hand in Rhodesia and southern Africa.

Rhodes employed this skillfully obtained, unprecedented, and largely unquestioned measure of decisive political power to continue rearranging relations between blacks and whites. He had introduced radical notions in this domain during the legislative years from 1890 to 1892. From 1893, and dramatically after his electoral triumph in 1894, much of Rhodes' considerable political energy was directed to the rewriting of the Cape's statute book in ways which might have appeared limited and parochial at the time, but which were profoundly to alter the contours and reach of discrimination throughout South and even southern Africa. Rhodes was allied to Hofmeyr. He and the Bond viewed burgeoning African numbers as a clear danger to white superiority and to the emerging coalition of Dutch- and English-speaking colonialists. Together Rhodes and Hofmeyr acted to undercut the established tradition of Cape liberalism.[6]

Even the most antagonistic of the Cape's legislators, and the most diehard leaders of the Bond, had hitherto been hesitant to erode the principle that all persons, irrespective of color, were equal before the law—one of Britain's priceless nineteenth-century gifts to the Cape (and thus to South Africa.) During Rhodes' premiership, however, other, more expedient, objectives achieved precedence. It is not wholly unfair to suggest that Rhodes' legislative victories in the early 1890s proved essential precursors to apartheid. But it was not so much his successful emphasis on segregation and differentiation on account of color which was formative; rather, by subordinating inherited values to the solving of immediate problems, by gaining parliamentary approval for questionable means because they served objectives which were less suspect or more threatening, Rhodes overcame the inherent traditional liberalism of the day. Rhodes elevated local above broader considerations, encouraged a frontier atmosphere of aggravation, and rewarded cynicism rather than humanity. That Rhodes personally could do so much which might affront his own presumed personal system of values may be explained less by an elemental vein of prejudice than by his instinctive awareness of how his own power, and that of the Cape and of whites generally (his own expanding power base), could best be enhanced. Rhodes was less evil than single-minded.

Rhodes had always been aware of the African issue. He was remarkably unaffected by antagonism to Africans during his farming year in Natal. Nor was he noticeably aggrieved by the "native question" during his early years in Kimberley (except insofar as he was aware of, and concerned by, the problem of attracting a steady stream of unskilled labor away from agricultural pursuits). Yet, over Stellaland and Goshen, Rhodes demonstrated an active disinclination to permit African prerogatives to interfere with the expansion of the Cape's or whites' sovereignty. For him the battle for southern Africa was between a British and an alien (a Transvaal, a German, or a Portuguese) hegemony. It was a conflict to be won or lost on imperial fields, between competing modes of expansion. The inevitable impact of these clashes upon African entitlement, African presumption, and the African way of life, were to him inevitable, unavoidable, and—to a large degree—irrelevant. Africans were important for their labor but otherwise largely in the way. Indeed it may be supposed that Rhodes, a man who both compartmentalized and rationalized with ease, rarely experienced a troubled conscience because of Africans. Merriman, Innes, Schreiner, Sprigg, Sauer, even Hofmeyr, and others of the day clearly worried about what would become of Africans, and whether their actions (and their votes) were fair. But not Rhodes. In this respect—especially by late twentieth-century and not late nineteenth-century standards—Rhodes ought to be considered less immoral than amoral.

Rhodes always protested that he knew Africans well and had lived among them all his adult life. In 1894 Rhodes reminded the House that "a great part of his life had been spent amongst the natives. At the diamond-mines he had ten thousand natives under his charge, and he was with them day by day." He had to deal with African problems in Basutoland, in Bechuanaland, and in the Transkei. "A human being who had been with the natives throughout the best portion of his life," he said grandly, "should have gained some thoughts regarding them."[7] He was quick to assure his auditors that he harbored no hostility toward Africans. Even before the 1890s, however, his political and his imperial attitudes had coalesced. Rhodes joined the Bond in seeking to limit the African franchise in 1887 and 1892. He favored corporal punishment for Africans—the infamous strop bill. He sought labor efficiency over indigenous freedom; he expanded the compound system in Kimberley and supported other efforts to control and channel the working lives of Africans. Outside the old colony he organized a new regime based on a usurpation of indigenous rights. By 1893 all of those maneuvers had turned Rhodes toward a fuller consideration of and a more energetic, carefully supervised attempt to devise a comprehensive settlement of the African "problem" in its broadest aspect.

For that reason Rhodes, in 1893 busier than ever, abruptly sought direct cabinet control of African affairs. He had understandably argued in 1890 and 1891 that premiers should not be expected to direct a ministry as well as the country. Yet in 1893 he demanded a portfolio which would give him wide control over Africans and the prerogative of introducing legislation affecting them and their place in the future of the colony. Admittedly, Rhodes sought this authority in the course of introducing and arguing for the creation of a separate agricultural ministry. Merriman, as treasurer-general, had been given responsibility for agriculture, as well as mines and industry, during Rhodes' initial premiership. Sprigg, Merriman's successor, continued to discharge those functions. It was clear that, after diamonds, agriculture was the Colony's chief industry. If diamonds were to disappear or slide in price, the Cape would always depend on the products of the soil. Moreover, at least twenty-six of the constituencies held by Bondsmen were districts dependent upon intensive agriculture. Sympathetic both to modern agriculture and to the Bond, Rhodes naturally sought to emphasize his and the Cape's maturing focus and concern by creating a cabinet slot solely for agriculture. Merriman and a few others were happy in principle, but sought to prevent the enlargement of the cabinet (as well as the consequent extra expenditure of at least £1,500—a minuscule sum for some but not for others). In order to keep cabinet numbers constant, thus mollifying the House, and to avoid merging African affairs with agriculture (a further possible solution), Rhodes (after much thought and a productive early morning ride) decided to shift oversight of African affairs from the existing minister to the office of the prime minister. Rhodes would take over.

"The Prime Minister should have the responsibility," Rhodes declared. There were one million "human beings whom they [Parliament] had under their charge, and whom they termed natives. . . ." They should "have a representative" in parliament. Some minister should "be the father of the natives, for the majority of these were merely children," and it should be himself. Rhodes explained his new notion at length: "Let the Prime Minister have responsibility thrown upon him for every act taken with reference to the huge number of natives under . . . care." The "most extreme negrophilist," Rhodes said, would welcome the transfer to the prime minister of paternal care for blacks. Because "there was not much detail work" involved, but rather "thought and consideration," Rhodes asserted that he would "have plenty of time to consider questions of native policy." The questions included "how to deal with this increasing—he would not use the word hordes—. . . native population"; the future of individual title; and the supply of labor. "Natives could not go on living in areas doing nothing but tilling the soil," he declared. Rhodes said that he was prepared to seek solutions for these and similar issues of enormous consequence. For those who "had strong feelings," he suggested that the "best thing that could happen to the natives would be that [he] . . . should be responsible." He would make the time. Moreover, Rhodes pleaded, he was enormously capable. He claimed "exceptional training," and "he was personally responsible for about two hundred thousand natives in Mashonaland. . . ." If he joined his oversight of the northern Africans to those of the Cape he "could then follow one train of thought" and create a single native policy.

Opposition to Rhodes' proposal was limited. Innes wished to retain the existing division of duties. The time was not opportune, especially when Africans were becoming more restless, better educated, and therefore more difficult to deal with than in the past. Hutton "always had the welfare of the natives sincerely at heart. . . ." But he had begun to despair; the House was approving "class" legislation against the interests of Africans. "It was one of the brightest points in the British character . . . that there should be an equal law for all classes of Her Majesty's subjects. The tendency should rather be in favour of the poor and degraded, who should be more tenderly treated than those who . . . could take care of themselves." Therefore, Hutton argued, one cabinet minister should devote his whole time and effort to the protection and uplift of Africans. Only by so doing could the House discharge its duty of "taking a higher, nobler and truer view of [its] responsibility to the . . . natives. . . ."[8] A few other members of parliament grumbled about giving oversight of Africans to Rhodes, but his wishes were speedily granted.

Rhodes' estimate of the vast dimension of the problems facing the Cape, and thus South Africa, differed little from Innes'. In a debate in the House on whether or not to encourage an influx of white immigrants, particularly juvenile boys, Rhodes raised a host of what he termed "practical" objections. Since South Africa's fundamental crisis was the growing competition between whites and blacks for the available jobs, why exacerbate this clash by inviting more whites without skills to settle in the Cape? "We called ourselves a dominant race among a native race," reminded Rhodes, "and that was really our position. What our position might be a hundred years hence [he] would not say." In South Africa whites were "surrounded and outnumbered by the native." Therefore it was beginning to be difficult for whites to find positions, even on farms, for their children. "We had an enormous competitor in the native and mixed class, who were very able and very efficient." Black labor would remain essential for the mines, as well as the farms, thus "recklessly" inviting young whites to the Cape was wrong, for it would increase the population of "poor whites." (In an entirely different context Rhodes believed that the perpetuation of the poor white problem was caused by the failure of rural whites to send their many children to school. Without schooling, these descendants of the first settlers "had no capacity for competing with the pushing Englishman or the clever Jew." Therefore the government must compel Afrikaners to educate their children.)

On still a third, connected, issue Rhodes urged the House not to tackle questions concerning individual title for African-occupied lands, or to legislate piecemeal for the large areas of the colony occupied by Africans. "Many members . . . wished to give natives all the privileges of citizenship without any of the obligations. They would give them the vote and the land," he said sarcastically, but at the same time they wished to protect Africans from white avarice. As secretary of native affairs, Rhodes promised to bring in comprehensive legislation to settle all of these outstanding and prickly issues.[9]

These and similar complexities affecting Africans Rhodes could defer until 1894, for the Franchise and Ballot exclusions were sufficient to curb their existing voting strength. In the case of Coloureds, however, there was some real concern, for a Muslim of local birth and Turkish descent stood for parliament from Cape Town in the 1894 elections. Because Malays of Muslim faith lived there in number and because, by a local constitutional peculiarity, each Cape Town voter could "plump"—cast four votes for any four candidates for the capital's four seats or give all four to the one favored by himself—the election of a member of the House who was not white was both a worrisome and a real possibility in the southern African winter of 1893. Only whites had ever sat in the House, and, although many representatives, notably Hofmeyr, assured their fellows that they would not personally mind sitting with Ahmed Effendi—who had put his name forward—they thought that it was anomalous that Cape Town alone should retain its cumulative voting method. James Tennant Molteno reminded the House that "the Malays and people of that class were . . . invading the town, and occupying the streets not occupied by them in times gone by. . . ." Joseph Millerd Orpen, from Wodehouse, thus moved to abolish plumping so that "some class that had interests adverse to the interests of the community [could not], by organisation, obtain a power which they had no right to at all." Moreover, Orpen claimed that his proffered change was not unfair to Malays "because if the people of Cape Town were all equally organised and determined to vote for certain men, they could do so equally well under the simpler system he proposed."[10]

Leander Starr Jameson, c. 1900.
(Sibbett Collection)

Charles D. Rudd, from a painting
in Gold Fields Collection.

The Houses of Parliament, Cape Town, 1890.
(McMillan Collection, Jagger Library, University of Cape Town)

The Cape Peninsula, from the air, looking south, c. 1966.
(McMillan Collection)

Groote Schuur: Rhodes' bedroom, from a photograph in an album, "Photographs of the Groote Schuur Estate," at Groote Schuur. *(Courtesy of Harry White)*

Groote Schuur: Rhodes' bath, from a photograph in an album, "Photographs of the Groote Schuur Estate," at Groote Schuur. *(Courtesy of Harry White)*

Groote Schuur, from the slopes of Table Mountain, from a photograph in an album, "Photographs of the Groote Schuur Estate," at Groote Schuur. *(Courtesy of Harry White)*

Olive Schreiner, c. 1893.
(De Beers archives)

On the stoep at Government
House, Salisbury (c. 1897):
Rhodes, A. Weston Jarvis,
Sir Charles Metcalfe, and Albert Grey.
(De Beers archives)

Opposite

Top. Groote Schuur, the stoep, from a photograph in an album, "Photographs of the Groote Schuur Estate," at Groote Schuur. *(Courtesy of Harry White)*

Bottom. Groote Schuur, the library, from a photograph in an album, "Photographs of the Groote Schuur Estate," at Groote Schuur. *(Courtesy of Harry White)*

On the veld, Rhodesia, 1896, Johnny Grimmer, Antonio Cruz, Cecil Rhodes, Ernest Rhodes, A. Weston Jarvis. (*De Beers archives*)

Directors of De Beers, 1893. Top: William H. Craven, Gardner Williams, George W. Compton. Bottom: Charles Edward Nind, Cecil Rhodes, Henry Robinow, David Harris. *(Sibbett Collection)*

Cecil Rhodes, c. 1900. *(Sibbett Collection and Zimbabwe archives)*

Opposite

Top. Bourchier F. Hawksley, c. 1905, from a painting in Rhodes House, Oxford.

Bottom. Rhodes and the Wedding Party, 1893; Dorothea Agnes Alexander, Rhodes, Eleanor Alexander. Standing, left: George Bowen, who married Dorothea, and an unidentified man. *(Sibbett Collection)*

The World's View (1897): Joseph Orford Williams Jerrard, Thomas William Smartt, Rhodes, and (behind Rhodes) Hamilton Hall, an American mining engineer. To the left are two unidentified Africans. *(Sibbett Collection)*

The World's View (1897): Joseph Orford Williams Jerrard, Hamilton Hall, Thomas William Smartt, Rhodes, and two unidentified Africans. *(Sibbett Collection)*

Rhodes at the Siege of Kimberley, 1900. *(De Beers archives)*

Rhodes at the center of a group of political supporters in Kimberley, 1898. *(Sibbett Collection)*

Siege of Kimberley, 1900: The searchlight, also Julia Maguire and Rhodes. *(De Beers archives)*

Siege of Kimberley, 1900: Meat supply announcement. *(De Beers archives)*

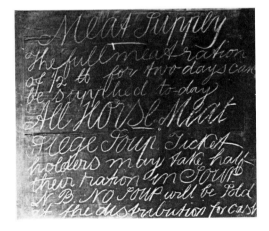

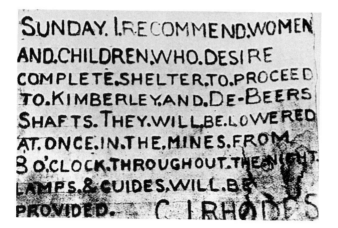

Siege of Kimberley, 1900:
Rhodes' announcement
of Shelter.
(De Beers archives)

Siege of Kimberley, 1900: The inauguration of the Soup Kitchen, Julia Maguire and Rhodes in the background. *(De Beers archives)*

Rhodes in Egypt, 1901: Rhodes is in the center and Philip Jourdan is hatless to the extreme right. Second from left is Sir Charles Metcalfe. In front is Leander Starr Jameson. The wall of the first Aswan dam is to the left. *(Sibbett Collection)*

The World's View, 1902: Readying Rhodes' tomb. *(De Beers archives)*

Hofmeyr, who favored the restriction, did not think that Malays deserved any "special consideration." Nevertheless, "his objection to colour was not so strong that he would object to see a well-educated man like the Effendi sitting in that House." Effendi was a teacher in the Muslim school in Kimberley; in 1862 his father had come to South Africa from the Ottoman Empire to teach Muslims in Cape Town. The Ottoman Empire paid his salary and may have made contributions to the support of his son.

Both Olè Anders Ohlsson, the brewer, and Thomas O'Reilly, two of the existing four representatives from Cape Town, scorned Orpen's proposed abridgment of the Cape constitution. They accused him of introducing it for the government, that is, for Rhodes and the Bond, and they challenged him to call his amendment the narrow class legislation that it was. "A more base attempt had never been made," said O'Reilly, "to take away the rights and privileges of a constituency." Moreover, asked the indignant O'Reilly, if Orpen wanted to keep Effendi out, "Why did he not say so like a man[?]" It was hardly just on the eve of an election to "bring in a measure of this magnitude. . . ." Herbert Travers Tamplin, representing Victoria East, urged the House to pause before depriving the Malay electors "of the power of voting for the man of their choice." "The Hon. the Premier," he continued, "was very fond of referring to the 'mother of nations,' but let them be careful not to do anything unworthy of that mother of nations." Tamplin appealed to the "liberty-loving" people of the Colony to "throw out this measure. . . ."

Sauer wanted no part of Effendi, and certainly opposed his sitting in the House. But Sauer, Richard Solomon, and Fuller opposed keeping a particular man out of parliament. Innes called it an "infamous precedent." It was not dignified. Merriman worried that Effendi would become a martyr.

Rhodes argued heatedly in favor of the amendment. It was "illogical" for Cape Town alone to vote cumulatively. He could not agree that removing such multiple votes would harm or reflect fear of the Malays. Either way they had four representatives in the House who could reflect their concerns. If plumping were retained and Effendi were elected, the other three Cape Town legislators would have less rather than more regard for Malay interests. "In so far as the Malay population was concerned they had not suffered in the past," but if the amendment were not passed and they returned Effendi, Malays would receive less rather than more "consideration" from the House. "It was not in the interests of the Malay population that the cumulative voting should remain," Rhodes asserted tendentiously.[11] Orpen's amendment passed its second reading by forty to twenty-four and its third and final reading by thirty to fifteen. Effendi was effectively kept out of the House, losing by 699 to 2356. Plumping might well have helped his candidacy.

The discussions of the parliamentary session of 1893 may have helped advance Rhodes' implicit legislative program. Yet they were but a prelude to his spectacular and far-reaching determination to reshape the African policies of the Cape and, hence, of South Africa. It is not as if Rhodes lacked projects and compelling interests. During the first half of 1894 he was also negotiating with Britain over Rhodesia, with Britain and Germany about telegraphic extensions, with Natal, the Transvaal, and the Free State about tariffs and a customs union, and with the Ottoman court about goats. He was concerned about administering or at least providing for the governance of trans-Zambezia, Nyasaland, and Rhodesia from afar. He was extending his monopoly over diamonds and recapitalizing his stake in gold, reconstructing and refurbishing Groote Schuur, and traveling extensively—to Europe every autumn. Rhodes was intimately concerned with his government's mundane as well as its precedent-shattering agenda. Moreover, in 1894 there was no shortage of contentious domestic issues upon which his coalition regime would need to pronounce. Yet, above all, African questions captured Rhodes' immediate attention.

When the Cape annexed the Transkei in 1878, and as it gradually extended its magisterial authority to Tembuland and East Griqualand through 1885, the coastal territories of the Mpondo remained autonomous, though under British protection. In the early 1890s there were about 200,000 Mpondo, under Chief Sigcawu, who ruled eastern Pondoland, and Chief Nqiliso, who ruled western Pondoland. For some years both Mpondo chiefdoms had been harassed by their African and Griqua rivals in the now-British Transkei, by white traders in Griqualand, and by the Cape officials—the magistrates—who governed the Transkei (largely by proclamation) on behalf of the secretary for native affairs and the governor. The Mpondo were regularly accused of raiding for cattle in the Colony.

British-appointed observers in Pondoland and Colonel Charles Duncan Griffith, the member for Tembuland, who made a report to parliament in 1891, affirmed that the Mpondo were "unfitted to govern themselves" and of "inferior stock." Major Henry Elliott, the resident magistrate of Tembuland in 1892, recorded that the appalling state of Pondoland affected "the whole of the Transkei in the same manner as a canker would an otherwise healthy body."[12] Later that year Natal complained that Sigcawu and his followers were repeatedly violating the Natal border, raiding the inhabitants of the smaller colony and causing expensive patrolling by the police. These complaints were directed by the governor of Natal to Loch, the Cape's governor, and from Loch to Rhodes' cabinet. Its members, acting collectively in Rhodes' absence in Europe, wanted no war as yet with Pondoland. Nevertheless, the problem persisted, with Natal growing more heated and Loch more exercised at his elected government's refusal to act. Loch himself even attempted to deal with Sigcawu directly, in late 1893, but Sigcawu kept the governor waiting for three days before seeing him.

Loch knew that Natal might demand to act itself, or might even send a private filibustering expedition against Sigcawu if Rhodes, in 1893 more concerned in Ndebeleland, continued to temporize. Loch wanted to maintain good relations with Natal, particularly after late 1893, when it achieved responsible government or settler control. Equally he wanted the Cape to assume authority over the Mpondo. Thus, by 1894 there was significant local pressure throughout the eastern Cape to end the independence of Pondoland. Loch had an equal incentive. He merely needed a fresh incident which could serve as a pretext, and require Rhodes' full attention. The first arrived when Mhlangaso, a subordinate chief in eastern Pondoland, revolted against Sigcawu, battled fiercely, and, unsuccessful, established an armed fiefdom on the border with Natal and then asked that colony for support and refuge. Natal would want to intervene. But Rhodes was also free to act. The crisis in this farthest and most distant corner of the Cape took on a dimension and a significance which was bound to concern the prime minister.

Rhodes had refused in 1890 to add the troubles of Pondoland to those of his newly established government. In 1894, however, as he had forecast to the electors of Barkly West in January, it was both necessary and logical that Rhodes and the Cape should act. Otherwise, Natal, newly enfranchised and seeking to demonstrate its power, would do so itself. As Rhodes subsequently told parliament, "Success had attended our efforts in the North, and [I] thought . . . it was one of those happy moments for dealing with the position." Because Natal had offered to handle the Mpondo, Rhodes declared that "the opportune moment had arrived." Early in February, alerted by telegrams from Natal's governor to Loch, and by Loch's own prodding, Rhodes acted forthrightly, but hardly rashly or boisterously. Taking advice from Elliott, Rhodes planned a limited initiative which could not commit the Cape to any irrevocable course of martial action. He asked Loch to appoint Elliott as a special resident commissioner for Pondoland, and then sent him and Walter Stanford, the magistrate in Griqualand, to Sigcawu.

Armed only with firm instructions from Loch and Rhodes, but backed by the potential might of the Cape's army, Elliott easily procured the cession to the Cape of first eastern and then, from Nqiliso, western Pondo. "In dealing with natives," Rhodes subsequently explained, "if [whites] showed physical force behind them they gained a great deal." Finally, there was Mhlangaso, whose insurrection had provided the excuse for intervention. In mid-March, Rhodes told Stanford to inform the sub-chief that his corner of eastern Pondo had been annexed, and that "any act of opposition [would] be treated as rebellion. . . ."[13] Rhodes, again impatient, sent 200 men of the Cape Mounted Rifles to reinforce this demand. But Mhlangaso was no fool; he submitted on 1 April.

In order to see for himself, to put his own stamp on the endeavor, and because he was now accustomed to take vast African hinterlands under his own aegis, Rhodes immediately set out for Pondoland on a triumphant journey that echoed the processions of Roman Caesars. Traveling in great state in a fancy coach drawn by eight cream-colored horses, and accompanied by 100 men of the Cape Mounted Rifles, Sir William Milton, his secretary, and Stanford, Rhodes went for what Merriman was to call his "scamper through the Transkei." First he visited and endured the white residents of Kokstad, some of whom owed their allegiance and had their trading connections to Natal, and one or more of whom may have presumed to praise Natal at a banquet in Rhodes' honor. This "agitation," as Rhodes called it, on behalf of Natal, produced an uncharacteristically violent speech by Rhodes. He attacked the financial stability of the Cape's smaller neighbor and ridiculed the pretensions of its tiny white population and its recently enfranchised legislative assembly at a time when Rhodes and the Cape still sought a united South Africa.

Having expressed himself intemperately, Rhodes insisted on completing the journey to Nqiliso and Sigcawu that Stanford and others advised him was both rash and dangerous. Near what is now Umtata, Rhodes met Nqiliso on 8 April. He chastised the chief for permitting his subordinates to fight and cause disorder in the rest of the Transkei, and for governing poorly and cruelly. But then he promised that white settlers would not be allowed into his territory, and that Pondoland would be governed as Tembuland was being governed. Nqiliso countered with complaints and demands of his own, but Rhodes stood on his dignity, refusing to accept such language. According to what Rhodes told parliament, Nqiliso and Sigcawu both assumed (or had been so informed by Elliott) that they would be ruled indirectly on Basuto lines. The chiefs would continue to hold power, but would be advised by white magistrates. Rhodes, however, bluntly told the chiefs that they were unfit; their territories were to be annexed, and ruled directly by magistrates. Rhodes had also told both chiefs that if the Mpondo rose in rebellion he would take their country from them and give it to whites, confining them to a coastal strip of land which was suitable for maize growing but not the grazing of cattle.

Ultimately, Nqiliso submitted entirely, Rhodes was satisfied, and the premier and his coach and soldiers moved rapidly on to Port St. Johns on 9 April, and then to the Palmerston Mission Station, five miles from Sigcawu's village, on 11 April. After breakfast that day, Sigcawu submitted to government control, saying that he was merely following in the footsteps of his father and grandfather.[14] Rhodes, in exchange for such compliant obeisance, granted him a yearly annuity. But Rhodes refused to put the two Mpondo chieftaincies under Sigcawu as they had once been joined under Sigcawu's grandfather. Having successfully explained why he could not and having indicated how the Mpondo would be ruled, Rhodes concluded his flag waving and returned in haste to the Cape, where parliament was soon to open. (En route, near Kokstad, Rhodes had his second "nasty fall." This accident adds to the catalogue of Rhodes' medical history.[15])

John Smith Moffat, then in Cape Town, provided a wry, skeptical, reflection: "The great Rhodes is prancing round. He returned last week from Pondoland. He has too much on his shoulders, and will probably end by making a mess of it, but meanwhile everybody here is bowing down and worshipping him as the wisest of men. The popular tide is with him. Great is success! I wonder the old Greeks and Romans never had a God of Success—that is the sort of god which would be popular nowadays. I suppose there will be a crash some day—and men will suddenly recollect that there is still such a thing as justice even to niggers."[16]

Rhodes formally asked parliament to annex Pondoland to the Cape in May. Having "a barbarian power between two civilised powers" was almost impossible in Africa, as it was in Central Asia, between Russia and India. The boundaries of Natal and the Cape should now meet. Rhodes explained the direct basis on which he had undertaken to rule Pondoland. Indeed, he told the House, magistrates were already in charge and the "common people" were "delighted with the change, because . . . they would not be at the mercy of a drunken savage."

Rhodes, as he had told the chiefs, informed parliament that he would grant or recognize no concessions. That meant that whites could not buy land from Mpondo, prospect for minerals, or carry on in the manner of Rhodesia's whites. It also meant that Pondoland would remain an African district, the costs of which (so far about £7,000, possibly another £8,000 in the next year, plus £15,000 a year for the Cape Mounted Rifles) would be borne by a hut tax—what Rhodes coyly called "civilised payments." Rhodes hoped "it would be only a question of time—to see the Transkei self-supporting. . . ."

There was a further policy question. Should the Mpondo be disarmed? Rhodes had seen at first hand the consequences of disarming the Sotho. Regarding the Mpondo, Rhodes reminded the House that they had submitted peacefully. Not a shot had been fired. Had they been disarmed, compensation would be merited. "What was the use of paying away good Colonial money for those useless weapons?" Moreover, he was confident the Mpondo would no longer use their guns in anger. "If the Government treated them with justice and consideration—which they were determined to do—the Pondos would not break out." And they never did. To Sprigg, Rhodes also confessed another motive for neither disarming nor moving the Mpondo into older districts of the Transkei. He was "anxious not to prejudice future land sales to whites. . . ."

What of the consequences of numbers? The Cape Colony now contained 1.4 million people, including 700,000 "savages and barbarians." Contrary to Rhodes' usual dictum, he was proposing to annex Africans, not just land. But Orpen welcomed the Mpondo—"a fresh labour supply for the Colony." "It made one feel overweighted almost with responsibility," said Rhodes. "But having taken the step of extending the Colony across the Transkei, it must go on. . . ." Rhodes stoutly defended the record of the Cape. "It was often believed . . . that the Cape people were . . . unfair to the natives." However, said Rhodes, "our progress in the Transkei was a bright record." His government had been and would continue to be unselfish, freeing the Transkeians "from the seething cauldron of barbarian atrocities." Pondoland would benefit from the "kind and beneficent sway of the Cape. . . ." Though the inhabitants of the Transkei had repeatedly rebelled—Rhodes ignored the contradiction—the Cape had left them in "sole possession of the land." It had given Africans good government "at a loss to ourselves." (John Charles Molteno objected, claiming that the people of the Transkei already paid more in taxes and customs duties than they received in services. "It was not fair to . . . say that these people were a burden. . . .") Rhodes asked (in the insouciant manner of so many later South African governments) if "any civilised nations in Europe could show such a record."[17]

Although parliament offered little opposition to the annexation of Pondoland, some of its members worried about the precise way in which the Mpondo would be ruled. They would be subject to the laws of the Cape as applied to them by the governor's proclamations. The House would have little oversight of this process, except through Rhodes. Sauer and Scanlen worried particularly that the Mpondo would not be protected by British common law, for its application could be denied. Rhodes, in reply, urged Sauer and others not to concern themselves too much with people living in such a state of "pure barbarism." Rhodes did not want to tie the government's hands too tightly. Since the Mpondo were not civilized, it was unreasonable to try to temper the extension of straightforward executive power to them. Over and over again Rhodes defended his decision not to extend the laws of the Cape to Pondoland. Repeatedly he justified such a limitation on the powers of parliament by calling the Mpondo naked savages. They would be ruled by him, through magistrates reinforced by soldiers and either Maxim or Nordenfelt guns, and that was that.[18]

And so they were. In mid-1895, while parliament was sitting in Cape Town, Rhodes sent 200 men of the Cape Mounted Rifles to arrest Sigcawu and detain him in Kokstad. Although Sigcawu and other Mpondo chiefs, especially the hapless Totwana, were subsequently accused of conspiring to defeat the ends of justice and being thoroughly uncooperative, Rhodes in fact persistently provoked a confrontation and, uncharacteristically, thirsted for decisive action. Even when his normally anti-African magistrates in the field sought to move circumspectly, cautiously, and justly, Rhodes bullied for closure.

What, were it not for Rhodes' serious role, would have been a sequence of events in Pondoland worthy of a comic opera, began in January 1895, when three Mpondo stock thieves escaped not once but three times in succession from the jail at Kokstad. Fleeing to Sigcawu's "Great Place," they found no sanctuary there. Indeed, Sigcawu appears to have cooperated fully with the initial request that the prisoners be returned to Kokstad. Nevertheless, the telegraphed messages from Cape Town were truculent, especially after the local whites began to suspect that Sigcawu was prevaricating, procrastinating, and behaving in all those devious ways in which they assumed chiefs would (and sometimes did) act. Yet, after the prisoners were re-committed to jail, Sigcawu appeared at a meeting with Stanford, the chief magistrate, accompanied by a large armed detachment, contrary to orders. This triggered Rhodes' ire. "He is amazed," telegraphed the undersecretary for native affairs, "that on the first occasion that Sigcau appeared before you with armed men you did not at once call upon them to lay down their arms. . . . Such conduct must not be repeated. . . ."

In March several other chiefs and their followers behaved in ways whites called insolent. Totwana was one of the most recalcitrant. It was supposed that Sigcawu was fomenting this dissent; rumors were rife in Pondoland. By the end of March, acting on orders from Cape Town, two patrols of the Cape Mounted Rifles arrested Totwana. He and his soldiers had given the people of chief Totwana "a severe lesson," crowed Stanford, "and they appreciate it." Yet, a few days later, Stanford told Rhodes that "so far evidence exonerates Totwana." A little later Stanford telegraphed that "Totwana's arrest cannot be regarded as just. . . ." A chief Mbemi, Totwana's nephew, was the real culprit, and he was believed to have been acting on Sigcawu's orders.

Rhodes instructed Stanford to warn Sigcawu to behave, or else. Stopping his subsidy would not be sufficient, said Rhodes. "If he obstructs . . . officials in carrying out the law you should deal with him as I told you at Lady Frere" (where the two had met). Stanford reminded the prime minister that some legal provision would have to be made to authorize Sigcawu's detention. Rhodes' telegraphic response was straightforward: "Please move with promptitude." Sigcawu also cabled, begging the premier for ten days. But Rhodes said he would give no time. Arrest Sigcawu, he demanded, and prepared a proclamation for the governor's signature, on 7 June. Stanford asked for reinforcements and prepared for hostilities. Rhodes demanded to know why. Get on with it, he wired. By 8 June, Stanford's assistants reported that Sigcawu denied any intentional rudeness, expressed regrets, and so on. On the next day, Stanford told Rhodes that there may be a "serious misapprehension" about the facts. Perhaps Sigcawu was not a fomenter, after all. But Rhodes still demanded the chief's arrest. By 10 June Rhodes was clearly exasperated. Be decisive, he wired. Two days later, the premier added that Sigcawu's village should be occupied. "Such a step will have a good effect on the Pondos. I did the same at Bulawayo, and have built my house on the spot where Lobengula's Kraal stood." On 16 June Stanford reported that Sigcawu had agreed to surrender. Rhodes, however, demanded an "unconditional" surrender. Rhodes wanted to show the Mpondo that "the rule of Sigacawu is at an end. . . ." After Sigcawu's arrest on 18 June, Rhodes reminded Stanford that the chief should be closely guarded night and day. "Guard him strictly."[19]

After the fact, Rhodes sought approval for his actions from parliament. He told its members that Sigcawu had been "giving trouble" and refusing to cease agitating against the previous year's annexation of Pondoland. What Rhodes neglected to mention, and what the House never learned officially, was that Rhodes had decided to victimize Sigcawu, whether Stanford or the House liked it or not. Over intense parliamentary opposition, Rhodes persuaded his colleagues to permit arrests in Pondoland by proclamation with or without subsequent trials. Sigcawu was detained at Kokstad, although the report of the commission which "tried" the chief and other accounts of his arrest were never laid before the House and discussed, as Rhodes had promised.

Merriman marveled at Rhodes' myriad talents. "What an amazingly clever fellow Rhodes is. The only person I ever knew who combined patriotism &

plunder. . . . He is a sort of Trinity—Premier, Managing Director & Finan-cier/Millionaire . . . he poses as a sort of beneficient patriot—Extending the Empire, ruling the Cape . . . amalgamating S. Africa & what not . . . he grants concessions of huge value to all sorts of companies and syndicates . . . and finally as [premier] he will induce the people of this colony through the agency of . . . Hofmeyr to take over his liabilities. . . ."[20]

Rhodes abused his powers as secretary for native affairs and misled the House. But his breach of faith and arbitrary actions beyond the scope of the law did not, for once, go unchecked. When the Sigcawu case came before Chief Justice Sir Henry de Villiers, the onetime would-be prime minister shredded any pretext that the arrest could have been either legal or fair. Sigcawu, said his judgment, had been "arrested, condemned and sentenced . . . without the intervention of any tribunal, without alleging the necessity for such a proceeding, without [any alteration of] the general law to meet the case of the individual" and without being heard in self-defense. The procla-mation had not even specified the offense. It had merely charged him with "obstruction" and declared him a "public danger." Although Rhodes at-tempted to plead that the proclamation had the force of law in Pondoland and could not be set aside by any court, de Villiers, supported by Justice Sir Thomas Upington, whom Rhodes had elevated to the bench, answered boldly: "Sigcawu, it is true, is a native, but he is a British subject, and there are many Englishmen and others resident in the territories who . . . [might] be liable to be deprived of their life and property, as well as their liberty . . ." in the same manner.[21] Thus Rhodes was rebuffed by the Supreme Court of the Cape (but only after other demonstrations of unchecked authoritarianism in parliament in 1894), his arbitrary actions curbed, and Sigcawu returned home to Pondoland.

In 1894 Rhodes had acquired Pondoland and filled out the eastern cor-ners of the Cape. He had begun to administer it. Next he had to assimilate its numerous Africans into a Cape polity already acutely aware that for the entire Cape Colony and for South Africa more widely the African problem was the single most important and potentially disruptive issue of the 1890s. Not only was its harmonious resolution essential to the maintenance of good relations among whites—in the Cape between the Bond and Rhodes' English-speaking followers, and in South Africa between at least the Transvaal and the Cape—but the very development of the Cape's agriculture and industry depended upon a workable answer to a series of significant subordinate questions which were customarily bundled together as "the native question." The Cape had long since ceased to be a white outpost of Europe. Thanks to frontier wars and annexations, of which that of Pondoland was but the most recent, the Cape had become a sub-imperial power with a white core and a vast black periphery that accounted for about 80 percent of the whole.

Already, Rhodes and Hofmeyr had largely dealt with the problem of po-litical control. By raising the property and earnings gates to the franchise they had curbed the real and potential influence of the growing black bourgeoisie.

By effectively excluding access to the franchise through communally held tenure, they had dramatically slowed any extraordinary growth in black power. It was thus possible politically to add significantly (the 200,000 Mpondo, for example) to the subordinate population of the Cape. Yet, progressive and satisfactory as these adjustments seemed to Rhodes and his ilk, they constituted but a partial solution to the short- and long-term problem of thorough assimilation. As Rhodes had earlier suggested, any long-term solution had to ensure adequate supplies of black labor for the mines and the farms and had to decide whether and how Africans could be acculturated. Under what conditions and with what safeguards could Africans move from traditional to modern forms of tenure? Should whites be allowed to intermingle with Africans in the frontier districts? Should Africans be protected from white capital, particularly in situations where Africans could lose their land? Hard liquor had proved destructive in an African setting; should the demon drink be proscribed in the African districts? How, finally, should the newer additions to the Cape be governed? The power of the chiefs had receded or been destroyed. In a colony where segregation was a continuing fact, what institutions should replace the rule of chiefs?

Rhodes consciously sought to legislate an African policy which would provide workable answers to these and a host of cognate questions. For him the answers had to be realistic, progressive, innovative, and politically palatable. They could be paternal, but they could not be motivated by sentimentality, or by any obsessive concern for the sensibilities of Africans or Negrophilists. Rhodes sought to do what was best for the Colony and to prepare for a future United South Africa. His definition of what was fit and proper, however, although popular among local whites, was molded both by conditions on the African frontier and by his (and it was not solely his) basic presumption that whites would always rule southern Africa and that no successful merging of Dutch- and English-speakers and tendencies to form a wider South Africa could ever occur if blacks played significant political roles in the Cape but were barred from a similar status in Natal, the Free State, and the Transvaal. Once again, Rhodes' larger objectives shaped his honing of intermediate instruments.

The Glen Grey district was a tiny section (250,000 morgen) of the eastern Cape north of Queenstown and St. Marks, nestled under the foothills of the Drakensberg mountains. In 1852 the Cape had assigned it to the Xhosa-speaking Tambookie branch of the Thembu people. Although sections of the Cape had been given to Mfengu and others under individual tenure, many of these experiments had been opposed by the chiefs, and had lapsed. Glen Grey was settled in communal tenure, even after 1864, when the government attempted to push the Thembu off their land to make way for whites. In 1881, the Thembu rebelled and were subdued, and settlement in what was popularly called the reserve was restricted to those Thembu who had remained loyal. However, by 1892, when a three-man commission appointed by Rhodes examined the conditions of the Glen Grey district, it was clear that the rebels had returned in great number and become indistinguishable from the so-called loyalists. The commission discovered a total population of about 40,000, a few mission stations and white settlers, and a preponderant desire among the Thembu for individual tenure, conceivably with safeguards against the transfer of their lands to whites.

Like most reserves, Glen Grey was overcrowded and overgrazed. Many of its male inhabitants had already begun to seek work from whites in the Colony. Others meanwhile had crowded into Glen Grey from more distant or less settled frontier areas. Whites, especially Dutch-speaking farmers, coveted its fertile valleys. In a microcosm, Glen Grey presented most of the problems found in the recently if only partially assimilated frontier districts. There was a clear need to remove sources of friction among Africans and between Africans and whites. Land was at the root of most disputes, but to grant individual tenure meant at least the possibility of a flood of newly entitled black voters, conceivably less pressure on Africans to seek work, and a host of ancillary questions with local and Cape-wide budgetary implications. There also was the danger that whites would purchase the newly salable black-owned farms and thus thrust vast numbers of landless black families onto the Colony.

The Holland commission on African labor, reporting in 1893, favored a total shift in Glen Grey from communal to individual tenure, albeit with provisions to prevent the swift transfer of these new freeholds to whites of comparative wealth. It said that each black family, of which there were approximately 8,000 in Glen Grey, ought to receive farms of 55 morgen each, an allotment which could well have satisfied the existing £75 property requirement for the franchise. By thus allocating all of the land of Glen Grey to existing families, newcomers would be unable to settle there and would be compelled to seek employment in the Colony. Such a provision pleased the Bond, but not the possibility that many of the 8,000 families of Glen Grey would, if literate, automatically be added to the voter's rolls. The Bond's members mostly welcomed individual tenure, for they saw opportunities for subsequent acquisitions by their compatriots, but they naturally deprecated any restrictions which would make such purchases difficult, if not impossible. As Innes recalled, "The Bond favoured free title, hoping to break up the locations; Sprigg, Frost and others favoured it, indifferent to that result. . . ."[22]

His hand at least somewhat forced by the commission, by a sharp debate in parliament in 1893, by the consequent anticipation of change by Africans and whites, and by the fact that he had assumed the mantle of czar for African affairs, Rhodes in 1894 was obliged to present a bill for Glen Grey and for African issues generally. It had to be crafted with unusual care if it were to satisfy the full range of his supporters, especially the Bond, serve his own interests as a political and industrial leader, exemplify his philosophical approach to matters African, and prove roughly congruent with what he was doing and expected to do beyond the Limpopo. For all of these reasons, but possibly because Rhodes was uncertain about precisely how to formulate some of its provisions until the last moment, he introduced the momentous and complicated Glen Grey bill at the very end of the session of 1894, with less than a month remaining. Conceived by Rhodes, the bill was drafted by Milton. It also grew out of extensive consultations with Hofmeyr. A number of its restrictions on tenure also reflected the advice that Victor Sampson, a Bondsman from Tembuland, had given Hofmeyr. Juta, the attorney general, who was responsible for all government legislation, saw the finished bill only when it was presented to Rhodes' caucus on the eve of its introduction to parliament. (Juta subsequently resigned because of the "public and continued manner in which as the Law Minister I am entirely ignored. . . . I really cannot sit [in the House] to be the laughing stock of everyone."[23]) The rest of the cabinet read the bill's detail only then, too.

In creating his draft, Rhodes had struggled to produce an integrated plan which would prove acceptable as an answer to the issues of Glen Grey, could be extended subsequently to other districts of the Cape, and could provide a basis for relations between black and white within a United South Africa and farther north, grandly, for Africa. "The whole of the North will some time or another come under this bill if passed by the House. . . . I would not be surprised to see Natal . . . come under this Bill," said Rhodes at the time. "This is a Native Bill for Africa."

When Rhodes introduced his bill in parliament—at an evening sitting—he spoke for an hour and forty minutes. What he believed about the place he intended Africans to fill, and the role in the colony and in Africa that he wanted them to play, achieved due exposure in his prolix, repetitive, but nevertheless compelling speech. As Innes said, Rhodes' speech was "long, rambling, and full of detail (he was a master of detail when detail mattered), but very able and effective." George Green, fresh from Britain and later the editor of the *Cape Times*, thought otherwise. "Being an irreverent newcomer, who had not yet fallen under the spell of the magician," Green explained, "I was not very favourably impressed. . . . My sense of propriety was startled by his careless, informal style of oratory. While the House listened breathlessly as to the voice of the Oracle, I . . . could but marvel at his bald diction and rough, unfinished sentences. At intervals he would jerk out a happy, illumining phrase or apt illustration; but the arrangement of the speech was distressingly faulty, and his occasional lapses into falsetto [and] . . . his flounderings rather resembled those of a schoolboy trying to repeat an imperfectly learned lesson."[24]

Rhodes opened his exhortation by asserting that Africans in their millions should be neither a source of trouble nor anxiety to the Colony. "Properly directed and properly looked after . . . the natives would be a source of assistance and wealth. At any rate, if the white population maintained its position as the supreme race . . . the day would come when they would all be thankful that they had had the natives—in their proper position. . . ."

The premier did not intend to minimize the existing problems. He was conscious that Africans were "increasing enormously." The Cape had established locations for Africans where "without any right or title to the ground, they were herded together." They were "multiplying to such an enormous extent that these locations . . . had become too small for them." Without war and pestilence, which had been ended by white rule, they were outgrowing their agricultural lands. Instead of war, all whites had offered was liquor. Because whites had not instructed Africans in "the dignity of labour," they lived "in sloth and laziness"—which Rhodes abhorred more than anything else—"and never went out to work." Using partial facts, Rhodes contended astonishingly that "the Kafir's wages were 50 per cent. in advance of those of the agricultural labourer in England." It was the government's duty to "give them some gentle stimulants to go forth and find out something of the dignity of labour," said Rhodes with "rapt expression."

Simply giving land to African families, and then allowing that land to be subdivided and Africans to "increase upon it" was a "ridiculous" proposition. Equally preposterous was the notion that Africans could deal with and be a part of the politics of the Cape. "It was really ridiculous to suppose that these poor children could be taken out of this absolute barbarism and . . . come to a practical conclusion on . . . politics." The prime minister worked from a premise, common to many of his peers, that "natives were different." Their brains were different. They were built differently. Yet "he did not despise them—far from it. . . ." Thus the essential four premises of his new bill were: "to give the natives interest in the land, allow the superior minds amongst them to attend to their local wants, remove the canteens [saloons], and give them the stimulus to labour." Moreover, Rhodes promised that if the bill were approved he would apply sections of it well beyond Glen Grey, to many of the other African areas.

Rhodes' detailed proposals included the granting of farms of four rather than fifty-five morgen on individual tenure, eliminating partible inheritance, and insisting that the farms should pass down the generations intact, by primogeniture. Doing so would both keep these small plots complete and also throw sons other than the eldest off the land; they would presumably seek work elsewhere. Moreover, farmers would lose the land if they failed to cultivate it. It was wrong, Rhodes suggested, for African heirs to be on a par with white heirs. "Wanting . . . to make the natives as themselves . . . was not a tenable position." Moreover, Rhodes' proposed legislation included a provision preventing the sale of their freeholds to whites. Whites should not be allowed to buy land in the midst of Africans. That would only accentuate the poor white problem. "The natives should be in native reserves, and not mixed up with whites." Communal grazing rights were preserved. As to the franchise, Rhodes contended that the mere possession of farms should not make individuals eligible. "They were dealing with 'citizens' who were children, and as the Government protected their land the natives had no right," said Rhodes, "to claim a vote upon it." The bill simply barred all those who would be newly enfranchised by the Glen Grey bill from voting in Cape elections.

Rhodes' "gentle stimulant" was a newly devised labor tax of 10 shillings a head. It was not "slavery," the premier declared. What he wanted to do was to clear out of the locations all those young men about town who spent their idleness at beer drinks and sponged off their brothers or fathers for food. They never did "a stroke of work." He was against loafing and the immorality to which it led. Even the owner of the four-morgen plot would not be exempt, for Rhodes thought that he would spend only three or four weeks sowing his maize, and would truly not be working hard enough. "It would be wise if such a man also went out and worked for a certain period." As Innes commented sarcastically, "No toil, however strenuous, upon a Native's own land, was dignified enough to satisfy the tax collector."

Stimulated by the labor tax, Rhodes the Social Darwinist suggested, Africans would change for the better. "Every black man could not have three acres and a cow in the future." Africans would have to change as the English had changed. "It must be brought home to them that in the future nine-tenths of them would have to spend their lives in manual labour, and the sooner that was brought home to them the better." Additionally, Africans would find that they were better off when they went to work. Rhodes promised to spend the funds from the labor tax on industrial schools, where Africans could be taught trades and vocations. South Africa had too many schools which specialized in "turning out a peculiar class of human beings—the Kafir parson. Now the Kafir parson was a most excellent type of individual," said Rhodes, "but he belonged to a class that was overdone." They became agitators, and accused the government of oppressing the common people. They constituted "a dangerous class."

Admitting that it was essential, in blunting the appeal of such men and in making his new program of freehold successful, to "keep the minds of the natives occupied," Rhodes sought to introduce local government to African areas. The district council of Glen Grey, and the boards of the eighteen locations into which the district would be divided, would be responsible for making and maintaining roads and bridges and planting forests. Moreover, by allowing the council to levy its own assessments on the new property owners, the Cape budget would be relieved of such local expenditures. Africans in general occupied, according to Rhodes, the "best portion" of South Africa. They should bear their own costs. But Rhodes proposed that the members of the boards and the council be nominated rather than elected. Although at first intending to have whites and blacks rule the district together, in what would have been an important and useful South African experiment, Rhodes subsequently excluded the area of Glen Grey in which whites lived on ten farms, and limited the council's jurisdiction to the African locations only.[25]

As it was offered to the members of the House—Rhodes suggested that they were "sitting in judgement on Africa"—the Glen Grey package envisaged a compact class of indigenous producers working their small farms, growing sufficient crops to feed their district and yielding extra cash with which to pay for local infrastructural needs. Governing themselves under the watchful eye of a white magistrate, they would watch their surplus kin go off to work for whites. The locations would be a place "where the people could go back to after working." But because no African could own more than one allotment, each producer would be unlikely to compete successfully with white farmers. Lacking the vote on the Cape franchise, they would eschew the politics of the Colony and busy themselves with district affairs like the sober peasants whom Rhodes idealized. "Those who knew the natives knew that they only wanted telling what they had to do, and they would do it."

Whatever Rhodes' underlying motives, Glen Grey was a bold, all-embracing plan which promised to alter the framework by which whites governed Africans and Africans lived their lives in the Cape. As Rhodes intended, it also offered the kinds of solutions to African problems which were to suggest themselves to South Africa's governments thereafter. In that sense, certainly, the Glen Grey bill was a forerunner of the segregationist legislation of the twentieth century, and of the combination of laws which together constitute apartheid. But it was not so much the content of the bill as it was Rhodes' rhetoric and rationalizations which prefigured the future. What modern readers appreciate as fatuous and sophistic arguments—mere fig leaves for white supremacy and denials of African rights—were those that Rhodes and all subsequent rulers in South Africa have used to justify their departures from the natural law and political culture of the Western world. It is a testimony to Rhodes' force of character and quality of persuasion that he, alone of likely Cape leaders, was able to arrange such shifts away from previous norms with ease. It delineates his character, too, that he did so with equanimity, without shame, and even with self-righteous determination.

That Rhodes prevailed is not to imply that the Glen Grey bill slid through the House. Rhodes' usual critics sharpened their knives, attacking both the principle and the details of the bill as well as the haste with which it was being rushed through parliament's deliberative stages. They knew what it meant for Africans, and how some of its seemingly innocuous provisions could be misapplied to their detriment. They worried about Rhodes' penchant for proclamation, not considered legislation. Sauer wanted the House to deal with Africans as grown-up men. Rhodes should not try to take away their votes "by a side wind, as in the present Bill. . . ." He laughed at the prime minister's suggestion that a black farmer could deal with his maize in three or four weeks. Moreover, why should the premier drive such a member of the producing class out to work? "By what right?" he asked. Rhodes said that women could work the plots, then. Sauer hoped that "the father of the native population was not going to say that native women should be made to work." Sauer further thought that the proposal to nominate all the members of the district council unfair. Africans would lose interest in their local government. Finally Sauer reminded his former colleague that whites could maintain their supremacy only by "just legislation . . . and by showing by their laws and civilization that the whites were the superior race."[26]

Additional determined opposition came from Hutton, Merriman, Innes,

Dr. William Bisset Berry, J.C. Molteno, Fuller, Tamplin, and others. Berry, from Queenstown, reminded the House that there was no need to stimulate labor beyond "fair treatment and fair wage." Innes instructed Rhodes that the object of individual tenure was to encourage, not discourage men who were prepared to devote their whole time to the land. Moreover, they could grow two crops on it within a year.

Merriman blamed the shoddy quality of the bill on the premier's refusal to fight it through the House properly. He accused him instead of taking refuge in the caucus and the lobby, where it had been agreed upon in an underhanded way. Moreover, as far as Merriman was concerned, the bill was vague and sketchy. It reflected Rhodes' recent "scamper through the Transkei . . . [where] he had gained a few ideas, put them into a Bill, and thought he was going to settle Africa." Africans were not lazy. Where would the diamond mines be "but for these lazy Kafirs?"

When Innes attempted to persuade the prime minister to let such an important and controversial bundle of ideas lie before the House for a year, Rhodes said it could not wait. His intention was to keep the House sitting until the bill was passed. Later Innes argued that the bill should not be pushed through "by mere force," with only the opposition speaking. "They were approaching a state of things in this matter which might very well fill those who had a desire to see Parliamentary institutions carried out in their integrity with alarm." Rhodes promised to let the bill wait after the second reading, and save thorough deliberations until 1895, but then he abruptly changed his mind, and sent it forward.

At the committee stage, Rhodes tried to make it clear what he would and would not accept as amendments and challenges from the opposition. When individuals pressed him too hard, over and over he yelled "obstruction," and threatened to "pursue a different course." Merriman called Rhodes' actions "disgraceful." "So far from showing obstruction," Merriman tutored, "we are only doing our duty. . . ." He also accused Rhodes of muzzling those of his supporters who usually spoke out on behalf of Africans. Later, after a number of other challenges, and with the evening sitting commencing, Rhodes flew into a rage and declared that "he was going to sit there all night. The members of the Opposition had obstructed the whole afternoon on one clause. It was perfectly clear."

Rhodes promised to "do his best to carry the Bill as it stood." Innes chided him for having "got into a temper, because it was the worst way of getting through business." But Rhodes replied that he had "made up [his] mind for a night of it." And for the remaining hours of the night and well into the following morning, Rhodes petulantly rammed the Glen Grey bill through nearly all of its committee phase, clause by clause, occasionally accepting minor alterations, but largely keeping his (or Milton's) phrases intact. Parliament adjourned on that fateful morning of 7 August 1894 at 7:17 a.m. Rhodes, recalled Innes, "for the first time had publicly displayed that dictatorial and impatient vein with which, in the near future, we were to become familiar."

The Kimberley *Advertiser* was even more acerbic: "Parliament is utterly demoralized. Mr. Rhodes' dictatorial demeanour, and even insulting methods, are in a great measure responsible. . . . No man with any spirit of independence will stand the pecular tendencies of the only Cecil to overrule everybody and all things. . . . Whatever Mr. Rhodes may have done for his self-aggrandisement during the past 12 or 15 years, he has at least achieved a record for unparallelled selfish dominance, impatience and grasping."[27]

The final discusssions of the committee stage of the bill took place two days later. During them Rhodes refused to deny the Africans of Glen Grey their liquor. Despite their supposed state of barbarism, Rhodes—influenced by the Bond's desire to sell wine and brandy to Africans—argued in a convoluted way that the canteens should not be removed. According to Merriman, the premier "pointed out what an evil the drink was, and then bound it on the natives." Finally, on this alone of the substantive clauses, Rhodes lost an amending vote by 33 to 25.

When, at the wearying end of a long session, in August, it was clear that Rhodes would get what he wanted, a largely unemasculated Glen Grey Act, he explained why he had decided to go beyond the second stage. He said that "it would be a very grievous mistake to allow a native agitation throughout the country." He feared an outcry of such proportions that the House would take fright and undo his clever work. It was most unwise to "allow a year to elapse and give the native mind time to be agitated." Earlier he had protested that he had never broken his word. "If there was one thing which he valued it was his word, and he had not broken it."[28]

Julia Merriman, the politician's sharp-tongued mother and the Bishop of Grahamstown's widow, had a different perspective. "One would imagine," she wrote to her daughter-in-law, "that Rhodes' public exposure over the Glen Grey bill as a man not of his word and ready to sacrifice principles at the bidding of men who avowedly had a sinister object in view, that he would lose respect and influence in the country, but judging from the tone of the Cape Town papers, it is not so."[29] The papers (to which Rhodes contributed financially) were calling him a hero.

Over Glen Grey Rhodes had shown a single-minded dedication to expediency which was more ruthless, or employed ruthlessness more openly, than ever before. In his exposition he had carried the day with innuendo, half-truth, confident but unsupported generalization, and sneering scorn for Africans. When cornered he had waxed intemperate, even bullying the usually gentlemanly House. He used hard-handed tactics and turns of phrase which would have been impossible in the early 1890s and before. Indeed, anyone who had behaved as had Rhodes over Glen Grey would earlier have been drummed out of the House. But in 1894 Rhodes controlled the men of his coalition, most through Hofmeyr, the remainder through his own powers of patronage as well as persuasion. The debates over Glen Grey, a year after the conquest of Ndebeleland and a year before the Raid, display Rhodes at the peak of his parliamentary power—a power he chose to deploy high-handedly, if not necessarily for narrow, personally self-serving ends.

Rhodes was "prepared to stand or fall" by Glen Grey. Its lasting provisions were those which introduced a differentiated franchise, limited home rule, individual tenure, and territorial partition. By the first arrangement, Rhodes could advance assimilation and settle the future of Africans in the frontier districts of the Cape without "swamping" the white vote. "The possession of land under the Glen Grey system," wrote Brookes, was "specially ruled out as a qualification for the Parliamentary franchise, which [had to] be qualified for in some other way." As Brookes went on to admit and then to excuse, "This [was] virtually a permanent disqualification of the majority of tribal Natives. . .," which Rhodes had indeed intended.

As a partial substitute, Rhodes introduced district councils. This experiment in governmental devolution, an idea which Rhodes borrowed and adapted from suggestions current in the Transkei a decade before, was extended beyond Glen Grey first to the Mfengu and then to four and then gradually to the majority of the districts into which the Transkei had been divided. Rhodes further authorized general councils for both the Transkei and the Ciskei; the district councils sent representatives to these senior bodies beginning in 1895 and 1898 respectively. The district councils met every other month under the chairmanship of a white magistrate to discuss and advise on local matters, particularly the allocation of local levies for public works, schools, clinics, and scholarships. (The South African Native Affairs Commission of 1921 regarded the council system as "the most valuable means of ascertaining representative Native opinion.") In 1931 the Transkeian Territories General Council was expanded in name and responsibility to become the United Transkeian Territories General Council, or Bunga. It met annually until 1956 to discuss parliamentary actions affecting Africans and the disposition of tax revenues. Rhodes' innovation thus led to more than sixty years' worth of formal talk about local and African rural matters (but not much more). In the Transkei, too, it led unexpectedly to an experience with partial home rule which helped to ease the decision on the part of chiefs to accept the first tribal authorities under the National party's Bantustan policy and then, in 1963, a territorial authority for the Transkei under apartheid.

The tenure provisions of the Glen Grey Act were also extended throughout the 1890s to the various Transkeian districts and eventually to Pondoland. Individual Africans received tenure, but such tenure was the grant of less than complete freehold. Africans had the permanent use of a plot of four or more morgen, but without full ownership. And each year they paid a quit-rent fee for it. Rhodes arranged that these farms could not be sold without the consent of the governor (through the district magistrate and the secretary for native affairs). In fact, by 1924 such consent had never been granted for transfers to whites, and only rarely from Africans to Africans. Nor could the land be mortgaged, sub-divided, sublet, or given away after death except to a single heir. Rhodes intended and his successors maintained that Glen Grey and the Transkei districts should remain "purely Native territories."[30]

By providing only very small farms for his new class of freeholders, and by limiting any accumulation of such land in African hands, Rhodes reduced the growth of an existing class of prosperous African smallholders and eliminated competition between African and white producers. As Charles Pamla, one of these gifted African entrepreneurs, commented at the time, "No man is allowed to occupy more than *one* lot. This shuts out all improvements and industry of some individuals who may work and buy. . . . Surely Mr. Rhodes can't expect that all the Natives will be equal. He himself is richer than others; even trees differ in height."

Diminished access to land by all Africans also succeeded in driving out numbers of men—Rhodes called them "Kafir mashers"—to work for whites, as Rhodes had intended.[31] Yet the labor tax itself quickly became a dead letter. It proved an irritation, not a stimulus. Africans, reviling the tax, overwhelmed sympathetic white magistrates with their claims for exemption. Understaffed and lacking any kind of administrative machinery, the magistrates found it almost impossible to verify or deny such requests. As a result, exemptions were granted widely (4,000 of an eligible 5,400 in Glen Grey), the tax being applied mostly to young unmarried men. Rhodes' intentions were subject to widespread evasion. The labor tax consequently fell into disuse and was repealed in 1905. A byproduct of Rhodes' edicts on labor did last, however. After passage of the Glen Grey Act, Rhodes appointed a labor officer to recruit and regulate the migratory labor from the district. South Africa's labor bureau system began there, in the office of the Glen Grey district council.

Even more fundamental and enduring, Rhodes gave the informal nineteenth-century reserve a secure and expanded footing. Much of his approach was accepted and given fuller elaboration in the report of the South African Native Affairs Commission (1903–1905); it espoused territorial partition as the only basis for the development of South African society and politics. The growth of a mixed society, it echoed Rhodes, was to be avoided. These conclusions led, after union, to the parliamentary compromise which justified and produced the Natives Land Act of 1913 (and the African National Congress, which grew out of indigenous opposition to the passage of that Act). The primary object of the 1913 Act was to segregate—to confine Africans to the lands which were set aside for them and to which, henceforth, their holdings would be restricted. Thus the Natives Land Act, the Native Trust and Land Act of 1936 (which added new territory to the reserves), the Bantu Authorities Act of 1951, the Promotion of Bantu Self-Government Act of 1959, and bantustans, homelands, and territorial separate development more generally, owe their original ideological underpinnings to Rhodes and the devilish compact he made with the worst instincts of the Bond. Certainly it was his rejection of the fundamental tenets of Cape liberalism which eased the Cape's fateful acquiescence in the distinctly discriminatory organization of modern South Africa in 1909.

The passage of the Glen Grey Act loosened white tongues and deepened the distrust of Africans among legislators. During the 1895 session of the Cape parliament, members of the House, led both wittingly and unwittingly by Rhodes, showed how antagonistic they were to Africans and how far they were prepared to translate those antagonisms into discriminatory—"class"—legislation. Rhodes took an unwavering hard line: to make a distinction in law between white and black was proper. "[the] general tendency of this country, and the feelings of this country were in the direction of a difference in the legislation between blacks and whites. And naturally so." Whites in the Cape "could not put the natives on the footing of the whites. We could not do it. Therefore we were now continually legislating in the direction of giving them special protection, and in requiring them special obligations."[32]

Special obligations included pass laws and other restrictions on movement and residence. The East London Municipal Act Amendment bill gave that city authority to set aside and regulate locations for Africans and Asians, impose curfews on them, and—in a departure from existing patterns in the Cape—to decide where Africans and Asians might or might not walk and "be found." Moreover, it gave the city council what Sauer called the extraordinary power to fix times after which it was illegal for Africans to be out of doors. Schreiner, the attorney general, strongly supported the bill, Innes and Charles Tennant Jones equally hotly disputed its value. Both suggested that such clauses, especially the last two, penalized educated Africans and discouraged the uplift and development of Africans in general. Sauer called the proposals blots on the statute book and shameful, but the bill was easily enacted into law.[33]

In the same session Rhodes accepted a motion to permit all the cities and towns of the Cape to impose evening curfews on Africans. Haarhoff, from Kimberley, proposed that municipalities should be able to declare the movement of Africans—"the aboriginal," and not " 'Colonial-born' coloured people or half-castes"—unlawful on public thoroughfares, in the streets, or in other public places between the hours of 9 p.m. and 4 a.m. without a written pass from their employer or a magistrate. Kingwilliamstown and Kimberley had enacted similar laws in 1872 and 1879, respectively. Sivewright, voicing the sentiments of many, declared that such a bill was needed to protect whites. "The streets of the . . . [Cape's] towns and villages should be as safe for women and children as the streets of the towns of the [Dutch] Republics." Hutton, however, called the bill "unworthy, depressing, and dishonourable." Although Innes and others argued that bills like this one should distinguish between "loafers" and "respectable natives," between clad and unclad, and Christian and "uncivilized" Africans, and such an exemption, if a narrow one, was ultimately accepted by the House, its provisions were intended to extend the restrictive and antagonistic "class" character of the East London legislation to the entire Colony.

Rhodes sat silently for much of the debate on this bill, even when taunted. Finally he spoke: "The House would be wise in passing the resolution." Kimberley, which had long enjoyed similar privileges, was a safer city on account of such discrimination. Rhodes helped pass the bill, 40 to 18, and thus to extend the Cape's net of ever-tightening segregation.[34]

During lengthy debates on a bill to regulate and organize the civil service, Abraham Stephanus Le Roex, a Bondsman from Victoria West, attempted to amend the bill so as to prevent Africans from being appointed magistrates or magistrate's clerks. "The natives were pushing themselves forward," he said, "and if [we] did not stop them they would soon pass the [committee] chairman's seat." Le Roex had been astonished that very afternoon to have seen "a Kafir" sitting between two ladies in the second row of the Speaker's Gallery of the House. "All the years he had sat in the House, he had never seen such impudence on the part of any black man. . . ." Rhodes' reaction was that "of course . . . it was not advisable to appoint a member of the coloured race to . . . office and he did not think that anyone in the positions that he held had done so, or would do so." Yet, seemingly sensitive to any suggestions that he might, nonetheless, favor or cosset Africans, Rhodes elsewhere in the debate reacted in an uncommonly defensive manner to suggestions that he had employed an African in his own Native Affairs Office. Merriman had read about such an appointment in the press, and had presumed that the prime minister welcomed the credit which he was deriving from such a progressive act. Rhodes protested that he had appointed no Africans. Merriman cited the individual by name, and said that he had been recruited from the Transkei. "The actual fact," retorted Rhodes, "is that this man came to me and said that he should like me to give him a job, and I put him into the kitchen. He got sick of it and ran away." Merriman persisted in believing that the person in question had been brought to Cape Town to assist the premier "in his native policy." With asperity, Rhodes said, "I tell you he was in the kitchen . . . in the kitchen at my house."[35]

Another of Rhodes' parliamentary accomplishments was achieved partially at the expense of the Bond. Although the modern reader may have difficulty appreciating why Rhodes and the House took the dipping of sheep so seriously, no proposal—not the Ballot and Franchise Act nor the Glen Grey Act—so divided the House. No other bill occupied so much debating time—nearly the whole of the 1894 session—or threatened so openly to destroy Rhodes' coalition. At stake was the future of the Cape's (and South Africa's) wool industry; for a mining entrepreneur and imperial expansionist, Rhodes had a keen interest in agriculture generally. An intuitive reformer, he attempted throughout his parliamentary and extra-parliamentary careers to improve local farming and husbandry practices—to adapt American and other modern practices to the needs and problems of the Cape.

By the 1890s, the amount and value of wool shorn from sheep grazed in the drier parts of the eastern Cape, in the Karoo, and in Namaqualand had decreased markedly from its peak in the 1870s. The annual loss to the Cape was estimated between £500,000 and £1 million. Moreover, overseas buyers had come to distrust the quality of Cape wool, instead preferring Australian and American shearings. Once a mainstay of the Cape (after diamonds), the wool industry was being destroyed. The cause of the decline, everyone agreed, was an insect that caused a scab disease in sheep and goats, disfiguring and destroying wool, mohair, and sheep and goat skins, and sometimes killing large numbers of stock.

The disease was endemic in the Colony, having been combated as early as the seventeenth century by the Dutch government. By the late nineteenth century it had been established that progressive farmers could control scab by dipping sheep in a pesticide solution and limiting the passage of herds across the countryside. As early as 1874, the Cape had provided for voluntary dipping. In 1886 dipping was made compulsory in the Eastern and Midland districts. In 1891, divisional councils controlled by white voters could decide to enforce dipping regulations in their areas. The Scab Commission, reporting early in 1894, found that those districts which had accepted compulsory dipping were largely free of the disease. Likewise Australia had freed itself of scab by dipping. The Commission recommended compulsory and simultaneous dipping of sheep and goats throughout the Colony, and a strengthened inspectorate to enforce new regulations.

Rhodes was easily persuaded that the Cape's wool industry could only be saved by strong anti-scab legislation. He had long favored such a sensible and seemingly irrefutable measure. But first he had to bridge a deep pool of ignorance and antagonism. Many graziers doubted that scab was contagious or that it could be eliminated or even controlled by dipping. They blamed dipping, or at least the long journeys to the dipping tanks, for deaths among their (already weakened) flocks. A legion also construed dipping as an infringement of their sacred liberty. They wanted to remain masters of their own separate destinies, whatever the scientific evidence or the effect refusals to dip could have on district-wide or Colony-wide collective efforts. To Rhodes' discomfort, much of the agitation against making scab eradication mandatory came from hardcore members of the Bond.

Frost, the secretary of agriculture, introduced a scab and dipping bill in June 1894. It embodied the recommendations of the commission, which Dr. Thomas William Smartt, its chairman, a Bondsman, and a leading sheep farmer, reminded the House had been arrived at unanimously and after deliberations and investigations lasting more than two years. "It was unjust," he chastised the libertarians, "that people who were trying to keep their sheep clean should not be protected from their careless neighbours." Drastic legislation was necessary at once. Fuller, a wool exporter, said that unless the Cape cleansed its flocks it would be out of the wool race—"our wool industry would be doomed." But others, primarily but not exclusively from farming districts, called the proposed legislation "cruel and tyrannical," impracticable, difficult, and a hardship. It was immediately evident that Rhodes would have difficulty steering a strong bill through the legislature. Indeed, since the Bond, his other supporters, and even his cabinet were divided, and the opposition equally so, obtaining all that Frost and Smartt wanted would be difficult if not impossible.

According to Innes, the bill was flawed in many ways, but its defects could be remedied at the committee stage and then receive assent if Rhodes had "the courage of his opinions." Alas, said Innes, the premier was wavering. Because of opposition from twenty hardcore Bondsmen, he was afraid to "put his foot down." In July, Rhodes' party caucused almost daily, for the prime minister did not like "the angry feelings of his Dutch supporters" and was attempting to talk them round.

Rhodes continued to insist on a bill which made dipping mandatory and refused to draw a dividing line across the country to separate those who favored permissiveness from those who were prepared to accept compulsion. But on other questions, including the recruitment of inspectors, he remained flexible. "His desire," Rhodes said, "was to have a workable Act, and the theory he went on was that they could get nothing unless they worked through the people." Later, after moving and supporting a number of amendments to the original bill in order to dampen the cries of his opponents and simultaneously defending himself against charges (from the usual opposition, now the bill's proponents) that he was emasculating the impact of scab legislation, Rhodes explained that he still wanted a strong bill, but a bill which "would be amenable to the wishes of the mass of the people," that is, to the Bond's hard core. Rhodes thus voted against Frost and Smartt over such details as double rather than single dipping, and temporized in other ways.

After seven weeks of hullabaloo and confusion, and much caucusing and horsetrading, the final version of a still compulsory, but otherwise weakened scab bill came before the House for a final vote. Innes called the result a humiliation for the ministry, a disaster to the cause of good government, and a disappointment. It was "prejudicial to the best interests of the country." Sauer said that the report of the commission had been "torn to shreds and tatters" by the bill. Moreover, he urged the House to "mark its sense of the manner in which the Government had conducted [the] bill, because anything more derogatory to Parliamentary institutions he had never seen and hoped he should never see again." Sauer continued his critique of Rhodes: "If the Prime Minister . . . thought his only duty was to secure his position . . . by lobbying, by throwing his colleagues overboard, by sacrificing his own views, and throwing over his own Bill, he did not envy him his happiness." The way that Rhodes "had conducted the Bill through the House had done a great deal to damage the interests of Responsible Government," Sauer charged. But Rhodes never cared terribly much for abstractions like responsible government; he wanted to save the wool industry without forfeiting too much of the support of the Bond. When forty-two members voted in favor of the bill and only twenty-three opposed it, Rhodes felt his tactics justified. He had retained the core requirements of effective legislation, its compulsory quality, even if other desirable provisions had been removed or moderated.

Ultimately, too, in 1895, Rhodes' government weathered massive opposition by petition and new legislative assaults on its integrity by agreeing to an inquiry into the workings of the Act. Innes called this search for a pacifying compromise an astonishing feat of "political agility." Rhodes also promised personally to visit the Karoo and other aggrieved districts to hear complaints.[36] The Jameson Raid eliminated any such a personal investigation. By then, at the end of 1895, opposition from farmers had begun to fade. By the middle of 1896 it was clear that dipping was reducing scab, numbers of infected sheep were falling dramatically, and the amount and value of wool being exported had already increased significantly. Despite, or because of, political maneuvering, Rhodes had managed to resuscitate an ailing industry.

Rhodes proved a tireless advocate in and out of parliament of farming and farmers. Genuinely interested in improving agricultural prospects, he also remained aware of and partial to the narrow self-interests of the Bond. Thus, although he had originally taken office because of Sprigg's wasteful and blatantly political proposal to provide farmers and voters with expensive rail lines, in his final years in the premiership, Rhodes, too, urged the construction of uneconomic railways to provide farmers with cheaper access to their markets. During one exchange he defended proposed branch lines to Graaff-Reinet and Oudtshoorn, but his production statistics were suspect. Merriman accused the premier of finding the hard facts inconvenient, and therefore of trying to sell the House on extensions to lines that were already losing money and would continue to do so. "I say that these arguments are puerile," Merriman attacked Rhodes, "and if the Prime Minister takes my advice he will remain perfectly quiet and trust to his log-rolled majority because when he tries hard facts he makes a most dismal display of this railway business."[37] Farming was a political game and, as Merriman insinuated, Rhodes wanted to keep his farmer-voters happy and those of his other supporters in the House who came from particular farming districts happy as well. As a result, the rail network of the Cape was extended in Rhodes' day almost as far as it would have been under Sprigg, but in a more piecemeal fashion, with each project scrutinized more carefully.

Politics aside, Rhodes continued genuinely to promote progressive agriculture. In parliament he worried out loud about how most efficiently to bring affordable irrigation to white farmers, sought new methods of eradicating plant as well as animal pests, and promised to continue his search for new varieties of fruit that could be grown profitably in the western Cape. Packing methods imported from the United States also helped. He improved the quality of horses in the Cape by importing stallions in 1893 from the Arabian peninsula at a cost of £700. In 1895, he established the Cape's mohair industry.[38]

The Bond, and most of the Cape's farmers, like insecure producers almost everywhere, sought through tariffs protection from price and other forms of commodity competition. Yet Rhodes was a free trader; he had long advocated colonial cooperation and inter-reliance as one means of maintaining and strengthening links between imperial outposts and the mother country and among the far-flung subjects of the metropole. Moreover, Rhodes the amalgamator knew that the economic future of South Africa could best be served, and his dream of a United South Africa best advanced, by a customs union— by expanding the internal free-trade area beyond that which in 1893–1895 existed between the Free State and the Cape only. Thus appeasing the Bond could prove costly, damaging Rhodes' broader and longer-term objectives. Consequently, as premier Rhodes actively promoted and pursued the aims of imperial free trade while simultaneously seeking to nurture the Cape's wine, maize, and sheep industries by giving them what he called moderate protection. Moderate protection would encourage a local landed class, but intense protection—in effect prohibition of, say, Australian meat and Canadian or American flour—would prove costly for the Cape as a whole and would retard its development.

Rhodes admitted that he sought to "preserve the landed classes . . . as a conservative element" for the good of the country, but he always distinguished between products of the soil and manufactured goods. He did not want the Cape to back "bastard" factories "at the expense of the whole community." He was adamantly opposed to subsidizing the Cape's infant manufacturing industries, firmly believing that Britain would remain the workshop of the world, and that it was both frivolous and wasteful—"a cause of burden to the State"—for a colony to try to compete with the mother country. Doing so would, from his point of view, sunder significant, if incipient, imperial ties. Anyway, in the Cape, there were few votes in the factories and more on the land.

In 1894 and 1895 Rhodes both opposed and supported moves in the House to put high tariffs on imported meat, wheat, and flour. He was attacked for being inconsistent. His reply was typically disingenuous: "The best course for a politician to take was to be consistent."[39] He was for moderate protection, but moderate protection only. That is, as a free trader with wider imperial objectives and important local political considerations, he had to seek a balance of interests which might appear contradictory but which could be rationalized in his own mind, at least, as being consistent.

So compromised was Rhodes the politician that, despite fine protestations, he voted in 1895 with the Bond and against half of his own cabinet for restrictively high tariffs on wheat, grain, and flour. That motion passed by 44 to 26, with even Sprigg, Sivewright, Frost (the secretary for agriculture), and Laing, as well as Merriman, Innes, and Sauer, casting negative votes. On another occasion Rhodes agreed to a special duty on frozen mutton to prevent the arrival of meat at prices which would undercut Dutch-speaking stockmen in the Cape. In these matters of detail Rhodes demonstrated flexibility, being more than willing to sacrifice his better judgment for parliamentary advantage.

Rhodes' critics hammered him hard over his decision to send delegates to the Colonial Conference in Ottawa in mid-1894. Obviously, Rhodes, envisaging as he did the eventual fruitful merging of Britain's colonies into a functioning and mutually supportive Empire or Commonwealth organization, would have wanted to be represented. However, neither the legislative season nor his other commitments permitted his own attendance. Hofmeyr, his political alter ego, was a logical substitute along with de Villiers, the chief justice, and Sir Charles Mills, the Cape's agent general in London. The conference was valuable, Rhodes explained to skeptics, because it would "improve the good feeling between the colonies." Moreover, Rhodes indulged his prejudices and amplified his motives: Australia and Canada represented 8 million British subjects, all of them white, and all of "a higher intelligence than the ordinary English population." There were 35 million Britons, but among them "was a large class of ignorant people." The standard of intelligence in England "was nothing like the standard of those who lived in the colonies . . . ," including the Cape. Therefore the deliberations in Ottawa would influence significantly the thinking of the British government in favor of the imperial preference that Rhodes and the governments of most of the other colonies desired.

Britain's treaties with Germany and Belgium prevented the entry of colonial goods at rates more favorable than those accorded the continental countries. These agreements also prevented the transfer of commodities between the British colonies themselves at advantageous tariff rates. Rhodes, and his fellow premiers in Ottawa, thus sought to free themselves from being bound by Britain's own trade arrangements at the same time as they wanted Britain to return to the mercantilism of the seventeenth and eighteenth centuries, when colonial preference was enforced by those European powers which dominated the seas. (In mid-1895 a Liberal colonial secretary conceded some of the freedom which was desired; in 1897 Lord Salisbury renounced the German and Belgian treaties. Nevertheless, Sir William Harcourt's earlier parsimony regarding true imperial preference remained a prevailing sentiment for some years longer.)

By sending representatives to Ottawa, Rhodes also put the Cape (and his own premiership) on the imperial map. He had earlier corresponded with Canada's leaders about tariff questions and purchased the scrip of impoverished Australian states in order to express confidence and solidarity. He had specific objectives, too: less expensive cable rates and an expansion of the Cape's trade with Canada. He wanted the interests of the Cape to be safeguarded when the colonies planned their new cable between Canada and Australia; Rhodes specifically desired the cable to be extended beyond New Zealand and Australia to the Cape. There was too little prospective trade between Canada and the Cape to justify a subsidized steamship line (which Canada and Australia were planning), but Rhodes told his delegates and parliament that he sought to exchange the free export of Canadian timber to the forest-poor Cape (where it would be used for supports in the underground mines) for the export of Cape wines into Canada. (Unfortunately French wines were better and more accessible to the Canadians.) When Rhodes himself was in Britain in 1894, he attempted to persuade Canada's prime minister to contemplate a treaty along these lines. It came to nought for economic as well as political reasons. Even so, as Sauer chided Rhodes, it was far more important to sell the Cape's wine and brandy in Johannesburg than to chase overseas after the impossible.[40]

Alas, Rhodes found it easier to talk to the Canadians than to do a deal with Kruger's Transvaal. The two leaders disliked and distrusted each other, with reason. Whatever Kruger's personal reaction to the brash youngster who repetitively harassed and challenged him, for Rhodes the craggy patriarch was an all-too-familiar figure. Kruger's deep-seated intransigence, the implacable nay-saying which obstructed Rhodes' cherished dreams, and even his gloomy visage, would have been fatally reminiscent of the paternal vicar. Without in any way discounting the myriad issues of territoriality, geography, and culture, or the conflicting aspirations of peoples, the contest between Rhodes and Kruger was a struggle between the implacably angry son and his aloof and frustrating father. Thus far Rhodes had bested Kruger over Stellaland and Goshen, and then had assisted but also patronized him when the Transvaal needed cash to complete its railway from Delagoa Bay.

Kruger naturally felt his and his people's security threatened, rightly suspecting that Rhodes' Cape had designs on the Transvaal's independence. A discussion with Rhodes at 5 a.m. in October 1894, when Rhodes was returning from a survey of Rhodesia, allayed few fears on either side. By this time the Cape's rail connection to the Rand had captured about 85 percent of traffic of the Transvaal, which Kruger and his railway managers naturally thought an intolerable threat to the state's autonomy and the Delagoa Bay railway's prosperity. Thus, when the Cape at the end of 1894, on the eve of the completion of the Delagoa Bay connection to Pretoria, appreciably lowered its rates on goods destined for the Transvaal, the Transvaal railway retaliated by trebling its own rates for the fifty—mile run from the border to Johannesburg. In order to avoid these charges, Rhodes' government ordered the off-loading of freight at the Vaal River border between the two states and then encouraged the merchants of the Rand to charter a flotilla of ox-wagons to carry it competitively to the Rand. Gold was booming, traffic was thick, and the miners were able to dig deeply into their pockets to pay for the imports from Europe and the Cape.

At the end of August Kruger decided that his control over a complete rail system to the east, a newly forged rail tie to Pietermaritzburg and Durban in Natal, the growing wealth of the Transvaal, and his own unquestioned dominance in the Republic would permit him to close down this clear affront to his authority and hegemony. A conference about the rail rates of the four states of South Africa had ended without either compromise or any sense of mutual interdependence. Kruger therefore notified the Cape that in October he would shut the drifts or ford over which the ox-wagons crossed the Vaal, throwing Rhodes and the Cape into acute consternation, and also giving Rhodes a superb justification to continue his ongoing preparations for the ouster of the Transvaal's president. Despite strong protests from the Cape and London, Kruger did block the drifts to Cape traffic. In November, however, British troopships were ordered to sail for South Africa, and Joseph Chamberlain, secretary of state for the colonies, issued a stiff ultimatum. Kruger backed down a few days later and let the wagons cross the Vaal. The open breach, and the war that Rhodes had wanted and for which he was so assiduously readying, was averted.

A direct clash between Rhodes and Kruger was avoided, if merely for a moment. Yet Rhodes spoiled for such a confrontation and had begun engineering an assault on Kruger's power about a year before. First he had used his position as premier of the Cape to complete the western encirclement of the Transvaal. Thus in 1895 he moved to annex Bechuanaland. He sought to complete his earlier embrace of Stellaland and Goshen, incorporating them, and the broader successor territory surrounding them known as the Crown Colony of British Bechuanaland, into the Cape Colony. Doing so would, as Britain had long desired, relieve the Crown of administrative expenses and end the ambiguous status of a large swath of largely desiccated land abutting on German Südwest Afrika as well as the Transvaal and the Free State. British Bechuanaland comprised a land area one-sixth as large as the Cape Colony. To its north, beyond the terminus of the railway at Mafeking, would remain the Bechuanaland Protectorate proper, on which Rhodes also had designs and substantial claims.

From the moment that he had entered parliament, Rhodes explained, it had "struck him that the proper course to pursue would be . . . the steady expansion of the Cape into the Hinterland. . . ." In the ten years since he had helped forestall Transvaal rule there, about 12,000 whites had settled along the road from Kimberley to Vryburg and Mafeking. They produced about £60,000 in tax revenue, exclusively from working the land, a sum which was only slightly less than the cost of administering it. Moreover, 20,000 square miles of, albeit, not the best-watered terrain, remained capable of being sold for profit. Because of the growth of Johannesburg, the Crown Colony might provide a reasonable living for cattle and sheep graziers. Chiefs Montshiwa and Mankurwane were opposed to annexation, but Rhodes thought that "the natives would find that they would receive the same justice from the Colonial Government as they had received . . . from the Imperial Government."

Missionaries and others at home in Britain also believed that annexing the Crown Colony would mean oppressing Africans, but, Rhodes declared sententiously, "they who lived in the [Cape] knew that the natives were as fairly treated . . . as by any country in the world." The British government feared that Rhodes' administration might diminish the extent of the existing African areas; but, assured the premier, "they had been extremely lenient with the natives." After all, he said, 60,000 Africans lived satisfactorily on 4,300 square miles of the total 51,000 square miles of British Bechuanaland. (To his compatriots, who might have worried that the 60,000 Africans would become voters, he offered reassurances that no more than a few hundred Africans would then or in the foreseeable future qualify for the franchise under the new, higher stipulations imposed in 1892.)

It was logical for the Cape to round out its domain by incorporating British Bechuanaland. In his speeches to parliament, however, Rhodes never explained why he moved so hurriedly and determinedly to annex the Crown Colony in 1895. There was little imperial pressure, and no particular problems in or with the administration of the area. Nor was there unusual opposition from his usual parliamentary antagonists. Nevertheless, suspicion was rife. J.C. Molteno spoke angrily about what he called the prime minister's "underhand intrigue." Others, especially Sauer and Merriman, complained, and rightly, that Rhodes was taking British Bechuanaland so that he could move by another route against the Bechuanaland Protectorate—the vast African territory that spread from the Molopo River to the borders of Ndebeleland—on behalf of the British South Africa Company. Indeed, that was at least one important part of Rhodes' increasing intrigue during 1895. He needed control over both territories before the end of the year, and thus slammed the easier annexation through the House (and past Chamberlain, the new Unionist/Conservative colonial secretary) during the waning days of the session.

Members of the House had never appreciated that the British South Africa Company's writ ran from Mafeking across the entire Protectorate. Yet that is what Rhodes now correctly insisted that the charter of 1889 had granted. "The minerals, railways, telegraphs, and so on belonged to the charter," he said.[41] He intended to impose a single political and economic system from the Cape to Lake Tanganyika. The administration of the Protectorate by the Company was an essential part of that effort. Moreover, Britain had always intended that the Protectorate should be governed by the Company, and, when Rhodes began annexing the area south of the Molopo River, so he attempted also to gain what had been promised, if quietly, by the British government in 1889. Lord Ripon, Chamberlain's predecessor, implied a willingness to do as Rhodes bid, but when the debates in the Cape House and rumors in London alerted the leading chiefs of Bechuanaland and their missionary supporters, Chamberlain was compelled to pause, reflect, and reconsider. "As far as I understand your main lines of policy I . . . am in general agreement with you," said Chamberlain. Nevertheless, he had found it necessary to heed the friends of the Tswana in ways which, Chamberlain asserted, would not "hamper" Rhodes' "operations."[42]

Kgama, Bathoen, and Sebele wanted to remain under the Queen's aegis, not Rhodes'. The demise of Lobengula was within recent memory. They feared that the Company would take their lands and sell them to whites, and that the Company would fill their country with shops selling liquor. They petitioned Chamberlain, and then they traveled to Britain and literally took their case to the country. Speaking in churches throughout Britain, they stirred a sizable opposition to Rhodes' takeover. So potent was this antagonism that Chamberlain, who a decade before had been allied to John Mackenzie and others who deprecated Rhodes' influence, in November 1895 arranged a compromise that distinctly favored the chiefs and gave Rhodes apoplexy. Despite furious telegrams from Rhodes, Chamberlain allotted the main Tswana chiefs extensive reserves corresponding to their existing claims. A representative of the Queen would continue to "protect" and advise there, and no drink would be permitted. Beyond, over the Kalahari wastelands, and along a thin strip of land paralleling the Transvaal border, Rhodes would gain control. He would construct a railway within the narrow strip. An individual chief was also persuaded by Frank Rhodes and Shippard to transfer a small chiefdom in the southeast corner of Bechuanaland to the Company. This corner was within 176 miles of Johannesburg. Otherwise, the whole of Bechuanaland, the future Botswana, remained a protectorate, coming under neither the Cape nor Rhodesia. Its Tswana inhabitants narrowly escaped being dispossessed or pushed aside.

"It is humiliating," Rhodes told Rutherfoord Harris, "to be utterly beaten by these niggers. They think more of one native, at home, than the whole of South Africa. . . ." Later he said that he objected to being beaten by "three canting natives. . . . The whole thing makes me ashamed of my own people."[43] Rhodes had suffered his first significant hegemonic defeat since his failure to oust the Portuguese from central Mozambique, but there was a more ominous setback on the horizon.

At the highest peak of his very considerable powers, after five full years during which the statute book of the Cape had been revolutionized and the hoary tenets of Cape liberalism partially overturned, Rhodes—supreme in Cape Town, Kimberley, Salisbury, beyond the Zambezi and even across the wastes of the Kalahari—was about to employ his genius for human affairs, for manipulating others, and his fierce concentration upon ends, not means, against the obstinacy of Kruger. A Greek chorus in the wings chanted caution, but Rhodes, ascendant, surrounded by sycophancy, and buoyed by an almost uninterrupted succession of triumphs, heard it not.

"Simply a Fairy Tale"
The Money Game and Other
Profitable Pursuits

T HE GREAT AMALGAMATOR had collected the sinews of war during the frantic 1880s, when he consolidated the diamond mines of Kimberley and
attempted, with mixed success, to establish a central position on the Rand.
During the first half of the 1890s Rhodes dominated the De Beers conglomerate and remained a key figure in Gold Fields; despite his increasing political
and imperial responsibilities, Rhodes never relaxed his hold on the financial
institutions that he had created, nor diminished his detailed oversight of the
diamond business, his principal and, in the earliest of those years, most remunerative source of wealth. A lesser man, someone with narrower ambitions
or someone whose personal passions lay in other directions, might conceivably
have capitalized his existing resources or employed financial managers to safeguard those interests while devoting himself to the accumulation of power
within the Cape and the Empire. But Rhodes could not afford to chance im-
providential errors. Nor did he wish to share with others the responsibility
and the pleasure of personal involvement in realizing the dreams which were
the principal objects of his affection. In this attention to detail he resembles
modern corporate leaders whose style frequently includes a surprising combination of overarching strategic activity and practical attention to the minutiae of everyday operations. The generation of healthy returns from diamonds and gold thus had significance beyond the mere accumulation of
wealth.

Control of personal riches was important in itself and because it gave him
entrée to the corporate and banking backers who were crucial for the success
of his growing enterprises. Such access gave Rhodes an ability to leverage and
cross-subsidize his much more speculative and more directly ego-gratifying
activities, such as the British South Africa Company. His role as an entrepreneur and industrialist furthermore gave Rhodes a stature in, and therefore

an influence upon, the British social circles which could either promote or destroy the realization of his grandest ideas.

Rhodes was different from Joseph Robinson, Barney Barnato, Alfred Beit, and Charles Rudd. Building upon initial holdings in diamonds, the latter (joined on the Rand by Hermann Eckstein and Julius Wernher) invested wisely if speculatively in gold and concentrated their energies entrepreneurially on the making of money. These were the new plutocrats, whether they lived ostentatiously like Barnato, or more quietly like Beit. For them the money game was of prime interest; they were consummate exploiters of inside information and shrewd players of hunches. They calculated their margins well, manipulated stock markets with unsurpassed skill, and tried consistently to make decisions which would enhance their own self-worth, as measured by a personal control over assets. They were single-minded. With regard to riches, however, Rhodes was not. For him in the 1890s (as distinct from earlier decades) the pursuit of riches was but a part of the larger pursuit of personal aggrandizement. Making money was not his sole object, for Rhodes' goals were more extensive and more grandiose and, in the early 1890s, less immediately gratified, than the much more straightforward goals of his peers. As financiers, they far surpassed him in wealth but, because of their more bounded horizons, not in fame or glory.

It is not that Rhodes, admittedly a man of little ostentation and fewer personal pretensions, was somehow averse to capitalizing upon his early gifts or remained content with fewer millions. Nor, in a buccaneering age, is it suggested that Rhodes was more abstemious or less avaricious than his contemporaries. Rather, in the early 1890s, with the invasion of Shonaland and the subsequent assault on Ndebeleland, railway building, telegraphic construction, and myriad expenditures on patronage and entertainment, Rhodes was rarely capable of devoting his capital exclusively to mining. Unlike Beit and Robinson, anyway, he was also highly leveraged, employing funds lent by the banking house of Rothschild, by Beit, or, unsuspectingly, by those who purchased ordinary shares in De Beers or Gold Fields. The Chartered Company's thrust into the interior and the war against the Ndebele would have been impossible without financial help from both of his mining houses. Nor would his railways to Mafeking or Salisbury have been built without the pledging of mining shares against overseas loans.

To maintain the financial momentum of his southern African empire in the 1890s, Rhodes was compelled to safeguard if not to improve the economic health of the original sources of his power. Without investor confidence in De Beers and Gold Fields, the progress of his other projects would have faltered or halted. Maintaining a liquid stream of cash for himself was also increasingly important: restoring Groote Schuur and entertaining there on a lavish but purposeful scale was costly. So was political patronage, although the bestowing of shares (or jobs) was personally less expensive for Rhodes, and certainly less subject to criticism, than the giving of gifts of cash (although Rhodes sometimes did distribute largesse openly).

A letter to Lady Sprigg, wife of Sir Gordon, conveyed a combination of friendly messages that could hardly have been lost on her and her husband, or, for that matter, on the many other recipients of similar missives from Rhodes: "I bought some De Beers the other day at £23. They are more than I want. So I thought you would like a little interest in the Company and during the next year . . . I shall be pleased to let you have 300 at any time, at price I bought. If you are very particular you shall pay me, if you take them, 4 per cent from date of purchase to date of taking."[1]

Rhodes, both sensitive to criticism and acutely aware of the virtues of a good press and public backing, required ample resources so that he could control or at least influence many of the major newspapers, especially those in Cape Town and Kimberley. Doing so both gratified him and satisfied his need to control. So did charitable giving boost his own ego and serve his sense of what was politically advantageous. Throughout the 1890s he devoted the profits (about £10,000 a year) from the company-owned stores in the Kimberley compounds to good causes there. But those good causes were the good causes of the white man's city—its interdenominational school, its churches, its sanatorium, and the lavish city exhibition of 1894. (He also hoped to construct a university in Cape Town with profits from the compounds, but the university was built after his death.)

Complaining bitterly when the Company's Kimberley board attempted to interfere, Rhodes made it abundantly clear that the profits were his to apportion; he would brook no interference in the distribution of this other form of patronage. In April 1895 he ordered Craven to "summon" the board of directors together to approve his "proposed" gifts to the local charities. When it refused to comply promptly, Rhodes fired off another letter from Cape Town to Craven. "Kindly call the local board together," he wrote, "and let me have their resolution before Parliament meets." Rhodes said that he was "simply tired out with endless opposition to me and will write no more on the question." What hurt the most, he told Craven, was that he had created the wealth and now his colleagues "simply spent their time in opposing. . . ." "I know," he said, what "must be done to meet the sentiment of the country."[2]

Mere dreamers often exceed the reach of their resources. Charisma was no permanent or reliable alternative to what Rhodes called "the ready." The great amalgamator, by contrast, remained ever-conscious that the exercise of his considerable gifts of persuasion and leadership depended ultimately upon access to tangible rewards. A visionary who was firmly grounded in pragmatic reality, Rhodes rarely ventured beyond the reasonable financial limits of his backers. Thus, in the early 1890s, as seemingly omnipotent as Rhodes could appear within the political and imperial spheres, he was still insecure financially. To a degree which was for him surprising, he remained responsive, if not subservient, to the London board of De Beers, to Rudd and the London board of Gold Fields, and to Beit and Rothschild. Having realized his youthful dreams to an uncommon extent, Rhodes had negotiated with grace the mid-life crisis of generativity in which, as with other men of his age, reassessment of his accomplishments served as a springboard to the future. If he had an ostensible weakness during the pivotal years running up to and slightly beyond his fortieth birthday, it was his lack of deep and liquid means with which to underwrite that important transition. As wealthy as he was, and as globally dominant in diamonds as he had come to be, what he was additionally attempting to achieve was so inherently risky, and so adventurous, that increasing infusions of capital were required on a regular basis. Rhodes therefore existed throughout the first half of the 1890s in a state of creative tension with the British financial market, the diamond-buying syndicate of Kimberley, Britain, Holland, and Belgium, and his boards of directors, each member of which was more narrowly and exclusively focused than he.

Although De Beers' net profit in 1892 was £1,137,308, great, unprecedented returns from diamonds came to Rhodes only after 1896. Until then—until the industry had become "a matter of course and uninteresting" and began to go "like clockwork"—the minds of the founders never rested easy, or "slept quietly." Rhodes, primarily, remained vigilant, safeguarding its essential short- and medium-term viability. To this end he insisted on as nearly complete an oligopolistic hold as possible on the diamond production of South Africa. This meant, as it had during the mid- and late 1880s, that no mines, even those which were too poor to pay, could be left out of the De Beers net. Bultfontein and Dutoitspan, in Kimberley, were therefore purchased in part by De Beers and their workings leased from the London and South African Exploration Company. In 1891 Rhodes demanded, over the bitter objections of Stow and Rothschild, that the Premier or Wesselton mine, near Kimberley, also be acquired. (The house of Rothschild, much later, agreed that buying it had been correct—a stroke of genius. It had been a wise and brilliant purchase, Carl Meyer finally wrote to Rhodes in 1899.)[3]

The supply of diamonds from the New Jagersfontein mine in the Orange Free State and the smaller Koffiefontein mine in the Cape posed a threat to Rhodes' designs for a successful cartel. Without telling the De Beers' board—for several of its members had interests in both—Rhodes encumbered the output of both mines by an intricate interweaving of shares. "When Koffyfontein was sold," said Rhodes, "we deemed it wise to obtain such an interest in the mine as to prevent it ever being formed as a whole mine." Jagersfontein had been producing diamonds worth £30,000 a month, but at little profit. So Rhodes quietly gave its directors shares in De Beers "in order to check the wild production . . . on the basis that the production should be reduced otherwise they threatened still further to increase . . . though the large production was no benefit to the Company as there was no profit being made."

By the time that Rhodes wrote to Stow, he had reduced Jagersfontein's production to £12,000 a month. "We now have entire control of the mode of working New Jagersfontein." Rhodes believed that De Beers would be working Jagersfontein in the best interest of the mine by reducing its output, but, he continued "as you well know shareholders in Jagersfontein will not believe that, [particularly] if it was once known that the Jagersfontein local board was practically De Beers." Rhodes reiterated: "By this stroke I have changed the Jagersfontein Board from being our opponents, to heartily co-operating with us. . . ." Yet, Rhodes demanded, Harry Mosenthal, a major shareholder in that mine and a member of the De Beers London board, should not be told. He might object. So, Rhodes told Stow, keep the news "profoundly secret."[4]

Rhodes preferred to let no potentially threatening Kimberlite pipe escape his net. Hence De Beers prudently acquired farms throughout the eastern Cape, primarily near Kimberley. By 1900, De Beers thus owned more than 500,000 acres of farmland. Farther afield, in the Orange Free State and the Transvaal, Rhodes and his associates investigated all new discoveries. "We can assure you," Rhodes told his shareholders in 1898, "that whenever a mine is discovered or heard of, either close to or at a distance from Kimberley, we always think it our duty to try to acquire such information as we can. . . [and] by different means we generally get at a certain acquaintance with the results of the new mine." If diamonds were ever found in Rhodesia, they would also belong to De Beers. "When I formed the Charter," Rhodes wrote later, "I desired to exclude diamonds from the trust deed as we know no new diamond mine will help us or the world. We have too many diamonds."[5]

Even so, at no time did Rhodes and his company control all diamonds; until his death they dominated merely 98 percent of South Africa's output, roughly £4 million a year throughout the 1890s (more than gold in 1891, but a quarter of gold by value in 1898). Outside of Rhodes' substantial net were the old alluvial diggings along the Vaal and nine very minor dry land producers. De Beers paid a 20 percent dividend in 1890, 25 percent in 1893, and 40 percent in 1896 (and thereafter to 1902). It doubled its payout from £789,682 in 1890 to £1,579,582 in 1896 (during an era of low inflation).

As assiduously as Rhodes protected his control of the total supply of diamonds, he never could exercise complete authority over the distribution of diamonds from Kimberley to the main cutting floors in Europe. De facto control of this phase of the diamond business belonged to a syndicate of financiers—the old diamond buyers—based in Kimberley. Three of the five major buyers sat on the Kimberley board of De Beers; their own interests as merchants of the syndicate were not always those of the company as a producer, nor of Rhodes as a capitalist and imperialist. Yet Rhodes was never able to work De Beers free of the syndicate, and thus to achieve a vertical integration of the industry. In 1892 and 1893 he contemplated selling substantial supplies outside what he called the "pool," but Rothschild and many of the directors (several of the London ones also had conflicts of interest) effectively persuaded Rhodes that he had no choice but to continue to work through the syndicate.

Such outside control was deeply distasteful to Rhodes. He had earlier experience with uncongenial elderly naysayers. If much of his organizing fantasy—his ego ideal as expressed in the "Confession of Faith"—was a persistent protest against such control, he could not help but react to the syndicate as if its interference might harm his far-reaching objectives. That there was reality to the danger hardly mitigated the personal roots of his disinclination to be under its sway. That he only chafed, acceding to no more than short-term contracts, and worked more within the system than without during the first half of the 1890s was evidence of his capacity to resist the pressure of his childhood at least during that relatively constructive period of his life. Overall, during the early 1890s, Rhodes worked with the syndicate, and the market stayed steady. Rhodes was spared those volatile financial fluctuations which would have or could have destroyed the more ambitious of his many imperial advances through 1895.

In mid-1893, Rhodes gave Barnato's syndicate an option on 300,000 carats at the end of two months and then persuaded it to take 400,000 carats at what he decided was a fair price. The condition of the contract, however, was that the final price should remain "absolutely secret," even from R.E. Wallace, who was part of the syndicate. Later in 1893, Rhodes took a week away from his pursuit of the Ndebele war to dash down from Tuli to Palapye to hold two vital telegraphic conversations about diamond pricing and sales to the syndicate. The first was with Craven and Gardner Williams. Rhodes questioned them closely about De Beers' overseas assets, debts to the local Standard Bank, numbers of carats available, the number of loads (3 million) being produced by the consolidated mines, and the likely next offer by the syndicate. The second, decisive, chat up and down the line was between Rhodes at the northern end and Barnato, Oats, and Craven in the south. Barnato and Oats represented the syndicate, which desired to purchase all of De Beers' accumulated stock plus three months' production. After a period of haggling limited mostly by Rhodes' impatient desire to return to the war and the inconvenience and slow pace of Samuel F.B. Morse's primitive device, Rhodes agreed to let Barnato buy about £700,000 worth of rough diamonds for 25 shillings a carat. In turn, Barnato and Oats promised Rhodes 26 shillings a carat for diamonds after January 1894.

"My point," Rhodes pressed Barnato, "is that if the market is good, you will only be too glad to give [26 shillings], and if it is bad, well, we shall have another deal; but we must get this price up now." Finally they closed on a price, although "for form's sake" Rhodes had to tell his London board. "I know they will agree," he tapped the telegraphic key, "but they like to be consulted." He concluded: "Now get the thing through quickly, as I [will] want to go to Tati to meet Jameson if he beats Lobengula . . . and it is better to get this sale through whilst I am at the wire."

Nearly a year later, when the syndicate proposed a price for 100,000 carats that Rhodes thought absurdly low, he suggested selling overseas on the open market. "You must be off your heads," Rhodes told Craven, Henry Robinow, Williams, and Charles Edward Nind, "to suppose I will agree for the sake of a sale . . . to tie our Coy. up indefinitely. On the whole I should . . . take the daily market . . . [since] a wider circle of buyers creates business." Rhodes was striving to avoid granting options of more than three or four months' duration. Otherwise, he said, "you give away your whole position."[6]

The ultimate compromise in this case was a sale, at 24 shillings a carat, with an option for a limited period, and the retention by the company of the right (which it never exercised) to sell stones on the open market.

Cautious entrepreneur that he was, Rhodes also contrived throughout this period to sell stones on the open market anyway and thus to build up a secret reserve fund against which De Beers could borrow if the syndicate's diamond market ever collapsed. Secrecy was essential for two reasons: to keep the shareholders from claiming the reserve fund as dividends and to minimize the impact of the sale of extra diamonds on De Beers' overall return from its regular shipments. With a youthful love of conspiracy, Rhodes in 1890 unveiled his special reserve plan to Stow, who had gone home to London to represent De Beers there. "I am anxious," he explained, "to make an attempt to slowly realize a private stock of diamonds which we have accumulated." When the syndicate and board had agreed to reduce output to 100,000 carats a month, Rhodes had "arranged" to produce 125,000 carats. "The plan succeeded without being noticed and we now regularly produce about 20,000 carats per month which do not appear in the returns. . . ." Rhodes wanted to add a further 60,000, "as we have plenty of blue pulverized and the staff to produce 200,000 carats per month . . . with little if any more expense."

Diamonds in the blue ground were separated naturally from their earth surround when exposed to the weather for several months. Rhodes was proposing to take advantage of this occurrence, since the blue ground was being excavated anyway thanks to Gardner Williams' new incline shafts. He would not need to reduce his work force (something he had always tried to avoid since the cotton days in Natal). The result would be shipments of 10,000 to 20,000 carats a month to Britain. But who was to sell them overseas, and how? Rhodes suggested sending Charles Edward Atkinson to Amsterdam and setting him up there as an owner of a small diamond cutting factory. Atkinson could be their front. His sales could then be converted into Bank of England consols (paying about 2.7 percent a year), the most secure (and conservative) form of investment that Rhodes could imagine.[7]

Even before revealing his ingenious idea to Stow, Rhodes had commenced caching extra carats. Having begun in March, perhaps prodded by Beit, Rhodes had marshaled stones worth about £200,000 by July, and intended to continue adding to his private hoard throughout 1890 and 1891, by which time he would have collected diamonds worth £1 million. Although he appreciated that the provision of the De Beers' trust deed technically prevented him from dealing privately in diamonds, the deed could be amended. Characteristically, Rhodes believed that his end, sensible and plausible, would justify any dubious means. Stow suggested that Rhodes should seek the sanction of the directors, but Rhodes understandably feared that if the scheme became publicly known the shareholders would be "sure to object and demand increased dividends." He and Stow would not need to say anything to the shareholders until the end of 1891, by which time Rhodes would reveal the reserve which he had secreted. That seemed easy to Rhodes, if suspect to

Stow. Anyway, Rhodes reminded Stow, in addition to what he was proposing, his men at Kimberley already, with the knowledge of the board, picked out larger stones and sold them separately.

"To be in a sound position," the company, Rhodes declared, "must have a million reserve," whatever the London board mistakenly thought. As Rhodes had instructed Craven, "It is all nonsense reducing production. It is quite right to do so publicly but you should produce privately. . . . My advice is produce all you can and put them in the safe. . . . Just take responsibility and keep it confidential." "The point I wish to impress upon you," Rhodes told Stow, "is that if I had not conceived the idea the Company would be at the present moment nearly £200,000 poorer or rather with £200,000 locked up in the ground, instead of held in the safe as diamonds and capable of immediate realisation. I could realise the whole tomorrow." He pleaded with the more upright, older Stow: "I am responsible for the production. Cannot you help me with the realisation?" If necessary, Rhodes added, Stow should consult Rothschild, who had always proved himself "loyal," that is, supportive of Rhodes' questionable ideas. In conclusion, Rhodes reverted to wheedling: "I should certainly like some support . . . from your side as between the Charter Company, De Beers and the Cape Colony I have quite enough to carry."[8]

Stow was nervous. "I find it difficult to enter upon a policy which I should strongly condemn were [others] to follow it." By early in 1891, however, Rhodes was starting to ship diamonds to Stow. Most of the London directors had a partial knowledge but had agreed, Rhodes assured Stow, "not to ask questions and to let you and I do as we like." By February, however, Stow was conscious that Meyer and Rothschild's firm looked upon the reserve scheme with "exceeding disfavour." Meyer told Sir Hercules Robinson, who told Stow, that the secret reserve was immoral and unfair. By April, Rhodes agreed to let Stow tell the other directors openly what they were doing. De Beers shares had started to slide precipitously, and Rhodes, unaware of the effect that the Barings bank crisis was having on world markets generally, wanted Rothschild's help in steadying the price of his firm. (Rothschild, in turn, asked Rhodes to make a "brilliant speech" and thus restore confidence in the company, and to husband its resources and continue to make it financially strong—conceivably by some such artifice as the secret reserve.) Yet when the diamond merchants on the London board learned officially of the existence of the special hoard, they tried to thwart Rhodes. He in turn cried "unfair" and ultimately bullied the Kimberley directors to get his way. "You better produce 10,000 carats a day," he told Craven in June, "and declare if necessary 6 or 7 . . . but you must not reduce work or men. . . . You must not stop Stow's shipment until he has a million pounds worth." Later he told Stow that under no circumstances should Stow follow Wernher's suggestion of investing the return on extra diamonds in De Beers obligations or debentures. "You must have it either in gold or English consols. We are not making this reserve to reduce our obligations but in order to maintain our position with the diamond buyers and if they will not buy at our price," Rhodes explained again, "to have securities against which we can borrow and continue our work independent of an immediate sale of diamonds." Rhodes reminded Stow, as he had told Rudd in the early days, that if he had been backed by a £1 million reserve in securities he would not recently have been compelled to sell diamonds to the syndicate, as his De Beers' obligations necessitated, at a price lower than that which he had sought.[9]

By November 1891 Stow was angry over the Wesselton purchase, over "disgraceful" dealings in De Beers' shares on the London exchange, and over what he construed as Rhodes' refusal to buy out his own life governorship for £35,000 (a decision which Stow believed that he and Rhodes had concluded in late 1890). When he began negotiating for the purchase of Wesselton, Rhodes was simultaneously selling as many diamonds as possible so as to depress the value of that mine. He told Stow, "Please oblige me and force [the] market by large sales. I want to depress diamonds. . . ." But Stow refused. "Smashing the market now . . . would be madness." He judged that the syndicate would refuse to take the whole of De Beers' production. (Rhodes attempted to oversell so as to reduce the price of his diamonds in mid-1893, too, for he feared that buyers of precious jewels would otherwise be driven into pearls. Moreover, his correct, if untutored, macroeconomic view was that inflated prices encouraged new prospecting.)[10]

Stow decided to receive no more reserve stones. Rhodes reminded Stow that it was important to keep a back channel open for diamonds, particularly since Rhodes had stopped holding diamonds in Kimberley. "It is a great thing to keep the channel open by small shipments," since the bulk of the trade in diamonds "must eventually go home," that is, be sold directly in London, avoiding the purchasing syndicate in Kimberley. Rhodes wanted thus to become independent "of the ring."[11]

By late 1892, Rhodes' reserve amounted to £650,000. By the end of 1894, belatedly approved by the London board, it had grown to £724,000, and by mid-1895 it had soared to £998,000. As Rhodes explained, whenever the diamond market was shaky, De Beers used its special fund as security against advances.[12] It gave strength to the pool of buyers who knew that De Beers had no need to dump diamonds on the market in periods of depression. Rhodes had succeeded, despite the opposition of the more orthodox directors, and despite a profound suspicion of his suspect procedures, in creating a fund which had served to steady the market.

Rhodes' mastery of the diamond industry was demonstrated repeatedly in the 1890s. He made most of the critical decisions about when to sell, to whom, in what quantities, and at what prices. He imposed his views upon the Kimberley board through its secretary, and by 1892 or 1893 was at least influencing if not always controlling the policies of the London board and the syndicate.

From late 1891, after severe difficulties with white mine labor, Rhodes demanded monthly statements from Kimberley of diamonds found and washed, balanced against expenses. "You must remember always that our expenses are with interest and sinking fund £160,000 per month and that anything under £125,000 per month will not give 12 1/2 per cent," he calculated. Therefore De Beers could not afford to sell diamonds under 27 shillings 6 pence a carat. He specified the number of loads which were required from the blue ground, and the number of carats that had to be sold. "These are facts," he reminded Craven. Moreover, the odd five pence on the price made "all the difference." An undated letter from this period further instructed Craven to produce more than 160,000 carats a month, "otherwise you carry on the industry for . . . the diamond buyers."[13] In 1894 he strongly opposed a discontinuation of the round-the-clock working of the mines. "After thinking it over," he telegraphed Craven, "I am strongly against stopping night hauling unless you can haul during the day as much as you wish." The sum of these messages—attempts to manage the company from the Cape—epitomized Rhodes' firm grip on his prime source of substantial capital.

Rhodes' imperiousness was opposed primarily by the directors in London. Sir Donald Currie, chairman of the Union Castle steamship line and the first London chairman of De Beers, objected to Rhodes treating the diamond company as a personal fief, as did the punctilious Meyer, who represented prudent management and the propriety of the new bankers of London. Rhodes regarded him as a very unpleasant obstacle, but knew that he could appeal over Meyer's head to Rothschild on matters of significance, and that he could and would outmaneuver Currie. Rhodes had his differences with Rothschild, too, especially over the extent to which De Beers' capital could be used to advance Rhodes' other projects. "De Beers," reminded Rothschild, "is simply and purely a diamond mining company." If Rhodes wanted funds for Rhodesia he would simply "have to obtain [them] from other sources than the cash reserve of the DeBeers Company." Rothschild continued: "It is quite possible that the Articles of Association [of De Beers] may give you a loophole." Rhodes, Rothschild knew, would employ any loophole he could find. However, "nowadays people are disposed to construe all articles of association more severely than they used to do," Rothschild said, "and if it became known that the Debeers Company lent money to the Chartered Company, some . . . shareholders might . . . get up an agitation to turn out the Board and put in their own nominees, which would be most undesirable." Rothschild was being practical: "Apart . . . from the question whether it is right or wrong to use the funds of the Debeers Company in this way, it would be very injudicious. . . ." Rothschild feared that Rhodes would damage the credit of his bankers and the reputation of the London directors.[14]

In 1892, Rothschild also wished to distribute to De Beers' shareholders 158,000 of the 210,000 shares that De Beers had initially purchased in the British South Africa Company as a way of strengthening the diamond concern's asset base. Rhodes strongly resisted such a move, but lost. By mid-1892, when the Chartered shares were worth only 16 shillings each, he admitted that De Beers had suffered only a small setback. But the firm, Rhodes spoke for the company as if it were himself, had "done a great public act, shewing it [was] not merely a mercenary corporation but recognise[d] the obligations connected with its great wealth." "As far as my share in it goes," he continued, "I have nothing to be ashamed of. . . ."

Still later, in 1894, Meyer, on behalf of Rothschild, promised to continue to advance funds to Rhodes with which he could purchase additional De Beers shares. Meyer also assured Rhodes that he would continue putting his hands in his pockets "and gladly" help finish the railway from Beira. "I always take the keenest interest in all your plans and ideas," he said, "and in my small way I shall always be proud to contribute towards their success." Concerning their differences, about which Rhodes had often complained, Meyer said that all he had "fought for was the separation of De Beers and Chartered and now that I see finality in that connection I am quite easy about it."[15]

Despite Rothschild's conservative influence on the board, Rhodes usually had the final word on the amount of dividends to be declared annually. In 1895, by which time he had only now and then subordinated the London board to his own methods of absentee management, there was an internal disagreement about how much to declare. Atkinson and Oats favored 17 shillings 6 pence per share; Meyer, Currie, Baring Gould, English, Thomas Shiels, John Morrogh, Stow, and Rothschild wanted 18 shillings; and Wernher, Beit, Mosenthal, Robinow, Nind, Woolf Joel, and Barnato sought a 20 shilling-per-share payout. Rhodes' opinion was decisive. He opted for the middle figure, both as a compromise and because doing so promised best to establish the claims of the life governors for whom there had thus far been no returns. He was also influenced by the fear that diamonds might suffer from the collapse in the European bourses; De Beers ought, he thought, to keep reserves back for future dividends, but they were never used for such a purpose.[16]

As Rhodes had boasted in 1888, "The Mines [were] simply perpetual. . . ." By late 1895 diamonds had proved a bonanza for him and for other large investors. With help from the syndicate and advice from Rothschild and others, and even the stimulus of a long memorandum from Charles Roulina, a French buyer, Rhodes had seen the demand and supply curves for diamonds smoothed and increasing profits returned to the principal backers of De Beers. The big returns were to come over the next seven years, but by late 1895 De Beers had demonstrated that prices could be stabilized by controlling all serious sources of production and by selling exclusively to a syndicate of buyers based in Kimberley. Rhodes never dumped, panicked, or forced the market up unreasonably. Indeed, he could not, for much of the power to do so was in the hands of the syndicate and the London board, not in his own.

Rhodes knew that diamonds were an unusual commodity with a more inelastic demand than most raw materials. Those who wanted them as a hedge against inflation or for adornment would purchase polished diamonds of quality only within a narrow band of price. Rhodes catered to these ultimate buyers, after an early antagonism worked successfully with the various middlemen,

and helped establish and maintain diamonds as a reliable investment. His secret reserve added to De Beers' fiscal and economic strength, and thus to the
strength of diamonds as an exceptionally stable commodity in the 1890s.

Rhodes was helped in the second half of the 1890s by a rising market
generally. But Rothschild's praise was nevertheless fully merited. Acting assertively, and as far as De Beers was concerned with a fundamental conserva-
tism compromised only by his substantial assistance to Rhodesia, Rhodes managed to establish a remarkably successful money machine. "The history of the
De Beers Company," Rothschild declared with unwitting metaphorical accuracy in 1900, "is simply a fairy tale." He told Rhodes: "You have succeeded
in establishing a practical monopoly of the production of diamonds, you have
succeeded in establishing a remarkably steady market for the sale of your
productions, and you have succeeded in finding machinery capable of carrying this through. . . . In short, the fact of a powerful Syndicate existing means
stability for the diamond market itself, the assurance of a dividend, . . . and
the fact that those who are selling the diamonds are quite as concerned in
maintaining the price as the purchasers."[17] Rhodes' monopoly was a fact, even
if it still sold to and never competed with a "ring" of purchasing intermediaries whom Rhodes could influence only informally and indirectly rather than
as part of an integrated producing and sales organization.

It was not the same for gold, a commodity with a fixed, monetized price,
and an industry with a broader geographical base and far greater demands
on capital. Critically, too, Rhodes from the first was in gold as a speculator
and not as an entrepreneur. He looked upon gold as a sideline to diamonds.
He believed that there was too little water on or near the Rand for mining
even at shallow depths to be carried out profitably for long. He had been
persuaded by Williams that the surface gold would soon be bound up in unworkable pyrites. Indeed, much of Rhodes' early money from Gold Fields was
made as a result of astutely timed sales of shares and from investments by
Gold Fields in De Beers.

Much smaller returns would have accrued to Rhodes and Rudd had the
two founders not structured the original Gold Fields concern in a manner
which favored them overwhelmingly. This was the common pattern on the
Rand, and did not originate with Rhodes' fertile brain, but Rhodes, Rudd,
and their closest cronies never hesitated to benefit from their inside knowledge and the theoretically significant attributes which they, as originators or
vendors, brought to their companies and the ordinary shareholders. Even so,
for reasons that have earlier been explained, when Rhodes purchased land
and pegged claims on the Rand in the late 1880s he did so haphazardly and
unwisely.[18] The Luipaard's Vlei and Witpoortjie claims produced poorly from
low grade or non-existent outcrops; by the standards of the day, Rhodes' initial forays into gold outcrop properties were disappointing. He had cornered
the dregs.

Rudd told the company's shareholders in 1889 that their anticipations
"had not quite [been] fulfilled." He and Rhodes had not "got on to the main

reef" because they (mostly Rhodes) had thought the main reef too small. Rudd blamed himself for supposing that the more extensive reefs of low-grade ore would pay more readily. But he had been wrong. "Rhodes and I . . . had not done as well as men of our experience and knowledge might have done. . . ."

Yet by then (the good results to be declared in the next year), Rhodes, followed by Rudd, had capitalized superbly upon an early knowledge that shares on the Rand would soon suffer a catastrophic collapse. In the first half of 1889 those who were exploiting the gold-bearing surface bodies on the main reef struck unweathered pyritic ores. "I think the change is very unfavourable," James Benjamin Taylor wrote urgently to Jules Porges & Co. in 1889, "as it comes so much sooner than we expected." There was no "free gold" in the quartz pebble conglomerate below 120 feet, Taylor concluded. It would be difficult to show a profit.

The existing basis of the gold industry in the Transvaal had been undermined. If resistant pyrites were found to be general, those who mined gold could no longer simply crush the surface conglomerate and then extract free gold by running it over copper plates covered with mercury. In the deeper pyrites, gold was encased in a matrix of iron, sulfides, and silica. To extract gold a much more costly chlorination process would be required; the low-grade mines would suffer the most; and margins everywhere would be very tight. By May, Rhodes had begun bearing gold shares overseas and refusing to make purchases on the Rand. Rudd followed him and before the end of 1889 Gold Fields had profitably divested itself of all but 57,000 of nearly 400,000 of its holdings on the Rand. The proceeds were invested in De Beers, which paid handsomely (and in Charters, which paid nothing) until Rhodes and Rudd were prepared to move back into gold. Rudd claimed that he still believed in the prospects of the Rand, but Rhodes, his energies and intellect focused elsewhere, remained skeptical, removed, and content in 1889 and 1890 to draw a steady return from Gold Fields' holdings in diamonds. Rothschild cynically called Gold Fields a land company.[19]

Rhodes never showed his face at meetings of either the original Gold Fields Company or its successor. In late 1891, Thomas Rudd, Charles Rudd's elder brother and the chairman of Gold Fields, was forced to confront irate shareholders. The company had decided not to declare a regular dividend, although the founding partners would, in accord with the original arrangements, divide a third of the concern's annual, if diminished, net profit of £16,000. Spokesmen for the ordinary investors called the London directors mere lackeys of Rhodes.[20] Indeed, what had not been revealed to the investors was even more disturbing: Rhodes had taken Gold Fields off the Rand. He planned to go with Rudd to the more promising "virgin" country of Shonaland in August; all of Gold Fields' capital would henceforth be expended there. Gold Fields would even close its office in Johannesburg.

That was Rhodes' plan. He was intent upon shoring up the infant colony of his dreams, and, to do so, it and he desperately needed capital. Yet Rudd, a conservative and conventional businessman with profit as his main motive, had never invested in Rhodes' dream. Pressed as much by his brother as by his own sense of responsibility to the City connection and the ordinary share-holders, Rudd was prepared to work with Rhodes only so long as the profit motive remained paramount. Rudd, as his diverse business adventures in early Kimberley suggest, was pre-eminently a practical entrepreneur who had been buoyed by Rhodes' lofty perspectives and, to some extent, by Rhodes' sound commercial and engineering instincts on the diamond fields. He had even condoned and profited from Rhodes' sharp practices in the 1870s regarding pumping contracts and the buying of diamond plots. But, without breaking from Rhodes, whose contacts with Beit, politicians, and others were still vital, Rudd was far quicker than his partner in appreciating the importance of two technological advances on the Rand.

The use of a solution of potassium cyanide to dissolve auriferous ores had been invented in the late 1880s by John S. MacArthur, a Glasgow chem-ist, and the brothers Robert and William Forrest, two medical doctors. Once dissolved, the gold in the ores could be precipitated out upon a bank of zinc dust as efficiently and cheaply as the older mercury method. By 1889 the MacArthur-Forrest technique had reached Barberton, and tailings were treated successfully there. At the end of 1890 it was brought to the Rand, and by mid-1891, just before Rhodes proposed to take Rudd to Rhodesia and focus Gold Fields on the search for a second Rand, nearly all the reef mine-man-agers were finally persuaded that cyanide would treat refractory ores easily.

Joseph Robinson had meanwhile erected a chlorination plant under the supervision of Charles Butters, a metallurgist from Haverhill, Massachusetts, and the University of California. It produced its first bars of local gold satis-factorily about the same time as the MacArthur-Forrest method was becoming better known, but was superseded completely by 1893–94, when nearly every-one on the Rand—even Butters—conceded that the cyanide process provided far better returns per ton than either the older processes or chlorination.

Equally if not more important for the future of South Africa, gold min-ing, and Rhodes, several more perceptive, imported experts began to suspect that the reefs of the Rand were not the tips of buried mountains of ancient alluvial conglomerate but finite shafts of gold-bearing ores that inclined downward at fairly shallow angles from their surface outcrop. They were thus less likely to be confined to a precise and known perimeter; rather, they could be followed for miles southward from the original main reef, but at increasing depths the farther from the surface outcrop.

Lionel Phillips of the Wernher, Beit company had begun pegging claims south of the outcrop in 1889, but there was no clear evidence until 1890 to support the theory of Joseph Storey Curtis, a Boston-born, Harvard- and Freiburg-educated mining engineer, that the main reef dipped out of the ver-tical confines of existing claims and headed south for 170 miles. His prede-cessors and the early miners in general, trained in diamond diggings or Brit-ish coal seams but not in gold conglomerates, had assumed that they would be digging deeper and deeper holes, not following a vein as it angled away from its visible manifestation.[21] When Curtis, employed by Wernher, Beit, bored earthward 1,000 feet south of the outcrop, his drills struck rich ores at 571 feet and the main reef at more than 600 feet. In great secrecy Phillips and Curtis thereafter began to buy farms through which the deeper levels would pass on their way to the distant Orange Free State, and thus to lay the basis for the great industry which was soon to transform South Africa's golden prospects. (Even so, it was because of the persistence of Henry Cleveland Perkins, Lord Randolph Churchill's partner in Rhodesia and the general manager of Rand Mines from mid-1893, that deep-level mining truly became popular. By late 1893, his laborious drilling had established that the main reef continued underneath what became Crown Deep, 1,600 feet from the outcrop, and that the gold there was very rich—nearly 14 ounces to the ton of debris.)

Percy Tarbutt, a British mining engineer in the employ of Gold Fields, tried to persuade Rhodes to invest in deep-level claims. But Rhodes was unaware of the MacArthur-Forrest process and was committed more to the possibility of a second Rand in the north than to a renewed exploitation of the first. Tarbutt formed his own company and pegged claims wherever he could.

Gold Fields would have lost all real opportunity in gold and been reduced to an insignificant financing shell had its access to capital and Rhodes' manipulative skills not been desirable commodities. Rhodes and Rudd began to realize the significance of the deep levels only in mid-1892, by which time Beit's firm had plunged very heavily into what could be considered a new and truly realizable Rand, and the first bores had confirmed gold at depth. Rhodes asked Beit for "an interest," and Beit agreed.

Why would Beit have let Rhodes and Gold Fields into what would in 1893 become the vastly powerful and, subsequently, immensely profitable Rand Mines Ltd.? On its 1,357 claims ten mines were soon established; an original investment of £200,000 was to be worth £50 million by the end of the decade. Several authors follow their predecessors and suggest that Beit "hammered away at Rhodes and Rudd until at last they were persuaded," but the evidence for this view is thin and inconclusive. Rhodes begged to be let in, and Beit believed that it was prudent to agree. Beit wanted the solid backing of his old friend and fellow schemer, especially now that Rhodes had become so well-placed politically. Who, after all, could ignore Rhodes' influence? In mid-1892 Beit said that he would "make some arrangement with Rhodes and Rudd. . . .I think it would be wise to do so. Rhodes' brains are not to be despised and if we had interests apart from theirs there would always be friction. . . ." Certainly, too, Beit wanted no recriminations from a friend with whom he had shared so much and invested so much emotionally as well as financially.

Beit may have wanted to allay Rhodes' long-nurtured anxieties. For some time, Rhodes had clearly been concerned about losing Beit, whether to gold or personally. Taylor, one of their contemporaries, wrote that "Rhodes never ceased trying to wean . . . Beit away from the lure of the Rand." He quotes Rhodes as admitting openly that it would never do " 'to let Beit forget that

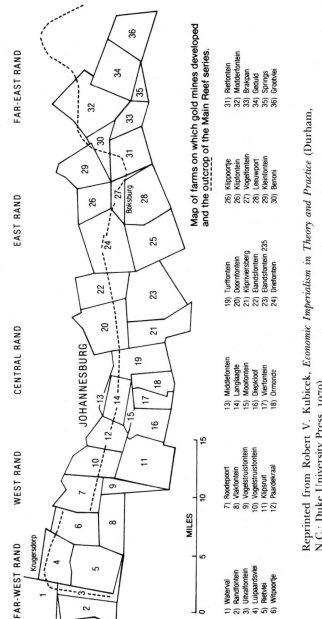

FAR-WEST RAND   WEST RAND   CENTRAL RAND   EAST RAND   FAR-EAST RAND

JOHANNESBURG

Krugersdorp

Boksburg

**Map of farms on which gold mines developed
and the outcrop of the Main Reef series.**

MILES

0   5   10   15

1) Waterval
2) Randfontein
3) Uitvalfontein
4) Luipaardsvlei
5) Rietvlei
6) Witpoortje

7) Roodepoort
8) Vlakfontein
9) Vogelstruisfontein
10) Vogelstruisfontein
11) Klipsruit
12) Paardekraal

13) Middlefontein
14) Langlaagte
15) Mooifontein
16) Diepkloof
17) Vierfontein
18) Ormonde

19) Turffontein
20) Doornfontein
21) Klipriviersberg
22) Elandsfontein
23) Elandsfontein 235
24) Driefontein

26) Klippoortje
26) Klipfontein
27) Vogelfontein
28) Leeuwport
29) Kleinfontein
30) Benoni

31) Rietfontein
32) Modderfontein
33) Brakpan
34) Geduld
35) Springs
36) Grootvlei

Reprinted from Robert V. Kubicek, *Economic Imperialism in Theory and Practice* (Durham,
N.C.: Duke University Press, 1979).

his diamond interests were calling him. If Beit becomes too deeply involved in this gold business I may risk losing his support, which I absolutely need for the fulfillment of my dreams in the north and the acquisition of the political power that I must have behind me when the moment arrives.' " One night when Rhodes and Taylor were together in 1889 or 1890, and after they had been drinking and talking until late, but Taylor had gone to sleep, Rhodes suddenly burst in at 2 a.m. Roused from slumber, Taylor found Rhodes in his dressing-gown, with a candle in his hand. "For two solid hours," said Taylor, "he sat on my bed declaiming against Rand gold-mines and declaring that the only mining worth undertaking was diamond-mining. . . . He kept on repeating in his high-pitched voice that we ought to seize the opportunity to sell all our gold-mining interests and return to Kimberley." Rhodes, deduced Taylor, was attempting to prevent Beit from "wandering away from his control and devoting his firm's capital to furthering interests in which . . . Rhodes . . . had no share." The band of brothers must stay together.

Beit knew that Rhodes and Rudd were adept at floating companies. They could help attract British capital (Beit had hitherto relied more upon German, Austrian, and French investors) for his firm's ten new mines. Beit also wanted to spread his firm's risk. (Rhodes was later to claim and Julius Wernher to deny that Beit had offered De Beers a half-interest in Rand Mines for a mere £150,000, but that the London board had turned it down. A half-interest would have been worth a tidy £10 million by 1900.) By the time that Rhodes and Beit had finished dickering, Gold Fields (not De Beers) owned 10 percent, Rothschild 20 percent, and Wernher, Beit 60 percent of Rand Mines (with a further 10 percent allocated to miscellaneous interests). Moreover, Beit gave Gold Fields 10 percent of Wernher, Beit's founder's share of Rand Mines. (It entitled his firm to 25 percent of all profits once the total subscribed capital had been repaid in the form of dividends.)[22] This slice of the vendor's portion would soon be worth more than £1 million to Gold Fields. Thanks to Beit's need of new capital and the backing of Rhodes, Gold Fields, and therefore Rudd and Rhodes, were not shut out of the best of the new, deeper developments on the Rand. By early 1893 Rudd was busily focused on expanding the firm's interests there.

Beit had helped save Gold Fields from oblivion. But to make it possible for Rhodes and Rudd to join him, they had to raise new capital. Tarbutt and his partners in the other set of extensive deep holdings also required an infusion of financial support. The result of these various requirements, and Rudd's enthusiasm for selling shares in deep mines—"There is no doubt that [Beit's] deep-level scheme will be a grand one and very popular," Rudd wrote to Harry Currey—was the complete corporate restructuring of Gold Fields.[23] Tarbutt and Herbert Davies, secretary of Gold Fields and a holder of mining properties on his own, offered to merge their deep-level holdings into the original company. The product, beginning in August 1892, was the Consolidated Gold Fields of South Africa, Ltd. Its authorized capital of £1,250,000 was divided into £500,000 for the old Gold Fields stockowners on a one-for-one basis, and £246,000 for Tarbutt, Davies, and their partners. More than 336,000 shares were held for the purchase of additional deep-level prospects in 1893. After extensive bargaining sessions, Davies and Tarbutt compelled Rhodes and Rudd to give up their founder's rights to the first three-fifteenths of any profits.

As Rudd explained, although he had been very reluctant to agree to such a bargain, given Gold Fields' liabilities, the only alternative to a merger became the sale either of their De Beers holdings or their shares in gold properties. Rudd told Rhodes that "the only possible way to carry out [their] views [was] to register a new company" minus the founder's shares.[24] In exchange for their loss of the first 20 percent of profit before dividends, the two managing directors received 80,000 shares, or 8 percent of ordinary dividends, and the right to purchase 25,000 more at par. They also retained two-fifteenths of all profits in lieu of salary, not an altogether uncomfortable compromise. In 1892, however, they could not conceivably have guessed the real value of Tarbutt's (and Beit's) second and third tier deep-level properties.

In that year the total output of the Rand was 100,000 fine ounces a month, three times more than in 1889. Within three years total production doubled again, to 2.25 million ounces, worth £8.5 million. The Transvaal exported a quarter of the world's gold and was the world's third largest producer after Australia and the United States. By 1897 South Africa was the world's largest exporter of gold. Its mining companies paid out more than £2 million annually in dividends; by value, half of the total exports of South Africa were gold ingots.

In 1893 the Consolidated Gold Fields showed a profit of more than £207,000, in 1894 nearly £309,000. These were speculative, not industrial profits, but the latter were on their way. In November 1895, after 350,000 shares in old reef properties had been unloaded at inflated levels, the company announced a profit of £2,540,918—a larger return than had ever been shown in one year by a limited liability concern registered in London.[25] After earlier dividends in 1893 and 1894 of 10 percent and 15 percent, the 1895 declared return was a whopping 125 percent, or a payout of £625,000. Of this total, Rhodes' share was about £112,000. On the eve of the Jameson Raid, Rhodes was hardly short of the "ready."

Consolidated Gold Fields then owned 25,000 shares in De Beers, 47,000 in Charters and another 87,000 in other Rhodesian concerns, 50,000 in underdeveloped outcrop properties, and 1,200,000 shares in existing or prospective deep-level mines. Speculations in shares provided another huge 125 percent payout in 1896; thereafter, Gold Fields lived off its mines, then starting to produce well and efficiently. But, by then, Rhodes' one-fifteenth share had been annulled.

Little of this new wealth had been developed directly by Rhodes. In that sense he had largely remained a passive participant in the great shift of local resources toward the Rand after 1892. His connections and premiership had been worth 10 percent to Beit and about the same amount, but for very different reasons, to Tarbutt and Davies. Ostensibly, he took little firsthand interest in the old company in the early 1890s and even less in Consolidated Gold Fields. In contrast to De Beers, where he tried to be active managing director, in the gold firm his word was important but not always decisive. After 1893, Davies effectively ran the company from London, with Rudd being the critical other figure whether he resided in South Africa or visited Britain.

Yet Rhodes' correspondence with Davies, notably in 1893 when he was traveling back to the Cape from London via Florence, Cairo, Luxor, and Zanzibar, demonstrates how forcibly Rhodes intervened in the gold as well as the diamond businesses. After receiving a letter from Davies enclosing a cable that revealed Rudd's reluctance to invest broadly in the deep levels, Rhodes agreed that Rudd had given "no reasons for change of view. I think myself he is suffering from . . . one of those sick headaches to which he is liable. . . ." Overruling Rudd, Rhodes urged Davies to continue buying on the Rand. "Tell Rudd," he instructed, "to watch the deep levels of Rietfontein [mine]."[26] In 1893 Rhodes also installed his brother Ernest as the representative of the joint managing directors in Johannesburg (replacing Harry Currey) without consulting Rudd or checking with Davies. (Ernest Rhodes, thought Rudd, was "very pushing . . . but without the ballast and shrewdness of his brother."[27]) Rhodes also gave Frank, his other brother, a job in the Johannesburg office of the firm on the eve of the Raid. Both gifts of position were nepotistic, but the place for Frank was also intended to assist the Raid.

Nothing showed Rhodes' residual powers more completely than his ability to thrust John Hays Hammond onto Gold Fields. Hammond, San Francisco-born and Yale- and Freiburg-educated, was an ebullient, thoroughly self-confident mining engineer of world reputation. Like the many other important Americans who had been enticed or attracted to the Rand because of their expertise in the hard rock conditions with which European and South African miners were unfamiliar, Hammond's experienced eye and geological judgment were desired as the owners began to grapple with problems of developing a new kind of mine. They would have to decide on which properties to sink shafts deeply and expensively, and the Americans possessed a knowledge which was prized.

Brought to the Rand by Barnato for a high fee, Hammond was soon talking vigorously with Rhodes. According to Hammond, whose autobiography may contain more hyperbole than most, early in the South African autumn (like most Americans, he wrote "spring" when he meant the sub-equatorial autumn) of 1894 Rhodes sat with him on a stone bench near Groote Schuur. "Mr. Hammond," Rhodes supposedly began, "I take it you are not in South Africa for your health?" "With due appreciation of the climate of South Africa," Hammond replied, he preferred California. Rhodes believed in experts, especially Americans. He offered Hammond complete charge of Rhodes' mining interests on the Rand, and agreed to pay him £12,000 a year, then worth about $75,000, a salary greater than anyone else's in South Africa. Moreover, because Hammond had no high regard for Rhodes' subordinates, including

Ernest Rhodes, the prime minister and magnate picked up a scrap of paper only a few inches long and wrote: "Mr. Hammond is authorized to make any purchases for going ahead, and has full authority, provided he informs me of it and gets no protest." In this manner Hammond became Rhodes' chief consulting engineer for gold. Rhodes' other instructions to Hammond were epigrammatic: "Do not buy deeps with poor parents. Drunkards' children are no good. Go always into good things, not doubtful ones unless they cost you nothing. Remember poor ground costs just as much to work as rich ground, the only difference is the first cost. . . ." In other words, purchase only ground near areas of proven value, and be frugal.

In Johannesburg, Ernest, "fine and high-principled," according to Hammond, but knowing "little" about mining or finance, let Hammond do what he wanted and spend lavishly on new claims, new staff, and new techniques. Hammond ignored Rudd, too, insisting upon doing what he alone thought best and consulting only with Rhodes, and sometimes not even with him.

Hammond successfully advised Rhodes to sell all of Gold Fields' outcrop holdings and to invest everything in distant deep-level claims, a very winning strategy in 1894–95. He was instrumental in taking Gold Fields into the Robinson Deep mine south of Johannesburg, in developing for Gold Fields the very profitable Simmer and Jack mine, between Johannesburg and Germiston, and in obtaining and opening what eventually became the equally remunerative Sub Nigel mine, thirty miles farther east. Tarbutt and Cecil Quentin already held land there near a great dip in the outcrop reef; Hammond understood its potential and insisted that Gold Fields purchase land extensively in the area.

Hammond claims that even after there was a general recognition that the leaders of the main reef could be followed for miles away from the Rand, the mining of deeper and deeper levels worried old-line entrepreneurs. Their engineers mistakenly believed—as did financiers overseas—that the deeper levels would be too torrid to exploit. Based on the conditions at a famous gold mine in Nevada, the faint-hearted believed that the thermal gradients in the Johannesburg mines would prove too steep to be worked even by Africans. Hammond guessed otherwise, based on the different conditions on the Rand. (So had Hamilton Smith, who worked for Beit in early 1893.) Hammond's other major contribution was the employment of American methods to sink shafts two and three times faster than had ever been done in South Africa. Not only were these imported techniques swifter than the old; they consumed great quantities of money and labor. (The gold mines employed 14,000 Africans in 1890 and 100,000 in 1899.) In order to retain good workers, Hammond tried to persuade Rhodes to extend the usual compound system by establishing traditional villages near the new mines. Doing so would ensure a ready supply of well-trained, contented African labor.[28] But such a rational plan was never adopted by the mine owners.

Hammond was Rhodes' type. Smart, decisive, possessed of opinions and prejudices, forthright, and egocentric, he appealed to Rhodes' assertive, problem-solving, non-passive side. Like Rhodes, Hammond was in a hurry, and rarely scrupled for details. Moreover, he produced results and had an excellent intuitive sense of where to buy likely land and where to set down shafts. Even so, Julius Wernher called Hammond a "windbag." Major Herbert Langton Sapte, who replaced Ernest Rhodes in the Johannesburg head office after the Raid, said that Hammond had also been careless and needlessly extravagant. Others who followed him suggested that Hammond had underestimated the costs of opening the new mines.[29]

Rhodes worked hard at diamonds, knew the business and the market, and continued to prosper even while he devoted at least half of every year to parliament and the other half to the intrigues of imperialism as well as high finance. Paradoxically, by the mid-1890s his returns were becoming better from gold, where he contributed less to the enterprise than to diamonds, but still more than has generally been appreciated. (Rhodesia paid nothing directly, although Rhodes may have made tens of thousands of pounds from the buying and selling of those shares.) His amazing returns from gold in 1895 and 1896 continued throughout the decade. Admittedly, they were his first substantial profits from Gold Fields, but that firm had earlier backed his venture into Shona country and thus heavily subsidized Rhodes' imperial expression of himself. What is significant is that Rhodes was growing rich in cash as well as in paper assets precisely at the moment when he was about to gamble his prestige and probity on a madcap adventure for which the gaining of further economic control of the wealth of the Transvaal would prove an insufficient and inadequate explanation.

Rhodes planned and schemed much more for his generous returns than his friendly biographers have suggested. He dealt supremely in shares, as his critics from time to time suggested. For example, in commenting upon Rhodes' activities on the world's stock markets, and the great increases in market valuation for all of his properties, the *Economist* paid him a supremely backhanded compliment: "The philanthropy and national spirit of the Cape Premier and his friends are of the distinctly profitable kind."[30]

Rhodes watched over his myriad investments well, firing off letters and telegrams to colleagues, subordinates, and opponents with dispatch and purpose. Rhodes also served his growing financial stature and his continual need for renewed infusions of capital from both discerning and gullible share buyers in Britain (and occasionally on the Continent) by visiting London yearly throughout the 1890s. His long sea voyages were always required for other reasons, too, but his golden-tongued ability to charm and impress financiers directly and exhort and ennoble both crotchety boards of directors in conclaves assembled and serried ranks of stockholders sitting in annual meetings, necessitated one journey after another. When he went home, Rhodes naturally also dabbled in the high politics of imperialism, pushed pet projects in a variety of spheres, and indulged his curiosity about places fabled and mysterious.

In late 1892 Rhodes was in London to persuade the directors of the British South Africa Company to find the funds to pay for the northern railway's extension from Vryburg to Mafeking, and to address the shareholders of that Company. But he used the occasion, as always, to promote the additional, sometimes grandiose ideas that happened to be on his mind, were timely, or were what he assumed to be helpful responses to perceived national and popular needs. In 1892 he talked about his transcontinental telegraph line, which earlier in the year had reached Salisbury from the south, and was threading its way across the Zambezi River toward Zomba and the shores of Lake Tanganyika. Rhodes had long planned to tie his own possessions together by telegraph and then to extend his own system northward across German-controlled Tanganyika toward Lake Victoria, Uganda, through the massive Sudan (where the unfriendly Mahdi unfortunately still ruled), and down the Nile to Cairo.

"I always had the idea of an overland telegraph to Egypt," Rhodes told the Company's shareholders in late 1892. What Harry Johnston called "this astounding scheme of a cable through the length of Africa" may well have been an integral part of Rhodes' "big idea" for years, and its genesis could well be ascribed to the Confession of 1877.[31] However, other, larger, projects made prior claims on his time and energies. Only the occupation of Rhodesia, and preparations for a war, gave urgency to the extension of a line 1,000 miles from Vryburg to Salisbury. This task he accomplished in a mere eighteen months, and had begun to turn a small profit on the endeavor. But until late 1892 Rhodes had no immediate plans to take the telegraph much beyond the southern waters of Lake Tanganyika, the farthest edge of the Company's sphere. In November of that year, however, when Rhodes was in London seeking renewed support for the Company and his dream of a white, wealthy Rhodesian colony, Britons were arguing bitterly about keeping or abandoning their predominant position in Uganda. Although the Imperial British East Africa Company had begun to occupy and develop what was to become Kenya, and was seeking funds for a railway upcountry, the task of pacifying Uganda, the locus of religious and indigenous interstate conflict deep in the heart of Africa, was proving impossibly expensive for the severely undercapitalized entity.

Lord Salisbury's Unionist/Conservative government had advanced Britain's hegemony in Egypt since the 1880s and had fostered the East Africa Company's recent expedition of pacification into Uganda. In Egypt, where Lord Cromer was Britain's viceroy in all but name, Britain was still ostensibly yoked with France in shared influence, but the French were also menacing the upper reaches of the Nile and therefore Uganda. When Gladstone's last Liberal government succeeded the Tory Unionists in the summer of 1892, imperialism divided a distinctly fractious cabinet. Sir William Harcourt, at the Treasury, wanted above all to conciliate the French and retreat from unnecessary overseas resonsibilities. Sir Henry Campbell-Bannerman, at the War Office, and Lord Asquith, the Home Secretary, largely agreed with Harcourt. Gladstone, a visceral anti-imperialist more concerned about home rule for Ireland than about the conduct of foreign affairs, felt the same way. Gladstone vividly remembered how General Gordon's masochism at Khartoum had hurt the Liberal cause in 1885. But Lord Rosebery was foreign minister largely at Queen Victoria's request, and he was intent on expanding the empire in Salisbury's wake.

Before a cabinet meeting in September Rosebery declared that he would never support a policy of "uninformed abandonment of the sphere of British influence and of leaving our missionaries & their converts to chance & the Arabs."[32] Rosebery was determined to resign before submitting either to the cabinet or to Gladstone over the Nile; he distrusted the French even more than he disagreed with Harcourt. Throughout the autumn of 1892, with the Liberals split and with the East Africa Company unable to afford further expenditures in the interior, Britain thus heatedly contested the Uganda question. Rhodes could hardly avoid injecting himself into the debate.

Alarmed by the possibility that Britain should limit its imperial reach, shrink from annexation, and appear weak in the eyes of other European powers, Rhodes naturally offered to assist. He proposed to administer Uganda for Britain in exchange for a subsidy of £25,000 a year. "Rhodes was with me yesterday," Harcourt told Wilfred Scawen Blunt. "He has offered to run Uganda for £25,000 a year, though he admits there is nothing to be made of it commercially."[33] Presumably Rhodes contemplated raising an expeditionary force under Lugard or his own brother Frank, and thus doing direct service for the empire and his own notions of personal destiny. It was fortunate for the British South Africa Company, which would have been employed as the vehicle of this far-flung administration, that Rosebery refused the brazen offer. Instead, in substitution for the grander gesture, Rhodes offered to extend his telegraph line overland to Uganda, and thence to Egypt. By so doing, he imagined that he could help ensure that the head of the Nile remained British red. Following discussions with Lord Rosebery and Lord Rothschild, Rhodes declared officially to the foreign secretary that he was "prepared to extend at once the line of Telegraph from Salisbury . . . to Uganda without asking Her Majesty's Government for any contribution." Sanction from the German government would obviously be necessary if the telegraph were to be carried to Uganda by the most direct route. He therefore urged the British government to intercede with the young kaiser. If these arrangements were concluded soon, he could be in Uganda—a distance of 1600 miles—within eighteen months. "My ultimate object," he informed the foreign secretary, "is to connect with the Telegraph system now existing in Egypt . . . but I am fully aware that under existing circumstances at Khartoum such an undertaking cannot at present be carried out."[34]

Rhodes believed that he could reach Uganda for about £150,000. There were "no difficult tribes to deal with." Going further, to Wadi Halfa in upper Egypt, would cost another £300,000 to £400,000. The whole would be cheaper than the cable systems along both the East and West African coasts. As a result, instead of charges that approximated 10 shillings a word to cable users, Rhodes expected that his transcontinental line would be able to make a profit by charging only 2 shillings a word. He proposed that this grand undertaking should be financed by the 14,000 persons who owned shares in the British South Africa Company, De Beers, Gold Fields, and his other concerns. If each invested £10 in the telegraphic endeavor Rhodes would obtain £3 million with which to work, and then "the cable companies, when I get to Uganda, would have to consider their position." Although the City, and Sivewright in the Cape parliament, were intensely skeptical, Rhodes had no doubts about the likely success of such a project. It was a much easier undertaking, he told the annual meeting of the Company, "than amalgamating the Kimberley diamond mines, or governing the Cape Colony." Moreover, he added curiously, "it will be a little relaxation from my work out there." A man like Rhodes clearly required the stimulus of a future-oriented project to protect him against the potential boredom of even *his* daily routine.

There were more salient arguments for the telegraphic extension. Doing so would help end the slave trade and "give us the keys to the continent. . . . If I extend the telegraph to Uganda we shall certainly not hear any more about the abandonment of that place." Moreover, once having attained Uganda, it would be easy to "get the money with which to extend the line to Egypt." Admittedly, the Mahdi and his warriors barred the way, and Rhodes would not wish to contest his reign militarily. But the Mahdi "could never exist between two civilized powers in Egypt and Uganda," thought Rhodes. "In such a case the Mahdi would be like a nut between the crackers." Better yet, Rhodes would " 'deal' " with him. He uttered his oft-quoted dictum in this context: "I have never met any one in my life whom it was not as easy to deal with as to fight."[35]

A month later, when Rhodes was in Cairo en route home to the Cape and the Logan/Sivewright controversy, he wrote a private letter to Rosebery urging him to "get . . . me the right of way for the telegraph through the German territory." If the British ambassador was "worth anything he would be able to explain to the young Emperor the advantages of the telegraph . . . and the alternatives through the King of the Belgians' territory." Rhodes was confident of the ultimate success of this project. If "the English people [did] not scuttle out of Uganda and Egypt," he predicted, ". . . I feel certain with the increasing prosperity here [in Egypt], almost entirely due to our rule, settled government will steadily spread up the Nile . . . and by the time I reach Uganda there will be little difficulty here." Gladstone had contemplated lessening or removing Britain's influence in Khedive Abbas II's Egypt, where that month a local coup had been attempted.

Rhodes, who had as early as 1891 and again in 1892 expressed himself strongly against Gladstone's "mad step," which would "bring ruin and misery on the whole of Egypt," now counseled Rosebery, who hardly required the new stiffening, to resist Gladstone at all costs. Rhodes had insisted that his earlier gift of £5,000 to the Liberal party be devoted to charity if Gladstone remained "obdurate" and "scuttled" Egypt. Now he countered the arguments of both Gladstone and Harcourt in a long letter from Cairo, where he had talked with Lord Cromer. "If you go out you will have greater difficulties . . . with your neighbours [the French]. . . . By remaining," he urged sagely, "you keep order and give no excuse for raising the Egyptian question. If you retired disorder is bound to arise, followed naturally by European complication, and as to the argument that it will remove all misunderstandings with France and promote a cordial feeling between the two people I do not believe one word of it." The French would continue to dislike the English "in proportion to our prosperity."

Britain stayed in Egypt, gradually exercising more and more direct power. In late 1892, partially as a result of Rhodes' urgings, Rosebery dispatched a commission, led by Sir Gerald Portal, former consul general at Zanzibar, and including Frank Rhodes, to ascertain whether or not Britain should keep Uganda. The commission's composition, Rosebery's firm instructions to Portal, and the inclusion of Frank Rhodes ensured but one result—a positive one that led to a major addition to Britain's empire and its inner African responsibilities. Rhodes, for his part, hoped that Rosebery would ask Frank to remain in Uganda as an administrator so that Rhodes would "be able to deal with him from the South and help him privately if he wants aid beyond your parliamentary vote." Rhodes was spreading familial imperial wings. "I think my brother will do far more good in working in Uganda," he gave paternal counsel, "than wasting his life in London." Following Marcus Aurelius' strictures, Rhodes feared random, goalless activity as much as he feared passivity and inaction, and feared it in his kin as well as in himself.

Britain kept Uganda officially in 1894. But Cecil Rhodes failed immediately to receive the blessings of the Germans or King Léopold for a telegraph line along either the eastern or western shores of Lake Tanganyika. At one point he pleaded with Henry M. Stanley, the explorer: "Kindly go to the King . . . and get me the right to come up his side of the Lake Tanganyika. . . . Be good enough to do this at once as it will influence me as to which side I shall take. I prefer the Belgian's territory," he dissembled.[36]

That ploy failed; so did more direct entreaties. And the Germans turned a deaf ear until Rhodes undertook personal negotiations in 1899. Rhodes never lived to make the final transcontinental connection by wire.

But he did live to see the ruler of all the Ottomans, to make his way through historic Italy and Egypt, and to see the glorious ruins of Greece. In London, the focus of his many overseas trips, he was fêted as royalty during the first half of the 1890s, implored to dine or stay with political and financial barons, and even commanded to appear before the Queen, who admired his insouciant energy and his ability to extend the empire. During 1894–95, Rhodes arrived in London in mid-November, spoke to a wildly enthusiastic and overflowing audience at the annual meeting of the British South Africa Company, busied himself with negotiations at the Foreign Office, where he was described as a "hustler," and was endlessly in demand. "I met Rhodes at dinner last night," Sir Hercules Robinson reported. Overlooking Rhodes' "haggard" and "worn out" appearance, he said in December that Rhodes was "in great form and being made much of all round." He had been to Windsor and was on his way to Mentmore, Lord Rosebery's estate. Harcourt, the chancellor of the exchequer and in some ways Rhodes' nemesis, tried to persuade him to spend Christmas at the family estate in the New Forest. "You cannot transact any business in London at Christmas . . . and we could sell you any number of telegraph poles here."[37]

Even Sultan Abdul Hamid of the Ottoman Empire wanted to see Rhodes. In early 1895 Rhodes traveled to Constantinople (Istanbul) for the sake of goats. The Cape already raised Angora goats for their wool, but the mohair of South Africa was poorer in quality than the true Angora wool which was spun from the purebred goats of the Anatolian steppes. The Ottomans closely protected their monopoly of such stock. It was Rhodes' intent to persuade the sultan to let him take Angora goats back to the Cape to improve the colony's breed. Many in the Cape and Europe doubted that even Rhodes, possessed of a smooth tongue and abundant other charms, could accomplish such a deed. The British ambassador to the Ottoman court, shocked that Rhodes would arrive for such an important interview in an old flannel suit instead of morning dress, also wondered how his errand could possibly succeed. After Rhodes slipped into the ambassador's dark overcoat, using it as a substitute for the prescribed attire, he then suffered the unaccustomed indignity of cooled heels. "[I] had to wait nearly half an hour," Rhodes confessed, "because the Sultan was engaged with an Indian rajah." He nearly walked out, so great was his indignation. But he realized that he had submitted [himself] to that indignity by going to see the Sultan in the first place, and waiting impotently on a potentate was worth the chance to improve the Cape's strain of goats.[38] The sultan liked the young magnate and consented to the export of prized Angora stock to the Cape. It is to this visit that South Africa owes its success as an exporter of mohair in the early years of the twentieth century.

At the beginning of 1895 Rosebery also made Rhodes a member of the Privy Council. The only flaw in this swath of triumph across Europe was that some member, probably Blunt, blackballed his admission to the Traveller's Club, for which Rhodes had not applied. Later, another, even more prestigious London club, the Athenaeum, was pleased to enroll him.

Immediately before Rhodes came to Europe in 1894, he and Hammond had inspected the mining prospects of Rhodesia. That journey was fateful, for it focused Rhodes the entrepreneur on the real promise of the Rand and away from the mineralized chimera of his interior colony. Rhodes had wanted Hammond's opinion of the potential of the newly conquered country of the Ndebele. Although he still believed in a Rhodesian Rand, Churchill's experts had earlier spoken and written negatively. Rhodes perceived that he could hardly continue praising its prospects, and those of Shonaland, if there were none. An objective appraisal by a recognized expert was essential.

In September 1894, as soon as parliament was adjourned, Rhodes, Jameson, Sir John Willoughby, Maurice Gifford, Robert Williams, Hammond, and three of Hammond's associates started on their survey. They visited ancient workings, including Great Zimbabwe. Hammond took careful note of the overall geology of the young colony. Rhodes refrained from interfering. Ultimately, Hammond decided that the promising portions of Rhodesia contained many true fissure veins which probably persisted in depth, but in no way resembled those of the Rand.

Hammond believed his report cautious. Rutherfoord Harris called it a disaster. Rhodes, his pessimistic fears supported, took the analysis by Hammond with stoic equanimity. "It's the report of a conscientious engineer. . . ."[39] Others, notably Jameson, used it to paint a promising future for the territory. In its generalities and in its weak encouragement to prospectors, it proved accurate. Rhodesians did discover very rich, if limited, gold mines and large deposits of chrome, nickel, copper, and coal. Substantial industries later developed. But what Hammond correctly discerned and Rhodes assuredly noted was that no second Rand—no vast, long stretching seam of payable ore—would be found in Rhodesia. The Witwatersrand deposits were unique and were unlikely to be duplicated. Hence Rhodes would be wise to focus his considerable financial energies on the as yet imperfectly cornered, still greatly underdeveloped Transvaal. There the gold would last for decades, if not a century or two. It would make Beit, Wernher, Eckstein, Barnato, Joseph Robinson—even Rudd and Rhodes—incredible fortunes. It would also enrich the coffers of the otherwise weak, poor, and isolated but pretentious Boer state. If President Kruger and his Afrikaner allies shed their poverty and after a few years emerged secure and strong, then federation, a united South Africa under British rule, and the enduring legacy of what Rhodes was bent on creating would be shattered. Hammond's report was the first of the significant catalysts which were to propel Rhodes toward the crisis of conspiracy.

"*Jameson Must Be Mad*"
The Raid and Its Consequences

R HODES TURNED FORTY-TWO in mid-1895. The easy-going, wide-eyed vicar's son who had walked boldly down the *Eudora*'s gangplank in 1870
had become an imperious, steely-looking, determined potentate of unrivaled
economic, diplomatic, and political influence. Descended from a long line of
prosperous yeomen and bankers, and a single clergyman, Rhodes had already
outstripped them all in accomplishment, affluence, and sheer power. He was
famous and renowned beyond all expectation; an empire builder as well as
an entrepreneur and amalgamator without peer, he had created states and
ruled them still. He had made war and won against heavy odds. He had claimed,
brutally acquired, and both occupied and governed interior territories on behalf of the Crown. After the triumph of De Beers and the successful investment in gold had come the Royal Charter, the invasion of Shonaland, and the
simple, wildly victorious campaign against the numerous Ndebele. He had a
railway and a telegraph line. Siding with Sivewright, he had risen politically
above the principled trio of Merriman, Innes, and Sauer in 1893 and tightened his already powerful alliance with Jan Hofmeyr's Afrikaner Bond. On
their joint behalf, and to the acute distress of Africans, he had pushed through
parliament laws restricting the exercise of the African franchise and the growth
of large-scale African farming. He was credited with having resolved the "race"
question—the antagonism of English- and Dutch-speaking South Africans. He
had a country named after him, and the ear of everyone important in Britain.
Before the end of 1895, Britain was to give him a measure of influence over
the destiny of Bechuanaland (Botswana). An object of widespread idolatry, he
was the lion of every season, a favorite of the Queen, a true and worthy Roman possessed of territory, talent, ego fulfillment, and riches. Even his wildest
dreams were being realized. Posterity was his to acquire. Objectively, Rhodes
required little more.

Yet it was his very success—the unusual degree to which his imaginings had become real—that sowed the seeds of disaster. The primitive omnipotence which lies at the heart of narcissistic grandiosity and, with an assist from biological predisposition, drives clinical mania, is held in check for most people by the relentless returns of less-than-perfect success. Those with expansive tendencies whose expansiveness succeeds can easily be persuaded of their invulnerability to failure. The critical powers of analysis and calculation of the odds which underwrite the transformation of possibilities into certainty can be paralyzed by success, especially if it comes early and easily. So it may have been that Rhodes and his associates, having so frequently accomplished the barely possible, began to feel that whatever they tried would be achieved.

William Thomas Stead, Rhodes' confidant and admirer, and Sir H. Rider Haggard, the celebrated author, both remembered Rhodes being at "the zenith of his power" or the "height of his success" in 1894–95. "I saw Rhodes several times," recalled Haggard. "I remember going to breakfast with him at the Burlington Hotel. . . . Already before breakfast a number of people, some of them well known . . . were waiting about in ante-rooms on the chance of getting a word with or a favour from the great man. It reminded me of . . . Dr. Johnson and others hanging about in the vestibule of . . . Lord Chesterfield's apartment for a like object. There was the same air of patient expectancy upon their faces. In a china bowl on a table I observed a great accumulation of unopened letters. . . . It was . . . one of the habits of the Rhodes entourage not to trouble to open letters that came by post. . . . They only attended to those that were sent by hand, or to telegrams. . . ."

"Alike in London and in South Africa," said Stead, "every obstacle seemed to bend before [Rhodes'] determined will. . . . In Rhodesia the impis of Lobengula had been shattered, and a territory as large as the German Empire had been won for civilisation. . . . When he left England everything seemed to point to his being able to carry out his greater scheme, when we should be able to undertake the propagation of 'our ideas' [of a Jesuitical secret society] on a wider scale throughout the world."[1] Rhodes hardly needed a fiasco like the Raid.

Nevertheless, beginning a year before and continuing throughout the balance of 1895, Rhodes and Jameson, and Rhodes, Beit, Rosebery, Chamberlain, and dozens of important others, hatched a tendentious and risky scheme to subvert President Kruger's hold on the Transvaal and make, by an invasion linked to armed revolt, that interior Afrikaner stronghold British. Ostensibly, there were grievances sufficient to justify an attack; the Rand mines had attracted (or so it was believed) more Britons and other English-speakers to Johannesburg than Kruger could count Afrikaners throughout the whole of his territory. The labor of these immigrants thus funded Kruger's autocratic rule. But he had refused to give them the vote. They were taxed without adequate representation. Rhodes could argue that he alone was capable of creating conditions favorable to the Transvaal's true manifest destiny; only he and his associates could fold the new province of gold into the empire where it and all of its people naturally belonged.

These were among the arguments which were mustered at the time and since to justify a planned incursion led by Rhodes' closest associate and carried out by a small force of volunteers and police. It was supposed to rendezvous with rebels in Johannesburg. But it proved a debacle and earned the pejorative sobriquet "Raid," derailing much of what Rhodes had set so magnificently in motion. Ever since, it has baffled those who seek answers to the tough questions posed by events. Was it necessary? Was the moment opportune? How could it have happened? Rhodes himself in 1899 told a tutor from Oriel that the Raid would not be "understood" in his own lifetime, "perhaps never." "Only psychiatry," Blainey suggested, ". . .could explain why Rhodes, for so long a brilliant seeker and creative wielder of economic and political power, should have become in 1895 a capitalist who half forgets where his capital is and a politician who tries to destroy himself."[2] Or did he?

Similar arguments to those advanced by Rhodes were powerful and persuasive in local and British circles when the country of the Mpondo or the Ndebele had been at risk. Yet the Transvaal was not another Pondoland, and, however barbaric Kruger might have seemed to visitors from afar, he could never be dismissed as a naked savage like Lobengula. His was a recognized nation-state—an interior outpost of pastoralism which had gained German as well as Cape Dutch sympathy. To invade the Transvaal would be piracy. For a British subject to do so was a violation of the Foreign Enlistment Act. The Transvaal may have looked and felt like yet another obstinate obstacle to Rhodes' union of South Africa—a South Africa dominated by English-speaking whites and their Cape Afrikaner allies—but Britain was bound by past policy to respect the Transvaal's autonomy. So was the Cape. Whereas Rhodes could transgress moral norms with comparative impunity so long as only indigenous Africans were involved, abusing the rights of states and attacking indigenous whites would flaunt both propriety and law. Privy councillors and prime ministers were expected to be more punctilious and upright. Moreover, Rhodes had promised not to abuse his dual position as premier of the Cape and managing director of the British South Africa Company.

Rhodes knew right from wrong and risk from certainty. The invasion of the Transvaal was premeditated, long incubated, connived at extensively and expensively, and was not merely opportunistic. In its complexity, it was no sudden aberration of a brilliant mind temporarily deranged. Although the English-speaking bourgeoisie of Johannesburg—the mine managers, retailers, and wealthier diggers—had agitated periodically from 1890 against the supposedly cruel exactions and iniquities of Kruger's government, their combinations and mobilizations of sentiment would have led nowhere, especially in the unusually prosperous months of late 1895, without the forcing hand of Rhodes (and Beit). Rhodes and Beit possessed material as well as potential political interests in the outcome of the agitation for change on the Rand. They owned the risky new deep-level mining properties and stood to profit appreciably by a radical change of regime. By contrast, the owners and managers of the older outcrop properties largely kept aloof from the rebellion; they were making money from stock exchange manipulations or had been able to make their own deals with Kruger. Those whose fortunes were tied up with the future profits of Rand Mines, Consolidated Gold Fields, and other deep-level estates formed the core of the conspiracy that was promoted and funded by Rhodes and Beit.

Because exploiting the deep levels tied up so much capital and was initially much more expensive than outcrop mining, the high costs imposed by Kruger's dynamite monopoly worried those who sought their gold well below the surface, where the compact conglomerate demanded increased quantities of gelignite. Labor costs as a percentage of total costs were also higher underground, and the deep-level firms, in particular, desired governmental controls which would increase the supply and efficiency of their labor. Kruger's refusal to join Rhodes' railway rates union raised the price of coal, which affected the deep-level mines adversely. Kruger's taxing policy also favored the outcrop over the deep-level firms. Several of the leading rebels believed that if they could produce a more efficient administration in the Transvaal, then they could reduce their expenses (and increase their profits) by up to 20 percent.

Because Rhodes' largest source of income by 1895 was gold, he certainly might have had a "strong incentive to rescue his company from the dangers of Krugerdom." Blainey suggests that the Raid "was essentially the revolt of the two big companies that were heirs to the treasures and problems of the deep-levels," and Mendelsohn suggests that these same firms stood to lower their costs to achieve better financial terms if the behavior of the Transvaal's government could be influenced substantially.[3] Certainly Rhodes and Beit would have been economically advantaged by a successful rising which resulted in a new government led by Rhodes' henchmen. But was such a result inevitable or even likely? Until the very eve of the Raid, leading Uitlanders, or foreigners, in Johannesburg disagreed about whether they sought to achieve a reformed Transvaal, an autonomous but non-Afrikaner and only informally British-dominated Transvaal, or a state which would form a part of a Cape-influenced united South Africa.

Although Rhodes and British officials worried about a revolution, the results of which they could not control, and thus sought to harness its energies for their own purposes, those purposes were not exclusively financial. Moreover, was the economic motive as sufficient as it may have been necessary? And would the web of conspiracy have stretched as far as London if Rhodes' primary grasp had been merely capitalistic? Would he have risked political primacy and imperial standing, much less real power, for cash alone? The naked economic argument is too simplistic.

British imperialists, whether Liberals, Conservatives, or the Unionists who followed Joseph Chamberlain, clearly favored a coup which would oust Kruger and knit the Transvaal into the empire. They regarded the autonomy of the Transvaal as temporary and anomalous—an unfortunate legacy of previous British policy errors. Given the menacing pretensions of Germany, they believed that the Transvaal belonged within the empire. They had no particular desire to see it annexed to Rhodes' sub-imperial conglomerate, but to achieve their own ends without antagonizing him they had little choice but to avail themselves opportunistically of Rhodes' energy, capital, and strategic position.

Even in the 1890s Britain sought territory and hegemony only on the cheap, as a byproduct of other initiatives. Moreover, as much as British statesmen might align themselves with Rhodes, they were distinctly unprepared to do so publicly. Over the Raid their involvement was intended to be covert, deniable, accessory, and, if necessary, hypocritical. "It would be better," Lord Salisbury, Britain's careful and upright prime minister, told Chamberlain, "if the revolution which transfers the Transvaal to British rulers were entirely the result of the action of internal forces, and not of Cecil Rhodes' intervention, or of ours."[4]

As they conspired together, Rhodes and Jameson could not have ignored the consequences of failure. Yet, as true buccaneers with an astonishing string of successes—the invasion by pioneer column, the conquest of Ndebeleland, the grabbing of trans-Zambezia—they gambled wildly on success. Their hubris was to assume that the smash-and-grab tactics that worked across the Limpopo would work across the Vaal. They also gambled (as they had before) that the consequences of anything less than a clearly positive result could somehow be parried by the exercise of their still formidable interpersonal skills, Rhodes' extraordinary world prominence, and—not least—the web of intrigue into which they had ensnared persons of prominence in official and political circles. Butler concludes that Jameson "crossed the border confident that he would stir Johannesburg to revolt, and that the British Government would have to back him."[5] But when Jameson bolted he possessed substantial indications that the rebellious reformers of the city of gold would not and could not stir. Signals from London via Rhodes might have misled him about Britain, but if they had, it would have been Jameson's willful misreading of the signals rather than the signals themselves. Possibly, too, propelled as they were by their victories, the conspirators simply excluded prospects of failure from their calculations. If so, Rhodes had indeed become a true Roman. Blinded by his rapid rise to greatness, he no longer planned against defeat, but instead presumed upon fate and the gods. Hitherto Rhodes had been disciplined, cautious, invariably fastidious about preparing the stages of any consequential advance. Was he suddenly careless or foolhardy in 1895?

Much more than the original circumvention of Lobengula or the conquest of Ndebeleland, the Raid depended for its success upon a long chain of carefully interlocking circumstance, each link of which was in turn dependent upon the actions and initiatives of one or more individuals or groups over which Rhodes could exercise less than his usual control and surveillance. Too much was left to chance.

For the Raid to prove effective, English-speaking Johannesburg had to rise in an outburst of indignation and take the city of 51,000 whites (40,000 of whom were Uitlanders), 4,000 Asians, and 42,000 Africans against Kruger's Boer commandos. The English miners had to be united, numerous, and well armed. Rhodes and his henchmen supplied the arms, crates of which were hidden under loads of coal or in false oil drums shipped into Johannesburg in the weeks before the rising. But instead of 7500 armed men, secretly prepared to precise temper for months beforehand, hapless, charming Frank Rhodes and the other conspirators in the city could recruit only a half-hearted 200 to 400, and Colonel Rhodes admitted to one participant that he himself could count on no more than 100. Even that small crowd hardly ever drilled together, and nearly all of them—especially their leaders—lost interest well before the assault. Cecil Rhodes himself told Garrett later that the performance of his brother Frank demonstrated "the difference between a brave soldier and a *man for a crisis.*"[6] Indeed, rather than emboldened, frustrated, sorely aggrieved patriots, like the Minute-men of Lexington and Concord in 1775, the reform crowd of late 1895 Johannesburg was enjoying wealth and the good life of midsummer, while Jameson drilled in forlorn Pitsani, 176 miles to the west. Choosing the Christmas season for a revolt was folly. Moreover, F. Rutherfoord Harris, Rhodes' prime purveyor of arms and much else, purchased only 3,000 rifles, and no Maxims. By the time that Jameson marched, none of the arms had even been unpacked from its protective grease.

In addition to a successful rising, Jameson and Rhodes assumed that the men of Johannesburg would be able to mount a lightning assault on the thinly defended Pretoria armory, thus destroying or capturing the bulk of the Transvaal's arsenal and limiting Kruger's ability to defend his state. This aim was not as inherently absurd as hindsight would suggest. But the conspirators forgot or omitted to note that the celebration of a Dutch festival would occur at Christmas, and would attract to Pretoria thousands of Kruger's armed faithful from the near and far reaches of the Transvaal. Those who rose in Johannesburg could not invest the arsenal and capture its 10,000 rifles, ten or twelve field guns, and 12 million rounds of ammunition with so many defenders about. Nor could the Johannesburg cabal count upon or even attempt to recruit the kinds of English-speaking numbers which would guarantee the success of the Pretoria caper. Without such a planned-for immobilization of Afrikaner defenses, Jameson might well have never started.

At the Pitsani end, too, Jameson had enlisted fewer soldiers and police than he had hoped. His plan called for 1500 mounted men and 3000 rifles. Many who knew about the Raid assumed that he had marched with 700, but at the final hour only 494 started with him for Johannesburg. There were few spare weapons. Jameson, no soldier, believed or at least boasted that he could best the Boers with 500 men armed with bull whips—that he could simply "blow them away." ("Simply" was his favorite word.) The easy victory over the Ndebele had given him confidence and overconfidence. Much of it was based on the Maxim gun. It had mowed down the spear-wielding Ndebele like a scythe among the corn. The Afrikaners had a few cannon, lots of trusted rifles and elephant guns, but no machine guns. Jameson thus based his insouciance on the eight Maxims that he had hauled from Rhodesia. "You do not know the Maxim gun," Jameson told the doubting Frederic Hamilton. "I shall draw a zone of lead a mile each side of my column and no Boer will be able

to Bulawayo
c. 65 miles

SOUTHERN RHODESIA
(ZIMBABWE)

SOUTH AFRICA
NORTHWESTERN AREA

Francis-
town
TATI
DISTRICT
Tati
Shashi
Tuli

TATI

Macloutsie

Limpopo

ZOUTPANSBERGE

Louis Trichardt

Letaba

Olifants

MOZAMBIQUE

Serowe
Palapye

NGWATO

Shoshong

Magalakwin

Patala

Pietersburg

DRAKENSBERGE

Pilgrim's
Rest

Lydenburg

Komati-
poort

Crocodile

BECHUANA-
LAND
(BOTSWANA)

KGATLA

TULI BLOCK

Limpopo

Crocodile

Nylstroom

Barberton
Komati

Mbabane
SWAZILAND

KWENA

Molepolole
Gaborone

Notwani

Marico

T R A N S V A A L

Middelburg

Pretoria

Vaal

Rustenburg

Johannesburg

Heidelberg

Standerton

Volksrust

NGWAKETSE
Pitsani

Lobatse

Zeerust

Vaal

Vrede

Newcastle

Mafeking

Lichtenburg

Potchefstroom

Frankfort

Malopo

GOSHEN

Klerksdorp

O R A N G E

Harrismith

Ladysmith

Valsch

Kroonstad

Bethlehem

NATAL

Vryburg

STELLALAND

Harts

Bloemhof

Vaal

Vet

Zand

Winburg

Leribe

BASUTO-
LAND
(LESOTHO)

Taung

Christiana

F R E E

Kuruman

Fourteen
Streams

Brandfort

Maseru

Hebron

Boshof

Modder

Barkly West

Bloemfontein

Pniel

Kimberley

C A P E

GRIQUALAND

WEST

Riet

Riet

Bethanie

Mafeteng

Jagersfontein

DRAKENSBERGE

Griquatown

S T A T E

Caledon

Orange

Hopetown

Orange

Bethulie

C O L O N Y

Orange

Colesberg

0   km   150
0   Miles   100

to live in it."[7] But Jameson forgot that the Afrikaners were good marksmen and might command the heights. Moreover, the Maxims overheated and burst if they were not cooled by water. Would Jameson be able to keep his Maxims in service? Would he be able to carry enough ammunition for the Maxims, rifles, and small arms, or would he and his men exhaust themselves and their supplies in combat with determined defenders? Jameson told Rhodes that he would be able to cover the 176 miles to Johannesburg in two days when four or five—dragging cannon and machine guns, bivouacking, and caring for horses, there were never enough of those—was a closer approximation. Why did Rhodes believe Jameson?

There were a host of exuberant miscalculations. One of the most damaging was the easy assumption that the rising in Johannesburg and Jameson's massing at Pitsani could remain secret. As Lord Bryce reported, "People . . . talked of a conspiracy, but never before was there, except on stage, so open a conspiracy. Two thirds of the action . . . went on before the public. The visitor had hardly installed himself in a hotel at Pretoria [in December 1895] before people began to tell him that an insurrection was imminent, that arms were being imported, that Maxim guns were being hidden. . . ."[8] Kruger and Kruger's adjutants learned that something was awry, certainly by 24 December. They had even begun to appease the settlers in Johannesburg with concessions, when the Raid interrupted a meeting of the Volksraad, or Transvaal legislature. Moreover, Jameson's program of action was predicated on his ability to slip away from Pitsani without Kruger knowing. Surprise was a key variable. But to arrive stealthily in Johannesburg, without interference, and with the Maxims still cool, depended upon the telegraph lines being cut. This task Jameson's men accomplished as far as the lines to the south. But either the assigned man, as received word would have it, was so drunk that he cut and buried a farmer's fence instead of the telegraph lines, or Jameson's reconnaissance omitted to note that a branch line went north via Zeerust to Rustenburg to Pretoria; it was never sundered. Kruger was apprised hourly of Jameson's movements.

Everything surprised Jameson, who had no intimate knowledge of the ground between Pitsani and Johannesburg, and very little astonished Kruger. Jameson asserted that his raw recruits were trained well enough for the rigors of the march and could give a good account of themselves in battle. Jameson (and Rhodes) assumed that Lieutenant Colonel Sir John Willoughby, an arrogant thirty-five-year-old fashion plate who had been a transport officer in Rhodesia, could lead troops and had the tactical sense to outwit and outflank the wily Afrikaners who would be apt to comprise the bulk of Kruger's tenacious defense. Jameson depended upon supplies of food cached along the way and fresh horses stabled there to replace his men's tired mounts. But these logistics were not directly in Jameson's hands; the men of Johannesburg detailed one of their own to provide provisions, and he was among those many in the city of gold who were dumbfounded when Jameson actually trekked. Likewise, just as Jameson's invasion was intended to respond to a widespread rising, so did Jameson's progress depend upon assistance from men coming out from Johannesburg to meet and strengthen the raiding column.

Each of these details provided a crucial link in the chain of circumstance that would make the Raid possible. Each broken link weakened the chain and made a decisive Raid less likely. But the weakest link was the first, the one on which Rhodes, Chamberlain, and the men in Johannesburg so depended. As Garrett wrote after the Raid, "Jameson has spoiled all—given us all away—damned Rhodes and himself and the future of South Africa." Jameson was the heart of the matter. All the preparations for the rising, the interplay of each of the complex variables that made up the plot's seamless web, focused on Jameson. His good sense, his critical judgment, his timing, and his leadership were all essential to the Raid and its objectives. The reformers in Johannesburg, Secretary of State for the Colonies Joseph Chamberlain, others in London, and even Harris and Rhodes in Cape Town, professed never to have believed that Jameson would attack before there was an uprising. Nor could they have assumed that he would commence the long march despite explicit pleas from Johannesburg and Cape Town to desist. Rhodes relied ultimately upon Jameson's patience, if not his sense. But neither Jameson nor Rhodes could handle inaction. Little Jameson was impulsive at the best of times, headstrong, and determined to play the hero. Brazen before, he had always received congratulations for intuitive calculations against overwhelming odds and enemies. Why not also against the Boers, whom he had always underestimated? Rhodes was Jameson's dearest friend, his confidant, his co-conspirator, his patron, and his leader. Yet in all of those capacities Rhodes' fate was hostage to Jameson's confidence, common sense, and, decisively, caprice. As Rhodes exclaimed on the horrible day: "Old Jameson has upset my applecart. . . . Twenty years we have been friends, and now he goes and ruins me."[9]

Rhodes failed to appreciate that not only Jameson's character but his early years of training as a surgeon added substantially to their mutual risk. Surgeons then, even more than now, were trained to make decisions on inadequate information. Once a surgeon decided to operate, his task was to carry out the procedure without hesitation or equivocation, either of which could be hazardous to the patient. Jameson, by nature a man of action who was confident of his surgical skills, understandably may have transferred that familiar style to his African adventures.

Even if Jameson's temperament and training induced disaster, Rhodes—the master of detail, the careful planner, the patient squarer—should have realized months before the Raid that too much was being left to chance, and that the statistical odds were defiantly poor. Any manager as good as Rhodes would have regrouped. He would have done so in November and certainly in early December, when his Johannesburg confidants, including his brother Frank, cast doubt on the reliability of the revolutionaries, on their preparations, and on the eagerness of the participants to do anything other than go to the "horse races," and on the general mood of lassitude. "So long as people are making money," Frank warned Cecil, ". . . they will endure a great many political wrongs. . . . Nothing is being done beyond a few desultory telegrams and deputations. . . ."[10] Thus wrote the man in charge of fomenting the local disturbances.

If Rhodes had questioned Rutherfoord Harris he would have learned that the guns and men were vastly fewer than had been assumed in the original blueprint. Until the very day and, indeed, the very hour of the rising, Rhodes was given opportunity after opportunity to call off or at least postpone the Raid. In the final moments before the wires were cut and communications became impossible, Rhodes received ample evidence that disaster was likely. Yet he never personally pulled Jameson back. Masochistically, cavalierly, absurdly, foolishly, or because of his love for Jameson and that part of himself which was grounded in the childhood defiance of the bearded, patriarchal Kruger, Rhodes let Jameson plunge them both into the abyss of renegade despair.

If there remain lingering questions about Rhodes' behavior at the very end, when Jameson was about to march, Rhodes' responsibility for the Raid—whatever he told the Select Committee of Inquiry of the House of Commons and however much Chamberlain and imperial officialdom share his culpability—is fully established and damaging. The research of the last fifty years has largely satisfied most remaining doubts about how best to apportion blame among the many significant conspirators and fellow travelers. What remains murky is not their motives, for most have been properly discerned, but the reasons for the ultimate irrationality and foolhardiness of Rhodes and Jameson, and particularly Rhodes. The bizarre quality of the final catastrophe becomes apparent the more the careful, early preparations for the Raid are contrasted with the progress of the Raid itself. Doing so also adds to an appreciation of Rhodes' harsh methods during the mid-1890s, when all his other endeavors were coming up trumps.

The trail of deceit begins in late 1894, stimulated or aroused by John Hays Hammond's modest assessment of the auriferous prospects for Rhodesia. (Even earlier, Lionel Phillips discussed a possible revolution with Beit and asked if he should consult Rhodes. He had been urged to do so by "the Gold Fields people," but he wondered whether he would be wise "to trust Rhodes's advice." He asked Beit to cable " 'See Rhodes' " if Beit "trusted Rhodes." Then Phillips would run down to Cape Town, but his own feeling was to be cautious, "to wait and watch" and to "spend some money in trying to improve the Raad," the Transvaal's legislature. Beit may have talked to Rhodes, but there is no evidence that Phillips saw Rhodes as early as mid-1894.)[11]

There would be no second Rand, Hammond concluded. Rhodes ought to stick with the first, where the deep levels were expected to prove immensely rich. With taxes on gold and gold mining operations cascading into Kruger's once empty treasury, and the prospect of much more to come, it was obvious to Rhodes and Hammond that the Transvaal would soon grow too wealthy to subvert. The capitalists of the Rand might even become content and complacent, particularly if Kruger were to accede to some of their requests. When Hammond told Rhodes of the sentiment in Johannesburg that favored and might lead to a homemade revolution, Rhodes grew equally alarmed. Remembering the Black Flag agitation twenty years before in Kimberley, Rhodes feared the unpredictable consequences of any local rising not inspired by him or beholden to his aims. "You might be sure," Rhodes remarked after the Raid, "that I was not going to risk my position to change President Kruger for President J.B. Robinson," long an arch-rival. Bower remembered him saying specifically that if there were a revolution, he meant to control it. Otherwise, South Africa was "done for." If Rhodes were to realize a unified South Africa in his lifetime, early and concerted intervention was essential. He told Low in early 1896 specifically that he had " 'joined with the wealthy men [in Johannesburg] who were ready to give their money to overthrow Kruger so that we might be able to turn the revolution in the right direction at the right time.' " He " 'went into the movement" because the revolution, without him, would have sooner or later succeeded. "Then the money of the capitalists, the influence of the leading men of Johannesburg, would have been used in favour of [a] new and more powerful Republican Government, which would have drifted away from the Empire and drawn all South Africa—English as well as Dutch— after it.' " The last consideration was overriding. Rhodes, concluded Low, "considered it necessary that the overthrow of the Kruger tyranny should *not* be the unaided work of the oppressed Uitlanders themselves." [12]

Rhodes' meeting with Kruger in 1894, after returning from Rhodesia, advanced his growing determination to seize the Rand while Kruger remained comparatively weak and isolated. Earlier, Carl Meyer had described Kruger as a "queer old Boer, ugly, badly dressed and ill-mannered, but a splendid type all the same and a very impressive speaker." Lionel Phillips, president of the Chamber of Mines, called him a "peasant farmer of acute intelligence and dominating will, but unhappily of little education." Others noted that he spat profusely and unashamedly, spraying onlookers intemperately. Uncouth, and also stern, irascible, remote, paternal, and uncompromising, Kruger could fatefully have challenged Rhodes' sense of control and maturity. As far as Rhodes was concerned, Kruger was a negative obstructionist, like his own father.

Although there is no surviving record of their interview early on a warm October morning, Kruger apparently shook his fist at Rhodes. The two men of strong will intensified their existing dislike and distrust of one another. Kruger clearly would not be squared. Rhodes, in turn, appeared to personify what Afrikaners call "slimness." To quote Olive Schreiner again, Rhodes simply "wriggled, wriggled, wriggled." [13] The dynamism of their discord propelled Rhodes, the supremely successful man of action, to do what he did best: to conspire and then to act decisively. Kruger then and at later points in the days before the actual Raid was content to wait patiently until the tortoise ventured out of its carapace. "When I want to kill a tortoise," Kruger was wont to caution his colleagues, "I wait until he sticks his head out." [14]

Precipitated by Hammond's report, the news of Johannesburg, and the impulses aroused within him by Kruger, Rhodes' activity was also impelled by conversations in London in late 1894. The Marquess of Winchester specifically suggests that the Raid was planned in the Burlington Hotel in London by Rhodes, Jameson, Maguire, and others.[15] The Liberals were still in power and were Rhodes' allies. He felt particularly comfortable with Rosebery, because they were both imperialists and believers in a strong and all-powerful Britain, and possibly also because they both tended to prefer the company of men like themselves. Ripon, at the Colonial Office, was a pushover. Many of his officials, like Sir Robert Herbert, Sir Robert Meade, and Edward Fairfield, had been won over by Rhodes' boldness and bullying. Rhodes could anticipate cooperation so long as the Liberals remained in office. If Lord Salisbury returned at the head of a Conservative/Unionist regime, unctuous rectitude might prevail, and conspiratorial involvement prove impossible. The hatching of likely schemes was thus influenced by Rhodes' affinity for the Liberals, by the romantic support of sympathetic opinion-makers such as Stead and Flora Shaw, by what Rhodes sensed to be a sentiment favorable to himself in London, and by the lavish attention that he received in 1894–95 from the Queen and her worthies. That the Liberals easily acceded to the first of his overt maneuvers only strengthened Rhodes' faith in what he might originally have viewed as a simple little enterprise.

Governor and High Commissioner Sir Henry Brougham Loch was an obstacle. If Rhodes were to loosen Kruger's hold on the Transvaal, Loch must go. Not only did they detest each other personally, they were also rivals, representing opposed approaches to approximately the same objectives. If Rhodes inspired or arranged a coup, he wanted his own sub-imperial system to benefit. Loch vastly preferred direct intervention by the Crown. He was a metropolitan imperialist. That he had failed in 1893–94 to substitute the Crown for the Company in Ndebeleland gave Rhodes no confidence that Loch, or any like-minded successor, would not succeed in the more propitious circumstances of a Johannesburg rising. Loch, an ex-cavalryman more rash even than Rhodes, was as anxious as his premier to oust Kruger and annex his state. Graham Bower, Loch's deputy and long-serving imperial secretary, described the governor as "hot-headed, vain, impulsive, and with strong likes and dislikes. . . . I spent my time . . . figuratively holding on to his coattails."[16]

Rhodes wanted Loch out of the way, not least because Loch had his own imperial plan for a fomented rising and British military intervention from across the Transvaal border. Loch's tumultuous and triumphant visit to Johannesburg in June 1894 had stiffened the high commissioner's desire to arrange a rising and a coup. Rhodes, who made Loch's endeavor his own, wanted no competition. Nor could Rhodes have countenanced Loch's independence. Their temperaments clashed; most of all, Loch refused to subordinate himself to the premier's will.

Within days of his arrival in Britain in 1894, Rhodes had therefore moved against Loch. "I have done well," Rhodes told Sprigg, "and I think H.M. Government will carry out our views. The Governor will return home almost immediately and will not come back." Two months later, from the R.M.S. *Athenian* steaming for South Africa, Rhodes wrote more diplomatically to Earl Grey that "H.M. Government wish to see Sir H. Loch leave . . . as he would naturally oppose [the transfer of Bechuanaland] as he likes to have large tracts of country . . . under his direct government, and the policy I am sketching would be clipping his wings."[17] Loch's term was over anyway. He was not reappointed, a rejection for which he was consoled with the conferment of a baronetcy.

Even more audacious than Loch's removal at Rhodes' behest was his replacement by a doddering, dropsy-inflicted, clearly compliant, aging sycophant who was almost literally in Rhodes' pocket and could be counted upon to do his bidding. Sir Hercules Robinson (later ennobled as the first Baron Rosmead) had been removed as governor of South Africa in 1890 because of his ties to Rhodes and because it was suspected that he had been bought. Chamberlain loathed him. As early as mid-1894, Rhodes flattered Robinson with the suggestion that he should come back to the Cape. When the rising occurred, a friendly British arbitrator would be required.

Even the Queen believed such a blatant appointment unwise, and Rosebery and Ripon were so skeptical that they kept the nomination from the cabinet until it was too late to be stopped. Sir William Harcourt read about Robinson's return in the press in March 1895 and was enraged. Clearly, said Harcourt, the chancellor of the exchequer, Robinson was "the nominee of Rhodes to carry out his political ideas and financial interests." Chamberlain uttered a sharp criticism in the Commons. Innes called Robinson's return wholly inappropriate: "Rhodes and his friends may talk till they are black in the face," Innes wrote to his brother, "but no impartial man can say that it is a proper thing to appoint as High Commissioner . . . a man who is involved in the business transactions which Sir Hercules took part in. . . ."[18]

Only a well-connected leader who was capable of deploying the strong support of most of the whites in the government of the Cape Colony could so brazenly have subordinated the custom and usual prerogatives of imperial oversight to the exercise of his own will. Rhodes was riding hard in the saddle of his own power. It was difficult for the panjandrums of London to bar his way or to have exchanged Loch for someone a shade more independent than Robinson. They were in nearly all cases familiar with and sympathetic to his ultimate object.

Thus, too, came the incorporation of British Bechuanaland into the Cape Colony, the curious cession of the Pitsani strip, and the near transfer of all of the Bechuanaland Protectorate into Rhodes' sphere. Rhodes offered to take the Protectorate off imperial hands as early as December 1894, and insisted at the very minimum—doing so was critical to his conspiracy—that the Crown Colony of Bechuanaland be annexed. In an anodyne and misleading letter to Grey, Rhodes explained that he was anxious to acquire the Crown Colony, but the British government hesitated. "I should not be annoyed if this course was not delaying the whole advance." Rhodes' rails had reached Mafeking and, in accord with the understanding reached in 1892 with Lord Ripon, he could at last ask for the transfer of the Protectorate into the keeping of the British South Africa Company. That was an arrangement which would have permitted Rhodes to continue the railway north along the old missionary road on the Transvaal's western flank. But even more urgently, Rhodes required a secluded jumping-off point for Jameson. The intervention could not occur from British-administered soil. Thus Rhodes had to move precipitously in the Cape parliament to annex British Bechuanaland and to add its pressure to his own attack on the precarious autonomy of the Protectorate.[19] As Merriman and others in the parliament assumed at the time, Rhodes did have ulterior motives. But those motives were both less and more suspect than the Cape opposition at first appreciated.

After June 1895, when the Liberal government lost a vote of confidence in the House of Commons and Chamberlain, earlier an ally of Mackenzie against Rhodes over Bechuanaland, replaced Ripon at the colonial office, the conspiracy depended largely upon the ability to square a man who was as independent, ambitious, strong-minded, and imperialistic as Rhodes. There is circumstantial evidence that Chamberlain already knew the outlines of the plot. Certainly he appears to have done so by August, when Harris and Grey went to press the colonial secretary over the transfer of the Protectorate. They were compelled to discuss it with him in some depth, and received a sympathetic response. Indeed, according to a secret cable that was suppressed at the time of the parliamentary inquiry, during that interview it was Chamberlain who suggested something like the transfer of the Pitsani strip.[20]

Even so, because Chamberlain was temporizing, that month Rhodes also wrote in modest desperation to Beit, who was in London and capable of influencing Chamberlain. Beit himself had been brought into the widening cabal in June, presumably subordinating his own mature judgment about its probable success to Rhodes' grandiloquent reasoning and pleading. Rhodes had recently seen Phillips (who worked for Beit) and Charles Leonard (a lawyer employed by Beit and another of the leading conspirators in Johannesburg, and chairman of the National Union and the Reform Committee). "Everything is all right and I am ready for the last fence if we get the Protectorate it is in my quiet judgement easier than Matabeleland. I hear Hammond is enthusiastic and . . . I hope that you will arrange to send 2000 or even 3000 affairs [guns] they will get through all right. They should be supplied with necessary things to fill them. I do hope after your telegrams that Chamberlain will rise to the situation for the Protectorate is essential. I assure you if we have the Protectorate I do not feel one atom of doubt as to matter. As a last resort," Rhodes suggested, "if everything else fails go yourself and see Chamberlain. You are more convincing than most people and shew him the whole position of England in the South depends on it and that next year may be too late. . . . Our shares [of the total mining industry] are going both at Johannesburg and Charter to the French and Germans." Beit's firm was indeed largely responsible for the Continental involvement in the Rand.

Rhodes asked for a clear accounting of his assets, "especially with the final effort coming." Then he continued in a revealing manner: "For goodness sake make him understand what it means and the whole thing may fail because he has not the courage [Rhodes' favorite gibe] to face Arnold Forster [Hugh Arnold-Forster, a Unionist member of parliament who protected the rights of Africans] and give us the Protectorate and he has all the assurances of his predecessors . . . and can ask any guarantees he likes . . . but we must have the right of administration to collect our force at Gaberoones [sic] . . . I am told Chamberlain is a strong man and a far seeing man and we can give Africa to England if he will only take one step." However, if Chamberlain persisted in standing still, Rhodes was at a loss to understand how the intervention could possibly succeed. From Rhodesia's closest point it was 400 miles to Johannesburg—too far for a filibustering expedition. From Gaberone, eventually the capital of modern Botswana, it was about 200 miles—a ride of three or four days. Beit was Rhodes' trusted accomplice. Certainly he could make Chamberlain comply. "Surely Chamberlain should see all this," Rhodes underlined his own logical appreciation of the problem for Beit. "He risks nothing. I risk everything and yet he will not budge an inch to help a big idea which [could] make England dominant in Africa, in fact [would give] England the African Continent."[21]

Rhodes pushed the annexation of the Crown Colony through the Cape House, and Chamberlain acceded to that part of the pre-Raid arrangements. But Chamberlain had political problems. He could not simply give Rhodes the Protectorate. Moreover, what if the Raid should fail? Chamberlain was appropriately cautious, refusing to rely on the sheer bravado of Jameson's reputation or the rumors of discontent in Johannesburg. It was not until early November, after the rousing tour of Britain by Kgama, Sebele, and Bathoen (see Chapter 17), that Harris was finally able to arrange terms which Chamberlain could accept. While Rhodes' gall had been rising, the colonial secretary had been cruising off Spain. The ultimate compromise, which preserved the Protectorate to its indigenous inhabitants but gave Rhodes a railway strip as well as a temporary base for Jameson, has already been discussed. In order to bring Chamberlain to this point Harris and Rhodes had wielded the weapon of public opinion. At their behest, Flora Shaw had assured Chamberlain of the backing of *The Times*. Rhodes was compelled to accept a "liberal native reserve for Native chiefs," in exchange for control over the Protectorate's police. Rhodes also forfeited a subsidy for the railway.[22]

Why was Rhodes so determined to press the imperial government to bow to his own will? Was Rhodes drawn into an unconscious struggle for primacy with not one father figure, the obvious Kruger, but with Chamberlain and the British government as well? What did Rhodes really think that he was doing throughout 1895? Why did he so unnecessarily, unwisely, carelessly, tempt fate?

He had already confirmed the immensity of his vision and the virtue of smash and grab tactics if they furthered laudable goals. Moreover, violence worked. In August 1895 he copied an aphorism attributed to Marcella into his "Commonplace Book": "Humanity is too apt to forget that the world yields itself only to the *violent.*" A few months later, on the eve of the Raid, Rhodes enigmatically wrote in the same book that when a person had a difficult decision to make he should "compare the vastness of nature and the pettiness of the human atom," and the process of doing so would provide "the right decision." A person should stick to one good idea and pursue it ceaselessly. Rhodes believed that he was acting for nature; by the mid-1890s he had also come to believe that he could interpret the designs of nature better than anyone else.[23]

Clues to enigmas are often buried in off-hand comments. "I am willing to risk my whole position," Rhodes told Beit and others in mid-1895. "Is it not awful to think that the whole future of the British Empire out here [in Africa] may turn on a wretched caffre [Chief Kgama] and a Secretary of State [Chamberlain] who listens to some fanatic in the House of Commons? The fact that I have got everything the world can give me and am willing to risk it all does not weight one bit as against the vote of one abusive fanatic. . . ." He conceded that Beit might appropriately urge him to be patient. "You might say Oh yes wait but as you know we will wait too long, and with its marvellous wealth Johannesburg will make South Africa an independent Republic, which you and I do not want."

For his "big idea," an idea which would make "England dominant in Africa," Rhodes would risk everything. Since her statesmen (like Chamberlain) were unwilling to take the kind of great chances that Rhodes, in 1894–95, proposed, he wondered out loud how it was that "the English Empire still retain[ed] so much of the world." For the world was his object and the Transvaal a means to that end.

The language of Rhodes' cry to Beit thus echoed the Confession and hence his childhood longings. It was consonant with the various wills, embodiments as they were of his attempts to control the future. It was consistent with the grandeur for which the great man yearned. The soaring rhetoric, and the aspiration behind the rhetoric, was as much the real Rhodes—his mother's magic child—as were the unhappy methods which he sometimes employed. Rhodes rationalized as much as he philosophized, and deceived others as well as himself. But not every facet of his quest for overarching, universal purpose—for a pantheistic Social Darwinism—can be considered mere flim-flam and hocus-pocus.

On the eve of the Raid, Rhodes explained his motives well to Frederic Hamilton, then a young, skeptical editor of the Johannesburg *Star*, in much the same vein that he had earlier written to Beit. (Beit was also in the room, slumbering away in a chair.) After persuading Rhodes to postpone the Raid, and believing that Rhodes had given Harris instructions to so order Jameson, Hamilton asked the prime minister why he had involved himself in the business of promoting a revolution in a nominally friendly state. Rhodes, reported Hamilton with apparently good recall many years later, showed no fatigue. "'I am glad you ask me that question,'" he began to reply in a high falsetto.

" 'You may well ask. Here am I, with all the money a man can possibly want, Prime Minister of the Cape, a Privy Councillor—why should I run all these risks? Well . . . I don't want to annex the Transvaal, but I want to see it a friendly member of a Community of South African States. I want equal rights for the English language, a Customs Union, a common Railway policy, a common Native policy, a central South African Court of Appeal, [and] British coast protection. I have tried to do a deal with old man Kruger and I have failed. I never shall bring him into line. . . . What I want to do is to lay the foundations of a united South Africa. I want men to associate my name with it after I have gone, and I know that I haven't much time.' " (Usually associated with his personal health, Rhodes' allusion to "time" reflected his fears of a successful local rising.)

After the Raid, when he was combating the rebellion in Ndebeleland, Rhodes explained to Harcourt that he had tried to unite South Africa, and "no sordid motive" influenced him. That he had "no sordid motive," meaning no underlying naked financial or economic motive, is a theme that occurs thrice, and in two relatively brief letters. It constituted a refrain of exculpation that was obviously of significance for Rhodes in his mental agony.[24] Does one discern the little boy, ambivalent about opposing his father, and unable to acknowledge how much he wants his mother and her love, denying an oedipal motive for his acts? If so, if Rhodes were emotionally in the grip of an earlier, intense situation from childhood, it is hardly surprising that his judgment strayed, that he was impulsive or ambivalent, that he perhaps misread Jameson, and may have wandered, half-mistakenly, into profound punishment.

Hamilton, admittedly with the benefit of great hindsight, describes Rhodes a few days before the Raid as already obviously ill, with a "purple complexion" that plainly "pointed to heart trouble." However, contemporary reports both before and after the Raid cannot confirm this circumstantial suggestion of debility. Nor did Rhodes suffer another full blown cardiac episode as a result of the Raid's failure. Yet, as several recent biographers assert by way of extenuation, declining physical health could certainly have affected his judgment and precipitated a descent into irrationality. The great man was to die from cardiovascular insufficiency—from dilated arteries and a strained heart—six years and four months later. He had suffered disabling falls from a horse and cart, had difficulty breathing as early as 1891, and as recently as August 1895 had endured a bout of what was called serious influenza but which could have been a pneumonia-like breathing difficulty associated with cardiovascular problems.

In appearance, he was aging rapidly. In late 1894 friends in Rhodesia and London noted his haggard visage and strained eyes. But, without solid evidence, it is a giant leap to assume, as do several biographers, that Rhodes' mental acuity had suddenly waned, or that his illness had so paralyzed him into inaction that he simply could not summon the mental energy to recall Jameson or think clearly about the consequences of a failed conspiracy. No one—not even Hamilton, who was with him during the crucial weeks and days before the Raid—subsequently recalled anything but the typically energetic Rhodes. Certainly his weakness of heart, and any recurrent pain which would have reminded him how short his life could become, would have spurred him to greater, more relentless activity, not the reverse. Rather than succumb as he might to a neurotic cosseting of himself in anticipatory invalidship, Rhodes' awareness of his ultimate physical fragility hastened his initiatives and contributed to the ruthlessness which so typified his actions in the early 1890s.

Simply wanting to do the deed—symbolically to "strike a blow and die" in the manner of John Brown at Harper's Ferry—was not Rhodes' way. As much as he knew that his earthly time was limited, he had comparatively recently expressed buoyant confidence in his gifts and his ability to see various schemes to fruition. "I am still full of vigour and life," Rhodes told Stead defensively in 1894, "and I don't expect that I shall require anyone but myself to administer my money for me for many years to come."[25] The madness of the Raid cannot primarily or even in major part be ascribed to physical or mental deterioration. That it was flawed from inception, and that it failed, testifies more to the fatal insufficiency of its overall conception than to the flaws of its detailed execution. The collapse at Doornkop, where Jameson was halted in 1895, cannot be laid exclusively at the door of a diseased heart.

There is a theory that Rhodes was bluffing, that he expected to move Kruger sufficiently by the threat of a combined rising and intervention to bring the Transvaal within a negotiated greater South Africa. Since tight secrecy was impossible, Kruger would surely learn of the preparations, recognize how precarious his own position could become, and begin parleying with Rhodes. Thus there would be no ruthlessness involved, merely a modest measure of comparatively gentle pressure. Rhodes would appear, and take credit for being, the wise statesman. Such a hypothetical reconstruction of the events of late 1895 is plausible, and could conceivably explain the way in which Chamberlain quietly cooperated with Rhodes, even sending troop reinforcements to the Cape in a timely fashion. It would accord with a mode of operations often employed by Rhodes. Given Rhodes' surgical success in early November 1895 over the Drifts crisis, when Kruger backed down before a stiff British ultimatum, a further series of sharp verbal assaults, and perhaps a timely threat or two, might (Rhodes could have believed) have brought Kruger to a bargaining table. Bower and Chamberlain apparently thought that Rhodes' forcefulness would not lead to hostilities—that Kruger would back down before shots were fired. Rhodes could have believed so, too, and the main conspirators on the Rand certainly gave many indications that they were really engaged in a great game of bluff.[26]

Unhappily, such a hypothesis fails to accord well with the prolonged duration of Rhodes' preparations, beginning more than a year before the Raid. Nor can it explain the complicated involvement of Chamberlain and others in Britain. If he had been only bluffing, Rhodes would not have fought so hard for Jameson's jumping-off point, and for the transfer of Bechuanaland, which was difficult for a politician as astute as Chamberlain to grant. Despite the victory over the Drifts, neither Rhodes nor Chamberlain really expected that Kruger would undercut the base of his own power (a few months before he had won but a very slim victory over a less narrow-minded Afrikaner opposition group) by extending the franchise to English-speakers. Nor was he likely to limit the exercise of the Transvaal's sovereignty through enrollment in a Rhodes-dominated union of the South African states. Rhodes had no illusions about the great patriarch's implacable obstinacy. Over the Drifts, Rhodes and Chamberlain had legality on their side; regarding votes for English-speaking immigrants, Rhodes could claim the authority of natural justice; but for a customs union and a common railway policy and all the rest, Rhodes could bluster with little generally recognized authority. Moreover, and most telling, no one (not even Rhodes) advanced the defense of bluffing before the parliamentary inquiry or anywhere else. If Rhodes had intended to pressure and not to steal the Transvaal, then the conspirators in Johannesburg had not been informed. Nor, obviously, had Jameson.

Jameson was determined to remain the hero, to do the bidding of and earn glory in the eyes of his scheming master. In relation to Rhodes, Jameson had become the personification and cutting edge of fantasy. What Rhodes sought, but was too cautious and well-grounded to demand or take, Jameson grabbed. He knew how both to excite and to please his master; more than that, Jameson knew that Rhodes preferred to live and act beyond the bounds of conventional morality, where the greater goals, the big ideas, overcame otherwise objectionable methods, and victory and success were the sole criteria by which merit would be judged. Success achieved its own morality. Closely attuned to the inner rhythms of Rhodes' psyche, Jameson even presumed to override the formal restraints that Rhodes might impose. Schreiner concluded that Jameson rode "because he had thought that he was thereby fulfilling Rhodes's unspoken wish. . . ."[27]

The key questions about the Jameson Raid are not why it was devised, for likely explanations are at hand, nor why it was pursued so haphazardly and sloppily, leaving so much to chance and to the inefficient and lackadaisical labors of Frank Rhodes and Rutherfoord Harris. The successes of recent years, many of which involved Harris, Jameson, and also Beit, had been prepared with equal bravado and similiar slack staff work. The crucial question remains: why did Jameson catapult himself and his men from Pitsani when every sign said stop, when Rhodes' intermediaries had cried desist, and when Rhodes had given no specific orders to spring? Answers must be sought in the events of the last seven weeks, and in an appreciation of the manner in which the personalities of the two principals had merged.

The long-nurtured conspiracy became an immediate plan of action in October 1895. By closing the drifts over the Vaal, Kruger provided Britain and the Cape, and Chamberlain and Rhodes, with more than a pretext. Indeed, Kruger gave them a superb opportunity. Not to have exploited it would have been unlike Rhodes. If the men of Johannesburg rose, and a filibustering expedition intervened to save the Transvaal from Kruger, the world would understand. Rhodes relished the tension. So did Chamberlain, who could at last authorize the territorial maneuvers which were essential to Rhodes' scheme. In mid-October Chamberlain knowingly permitted Sir Hercules Robinson to give the territories of Chiefs Ikaneng and Montshiwa to the British South Africa Company. Rhodes had a detailed private discussion with Bower and then with Robinson. Frank Rhodes, bon vivant and good sportsman, was sent up to Johannesburg to take charge of the rising. "Cecil wanted him and that was enough."[28] On the same day, Robinson appointed Jameson, the administrator of Rhodesia, as resident commissioner of the newly transferred tiny little strip of insignificant territory along the Transvaal border. Robinson also approved the transfer of several contingents of Company mounted police from Bulawayo to the strip and gave permission for British forage dumps to be used to feed the Company's horses. By the end of October, 250 men were on their way south. Jameson inspected and approved the camp at Pitsani on 1 November.

During the next week Rhodes put extraordinary pressure on Harris in London, who in turn badgered Fairfield and, ultimately, Chamberlain, to give the conspiracy the fullest possible territorial room within which to operate. In addition to the Pitsani strip, Rhodes still demanded the whole of the Bechuanaland Protectorate. It was essential, he said, that the entire length of the Transvaal border should be under Company control. Rhodes wished to have the 1000–man Rhodesia Horse volunteers battalion at his disposal, as well as those members of the Bechuanaland Border Police who might wish to join Jameson. But first Chamberlain demanded specifically to be reassured that Rhodes would place a conquered or usurped Transvaal under the British flag. He had been correctly informed that many of the conspirators were indifferent to an imperial standard and simply wanted their rights. But for Rhodes (though subsequently he hedged when a deputation of Johannesburgers came to see him), Her Majesty's dominion was the whole point. "I of course would not risk everything as I am doing except for British flag," Rhodes replied. Immediately afterwards Chamberlain personally drew lines on a map and gave Rhodes a border zone running from Mafeking to Bulawayo. It included 100,000 square miles of the Protectorate. The Company would administer (and have free run in) this vast and ostensible railway zone. Chamberlain also instructed Robinson to release the Protectorate police and sell their equipment to the Company. In exchange, Rhodes gave up his rail subsidy. A day after all these deeds were quietly done, Kruger capitulated unexpectedly over the Drifts.[29]

As Kruger retreated, Rhodes and Britain lost their diplomatic cover. Yet, because preparations for a coup were in train, because Rhodes calculated that Kruger's retreat was only tactical, or because he hated to give up a good joint project of "the boys" when so much had already been achieved, Rhodes let the conspiracy roll. When Schreiner later asked Rhodes why he had been in such a hurry to overthrow Kruger, Rhodes replied that, although Kruger's reign was "temporary," there would soon be "a huge English speaking republic in Transvaal which will absorb the North and leave the Cape out at the shank end of the Continent. My idea has always been union under the English flag under responsible government."

Jameson, who had visited Johannesburg in September to discuss tactics, arrived again on 19 November. He procured a letter of invitation from Leonard, Phillips, Frank Rhodes, Hammond, and George Farrar, the representative of a French mining syndicate. It summoned him to the rescue of unarmed men, women, and children in beleaguered Johannesburg. Its date was left blank so that Jameson could later fill it in, as required.

The local committee told Jameson they would rise on 28 December, just after Johannesburg's annual Christmas horse races. Jameson was to start two days before. During Jameson's time in Johannesburg, Phillips, a little, formal man, also made a strong speech demanding that the Transvaal government should cease ignoring the grievances of those men of property and skill whom the Afrikaners persisted in calling Uitlanders. Otherwise, Phillips declared turgidly, the immigrants might be driven to engage in extreme action. Jameson also lunched with Hamilton and Frank Rhodes. Hamilton claims to have told the other two that they would meet tough opposition. Jameson declared Hamilton dead wrong. "I shall get through as easily as a knife cuts butter. You people do not know what the Maxim gun means. I have seen it at work."[30]

Jameson traveled to Groote Schuur to make final arrangements with Rhodes and to have a long private chat with Robinson. Leonard and Phillips joined Jameson. They, too, wanted to confirm with Rhodes, to go over the flag question once again, and presumably to ascertain that the supplies from Harris (who had only recently left London) were still on their way. Rhodes satisfied these leaders of the English-speaking reformers; he did so apparently by trimming or making ambiguous his insistence on the British flag. All he asked of them, it was said, was a strong insistence on free trade.[31]

This meeting of 24–25 November launched the conspiracy into its highest gear. None of the participants—not Chamberlain, Robinson, the reform crowd in Johannesburg, or Jameson—could afterward have doubted that Rhodes remained intent upon upsetting Kruger's applecart despite the president's improved attitude over the Drifts and his willingness to talk about railway rates. Presumably everyone involved still believed, or had come to be persuaded by Rhodes, that dumping Kruger by means of a trumped-up rising, an intervention from afar, and the mock arbitration of the high commissioner and himself, would be accomplished easily and appear genuine. True, *The Times* at home and its man in Johannesburg were primed to applaud, as would most local newspapers that counted. But could a small-scale conspiracy overthrow an established state?

The days of December were notable for their desperate drama. Or was it high farce? Jameson, Willoughby, and the men assembled at Pitsani readied themselves as best they could, mostly by talking and idling, occasionally by drilling. As the hot days dragged on, what little patience Jameson possessed leached away amid fears that his men would blab, indiscretions would become a cascade of confirmation, and Kruger would learn the intimate details of the conspiracy. Moreover, what Jameson heard from Johannesburg could hardly have given him confidence. By the end of the first week of the month Jameson learned that Frank Rhodes and other reformers had been able to arouse little enthusiasm for real action among the contented revolutionaries. The "polo tournament," Frank Rhodes telegraphed in childish code, should be postponed until the new year. Jameson's ride should not clash with race week.

The response from Pitsani was "Have everything ready here." "Any delay would be most injurious." On 12 December Jameson reminded Cecil Rhodes that tarrying meant danger and premature discovery. Surely, he asked the master, his ride and their plans were more important than the races? *The Times,* pumped by Flora Shaw, its forty-five-year-old expert on colonial issues, was simultaneously urging Rhodes to hurry, lest the capitals of Europe learn of the plot. (Shaw, cool, decisive, and unique as a female "special correspondent," had been a disciple of Stead's on the *Pall Mall Gazette.* She later married Colonel Frederick Lugard and became Lady Lugard.) Rhodes so informed Frank Rhodes. But (and it was clearly late, but unerringly wise) Hammond, on behalf of the other Johannesburg conspirators, telegraphed Rhodes on 18 December that "the flotation" should be delayed until Beit (only then landed at Cape Town with Harris) could give them counsel.

Instead, Rhodes, with his hand on Beit's elbow, urged "immediate flotation." He did so not despite but because U.S. President Grover Cleveland had invoked the Monroe Doctrine over Britain's boundary dispute in South America between Venezuela (an ally of the U.S.) and British Guiana (later Guyana). Cleveland threatened to impose a U.S.-determined demarcation line. However anachronistic it may seem after the passage of ninety years, for a few weeks renewed war between Her Majesty's government and the United States appeared a distinct possibility. Shaw and Charles Moberly Bell, the assistant manager of *The Times,* both in touch with the mood of London, had advised Rhodes not to brook delay. So had Chamberlain, if guardedly and indirectly. In six months Britain and Venezuela, and hence Britain and the U.S., might be engaged in heavy recrimination, if not hostilities. If the deed were to be done, it had better be done at once.[32]

Jameson, ever impatient, could not wait forever, Rhodes thundered up the line to his brother on 21 December. Advise "when you can float," so that Jameson could be informed. A week before Rhodes and company were intending to provoke and capitalize upon an incident with profound imperial and international implications, the men at the helm and the tiller had not yet decided upon the best moment to launch their ship of insurrection (or of fools). Indeed, by this time the men responsible for the rising clearly wanted nothing of the kind. They had enlisted too few men; their arms were insufficient.

The force that was to be dispatched on 27 December to take the Pretoria armory was still a figment of an earlier imagination. Yet how could these earnest, honorable patriots, every man true blue, let down the side? How would good old Jameson feel? And what could Frank tell his imperious younger brother? Naturally, the men who were to mount the barricades faltered, temporized, and blamed a residual concern about putative sovereignty for the focus of delay. Would Rhodes let them, as the Americans wanted, seize Johannesburg under the Transvaal flag or would Rhodes and the high commissioner demand only the Union Jack? They initially put back Jameson's departure until 28 December. And to Cape Town they dispatched Colonel Francis Younghusband, the local correspondent of *The Times*. On 22 December Rhodes hurried Younghusband away from a mass of friends on his back verandah. Taking him amid the blooming hydrangeas, Rhodes learned the sad news about Johannesburg's unready state of mind. "All right," he responded, "if they won't go . . . they won't; . . . I shall wire to Jameson to keep quiet."[33]

These assurances were clearly regarded as insufficient by some of the strongest-minded reformers. On Christmas Day the Reform Committee dispatched a delegation of Hamilton and Leonard to persuade Rhodes that the rising absolutely must be postponed until 6 January. (Johannesburg and Cape Town are 900 miles apart. Sending delegates to Rhodes was no lighthearted endeavor, as even reliable trains took three nights each way to shuttle the conspirators. It is obvious the reformers, and Frank Rhodes, had reason to believe that Cecil Rhodes might ignore telegraphic messages, or—plausibly—that Harris would shield him from their import.) The next day, 26 December, Jameson received a telegram from his brother Sam, in Johannesburg: "It is absolutely necessary to postpone flotation. . . . We will endeavor to meet your wishes as regards December, but you must not move until you have received instructions to." Harris telegraphed Jameson on the same day: "You must not move till you hear from us again. Too awful! Very sorry."[34]

Hamilton and Leonard reached Cape Town as dawn was breaking on 28 December. Jameson was intending to ride the next day. Going directly from their train to Groote Schuur, Hamilton and Leonard found Rhodes attentive and receptive. The men from Johannesburg told Rhodes that the city was unready, that arms and men were too few, and that the reformers would need time, perhaps six months or more, to reorganize the cabal. They must have hinted, or Rhodes inferred, that a postponement would surely mean the end of the scheme. There would never be a rising, and Jameson would have to beat a conspicuous retreat to Rhodesia. There was the danger, moreover, that Jameson's withdrawal would not end the question of Rhodes' complicity. The aborted conspiracy would surely be uncovered, and then where would they all be? Nevertheless, Rhodes responded decisively. He would wire at once, halting Jameson. Then he hustled them out of the house. "I am closely watched, and if it were known that you had come straight off the train to me, tongues would get busy."

Hamilton believed Rhodes. That morning he cabled J. Percy FitzPatrick, the future author and another key conspirator, that the delegation had received "perfectly satisfactory assurance" from Rhodes, that Jameson had been advised accordingly, and that the reformers should continue their preparations, but without any particular urgency since an "entirely fresh departure" would be necessary.

In the afternoon Rhodes asked Bower to stroll over from his nearby house. Although he and Bower had quarreled bitterly about the propriety of the prospective Raid, Rhodes was affable when they talked in the gathering dusk on Groote Schuur's old tennis court. "You will be glad to hear," Rhodes told Bower, "that the revolution has fizzled out like a damp squib. You can tell the Governor: he will be glad to hear it." Rhodes, seemingly relieved, blamed the collapse of their efforts on quarreling among the reformers over which flag to raise. In his view the revolutionaries had never really meant to fight; they had merely wanted to put pressure on Kruger. At Pitsani, Jameson would gradually reduce his troops. Although he and Beit had spent vast sums of their own money on the proposed coup, he was still rich. He expected to "spend the rest of his money in developing the North."

Later, on the evening of 28 December, when Hamilton and Leonard, and, it seems, Rhodes, confidently believed that Jameson had been stopped, the first two returned to Groote Schuur. They found Rhodes in his study, sitting in a high-backed chair and looking "rather like a Roman emperor in a rumpled shirt and an ill-fitting dinner jacket." Beit was also present. Everyone was relaxed; Rhodes was sympathetic. Hamilton and Leonard detailed how unprepared Johannesburg had been. "Not only were we hopelessly unready," Hamilton explained, "but the intervention of the Chartered Company . . . would [have] antagonize[d] all the Afrikanders and many of the English." Such a lengthy explanation had not been possible in the morning. When they finished, Rhodes reported that he had sent Jameson a wire to tell him not to move. Knowing Jameson's impulsive character, he promised an even stronger one in the morning. Rhodes went on: "Jameson shall stop on the border for six months if necessary and he shall not cross until you fellows tell him to." Rhodes, reported Hamilton, "was sincere."[35]

Was Rhodes sincere? He naturally could not send the telegrams himself, but would have dictated them to Harris. Or perhaps he only waved at Harris and, in some general manner, said "stop Jameson." Did he convey a sense of dire urgency to Harris? Or did he shrug and imply that Harris should cover their tracks with misleading missives that would give the world one message, but which would not deter the restless Jameson? Could he have told Jameson, possibly in late November, to ignore any recalls unless they came in some special peremptory code? Or did Rhodes rely or bet on Jameson's temperament, knowing that nothing could hold his friend at the eleventh hour?

The evidence of the cable traffic is that on 27 December Jameson was wildly attempting to attract attention and positive responses. Straining at the leash, aware that the reformers had lost heart, seemingly determined to find an excuse, any excuse, to jump, he warned his brother Sam that his men had already gone forth to cut the telegraph lines. "Let Hammond telegraph instantly all right." He asked Harris for explicit authorization. A few hours later he insisted to Harris that the original plans must be put into effect. It was too late to change. If the reformers refused to rise, he would issue the blankly dated invitation in their name, and come in.

On the same day, Hammond replied very firmly. "Expert reports decidedly adverse. I absolutely condemn further developments at present." Phillips cabled in the same vein. Then, on the fateful Saturday, 28 December, Harris (for Rhodes) wired, "It is all right if you will only wait." Hold on. Panic not. See us through. Harris sent another message the same morning which said that all their foreign friends were opposed to a "flotation." He used the words "dead against it." A third wire from Harris (was this the supposedly strong one?) told Jameson, "We cannot have fiasco." He also told him that Heaney and Holden were on their way. But there was no message from Rhodes personally, and nothing ordering Jameson to come to Cape Town.

In Johannesburg, the men who knew Jameson well had already suspected that he might not heed their cables, or even the messages from Cape Town. The day before they had sent Captain Harry Holden by one route and Major Maurice Heaney, an American, by another. Holden rode to Jameson in seventy hours, arriving late on Saturday. Heaney came by train (via Bloemfontein, Kimberley, and Vryburg), reaching Mafeking early on the morning of 29 December. There he hired a cart, and pushed it hard toward Pitsani. Holden on Saturday and Heaney on Sunday told Jameson that there would be no rising. He should do nothing. On the Saturday Jameson responded to Harris' telegrams, and possibly to Holden, with a twisted "Received your telegram . . . re Heaney. Have no further news I need to know. Unless I hear definitely to the contrary shall leave tomorrow evening and carry into effect my [plan to release the invitation] . . . and it will be all right." He also wired curtly to Sam. He would "start without fail" Sunday night. Jameson may have cannily calculated that no one would be in Cape Town to receive that cable. The South Africa Company offices in Cape Town to which he had addressed the wire were closed. Harris had locked the doors and gone off to Three Anchor Bay, two miles distant. Did Harris think that Jameson had truly been halted and that there was no urgency? Did Rhodes? Or, as Flint suggests, was it all an elaborate charade? "Rhodes could have stopped Jameson and did not do so," says Flint.[36]

When Heaney arrived on Sunday morning Jameson received his message and then "walked up and down for some little time." Finally, he told Heaney, "I'm going." "Thought you would," said Heaney, who went with him, and later told the South Africa Committee in London that he knew Jameson "intimately," and knew that once Jameson made up his mind "to do a thing, he usually [did] it." They believed that a fait accompli would lead automatically to victory. According to one report, the doctor had been reading Thomas Babington Macaulay's essay on Robert Clive of India. He sensed that Clive's position as the conqueror of India was analogous to his own. "You may say what you like but Clive would have done it," Jameson declared. At the parliamentary inquiry he answered Henry Labouchere that he had "felt sure that it would be all right supposing we were successful, and I never had a doubt that we would be successful. . . ." Moreover, Jameson reminded the committee that he had been confident that success was its own reward. "If I had succeeded I should have been forgiven" for perpetrating an improper act, indeed a crime. In the context of Jameson's time, he was right. He never said that he was doing it for Rhodes, or that he knew or felt or sensed that Rhodes wanted him to go, whatever other signals had been received.[37]

At five minutes past nine on Sunday morning, 29 December, Jameson wired to "Charter," as he habitually did, and not to Rhodes specifically. He was leaving that evening. "We are simply going in to protect everybody while they change the present dishonest government. . . ." The telegram arrived at 10:52 a.m., the previous one at 6 p.m. on Saturday. Harris' clerk collected both messages at about 11 a.m. He decoded them and then rushed them by horse-drawn cab to Harris' home on Three Anchor Bay. Harris, despite what van der Poel suggests, understood what must be done. He sent his clerk back to the telegraph office to try to keep the line open to Mafeking (it had already closed) throughout the remainder of the morning if not the day. (There was another route for telegrams to Pitsani via Kimberley and Macloutsie, but Harris may not have known about it.) If Harris had replied immediately, as Longford says, Jameson probably could have been stopped. But Rhodes had to be consulted. Harris dashed in the cab to Groote Schuur, a distance of about eight miles. Flint surmises that Rhodes would have received the critical cables as early as 10:30, but that is surely wrong. Longford suggests he read them at 11:30, which is still a little early. Van der Poel offers 1 p.m., probably half an hour or so too late. The line to Kimberley closed at 1:20 p.m. But Rhodes was premier as well as high everything else. Could he not have opened the telegraph offices? Was there no way to arouse operators in Kimberley and Mafeking in an emergency? What about the police network?

Arguably, Rhodes had an hour, or possibly two, to recall Jameson *if* he had known that Pitsani would remain in communication with Kimberley by the roundabout route until lunch time. However, says Flint, Rhodes dithered, and, when it was obviously too late to do anything, he drafted an absurdly muddled telegram which ended with a mixed message: "Things in Johannesburg I yet hope to see amicably settled, and a little patience and common sense is only necessary—on no account must you move, I most strongly object to such a course." Harris' clerk tried to send this message from about 4 to 7 p.m., or so he subsequently said. Van der Poel asserted that it was never intended to be sent. Indeed, she believed that the wire was forged afterward and inserted in the South Africa Committee's dossier of evidence. Yet Bower recalled Rhodes showing him Sunday's telegram that very evening. If the telegram were bogus (perhaps Bower's memory played tricks), Rhodes would have intended it to provide retrospective cover. Longford argues that the wire could nevertheless be regarded as genuine *if*—a great imponderable—Rhodes had actually assumed that the key message had been or would be sent in time to curtail Jameson. Otherwise, Rhodes consciously did nothing, believing that he and Harris possessed no means by which to undo Jameson's desperate act.

He let Jameson go and willed the best. At first determined to ride out the storm, he also hoped by some miracle or other that Jameson could still succeed against all odds.[38]

Rhodes simply had no wish to recall Jameson. Bourchier F. Hawksley, Rhodes' austere but combative London solicitor, on 27 December had warned Fairfield of the Colonial Office that Rhodes "might be driven into an attitude of frenzy and unreason, and order Dr. Jameson to 'go in' . . . and manipulate the revolution. . . ."[39] Rhodes knew Jameson's temperament; he must have appreciated that the messages of Saturday would be insufficient to check his headstrong accomplice. He anticipated the decision announced by Jameson on Sunday, indeed exulted in it. This is a plausible reconstruction of Rhodes' role in the precipitating of the final debacle. But it depends upon a charge of base duplicity. Were Rhodes' reassurances to Hamilton and Leonard, and to Bower sheer subterfuge or masterful acting which controlled devastating anxiety?

True, Rhodes could be deceitful when cornered, a characteristic from childhood. But he had no need to mislead his associates and Bower directly. Temporizing or stalling, or greater verbal indirection, might have done just as well. And what if Harris' cables, or the messages carried by Holden and Heaney, had been obeyed? Rhodes was aware, if Jameson were not, that Johannesburg was simply unready. To have sent his own alter ego toward Johannesburg was suicidal and sadomasochistic. When Rhodes exclaimed that Jameson had ruined him and upset his applecart, he spoke of the decision to bolt, not the capitulation.

The Raid was designed and prosecuted by Rhodes, but he lost control at the end. He had placed Jameson in a position where Jameson could act for Rhodes, even if Rhodes' caution had ultimately prevailed. To do the deed was Jameson's effort for Rhodes. It mattered too little that Rhodes had used every means but a precise personal plea to keep Jameson at Pitsani. Flint may not be correct to suggest that Jameson would have obeyed a direct order from Rhodes. Jameson often believed that he alone knew best. The circumstantial evidence—conceivably a slimy trail left consciously by Rhodes—cannot demonstrate that Rhodes sent or willed Jameson into the Transvaal. Indeed, nearly all of it points the other way.

Blake believes that Jameson's "reckless act" took Rhodes "by surprise." That is a reasonable if too strongly affirmative reading of the available evidence. It still cannot explain precisely why Rhodes did so little (or did he believe that he had, in fact done enough?) on Sunday to stop Jameson when he might still have managed to halt the precipitous ride. Nor does it explain why he refused to recall and then condemn Jameson. But it does fit the corroborating explanation Rhodes gave in an unguarded moment to Alfred Sharpe in Cairo. "Mr. Rhodes was very open on the question of the Raid, and spoke freely," Sharpe reported. "He made absolutely no secret of the fact of his having been at the bottom of it. I did not of course *question* him, and most of what he said to me was spoken openly and not in any way confidentially. The *immediate* start by Dr. J. was evidently on his (J.'s) own responsibility but Rhodes had been, *avowedly* from the beginning the instigator and designer." Furthermore, Jameson allegedly told Beit, who told Taylor, that he had started for the Transvaal "on a sudden impulse, because he was convinced that the game was up and that President Kruger knew everything." He told Beit that "in order to draw all the blame upon himself and save Rhodes, he had dashed into the Transvaal." He further believed that he could enter Johannesburg without fighting. He hoped that Robinson would go to Johannesburg, as arranged, and prevent the outbreak of further hostilities. Jameson felt that "he could not be expected to wait and allow the blow to fall on Rhodes's head." Taylor also asserted that Willoughby was just as impulsive as Jameson; the two together were an impetuous duo.[40] For Rhodes the rising was intended to precede the Raid. When the Raid was thrust upon him, and aware as he was of Chamberlain's mutual designs upon the Transvaal, Rhodes could well have hoped to make the best of an unfortunately ill-timed folly. So he did too little, even to protect his name and position. Jameson sauntered unhindered into Afrikaner hands.

Jameson had decided, Clive-like and surgeon-like, to do it or be damned. Rhodes later was said to have exclaimed that Jameson, "at any rate, tried to do something."[41] Jameson's mind had probably been made up by Saturday, before he sent that late and never answered wire to Charter. In the bare square at Pitsani, Jameson paraded his 372 men in mid-afternoon on Sunday. At 6:30 p.m., when the sun would have been setting rapidly, they marched for Malmani, where 122 additional men of the Bechuanaland Border Police were to join them from Mafeking. By midnight both columns had penetrated deeply into the Transvaal. They joined forces at 5 a.m. By Monday evening, when Jameson's raiders had passed north of Lichtenburg, all of the Transvaal, indeed, most of the world, knew that Jameson had invaded Kruger's state. Already he was being trailed by Boer commandos, and the rising in Johannesburg had fizzled into nothing more than extended discussions with Kruger, the old man baiting a perfectly obvious trap for the earnest reformers. Fiasco is the correct descriptive noun.

Rhodes should have repudiated Jameson on Sunday if not Saturday. For the sake of what he valued most—his reputation, his works, his dreams, his history, the safety of his brother and Jameson, and the future of Rhodesia—Rhodes should have sent men after him. He should have reached Jameson via any of the towns east of Malmani and west of Krugersdorp. Wiring via Zeerust would have worked. If not only to save himself, Rhodes should have done more to save the reformers from jail, his cabinet's reputation and existence, and Chamberlain from suspicion. Instead, behaving like the gambler he hardly ever resembled, Rhodes let Jameson ride, presuming or praying that the Maxims would humble the Boers as they had destroyed the Ndebele. Was he so caught up in the oedipal struggle with Kruger that he allowed himself to drift into disaster? Or, more simply, was he so plump with grandiosity, so sure that he could not fail, that he denied the import of the news from Johannesburg and assumed that Jameson could defy all human odds?

Sunday would have been the day for denial. If Rhodes understood (he must have, but did he?) that his final message would not reach Jameson in time, he should have been obviously fretful and worried. If he had never honestly attempted to curtail Jameson, and was positive that Jameson would soon cross the border, he should have betrayed anxiety, even acute anxiety. At the very least he might have taken his horse onto the mountain or started evasive measures, warning Chamberlain and the governor, even telegraphing his brother. But Rhodes carried on calmly. Could he have assumed that Heaney would hold Jameson, that sense would prevail, or—knowing Jameson so well and believing him completely under his own sway—that Jameson was mostly gesturing, posturing, and bluffing to get his own way? To rail at Rhodes, and to wait for permission, would have conformed to the normal rules of their special relationship.

Rhodes seemed serene on Sunday. William P. Schreiner, his attorney-general and warm admirer, joined a vast crowd of guests on Groote Schuur's verandah as the sun fell behind the mass of Table Mountain. Nothing seemed amiss. When Schreiner warned Rhodes to keep clear of Leonard and the conspiratorial crowd in Johannesburg, Rhodes cheerfully replied, "Oh, that will be all right." Later that night he wrote a friendly letter to Schreiner's mother in Grahamstown. (When, the next day, Schreiner asked Rhodes why he had said nothing about Jameson, Rhodes lamely said that he believed that the message had arrived. But could he genuinely have believed such a thing?)

Between 7 and 11 p.m. some internal or, conceivably, external occurrence concentrated Rhodes' mind. He could have received no new telegraphic messages or other information about Jameson. No unexpected visitations have been discovered. Did the influence of his usual evening's heavy drink wear off? Did he learn that Kruger knew everything? When the household finally became quiet did he suddenly realize the enormity of his and Jameson's joint responsibility? Had Harris' clerk finally reported the failure to send the last message? Did he make some rapid calculations and suddenly appreciate that Jameson could not conceivably win through? It is hard to reconcile the change in Rhodes' demeanor from serene to panic-stricken with the notion that he had never tried to recall Jameson.

Bower heard horses' hooves outside his house about 11 p.m. A messenger said that Rhodes was anxious to speak to him at once. Bower went up to Rhodes' bedroom. "Jameson has taken the bit between his teeth and gone into the Transvaal," he said. "I've sent to stop him [had he?] and it may yet come out all right." "I will take the blame." He himself was ruined. He would resign as premier. Bower believed him genuinely crushed; his face was ashen and his distress indubitably genuine. Early the next morning, 30 December, when Bower reported the dreadful news to Robinson, he declared that Jameson had "disobeyed" Rhodes. Certainly that was the inference which Rhodes had clearly conveyed to Bower. At 11 a.m. Rhodes summoned Hamilton and Leonard from the city to Groote Schuur. He looked "ill and haggard." (Had Rhodes slept?) He told them that Jameson had crossed the border. "This is the finish of me," he explained to Hamilton. Although Hamilton was young enough to recover his position and promise, Rhodes said that for himself it was "the end." He was absolutely right to conclude that "the Dutch will never forgive me."

About 8 p.m. on 30 December, Schreiner saw Rhodes, who had spent much of the afternoon riding alone on the mountain. In the library, Schreiner found a Rhodes he hardly recognized. Rhodes appeared "absolutely broken down in spirit, ruined." "It is all true," he repeated over and over again. They talked for hours. "Poor old Jameson, twenty years we have been friends and now he goes and ruins me." Yet Rhodes told Schreiner that he could not now attempt to "hinder" Jameson. "I cannot go and destroy him." The next day Rhodes repeated that same refrain to Hofmeyr, who, Rhodes wrote, wanted his death. "It is death and nothing else." About midnight Sauer went home, convinced that Rhodes was indeed a broken, even a contrite, leader. So was Colonel David Harris, who saw Rhodes a day or two later. "I was shocked to see the change that had taken place in his appearance in so short a time. He seemed to be in a terribly depressed and agitated condition. He looked quite ten years older. . . . He seemed overwhelmed by what had taken place."[42]

One part of Rhodes was crushed. The other acted as if Jameson's raid could still be turned to positive advantage. Not one to allow himself to be overwhelmed for long, Rhodes mustered his adaptive powers and set about vigorously to minimize the damage. At noon on Monday, before socializing with a visiting English cricket team that had been invited to lunch at the house, and after unburdening himself to Hamilton, Rhodes pivoted to the attack. " 'We have twenty-four hours start of public opinion,' " he instructed the youthful editor. He advised Hamilton to write every editorial in the Cape papers, an order which was largely fulfilled. To London, for publication in *The Times* on New Year's Day, Rhodes dispatched an altered and purposely misdated text of the (concocted) letter of justification. The plight of the supposedly distraught "women and children" of Johannesburg successfully aroused sympathy; Jameson was depicted as a chivalrous hero rescuing a community in great peril.

Rhodes himself sent a sham cable to the London offices of the British South Africa Company explaining that Jameson had entered the Transvaal to assist oppressed English-speakers. "We are confident of success," he cabled. "Johannesburg united and strong on our side." He also cabled indirectly to Chamberlain via Shaw that he would "get through all right" if Chamberlain supported the cause. "To-day the crux is, I will win and South Africa will belong to England." Refusing to face Robinson or Bower by going into town, he replied to their messages by saying that Jameson had entered the Transvaal without his authority. "I hope our messages may have stopped him," he said disingenuously.[43] Then Rhodes took to the wooded slopes of the mountain.

Rhodes only stirred on Tuesday, when Rutherfoord Harris alerted him to the fact that Robinson, impelled and counseled by Hofmeyr, was preparing a proclamation denouncing the Raid and Jameson and calling upon British subjects in the Transvaal to resist the invasion by force of arms. Rhodes rushed into town and badgered Robinson to desist. "It's making an outlaw of the Doctor," he complained. He also attempted to persuade the old and much-tried governor to go to Johannesburg to carry out his previously defined role as the embodiment of British authority and the sanctification of the rising that never was. That same day Rhodes cabled Shaw to "make" Chamberlain "in-struct" Robinson to proceed "at once" to Johannesburg. Unless Shaw could do that—he shifted some of the blame—"the whole position [was] lost." Rhodes predicted a "splendid reception" for the high commissioner. He could "still turn position to England advantage." When this gambit proved unproductive, Rhodes, on the offensive, proposed to steam in his own special train to Pre-toria and Kruger. Rutherfoord Harris urged him on. But Hamilton suggested that the Afrikaners would hang him. "Hang *me!*" Rhodes is said to have re-plied. "They can't hang me! I'm a Privy Councillor! There are only two hundred of us in the British Empire!"

Hamilton had a few further words with Rhodes before himself traveling up to Johannesburg. Rhodes indicated that his only satisfaction was that he had "got Chamberlain by the short hairs." Hamilton asked for confirmation. "In it?" Rhodes responded. "Up to the neck!" Could Rhodes have prevari-cated on Sunday and Monday mostly to protect Chamberlain? Certainly there can now be no doubt that Chamberlain was profoundly implicated in the plot. Hawksley later said that Chamberlain had "deceived the House of Commons & the country. . . ." But Chamberlain's complicity is important here only to the extent that he had a private understanding with Rhodes which drove the prime minister and his closest friend to do the deed regardless. "Jameson . . . must be mad," Chamberlain cabled upon learning of the dash into the Trans-vaal.[44] Rhodes could well have pursued his Transvaal object in the days before Christmas because Shaw and Bell influenced him to believe that Chamberlain desired immediate action. But there are no indications that "pushful Joe" trig-gered the actual intervention or that Rhodes received any promise which would have or should have resulted in official British military or even diplomatic backing at all costs. Jameson did not ride, nor Rhodes provoke the Raid, be-cause Chamberlain was committed to come to their aid, rising or no rising.

The raiders reached Doornkop, fourteen miles from Johannesburg and just south of Krugersdorp, before Kruger's commandos tightened the noose. Even the Maxims were unable to compensate for Jameson's poorly prepared, ill-arranged, headlong rush into a narrow valley where Boer marksmen could command the hills. The curtain clattered down on this crucial phase of the deadly serious comic opera.

On Thursday morning, 2 January, one of the raiders seized an apron from a Khoi nursemaid and held it up as the white flag of surrender. That evening Jameson and most of his men were bundled into Pretoria's prison. In Johannesburg the reformers had not risen. "Tonight," one of the key con-spirators wrote on 3 January, "we are all hooted and howled at by the crowd because they say we have deserted Jameson. We have done nothing of the sort but he has failed to reach this [sic] and, as far as we can learn has had to surrender to the Boers. It is the blackest and most cruel game of treachery ever played. Chamberlain sold Jameson and the High Commissioner or Rhodes sold us both. . . ." By 9 January, after a week of revolutionary atmosphere which approximated "a combination of Armageddon and a psychopathic ward," Kruger confidently collected the English-speaking ringleaders and their many also-rans and tossed them into prison, where they were united with Jameson at last.[45]

Chamberlain managed skillfully to disassociate himself from the mess. Rhodes resigned as premier (but not his parliamentary seat), taking his cabinet with him, although Merriman felt that "every engine of corruption and intrigue [was] being worked to keep either Rhodes in power or else to form some [other] government . . . that would be the same thing with another name." Then for five days the colossus spent his waking hours roaming the great mountain, his nights pacing his bedroom floor, hardly sleeping. Dr. Jane Waterston found him during a quiet interlude staring at a luxurious bank of blue hydrangeas. It all means peace, he told her.[46] But there could be no real peace, and no real acceptance of fate, once he learned that Frank Rhodes would be tried for treason in Pretoria and Jameson shipped home for judgment in Britain. Moreover, the Queen's government might strip him of his Charter, and the directors of De Beers and Gold Fields deny him continued influence over their companies. There was much to defend and recoup.

Rhodes continued to wriggle, grieving for his lost life—but only for a week. "I [was] dead in a way," he told Schreiner later. Yet by 7 January he was bombarding Chamberlain with strongly worded cables of advice. That he rapidly decided on a course of vigorous action testifies to his personal strength and continued psychological agility. Subsequently, defending himself in a speech at Kimberley, he said that the Raid had been the beginning of great events, not their end. Given his own strong commitment to himself and his big ideas, it was required that he seek to save what he could of his life's mission and salvage something as well of his own power.

Rhodes sailed to Britain in late January to make what he could of the calamity. A week after Rhodes' arrival, Sidney Low called on him early one morning at the Burlington Hotel. Low, a London editor and journalist, had interviewed him in 1892 and, was no acolyte. The great man was in his bedroom, and not quite dressed. "As he talked he walked feverishly up and down the room, awkwardly completing his toilet. He had been dining out the evening before; the dress clothes he had worn were scattered in disorder about the room. . . ." Low, like Schreiner and Waterston a month before, found a "pathetic, almost a desolate figure." His hair was grey-brown and much changed. "Through the ruddy bronze of the sea wind and the veldt breezes his cheeks showed grey and livid; he looked old and worn." Although Low recalled raising questions about the Raid diffidently, Rhodes was "full of it—too full to keep silence." Low had hitherto found him candid. Now he found Rhodes almost too free with his words. Rhodes apparently wanted to talk. "We have made a mistake," he said several times.

Despite his battered appearance, Rhodes remained resilient. In London, in consultation with Rochfort Maguire and Hawksley, he chose most of all to secure the Charter, which, in the enforced absence of Jameson, was the closest approximation he had of himself, as well as the key to his continuing power and influence. Using Reginald Brett, that fellow homosexual crusader for a secret solidarity, as an intermediary, Rhodes held a private conversation with Chamberlain and Lord Selborne, minister of state in the Colonial Office and Lord Salisbury's son-in-law. Rhodes intimated that he would be loath ever to implicate Chamberlain (whose commanding role was not yet suspect), providing that Chamberlain protected the chartered company's position in Rhodesia (not Rhodes personally) and did what he could to advance the interests of closer union in South Africa. As Julia Merriman commented acidly, "Mr. Chamberlain appears to have been talked over by Mr. Rhodes. His personality is something marvellous!" Only Blunt really understood that Chamberlain was intent on saving his own as well as Rhodes' "bacon." "It is. . .obvious," Blunt said at the time, "that [Chamberlain] was in with Rhodes and Jameson, though they possibly acted without his exact knowledge at the last moment."

Hawksley threatened to reveal the secret cables more than once to secure Rhodes' interests and Jameson's future. Yet Chamberlain could always employ the power of the state to compromise Rhodes' sub-imperial ambitions. Together the two vigorous, canny, and unscrupulous adversaries arranged a mutually beneficial conspiracy of silence. Their weapons of blackmail were reputation and status, and neither—men of future rather than past bent— could afford to forfeit either. As Rhodes soothingly reminded Chamberlain in early 1897, "Nothing is impossible; everything is impossible until you are confronted with something more impossible still, and you must choose between them. It is better to lose your arm than your life." Hawksley wanted Chamberlain to have the "courage" to admit his complicity. Much later Stead berated Rhodes for covering up for Chamberlain. Rhodes' mistake in trying to overthrow Kruger was a "mere venial sin," said Stead, compared "with the monstrous crime which was committed against the Empire when Mr. Chamberlain succeeded in inducing you to suppress all evidence of his guilt. . . ."[47]

By mid-1896, Rhodes and Beit had been compelled to resign their directorships in the British South Africa Company. (The Company lost its commanding position in Bechuanaland, too.) By then the Cape parliament had held its own investigation, the results of which were thoroughly critical of Rhodes. The Transvaal had also issued damning documents in connection with the trial of the reformers. The ringleaders of that group were sentenced to hang, but Rhodes purchased their freedom and those of the others for a total of £400,000, and Kruger commuted their sentences to banishment or a kind of internal political exile. (About £8,000 of Rhodes and Beit's money was additionally channeled through a secret Relief Fund, administered by Edward Ridge Syfret in Cape Town. These funds were devoted to remunerating Jameson's troops and, especially, those who were wounded.) In July, Jameson and Willoughby were brought before a special jury in London and sentenced to fifteen months in Holloway prison. Rhodes was in the Matopos when he learned of the verdict. Milton watched Rhodes sitting silently, thinking. He then exclaimed: " 'A tribute to the upright [or did he say 'unctuous'?] rectitude of my countrymen who have jumped the whole world!' "[48] Jameson, however, served only four of those months because of a bad attack of gallstones and because of his many sympathetic and well-placed connections. Oddly and still inexplicably, Rhodes appears not to have communicated with Jameson at all until 1897.

Despite the detailed inquiries and the two trials, Rhodes and Jameson had broadly recovered public sympathy and regard by mid-year. The opportune outbreak of war in Rhodesia had helped. So had the steadfast support of *The Times*. Later, Kruger's maladroit attempt to advance local legislation harmful to Uitlanders also assisted in evoking support for Rhodes. What neither Rhodes nor Chamberlain could totally avoid, however, was an official investigation by the House of Commons. At various times during 1896 Chamberlain endeavored to threaten the Transvaal with British troops, and possibly even sought to foment a war. One result would have been an end to the inconvenience of an inquiry.

The South Africa Committee was finally constituted in late January 1897. Rhodes would at last be summoned to account for his misdeed. This was the bar of justice before which Olive Schreiner had wanted to propel Rhodes since 1891. The Committee included prominent front-benchers. Harcourt, Labouchere, Sir Henry Campbell-Bannerman, Sydney Buxton, and John Ellis were the five Liberals who theoretically would be counted upon to seek the truth. The Conservatives were Sir Michael Hicks Beach, Sir Richard Webster, and William Jackson, the inoffensive chairman. Hawksley succeeded in adding George Wyndham, a Tory parliamentarian partial to Rhodes. The strange surprise, however, was that the tenth member was Chamberlain. He would influence the way in which his own role was portrayed, and be there to help the witnesses remember what he wanted them to remember.

Rhodes—"stout and like a big farmer"—appeared before the Committee for six days in February.[49] Beit, Harris, Hawksley, Jameson, Willoughby, Bower, Shaw, and a host of other conspirators endured the questions of the Committee. Inability to remember, refusals to talk about the doings of others, clever but uninformative ripostes, gibes, parryings, and partial replies were the accomplishment of nearly six months of testimony. Rhodes even charmed Labouchere, who called him " 'an entirely honest, heavy person.' " Harcourt, who later termed him "an astonishing rogue and liar," cross-examined Rhodes tolerably well and savaged Bower and a few of the hapless witnesses, but for the most part the leading participants, especially Rhodes, were allowed to evade the tough questions and thus avoid giving away the real involvement of Chamberlain, Robinson, and others. No one ever sought the critical cables in the Colonial Office files with vigor, or explicitly asked Chamberlain what they contained. Rhodes effectively shouldered the blame, as he had said he would. But by so doing he connived with the Committee and others, notably the clever Shaw, to provide prevarication and deceit in lieu of helpful testimony.

THE END OF THE GAME.

Chorus (all except Mr. Blake and Mr. Labouchere): "Well, if we can't safely do anything else, we can all sit on Rhodes. That won't hurt anyone." (Left sitting.) (*Westminster Gazette,* July 15, 1897.)

As Rhodes exulted afterwards, "The great thing is England is not implicated. There will be all sorts of surmises, conjectures, and suspicions for a week or so and then indifference and forgetfulness. The only thing that will be remembered will be that before the world England is not implicated, and that you and the other men with you," he wrote to Grey, "dared boldly and suffered silently for England." Earlier he had predicted that his own role was to play "the sacrificial lamb to save Chamberlain. . . ." Indeed, he said, the "public may respect one for it."[50]

The Committee condemned the Raid and concluded that Rhodes was responsible for it, although Jameson had bolted on his own. It said nothing about the activities or the administration of the Company. Nor did it indicate how Rhodes should be punished for his nefarious activities. Yet, despite the Committee's conviction, it never discovered why Jameson rode, or what motivated Rhodes on that fateful Saturday and Sunday while Jameson was saddling up in Pitsani. A cartoon in the *Westminster Gazette* summed up the proceedings: the Committee, blindfolded, was sitting upon the prostrate body of Rhodes, saying, "Well, if we can't safely do anything else, we can all sit on Rhodes. That won't hurt anyone." Rosebery said that he had never read a document "at once so shameful and so absurd." Blunt called it "the most scandalous [report] ever jobbed." Arnold Morley termed it "The Lying in State at Westminster." Rhodes' own comment was contained in a letter to Michell: " 'I notice the Home Committee have made me the sacrificial lamb. I wonder whether the decay of our race will come through unctuous rectitude."[51]

Rhodes had not only survived. In many respects he had won the battle for respect and command. Having failed to oust Kruger easily, he had emerged from the debacle of the Raid with the remainder of his empire largely intact. Gold and diamonds were doing well. He may have regretted the loss of political control in the Cape, but he hardly needed it. The risings in Rhodesia (see the next chapter) and his own role in returning peace to a troubled territory had further re-emphasized his own sense of self-worth. If the collapse of the trumped-up white rebellion had driven Rhodes briefly to despair, the quelling of authentic black revolutions granted him a sense of renewed positive accomplishment. As Rhodes told the Committee when asked whether he had fomented the Raid as prime minister or as managing director, Rhodes had replied "neither." He had done it solely "in my capacity as myself."[52]

Even so, Rhodes had forever forfeited the realization of his "noble" dream. The reunion of the white "races" in South Africa was henceforth impossible. Afrikaners would never again trust Britons. The betrayal of the Dutch in the Cape, and Rhodes' refusal to renounce Jameson at Hofmeyr's behest, doomed the Founder to jingoism. Thereafter he could count only on the sectarian support of English-speakers. No longer could he conciliate, merge, and amalgamate politically. In consequence his power in the Cape and in South Africa was fatefully diminished. Only in the Rhodesias could he exert himself fully. The red line to Cairo and other peripheral pursuits like fruit farming took on a new importance. Moreover, even as he retrieved much of his reputation and lost none of his wealth, he destroyed his image as a great South African. He would be remembered among the descendants of the Dutch primarily as an English-speaking, white, much-flawed leader of a treacherous conspiracy.

20

"The Eyes Are White"
The Risings and Redemption

RHODES HAD FAILED ignominiously to usurp the Transvaal's autonomy. It was a startling contrast to the ease with which he had first suborned and then overwhelmed the Ndebele, gulled the Lozi, outwitted the Tswana, and punished the Mpondo. Rhodes was a white capitalist of imperial reach whose callous disregard for African aspirations was consonant with the prevalent European attitudes of the times. An entrepreneur whose horizons were not narrowly bounded by mere mineral riches but instead expanded to encompass vast dreams of English glory, he saw Africans in their ethnic arrays both as obstacles to be pushed aside and as strategic pools of available labor. "The native question" was for him largely a factor in the smooth running of the mines and a major source of tension between Dutch- and English-speaking voters. As a young man he had related directly and well to unlettered Zulu. Throughout his life he remained sympathetic and responsive to the needs of individual persons of color. But to Africans as a group Rhodes reacted tactically, subordinating any rights that they might be said to possess to his overarching imperial design—the creation of a united, Cape-dominated, British bulwark in southern Africa—and to his own intense search for personal fulfillment through power.

In Rhodesia the Founder had never elaborated nor, as far as can be discovered, even thought much about the particular manner in which his African subjects should best be ruled. He left the articulation of a point of view on this subject and the detailed application of any intellectual result to subordinates—to Jameson and others. In turn, they had only primitive notions of how best to ensure order and compel obedience while obtaining a ready supply of unskilled labor. The only model readily at hand was the direct method of South Africa, with white native commissioners imposing their own rough, hardly impartial, notions of right and justice on Shona and Ndebele with little subtlety and hardly any differentiation between the recently conquered and their former tributaries. They behaved as colonial whites nearly everywhere in Africa behaved: arrogantly. They alienated land, appropriated property, and abused their tenants and laborers. They were brutal and unfeeling; rude and insensitive. With rare exceptions they made the indigenous inhabitants of the newly seized territories feel rejected, unclean, defiled, and humiliated. Objectively, too, whites deprived Africans of their livelihood and primary means of subsistence.

In the specific case of Rhodesia, in 1893 Jameson had promised his volunteers a significant share of the loot—cattle and land. For that reason, and because the Company had no resources, Jameson's men quickly confiscated Lobengula's cattle. They made little distinction, indeed, between the king's beasts and individually held cattle. Vast herds (possibly 200,000 in all) were taken by the Company between 1893 and 1895. An ordinance of mid-1895 declared that all cattle in Matabeleland and their offspring held by Africans were the property of the Company. Proportionally, very few cattle were redistributed to indigenous individuals before 1896; yet for the Ndebele, like other Nguni-speaking people in southern Africa, cattle constituted wealth (both assets and income), and contributed to status and well-being. It was a "fatal mistake" so thoroughly to have looted the beasts of the conquered, and then to have confiscated cattle from the Shona, too, on the grounds that they had held or acquired portions of Lobengula's herd. "Next to burning the home of a native," Colonel Colin Harding later explained, "you cannot inflict a greater injury than to deprive him of his cattle, which are really a part of his family. Besides this, it is a suicidal policy to cripple a native farmer's prospects by taking for slaughter cattle which can be and are used for breeding purposes."[1]

Except in the Melsetter district, there was no appreciable competition for land between whites and blacks in Shonaland. In Ndebeleland, however, white volunteers had been promised 3,000 morgen each. By 1895 more than 1,000 white-owned farms covered over 10,000 square miles in the very heart of what had been Ndebele country. When the Ndebele crept back to their homes after the 1893 war, their villages and fields had been taken by whites; many now resided as tenants or serfs, but were subject to arbitrary expulsion, labor brigades, and the orders of persons with white skins. These were the suddenly dispossessed, aliens in their own land. Nor, without some tenure of their own, could the Ndebele grow food for themselves or for sale. Whites complained that the Ndebele were too numerous in and around Bulawayo and on the newly pegged white farms in the vicinity. After 1895, when the Gwaai and Shangani reserves were established north of Bulawayo and Africans unwillingly shunted onto the rougher, drier terrain there, a further focus of indigenous discontent was created.

A hut tax was imposed on the Shona, as it had been imposed earlier on the Zulu and the Tswana. Although justified as a modest recompense to a British administering authority for its efforts in ending local wars and imposing peace on the countries in question, such taxes were intended to propel African men out of their huts to seek work on white-run enterprises. Labor was short everywhere at the beginning of the colonial occupations in Africa; Africans were reluctant to work for whites, for wages, or for the material wants which initially interested them little. Working for whites also took them away from their families and their fields. Thus the first impress of the tax could be onerous. Moreover, in Shonaland whites and their African collaborators never collected the tax (in cattle, goats, grain, or cash) gently. Not infrequently, too, they took the tax in labor, marching whole villages off to work on a road, on a farm, or at a mine. Chiefs and headmen who resisted on behalf of their followers were fined, lashed, beaten, and humiliated.

The tranquil Shona were aroused in 1894 and 1895 in direct response to the brutalities and indignities heaped upon them and their leaders by Jameson's appointees and by the settlers with whom these local officials naturally associated and were affiliated. Even John S. Brabant, the chief native commissioner for Mashonaland, contributed little but offense to the Shona from whom he sought to collect taxes. Early in 1895, for example, he traveled to the Mtoko district, where the chiefs had resisted the payment of taxes and the confiscation of cattle. He stripped and flogged the African collaborators who had failed to keep order and obtain the tax, beat a chief's councillor who said something to which Brabant took offense, spurned a peace offering from Chief Gurupira, and then explained to the chief that he should tell his people that Brabant and his men were "going to burn and shoot and destroy everything [they] saw until he sent to stop [them] and ask for mercy, but that before [they] would cease he would have to fill the valley with cattle for [them] to pick from for hut tax and that he was also to furnish [them] with 200 of his picked men to go and work in the mines." Brabant's team "scattered over the hills" and burned down villages "until the whole atmosphere was dense with smoke. . . . The whites amused themselves meanwhile with a 'pig-sticking match on foot and horse-back.'" On the following day Brabant collected tax in cattle and goats, a further fine in cattle, and 500 men for work on the mines.[2]

The Ndebele may have been treated even more insolently. When their leaders later complained to Rhodes that they had been made "dogs" by the whites, they told him that white native commissioners had deflowered their wives and daughters, behaved harshly in other ways, and in every manner heaped abuse upon their unsuspecting heads. One chief explained that he had once gone to Bulawayo to pay his respects to the chief magistrate. "'I brought my induna with me, and my servants,'" related Somabhulana. "'I am a chief. I am expected to travel with attendants and advisers. I came to Bulawayo early in the morning before the sun had dried the dew, and I sat down before the Court House, sending messages to the Chief Magistrate that I waited to pay my respects to him. And so I sat until the evening shadows were long. . . . I again sent to the Chief Magistrate and told him that I did not wish to hurry him in any unmannerly way; I would wait his pleasure; but my people were hungry; and when the white men visited me it was my custom to kill that they might eat. The answer from the Chief Magistrate . . . was that the town was full of stray dogs; dog to dog; we might kill those and eat them if we could catch them. So I left Bulawayo that night. . . .' "[3]

In the years after 1893, important sections of Rhodesia had also suffered from drought, neither maize nor grass for fodder growing as tall and as lush as they had before the white men had conquered their country. Accompanying the drought were great clouds of locusts. They ate their way south, devastating cereal crops of all kinds. During the southern African summer of 1895–96, the locusts swarmed with unusual ferocity. Moreover, a third natural disaster contributed to the economic as well as the psychological unease of the Africans. Rinderpest, an inflammatory epizootic disease which had spread southward from Somalia and Uganda, jumped the Zambezi River in 1895 and began to destroy cattle and transport oxen in great number by early 1895. Once it reached Ndebeleland it spread quickly, moving twenty miles a day. Cattle that were spared were often killed by government order so as to prevent a further dissemination of the deadly fever. Thus the Ndebele, and the Shona as well, experienced a host of calamities at a time when they were also chafing under the man-made exactions of the English-speaking intruders from the south. Some of their religious leaders may well have ascribed these events to the evil influence of the whites and treated the locusts and the rinderpest, particularly, as omens and as spurs to a profound indigenous response. (This was the pattern common to the Zulu rebellion of 1906 and the Maji Maji uprising of the same year in Tanzania.) But the Ndebele and the Shona already possessed grievances aplenty, and several crucial areas of Rhodesia had been visited before 1896 by none or only one or two of the four horsemen of the apocalypse. Rinderpest had not reached several critical districts when the Ndebele acted. Other areas had escaped the drought or locusts. Nevertheless, the onset of natural crises assisted in the mobilization of Africans against whites. Resentful of and embittered by the brutality of the white occupation, and blighted by drought, locusts, and rinderpest, the Ndebele needed only the unexpected and fortuitous weakening of the white state to transform a conspiracy of antagonism into a concerted attack of revenge.

Jameson had taken 372 police to Pitsani, leaving 63 whites to patrol Rhodesia, only 48 of whom were posted in Matabeleland. There were nearly 1,000 additional white men of the two regiments of the Rhodesian Horse volunteers who had been expected to join Jameson after the insurrection in Johannesburg had succceeded, and 600 resided in Matabeleland, but when the rebellion broke out they were scattered throughout the province. Jameson's Raid had left the territory defenseless. Moreover, the Ndebele were aware that Jameson, their conqueror, had been defeated and he and the ex-police jailed by President Kruger. The strong back of British power in their conquered land had been broken. If the Ndebele were ever to do the great deed and rise up against their overlords, the months after the fiasco of the Raid were obviously ideal.

Like the Mau Mau in Kenya in the 1950s, and the modern Chimurenga in Zimbabwe in the 1970s, the Ndebele first killed African collaborators and then turned against whites. In late March 1896, an early, even premature Ndebele war party killed a policeman. Three days later fifteen whites were murdered in isolated parts of Matabeleland. About 200 were killed in the weeks that followed, along with Africans in greater number. Quickly Gwelo (Gweru), Belingwe, Gwanda, Inyati, and other tiny settlements found themselves under attack. Bulawayo, housing the only sizable collection of whites (about 1500), was the main target. It armed itself on 25 March and began building a formidable laager the next day. By then the rising of the Ndebele against Rhodes and the rule of his Company was undeniable. About 5,000 warriors had clasped their assegais, being joined by numerous white-trained African police bearing arms. Unlike 1893, the Ndebele were not completely without modern weapons. Wary of direct confrontations with whites, they mounted guerrilla attacks and kept to the hills and rocky kopjes along the routes between Bulawayo and the outlying white settlements. Aside from the advantage of surprise, the rebels burned with the fire of bitter resentment. They sought the recovery of their land and sovereignty, a reinstatement of their shattered dignity, and the obliteration and ouster of whites.

The rising of the Ndebele threatened to deny life to Rhodes' infant off-spring, and to destroy the centerpiece of his African empire. "Rhodesia was . . . to him," reported Stent, "as her first-born [was] to a woman. . . ."[4] After the Raid, Rhodes had naturally focused his heart and his energies on "the north," where he had intended to seek solace and a spiritual revival. Now even that was to be torn from him, a dream and a desire menaced by the cruel hostility of Lobengula's murderous, avenging, aggrieved subjects. The settlers, Rhodes discovered only later, had brought this retribution upon themselves. Together with the native commissioners and the suddenly all-powerful African police, they had taken cruel advantage of the Ndebele. Deprived of their self-respect as well as their land, cattle, and traditions, the Ndebele (joined before too long by the Shona) became determined to reassert their proud heritage. They went boldly to war.

Rhodes learned of the mortal threat to his colonial creation at the end of March. Providentially, he had returned from his rescue mission to London, and his audience with Chamberlain, via Naples, Egypt, and the African east coast. In Egypt he had purchased donkeys to see if they could help replace slower oxen as the territory's prime source of transport locomotion. (Because of rinderpest, the steady shipments of donkeys were to help rescue white Rhodesia at a time when transport was essential.) He would also have learned of and even seen the preparations for Britain's attempted reconquest of the Sudan. General Sir Horatio Herbert Kitchener had begun mobilizing troops and equipment for the long assault on the domain of the Mahdi. When Rhodes and Sir Charles Metcalfe, the railway builder, landed at Beira on 20 March, Rhodes was concerned about accelerating the construction of the railway from that port to Umtali and Salisbury. He worried about the impact of rinderpest, its deadly result being visible all along his route up from the coast and through the highlands to Salisbury. Soon he was also suffering from a severe attack of malaria, which affected him for several weeks. By the time he reached Salisbury a louder klaxon of alarm had sounded shrilly throughout the colony, southern Africa, and the empire. The Ndebele had attacked.

Rhodes assumed charge, determined—as his contemporaries reported—to rescue the beleaguered white population and save his offspring from destruction. Rhodes telegraphed orders to Bulawayo, where the acting administrator of the province was told to "hammer away" at the Ndebele until Rhodes could arrive with reinforcements. Then they would together sweep the Matopo hills. Shortly thereafter Rhodes dispatched arms and ammunition to Gwelo. On 6 April he joined a column of 150 white troops (leaving only 60 to defend Salisbury) as it set out on a long march to strengthen the defense of Bulawayo. At this juncture, Rhodes and his associates in Salisbury apparently believed that they were confronting a comparatively contained rebellion that the Company could suppress through the efforts of local volunteers and new recruits from the south. Rhodes hardly wanted to involve Britain for fear that he would lose control of the military effort and therefore of his colony, and also because he knew that Chamberlain would make the impoverished entity cover the full cost of imperial troops.

Lieutenant Maurice Gifford, in Bulawayo, gave Rhodes the first solid warning when he telegraphed, "Much more serious than you think. To go into Matopos with less than 500 is madness."[5] Indeed, the 1500 whites largely but never completely surrounded in Bulawayo were in acute danger for another month. The high commissioner's office in the Cape realized the seriousness of the rising even before Rhodes had reached Gwelo on his way south, and a relief force was rapidly raised and assembled at Mafeking, at the end of the railway, by mid-April. By then, too, Chamberlain had insisted that the ending of the Ndebele rebellion must be entrusted to British troops under a regular army general. Although Rhodes would have preferred to have tried to destroy the Ndebele on his own, the war was serious, and Rhodes and Rhodesia really had no other viable options.

By mid-May Rhodes and the relief column from Salisbury were safely inside the laager at Gwelo. Rhodes had hitched a field telegraph apparatus to the telegraph lines from the Cape, and had thus sent and received masses of telegrams every day all along the route of march. It was in Gwelo that he received a message from Chamberlain asking him, because of the Raid, to resign his directorship in the Company. "Let resignation wait," he thundered back. "We fight the Matabele again tomorrow." It was from Gwelo that he wrote to Harcourt about his lack of "sordid" motives for the Raid, concluding with "I know that I haven't much time." There, too, he installed himself as a full colonel so that he could resolve the inevitable bickering between the lieutenant colonels who commanded his column and the one in charge of the laager. It was on account of this illegal assumption of rank that he cabled Chamberlain with bravado, genuine horror, and a tinge of fatalism: "There is no colonel more unhappy than I am; obliged to take position to smooth over individual jealousies as to rank between various officers. The result is I have to go out into the field and be fired at by the horrid Matabeles with their ["beastly"] elephant guns, which make a fearful row. It is a new and most unpleasant sensation."[6]

Rhodes never took refuge in inaction. With typical gusto, he seized the opportunity to reassert himself in the aftermath of the humiliation of the Raid. Just as he told Chamberlain that the resignation could wait and assumed the position of colonel, so he sent orders to outlying field commanders and busied himself with the details of his own column's movements through a hinterland largely controlled by Ndebele war parties. Later, too, he was to preach reconciliation and to demonstrate a generosity of spirit that was positively redemptive for himself and for the Ndebele. But Rhodes' initial and for many months predominant reaction to the rising was harsh and vindictive. "Your instructions are," he told a major, to "do the most harm you can to the natives around you." He ordered a police officer to "kill all you can," even those Ndebele who begged for mercy and threw down their arms. Doing so "serves as a lesson to them when they talk things over at night." Eyewitnesses described the way in which Rhodes would descend upon a battleground after the warfare had died down in order to count the corpses. Jarvis remembered how he and Rhodes accompanied a patrol which had been burning crops and villages and capturing cattle and wives. "I have been out with Rhodes looting corn all the morning," he wrote, "and he is now keen to be off again."[7] One of the reasons for the successful repression of the Rhodesian rebellion was the adoption of such scorched earth tactics. By destroying crops and whole villages, whites drove the Ndebele quickly to realize their desperation. Olive Schreiner captured the venom of Rhodes and his contemporaries in *Trooper Peter Halket of Mashonaland*, a novelistic denunciation of white-perpetrated cruelties that appeared in 1897. Its original edition contained a photograph of a row of Africans hanging from trees, with armed and smiling whites posed beside them.

By the third week of May, Rhodes' reinforcements, proceeding southward from Gwelo, linked up with a column sent out from Bulawayo under Colonel William Napier near the Shangani River. Together, these two detachments swept through the Insiza and Filabusi districts, where Ndebele had initially attacked whites. Rhodes noted a total absence of Africans. "Our difficulty now," he cabled on 22 May, "is that the natives have disappeared."

It was about this time that a young trooper met the Founder: "We were camped on the veldt some miles out of Bulawayo, and with a comrade I was sitting by our fire when a wagon lumbered up and halted near us. Presently a big, shuffling figure, followed by two or three others, strolled over to our fire. The big man . . . was Rhodes, and . . . what a very red face he had, and what shocking bad clothes he wore." C.H. Instrap and his companions entertained Rhodes with stewed tea and adamantine cookies. They also talked about books, for a novel was near the fire. " 'Fond of reading?' " Rhodes asked.

"'Very,'" but mostly novels, Instrap replied deprecatingly. But Rhodes was unconcerned. "'Humph!'" he uttered. "'Nothing like a good novel sometimes. When I was a lad I spent all my money on books,'" Rhodes embellished. Rhodes ended the conversation by recommending a great book by a Dr. Theal. "'You ought to read it . . . good book . . . very good,'" he declared. Rhodes referred, amid the guns of war, to what probably was George McCall Theal's five-volume *History of South Africa*, which had been published in 1889.

On 1 June Rhodes' reinforcements and the Napier column made their way into Bulawayo without difficulty. "Rhodes," recalled one of his contemporaries, "looked well, but his hair is turning grey and the strong face tells a tale of excessive mental strain."[8]

Within a day, Major-General Sir Frederick Carrington had arrived from the south to take charge of the military effort. Fortunately for him, the Ndebele were now on the defensive. They had lost the initiative and had failed to achieve their objective of annihilating whites and ousting the Company. A military check at the Umguza River in late April, where their belief in the protection of magical potions had been critically undermined, and a succession of rebuffs in May reduced Ndebele ardor. The whites were able to stiffen their resistance appreciably. Moreover, reinforcements arrived from the south, together with machine guns and rifles, and soon Carrington could confidently contemplate an attack on the most determined Ndebele warrior groups. They had regrouped in and around the desolate Matopo hills to the south and the wilder Taba zi ka Mambo kopjes to the north.

Hubert Hervey, the young Etonian trooper who had accompanied Rhodes from Salisbury, wrote home on 1 June that ". . . the main force of the rebellion is quelled, but a lot of work remains to be done, as it would certainly be unsafe to travel about the country at present alone. . . . The mail route to Salisbury is still closed. . . . all townships are perfectly safe, but then natives still hold a good deal of the open country. The great difficulty is that they won't stay to fight any large force, so that the whole thing is being gradually reduced to a tedious guerrilla warfare. . . ." Fifteen days later Grey told his son that the end of the Ndebele rising was in sight. All that remained was the steady pursuit of the outstanding recalcitrants. "We must go on hammering and hunting them," he said, until "we . . . thoroughly convince them that this country is to be the country of the white, and not the black. . . ."[9]

Carrington and Rhodes (for Rhodes continued to exercise authority despite Carrington's arrival) thus were faced in June with the urgent need to make the countryside safe, to reassert the suzerainty of whites, and to flush the mass of rebels from their distant and impregnable retreats. These tasks they soon undertook but with the knowledge, at first incomplete and not as alarming as it should have been, that the Shona near Salisbury, south toward Gwelo, and east to Marandellas and beyond had also begun killing isolated white farmers, miners, administrators, and even missionaries with unexpected ferocity.

Aroused by their manifold grievances, the Shona had begun to settle scores against whites. Some of the Shona who rose clearly waited to attack until the whites had become fully engaged against the Ndebele. There were but sixty soldiers and fifteen white police to defend the country north of Gwelo. The Shona may also have believed that the Ndebele were achieving more than was in fact the case. Another group of the Shona was influenced by messages of encouragement from the main Ndebele spiritual leaders; those leaders sought the opening up of a second front against the whites, particularly when the momentum of Ndebele attack had begun to falter.

Shona murders and mutilations, the coordinated and clandestine nature of their assaults, and the prominence in the leadership of the rebellion of chiefs and spirit mediums all surprised the whites of Rhodesia. They had known and treated the Shona as pusillanimous serfs long subject to Ndebele dictates. Not all the Shona ever rose, but the whites of Salisbury and the other, smaller, settlements of the northern part of Rhodes' colony were soon as anxious and endangered as those of the Bulawayo region. By the end of June, sixty whites had lost their lives. "We were just getting abreast of our Matabeleland troubles," Grey wrote ruefully to his son in early July, "when this buffet came from Mashonaland. It is most provoking; it throws everything back and will cost the Company more money than it is pleasant to spend not to speak of the many poor fellows that have been killed." By the end of July, another 300 had been killed. As one of the native commissioners later admitted, "whites had under-rated the Mashona native. They were certainly not a warrior race like the Zulu, but they were steeped in superstition, and were cunning and clever, far more so than their late over-lords, the Matabele. . . . We were sitting on a smouldering fire and didn't know it."[10]

Throughout June and July 1896, Rhodes characteristically fought three critical wars simultaneously: against the Ndebele and the Shona; against British opinion, Chamberlain, and others (even members of the British South Africa Company's board of directors) who might seek to deprive the Company of its civil powers in Rhodesia as a way of pillorying him for the Raid; and to boost the morale of the anxious and genuinely threatened whites in the country. His first priority was to subdue the Ndebele, and for six weeks Rhodes was in the field, accompanying flying columns of white troops and participating in their battles as they scoured the countryside. From these bivouacs he sent back a stream of exhortations and instructions to Grey and Carrington, both of whom were establishing themselves in Bulawayo.

As early as 13 June Rhodes was persuaded that the rebellion was over. "You must be worried but I see daylight," he told Grey. Then and later he urged Grey to establish a series of police posts as soon as possible. "It is hopeless," he said, "hunting these natives with huge columns." After giving orders to construct a chain of stations to "protect the whole of northern frontier," he suggested that a war of attrition would be the only way to flush the mass of armed Ndebele from the Matopos. "Please tell Carrington," he wrote, "that in this part of the world the natives wont fight the whole country is stony koppies [hills] where you cannot move horsemen and you can only catch stray bodies along the rivers and they bolt as soon as they see us. . . . I am very sorry but the natives will not *fight*." Later, at his repetitive best, Rhodes again told Grey to inform Carrington that "chasing natives with these huge columns is not much permanent good though at same time I think we should complete this movement of three columns which will take another three weeks. It does good to natives seeing how many we are but I think they have given up the offensive on any large scale and will only make an attempt on a *small body of men*." On the next day, 17 June, he wrote that "the native rebellion [was] over and a bugbear, but nature abhors a vacuum and a few police in these outlying districts prevent further trouble."

There is evidence that Rhodes was no sideline observer of encounters with the Ndebele. His self-appointed role was to help the nominal commanders lead their mounted troops, not to man a gun. On 16 June, several hundred white and African troops sought a Ndebele war party about fifty miles north of Bulawayo. Rhodes' report to Grey was simple: They "had an engagement in bush this morning the firing was heavy and I dare say 20 or 30 natives were killed but you never can tell in bush. . . ."

A subsequent account by a friendly eyewitness provides a more detailed and much more favorable account of Rhodes' own role. The column attacked at dawn and found the Ndebele waiting for them. The Ndebele "opened up a brisk fire. As often happens with irregular and half-disciplined troops, the advance and flank guards galloped forward to meet the attack, leaving the wagon convoy halted in the road, and protected only by a small dismounted escort. . . . They came under fire at short range from some of the enemy. . . . It was a critical situation, for, owing to the long grass and dense scrub, the attackers could not be seen, and it was impossible to detach any men from the small escort to clear the bush. . . . At this juncture Rhodes, who had dashed ahead at the first contact with the rebels, reappeared with Metcalfe. He took in the position at a glance, and said to the officer in charge of the guns, 'We must clear the bush or these fellows will get our guns and mules.' " Rhodes knew that none of the whites could be spared, but hoped that the locally recruited African soldiers, armed only with spears, might be persuaded to enter the bush. But they refused. " 'Will they follow me if I lead the way?' " Rhodes asked. "Without waiting for a definite 'yes,' " reported Hole, and despite a warning from Metcalfe that Rhodes should not " 'go in there . . . they'll get you for certain,' " Rhodes "turned his horse and rode forward." The African recruits "plucked up courage and followed, beating the bush and yelling some sort of war-cry." The Ndebele wavered and "were soon in full retreat." Rhodes had saved the day.

Rhodes also participated in a major assault on the "confused" mass of granite kopjes of Taba zi ka Mambo in early July, when Lieutenant-Colonel Herbert Plumer and 752 soldiers (with four Maxim guns and two five-inch mountain guns) routed 1,000 Ndebele from strongly defended positions eighteen miles north of Inyati. Plumer said afterwards that Rhodes, Colonel

Frank Rhodes (recently released from prison in Pretoria and ordered by Chamberlain to participate in no official way in the campaign), and Captain A. Weston Jarvis joined the column an evening before the assault. "They had their own wagon and mess . . . and did not draw on us for . . . transport or supplies, but while quite independent . . . they conformed in every way to the arrangements of the march. . . ." Stent remembers Rhodes before this engagement, sitting on a camp stool next to his tented wagon, which was parked under "the friendly shelter of a klomje of mimosa." Plumer's column had been marching about twelve miles a day. In order to surprise the Ndebele at dawn, Plumer planned a forced night march of twenty-five miles. Rhodes joined the march although he had "no business" with it. "The staff were not over pleased to see him. He was a responsibility and not a fighting unit. But they understood his feelings, and their sympathy went out to the man in the hour of his travail. . . . He went merely as onlooker, a voluntary hostage, knowing that his presence would greatly encourage and hearten his own people of Rhodesia." He was, said Stent, a special kind of "camp follower." As Selous had commented about another engagement when he was contemplating an attack on several well-armed impi (war parties) with too few men and rifles of his own, "I had to consider the safety of Mr. C.J. Rhodes, for whose very valuable life I felt myself more or less responsible." (Selous did admit, however, that "whilst under fire Mr. Rhodes and his friends behaved with perfect coolness and seemed to be thoroughly enjoying themselves.")

As the march began, Rhodes' party, which included the boyish Johnny Grimmer, took a position midway along the column. "All night we rode—a stealthy band of khaki-grey intruders. . . . The small hours grew longer. Then the picket fires of the rebels lifted through the cumber of the night. . . . Rhodes and his friends followed a flanking force . . . and I followed him." At 3 a.m. this little force reached its appointed station, unsaddled, and the troopers rested next to their horses. Stent walked around the camp. "Returning alone I crossed the open centre of the horse ring and stumbled over some one lying asleep amidst the roots of a tree." That someone was Rhodes, wearing "a short ridiculous overcoat, reaching hardly to his knees" in the cold of a July night. He had been sleeping on his hat, with an inverted saddle as a pillow. He had no blanket, and was shivering.

The battle began at dawn, with the Ndebele making a stand on a central kopje. Rhodes, recalled Plumer, came "under a pretty warm fire." A few Ndebele fired on Stent and Rhodes and then ran. Indeed, at least one shot struck the ground directly under Rhodes' horse. (" 'If I had been shot through the leg,' " Rhodes complained, " 'I should have been very much annoyed; in fact, very angry.' ") "The squadron trailed after them in pursuit," said Stent. "One man drew out ahead, in spite of warnings and expostulations. I spurred to see. It was Rhodes himself, riding unarmed, switch in hand, leading the hunt."

What was remarkable about Rhodes during this second Ndebele war, if psychologically explicable, was that his exploits in or close to combat occurred despite a life-long fear of physical injury. "He had a remarkable dread of any mutilation of his person," Sauer remembered, "and it must have been by the exercise of the highest form of moral courage that he forced himself into position where he was constantly under fire at close range from rifles and elephant guns loaded with slugs and other projectiles which make ghastly wounds." Or did Jarvis, who had known Rhodes before but was in his camp for many weeks, provide a simpler explanation which in no way contradicts the first? He described Rhodes as "very like Napoleon. He quite thinks that he was not intended to be killed by a damned nigger. He is also a great fatalist." [11]

Another contemporary observer and subsequent hagiographer reported that Rhodes was frequently in action. But he seems never to have fired a gun against the Ndebele; rather, he strode around near the attacking lines in white flannel trousers, holding a riding crop. Obviously he was "an easy mark for a Matabele bullet," but "the marksmanship of the enemy snipers was bad. . . ." According to this same source, Rhodes' "extreme coolness under the hottest fire, coupled with the recklessness with which he would ride in advance of the column, was remarked by all his companions, and proved, had it been necessary, that his physical bravery equaled the moral courage he had so often shown." Or did it show that Rhodes, after the Raid, worried less about whether his life would end than in what circumstances that finality would occur? To be killed in battle might well improve his standing in the eyes of posterity.

For the whites, who nevertheless lost three of their own, the battle of Taba zi ka Mambo was a great victory. Plumer's plunder included 1,000 head of cattle, 2,000 sheep, and 600 prisoners. About 200 Ndebele were killed. "Plumer has done excellent work," Rhodes told Grey. The Ndebele had been "utterly smashed." Yet Rhodes was overconfident. The Ndebele maintained their resistance at high levels throughout the remainder of July and well into August. By then, too, Rhodes had learned about the revolt of the Shona. On 24 June, when Rhodes was forty-four miles northeast of Bulawayo, Grey informed him that the Shona had unexpectedly copied the murderous tactics of the Ndebele. At this time Grey and others were confident that the Shona could not sustain a prolonged war, even against the vastly outnumbered whites of Salisbury, Enkeldoorn, Hartley, Beatrice, Mazoe, Marandellas, and elsewhere. Rhodes therefore focused on the Shona problem only belatedly.

Rhodes was by now busily battling his own second war, too, against his political enemies in Britain and the Cape. He had tendered his resignation as managing director of the Company in February, and it had been refused. Chamberlain had demanded it later as the minimal price which had to be paid to protect the Charter itself. The tenor of the parliamentary inquiry in the Cape made such a resignation more imperative by mid-year, Rhodes being easily reconciled to the loss of his official position. Content to become a private citizen, he knew that his massive shareholdings in the Company as well as his aura as the Founder would ensure a continued position of immense influence in the Colony. Thus it was only a matter of time before the Company's board would agree to accept the resignation which Rhodes had again tendered in May. Rhodes' concern was that Chamberlain would demand or the board itself decide to strip the Company of its administrative authority. That was a prospect too chilling to contemplate. If it happened, there would be no role for him. It would mean the collapse of his "big idea"—the loss of that sustaining presence upon which his sense of purpose and self-worth were so dependent.

Rhodes' letters to Grey reveal the intensity of his feelings about Rhodesia the country—and as an essential part of himself. "If we keep civil administration," he wrote from an outlying farm, "I will remain and help the country but my position would be hopeless with an Imperial officer—with a Company officer I would work . . . to the end namely self government. . . . The key of Africa in the future is a great self-governing English state here. If I have to retire I promise to work with Companys representative here . . . but . . . with an Imperial representative it would be hopeless. I must go elsewhere." On 17 June, Rhodes received cables from Hawksley and Maguire and a letter from Grey. All informed him that he would have to resign as managing director. Again he wrote that he would leave the country if the Company lost its civil powers. If not, he was sure he could "pull the matter through." At about the same point in June he received messages from the Cape that its committee of inquiry wished him to testify. Conveniently, he felt unable to leave Rhodesia "until this war is through the crux." He decided that it was his "first duty to see matter through and I do not think I am doing bad work in field. As to not *facing the music,* which is the pet term of my opponents, in my judgement there is no further music to face at any rate from them. I leave it to the future to calmly judge my action," he concluded defiantly—or was it despondently?[12]

Rhodes elaborated upon this sense of future justification in a long, unusual letter (with numbered paragraphs) to William P. Schreiner. He penned it while accompanying Plumer's troops near Shiloh, north of Bulawayo. Rhodes thanked Schreiner for proposing to persuade the House of Assembly to give him a leave of absence for the 1896 session; otherwise Rhodes would lose his seat. But he urged Schreiner to do nothing of the kind until the committee of inquiry's report had been tabled. It would, he explained to Grey, "not be fair to members" and to Schreiner. It might somehow turn a less defiant face toward the committee, or show tactical weakness. (Schreiner nevertheless obtained the necessary leave for Rhodes.)

Rhodes was intent on assuring Schreiner that the future would be good to him. Indeed, that was the central reason for such a long letter from the battlefield. "You need not fear as to North the people are fond of me and I will fulfill every pledge I gave in the house as to closer union. . . . You said once supposing you died. I am dead in a way, but everything will be carried out as I foretold by my presence here. I am not going physically to die. . . . I am not going to run away from Africa and I will remain here unofficially and carry out the big idea. You may have for policy [personally] to repudiate me. I am very glad I have considerable wealth, it will be devoted to the one idea that is closer union." He urged Schreiner not to tire of politics. "It's your duty. Please be firm and continue. I am not thinking of yourself, but of the country. Really you and myself are nothing, it is the country." Significantly, he explained that such was the "thought that has put me through the late troubles." After giving a reason for the timing of the Raid, Rhodes explained that he was writing to Schreiner in this unusual (and revealing) manner because Schreiner could give him "nothing" and because writing to Schreiner offered Rhodes an opportunity to explain his thoughts and clear "some doubts" in Schreiner's mind. He closed the letter with an aphoristic golden rule: "Possess your soul in patience."[13]

There could be no more persuasive evidence of Rhodes' psychological resilience than the way that he could sustain himself by regressing to earlier positive experiences. In the face of a crisis which destroyed many of the attributes and activities upon which he was most dependent, he managed ultimately to preserve his self-esteem and psychological balance, as well as much of his reputation, power, and influence. Echoes of the vicarage in the Biblical tone of the letter, the hints of identification with Christ, the "son with whom I am well pleased," who, also, was "crucified, dead and buried" and yet rose from the grave, all reflect, in Rhodes' life, sustaining earlier images and the attendant positive emotions which helped him to survive and renew himself. These were deep intimations of times when he felt safe and loved, expressed in church language and in conscious recollections of the ideas which had made him feel wanted. They were a solid protection against depression, despair, and psychological dissolution. They constituted a platform of stability and confidence from which he could launch a vigorous defense, even a counterattack.

Rhodes' third battle was for the hearts and minds of his colonials. When he spoke to them in assemblies at Bulawayo both before and after his exercise in peacemaking, he sought as well to bolster his own spirits and strengthen the continued significance of what could otherwise be regarded as a dramatically weakened personal justification of leadership and wealth. As far as he was concerned, Rhodesia was not a tropical country: "The population could not always remain purely native . . . this country will be the abode of a white race. If I am allowed to remain and work with you," he said while his resignation was still pending, "I look in the future for the Charter to lapse, and for you to become a self-governing body, and that as speedily as possible." Rhodesia would "become another state in South Africa," he said, "and it will be my duty," he declared, "to think out the plan by which that self-governing state may be created with the greatest advantage to yourselves; but as to Transvaal or Cape absorption, that is impossible." He suggested that Rhodesia was not bounded on the north by the Zambezi River. "The country north of that river you must look on as your own." He prophesied a white-governed Rhodesia within a southern African federation. "If I have a say in the country, my policy will never change."

In a second speech, Rhodes thanked the audience for its expression of sympathy. However, he said that no sympathy was needed: "If I were to look to find what is the pleasantest work in life, I think you would find it in the development of a country as big as France, Germany, and Spain combined. You have been good enough to give my name to the country which you occupy." Later he said that "one can have no more attractive occupation than the development of a country from barbarism to civilisation." On a third occasion, Rhodes told the whites of Bulawayo that being among them had made him a happier man than ever before. "The great secret of life is work."[14]

Ultimately, Rhodes rose to the striking challenge of a country fractured by conflict, rent by the great division of color, and convulsed by legitimate indigenous grievances. He crossed the great gulf between imperial and indigenous man, radically reversed his own previous approach to the Rhodesian question, discarded prejudices of his own and of his contemporaries, and created conditions of compromise. A man of war as far as Africans and Afrikaners were concerned, Rhodes sought and gained peace. It was a supremely worthwhile achievement that restored his faith in himself and his belief in and for his colonial namesake. That was the happiness of which Rhodes had spoken, but its realization—like all redemptions—proved arduous.

Even after their massive defeat at Taba zi ka Mambo, when Rhodes believed that the Ndebele had been "utterly smashed," the Ndebele fought on. Carrington's troops even suffered a few annoying setbacks toward the end of July and throughout August 1896. A stalemate was developing, particularly since the main group of Ndebele warriors had retreated into the Matopos, where the imperial troops could but move them from one rocky fastness to another. Fighting in the Matopos, Lady Grey concluded, was "practically throwing away valuable lives for no adequate gain. The [white] men are simply shot at from behind rocks without ever really a chance of an open fight. . . ." Her daugher underlined the point: "Our men are quite helpless, for they can only hear the bullets whizzing and they never see the niggers who fire out of these hidden caves."[15] Carrington lost heart, concluding that to flush the Ndebele out of the Matopos without too much loss of white life, he would need up to 3,000 more troops, and vast numbers of carriers, engineers, mountain guns, and so on. Since gathering together all these men and supplies would take months and the normal summer rains would soon descend upon Rhodesia, the final campaign would of necessity be deferred until the dry season (April to November) of 1897.

Rhodes could neither contemplate such a long hiatus personally, on behalf of the country and its settlers, or on behalf of the Company. Paying for the reinforcements and their supplies, as well as for the soldiers who would remain comparatively idle for six months, and forgoing any return to a semblance of prosperity in Ndebele country, would bankrupt the Company and drain his own capital. Moreover, Rhodes may have calculated that delay in Ndebeleland could contribute little to the pacification of the Shona.

There would have been a dozen good reasons why Rhodes (and Grey) found Carrington's cautious assessment of his available options unsatisfactory and disconcerting. Most of all, Rhodes must have wanted the war well behind him, and won, when he appeared before the British committee of inquiry into the Raid in early 1897. Its mandate also included an investigation of the Company and its performance under the Charter. Since he could trust Chamberlain only up to a point, for Rhodes it was essential to remove Carrington and the other imperial commanders from Rhodesian soil and to reduce the relevance of Sir Richard Martin, the high commissioner's representative and nominal overlord of post-Raid Rhodesia. Rhodes further knew that an amnesty, which Martin had proclaimed for Ndebele rebels who turned in their arms by 10 August, later extended to 25 September, was accomplishing little. Fewer than 3,000 Ndebele, predominantly women and children, ever took advantage of the offer; they turned in a total of 79 guns.

If Rhodes were to save his state and, he may have realized, save or restore his good name and his reputation for nimble, innovative genius, he must devise a bold, strategic stroke as well as a series of tactical breakthroughs. Letting the war drag on, and exulting in what must inevitably be incremental, possibly petty, successes, would not suffice. " 'It is enough,' " Rhodes decided. " 'As rebels, [they] . . . have been sufficiently punished. Let us outlaw the murderers, but to the rest let us give peace.' " With the rains due in October or November 1896, the Shona insurgency surprisingly intense, Jameson on trial in Britain, and Rhodes undergoing a profound personal inquisition in and around Bulawayo, there was an intense need to think out a masterful pre-emptive move and then to act.

Stent, who was there, asserted that Rhodes conceived his alternative approach to continued war with the Ndebele after witnessing the successful assault on Taba zi ka Mambo. Depressed by the deaths of white pioneers (not to mention the many Cape Africans and Coloureds), Rhodes afterwards "sat over a fire, his shoulders . . . hunched up. He was not restless. He was thinking; gazing into the coals—the little flickering flames—silent." The result of this silent contemplation was the decision to try to meet the Ndebele themselves, "learning what they fought for," in order to search for peace.[16] Rhodes determined to use his own considerable empathic gifts to save Rhodesia. Whether or not Rhodes began thinking then about negotiations rather than combat, the notion (like so many of Rhodes' ideas in the past) that at least some of the Ndebele might be induced to lay down their arms was implicit in the official amnesty and in the efforts of a small handful of native commissioners, interpreters, and scouts, all of whom were seeking to contact the Ndebele leaders through intermediaries in late July and early August.

The military command among the whites, however, still regarded anything short of unconditional surrender by the Ndebele to be anathema. Martin, in particular, and Carrington also, believed that a cease-fire or a compromise arranged by talks would permit the Ndebele to regroup, ultimately prolong the war or lead to a subsequent rebellion, and set the wrong example. Most whites in Rhodesia probably accepted the wisdom of Martin's approach. By seeking an end other than outright submission or annihilation to the Ndebele phase of the Rhodesian revolt, Rhodes had to pursue an unpopular path, and to do so devoid of any official status. He had been a private citizen since the end of June. In theory he possessed no standing other than his ordinary directorship of the Company. In practice, of course, he was still regarded as lord high everything except by Martin and, possibly, Carrington. Grey was Rhodes' front.

By the end of the first week of August, Rhodes had committed himself to an all-out attempt to make contact with the enemy. He fully appreciated that the Ndebele food supplies were beginning to run low. He knew that so long as the main mass of Ndebele remained in the rocky fastness of the Matopos they would be unable to sow maize and sorghum on the fertile plains. Even though the Ndebele might confidently expect to fight off the whites from the mountains throughout the coming rainy season, hunger would prove a problem. Certainly by October they would be compelled to forage or starve. Thus the Ndebele were vulnerable; perhaps their elders were also tired of fighting. Rhodes was anxious to avoid the expense and loss of white life of a prolonged war. Perhaps a deal could be struck. Could Rhodes employ his vaunted powers of persuasion to square the proud Ndebele warrior chiefs?

The puzzle was to discover, without being killed in the process, whether the Ndebele leadership was willing to talk. The accidental capture of an aged widow of Mzilikazi, the first Ndebele paramount chief, who was also the mother of one of the important chiefs in the hills, and her subsequent release with messages and a white flag of peace, may have initiated the exchanges that led to talk. Or the critical emissary may have been Jan Grootboom, a Mfengu scout from the Cape, who bravely ventured several times into the hills to parley with the Ndebele on behalf of Johann Colenbrander, the Company's chief interpreter, and Rhodes. The Ndebele also sent messengers to Rhodes on 18 August; Rhodes suggested that they return in three days with a definite answer. Could serious discussions begin?

Grootboom and James Makhunga, another Mfengu interpreter, came down from the hills in the early afternoon of 21 August. The principal Ndebele chiefs were prepared to meet Rhodes, unarmed, well up in the Matopos with but a handful of other whites. Colenbrander, Hans Sauer (released from Pretoria prison after participating in the abortive Johannesburg rising), and Stent of the *Cape Times* were selected to accompany Rhodes, Grootboom, and Makhunga. Stent remembered it lyrically as a "lovely winter's day, the sun just beginning to western; comfortably hot; the grasses, bronze and golden, swaying in the slight wind; the hills ahead of us blurred in the quivering mirage of early afternoon." The group talked little among themselves. "We were all a little nervous."

Once having entered the hills Rhodes and his men made for a tiny open basin ringed by kopjes. "Looking round the vast amphitheatre of granite mountains [Sauer] saw thousands of Ndebele . . . dodging about among the boulders. Our position was such that, in the event of trouble arising, escape would have been impossible." Stent remembers wondering out loud whether they should, for safety's sake, remain on their mounts. Sauer and Colenbrander looked at Rhodes. " 'Dismount,' " he said. " 'It will give them confidence. They are nervous, too. How do they know that we have not an ambush ready for them behind the hill?' " Rhodes had refused to carry a white flag. He asserted that he was meeting the Ndebele at their request; the warriors must show the white flag. They did, and a small procession came toward the whites. "The wonderful smile broke out over Rhodes' face as he said, 'Yes, yes, there they are. This is one of those moments in life that makes it worth living! Here they come!' "

Rhodes uttered words of peace in Sindebele. " 'The eyes are white,' " he said, and Somabhulana and the other great Ndebele chiefs responded in kind. " 'Is it peace?' " Rhodes asked. " 'It is peace, father,' " was the reply. In the African manner, Somabhulana explained how whites and blacks had become such bitter antagonists. He started at the beginning, with the great wars of Shaka and the raids of Mzilikazi eighty-five years before. "It was a fascinating story," recalled Stent, "and took time in the telling. . . ." Rhodes was patient. The whites listened when Somabhulana gave a vehement Ndebele version of the first Ndebele war. " 'You came, you conquered,' " the chief supposedly said. " 'The strongest takes the land. We accepted your rule. We lived under you. But not as dogs! If we are to be dogs it is better to be dead. . . .' " "The moment," said Stent, "was inflammable. The least indiscretion might precipitate a massacre."

Rhodes calmly urged Somabhulana to continue talking. Thus Rhodes learned how this chiefly figure had been humiliated by the chief magistrate in Bulawayo, of the brutality of the African police, of forced labor, and of particularly offensive officials. Rhodes taxed the Ndebele with having killed innocent women and children rather than simply protesting against injustice. But the chief replied that the whites had in fact first begun killing Ndebele women and children in the course of tax collecting. Colenbrander urged Rhodes to accept that contention and not to pursue the subject. Rhodes wisely told the Ndebele that " 'all that is over.' " The time for peace had come.

It was late in the afternoon. Somabhulana stood up, signifying that the indaba or negotiation was concluded. " 'But is it peace or war?' " Rhodes demanded. "An intense silence followed," recalled Sauer. Finally Somabhulana said " 'It is peace.' " " 'You have [my] word. . . .' " Rhodes was soon surrounded, but it was only a clamor among the chiefs to share Sauer's tobacco. The first quarter of Rhodes' finest hour had passed safely, and successfully.

Sauer pointed out to Rhodes that his successful peacemaking with the Ndebele, "under conditions that had hitherto always proved disastrous, would go a long way to rehabilitate him in the minds of his countrymen, both in South Africa and England."[17] But Rhodes refused for once to send off a flurry of telegrams crowing about his achievement. Admittedly, he let Sauer and Stent rush into Bulawayo and send word to the press (and to buy Company shares); Stent wanted the journalistic scoop and had been added to the white side of the indaba primarily so that he could record it for posterity.

Stent, a writer with known pro-African sympathies, had been a last-minute addition to the party, but had hardly been chosen at random. Nevertheless, all that Rhodes himself wished to tell Grey was "I have been sitting with all the rebel chiefs for about four hours and the war is over as [far as] this part is concerned."

Martin, Carrington, and their superiors in Cape Town and London were, however, less than delighted. A private citizen had been negotiating the end of a war which, officially, was in imperial hands. What had Rhodes offered and what were the next steps? Martin needed to be involved in the subsequent talks, for only such a personage as the deputy high commissioner could give the Queen's word. But Rhodes and Grey were worried, even paralyzed by the fear that Martin might very well demand the unconditional surrender that he was known to want, or otherwise throw his imperial might about in ways which would destroy Rhodes' carefully crafted and delicately balanced initiative.

Rhodes wisely appreciated that the first session in the hills had constituted no more than an exercise in the building of confidence. He had promised the Ndebele a fresh start, a reformed white administration and, explicitly, to cease employing Africans to enforce the white man's laws. The Ndebele chiefs resented African police, for they became the "masters of their fathers." The Ndebele had not yet given up, even though, as Rhodes had told Grey, the war was probably over.

In the days that followed the first indaba, Rhodes continued listening sympathetically with a "third ear" that was uncharacteristic of him, or at least had long lain dormant. He held court in his tented wagon at the foot of the Matopos. "The natives come in daily," he told Grey, "and everything is going most satisfactorily. There will be no more war unless we make it. The natural suspicion of the natives makes them slow to move out of the hills at once for fear of being killed but the position is clear if we only leave them alone." He wisely asked Grey to return the wives of a particular set of Ndebele warriors; the women had been "appropriated" by African "friendlies"—wartime collaborators. "Please give them food," Rhodes also asked. "A few tins [of beef] . . . may stop any expenditure of £100,000 per month." Rhodes had also become a confident peacemaker, or was he more simply the fatalist that Jarvis had described? "I should feel perfectly safe," he told Grey, "if I went into the hills and lived with them."[18]

The second indaba took place on 28 August, fortunately without Martin and his thirty armed escorts. With Rhodes under a large tree on a hillock about a mile southeast of Fort Usher at the foot of the Matopos were Plumer, Metcalfe, Herbert J. Taylor, James G. McDonald (Rhodes' biographer), Grimmer, Stent, Mollie Colenbrander, and her sister Mrs. Alphonse Colenbrander. The Ndebele party of chiefs and induna was larger than the first, and included a broader cross-section of the different rebel age groups and factions. "I remember how the chiefs . . . began to arrive, dressed mostly in skins," said the second Mrs. Colenbrander. "They were in a miserable, wretched condition." The African spokesmen were Dhliso and Babyaan, elder induna, but they were interrupted continually by representatives of the younger warriors. Although the Africans were armed, and most of the whites exceedingly nervous, Rhodes appeared casual, even crossing from the white side of the gathering to the African side, and sitting with them and taking their part. He tried to assure them that the past was behind them. " 'It is peace now.' " When a younger induna asked where the Ndebele were to live now that the whites claimed all the land, Rhodes promised them settlements and locations. " 'You will give us land in our own country! That's good of you!' " came a retort from the Africans. But Rhodes persisted, turning aside their wrath with humor and clever ambiguity. Stent also suggests that Rhodes distributed cash to some of the young hotheads.[19] Whatever he did, and however he communicated his sense of destiny, greatness, authority, and vision to the induna, Rhodes somehow persuaded the once-hostile Ndebele that he could be trusted—that he would be their friend and that they no longer needed to achieve their objectives on the battlefield. This was a considerable achievement, more significant and more difficult than the accomplishments of the first indaba.

Yet settlers, the press, and officialdom were still disturbed. Rhodes had given away too much to murderers and villains. He had treated the Ndebele like patriots when they were despoilers. He was defeating the ends of justice. Only a complete conquest would safeguard Rhodesia and permit a fully just administration to be reconstructed. Martin worried that the attitudes of the leading Ndebele had not really changed, that the Queen's dignity was being compromised, and that no good could come of these ill-considered, privately arranged talks between whites of no standing and chiefs of ill-repute.

Merriman, alone of so many southern Africans, knew how extraordinarily difficult going into the Matopos must have been for Rhodes, never physically intrepid. He also appreciated more than most of his contemporaries, how signally important Rhodes' intervention was and would be. "I feel bound [as a critic of Rhodes]," Merriman wrote to the *South African Telegraph*, a Cape Town opposition newspaper, "to express . . . strongly my sense of the physical and moral courage shown by [Rhodes]. . . . Many will be found ready to face danger when called upon, but there are not so many who can . . . incur the responsibility of doing an unpalatable and an unpopular action from a sense of duty."

Chamberlain also appreciated the significance of Rhodes' exercise in pacification. Siding with Grey, who had reported that Rhodes was "looked upon by the Natives with the greatest respect as the big white chief and the conqueror of their country," Chamberlain instructed General Sir William Goodenough, the acting high commissioner, to overrule Martin. "Rhodes," said Grey, had "been successful beyond our most sanguine hopes. . . ." Chamberlain accepted this fact. "There would be great difficulty," he cabled, "in defending an attitude of less leniency than that advocated by representatives of the . . . Company."[20] Chamberlain knew how foolish he and the British government would have appeared if they had even tried to cross Rhodes on—strange idea— a humanitarian issue.

By taking the high road, seizing the initiative, and understanding the impact of generosity on British public opinion, Rhodes restored himself to a position of leadership which Chamberlain, and hence Martin, was compelled to acknowledge. He rose, in a sense, from the dead. It was Rhodes' war, if not Jameson's, and Rhodes could be allowed to conclude it. As Rhodes ended a long letter to Beit matter-of-factly on 3 September, he was "now in the Matoppos, settling with the natives. The war is practically over but it will take a little time to make a complete agreement." By 9 September, the day of the third indaba, a great number of Africans had "dribbled in" daily to Rhodes' camp, consulted with him, aired their grievances, presumably accepted presents, and obviously spread the word of satisfaction. At the third meeting near Rhodes' camp, the Founder was joined by Grey, Martin, Johann Colenbrander, and five other whites. Six principal Ndebele chiefs and thirty-eight induna comprised the party of warriors. Grey told the chiefs that they and their followers must come out of the hills, lay down their arms, return to their farms and plant their crops. He confirmed the promises that Rhodes had made. Martin—"that consummate ass"—hectored, but Rhodes was able to smooth over the rough spots. "Come and help me," he asked them. They hardly wanted to give up their arms "and die like dogs," but they were hungry, and, as Rhodes hoped, the older Ndebele were thoroughly committed to peace.[21]

The war was over in Ndebeleland, and Rhodes had procured peace. Or was it? And had he? Even after the third indaba, Rhodes' only tangible result was immense goodwill. The warriors were still in the hills, loath to return to their farms and give up their arms until the white army was withdrawn and demobilized. Rhodes attempted to persuade Carrington to take his troops home. But Martin and Carrington still demanded submission; then they could stand down the soldiers. Few whites in Rhodesia other than Rhodes, Grey, and their associates believed that the Ndebele would submit. Many thought that they were simply stalling for time, like the cunning thieves the whites believed that they really were. Martin insisted that there could be no secure peace until every rebellious African had flung his rifle and spear at a white commander's feet. If Rhodes had ever wavered, the firing might have begun again in earnest, and his finest hour might never have been consummated.

Throughout September and well into October Rhodes employed all of his powers of example and persuasion on the chiefs and induna. "I marvelled at Mr. Rhodes's patience," remembered Philip Jourdan, Rhodes' new secretary. "The native mind moves slowly, and even when the chiefs had grasped a simple fact they always returned to their people in the hills, where they would sit round their fires and repeat and repeat what they had heard . . . till everybody understood the position. The chiefs would then take their own time about returning to camp. They had no conception of the value of time. . . . In the meanwhile Mr. Rhodes would anxiously await their return to know how the men of each particular chief took their messages. . . . It was a very hot time of the year . . . but Mr. Rhodes never heeded the heat.

He used to sit day after day in the blazing sun talking to the chiefs and crack-
ing jokes with them until we were all tired to death of them. . . . He inspired
the chiefs with confidence. . . ."

Over and over again he rode unarmed into the Matopos, on one occasion
stumbling upon the granite dome of Malindudzimu, from which Rhodes could
see one of what he called the "views of the world." He chose it then for his
place of burial. These rides were often prolonged. Jourdan admired his
"physical strength and powers of endurance" during these weeks of aroused
and focused attention. Rhodes rode each morning, for up to seven and usually five or six hours, often shooting small game. "Sometimes I felt almost too
tired to dismount," said Jourdan, "but Mr. Rhodes never seemed to feel the
strain of a long ride in the least." He would "hurry through his breakfast, and
then start talking to the chiefs right through the heat of the day till four in
the afternoon, when the horses would be saddled again and he would ride till
dusk. After dinner the chiefs would turn up again, and he would chat with
them till late at night." Sometimes, after an unusually long ride, he would
"quietly rise from his chair at the breakfast table, throw himself down under
the nearest tree on the bare ground, and fall asleep at once . . . for about
half an hour. . . ."

At his camp at the foot of the hills Rhodes played generous host and
ready listener. There he accepted the submission of the great and minor chiefs.
There he dispensed advice, and in a few instances gave them ultimatums. He
warned them that his railway was coming from the south. Troops could arrive
easily. They now had no choice but to submit and bring their arms. "Things
are really looking bright," he wrote to Grey on 21 September. Babyaan, Dhliso,
Unthwani, and other important chiefs were with him. "Large numbers [are]
already out. In fact . . . the matter is over as far as these hills are concerned. . . ." The Africans at last understood that they simply had to give
up their guns. "It has required immense patience on the part of Mr. Rhodes
to persuade the natives to come out and to reassure them that they are not
all going to be shot by the Queen's soldiers," Alice Grey wrote, "and without
him it would never have been accomplished for no other man could secure as
he can the confidence of both the whites and the natives."

In October, Rhodes told Albert Grey that the chiefs had been interviewing him all day. "Their surrender is complete, but the suspicion of the natives
at the huge white impis that we are retaining along the Matoppos prevents
absolute surrender of guns." He reminded Grey that it was "very easy to begin war again, but the responsibility rest[ed] with the Imperial authorities."
Rhodes believed that the Ndebele were "absolutely submissive. . . . I would
go and live among them in the Matoppos by myself, but . . . if the Imperial
authorities persist in commencing the war again, let them do so and take the
responsibility." He went on: "I myself will have nothing to do with it. The
Matabele are a lot of children. They know that they have done wrong. They
have submitted, but are afraid of the huge white forces and fear being slaughtered by our people. It is wonderful how they came out into the flats and

trusted my word." The magic was that the Ndebele had, indeed, put their trust in Rhodes' words, a conclusion in which Colenbrander concurred. At the very end of this letter, after again thrusting responsibility for any war onto the shoulders of the empire's officials, Rhodes repeated himself: "If necessary tell the Secretary of State that I am prepared to go and live in the Matoppos with the rebels."[22]

Rhodes concluded his finest hour on 13 October, when all the rebel leaders submitted themselves and their arms to Grey and Rhodes. Grey heard their grievances. He restored the authority of which they had been deprived in 1893; he promised them positions and salaries as retainers of the state. The chiefs worried that they would have no way of reaching Rhodes, their overlord. Grey gave them a channel through himself, the administrator. Rhodes told the chiefs and induna to "forget the past . . . be loyal to your Queen, and to the promises you have made me. I don't think you will want to fight again." Somabhulana had the last word; he called Rhodes "Umlamulanmkunzi"—"The bull who separates the two fighting bulls," the Peacemaker.[23]

Ultimately, Rhodes' great achievement was less in cajoling the Ndebele to give up a battle that they had lost and a severe hunger that was coming (and came anyway) than in singlehandedly restraining the martial instincts of his nominal superiors. It was a very strange part for Rhodes to play and essentially out of character. Or was it? Rhodes was an accomplished solver of problems and a master tactician who had never followed the easy or accepted paths to a conclusion. In this case he perceived that concluding a peace inexpensively was his only real choice. Otherwise Rhodesia and the big idea would perish. And so would he.

Rhodes came face to face with himself, with the real meaning of his life, and with high purpose, in the Matopos. It is said that at some point during the long days of September and October Rhodes told one of his companions that prosperity in southern Africa depended upon the establishment of " 'complete confidence between the two [white and black] races, and henceforth I shall make that part of my work, but all must help, all must help.' "[24]

Rhodes played little direct part in the pacification of Shonaland. By the time that he had ended hostilities in the central core of Ndebeleland (a few outlying warrior groups had still to be subdued by conventional means), the revolt of the Shona had been contained, if not suppressed, by a detachment of imperial troops and the energetic efforts of locally raised volunteers. Rhodes wanted to believe that the outstanding Shona rebels no longer represented a serious threat to the colony. Along with Carrington and Grey, he wished to reduce expenses and to be in position to face the new year's parliamentary inquiry with the Rhodesian war at his back. "As I told you," Rhodes wrote to Grey in early November, "we found rebellion all along the road practically over except in a few natives here and there in the caves. . . ." One unreconciled Shona leader lived in a granite fastness about seven miles from Enkeldoorn, but Rhodes participated in his defeat. "We went out and destroyed his kraal, killing a good many natives," Rhodes reported. "With these facts before us I think it would be possible to wind up matters. . . ." Carrington agreed, cabling at the end of November that the rebellion was at an end. There was no further need for British-officered troops; the newly organized police could continue their patrols.[25] The rains were due soon, too. Few in Rhodesia then expected that significant sections of the Shona would remain hostile to settler rule throughout the wet season of 1896–97 and well into the next southern African winter. It was not until July and August 1897, long after Rhodes had ceased to pay proper regard to the Shona question, that white-led legions managed to achieve decisive victories over the last important Shona protagonists. Only then could whites begin to move freely within all sections of northern and eastern Rhodesia.

Rhodes' contribution to the restoration of white rule in this part of his country was largely indirect. Even while he was living among the Ndebele and wrestling mightily there with the conundrum of peace at any or at what price, he remained conscious of the crucial importance of stiffening the always-weak fiber of the settler element in Salisbury and other colonial centers. Whites needed to be assured that the railway from the Pungwe mouth to Umtali and Salisbury would be rushed forward, and Rhodes sympathized with their worries. (Only the availability of comparatively sure and rapid transportation access to the outside world would link the whites securely to reinforcements and supplies in case of a further emergency.) He also wanted "the people of the country to be unanimously in favour of Charter when the London Committee [sat] next February" in judgment. For those reasons, and because he had already planned to complete that rail connection as well as the rail line from Mafeking to Bulawayo as rapidly as possible (at a speed of about a mile a day), Rhodes urged Beit to help him raise the £500,000 which he estimated it would cost to lay rails 174 miles from Umtali to Salisbury. He pledged £100,000 himself. "I feel certain that this railway will pay," he said, since "in future the heavy stuff must come from East Coast." Anyway, he told Beit, the money would simply be a guarantee—"a temporary matter." The important point was not the amount of money but the rapid completion of final arrangements for this last stretch of rail. "I wish to get the whole country with us."[26]

In late October, notwithstanding his efforts on the railway, when Rhodes arrived in Salisbury en route to the Cape and then Britain, he faced a disgruntled hubbub of whites. The best and the brightest of the settlers were antagonistic to the Company's rule, blaming it for the Shona rising and their initial defenselessness. Rhodes still retained sufficient éclat to command their attention, but now they sought self-government. The settlers wanted to manage their own destiny. Yet since Rhodes had already tackled this issue in Bulawayo, and since he retained his faculty for persuading whites (as well as Africans) of his positive intentions, he needed to employ no special suppleness to hold their loyalty a little longer. According to Milton, the whites of Salisbury were full of grievances, and asked for redress and assistance "on every conceivable pretext." Rhodes, said his secretary, "felt sorry for them. . . . We stayed . . . for three weeks, [and] there was literally a string of applicants winding their way to [Rhodes]. . . . They all wanted something, and I do not think there was a single applicant . . . who did not get something. My time was fully occupied writing out cheques. . . ." "They have simply plundered him, deserving and undeserving alike. They have really disgusted him," his secretary reported. Milton reckoned that Rhodes gave away £10,000. " 'I must encourage them so that they should not leave the country,' " Rhodes explained.[27]

The Founder promised the politically active that he would support their agitation for home rule. He would see that settlers could be elected to the new council which would run the colony. Rhodes envisaged a stage of semi-responsible government with both elected and appointed members of the council, leading before too long to full self-government. However, they should not expect the last until they were prepared to pay the costs of running the country. (Neither Rhodes nor the settlers ever—even after the rebellion—referred to the role of Africans. When they spoke of giving the vote to the "inhabitants" of Rhodesia they talked in their colonial blindness of whites only.)

In 1897, in line with these promises, when Rhodes and the Company were still subject to examination and censure in London, he pressed Sir Alfred Milner, the new high commissioner, and Chamberlain for changes in the way Rhodesia would henceforth be governed. Milner, who gave his views privately to Lord Selborne in the Colonial Office, read Rhodes' motives well: "He looks to making the territory . . . into a separate Colony ultimately self-governed." But, said Milner, such a colony, even if nominally self-governed, would virtually be "an absolute monarchy with Rhodes as monarch." Rhodes intended (in keeping with the "big idea") to unite the Cape, Natal, and Rhodesia, and then to bring *"peaceful* pressure upon the Republics to drive them into a S. African federation." As to Rhodesia itself, "Rhodes' game is to get rid of Imperial control. . . . He hates it, as he hates all control." Milner was in favor of a representative element in the future govenment of Rhodesia. The settlers wanted it, and Rhodes was "going for it 'hot and strong,' avowedly with the object of strengthening his own position in any differences with the Imperial Govt. They may bully the Company, he says frankly, but they won't dare to bully a representative Council. At the same time . . . this representative council will simply be Rhodes, even more completely than the Company is."[28]

After long discussion and many drafts, a new Order-in-Council was promulgated for Rhodesia in late November 1897. It gave the colony legislative and executive bodies to replace the old administrative council. Four of the members of the new legislative council were to be elected and five appointed by the Company. The administrator, also a Company man, would preside. The Company lost its power to make laws from London through its board of directors. In its place the High Commissioner obtained what amounted to final veto powers, but those were only very rarely employed in the years before 1980.

One of the signal results of the risings of 1896–97 was the rapid shift in power from the Company to the settlers. It was a transfer which served Rhodes' larger purposes, but which would not have been on his immediate agenda if the Raid, the rebellions, and his own intense need for white support had not made virtue of necessity. For Rhodesia and then Zimbabwe, Rhodes' most important legacy was an almost completely unfettered dominance by colonial whites from 1898 to 1980, the consequent official neglect and abuse of the mass of the indigenous inhabitants of the Colony (in practice, imperial oversight proved unhelpful to Africans), and the creation of an entity that revered him and his name as the Founder, but neglected for more than eight decades to expand upon the lesson of reconciliation that he had taught himself high in the Matopos.

Rhodes' gift to his adolescent offspring could also be measured in steel. Rhodesia could hardly have prospered without strong rail connections to both the south and the east. Morever, to construct a railway was a solid and enduring achievement. A staunch believer in the obvious economic as well as the more intangible but critical political contribution of rail ties, Rhodes pushed the rails toward Bulawayo and Salisbury with all the determination of his character. By late 1896 the extension from Mafeking had traveled ninety-two miles to Gaborone. By February of the next year a light line, initially without bothering to bridge streams properly, reached Palapye, and by November a locomotive could steam into Bulawayo itself.

Rhodes did not himself open the line ceremonially, either because he was avoiding Milner, who officially did so, or, more plausibly, because he was too ill from "fever" to travel. (Rhodes and Milner met a few weeks later, "in the veld" near Umtali. They had a "perfectly frank talk" and, according to Milner, ever afterwards they "understood & trusted one another. . . .") On the day of the celebrations Rhodes was "still bad," with a need to "keep quiet." He had experienced some kind of heart attack. After the opening ceremonies Rhodes himself wrote that his heart was "better," but that he had to "keep quiet."[29]

At that moment in 1897, because of the more difficult terrain, because of its even more narrow gauge, and also because of the financial weakness of the main contractors, the Indian Ocean railway was running only to Macequece in Mozambique. Rhodes had promised at the earlier meeting in Salisbury that the rails from the sea would reach Umtali by May 1898; in fact the first train steamed there in February 1898, but only after Rhodes and George Pauling, the railway builder, persuaded the inhabitants to move their town several miles closer to the line of rail (in order to avoid steep gradients and an expensive tunnel).[30] Meanwhile, as Rhodes had planned with Beit, a separate company had been formed to extend the rails from Umtali to Salisbury. The full line to Salisbury was opened in May 1899, but with a change of gauge at Umtali. That last obstacle to smooth communications was eliminated in August 1900, when the Portuguese portion of the railway was converted to broader gauge. As far as Rhodes was concerned, once the rails were in place his colony could be secure. His own place in history was riveted firmly by those long lines of steel and the white sense of prosperity which, he had always assumed, would follow.

Rhodes rebuilt Groote Schuur after the catastrophic fire of 1896, and from 1898 he resumed a central role in Cape politics. But the Raid and the rising shifted his personal allegiance several degrees toward Rhodesia—where he intended to be buried, where his name would remain, and where his actions and influence were and would be less subject to controversy. After the rebellion Rhodes had purchased Hans Sauer's large block of farms, called Sauerdale, on the northern edge of the Matopos and, at McDonald's urging, nearly 100,000 acres of the finest land and views (including the Pungwe Falls) in the elevated Inyanga district north of Umtali. He loved the second and lived there for three months in late 1897. "Do you not think [it] the best place in Africa for farming?" he asked later. He began trying to grow wheat and to raise Cape sheep, cattle, and ostriches. He found the local Africans "backward," and so sought thirty or forty Ndebele to labor for him. Subsequently he settled Grimmer and John Norris as managers, sending them detailed instructions on how to develop his estates, but all that he harvested was a great anger at them both for their waste and inefficiency. At Sauerdale, he tried to grow maize, alfalfa, and potatoes, and to raise Angora goats and cattle. Six months before his death Rhodes was still giving precise orders to McDonald about how Sauerdale (under Percy Ross) could best be farmed and irrigated.[31]

But that great block of land was also purchased for Ndebele and their chiefs, as partial payment of his promise to provide them with decent land. He settled a number of former rebels there in 1896 and 1897 and was thus able, if from a distance, to play the kind of paternal role which he best enjoyed. He would be their laird. He would provide for their welfare. He would hear their grievances, as he did so masterfully once again in June 1897, when 150 induna sat at his feet during the celebration in Bulawayo of Queen Victoria's jubilee. They said that they were inhibited by the white man's regulations from controlling land and planting as they had been accustomed to do. Rhodes promised to investigate. As the *Chronicle* reported with awe, "Coming to speak to the indunas individually Mr. Rhodes' manner underwent a startling change, it assumed a boyish exuberance and aspect of pleasure, which was immensely gratifying to the indunas personally known to him and . . . there was a suggestion conveyed to each of the circumstances under which they had last met, which indicated an extraordinarily capable memory." Subsequently there was a birthday bash at Sauerdale for 1200 Ndebele and a crush of whites. The party was one that Rhodes threw, very unusually, for himself; it was his forty-fourth birthday. Two hundred sheep were slaughtered, blankets and tobacco were distributed, grievances heard, and promises made. What the *Chronicle* never knew was that Rhodes, wanting to experience the special relationship that had once been enjoyed by feudal lords, had planned every detail himself.[32]

Rhodes' other gifts to his created country were many. He urged McDonald to construct a dam to collect and contain the water from the Matopos, and to provide supplies for irrigation. "The whole thing hinges on proper valves," Rhodes instructed McDonald in the course of an explicitly detailed letter. He purchased Maltese goats for Shonaland and personally restocked the cattle herds of the country by importing cattle from Madagascar and Argentina. He ordered the administrator of Mashonaland to plant avenues of trees in Umtali and Salisbury, specifying red flamboyants (royal poinciana or *Delonix regia*) from Madagascar. "If the government cannot pay I will pay myself," he said. In 1899 he took a strong position against government-controlled rather than voluntary or mission schools. "You should only start a government school where you think it is absolutely necessary. . . ." He recommended grants per pupil to church schools, but only after an inspector certified that the pupils had attained uniformly high standards. He agreed to permit religious instruction each morning.[33] For so long as he lived, Rhodes was concerned for and interfered directly in the development of white Rhodesia. He was far less interested in what happened to Africans.

There is little doubt that Rhodes felt redeemed by his successful change of direction in the Matopos. There can be little question that his sense of accomplishment was real, that he felt personally renewed, if not cleansed. Whatever had been lost by the Raid had been or could be made up. He was still capable of seeing what he regarded as high purposes through to fruition, if only his body would permit. An impromptu speech in Port Elizabeth, where he docked after traveling from Beira in late 1896, expressed Rhodes' own conclusions about himself and his life's work. "I have had a troublesome year," he began with understatement. He had learned through adversity that "the man who is continually prosperous does not know himself . . . his own mind and character." He accepted the meaning of his unexpected reception in Port Elizabeth—"that I have done my best in the interests of the country." Rhodes reminded his listeners that after the Raid he had been told that his public life was at an end, but in fact "it was only beginning." "I do not feel that my public career has closed." He promised to retain his seat in the Cape parliament because, he said, it was part of his program to show to the people of South Africa that he did not undertake a career of isolation. He went on: "You may tell me my faults, you may condemn me, but until you turn me out, I mean to remain with you."

At Kimberley, where he presided over De Beers' annual meeting, and even at Paarl, the center of Dutch life in the Cape, Rhodes received a royal welcome as he progressed by train to Cape Town, where a reception had been organized in his honor. When he arrived, on 1 January 1897, "the crowds ran after him and before him, shouted their welcomes and gripped his hands." Rhodes had not returned to Cape Town since the week after the Raid. He was moved by all the adulation. When facing the large crowd that had come to pay him tribute and hear him speak, Rhodes told Fuller exultingly that "such appreciation as this generally comes after a man is dead."

Six hundred citizens of Cape Town dined with Rhodes at a vast banquet in the city's drill hall on 5 January. As he entered the building a band played

"See the Conquering Hero Comes." Sir John Woodhead, the mayor, presided, and Sir Thomas Fuller, his legislative colleague, friend, and later biographer, proposed Rhodes' health "amidst a scene of wild excitement," reported the local press, "the like of which has never been witnessed in Cape Town." In the course of his hour-long reply, Rhodes apologized for using the pronoun "I." "But how can I help it?" he asked. The philosophy that had guided him for years, he explained, was "that the world was limited to its surface, that it was probably that the colony he belonged to would in the future be limited to its hinterland. Having read the history of other countries, he saw that expansion was everything, and the world's surface being limited, the great object should be to take as much of that world as it possibly could." That accounted for Rhodesia, at least. Closer to Cape Town, Rhodes' principal object was still a closer union of the principal provinces of South Africa. He refused to be tarred with the dirty brush of racism; the Raid into the Transvaal was not anti-Dutch, nor was he.

" 'Every man must do something,' " he proclaimed. " 'Some people grow orchids. Others have great delight in masonry. But, whether rightly or wrongly, my hobby,' " he called it, " 'has been expansion and unity in this country. Faults one must have, and I would like to know any man in this room who has not committed any faults!' " " 'The future,' " he went on, " 'may take many things away, but I have succeeded in obtaining, owing to the paramount idea, many things which I deem valuable.' " He thanked the citizens, as would any triumphant emperor, for appreciating his work and his contribution despite his faults. " 'Your greeting,' " he concluded, " 'expresses, in a more marked degree than it was ever before expressed in the course of my life, the trust and confidence of my fellow-citizens.' "

Fuller arranged a final meal at the City Club on Queen Victoria Street for Rhodes and thirty of his parliamentary colleagues. "I do not so much regret joining in an attempt to force President Kruger into a juster and more reasonable policy," Rhodes said, "but . . . I was Prime Minister at the time, and . . . I had given a promise that I would not do anything incompatible with the joint position I held as Director of the Chartered Company and Premier of the Cape Colony. . . . I can only say that I will do my best to make atonement for my error by untiring devotion to the best interests of South Africa." This is the only known record of an apology by Cecil Rhodes. The intimate nature of the gathering, the fact that he was about to sail for London and the parliamentary inquiry, and the spiritual quality of his achievement in the Matopos may all have contributed to its easy expression. There is a final image of Rhodes leaving Cape Town. Aboard the SS *Dunvegan Castle* as it weighed anchor for London, Rhodes is on deck, "smoking a cigarette, and raising his hat in acknowledgement of the [wildly enthusiastic] cheers [of the enormous crowd on the quay], which were continued as long as he was in sight."

Despite this private voicing of humility at the City Club, Rhodes hardly appeared chastened when he was questioned by the select committee. Nor did he during the next few months, when he tried to bully both Milner and Chamberlain into giving the Company control over all of Bechuanaland, as had been agreed upon on the eve of the Raid. Rhodes audaciously professed to believe that the Raid had made no difference, and that since he had been promised Bechuanaland, it should now be his. He wanted it in order to strengthen his hand within southern Africa should there be negotiations over closer union, and as a broader buffer against any attack on the Charter. Milner, with a good but still incomplete understanding, explained that Rhodes wanted the Protectorate because when Rhodes looked at a map "he sees on the one side the Cape Colony, of which he once was master and hopes to be again, on the other side Rhodesia, of which he is master. Between the two he sees that huge patch, which he all but got once and is still without. It makes his mouth water and he will do all he can to get it." Moreover, "Men are ruled by their foibles, and Rhodes's foible is *size*." Milner wanted to hold Rhodes to ransom over Bechuanaland, but Chamberlain could hardly afford ever to give it to him for fear of political retribution. It made no difference to Chamberlain that Rhodes was sponsoring a small trek toward Lake Ngami, where there were grazing lands around Ghanzi on which Afrikaners would settle.

Milner found Rhodes essentially unchanged. He regarded him in mid-1897 as still "too self-willed, too violent, too sanguine, and in too great a hurry. He is just the same man he always was, undaunted and unbroken by his former failure, but also untaught by it."[34] The real Rhodes was a pragmatic problem-solver whose ethical sense was subordinate to, and organized by, his great idea. This is not to say that he was incapable of feeling shame and guilt (though rarely), nor that he would not prefer to do what others would regard as just if he only had the choice. But it does mean that his choices were dictated less by general humanistic values, and by no specific commitments to protect Africans from cruelty and greed. More often, his choices were driven relentlessly by the relationship of the issue at hand to the furtherance of the paramount idea. Thus peace with the Ndebele would conserve the Company's resources and improve his public standing. That it would reduce the racial conflict which threatened Rhodesia's survival was an additional, desirable outcome. That it might save white and black lives as well was also welcome, but an ancillary benefit.

The real Rhodes remained. This is not to dim the importance of the reconciliation in Rhodesia, nor to deny the profound impact that the negotiations with the chiefs had on Rhodes. But that formidable experience did not remake the man. His life was not inwardly altered by the events in the Matopos. Rhodes ended a war expeditiously, but without transforming his own character to the extent that has usually been suggested. The real Rhodes of the late 1890s was driven by the same needs and dreams as the Rhodes of the first half of that critical decade.

"What a Man He Is!"
Across the Zambezi and
Through Africa

R HODES' AMBITIONS had never been bounded by the Zambezi. Beyond South
Africa, the southern half of Rhodesia—the land of the pioneers, the war,
and the rebellions—had preoccupied him and would prove the dominant focus of his imperial concern and energies in the waning years of his life. Yet
Northern Rhodesia, that vast, kidney-shaped territory—stretching from the
thunderous Victoria Falls northwestward to the headwaters of the Zambezi
and northeastward to the shores of Lake Tanganyika— also carried his name
and represented the farthest reaches of the British South Africa Company's
jurisdiction and responsibility. So, too, did the long arm of Rhodes and the
Company extend itself in the 1890s to the occupation and settlement of the
Nyasa Districts (from 1893–1907 the British Central Africa Protectorate)—
what became modern Malawi.

Although Nyasaland remained under Britain's parsimonious Foreign Of-
fice after 1891, Rhodes had granted Commissioner and Consul General Henry
Hamilton (Sir Harry) Johnston £10,000 a year to extend and administer Her
Majesty's dominions as well as those in neighboring Northeastern Rhodesia
(Zambia) which had been allotted to the Company in 1891.[1] In effect, Lord
Salisbury and Rhodes had created a dual mandate, for Johnston initially derived nearly all of his regular funds from the Company, and thus reported to
its officials in London and Cape Town. But he owed his office and his livelihood to the British government, which made the rules. Johnston therefore
contracted a bad case of divided loyalty, of which Rhodes never approved.
Nevertheless, with Rhodes' funds and whatever he could worm out of the
British government, Johnston proceeded between 1891 and 1894 to create a
rudimentary government amid the southern highlands of his elongated entity
south and west of Lake Nyasa. This new province of empire should, Johnston
considered, "be ruled by whites, developed by Indians, and worked by blacks."[2]

Johnston (and Rhodes would have approved) thus sought to encourage the immigration of whites, who would make their fortunes from the growing of coffee, and Sikhs and other Indians to operate trading stores and serve as policemen. Johnston expected to obtain the willing cooperation of Africans and, if not, to subdue them. Indeed, once it became clear that the more powerful chiefs in the Protectorate intended to resist Johnston's sub-imperial grasp, Rhodes' money was used to purchase weapons and recruit an army of pacification.

The campaign of conquest began in mid-1891 when Chikumbu, a Yao chief who had attempted to prevent the settlement of white coffee planters near Mount Mlanje, found that his own weapons were no match for those wielded by a little army of Sikhs and Muslims from Hyderabad and commanded by Captain Cecil Montgomery Maguire. A few months later, Johnston, Maguire, and the army constructed a fort (named after Johnston) near Lake Nyasa's outlet into the Shire River. They then moved against Makandanji, a Yao chief who had earlier imprisoned envoys sent from Zomba, the white capital. Soon Makandanji's forces were scattered. But Mponda, a more powerful Yao chief who resided near the fort, enslaved those who had been "scattered." Johnston was a man in Rhodes' mold: "Over seventy of the captives [Mponda] had the insolence to drive through our . . . Fort," Johnston wrote. Since Maguire was absent Johnston could initially do nothing. But when his troops had returned, Johnston "summoned Mponda to set all these slaves at liberty. He declined to do so, and commenced warlike proceedings against us." Thus, in October 1891, Johnston and Maguire shelled Mponda's town until the chief capitulated. Two weeks later, emboldened by this easy victory, Johnston borrowed a steamer from the African Lakes Company, steamed up the great lake, and destroyed the villages of Chief Makanjira, a "notorious" slave-raiding Yao chief who lived along the lake's eastern shores. As far as Johnston was concerned, these punitive actions made his protectorate "a reality."[3]

It was not always so easy. Resistance to white rule intensified rather than diminished. Kawinga, who lived near Zomba, managed to kill several Asian soldiers and wound Maguire before being humbled. In early 1892, Maguire and two other Britons lost their lives in an abortive attempt to capture Makanjira, whose men had regained their command of the southeastern corner of Lake Nyasa. Zarafi, another Yao chief, attacked Fort Johnston and captured the seven-pound gun which had been the conquest's most formidable weapon. Later Makanjira expanded his own sphere of influence along the eastern and western shores of the lake. Led by him, the various antagonistic Yao chiefs maintained their independence until the last months of 1893, by which time Johnston had obtained three small gunboats for his lake patrol; additional Sikhs from India; help from the Admiralty, the War Office, and the India Office; and the promise of further funds from Rhodes.

By early 1893 it was clear to Johnston, if not Rhodes, that imperialism on the cheap simply compromised and confused his own and Britain's administrative options. Rhodes had intended Johnston to expend at least a reasonable portion of the Company subsidy on the administration of Northeastern Rhodesia. But, except for the establishment of a lone, distant outpost on the shores of Lake Mweru, Johnston was acutely aware by 1893 that he had done nothing to advance Rhodes' or Britain's claims there. The slave trade still continued. Belgians from the west or Germans from the east might conceivably lay claim to its high plateau. Johnston had been compelled to employ Rhodes' subsidy fully against the Yao in Nyasaland. He had not even satisfied the Company's lust for land and mineral rights within the Protectorate, the Company's claims being "inferior from a legal point of view to the most spurious claims of the private settlers."[4] Moreover, missionaries and settlers were continuing to oppose the extension of the charter of the Company to Johnston's sphere, and so doubtless did he. Johnston tried to obtain £20,000 more from the Foreign Office and the Treasury. But his hopes were unmet, and so he was compelled to try to secure more money for his own tiny empire from Rhodes, busy in the adjacent, larger, sub-imperial sphere.

Johnston, a bantam of a man, was never comfortable as anyone's subordinate. Rhodes, on the other hand, had originally intended that Johnston, still unmarried, should primarily be an instrument of a Rhodes-led, not Johnston-devised expansion. Clearly their objectives were similiar, but Johnston had a British focus and Rhodes a South African one. Johnston was unprepared to serve as an acolyte; Rhodes, not unnaturally, was uncomfortable paying for projects over which he had increasingly less control and nearly no tangible or psychic benefit. These differences of purpose and personality became evident when Johnston was pushed by circumstances—the cost of the wars and the stinginess of the Treasury—to beg Rhodes for an additional grant in 1893.

Johnston's troubles began when Rhodes summoned him to a meeting on Mozambique island in February 1893. (Rhodes was then returning from Britain, Cairo, Luxor, and Zanzibar, en route to the cabinet crisis in the Cape.) Rhodes wanted to talk about the extension of the trans-continental telegraph to the Protectorate and beyond. He also suspected Johnston (falsely) of fomenting anti-Company sentiment among the planters, missionaries, and other white settlers of the Shire Highlands.

But Johnston could not and would not go. Rhodes' cable had to be delivered by steamer and runner from the coast. Had he been given longer notice, or had he been down country instead of at Zomba, his hill retreat, Johnston might have contemplated the long trek to the coast. But the war with Makanjira, worries about the safe arrival overland of the new gunboats (carried in sections), and the coming reinforcements of Sikhs made it imperative that he remain at Zomba. Also, he was feeling strangely unwell. He felt "as though [he] should go to pieces—come unglued, in fact, like all the toys and boxes do in this damp climate." He would not meet the Founder, but as soon as he thought that he could safely leave, he would go to the Cape, or wherever Rhodes then was.

Alternatively, Johnston audaciously proposed that Rhodes should travel up-country. "Such a visit would, I am sure, teach you more about Central Africa than the letter-writing and conversation of ten years' duration." Johnston proposed that Rhodes "might make a brief stay at Zomba" and then travel with Johnston to Lake Nyasa or beyond. If so, Johnston would throw himself "into the project heart and soul, and make it as comfortable for you as travelling can be made in Central Africa during the Rainy Season." "If you are really bent on this astounding scheme of a cable through the length of Africa," Johnston continued, "I think this excursion is worth your while." But, he cautioned quaintly, "bring no mass of luggage and no alcohol," for liquor and chills were "the main source of ill health and fever in Central Africa." The provocative little consul indicated that a trip to the coast to see Rhodes would only duplicate his letters. But a visit to him by Rhodes "would be productive of enormous results." If Rhodes really, really cared about Central Africa he should see it for himself. However, Rhodes could not then detour up the Zambezi or Shire rivers. Although he urged Johnny Grimmer to join him in an expedition to trans-Zambezia in 1897, Rhodes never found the time or, realistically, had the inclination to experience at first hand the problems of underdevelopment north of the Zambezi.

Johnston asked Rhodes for another £5,000 for the development of Northeastern Rhodesia and a further £2,500 to cover the cost of water transport, which was still controlled by the African Lakes Company. Johnston admitted that it was "of course . . . extremely hard on the . . . South Africa Company that, in order to retain Nyasaland amongst the possessions of the British Empire, it has got to pay out £10,000 a year with no very clear prospect of getting any return for its expenditure. The only consolation I can find . . . are . . . that if your main object was the Britannicising of Nyasaland . . . your object is being effectually accomplished . . . and . . . that if you intend to develop [the Company's sphere] you can only do so through Nyasaland. . . ." Johnston told Sir Percy Anderson that only by the "vigorous development of the magnificent territories" to the north and west of the Protectorate could the Company hope to obtain a decent return on its investment in the Protectorate. (By then Johnston had spent £55,000 of the Company's funds.) Johnston could not tell Rhodes "too emphatically" that if he wanted to keep his own sphere of influence across the Zambezi, he "must fork out an extra £5000."[5]

Rhodes scrawled acerbic comments in the margins of Johnston's letter. When he replied fully it was with impatience. He was cross that Johnston had not confirmed the land claims of the African Lakes Company, because the British South Africa Company, Johnston's paymaster, in fact owned those claims. "This, you will admit," wrote Rhodes, "is absurd." Rhodes argued at length that since Lord Ripon had promised Rhodes' Company all land and mineral rights in Bechuanaland, then the same logic applied to Nyasaland, where Rhodes, not Britain, paid the cost of administration. It was even clearer that in Northeastern and Northwestern Rhodesia chiefs could give their land only to the Company, not to others, yet Johnston was worried about contend-

ing concessionaires. "I would impress . . . upon you," Rhodes wrote to Johnston, "The Chartered Company have been paying and are still paying £10,000
a year to you for nothing." Rhodes was prepared to give Johnston another
£5,000, but only if his Company thereby secured the reversionary rights in
the land and minerals of the Protectorate and Northeastern Rhodesia. "These"
it would "take up and develop so soon as civilisation [were] sufficiently advanced and the administration of law firmly established. . . ." Rhodes did
not object to the land grants already made by Johnston, for they had been
made in favor of men who were residents. He simply wanted it understood
that only the Chartered Company possessed the right to acquire concessions
of land and minerals.

Johnston had wished to distinguish between his zone north of the Zambezi and Rhodes' sphere. He advocated distinctive official imprints and post-
age stamps. Rhodes regarded this eminently sensible and comparatively routine proposal as sinister. "I am quite unable to agree with you," he wrote with
prescience. "It is clear to me that in the future North and south of the Zambesi will be united in one harmonious whole and the tendency in all things
should be towards unification and not to separation. . . ." He urged Johnston, as before, to use the Company's stamps and symbols. And to Lord
Rosebery, Johnston's employer, Rhodes complained that "though we pay for
everything I think [Johnston] is like all imperial officers, somewhat small minded
and does not like to be considered as connected with a Chartered Co. It is
human nature so I reminded him . . . that whether he liked it or not he must
remember that the oil that kept the wheels going came from us."[6]

Rhodes instinctively grabbed for the fullest territorial and economic stake.
In the case of Nyasaland, he copied the British government's imperialism by
proxy and on the cheap. The acquisition of all of Nyasaland for even £20,000
a year, and its incorporation into the Company's sphere, would truly have
represented an inexpensive and aimless accretion to Rhodes' then-unchallenged
power in southern Africa. He wanted Nyasaland, and its lands and minerals,
not because he expected to make a quick profit for himself or the Company
but as an extension of his "big idea," and a rounding-out of his dreams. As
he told Rosebery in another context, "Never expect a return from the development of a new country."[7]

When Johnston visited Cape Town in May 1893, he did so as reluctant
supplicant. Rhodes was then deviously engaged in suborning his old cabinet
colleagues and reconstructing the government of the Cape. Johnston thus found
him irritable and, sometimes, almost "drugged." They ate silent dinners opposite one another. Johnston also endured abuse and invective. Rhodes suspected that Johnston was disloyal—not to the dream of an expanded British
empire but to Rhodes' specific vision of an empire that he would fashion and
lead. They nevertheless parted with an agreement, dictated by Rhodes, for a
£17,000 subsidy each year for five years, plus additional money for steamers
on the lake. In exchange Johnston gave Rhodes the conditions which Rhodes
had earlier set out in his letters. Rhodes acknowledged that the Foreign Office

might refuse to ratify such a bold assertion of the Company's prerogatives. Johnston nevertheless campaigned for this devilish bargain. "In this world you get nothing for nothing," he said. "Money, I am afraid I must have," he told the Foreign Office.[8]

Had Johnston showed too much independence in Cape Town? Had Johnston crossed F. Rutherfoord Harris, Rhodes' confidant and assistant there? No one, not even Jameson, liked Harris, whom Merriman called "Cactus." Harris labeled Johnston a "little, prancing Proconsul." Was jealousy and misplaced affection at the root of the incipient rupture between miniature Johnston and big Rhodes, two opinionated men with many similiar tastes and proclivities?

The Foreign Office approved the Rhodes-Johnston agreement in late August, but only after stipulating (on advice from the Colonial Office) that the whole of the subsidy should be expended within the Protectorate and that it should run for ten, not five years. Furthermore, Rhodes was to pay for any of Johnston's added expenditures in the Company's territory. Johnston was also given permission to tax properties of the Company.

Johnston had no hand in these alterations, but Rhodes—not unnaturally—thought that Johnston had double-crossed him by writing privately to officials in the Foreign Office. Harris called the draft agreement "pure mockery." Rhodes, livid, stopped all extra subsidy payments to Johnston. "What I feel deeply is your disloyalty, though it was not altogether unexpected. . . ." To others Rhodes thundered that he was not "going to create with my funds an independent King Johnston over the Zambezi." That was the nub of the dispute. Taken unfairly as a traitor, Johnston demanded an apology.[9]

Johnston never received a clear apology, but he insisted upon and received the full amount of his promised subsidy for 1893 and 1894. He used those funds to smash the Yao lords around the lake. Chiwaura, a Yao ally of Makanjira who had constructed a fortified town about five miles inland from Kota Kota (Nkhota Khota), was soon bombarded by gun boats, and his legions overcome in hand to hand combat. Makanjira's town was stormed and burned, although the chief escaped. Along with Zarafi, he led attacks on Johnston's administration throughout 1894 and murdered collaborators. There was more warfare in 1895 against British settlements in the Shire Highlands, but, after an intensive campaign, the Protectorate's little army defeated Kawinga, disarmed chief Matapwiri and, after heavy fighting, compelled Zarafi and his legions to flee into Mozambique. Soon Makanjira, too, was overwhelmed. "A sense of security," Johnston later wrote, "spread over the Southern portion of the Protectorate which was quite pleasantly unfamiliar."[10]

After the final victory over Makanjira, Harris wrote on Rhodes' behalf to congratulate Johnston. "Mr. Rhodes has no wish to abandon what you have already done" along the lake and west as far as the Luapula River. Harris asked Johnston simply to spend as little as possible until the Company found gold in Rhodesia. Rhodes had defeated Lobengula's Ndebele and was busily constructing his transcontinental telegraph line toward Zomba. He still needed Johnston's cooperation.

Even so, the rupture between Johnston and Rhodes was complete and in 1894 led to the end of Rhodes' hold on and hopes for a significant influence over Nyasaland. Johnston preceded Rhodes to London and persuaded a very reluctant combination of civil servants and ministers to put British Central Africa on a proper financial basis. Rhodes accepted the new dispensation, despite his renewed anger at Johnston. The Company would from mid-1895 undertake to administer its own sphere north of the Zambezi. It would cut itself off from Zomba, while still paying the basic £10,000 subsidy to the Protectorate for another year. There were further agreements about the Company's land holdings in northern Nyasaland and about outstanding financial questions, but by an official accord of late November 1894, Rhodes renounced his personal and imperial claims to the whole of Nyasaland. He also told Johnston that he never wished to see him again, and he never did.[11]

Although Rhodes sent Major Patrick William Forbes across the Zambezi in 1895 to take charge of the Company's territory west of Nyasaland and east of the Kafue River—Northeastern Rhodesia—Forbes' administration was initially separated from Johnston's only in financial terms. Because his imperial extension lacked roads and outposts, and because so few of the important peoples within it had acknowledged Company or British rule, Forbes controlled precious little. Moreover, only by borrowing Johnston's little army (for which the Company paid an annual retainer) could Forbes make the writ of the Company known within his domain. Johnston called Forbes "excessively disagreeable." Sharpe labeled him a "horrid nuisance." Even Rhodes later complained that Forbes was a "slacker."[12]

Missionaries had anticipated the Company. There were London Missionary Society stations south of Lake Tanganyika by 1883 (permanently from 1887). The first outpost of the Roman Catholic order of White Fathers was established nearby in 1891, and emissaries of the United Free Church of Scotland, which operated on and around Lake Nyasa, moved westward into Northeastern Rhodesia in 1895.

Johnston and Alfred Sharpe, his deputy commissioner, followed the missionaries. After having established "Rhodesia," subsequently called Kalungwizi, in 1890 south of the outlet of Lake Mweru into the Luapula River, Johnston's men in 1893 placed themselves on the highlands overlooking Lake Tanganyika, near the London Missionary Society station of Fwambo, and called their fort Abercorn after the chairman of the Company. In 1894, they opened the Fife station (after the deputy chairman of the Company) midway between Abercorn and the northern end of Lake Nyasa. Just as Kalungwizi existed as a counter to Belgian predations from the Congo (Zaire), so Abercorn and Fife fixed a British presence in the region, responded to missionary calls for secular assistance, and countered any ideas that the Germans might entertain about this otherwise pristine border region. By 1895 there were no more than forty whites resident in all of Forbes' province. There were no mines, no railways, and little of Western commercial importance. Aside from foot traffic along the Stevenson Road from Lake Nyasa to Fwambo and Abercorn, the traditional trade in copper, ivory, and slaves carried by Lunda, Bisa, and Arab entrepreneurs between Katanga (Shaba) and Lake Nyasa and the Indian Ocean still dominated the central highlands of the territory.

The powers of the province were Chief Mwata Kazembe, leader of the Lunda from a fortified village south of Kalungwizi on the east bank of the Luapula River; Paramount Chief Chitimukulu Sampa of the Bemba, who ruled the uplands from a stockade near what is modern Kasama; and Chief Mpeseni of the Ngoni, whose word was law along the eastern marches of the Company's land. There were a few Arabs, too, whose guns and capital had carved out zones of independence along the northern fringes of the territory. These interlopers were opposed and their caravans attacked by whites throughout the latter half of the 1890s; the Arabs then moved their slaving operations into the farther recesses of the Congo. But at first Johnston was reluctant to move against the Bemba. They were too strong, he told Rhodes. Instead, he urged, "Let's go at the obnoxious half-breed Angoni," and only eventually against the Bemba, whom he called a "fine people." Both the Bemba and the Ngoni in fact remained unmolested, along with most other indigenous chiefs, until the regime of Robert Edward Codrington, Forbes' successor, felt itself strong enough to assert its own authority as the newest power in the land. (Codrington, thirty-one, had been a sergeant-major in the Bechuanaland Mounted Police, had fought against the Ndebele in 1893, and was an assistant collector in Johnston's administration of Nyasaland.)

By 1896, the Ngoni had begun to resent the demands for labor made upon them by white recruiting agents, by planters from Nyasaland, and by the handful of white settlers who entered their domain in the 1890s. They particularly feared the intrusions of the North Charterland Company, an early claimant to Mpeseni's kingdom which Rhodes had folded into the British South Africa Company. As Sharpe, Johnston's successor as commissioner and consul-general, wrote home, "Matters in Mpeseni's country are far from satisfactory: These expeditions organized by the British South Africa Company or their sub-concessionaires keep dropping into the [Ngoni] district, and Mpeseni and his . . . warriors are evidently beginning to get a little uneasy." That was an understatement. The Ngoni rightly sensed a clear and present danger to their position as the leading African power to the west of Nyasaland. Moreover, the tension between traditional African might and growing white power could not long endure.

"I hear the Angoni have broken out," Rhodes cabled in early 1898. He suggested ways of moving reinforcements across Portuguese territory ("We have permission. . . ."). Separately, from a base in nearby Nyasaland, a force of 100 Sikhs and 350 local Tonga and Yao recruits, led by Colonel William Manning, invaded Mpeseni's country, finding a defending army estimated at 10,000 warriors. The attackers employed two Maxim guns and two seven-pound cannon to good effect, as had Jameson against the Ndebele, and soon humbled the Ngoni and their muskets. The British loot included 12,000 to 16,000 head of cattle, 10,000 of which were confiscated on Rhodes' orders and walked to Umtali, the remainder being returned to the Ngoni. Hays Scott

Turner, the local magistrate, later had the task of selling off the "miserable" Ngoni cattle for £5 each, for "no one in Umtali [had] any money."[13]

During the next year, an equally large force of British-officered troops, reinforced with Maxims, ended Kazembe's freedom. Kazembe, reported Codrington, had "received European traders in a hostile manner." Sharpe reported that Kazembe's town was a refuge for "malcontents and bad characters." The Foreign Office implored Codrington to avoid military action. But Sharpe was determined to strike "the final blow for order in Northeast Rhodesia." After marching the Protectorate's army to the outskirts of Kazembe's kingdom, Sharpe "informed Kazembe of the foolishness of his actions. . . ." Sharpe told the chief that he "did not want to use force. . . . [Kazembe] was told to destroy his stockade. . . . He replied that he was ready for war." Sharpe decided that further negotiations were useless.[14] Kazembe fled, and the army of occupation entered his village of 1700 huts unmolested. Five thousand Lunda scattered. Similarly, the various Bemba and Bisa chiefs offered no serious resistance when, after the deaths of Chitimukulu Sampa and Chief Mwamba in 1896 and 1898, Sharpe's soldiers and Codrington's magistrates and collectors gradually imposed Rhodes' territorial ambitions upon the remaining rulers of Northeastern Rhodesia.

Northwestern Rhodesia had meanwhile existed as little more than a designation since Frank Elliott Lochner had obtained the supposed treaty of cession in 1890 from Lewanika, Litunga of the Lozi. Subsequently, Lewanika had begged the Company for a resident administrator and some evidence that it meant to bring to his kingdom the accouterments of white rule—roads, a postal service, weapons, and economic advances. Rhodes was conscious of this request, but in no hurry to spend money on an unproductive region which had been acquired largely in order to prevent others from taking it. However, he had finally decided to show the Company's flag in 1896. Hubert Hervey had been destined for service there when an untimely Ndebele bullet took his life. Finally, in 1897, under pressure from François Coillard, the Paris Missionary Society leader, from Lewanika, and from the Foreign Office, Rhodes despatched Robert Coryndon, one of his "lambs" from the early Rhodesian days, as the Company's first resident administrator for Barotseland and Northwestern Rhodesia.

Coryndon was only twenty-seven. He had guarded the pioneer column and had fought twice against the Ndebele and once against the Shona. For Rhodes and the Company his primary task was to induce Lewanika, annoyed over the treaty of 1890 as well as his subsequent neglect, to grant the Company substantive new powers. Otherwise the Company would have no civil authority and no ability to license prospectors or traders. In this period after the Jameson Raid, the British Foreign Office intended strictly to regulate Rhodes' rights beyond the Zambezi. It was no longer inclined to be permissive or to be bullied, and Lord Salisbury was content for Coryndon to be a comparatively passive presence among the Lozi. Rhodes, too, in his post-Raid and post-rebellion mood, was willing to leave the oversight of his northernmost territories largely to Britain. As far as he was concerned, the situation there would only change, and the Company's position be enhanced, when the projected railway from Bulawayo crossed the Zambezi. Only then would Northern Rhodesia "practically become part of Southern Rhodesia." Even so, he had been impressed with what he had heard about the abundance of wild rubber vines to the west of Lewanika's kingdom. "Do not forget," he instructed Grey, "to impress on Chamberlain the importance of the western boundary of Barotseland in connection with India rubber and its future enormous price owing to bicycles." Coryndon predicted to Rhodes that gold would be found in the Ila and Toka countries near the Kafue River in the easternmost sections of Lewanika's territory; in 1900 Rhodes despatched A. Val Gielgud, a Southern Rhodesian native commissioner, and an armed escort to the Hook of the Kafue region to see if he could discover more about this rumored gold, but Gielgud returned empty handed. Rumors or not, Rhodes was pleased when, in 1898, Lewanika conceded administrative, mining, and commercial rights to the Company in exchange for an annual subsidy and the reservation of large tracts of land to the Lozi. Unhappily for Rhodes, the Foreign Office ratified this agreement only in 1901.[15]

Had Rhodes lived longer, his innovative genius and bold approach to developmental problems might have accelerated the gradual intrusion of Europe into both of his territories across the Zambezi. Those trans-Zambezian hinterlands therefore might have carried more than his name, and been affected in perpetuity by much more than his earlier insistence on their annexation. Had the Raid not sullied his reputation and dimmed his direct power, Rhodes might have forced the incorporation of the northern provinces into the southern bastion of his empire. Instead, Rhodes had little choice but to accept the two British orders-in-council which put an official stamp on and thus legally established the Protectorates of Northwestern Rhodesia in 1899 and Northeastern Rhodesia in 1900. For Northwestern Rhodesia, Rhodes failed to obtain the wider border in the west that he coveted, but for both territories his preferences for a future tariff protocol favorable to Britain naturally prevailed.

The two agreements subordinated the Company to the Crown. The ultimate authority for the western segment was given to the British high commissioner in Cape Town on behalf of the Colonial Office; responsibility for the eastern section flowed to the Foreign Office via Her Majesty's Commissioner for British Central Africa in Zomba. The Company would continue paying for the administration of both territories, but it shared civil authority with Britain's representatives. In practice, however, Rhodes was assured by his representative in Bulawayo that the high commissioner would make laws only "after suggestions" from Rhodes. Furthermore, Rhodes was promised, no expenditures could be undertaken without his consent. Sir Arthur Lawley, administrator of Matabeleland, said that he would advise Codrington in the same way to consult Milton, administrator for Mashonaland, before sending any proposals to Zomba. Milton would doubtless confer beforehand with Rhodes, and no loss of real power or control would ensue.

By labeling the Company's territories "protectorates" and not colonies, the orders-in-council implied that they were held in trust by the Crown until the indigenous inhabitants should be ready to resume their independence in some modern guise. Although settlers later fought this presumption with vigor, Rhodes himself appears to have understood that for a long time whites could not be so favored in the north as they were south of the river. Malaria was a problem, for whites succumbed quickly to fever when away from the high plateaux of the more southerly portions of the continent. Rhodes hence recommended that Codrington and Coryndon recruit African rather than white police. Whites would take to their stretchers, read social magazines and devote their time to "cursing the country and the Chartered Co." Rhodes would not blame them, for they were constitutionally unable to "walk like natives in the sun and so they [would] lie on their backs," overeat, and become feverish.[16] That was his tidy analysis.

Rhodes possessed a wry understanding of the type of men who were drawn to his service in southern Africa and over the Zambezi. He knew that the comparatively healthy lands near the Kafue River would attract white farmers, and he may well have guessed that the mining of copper, lead, and zinc would also prove profitable for whites. But these developments were for the future. It was well after Rhodes' death, and after Northestern and Northwestern Rhodesia had been fused in 1911 under the Colonial Office as the Protectorate of Northern Rhodesia, that its administration began treating the territory as an extension of the conquered areas south of the Zambezi. In 1911, only 500 whites lived in the country, mostly administrators and missionaries, but soon their numbers increased. Local officials granted them important measures of political influence, tying the immediate future of the Protectorate, as Rhodes had predicted, not to African aspirations but to a white-defined perception of the country's future.[17]

Rhodes' ultimate legacy was the territorial outline of what was to become modern Zambia. In this region he left no precise governmental imprint, although the Southern Rhodesian model, with its emphasis on settler representation, heavily influenced that of Northern Rhodesia and led to the conflict between Africans and whites. He also left a Company which, until 1964, controlled mineral rights and therefore the foundations of the country's great copper industry. Most of all, Rhodes decided before his death to extend the main rail line from Kimberley, Mafeking, and Bulawayo north through the desolate country of the Ndebele and thence across the Zambezi at the Victoria Falls.

"I want to get there at once," he said in 1897. "There is little satisfaction in knowing the railway will reach there after one's death."[18] Rhodes referred to the Victoria Falls, 200 miles north of the main Rhodesian rail line's terminus in Bulawayo. Rhodes wanted his rail line to cross the Zambezi slightly downstream from the Falls, but sufficiently close by so that travelers could view the magnificent 355-foot drop, hear their mighty roar as the one-mile-wide Zambezi funneled down a very narrow chasm, and even be sprayed by them during the seasons when the Falls were full. But the Falls were less a final destination than a way station en route to Lake Tanganyika, Uganda, and Egypt.

Rhodes' fantasies had hardly been destroyed by the Raid or the rebellions. By mid-1897, after it was absolutely clear that the House of Commons would do little more than censure him mildly, Rhodes was again free to resume his dreams. Given the attention he was beginning to pay to trans-Zambezia after 1895, and given his own sense of personal foreboding and doom, two colossal projects close to his heart—dramatic extensions to his already successful rail and telegraph networks—naturally focused his not inconsiderable remaining energies. With crucial assistance from Johnston, Sharpe, and even Forbes, Rhodes' persistence and eye for detail propelled the telegraph line from Umtali to Tete in Mozambique and on to Blantyre, in Nyasaland, by April 1898. Poles and wire had to be carried in freighters from the Cape to the mouth of the Zambezi River, transshipped in shallow-draft river steamers, and then off-loaded along the Shire River and carried inland. By the end of 1899, Rhodes' men had erected these poles and strung the bare copper wire to Zomba, Fort Johnston, up Lake Nyasa, to Fife, and finally to Abercorn overlooking the southern end of Lake Tanganyika.

If Rhodes were to achieve his goal of forging transcontinental communications links from Cape Town to Cairo, he next had to find a route across King Léopold's land to the west of the lake, or through the domain of Kaiser Wilhelm of Germany, who controlled the vast territory between the lake and Zanzibar. Johnston, for one, had been bowled over by Rhodes' ambitious plans for his telegraph line. "I must confess," he had written in 1893, "I find myself rather staggered at the idea of carrying an overland line from the north end of Tanganyika to Victoria Nyanza, because the people between the two Lakes are very hostile to Whites, and would certainly regard the telegraph line as an embodiment of witchcraft." [19]

Rhodes had earlier attempted to surmount both the Tanganyikan obstacle, as well as to find a way through Uganda, across the Mahdi's Sudan, and into Egypt. Fortunately, by 1899 when it was timely and imperative, the Mahdi had died and General Sir Horatio Herbert Kitchener, Rhodes' friend and ally, throwing rail and telegraph lines before him, had reconquered the Sudan from the Mahdi's successors. On the occasion of Kitchener's victory Rhodes had wired saucily: "Glad you beat the Khalifa. . . . My telegraph will shortly be at south end of Tanganyika. If you don't look sharp in spite of your victory I shall reach Uganda before you." Kitchener's answer was equally imperious. "Hurry up," he wired. [20]

Already Rhodes had planned a rail line which, following a somewhat different route, would ultimately also connect (at least in Rhodes' mind) to Kitchener's terminus in the Sudan. Rhodes, who sought financial guarantees from Her Majesty's Treasury, detailed his plans to Chamberlain and the British cabinet in 1898. First he wanted to take the rails across the belly of Northern Rhodesia and then north around Lake Tanganyika, through the German-held zone, to Uganda. He supposed it could cost £2 million (although Beit suggested to Rhodes that his estimates were £1 million to £2 million too low). From Bulawayo and Victoria Falls it would run through "excellent cattle country, densely populated by natives, and [would] absorb the greater portion of the trade of the upper Zambezi [and] upper Congo [rivers] and the western portions of German East Africa." Rubber and copper would be exported and, equally important, labor would be drawn expeditiously to the mines of Kimberley and Johannesburg. It might also help dampen the slave trade of the Congo basin. As a result, Rhodes prophesied, there would be no further need for Britain's anti-slave trade blockade of the East African coast, a saving of expenditure for the Treasury.

Rhodes advanced another part-tactical, part-philosophical reason why backing his railway scheme made good sense. "The question of the future Government of the vast native populations within the British sphere must also be considered. Experience has conclusively shown," he argued by analogy from his Southern Rhodesian experience with the Ndebele and Shona, "that the contact of European civilisation with barbarism will always result in Native wars and disturbances unless authority can be effectively exercised." A railway was thus essential for the proper administration and pacification of Northern Rhodesia. He declared that the 1896 rebellions would not have occurred if a rail connection with the Cape (where reinforcements had been available) had then been in place. The governance of Nyasaland would be eased, too, for Rhodes would drive his rails as close as possible to that Protectorate. (Later, after the rail line to Umtali had been reconstructed at a 3'6" width, he gave orders to retain the original two-foot-wide light line so that it could be used, if necessary, between Beira and Blantyre. "Such a railway . . . will give us the control of Nyasaland and meet the aspirations of the planters," Rhodes argued.)

Rhodes was obsessed, good capitalist that he was, with mining diamonds profitably. Contributing significantly to broad margins and satisfactory returns were the real costs of labor. In his appeal to Chamberlain and, during the same year (1898), in impassioned presentations to the Cape parliament, Rhodes explained how a railway to the north would benefit industrial development in South Africa. As far as Rhodes was concerned, the "enormous demand" for workers in Kimberley, in Johannesburg, and in Rhodesia had forced African wages to "reach an unduly high figure." Africans were still reluctant to leave their fields for the pits, shafts, and fenced-in compounds of South African industry. Rhodes was paying the princely sum of £1 a week to miners in Kimberley; north of the Zambezi River he understood that Africans were prepared to work for a shilling a week. The proposed railway would thus reduce costs in South Africa and Rhodesia by expanding the available supply and by using a railway to link the low-wage and high-wage regions. Rhodes assumed that the "natives in [the] northern districts [were] anxious to obtain work," but were deterred by the vast distances to be covered on foot. Carrying workers would enrich the rail company and boost his own profits. What could be stronger arguments for his scheme?[21]

Although he hardly could say so to Chamberlain, Rhodes was being driven by a vision. Some of Rhodes' critics may have supposed that the only object of the railway was to transport passengers from Cairo to Cape Town. "This is of course ridiculous," he wrote. "The object is to cut Africa through the centre and the railway will pick up trade all along this route. The junctions to the East and West Coasts, which will," Rhodes imagined, "occur in the future, will be outlets for the traffic obtained along the route of the line as it passes through the centre of Africa."[22]

Although Chamberlain backed this ambitious rail proposal, others in the British government believed it fanciful and fantastic. Sir Michael Hicks Beach, at the Treasury, and the rest of the cabinet, savaged it. Hicks Beach, Rhodes had foreseen, would sell him "a dog. I *know* he will." Rhodes, claimed Hicks Beach in turn, could raise the loan himself; alternately, he had sufficient capital to pay for it all. "The more I think of that Beach the more angry I am," Rhodes complained. "Fancy his bullying me. . . . He is not fit to be treasurer to a village council and yet is in charge of the empire. I often wonder how we [the Empire] get along. I suppose his recommendations for the principal seat in the cabinet are that he has the worst temper and the smallest mind."

The guarantees that Rhodes requested would have to be for several decades. The cabinet could not think of committing the British government for so long. Instead, it offered Rhodes a direct loan to the Bechuanaland Railway Company, the concern which would actually extend the rails beyond Bulawayo. But it tied such a loan to a guarantee from the Cape Colony and to other strict conditions which Rhodes rejected. In the event of default he did not want the railway to revert to the Cape, "should the federation of the various states of South Africa not be accomplished."[23] As much as Rhodes sought to serve his federal objectives by tying territories together by telegraphs and rails, in the darkening days of 1899 he hardly wanted the future prosperity of Southern and Northern Rhodesia to depend wholly on the Cape's position in or outside of an amalgamated South Africa. By then, too, Rhodes feared that he might no longer remain in control.

Rhodes raised the funds for the railway to the Falls and through Northern Rhodesia from De Beers, Beit, and others, and by persuading the board of the British South Africa Company to forgo dividends once again in 1899. (It finally paid dividends only in the 1920s.) "Surely I am not going to be beaten by the legs of a Cambridge undergraduate," he wrote about his own transcontinental efforts after Ewart Scott Grogan, an intrepid ex-University of Cambridge man, had tramped through Africa from the mouth of the Zambezi to Cairo between 1898 and 1900.[24] By then, too, Rhodes and the directors of the Company could cite a real and not simply a supposed economic rationale for the vast extension northward. Rhodes originally intended to take the rails toward Lake Tanganyika via the valley of the Luangwa River, but the confirmation of good coal at Wankie and copper riches due north of the Falls altered the direction of the line and the entire economic destiny of modern Zambia.

The Tanganyika Concessions Company, a speculative prospecting entity to which Rhodes had given exploring rights in trans-Zambezia, had located a serious copper deposit along the Rhodesian-Congo border (near modern Solwezi). That is, George Grey, who led an expedition on behalf of Sir Robert Williams, a friend of Rhodes from his Kimberley days, had confirmed the traditional tales of copper there, located a deposit that had been worked by Africans, and guessed that it would still prove economically exploitable. Where one mine had been located, others, it was correctly surmised, would also exist. "Beit and I look to your copper to pull us through," Rhodes, in failing health, told Williams about the railway. "You have a mine worth probably five million, but it is no use without a railway. I am taking my railway to assist you. That is what I am doing for you."[25]

Rhodes never saw the Falls from his rail cars, or at all. The main line of rail crossed the Zambezi in 1904, reached the lead and zinc mine at Broken Hill (Kabwe) in 1906, and Ndola, on the edge of Northern Rhodesia's copperbelt, in 1909. By 1910 it had entered Katanga, there to join a railway to the Angolan coast that was eventually constructed by Robert Williams' Concessions Company.

For Rhodes it was never fantastic to think that the still-raw continent of Africa should be tamed by copper and steel. After all, the Mahdi was gone, the two Rhodesian rail lines were progressing north from Bulawayo and west from Umtali to Salisbury, and Grey's finds of ore augured well. Rhodes was confident that he could persuade King Léopold II of the Belgians to adhere to an earlier agreement that gave a British company access to Congolese territory west of Lake Tanganyika for the specific purpose of constructing a telegraph line from south to north. Unhappily, the monarch was susceptible neither to Rhodes' charm nor to his logical arguments.

Rhodes had earlier been reluctant to visit the king, having told the British ambassador that he was "very busy" and could not spare the time. Thus Rhodes' manner at a state luncheon early in February 1899 in Brussels may not have been as cooperative as the conspiratorial Léopold might have wished. It is alleged, too, that Rhodes arrogantly suggested a merger of their territories— that Rhodes' and Léopold's possessions should be joined and their civil services amalgamated. Rhodes could then connect his telegraphic line to Kitchener's in the Sudan and drive his railway through the Congo to Cairo. (Rhodes deprecated Léopold's own telegraphic initiatives on technical grounds.) Together the two promoters, one royal, one secular, would control a massive central African colony larger than western Europe.

However plausible Rhodes may have made this majestic proposition sound, and however intrigued the king may have been by a rail connection through the Congo, Léopold had many reasons to refuse Rhodes the telegraphic right-of-way that he required. Although Article V of Anglo-Belgian treaty of 1894 specifically authorized the construction of a telegraph line by Britain from its southern African to its Nilotic territories through the Congo, that treaty had in practice subsequently been voided. The central clauses of the treaty had exchanged British access to Lake Tanganyika via a strip of land through the Congo from Uganda for a swath of territory on the west bank of the Nile from Lake Albert to Fashoda (Kodok). But the Germans objected to some of these provisions, and Léopold ceded the crucial strip along the Nile to France, an action which Lord Rosebery, who had originally negotiated the 1894 treaty, had refused to countenance. In 1898 Britain had ended French pretensions to a cross-African sundering of its own longitudinal empire along the upper Nile; the French were forced by ultimatums from Lord Salisbury to withdraw from Fashoda and concede total hegemony to Britain in the Sudan and the entire watershed of the Nile. In these various diplomatic maneuvers Léopold had sided with and cooperated with the French. Thus Rhodes' requests a few months later carried with them far broader implications for Europe's struggle for power in Africa than might be assumed by a focus on Rhodes' machinations in isolation.

Rhodes was not unaware of these complications. Indeed, if he entered Léopold's palace with any illusions, the willful monarch soon acquainted Rhodes with the facts of intra-European conspiracy. Although the king had in fact defaulted on the 1894 treaty, he told Rhodes that he could give him neither telegraphic nor rail access until and unless Britain reinstated the Congo's putative rights to land along the upper Nile. Rhodes understood that, "after such a struggle with the French," Britain would never give the area back to the Belgians. Rhodes' telegraph would thus "go to the wall," he told the Prince of Wales, unless he took it through German territory. "My own opinion of the King of the Belgians is that it will be very difficult ever to get him to any practical conclusions unless he has by far the best of the bargain." Léopold, in other words, would not succumb to Rhodes' soft blandishments. He could not be squared. "I couldn't get on with him at all," Rhodes told Williams in 1900. "He is an old Jew. . . ." In conversation with Lascelles, he accused Léopold of haggling "like a Jew," a descriptive epithet that Rhodes had frequently used to describe his rivals in the Kimberley diamond days. Shortly after the interview with Léopold, Rhodes informed Julia and Rochfort Maguire that as soon as the door had closed and the talks had begun Rhodes "felt that the King had disappeared and that his place had been taken by a commercial traveller."[26] In fact, however their personalities had failed to mesh, Léopold could hardly have met Rhodes' wishes without seriously compromising his own position in the complicated games of diplomatic chess on which the powers of Europe were then concentrated. Only a Rhodes whom Léopold found attractive could have overcome such formidable obstacles.

Léopold's intransigence compelled Rhodes to request a meeting with Kaiser Wilhelm II, emperor of Germany. There was every expectation that the kaiser, although half-English, would be just as antagonistic as Léopold. After all, Britain and Germany were competitors. Germany had supported President Kruger in the Transvaal. It could hardly have been assumed that Rhodes would or could provide the kinds of incentives or opportunities that would bring success to the Founder's entrepreneurial enterprises. Two years before,

Rhodes had told the foreign minister of France that he "hated" the Germans. Primed by Britain's ambassador, however, Rhodes was ready to promise the kaiser anything within reason. He agreed to use his influence to advance German claims to Samoa, and supported the kaiser's dreams of an expanded German empire in the Middle East, in what is now Syria and Iraq. Indeed, the two visionaries happily discussed how best to build a German railway to Baghdad, and the importance of using the waters of the Tigris and Euphrates rivers to irrigate the proposed addition to Germany's empire. That, Rhodes told the kaiser, was "Germany's task"; his was the Cape-to-Cairo line. Moreover, Rhodes was willing to construct the trans-continental telegraph with his own funds, but after forty years to cede ownership of the portion within German East Africa to the emperor. In March 1899, Rhodes with surprising ease obtained permission to continue raising wire beyond Abercorn along the east side of Lake Tanganyika. "What does this *rapprochement* between Rhodes and the Germans mean?" worried Merriman. "Are they humbugging him or is he humbugging them, and what is South Africa to pay for the bargain?" Rhodes had squared the kaiser, and anxiety levels rose.

By the end of 1900 Rhodes' line had penetrated fifty miles into German territory. It reached Ujiji, on the northeastern shores of the lake, in 1903. Yet the telegraph never in fact followed the crow's flight to Uganda—what Rhodes had earlier called "a very little distance"—for the British government worried about communications connections through German territory and preferred an all-red line from Zanzibar up-country to the interior lakes.

The kaiser and his officials were also forthcoming over Rhodes' railway. Although Rhodes promised the kaiser that he would "be up in your country in about five years' time," the final agreement between Germany and Rhodes was not signed until October 1899, and both the magnet of copper and Rhodes' death ended dreams of a rail route from Cape to Cairo. Nevertheless, Rhodes always extolled the kaiser personally. "He is a big man," Rhodes said. "The German people are very fortunate in having such an emperor, who spends his whole day in efforts for his people." Rhodes liked the "broad-minded" kaiser so much that he later altered his will to include Germans within the otherwise exclusively English-speaking ambit of his great scholarship scheme. And the feeling was mutual. "What a man he is," the kaiser, an admirer of appealing young men, told Sir Frank Lascelles, Britain's ambassador. "Why is he not my Minister? With him I could do anything."[27]

Rhodes found it hard to give up his dreams of a trans-continental connection of riveted rails. Even in late 1900, after enduring the siege of Kimberley and sending Robert Williams to treat again with Léopold, Rhodes debated the advantages of a 4′ 8½″ rail width for his African lines instead of the prevailing southern African standard gauge of only 3′6″. The advantages of a broader gauge were obvious. Trains could travel through Africa at about twice their existing speeds, and costs would not double. "I am inclined to make the change," he wrote. "We should then go through Africa (5,500 miles) at a rate of 50 m.p.h. rather than 20 m.p.h. . . . [or] in 110 hours instead of

270." As he pointed out, Egypt already employed the wider gauge, and so did the Americans—"the cleverest people in the world. . . ."[28] But this was pure fantasy. International rivalries and boundaries were becoming important with the end of the era of the scramble. There would still be scope for buccaneering and plunder, but hardly on Rhodes' earlier scale. Unbounded entrepreneurial opportunity was receding. Even so, a year later Rhodes attempted to strike a deal with Williams. Rhodes would extend his main line (still south of the Zambezi) to the borders of Katanga, where Williams held a major concession, in exchange for 50 percent of the mineral rights: "And in case of extension through the Congo State to the Nile," Rhodes wrote grandly, "an interest equal to 50% of the mineral rights of the country for fifty miles on each side of the line and such wood, free of charge, as may be required for mining. . . ."[29]

Without Rhodes, smaller men might complete his projects, but they could hardly substitute their own narrower visions and lesser statures for his ability to think and plan on a continental scale. Rhodes was dying, and so were those of his epochal efforts which, thwarted by distance and time, he left undone.

⎯⎯⎯⎯ ·•◄ 22 ►•· ⎯⎯⎯⎯

"Equal Rights for Civilized Men"
The Last Hurrah and the
Guns of October

"Y OU WANT *ME*. You can't do without me," Rhodes declared in early 1898. "The feeling of the people—you may think it egoism, but there are the facts—is that somebody is wanted to fight a certain thing for them, and there is nobody else able and willing to fight it."[1]

Rhodes refused to renounce the politics of power. His enemies in the Cape wanted him to become a reclusive hermit along the Zambezi; Innes wished that he would "stay in the North and do his work there."[2] But, in the aftermath of more difficulty with his heart and a troubled convalescence in Inyanga, Rhodes decided to dash headlong from the political wilderness back into the very eye of controversy and, he envisaged, to the summit of restored influence. Stirred by strong intimations that his time might fast be running out and stimulated by the earnest pleas of political busybodies, matchmakers, and old and new acolytes in the Cape, Rhodes decided that he ought to heed their call and his own otherwise difficult-to-fulfill lust for action, for intrigue and conspiracy, and for centrality. Rhodes exulted in his ability to manipulate men and events. Rhodesia, rails, and the telegraph should have been enough (along with diamonds, gold, and new entrepreneurial projects) to keep him busy, but Rhodes in late 1897, after being emotionally exonerated if technically chastised by the parliamentary inquiry, sought a mission to which he could devote himself passionately, idealistically, intellectually, and, if necessary, deviously.

Rhodes was a genius of adaptation. Like a great artist, he brought a rich technique and a full palette to the challenge of creating his life. The power of his technical gifts and his palette's breadth and subtlety had been amply displayed in the aftermath of the Raid. It had served him well when the opportunity presented itself to portray the peacemaker by negotiating with the Ndebele. Now, again, he displayed his polychromatic repertoire, with perhaps

599

some underpainting of somber tones occasioned by past sad events and the evidence of advancing physical infirmity. Still, abhorring a canvas empty of action and relevance, in 1897 and 1898 he poured what was left of his energy and creativity into an object which was important enough to provide sizable rewards—tangible power for its own sake and to further the realization of his "big idea." It was, as well, for the satisfaction of exercising his capacity to make things happen—the artist taking pleasure in the exercise of his craft. As Rhodes told a crowd in Cape Town, "The best service I can render to the country is to return here and to assist you in your big aims of closer union." Without his own renewed intervention in the politics of the Cape colony, Rhodes asserted, "Kruger will be supported and the Northern development damned."[3]

Rhodes refused to admit that he was anxious for a return to the hustings. "Don't talk as if it was I who want your Cape politics," he boomed at Garrett. "*I* am quite willing to keep out, but you have to take the feeling of the people," he said. He denied wanting to return to power. As to ambition, "humanly speaking, *qua* ambition at the Cape, one has had everything. There is no more to offer, only work and worry." He spoke of the real labor in the North—the creative opening up and developing of a country. He spoke proudly of his railway and telegraph lines to Cairo. "Really there are many other things to think of besides the Cape Town parish pump."[4]

There was a measure of truth in Rhodes' denials. He doubtless could persuade himself that the Cape needed him. The people needed him. The big idea of closer union required his talents and promotional abilities. "During the next five years the States of South Africa will crystallise one way or the other." The Uitlanders would probably triumph in the Transvaal and then amalgamate with Rhodesia against the Cape and Natal. Or Kruger would win, and end all notion of union. Or, best of all, Kruger's defeat would permit all of the states of southern Africa to federate. That was Rhodes' dream; that was sufficient reason to set aside his worries about a failing heart, and his other cares and projects, for a further intervention into the affairs of the Cape.

An undoubted measure of self-justification entered into Rhodes' decision to re-enter the political jousts of the Cape. "I do think that if I have ever so many faults to atone for—and I have many—the best atonement I can make is to work for this big object [of federation]," Rhodes declared. But Rhodes also protested too much. In 1898, sensing that the conflicts between English- and Dutch-speakers south of the Limpopo, between Britain and the Transvaal, and between local forms of autonomy for whites and the absorption of republics into a European-centered empire were still to be resolved, he determined to play an influential role in that struggle. He did so in order to advance his own vision of the proper outcome. He did so, too, for revenge—against Kruger, against Jan Hofmeyr and the Dutch Bondsmen of the Cape who had spurned him in his agony, and against all those who had proven disloyal and had kicked him when he was down. "It is not a case of whether the Bond will forgive me," Rhodes told Garrett on the eve of the 1898 campaign. "It is I who will have to compromise with them and their continental gang [from Pretoria]. . . . Some of my greatest friends are Dutch. . . ." He accused Hofmeyr and the Bond of supporting "everything rotten at Pretoria," and of "simply spreading hatred as hard as they can spread it." Rhodes was resolute and pugnacious: "Those are the people we are going to fight," he said. "We shall want all our discipline and all our organisation and unity for the fight. But it will all come right later on. I may not live to see it," he worried, "but you will all be putting up statues to me."[5]

Rhodes' resurgence was in every sense remarkable. Admittedly, he had never resigned his seat in the House or retired from the imperial stage. In 1897, after testifying before the Select Committee in London and before learning of its outcome in the distant reaches of Rhodesia, Rhodes had even flexed his political muscle in the Cape assembly. There an ideologically muted, mixed, and effectively caretaker ministry headed by Sir Gordon Sprigg had replaced that of Rhodes. Containing Sir Thomas Upington, Sivewright, and two other Bondsmen, it was initially kept in office by the Bond. Opposed were the liberal independents, guided in their separate ways by Innes, Sauer, and Merriman, and the British supremacists, led at first by Fuller. As always, Sprigg's leadership was hopelessly opportunistic and maddening in turns to the Bond and to the opposition. The fundamental cleavage between the two blocs of opposition, and even among the hardy liberals, was over how best to preserve southern African peace. The Dutch and men like Merriman sought reconciliation; others, including Innes, wanted to pressure Kruger to redress the real grievances of the Uitlanders. There were appeasers and jingoes. Where Rhodes once marched with the appeasers and the Bond and had demonstrated his faith in reconciliation in the Matopos, now he harmonized with the most raucous jingoes. Sprigg both attacked Kruger and voted with the Bond to keep his position. Thus, in April 1897, Merriman, Sauer, Innes, Schreiner, and others plotted Sprigg's downfall. On their behalf, Merriman moved a vote of no confidence.

Rhodes was not ready for Merriman to become prime minister, or for Schreiner to lead a ministry on behalf of Hofmeyr and the Bond. "Feeling of course ran very high," reported Innes in May 1897. "And it was made very much a question of English and Dutch. Rhodes was awfully put out, and all his men kept spreading the report that if a new Ministry [came] in now, it would 'hamper the Imperial Government.' " "But for some traitors who were brought over by C.J.R. at the eleventh hour," said Merriman, Sprigg's cabinet would have fallen. Rhodes, it appears, distributed promises and money and called in financial chits from earlier years in order to prevent Sprigg's demise.

Rhodes also sidled up to Innes during the debate and "said that Sprigg would advise the Governor to send for [him] (not for Merriman) if he was beaten. . . . 'You will have thirty-two men who voted with you on the Peace Amendment,' " Rhodes said quietly. " 'I can get you six [additional] Dutchmen, and you will have four of the present Ministry; so just think it over.' " But Innes would not enlist under Rhodes' banner. Nor would he support

Sprigg. So Rhodes' persuasive powers and Innes' imperialistic and personal reluctance resulted, when the votes were cast, in a solid tie. The Speaker sided, following custom, with the "noes," and so Sprigg was saved, as Innes wrote, "for a time longer."[6]

The attitudes of the old Rhodes, unreformed by the indabas in the Matopos and his loss of Bond support, were apparent once more during the 1897 session of the Cape parliament. Sprigg, recalling Rhodes' illegal arrest of Chief Sigcawu in Pondoland in 1895, introduced a Transkeian Territories bill in June, at a time when the government was with great difficulty quelling an African insurrection in the Kuruman area of what had been the Crown Colony of Bechuanaland. Sprigg wanted powers to intervene in African areas before rebellions or other troubles occurred. The new bill included an amendment which enabled the governor to authorize by proclamation the summary arrest and detention of any person in the Transkei who was deemed dangerous to the public peace. Such persons could be detained without appeal for three months or, by a variety of legal dodges, even longer. As Sir Alfred Milner, the newly installed governor and high commissioner, wrote to the Colonial Office, there was a "great difference—no use blinking it—. . . between British ideas as to the treatment of native races and colonial ideas. . . ." Merriman and Sauer were also appalled, and fought the bill bitterly, but Schreiner, Sivewright, and Rhodes all delighted in its draconian certainty. Indeed, Merriman blamed the easy passage of the act, and the discriminatory clause that had, he said, been proposed by Rhodes, on Rhodes' lobbying. Thus began South Africa's long-term reliance on detentions without trial, and another of Rhodes' political anticipations of the excesses of apartheid.

It was clear that Rhodes remained a man of profound influence in the House. As Innes admitted a year later, Rhodes, "if not the biggest, . . . was one of the biggest men in Africa. The restless energy of his genius, the material resources at his command, the position he held here, and the position he held in England, could not but make him one who must exercise a very great influence both in the House and the country if he cared to do so."[7]

Having exerted himself against Africans as well as to save Sprigg, Rhodes chose neither to supersede him as premier in 1897 (which he might just have engineered) nor to participate in any other significant manner in the affairs of the House during that session. As far as vaulting ambition, his aims were largely leashed until the mother of parliaments completed its examination of the Raid. Yet the sharp division of the Cape assembly over Sprigg, and whether he should survive as premier, marked the beginning (really the public acknowledgment) of acute political divisions within both that body and the Cape generally and the rise of new political organizations—protean parties—among English-speaking whites of the Colony.

Innes' true liberals or moderates were affiliated to the South African Political Association. The South Africa party (of 1898) was to form an umbrella for the aspirations of those English-speaking parliamentarians who sought, like Merriman, to oppose jingoism and Transvaal-baiting and, as a result, work with the Bond. Those inside and outside of parliament who were determined to preserve British supremacy in South Africa were members of or friendly to the aims of the South African League, formed among loyalists in the strongly English frontier districts of the eastern Cape in 1896, shortly after the Raid. The League grew rapidly within the Colony, in Natal, and even in the Transvaal, and also welcomed the establishment of a sister association in Britain itself. The League was anti-Bond, anti-Dutch, and anxious to advance British hegemony within the sub-continent.

In order to exert its influence in a politically direct manner, the League in 1897 established the Progressive party. Earlier, the name had been used to group those members of parliament who had opposed Rhodes and his Bond allies in 1890–91, but, as a party in 1896–97, its members sat initially on the opposition benches. Rhodes joined them in spirit and became their unofficial leader in 1897; Sprigg shifted to their cause from the Bond at about the same time that Rhodes returned to parliament. After the crisis of confidence of April 1897, when the Bond realized that Sprigg was tilting away from conciliating and now, stiffened by Rhodes, favored a tough stance toward the Transvaal, it broke with him entirely. Sprigg thereafter governed as a Progressive, backed and guided by Rhodes. As Milner explained to Chamberlain, "The present Ministry, a weak one, . . . has hitherto leant . . . upon the Bond, though with mutual distrust. . . . *Now* there is something like an open rupture, and at the next election the Ministry will stand boldly upon the 'no more Bond dictation' platform. On that platform they will have all the English on their side, and some Dutchmen, corrupted by Rhodes. But they cannot quite afford to show their hand yet. . . ."[8]

Rhodes was not yet ready to push Sprigg aside and seek the premiership. But he was set to do so in early 1898, when he resumed his political pursuits with a clarity of purpose and burst of energy that belied the curt disdain with which he dismissed Garrett's friendly questions. After assuring himself of the allegiance of most of the Progressives in parliament and attempting to gain the support of friends among the liberals and the Bond alike, Rhodes took his resumed cause to the country. Unwittingly echoing a sixteenth-century professor at the University of Salamanca who, having survived a five-year incarceration under the Spanish Inquisition, again stood before his students and began, "As I was saying . . ," Rhodes enunciated his objectives with a fervor which was as usual as his policies were heretical.[9] Although he denied being inconsistent, the new Rhodes, the Progessive Rhodes, no longer sought tariff protection for farming interests. Nor did he propose to square Kruger. The new Rhodes was mostly an imperialistic jingo, with new and appealing proposals for segments of the Cape population that he had hitherto ignored.

"Now I am back at a crisis of your country," Rhodes prefaced a long exposition of his views in Cape Town in March 1898. Rather than talk as he might prefer about northern questions, he spoke specifically about matters of the parish pump—"those things that burden . . . families." Prior to elections to the Cape's upper legislative chamber, Rhodes took to the national campaign trail as never before. He also charted a course for Progressives which would carry them through the likely polling later in the year for seats in the Cape's more important lower house of assembly. "On your votes at this election," Rhodes declared, "rests very probably the future of South Africa. That is what I wish to bring home to you. . . ." Then he admonished: "And I can only do so if you will be perfectly silent."

"You are troubled about meat and bread duties." (Rinderpest had devastated local herds of cattle.) Rhodes, the sometime champion of Dutch farming interests, pledged himself to abolish duties on imported meat. He favored reductions in the cost of wheat and lower excise taxes on liquor, mostly to be collected from drinkers, not producers. As Garrett, who also influenced them, characterized Rhodes' views in a summary of that portion of their interview, "On food-stuffs apart from meat he is evidently prepared to make something of a new departure, though not nearly so large a one as his urban admirers would like." Rhodes refused to accept that he was inconsistent with his past. "I suppose you say you are hearing a recantation, but you are not," he pleaded with the Cape Town audience.

Politically, Rhodes lent his support to a radical redistribution of seats in the House. Based on the report of a recently concluded commission, removing the rural weighting (which Rhodes had hitherto favored to please the Bond) of the Cape's constituencies could give the towns further members. "I have never altered my ideas, and shall never alter them so long as I have life," he said. The Progressives would obviously benefit, and the Bond lose its long-cherished advantage. "We must give representation of this country on the basis of the number of people who live in it. . . ," Rhodes said reasonably. The key qualifications, moreover, for the vote should be "proper intelligence" and an elevated position based on "inheritance of means or by the work of their hands." Rhodes had still not become a populist or a true democrat. He still abhorred "loafers."

In terms of domestic legislation for the Cape, he now favored (as he could not when he was working with the Bond) compulsory education, confusingly on what he called a permissive basis. He envisaged a locally based system similar to that customary in the United States but rare in the empire. "With education," he proclaimed loftily, "will disappear that race hatred [between English and Dutch] which is inspired by ignorance, and with education will come better thoughts and grander conceptions." By "education," Rhodes clearly meant state-controlled, English-dominated, secular education.

Despite that plea for a future fusion of the two white linguistic groups in the Cape, Rhodes immediately launched a vicious attack on the Bond. He also attempted to separate the goals of the Bond from the real political aims of the mass of the Dutch-speaking whites of the Cape. He characterized the policies of the Bond as being against education, in favor of keeping Coloured labourers drunk on cheap, Dutch-produced brandy, against loyal contributions to Her Majesty's fleet, against his own northern expansion, and favorable to Kruger and his misguided initiatives. He accused Hofmeyr of establishing an "enormous" one-man "terrorism" over the Dutch farmers of the Cape. "Many . . . are resenting it. I say it is wrong," Rhodes declared with a new virtue. Regarding the Transvaal, Rhodes said that, although he did not "wish to indulge in an antagonistic policy which would bring bloodshed," what good could come of "supporting all these barbaric actions of the Transvaal Government?" Statesmanship, Rhodes suggested, was not "rubbing along somehow" with the Transvaal, but doing everything "to promote the union of the country" by sympathizing with the Uitlanders.

Rhodes, furthermore, was allying himself sternly with Milner, whose private views ("There has got to be a separation of the sheep from the goats in this sub-continent") were widely suspect but who had hitherto carefully kept them from the public ear. A railway opening ceremony in Graaff-Reinet finally gave Milner an opportunity to express himself in what was viewed by the different white communities as either a notorious or a celebrated speech. Nine days before Rhodes spoke, Milner told an audience primarily of Bondsmen that there could be no reason in the Cape for disloyalty to the Queen and her government. "You have thriven wonderfully well under that Government . . . [and] live under an absolutely free system of government . . . [which was] freely and gladly bestowed upon you, because freedom and self-government, justice and equality are the first principles of British policy. . . ." "Of course," said Milner, "you are loyal. It would be monstrous if you were not." As regards the Transvaal, Milner suggested that Britain harbored no "occult design" on its independence. Rather, Britain insisted only on a minimum of control consistent with the London Convention of 1884. Britain wished to enhance the "future tranquillity" of South Africa. It desired to induce the Transvaal "gradually to assimilate its institutions, and, what is even more important . . . the temper and spirit of its administration to those of the free communities of South Africa. . . ."

Rhodes echoed Milner. He urged his listeners to elect Progressive majorities to both the upper and lower houses of parliament because that would give them a "great United South Africa." By backing the Bond, union would be put off and Krugerism would triumph. The Bond, he said, was "afraid to lose the oligarchical domination which exists [in the Cape] and in the Transvaal, which is out of sympathy entirely with republican ideas and Imperial ideas, which preaches that the government of the few shall run a State. That has to be fought, and I am anxious," said Rhodes, "that the system of government by the few, established through the excitement of race feeling, shall not exist here." By backing the Bond the North would be driven away and the new English-speaking population in the Transvaal utterly isolated. "When the one gets its wealth and the other its rights, it is probable that the two will go together, and leave [the Cape] at the shank end of the continent." That was his old, recurring fear—that the Cape (and Rhodes) would be left out (and left out of the family) and denied room for expansion and opportunity.[10]

"If I followed my own wishes," Rhodes jabbed at Garrett, "do you think

I should be messing about down here?" But he was "waiting about" in order to help the Progressive party win the elections to the upper house. His speech at Cape Town and another at Salt River, Milner's at Graaff-Reinet, a press campaign which he and his followers orchestrated, and infusions of cash to counter funds supposedly supplied to the Bond from the Transvaal's secret service fund were all meant to assist in the prosecution of what had become his new crusade. That they did, and that the Progressives obtained a small 14 to 9 majority in the upper house, may have been due largely to Rhodes and his purse, and even to a substantial disbursement wired from Madeira in the closing days of the campaign.[11] By the time that the final results were achieved, Rhodes had arrived in London to address an annual meeting of the British South Africa Company (where he was reinstated as a director).

Paramountcy in South and southern Africa was the central focus of what during the remainder of 1898 ostensibly was but a continuation of the usual struggle in the Cape over parochial advantage and the policies of the parish pump. Those in political life, such as Rhodes, who understood the immediacy of the renewed battle with Krugerism and who stood for vigorous imperial expansion (after all, the English were the "best race" in the world) could hardly have appreciated how swiftly Milner and Chamberlain were propelling South Africa toward the cataclysm of war. Rhodes thought that he and South Africa had a few more years of peace, possibly five or more. In early 1898 even he could not have imagined that the great rupture would come in a year and a half. Furthermore, as Rhodes strove to reassert his own mastery over southern Africa, so he assumed that the tide of events could be shaped and stemmed, as always before, by the force of his own leadership and will. Otherwise, why had he chosen to come out of the political wilderness?

Rhodes returned from Britain in time to participate in the second half of the opening session of parliament of 1898—what Innes called "the preface to the most unpleasant chapter of parliamentary history within my experience."[12] Sprigg, with naked expediency, had introduced a radical redistribution bill which, if passed, would have given a mighty assist to the electoral fortunes of the Progressives. By adding eighteen urban seats to the seventy-nine existing seats in parliament, two-thirds of which were rural, Sprigg would strike a blow for democracy, for his party, and for Sprigg. If the bill passed, he planned to dissolve the house, win the new election on the back of the now fully enfranchised urban voters, and—very possibly—hand the premiership back to Rhodes. "All this redistribution nonsense has only one object," Merriman wrote, "to set Rhodes up again and to make him a sort of dictator, in which case—woe to the Transvaal and woe to the Natives. . . ."[13] Sprigg understood that the Bond would retaliate. Its leading representative in his cabinet promptly resigned. Schreiner, on behalf of the Bond, introduced a motion of no confidence. If successful, that motion would oust the sitting premier before Rhodes should be riding hard, and compel a colony-wide contest at the polls. Schreiner and the Bond, unaware of the precipitous bent of Milner and Chamberlain, saw Rhodes as Africa's wildest war-monger and as the single major threat to the Cape's pacific policies toward the Transvaal. "It is all wretched," Schreiner groaned, "wherever the work or influence of Rhodes comes to be seen or felt."

The debates in the House on redistribution were notable for Schreiner's snarling at Rhodes, and Rhodes' tactful and quiet replies. By calling Rhodes a man who "not by any platform utterance, not by anything you can lay hold of, exercises and brings to bear throughout this country an influence which is keeping alive . . . racial feeling," Schreiner played directly into the great man's hands. There were loud cries of "No, no" and "Shame" and "cheers and uproar," according to the parliamentary report. The Speaker called for order. Indeed, Innes reported that Rhodes "for the most part sat silent, egging . . . on" his and Sprigg's supporters. He rose to say merely that Schreiner was incorrect. Earlier, when Merriman said that as much as he admired Rhodes' "great talents," the former premier's methods and the man himself were a "demoralising force in their political life," Rhodes held his usually voluble tongue. Before Sprigg's bill came to a vote he spoke at length only once, to protest the inconvenience of a suddenly arranged evening sitting. "A number of people were dining with him" that very evening. He also indicated that he for one was "only too ready to go to the country"—to put his policies to the test of a natural poll. When the House finally divided on redistribution, the bill passed by 42 to 35. Yet, two days later, so did the motion of no confidence, by 41 to 36. John Charles Molteno, Richard Solomon, and William Hay were among the key defectors; Innes, opposed as he was to Rhodes' policies, nevertheless voted with him. Parliament was promptly dissolved and a general election scheduled.

Innes and his band of hardy liberals had wanted redistribution. " 'The true inwardness of the present situation,' " he said, " 'turned upon the position, plans, and prospects. . .' " of Rhodes. Innes absolutely refused to become "a Rhodes man." As Innes had recently written, "I am not a Rhodes man; and do not think I am ever likely to be one. I have no confidence in Mr Rhodes' policy in Colonial politics. I do not think he cares about them, and he is prepared in my opinion to use them in any way which will serve his policy in the North. I am prepared to support him in the North, but I am not prepared to put myself as a Colonial politician under the banner of any man who is a mere opportunist."[14] Innes' conclusion was broadly fair.

The ensuing election was the most bitterly contested, corrupt, and corrosive that the Cape had ever known. Much more was at stake than before. Both Rhodes and Hofmeyr thought so, and the vitriol and calumnies of the partisan press (much of it beholden to Rhodes) were matched only by the discreditable rumors spread by both sides and the personal invective that laced the campaign speeches of many candidates. Rhodes was determined to secure a Progressive majority, and to return to the premiership. He imported C.A. Owen Lewis, an astute and experienced campaign manager from Britain, secured (if he did not already control) the backing of virtually all of the English-language press, and was prepared to spend money as lavishly and as tellingly as he had once distributed shares to men and women who thereby became obligated. There is clear evidence that he even paid individuals for not signing Bond registration lists, and to stand against Bondsmen in solidly Dutch-speaking districts. As Innes commented, "The Rhodes people will spare no effort *and no expense* to return Rhodes men."

The surviving telegraph and letter traffic of this hectic period testifies to Rhodes' concentration on the detailed management of a comparatively complicated campaign. It makes plain his wily appreciation of individual vulnerability and strength and the unscrupulous manner in which he targeted former allies (like Merriman and Richard Solomon) for defeat. He employed underhanded methods (leaked letters, innuendo, and so on) and was blatantly willing to purchase favor and unexpected advantage. Olive Schreiner's support of her brother, the prospective prime minister, was strong. So was her acutely defined critique of Rhodes. "I sometimes fear Rhodes is coming near the end of his course," she wrote. "And it need not have been! He might have had all that was best . . . in South Africa to his side. We that would have loved him so, honoured him, followed him!—but he has chosen . . . not only the worst men as his instruments, but to *act on men always through the lowest sides of their nature,* to lead them through narrow self-interest instead of animating them with large enthusiasms." Rhodes, meanwhile, poured on the money. "Fuller wants more," he told his banker early in the campaign. "Well it is the crisis of the country. He wants £11,000, so kindly draw draft on Beit." On another occasion Rhodes told Michell to give Fuller a further £10,000. Later, in a startling departure from previous practice, he cautioned Rutherfoord Harris to keep spending, but to charge the bills to him, not to De Beers (except in and around Kimberley).[15]

Rhodes stood, as was then permissible if unusual, for two seats, his own at Barkly West (where there had long been a Dutch-speaking majority and where he feared defeat) and Merriman's safer one in Namaqualand. "The course I am pursuing has precedents in the old country and in adopting this I feel sure I have your support," Rhodes sought assurances from an influential voter in his second district.[16] Merriman and Solomon were compelled to seek new constituencies, while Rhodes dispatched loyal Progressives into those districts which he thought the power of his purse and rhetoric could command. Rhodes spoke widely and frequently, but mostly in and around Kimberley, in Port Elizabeth, and, when it was critical, in Taung and Vryburg. He never ventured into hard-core Bond territory. Nor did he appear before Africans. He said little in his speeches about redistribution, and nothing new about tariffs and protectionism. For the most part his election addresses consisted of long reviews of his accomplishments in the north and recitations of his dreams for and explanations of the urgency of South African union. Merriman thought that the content of his speeches showed that Rhodes was "clean off his head, for his egotism rises to a pitch of mania. . . ." "Surely," said Merriman, "English folk will not continue to be blinded for ever by such self-conceited rant."

Was Merriman simply partisan and sour, or was he reacting unwittingly to a new phase of Rhodes' self-assessment? Was the Rhodes who ranted repetitively about his past accomplishments a man who knew himself to be embarked on the downslope of life? Was he thus impelled to rehearse the past, to rewrite history in order to feel worthy in the face of early but tangible physical and emotional decline? Was Rhodes prematurely demonstrating the defensive reminiscing of the aged?

Rhodes' criticism of the Bond and Kruger were steady themes. "It is not Rhodes that is causing unrest in Africa," he told voters at Longlands. "It is the Transvaal position that is causing unrest in Africa, and if I were dead tomorrow" (a constant theme), "the same thing would go on. The same thing must go on until the new people in the Transvaal receive similar privileges with the old. . . ." At Port Elizabeth, Rhodes warned the electors that, if the Bond became supreme, the Cape would be "under the domination of Krugerism for the next five years." Rhodes saw "the danger" that was coming. His northern country would be "all right." But he would not retire there until he saw that the south was "clear of the risk of being dominated by Krugerism."[17]

Rhodes insinuated that the Bond was being financed by the Transvaal: "Was there ever a greater perversion of capital than the action of [the South Africa party] . . . in using money from a foreign state, a state that is very unfriendly to Her Majesty. . . ?" Although Rhodes thus excused his own excessive financing of Progressive candidates, his allegations, though widely believed at the time, were almost certainly false. In fact, Stow, Rhodes' old colleague and recently turned enemy, was secretly supplying funds to an anti-Rhodes newspaper in the Cape and to the South Africa party.

Speaking in the heart of his old constituency on the eve of the poll, he told the predominantly Dutch electors that they might well think that it made little difference whether they voted for or against him. "But," he said, "it makes a great deal of difference." If he received Dutch support he would be heard in the House when he advocated the kinds of imperial policies to which the Bond were opposed. "I may then lay claim fairly to represent not only the English but also the Afrikanders, and that will be the best answer I can make to the charge that I have no longer the confidence of the old population of this country. You must," he implored, "give me your confidence, because your hinterland is at stake, and I am the only man who can work the North with the South." He was against Kruger, for a healing of the supposed antagonism between Dutch and English, and for union. "My great anxiety during the next five years," he concluded one speech, "will be to keep the Dutch people with us, but it rests with the Afrikander people themselves," he threatened, "to see that we are not divided into two camps."[18]

Rhodes saturated his listeners (those patient people of the nineteenth century who were entertained by harangues rather than by television screens) with talk of union—its importance, its economic benefits, and its attainability. A union of territories and of peoples was an objective first sketched in the Confession as a mystical ideal and since elaborated upon as a goal of practical benefit to farmers, miners, and settlers in the distant interior. Rhodes' rails and telegraphs served such goals; a federation or some other kind of southern African amalgamation would ensure, or so Rhodes reiterated, the peace and prosperity of its white population. Common tariffs, common rail rates, common representation, and a single "native policy" would serve whites well. "If I continue to live, although I know another wish has been expressed, I have hopes," Rhodes said, "that union may be brought about."

It was in the context of a speech about such a union during the 1898 political campaign that Rhodes first enunciated the doctrine of equal rights. His modern defenders use Rhodes' pronouncements on this subject to salvage his reputation, but no clear description of what he said and what he meant has hitherto been readily available. Much, too, on this question has been seriously distorted to favor the Founder. "It is only when you accept the idea of the equality of human beings that you can consider seriously the union of Africa," he told an audience near Barkly West. Virtuously, he billed himself as an "exponent of a united South Africa" who was capable of rising above "race feeling." At Vryburg, after explaining that the "party of Progress must govern South Africa . . . become supreme in Cape Colony . . . [and] have its union with the North," Rhodes said that it would have "its relations" with the Transvaal, which would therefore "have to consider equal rights for every civilised man."[19]

These were equal rights for whites. Throughout the 1898 campaign Rhodes sought to conciliate Dutch-speaking voters. Although he spoke the taal appallingly (despite twenty-eight years among the Dutch), and often used an interpreter, Rhodes had hitherto always won the votes of his own predominantly Dutch-speaking constituency and, until the Raid, had consorted with and been a staunch ally of the leading farmers and burghers of the Cape. He had supported the Dutch when they wanted their language, religious preferences, and customs to receive respect and legal equality. Now he sought equal standing for the language, culture, and political aspirations of Uitlanders. His slogan of equal rights, even equal rights for "every civilised man," was not initially intended to appeal to African or even Coloured voters in the Cape. Given the closeness of the parties throughout the Colony and the strong possibility that the casting of ballots by Africans and Coloureds could easily decide several critical seats (like Wodehouse), Rhodes certainly would have wanted and been advised to make naked appeals for their support. After all, he had been no friend of either Africans or Coloureds, and his recent vote in favor of the Transkei Territories bill would have helped his reputation little. Yet, throughout the busy campaign, Rhodes never spoke in a marginal constituency; he left it to others to appeal to Africans.

Plomer, followed by Innes, suggested that at some point along the campaign trail Rhodes told an audience that he believed in "Equal rights for every white man south of the Zambesi." An association of Coloured voters immediately asked Rhodes whether the newspaper report that they had read was accurate. In his reply, Rhodes sent the association a copy of the newspaper, in the margin of which he had written: "My motto is—Equal rights for every civilised man south of the Zambesi." He defined a civilized man as a man, white or black, " 'who has sufficient education to write his name, has some property, or works. In fact, is not a loafer.' " Innes' memory, jogged by Plomer, was the same as Plomer's. "Rhodes, intent upon his duel with Kruger, quite lost sight of the Native and Coloured voter at the Cape." Those who were running the Progressive party grew concerned. Indeed, "there was consternation." Rhodes executed a rapid reversal. He introduced, as a "vote-catching device," the additions "civilised man south of the Zambesi," and then defined what he meant, albeit crudely and inconsiderately.[20]

Vote-catching devices are meant to be deployed. If Rhodes' famous phrase, hitherto interpreted as demonstrating responsible feeling toward Africans, was anything more than a slogan meant to influence Dutch-speakers, evidence is lacking. Urged upon him by Fuller, Edgar Harris Walton (the editor of the *Eastern Province Herald*), his campaign manager imported from Britain, or even by Rutherfoord Harris, the phrase was not widely (or even narrowly) disseminated. There is no proof that it swayed electors. There is nothing in the contemporary correspondence of Rhodes, Garrett, Innes, or Merriman which refers to this presumably noteworthy addition to the campaign rhetoric. True, in a speech in mid-1899, Rhodes said that the policy of the Progressives in 1898 had been "equality of rights for every civilised man south of the Zambesi." In 1899, too, he said that they had presumed that all men who could write their name, place of residence, and occupation, and who worked or held property, were civilized. "Quite irrespective of colour," they would be "entitled to equality of rights." But at the same time, in Claremont, he said deprecatingly that the "pure natives" of Tembuland had voted with the Bond and that the Bond was still "hungering" for black representatives to sit with them on their side of the House. He did not cast about for African votes, since the Bond had them; and, though he praised Coloureds, he did not seek their votes since the "Progressives [had] them already." In fact, Rhodes employed the "civilised man" catch phrase frequently in his speeches only in 1899, after he had returned from six months in Europe. Even then he had whites and Coloureds, but hardly Africans, in mind. He had made a strong case in the House that Kruger was mistreating Coloureds from the Cape. He seems to have framed his appeals to Dutch-speakers as before, and now also to their Coloured brethren in case another election might be forced upon the country.[21]

In mid-July 1899, immediately after landing at Cape Town, he referred to the Raid: "Notwithstanding my past little temporary difficulty, if we were all to accept equal rights, I feel convinced that we should all be united on the proposition that Africa is not, after all, big enough for us." British supremacy could alone deliver equal rights to South Africa; once united, the whites in southern Africa could spread their accomplishments and advance their mission more broadly. Rhodes feared that whites in the Cape would lose the idea of union. "We must try . . . to keep the continent together." Rhodes envisaged a "great commonwealth" of the states of Africa where there would be "equality of rights," implicitly again, among and for whites. He rambled on. After telling his audience of the great number of telegrams of support he had received from Dutch-speakers in Paarl and elsewhere, Rhodes indicated that he and they were all working "for not only . . . union of the country but union of the races." He meant the union of the white race. "That will come right," he explained, "once the principle of equal rights is accepted—equal rights for every civilised man south of the Zambesi." That was the renowned formula. His next words were an elaboration: "Once the competition between us is on the basis of the best man, . . . be he a German . . . a Frenchman . . . a Russian . . . a Dutchman, or be he an Englishman, the question is over." He wanted to leave behind him a union of states in which both English- and Dutch-speakers would together enjoy "liberty." Coloureds and Africans were hardly included. At Claremont, where Coloureds might have been in the audience, Rhodes congratulated himself for having worked in the north "on the basis of equal rights for every class of citizen," that is, for both English- and Dutch-speakers.

Although Rhodes spoke feelingly of all the help Coloureds had given him during the battles against the Ndebele and Shona in Rhodesia in 1896, he said nothing about Africans, except that the Bond relied upon their vote. When he demanded that "the best men [should] come to the front, independent of race or the accident of birth [overseas]," he spoke only of whites. The whites of the Cape "must fight for equal rights." Practically, the result would be "the federal union of South Africa." [22]

Throughout his speeches, Rhodes' appeals in 1898 and 1899 were to whites, and particularly to those in his audiences who spoke Dutch. At no point can Rhodes be said to have envisaged, contemplated, supported, or advocated fundamental human rights, or anything like improved treatment for Africans within the Cape, or even within the realm of his projected union. Throughout his career, and even at its end, Rhodes sought to bridge the gap of history and sentiment between the original white settlers—those who spoke Dutch— and those like himself who were English-speaking newcomers. He sought fusion, but among whites and in order to further his own narrow, white-bounded, political conception of an enlarged, unified South Africa.

There is a sequel. When the South African war had broken out, and after Rhodes had survived the four-month-long siege of Kimberley, he spoke (in 1900) at an annual meeting of the De Beers shareholders in that city. The guns still fired. After thundering away at the self-serving, corrupt, oligarchical cliques who had plunged the Transvaal and the Orange Free State into conflict, Rhodes refuted any notions that those so-called republics belonged to persons who spoke Dutch. That "contention" would "be over with the recognition of equal rights for every civilised man south of the Zambesi. That principle for which we have been so long striving is the crux of the present struggle." Rhodes explained: "My own belief is that when the war is over, a large number of Dutch farmers in this country will throw in their lot with us on this basis, that neither shall claim any right of preference over the other. . . . We find—owing, I suppose it is, to the race affinity—there is not much between us." The Dutch had been misled by the "gangs" in Pretoria, Bloemfontein, and even in Cape Town. Thus, even during the war, Rhodes' civilized man south of the Zambezi was purely white. Moreover, Michell asserts that it was only after this speech, and not in 1898 or 1899, that "when approached shortly afterwards by the coloured community [presumably of Kimberley] . . . he wrote his views . . . on a scrap of newspaper. . . ." It was on this occasion, reports Michell, that he reiterated his motto and provided the definition, word for word, supplied by Plomer. Indeed, Michell printed a facsimile of the famous motto and definition, set out, in Rhodes' clear hand, on a scrap of newspaper. Two conclusions are inescapable: Rhodes only included Coloureds (and never blacks) in his definition of the already "civilised" as an afterthought, and firmly only in 1900. Moreover, to the end of his days Rhodes, as before, was primarily concerned—for he had been the cause of their split—to put the Humpty Dumpty of Dutch and English feelings back together again.[23]

Despite all of Rhodes' efforts and money, the final results of the poll of 1898 proved perverse. It had been fought on the basis of the old constituencies; redistribution had not yet occurred. Thus, although the Progressive party obtained many more votes than its rival—about 44,000 to 37,000—three Bondsmen scraped home by tiny pluralities of 2, 10, and 20 in marginal seats, and most of the "Mugwumps," true liberal followers of Innes, lost. Rhodes achieved the high vote that he wanted in Barkly West, and also won easily in Namaqualand (which he promptly resigned). Despite Rhodes, Merriman was returned more easily than he had expected in Wodehouse. Garrett, a newcomer, was elected from Victoria East. Innes had no competition in Cape Division (the Cape Peninsula, excluding Cape Town and Sea Point), Sprigg very little in East London. Overall, despite the decisive Progressive mandate in the popular vote, they took only thirty-nine to their opponents' forty seats.

Rhodes and Sprigg tried desperately to avoid the obvious consequences of their defeat, however narrow. Rhodes believed that he might be able to persuade three Bondsmen—two by promises of railways for their districts and a third by blackmail—to cross the floor. But Milner was a problem. Despite his own personal preferences, he had a constitutional obligation to summon Schreiner, the putative leader of the majority, to form a new government. Rhodes pleaded for room in which to maneuver. "I know the House and if the new lot come in wild horses will not move them at any rate for five years. Let us have a little time for consideration. . . . I feel sure the right course is that Sir J. [Gordon] Sprigg should hold on as long as there is a chance of a majority and with the various changes now before him [as well as Rhodes' prospects]. I think he has a fair chance of success." As Milner later wrote home, "In spite of interminable arguments to the contrary addressed to me both by the nominal (J.G.S.) and the real (C.J.R.) head of Government," Milner told them that parliament must be summoned without delay.

Rhodes sought to escape defeat, and Milner, although admitting that he wished to see Sprigg stay, "disbelieve[d] absolutely in the policy of such tactics." He accused Rhodes of refusing to see that there was a "moral side to such matters or even that *straightforwardness* may have a tactical value." "As to Rhodes, he is doing all he knows to make Sprigg stay in, not caring two pins how ridiculous he makes him look in the process." Rhodes, said Innes, "has no moral courage, and never had." Milner suggested that the scheme for keeping office "is just the Raid over again." "I mean," the governor wrote, "it is the same attempt to gain prematurely by violent and unscrupulous means what you could get honestly and without violence, if you would only *wait and work for it*." In other words, "Captain of XI to umpire: 'Unless you cheat, I won't play.' What rubbish!"

Milner convened parliament again in October, after finally compelling Sprigg to come to terms with his possible defeat. By then the two seats in Vryburg had been declared for the Progressives (Rhodes' renounced seat in Namaqualand was claimed by the Progressives a week later). Still Sprigg and Rhodes tried to wriggle, and Milner felt called upon to prevent "so great a public disaster." Firmly he told Sprigg, and through Sprigg, Rhodes, that "no Ministry [was] justified in holding office," unless it could be sure of passing a budget or of obtaining a vote of funds.[24] This was elemental parliamentary behavior. On the next day Sprigg's ministry plunged to defeat by two votes (Dr. Bisset Berry, a Progressive, had been elected speaker of the House). Sprigg resigned, Schreiner formed the new Cape government, and Rhodes assumed Sprigg's position as leader of the opposition. It was a new and strange role for the former prime minister, accentuated by the composition of Schreiner's cabinet. Since it included Merriman, Solomon, and Sauer, the new government was not so much a Bond front (although it was that) but a coalition of men opposed to the personal domination of Rhodes and everything for which their once so esteemed leader stood. Obviously, too, the nature of the campaign had only deepened enmities. As Milner had so correctly suggested, straightforwardness would have proven a much more successful tactic.

One of Rhodes' first efforts was to pressure Berry, who had been elected from Progressive party ranks, to resign as Speaker so that Schreiner's majority would be cut to one; Rhodes anticipated slipping David de Waal, a Bondsman and an old trekking companion, into his own camp, and thus securing a thin majority. At a Progressive party caucus where his maneuver was discussed, Innes opposed any attempt to bombard Berry; doing so would demean the status of the office and offend parliamentary traditions. "Rhodes," reported Innes, "was in a white heat, and did nothing but talk at me. . . . Rhodes hates a spoke being put in his wheel and is frantic with me. Abuses me like a pickpocket I am told." The Speaker stayed. "Rhodes and his friends don't care how they drag the Constitution through the mire, if they only get their own way," concluded Innes.[25]

It has often been said that Rhodes felt uncomfortable as uncrowned leader of the opposition, and performed that role, so difficult and taxing even in the happiest of parliamentary climates, irascibly. In fact, a close reading of the proceedings of the House shows that Rhodes enjoyed himself tremendously, twitting and frustrating the government at every turn, and remaining—to the great annoyance of the new government—the continued orbit around which all parliamentary debates swirled. He and Merriman were on opposite sides and clashed, in the manner of British-influenced parliaments, incessantly. So did Rhodes and Jacobus Sauer. But Rhodes saved his best sallies and his hardest thrusts for Schreiner. When Rhodes was demanding intervention on the part of the Cape government to protect Britons, albeit Coloured ones, in the Transvaal—"let them dismiss the case of their being white, or almost white, or very nearly white . . . let them say they were their fellow-subjects"—Rhodes (the new convert to democratic procedures) accused the premier of having run away twice from the debates, of having "disregarded and despised" the House, and of being "afraid" to talk to the Transvaal. Rhodes said (with tongue in cheek) that he had been prime minister for many years, and would not have "dared to treat the House" in the same manner.

During an earlier discussion of a very different subject, Sauer accused Rhodes of addressing parliament as if he were talking to a board of directors. "But they in the House were free men, and would not be dictated to," declared his old colleague. Nevertheless Rhodes compelled Schreiner's ministry to defer consideration of the Colony's budget until after it had been maneuvered into accepting a compromise redistribution bill which granted the townspeople of the Cape sixteen extra seats and was inimical to the interests of the Bond. "The House might congratulate itself," Rhodes said at the end of the bitter, rancorous session, "on the fact that . . . they have got the wretched Redistribution Bill out of the way." In other words, Rhodes had obtained what he had wanted, in this case by plying vigorously the craft of political intrigue and vituperation within and around parliament.

The opposition and Rhodes managed to win a number of important divisions and therefore to alter both the agenda and the legislative intent of Schreiner's government. In keeping with Rhodes' campaign pledge, they rewrote a government bill and thus reduced duties on imported meat and, incidentally, spurred his personal and corporate intervention into the cold storage and slaughterhouse industries in the Cape. The Progressives, with Rhodes leaping to attack Merriman, the treasurer general, overcame official reluctance to put ocean mail contracts out to tender, or bid. Rhodes accused Merriman of having no idea "of the expansion of the world. . . ." He attacked others for seeking the vote of literate Africans, and vigorously defended his actions regarding the earlier detention of Chief Sigcawu. Reminding Schreiner that they had then been colleagues, and that—whatever he currently thought—they might be colleagues again, or "dead, . . . but time would show," he urged the prime minister to be moderate and reasonable. Regarding new laws for Pondoland, Rhodes favored their application to chiefs only, and not to Transkeians or Africans as a class. Rhodes declared that he was being consistent, but those in the House who could remember his days as premier would have snickered.

Rhodes managed to obtain attention (although not passage) for an ingenious forward-looking plan to construct dams on the Harts and Vaal rivers in Griqualand West and thus bring modern concepts of water conservation and the benefits of large scale irrigation to his constituents. Rhodes was also moved by the inept handling by Schreiner of an otherwise non-contentious measure on judicial jurisdictions to remind the House that he alone "represented" Rhodesia, and should have been consulted. Since Schreiner was in a hurry, Rhodes offered to telegraph the contents of the bill to the judges in Rhodesia. But "that would be a great waste of money," Schreiner retorted to the millionaire. Rhodes replied firmly: "That is my business." He had the final put-down.

During the spring session of 1898 and the autumn session of 1899, Rhodes possessed a number of advantages. Given Schreiner's slim majority and the possibility of defections on particular issues—a potential which Rhodes exploited politically and financially—and given the opposition's consummate ability to obstruct, annoy, and delay, the Progressives were not without considerable influence. Given Schreiner's inexperience and naïveté, Merriman's unpopularity, and the fear of the Bond even among the ranks of English-speaking supporters of the South Africa party, there is little wonder that the ministry led by Schreiner bumbled and stumbled along and was steadily held hostage by its opponents. The Progressives also had a majority in the upper house, so crucial items, such as the budget, could be altered or vetoed. Rhodes, often behaving as if he were premier again, claimed too much when he crowed to Beit that "the Government are entirely in our hands. . . ," but he was close.[26]

Contrary to what has been written about Rhodes' lack of enthusiasm and stamina for the task of opposition leadership during the parliamentary session of 1899, which opened as he returned from six months in Britain, on the Continent, and in Egypt, the ex-premier actively led his side of the House. He steadily harassed Schreiner and Merriman on a variety of issues and defended himself vigorously against their personal attacks. He spoke strongly and frequently against a bill which might inhibit the registration of African voters, lectured the government on its fiscal responsibilities, and—throughout—appeared to be biding his time until the moment arrived when he could overthrow Schreiner's ministry and rule the Cape in its stead. "I will again be Prime Minister," he told David Harris. Rhodes can be faulted for never succeeding—for never overthrowing the government—but, given his worsening health and his many other projects, not for "virtually abandon[ing]" the leadership of the party.[27]

The two sides of the House divided over continuing to appease the Transvaal (in the matter of tariff arrangements, for example) or, as Rhodes suggested, "begging no more." This division led to clashes over such seemingly esoteric but, in fact, meaningful matters such as duties on tobacco and whether Transvaal tobacco could enter Rhodesia free. (Rhodes advocated using the tobacco question as a "lever" on the Transvaal. "He would put on duties upon Transvaal products until the Transvaal took them off Colonial goods.") In the same debate, and regarding the accusation that Rhodes had "cheated" the Colony over his earlier rail contract, he accused Merriman of "misleading" the House. "You think so?" asked Merriman. "Well, yes, I think so," replied Rhodes. Merriman was called either "a knave or a fool . . . and he was certainly not a fool."

Back and forth the accusations flew, John Laing complaining that parliamentary manners had deteriorated. "Let them try to respect each other." He admitted that Merriman had provoked Rhodes and marveled that Rhodes had generally sat silent when "gibed and jeered at during the past two years." Herbert Tamplin accused the government of "magnifying . . . the Transvaal" and belittling and attempting to obliterate Rhodes. He was "getting rather tired of this constant vituperation." He and others thought that the House should put the Raid behind them. But Schreiner, Merriman, and others on the neo-Bond side of the House refused throughout the entire session to drop their major weapon against Rhodes and all the calumnies and arousal of anti-Dutch feelings with which he could justifiably and forever be charged. "You deceived the Dutch people. You deceived others who trusted you, with whom you had supped," said Sauer. Merriman accused Rhodes of being a good judge of "what is conduct worthy of a Minister of the Crown." At least, the ex-premier replied, "I never encouraged a rebellion and then hid my head and disavowed it," he said. "Those are facts."[28]

When Captain Edward Yewd Brabant, a jingoistic Boer-baiter, accused Schreiner and his colleagues of employing governmental funds to tour the Colony for political purposes—"no one was better able to bring forward . . . [a Parliamentary Elections Corrupt Practices] Bill because they had studied it from the inside," he said—Schreiner bounded to the offensive by slurring Rhodes. His presence "was always signified by a return to the attitude of the human pigstyes. . . ." He reminded the House that Rhodes had been ordered in 1898 to pay libel damages for making the same insinuation of corruption outside the House. Rhodes rose to a point of order. Later he explained that he still believed that several contests had been influenced by funds from Kruger, and that one of his own opponents had in fact come straight from the Transvaal and, after losing, had gone back to Pretoria for good. He reminded Schreiner that a jury judged Rhodes libelous only to the extent of £5. "I should have been mulcted in heavy damages unless the surrounding circumstances had made the jury believe that practically it was a case of not proven," Rhodes contended. Schreiner had also commented adversely when the ex-premier had seemed to slumber during a debate on the pro-Transvaal bias of the government. "Am I to be attacked because I shut my eyes?" asked Rhodes. "I call upon my friend to stop his ebullitions of temper." Be dignified, he advised.

There were bitter battles between the two political parties, and between Rhodes and his former close colleagues, not only over which group had more corruptly influenced the 1898 elections, but over the Bond's loyalty to Kruger, over the intentions of the Transvaal on the eve of a possible war, and over the significant question of whether Schreiner's ministry was doing enough to keep guns and ammunition from falling into the hands of Kruger's regime via the Free State. Rhodes lectured Merriman and others regarding the proper manner of framing and passing an appropriations bill, thus demonstrating his side's power of delay. He waspishly urged Schreiner to be "more concise in his answers." It was a "disease that was growing upon the Prime Minister." Otherwise the House would never complete its business.[29]

The Parliamentary Registration Law Amendment bill proposed to reduce constituency residency requirements for voters from twelve to six months, radically to alter the manner in which returning officers compiled voters' lists, to give officers in charge of revising such lists strengthened powers, and— controversial and strikingly new—to restrict voters from casting ballots in constituencies other than the one in which they were registered. (In 1898 the Progressives and the Bond had both moved phalanxes of voters into strategically placed contests.) Rhodes attacked a seemingly innocuous clause in the bill which would have permitted voters to be examined about their educational qualifications and which could have had the effect of disqualifying numerous Africans and some Coloureds. "They could be put to an examination on almost every subject by a hostile registering officer," said Rhodes, since revising officers or other officials could invent their own tests for educational attributes and the party in power would appoint such men. He reminded the House that Jan Hofmeyr, on behalf of the Bond, had accepted less taxing requirements for Africans in the 1893 debates on the subject. Now a Bond-dominated assembly was reneging on the earlier agreement. "The effect of the clause would be to remove practically the whole body of natives. . . ." Since Africans were at last "emerging from barbarism to civilisation," being able to vote without too much hindrance was a good incentive. "I shall fight this . . . to the end," Rhodes declared as a momentarily reborn champion of the Africans and as one who knew how to discern the real intentions of bills designed to harm Africans and therefore Progressives.

Rhodes claimed that he had consistently held similar views. "I have always differentiated between the raw barbarians and the civilised natives," Rhodes declared. When Africans were "civilised," they should vote. They should be included, he said, in the principle "of equal rights to every civilised man south of the Zambesi." That was the position he "had always maintained," said Rhodes to ministerial laughter and the subsequent reading of his old speeches by Sauer and others. Yet, what Rhodes was quietly affirming in his own way was the inescapable fact that circumstances had changed. He was no longer chained to the Bond and could still easily persuade himself of his own logical and rational continuity.

Rhodes also objected to the clause which would prevent persons from voting whose occupations caused them to move about the country. Schreiner's ministry wanted to prevent another Vryburg scandal, but Rhodes wondered about soldiers and railwaymen. Then there were nomadic diamond diggers, like those in the 150 mile-long Barkly West polling area. The diggers employed Coloured assistants, and they, too, could be disenfranchised by the new residence requirements. The bill was intended to hurt the Progressive cause, particularly since a general election could come at almost any moment. Why, Rhodes wondered in the most partisan manner, should such mobile men have to prove residence in a particular constituency? On his own fruit farms in the Paarl district there were laborers from beyond Wellington. How could they vote where they worked?[30]

Rhodes and his Progressives put up a strong and prolonged battle against the bill. Nevertheless, it passed, largely unaltered, by 43 to 34, on 3 October 1899. Rhodes spoke about taxes on mines and the Bechuanaland railway on 6 October. Although the House remained in session for another six days, Rhodes never spoke again. Nor did he stay in his seat until the Assembly adjourned.

Kruger and Milner together ended Rhodes' active political ambitions. Although Rhodes may have wanted war, throughout the local winter of 1899 he professed to believe that Milner's huffing and Kruger's puffing would shake but not topple the foundations of South African stability. It was less that Rhodes feared a military struggle for the sub-continent or failed to understand the seriousness of Milner's threats and the stiffness of the Boer response than he presumed on the basis of his own past experience that the wily old Transvaal president would march to the brink and then back down, as he had over the Goshen and then over the Drifts. "Her Majesty's Government are determined to have a redress of the Uitlanders' grievances. The President is doing the usual thing, he is playing up to the Raad," said Rhodes. As a result, there was "not the slightest chance of war. . . ." The troubles of South Africa were, he suggested, only temporary. "The opinion is rapidly growing here," Maguire wrote to Rothschild in September, "that war is inevitable though many of the best heads, including Rhodes, believe that the Boers will give in at the last but of this there is as yet no sign." Privately, in conversation and in letters, Rhodes assured those (like Milner) who knew better that there would be no bloodshed. "I feel so absolutely sure Kruger will concede everything H.M.G. demand. . .," Rhodes said in recommending a particular post-settlement franchise scheme to Milner. Kruger would "climb down at the end," he told parliament. He tried to prevent David Harris from leaving parliament for Kimberley in September. There would be no war. He even made several small bets against the likelihood of war. Kruger, after all, knew that Britain was the world's dominant military power, and understood that the outbreak of hostilities would certainly mean the ruin of the Transvaal. When associates who were staying with him at Groote Schuur insisted that war was inevitable, Rhodes doubled and tripled his wagering stakes.[31] Kruger would ultimately succumb.

Innes argued that Rhodes, often disingenuous, was so anxious for the Transvaal's demise and Kruger's humbling that he positively must have played a decisive part in propelling, or at least hastening, the acceleration of South Africa's plunge into battle. Indeed, by the time that Rhodes had returned from Britain in mid-1899, he must have been astute enough to have appreciated that there was no turning back. Both Britain and the Boers were bent on a trial by blood. Thus, as Innes and others urged, Rhodes spoke confidently of an eventual "climb down," and of "temporary" difficulties in order to accentuate the pitch and pace of Milner's demands, to help force the inevitable result—a war for supremacy, for union, and for the realization of Rhodes' dreams before his own heart should go. Wilson, then a reporter on the *Cape Times*, recalls Rhodes admitting after war began that he had felt "certain" that Kruger would declare war, but had also thought that "if I said he wouldn't, it might make him change his mind." Hence the meaning of a letter authorized by Rhodes from his secretary to Stead is clear. "He himself, though wholly quiescent on account of his past bad conduct in connection with the Transvaal, still wishes to place on record . . . that he sides entirely with Sir Alfred Milner's views. He does not advise him for the very good reason that Sir Alfred Milner takes only one person's advice and that is the advice of Sir Alfred Milner."[32]

Since Milner was a war-provoker without peer and Kruger was playing his own obstinate part well, Rhodes hardly needed to help. Furthermore, there is no logical or psychological incompatibility between Rhodes' consciousness that war could come, his own mental preparation for such a result, and his enduring conviction (for he had always believed and still, in the aftermath of the hash of the Raid, needed to believe) that Kruger, like most up-country Dutch-speakers, or Afrikaners, was a bully who bluffed and then gave way. As much as he may have desired a British trouncing of the Transvaal in 1899, as in 1895, the Anglo-Boer war was not Rhodes' war. However much the Raid was a critical prefiguring, and however much he added to an atmosphere of bellicosity in 1899, it unnecessarily magnifies Rhodes' importance to suggest that he played other than an ancillary role in triggering the conflict.

Rhodes had been responsible for defining the underlying issue. From the 1880s, and directly during his premiership in the 1890s, Rhodes had declared Krugerism an obstacle to progress in southern Africa. "Progress" for Rhodes and the imperialists who subsequently echoed his analyses consisted of unfettered opportunity for expansion throughout the subcontinent of British ideas, British values, British capital, the English language, and Britons. The good was meant to drive out the bad, whether construed in terms of a reverse of Gresham's law or of Social Darwinism. Rhodes, Progressives, and imperialists like Chamberlain and Milner believed strongly in the God-given gifts of Britons, in their manifest destiny, and in the essential humanism of British domination. Only Lord Salisbury, the prime minister, demurred. "We have to act," he protested, "upon a moral field prepared . . . by [Milner] and his jingo supporters. . . . I see before us the necessity for considerable military effort—and all for people whom we despise, and for territory which will bring no profit and no power to England."[33]

The approaches of Chamberlain, Milner, Rhodes, and others, no matter how arrogant, chauvinistic, and distasteful they appear to modern readers, were broadly accepted as noble and just by Britons in late Victorian times. The backward quality of Kruger's government, especially its refusal to give the Uitlanders the vote, confirmed Rhodes and others in these beliefs. That the Transvaalers should even trifle with Britain affronted and antagonized those, like Milner, who believed fundamentally that the empire would suffer if Kruger's contemptible challenge were not met. Gold was important, for the Transvaal could not have defended itself without profits from its auriferous reefs, and Rhodes and others would not otherwise have viewed that state as a force capable before long of rivaling the Cape within South Africa. Yet it is much too simple to suppose that Rhodes, Milner, or any other imperialist antagonists simply wanted to control the gold mines themselves.

The struggle for supremacy in South Africa at the end of the nineteenth century extended the ideological and cultural battles of the early years of the century, and, essentially unresolved by the Anglo-Boer war, remain central to the bitter contestations of today. Would the whites who had made homes for themselves in the Cape and then trekked into the interior to escape the more modernistic and liberalizing demands of the world's then dominant power be permitted to control their own destiny, or would they once again (despite the victory at Majuba in 1881) become subordinate to the alien views of a European power? Would the Afrikaners be "wood-cutters and water carriers for a hated race," as Jan Christiaan Smuts asked in 1899, or would they become the "founders of a United South Africa, of . . . an Afrikaner republic . . . stretching from Table Bay to the Zambesi?"[34] Would Britain, as Milner and Rhodes wanted, compel the Afrikaners to be more tolerant, more open, more accommodating to English-speaking miners and traders—to subordinate their autonomy to an English-denominated excellence, humanity, development, and prosperity? Although Rhodes had long sought a "common native policy" in order to further federation, African rights never were or became more than a rhetorical issue in the war.

Milner had thrown down the gauntlet at Graaff-Reinet. If Kruger would recognize the legitimate grievances of the Uitlanders, all would be well. But Kruger knew that if he gave those English-speaking foreigners the vote, he would soon lose control of his country. As far as Milner and the Uitlanders were concerned, Kruger further provoked the British sense of fair play when he dismissed a chief justice who had dared to assert the right of the court to challenge legislation and had refused to diminish the power of a state-controlled dynamite monopoly to impose "unfairly" high costs on the gold-mining industry. The Uitlanders and Milner complained about the harsh and arbitrary quality of the police, the prohibition of open-air protest meetings, and taxation without representation. When Kruger, like President P.W. Botha nearly ninety years later, proposed reforms in 1899 which would have gradually settled some of the grievances of the Uitlanders, Milner sensed subterfuge and prevarication. Kruger was prepared to grant privileges only so long as he and his people retained real power.

In an important and lengthy dispatch Milner reminded the colonial secretary that Britain was dealing with a popular movement among the Uitlanders similar to that of 1895, "before it was perverted and ruined by a conspiracy of which the great body of the Uitlanders were totally innocent." Rhodes had acted rashly and prematurely, but not in a wrong cause. "None of the grievances then complained of . . . have been remedied, and others have been added. The case is much stronger than it was." Those persons making "vehement" demands for enfranchisement (Milner might have been rephrasing Thomas Paine) were "mostly British subjects, accustomed to a free system and equal rights; they feel deeply the personal indignity involved in a position of permanent subjection to the ruling caste which owes its wealth and power to their exertion. The political turmoil in the Transvaal Republic will never end till the permanent Uitlander population is admitted to a share in the Government, and while that turmoil lasts there will be no tranquillity or adequate progress in Her Majesty's South African dominions."

Milner's analysis continued along lines which Rhodes (still in Britain) would have cheered (and articulated less persuasively). Progress and harmony in the region could only come when differences between the two conflicting social and political systems of the region were reconciled. Conditions in the Transvaal were thus of vital interest to Britain. "The right of Great Britain to intervene to secure fair treatment of Uitlanders is fully equal to her supreme interest in securing it." Britain was duty bound to protect her subjects. The number of those subjects and the endless nature of their grievances made protection by ordinary diplomatic means "impossible." "The true remedy [was] to strike at the . . . political impotence of the injured." Fair representation would do it. Although biding Britain's time might help, the Transvaal was preparing for war. It was arming itself. Time was running out.

Milner tightened the snares of emotion: "The spectacle of thousands of British subjects kept permanently in the position of helots . . . and calling vainly to Her Majesty's Government for redress . . ." undermined the "influence and reputation of Great Britain and the respect for the British Government within its own dominions." Milner wanted his government to demonstrate that it would not be ousted from South Africa. Only by an ultimatum of intention could the existing "race feud be eradicated."[35] At a conference in Bloemfontein in late May and early June 1899, Kruger declined to give away his country by enfranchising the newcomers, and Milner refused to talk about other issues until Kruger conceded what he would not. Milner ended the meeting prematurely and telegraphed Chamberlain that the case for intervention was "overwhelming." Unless Kruger backed down, war would soon come. By the time that Rhodes returned from Britain in mid-1899, nearly everyone understood where the escalations of both sides could lead.

Schreiner and his colleagues in the Bond-backed government of the Cape attempted to dampen the fires of war. Until he was replaced, so did Lieutenant-General Sir William Butler, who initially commanded the British troops in South Africa and was virulently anti-Rhodes and pro-peace. Britain only began reinforcing its detachments in the southern African spring. Thus there was a window of opportunity for peace in September, when the Transvaal agreed, albeit ambiguously, to consider ways to alleviate the problems of the "helots." Milner and Chamberlain insisted, however, upon the enfranchisement of adult whites after they had lived in the Transvaal for five years. Kruger called the British reply "insolent" and stuck to seven years, with qualifications. Britain threatened a drastic ultimatum. "Every attempt at *rapprochement* from our side," wrote Smuts, the attorney general of the Transvaal, "has been haughtily rejected. . . . War between the Republics and England is certain." Chamberlain told a still skeptical British cabinet that "at stake [was] the position of Great Britain in South Africa and with it the estimate formed of our power and influence in our Colonies and throughout the world. . ."—an expression of the domino theory. Chamberlain also wished to safeguard the sea route to India. Milner wanted Chamberlain to demand "absolute" political equality for all whites in the Transvaal, recognition of British paramountcy through a ceding of control of the republic's foreign affairs and the right to interfere internally, and partial disarmament.[36]

Chamberlain was utterly sanguine. Governor Sir Walter Hely-Hutchinson of Natal doubted that the Afrikaners would be so "crack-brained" as to strike first. Although Smuts calculated that the two republics could muster 40,000 commandos—locally raised detachments of cavalry, accustomed to frontier fighting—Chamberlain believed that the 12,000 British troops already in South Africa, plus 10,000 due to arrive in October, would suffice. Forgetting that Britain had fought no recent wars against well-armed and determined opponents, and that its commanders were hidebound by tradition and untrained in the arts of counter-insurgency, Milner, Rhodes, and Britons in general expected a short war of easy triumph. If the Transvaalers precipitated the conflict, Chamberlain was confident that the "Lord will have delivered them into our hands—at least so far as diplomacy is concerned." Yet the delivery was robust. On 9 October 1899, Kruger demanded that the British government settle all differences by arbitration, withdraw its troops, and not land any of its reinforcements. Otherwise, the note said, there would be war. Milner replied that his government deemed Kruger's conditions "impossible to discuss."

"War dates from to-day, I suppose," Milner wrote laconically on 11 October. The first shots were fired near Newcastle, in Natal.[37] By then Rhodes had returned to Kimberley, to protect his mines and to remain with "his" people. Was it fatalism or bravado which drove Rhodes, brushing protests of friends and of Kimberleyites aside, to forsake the safety of Cape Town for the targeted dangers of a prominent city on the borders of the Free State? Its telegraph and railway links to the Cape could easily be cut. It was endlessly flat, difficult to defend, and a likely target, whatever happened.

The mayor of Kimberley had urged Rhodes to stay away. The mayor, Michell, Jourdan, and others suggested that he was needlessly exposing the town and himself, for Rhodes' presence would surely invite attack. Milner, the Progressives, and almost every individual and group one could imagine, all for different reasons, wanted Rhodes to remain in Cape Town. But the Founder had other ideas. "My post is at Kimberley—yours at Cape Town," he told Fuller (who then lived in Kimberley as a member of the local board of De Beers).[38] Rhodes decided to go there when war seemed unavoidable mostly in order to safeguard the prosperity of the mines (and the source of his own wealth), and because he calculated that the town might be protected, and certainly relieved rapidly, if he were there. It was his home base and had to be secured. As Jarvis suggested in another context, he may still have believed that he was invulnerable to mayhem and bullets and would succumb, when the day was right, only to the weakness in his heart. Or was it more simply that Rhodes could not bear passively to observe a war from the sidelines, even if, or because, it was no longer his to run? As much as he feared personal injury, he could abide inaction and futility far less. Moreover, he needed to express his instinct for leadership. Awkward and even dangerous though it might be, his place was in Kimberley. Were he anywhere else, his internal credibility would be sorely strained.

Kimberley lies 600 miles from Cape Town. When Rhodes' train steamed into the city late on 10 October, a day before the Boer ultimatum was to expire, he was accompanied by young Jourdan, his secretary; Dr. Thomas William Smartt, an Irish-born physician turned farmer who had served in Sprigg's recent cabinet and, in the 1898 elections, had been badly beaten at Wodehouse by Merriman; his old crony Rochfort Maguire, recently a Liberal member of the British parliament from Ireland; and Julia Maguire, Rochfort Maguire's wife and the eldest daughter of Arthur Wellesley, first Viscount Peel and sometime Speaker of the House of Commons. Julia Maguire was the temporary reporter for *The Times* in Kimberley; her husband was one of Rhodes' few enduring friends who had ever married and been welcomed back with his wife. (But she came from a family which could not be ignored.)

Rhodes and his friends received only a tepid reception from worried townsmen, many of whom correctly supposed that the Boers would do almost anything to capture Rhodes, their most hated enemy. "People were wild with indignation," yet Jourdan remembered being "very much excited." Hostilities were not regarded as a serious possiblity. "It was believed that in a few days' time the Boers would either withdraw . . . from Kimberley or would be driven away by . . . British troops."[39]

Kimberley was a company town. About 90 percent of the world's diamonds were produced there. Nearly 10,000 of the town's 18,000 Africans were employed by or in other ways dependent upon De Beers Consolidated Mines, Ltd. A much smaller proportion of Kimberley's 27,000 whites and Coloureds worked for the company, but nearly all owed their livelihoods, and their reason for settling in the large town baking in the middle of a dusty plain, to the discovery of diamonds. To defend themselves against attack, the people of Kimberley could put about 1,100 local men under arms. Once Lieutenant Colonel Robert George Kekewich, a hitherto undistinguished regular officer, had assessed the town's precarious military position in September, he requested four companies of British troops from Cape Town, raised a "town guard," and constructed over thirteen miles of ramparts around the mining complex and its principal suburbs. Fortuitously and unexpectedly, De Beers was able to supply six Maxims, 422 rifles, and 700,000 rounds of ammunition from stores laid up for Jameson's attack. The Company, possibly on Rhodes' orders, had also stockpiled a vast hoard of provisions on which the firm's managers, many of the white townspeople, and, marginally, Africans, were to depend throughout the long weeks when Kimberley was almost completely cut off from the rest of the country and otherwise dependent for food upon such expedients as the slaughtering of local horses.

It is clear that Rhodes expected to keep the mines working and his wealth flowing. He may have wished to secure the stockpiles of diamonds in the town. (He sent his share certificates south for safekeeping.)[40] He would certainly have wanted to keep De Beers' valuable properties out of enemy hands. He must have known that he could not really expect to shield them and his investments by the sheer force of his personality. But he probably harbored some hope, latent or otherwise, that his presence would affect positively those who could protect them—that the great man cared enough about Kimberley, its white people and what they did, to risk his life to be there. His presence might give a sense of significance and meaning—the essential gift from a leader to the led—to Kimberley in stress. That his being there turned out to be a hindrance and, ultimately, a divisive force, was one of those miscarriages to which overweening self-importance is prone. It was also another sign that Rhodes' touch, the melding of his grandiosity with reality, was failing as he was failing, for his health deteriorated during the siege.

Whatever he had planned, and whatever he had anticipated, he could hardly have expected so completely to lose control over his own destiny for so long. Rhodes, however much he craved a chance for further Matopo-like heroism, hardly enjoyed being dependent upon others, being largely (but never completely) deprived of access to his networks of power and influence, and being subordinated in terms of command to someone like Kekewich. In Rhodes' eyes, Kekewich was a jumped-up ordinary officer who could be bullied, and thus was weak, but who in fact insisted on retaining his authority and refused to be obsequious. Possibly Rhodes, as Jourdan suggests, hardly expected to be subjected to siege, and doubtless not for very long. Like so many others, Rhodes vastly underestimated the enemy, and vastly—but it was a common failing— overestimated the capacity of Britain to humble the upstart Boers.

Although Kekewich put Kimberley under martial law on 15 October, and the state of siege began from that date, more than a week went by before there was any fighting near Kimberley. The Boers had lost their chance to capture Rhodes. It was only in early November that the town was finally surrounded by about 5,000 Afrikaners from the Free State, later supplemented by Transvaalers. Kimberley was thereafter shelled almost daily from positions in the hills five miles southwest of the city. But the shelling was largely harmless, because of distance and the poor quality of the projectiles, and, aside from occasional skirmishes, the besiegers and the defenders rarely engaged each other. Food was not at first short, either, although claustrophobia was a

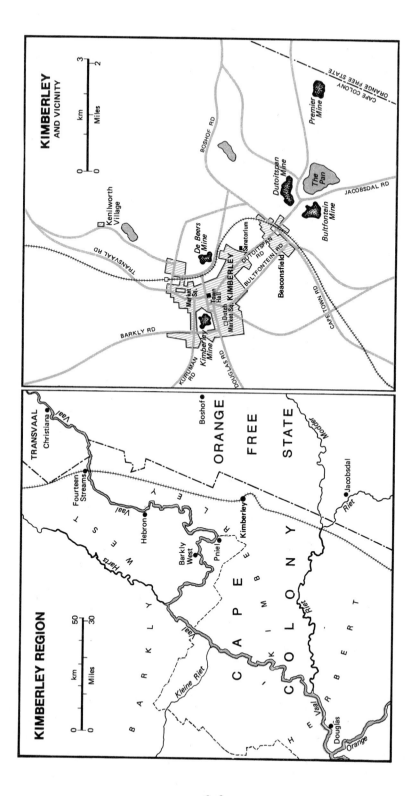

commodity in increasing supply. Certainly Rhodes felt it and his own state of enforced ennui very early, well before the town was in any danger. From mid-October, when there could have been no real cause for alarm, he began bombarding his official and political friends in Cape Town, the local and British press, and even such worthies as Lord Rothschild with what Milner called "panicky" messages about the city's and the diamond industry's peril.

The mines had, it is true, stopped working because of the shortage of coal, usually supplied by trains along lines that were now cut. But although this to some extent vitiated Rhodes' rationale for remaining in Kimberley, life remained comparatively comfortable and routine, if tense, for many weeks longer. Rhodes thus magnified the apparent dangers and demanded relief. He railed against the incompetence of both the local command and the British forces in South Africa, being simply unable to comprehend why Kimberley, "helpless," was being left to its own devices. He could not understand why a regiment or two had not been sent marching up from the Orange River, seventy-four miles away. "I can assure you [it is] . . . quite an easy matter," he wrote in a smuggled note to Sprigg in November. A few days later he sent two coded messages to Milner by dispatch rider (money could buy almost anything, even communications during a time of siege). "We are absolutely surrounded by hordes enemy," said one. Another urged help, "otherwise terrible disaster."[41] In other words, how could the empire leave Rhodes shut up for so long without coming to the rescue?

How indeed? Because of Rhodes' outcries, the British army gave the relief of Kimberley an early and high priority. There would be widespread shame if a privy councillor were captured or the richest resource in the empire were lost to the ragged Boer veld fighters. Thus General Lord Methuen moved with urgency, even undue haste, in November. He assembled 8,000 men at the Orange River later in the month and set out by forced marches along the rail line, directly for Kimberley and, as he learned four times painfully, straight into a series of well-thought-out Boer ambushes. By mid-December, despite two of these brutal engagements, the titled but militarily naïve general, still ignorant of the innovative nature of his foe, gave little thought to varied tactics. Methuen had served in South Africa a decade before and was not totally inexperienced. Nevertheless, he confidently expected to cross the Modder River, twenty miles from Kimberley, overcome Boer defenses in the Magersfontein hills, and arrive in Kimberley within a day or two. Similarly insouciant, Kekewich and Rhodes happily believed that the city could soon return to normal; Rhodes was pleased that his demands had brought results, although he could still not understand why the incompetent military leaders were taking so long to move so many troops across a flat terrain (with occasional outcrops) defended by presumably outnumbered and outgunned, and certainly outgeneraled, frontier fighters.

Kekewich, his hours usually spent surveying the ramparts and watching for attacks atop a 155–foot watchtower constructed above the huge steel wheel of the winding headgear of the main mine, expected Methuen to follow a flanking maneuver and, at any moment, to reach the town from the southeast. Once he arrived, Kekewich could be excused from his terrible chore of commanding a town Rhodes would not let him command fully, even under martial law.

Methuen never arrived in Kimberley. First along the Modder, where the British legion was severely checked and badly mauled by 3,000 Boers dug in along the river banks, then at the foot of the Magersfontein kopje, where it suffered a signal defeat, the finest of Her Majesty's forces were stalled by defenders whom they disdained. At the battle of Magersfontein on 11 December 1899, 6,000 Boers in a cannily camouflaged ten-mile long horseshoe curved trench at the foot of the hills slaughtered 220 British soldiers in khaki and kilts as they threw themselves forward in wave after suicidal wave. Another 800 were wounded or captured. (Many of the individual actions in the Anglo-Boer war, like trenches and the use of barbed wire, represented new advances in warfare. The painful lessons learned at Magersfontein and elsewhere were remembered during World War I.) Having suffered an unimaginable reverse, Methuen and his decimated forces withdrew to the Modder River, where they remained, a short series of marches from Kimberley, until reinforcements under a new commander could arrive in February. As the British regrouped, licking the wounds of empire, so Rhodes paced the besieged town, fuming, short of temper, and irascible as never before.

Two more months confined to the laager were hard on everyone. After Methuen's debacle, tensions rose as the days of desperation lengthened and the possibility became more certain that life inside would become even nastier. They might even be invested by the barbarians at the gates. As his friends would have supposed, Rhodes responded badly to this enforced confinement. Although early in the siege he had accepted appointment as honorary colonel of the newly raised Kimberley Light Horse brigade, Rhodes meddled militarily more than he assisted the town's defense. He infuriated Kekewich by evading curfew, censorship, and other restrictions that had been imposed on the citizens under martial law. Blithely ignoring the commandant's orders, he organized his own communication system with the outside world, using runners, heliographs, and—when he could—the town's official searchlight for his own purposes. In this way he sent streams of orders to London about diamond sales and the activities of the Chartered Company, to Groote Schuur about his guests and their social life, to his old friend Lieutenant General Robert Baden-Powell, stuck in charge of Mafeking during that town's untroubled siege, to Lord Methuen (who, deeply offended, replied to Kekewich that Rhodes should have "no voice in the matter"), to his toadies and hangers-on in Cape Town, to the titled and ennobled throughout the empire, and even to the Progressives who were still contemplating an entrapment of Schreiner.

Rhodes attempted to be a law unto himself. After all, it was *his* town. "The main streets were barricaded," a local physician reported, and the guard had orders to allow no one to pass in or out. But "on more than one occasion Rhodes [was] stopped at the barrier and asked for his permit, and at one barrier where the orders were to search everybody . . . Rhodes fumed and blustered and said he had never heard of such damned insolence, but the guard was firm, so Rhodes burst out laughing and produced a permit. . . . He was just testing the men's discipline."[42] Moreover, he may have written out the pass himself.

Although endlessly annoyed, due in no small part to the condition of his worsening heart, Rhodes, Jourdan recalled, was "more energetic up-country than when at Cape Town." Jourdan said that Rhodes took long rides almost every morning and evening. "He liked visiting the different forts and chatting to the men." Not necessarily to make himself an easy target, although that was the result, "he always wore a pair of white flannel pantaloons, and it was very easy for the Boers to see him for miles on horseback." Although warned not to be so conspicuous, Rhodes had always worn white trousers in South Africa, and saw no reason to stop. He also wore his usual brown tweed coat, and a comfortable, narrow-brimmed felt hat.

Julia Maguire claimed to have eaten every meal during the siege with Rhodes. She recalled little of note about the food, but had never known such good conversation. Indeed, she had wished each meal to go "on and on," so "fine and exhilarating was his talk."[43]

Rhodes remembered that he was all things to all persons during the siege. He was generous with De Beers' supplies, although saving secret caches of food and wine for himself and for the officers who eventually relieved the town. "His was the only house in Kimberley," Kekewich criticized afterward, "where during the whole siege there was a luxurious table, with abundance of all kinds of food and drink." To the garrison Rhodes gave grapes from the Company's newly planted arbors. There were nectarines and peaches in February. He also credited himself with inventing and distributing a nourishing soup concocted in the depths of the siege from (it later transpired) horse bones and other unsavory remnants. He devoted the resources of De Beer's workshops to the fabricating of homemade artillery shells.

George Labram, Rhodes' ingenious, young American engineer, managed somehow to take a piece of steel shafting and improvise a 4.1 inch gun which could throw a fearsome twenty-eight-pound projectile nearly five miles. Nick-named "Long Cecil," this hefty ordnance piece startled the Boers around the town when it was first fired in mid-January, and helped to keep the besiegers distant. Labram also built a 1400 cubic foot refrigeration unit to chill and keep whatever could be slaughtered for food, as well as Rhodes' champagne.

Rhodes took credit for pumping water from the mines to help the town, for supplying mules when the Boers took those which had been carting night soil and trash, for purchasing horses for the local cavalry, and for finding employment for whites as well as blacks. In February, when French mercenaries dragged a "Long Tom," a six-inch Creusot gun (earlier used to harass Ladysmith), into the surrounding hills and began pounding the city with an accuracy that was new, Rhodes hustled women and children down his mine shafts, and cared for them there.[44]

Rhodes tried to deal with African problems, too. With the mines shut, Rhodes and others realized that the Africans who lived in his covered compounds and those who had come into the town because of the war would present a security issue. First he attempted to send thousands away through the Boer lines. But the Boers sent them back. All that Rhodes could then do was to encourage small groups to flee at night. In order to keep the Africans occupied in the meanwhile, he organized public works projects, like the planting of trees along the town's main streets, the breaking of stones for cart roads, and so on. But Rhodes presumably could do little for the Africans and Coloureds who grew hungry or sickened (many from scurvy) and died. When Kekewich began investigating the prevalence of deaths among Africans, he discovered that De Beers had stopped feeding large numbers. "I talked to Mr. Rhodes about it," Kekewich recalled, "but he got very angry with me, asked me not to meddle in his affairs, and said that if they would not leave the town, they must be forced to, and giving them only bread and salt had this effect." Although Kekewich should be considered highly partisan, his explanation fits with what is known of the siege: "We [whites] were never short of provisions and I thought this action on his part most heartless." The neglect of Africans was a natural if inhuman response by Rhodes and others to the supposedly greater needs of whites, who had felt the restrictions of rationing in early January.

Kekewich was "a well-built handsome man," according to Rhodes' friend David Harris, and a "splendid" and well-liked fellow, according to Ashe. He was "fair-minded, painstaking . . . and devoted to duty." He was also a bachelor, and Rhodes usually befriended bachelors and was able to persuade most to become allies. But in this case their mutual struggle for control brought out the very worst in Rhodes at a time when his good humor was anyway in parlously short supply. Kekewich was a proxy, too, representing for Rhodes every kind of force that he had always fought to overcome—the mugwumps of British officialdom, and the constraints and bureaucratic obstacles that seemed so idiotic and unnecessary to a man now long accustomed to making his own rules and breaking those of others. "I verily believe if God Almighty even was in a fix you would refuse to get Him out of it should the doing so interfere with your damned military situation," Rhodes shouted on one occasion.

When Kekewich gave Rhodes military information in strict confidence, Rhodes told the town. When Kekewich informed him of plans prepared by the military authorities in Cape Town that Rhodes opposed, he promptly raised local and Colony-wide ruckuses by leaking the unacceptable news to the press. When Kekewich remonstrated, reminding Rhodes of his "solemn promises," Rhodes replied that Kekewich was talking "a lot of nonsense." "I am not going to be told that by you again," he bellowed. Later, when "Long Tom" had begun to frighten the town severely, Rhodes grew positively mutinous. Worried personally by the newly accurate heavy shelling, livid at the British for so languidly sitting in their serried ranks a mere twenty miles away, Rhodes threatened local meetings and hinted at the possibility of surrender. He slurred Kekewich repeatedly, and suggested that he would later ruin his career—that he would "crush" Kekewich.

"He is quite unreasonable," Kekewich heliographed to the second relief expedition that was now readying itself along the Modder River. Kekewich had official permission to arrest Rhodes. But how could he call the King of Kimberley to account? Who would enforce such an edict? Rhodes knew that he was above the law; Kekewich was too unsure of himself or his position to act decisively or dramatically. Their enmity plunged to a new low a few days later. Kekewich, valiantly attempting to hold on to his authority, refused to send messages by heliograph from Rhodes to Colonel Elmhirst Rhodes, his brother now with the expeditionary force under Field Marshal Lord Roberts. Rhodes flung himself at Kekewich, calling the colonel a "low, damned mean cur, . . . you deny me at your peril." The mayor of Kimberley prevented the two men, both forty-five, from throwing punches across a desk.[45]

The shelling of "Long Tom," Rhodes' renewed panic and exasperation, and Kekewich's ambiguous flashes across the intervening twenty miles impelled Lord Roberts to relieve Kimberley days faster, and with a greater vigor, than he had planned. When Rhodes learned that Roberts had finally arrived and taken charge along the Modder, he wrote insufferably that it was "high time you did something." Having assembled 34,000 white troops and 4,000 African drivers, and trained the cavalry that Methuen had lacked, Roberts employed flanking, diversionary, and other obvious tactics that the inflexible Methuen, like hapless General Sir Redvers Buller in Natal, had failed to initiate during his humiliation by Boer marksmen in December.

Kekewich, straining in his watchtower, suddenly could see a great cloud of dust, moving steadily forward. It was a division of cavalry under Lieutenant General John French. Five thousand strong, it charged and broke through the ranks of the enemy at Abon's Dam, north of the Modder River, and was soon in Kimberley. On 15 February, French's heroic riders clanked into the now shell-marked, exhausted, and truly beleaguered city and lifted its 124-day siege.

Rhodes lifted toasts of champagne to the general and his men, while the press of the empire cheered both the new and the presumed old savior of the town. "Kimberley is won, Mr. Cecil Rhodes is free, the De Beers shareholders are all full of themselves, and the beginning of the war is at an end," said the *Daily Mail*. Rhodes himself told the same newspaper, "Glad to have Kimberley relieved? Of course, we are all glad, but, in Heaven's name, why was it not done sooner?"

There were other opinions of Rhodes' contribution to Kimberley's defense and relief. "I consider he held his own, and the interests of Kimberley, far above those of his country, and that he did much during the Siege to imperil the success of our armies. . . ," concluded Kekewich. Conan Doyle, then a war correspondent, agreed: "Every credit may be given to him for all his aid to the military—he gave with good grace what the garrison would otherwise have had to commandeer—but it is a fact that the town would have been more united, and therefore stronger, without his presence." As the jingoistic *Morning Leader* commented acidly, Rhodes surely "expected the whole strength of Her Majesty's forces to be incontinently directed to the relief of him, the mighty Cecil Rhodes. . . ." Of course![46]

The siege was not Rhodes' finest performance. Troubled by the miscalculations that had imprisoned him there and endangered his life, comparatively devoid of responsibility and efficacy while so much in life remained to be done, totally uncomprehending of military matters, and blunted by Kekewich's attempts to take charge, Rhodes had merely endured when he was accustomed to being ingenious and creative. Pleased to perceive on a grand scale, he had been compelled to think small, and then to think smaller still. Pacing the ramparts in his white flannels in the heat of midsummer was far less invigorating than the command performance in the Matopos.

What Rhodes told the shareholders of De Beers a mere eight days after the lifting of the siege, however, was altogether different. Again he reinterpreted and reconstructed reality so as to feed his own self-esteem. "During the past four months we have not been miners: we have been warriors, fighting for the preservation of our homes and property." "We merely did our duty . . . [and] . . . materially helped to maintain the defence of this town." "The brunt of the work" connected with the defense of Kimberley fell upon "citizen soldiers" of the town. "For four weary months . . . [citizens] . . . cheerfully carried out the obligations" of defense. Then the town was assaulted, Rhodes said. "We all know how unpleasant it was to be shelled all day by a gun throwing a 100–pound shell. . . . We were right to put the women and children down the mines. But . . . there was no thought of surrender. . . ."[47]

Rhodes had not surrendered to the enemies without. He had survived the siege and saved his mineral properties from capture and destruction; the mines even resumed washing already-excavated ground for diamonds in March and actual mining in April. But the enemy within had, despite Jourdan's positive memory, grown stronger. At Kimberley he had suffered a heavy fall from his horse, perhaps the result of another heart attack and "the growth of an aneurism." The struggle to breathe had become more severe.[48] When Rhodes traveled down country to the Cape in March he was weak, and gasping for breath. Instead of returning to Groote Schuur, which was filled with important invalids from the war and titled men and women from Britain on whom he doted, Rhodes settled with Jameson into a small cottage south of Muizenberg, where his heart might rest. There he could look out upon the warm waters of False Bay, stare at the Hottentots Holland peaks in the eastern distance, and remember his rides long ago in the same area with Merriman, Sauer, and Innes. His musings were interrupted only by noisy locomotives steaming down the Cape peninsula toward Kalk Bay and Simonstown, and by a stream of acquaintances who expected and wanted him, the self-promoted hero of the siege, to resume his rightful place as the uncrowned monarch of the Colony.

The Progressives and the South African League had continued to agitate and organize. Since the Bond was associated with an enemy that had actually declared war, there was every expectation that Schreiner's government could not long endure. Rhodes, in the minds of his supporters as well as his enemies, was hence set to scale the heights of political leadership from which he had plummeted so abruptly four years before. The onset of war had dimmed the stain on his character. So, too, the war, and expectations that the relief of Kimberley and Ladysmith would soon be followed by a Boer surrender (Kruger and his cronies had already fled to Holland), promised to provide a perfect opportunity for the realization of Rhodes' "big idea." Annexation of the two republics, which Chamberlain contemplated, would surely prove a precursor to federation along the lines that Rhodes had long advocated. Greater South Africa, including Rhodesia, would be Rhodes' gift to the empire and the world. A total resurrection of his political fortunes seemed at hand.

For the first time in his life, Rhodes was not ready. After two weeks in Muizenberg he sailed to Britain to consult Sir James Kingston Fowler, a British physician and authority on diseases of the chest. Fowler was not a cardiologist, but he was unmarried and noted for his numerous male friends "of distinction in walks of life other than medical." "We hope to get him thoroughly overhauled by the doctors," Hawksley wrote to Michell from London in April.[49] Rhodes also had a long talk about the war with Stead, to whom he expressed his thorough support for Milner and Milner's policies. Then, after no more than three weeks in England, he rushed back to Africa (the sea voyages then averaged eighteen to nineteen days), partially to avoid Princess Catherine Radziwill (who adds confusion to Rhodes' life in the next chapter), and mostly to attend to the nurturing of the still-infant Rhodesia. Indeed, Rhodes remained in Cape Town only a few days before chartering a small steamer and sailing up the African coast to Beira.

Rhodes was in Bulawayo, having visited Salisbury and Melsetter, when Schreiner resigned in sorrow in mid-June. Although still a conciliator, Schreiner and Solomon believed in punishing ordinary citizens of the Cape colony who had helped the commandos and thus rebelled, committing treason and aiding the enemy. The Bond, Merriman, and Sauer, in caucus with the South African party, wanted a complete amnesty, refusing even to accept a temporary loss of the vote for those who would be convicted of aiding and abetting "treason." The ministry, tottering ever since the war had begun, thus became a casualty of the sharp, now exacerbated, ethnic division in the country—what Rhodes and others called its fundamental "race hatred."

Rhodes could have become prime minister again. It is not that he had lost interest or ambition, for he even asked Owen Lewis in May by urgent cable for an analysis of the votes cast in 1898 in several key Cape constituencies "showing what extra votes are required to ensure success." He demanded details of the "native vote" too, for it would be critical in marginal districts like Aliwal North and Wodehouse. He did not demur for fear of objections from Milner, nor because he preferred one of several attractive offers to stand for the Liberals in Britain (as Rutherfoord Harris soon did successfully for the Conservatives in Wales).

His reasons, in fact, were sound: "I hope Parliament will do without me," he told Milner. He doubted whether the time was ripe for a general election. He was not sure of winning a majority. "We are not ready," he thought. Furthermore, "the personal" weighed heavily. He said nothing about his health. "Though nominally not leader I know I should be dragged into the matter and have to do the whole work and I want to settle the colonials start the railway to Victoria Falls, see the mines personally and form my judgement as to gold prospects help Milton to start his North Eastern Rhodesia and see to the telegraph to Egypt, besides many other minor details."

Milner had painstakingly persuaded Rhodes that their visions of the future of South Africa were congruent, that each dominant personality had an important, contributory, role, and that so long as the war raged, Milner's efforts must precede and take precedence over those of Rhodes. As Milner wrote to Philip Lyttelton Gell, his bosom friend, former journalistic colleague, and now associate of the Chartered Company, he and Rhodes had their "separate & successive parts to play in *one* policy—mine is to make a British S. Africa, including the Afrikander, but as a real British subject, possible (in order to do that the Imperial harrow may have to pass over the whole field). His is to govern & *consolidate* the new community, when my work is done." A danger was that the second chapter might begin before the first was finished—"that we should begin sowing before the field is prepared, conciliating, harmonizing, self-governing before the only possible basis of a *self-governing, all-embracing nation* here, the basis of clear unquestioned & unquestionable membership of the British group of nations is firmly laid." Rhodes' influence could not be eliminated during the first stage. "It would be impossible." Milner had "to set the tune," or there would be "chaos." Milner also acknowledged a danger—that Rhodes might become impatient.

In earlier times Rhodes would not have let Milner choose the score and perform the sonata himself. But Milner had judged the Rhodes of 1899–1900 well. In his present time of physical stress, Rhodes was content to observe Milner's results from afar, and also to play kingmaker from a distance. Specifically, he sanctioned the participation of his associates in another government cobbled together by the irrepressible Sprigg. Although Rhodes accepted that Sprigg was a "mediocrity," he had an affection for the "good little fellow." Rhodes also told Walton that Sprigg suited the "present position," which Rhodes hardly thought ripe for his own talents. Before accepting the governor's call to shape a government, Sprigg asked whether Rhodes would object to including Innes in the new cabinet if that were the only way to obtain a certain majority. "I have no objection and can swallow a mugwump if it will help the governor," Rhodes replied. A few days later, when Smartt and Thomas Graham asked Rhodes' permission to accept places in Sprigg's cabinet, Rhodes conferred his blessing. "You must do everything to help the governor through," Rhodes telegrammed. "I hope you will not want my vote as I am very happy building railways importing stock and in fact creating and you must remember I am like a red rag to a bull especially to Schreiner and Innes."

Rhodes consistently refused to return to the political fray. In early July, when de Waal, Louis Abrahamson, and Fuller all implored him to occupy his seat when the House met in mid-month, Rhodes was torn. They believed that Rhodes' presence would be necessary to help the Progressives administer a sound defeat to the Bond. Edward Ridge Syfret, one of Rhodes' financial managers, wanted Rhodes to return because "The Mole [Hofmeyr] & his crew [were] most active and [would] want a great deal of watching." But Rhodes strongly preferred to stay in the north. He was prepared to come south only if his vote were truly essential. Was he "really necessary?" he asked Fuller by wire.

Smartt, Fuller, and Jameson, who had recently won a by-election for Rutherfoord Harris' old seat in Kimberley, agreed that the casting of his own vote technically might not be required to secure a majority, but his "hospitality"—his ability to find the means to assure the necessary backing—would surely be missed. Nevertheless, Rhodes decided to remain in Rhodesia, away from the manipulative life he had formerly loved so much, out of the clutches of the princess, and confident that when and if the cataclysm of war ever ended he would be available to help Milner reconstruct South Africa along imperial lines. When Walton wrote to Rhodes from Groote Schuur in August he regarded the parliamentary scene, where Hofmeyr was still trying to prevent a strong treason bill from being passed, as profoundly "depressing." "We have the knife at the throat of the Afrikander nation," exulted this leader of the South African League, ". . .and he has got to die. He squeals and kicks . . . [but] . . . we have to drive the knife home . . . soon. . . . [The] squealing gets on my nerves and I am rather glad you are not there."[50]

So was Rhodes. He stayed in Rhodesia, preferring the calm of the veld to the anxieties of the Cape. For five months he trekked with Jourdan, Grimmer, Metcalfe, and de la Cruz from one end of the territory to the other, covering thirty miles a day on horseback, and walking another ten or so each day in pursuit of game. He remained in the interior until a few weeks before parliament rose in October and, oddly, never entered the House during those brief days before the end of the session. However, he had earlier been persuaded after long negotiation to accept the presidency of the South African League. According to Brabant, the most characteristic interview with Rhodes took place in May in his bedroom: "He took off his coat and waistcoat strode up and down the room in his shirt sleeves, arguing with great vigor. . . ." Eventually Brabant won his point, and, in October, Rhodes gave a presidential address which focused on winning the battle against Krugerism, not the Dutch. Rhodes would have "none" of "this wretched racial feeling." "Let us drop disputes, evacuate our hostile camps and work for closer union with one another and the mother country," he urged plausibly and characteristically.[51]

Rhodes' zest for advocacy and combat had not been entirely lost, but he was biding his time, knowing that winning the war was the responsibility and province of others, and that he ought to remain as unimplicated as possible in the political bitterness between Dutch and English speakers. Where he had always been hurried, the experiences of the siege and the recurring pains in his heart—he had another bad bout of "fever" in November—combined to counsel patience.

Stead and Major General John Fielden Brocklehurst, the queen's equerry, believed that only Rhodes could "save South Africa." Rhodes would have continued to believe so himself well into 1901, while the much-vaunted peace still escaped the parties of war. In May, he even toyed with the possibility, veteran that he now was, of again taking charge. He may have made overtures to the Bond in the hopes of forging a coalition government above "race" considerations. Milner noted that there had been a determined effort to bring Rhodes and the Bond together. "I don't think it is possible," Milner had earlier commented caustically, "even in this world of absolute political unscrupulousness. But if they come crawling on their bellies to him, it may be a temptation, especially as the British press & public have been rather unfair to him lately and the Bond in their present whipped cur . . . state are capable of crawling very humbly. Ugh! What a country!"

To Rhodes, Milner conceded in May 1901 that Sprigg was "aging." Furthermore, he agreed that many in the Cape desired "a more vigorous hand at the helm. . . ." Doubtless Rhodes could become premier if he wanted to "come in." But did he? Milner soothingly and smoothly doubted whether Rhodes really wanted the position so "long as things go decently without. . . ." He assumed—which was still correct—that Rhodes wished to "reserve" himself for Rhodesia and for the larger questions of South Africa's future. True, possibly only Rhodes' "coming in" could keep parliament together, but Milner intended to defer any resumed sittings of the House, and any elections which might then result from a return of Rhodes, as long as possible. On his part, Rhodes did not object too strongly, for he admitted that his heart was "dickey" and had given him increasing "trouble."

For that reason as well as his own intention to continue "reserving" himself, he advised the Progressives in June not to agitate for a suspension of the constitution, which he otherwise favored (Sprigg and Milner were already governing by proclamation). "Better leave it alone," he said. "Agitation will not help and it will probably come automatically." Rhodes received an overture from a political association in Natal in September, asking him to stand for that colony's legislative council from the Newcastle district, but Rhodes rebuffed it. As late as December, Michell, who usually safeguarded Rhodes' health and followed a generally cautious, bankerish approach, urged him to come home. So did Syfret. There had been runs on a savings bank. An atmosphere of crisis pervaded the Cape. Only Rhodes could save the day. Sprigg was "old and impractible [sic] and [would] not see his position. The governor has lost all confidence in him and would take strong measures to change his

. . . administrator were you here." Michell expected major surprises soon. "I should extremely regret to see the earthquake in your absence."[52]

Michell, usually persuasive, would not have troubled Rhodes if he had not believed that the Founder was still ambitious and tolerably well. But Rhodes had already experienced his last hurrah. He had fought his last political campaign and was no longer a possible premier. The war was still unwon, and, until it ended, he could do nothing. More decisively, Rhodes was losing the world's fight. His heart was no longer in the game of life.

·◄ 23 ►··

"Sex Enters into Great Matters of State"
Of Dreams and Deeds

R HODES WAS both a dreamer and a doer. To the end of his days the Founder never ceased asking "what if . . . ?" and then seeking practical, entrepreneurial answers to questions both profound and mundane. He did so despite increasing concerns about the ability of his body to endure the uncommon strains placed upon it by both stress and physical deterioration, and despite the repeated pains that came from his heart and the "fevers" which sent him so often to bed. Refusing until near the end to slow down or to succumb to this most unsquarable of enemies, Rhodes set his usual fast and varied pace, imagining, conceptualizing, delegating, and nagging by telegraph. He sought new economic opportunities and to promote and further those which had already been initiated. His energy levels remained astonishingly high almost to the end, and so too did his ability to translate even the most seemingly far-fetched ideas into accomplishment.

In addition to his hitherto little-acknowledged heavy involvement in the political transformation of the Cape both before and during the Anglo-Boer War, Rhodes propelled his telegraph and his rails toward Cairo and toward more directly realizable but still challenging goals like Ujiji and the Victoria Falls. He presided over the emergence of settler Southern Rhodesia, and encouraged and assisted its development. He directed the occupation and initial administration of Northern Rhodesia. He continued to guide De Beers and the diamond industry (as well as the British South Africa Company), and never simply sat back and counted his growing wealth. Nor did he resort to the narcissistic exercise of erecting empty monuments to his own genius. Instead, his active brain fostered a stream of new projects, both in the Cape and in the north, which were to lead to industries of benefit to South Africa and the Rhodesias. He traveled the world and thought and planned constantly for an empire which comparatively soon would be deprived of his guiding gifts.[1]

Of the schemes in the late 1890s which had a lasting impact on the Cape, none was more basic than the establishment of experimental fruit farms. Nevertheless, Rhodes almost killed what he had begun. In 1891, when he was prime minister, Rhodes attempted to put the Colony's infant and primitively organized fruit industry on a modern basis. He recognized the need to introduce new and better varieties of fruit into the Cape and improve traditional methods of cultivation. Scientific fruit growing, and advice from American and British pickers and packers, could create new export crops, and thus benefit the exchequer of the Colony. When Merriman became Rhodes' minister of agriculture, he enthusiastically advanced this idea, and sowed the seeds of what ultimately became a thriving and profitable supplement to the Cape's economic dependence on diamonds.[2] By 1897, however, the agricultural schemes which had been sponsored by the government were starved of capital and leadership and were still unproven. Rhodes therefore determined to undertake and underwrite his own experiment. A great believer in the advice of authorities, especially those who had gained their knowledge overseas, Rhodes at the end of 1896 (during and immediately after his triumphant return from Rhodesia) persuaded Harry Ernest Victor Pickstone to help him establish a vast scientific fruit industry in the western Cape.

Born in Lancashire in 1865, Pickstone first became acquainted with the Cape as a soldier with General Charles Warren's expedition to Bechuanaland in 1884–85. Subsequently, he worked in Canada, and in southern California as a railway laborer. Soon unemployed and with no experience with fruit cultivation, he obtained a job budding orange trees near Riverside. Later he went north, and found similar work as a propagator on fruit farms in the Santa Clara valley of California. During this period he determined to introduce fruit growing to South Africa. On his return to the Cape in 1892 he became acquainted with Merriman, and met Rhodes as well. Pickstone was soon advising the department of agriculture and a select committee of parliament. For the next few years he also acted as extension agent for the department. Visiting different areas of the colony, he counseled farmers and compiled technical reports for publication in the journal of the ministry. Meanwhile, in 1893 Rhodes and Rudd together gave him £300 to establish modern nurseries in Wellington, Hex River, and Constantia. Pickstone's aim was to "help in changing our little amateur retail orcharding into such wholesome development as the export trade requires."[3] He did so by developing and providing varieties of citrus and deciduous fruit suitable for the conditions of the Cape, and by issuing descriptive catalogues containing careful instructions as well as sales information. Subsequently, too, he established two demonstration orchards in the Groot Drakenstein valley.

Pickstone had earlier tried to obtain backing from Rhodes for a truly grand spread of orchards, and thus the establishment of an export industry. By the beginning of 1897 Rhodes was ready, and Pickstone began purchasing farms throughout the wine-growing areas of the western Cape. At Rhodes' death, twenty-nine of these properties had been consolidated into at least thirteen and probably nineteen fruit and wine farms in the Paarl, Groot Drakenstein, Franschhoek, Stellenbosch, Tulbagh, and Wellington districts. The principal farms on which innovative orchards were planted were in the valley of the Drakenstein, in Franschhoek, and Paarl. There Pickstone planted 134,000 pear, apple, plum, apricot, nectarine, quince, and peach trees and, as Rhodes ordered, arranged for an irrigation system to bring them steady water.

By the end of 1900 this experiment had cost De Beers, Rhodes, and Beit £53,000 each. Rhodes anticipated further expenses of £12,000 a year for three more years, by which time the trees would begin to bear and a return be realized. "Pickstone who is in charge is confident as to the future," Rhodes wrote Beit. Yet, a year later, it was clear that Pickstone was devoting time and effort to his own nursery business as well as to the fruit farms. "It seems to me he cannot do justice to both . . . and if he has confidence in the fruit, which he says he has, he should jump at my offer . . . [and] . . . devote all his energies to making a payable matter of the venture which I have undertaken solely on his representations." Rhodes was ready to purchase Pickstone's own business and its goodwill and give him a good salary as full-time manager of the fruit farms. Rhodes was also prepared to fund the development of this experiment for a prospective sixth year as well as the five to which he was already committed. He was anxious to see it succeed. Indeed, like a nervous parent, he watched over the fruit farms as he managed diamonds.

In 1901 and early 1902, Pickstone, who had finally accepted Rhodes' generous offer, received a steady stream of advice and instruction from the Founder. More vines should be planted and no more fruit trees, for, Rhodes declared, "we have quite enough." Should the fruit "not pay it will certainly pay with the vines." By late 1901 Rhodes was becoming more and more nervous about Pickstone's extravagance and about the possibility that the fruit farms would not begin to cover their costs. "We should make an insurance fund in vines," he ordered from Egypt. From Wadi Halfa, up the Nile, after gleaning advice somewhere in Europe, he instructed Edward Ridge Syfret to tell Pickstone precisely how far apart the new vines were to be planted, how many should be planted, and on which farms. He specified the soils into which they should go, too. A total of 685,000 vines were ultimately planted. "I have always felt doubtful about the fruit," Rhodes said in late 1901.

On the site of the main fruit farms, Rhodes nevertheless had attempted to solve the question of obtaining adequate labor, primarily Coloured, to work his farms. Characteristically, he had decided to build 140 cottages (designed by Baker) of a model style for the time, create a school and a church, and import both a teacher and a minister. Rhodes would once again be a laird, if largely by proxy. "The cottages were essential," he told Beit, "so as to enable us to keep good men for the fruit culture." But the new village of Languedoc cost £25,000 and annoyed the Bond; the Coloured men were all qualified voters, and, Rhodes wrote with some glee, "their votes would probably change the result of the Paarl constituency at the next General Election." The village, modernized again only in the 1980s, was in fact an example of Rhodes' paternalism and his generativity. Like other creative persons, Rhodes' impulse was to create a world according to his own vision of how things ought to be. That urge in some instances led him to offend ethical norms. In others, it led him to create works of lasting value. In the case of the village, besides creating a local setting for his workers, construction spawned another important local industry. Good clays were found on Rhodes' farms in the Stellenbosch district, and the bricks and tiles for the workers' cottages were all made there.[4]

In late 1901 and 1902 Rhodes had faith neither in the profitability of his fruit experiment nor in the brick and tile works. He favored taking "the first loss" and then closing down the latter, and believed more in wine from grapes than in the apricots, plums, and so on which were beginning to fruit as he lay dying. Pickstone claimed a return of £5,000 in 1901, and Rhodes' Fruit Farms were officially incorporated in 1902 as a joint stock company owned by De Beers, Beit, and Rhodes. It was still losing large sums, although Rudyard Kipling, for one, praised the grapefruits and the tangerines that Pickstone was sending to London. "It is a great joy to taste clean fresh grape fruit again," he wrote.[5]

Only after his death did Rhodes' vision and initiative produce rewards. At the Royal Horticultural Show in London in 1906, Rhodes' estates received a gold medal for their fruit. In that year they shipped 120 tons to Britain. The balance sheet also improved, and a cannery and a jam factory were constructed to process the raw fruit. It had been demonstrated that South African varieties could be landed in Europe in good condition. Although the Cape as a whole was still importing far more fruit than it exported, an example was beginning to be set by Rhodes' estates for the farmers of the Colony. Indeed, in 1910 the Cape exported 2,705 tons of deciduous fruit (mostly apples) to London. By 1921 Cape fruit was on sale in New York, and in 1923 a million boxes of apples and pears were shipped from Cape Town for the first time.

Rhodes had long wanted to reduce the costs of diamond and gold mining by producing his own dynamite. By the mid-1890s De Beers alone was consuming 30,000 cases of dynamite a year, worth about £60,000, all of it imported initially from Britain and the United States and, later, when the Nobel Trust had established an effective monopoly over world-wide production, from Britain and Germany. Nobel refused to give Rhodes any discount, despite the massive size of his annual purchases. Nor did De Beers wish to import from the Transvaal's expensive dynamite repackaging concern at Modderfontein. All of the gold mines were compelled to purchase their supplies locally; its exactions were among the grievances that helped rationalize the Raid, and gave the Uitlander businessmen cause to agitate for and welcome the Anglo-Boer War.

A year before the war, Rhodes, rebuffed by the Raid's failure to unify the Cape and the Transvaal, decided to seek his own solution to the separate but related question of dynamite manufacture. Given Nobel's cartel, this was a bold undertaking worthy of Rhodes' earlier days as a decisive entrepreneur.

In late 1898 he persuaded Beit and De Beers to commit £500,000 to such a quest for economic independence. (Costs later increased to £1.5 million.) Delegating the details to Gardner Williams, the American manager of De Beers, Rhodes was content amid the flurry of his political and Rhodesian activities, and his extensive travels in early 1899, to supervise from afar. Williams, in turn, sought out another American, then employed by a branch of the Nobel firm in California.

William Russell Quinan, a West Point graduate and for a short time an officer in the U.S. army, for fifteen years had manufactured dynamite in California. For a trebled salary and the challenge of creating an entirely original explosives works in the southern hemisphere, Quinan agreed to work for Rhodes. Arriving in Cape Town a few months before war broke out, Quinan and the five American engineers who accompanied him chose a site for the factory near Somerset West and, during the war, overcame fearsome local opposition to its construction because of presumed danger and on political and social grounds. (The Dutch-speaking farmers of the area were opposed on grounds of principle to any enterprise connected with Rhodes. They also feared an influx of "kaffir" workers.) Just before the war broke out Quinan received a boatload of supplies from the United States: 1,000 tons of bricks, redwood timbering, iron, and caustic soda. He expected to purchase 100 tons of quartz for his sulphuric acid plant in South Africa and whatever structural steel he required.

Quinan's initial plan called for the production on the site of both nitric and sulphuric acid in great quantities, and their combination into 100,000 cases of year of nitroglycerine. He anticipated manufacturing blasting dynamite for Kimberley at 32 shillings per case; the mines were then paying 55 shillings a case for imports. He would need to build his own power station, refrigeration plant, retort building, box unit, and printing house. He also decided to import crude glycerine from overseas and to refine it locally, thus saving large amounts of money. In supporting Quinan and the escalating level of his probable expenditures, Rhodes reassured an increasingly nervous Beit. "When Africa federates, which it is sure to do," he wrote in his characteristically expansive manner, "the Home Government will probably have an external duty on dynamite, but there will be no duty between the different states." To the London board of De Beers he wrote encouragingly that the production of dynamite would prove "exceedingly profitable." "We may calculate fairly on supplying the whole of the mines of Africa with dynamite in the future." Indeed "the thing [was] altogether too good to part with." Labor would prove no problem for there was an abundant supply of Coloureds in the Cape. "We have excellent labour in the yellow man," Rhodes reminded Beit. In 1901, as the war appeared to be winding down, Rhodes wrote supportively to Quinan from Salsomaggiore in northern Italy. It was essential to complete the works at Somerset West so as to provide a viable alternative to the restarting of the Modderfontein assembly. "De Beers has plenty of funds so it rests with you now. . . . Spare no effort," he exhorted.[6]

Once again Rhodes died too young to know that he had beaten the Nobel Trust and established the beginnings of a very successful, if temporary, local monopoly of his own. Quinan shipped the first 400 cases of dynamite to Kimberley in 1903. Seventy thousand cases were manufactured in 1903–04, and 350,000 cases each year through 1909, when production was increased further and exports shipped to Australia. Refined glycerine was supplied locally for pharmaceutical purposes as well, and the factory subsequently produced fuse igniters, detonators, agricultural chemicals, insecticides, fertilizers, and so on. In 1924, Rhodes' Cape Explosives merged with the Modderfontein firm to form African Explosives and Industries, subsequently the African Explosives and Chemical Industries, long the supplier of all explosives to the mines of southern Africa—as Rhodes had predicted and wished.

Rhodes sponsored another far less capital-intensive but equally important and profitable project. After rinderpest had halved the cattle herds of southern Africa in 1896, and the then-existing cold storage firms in Johannesburg and Cape Town had taken advantage of scarcity to raise the prices of meat, Rhodes attempted to persuade the government of the Cape to challenge their market dominance by constructing its own refrigeration facilities. The price of meat, Rhodes told the House, "had enormously risen. It had almost doubled . . . to the embarrassment of the working-man. . . ." The cost of meat had also affected him "most seriously." If it affected him "in connection with his animals, how much more must it affect poor people . . . ?" Moreover, he was responsible for feeding 10,000 people at the Kimberley mines, and expensive meat added to the costs of running that diamond center. He said that he was "determined to work for the reduction of the cost of meat" for the people of the country. Although mutton and beef were available comparatively inexpensively from Australia, no one could import either because of the lack of guaranteed chilled storage space. "The question of spending [only] £50,000 in dealing with the growing evil of the monopoly in frozen meat was not too much," Rhodes urged the House in late 1898. Finally, when it was clear that the government would not heed his pleas, Rhodes declared that if Schreiner's ministry would do nothing, he would act alone. "This close monopoly must not be allowed to go on," the diamond monopolist declared ringingly.

At the end of 1898, Rhodes instructed De Beers to build cold storage depots at the Cape and in Kimberley and to import meat from Australia for sale to the mines and to the public. With the diamond company as a guaranteed customer and the leverage that flowed from his firm's significant position within the overall economy of the Cape, the Kimberley branch quickly turned profitable, and, by 1900, the depot in Cape Town was breaking even. "We thought it wise," Rhodes told De Beers' shareholders in 1900, "wise for both ourselves and the people of the country, that we should . . . endeavour to check too gross a monopoly in the purchase and distribution of meat." Although the Bond regularly attacked his monopoly in diamonds, it had sanctioned the existing meat cartel. "The distinction between the luxury of diamonds and the necessity of meat," he continued, "I leave to you."[7] The Progressive parliamentarian, and convert to lower duties on meat, had started to see the results of enlightened free trade. He had also begun successfully to take business away from David de Villiers Graaff's Imperial Cold Storage and Supply Company, the Cape's pioneering firm. His company also began purchasing most of its supplies locally. Rhodes could certainly credit himself with restoring competition to the wholesale meat industry, and with adding to De Beers' profitability as an emerging conglomerate.

There is a further reason why Rhodes sponsored these three significant new ventures when he did. Barney Barnato had committed suicide in 1897, leaving Rhodes and Beit, as the remaining life governors of De Beers, in receipt of the profits from his share as well as their own. From the life governorship arrangement alone, Rhodes thereafter received £140,000 in 1896 and 1897, £159,000 in 1898, and in 1899 and 1900 about £317,000 each year. He fought off Frederic Philipson Stow's attempt in 1898 to give Barnato's life governorship to Francis Baring Gould, who—despite a promise from Rhodes—had been barred by Barnato from becoming one of the original governors. In 1892, Rhodes told Stow curtly, "After your sale to me" of Stow's own life governorship, "I made arrangements . . . with others which cannot now be altered."[8] Stow, who formally resigned from the De Beers' board only in 1898, always believed that he and Baring Gould had been double-crossed.

De Beers had been highly profitable for five years, and Rhodes desired to give up no shares in that bonanza. Since the number of diamond carats sold yearly had soared to 2.7 million in 1896–97, and costs had been prevented from escalating, De Beers then and until 1899, and again in 1901, declared dividends of £1.6 million a year, or 40 percent on each share. From 1902 to 1904 the yearly payout was about £2 million. Rhodes owned 20,337 shares, and in 1899 was the Company's second largest shareholder, well behind Lord Rothschild, but ahead of the brothers Isaac and Solly Joel, Barnato's heirs. From these ordinary dividends he received another £41,000 a year.[9] (Bemusedly, it was about this time that Rhodes fired off a peremptory, sarcastic note in his own hand to John Norris, the manager of his expensive estate in Inyanga: "I cannot do everything. It appears to me I am supposed to be a class of animal which everyone has a right to feed upon. I would remind you that just at present my extinction by pecuniary exhaustion does not suit my friends.")[10]

He was still De Beers' chairman, too, and despite his intense political machinations of 1898 and 1899, his steady involvement in the affairs of the Rhodesias, and his extensive travels, Rhodes never relaxed his detailed oversight of the affairs of the great mines of Kimberley. "If you dont look out you will get your mines shut down for want of labour," Rhodes in late 1900 warned William Pickering, the company's secretary in Kimberley. He told him how he should go about removing wartime restrictions on the recruitment of workers from the Transkei. Even if they refused to go down the mines they could work De Beers' tailings and debris dumps (where diamonds could still be picked out). "Get as many boys as you can," Rhodes telegraphed from Groote Schuur. "The price of diamonds is gigantic. . . ." A few weeks later, when Rhodes learned that the supply of coal was short, he berated Pickering. "You appear to be always running out. I suppose no one thinks a fortnight ahead. You have been free from blockade for nine months," said the survivor of the siege, "and seem to live from hand to mouth," even though a town of 50,000 and the Cape's prosperity (not to mention his own) depended upon the efficient mining and washing of diamonds. As to the possibility that war-forced constraints were hampering Pickering, Rhodes declared that excuse "absurd." "Few human beings," he fumed, "ever think excepting of the next meal." After Gardner Williams, the manager of De Beers, had produced a long enumeration of water consumption in the company's gardens, Rhodes wished that he could show "the same activity of brain in keeping up his mine supplies." Imagine, he exclaimed in horror, being reduced to one case of dynamite! "Tell Williams from me to go through his morning catechism daily. . . ."

Later in the year Rhodes worried about the timbering of the mines, and about every small detail of the production of diamonds. After all, he was the Founder. At the end of 1901 he even wrote from a river boat up the Nile that he had heard about renewed outbreaks of scurvy in the mine compounds. The cure, he related not unreasonably, was for De Beers to make and sell "kaffir beer." "Allow the natives," he instructed, "when they come up from the mines, . . . one or two mugs of beer. You will find it will be very popular." Not only would the nutrients in the beer prevent scurvy; providing the beer would also increase the availability of labor. "The way you will proceed is to buy some kaffir corn and give out to some women at the location to make beer with. They would bring it in jars to the compounds and it would be sold by the store keeper in the evening." The workers should be limited to whatever amount the mine physician decided would "cheer but not inebriate." It could well be difficult to procure adequate supplies of labor after the war. "Everything that we can do for the comfort and pleasure of our boys will be an assistance," Rhodes declared solicitously.[11]

Until the very end of his days, Rhodes never relaxed the careful attention he paid both to his gold properties and to the marketing of De Beers' diamonds. In 1899, for example, he agreed to sell 7,397 claims in the City and Suburban Deep mine for £40,683 to Consolidated Gold Fields; two months later, when he learned that Gold Fields planned to offer those same claims through a stock offering to public subscribers, he demanded that Gold Fields rescind his original transaction. Since Rhodes was still such an influential figure in the company, the board finally agreed and Rhodes, through a complicated series of transactions, quietly turned his minor attempt to realize profits into a significant windfall. By annulling a single transaction, he pyramided his paper profits to £260,000.[12]

The sale of diamonds to the trade was still accomplished through multi-year contracts specifying six-month sales to the syndicate of buyers in Kimberley. Rhodes always resented the interference and dilution of his power that the syndicate represented. Now and then throughout the late 1890s, especially in 1898, Rhodes thought that De Beers could do better by selling the diamonds directly in London and bypassing the syndicate, by selling on commission through one or more brokers, or by auctioning diamonds to the highest bidder. In 1899, Rothschild and the members of the syndicate who sat on De Beers' London board successfully argued against Rhodes' proposal to charge the syndicate higher prices and, further, to claw back a portion of the profits of the syndicate.

The Anglo-Boer War and the siege of Kimberley effectively limited Rhodes' and De Beers' leverage until late 1901, when the contract with the syndicate again came up for renewal. Rhodes then informed the London board of its considerable flaws. The price was poor and below existing market rates: "I grudge no one his fair due but I do consider that one million and a half to the middle man for the distribution of a product worth five millions is excessive. . . ." Rhodes "absolutely protest[ed] against such a transaction."

Rhodes encountered serious opposition, however, from Rothschild. Along with others he argued that it was best to "leave well alone," especially when the "well" had produced such extraordinary riches. The history of De Beers, he reminded Rhodes, was "simply a fairy tale." Rothschild hardly wished to interrupt the steady market for the sale of diamonds—was he preaching to a convert who had become an apostate? The substitutes that Rhodes had suggested could produce a "disorganized" market, the antithesis of a satisfactory cartel.[13] After much debate, a compromise was forged which largely accepted Rhodes' evaluation of what would be best for De Beers. A five-year contract, signed by the end of 1901, revised the way in which diamonds would be valued and export quantities determined. The company and the syndicate were to share profits and losses. Rhodes also demanded and obtained for De Beers the right to switch classes of stones in order to maintain value in terms of annual sales.

The struggle over the syndicate was but one aspect of a contest for control of De Beers as a capitalistic entity. Long accustomed to running the company as if it were privately owned, his to manage as he wished, Rhodes objected vociferously to attempts, more and more open as they were in the years after the Raid, to restrict his powers as chairman. The central question for big shareholders and their representatives was clearly one of money, and the fear that Rhodes would again extravagantly risk their yields and gains on speculative new projects like the decade-old British South Africa Company, or on madcap adventures like the Raid. The issue for Rhodes, however, was one of autonomy; he took substantial challenges to his leadership, and his continued capacity to direct, very hard. Lord Rothschild and the London board wanted to curtail his freedom to act decisively—to operate with entrepreneurial alacrity. The London board also had begun to threaten his returns as a life governor. Rhodes had little leverage—for, even if he held 20,000 shares, there were several hundred thousand outstanding—the board could hardly do without the Founder and De Beers' champion promoter. Nevertheless, its members wished to cling to what Rhodes called their "unimaginative" profits, and deny him his "big ideas."

In April 1899, when he was in London discussing investments and seeking funds for his telegraph and railway to Cairo, Rhodes protested at length to the governing board of De Beers "against the persistent manner in which the whole of my policy has been opposed . . . ever since it [was] created. . . ." He explained the famous trust deed. "When we created . . . de Beers . . . we . . . took power to deal in matters other than diamonds. My reason . . . was that I felt it was risky to confine ourselves entirely to diamonds." The life of the mines was limited, and new kimberlite pipes might be discovered elsewhere. "Now I do not for one moment claim," Rhodes said, "that I should have the power to make heavy investments in undertakings other [than] diamonds, without consultation with the Board," although he did. He mentioned several transactions where the board had overruled him and good opportunities and handsome profits had been lost. "I would have thought that the continued proof of the wisdom of my suggestions . . . would have led [the board] to view . . . further suggestions [favorably] but this persistent and untiring opposition appears to me to be more continuous than ever." It was particularly objectionable "in view of the enormous expansion going on in Africa and the special opportunities that I have for wise and judicious investment; and," he wrote from the heart, "considering the limit of life which every one must agree is the fate of all mines." "I always feel that it is no small thing," Rhodes told the company's shareholders in 1900, "to be able to say that [De Beers] has devoted its wealth to other things besides the expansion of luxury." If the board maintained its opposition to him in the matter of financing his railway to the Zambezi, Rhodes threatened to go public—to call a meeting of the shareholders. If for some reason the shareholders refused to support him, he further threatened to retire from De Beers.

Rothschild, to whom Rhodes had sent a copy of his letter, replied suavely as "an admirer" of Rhodes' "genius." Rothschild was opposed only to injudicious investments which might threaten the financial stability of the company. "The first duty of the directors . . . is to make their financial situation quite strong." Pointing out the large stake—450,000 shares—now held by French shareholders who cared little for Rhodes' imperialism, he urged the Founder not to call a meeting of shareholders. But Rhodes was still angry, resenting the suggestion that he and Beit had drawn their life governorship remunerations illegally. He threatened to seek a judicial opinion. "There can be no question of a law suit, amicable or otherwise," Rothschild cautioned. He suggested that the directors sit down and talk. In May, thanks to Beit's intervention, Rhodes and the board compromised. Rhodes could use surplus funds for new South African investments, but with the approval of the London board. The Kimberley board—that meant Rhodes—could invest amounts of up to £100,000 on its own, without reference to London. He also received backing for the railway to the north.

Even so, the fundamental issue of control—whose company was it?—remained unresolved a little longer. Rhodes was accustomed to the comparatively loose accounting methods of his pioneering days, and Rothschild wanted the kind of precise bookkeeping which would expose, and therefore curtail, Rhodes' ability to use De Beers' cash as well as his own when he seized new opportunities. "I am bound to point out to you my dear Rhodes," he said, "that it will be impossible for the accounts to be kept in the future in the same manner without certainty of . . . litigation." Otherwise, Rhodes could be accused of not dealing honestly with his shareholders. Rothschild told Rhodes that he could no longer employ surpluses for outside investments. "You must not use the annual profits of the Company for Capital Expenditures" like those on the dynamite factory and the fruit farms.[14]

Rhodes and Beit ultimately lost the profits of their life governorships. Although Rhodes knew that by so doing he would forfeit substantial returns, in late 1901 he and Beit traded their governorships for 80,000 shares each. "I have been made by pressure to agree," he told David Harris, and asked him to read his objections out to a meeting of the board in London.[15] Rothschild and the other directors had finally managed to revise the original arrangements that they, like Stow, had increasingly found unfair. They had, in fact, successfully reduced Rhodes' role as the company's originator.

What no one could reduce was Rhodes' idea of himself as founder, creator, and empire builder. He had spent half a short lifetime constructing that edifice, applying his unusual personal capabilities to the raw material of his talents and the circumstances in which he found himself. As he exercised his capacities, they grew in strength and complexity. The result was that his ability to deal with the world, to make his way and to prevail, was as formidable as was his determination to perpetuate himself, his contributions to Britain and the empire, and his ideas. He had reserved a place in history for himself; contemplating that place became a soothing influence as he aged and felt himself to be dying.

As his cardiovascular system grew more troublesome, Rhodes naturally focused much more of his attention on the permanent forms by and through which he would be remembered. Entombment in the granite of the Matopos would prove secure. So, he hoped, were the countries named after him. His companies would remain, whether or not women later looked at the ring fingers of their left hands and murmured "Rhodes." His rails and telegraph were solid achievements. By the 1890s he was contemplating the establishment of some kind of educational monument. Since he often thought of himself as a latter-day Caesar and was an obvious target for artists who lived by commission, it is no wonder that he sat for innumerable portraits and posed for plaster busts, copper castings, and great stone carvings.

Rhodes was vain enough—Grey called him "the vainest of the vain"—to accept the attentions of painters and sculptors, and also to criticize their results. He was always impatient, too, insisting on interviewing, dictating, and meeting others during his supposed sittings, and just as frequently dashing away in the middle of what had been intended to be a concentrated time alone with an artist. (He sometimes slashed or stomped on paintings of himself which he disliked.) P. Tennyson Cole, Luke Fildes, Mortimer Menpes, and Sir Hubert Herkomer were among the British painters who caught or tried to catch Rhodes full-length, head and shoulders, or facially in oils. Always they had to do so frontally, never in profile, the sketch by Violet Granby of Rhodes in London in 1898 being a conspicuous exception. Rhodes believed that "no man should be painted [in] . . . profile. A man is known full face if he is an honest man." "I took out my paint-box," remembered Menpes of their dealings in 1900, and Rhodes drew himself up to his full height. "Sir," he began, "do you intend to paint me full-face? If not, you don't paint me at all—unless it is the back of my head."

Another painter was George Frederic Watts, who first sketched him— Rhodes felt it made him look "too severe" and too "imperial" when he wanted the "happy young side to show." Later Watts, a celebrated sculptor, prepared *Physical Energy*, the bronze rider on horseback which looks north from the side of Table Mountain high above Groote Schuur. The horse is reined in after speed and the rider is scanning the distance for the next deed beyond. Watts called it "an emblem of energy and outlook, so characteristic of him." (A second bronze casting was installed in Kensington Gardens, London.) In 1898 Earl Grey prevailed upon Watts to make the face of the rider resemble Rhodes. Watts took Grey to the statue and said, "Well, that is Rhodes."

Charles Wellington Furse, an eighth British painter, attempted to capture Rhodes in all his greatness in 1895. He was fascinated by the plastic qualities of Rhodes' massive, leonine head. But, although Oriel College, Oxford, wanted the portrait, Rhodes was reluctant. He had disliked Herkomer's efforts, being "awfully down on the painter as a class after his experience with Herkomer." Furse persisted. "It is rather fun dealing with a barbarian like this," he wrote home. "I must get his force and his silence, and all this will have to be arrived at with no theatrical accompaniment. . . . He is a man whose type of head would never be dealt with by half measures." Furse reported that one among many of Rhodes' schemes was the building of a facsimile of Oriel on the side of Table Mountain (where the University of Cape Town now sits). The actual idea Furse called "rotten, but the purpose behind it awfully deep and touching."

"Confound Rhodes!" Furse wrote a little later. "He will not make up his mind about being painted, he liked the notion of Oriel wanting his picture, and he hates the idea of sitting, so things are at a deadlock. . . ." Finally, Rhodes agreed to be painted, but not for a month. "I have had to agree to very hard terms, namely that if he disapproves the picture shall not go to Oriel, and that if . . . I disapprove, it shall be knifed. . . ." In the end Oriel never obtained this painting. Rhodes put Furse off for a month and the Jameson Raid intervened.

One of the more prolific sculptors who worked for Rhodes was John Tweed, a young Scot. As early as 1893, Sir Edward Lutyens brought Tweed to the attention of Herbert Baker, Rhodes' architect, and thus of Rhodes. Tweed prepared a bronze panel of Jan van Riebeeck's landing at the Cape for Groote Schuur. After several more commissions over the intervening three years, including a larger-than-life-size bronze of Rhodes for Bulawayo, Rhodes sat for Tweed in his studio in London. They also went on tours of the London art galleries together, Rhodes wishing thereby to acquire taste. "Let me say what's good and bad, and then see if I'm right," he cautioned Tweed. (In his memoirs Tweed tactfully does not discuss the breadth of Rhodes' aesthetic philistinism.) However, despite their camaraderie, Rhodes objected to the likeness of himself that Tweed eventually wrought. "I know it is quite hopeless to venture an opinion about your work as you are so exceedingly pleased with yourself that no criticism is possible. However as the work has a long life before it I venture to ask you to call in some sculptor of repute who would give you his candid opinion. As to the Guy Fawkes of myself you are creating I simply say I shall do my best to prevent its being located in my country." [16]

It was in 1899, when Rhodes was still ostensibly at the height of his influence, that he returned to Britain from Cairo in time to quarrel with the directors of De Beers and Rothschild over his prerogatives as chairman, and with Sir Michael Hicks Beach and the British cabinet over the financing of the Cape to Cairo railway. In May he nevertheless spoke enthusiastically to a noontime meeting of the shareholders of the British South Africa Company about their still exciting if not as yet fully realizable prospects. He and they were building; dividends would have to deferred for the sake of the lofty goals of imperial expansion. The meeting rooms in the Cannon Street Hotel were packed, individual holders of stock having begun arriving early in the morning to find places. After his main speech the fervor was such that he was compelled to address an overflow crowd of applauding shareholders on the stairs of the hotel. Only with the help of the police could he eventually extricate himself and go off to the De Beers' office in the City, London's financial district.

Throughout the same spring in London he renewed his acquaintance with General Kitchener, now Lord Kitchener, the liberator of Khartoum. Like Rhodes, the stern-faced Kitchener, then forty-nine, was devoted to a coterie of young male acolytes and assistants. They were known as his "band of boys," and corresponded to the childhood "band of brothers" that Rhodes often sought to recreate in his own adulthood. Rhodes liked Kitchener, although others found him remote and dour. They were both imperialists of the conquer-and-then-civilize school. They both had similar views on the importance of education, especially of "subject races." They shared a common belief in the possibility of Cape-to-Cairo communication links; Kitchener had only been half-joking when he had urged Rhodes to "hurry up!" in 1898. Rhodes confidentally expected him soon to continue onward to Uganda, presumably with funds supplied by Rhodes or one of Rhodes' companies. Although Rhodes usually found military men ineffectual and priggish (was General Charles Warren his prototype?), for him Kitchener was a model of decisive energy. Together they rode in Hyde Park, Rhodes looking like Napoleon as he tucked one arm into his jacket and cantered off to Rotten Row. "Horse exercise," Rhodes remarked shortly thereafter, "increases the activity of the brain."

In June, Rhodes and Kitchener together went up to Oxford and received honorary doctorates, along with five others. Kitchener's was new, but Rhodes' Doctor of Civil Laws degree had been awarded in 1892, when he was much more popular and also much too busy to take it. Late in that year the Master of Pembroke College had moved in Hebdomadal Council, Oxford's ruling body, that Rhodes should receive such a degree. The principal of St. Edmund Hall further proposed that Governor and High Commissioner Sir Henry B. Loch be awarded the same degree. As Newbury suggests, the Council or the two movers were inspired in recommending identical awards to two competitors who intensely distrusted each other "either by a fine sense of imperial protocol, or by a malicious sense of humour." Rhodes stayed in Britain for some weeks beyond the end of Oxford's Michaelmas or autumn term in 1892, but for reasons now unknown could not or refused to come to obtain it in person until 1899, when—according to *The Times*—"a leading member of the University" (probably the provost or some other official of Oriel College) suggested that the "proper time" had arrived for him to assume the degree.

Rhodes now wanted and had the leisure to appear in person, but the initiative was not his own. It was alleged that he had uncharacteristically remained "entirely passive," taking no action except in "agreeing to attend." Nevertheless, upon learning that Rhodes intended returning to the university to take his degree, at least ninety-four dons publicly deplored the notion of conferring an honor on a man responsible for the odious Raid. The master of Balliol College and the principals of Pusey House and Mansfield and Manchester colleges, three theological foundations, were among the angry dissenters. So was Bodley's Librarian; Professor Albert Venn Dicey, the law codifier; and Herbert A.L. Fisher, the historian and future master of New College and future member of the Rhodes Trust. They and their fellows campaigned against Rhodes and the degree. The university's two elected proctors, who also signed the protest manifesto, contemplated exercising a veto that was within their traditional but rarely used prerogatives.

Even so, the ceremony in the Sheldonian Theatre proved entirely peaceful. *The Times'* correspondent called it "particularly brilliant." In addition to Rhodes and Kitchener, doctorates of civil law were received by the Earl of Elgin, viceroy of India; Sir Charles Hubert Parry, the composer, musicologist, and director of the Royal College of Music; Frederick William Maitland, the medieval historian and Downing Professor of the Laws of England at the University of Cambridge; Frederick Godman, zoologist and trustee of the British Museum; James George Frazer, the anthropologist from the University of Cambridge; and the Rev. Francesco Ehrle, prefect of the Vatican library and a Jesuit.

Rhodes and Kitchener received "the most uproarious welcome," Kitchener's a distinct second to that of the Founder. The university cited Rhodes as an alumnus "hujus academie, vir per totum orbem nomine celeberrimus. Sci-pionibus haud imparem, tertium hodie Africanum salutamus." In other words, the university welcomed him as a graduate of Oxford whose name was well-known over all the world. It compared his achievements to those of the two Scipios: Publius Cornelius Scipio (235–183 B.C.), known as Africanus for his defeat of Hannibal at the end of the Second Punic War, and Publius Corne-lius Scipio Aemiliamus (185–129 B.C.), also surnamed Africanus because of his victory at the end of the third and final Punic War in 146 B.C. "We salute him as a veritable third Africanus," declaimed the university orator, thus either grandly or conceivably waspishly equating Rhodes' aggrandizements with the sanguinary brutalities of the Scipios. Despite his monumental errors, Oxford pronounced itself proud of Rhodes.

"Talking of Oxford," Rhodes subsequently told an audience in Cape Town, "really one sometimes feels fortunate in having done very wrong because it brings out the affection and support of one's people. Some possessed of the most complete rectitude . . . thought I was unworthy of receiving the de-gree." Yet their opposition was fortunate. Rhodes reported that he went up to Oxford with the eyes of the world fixed on the great general. "I should have been almost nobody if it had not been for this opposition to me. But I can assure you . . .they gave me a greater reception than . . . Kitchener." At least that is what Rhodes said, and presumably how he felt about overcoming the first overt public displeasure of his career.

After the award ceremony Rhodes gave a luncheon speech in Oriel Col-lege. He admitted that in pursuing the enlargement of the empire he had adopted "means in removing opposition which were the rough-and-ready way and not the highest way to attain that object." "I do not deny that I have made mistakes," he said, "and there are certain events in my life which, if they occurred again, would have been arranged differently." He excused such methodological lapses: "In South Africa . . . the laws of right and equity are not so fixed and established" as in Britain. Once or twice he had "done things which savoured rather of violence than of . . . peaceful striving." Yet there were parallels in early English history, and it was among those good men that "my own life and actions must be weighed and measured," he suggested with-out a twinge of modesty.[17]

After taking the degree, and completing his business in London, Rhodes sailed to Cape Town and his final parliamentary session. Aboard ship, not by coincidence but as a result of her careful calculations, was the woman with whom Rhodes would soon be linked romantically and enmeshed financially, and, before too much longer, by whom he would be endlessly embarrassed and bothered. Ekaterina Adamevna Rzewuska, the daughter of an aging Pol-ish count who had ingratiated himself into the Russian court of Czar Alex-ander I and a young woman of Tartar descent who had died as a consequence of childbirth, was the improbable person who schemed for Rhodes' notice and possibly his hand. She grew up in the Ukraine, but had also traveled to Odessa, St. Petersburg, and even Paris before she was given in an arranged marriage to Prince Wilhelm Radziwill, whose Polish family was well known to the imperial German court in Berlin. Prince Wilhelm, an officer in the Prussian army, was twenty-eight; his bride, who soon took the name Catherine Marie, a mere fifteen and a half. Within a year she was pregnant with their first child. Four more followed, in all of whom she took little interest. In her mid-twenties she wrote a series of barbed and gossipy articles about court life in Berlin. Published under a pseudonym in a French review and as the book *Berlin Society* in 1885, they greatly annoyed the household of the German emperor. A few years later, after she was unmasked as their author, the Radziwills were forced to leave Berlin for St. Petersburg. Barely thirty, Princess Radziwill fashioned a salon, met the best and the brightest in Russian society, and lived "brilliantly." She doted on political intrigue. It was in 1888, through a politically active Russian woman who wrote both for the Russian and the English press, that she met W.T. Stead, editor of the *Review of Reviews* and Rhodes' longtime admirer and friend. It was at about the same time that her love of conspiracy and mystery became fully apparent.

With the death of Czar Alexander III in 1894, Princess Radziwill lost her position in Russian court society. By then, too, she was estranged from her husband. Her fluency in French and English as well as German, Polish, and Russian permitted her to spend the succeeding two years largely in Paris and London, living as a journalist with a refined taste for personalities in politics. When Rhodes dined at the house of Charles Moberly Bell, manager of *The Times,* in early 1896, Radziwill was sitting on his left. Although Rhodes could not at first remember meeting her when she wrote to him in early 1899, he shortly thereafter recalled who she was. "She was quite interesting, a vivacious talker." Indeed she was. Sharp-tongued, a superb name dropper, with great energy and verve, it was still surprising that she made any impression whatsoever on Rhodes. Perhaps the Raid had blurred his instincts more than anyone suspected at the time.

Radziwill wrote flatteringly to Rhodes after the House of Commons inquiry into the Raid; she claimed second sight, and said that she feared for his safety. Receiving no answer from Rhodes' campsite at Inyanga, her letter at least escaped being thrown onto an open fire along with those of hundreds of other correspondents. She wrote again in early 1899 (when Rhodes was in London) to seek advice on investments. Radziwill was attempting to live by her wits, and, like so much that she did, this excuse to become reacquainted with Rhodes was contrived. She had nothing to invest, having lived far beyond her means ever since being separated from her long-suffering prince. Rhodes, however, replied to her himself, albeit perfunctorily. After all, she was a princess, and Rhodes still had a juvenile Briton's weakness for royalty.

She learned that Rhodes would be sailing for Cape Town on the S.S. *Scot,* booked her own passage on the same ship, and arranged to flounce into the dining salon at the first dinner and, by "coincidence," make her way to his table. There she joined Philip Jourdan and Sir Charles Metcalfe, Rhodes' traveling companions, for eighteen days as the *Scot* steamed toward Madeira, crossed the equator, and headed home. Vivacious, forty-one, and appealing if not especially attractive, "she was quite an acquisition," Jourdan remembered. "She was a bright and versatile conversationalist. There was not a subject she could not converse upon. . . . She appeared to know everyone, and kept us all amused during the whole voyage." Occasionally she "expressed herself rather bluntly on delicate matters." Even Rhodes blushed. Colin Harding, also aboard the *Scot,* appreciated her "strange fascination, and wonderful powers as a linguist." Wilson, of the *Cape Times,* found that she had "a certain charm," although she was "by no means beautiful."

Although it would be claiming too much to describe Rhodes as captivated, he apparently found her intriguing and intelligent. He invited her to dine. Possibly she was initially bent on using Rhodes and Rhodes' contacts to further her journalistic enterprise on the eve of a war which might soon break out, or she was intent on trapping Rhodes, or the one led to the other, or both. Whichever, Radziwill was soon a frequent visitor to Groote Schuur. She rode, joined a multiplicity of guests for meals, and generally became an accepted part of the ménage surrounding Rhodes. Radziwill seemed to be in love with the Founder; that was Harding's impression. She also led him to believe that Rhodes intended to marry her.[18]

Radziwill was not the only woman admitted to Rhodes' circle of confidants during these last years of life at the court of Groote Schuur. Lady Sarah Wilson, Lord Randolph Churchill's younger sister and Winston Churchill's aunt, coincided with Radziwill. So did Lady Edward Cecil, the future Viscountess Milner, who dismissed Radziwill as a vulgar adventuress. Nearly contemporaneous was the Countess of Warwick, former mistress of the future King Edward VII, whom Rhodes saw in London and Scotland. With them, as with the men arrayed along Groote Schuur's polished mahogany dining table, he discussed his political struggle with the Bond, the possibility of war, and doubtless dilated upon his dreams of union. Agile and alert, the princess may have responded brightly. Soon, however, she became tiresome, persisting in expressing political opinions too forcefully or being too inquisitive. She may also have interested herself too much in his return to power, and attempted to promote it. Whatever it was, within a month or so, Rhodes began trying to avoid her. One morning he told James G. McDonald, at Groote Schuur on a visit from Bulawayo, "on no account leave me alone with her. Never mind what she may say to you or how she may look at you. You must put up with it till Metcalfe, [Dr. Thomas William] Smartt, or Jourdan returns."

McDonald suggests that Radziwill had begun antagonizing Rhodes' male friends. Rhodes may also have heard rumors, doubtless spread throughout the Cape Town society in which the wily princess was now gliding, that they were linked romantically. Leo Amery, correspondent of *The Times,* recalled the guests a few months later at the Mount Nelson Hotel in Cape Town: "Not the least conspicuous was the once lovely, still decoratively imposing, . . .

Princess Radziwill, who had conceived an infatuation for Rhodes and had come out in the vain hope of vamping him into matrimony. . . ." The local gossips were doubtless titillated; indeed, even newspapers as far afield as Grahamstown in 1900 published "authoritative" rumors of their pending matrimony.[19]

When the war broke out, Rhodes hardly invited her to accompany him to Kimberley. Indeed, he was delighted to escape the princess' continued attempts at friendship and intimacy. Once curious about her, his interest had slipped from attraction and amusement to annoyance. During the siege she intrigued politically in Cape Town with the Bond and others. It is therefore likely that when Rhodes returned to the Cape he was as irritated with her as she suggested. But Rhodes was ill, and spent little time at Groote Schuur before sailing to London to consult Fowler. Even so, informed of the dire state of her finances, and either sympathetic or fearing embarrassment, he paid her mounting hotel bills, purchased her passage to London, and hoped or urged that she would leave South Africa. At that time Syfret, Rhodes' paymaster, found her grasping and inconsistent. He, at least, was very suspicious, and so informed Rhodes.[20]

She indeed sailed to London shortly after Rhodes. That might, or should, have been the end of the episode of Rhodes and the princess. But she was both clever and desperate. During her days in London she wrote a number of articles (published in Britain and the United States) defending Rhodes' role in the Raid and his leadership of Kimberley during the siege. She seems to have been inspired and certainly encouraged by Stead, who had a separate political agenda of his own. It is not certain that Rhodes knew immediately of her political journalism or the extent to which she persisted in trading on their association. She was a mistress of innuendo, however; Stead and others in London could have been impressed by her panache and her supposed friendships. Unfortunately, ordinary tradesmen and hoteliers were not. Living high as she had to do, Radziwill took chances. Indeed, during her time in London she attempted to fake the loss of supposedly expensive pearls, and thus came to the attention of the London police. To Inspector Edward Drew, she alleged that she and Rhodes were engaged, and that he was helping her to obtain a divorce.[21]

Rhodes represented Radziwill's only plausible opportunity to recover fortune and glory. After the brush with the London police, she doubtless was anxious to try her luck at the Cape once again. When she reappeared there in mid-1900, Rhodes was in Rhodesia, where he remained until early October. She made no attempt to follow him, but she successfully insinuated herself into circles of political intrigue in Cape Town, where Milner, at least, saw through her. "She is a beast," he informed Sir Philip Lyttelton Gell. "Strange," Milner wrote in a second letter, "how sex enters into these great matters of State. It always has, it always will. It is never recorded, therefore history will never be intelligible. Princess R——," he continued, "works on that tremendously. She is to me . . . the most repulsive animal imaginable. . . . But there is no doubt . . . that she did have . . . (not in any coarse sense) a hold over Rhodes. 100 to 1 she has it over Stead—the most susceptible mortal . . . to the most fleshly type of feminine 'charm.' . . . She is Dangerous." Even so, Milner suggested that her influence would surely weaken once it were widely known that she was a "perfect liar."[22]

Whether out of sympathy or weary reluctance to row openly with a woman, Rhodes let Radziwill back into Groote Schuur occasionally during the last few months of 1900. She drove Rhodes' young male secretaries and associates to distraction and irritated Jameson. Given their displeasure, as well as the earlier warnings from Syfret and Milner, it is a wonder that Rhodes tolerated her return. Yet he never sufficiently feared her, or took her seriously enough, to suppose that he wished to keep her under observation or out of trouble. He refused to help her start *Greater Britain,* a Cape Town weekly of political comment, which she began planning early in 1901 and which carried the same name as a British weekly. (It finally appeared in June and lasted until August.) Shortly thereafter Rhodes and the princess had a major argument—at least Radziwill said that they did. Was it over papers and telegrams that Radziwill had stolen from Rhodes implicating Chamberlain in the Raid? Or were there other incriminating documents? Rhodes banished her from Groote Schuur and his sight forever. That should have been and, in terms of biographical content, was the end of Rhodes' only extended involvement with a woman (and the interaction between them could hardly be described as substantial) since his intellectual flirtation with Olive Schreiner.[23]

But there was a coda. Beginning in June 1901, Radizwill's confidence game began to fail. She started to forge Rhodes' signature to promissory notes and bills. "I knew you had been good to her," Michell warned Rhodes in Rhodesia, "but I doubted your giving her *carte blanche*. . . . My lady appears to be a dangerous character and if she has forged . . . one document, there may be others afloat." Indeed, forgeries of letters from others as well as Rhodes soon appeared. Michell ordered Harry Currey to lock Rhodes' bedroom and Jourdan's secretarial office at Groote Schuur "and keep the keys." "You may say it is none of my business," wrote the prudent banker, "but the parties . . . were likely . . . to be prying around Groote Schuur and laying ungodly hands on your private papers with ulterior motives. The affair is serious." Rhodes' own answer was simple, if belated. "I really think the best course is to make her leave the country as you never know what a criminal woman of her class will do."[24]

In November 1901 Radziwill was arrested and charged with twenty-four counts of fraud and forgery, and released on bail. By the time that she was tried, found guilty, and sentenced to two years in jail, Rhodes was unable to explain why his intuitive appreciation of people's characters had, in this particular case, proved so deficient. He had more enduring problems.

24

"You Like to Put Your House in Order"
The End of the Beginning

"**Y**OU WILL NEVER HAVE another chance," Rhodes told Beit. We should see the world "before we die." It was early 1901, the Anglo-Boer War was "dragging on in an irregular fashion," and, Rhodes predicted, it would do so "for months." Jameson was with him in Cape Town. Beit was in London. "My proposition is that about the end of February you should meet Metcalfe, Jameson and myself at Aden or Cairo and we go to India, China, Japan and America. . . . You must want to see those places before you die." Rhodes certainly did. "Kindly cable me," Rhodes asked. "Please remember there will always be business in your office out of which sovereigns are to be made which requires supervision but the broad point is that you and I have not seen the world, that we should see it before we die and that the four names mentioned, plus bridge of an evening would be a very good party to see the world with and once peace is restored we shall never have another chance."[1]

From his young adulthood, if not even earlier, Rhodes had a yearning both to see and to encompass the world. Egypt had become fashionable by the 1890s. Rhodes went to Cairo first in 1892 and to Luxor and Aswan, up the Nile, in 1893. He saw Florence and its Renaissance galleries in 1893 and the classical ruins of Athens in 1894. He went to Constantinople to see Sultan Abdul Hamid II in 1895. He had been to Paris in 1889, on business, and was in that cultured city several more times. In 1897 he called at the Quai d'Orsay and lectured the French foreign minister. Despite his affinity for emperors, Rhodes toured Rome only in 1896 and 1897. He stopped in Naples in 1897 but omitted a glance at Vesuvius before sailing with Jameson, Beit, James B. Taylor, and others to Marseilles. He came down the east coast of Africa in 1893, and halted in Zanzibar, but all of his other voyages were from the Cape to London direct; he never glimpsed more than the coastline of West Africa, nor much else of East Africa north of Mozambique island.

By the beginning of 1898 Rhodes had traveled widely, often but not invariably with an imperially or commercially related purpose. He was genuinely intrigued by past glories, by the heritage of empire, and the rise and decay of civilizations. Conscious of his own place in the modern imperial saga, he sought examples and instruction from the monuments of earlier eras. Unfortunately, Rhodes' reactions to the contents of the Ufizzi gallery, to the Sphinx and pyramids, to Ottoman Constantinople, or even to Paris, are lost. So are his aesthetic judgments, and his feelings about the sights and smells, food, and people of the unfamiliar places he visited as a gilded, but monoglot, tourist. It is clear that Egypt impressed Rhodes, but what particulars other than waterworks excited and entranced him are imperfectly understood. Nevertheless, the young magnate who in 1883 had first talked about strolling "around the world" and then indulged himself with an orgy of sightseeing after he became prime minister, was doubtless sincere when he implored Beit to join his tour of the globe.[2]

By then, indeed as early as 1898, much of what Rhodes did, including his ruthless quest for renewed political power, was driven by premonitions of early mortality. During his youth his supposed "delicacy," coupled with a vague family history of doubtful health, had given him and his parents the idea that he might be susceptible to afflictions of the lungs. "Delicacy" was a term applied to slim young people of above average height with a history of physical symptoms and anxiety attacks. During Rhodes' youth there had been periods when his health had been considered poor, or it may actually have been poor. Although he was not sent to Africa because of consumption or some other immediate health problem, his family was concerned about his physical condition.

In 1872 his "delicate constitution" necessitated a prolonged period of convalescence following a serious but unspecified heart-related illness. The frequently cited "chill while rowing" incident at the end of his first term at Oxford in 1873 may or may not have occurred. If it did, the illness may have been an autumn virus complicated by grief at his mother's death. Virus infections can cause pericarditis (inflammation of the lining of the sac surrounding the heart), pneumonia, or severe upper respiratory infection with subsequent weakness. If it is true that Dr. Morell Mackenzie told him that he had "not six months to live," then there may have been some physical finding of significance—a cardiac murmur, a friction rub from pericarditis, or abnormal chest sounds (rales) from pneumonia.[3]

In 1872, only the classic quartet of physical diagnosis was available: inspection, palpation, percussion, and auscultation. Listening to the heart was direct—the experienced ear applied to the chest—and then indirect, by means of the stethoscope, the diagnostic usefulness of which had been described in 1819 by its inventor, René-Théophile-Hyacinthe Laënnec. By the 1870s stethoscopes were an accepted part of the evaluation of the heart. Routine measurement of blood pressure came only after the turn of the twentieth century. A crude sphygmomanometer, which for the first time could measure the blood pressure without breaking the skin, was invented by Samuel Siegfried von Basch in 1876. It was refined in 1896 by Scipione Riva-Rocci, but modern measurements of both systolic and diastolic pressure were not possible until the work of Nikolai Korotkoff in 1905. The electrocardiogram was developed only in 1903 by Willem Einthoven.

Without the results of these procedures, access to original clinical records, or even a complete autopsy report, a confident diagnosis of Rhodes' physical history is impossible. However, the evidence of admittedly sketchy, anecdotal accounts from his associates, his life course, and the autopsy material which is available is sufficient to develop a set of possible hypotheses to explain the health problems which plagued him for so many years and which finally overcame even his extraordinary will to achieve and to persist. Given his gargantuan appetite for food and drink, the extraordinary extent to which he was poisoned daily by nicotine, and his regular acquaintance with stress, it is a wonder that someone with a "dickey" heart survived for so long, and remained busy almost until the very end.

Photographs and paintings from his last few years show a bloated, jowly, ponderous man of great age and girth. The slim youth of the 1870s and the trim young adult of the 1880s had been succeeded in the early 1890s by a large-headed man of imposing stature, always described as massive or big. The Raid took its toll, doubtless on his heart and visibly on his outward appearance. Olive Schreiner, who had loved him in the early 1890s, saw him on shipboard and in Britain in early 1897 and then again in August 1898. "Yesterday evening as Cron & I were driving home in our little trap from Kimberley," she wrote of a tour with her husband, "we passed a cart full of people from Barkly, they bowed to me, & though I didn't recognize him I noticed a fat man take off his hat & bow very markedly." After they had gone "it flashed" that "it was Rhodes!!!" "He has changed tremendously since I saw him in England. Such a miserable bloated heavy face."[4]

Within a year someone had introduced Rhodes to bridge (actually bridge whist), a precursor of both auction and contract bridge. "I am learning the mysteries of Bridge," Rhodes confessed to Lady Randolph Churchill in 1899. "Even with shilling points am only thirty shillings to the bad. I quite see that it is an assured income to a thinking player. Of course the annoyance—I would say amusement—is playing badly and seeing your partner's face; it sometimes changes their manners." Jourdan, certainly not an expert or impartial witness, blames bridge—of all things—for accelerating Rhodes' physical deterioration. "It entirely changed his habits," said Jourdan. "Many said that bridge was good for him, that it was his Recreation, and served to rest his brain and take his mind off other matters." Jourdan recalled, however, that Rhodes "derived no benefit from sitting in a smoky atmosphere—sometimes till the early hours." Before taking up bridge, Rhodes rode morning and night, and at least took that kind of exercise. But as Rhodes grew "passionately fond of bridge," which he began playing regularly every night, so he rose later in the morning, missing his rides. "Sometimes days passed when he did not ride at all." From that

time on, Jourdan claimed, Rhodes' heart "began to trouble him more frequently." Physically, he became "quite a different man." In the latter half of
1899 he began to leave his room only at breakfast time. "Sometimes his face
appeared swollen and had a bluish hue."[5] Or could Rhodes' new sedentary
passion be better explained by his increasing cardiac difficulties?

Rhodes had been conscious of his heart since the 1870s, when he became
aware that it was his heart and not his lungs that were affected. But it was
only in the late 1890s when he confessed to Grey and Michell that his heart
would prove his undoing. He also worried with Garrett. Rhodes and Garrett
were alone one evening at Groote Schuur in the late 1890s. Suddenly the
great man yanked up the sleeve on his right arm, and rested his hand palm
upwards. "'Look there,'" he commanded. Garrett looked at Rhodes' wrist.
"Where a doctor feels one's pulse, there stood out . . . a knot, and as the
artery pumped and laboured one could count the throbs by the eye, without
laying a finger there." Rhodes told Garrett that what they saw was not simply
an errant pulse. They were glimpsing his "'heart.'"[6] The allusions to finality
and doom in his speeches and letters become more and more prominent as
Rhodes, having thus far escaped the scenes of judgment that Olive Schreiner
had sketched much earlier, and avoided punishment from his peers in the
British and the Cape parliaments, gradually reconciled himself to an abbreviated life. Even so, until the very end, Rhodes believed that he would be
spared for several more years, not just one or two. The rapidity of his demise
took him and his world by surprise.

Rhodes expressed unmistakable anxiety about the numbering of his days
from the opening of 1898, although many earlier intimations can also be discovered. Will Stuart, who as a teenager had the run of Groote Schuur in the
late 1890s, remembered being twice alone on the mountain with Rhodes, and
"once in the bird cages of his zoo when he had been trying to catch a crow,"
when the Founder was prostrated by attacks and "lay down like a very drunken
man."[7] He had suffered a heart attack of some kind in Bulawayo in June or
July 1897, and a much more serious attack in November, when he was at his
Inyanga estate for three months. While Jameson was away arranging the construction of the trans-continental telegraph line from Umtali to Tete and buying goats and cattle, Rhodes "started ailing." Le Sueur at first assumed that it
was "a mere attack of fever," but Rhodes "got worse and worse. . . . [He]
did not take much care of himself either, but would lie under the blankets
until in a bath of perspiration, then jump up, strip himself stark naked, and
expose himself to the draught from door and window. He would not allow us
to send for a doctor, saying that when Jameson arrived he would be all right."
Finally, however, Le Sueur sent an emissary to fetch a physician from Umtali.
Two days later that doctor arrived, administered doses of digitalis, and Rhodes
"was soon on the way to recovery." Rhodes instructed Le Sueur to "get a
supply." "That's the stuff," he said with pleasure. This episode probably began with a recurrence of malaria (accounting for the sudden high fever), which
tipped him into cardiac decompensation. His heart, unable to keep up with

the stress imposed by the increased metabolic demands of the fever, began to fail. Or the fever might have precipitated cardiac irregularity—atrial fibrillation. Either condition would have been improved by the administration of digitalis. A few weeks later Rhodes informed Grey that his heart was better, "but like the coffin of the Egyptian feast [it] warns me that we are mortal."

In March 1898, Rhodes supposed that he would survive for five more years or so, but that dying while he was still young was probable. "The temporary nature of human life is very depressing," he told his lawyer in May. Rhodes feared that "some hidden devil may whip me off before my worldly depositions are signed." During the tumultuous political campaign of that year he boasted that his public life was "only just beginning." It was not yet "over." "It cannot be over. I must go on. . . ." Even so, he admitted that his life was but "a temporary one." Rhodes was preparing himself, more than his largely unconcerned constituents, for an early end. He could foresee it with greater prescience than any of his associates or acolytes.[8]

After parliament recessed at the very end of 1898, Rhodes sailed for London, and then briefly went back to Egypt. After seeing King Léopold in Brussels in February, he visited Kaiser Wilhelm in Berlin in March, recording nothing himself about either city. According to Wilhelm, however, Rhodes "admired" Berlin and its "tremendous industrial plants," which he visited "daily." He returned to London in April for railway finance negotiations and his tense arguments with the London board of De Beers. Addressing its crowded annual meeting in May, he began his long speech very curiously but, given the worries about his heart, understandably: ". . .the most unhappy thing in the world is for a public man to make a speech, especially the night and day beforehand. The only simile I can think of would be, perhaps, the night and morning of one of our forefathers just before he went to a state execution." After receiving his honorary degree at Oxford in June, he returned to the Cape and to the platform. He reminded an audience in the drill hall that "we do get older" and time tends to progress. Time was a terrible thing. "You can conquer anything . . . even raids, but time you can never interfere with. . . ."[9]

During the siege of Kimberley, Rhodes suffered another heart attack of some kind. He again fell off his horse, and was sufficiently worried by chest pains and shortness of breath that he sailed to London in March 1900, largely if not exclusively to consult Fowler. It is not known what Fowler, a chest specialist, told him, and whether or not Fowler gave him reassurances or further causes for anxiety. But he was advised that rest would help. His return to the Cape was thus brief. Anxious both to avoid stress and to examine his colony of Rhodesia with some care, he sailed in haste for Beira. If his name were to live on and his deeds be celebrated after his own departure from life, Rhodesia must prosper and grow strong. Rhodes sought those reconfirmations during a five-month trek by horse and mule-wagon from Umtali to Melsetter, Salisbury, Bulawayo, and Gwanda. He loved the "nature and the simple life" which he and his party led on the open veld as they moved from town to town across the highlands of the future Zimbabwe. It was a time for the conscious renewal of his own soul as well as a further first-hand analysis of Rhodesia's prospects.[10]

Rhodes had traveled, but he had done so restfully. After returning by train to Kimberley from the north, and addressing the South African League in Cape Town, he continued to take it easy, both at Groote Schuur and, increasingly, at Kalk Bay, below Muizenberg on the warm waters of False Bay. "Rhodes is doing nothing in particular," Edward Ridge Syfret reported matter-of-factly in late November. Such a laconic entry about another's life would occasion no comment. But for Rhodes to be so described, even at the end of 1900, indicates both the extent to which the grinding on of the Anglo-Boer War had driven him into watchful inactivity and the intensifying nature of his infirmity. Furthermore, he experienced more "fever" in November, probably the result of recurring malaria. He was affected for several weeks. It was a period, too, when Princess Radziwill was chasing him again. Rhodes tried to avoid her, either fleeing to his bedroom or escaping on his horse to houses nearby when he saw her trap coming up the drive at Groote Schuur. Sometimes they quarreled, and Radziwill reports that he was once sufficiently angry to smash furniture.[11]

Rhodes was restless. When he implored Beit to travel the world with him he was still unable to leave Cape Town. Boer irregulars were within 150 miles of the city, having succeeded in menacing the towns and villages of the western Cape. He had his fruit farms, the dynamite factory, the cold storage facilities, the production of diamonds, and a network of other business activities to supervise, and an editor of the *Cape Times* to choose, but taking his "last chance" to see the important nations of the Far East and the Western Hemisphere was still possible. Although he still expected to run the Cape again— "'It may sound conceited but I will be Prime Minister of this Colony again before very long'"—South Africa was still embroiled in war and not yet ready to be transformed politically along Rhodes' lines, and at his direction. He therefore could have continued to delegate to others the amassing of more and more sovereigns, and could have sailed to the east. At the end of February, Rhodes still planned to travel the world but, in fact, never did. Was he deterred by the potential unavailability of both Beit and Jameson, now an elected member of parliament? Or—ultimately—did he distrust his heart? As he told the Anglican archbishop of Cape Town, he was still not quite himself. His physicians had instructed him to "keep quiet."[12]

Instead of touring, Rhodes continued to contemplate the most noble uses for his wealth. He had begun doing so in 1877, with the "Confession of Faith" and the second will that accompanied it. At no moment thereafter had he ever ceased wondering how his riches could best be devoted to mankind's enrichment and to the perpetuation of his own visions and ideals. In 1898, after a friend's death, he wrote that it was a "pity you cannot carry your wealth to next world. The moral is spend some on public objects in this one." Rhodes did so, also regretting that occupying oneself with politics hindered the amassing of great riches. "I should have liked to take more," he told De

Beers' shareholders in 1899, "but during the last ten years I have devoted my mind to politics, and politics and the accumulating of money do not run together."

In fact, living as he did in an age that may have welcomed but hardly encouraged giving by the rich, Rhodes proved unusual. He helped individuals, hospitals, and missions, and liked to do all manner of good works. He was never mean and often indulged in gestures of kindness which were both clever and unexpected. In 1897, for example, he planted 100 orange trees around the official government residence in Bulawayo, dedicating 10 percent of the fruit of the trees to the patients of a local mission hospital. He called such tithing of the tree's product a "servitude." "Naturally," he wrote, "it will be several years before the trees make any return but time passes very speedily and I think the idea is a good one and may be adopted by others." He apparently learned that the Pharaonic Egyptians had dedicated trees and gardens for the support of their temples. "I venture to say there is no better Temple than that over which you preside," he wrote to Mother Jacoba Zirn. "If you obtain as I hope a servitude over many homes it will be a pleasure to think that it is due to a passing thought." [13]

Rhodes wished most of all to perfect his place in posterity. "I find I am human and should like to be living after my death," he told Stead in 1891. An undated note in Rhodes' hand further made it plain that Rhodes wanted to "leave a monument to posterity which shall convince mankind that [he] had really lived." Rhodes' success in diamonds and gold, his stock manipulations, and his other financial adventures would make that possible. He worried that his works were "perishable" and that time would destroy them. "My discoveries too will be found fault with," he said. Rhodes' second will would have expended his then slim but not inconsiderable assets on the establishment of a secret society. That Masonic-, Jesuit-like entity would have had as its object the extension of British rule and emigration throughout the globe, the reattachment of the United States to the empire, and the "foundation of so great a power as to . . . render wars impossible and promote the best interests of humanity." A third will, of 1882, left everything to Neville Pickering, but indicated that Rhodes' young friend should nevertheless attempt to carry out the designs of the second will. After Pickering died, a fourth will put his money and his plans into the care of Lord Rothschild. [14]

By the time that Rhodes drafted his fifth will in 1891, De Beers had been amalgamated and Gold Fields had timed its sales well and invested wisely. Rhodes possessed a growing fortune. He still spun elaborate plans for a secret order of helpers—a band of brothers—mystically joined by ritual bonds. But his mind construed its realization in a more practical direction. His sixth and seventh wills, of 1892 and 1893, focused for the first time on another of his ruling passions—the education of young colonials. Out of the visionary crucible of idealistic fraternity came plans to acculturate callow sons of settlers by establishing Oxford-like institutions in South Africa and then sending them home to the mother country to be tutored properly. Even if Rhodes himself had played more than studied at Oxford, he had come in his middle years to revere its atmosphere and its passion for learning as much as he had once praised the contacts with Britain's ruling class that could come through years spent beneath its dreaming spires.[15] The sixth and seventh wills would have expended a portion of Rhodes' estate on the founding in Cape Town of a residential college on the Oxford and Cambridge model. They added scholarships specifically to Oxford, initially for South Africans only, and then for whites from the older parts of the empire.

Rhodes almost certainly derived his ideas for these scholarships from J. Astley Cooper, editor of the London weekly *Greater Britain,* and Professor Sir Thomas Hudson Beare, a South Australian engineer who held chairs at University College, London, and the University of Edinburgh. Cooper, another of Rhodes' many contacts who was an active homosexual, introduced his scheme for a "Pan-Britannic contest of our social pursuits" in a July 1891 issue of *Greater Britain* and elaborated upon it in a long letter to *The Times* in late October. He advocated a "periodical gathering of representatives of the [English] race in a festival and contest of industry, athletics, and culture." Cooper wished by these means to increase "the good will and the good understanding of the Empire. . ." and to strengthen the "family bonds between the United States and the Empire. . . ." He suggested the awarding of "national scholarships" throughout the Empire, based on examinations held simultaneously in its major capitals. Cooper envisaged sixteen such annual scholarships worth £200 each, or £80,000 a year, and tenable in Britain. Competition for them would "encourage intellectual attainments in the colonies and tend to discourage growing materialism there." Stead urged a provision for the Americans, but Cooper could not immediately understand how they might be included. On 15 November 1891, *Greater Britain* carried Cooper's "The Proposed Periodic Britannic Contest and all-English Speaking Festival," which added to his proposal. "I suggest the foundation of national or Imperial scholarships (there are none in existence yet)," wrote Cooper. He envisaged that the endowment for this scholarship scheme would come from the "Mother Country." He suggested that proficiency in athletics be a factor in choosing scholars since "the future relationship of the various portions of the Empire rests chiefly in the hands of the young men of the Empire. . . ." A month later Beare added modifications to Cooper's scheme; he thought that they should be called "British Scholarships."

Cooper and Beare distinctly wanted to strengthen "those invisible ties, stronger than any which can be devised by the cunning of law-makers, which will keep together, for good or ill, the Anglo-Saxon race." This was a splendid expression of Rhodes' own as yet underdeveloped philosophical and theological leanings. Moreover, in his very first article Cooper suggested that "in the life of every individual there comes a time when a sufficiency of this world's goods are attained; when the man, having no longer a necessity to work unceasingly for a living, looks round for further interests upon which to spend his leisure and his gold." Rhodes would have taken this message to heart,

coupled as it was with a plea by Cooper for the British nation to "brace ourselves to actions for the benefit of mankind. . . ." Since Cooper was an ally
of Stead, Rhodes doubtless learned of these ideas from and was probably
given the various articles by his then close confidant.[16]

Throughout the ensuing decade Rhodes thought more and more about
this educational "big idea." He became persuaded that the creation of a widespread band of brothers and the unification of the empire's possessions could
best be achieved through a single scholarship scheme tenable at only the oldest and largest of the universities of the English-speaking world. The problem
with expending his funds solely on a South African college, Rhodes told
Hawksley, his solicitor, was that doing so would discourage South Africans
from attending British universities and thus promote "separation" from the
mother country. Instead, South Africans should go to Oxford for three years,
and be handsomely kept and rewarded while they were there. "The conditions for election," the Founder decided in 1893, "should not only be for
literary attainments but also . . . [for] character and social qualities . . . especially being moderately fond of field sports say cricket and football. I do
not want simply 'bookworms,' " he wrote from Aden. "You might put it in the
will that I consider such a course of great advantage to young colonists for
giving breadth to their views . . . and for the instilling into their minds the
advantages of the colonies as well as to England of the retention of the Unity
of the Empire."

Rhodes favored the Oxford residential system. "I think it most disastrous
that young fellows should at the most critical period of their lives be left without supervision it leads to the ruin of many especially young colonists from
abroad who have no family circles . . . to . . . check . . . free living and
dissipation." Rhodes liked the University of Edinburgh medical school, where
David Livingstone and Leander Jameson had matriculated, but refrained from
including it in his will; Edinburgh lacked the residential system.

Three yearly scholarships were set aside for South Africans, two for Canadians, one each for the six colonies of Australia and Tasmania, and one for
New Zealand. The scholarships were all to be drawn from national universities. In South Africa two were allocated to South African College (the forerunner of the University of Cape Town) and one for Stellenbosch College
(the precursor of the university of the same name); the students of the latter
were of Dutch descent and Rhodes wished specifically in 1893 to "shew no
distinction as to race." At Oxford, Rhodes wanted the successful candidates
to choose any of the colleges. He deemed it a mistake "for them to crowd
together at one college they would get too local they should be spread through
the University." He wanted them to have a yearly dinner "to compare and
celebrate their successes in the schools and in field sports."[17]

Rhodes' intent, at least in 1893, was to create "a monument more durable
than bronze/taller than the majestic design of the pyramids, which neither
rain can wash away nor the north wind's impotent cage bring down/nor the
innumerable sequence of centuries and the sheer passing of time." In a post-

script to his will of 8 September 1893 he quoted (not completely accurately) one of the odes of Horace that he had read in Latin in school. He then determined, following Horace, to strive to ensure that not all of himself should perish (non omnis moriar).

The same postscript further explained that his belief continued to be that "the active working of the soul in pursuit of the higher object is a complete life." Although he considered that he had "dismally failed" in achieving such a goal, for him the "highest object" had continued to be the "greatness" of his country, that is, Britain. "I expressly hope," he went on piously, "that the colonies and the mother country may never separate." He declared that "permanent union" meant the "permanent peace" of the world. Rhodes had earlier sought to join the House of Commons to the Congress of the United States. Once accomplished, "the peace of the world would," he imagined, "be secured for all eternity." His was an Anglo-American scheme to "take the government of the whole world." In the enthusiasm of perpetual boyhood, he had discovered "an idea which leads to the cessation of all wars and one language throughout the world." He dreamed of a federal union which would bring the United States back under Britain's aegis. Certainly this mystical search for union was a passion which Rhodes communicated throughout the 1890s to persons with whom he thought he could entrust his secret hopes. The Countess of Warwick, a great pursuer of causes and men, began to understand "everything" in 1898. After a talk with the irrepressible Stead, she agreed to be "a silent worker for the cause." She knew Rhodes' mission to be the reunion and reconsolidation of the English-speaking universe so as to improve the world.[18]

Rhodes made wills comparatively frequently. But there was an unusual hiatus during the 1890s in the written discussion of how his life and ideals would best be commemorated. Only in 1898, while pondering his scholarship scheme during a voyage back to the Cape from Britain, did he hit upon the key qualification. " 'Great consideration,' " he wrote from Madeira, should " 'be given to those who have shewn during their school days that they have instincts to lead and . . . which . . . will be likely in after life to guide them to esteem the performance of public duties as their highest aim.' " "The last thing" Rhodes said that he wanted was "a book worm." "I do not think you will beat the above the thought came from the sea."[19]

The will that created the magnificent scholarships bearing the Founder's name was his eighth, signed as Rhodes was about to embark on another voyage back to the Cape in mid-1899. It drew in large part on the seventh. He had just completed the financing of the first sections of his Cape to Cairo railway, received an honorary doctorate at Oxford, and been fêted at his old college (which received a bequest of £100,000). The first fifteen clauses of the will dispose of his real properties in particular ways, for example, giving Groote Schuur to the government of a future federal South Africa as a residence for its prime ministers. Clause sixteen explains that since educating young colonists at Oxford would give "breadth to their views for their instruction in life and manners and for instilling into their minds the advantages to the Colonies as well as to the United Kingdom of the retention of the unity of the Empire," Rhodes directed his trustees to establish "Colonial Scholarships" for "male students." He emphasized the advantages of a residential system and the need for Americans to be brought under the umbrella of his imperially unifying idea. He detailed the number of scholarships to be awarded from each colony each year, adding three for Rhodesia, distributing the South African ones to named secondary schools in the Cape and to Natal, and including the provinces and colonies of Australia and Canada (but omitting the province of Nova Scotia, about which he was presumably ignorant), Jamaica, and Bermuda. The American scholarships were specifically allocated to each of the then-present states and territories of the United States.

Rhodes repeated his qualifications: no bookworms (no Latin and Greek "swots"). Due regard, however, was to be paid in choosing scholars to their literary and scholastic attainments, their "smug" as he called it; their "fondness of and success in manly outdoor sports," their "brutality," he said; their qualities of "manhood truth courage devotion to duty sympathy for and protection of the weak kindliness unselfishness and fellowship," what he deprecatingly called their "unctuous rectitude," and their demonstration during their schooldays of "moral force of character and of instincts to lead and to take an interest in [their] schoolmates," in his summation, their "tact." Such attributes would be likely, Rhodes still believed, "in afterlife" to guide them to "esteem the performance of public duties" as their highest aim.

In settling on these qualities for his scholars, Rhodes was influenced by discussions in 1899 and earlier with Stead and Hawksley. Rhodes and Hawksley drew, Stead reported, on their memories of their own schooldays. As a result, Hawksley insisted that the scholars should share a knowledge of Greek, Roman, and English history. Stead thought that moral qualities of leadership should prove of equal value in the selection of recipients. Rhodes accepted that suggestion, but Hawksley reproached him for "being always ready to make a deal," even over his future scholars.

Rhodes had only men in mind. A posthumous explanation by Stead, who was close to his ideas, confirms that women were never believed to be fit for consideration as scholars. "He refused to open this scholarship to women." Rhodes furthermore suggested the proportions which ideal candidates should attain: four-tenths for scholarship, two-tenths for athletics, two-tenths for manhood, etc., and two-tenths for leadership. Rhodes subsequently continued to ponder both the attributes that he wished his scholars to demonstrate and the way those attributes were to be rated. In late 1901 he decided that literary abilities should count three-tenths and that moral force of character should be lifted from two-tenths to three-tenths. However, Rhodes never specifically envisaged the kind of interviews by committee which subsequently became standard for the selection of scholars. Indeed, he originally wanted the votes of classmates to be cast for potential winners.

Clause twenty-four of the will specified that no student should be qualified or disqualified on account of religion or race. Rhodes was thinking of the English-Dutch division, not of overcoming color bars. He again indicated that his scholars should be distributed throughout the Oxford college system. Clause thirty-four ordered an annual dinner. A codicil in 1901 added five scholarships for Germans because Kaiser Wilhelm had made instruction in English compulsory in German schools, and because Rhodes liked Wilhelm. Perhaps Rhodes also favored the Teutonic idea of an eventual union of the white Anglo-Saxon entities (including Germany). If so, there is no direct evidence for such an assumption.

In a note to Hawksley that immediately followed the drafting of the final will, Rhodes indicated that he had not completely discarded his earlier notion that men in imperial holy orders should propagate the faith of Britain's dominions. After completing their Oxford years he wanted the best of his scholars to be distributed around the globe "to maintain the Imperial thought." He favored unmarried men for this purpose "as the consideration of babies and other domestic agenda generally destroys higher thought. Please understand I am in no sense a woman hater but this particular business is better untrammelled with material thought." Later he told Grey to use the excess income from his estate to encourage the emigration of "our people, women especially, to Africa." "We shall never be safe . . . until we occupy the soil equally with the Dutch," he said. To an editorial writer on the *Daily Telegraph,* Rhodes suggested that the gravity of the potential postwar problems in South Africa should be "brought home" to the British public. Since "our whole future in Africa" depended upon a "proper land settlement," it was crucial that English-speakers be interspersed with Boers when Britain's 20,000 Dutch-speaking prisoners of war were returned to their farms after a settlement. "Unless we mix our people with them on the soil I say 'look out.'" Furthermore, Rhodes hinted to both Hawksley and Grey that some of his funds could be spent on the formation of an imperially oriented political party or interest groups within the existing British political parties. Or, as Merriman attempted to explain, "Rhodes left the residue of his vast estate for political purposes, unnamed. . . . It is no doubt an attempt to realize some of Rhodes's crazy maunderings to . . . Stead about an order of millionaires on the basis of the Jesuits!" [20]

Michell persuaded Rhodes to experiment with a mini-version of his scholarship scheme when he was still alive, and not merely to let the force of his ideas guide the eventual trustees. In 1901, when he might have been sailing to Aden to join Beit, but was instead confined to Cape Town by his doctors, Rhodes established a single scholarship for graduates of the Diocesan College School in Rondebosch, at the foot of Groote Schuur. Those selected would go to Oxford for three years. Giving prizes for literary attainments encouraged bookworms; therefore, he instructed that the Diocesan College grantees should, now in the proportions listed as two-fifths for the first and one-fifth for each of the others, possess the same ranges of gifts as those detailed in his main will. Fellow students would decide the marks of the various candidates for "athletics" and "manhood," the middle two criteria, "scholarship" to be decided by examination and "leadership" by the College's headmaster. "I do not know whether your governing body will accept this rather complicated scholarship," Rhodes wrote to the archbishop of Cape Town, "but it is an effort to change the dull monotony of modern competition. There must have been some pleasure in viewing the contests in the gymnasium, say, at Athens." Under the usual modern system of competitive examinations, he asked, "do we . . . get the best man for the World's fight?" "I think not," he answered. After the experiment had been running for a year and the first scholar chosen, the Founder commented to the prelate, "Who knows," his experiment might "be the grain of mustard seed which produces the largest tree."[21]

Rhodes began to put the rest of his house in order. From March to May 1901 he lived again in Kimberley, supervising the affairs of De Beers and resting. "My heart is dickey," he wrote to Milner early in May, "so you like to put your house in order." Nevertheless, and despite the possibility of attacks by Boer marauders, he took the train to Bulawayo and, in June, gave a significant speech about the future of his creation. Rule by the British South Africa Company, he reminded the settlers, was but a transient phenomenon. In being "purely temporary," it echoed his own predicament. Self-government was coming. Moreover, he wished the settlers to get their house in order, to be ready (which they never were) to enter the federation of southern Africa which he hoped would follow the conclusion of the Anglo-Boer war. "This great dominant North—including the Transvaal, will dictate the federation."[22] He also spoke of the mausoleum he planned for himself and others of Rhodesia's fallen in the Matopos.

In late June, Rhodes returned briefly to Kimberley, traveled to Cape Town, and began planning the construction of a new house at St. James near Muizenberg. He spent a day at Groote Schuur before sailing in July for Britain, where he dealt with the business of De Beers and the Chartered Company, saw Beit and Milner, and appeared before King Edward VII to be inducted again into the Privy Council. But Rhodes' most important appointment was with Fowler, whose records, alas, have not survived. Rhodes' heart was very weak. "At any rate," he supposedly asked Jameson, "death from the heart is clean and quick; there is nothing repulsive or lingering about it; it is a clean death, isn't it?" Fowler recommended a long rest and, in keeping with the practice of the times, a constant change of surroundings.

Rhodes rented a luxurious lodge near Loch Rannoch in northern Perthshire for August and September, during grouse shooting season. There he surrounded himself with his cronies—Jameson, Metcalfe, the Maguires, and Jourdan. Ernest Rhodes took an adjoining estate. Beit and Grey visited. So did Gardner Williams and Robert Williams, the Countess of Warwick, Abe Bailey, and Winston S. Churchill, then twenty-seven, who sixty years later remembered a holiday spent riding ponies, carrying guns, and engaged "in various affairs, nominally sporting." Rhodes, reported Jourdan, enjoyed shooting grouse. "He was always very keen on getting a good bag." "He revelled in the open life, and loved having his lunch on the heather, where he was always in good spirits and forgot all about his heart trouble."

Frances Evelyn Maynard, the slim, fair, poised, captivating young woman who had become the Countess of Warwick and moved easily among the politically and imperially active, remembered a Rhodes who was too ill at Rannoch to join his own shooting or fishing parties. She spent a week with him. When the others went out after grouse she and Rhodes mounted hill ponies and trotted along the moors. "There we would dismount," she wrote romantically, "and let the ponies wander, while we sat and talked, he telling me of all his wonderful ideas, while before us stretched the beautiful Loch, and the heather-covered hills beyond glowed and deepened with sunshine or cloud." He told her about the scholarship scheme—"his aim being to build up Citizens of the Empire." He spoke of the empire, "which seemed much nearer to him than his own daily existence." He spoke of it "where another man would have talked of his family life, or his own predilections."

Warwick accused Rhodes of being a dreamer. " 'It is the dreamers that move the world!' " he retorted. "'Practical men are so busy being practical that they cannot see beyond their own lifetime. Dreamers and visionaries have made civilizations. It is trying to do the things that cannot be done that makes life worth while. The dream of today becomes the custom of to-morrow. But if there had been no dream . . . we should still be living in caves, clubbing each other to death for a mouthful of food."

Warwick asked Rhodes whether he had ever been happy. " 'I am happy when I am planning and dreaming of things that can never come to pass in my lifetime,' " he allegedly replied. But had he ever been happy "with things just as they were?" Rhodes "shook his leonine head vigorously," reported the countess. " 'No . . . I was too busy when I was young. . . . I have had no time since.' "

William Bramwell Booth had asked Rhodes the same question in 1898 when they traveled together in a railway carriage to London after a moving day at the Salvation Army's Land Colony for Men in Hadleigh. "I shall never forget," Booth wrote, "how he threw himself back against the cushions of that first-class compartment, gripped the arm of the seat, and [tensely] . . . looked at me with that extraordinary stare of his. . . . 'Happy? I—happy? Good God, no!' " He went on to say that he would " 'give all I possess to believe. . . .' "

At the end of their talks Lady Warwick would catch the ponies and bring the one that Rhodes was riding near some large boulder so that he might mount with ease. "The slightest exertion made him breathless." Even so, he would say, in a "touching, child-like way . . . that he was sure that God would not let him die before he had done his work. . ."—bringing the union of southern Africa into being.[23]

From Perthshire, Rhodes traveled by chauffeured automobile with Beit, Jameson, Metcalfe, and Jourdan to Paris and Lucerne, and then into Italy. The saline baths of Salsomaggiore, near Fidenza, were supposed to be beneficial for inflammatory disorders, so Rhodes spent a week there in unhappy idleness. The sight of so many of the sick depressed him. The party went on to Bologna, Verona, and Venice. Toward the end of November, the tight little group, minus Beit, who refused to go any further, sailed from Brindisi to Port Said. Near Cairo, Rhodes revisited the great pyramids of Giza and then boarded one of Thomas Cook & Son's large river sailing vessels for another voyage up the mighty Nile. "I am better," Rhodes wrote to Michell. "The heart has quieted down, though I still have pain, which they say is the enlarged heart pressing on the lung. The great thing is to rest."

As he sailed upstream Rhodes renewed his fascination with the irrigation works along the river. But he was even more entranced by the details of the construction of the first Aswan dam, then growing more and more massive. (He sent a flurry of instructions to McDonald about his own, much smaller dam in the Matopos.) The original Aswan dam, completed in 1902 at the first cataract, was built of red granite. It stood 177 feet high and was one and a quarter miles wide. Its reservoir was nearly 200 miles long, although Rhodes would have seen a smaller lake. As much as 1500 tons of water a second could be released for irrigation purposes. "His great delight was to lie all day at the barrage in the grass under the shade of trees and rest."

Jourdan recalled a "most enjoyable" time on the river, with short excursions to places of interest and bridge in the evening. Yet of Rhodes' reactions to the Temples of Isis and Ramses, for example, the record is silent. For Dicey, who traveled in Egypt with Rhodes in the 1890s, it was indeed clear that the Founder had little interest in "relics of bygone grandeur." It was Rhodes' nature to "live in the present rather than in the past." The aspect of Egypt which interested him most, according to Dicey, was "the marvellous productive power of the . . . annual Nile flood. . . ." Fascinated by the possibilities of irrigation in southern Africa, he was far more entranced by the dam at Aswan and the barrage below Cairo than by Egypt's history. Dicey, a prominent journalist and the brother of the eminent law don at Oxford who had opposed Rhodes' honorary degree, had earlier edited *The Observer*.

In 1901, Rhodes planned to sail upriver until Wadi Halfa, at the second cataract, and then to proceed by train along Kitchener's rail tracks to Khartoum, capital of the recently reconquered Anglo-Egyptian Sudan. But Jameson vetoed this idea. He feared that the unrelieved heat of the upper Nile region would strain Rhodes unduly.[24]

Le Sueur remembered meeting Rhodes' ship when it arrived in London during the first week of 1902. "His face was bloated, almost swollen, and he was livid with a purple tinge in his face, and I realized that he was very ill indeed." This description is consistent with a superior vena cava syndrome, which was to be a major contributing cause of Rhodes' death. Two months later, while he lay mortally sick in South Africa, there were daily cables from Jameson to Hawksley, who then showed them to Fowler. The cables were transmitted in cipher to prevent the stock market from being adversely affected by Rhodes' illness. From the more than fifty secret cables it is clear that his doctors diagnosed the compression of Rhodes' vena cava by a large aneurysm (confirmed at autopsy) of the thoracic aorta, the major vessel carrying fresh blood from the heart. It arches over and then down behind the heart toward the abdomen and legs. The aneurysm, a large swelling of the vessel, created a blood filled sac, "the size of a child's head," which pressed on the superior vena cava, the great vein which returns blood from the head, neck, chest and arms. The result was backup of blood in all of the tributary veins, with congestion and swelling of his head and face and purpling of his skin. The aneurysm also pressed upon his trachea and lungs and caused him difficulty in breathing. The cables refer to Rhodes' "air hunger."

Despite these terrible problems, Rhodes had sufficient strength of will to negotiate the purchase of Dalham Hall, six miles from Newmarket, north of Cambridge, where there were cool breezes and where he hoped to recover his strength or at least endure the growing pains in his chest and heart. He paid about £103,000. It was to be a home for his family as well. After learning about the new estate, Bernard Rhodes, a younger brother, said that it would want eleven gardeners. "If your poor pa could see us," he wrote. In a codicil to his will Rhodes left Dalham to his brother Frank and then to his brother Ernest. But he specifically objected to expectant heirs developing into "loafers." The "strength of England" had been ruined by weak-kneed hereditary idlers. Therefore, Rhodes directed that no one could inherit Dalham Hall who had not for at least ten consecutive years engaged in a profession or business (and not the army), or was not so occupied within one year of gaining control over the estate.[25] Rhodes was concerned to the end of his days about wasting his earnings on descendants who were layabouts. Life was too precious and activity too prized.

Rhodes meanwhile decided to return to Africa to "face the music." Rather than depress the price of shares in his companies by pleading illness, he chose, despite the advice of Jameson and all of his associates, to travel back to the Cape to give evidence against Princess Radziwill. He could have sent a deposition. But Hawksley had advised against it, not much liking "the idea of sending medical evidence and suggesting that [Rhodes] should be examined and cross-examined on this side before a . . . commissioner. . . ." Rhodes also wanted to be there to prevent new rumors and to testify against otherwise incriminating letters and documents that Radziwill might forge on the eve of the trial. Hawksley cabled to Michell that the trial "must not be held without Rhodes' evidence."[26] Rhodes' reputation was in jeopardy. He may also have wanted to see the Cape one last time.

When Rhodes sailed south in January a bed was rigged up for him on the upper deck; he could not breathe in his cabin. The voyage was ostensibly uneventful, but at least once he was tossed out of his makeshift bed onto the deck. Another time he tumbled from his cabin berth. Rhodes was hardly robust by the time he arrived back in his adopted land.

Although Rhodes visited Groote Schuur during the day, he chose to spend all of his February evenings in Muizenberg, where the cool breezes might blow off False Bay. At first he drove nearly every day to Cape Town in his new automobile (having been entranced by Metcalfe's own motorcar when they had all been together in Scotland). There he testified in the Radziwill case. He also led a large deputation of members of parliament to see Sprigg about the costs of militarily defending the Cape. "Really I was shocked to see him," Innes told his wife. "He has become stouter, and his face is a deep red and half again as big as it was when I saw him last. His breath also is very short. I understand that his heart is so dilated that it presses upon one lung, and that accounts for the flushed face and laboured breath. . . . He really is a pathetic spectacle. . . ."[27] Rhodes' final journey into the great city at the foot of Table Mountain took place on the very last day of February, when, while again giving evidence, he munched sandwiches in the court house as he had once chomped his way through similar fodder before the South Africa Committee of the House of Commons.

Rhodes spent his last month in the tiny cottage by the sea that he had earlier used in 1900. There he fought for each breath, as his failing heart "thumped" tremendously. Jameson let ice boxes into the ceiling and ordered Indian-type punkah fans to be kept going day and night. He also enlarged the windows to "catch prevailing winds." But the air in the house remained terribly tight, and Rhodes suffered when, arguably, he could have been made more comfortable in the far more spacious Groote Schuur. But he insisted on staying by the sea if his doctors would not let him return to Britain. Jameson and Sir Edmond Sinclair Stevenson, the physician in charge, treated their patient with morphia for pain and digitalis and strychnine for his heart. (Three years older than Rhodes, Stevenson had been trained in Edinburgh as an obstetrician. He had a "high class" family practice in Rondebosch, near Cape Town, and wrote articles on abdominal surgery.)

From the middle of the month Rhodes' lungs "hardly worked at all." His physicians gave him oxygen and began trying "gelatine" (presumably blasting gelatine, containing nitroglycerine) for his heart pains. According to the cables, Fowler had recently seen a case of an expanding aneurysm, the symptoms of which had been helped by the administration of gelatine. Jameson and Stevenson were apprehensive about prescribing what they regarded as a dangerous treatment for a patient in such poor condition. Fowler wired back, through Hawksley: "No condition too grave," and they gave the gelatine. They drained his legs with silver Southey tubes to relieve the fluid which was accumulating from progressively worsening heart failure and tested his urine for albumin to keep track of the increasing failure of his kidneys.

Jameson and Metcalfe never left Rhodes' side. Smartt, Michell, Grimmer, McDonald and a host of lesser intimates were there frequently. A phalanx of old friends and enemies came for concluding words (Merriman was forbidden to attend) and went away saddened by the sight of the colossus immobilized and decaying. "On the narrow stoep of that tin-roofed cottage," Innes later remembered a visit at the beginning of March, "sat, mortally stricken and in sore need of spacious and airy surroundings, one of the most famous and wealthiest men in the British empire." Innes continued to see him. "I am glad of the wind," he wrote on 9 March, "because it will relieve Rhodes who suffers a great deal when there is no air. . . . He is in a *very* bad way; and in the absence of some miraculous rally, I do not see how he can last much longer. His heart has taken a much worse turn of late, and . . . now he is too ill to be moved even if he wanted to go." There was "something strange and pathetic," Innes and others said at the time, "at seeing a man of his wealth breathing away in a miserably airless little box of a cottage; he will have no nurse or personal attendant; but Jamieson [sic] is very devoted. . . ." A week later Rhodes appeared "about as bad as can be; the extreme weakness of his heart impairs the use of both lungs, and he is becoming dropsical. He sits up in bed day and night" (as he had begun doing in order to breathe as long ago as his first journey to Rhodesia in 1891). "I hardly think he can last long," wrote Innes. "He has gone steadily downhill during the last week."

The cables told the same story: 14 March 1902: "Communicate the following to Fowler from Stevenson begins stop Lungs scarcely acting at all stop Frequent attacks of heart failure only overcome by administration of oxygen. . . ." 17 March 1902: "Confidential Stevenson says tell Fowler pressure on vena cava increasing rapidly Cyanosis increasing necessitating constant supply oxygen otherwise getting steadily weaker. . . ." 18 March 1902: "Confidential A fair night with a good deal of restless sleep. Lung condition certainly not worse for last two days but dropsy now extended to abdomen. . . ."

Rhodes insisted on returning to Britain, and passages were booked during the middle of March on the S.S. *Saxon*, in case he "rallied." He never did, and shortly thereafter Jameson and Stevenson became convinced that Rhodes' case was "hopeless." He had "lasted longer than we expected owing to extraordinary vitality," they cabled on 21 March, "but the end is certain. . . ." He was "in fact dying," as Innes wrote on 23 March. "He suffers a good deal and is only kept alive by injections of ether and inhalations of oxygen gas. There is something very sad in seeing a strong man fighting for life when one knows that there is only one end to the struggle." The next day Le Sueur reported that "the chief" had been "very bad all day. I fear the end is not far off. It is the saddest sight in the world to see him now. He knows the case is hopeless but is fighting hard." Syfret called Rhodes' fight "plucky." Michell sat by his bedside on 26 March while Jameson, "worn out by persistent watching day and night" took a nap. Rhodes was restless. Once, Michell reported, he murmured: " 'So little done, so much to do.' " After a long pause Michell heard him singing to himself "maybe a few bars of an air he had once sung at his mother's knee." Rhodes was "dying by inches," Syfret wrote on the same day. "There is absolutely no hope."[28]

Nor was there. The heart failure progressed, the backed up fluid crept inexorably up his legs and abdomen. He steadily weakened. The Founder died at 6 p.m. on 26 March 1902. "The news created a great sensation," Innes wrote from the Civil Service Club in Cape Town, "and has depressed the community a great deal." Milner anticipated Rhodes' death and called it "a great blow." The Progressive party had lost its banker, brains, and guiding spirit. Milner feared a resurgence of the Bond. "Certainly there has never been a time since first I came to South Africa when I have wanted him more . . . I mean when *the work* has wanted him more. It is like the Evil Fate, which has dogged us all along. . . ."[29]

According to the autopsy performed by Dr. Stephen Boxer Syfret, and observed by Stevenson, Jameson, and Smartt, late on the evening of the day of his death, both of Rhodes' lungs were highly oedematous, congested, and compressed. (Syfret was the younger brother of Rhodes' financial agent and Cambridge-educated. He served for a time as the additional district surgeon of Mowbray, a suburb of Cape Town, but devoted most of his efforts to a typical large family practice.) The major finding of the report confirmed the clinical diagnosis of a dilation of the ascending aorta the "size of a man's wrist" with a "saccular dilation from the transverse portion as large as a child's head." The descending aorta was also much dilated. There was no dangerous thinning of the aorta nor any ulceration, such as one might see in a dissecting or about-to-rupture aneurysm. The aortic walls showed extensive arteriosclerosis. Stevenson's published account merely reports that the surgeons "found what [they] expected, a large cardiac aneurysm, which blocked the circulation."[30]

The heart was enlarged, indicating the results of its increasing load and failure near the end. The pericardium, the sac surrounding the heart, was thickened and was adherent to the heart, although the adhesions were easily separated. The lungs were filled with fluid, congested with blood and compressed, doubtless by the aneurysm. The pleura, the membrane surrounding the lungs, was thickened, but no mention was made of tubercular lesions which, if significant in his earlier history, would doubtless have been noted. The brain, all forty-nine ounces of it, was pronounced "normal in all respects." Except for a brief, descriptive note that the abdominal walls were distended, there is no information on the body below the chest. And there is no report of findings in the heart except for the existence of a clot in the right auricle, indicating that the heart was opened and examined. A second page of Syfret's autopsy report is probably missing. Although the autopsy was done privately and informally, and in the early twentieth century, it reflects a disciplined, if limited, appraisal.

The information supplied by two contrasting versions of the Rhodes' autopsy (an official report by Syfret and a cable from Stevenson to Fowler which ends, frustratingly, "full details by letter") is insufficient for modern clinicians to arrive at a confident single diagnosis to explain Rhodes' nearly life-long health problems. But it is possible to draw certain conclusions, as well as to construct hypotheses about matters which, without further evidence, must remain mysterious.

The immediate cause of death was congestive failure of both the left and right ventricles of Rhodes' heart. The size of the aneurysm makes it likely that the aortic valve, which prevents blood from regurgitating back into the heart, had become insufficient for its task. Thus the heart was, at least intermittently, pumping ineffectively and leading directly to its ultimate failure. Hypertension could well have been associated with Rhodes' problem, particularly earlier in his life. It is also possible that episodes of atrial fibrillation, paroxysmal irregularity of the heartbeat, could have been a feature of the case. An undated cable from Jameson to a Dr. Davis in Johannesburg begins, "Heart always extremely irregular." Atrial fibrillation could help to explain the heart failure which was precipitated by a bout of malarial fever and could account for the rapid improvement of the functioning of his heart with digitalis. It slows the heart rate and helps resume a normal rhythm. It is also true that fever alone, including that due to malaria, can precipitate episodes of congestive heart failure in persons with underlying chronic heart disease, even without atrial fibrillation. The increased metabolic demands of a fever can strain the heart to the point of decompensation.

The aneurysm occupied considerable space in the chest cavity, compressing the great veins, the lungs and the trachea. Pain, which was one of Rhodes' most agonizing complaints, regularly accompanies thoracic aortic aneurysms because of the erosion of surrounding structures by pressure from the swelling. There are at least two possible causes of such aneurysms; The first is syphilis. The standard textbook of Rhodes' day noted that "healthy, strong males who have worked hard and have had syphilis [were] the most common subjects of aneurism." Although a syphilitic aneurysm classically affects only the ascending aorta, it sometimes extends to the transverse and descending portions as well. Rumors that Rhodes had acquired syphilis abound but there is no evidence that he ever received treatment for the disease.

The first clear descriptions of syphilis were recorded at the end of the fifteenth century, when a pandemic swept Europe. Its sexual mode of transmission was known from the first but its multiple manifestations, which affect the skin, heart, liver, kidneys, gastrointestinal tract, and central nervous system, were only gradually recognized as parts of the same illness during the eighteenth and nineteenth centuries. The organism causing syphilis, *Treponema pallidum,* was discovered in 1905. It was in 1910 that the complement fixation test made it possible to diagnose the disease with laboratory certainty. However, in Rhodes' time, physicians were familiar with the clinical manifestations, felt assured of their ability to diagnose it from its major symptoms of chancre, rash, fever, and mucous lesions. They regarded it as "one of the most amenable of all diseases to treatment." The major problem in achieving a good result was the reluctance of the patient to cooperate with the treatment, which consisted of the administration of mercury and/or potassium iodide. These "cures" were given by mouth, by injection, by rubbing on a salve containing mercury, or by fumigation, during which the patient breathed volatilized calomel. Such a prolonged regimen could take up to two years. It was a course of treatment which Rhodes would have found intolerable and which, if applied, could hardly have escaped public attention. Furthermore, there are no indications from the autopsy or clinical accounts of any of the other signs or symptoms of syphilis other than the aneurysm.

Aneurysms like Rhodes' are more commonly due to advanced arteriosclerosis. His lifestyle—the heavy use of tobacco and alcohol and his enormous appetite for food—certainly constitute impressive risk factors for this condition. The autopsy finding of chronic pericarditis with adhesions, binding the heart to its surrounding sac, could have been a late result of several causes, including earlier episodes of acute pericarditis, most likely caused by bacteria or viruses.

The clinical course of his last illness and the autopsy findings do little to explain with any assurance the cause of his "heart attacks," especially those in 1872, 1877, and the 1880s. Nor can they reveal why Mackenzie gave him six months to live in 1873. It is possible that Mackenzie picked up a murmur or friction rub associated with acute pericarditis, which is more common in young men in the late fall or early winter, when Rhodes suffered his "chill." Other, less frequent causes of Rhodes' symptoms could include acute myocarditis, an inflammation of the muscle of the heart caused by a virus.

Earlier efforts to explain Rhodes' illnesses are unconvincing. Shee reviewed the clinical information available to him and the autopsy reports and concluded that Rhodes' history and the autopsy findings were not consistent with pulmonary tuberculosis. He felt that Rhodes' health problems could best be explained as the result of an auricular septal defect—a "hole in the heart." This congenital defect in the wall between two of the chambers of the heart, the auricles, could, according to Shee, explain the fact that Rhodes' medical problems were life-long but intermittent, and that he grew to normal size. The episodic nature of his attacks of illness in adult life, and his slowly progressive decline in later years were also, according to Shee, explicable by this defect, which leads to heart failure in later life, with the average age of death being forty-nine years.[31]

More recent reviews of the evidence find the history of alternating ill-health and full activity to be inconsistent with auricular septal defect. A second page of Syfret's autopsy report, if ever located, may contain a description of the results of the dissection of the heart and thus settle the question conclusively.

Rhodes died a man of wealth, but compared to the spectacularly gilded such as John D. Rockefeller, J. Pierpont Morgan, Andrew Carnegie, Beit, Barnato, and Joseph B. Robinson, his riches were hardly fabled. At the end of the century Rhodes believed that he "represented personally an amount of State equivalent to the amount possessed by almost all the hon. members on the other side together in this colony." Yet he was never fond of account books, and never knew his real net worth. Moreover, Rhodesia was a drain. So were the railways. Michell, his banker, valued Rhodes' assets in 1899 at only £2.8 million. By his death Rhodes was worth nearly £5 million, although after death duties the Rhodes estate netted only £3.9 million (each contemporary £1 then being equivalent to nearly $5). Of this total, and despite the restructuring of Rhodes' financial relationship to De Beers in 1901, his holdings in that diamond mining firm still constituted £2.7 million, the predominant share (68.5 percent) of his assets. Consolidated Gold Fields and other gold mining properties on the Rand and in Rhodesia constituted far less—

only about £400,000 worth of the estate. Dalston and Dalham, and Rhodes' 1,584 other properties in Britain, were together appraised at only £146,000; his vast farms in Rhodesia and his land and houses (including Groote Schuur) in South Africa were worth only £141,000. British South Africa Company shares were valued at a mere £69,000. More valuable was his stock in Rhodesia Railways, at £172,000. Altogether, Rhodes owned shares in about 125 companies. Forty were mining or prospecting ventures; twenty were service companies, including the *Cape Times* and various printing works in South Africa and Rhodesia; eight were transportation and communication concerns (his holdings in the African Trans-Continental Telegraph Company were worth less than £5,000), and a few were in agriculture.[32]

Aside from comparatively minor personal and family legacies, Rhodes intended the proceeds from the bulk of his estate to power the vision which had been articulated in the Confession and elaborated in successive wills. Lord Rothschild provided an epitaph which extolled Rhodes more than he would have done in life. It offers a contemporary appreciation of how those close to the Founder understood his special vision, and how they understood that Rhodes wished his legacy to be employed to propel his big ideas forward. "Although his work was not done, he had lived a great life and left a name behind him which untold generations of the future will revere and will be grateful that he lived," wrote Rothschild. "I have not seen his last will, but I know the contents of it—it is a magnificent Will of a truly great and magnificent man," wrote Rothschild, one of the eminent persons whom Rhodes had originally designated as a trustee. (The others, far more recently appointed by Rhodes, were Jameson, Rosebery, Milner, Grey, Michell, and Hawksley. Stead had been dropped in favor of Milner because of the impulsive, idealistic editor's impassioned defense of Boer rights during the war. Rothschild had been replaced by Grey.)

Rhodes' primary bequest, continued Rothschild, was to the University of Oxford, which will henceforth be able to offer "inducements to Colonials and even Americans to study on the banks of the Isis and to learn . . . to love [England] . . . and make it big and prosperous." Rothschild knew that Rhodes wanted his trustees to provide scholarships worth about £60,000 a year. The interest on the remainder of Rhodes' fortune "his Trustees will have to spend in the interest of, for the development of the Anglo Saxon race," he said. But that was a desire which ultimately proved impractical except through the scholarship scheme—what, unintended by Rhodes, became his main and overarching bequest.

"Rhodes was a very great man, he saw things as no one else saw them and he foresaw things which no one else dreamt of—. . . his great generosity bewitched those who came in contact with him." Rothschild declared that "his loss would be irreparable, were it not for the fact that he put in motion ideas which have taken root, ideas firmly established . . . which will continue to grow and to flourish."[33]

·◄ 25 ►·

"A Man of Compelling Potency"
Enigma and Resolution

R HODES DIED both genius and rogue. Even before an aneurysm led to the collapse of his bloated body in middle life, the very magnificence of Rhodes' successes had begun to subordinate the facts of his kaleidoscopic years to the idealistic apotheosizing of his acolytes and himself. His death occasioned an outpouring of part-remembered, part-fanciful, part-true, part-wishful retrospection. Those of his contemporaries who wrote soon afterward were concerned to improve a glorified memory. So were most of their successors. Others, equally determined, offered appraisals that were as venomous as those of his admirers were adulatory. Those who saw hardly anything but the good were invested in myth. But so, too, were those who could still see the very twitch of the devil's tail.

A century after the decade of his greatest glories, it is important to push aside the veil of myth to reveal the real Rhodes, the man who served both god and mammon, who was as human, fallible, gentle, charismatic, and constructive as he was shameless, vain, driven, ruthless, and destructive. He deserves to be seen in both the bright and the somber hues of the rainbow. As Colvin, biographer of Jameson, wrote, Rhodes was "such a great example to Englishmen and has been so abominably analyzed that the truth cannot be too often told."[1]

In Rhodes' case, what is that truth? Certain of the cobwebs of misconception can be removed without arousing ire among the faithful—those generations of Rhodes scholars, South Africans, Rhodesians, and even Britons who were taught to enshrine Rhodes as a heroic, nearly perfect, far-seeing, fundamentally idealistic colossus.

Rhodes was never tubercular. He was not sent to Africa primarily for his health and thus never had to overcome a debility. Still, the presumption that his lungs were weak preyed on his mind and was dealt with by restless energy

679

and a striving for manly success. Yet it was his cardiovascular mishaps which later worried the Founder, and spurred him to action. The main point is that Rhodes was physically at least of average strength until the 1890s, when he still accomplished prodigious feats despite a circulatory system which was ultimately taxed beyond its capacity.

Rhodes was not the short, fat curmudgeon of many imaginations. About six feet in height, he originally was fair-haired and slim. A good-looking youth, he became an attractive adult. Only the growing ballooning of his aorta, which progressively restricted the return of blood from his head and upper body, transformed the lithe figure into someone swollen and prematurely gray-haired. Syphilis may have caused his aortic weakening, but it is more likely that arteriosclerosis was the primary culprit. Throughout his forties Rhodes filled out his large frame. He ate voraciously, drank copiously, and smoked constantly. The strain on his heart was severe, and, in ways which are difficult to calculate precisely, the premonition of early death drove Rhodes onward at what was often a reckless pace. But his physical deterioration cannot totally explain the irrationality of the Jameson Raid in 1895 any more than it alone can explain his unaccustomed patience and deft feel for reconciliation amid angry Ndebele in 1896.

After his mother died in 1873, Rhodes loved only men, usually his social and intellectual inferiors. Whether or not he expressed that love physically, and there is modest circumstantial evidence that he did, his emotional attachments were to men. His closest friends and warmest supporters were men who themselves consorted with men and, in a few cases, were widely known in British homosexual circles. In keeping with an image of his age, Rhodes could well have repressed his urges and behaved wholly latently. Or he might have been asexual. In fact, Rhodes surrounded himself with men who were unmarried and, in most cases, were never to marry. Without being at all flamboyant about his tastes, Rhodes usually preferred to spend his days and nights with congenial men.

The product of a mother's uncommon affirmation and a father's disagreeable challenge, Rhodes adapted impressively to the demands of school and family, and managed his teenage transition to Africa with panache. From there the alert, canny, young cotton farmer joined thousands of others seeking their fortunes from diamonds in Kimberley. His imagination and energy were important; so were his skillful uses of the talents of others. Whether pumping water or selling ice cream, Rhodes searched restlessly for opportunity, and employed many of his nine terms at Oxford both to consolidate his post-adolescent sense of self and to make useful contacts among the gentry. His personal epiphany and quasi-religious self-dedication came in 1877, after completing the first half of his Oxford career. Its expression, the "Confession of Faith," is a jejune effervescence, hardly to be taken seriously as a philosophical document. But it has great significance as a sign that he was maturing psychologically and was prepared to seek a self-defined destiny. Rhodes believed that Victorian men should have objects in life. His was a truly grand affirmation: to unite the present and former English-speaking colonies to the mother country and to bring as much of Africa as possible under the British flag.

It is a measure of Rhodes' magnetism that the men on the frontier to whom he revealed these secret dreams in the late 1870s and thereafter believed in him and in those dreams. So did a range of supposedly skeptical Britons. No matter how wildly grandiose his dreams may appear today, Rhodes' own sense of conviction—his utter self-confidence—commanded a growing legion of followers. Rhodes, articulating his plans in a high voice that broke occasionally into falsetto, inducted men both older and more experienced than himself into a growing fraternity of believers. Even men otherwise cynical seemed to accept the compelling magic of Rhodes' charisma. When he angled for the amalgamation of the diamond mines, sought hegemony over the north, or attempted to oust the Portuguese from Mozambique, Rhodes enrolled supporters from all backgrounds. Not least, the Founder crucially gained the support of men more powerful, wealthier, and better-connected than himself.

Rhodes' genius is rooted in the family soil of Bishop's Stortford, especially in his mother's strong acceptance and reassurance. But since so much of his genius was his gift of persuasion, it is clear that Rhodes at some early moment discovered that he could make men believe both in the rightness of his cause and in his ability to realize it. Yet his intelligence was not of the type that impressed his contemporaries. It is unlikely that he would have done well on modern tests of intelligence, which for the most part correlate with academic performance rather than achievement in a broader sense. His intelligence was more centered in the capacity to discern relationships among objects and to project forward in time the outcome of various new arrangements. His ability to analyze the elements of a situation and to be decisive was no better than that of others in Kimberley. Nor could he manage capital or make business decisions any better than dozens of others in that mining city in the 1870s and 1880s. But his longer range intuition proved exceptional.

A ceaseless energy was essential. So was attention to detail. More important may have been his ability to empathize—to appreciate the strengths and weaknesses of others. Rhodes called this talent "squaring"—he sensed what others wanted, what their dreams were, and thereupon made converts. Charm, which he had in abundance, bright blue eyes, a broad smile, and an impressively large head could not have been sufficient, but they assisted. Rhodes, said Low, "could conquer hearts as effectually as any beauty that ever set herself to subjugate mankind." An especial appeal to persons whose sexual preferences were similar to his own doubtless helped among a subset of men on the frontier, in parliament, and in positions of power in Britain. Many of Rhodes' strongest allies were homosexuals. But not all were.

Overall, and for men and women of either orientation, it was Rhodes' larger-than-life belief in his own destiny which transcended his human imperfections. One of Rhodes' physicians recalled how the first time they met he was struck by the great man's "leonine appearance, his large and broad forehead and his kind smile, but a face full of determination. That was the man: for nothing could alter his mind, if he thought that he was right."[2]

William Bramwell Booth, the son of the founder of the Salvation Army, met Rhodes in the late 1890s and was as staggered by the Founder's sheer presence as he was by the quality of his mind and the fervor of his idealism. "I have never met any one, always excepting [my father], who made such an impression on me. . . . His life was full of faith—though not, indeed, the highest kind of faith. . . . The moving force of his career was his faith in Britain's future. He believed in Britain as no man I have ever met believed in her. His patriotic faith took on almost a religious enthusiasm."[3]

Even as a youth, Rhodes exuded power and smelled of success. Thus it was not so much the content of his dream which attracted others but the fact that he dreamed magnificently that roused men who sought to invest their lives with renewed meaning and to dedicate themselves to a visionary purpose. Rhodes was a "romancer." "When you listened to his talk you found yourself carried away by the contagion of his enthusiasm," recalled Low. It is important that a part of Rhodes remained boyish; he appealed to the lost, dreamy youth of a legion of Victorian adults. He had the charisma to recall a golden age and to imbue individuals in number with a renewed faith. If they followed Rhodes, their lives would be as worthwhile as they once seemed to be in halcyon days of prepubescent glory.

Rhodes appealed to the idealism of men. When listening to him, recalled Low, "you remembered only that you were in the presence of a man dominated by an inspiring faith, and an ambition in which there was nothing narrow or merely selfish." A belief in Rhodes became "a substitute for religion." Indeed, "minds of more subtlety and more accurate intelligence . . . yielded to his sway." Low struggled to explain how someone so weak intellectually could fire the enthusiasm of so many. Others were "wittier talkers." Others were better read, more brilliant, and more logical.

Rhodes "was not a clear reckoner or a close thinker." He hardly originated ideas, but "took up the conceptions of others, expanded them, dwelt upon them, advertised them to the world in his grandiloquent fashion, made them his own." Rhodes had "compelling potency." Low describes his art: "It was the personality behind the voice that drove home the words—the restless vivid soul, that set the big body fidgeting in nervous movements, the imaginative mysticism, the absorbing egotism of the man with great ideas, and the unconscious dramatic instinct, that appealed to the sympathies of the hearer."[4]

Rhodes was a revivalist. But he also was an immensely practical problem-solver who enjoyed acquisitions for their own sake, who chortled at corporate coups, maneuvered adroitly in parliament, and took tactical advantage of bumbling businessmen, statesmen, and indigenous potentates alike. Indeed, his talents for finding common ground were equally well deployed and discerned in the legislative backroom with Jan Hofmeyr, in the boardrooms of the City, or high atop the Matopos with angry and aggrieved Ndebele. Rhodes' technique was to think aloud "without eloquence, without dialectics, . . . making admissions, making confidences; insisting, recapitulating, riding a phrase to death . . . but always going to the root of the matter—and often making a conquest by sheer frank force of personality." Unlike men of mere warmth, however, Rhodes drove relentlessly and ruthlessly for ends which made sense to some if not to all of those with whom he shared his dreams. He persisted, succeeded, and triumphed over and over again.

What did Rhodes want of life? The question is appropriate, but no short answer can suffice. For Rhodes wanted it all. He sought wealth from diamonds for its own sake, then for a professional education, then so that he could achieve the objects of the Confession, and, ultimately, to provide for the scholarships. He never counted his money obsessively and, in later life, never knew exactly how much he was worth. But it is foolish to suggest that he never wanted to control the diamond wealth of the world for its own sake, or that he did not relish the power, scope, and influence which immense wealth conferred. Merriman, never unbiased, asserted that Rhodes had a "double character." The one side was "given over to the worship of money—the worship of the golden calf." The other was "semi-religious, gentlemanlike, full of all sort of odd fancies and notions, a charming companion." Unhappily, reported Merriman, the first aspect "as life went on rather gained the mastery of the latter." Rhodes was never crass or ostentatious about his riches, although Merriman said that he sometimes could be "brusque coarse [and] ready to gain his ends by any ways. . . ." Rhodes was also no ascetic. Only Kipling described him as a "dreamer devout." Rhodes liked to be able to run a big house and keep a lavish table. He was pleased to purchase property for his brothers and sisters and to distribute it generously to charities and the less fortunate.[5]

Many men and women seek adulation as a narcissistic reward. Rhodes believed in himself, was enthralled by his own ideas, and was narcissistic in that dimension, but he was less interested in being famous than in being influential. " 'I want the power—let who will wear the peacock's feathers' " was one of his favorite sayings.[6] He sought power in order to shape events according to the contours of his own unique vision. Thus he desired power and would have called that power the power to do good. His decision to enter parliament, hitherto unrecognized as a component of his grasp for power, was but one example of the ways in which Rhodes positioned himself for greatness and ultimate influence. Oxford served that purpose as well. But whereas some persons may find sufficient satisfaction in minor displays of naked power—as bullies, policemen, or modern-day arbitrageurs—Rhodes was impatient with anything less than the power to be decisive. His arrangement with the Bond was a means to greater control, and, thus, even if the precise employment of that power could not have been predicted beforehand, he wanted its use to reshape South Africa and to remake all of southern Africa.

Rhodes derived a portion of power from others. Rudd, Beit, Stow, Rothschild, and a host of businessmen and financiers played critical roles in his rise as an entrepreneur. Each, especially the first two, contributed much more than an idea or two and more than what could be characterized as assistance at a few critical moments. Their efforts were consistently valuable, strikingly vital, and truly foundation-forming. Without Rudd, Rhodes might have amassed capital more slowly during the 1870s and therefore never been able to shift significantly from ice, ice cream, and pumping into diamond claims. Rudd had the better reputation. He was steady, cautious, and reliable. Rhodes absorbed commercial lessons from Rudd. He relied extraordinarily on Rudd's fundamental integrity and keen business sense during his long absences at Oxford. Later, making a success of investments in gold depended decisively on Rudd, on his contacts in London, and on his ability to gather in and then husband the resources of myriad investors. Not least of all his critical accomplishments, Rudd obtained Lobengula's assent to a concession, the remarkable cornerstone of the Rhodesian imperial edifice. Rhodes' great take-off might have been grounded, or at least more awkward, without Rudd.

Beit knew the value of diamonds, understood the workings of the world money markets, and advised Rhodes on how share offerings could be floated and debentures sold profitably. Rhodes learned from Beit as he learned from Rudd. He employed Beit's capital at crucial junctures and prospered even more from Beit's ability to tap the resources of European money markets. Beit was worth about £8 million—more than twice as much as Rhodes—when he died in 1908. He was a wise speculator and, like Rudd, was steady, solid, sober, free from scandal, and loyal. Again, it is hard to conceive that Rhodes would have achieved as much as he did in the world of commerce without Beit. Had he not had Beit's help, there would have been no consolidation of diamond mining interests, no (or a much smaller) stake in gold, few other corporate victories, and no surplus resources for Rhodesia and the rest.

Merriman reminded Basil Williams that among Rhodes' great gifts he took "other folks' ideas and work[ed] them out. . . ."[7] True, and Rhodes delegated masterfully while almost always managing to focus on the details at his feet as well as the far horizons. Yet, however much Beit's brains, Rudd's resolve, Rothschild's approval and insistence, and Stow's early wealth contributed to Rhodes' economic independence, Rhodes was both pupil and master. They joined him because they believed in his dreams and saw in the fervor of the youth and later in the man a bright gleam that was more than quicksilver.

Like most entrepreneurs, Rhodes was more creative than original. His talent was the marshaling of many pieces in the service of some larger whole. He was the architect, others such as Rudd and Beit the structural engineers. Just as great skyscrapers demand the talents of many but follow the vision of one, so Rhodes introduced several of the fundamental entrepreneurial ideas. He was largely responsible for the innovative life governorships, the trust deed, and the profit-sharing scheme for Gold Fields. It is hard to be sure whether Rhodes, Beit, or Gardner Williams suggested appealing to Rothschild and then to the French financiers for support during the struggle to amalgamate the diamond mines, but, once guided, Rhodes knew when and how to act decisively. He never really understood basic bookkeeping methods or international trade, but he had an instinct for brilliant, timely financial maneuvers. Again and again, Rhodes' conception of a larger future, and his innate talent for reading the contour maps of economic endeavor, proved decisive in developing a diamond mining monopoly in the 1880s. He failed to do so well in gold, possibly because he was distracted, already comparatively rich, and surprisingly cautious.

It was Rhodes' skills with people and his visionary capacity, not his intellect or a midas touch, which won the mines for the De Beers combine. Rhodes saw and believed in the larger, dramatic possibilities and gave others confidence in himself and therefore in his dreams. He promoted himself and his prospects well, and, without reducing the well-conceived unfairly to the flash of charisma, he made his fortune and the fortunes of others largely because his head for business could encompass vast sums and broad results and because he could sell those goals to men of consequence and ability. In all his endeavors, once he obtained support for defined objectives, he could persuade more scrupulous or more conventional men to take shortcuts, water stock, misrepresent prospects, set up secret reserves of diamonds, and disguise the underlying concessions on which floated companies were based. In 1892–93 he even condoned James Sivewright's crooked catering arrangements with James Logan.

Rhodes' lack of shame and guilt was intrinsic to his success. No one with conventional mores could have accomplished what he did in every sphere, especially financially. Rhodes, a man with "big plans and great ambitions," fell victim as politician, promoter, entrepreneur, and empire-extender to the persuasive belief that the greatness of the objective justified any method of achieving it. The more important Rhodes' plans seemed to himself, the more steadily did the significance of his techniques "dwindle by comparison to vanishing point."[8] The goal, wrote Innes, "alone fill[ed] his vision." Ends were everything; any means whatsoever could be justified if it served great goals.

Decades before the discipline of strategic management was defined, Rhodes was a superb strategist and skilled manager. Levitt defines management as "the rational assessment of a situation and the systematic selection of goals and purposes . . . ; the systematic development of strategies to achieve those goals; the marshalling of the required resources; the rational design, organization, direction, and control of the activities required to attain the selected purposes; and, finally, the motivating and rewarding of people to do the work. . . ." Rhodes would have felt at home among Levinson's corporate leaders. These chiefs of corporations merged their own values and sense of obligation to society into a collective ego ideal which they both purveyed and enforced in the company. Each saw their organization in relation to national and international issues; they were powerfully value-driven. They interacted constantly and supportively with customers, employees, and other constituencies. Like Rhodes, they were not remote figures but immersed themselves in their associates and their affairs. These contacts kept them in touch with reality; they constantly faced their own doubts and fallibility. Sensitive to people and to internal and external politics, they were flexible, intuitive, and imaginative. They took risks; they were not afraid to fail. All of the leaders faulted themselves for refusing to follow their instincts and intuitions as assiduously as they might have done. They were thinkers as well as doers.[9]

Although Rhodes lived before the age of the spreadsheet and rarely did his planning on more than the back of an old envelope, he managed his affairs strategically from the 1870s onward. Levitt's attributes, from assessment to rewards, fit Rhodes and describe his methods and much of the reason for his entrepreneurial and territorial conquests. When he "squared," cultivated, or manipulated powerful individuals, he organized resources. When he excited others with the power of his vision he motivated them to do his work. Rhodes' intuitive grasp of strategic management was displayed most dramatically during the struggle to amalgamate the diamond mines and, virtually simultaneously, in London during the months when he sought ministerial backing and royal patronage for the acquisition of Rhodesia. Rhodes possessed strategic acumen and flair.

As Rhodes began to perform on an imperial stage, his gifts became more and more apparent, his confidence ever more pronounced, and his vision ever more bold and daring. Rhodes wanted the lands beyond the Limpopo, the lands across the Zambezi, and a red line for telegraph and rails all the long way to Cairo. In this sphere he behaved like an Elizabethan, manipulating Her Majesty's ministers as much as he was willingly employed by them to paint southern Africa British red before the crafty Germans or the stubborn Boers could similarly deprive Africans of their lands and power. Although Rhodes probably had not thought specifically of imperial initiatives before 1882, he had mused about them conceptually and generally, and set imperial objectives for himself in the Confession.

As a young entrepreneur with grand ideas, Rhodes saw clearly that the "Suez Canal" of the interior must be kept open so that he and his enterprises would not be stifled by filibustering Boers from the Transvaal. That fundamental striving for scope, for not mortgaging his future, and for keeping all his options open led to the annexation of southern Bechuanaland to the Cape Colony, to the British protection and thus acquisition of Bechuanaland proper (modern Botswana), and to the placing of Rhodes and his imperial ambitions advantageously on the very borders of Ndebeleland. Once Rhodes had sufficient capital he could strive for a charter. With a charter he could raise funds under royal aegis from British investors and devote those proceeds to the conquest of the territory that was to comprise Rhodesia. Doing the actual deed depended less upon tactical cleverness than it did on manipulating overseas and local political environments. Suborning indigenous monarchs was a joint effort of Rhodes, British governors, highly placed civil servants in Whitehall, and even well-situated Protestant missionaries. But just as Rhodes believed that the greater good sanctified dubious means, so the strength of his vision, and only sometimes the wealth of his purse, captivated willing collaborators.

Rhodes' actual conquests were consummated with comparative ease. Relying on a special interpretation of the Rudd Concession and his own superb sense of the outer limits of bravado in a time of rapidly shifting power, Rhodes recruited mercenaries to settle the African-dominated interior. The resulting Pioneer Column skirted Ndebeleland and reached the Shona high ground without drawing hostile fire. Beyond the Zambezi, emissaries concluded ambiguous treaties with Lewanika of the Lozi and with other important leaders. By these different methods Rhodes and his employees acquired what became Southern and Northern Rhodesia (Zimbabwe and Zambia). Rhodes also funded Harry Johnston's forceful occupation of Nyasaland (Malawi). The era of traditional autonomy was everywhere passing. Rhodes' imperialist urge occurred when and how it did both because the scramble for Africa had been started by Europe and Europeans and because he had a vision and a sense of individual destiny.

The imperial Rhodes is hardly attractive. Lobengula of the Ndebele was tricked into providing a concession, his authority ignored by the Pioneer Column, and fine promises given to him—all with Rhodes' knowledge and approval—until the moment came when whites could overthrow him entirely. That moment, the war of 1893, was unprovoked by the Ndebele, and destroyed their independence. With Her Majesty's Government turning a blind eye, Rhodes personally approved the decision to attack; his troops had Maxim machine guns and the more numerous Ndebele had not. Rhodes also badly wanted copper-rich Katanga and the lands leading down to the Indian Ocean shores of Mozambique, but Lord Salisbury had to balance the needs of peace in Europe against an enhanced dominion under the British flag and in Rhodes' grip.

Without Rhodes, the Rhodesias, Nyasaland, and Bechuanaland—an area the size of western Europe including Great Britain, Italy, and Austria—might have become British anyway, if with fewer incentives for white settlers. But Rhodes decided when and how it did so, provided the organizational and capitalist framework, and personally sustained these young outposts of Europe during their difficult first years. For the Rhodesias, certainly, he justly was the Founder. For present day Zimbabwe and Zambia, he appropriately is the despoiler. Both designations pay tribute to the breadth of his conception and the energy, persistence, and care with which he made his dreams come true. The Rhodesias were his offspring, his conscious and half-conscious embodiment of immortality. Establishing them enabled him to serve the expanding family of English-speaking colonials that he sought to recreate as a way of conferring the benefits of Britain upon the world.

Rhodes actively fostered territorial acquisition by English-speakers with a Cape bias. He did so out of no hatred for Africans. Even dislike would be too strong a charge. Africans simply stood in the way of imperial progress. They represented an anachronistic barbarianism. Whites would take over, introduce Africans to higher things, and fashion colonies where a handful of whites would rule greater numbers of blacks and, naturally, rely on their labor. Rhodes was not alone in the 1880s and 1890s in regarding critics of such a program as sentimentalists. Africa was going to be deprived of its freedom; it was merely a question of whether Rhodes or some lesser being would take charge. He never doubted the superiority of whites nor reflected, even for a moment, on alternative fates for Africans. Rhodes' highly developed sense of injustice was reserved for rebuffs to his own territorial ambitions, not to the hurts inflicted upon Africans.

As a parliamentarian and a prime minister, Rhodes' approach to Africans was consistently antagonistic. Concerned as he was from his first months in Kimberley to secure abundant supplies of cheap labor for the diamond mines and for the Cape generally, Rhodes' legislative power depended upon an alliance with the Afrikaner Bond. That compact in turn was based on crimping the Cape's hitherto color-blind franchise. For the likes of the Bond, too many Africans voted and would overwhelm the polls as soon as the Transkei and Pondoland were incorporated into the Cape Colony in the 1890s. African numbers had to be reduced. Rhodes found a way—by denying votes only to those Africans who held communal property, and, later, by raising the financial qualification levels. He defied liberal thinking in the Cape and, through the Glen Grey legislation of 1894, laid the basis for twentieth-century rural segregation in South Africa. In defending his actions against Africans, Rhodes rationalized, persuading even himself that Africans would benefit neither by voting nor by freehold ownership of farms. So secure was he by the mid-1890s, when these fatal attacks upon African rights were mounted, that Rhodes may not even have paused to consider the long-term consequences of such policies for Africans or for the future of South Africa. Remarkably perceptive about some things, Rhodes (like so many of his contemporaries) never concerned himself about the forfeitures of African trust and respect, and the chasm that was widening between white and black.

True, as a capitalist, Rhodes depended upon an expanding frontier for unskilled labor. Without being able to tap vast reservoirs of manpower, his mines would shut and his ability to finance Rhodesia and his other quests for immortality would cease. His class interest thus inevitably influenced his thinking and his judgment regarding Africans as workers. It was less for glory than to safeguard the mines that he initially entered parliament, and it was partially to secure supplies of fuel wood and Africans that he pushed hard for the incorporation of Stellaland and Goshen, annexed the Transkei, and opened up the north. But Rhodes' financial greed was after 1880 subordinated to the service of a larger purpose. If Rhodes' actions were base, it is evident that his motives were never merely or wholly commercial.

Building upon the fantasy of 1877, and accumulating means and political influence in the 1880s, Rhodes in the 1890s was poised atop an Everest of accomplishment. As a politician and a visionary, Rhodes harbored aims which superseded any attachments to or even much thought about the place of Africans in South Africa. He firmly believed that the realization of his dream of a united South and southern Africa under his own and British leadership intimately depended upon an Anglo-Dutch alliance. The Afrikaners and the

English were the competing "races." Hence how to eliminate race conflict was the problem which Rhodes worked to solve through the end of 1895, and to which he returned from 1898 to 1901. His "equal rights" slogan was devised as an appeal to the Dutch, not to Africans or Coloureds. A leader of the nineteenth century, Rhodes was fully prepared to sacrifice the Cape's liberal tradition and the fullest range of indigenous human rights to cement an accord between the two dominant (white) races. Never anti-Afrikaner, and only antagonistic to the Transvaalers because of President Kruger's patriarchal, obstinate opposition to himself personally and to his dreams of unity under the spreading Crown, Rhodes firmly believed that his objective was commendably lofty. Any and all means were acceptable in the service of that objective. Rhodes, Plumb once declared, "lacked all sense of public morality." A contemporary of Rhodes placed such a judgment in a more fully rounded context. "Absorbed in the contemplation of great ends, he was indifferent to the means by which his results were to be attained." He judged right and wrong by cosmic standards, not by merely conventional rules of morality. "His vision of the future," thought Low, "was too vivid to be blurred by such considerations." [10]

The root cause of the disastrous Jameson Raid was Rhodes' fear that gold would fuel the growing independence of Kruger and his ilk and of republican-minded Uitlanders on the Witwatersrand. In either hands, the immense riches of the Rand would shatter Rhodes' hopes for a unified South Africa. Thus Rhodes enthusiastically and incautiously conceived a madcap cabal for the overthrow of the Transvaal government. He would fund and supply the Uitlanders and sponsor an invasion force led by Jameson. When the Uitlanders rose in Johannesburg, Jameson would come to their rescue. But the Uitlanders never rose, and Jameson, on his own initiative and to Rhodes' considerable horror, invaded anyway. Rhodes' applecart was upset, profoundly, his pre-eminent political position destroyed, his reputation sullied forever, and his treacherous (or merely self-serving?) goals exposed. No Afrikaner has ever forgiven Rhodes, and the terrible war that Britain and the Afrikaners fought from 1899 to 1902 was caused to some extent by the enormous distrust of the English and the great gulf between Afrikaans- and English-speakers which grew cancerously after the Raid.

Rhodes not only sought to monopolize the gold of the Rand and to right the grievances of the English-speaking foreigners who outnumbered the Boers on the Rand and in the Transvaal. He played for much higher, much more complex stakes. Rhodes' actions—even regarding the Raid—cannot be reduced to vulgar motives. Ruthless, unscrupulous, foolish he certainly was. Wildly overconfident he was, too, probably because of the ease with which the Maxims had decimated the Ndebele. Rhodes and Jameson had unfounded contempt for the Boer fighters. But so did Lord Methuen, General Sir Redvers Buller, and the entire British army at the beginning of the Anglo-Boer War. In late 1895, too, Rhodes had an unbounded faith in himself. Although he often compared himself to a Roman emperor, his fate was Greek. He (and his acolytes) had come to accept the annointed quality of Rhodes' vision. His successes had been so staggering and so recurrent that Rhodes seemed indomitable.

Rhodes miraculously recovered much of his reputation and a semblance of his old power in the years after the Raid. The ending of the Ndebele rebellion in 1896 took skill and courage. Rhodes solved an otherwise intractable problem of continuing guerrilla war by venturing unarmed into the Matopos mountains and negotiating a cease-fire with angry induna. Genuinely that was his finest hour. Later he modernized fruit growing in the Cape, expanded its dynamite industry, and improved its ability to store fresh meat. He almost became premier again, and played a significant role in Cape political life on the eve of the Anglo-Boer War. He died before the war ended, leaving the outline of a dramatic scholarship scheme that was designed to unite the English-speaking peoples of the world through education. He also left a great monopoly in diamonds as well as a solid position in gold, and colonies on either side of the Zambezi that bore his name. " 'Well, there is something that will live,' " he once said. " 'They can't take that away, can they?' "[11]

Rhodes' one colossal failure and his often forgotten but most enduring legacy is the fatal antagonism between white South African speakers of Afrikaans and English. Afrikaners in the Cape had trusted Rhodes, but Rhodes betrayed them. Lord Milner compounded that betrayal in 1899 and afterward. Rhodes achieved much for the education of English-speakers in the Commonwealth and the United States, but he killed the distant hope of Afrikaner-British comity in South Africa.

It is as easy to focus on Rhodes' entrepreneurial accomplishments as it is to condemn his supposed avarice. Likewise it is possible and not completely irrelevant to concentrate exclusively on the virtues embodied in his "big idea." It is not hard to show that his practices were sharp, his offenses against conventional corporate ethics many, and his expediency substantial. Milner, who knew Rhodes toward the end of his life, admired him, but still found him "enormously untrustworthy." They were on the "best of terms," but nevertheless Milner felt certain that Rhodes would "give away me or anybody else to gain *the least* of [his] private ends."[12]

It *is* appropriate to dwell on Rhodes' role in improving southern African agricultural practices, the efficacy of his mining amalgamation, and the good he attempted to achieve by unifying southern Africa politically and economically. It would hardly be amiss, however, to examine the vast costs to Africans of each of such attributes and to add up the harm to Africa and South Africa through franchise restrictions, rural segregation, the conquest of the Rhodesias, and so on. In a narrow normative sense, Rhodes acted, it is now clear, for both ultimate good and ultimate evil.

Rhodes' appetite was gargantuan. He first gobbled the mines, then swallowed the Rhodesias, and failed only to consume the Transvaal. Each meal served to prepare him for the next and, taken together, they fed a desire for immortality. Other persons of wealth have been content to enrich their descendants, improve the lot of anonymous unfortunates, endow unversities, or—bless them—create foundations. Rhodes, driven by his juvenile attachment to reunion, to the ingathering of the lost sheep of far-flung Britain, decided to sponsor the commingling of colonials under the intellectually invigorating spires of England's first university. That was to be a positive gift to the world. It would long outlive his eponymous colonies, and, indeed, since he never imagined that the scholarship committees would select the men (and women!) that they have, and since he desired a tightly knit, imperially centered universe, the fact that the scholarships have succeeded in defiance of the design of their founder is an ironic tribute to the final workings of his uncommon genius.

Rhodes is remembered for no original theorem, for no single invention, nor for any enduring idea other than his scholarships. Imperial expansion is deservedly out of fashion, too, and Rhodes today can hardly be revered as he once was as a conqueror of countries and an organizer of subject peoples. Even the kind of ruthless entrepreneurship which amalgamated the diamond mines and gathered gold hardly excites late twentieth century readers as it did but five decades ago. Rhodes failed Jane Waterston's test, too: Providence gave him "the grandest opportunities" in the arena of African advancement, and he "flung them away." He failed lamentably and destructively to rule "many thousands of natives wisely and well."[13] He deprived Africans in South Africa of their political rights in order to appease the Afrikaner Bond and further his political, and thus his entrepreneurial and imperial fortunes. He extirpated Zimbabweans, redeeming himself only by concluding a negotiated peace with the Ndebele. On the personal level, he manipulated acquaintances and friends, never really caring that once-close colleagues such as Merriman, Innes, Sauer, William Schreiner, even Olive Schreiner, and John Blades Currey felt rejected and betrayed. He largely ignored or derided his brothers and sisters, but patronized them. Rhodes had deep emotional needs, but he satisfied them almost exclusively through his loyalty and devotion to male intimates of questionable quality such as Jameson, Metcalfe, Rutherfoord Harris, Neville Pickering, and Johnny Grimmer.

Such is an unabashedly negative assessment, and, as the pages of this biography have shown over and over, there are many other terms and conditions under which the Founder can be vilified. But, there is no denying he was a "mighty force." His vast and grandiloquent vision cannot be dismissed as megalomaniacal. It inspired some of the best and the brightest of Britain's empire. It mesmerized a legion of white South Africans and Rhodesians. He was indeed the Founder—of countries and scholarships. Since Africa across the Limpopo and Zambezi rivers would have been occupied inevitably by Europeans, he saved it for Britain's kind of colonial domination. He dreamt of a union of all South African whites, and destroyed that dream by the Raid. But he did dream genuinely, and believed intensely in a federated future for southern Africa (under white control but for general development). He believed in progress in Africa and the empire on a broad scale and across a vast reach of geography and history. His scholarships embody and fulfill that part of the pertinacious vision which was always focused on giving to posterity.

Rhodes was not a good man, but he was great and far-seeing. He believed in himself and in his ability to leave the world richer than it was when he entered it. In the titanic struggle between self-absorption and genuine involvement with others, self-absorption almost invariably won. His love affair with his big ideas ultimately crowded out any lasting or deep concerns for most companions, associates, and friends. Rhodes' few long-term relationships were with those who were prepared to subordinate themselves to his dominating goals. The momentum and scope of his narcissistic dreams devoured the accomplishment of a fulfilling and rounded personal generativity. Yet however hollow he may have been in basic human terms, he left a rich and compelling heritage of achievement and philanthropy for humankind. In that soaring sense, which will hardly satisfy every modern reader, he did not, in fact, fling away the gifts of Providence. He amassed, he acquired, he savaged, he disrupted, and he presided arrogantly over the fate of southern Africa. But he also built lasting economic institutions, furthered transportation and communication, improved agriculture, enhanced education, and fervently believed and preached the doctrine that riches were his primarily to advance the positive interests of a modern southern Africa, and the farther flung English empire, and to uplift the colonies and ex-colonies by sending the very best of their young men to consort with and learn from one another in Britain's oldest cathedral of learning. Rhodes had always tried to find his way back home. The scholarships were meant to unify the original empire, to tie mystical bonds, and to provide a way in which Rhodes, the romantic boy and the irrepressible man, could live on, and do good works.

Notes

PREFACE

1. Jeffrey Butler, "Cecil Rhodes," *International Journal of African Historical Studies* X (1977), 260, 280. C.W. de Kiewiet, *A History of South Africa, Social & Economic* (London, 1941), 111.

2. Kipling to Basil Williams, October 1918, Mss. Afr. s. 134 *(27); Anthony Sampson, The Black and Gold* (New York, 1987), 48; Geoffrey Wheatcroft, *The Randlords* (New York, 1986), 283.

3. Waterston to CJR, 8 February 1893, Mss. Afr. s. 288 (C 227), Rhodes House, Oxford.

4. Butler, "Rhodes," 281.

CHAPTER 1

The Man and the Mystery

1. Philip Jourdan, *Cecil Rhodes: His Private Life by His Private Secretary* (London, 1911), 19–20.

2. Gordon Le Sueur, *Cecil Rhodes: The Man and His Work* (London, 1913), 20–24.

3. Sidney Low, "Personal Recollections of Cecil Rhodes: Some Conversations in London," *The Nineteenth Century and After,* CCCIII (May 1902), 829.

4. Perceval Maitland Laurence, "A Great Adventurer," *The Examiner* (9 October 1902), 255–261. This article was reprinted in Laurence, *On Circuit in Kaffirland and Other Sketches and Studies* (London, 1903), 43–69. It was written in Kimberley on 6 April 1902, a week after Rhodes' death. Le Sueur, *Rhodes,* 29; Low, "Recollections," 830.

5. Emil Ludwig (trans. Kenneth Burke), *Genius and Character* (New York, 1927), 27.

6. Imperialist (pseud. John Verschoyle), *Cecil Rhodes: A Biography and an Appreciation* (London, 1897), 9–15.

7. Basil Williams, *Cecil Rhodes* (London, 1921), 6.

8. James G. McDonald, *Rhodes: A Life* (London, 1927), 381, 387, 387, 392.

9. J.G. Lockhart and C.M. Woodhouse, *Cecil Rhodes: The Colossus of Southern Africa* (New York, 1963), 1, 3–4, 9.

10. John Gallagher and Ronald Robinson, "The Partition of Africa," in John Gallagher (ed. Anil Seal), *The Decline, Revival and Fall of the British Empire* (Cambridge, 1982), 67–68.

11. Gilbert K. Chesterton, "The Sultan," in his *A Miscellany of Men* (New York, 1912), 239–243. "The Sultan" was first published in the *Daily News* (London), 11 June 1910, under the title "The Orientalism of the Empire."

12. Ernest Bruce Iwan-Müller, "Cecil John Rhodes," *Fortnightly Review*, LXXVII (1902), 758.

13. Low, "Recollections," 830.

14. Laurence, "Adventurer," 256–257.

CHAPTER 2

Life in the Vicarage

1. Quoted in Ernest Jones, *Life and Work of Sigmund Freud* (New York, 1953), I, 5.

2. These quotations are from a mélange of reminiscences collected from survivors in Bishop's Stortford, the family home, who knew the Rhodes family well. The statements by Rickett, a servant; William Harrington, the church clerk; Mrs. Newman (née Wyhow), nurse to Arthur and Bernard Rhodes; and William Smith, the church sexton, have been quoted above and additional comments appear below. The longest description of Mrs. Rhodes comes from a curious document originally deposited in the Rhodes-Livingstone Museum (Zambia) and of unknown provenance. Its author and date are also unknown, but the information contained in the typescript about Rhodes and his family is of great circumstantial value. It is the account of a contemporary in the village who knew the family intimately or the reconstructed account of someone, possibly Lewis Michell, who was able to learn about the family in Bishop's Stortford not long after Rhodes' death. The prose is very florid. That document is called "Fragments on Rhodes." When I attempted in the 1970s through the Museum and its early curators to discover information about the "Fragments," I could elicit no new details whatsoever. The other statements are called "Ideas" and "Says." Both sets are now in Mss. Afr. s. 641, Rhodes House.

3. See Heinz Kohut, "Forms and Transformations of Narcissism," in Charles Strozier (ed.), *Self, Psychology, and the Humanities* (New York, 1985), 97.

4. "Fragments," 8. Susan Bankes, quoted in Norfolk *Weekly Standard* (10 May 1902).

5. James G. McDonald, *Rhodes: A Life* (London, 1927), 4.

6. Harry Levinson and Stuart Rosenthal, *CEO: Corporate Leadership in Action* (New York, 1984), 290. Levinson and Rosenthal interviewed the leaders of six major national and international corporations. A significant finding was the degree to which these men enjoyed leadership as a form of play.

7. Much of the information on Rhodes' ancestors is derived from an unpublished typescript prepared by Charles Cowen and filed with the Cowen Papers, Mss. Afr. s. 229(II), Rhodes House, and from excerpts from R.B. Prosser's unnamed articles in *St. Pancras Notes and Queries*, 1, 2 (3 February, 5 March 1897). Thomas William Baxter

pursued some of the same matters in 1971 and discovered that William's case also went to the House of Lords on appeal, where he lost. It was also tried in the Court of Exchequer, which found for de Beauvoir in 1834. The chancery records are at C.13/2184/22 in the Public Record Office; there is printed material in the Hackney Archives department; and the whole is summarized in a letter of 1971 (but undated) from the Borough of Hackney to Baxter. The letter and other correspondence are in Mss. Afr. s. 1647 (II, 122), Rhodes House.

   8. John Evelyn, *The Diary* (London, 1906), II, 98; Daniel Defoe, *A Tour through the Whole Island of Great Britain . . .* (London, 1753; orig. ed., 1710), II, 196; Annie Berlyn, *Bishop's Stortford and Its Story* (Norwich, n.d. but c. 1924); W.E.B. Ewbank et al., *Bishop's Stortford: A Short History* (Bishop's Stortford, 1969).

   9. See Dean Keith Simonton, *Genius, Creativity, and Leadership: Historiometric Inquiries* (Cambridge, Mass., 1984), 26–28.

   10. "Fragments," 9; "Mrs. Gervis Reminiscences," 4, Mss. Afr. s. 641, Rhodes House.

   11. "Fragments," 9; "Harrington's Ideas," 8–9, Mss. Afr. s. 641.

   12. W. Basil Worsfold, "The Boyhood of Cecil Rhodes," *The Blue Peter* (July 1934), 327; "Harrington's Ideas," 8.

   13. McDonald, *Rhodes*, 7–8.

   14. CJR to Mother, 11 September 1870, Mss. Afr. s. 1647, Rhodes House.

   15. Eleanor Alexander reported that Rhodes told her in the 1890s that when he first went out to Africa only his mother wrote to him. No other family members corresponded. "This partly accounted for his attitude toward women," she explained. Lady Alexander, interview with Basil Williams, 14 February 1920, Mss. Afr. s. 134, Rhodes House.

   16. For the full Confession, its context, and references, see Chapter 5. Harry Levinson, quoted in Daniel Goleman, "The Psyche of the Entrepreneur," *New York Times Magazine* (2 February 1986), 30. See also the detailed studies of Orvis S. Collins and David G. Moore, *The Enterprising Man* (East Lansing, 1964). The subjects of their interviews had fathers who were "unable and unwilling" to nurture. The mothers of the nascent entrepreneurs exerted a hold on them; they grew up prematurely, were little interested in formal education, and had intense desires for autonomy (68).

   17. "Mrs. Newman Says," 16, in Mss. Afr. s. 641.

   18. Fragments, 4; "Rickett's Ideas," 4; "Mrs. Newman," 15; Lewis Michell, *The Life of the Rt. Hon. Cecil J. Rhodes, 1853–1902* (London, 1910), I, 18; Violet Sparrow, *Yesterday's Stortford* (Buckingham, 1986), 43.

   19. "Mrs. Newman," 15.

   20. "Fragments," 11; "Mrs. Purkis (Purllis?) Says," 18.

   21. "Rickett," 5.

   22. Anon., "Cecil Rhodes," Ch. 1, 10, Mss. Afr. s. 641, Rhodes House.

   23. Worsfold, "Boyhood," 328; Yerburgh, interview with Basil Williams, 26 June 1914, Mss. Afr. s. 134 (Box 1, Notebook I), Rhodes House.

   24. G.T. Hutchinson, *Frank Rhodes: A Memoir* (London, 1908), 2–3.

   25. "Fragments," 11–12.

   26. Although Francis William's brother William Arthur is listed in an official genealogy as unmarried and deceased before 1860, W. Basil Worsfold, *Twenty Centuries of England: Being the Annals of Bishop's Stortford* (London, 1926), 131, states that the Arthur who lived with his wife and children at Twyford was that brother. He is said in one account to have moved from the Midlands to Twyford, in another from Leyton Grange, Cecil's grandfather's home. There is no other Arthur on the Rhodes' family

chart, aside from a distant collateral cousin who never married. See also "Fragments," 7; "Games Played," 4, Mss. Afr. s. 1647.

27. Assembly, *Debates* (1894), 419.

28. *Ibid.,* 12; Worsfold, "Boyhood," 328.

29. Alfred W.N. Barder to Charles Cowen, 9 October 1899; D.C.R. Banham to Cowen, 12 October 1899; in Mss. Afr. s. 229 (II) (Box 1, file 1), 10–11, 18–19, Rhodes House.

30. Worsfold, "Boyhood," 328; "Fragments," 7.

31. CJR to Aunt Sophy, 17 July 1868.

32. "Fragments," 15; Michell, *Rhodes,* I, 21.

33. Howard Hensman, *Cecil Rhodes: A Study of a Career* (Edinburgh, 1901), 6; Hensman was close to Edith, Rhodes' sister. See also Lockhart and Woodhouse, *Rhodes,* 29; "Fragments," 16. By the time we reach Robert Blake, *A History of Rhodesia* (London, 1977), 32, Rhodes at sixteen had been "taken seriously ill."

34. The gist of Herbert's letters to his family is quoted in a report written by the London secretary of the Colonisation Society, in turn quoted in Guy McDonald, "Cecil Rhodes in Natal," *Cape Argus* (6 June 1936). The new evidence is from an article in the *Natal Witness* for 1935 or 1936 which quotes a letter from Herbert Rhodes to Dr. P.C. Sutherland, 1868, Mss. Afr. t. 5(407).

35. On the family lungs, see Ernest Rhodes to CJR, 26 June, 14 July 1886, Mss. Afr. s. 228 (C28, 26–27), Rhodes House. The Morris report is Claude W. Morris to Lord Elton, 6 October 1955, Mss. Afr. t. 11 (101–104). However, in 1924, Edward A. Maund, who had known Rhodes in Africa, went to Bishop's Stortford. He interviewed William Smith, who had attended the high school at some point during Rhodes' tenure there. Smith told Maund that Rhodes was "certainly delicate. . . ." He remembered him being sent off to Africa. "It was like this. He was at home studying and his father thinking he looked ill sent him down to the doctor. . . ." Smith claimed to have been present during the interview when the physician asked Rhodes what ailed him. " 'You are all in a sweat . . . go off for a quiet walk and come back to me when you have calmed down.' " The corroboration of the Morris view ends at that point in the recollection, for when Rhodes had returned from his walk and had been examined, the physician "wrote" to the vicar, reporting distinct signs of tubercular trouble. A warm climate was best. And "so he was sent off." Smith, interview with Maund, 23 June 1924, Mss. Afr. s. 229(IV), Rhodes House.

36. McDonald, *Rhodes,* 10. For Rhodes' letters to his mother, see the next chapter, and references there.

CHAPTER 3
The Cotton Fields, a Testing

1. CJR to his mother, 11 September 1870. Mss. Afr. s. 1647, Rhodes House. Ernest Jones, *Life and Work of Sigmund Freud* (New York, 1953), I, 5.

2. Peter Cormack Sutherland, *Journal of a Voyage in Baffins Bay and Barrow Straits* (London, 1852), 2 v.

3. CJR to his mother, 11 September 1870. He never did make the collection since other priorities imposed themselves.

4. See Henry Slater, "Land, Labour and Capital in Natal: The Natal Land and Colonisation Company, 1860–1948," *Journal of African History,* XVI (1975), 257–271;

Alan F. Hattersley, *The British Settlement of Natal: A Study in Imperial Migration* (Cambridge, 1950), 229–231; B.J.T. Leverton, *The Natal Cotton Industry, 1845–1875: A Study in Failure* (Pretoria, 1963), 12–35.

5. CJR to his mother, 11 September 1870.

6. The precise sequence of events of the discovery of diamonds in South Africa is still remarkably tangled. A recent, well-researched source sets out much of the evidence, but without drawing any clear conclusions. What follows is based on that evidence, with an awareness that disagreements may still exist respecting a month-by-month chronology. Marian Robertson, *Diamond Fever: South African Diamond History, 1866–9 from Primary Sources* (Cape Town, 1974), 179, 221–223. This supersedes the older, popular sources and debunks many of the most racy myths about the circumstances in which diamonds were found.

7. Quoted in Guy McDonald, "Cecil Rhodes in Natal," *Cape Argus* (6 June 1936).

8. CJR to Mary Peacock, 13 February 1871, Afr. s. 115, Rhodes House.

9. CJR to his mother, 18 October 1870. Margaret Ballantyne, the rumors go, broke off her engagement to Rhodes and married Charles Taylor. But this tale may have originated very much later, after Rhodes had become famous. See Killie Campbell to C.J. Sibbett, 16 February, 27 February 1953, E. Hart to Killie Campbell, 14 March 1953, Mss. Afr. t. 5 (295–300), Rhodes House.

10. CJR to his mother, 11 September 1870.

11. An Amateur Cotton Planter, "The Cotton Fields, Upper Umkomanzi," in John Robinson (ed.), *Notes on Natal: An Old Colonist's Book for New Settlers* (Durban, 1872), 143.

12. *Ibid.*, 144.

13. CJR to his mother, 19 September 1870, Mss. Afr. s. 1647.

14. CJR to his mother, 18 October 1870, Mss. Afr. s. 1647.

15. CJR to Louisa and Edith Rhodes, 17 November 1870, Mss. Afr. s. 1647.

16. CJR to his mother, 17 January 1871, Mss. Afr. s. 1647.

17. CJR to Mary Peacock, 13 February 1871, Mss. Afr. s. 115.

18. Anon., "The Cotton Fields," 146.

19. CJR to Mary Peacock, 13 February 1871.

20. CJR to his mother, 17 February 1871; CJR to his mother, 11 April 1871.

21. CJR to his mother, 26 February 1871; 20 April 1871.

22. See Heinz Kohut, "Creativeness, Charisma, Group Psychoanalysis: Reflections on the Self-Analysis of Freud," in Charles Strozier (ed.), *Self-Psychology and the Humanities* (New York, 1985), 199–201.

23. Kohut, "Charisma," 196–197.

24. CJR to his mother, 20 April 1871.

25. CJR to his mother, 11 April 1871.

26. Leverton, "Natal Cotton," 35; McDonald, "Rhodes in Natal," 6 June 1936; CJR to his mother, 7 June 1871.

27. CJR to his mother, 26 February 1871.

28. CJR to his mother, 7 June 1871.

29. CJR to his mother, 16 July 1871; McDonald, "Rhodes in Natal." Killie Campbell heard a story that a man called Powys went with Rhodes to Kimberley. Campbell to C.J. Sibbett, 11 April 1953, Mss. Afr. t. 5 (300).

30. James G. McDonald, *Rhodes: A Life* (London, 1927), 16. See Lewis Michell, *The Life of the Rt. Hon. Cecil J. Rhodes* (London, 1910), I, 34–35. H.E. Norton to Harold Kennedy, secretary, Syfret Trust Co., 13 December 1960, Mss. Afr. s. 229 (VII). See

also J.G. Lockhart and C.M. Woodhouse, *Cecil Rhodes: The Colossus of Southern Africa* (New York, 1963), 40–41.

CHAPTER 4

Scraping Together the First Riches

1. CJR to his mother, 4 January 1872, Mss. Afr. s. 1647, Rhodes House. This well-known letter is excerpted in part, but not dated, in Williams, *Rhodes*, 26–29, and quoted from Williams by virtually all other biographers. Most follow Williams in implying that Rhodes wrote it "shortly after his arrival." Thus the narrative flow of their exposition is improved at the expense of questions concerning the long delay (given Rhodes' habits and the apology to his mother with which he begins the letter) between arriving and writing, the absence of any word about Herbert's departure, and, given the tenor of his previous letters to his mother, the absence of any discussion of what was to happen with the cotton plantation. This also is the most fully descriptive and powerful letter—five long foolscap pages in holograph—that Rhodes ever wrote. Unlike later ones, there is almost no repetition of themes and ideas.

2. George Beet, *The Grand Old Days of the Diamond Fields: Memories of Past Times with the Diggers of Diamondia* (Cape Town, 1931), 19–21.

3. "A Digger," "The Great Camp at Colesberg Kop," in Robinson, *Notes on Natal*, 211. Most modern sources date the discovery of the wealth of the Colesberg kopje to July 1871. For contemporary agreements, see Charles Albert Payton, *The Diamond Diggings of South Africa: A Personal and Practical Account* (London, 1872), 22–210; Beet, *Old Days*, 16–18. But Babe, writing a few months after the event, says that the rush occurred at the beginning of August. Jerome L. Babe, *South African Diamond Fields* (New York, 1872), 66. The anonymous account in Robinson, Notes on Natal, 210, agrees.

4. Charles Chapman, *A Voyage from Southampton to Cape Town . . . and Illustrations of the Diamond Fields . . .* (London, 1872), 122–123, 145–146.

5. See Robert Ross, *Adam Kok's Griquas: A Study in the Development of Stratification in South Africa* (Cambridge, 1976), 18–20; Phyllis Lewsen, *John X. Merriman: Paradoxical South African Statesman* (New Haven, 1982), 34–35.

6. John Xavier Merriman, Memoir on Rhodes, March 1922. The memoir was requested by the *Cape Times*, but later not used at Merriman's request. It is in file A90 in the Cullen Library, University of the Witwatersrand.

7. William Charles Scully, *Reminiscences of a South African Pioneer* (London, 1913), 126.

8. George Beet, handwritten memoir, in the Beet papers, McGregor Memorial Museum, Kimberley. The published version is virtually identical to the holographic description: Beet, *The Grand Old Days*, 163. Beet arrived in Africa in 1856 when he was three, the son of a soldier from Canterbury. Beet worked as a government clerk in Kaffraria (Ciskei) and in Cape Town, and then went to the diamond fields about the same time as Cecil Rhodes. Shortly thereafter, he helped run the *Diamond News*, the first local newspaper, and subsequently became a law agent and stock broker.

9. CJR to his mother, 4 January 1872.

10. Babe, *Diamond Fields*, 69.

11. Chapman, *Journey*, 135–136.

12. The above quotations, if not otherwise attributed, are from CJR to his mother, 4 January 1872.

13. Payton, *Diamond Diggings,* 232.

14. *Diamond News,* 2 March 1872. Quoted in Lewsen, *Selections,* I, 5–7.

15. Quoted in Lewis Michell, *The Life of the Rt. Hon. Cecil John Rhodes* (London, 1910), I, 44.

16. Frank Rhodes to his mother, n.d., quoted in Williams, *Rhodes,* 31. Another revealing letter is from about 1873, from Cecil to Frank, Mss. Afr. s. 1647.

17. Garstin, quoted in Michell, Rhodes, I, 41–42.

18. Francis Rhodes to his mother, 27 April 1872, quoted in G.T. Hutchinson, *Frank Rhodes: A Memoir* (London, 1908), 7; Lewsen, *Merriman,* 35–37.

19. Alan Rudd, *Charles Dunell Rudd, 1844–1916* (Ipswich, 1981), 7; Lewsen, *Merriman,* 36.

20. Digger Steytler, quoted in J.T. McNish, *The Glittering Road* (Cape Town, 1970), 29.

21. *Ibid.,* 31. The doubtful suggestion is in Robert V. Turrell, "Rhodes, De Beers, and Monopoly," *Journal of Imperial and Commonwealth History,* X (1982), 314.

22. See Colin Newbury, "Out of the Pit: The Capital Accumulation of Cecil Rhodes," *Journal of Imperial and Commonwealth History,* X (1981), 28. Turrell's revisionary view of Rudd the merchant has yet to be substantiated. Turrell, "Rhodes," 316.

23. McDonald, *Rhodes,* 20.

24. McNish, *Glittering,* 30.

25. Payton, *Diamond Diggings,* 19.

26. Nancy Rouillard (ed.), *Matabele Thompson: An Autobiography* (London, 1936), 198–199.

27. CJR to Rudd, 1 June 1876, Trinity College (Oxford) archives, printed in Rhodes House Christmas letter, 1972.

28. CJR to Sutherland, August 1873, Mss. Afr. t. 5; John Edward A. Dick Lauder (Rhodes' agent) to Sutherland, 10 September 1873; Dick Lauder to Sutherland, 3 December 1873; CJR to Sutherland, 28 May 1874; Michell, *Rhodes,* I, 57, says that Rhodes suggested this kind of charity because Sutherland wanted Rhodes to send a gift to the local church, but evidence for Michell's aspersion is lacking. For the new railways in Natal, see Robinson, *Natal,* xx. For Oxford and England, see Chapter V.

29. CJR to Sutherland, 28 May 1874, Mss. Afr. t. 5. The population figures are Merriman's. See Lewsen, *Merriman,* 39. The most coherent study of this period is William H. Worger, *South Africa's City of Diamonds: Mine Workers and Monopoly Capitalism in Kimberley, 1867–1895* (New Haven, 1987), 13–30.

30. But see Turrell, "Rhodes," 316.

31. Letters from Rhodes to Rudd (7 December, 8 December 1874), Mss. Afr. s. 134 (VI), precisely date and describe this event in an even-handed manner that is distorted and dramatized in the biographies, e.g., Michell, *Rhodes,* I, 65–66; McDonald, *Rhodes,* 42–43. Clive Mennell's copy (in Johannesburg) of the 8 December 1874 letter provides a clearer date than others. For the alleged bribery, see Brian Roberts, *The Diamond Magnates* (New York, 1972), 53–56; Turrell, "Rhodes," 317. Turrell, *Capital and Labour on the Kimberley Diamond Fields, 1871–1890* (Cambridge, 1987), 84, 82–87, puts an entirely revisionist twist on this episode. He also tries to downgrade Rhodes' role as a mining entrepreneur. But his attitude races ahead of the available evidence.

32. CJR to Rudd, 9 October 1874, Ms. 110/1, the Brenthurst Library.

33. Henry Caesar Hawkins, quoted in Michell, *Rhodes,* I, 64.

34. CJR to Frank, 19 August 1875, Mss. Afr. s.1647 (98). For the seller's market in wood, see Kevin Shillington, "The Impact of the Diamond Discoveries on the Kim-

berley Hinterland: Class Formation, Colonialism and Resistance among the Thlaping of Griqualand West in the 1870s," in Shula Marks and Richard Rathbone (eds.), *Industrialisation and Social Change in South Africa* (London, 1982), 106.

35. CJR to Thomas Rudd and Co., 8 May 1876; CJR to C.D. Rudd, 1 June 1876, Trinity College archives, printed in Rhodes House Christmas letter, 1972.

36. CJR to Frank, 19 August 1875. Imperialist (pseud. John Verschoyle), *Cecil Rhodes: A Biography and An Appreciation* (London, 1897), 8–9.

37. CJR to Frank, 19 August 1875. The deceased was John Cyprian Thompson, one of three commissioners who had administered Griqualand West before Southey. His friend was Captain John Carr.

38. *Diamond Fields Advertiser* (29 April 1932), cited by Phillida Brooke Simons (ed.), *John Blades Currey, 1850 to 1900: Fifty Years in the Cape Colony* (Johannesburg, 1986), 249.

39. This first will is not to be found in Afr. t. 1, the collection of wills in Rhodes House. It is mentioned, however, along with the "slight" heart attack, in McDonald, *Rhodes*, 25–26.

40. Michell, *Rhodes*, I, 49; McDonald, *Rhodes*, 26; Williams, *Rhodes*, 35; Scully, *Reminiscences*, 129. See also Colvin, *Jameson*, I, 48.

41. CJR to Sutherland, n.d. October 1873. In the late 1880s, this farm was being run for Rhodes by J.E. van der Merwe, who had interpreted for him in the Transvaal.

42. McDonald, *Rhodes*, 26; Williams, *Rhodes*, 35.

43. Merriman to Basil Williams, 4 July 1919, Mss. Afr. s. 134; Lewsen, *Merriman*, 36; Hutchinson, *Frank Rhodes*, 5, and quoted, 10; Imperialist, *Rhodes*, 5; Garstin, quoted in Michell, *Rhodes*, I, 46; Scully, *Reminiscences*, 128–129; Louis Cohen, *Reminiscences of Kimberley* (London, 1911), 46. The reference to Mirabeau was an allusion to Honoré Gabriel Riqueti, Comte de Mirabeau (1749–1791), orator, Jacobin, gastronome, and president of the Assemblée Nationale. Brian Roberts, *Cecil Rhodes: Flawed Colossus* (London, 1987), 19, calls Rhodes a "nervous exhibitionist" in his early Kimberley days, but such an interpretation seems vastly overdrawn.

44. Simons, *Currey*, 150. Currey composed his memoirs in 1899–1900.

45. CJR to his father, n.d. January 1874; n.d. March 1874. J.H. Hall (who had been up at Oriel with Rhodes) interview with Basil Williams, 5 July 1919, Mss. Afr. s. 134, seems to be the source for the "chill" notion, although Hall refers to "chest weakness," too. Williams, *Rhodes*, 37, says that Rhodes' chill was caught during a second term (very unlikely given his movements in early 1874), and that a doctor gave him only six months to live—a notation that Rhodes subsequently saw.

46. CJR to Aunt Sophy, n.d. September 1873. The Bennett story is usually assigned to 1870 (e.g., Lockhart and Woodhouse, *Rhodes*, 30), but the Albert Hall was not then built, and Rhodes would have been unlikely at sixteen to have spent his last night attending a concert. In 1873–74, however, with his mother recently dead and his father undergoing a "cure" at a Woodhall Spa in Northamptonshire, Rhodes could easily have gone up to the Albert Hall (in the right season, too) after a term at Oxford. Dicina A. Hurst to Lord Elton, 18 September 1955, Mss. Afr. t. 10, reported the memoirs of a Mrs. Bennett of Southampton, who related this anecdote to her in 1914. In a letter from Rhodes to Aunt Sophy, undated but written in 1873, Rhodes refers to having been given a concert ticket by his aunt, Mss. Afr. s.1647. The concert at the Albert Hall closest to December 15, his date of departure, was a performance by William Carter's choir on Thursday evening, December 11, of Haydn's *Creation.*.

47. CJR to Sophy, n.d. September 1873, Mss. Afr. s.1647.

48. George A. Shepperson calls him deeply emotional in "Cecil John Rhodes: Some Biographical Problems," *Rhodes* [University] - *Newsletter* (December, 1981), 2.

49. Lewsen, *Merriman*, 36; Merriman to Basil Williams, 4 July 1919.

50. Paton to Merriman, 20 September 1874, quoted in Lewsen, *Selections*, I, 9, 11. See also Josiah Wright Matthews, *Incwadi Yami: Or Twenty Years' Personal Experience in South Africa* (New York, 1887), 209. For the genesis and events of the rebellion, see Ken Smith, *Alfred Aylward: The Tireless Agitator* (Johannesburg, 1983), 49–65; Robert V. Turrell, "The 1875 Black Flag Revolt on the Kimberley Diamond Fields," *Journal of Southern African Studies*, VIII (1981), 194–235; Inez B. Sutton, "The Diggers' Revolt in Griqualand West, 1875," *International Journal of African Historical Studies*, XII (1979), 40–61. Turrell believes that the antagonism of the diggers directly reflected their own declining economic stake in the future of the diamond fields. He also questions the usual classification of Southey as pro-digger.

51. Cornelis W. de Kiewiet, *The Imperial Factor in South Africa: A Study in Politics and Economics* (Cambridge, 1973), 56.

52. CJR to Frank, 19 August 1875. For another view of Rhodes' attitudes, see Lewsen, *Merriman*, 37.

53. According to Simons, *Currey*, 150: "I set to work on a proclamation . . . suppressing public gaming houses; and while engaged on it—I fear it was on a Sunday—I first got to know something of Mr. C.J. Rhodes who was on a visit to us and I at once formed a high opinion of his quick intelligence and of his grasp of facts. We went over my work together and, knowing something of the subject, he gave me very material help."

54. Alexander Wilmot, *The Life and Times of Sir Richard Southey* (London, 1904), 253–254; CJR to Frank, 19 August 1875.

CHAPTER 5

A Band of Brothers amid the Dreaming Spires

1. John Flint, *Cecil Rhodes* (Boston, 1974), 23.

2. See the discussion in Chapter 4 and the letter cited there to his aunt.

3. Lewis Michell, *Cecil Rhodes* (London, 1910), I, 76; Sir Charles Metcalfe, interview 16 June 1914; Robert A. Yerburgh, interview with Basil Williams, 26 June 1914; Mss. Afr. 134 (Box 1, Notebook 1, 170–171), Rhodes House. St. Albans merged into Merton College in 1882. See University College, *Record*, IX (1984), 342.

4. George N. Clark, *Cecil Rhodes and His College* (Oxford, 1953), 3. J.H. Hall to Basil Williams, 5 July 1919; Mss. Afr. s. 134 (39–40), Rhodes House. Anon., "How Mr. Rhodes Went to Oriel," *Westminster Gazette*, (9 April 1902).

5. Walker, quoted in Clark, *College*, 4.

6. Butler, in Howard Hensman, *Cecil Rhodes: A Study of a Career* (Edinburgh, 1901), 23, 25; Basil Williams, *Cecil Rhodes* (London, 1921), 37; Hall to Williams, Mss. Afr. s. 134. See also above, Chapter 3. The main obituary in *The Times* (27 March 1902) says more directly, but without attribution, that Rhodes remained at Oriel for six months (!) "taking a great deal of athletic exercise. His heart became again seriously affected, and inflammation of the lungs threatened him with complete breakdown." Michell, *Rhodes*, I, 78.

7. Rhodes to Rudd, May 1876, Mss. Afr. t. 5 (540–543), Rhodes House.

8. J.G. Lockhart and C.M. Woodhouse, *Cecil Rhodes* (New York, 1963), 49.

9. Butler, in *Westminster Gazette*, 1902; quoted in Hensman, *Rhodes*, 24.

10. Williams, *Rhodes*, 4. See also Colin Newbury, "Cecil Rhodes and the South African Connection: 'A Great Imperial University'?" in Frederick Madden and David K. Fieldhouse (eds.), *Oxford and the Idea of Commonwealth: Essays Presented to Sir Edgar Williams* (London, 1982), 79.

11. Quoted in Clark, *College*, 5. The same story also appears with slight differences in Hall to Williams, Mss. Afr. s. 134 (38–39); *The Times* (27 March 1902). What may be the original, correct version of the same story is contained in the P.H. Ditchfield, "Famous Men of Oriel College," *The Oriel Record*, I (1911), 163. There Rhodes is quoted as saying to Butler: "You let me alone, Mr. Dean; I shall pull through somehow." Apparently this comment was provoked by Butler's suggesting to Rhodes that he was cutting too many lectures and that he therefore might find a more "congenial sphere" for the exercise of his "peculiar genius" at New Inn Hall, which was not then a true college foundation. For another version of the quotation, see Butler, quoted in Hensman, *Rhodes*, 24. See also Michell, *Rhodes*, I, 81.

12. Rhodes to Rudd, 1 June 1876, Trinity College archives.

13. Michell, *Rhodes*, I, 78; Yerburgh, interview with Williams, Mss. Afr. s. 134 (Box 1, Notebook 1, 173); Lord Desborough, interview with Williams, 18 May 1914, Mss. Afr. s. 134.

14. James Rochfort Maguire, interviewed by Basil Williams, 18 June 1914; Sir Francis Newton, interviewed by Williams, 4 July 1919, Mss. Afr. s. 134 (Box 1, Notebook 1); Lockhart and Woodhouse, *Rhodes*, 51; E. Ruggles-Brise, letter of 11 April 1902, in *The Times* (19 April 1902). Perceval Maitland Laurence, *On Circuit in Kaffirland* (London, 1903), 56.

15. Flint, *Rhodes*, 23. The quotation was cited first, slightly incorrectly, in Williams, *Rhodes*, 42. It comes from the memory of William Alexander, Archbishop of Armagh, reporting a conversation of 1898(?), in Eleanor Alexander (ed.), *Primate Alexander: A Memoir* (London, 1913), 259. For the Masons, see Rhodes, "Confession of Faith," 2 June 1877, in Flint, *Rhodes*, 249. The account of the masonic ceremony derives from Maguire's interview with Williams, 18 May 1914, Mss. Afr. s. 134, (Box 1, Notebook 1, 168).

16. Desborough, interview with Williams, 18 May 1914; Maguire interview, 18 May 1914; Metcalfe, interview, 16 May 1919 (Box 1, Notebook 1, 193–197), all Mss. Afr. s. 134. See also E. Ruggles-Brise, letter of 11 April 1902, in *The Times* (19 April 1902). The other reports are by unnamed individuals in Michell, *Rhodes*, I, 79–80. The Rev. A.L. Barnes-Lawrence's report appeared in Hensman, *Rhodes*, 27–28, 31. See also Ditchfield, "Famous Men," 163. For delicacy, see also Chapter 25.

17. CJR to blank, n.d. but September/October 1876, in *Diamond Fields Advertiser*, Christmas 1906.

18. Yerburgh, interview with Williams, 26 June 1914, Mss. Afr. s. 134.

19. CJR to blank, in *Advertiser*.

20. Felix Gross, *Rhodes of Africa* (London, 1956), 39, 43–44. According to W.W. Paddon, Rhodes wrote to Disraeli in 1876 from Kimberley, and not from Oxford in 1877. See Michell, *Rhodes*, I, 66–67. See also Lois A.C. Raphael, *The Cape-to-Cairo Dream: A Study in British Imperialism* (New York, 1936), 21, 50–51; William E. Gladstone, "Aggression on Egypt and Freedom in the East," *The Nineteenth Century*, I, 6 (1877), 158–159. The Arnold pamphlet of 1876 is mentioned in Henry Hamilton (Sir Harry) Johnston, "My Story of the Cape to Cairo Scheme," in Leo Weinthal (ed.), *The Story of the Cape to Cairo River Route from 1887 to 1922* (London, 1923), I, 69.

21. John Ruskin, *Lectures in Art* (Oxford, 1870), 41–44. Newbury, "Rhodes," 79; Williams, *Rhodes,* 42; Lockhart and Woodhouse, *Rhodes,* 49–50. But see Flint, *Rhodes,* 27. There is a report which contradicts Newbury, and which may stem from a conversation with Rhodes himself, in Frank Harris, *My Life and Loves* (New York, 1979; orig. pub. 1925, 1953, 1963, in five volumes), II, 444–445, 781.

22. CJR to Rudd, l June 1876, Trinity College archives. CJR to blank, in *Advertiser.*

23. CJR to Rudd, 1 June 1876, corrected transcription supplied by Robert V. Turrell, Mss. Afr. t. 14 (214–228).

24. CJR to Sophia Peacock, 26 February 1880, Mss. Afr. s. 1647; CJR to blank, in *Advertiser.*

25. CJR to Rudd, 1 June 1876. Williams, *Rhodes,* 39. Whether Rhodes sold the property then or later has never been clear. A footnote by Williams has led biographers to assume that Rhodes in fact realized his £800 profit. But there is no real evidence either way.

26. CJR to Rudd, 1 June 1876. See also Chapter 4, above, for the machinery and for Rhodes' nefarious pumping experiences.

27. Daniel J. Levinson, *The Seasons of a Man's Life* (New York, 1978), 56–58. The work of Levinson and his collaborators is based on intensive study of forty men of diverse ethnic, social, and cultural backgrounds between ages 35 and 45. It fills in the details of a relatively silent period in Erikson's developmental schema using data drawn from normal subjects rather than from persons undergoing treatment for psychological disorders. See Erik H. Erikson, *Childhood and Society* (New York, 1963; 2nd ed.), 263–269.

28. William Winwood Reade, *The Martyrdom of Man* (New York, 1874), 505, 512–515; Catherine Radziwill, *Cecil Rhodes: Man and Empire-Maker* (New York, 1918), 126–127.

29. The fullest printed text of the Confession is in Flint, *Rhodes,* 248–252. The original is in Mss. Afr. t. 1 (17), Rhodes House, Oxford.

30. Charles Warren, letter of 27 March 1902 in *The Times* (30 March 1902). See also Warren, *On the Veldt in the Seventies* (London, 1902), 254. Earlier, Warren, en route to Kimberley from Cape Town to serve as a special commissioner to settle white claims to land in Griqualand West after surveying the little colony's border with the Orange Free State, met Rhodes aboard the *Nubia.* Warren was impressed, and was pleased to see Rhodes again when he traveled by postcart from Dordrecht to Kimberley between 3 and 7 August 1878. Watkin W. Williams, *The Life of General Sir Charles Warren* (Oxford, 1941), 95–96.

31. W.T. Stead, *The Last Will and Testament of Cecil John Rhodes* (London, 1902), 61–62.

32. Michell, *Rhodes,* I, 67. No other early biographer mentions that Rhodes endured a heart attack in 1877. No primary evidence is available, either way. Michell conceivably could be confusing the incident with someone's memory of the 1872 heart attack, Rhodes' real first. It is not clear, either, when friends found Rhodes blue with fright.

33. Joseph Orpen to Sir Arthur Francis Thomas William Smartt, 24 June 1918, Smartt Papers, A 2, South African Library. It is possible that Orpen correctly dated the dinner but remembered 1877 instead of 1878. A briefer account of the same occasion is cited in Ian Colvin, *The Life of Jameson* (London, 1922), I, 52. See also Orpen, *Reminiscences of Life in South Africa from 1846 to the Present Day* (Cape Town, 1964; repr.), 2.

34. Lockhart and Woodhouse, *Rhodes*, 53.

35. On Herbert Rhodes himself, see George Shepperson, "The Literature of British Central Africa," *The Rhodes-Livingstone Journal*, XXIII (1958), 36–38; *idem*, "Cecil John Rhodes: Some Biographical Problems," unpub. ms. (1981), 7–16, published in part with the same title in *Rhodes Newsletter* (December 1981); Helga Kaye, *The Tycoon and the President: The Life and Times of Alois Hugo Nellmapius* (Johannesburg, 1978), 19–20, 32; Norman Etherington, "Frederic Elton and the South African Factor in the Making of Britain's East African Empire," *Journal of Imperial and Commonwealth History*, IX (1981), 264–268; James Frederic Elton (ed. N.B. Cotterill), *Travels and Researches among the Lakes and Mountains of Eastern and Central Africa* (London, 1879), 242, 246–250, 256, 307, 393. William Scully, *Reminiscences of a South African Pioneer* (London, 1913), 128. For Cecil Rhodes and Herbert, see the Shepperson articles above and: Williams, *Rhodes*, 146; McDonald, *Rhodes*, 49; Gross, *Rhodes*, 412; Alexander, *Alexander*, 81; Gordon Le Sueur, *Cecil Rhodes: The Man and His Work* (London, 1913), 708. CJR to Sophia Peacock, 26 February 1880, Mss. Afr. s. 1647.

36. See Chapter 21.

37. *Dictionary of National Biography*, 182; Clark, *College*, 4.

38. Hall to Williams, 5 July 1919, Mss. Afr. s. 134. For the numbers of students and for other help I am grateful to the archival persistence of Mark Curthoys.

39. Lockhart and Woodhouse, *Rhodes*, 53; Reminiscences of E.A. Maund, 25 May 1929, Mss. Afr. s. 229 (IV); CJR to Craven, 5 August 1892. Ms. 113, the Brenthurst Library.

40. Edward Dicey, "Cecil Rhodes in Egypt," *Fortnightly Review*, LXXVII (1902), 763; Newbury, "Rhodes," 79.

41. Assembly, *Debates* (1895), 451.

CHAPTER 6

Pursuing Position and Fortune

1. Howard Hensman, *Cecil Rhodes: A Study of a Career* (Edinburgh, 1901), 34. The period of Rhodes' life that is described in this chapter has escaped the close attention of his many biographers. Each has naturally wanted briskly to propel Rhodes from Oxford to politics and then on to the great drama of the amalgamation of the major diamond mines. The first biographers rushed along in this manner, their successors following in the same furrow. Admittedly, since the sources for this period are scattered, if not obscure, it has been difficult for the biographers to tarry over a matter of a few years, however formative, in the life of a man whose later accomplishments were many and much more striking than anything that happened between 1878 and 1881. However, a key to understanding the mature Rhodes lies in an illumination of his shadows as well as in a recitation of the well known.

2. Daniel J. Levinson, *The Seasons of a Man's Life* (New York, 1978), 41.

3. Anthony Trollope, *South Africa* (Leipzig, 1878), II, 174–176, 178, 159, 160, 168.

4. Gardner F. Williams, *The Diamond Mines of South Africa* (New York, 1902), 237.

5. See John Flint, *Cecil Rhodes* (Boston, 1974), 43.

6. Nancy Rouillard (ed.), *Matabele Thompson* (London, 1936), 201; A.P. Cartwright, *Gold Paved the Way: The Story of the Gold Fields Group of Companies* (New York, 1967), 10–11. For a pro-Rudd analysis, see Colin Newbury, "Out of the Pit: The Cap-

ital Accumulation of Cecil Rhodes," *Journal of Imperial and Commonwealth History*, X, (1981), 28.

7. Alan Rudd, *Charles Dunell Rudd* (Ipswich, 1981), 16.

8. Seymour Fort, *Alfred Beit: A Study of the Man and His Work* (London, 1932), 54.

9. *Ibid.*, 54.

10. Frank Harris, *My Life and Loves* (New York, 1979; orig. ed. 1925), IV, 824.

11. *Ibid.*, 825, 823.

12. Fort, *Beit*, 58, 89.

13. Frederic S. Philipson Stow, unpub. "Memoir of the Formation of the de Beers Mining Company Ltd., and Its Subsequent Transformation into the de Beers Consolidated Mines Limited with Five Life Governors," McGregor Memorial Museum, Kimberley. The ms. was written in 1898, and the quoted portions of a typescript made from the holograph contain dates which are suspect, if not incorrect. Robert V. Turrell's edition of the Philipson Stow Papers had not been published when this book went to press.

14. Ian Colvin, *The Life of Jameson* (London, 1923), I, 59. See also Worger, *Diamonds*, 56–57.

15. CJR to Merriman, 16 February 1880, quoted in Lewsen, *Selections*, I, 81.

16. CJR to Rudd, 1 February 1881, Ms. 110/3, the Brenthurst Library. See also Turrell, *Diamond Fields*, 152.

17. CJR to Sophy, 26 February 1880, Mss. Afr. s 1647, Rhodes House.

18. *Ibid.*

19. Josiah Wright Matthews, *Incwadi Yami: Or Twenty Years' Personal Experience in South Africa* (New York, 1887), 309. See also Charles Warren, "Cecil Rhodes' Early Days in South Africa," *Contemporary Review*, LXXXI (1902), 648–649.

20. Richard Southey, quoted in Matthews, *Incwadi Yami*, 308. For the understandable causes of the Thlaping rising, see Kevin Shillington, "The Impact of the Diamond Discoveries on the Kimberley Hinterland," in Shula Marks and Richard Rathbone (eds.), *Industrialisation and Social Change in South Africa* (London, 1982), 110–112.

21. Richard A. Moyer, "The Mfengu, Self-Defence and the Cape Frontier Wars," in Christopher Saunders and Robin Derricourt (eds.), *Beyond the Cape Frontier: Studies in the History of the Transkei and Ciskei* (London, 1974), 122. CJR to Sophy, 26 February 1880, Mss. Afr. s. 1647.

22. Merriman to Julia Merriman, 20 October 1878, quoted in Phyllis Lewsen, *John X. Merriman: Paradoxical South African Statesman* (New Haven, 1982), 79.

23. Trollope, *South Africa*, II, 171–172.

24. Cornelis W. de Kiewiet, *The Imperial Factor in South Africa: A Study in Politics and Economics* (Cambridge, 1937), 158–159.

25. CJR to Merriman, 16 May 1880, quoted in Lewsen, *Selections*, I, 81–82.

26. Matthews, *Incwadi Yami*, 319. On Matthews, see Louis Cohen, *Reminiscences of Kimberley* (London, 1911), 72–73.

27. CJR to Rudd, 1 February 1881, Ms. 110/3, the Brenthurst Library.

28. Trollope, *South Africa*, II, 152; Brian Roberts, *The Diamond Magnates* (New York, 1972), 109.

29. Lockhart and Woodhouse, *Rhodes*, 69, and Flint, *Rhodes*, 51, following them, suppose that Robinson's opposition prevented Rhodes from seeking a Kimberley seat. But this predates a conflict between the two men which began a few years later, when Rhodes' wealth and prominence made him seem a serious threat to Robinson's esteem.

30. For Rudd's refusal to stand for a legislative seat in 1878, see Rudd, *Rudd*, 17.

31. Flint, *Rhodes*, 50.

32. Elliott Jaques, *A General Theory of Bureaucracy* (London, 1976), 166.

33. Memorandum by Merriman, on Rhodes, March 1922, Cullen Library, A 90. See also Merriman to Basil Williams, 27 August, 4 July 1919, Mss. Afr. s. 134, Rhodes House. For the quotation, see also Chapter 4.

34. Colvin, *Jameson*, II, 5, 10, 14.

35. Cohen, *Reminiscences*, 269; Colvin, *Jameson*, I, 38.

36. Jameson, "Personal Reminiscences of Mr. Rhodes," in Imperialist (pseud. John Verschoyle), *Cecil Rhodes: A Biography and Appreciation* (London, 1897), 391–392.

CHAPTER 7
Forging Political and Personal Alliances

1. Quoted in Michell, *Rhodes*, I, 95–96. Williams, *Rhodes*, 58, began the biographical rumor that Rhodes had refused to wear the expected black coat and top hat upon entering parliament for the first time. But there was no expectation of sable clothing. Williams also mistook the correct allusion, in a speech of Rhodes to the House on 18 July 1883. See Vindex, *Cecil Rhodes: His Political Life and Speeches, 1881–1900* (London, 1900), 50.

2. Quoted in Thomas E. Fuller, *The Right Honourable Cecil John Rhodes: A Monograph and a Reminiscence* (London, 1910), 5–6, 17–19; Michell, *Rhodes*, I, 151; Williams, *Rhodes*, 58; McDonald, *Rhodes*, 50–51; Hensman, *Rhodes*, 51.

3. Ralph Kilpin, *The Romance of a Colonial Parliament* (London, 1930), 108. Quoted in Michell, *Rhodes*, I, 93–94.

4. Francis J. Dormer, *Vengeance as a Policy in Afrikanderland: A Plea for a New Departure* (London, 1901), 241–244. See also W. E. Gladstone Solomon, *Saul Solomon: "The Member for Cape Town"* (Cape Town, 1948), 285, 289.

5. For a new view, see Hermann Giliomee, "Western Cape Farmers and the Beginnings of Afrikaner Nationalism, 1870–1915," unpub. paper (1987), 9–15.

6. See Anthony Atmore, "The Moorosi Rebellion: Lesotho, 1879," in Robert I. Rotberg and Ali A. Mazrui (eds.), *Protest and Power in Black Africa* (New York, 1970), 3–35.

7. See Edna Bradlow, "The Cape Government's Rule of Basutoland, 1871–1883," in *Archives Yearbook for South African History* (Pretoria, 1969), II, 174. For Rhodes' speech, see Vindex, *Rhodes*, 33–34; Fuller, *Rhodes*, 18; de Kiewiet, *Imperial*, 291.

8. Saul Solomon, quoted in Lockhart and Woodhouse, *Rhodes*, 71. For earlier quotes, see Williams, *Rhodes*, 63; Michell, *Rhodes*, 95. On the sequence of maneuvers which turned out the Sprigg government, only J.H. Hofmeyr, *The Life of Jan Hendrik Hofmeyr* (Cape Town, 1913), 187, states it correctly. The biographies garble this critical early shift.

9. Perceval Laurence, "A Great Adventure," *The Examiner* (9 October 1902), 257; *The Independent* (27 July 1881), quoted in Roberts, *Magnates*, 114.

10. Robinson, quoted in Weinthal, *Memories, Mines*, 79; *The Independent* (19 September 1881), quoted in Roberts, *Magnates*, 132.

11. Roberts, *Magnates*, 131. For a vivid description of trapping, see Matthews, *Incwadi Yami*, 217.

12. Quoted in Roberts, *Magnates*, 133. For searching and other methods of corraling and curbing Africans, see Worger, *Diamonds*, 139–146, 166–167.

13. Matthews, *Incwadi Yami,* 216. For details and an excellent discussion, see Colin Newbury's unpublished book on Kimberley's diamond industry (Chapter 2). I am grateful to Newbury for an early opportunity to read his chapters in draft (1987).

14. *The Independent* (27 September 1883, 4 February 1884), quoted in Roberts, *Magnates,* 137; Randolph Churchill, *Men, Mines and Animals in South Africa* (London, 1892), 45.

15. Joseph Orpen to Secretary for Native Affairs (J.W. Sauer), 27 January 1882, quoted in Bradlow, "Basutoland," 175.

16. Lord Kimberley to Robinson, 2 February 1882, quoted in ibid., 178.

17. Lord Elton, *General Gordon* (London, 1954), 303.

18. CJR to Thomas Scanlen, 3 September 1882, Mss. Afr. s. 229 (V), Rhodes House.

19. Joseph Millerd Orpen, "Maj. Gen. Gordon's Visit to Basutoland in 1882 and My Administration of the Government of That Territory from Aug. '81 to March '83," (c. 1920s), 64, unpub. typescript, Ms. 1248, Cory Library, Rhodes University; Merriman to *Cape Times* (24 November 1896), quoted in Lewsen, *Merriman,* 105. For Rhodes' cryptic view of the matter, see CJR to Merriman, 8 April 1883, Mss. Afr. t. 5 (37–40). For a favorable description of Masopha, see Matthews, *Incwadi Yami,* 382. See also Edna Bradlow, "General Gordon in Basutoland," *Historia,* XV (1970), 232–236.

20. The lush quotation is from Elton, *Gordon,* 307. The information about the actual meeting place, otherwise obscure, comes from Orpen, "Basutoland," 60–61. The description of Gordon is from Harris, *Life and Loves,* II, 431. The quoted colloquy between Gordon and Rhodes comes from Imperialist, *Rhodes,* 22–24. It appears without attribution, occasionally misquoted, in virtually all of the subsequent biographies, the earliest of which were Hensman, *Rhodes,* 46; Michell, *Rhodes,* I, 135. Orpen's typescript indicates that Rhodes took Gordon to task about his attitude to Sauer at their very first meeting. See also John Widdicombe, *In Basutoland: A Sketch of Mission Life* (London, 1891), 204–209.

21. Maund, "Rhodes and Gordon," unpub. typescript, 18 December 1924, Maund Papers, Mss. Afr. s. 229 (IV, 78–98), Rhodes House. Elton, *Gordon,* 308–309, misquotes this account, and omits Maund's criticisms of Rhodes. See also Chapter 18, where Rhodes uses other methods.

22. Gordon, letter of 1 March 1881, quoted in "The Campaign Against Corruption," *Pall Mall Gazette* (22 February 1887). Gordon's unnamed correspondent probably was Reginald Brett.

23. CJR, speech to the House, 18 July 1883, in Vindex, *Rhodes,* 48–53.

24. CJR to Merriman, 8 April 1883.

25. CJR to Merriman, 8 April 1883, Mss. Afr. t. 5 (37–40); Lewsen, *Merriman,* I, 101.

26. Francis S. Dormer, interview with Basil Williams, 14 July 1919, Mss. Afr. s. 134, Rhodes House.

27. Colvin, *Jameson,* I, 79. The will and letter are in Mss. Afr. t. 1 (6), Rhodes House. Bower to Basil Williams, 15 November 1918; interview by Williams with the Solomons, 12 June 1914, both in Mss. Afr. s. 134. Irving Grimmer, interview with J.W. Garmany, 1949, Mss. Afr. s. 69, Rhodes House.

28. For details on the cottage, see Roberts, *Magnates,* 128–129.

29. See Bernard C. Meyer, "Some Reflections on the Contribution of Psychoanalysis to Biography," *Psychoanalysis and Contemporary Science,* I (1972), 381.

CHAPTER 8

Forestalling Bismarck and Kruger—An Imperial Prologue

1. For the Confession, see above, Chapter 5. For Rhodes, see Michell, *Rhodes*, I, 71. Jameson, "Personal Reminiscences," in Imperialist, *Rhodes*, 394–395. Sidney G.A. Shippard, "Bechuanaland," in William Sheowring (ed.), *British Africa* (London, 1899), 52. See also F. Edmund Garrett, "The Character of Cecil Rhodes," *Contemporary Review*, LXXXI, (1902), 770.

2. Francis J. Dormer, *Vengeance as a Policy in Afrikanderland: A Plea for a New Departure* (London, 1901), 242.

3. John A. Hobson, "Capitalism and Imperialism in South Africa," *Contemporary Review*, LXXVII (1900), 1–17.

4. David Livingstone to Pakington, 12 December 1852, quoted in Anthony J. Dachs, "Missionary Imperialism—The Case of Bechuanaland," *Journal of African History*, XIII (1972), 649.

5. Bramston, minute on Robinson to Derby, 7 December 1882, quoted in Cornelis W. de Kiewiet, *The Imperial Factor in South Africa: A Study in Politics and Economics* (Cambridge, 1937), 295; Anthony Sillery, *Botswana: A Short Political History* (London, 1974), 58; Dachs, "Missionary", 655.

6. John Mackenzie, *Austral Africa: Losing It or Ruling It* (London, 1887), I, 118. For a good discussion of the troubled state of affairs in southern Bechuanaland, see Kevin Shillington, *The Colonisation of the Southern Tswana* (Johannesburg, 1985), 130–143.

7. CJR to Scanlen, 26 May 1883; telegraphic exchange between CJR and Scanlen, 2 June 1883; 5 June 1883; G.D. Smith to CJR, 3 June 1883, Mss. Afr. s. 229(V), Rhodes House. See also Michell, *Rhodes*, I, 153–172. Letters to CJR from G.D. Smith, W.J. King, and Gervase Donovan, from Stellaland, of 10, 18, 20 June 1883, in GH 19/12, Cape archives.

8. CJR to Merriman, 25 October 1883, Merriman Papers (204), South African Library. See also Ake Holmberg, *African Tribes and European Agencies: Colonialism and Humanitarianism in British South and East Africa, 1870–1895* (Göteborg, 1966), 36, 40, 79–80.

9. Quoted in Cape *Argus* (31 August 1883), in Lewsen, *Selections*, I, 109.

10. CJR, speech of 16 August 1883; speech of 28 September 1888, quoted in Vindex, *Cecil Rhodes: His Political Life and Speeches, 1881–1900* (London, 1900), 62–69; 214. Shillington, *Tswana*, 157–160, examines Rhodes' narrow economic motives.

11. Hercules Robinson to Merriman, 8 August, 22 August, 11 September 1883; Scanlen to Merriman, 1 November 1883, all quoted in Lewsen, *Selections*, I, 133–139.

12. Rhodes later credited Robinson with persuading both Scanlen and Derby to approach the issue correctly. CJR, speech of 28 September 1888, in Barkly West, quoted in Vindex, *Rhodes*, 215. For the negotiations and the Convention, see Deryck M. Schreuder, *Gladstone and Kruger: Liberal Government and Colonial "Home Rule," 1880–85* (London, 1969), 385–427.

13. Mackenzie to Robinson, 8 February 1884; minute by Herbert, 9 February 1884, in Anthony J. Dachs (ed.), *Papers of John Mackenzie* (Johannesburg, 1975), 162–163.

14. Cables from Robinson to Mackenzie, 30 May or 30 July 1884, Mackenzie Papers, 777, Cullen Library. See also Robinson to Mackenzie, letter, 25 July 1884, quoted in Anthony Sillery, *John Mackenzie of Bechuanaland, 1835–1899: A Study in Humanitarian Imperialism* (Cape Town, 1971), 107. For Bower, see Mackenzie to his wife, 7 November

1884, Mackenzie Papers, 883, Cullen Library, University of the Witwatersrand. Thompson claimed credit for alerting Rhodes to Mackenzie's failure in Stellaland and for persuading Robinson to send Rhodes in his place. See Nancy Rouillard (ed.), *Matabele Thompson: An Autobiography* (London, 1936), 64–65.

15. CJR to Merriman, 25 October 1883, Merriman Papers (204); Robert Herbert and Edward Fairfield, minutes on Robinson to Derby, 30 August 1884, quoted in de Kiewiet, *Imperial*, 322.

16. Merriman to Charles Mills, 15 March 1884; Agnes Merriman to John X. Merriman, 14 March 1884; in Lewsen, *Selections*, I, 167.

17. Merriman to Currey, 7 May 1884, in Lewsen, *Selections*, I, 176; Rhodes, speech of 28 September 1888, quoted in Vindex, *Rhodes*, 117, 215; J.H. Hofmeyr and F.W. Reitz, *The Life of Jan Hendrik Hofmeyr* (Cape Town, 1913), 246.

18. CJR, speech of 9 June 1884, in Vindex, *Rhodes*, 77.

19. Report of speech in Cape *Argus* (16 July 1884), quoted slightly at variance in Vindex, *Rhodes*, xxiii–xxiv; Michell, *Rhodes*, I, 193. The original is Cape of Good Hope, *Debates in the House of Assembly* (1884), 342–352.

20. *Ibid.*

21. CJR to Merriman, 13 January 1885, in Lewsen, *Selections*, I, 188. See also Holmberg, *Tribes*, 83.

22. Rouillard, *Thompson*, 67–68.

23. Quoted in Hensman, *Rhodes*, 62 (and many subsequent biographies); J.A.I. Agar-Hamilton, *The Road to the North: South Africa, 1852–1886* (London, 1937), 335–336.

24. CJR to Robinson, 20 September 1884, C. 4213; CJR to Merriman, 13 January 1885, Lewsen, *Selections*, I, 187.

25. *Ibid.*

26. CJR to Robinson, 20 September 1884. For fascinating detail on this microperiod in Rhodes' career, see Agar-Hamilton, *Road*, 337–358.

27. But see Schreuder, *Scramble*, 111.

28. CJR to Merriman, 25 October 1883, Merriman Papers. Vindex, *Rhodes*, 91; Evelyn Ashley, parliamentary under-secretary, minutes on Smyth to Derby, 6 November 1883, quoted in de Kiewiet, *Imperial*, 315. See also Henry Ashby Turner, Jr., "Bismarck's Imperialist Venture: Anti-British in Origin?" in Prosser Gifford and William Roger Louis (eds.), *Britain and Germany in Africa: Imperial Rivalry and Colonial Rule* (New Haven, 1967), 47–82.

29. Scanlen to Merriman, 15 November 1883, in Lewsen, *Selections*, I, 142; de Kiewiet, *Imperial*, 320.

30. Kimberley to Chamberlain, 25 September 1884, quoted in Schreuder, *Scramble*, 163; Merriman to Mills, 31 December 1884, in Lewsen, *Selections*, I, 85.

31. Warren, quoted at length in *The Times* (22 October 1885); Fuller, *Rhodes*, 53; Warren to Robinson, 20 March 1885, quoted in Sillery, *Mackenzie*, 123. Phillida Brooke Simons (ed.), "The Memoirs of Henry Latham (Harry) Currey," unpublished typescript, 32.

32. Quoted in Williams, *Rhodes*, 86–87. For Warren's version of the meeting with Kruger, see his letter in *The Times* (28 March 1902); Watkin W. Williams, *The Life of General Sir Charles Warren* (Oxford, 1941), 161.

33. Ralph Williams, *How I Became a Governor* (London, 1913), 119.

34. Recounted in Marquis del Moral, memoir of 25 November 1952, Mss. Afr. t. 5 (259), Rhodes House.

35. Simons, "Harry Currey Memoirs," 29–33; Williams, *Governor*, 124. See also Rouillard, *Thompson*, 79. For the arrest of van Niekerk, see Williams, *Governor*, 124.

36. Warren, quoted in *The Times* (22 October 1885); Warren, address to the Royal Colonial Institute (10 November 1885), quoted in *The Times* (11 November 1885). Rhodes, letter to *The Times* (11 November 1885).

37. CJR to Warren, 21 February 1885. Cf. CJR to Warren, 17 January 1885, in Charles Warren, "Cecil Rhodes' Early Days in South Africa," *Contemporary Review*, LXXXI (1902), 650–651.

38. CJR to Robinson, 16 March 1885, C. 4432; speech of 30 June 1885, in Vindex, *Rhodes*, 124–125.

39. George Baden-Powell was the elder brother of the later, more famous Robert Baden-Powell, who founded the Boy Scouts. For the younger Baden-Powell, see below, Chapter 22. George Baden-Powell became a member of parliament for Liverpool.

40. CJR, speech in parliament, 30 June 1885, in Vindex, *Rhodes*, 126–127; Rhodes, letter in *The Times* (11 November 1885). Rhodes' several letters to *The Times* of late 1885 about his dispute with Warren were written in collaboration with Ralph Williams, first in a hotel in Chester and later in lodgings in London. Rochfort Maguire critiqued the latter efforts. Williams explained how the letters were written: "I wrote several sheets and then stopped and read them to Rhodes. He leaned against the chimneypiece and criticised." He sometimes took Warren's side and argued against what Williams had written, and sometimes objected to phrases because they had too much of the *Daily Telegraph* about them. "When warmed up to his subject, [Rhodes] would ruffle his hair, take off his coat and shy it on the ground, and, walking about the room, would pour out arguments against his own views so as thoroughly to sift the points for which he was contending." Williams, *Governor*, 134–135. See also Ralph Williams to Basil Williams, 8 January 1922, Mss. Afr. s. 134 (34), Rhodes House.

41. Williams, *Governor*, 123; Ralph Williams to Basil Williams, 20 June 1919, Mss. Afr. s. 134 (32), Rhodes House. Rhodes, letter to *The Times* (11 November 1885); Grant Duff, quoted in de Kiewiet, *Imperial*, 299. For Maund, see Chapter 11.

42. Robinson to Colonel F.A. Stanley, 7 July 1885, quoted in Schreuder, *Scramble*, 173.

43. John Eddie Mackenzie (the missionary's son) to Aunt Bessie (Douglas), 18 January 1885, Mackenzie Papers, 961, Cullen Library; Merriman to Currey, 20 December 1884; to Agnes, 14 January 1885; to Currey, 17 January 1885; his diary entry, 23 February 1885; CJR to Merriman, 21 February 1885; Merriman to Currey, 25 February 1885; to Agnes, 23, 24, 31 March, 1885; to Currey, 27 April 1885. Quoted in Lewsen, *Selections*, I, 184, 189, 192–194, 196, 197. Fuller, *Rhodes*, 55.

44. CJR to Merriman, 25 October 1883; Michell, *Rhodes*, I, 201.

CHAPTER 9

Seeking Dominion over Diamonds and Gold

1. Frederick Boyle, *To the Cape for Diamonds: A Story of Digging Experiences in South Africa* (London, 1873), 376–377.

2. Frederic Philipson Stow, "Memoir of the Formation of the De Beers Mining Company Limited" (1898), McGregor Memorial Museum, typescript, 14–15. Stow may have been thinking about Rhodes' 1886 (not 1881) scheme. The minutes of the De Beers' board reveal no such vote as Stow suggests. Colin Newbury has investigated the history of De Beers and kindly has shared his views. Also see his thorough "Technol-

ogy, Capital and Consolidation: The Performance of De Beers Mining Company Limited, 1880–1889," *Business History Review*, LXI (1987), 1–42.

3. *The Independent*, 14 March 1882, quoted in Roberts, *Magnates*, 131. See also Worger, *Diamonds*, 52–54.

4. CJR to Merriman, 8 April, 1883, Merriman Papers (102), South African Library.

5. Newbury, "Out of the Pit," 29.

6. Louis Cohen, in *Winning Post* (London), 22 February 1908, quoted in Roberts, *Magnates*, 60.

7. Hans Sauer, *Ex Africa . . .* (London, 1937), 42, 95–96, 377.

8. Edmond Sinclair Stevenson, *The Adventures of a Medical Man* (Cape Town, 1925), 12–13. On the epidemic, see also Robert V. Turrell, "Kimberley: Labour and Compounds, 1871–1888," in Shula Marks and Richard Rathbone (eds.), *Industrialisation and Social Change in South Africa: African Class Formation, Culture and Consciousness, 1870–1930* (London, 1982), 60. See also Edmund H. Burrows, *A History of Medicine in South Africa up to the End of the Nineteenth Century* (Cape Town, 1958), 259–262.

9. J.B. Robinson to Merriman, 5 January 1884, quoted in Roberts, *Magnates*, 173.

10. Merriman to Agnes Merriman, 18 January 1886, in Lewsen, *Selections*, I, 204. See also Worger, *Diamonds*, 195, 197. Turrell, *Diamond Fields*, 210, provides a slightly different interpretation.

11. Merriman to Agnes Merriman, 20 January, 27 January 1886, in Lewsen, *Selections*, I, 206–207.

12. Merriman to Agnes Merriman, 10 February 1886, in Lewsen, *Selections*, I, 208–209.

13. CJR, speech of 5 October 1888, in Lewis Michell's handwritten notes (1889), Michell Papers, A 540/37, Cape archives.

14. Sauer, *Ex Africa*, 96.

15. Rhodes, quoted in Colvin, *Jameson*, I, 61–62.

16. Stow, "Memoir," 20.

17. CJR to Stow, 12 July 1886, Stow Papers, McGregor Memorial Museum, Kimberley.

18. *Ibid.*

19. Quoted in Sauer, *Ex Africa*, 119.

20. *Ibid.* Merriman to Currey, 24 March, 14 October 1886, in Lewsen, *Selections*, I, 210, 220–221. In an editor's note to the earlier letter Lewsen reports that Pickering was dying from tuberculosis. Could he have had bone tuberculosis?

21. Colvin, *Jameson*, I, 81; Sauer, *Ex Africa*, 119, J. Percy FitzPatrick, *South African Memories* (London, 1932), 87–89; Roberts, *Magnates*, 250–254. The newspaper accounts of Pickering's fall and death, courtesy of Mrs. L. Brits of the Kimberley Library, from the "collapse" of his lungs, are in *Diamond Fields Advertiser* (28 June 1884, 18 October 1886), *Eastern Province Herald* (18 October 1886).

22. Unsourced, Roberts, *Magnates*, 255.

23. CJR, speech at the May, 1887, annual meeting of the De Beers Company, quoted in Colvin, *Jameson*, I, 62–63.

24. CJR to Rudd, 12 December 1886, Ms. 110/6, the Brenthurst Library.

25. CJR to Rudd, 6 April 1887, Ms. 110/9, the Brenthurst Library.

26. Simons, "Harry Currey Memoirs," 35.

27. CJR to Rudd, 8 January 1887, 5 February 1887, Ms. 110/8, the Brenthurst Library.

28. For details of the share offering and the origins of the Gold Fields Ltd., see

A.P. Cartwright, *Gold Paved the Way: The Story of the Gold Fields Group of Companies* (New York, 1967), 26–35; Robert V. Kubicek, *Economic Imperialism in Theory and Practice: The Case of South African Gold Mining Finance, 1886–1914* (Durham, 1979), 87–90.

29. CJR, report of the annual meeting of the De Beers Co., in *Daily Independent*, (7 May 1887), in Worger, *Diamonds*, 219.

30. Cohen, in *Winning Post* (22 February 1908), quoted in Roberts, *Magnates*, 193.

31. Williams, *Rhodes*, 99. For further details of the amalgamations, see Newbury, "Technology", 18–21. There is no echo of this standard tale in Andrew Porter's new biography of Currie, thus casting considerable doubt on its authenticity: *Victorian Shipping, Business and Imperial Policy: Donald Currie, The Castle Line and Southern Africa* (New York, 1986), 149.

32. Quoted in Alpheus F. Williams, *Some Dreams Come True: Being a Sheaf of Stories Leading up to the Discovery of Copper, Diamonds and Gold in Southern Africa, and of the Pioneers Who Took Part in the Excitement of Those Early Days* (Cape Town, 1948), 223–224.

33. Quoted in Gardner F. Williams, *The Diamond Mines of South Africa: Some Account of Their Rise and Development* (New York, 1902), 287. See also Newbury, "Technology," 30, 39; Robert V. Turrell, "Rhodes, De Beers, and Monopoly," *Journal of Imperial and Commonwealth History*, X (1982), 330. Stow was impressed by Rhodes' "coup d'état." See Turrell, "Stow," 67. For Rothschild's lower fee, Turrell, *Diamond Fields*, 217. Reginald Fenton, "The True History of the Amalgamation of the Diamond Mines," Mss. Afr. 138 (4), presents a different and very anti-Rhodes view of these events. Fenton was a part owner of Kimberley Central.

34. Rhodes, speech to the shareholders of De Beers, 31 March 1888, quoted in Vindex, *Rhodes*, 750.

35. Rhodes to Stow, 22 October 1887, Stow Papers, McGregor Memorial Museum, Kimberley. See also Newbury, "Technology," 31–32; Worger, *Diamonds*, 224–225, which differ about the amount.

36. Stow to Rhodes in Stow, "Memoir," 48. For Barnato's pre-amalgamation profits, see Turrell, "Rhodes," 332.

37. Stow, "Memoirs," 60, emphasis added. See also Turrell, *Diamond Fields*, 222, 227, on Barnato.

38. Quoted in Vindex, *Rhodes*, 752.

39. FitzPatrick, *Memories*, 34.

40. Cf., Stanley Jackson, *The Great Barnato* (London, 1970), 80–81; Flint, *Rhodes*, 89.

41. Barnato to CJR, 5 February 1890, Mss. Afr. s. 8 (70), Rhodes House; Stow, "Memoirs," 65.

42. CJR to Stow, 14 April 1888, Stow Papers.

43. Michell, *Rhodes*, I, 184. Williams, *Rhodes*, 103. Since both Michell and Williams couple this event with Pickering's much earlier death, Barnato's precise words, but not his sentiments, ought to remain suspect. See Stow to Caldecott, 3 May 1887, in Turrell, "Stow," 68.

44. For the judgment, see Harry Raymond, *B.I. Barnato: A Memoir* (New York, 1897), 44–48.

45. Stow to CJR, 4 October 1888, Stow Papers.

46. CJR to Rothschild, 26 August 1888, RAL B17/RH/1888-4, Rothschild archives; CJR to Stow, 25 August 1888, Stow Papers.

47. CJR to Rothschild, 29 October 1888, RAL B17/RH/1888-5.

48. Quoted in *Daily Independent* (5 June 1888), in Worger, *Diamonds,* 229. For unemployment, see Turrell, *Diamond Fields,* 226.

49. CJR to Stow, 8 February 188[9], 14 May 1898; Stow to CJR, 30 August 1888; Stow to Woolf Joel, 22 September 1897; MMK 3503, MMK 3493, Stow Papers, McGregor Memorial Museum, Kimberley. See also Minutes of the Meeting of the Directors of De Beers Consolidated Mines, 28 November 1889.

50. CJR to Rothschild, 29 October 1888, RAL B17/RH/1888-5.

51. CJR to Rudd, 4 March 1889, Ms. 110/11, the Brenthurst Library.

52. Rudd, quoted slightly differently in Cartwright, *Gold,* 53–54; C.G.F.S.A, *"The Gold Fields," 1887–1937* (London, 1937), 27.

53. CJR to Rothschild, 29 October 1888, RAL B17/RH/1888-5.

CHAPTER 10
Fashioning a Distinctive Destiny as the Solitary Springbok

1. Daniel J. Levinson, *The Seasons of a Man's Life* (New York, 1978), 139–144. Levinson, reporting a study of the early adult development of forty men aged 35 to 45, identifies the early thirties as the "settling down" period in which there are two tasks. The first is "to establish one's niche in society," i.e., to organize a stable life with a family, occupation, and community. This home base is necessary for the second task, "to work at advancement." Rhodes did not arrange a stable life style until 1891, when he acquired Groote Schuur. As Levinson puts it, "A man who wants desperately to make his mark, to attain great heights of power, virtue or achievement . . . cannot afford to make strong commitments to particular persons or place great value on stability" (140).

2. CJR to Sidney Shippard, 3 January 1886, RH 1, Zimbabwe archives.

3. CJR to Lord Harris, 7 June 1885, Mss. Afr. s. 229, Rhodes House.

4. *Telegraph* (27 December 1881); *Imvo* (30 March 1887), both quoted in T.R.H. Davenport, *The Afrikaner Bond* (Cape Town, 1966), 120–121.

5. Cape of Good Hope, *Debates in the House of Assembly,* 3rd session, 7th parliament (30 April 1886), 110–111, 113.

6. Assembly, *Debates* (6 May 1886), 148–149.

7. Assembly, *Debates* (13 May 1886), 222; Merriman to Currey, 10 May 1886, 8 July 1886, in Lewsen, *Selections,* I, 210–212, 217; Hofmeyr, *Hofmeyr,* 281.

8. Assembly, *Debates* (1886), 150, 253. For scab, see Chapter 17.

9. Matthews, *Incwadi Yami,* 218. James Bryce, *Impressions of South Africa* (New York, 1898), 204. For the origins of compounds, see John M. Smalberger, "I.D.B. and the Mining Compound System in the 1880s," *The South African Journal of Economics,* XLII (1974), 411–414. For the convict station, see Turrell, *Diamond Fields,* 155–158.

10. Assembly, *Debates* (16, 17 June 1886), 412. Merriman to J.B. Currey, 18 June 1886, in Lewsen, *Selections,* I, 215; Matthews, *Incwadi Yami,* 222–223. For the compounds, IDBs, and the "truck" question, see Robert V. Turrell, "Kimberley: Labour and Compounds, 1871–1888," in Shula Marks and Richard Rathbone (eds.), *Industrialisation and Social Change in South Africa* (London, 1982) 55–57, 61–66. Rhodes' maneuverings on the issues of compounds and "truck" were intricate and expedient. For a sensible analysis see Worger, *Diamonds,* 196–197, 209–211, 218, 228.

11. B.A. Tindall (ed.), *James Rose Innes: Chief Justice of South Africa, 1914–27, An Autobiography* (Cape Town, 1949), 58.

12. Merriman to Currey, 24 March 1886, in Lewsen, *Selections*, I, 209.

13. Assembly, *Debates* (15 June 1886), 399–400; Davenport, *Bond*, 119–123, 352–353; Merriman to Currey, 14 June 1886, in Lewsen, *Selections*, I, 214. Hofmeyr, *Hofmeyr*, 283.

14. CJR, speech at Paarl, 21 June 1886, in Vindex, *Rhodes*, 138–139.

15. Assembly, *Debates* (1887), 99–201; Jabavu, *Jabavu*, 29, both in Lewsen, *Merriman*, 132.

16. Innes to Richard W. Rose Innes, 21 March 1887; Innes to Sir Edward Yewd Brabant, 22 March 1887; Innes to Jabavu, March or April 1887; Innes to Mzimba, 2 May 1887, all in Harrison Wright (ed.), *Sir James Rose Innes: Selected Correspondence (1884–1902)*, (Cape Town, 1972), 52–58.

17. Assembly, *Debates* (23 June 1887), 101–107; Vindex, *Rhodes*, 150–166. The CJR quotations in the text are taken from Vindex, but have been compared with and supplemented by the material in the *Debates*. As texts, the Vindex and the *Debates* differ in phraseology, the *Debates* being in the third person and Vindex in first person. Verschoyle (Vindex) took his materials from the stenographic reports of the reporters and from their published articles. Even though the *Debates* are the official record, Vindex *may* be—it is impossible to know—the more accurate if not the more lively record of Rhodes' words in parliament.

18. Assembly, *Debates* (1886), 263, 265.

19. CJR, letter in *Cape Argus* (6 July 1887), in Vindex, *Rhodes*, 170–174. For Kruger's attitude, see Jean van der Poel, *Railway and Customs Policies in South Africa, 1885–1910* (London, 1933), 29–30.

20. See Chapter 8.

21. Quoted in J.G. Swift MacNeill, *What I Have Seen and Heard* (Boston, 1925), 260–266.

22. CJR, quoted in R. Barry O'Brien, *The Life of Charles Stewart Parnell, 1846–1891* (New York, 1968; orig. pub. 1898), II, 186.

23. Texts of both letters in Hensman, *Rhodes*, 120–124.

24. Quoted in McDonald, *Rhodes*, 96.

25. Merriman to Currey, 28 September 1887; Merriman to Agnes Merriman, 6 October 1887, in Lewsen, *Selections*, I, 268, 270.

26. CJR, speech of 28 September 1888, in Vindex, *Rhodes*, 209–210, 221–222. Excerpts from a very similar, if not the same, speech are contained in Lewis Michell's stenographic notes. Michell does not detail the place in which the speech was made, but dates it 5 October 1888. Michell Papers, A 540/37, Cape archives. For the cash transfer, see Ronald Currey to Dr. Allan, 2 June 1938, Mss. Afr. s. 228 (C 28), Rhodes House.

27. For the use of the first £5,000, and Parnell's relevance, see Conor Cruise O'Brien, *Parnell and His Party, 1880–90* (Oxford, 1957), 267–268, 349. The 1893 home rule bill was successful in the House of Commons but vetoed in the Lords. For the disposition of the second £5,000, see the discussion in Francis Stewart Leland Lyons, *Charles Stewart Parnell* (New York, 1977), 587–589.

28. Quoted in Ronald Currey, *Rhodes: A Biographical Footnote* (Cape Town, n.d.), 13–14.

29. Merriman to Currey, 28 October 1887, in Lewsen, *Selections*, I, 272. See also Jackson, *Barnato*, 86–89.

30. Will of 27 June, 1888; CJR to Rothschild, 24 June 1888, Mss. Afr., t. 1 (24), Rhodes House.

31. For the details, see Martin P. Harney, *The Jesuits in History: The Society of Jesus through Four Centuries* (New York, 1941) 101–109; Javier Osuna (trans. Nicholas King) *Friends in the Lord: A Study in the Origins and Growth of Community in the Society of Jesus* . . . (London, 1974), 104–141.

32. CJR, speech to the House, 23 June 1887, in Vindex, *Rhodes*, 164–165.

CHAPTER 11

Employing the Sinews of War in the North

1. For the pre-conquest Ndebele, see Richard Brown, "Aspects of the Scramble for Matabeleland," in Eric Stokes and Richard Brown (eds.), *The Zambesian Past: Studies in Central African History* (Manchester, 1966), 63–67; Richard Brown, "The Ndebele Succession Crisis," in *Historians in Tropical Africa* (Harare, 1960), 159–175; John D. Omer-Cooper, *The Zulu Aftermath: A Nineteenth-Century Revolution in Bantu Africa* (London, 1966), 129–155.

2. For the "Confession of Faith," the will, and the conversation, see Chapter 5. For Shippard and Jameson, see Chapter 8.

3. Maund, memoir, 26 May 1929, in Mss. Afr. s. 229 (IV, 415–425), Rhodes House. See also Chapter 8.

4. CJR to Ralph Williams, 12 July 1885, Mss. Afr. s. 134, Rhodes House. See also Ralph Williams, *How I Became a Governor* (London, 1913), 131–133; Williams, interview with Basil Williams, 11 June 1919, Mss. Afr. s. 134. See also Chapter 8. John S. Galbraith, *Crown and Charter: The Early Years of the British South Africa Company* (Berkeley, 1974), 40–41, following Maund, errs in suggesting that Rhodes believed Matabeleland to be "fever stricken." For Holub, see Emil Holub (trans. Christa Johns, ed. Ladislav Holy), *Travels North of the Zambezi, 1885–6* (Lusaka, 1975).

5. The Maund and Edwards reports are in Edwards (29 August 1885) and C.E. Haynes (5 September 1885), in Warren to Colonial Office, 26 October 1885, C. 4643 (1886); Maund to Compte Rodolphe Montgelas, December 1885; and Maund reports, in Mss. Afr. s. 229 (IV, 390–399), Rhodes House.

6. CJR, letter to *The Times*, 11 November 1885. Williams doubtless drafted the letter from Rhodes' dictation.

7. CJR to Shippard, 3 January 1886, Mss. Afr. t. 5, Rhodes House.

8. Frank Johnson, *Great Days: The Autobiography of an Empire Pioneer* (London, 1940), 36–48, 59–60; John Cooper-Chadwick, *Three Years with Lobengula, and Experiences in South Africa* (London, 1894), 90.

9. Shippard to Hercules Robinson, 21 May 1887, cited in J.L. Rademeyer, *Die Land Noord van die Limpopo in die Ekspansie-Beleid van die Suid-Afrikaanse Republiek* (Cape Town, 1949), 58–59.

10. For the English text of the Grobler treaty, see W.J. Leyds, *The Transvaal Surrounded* (London, 1919), 290–291. For the text and a severe critique, see Hugh Marshall Hole, *The Making of Rhodesia* (London, 1926), 59–62. For another dismissal of its authenticity, see J.E.S. Green, *Rhodes Goes North* (London, 1936), 64–65. The original is in the State Secretary files in the Transvaal archives.

11. Williams, *Governor*, 157–158. Williams fails to date his reminiscence precisely. The merchant's words might lead the unsuspecting reader to assume that they were exchanged before Grobler's initial sally north. But Williams was then en route to Pre-

toria. He arrived only toward the end of 1887, in time for the celebration of Queen Victoria's jubilee.

12. Grobler was killed in 1888 en route home from Gbulawayo. As a sometime horsetrader suspected of swindling the Ngwato court, the chiefs of that Tswana nation had a motive. Felix Gross, *Rhodes of Africa* (London, 1956), 147, asserts that Rhodes arranged to have Grobler killed, but there is no evidence to support such an assertion. See also Green, *Rhodes*, 73; Robert Unwin Moffat, *John Smith Moffat, C.M.G., Missionary: A Memoir* (London, 1921), 242–243.

13. Shippard to Lobengula, 22 August 1887, in Colonial Office to Foreign Office, 3 December 1887, FO 84/1875, Public Record Office. Moffat to Shippard, 12 December 1887; 30 January 1888; Shippard to Moffat, 26 December 1887, in Brown, "Scramble," 73–74. For Nellmapius' role, Arthur Keppel-Jones, "Rhodes and the Imperial Venture: The Rhodesias," unpub. paper (1985), 12–13. See also Ralph Williams to Basil Williams, 8 January 1922, Mss. Afr. s. 134 (34–36).

14. Moffat to Shippard, 10 February 1888, cited in Brown, "Scramble," 75.

15. The text is in Hole, *Rhodesia*, 54.

16. CJR to Shippard, 14 April 1887, Mss. Afr. t. 5, Rhodes House.

17. Shippard to Moffat, 30 July 1888, quoted in Brown, "Scramble," 76.

18. Harry H. Johnston, *The Story of My Life* (Indianapolis, 1923), 221. For the characterological assessment of Shippard, see William Plomer, *Cecil Rhodes* (London, 1933), 58.

19. CJR to Shippard, 1 August 1888, Mss. Afr. t. 5, Rhodes House. See also Charles Warren, "Cecil Rhodes' Early Days in South Africa," *Contemporary Review,* LXXXI (1902), 653.

20. CJR to Shippard, 1 August 1888, Mss. Afr. t. 5.

21. CJR to Shippard, 14 August 1888; another, 14 August 1888, both in Mss. Afr. t. 5.

22. CJR to Francis J. Newton, Colonial Secretary for Bechuanaland, based in Vryburg, n.d. (but prob. 14) August 1888, RH 1/1/1, Zimbabwe archives.

23. Cited in Galbraith, *Crown and Charter,* 62.

24. CJR to Shippard, 14 August 1888.

25. CJR to Rothschild, 29 October 1888, RAL B17/RH/1888–4, Rothschild archives.

26. Moffat to Shippard, 31 August 1888, 6 September 1888, quoted in Brown, "Scramble," 77.

27. Newton to Moffat, 26 August 1888, quoted in Brown, "Scramble," 78; Newton to Basil Williams, 7 July 1919, Mss. Afr. s. 134.

28. Rudd, diary entry, 21 September 1888, in V.W. Hiller (ed.), "The Concession Journey of Charles Dunell Rudd, 1888," in Constance E. Fripp and Hiller (eds.), *Gold and the Gospel in Mashonaland, 1888* (London, 1849), 181–182; Rouillard, *Thompson,* 124.

29. Moffat to Shippard, 28 September 1888, quoted in Brown, "Scramble," 78; Rudd, diary, 29 September 1888, in Hiller, "Journey," 187.

30. Maguire to Newton, 27 October 1888; Shippard to Newton, 29 October 1888; quoted in Galbraith, *Crown,* 68–69. For Shippard's aims, see the diary of Bishop Knight-Bruce, 18 October 1888, in *Gold and Gospel,* 95.

31. CJR to Rudd, 10 September 1888, Ms. 110/10, the Brenthurst Library.

32. Rudd, diary entries, 10 October, 21 October, 30 October 1888, in Hiller, "Journey," 193, 199, 200, 201–202.

33. Rouillard, *Thompson,* 131.

34. The text of the Concession is in *ibid.,* 219–220.

35. Rudd, diary, 30 October 1888, in Hiller, "Journey," 202–203; Helm to the London Missionary Society, 29 March 1889, in *ibid.,* 227. See also Maund to CJR, 25 December 1889, extract in Hole Papers; full copy in CT 1/13/8, Zimbabwe archives; Rouillard, *Thompson,* 127. For the promise to Helm, see Thompson to Helm, 9 November 1888, in Hiller, "Journey," 225.

36. CJR to Rudd, 10 January 1889, RU 2/1/1, Zimbabwe archives; Rhodes to Rothschild, 26 November 1888, telegram, RAL B17/RH/1888–6, Rothschild archives; Rudd to Currey, 4 August 1888, in Ms. 16.096, Gold Fields Papers, Cory Library; Flint, *Rhodes,* 104.

37. CJR to Shippard, 3 September 1889, RH 1/1/1, Zimbabwe archives; CJR to Grey, 30 August 1889, Mss. Afr. s. 78.

38. Hole, *Rhodesia,* 77; Green, *North,* 109–110; Arthur Keppel-Jones, *Rhodes and Rhodesia* (Kingston, 1983), 89; Galbraith, *Crown,* 77; Lockhart and Woodhouse, *Rhodes,* 140; Knight-Bruce speech of 8 December 1888, quoted in Fripp, "The Mashonaland Mission of Bishop Knight-Bruce," in Fripp and Hiller, *Gold and Gospel,* 138; CJR to Rudd, 26 December 1888, Ms. 16.097, Cory Library. See also Merriman, Assembly, *Debates* (8 August 1889), 438–439.

39. CJR to Rudd, 17 December, 26 December, 28 December 1888, 10 January 1889, Ms. 14997, Cory Library; Jameson to CJR, 4 March 1889, Ms. 111/2, the Brenthurst Library. Rudd to Thompson and Maguire, 4 February 1889, quoted in Keppel-Jones, *Rhodes,* 101.

40. CJR to Thompson, 14 February 1889, in Rouillard, *Thompson,* 153–158; Green, *North,* 93. Rhodes was replying to Thompson to Rudd and Thompson to Rudd and Rhodes of 15 March and 30 March 1889, McGregor Memorial Museum.

41. CJR to Rudd, 17 December 1888, 24 February 1889, RU 2/1/1, Zimbabwe archives; Rudd to Currey, 1 March 1889, Ms. 16.096, Cory Library, emphasis added. Henry Rider Haggard, *The Days of My Life* (London, 1926), II, 115. On the Leask concession, see Keppel-Jones, *Rhodes,* 56–57.

42. Maund, report of interview with Rhodes, Maund Papers, A77 (152), Cullen Library, University of the Witwatersrand; CJR to Thompson, 14 February 1889; CJR to Thompson and Maguire, 11 April 1889, in Rouillard, *Thompson,* 159–160; CJR to Rothschild, 20 January 1889, RAL B17/RH/1889–2, Rothschild archives; Cawston to Maund, 24 January 1889, Mss. Afr. s. 78. For these events, and Maund's approach, see Ake Holmberg, *African Tribes and European Agencies* (Göteberg, 1966), 191–198.

43. The message was dated 26 March 1889, in Knutsford to Robinson, 27 March 1889, CO 878/30/372. See also Hole, *Rhodesia,* 82. Blake, *Rhodesia,* 58, flatly declares Lobengula's letter of April a fraud, but it probably represented a genuine sentiment.

44. CJR to Cawston, 30 September, 4 October 1889, Mss. Afr. s. 73; Keppel-Jones, *Rhodes,* 111, 115. For the Maund comments upon which all writers before Keppel-Jones based their narratives, see Maund's memoir, 18–26 September 1923, Mss. Afr. s. 229 (IV, 13–23). The letter from the Society is in Mss. British Empire s. 22 (G.13). It is also quoted in Hole, *Rhodesia,* 84, as is Lobengula's response, on 111. The letter from Maund to Gifford, which Keppel-Jones and others did not see, is dated 29 August 1889, from Gbulawayo. It rues the failure in March to eliminate the troubling sentence. The letter is extracted in the Maund papers, Mss. Afr. s. 229 (IV, 301–310), Rhodes House.

45. Quoted in Ronald Robinson and John Gallagher, *Africa and the Victorians: The Climax of Imperialism* (London, 1961), 224.

46. A.L. Kennedy, *Salisbury, 1830–1903* (London, 1953), 229–230.

47. A.H. Weatherley, secretary of the Bechuanaland Company, to Maund, 14 June 1889, Maund Papers, A 77, Cullen Library, University of the Witwatersrand.

48. CJR to Rothschild, 20 January 1889, RAL B17/RH/1889–2, Rothschild Archives.

49. *Ibid.*

50. Lishy(?) to Mackenzie, 24 May 1889, Mackenzie Papers, Cullen Library, University of the Witwatersrand.

51. Keppel-Jones, *Rhodes,* 120.

52. Maund, reminiscences of 18–26 September 1923, in Mss. Afr. s. 229 (IV, 13–23), Rhodes House.

53. Galbraith, *Crown and Charter,* 84–86.

54. For Beit's role, see Keppel-Jones, "Rhodes and the Imperial Venture," 15.

55. CJR to Rothschild, 29 October 1888, RAL B17/RH/1888–5, Rothschild archives.

56. Quotations in Lockhart and Woodhouse, *Rhodes,* 165; Williams, *Rhodes,* 136; George H. Tanser, *A Scantling of Time: The Story of Rhodesia, 1890–1900* (Salisbury, 1965), 128.

57. For Shaw, see Chapter 19.

58. Johnston, *My Life,* 218, 219; Johnston ("An African Explorer"), "Great Britain's Policy in Africa," *The Times,* 22 August 1888, quoted in Roland Oliver, *Sir Harry Johnston and the Scramble for Africa* (London, 1957), 141, 143; Johnston to CJR, 8 October 1893, in Johnston to Rosebery, 8 October 1893, FO 2/55, Public Record Office. Harris, *Life and Loves,* II, 331.

59. Frederic Whyte, *The Life of W.T. Stead* (London, 1925), I, 270–271; Estelle W. Stead, *My Father: Personal and Spiritual Reminiscences* (London, 1913), 231–237; Chamberlain to Hugh Oakley Arnold-Forster, 10 July 1889, Mackenzie Papers, 2282, Cullen Library, University of the Witwatersrand. There are five short, friendly, even warm letters for this period from Rhodes to Stead, 3 April, 18 June, 6 July 1889, (?) July, and (?) August (n.d.), Afr. s. 413 (micr). See also Raymond L. Schults, *Crusader in Babylon: W.T. Stead and the Pall Mall Gazette* (Lincoln, 1972), 247–248. For the Crawford novel, see Chapter 10.

60. CJR to Shippard, 13 June 1889, RH 1/1/1, Zimbabwe archives. For Chamberlain and Salisbury on Robinson, see Joseph L. Garvin, *The Life of Joseph Chamberlain* (London, 1933), II, 466.

61. CJR to Knutsford, 1 June, 17 June 1889, C. 5918 (1889).

62. Quoted in Keppel-Jones, *Rhodes,* 135.

63. CJR to Maund, 7 September, 26 September 1889, Mss. Afr. s. 229 (IV), Rhodes House.

64. Text in Michell, *Rhodes,* I, 331–342; Edward Hertslet, *The Map of Africa by Treaty* (London, 1909), I, 271–277.

65. CJR to Cawston, 4 October 1889, Mss. Afr. s. 73.

CHAPTER 12

A Rush of Cynicism and Conspiracy—The Acquisition of Rhodesia

1. CJR to Sir Robert Herbert (Colonial Office), 9 December 1889, TAB A 1509, Transvaal archives, Pretoria.

2. Lobengula to Queen Victoria, 10 August 1889, in Hole, *Rhodesia,* 111; John

Smith Moffat to Shippard, 26 August 1889, Thompson to his wife, ?10 September 1889, both in Keppel-Jones, *Rhodes,* 140, 142; Maund to Lord Gifford, 29 August, 11 September 1889, in Mss. Afr. s. 229 (IV), Rhodes House. For Lotshe, see Chapter 11.

3. CJR to Maund, 7 September 1889, 26 September 1889, Maund Papers, Cullen Library, University of the Witwatersrand; CJR to Beit, 24 October 1889, Rand Mines; Colvin, *Jameson,* I, 115; CJR to Thompson, 28 September 1889, National Archives of Zimbabwe. On the controversial roles of Maund (who was intensely disliked by his contemporaries in Gbulawayo) and Thompson, who was thought foolish, see Hugh Marshall Hole's extracts of a series of late 1889 letters between Rhodes and Jameson, Maund, Thompson, Doyle, and others. Hole Papers, Micr. 1249, Cullen Library; HO/1/2/1, Zimbabwe archives.

4. CJR to Thompson, 28 September 1889, Zimbabwe archives.

5. Lobengula ceaselessly asked for a face-to-face discussion with Rhodes. See Colvin, *Jameson,* I, 116; Frederick Courtenay Selous, letter of 26 March 1890, quoted in J.G. Millais, *Life of Frederick Courtenay Selous* (London, 1918), 174. Merriman to John Blades Currey, 4 December 1889 (from Rome), in Lewsen, *Selections,* I, 294. For Thompson and gout, Jameson to Harris, 8 January 1890, copy in Rand Mines.

6. Jameson to Rutherfoord Harris, 12 December 1889, in Julian R.D. Cobbing, "Lobengula, Jameson, and the Occupation of Mashonaland, 1890," *Rhodesian History,* IV (1973), 42.

7. Frederick Courtenay Selous, *Travel and Adventure in South Central Africa* (London, 1893), 359; Millais, *Selous,* 175.

8. CJR to Sir Charles Dilke, 15 October 1889, Dilke Papers, Add. Mss. 43877, British Museum; Jameson to Harris, 1 November 1889, in Keppel-Jones, *Rhodes,* 154.

9. CJR to Cawston, 11 January 1890, Mss. Afr. s. 73, Rhodes House.

10. Johnson, in *Cape Times* (12 September 1930), in Brown, "Scramble," 89. The agreement with Rhodes is in the Johnson Papers (JO 3/2), Zimbabwe archives. The suppressed chapter of the Johnson autobiography which discusses the deal is also in those archives. Robert Cary, *Charter Royal* (Cape Town, 1970) 53–58, 175, provides a persuasive revisionary analysis of Johnson and his maneuvers.

11. Green, *Rhodes,* 173.

12. CJR to Beit, 11 January 1890, Rand Mines.

13. *Ibid.*

14. Fairfield, minute, date not specified, in Keppel-Jones, *Rhodes,* 158; Knutsford to Loch, 14 February 1890, C.O. confidential print, *Africa South* 392, quoted in Stanlake Samkange, *Origins of Rhodesia* (New York, 1969), 173.

15. Jameson to Harris, 30 January, 31 January 1890, Rand Mines.

16. Jameson to Harris, 5 May 1890, 27 July 1890, both in Cobbing, "Occupation," 49, 51.

17. Moffat to Rhodes, 16 January 1890 (Confidential), Rand Mines.

18. Rhodes to Herbert, n.d. but March, 1890, TAB A 1509, Transvaal archives. See also Foreign Office to Colonial Office, 7 March 1890; Knutsford to Loch, 10 March 1890, in Mason, *Dilemma,* 138. Salisbury, n.d. but March, 1890, TAB A 558, Transvaal archives.

19. Johnson, *Great Days,* 109–110.

20. Merriman to Agnes Merriman, 25 April 1890, in Lewsen, *Selections,* I, 301.

21. CJR to Loch, 19 May 1890, in Loch Papers, 16, Centre for Southern African Studies, University of York. The Loch Papers are now in the Scottish Record Office, Edinburgh.

22. Loch to Moffat, 12 June 1890; Lobengula to Loch, 24 June 1890, in Keppel-Jones, *Rhodes,* 167.

23. Pennefather to Harris, 12 September 1890, in George H. Tanser, *A Scantling of Time: The Story of Salisbury, Rhodesia (1890 to 1900)* (Salisbury, 1965), 26–27.

24. CJR to Abercorn, 31 March 1890, Zimbabwe archives.

25. Merriman to Charles J. Posno, chairman of the London and South African Exploration Company, 15 October 1890, in Lewsen, *Selections,* II, 17.

26. CJR, speech in Vryburg, early October 1890, in Vindex, *Speeches,* 249.

27. Quoted in Williams, *Rhodes,* 150–151.

28. CJR to Sprigg, 24 October 1889; Sprigg to CJR, 26 October 1889, 10.073, Cory Library. See also CJR to Beit, 26 October 1889, Rand Mines. Merriman to Currey, 4 December 1890, Lewsen, *Selections,* I, 293.

29. Harris to Beit, 14 April 1890, Rand Mines.

30. CJR to Beit, 11 January 1890, 24 January 1890; Rudd to Beit, 3 February 1890; all Rand Mines. In a letter to Sprigg, 23 January 1890, 10.073a, Cory Library, Rhodes agreed that a line from Walvis Bay eastward would not be a competing venture. See also Chapter 14.

31. CJR to Abercorn, 31 March 1890, Zimbabwe archives.

32. CJR to Herbert, 3 December 1889, TAB A 1509, Transvaal archives.

33. Cawston to CJR, 13 December 1889, Mss. Afr. s. 73.

34. Gwendolen Cecil, *Life of Robert, Marquis of Salisbury,* (London, 1932), IV, 263.

35. Johnston to CJR, 16 October 1889, Rand Mines.

36. CJR to Abercorn, 2 June 1890, RM 1/3, Zimbabwe archives. For the origins of the Stevenson Road, see Robert I. Rotberg, *Joseph Thomson and the Exploration of Africa* (London, 1971), 80.

37. Abercorn to Cawston, 5 April 1890, quoted in Alexander John Hanna, *The Beginnings of Nyasaland and North-Eastern Rhodesia, 1859–95* (Oxford, 1956), 165; *Hansard,* CCCXLVI (1890), 1268, quoted in Robinson and Gallagher, *Africa and the Victorians,* 249. For the best discussion of how the red route was lost, see John Galbraith, *Mackinnon and East Africa, 1878–1895: A Study in the "New Imperialism"* (Cambridge, 1972), 177–188. For the treaty, see Hertslet, *Map of Africa by Treaty* (1896), II, 642–657. See also Chapter 21.

38. CJR to Herbert, fragment, n.d. but 1890 (April?), John Oxley Library, Queensland; CJR to Abercorn, 25 June 1890, RM 1/3, Zimbabwe archives.

39. Robert Graham, quoted in Keppel-Jones, *Rhodes,* 199.

40. Johnston to CJR, 25 July 1890, Mss. Afr. s. 228 (3A, 18), Rhodes House; CJR to Board, Abercorn to Cawston, 21 September 1890, Mss. Afr. s. 74.

41. CJR to Johnston, 22 September 1890, JO 1/1/1 (130–133), Zimbabwe archives. See also Chapter 21.

42. Abercorn to Cawston, 25 September 1890, Mss. Afr. s. 74.

43. Currie to Cawston, 14 August 1890, Mss. Afr. s. 74.

44. CJR to Johnston, 22 September 1890; CJR to Herbert, early October 1890, fragment in the John Oxley Library, State Library of Queensland; Mss. Afr. t. 14 (135–136). The "fools paradise" is in Salisbury to Sir George Petre (H.M. Ambassador in Lisbon), 24 December 1890, in Cecil, *Salisbury,* IV, 270.

45. Archibald R. Colquhoun, *Dan to Beersheba: Work and Travel in Four Continents* (London, 1908), 277.

46. Green, *Rhodes,* 237–238. Arthur Glyn Leonard, *How We Made Rhodesia* (London, 1894), 150–151.

47. For Gungunyane's tactics, see Douglas L. Wheeler, "Gungunyane the Negotiator: A Study in African Diplomacy," *Journal of African History,* IX (1968), 587–591.

48. Jameson to Midge Jameson, 17 November 1890, in Colvin, *Jameson,* I, 170. See Johnson, *Great Days,* 118, for Colquhoun.

49. British South Africa Company to Foreign Office, 16 December 1890, quoted in Philip R. Warhurst, *Anglo-Portuguese Relations in South-Central Africa, 1890–1900* (London, 1962), 52–53.

50. Charles Mills to Merriman, 12, 20 February 1891; Merriman to Agnes Merriman, 28 March 1891, in Lewsen, *Selections,* II, 26, 45; Simons, "Harry Currey Memoirs," 46–51.

51. Simons, "Harry Currey Memoirs," 50. The fifth will is dated 5 March 1891, in Mss. Afr. t. 1 (10). CJR, quoted in W.T. Stead (ed.), *The Last Will and Testament of Cecil John Rhodes* (London, 1902), 102–104.

52. Jameson, in Salisbury to Petre, 17 April 1891, in Warhurst, *Anglo-Portuguese,* 89.

53. Speech of 11 June 1891, *Hansard,* XXXLIV (1891), 137, quoted in Warhurst, *Anglo-Portuguese,* 99.

54. CJR to Rothschild, 6 June 1891, RAL B17/RH/1891–9, Rothschild archives; second quote in Colvin, *Jameson,* I, 205.

55. Details in Hertslet, *Map of Africa by Treaty,* (1909), III, 1016–1025.

56. CJR to Salisbury, 12 September 1891, Mss. Afr. s. 75.

CHAPTER 13

Assaults Across the Zambezi

1. CJR to Beit, 11 November 1889, Rand Mines.

2. For the missionary period, see Robert I. Rotberg, *Christian Missionaries and the Creation of Northern Rhodesia* (Princeton, 1965), 12–24.

3. Kgama to Lewanika, in Kgama to Coillard, 17 July 1889, Royal Commonwealth Society archives; Coillard to Shippard, 2 January 1889, in Colonial Office to Foreign Office, 30 August 1889, FO 84/2002. See also Hole, *Rhodesia,* 212–214.

4. Coillard to John Smith, 19 April 1890, CO 5/1/1/1, Zimbabwe archives.

5. CJR to Grey, 30 August 1889, Mss. Afr. s. 73.

6. CJR to Beit, 11 November 1889, Rand Mines; Ware Concession of 27 June 1889 in MA 18/4/1, Zimbabwe archives; CJR to Robert Herbert, 9 December 1889, Mss. Afr. t. 14 (129–130).

7. Shippard to Coillard, 1 September 1889, Lochner to Harris, 27 November 1889, CO 5/5/l, Zimbabwe archives; Hepburn to Coillard, 23 November 1889, Royal Commonwealth Society archives.

8. Lewanika to Lochner, 3 May 1890, CO 5/5/1, Zimbabwe archives.

9. Coillard to CJR, 8 April 1890, MA 18/4/1; Coillard to Smith, 19 April 1890; Coillard to Mrs. Hart, 28 May 1890; Coillard to Smith, 10 June 1890; CO 5/1/1/1, Zimbabwe archives. Harris outlined all the benefits that could be showered on Coillard in Harris to Lochner, 5 July 1890, Royal Commonwealth Society archives.

10. Lochner to Harris, 23 April 1890, 10 June 1890, 30 July 1890, MA 18/4/1; Coillard to Smith, 20 June 1890; Coillard to Hart, 16 May 1890, CO 5/1/1/1, Zimbabwe archives.

11. Lochner to Harris, 27 June 1890, in Harris to Loch, 6 September 1890, in

Africa South, 392 (1890), 317, together with the Lochner Concession, at 320. For the treaty, see also Royal Commonwealth Society archives. For the circumstances of the signing of the concession, see Gerald L. Kaplan, *The Elites of Barotseland, 1878–1969: A Political History of Zambia's Western Province* (Berkeley, 1970), 50–54.

12. Coillard to CJR, 27 October 1890, CT 1/4/3, Zimbabwe archives.

13. Coillard to Hunter (Glasgow), 12 August 1890, CO 5/2/1, Zimbabwe archives.

14. Cawston to CJR, 6 February 1890, Mss. Afr. s. 74. Cawston warned Rhodes in even stronger terms about Léopold's lock on the Congo on 3 September 1890.

15. Arnot, diary entry, 17 February 1886, *The Life and Explorations of Frederick Stanley Arnot* (London, 1921), 183; 11 August 1886 in *Echoes of Service* (April, 1887), 59.

16. Cawston to Beit, 15 March 1890, in Rotberg, *Thomson*, 266.

17. Johnston to Cawston, 16 June 1890, Mss. Afr. s. 74. For a summary of Rhodes' discussion with Moir about the future of the African Lakes Company, and of Moir himself, see George Shepperson, "Cecil Rhodes: Some Documents and Reflections," *Rhodesian History*, IX (1978), 86–88.

18. Johnston to CJR, 25 July 1890, Mss. Afr. s. 228 (3A, 18); Johnston to Philip Currie, 21 July 1890, FO 84/2052; Cawston to CJR, 10 June, 2 September 1890, Mss. Afr. s. 74.

19. CJR to Abercorn, 25 June 1890, RM 1/3, Zimbabwe archives.

20. Sharpe to CJR, 1 August 1890, CT 1/16/5, Zimbabwe archives.

21. Quoted in Rotberg, *Thomson*, 280. For Thomson's route, see the map in *ibid*, 272–273.

22. Johnston to Rosebery, 18 October 1892; Johnston, Certificate of Claim, 25 September 1893; Percy Anderson to Colonial Office, 23 July 1894; H. Wilson Fox to Robert Codrington, 11 March 1904; Memorandum of a conversation between Rhodes and Anderson, 19 November 1894. For the location and provenance of these documents, see Rotberg, *Thomson*, 285–287.

23. Thomson to Cawston, 10 June, 17 June 1891; CJR to Thomson, quoted in Rotberg, *Thomson*, 288.

24. Salisbury to Queen Victoria, April 1891, quoted in Galbraith, *Crown and Charter*, 252.

25. Quoted in Robert Williams, "My Story of the Schemes," in Leo Weinthal (ed.), *The Story of the Cape to Cairo Railway and River Route* (London, 1923), I, 114.

26. Rhodes' rationale had been set out, as often happened, a year before. "Our policy," Rhodes told Beit, should not be "to enter into great obligations over the Zambesi but simply to hold our own. . . ." As far as expending funds on a small army, Rhodes said that he was "no advocate of expenditure and large Police Forces but . . . a judicious sum . . . will retain our position over the Zambesi meantime leaving the expenditure for the South. . . ," CJR to Beit, 11 January 1890, Rand Mines.

27. CJR to Johnston, 7 February 1891, JO 1/1/1 (144–147), Zimbabwe archives.

28. CJR to Abercorn, 2 June 1890, RM 1/3, Zimbabwe archives. See also Chapter 21.

29. CJR to Johnston, 7 February 1891, JO 1/1/1. For trans-Zambezia in the 1890s, see Chapter 21.

30. Randolph Spencer Churchill, *Men, Mines and Animals in South Africa*, (London, 1892), 198–199, 208–209.

31. CJR to Stead, 19 August 1891, Mss. Afr. t. 1 (19), Rhodes House.

32. CJR to Salisbury, 12 September 1891, Mss. Afr. s. 75.

33. Harry Currey to Beit, 21 May, 28 May 1891; Francis J. Dormer to Harry Currey, 22 May, 27 May 1891, Rand Mines. Moffat to CJR, 9 October 1891; Moffat to Loch, 26 August 1891, both in Moffat, *John Smith Moffat*, 257, 258. For the other accounts, see Keppel-Jones, *Rhodes*, 174–184; Galbraith, *Crown and Charter*, 271–277.

34. CJR to Stead, 19 August 1891, Mss. Afr. t. 1; "Special Correspondent," "Trekking with the High Commissioner," *Cape Argus Weekly Edition* (20 October 1890); Jameson to Midge Jameson, 1 December 1890, in Colvin, *Jameson*, I, 172. The final quotation is from Williams, *Rhodes*, 191. On official sanction for the name, see Joseph Chamberlain to Lord Rosmead, 2 April 1897, copy in Mss. Afr. s. 134 (27), Rhodes House.

CHAPTER 14
Ends and Means, the First Premiership

1. House of Assembly, *Debates* (1890), 63, 66, 67, 70; Merriman to Sir Jacob Barry, 5 June 1890, in Lewsen, *Selections*, I, 302.

2. Assembly, *Debates* (1890), 39.

3. *Cape Times*, 16 July 1890, quoted in Stanley John Jenkins, "The Administration of Cecil John Rhodes as Prime Minister of the Cape Colony (1890–1896)," unpub. M.A. thesis (Univ. of Cape Town, 1951); T. Rodney H. Davenport, *The Afrikaner Bond* (Cape Town, 1966), 132. See also Francis H. Dormer to CJR, 5 September 1888, Mss. Afr. s. 228 (c26/26); Hofmeyr to CJR, 3 October 1888, Rhodes House.

4. CJR to Stow, 9 July 1890, Stow Papers, McGregor Memorial Museum; CJR, speech at Kimberley, 6 September 1890, quoted in Vindex, *Speeches*, 241–242; Assembly, *Debates* (1890), 165. See also Fuller, *Rhodes*, 163–165.

5. CJR, speech at the congress of the Bond, 30 March 1891, in Vindex, *Speeches*, 272.

6. Vindex, *Speeches*, 243–244. For the question of the British flag, see also Chapter 19.

7. Lewsen, *Merriman*, 139.

8. CJR, speech at the annual conference of the Afrikaner Bond, 30 March 1891, in Vindex, *Speeches*, 267. For "the Mole," see Laurence, *Merriman*, 99.

9. Hofmeyr, *Hofmeyr*, 338–389.

10. Merriman to Charlotte Barry, 1 October 1890, in Lewsen, *Selections*, II, 13.

11. Merriman to Mills, 26 August 1891, in Lewsen, *Selections*, II, 65.

12. Assembly, *Debates* (1890), 149.

13. Assembly, *Debates* (1891), 168–169; Tindall, *Innes*, 82, 85.

14. Assembly, *Debates* (1890), 162–167.

15. Merriman to Agnes Merriman, 25 March 1891, in Lewsen, *Selections*, II, 45.

16. Merriman to John Blades Currey, 22 April 1891, Lewsen, *Selections*, II, 49.

17. Flint, *Rhodes*, 160.

18. Assembly, *Debates* (1892), 287; CJR, speech at the congress of the Bond, 30 March 1891, in Vindex, *Speeches*, 267; Merriman to Currey, 22 April 1891, in Lewsen, *Selections*, II, 49.

19. Tindall, *Innes*, 85–87. George A.L. Green, *An Editor Looks Back: South African and Other Memories, 1883–1946* (Cape Town, 1947), 39.

20. Edmund Garrett, *Pall Mall Gazette*, (1890), quoted in Gerald Shaw, *Some Beginnings: The Cape Times 1876–1910* (Cape Town, 1975), 29.

21. Assembly, *Debates* (1890), 230–231.

22. CJR, speech at the congress of the Bond, 30 March 1891, in Vindex, *Speeches*, 264, 268, 269, 270, 273, 277.

23. For the complicated details of these and other rail-related negotiations, see Kenneth E. Wilburn, Jr., "The Climax of Railway Competition in South Africa, 1887–1899," unpub. D.Phil. thesis (Oxford, 1982), 78–83.

24. Assembly, *Debates* (1892), 387–388.

25. Merriman to Charles Mills, 31 August 1892, in Lewsen, *Selections*, II, 103. See also Jean van der Poel, *Railway and Customs Policies in South Africa* (London, 1933), 55–62.

26. Assembly, *Debates* (1892), 64, 329. Merriman to Mills, 16 September 1891, in Lewsen, *Selections*, II, 68. See also Chapter 23.

27. Assembly, *Debates* (1891), 32. CJR to Harcourt, 18 January 1893; Harcourt to CJR, 2 February 1893, in Mss. Afr. s. 228 (C2A), Rhodes House. Merriman to Mills, 11 January 1893, in Lewsen, *Selections*, II, 122.

28. Assembly, *Debates* (1892), 329.

29. Michell, *Rhodes*, II, 29.

30. CJR, speech at the congress of the Bond, 30 March 1891, Vindex, *Speeches*, 276. Merriman to Henry B. Webb, director of the London and South African Exploration Company, who was living overseas, 29 April 1881, in Lewsen, *Selections*, II, 42–43.

31. Quoted in Williams, *Rhodes*, 195–196.

32. Assembly, *Debates* (1892), 307.

33. Tindall, *Innes*, 84–85.

34. Assembly, *Debates* (1890), 122–125, 220–224.

35. Merriman to Charles Mills, 29 October 1890, Merriman to Agnes Merriman, 18 March 1891, in Lewsen, *Selections*, II, 16, 45.

36. Jenkins, "Rhodes as Prime Minister," 20. But see another estimate, possibly for the late 1890s, in Stanley Trapido, "African Divisional Politics in the Cape Colony, 1884–1910," *Journal of African History*, IX (1968), 80.

37. Stanley Trapido, " 'The Friends of the Natives': Merchants, Peasants and the Political and Ideological Structure of Liberalism in the Cape, 1854–1910," in Shula Marks and Anthony Atmore (eds.), *Economy and Society in Pre-industrial South Africa* (London, 1980), 267–268, suggests that the British establishment had been responsible for imposing an orthodox liberal view of these events, but his case appears both insubstantial and unsupported by the empirical evidence of the day. See also Chapter 10.

38. Assembly, *Debates* (1891), 329–330, 333, 341.

39. *Ibid.*, 332.

40. Assembly, *Debates* (1891), 334–335, 342; Merriman to Mills, 6 August 1891, in Lewsen, *Selections*, II, 62.

41. Innes to Merriman, 21 January 1892, in Lewsen, *Selections*, II, 77.

42. Sauer to Merriman, 13 January, 27 February, and 3 February 1892; Innes to Merriman, 21 January, 27 January, 3 February, 24 February 1892; Merriman to Currey, 23 May 1892, in Lewsen, *Selections*, II, 77–81, 99. Innes to CJR, 3 February, 15 February, 1892, in Harrison M. Wright, *Sir James Rose Innes: Selected Correspondence (1884–1902)* (Cape Town, 1972), 96–97.

43. J.H. Lange reported to Rhodes on 22 December 1891 that he and his associate had managed to remove 180 Africans from the rolls and only 20 remained. Lange described the process as "knocking natives off." Mss. Afr. s. 228 (C2A, 40), Rhodes House.

44. Assembly, *Debates* (1892), 150–152.

45. *Ibid.*, 157, 158, 165–167, 182, 185, 194–196, 199, 202–203.

46. *Ibid.*, 160–161, 169, 170, 177, 179, 197, 204.

47. *Ibid.*, 246–247; Williams, *Rhodes*, 189; Grey to Dorothy Grey, 2 November 1892, quoted in G.M. Trevelyan, *Grey of Falloden* (London, 1937), 61.

48. Tindall, *Innes*, 95.

49. Assembly, *Debates* (1892), 6, 115–118, 119–121; Tindall, *Innes*, 92.

50. Tindall, *Innes*, 93.

51. See Ripon to Loch, 20 December 1892, despatch no. 308, C. 23359, found with Rhodes' marking in red, enclosed in CJR to Rosebery, 18 April 1893, in Rosebery Papers, copies in Mss. Afr. s. 1826. See also Rhodes, in Assembly, *Debates* (1894), 194; Paul Maylam, *Rhodes, the Tswana, and the British: Colonialism, Collaboration, and Conflict in the Bechuanaland Protectorate, 1885–1899* (Westport, 1980), 92–93. See also Chapter 12.

52. Mills to Merriman, 13 January 1893, in Lewsen, *Selections*, II, 120–121.

53. The *Cape Times*, 8 November 1892, quoted in Shaw, *Beginnings*, 35. Merriman to Mills, 7 September 1892, Merriman to Currey, 20 December 1892, in Lewsen, *Selections*, II, 106, 117–118; Innes to CJR, 21 May 1891, Mss. Afr. s. 228 (C27/20); Innes to CJR, 8 November 1892, in Wright, *Innes*, 100–101; Assembly, *Debates* (1893), 4–5; Sauer to CJR, 23 November 1892, in Mss. Afr. s. 228 (2A), Rhodes House. For Sivewright, see J.S. Marais, *The Fall of Kruger's Republic* (Oxford, 1961), 24; Agnes Merriman, diary, 25 April to 7 May 1893, in Lewsen, *Selections*, II, 137; Kenneth E. Wilburn, "Sir James Sivewright," *Dictionary of South African Biography* (Johannesburg, 1981), IV, 572–574. For Logan and Sivewright's characters, see Sauer and Merriman in Assembly, *Debates* (1893), 12–13, 29–31. For Sivewright's defense, see *ibid.*, 20–29, 104–107.

54. CJR to Sauer, 19 November, 25 November 1892, Mss. Afr. s. 228 (C2A), Rhodes House; Sivewright to CJR, cable, 25 November 1892, Merriman to CJR, 30 November 1892, quoted in Jenkins, "Rhodes as Prime Minister," 39; Innes, in Assembly, *Debates* (1893), 7; Merriman to Currey, 20 December 1892, 24 January 1893, in Lewsen, Selections, II, 118, 122.

55. CJR to Sauer, 28 November 1892, in Mss. Afr. s. 228 (C2A), Rhodes House. CJR to Loch (telegram), c. 13 December 1893, in Loch Papers, 9, Centre for African Studies, University of York (now in Scottish Record Office, Edinburgh).

56. Herbert Baker to Basil Williams, 1 April 1921, Mss. Afr. s. 134 (12), Rhodes House.

57. Sprigg, "Short Record of Negotiations . . . ," n.d. 1893, Ms. 10.536, Sprigg papers, Cory Library, Rhodes University; James Perry Vanstone, "Sir Gordon Sprigg: A Political Biography," unpub. Ph.D. thesis (Queens Univ., 1974), 336.

58. Merriman to Currey, 17 March 1893; Agnes Merriman, "Diary of a Ministerial Crisis," 26 April, 2 May 1893, both in Lewsen, *Selections*, II, 132, 137–141; Stent, quoted in Shaw, *Beginnings*, 37. Sprigg, in *Cape Times*, 2 February 1893, quoted in Jenkins, "Rhodes as Prime Minister," 45.

59. CJR to Sprigg, 2 May 1893, 10,076, Sprigg Papers, Cory Library, Rhodes University. See also Assembly, *Debates* (1893), 284–285, 339–341.

60. CJR to Henry de Villiers, 3 June 1893, in Eric Walker, *Lord de Villiers and His Times: South Africa, 1842–1914* (London, 1925), 229. De Villiers' puzzled reply to Rhodes of 5 May 1893 is in Mss. Afr. s. 228 (C2A, 65). See also J.H. de Villiers to Gordon Le Sueur, 17 November 1906, in Mss. Afr. s. 228 (IV, 299–306), Rhodes House. CJR to Merriman, 5 May 1893, in Lewsen, *Selections*, II, 142–143.

61. Agnes Merriman, "Diary," 5 May 1893; Barry to Merriman, 5 May, 18 May 1893, in *ibid.*, 142, 144, 145.

62. Julia Merriman to Merriman, 6 June 1893, Merriman Papers (95), South African Library; Tindall, *Innes*, 90.

CHAPTER 15
Creating a Castle and Courting the World

1. Ernest Jones, *Life and Work of Sigmund Freud* (New York, 1953), I, 5.

2. See Elliott Jaques, "Death and the Midlife Crisis," *International Journal of Psychoanalysis*, XLVI (1965), 513; *idem, A General Theory of Bureaucracy* (London, 1967), 139–160; Helen Tartakoff, "The Normal Personality in Our Time and the Nobel Prize Complex," in Rudolph M. Lowenstein, Lotte M. Newman, Max Schur, and Albert J. Solnit (eds.), *Psychoanalysis: A General Psychology: Essays in Honor of Heinz Hartmann* (New York, 1966), 222–252.

3. Assembly, *Debates* (1893), 350.

4. CJR to Stow, 24 November 1890, Stow Papers, McGregor Memorial Museum, Kimberley.

5. Fuller, *Rhodes*, 128; Hensman, *Rhodes*, 67.

6. Alpheus F. Williams, *Some Dreams Come True* (Cape Town, 1949), 361; Herbert Baker, "New Delhi: The Problem of Style," *The Times* (3 October 1912), in Robert Grant Irving, *Indian Summer: Lutyens, Baker, and Imperial Delhi* (New Haven, 1981), 277, and other quotations, 276, 278. Baker, "Reminiscences of Cecil Rhodes," typescript, 1 November 1918, Mss. Afr. s. 134 (44–64). For lavish detail on Baker's origins and inspiration as an architect, see Doreen E. Greig, *Herbert Baker in South Africa* (Cape Town, 1970), 11–26.

7. Baker, "Reminiscences," (48); Herbert Baker, *Cecil Rhodes, by His Architect* (London, 1938, 2nd ed.), 19, 21, 22. Henry Lucy, "Cecil Rhodes: Some Personal Reminiscences," *Chamber's Journal*, IX (8 February 1919), 145.

8. Sarah Wilson, *South African Memories: Social, Warlike and Sporting* (London, 1909), 9–11. Architectural historians are less generous with their comments on the house as it was reconstructed. See Grieg, *Baker*, 53–54, 58.

9. Fuller, *Rhodes*, 127–128.

10. McDonald, *Rhodes*, 340.

11. Will Stuart, "Private History of the Schreiner Family" (c. 1946), Appendix 1, South African Library. But see also Frederic Hamilton, *Here, There and Everywhere* (London, 1921), 275.

12. Baker, *Rhodes*, 81; Jourdan, *Rhodes*, 133–134; T.H. Cook to Lord Elton, January? 1953, Mss. Afr. t. 5, Rhodes House.

13. Hensman, *Rhodes*, 68–69; Reminiscences of Edward Arthur Maund, 19 December 1925, Mss. Afr. s. 229, Rhodes House.

14. Cecilia FitzPatrick Sauer to Leopold S. Amery, 7 March 1949, in Lord Elton's notes, Mss. Afr. s. 229 (VII, Box 1, 5–6). Rhodes' edition was George Long (trans.), *The Thoughts of the Emperor M. Aurelius Antonius* (London, 1880, 2nd ed.).

15. Simons, "Currey Memoirs," 52; Philip Jourdan, *Cecil Rhodes: His Private Life by His Private Secretary* (London, 1911), 129–130.

16. CJR, Commonplace Book, jottings, c. 1896, Mss. Afr. s 1647 (Box 1, item 6), Rhodes House.

17. Fuller, *Rhodes*, 133–136; CJR to Wehrner Beit & Co., 31 July 1898, in Letter Books, Mss. Afr. s. 227; Interview (n.d., but 1920) by Basil Williams with Arthur L. Humphreys, Mss. Afr. s. 134; Sauer, *Ex Africa*, 202; Lucy, "Rhodes," 146; Anon.

"Translator," in *Daily Express* (21 April 1902). A complete list of Rhodes' typescripts was kindly supplied (1 June 1971) by Mrs. Balthazar John Vorster, who then occupied Groote Schuur.

18. Quoted in Jourdan, *Rhodes,* 198. Despite the energetic detective efforts of Laura Highstone and the author, the precise Reynolds possessed by Rhodes has not yet been identified. Reynolds painted several dozen portraits of young, unnamed married women.

19. Fuller, *Rhodes,* 130. For Watts, see Chapter 23.

20. Baker, *Rhodes,* 30, 39, 77.

21. McDonald, *Rhodes,* 337–338; Mortimer Menpes (ed. Dorothy Menpes), *War Impressions: Being a Record in Colour* (London, 1901), 112. Herbert Baker to Basil Williams, 1 April 1921, Mss Afr. s. 134 (13).

22. Menpes, *Impressions,* 105, 111, 117; Hensman, *Rhodes,* 69–70.

23. It is often alleged that a deep archive of personal papers was lost in the fire. This report has been handed down from biographer to biographer, and may be true. But the real nature and extent of the loss, and of the contents of any personal papers, remains obscure. For a contemporary account, see "The Fire at Groote Schuur," *South Africa* (9 January 1897), 66.

24. Quoted in A.H. Holland, "Personal Memories of Cecil John Rhodes," *The Daily Dispatch* (East London) (10 November 1953); CJR to Stevens, n.d.; CJR to Hawksley (urgent cable), 15 December 1896, Mss. Afr. s. 227 (Telegrams, V).

25. Charlie Rickson, "I Was Rhodes's Valet," *The Outspan* (9 December 1949), 71.

26. Baker, *Rhodes,* 77.

27. Le Sueur, notes and reminiscences, Mss. Afr. s. 229 (III, 397–398).

28. Michell, *Rhodes,* II, 9–10; Fuller, *Rhodes,* 138–141; Menpes, *Impressions,* 105; Eleanor Alexander (ed.), *Primate Alexander, Archbishop of Armagh* (London, 1913), 253–254; Wilson, *Memories,* 67; quoted in Katharine Furse, *Hearts and Pomegranates: The Story of Forty-Five Years, 1875–1920* (London, 1940), 235. See also Chapter 23.

29. Alexander, *Primate,* 257; Menpes, *Impressions,* 105. Lucy, "Rhodes," 147; Rudyard Kipling, report of a talk with Herbert Baker, December 1932, Mss. Afr. s. 8 (36), Rhodes House.

30. Eleanor Alexander, interview with Basil Williams, 14 February 1920, Mss. Afr. s. 134; Alexander, *Primate,* 257–258; Williams, *Rhodes,* 228.

31. Palk is discussed and analyzed in CJR to Stead, 8 April 1891. For the break with Rhodes, see Palk to Stead, 16 June 1897, Mss. Afr. s. 413.

32. Simons, "Currey Memoirs," 61–62, 72; Cook, interview 1949, in Mss. Afr. s. 69; Jourdan, *Rhodes,* 8–9, 20–21, 242; Gordon Le Sueur, *Cecil Rhodes: The Man and His Work* (London, 1913), 194–196, 202–203, 207, 210; Williams, *Dreams,* 375; H.A. Myburgh, interview, 1949, Mss. Afr. s. 69; CJR to Grimmer, 27 September, 13 December 1898, Letterbook I, Mss. Afr. s. 227; Grimmer to CJR, 25 October 1898, Mss. Afr. s. 227, Box 13.

33. Johannes Meintjes, *Olive Schreiner: Portrait of a South African Woman* (Johannesburg, 1965), 57. *The Story of an African Farm* appeared in 1883.

34. Olive Schreiner to Mrs. Erilda B. Cawood, February 1890, quoted in Samuel C. Cronwright-Schreiner, *The Life of Olive Schreiner* (Boston, 1923), 198; Schreiner to Havelock Ellis, 16 March 1890, 15 April 1890, in Cronwright-Schreiner (ed.), *The Letters of Olive Schreiner, 1876–1920* (London, 1924), 179, 183. A fuller, more accurate transcription of the 16 March 1890 letter may be found in Richard Rive (ed.), *Olive Schreiner: Letters 1871–99* (Cape Town, 1987), 165–166. For liking Rhodes, and their meeting, Schreiner to Ellis, 22 June 1890, *ibid,* 175.

35. Schreiner to Jessie Rose Innes, 10 February 1893, D 131/58, Jagger Library,

University of Cape Town; Schreiner to Stead, 12 July 1890, in Cronwright-Schreiner, *Letters*, 191; Ruth First and Ann Scott, *Olive Schreiner* (New York, 1980), 198.

36. Merriman to Charlotte Barry, 1 October 1890, in Lewsen, *Selections*, II, 14.

37. Schreiner to Stead, 12 July 1890, in Rive, *Letters*, 175; Schreiner to Ellis, n.d., but May? 1890, in *Life*, 209–210; Jane Graves, introduction, to Olive Schreiner, *Women and Labour* (London, 1978, 2nd. ed.), quoted in Dale Spender, *Women of Ideas, and What Men Have Done to Them* (London, 1982), 470; Olive Schreiner to CJR, 15 November 1890, Mss. Afr. s. 228 (C28/40), Rhodes House. Richard Rive cannot believe that Schreiner implied deep affection.

38. Schreiner to Ellis, 29 November, 21 December 1890, in *Life*, 210.

39. Olive Schreiner to CJR, n.d. [May? 1891], Mss. Afr. s. 228 (C27/142/12), Rhodes House.

40. Schreiner to Stead [March 1892?] in Frederic Whyte, *The Life of W.T. Stead* (Boston, 1925), II, 26. Another version in Rive, *Letters*, 201.

41. Swift MacNeill, quoted in *Life*, 213; Schreiner to Stead, 24 September, 23 November 1891, in Cronwright-Schreiner, *Letters*, 206–207. The reports of Stead, Booth, and Jameson are contained in an undated anonymous account, possibly by Lewis Michell, "Stead's Idea," in "Fragments on Rhodes," Rhodes-Livingstone Museum, in Mss. Afr. s. 641, Rhodes House.

42. Schreiner to Stead, 13 March, 24 September 1891, in Cronwright-Schreiner, *Letters*, 204, 206; Adela Villiers(Smith), quoted in Meintjes, *Schreiner*, 110–111; Merriman, diary, 2 February 1891, in Lewsen, *Selections*, II, 29.

43. "The Salvation," in *Life*, 202–205. The skit was never published.

44. Olive Schreiner to William Phillip Schreiner, 13 September [1892], D 60/241, III, H 16, Jagger Library.

45. Schreiner to her mother, Rebecca Schreiner, n.d. but February 1896; Schreiner to her sister Ettie (Henrietta Stakesby Lewis), 25 May 1896; Schreiner to W.P. Schreiner, 13, 30 August 1895, D 67/1, BC 112, Jagger Library and Rive, *Letters*, 258, 268, 280. Schreiner to Mary Sauer, 10 January 1896, in Rive, *Letters*, 261.

46. Richard C. Pillard and James D. Weinrich, "Evidence of Familial Nature of Male Homosexuality," *Archives of General Psychiatry*, XLIII (1986), 808–812.

47. Lockhart and Woodhouse, *Rhodes*, 13–14. For syphilis and Rhodes, see Chapter 24.

48. Harris, *Life and Loves*, V, 947.

49. Jourdan, *Rhodes*, 23–25, 50; Le Sueur, *Rhodes*, 190, 192, 194–195, 199–200.

50. Brian Roberts, *The Diamond Magnates* (New York, 1972), 262–264; Jourdan, *Rhodes*, 135–136; Anon., "Stead's Idea," "Fragments," Mss. Afr. s. 641.

51. Robert Bernard Martin, *With Friends Possessed: A Life of Edward FitzGerald* (New York, 1985), 117. See also Roberts, *Rhodes*, 205–206.

52. Brian Reade, *Sexual Heretics: Male Homosexuals in English Literature from 1850 to 1900.* (London, 1970), 1–55. Montgomery Hyde, *The Love That Dared Not Speak Its Name* (Boston, 1970), 90–170.

53. Blake, *Rhodesia*, 36–37. See also Chapter 2.

54. For 1877, see Chapter V. For the wills, see Chapter 24.

55. Graham Bower to James Rose Innes, 16 November 1932, Innes Papers, 873, South African Library. Brian Roberts, *Churchills in Africa* (London, 1970), 71.

56. For 1894, see Chapter 17. Williams, *Rhodes*, 251. Williams offers no source of evidence for this paraphrase of Rhodes' own thoughts. See also Gardner Williams to Carl Meyer, 21 October 1895, RAL B17/RH/1895–27, Rothschild archives. See also Chapter 24.

57. John Hays Hammond, *The Autobiography of John Hays Hammond* (New York, 1935), 213; Furse, *Pomegranates*, 235; Wilson, Memories, 9, 65; Bramwell Booth, *Echoes and Memories* (New York, 1926), 147–148; Menpes, *Impressions*, 102–103; Jourdan, *Rhodes*, 19–20. Photographs in Sibbett Collection, Jagger Library, Univ. of Cape Town; Flint, *Rhodes*, 122.

58. F. Edmund Garrett, "The Character of Cecil Rhodes," *The Contemporary Review*, LXXXI (1902), 763–764. See also Hans Sauer, "Cecil Rhodes: As a Man and a Friend," *Empire Review*, III (1902), 366–367.

59. J. Keir Hardie (ed. Emrys Hughes), *Keir Hardie's Speeches and Writings (from 1886 to 1915)* (Glasgow, 1928), 97. See also Chapter 22.

60. Harry H. Johnston, *The Story of My Life* (Indianapolis, 1923), 281–283; Le Sueur, *Rhodes*, 24–25, 31; Baker, *Rhodes*, 82; Lord Winchester to Lord Elton, 22 January 1957, Mss. Afr. t. 10; Charles Mills to Merriman, 14 May 1891, Merriman Papers, 130, South African Library; G.H. Wilson, *Gone Down the Years* (Cape Town, 1947), 51; Charles Metcalfe to Basil Williams, 16 May 1919, Mss. Afr. s. 134 (Box 1, Notebook 1, 197); C.H. Instrap, "Rhodes in Matabeleland, '96," *The Sunrise* (29 March 1902). Henry W. Lucy, *A Diary of the Unionist Parliament, 1895–1900* (Bristol, 1901), 130; Hesketh Pearson, *Labby: The Life and Character of Henry Labouchere* (London, 1936), 279; John Norris, "Personal Servant's Stories of Rhodes," Mss. Afr. s. 8 (61–62); Harris, *Life and Loves*, II, 485, 447. See also Tudor G. Trevor, *Forty Years in Africa* (London, 1932), 104–105.

61. Douglas A. Parker, Elizabeth S. Parker, et al., "Alcohol Use and Cognitive Loss among Employed Men and Women," *American Journal of Public Health*, LXXIII (1973), 521–526; Douglas A. Parker, Elizabeth S. Parker, Thomas C. Harford, and Gail C. Farmer, "Alcohol Use and Depression Symptoms among Employed Men and Women," *American Journal of Public Health*, LXXVII (1987), 706.

62. Eugene Braunwald, *Heart Disease: A Textbook of Cardiovascular Medicine* (Philadelphia, 1984, 2nd ed.), 1406.

63. W.T. Stead (ed.), *The Last Will and Testament of Cecil John Rhodes, with Elucidatory Notes, to Which Are Added Some Chapters Describing the Political and Religious Ideas of the Testator* (London, 1902), 98.

64. Untitled, undated essay, Mss. Afr. s. 1647 (57–59), Rhodes House.

65. See also Chapter 12.

66. Reginald Brett to CJR, 15 November 1892, A 540/40, Cape archives. See also James Lees-Milne, *The Enigmatic Edwardian: The Life of Reginald, 2nd Viscount Esher* (London, 1986), 83–84. Lees-Milne misdates the visit. See also Chapter 19.

67. Stead, *Last Will*, 104–105, 113. For the scholarships, see Chapter 24.

CHAPTER 16
Making War in Rhodesia

1. Erik H. Erikson, *Insight and Responsibility* (New York, 1964), 130–131. Cf. John S. Galbraith, "Cecil Rhodes and His 'Cosmic Dreams': A Reassessment," *Journal of Imperial and Commonwealth History*, I (1973), 175.

2. See Heinz Kohut, *The Analysis of the Self* (New York, 1971), 1–34.

3. Robert Shenton, "The Chartered Company, 1889–1898: A Financial and Political History of the British South Africa Company," unpub. Ph.D. thesis (Harvard, 1961), 60–63.

4. Beit to Phillips, ? August 1891, quoted in A.P. Cartwright, *The Corner House:*

The Early History of Johannesburg (Johannesburg, 1965), 108. See also A.P. Cartwright, *The First South African: The Life and Times of Sir Percy FitzPatrick* (Johannesburg, 1971), 52.

5. Quoted in *South Africa*, 30 January 189[2], in Brian Roberts, *Churchills in Africa* (London, 1970), 48. See also Robert Rhodes James, *Lord Randolph Churchill* (London, 1959), 351–352.

6. Arthur Glyn Leonard, *How We Made Rhodesia* (London, 1896), 255, 273.

7. Randolph Churchill, *Men, Mines and Animals in South Africa* (London, 1892), 198–199, 206–207, 145.

8. CJR to Jameson, 4 November 1891, Mss. Afr. t. 5 (544). See also Chapter 14.

9. H. Wilson Fox to Milton, 14 October 1898, A 1/5/1, Zimbabwe archives, quoted in Galbraith, *Charter*, 281.

10. Middleton Jameson to Lizzie Jameson, n.d. but late 1891, quoted in Colvin, *Jameson*, I, 222. First quote at 220.

11. Quoted in Millin, *Rhodes*, 165.

12. David C. de Waal (trans. Jan H. Hofmeyr de Waal), *With Rhodes in Mashonaland* (Cape Town, 1896), 102, 122, 169, 211; Frank Johnson, *Great Days: The Autobiography of an Empire Pioneer* (London, 1940), 206–207.

13. Rose Blennerhassett and Lucy Sleeman, *Adventures in Mashonaland* (London, 1893), 191–192.

14. De Waal, *Rhodes*, 221–222; Johnson, *Days*, 206–207.

15. De Waal, *Rhodes*, 229.

16. Churchill, *Men, Mines*, 305–306. See also Chapter 21.

17. De Waal, *Rhodes*, 270.

18. De Waal, *Rhodes*, 283, 285. For Rhodes' view of the origins of Zimbabwe, see CJR to Stead, 19 August 1891, Mss. Afr. s. 413.

19. De Waal, *Rhodes*, 350; CJR to Cawston, n.d. but December 1891, CJR to Jameson, 9 December 1891, Cullen Library, University of the Witwatersrand.

20. CJR to Stow, 27 November 1891, Stow Papers, McGregor Memorial Museum, Kimberley. CJR, speech to the British South Africa Company shareholders, 29 November 1892, in Vindex, *Speeches*, 300–319.

21. Olive Schreiner to William P. Schreiner, n.d., 1896?, Jagger Library, University of Cape Town.

22. James Johnston, *Reality versus Romance in South Central Africa* (New York, 1893), 262–264.

23. Joseph M. Orpen to CJR, 10 September 1897, Mss. Afr. s. 228 (C 1), Rhodes House. Loch to Sir Marshall Clarke, Resident Commissioner of Zululand, 22 August 1893, in Loch Papers, 9, Scottish Record Office.

24. CJR to Jameson, 12 February 1892, CT 1/15/4, Zimbabwe archives; Report of Jameson, 1 June 1892, Report of Captain Charles Frederick Lendy, 24 March 1892, quoted in Terence O. Ranger, *Revolt in Southern Rhodesia, 1896–97* (London, 1967), 64, 65; Galbraith, *Charter*, 292–293.

25. Johannes Colenbrander to Harry Currey, 1 May 1892, quoted in Galbraith, *Charter*, 292.

26. Lobengula to Jameson, 13? May 1893, quoted in Stafford Glass, *The Matabele War* (London 1968), 64.

27. F. Rutherfoord Harris to Colenbrander, 9 February 1892, quoted in Galbraith, *Charter*, 288; Jameson to Samuel Jameson, 11 August 1892, quoted in Colvin, *Jameson*, I, 229.

28. Harris to London Board of BSA Co., 12 July 1893, quoted in Galbraith, *Charter*, 296.

29. Lobengula (written by James W. Dawson) to Lendy, 28 June 1893, quoted in Keppel-Jones, *Rhodes*, 237–238.

30. Jameson to Lendy, 9 July 1893, Jameson to Lobengula, 9 July 1893, Jameson to Harris, 10 July 1893, in Colvin, *Jameson*, I, 249–250; Jameson to Harris, 11 July 1893, Harris to London Board, 12 July 1893, in Ranger, *Revolt*, 93; Lobengula to Jameson, in Keppel-Jones, *Rhodes*, 241.

31. Jameson to Harris, 17 July 1893, telegram, Afr. Mss. s. 228 (C 3 B, 214a). See also Glass, *Matabele*, 88.

32. Jameson to Harris, 19 July 1893, telegram, Afr. Mss. s. 228 (C 3 B, 214b), Rhodes House; Harris to Jameson, 17 July 1893, quoted in Glass, *Matabele*, 96; Colvin, *Jameson*, I, 259–260. Arthur Keppel-Jones pins the decision to go to war on Jameson, "Rhodes and the Imperial Venture: The Rhodesias," unpub. paper (1985), 18. "Necessity and Curse" is Blake's apt adaptation of what Gladstone said about Disraeli's relationship to Lord Derby. Blake, *Rhodesia*, 57.

33. Harris to the London Board, 9 August 1893, quoted in Ranger, *Revolt*, 95.

34. Cf. Ian R. Phimister, "Rhodes, Rhodesia and the Rand," *Journal of Southern African Studies*, I (1974), 81.

35. Ripon to Loch, 28 September 1893, 12 October 1893, Ripon Papers, British Museum, quoted in Charles Allen Thompson, "The Administration of Sir Henry Loch as Governor of the Cape Colony and High Commissioner for South Africa, 1889–1895," unpub. Ph.D. thesis (Duke Univ., 1973), 186, 189. *The Economist* (4 October 1893). See also Anthony Denholm, *Lord Ripon, 1827–1909: A Political Biography* (London, 1982), 208–211.

36. Jameson to Maund, 24 July 1893, in Maund Papers, Cullen Library, University of the Witwatersrand; Jameson to Middleton Jameson, 10 August 1893, in Colvin, *Jameson*, I, 264.

37. Keppel-Jones, *Rhodes*, 249.

38. Lobengula to Harris, quoted in *The Times* (13 October 1894), and slightly differently in Philip Mason, *The Birth of a Dilemma: The Conquest and Settlement of Rhodesia* (London, 1958), 170. Lobengula to Moffat, 15 August 1893, in Moffat, *Moffat*, 272.

39. Lobengula to Loch, 12 October 1893, quoted in Galbraith, *Charter*, 306–307.

40. Leonard, *Rhodesia*, 321.

41. Sauer, *Ex Africa*, 227–228. Le Sueur, *Rhodes*, omits any mention of this journey with Rhodes. Michell, *Rhodes*, II, 87; *Rhodesia Herald* (14 October 1893).

42. Moffat to Robert Unwin Moffat, 12 October 1893, in Moffat, *Moffat*, 273. Hilaire Belloc, "The Modern Traveller," in Belloc, *Complete Verse* (London, 1970), 184.

43. Hubert Hervey to Mary Hervey, 3 January 1894, in Albert Grey, *Hubert Hervey, Student and Imperialist: A Memoir* (London, 1899), 90–91. Hervey was the grandson of the Marquess of Bristol and an Old Etonian. George Wyndham Hamilton Knight Bruce, diary, 24 October 1893, in his *Memoirs of Mashonaland* (London, 1895), 231–232. *The Times* (12 December 1893). There is circumstantial evidence that Ernest Gedge, the correspondent of *The Times*, derived his report of the battle from Rhodes. For Rhodes' own report, see a press report (4 November 1893), quoting Rhodes, in the Christopher Francis Harrison Papers, HA 2/1/2, Zimbabwe archives.

44. CJR to W.H. Craven, 26 December 1893, telegram, Ms. 113, the Brenthurst Library; John Smith Moffat to H. Unwin Moffat, 9 July 1903, in Moffat, *Moffat*, 346.

45. CJR to Jameson, 21 October 1893, 4 November 1893; CJR to Harris, 5 November 1893, all in Mss. Afr. s. 227, telegrams, Rhodes House.

46. McDonald, *Rhodes*, 162.

47. Quoted in Vere Stent, *A Personal Record of Some Incidents in the Life of Cecil Rhodes* (Cape Town, 1925; reprint, Bulawayo, 1970), 5, 7, 8. Also in Sally and Betty Stent (ed. Paddy Cartwright), *The Forthright Man* (Cape Town, 1972), 29–30. Stent's report originally appeared in the *Transvaal Advertiser*. Stent, from Grahamstown, became the editor of the *Pretoria News* in 1903.

48. Rhodes, speech at Bulawayo, 19 December 1893, in Vindex, *Speeches*, 328–335.

49. Although the official text in Vindex, *Speeches*, omits this threat, Stent, *Personal*, 8, who heard the speech, gives it prominence. Verschoyle, the compiler of the *Speeches*, probably thought it wise to purge Rhodes' published utterances of anti-imperial rhetoric.

50. Harris to Jameson, 6 January 1894, quoted in Glass, *Matabele*, 266.

51. Rhodes, speech of 3 January 1894 in Cape Town, in Vindex, *Speeches*, 336–360. Again, Verschoyle purged the offical text of the threat to Britain. It is quoted, from *The Times* (4 January 1894) and from other contemporary newspaper accounts, in Glass, *Matabele*, 266. See also the material in the Harrison papers, HA 2/1/3, Zimbabwe archives; *The Economist* (6 January 1894).

52. Julia Merriman to Agnes Merriman, 13 January 1894, Merriman Papers, 1, South African Library.

53. Loch to CJR, 23 October 1893, telegram, Afr. Mss. s. 228 (C 3 B, 218), Rhodes House; Ripon to Loch, 27 October 1893, Ripon Papers, quoted in Galbraith, *Charter*, 332; CJR to Sprigg, 22 November 1893, Sprigg to CJR, 24 (?) November 1893, in Mss. Afr. s. 227, telegrams, Rhodes House; Edward Fairchild, Assistant Under-Secretary of State for the Colonies, minute of 6 November 1893, quoted in Keppel-Jones, *Rhodes*, 330. See also diary entry 24 November 1893, William Scawen Blunt, *My Diaries: Being a Personal Narrative of Events, 1888–1914* (New York, 1921), I, 117. The telegrams that passed back and forth between Ripon and the Company in London, and Ripon and Loch, in late October 1893, are in the Loch Papers, 9, Scottish Record Office.

54. Quoted in Keppel-Jones, *Rhodes*, 336. See also Claire Palley, *The Constitutional History and Law of Southern Rhodesia, 1888–1965, with Special Reference to Imperial Control* (Oxford, 1966), 118–119. The details of the negotiations between Rhodes, Loch, and Ripon and the actual multiple drafts of the 1894 Order-in-Council are preserved in the Loch Papers, 9.

55. Alfred Lord Milner to Joseph Chamberlain, 1 December 1897, in Cecil Headlam (ed.), *The Milner Papers: South Africa, 1897–1899* (London, 1931), I, 140–141.

CHAPTER 17
The Second Premiership

1. Assembly, *Debates* (1894), 384–385.

2. Telegraphic conversation between CJR and Gardner Williams and William H. Craven (Rhodes in Macloutsie, the other two in Kimberley), 19 November 1893; CJR to Craven (letters), 7, 11 July, 9 August, ? August 1893, Ms. 113, the Brenthurst Library; CJR to Stephen Albertyn Le Riche, 3 February 1894, Royal Commonwealth Society archives.

3. Quoted in Gerald Shaw, *Some Beginnings* (Cape Town, 1975), 66.

4. Edgar H. Walton to Merriman, 14 November 1893, in Lewsen, *Selections*, II, 158.

5. Innes to G.A. Hay, 4 June 1894, in Wright, *Innes*, 139.

6. For an unromantic examination of the rootedness of and contradictions within this tradition, see Phyllis Lewsen, "The Cape Liberal Tradition—Myth or Reality?" *Race*, XIII (1971), 65–80.

7. Assembly, *Debates* (1894), 417.

8. Assembly, *Debates* (1893), 217, 218, 221.

9. *Ibid.*, 95, 374, 325.

10. *Ibid.*, 165, 201.

11. *Ibid.*, 202–206, 208.

12. Quoted in W.T . Ferguson, "The Native Policy of Cecil John Rhodes in the Eastern Province," unpub. M.A. thesis (Univ. of Cape Town, 1932), 29–30. For Loch's role, see Charles Allen Thompson, "The Administration of Sir Henry Loch as Governor of Cape Colony and High Commissioner for South Africa, 1889–1895," unpub. Ph.D. thesis (Duke Univ., 1973), 146–159.

13. Assembly, *Debates* (1894), 7–8. Rhodes, quoted in Ferguson, "Native Policy," 34.

14. Although the older biographies of Rhodes add considerable color to this visit, the reports which flow onward from Michell, *Rhodes*, II, 105–106; Williams, *Rhodes*, 209; McDonald, *Rhodes*, 167, are all concocted. Rhodes did not keep Sigcawu waiting three days to repay him for his "insult" to Loch. Rhodes did not take Sigcawu into a maize field to show him what would happen to him and his tribe if there were further trouble. (There machine guns supposedly blew the heads off the waving fields of grain.) Rhodes was not accompanied by either artillery or Maxim guns and the dates given in the text show that Sigcawu could not have been kept waiting. See Ferguson, "Native Policy," 37–38.

15. CJR to Stanford, 21 April 1894, in PMO 416 (Telegrams), Cape archives.

16. John Smith Moffat to Robert Unwin Moffat, c. May 1894, in Moffat, *Moffat*, 279.

17. Assembly, *Debates* (1894), 8–10, 13, 67. CJR to Sprigg, 17 April 1894, in PMO 416 (Telegrams), Cape archives.

18. Assembly, *Debates* (1894), 90–92, 225.

19. Under Secretary of Native Affairs to Stanford, 22 February; Stanford to CJR, 29 March, 30 March, 5 June, 9 June; CJR to Stanford, 25 May, 5 June, 7 June, 9 June, 10 June, 12 June, 16 June, 18 June; Sigcawu to CJR, 5 June; all telegrams printed in Cape of Good Hope, *Correspondence Relating to the State of Affairs in Eastern Pondoland* (Cape Town, 1895).

20. Merriman to Walton, 8 May 1895, Walton Papers, Cory Library, Rhodes University.

21. Assembly, Debates (1895), 220. Eric A. Walker, *Lord de Villiers and His Times: South Africa, 1842–1914* (London, 1925), 259–260.

22. Tindall, *Innes*, 105.

23. H.H. Juta to Sprigg (n.d.), Juta to CJR, 24 August 1894, both in CJR to W.P. Schreiner, 24 August 1894, Schreiner Papers, Jagger Library, Univ. of Cape Town.

24. Tindall, *Innes*, 105; George A.L. Green, *An Editor Looks Back: South African and Other Memories, 1883–1946* (Cape Town, 1947), 38.

25. Assembly, *Debates* (1894,), 362–369. Tindall, Innes, 105. The "rapt expres-

sion" was Innes' observation. Sampson's role, particularly important with regard to the detailed restrictions on individual tenure in Glen Grey, and the small size of the farms, are discussed in Davenport, *Afrikaner Bond*, 154–155; Ruth Edgecombe, "The Glen Grey Act: Local Origins of an Abortive 'Bill for Africa,' " in J.A. Benyon et al. (eds.) *Studies in Local History* (Cape Town, 1976), 89–90. Important letters are Sampson to Hofmeyr, 15 June 1891; 25 October 1892; 18 July, 3 November 1893; in Hofmeyr Papers, 15 F, South African Library.

26. Assembly, *Debates* (1894), 380, 382, 383, 418, 420.

27. Tindall, *Innes*, 106. *The Advertiser* (9 August 1894).

28. Assembly, *Debates* (1894), 434, 439, 461, 466, 467.

29. Julia Merriman to Agnes Merriman, 15 July 1894, Merriman Papers, South African Library.

30. CJR, speech at Queenstown, 3 April 1895, Mss. Afr. s. 228 (C 16/42); Edgar H. Brookes, *The History of Native Policy in South Africa from 1830 to the Present Day* (Cape Town, 1924), 114, 368.

31. Quoted in Colin Bundy, *The Rise and Fall of the South African Peasantry* (Berkeley, 1979), 136. Assembly, *Debates* (1894), 418.

32. Assembly, *Debates* (1895), 52.

33. *Ibid.,* 24, 25, 126.

34. *Ibid.,* 240–242, 427–428.

35. *Ibid.,* 137, 175, 176, 421.

36. Assembly, *Debates* (1894), 121–123, 154, 248, 357, 359; (1985), 472; Innes to W.H. Hockly, 2 July 1894, in Wright, *Innes*, 142.

37. Assembly, *Debates* (1895), 456.

38. See Chapter 18.

39. Assembly, *Debates* (1894), 280; (1895), 100, 156.

40. Assembly, *Debates* (1894), 210; (1895), 65–66. See also Lucien Wolf, *Life of the First Marquess of Ripon* (London, 1921), II, 216–221.

41. Assembly, *Debates* (1895), 203, 205, 206, 438, 558. See also CJR to Lord Ripon, 29 November 1894, in Paul Maylam, *Rhodes, the Tswana, and the British: Colonialism, Collaboration, and Conflict in the Bechuanaland Protectorate, 1885–1899* (Westport, 1980), 150; CJR to Earl Grey, ? February 1895, Mss. Afr. t. 6 (13–17); CJR to Chamberlain, 9 July 1895, Chamberlain Papers, Birmingham Univ.

42. Chamberlain to CJR, 31 July 1895. See also Lord Rosebery to CJR, 26 August 1895, both in Mss. Afr. s. 228 (C27/53, 58), Rhodes House.

43. CJR to Harris, 12, 23 November 1895, quoted in Joseph L. Garvin, *The Life of Joseph Chamberlain* (London, 1934), III, 50–51. See also Maylam, *Rhodes*, 168–170.

CHAPTER 18
The Money Game and Other Profitable Pursuits

1. CJR to Ellen Sprigg, 2 September 1895, Sprigg Papers, 10.078, Cory Library, Rhodes University.

2. CJR to Craven, 7 April, 20 April 1895, Ms. 113, the Brenthurst Library. For the university, see Chapter 14.

3. CJR, speech to the eighth annual general meeting of the De Beers shareholders, 1896, quoted in Theodore Gregory, *Ernest Oppenheimer and the Economic Development of Southern Africa* (Cape Town, 1962), 56. Meyer and other directors to CJR, 26 April

1899, in 4/1/1, De Beers archives; *The Economist* (26 November 1892), 1482. Turrell has a somewhat different view of the Wesselton purchase. See his "Sir Frederic Philipson Stow: The Unknown Diamond Magnate," *Business History*, XXVIII (1986), 69.

4. CJR to Stow, 22 November 1890, Stow Papers, McGregor Memorial Museum, Kimberley. See also Worger, *Diamonds*, 260.

5. CJR, speech to the tenth annual meeting of De Beers, quoted in Gregory, *Oppenheimer*, 54; CJR to Craven, n.d. but received 7 March 1892, Ms. 113, the Brenthurst Library.

6. CJR to Craven, 24 July 1893, telegram, De Beers archives; Records of Telegraphic Conversations, 19 November, 22 November 1893, Ms. 113, the Brenthurst Library; Record of Craven's telegraphic talk with CJR, 3 August 1894, 5/1/1, De Beers archives.

7. CJR to Stow, 19 May 1890, Stow Papers, McGregor Memorial Museum, Kimberley.

8. CJR to Stow, 19 July 1890 [often misread as 1891], Stow Papers; CJR to Craven, n.d. 1890, Ms. 113, the Brenthurst Library; CJR to Beit, 2 July 1890, Mss Afr. t. 14 (191–192).

9. Stow to CJR, 15 August 1890; CJR to Stow, 20 January 1891 [the date of this letter has often been misread as June for Jan.], 1 August 1891, Stow Papers; CJR to Craven, 19 April 1891 (telegram), 10 June 1891, Ms. 113, the Brenthurst Library; Stow to CJR, 13 Feb 1891, Mss. Afr. s. 228 (C7A/30); Rothschild to CJR, 7 August 1891, Mss. Afr. s. 228 (C27/23), Rhodes House; CJR to Stow, 11 March 1891, Stow Papers. See also Turrell, "Stow," 70–71; Worger, *Diamonds*, 261–262.

10. CJR to Stow, n.d. but late 1891, 5/1/1; Stow to CJR, 19 August 1891, 4/1/1; CJR to Craven, 30 June 1893, De Beers archives.

11. CJR to Stow, 27 November 1891, Stow Papers.

12. Quoted in Alpheus F. Williams, *Some Dreams Come True* (Cape Town, 1948), 328; CJR to Craven, n.d. but received 24 August 1895.

13. CJR to Craven, 29 November 1891, De Beers archives, Kimberley; CJR to Craven, undated, CJR to Craven, 10 July 1894 (telegram), Ms. 113, the Brenthurst Library.

14. Rothschild to CJR, 15 January 1892, RAL B 17/RH/XC, Rothschild archives.

15. CJR to Craven, n.d. but received 19 August 1892; Carl Meyer to CJR, 29 June 1894, RAL B 17/RH/XC.

16. W.H. Milton to William Pickering, 17 December 1895; Carl Meyer to CJR, 22 November 1895.

17. CJR to Rothschild, 29 October 1888, Mss. Afr. t. 14 (317–320), Rhodes House. See Chapter 9. Rothschild to CJR, 20 August 1901, RAL B 17/RH/XC. See also Stanley D. Chapman, "Rhodes and the City of London: Another View of Imperialism," *The Historical Journal*, XXVIII (1985), 655–656.

18. See Chapter 9.

19. Rudd, speeches to annual meeting of Gold Fields of South Africa, November 1889, 1890, quoted in Cartwright, *Gold*, 49, 53. Taylor to Porges, 22 March 1889, quoted in A.P. Cartwright, *The Corner House: The Early History of Johannesburg* (Johannesburg, 1965), 93.

20. Meeting of 30 November 1891, Cartwright, *Gold*, 60. See also Kubicek, *Economic Imperialism*, 92–93.

21. Lionel Phillips, *Some Reminiscences* (London, 1924), 116.

22. Beit to Lionel Phillips, 9 July 1892, quoted in Cartwright, *Corner House*, 130;

CJR to Beit, n.d. but 9/10 December 1892, Rand Mines archives; Rudd to Beit, 9 March 1893, Rand Mines archives; Cartwright, *Gold*, 65–66. James B. Taylor, *A Pioneer Looks Back* (London, 1939), 123–124; Kubicek, *Imperialism*, 65, 98.

23. Quoted, without date, in Cartwright, *Gold*, 66.

24. Rudd to Currey, 7 July 1892, Rudd to CJR, 14 July 1892, quoted in Cartwright, Gold, 68.

25. A slightly lower figure appears in Paul Johnson, *Consolidated Gold Fields: A Centenary Portrait* (London, 1987), 28.

26. CJR to Davies, n.d. (January), 17 January 1893, Gold Fields archives. For Frank Rhodes, see Chapter 19.

27. Rudd to Arthur Boucher, 9 February 1893, Gold Fields archives, quoted in Kubicek, *Imperialism*, 102.

28. John Hays Hammond, *The Autobiography of John Hays Hammond* (New York, 1935), I, 213–215, 293–294, 304.

29. Julius Wernher to Georges Rouliot, 18 December 1896; Sapte to Herbert Davies, 4 October 1896; Edward S. Birkenruth to James C. Prinsep, 1 November 1896, Gold Fields archives, all quoted in Kubicek, *Imperialism*, 103.

30. *The Economist* (29 April 1893), 504.

31. Francis William Fox reported that Rhodes had been influenced in his decision to extend the trans-continental telegraph line to Egypt by a reading of Fox's letters about the Mahdi's Sudan in Henry Russell, *The Ruin of the Soudan, Cause, Effect, and Remedy: A Resume of Events, 1883–1891* (London, 1892). One letter, to Russell, dated 18 March 1891, advocated building a railway to aid in the pacification and unification of the peoples of the eastern Sudan. Rhodes resolved to carry out such a policy by the swifter means of erecting a telegraph line, thus opening the Sudan to outside influence. A second letter, of the same date, from Fox and the explorer Verney Lovett Cameron to Lord Salisbury, advocated "handing the country over to a powerful chartered company, which should devote its whole energies to the important task of the pacification and development of the Soudan and its future Government." They advocated a British subsidy to such a company and asserted that the commercial prospects of the Sudan were "of the highest class." Therefore a chartered company would "not only prove of use to the world in a political sense, but also in a few years become self-supporting. . . ," help end the slave trade, and "tend to the civilization of Africa." The quotations and the letters are found on pp. 332, 335–336. Fox's account of Rhodes' interest is contained in Fox, "Narrative of Some Historical Incidents Connected with Right Honorable Cecil Rhodes and the African Transcontinental Telegraph Line, and the Central African Highway from the Zambesi to Egypt," unpub. typescript (London, 16 September 1907), in Michell Papers, A 540/31, Cape archives.

32. Rosebery to Lord Herschell, 27 September 1893, quoted in Robert Rhodes James, *Rosebery: A Biography of Archibald Philip, Fifth Earl of Rosebery* (London, 1963), 266.

33. Diary entry, 4 November 1892, Wilfrid Scawen Blunt, *My Diaries: Being a Personal Narrative of Events, 1888–1914* (New York, 1921), I, 82.

34. H.H. Johnston to CJR, 20 January 1893, in CJR to Rosebery, (n.d.) November 1893, in Michell, *Rhodes*, II, 63. CJR to Rosebery, 29 October 1892, FO 84/2252, Public Record Office. Cf. Williams, *Rhodes*, 236–237.

35. CJR, speech of 29 November 1893, at the annual meeting of the British South Africa Company, in Vindex, *Speeches*, 313–315. Rhodes, in Assembly, *Debates* (1894), 210. Sivewright's skepticism about the efficacy and economics of an overland line to Egypt were expressed in the Cape parliament. Assembly, *Debates* (1894), 212.

36. CJR to Rosebery, 22 January 1893, Rosebery Papers, Mss. Afr. t. 5 (494–505); CJR to Stanley, 17 April 1893, xerox of holograph; CJR to Francis Schnadhorst, 23 February 1891, Mss. Afr. t. 5 (496–499); CJR to Schnadhorst, 25 April 1892, in *The Spectator* (12 October 1901). See also Chapter 21.

37. Robinson to Lewis Michell, 7 December 1892, Harcourt to CJR, 20 December 1892, both quoted in Michell, *Rhodes,* II, 122–123; Lockhart and Woodhouse, *Rhodes,* 281.

38. Assembly, *Debates* (1895), 77; Lockhart and Woodhouse, *Rhodes,* 281.

39. Hammond, *Autobiography,* 277–278.

CHAPTER 19
The Raid and Its Consequences

1. William Thomas Stead (ed.), *The Last Will and Testament of Cecil John Rhodes* (London, 1902), 106; Henry Rider Haggard, *The Days of My Life: An Autobiography* (London, 1926), II, 116–117.

2. A.G. Butler to Edith Rhodes, n.d. 1899, Mss. Afr. s. 1647 (72), Rhodes House; A. Geoffrey Blainey, "Lost Causes of the Jameson Raid," *Economic History Review,* XLVIII (1965), 366.

3. Blainey, "Causes," 362–364. Richard Mendelsohn, "Blainey and the Jameson Raid: The Debate Renewed," *Journal of Southern African Studies,* VI (1980), 170. Donald J.N. Denoon, "'Capitalist Influence' and the Transvaal Government During the Crown Colony Period, 1900–1906," *Historical Journal,* XI (1968), 301–312, follows Blainey, but the arguments of both were countered effectively by Kubicek, "Randlords," 101–102; Arthur A. Mawby, "Capital, Government and Politics in the Transvaal, 1900–1907: A Revision and a Reversion, *Historical Journal,* XVII (1974), 392, 415. The historiography of this important controversy over the relevance of deep-level mine ownership to the Raid is summarized well in Peter Richardson and Jean-Jacques van Helten, "The Development of the South African Gold-Mining Industry, 1895–1918," *Economic History Review,* XXXVII (1984), 322–325. See also Alan Henry Jeeves, "The Rand Capitalists and Transvaal Politics, 1892–1899" unpub. Ph.D. thesis (Queens Univ., 1971), 143–146; Edward Fairfield to Joseph Chamberlain, 5 January 1896, Chamberlain Papers, in Ethel Drus, "A Report on the Papers of Joseph Chamberlain Relating to the Jameson Raid and the Inquiry," *Bulletin of the Institute of Historical Research,* XXV (1952), 42.

4. Lord Salisbury to Chamberlain, 30 December 1895, in Ethel Drus, "Papers of Joseph Chamberlain," 37.

5. Jeffrey Butler, *The Liberal Party and the Jameson Raid* (Oxford, 1968), 60.

6. Edmund Garrett to Agnes Garrett, his cousin, 8 January 1896, in Gerald Shaw (ed.), *The Garrett Papers* (Cape Town, 1984), 49.

7. Quoted in Sir Frederic Howard Hamilton to Howell Wright, 27 September 1937, Howell Wright Papers, Sterling Library, Yale University.

8. James Bryce, *Impressions of South Africa* (New York, 1898), 438–439.

9. Quoted in Eric A. Walker, *W.P. Schreiner: A South African* (London, 1937), 71. Edmund Garrett to Agnes Garrett, 1 January 1896, in Shaw, *Garrett,* 42. For the claim that Jameson promised to leave Pitsani *only* when instructed to do so by the Reform Committee and Rhodes, see John Hays Hammond and Alleyne Ireland, *The Truth about the Jameson Raid* (Boston, 1918), 29.

10. Frank Rhodes to CJR, 25 October 1895, Mss. Afr. s. 228 (C 102, 103), Rhodes House.

11. See Chapter 18; Phillips to Beit, 16 June 1894, Rhodes House (published in part in Select Committee report, the Transvaal report, and the Cape report).

12. CJR, quoted in Lockhart and Woodhouse, *Rhodes*, 308, 377; Bower to Montagu Ommanney, 11 December 1906 (49), Bower Papers, 71, South African Library; CJR, quoted in Sidney Low, "Personal Recollections of Cecil Rhodes: Some Conversations in London," *The Nineteenth Century and After*, LI (1902), 838–839.

13. For Schreiner, see Chapter 15. Meyer to N.M. Rothschild & Co., 23 March 1892, RAL B 17/RH 1892–28, Rothschild archives. Kruger's fist was cited by the Hon. Eustace Fiennes, who heard the story from Rhodes or Jameson immediately after the interview. This account appears in James Rose Innes to Graham Bower, 10 February 1932, Bower Papers, 288, South African Library. Lionel Phillips, *Some Reminiscences* (London, 1924), 136.

14. Kruger, quoted in Hamilton to Wright, 27 September 1937, Wright Papers. This aphorism appears in a variety of forms, probably because Kruger was fond of employing it, and did so distinctively on different occasions. For the varieties and an exegesis, see Vincent Harlow, "Sir Frederic Hamilton's Narrative of Events Relative to the Jameson Raid," *English Historical Review*, LXXIII (1957), 292–293.

15. The Marquess of Winchester, *Statesmen, Financiers, and Felons* (Abbeville, 1935), 181.

16. Quoted in Lockhart and Woodhouse, *Rhodes*, 298.

17. CJR to Sprigg, 18 December 1894, 10.077, Cory Library, Rhodes University; CJR to Albert Grey, ? February 1895, Mss. Afr. t. 6 (13–17), Rhodes House.

18. James Rose Innes to Richard W. Rose Innes, 4 April 1895, in Harrison M. Wright (ed.), *Sir James Rose Innes: Selected Correspondence (1884–1902)* (Cape Town, 1972), 151; A.G. Gardiner, *The Life of Sir William Harcourt* (London, 1923), II, 338; Lt. Col. Arthur Bigge to Queen Victoria, 26 February 1895, in George Earle Buckle (ed.), *The Letters of Queen Victoria: A Selection* (London, 1931), II, 483; Sir Hercules Robinson to CJR, 20 July 1894, Mss. Afr. s. 228 (C27/39), Rhodes House.

19. CJR to Grey, ? February 1895, Mss. Afr. t. 6 (13–17). See also Chapter 17.

20. Herbert Canning (of B.S.A. Company) to CJR, 2 August 1895 (telegram), Mss. Afr. s. 228 (C 3 B, 255), Rhodes House. Also printed in Lockhart and Woodhouse, *Rhodes*, 500.

21. CJR to Beit, n.d., August 1895, Ms. 114, the Brenthurst Library; Mss. Afr. t. 14 (352–359), Rhodes House.

22. Harris to CJR, 4 November, 5 November 1895, secret cables, Mss. Afr. s. 228 (C 3 B, 266), Rhodes House, also printed in Lockhart and Woodhouse, *Rhodes*, 500–501. For Bechuanaland, see Chapter 17. See also Albert Grey to Joseph Chamberlain, 17 November 1895, Grey Papers, GR 2/1/1, Zimbabwe archives, in Butler, *Raid*, 295–296.

23. CJR, Commonplace Book, 13 August 1895, n.d. late 1895, Mss. Afr. s. 1647 (Box 1, item 6), Rhodes House.

24. CJR to Beit, n.d., August 1895, Ms. 114, the Brenthurst Library; Hamilton to Wright, 27 September 1937, Wright Papers; CJR to Harcourt, 13 May, 14 May 1896, in Gardiner, *Harcourt*, II, 392.

25. See above, Chapter 15. Lockhart and Woodhouse, *Rhodes*, 312. CJR, quoted in "Conversations," in Stead, *The Last Will*, 105.

26. For the Drifts, see above, Chapter 17. For the bluff, see Jean van der Poel, *The Jameson Raid* (London, 1951), 36, 41, 64. Bower to Senator Francis William Reitz,

15 March 1915, Bower Papers, 145, South African Library. Edward Fairfield to Joseph Chamberlain, 28 December 1895, quoted in J. L. Garvin, *The Life of Joseph Chamberlain* (London, 1934), III, 81.

27. Summary of Schreiner's speech to the Cape House of Assembly, 24 July 1896, in Walker, *Schreiner*, 83.

28. G.T. Hutchinson, *Frank Rhodes: A Memoir* (London, 1908), 86. See also Chapter 18.

29. CJR to Harris, 6 November 1895 (telegram), quoted in Garvin, *Chamberlain*, III, 55. See also Maylam, *Rhodes*, 168; Chapter 17.

30. Frederic Hamilton to Howell Wright, 27 September 1937, Wright Papers; CJR to W. P. Schreiner, 3 July 1896, quoted in Walker, *Schreiner*, 81. The "shank end" occurs in a speech, too, 12 March 1898, in Vindex, *Speeches*, 521–546.

31. J. Percy FitzPatrick, *The Transvaal from Within: A Private Record of Public Affairs* (London, 1899), 122.

32. Printed versions of the above and other telegrams are easily found in Jean van der Poel, *The Jameson Raid* (London, 1951), 72, 74; Elizabeth Longford (née Pakenham), *Jameson's Raid: The Prelude to the Boer War* (Johannesburg, 1958), 69–75; Garvin, *Chamberlain*, II, 72, 75; Drus, "Raid," 35. The originals were included in House of Commons, *Second Report from the Select Committee on British South Africa* (London, 1897), Appendix. For Shaw, see also Chapter 15.

33. CJR, quoted in Williams, *Rhodes*, 267.

34. Samuel Watson Jameson to his brother, 26 December 1895, Harris to Jameson, 26 December 1895, quoted in Colvin, *Jameson*, II, 47–48.

35. Hamilton to Wright, 27 September 1937, Wright Papers; Hamilton to Fitz-Patrick, 28 September 1895, in FitzPatrick, *Transvaal*, 131; Bower to Montagu Omman-ney, 11 May 1906 (51–52), Bower Papers, 71, South African Library; Bower, "Rough Notes Written on His Sickbed at the Age of 85," 26 July 1933, Bower Papers, in Micr. Afr. 411, Rhodes House. Hamilton prefaced his long account with a distinctive caveat of which he, as a careful journalist, would have been unusually conscious: "I propose to reproduce certain conversations in spoken form as I remember them. I do not think you need have any doubts as to their general accuracy. The events naturally made a deep impression upon my mind, and occasionally a sentence or a phrase has fixed itself in my memory so firmly that I am sure of the actual words. I do not wish you to understand, however, . . . that I claim to record any conversation verbatim. Forty years is a long time, memory plays quaint tricks, and it would not be right to [rely] on the *ipissima verba* as I have set them down." Hamilton said that this conclusion was especially true regarding his talks with Rhodes.

36. Flint, *Rhodes*, 192. For the telegrams, see FitzPatrick, *Transvaal*, 131–132.

37. Colvin, *Jameson*, II, 49, 53, 165. Jameson's links with the Macaulay essay on Clive are based on Edmund Garrett and E. J. Edwards, *The Story of an African Crisis: Being the Truth about the Jameson Raid and Johannesburg Revolt of 1896 Told with the Assistance of the Leading Actors in the Drama* (New York, 1897), 29. Garrett and Edward's evidence for this connection, however, appears highly circumstantial. It has been accepted, nevertheless, by generations of scholars and biographers. They refer to Thomas B. Macaulay, "The Life of Robert Lord Clive," the *Edinburgh Review*, LXX (January 1840). If he indeed read it, Jameson must have seen the ninety-three-page article in a collection of Macaulay's reprinted essays, possibly an edition (of which there were about fifteen) of Macaulay, *Critical and Historical Essays Contributed to the Edinburgh Review* (London, 1843, 1852, 1860, 1870, 1874, or 1877–1880), in 3 or 4 v.

38. Van der Poel, *Raid*, 88, 91–92; Longford, *Raid*, 79, 222–223; Flint, *Rhodes*, 193; Bower to Ommanney, 11 May 1906, Bower Papers, 71, South African Library.

39. Fairfield to Chamberlain, 28 December 1895, in Garvin, *Chamberlain*, II, 81. Garvin italicized the part of Fairfield's letter excerpted here. Fairfield also claimed that Hawksley did not "much like" Rhodes.

40. Robert Blake, "The Jameson Raid and 'The Missing Telegrams,'" in Hugh Lloyd-Jones, Valerie Pearl, and Blair Worden (eds.), *History and Imagination: Essays in Honour of H.R. Trevor-Roper* (London, 1981), 327, 338; Alfred Sharpe to Sir Clement Hill (Foreign Office), 26 May 1896 (private), FO 2/106, 263–264; J. B. Taylor, *A Pioneer Looks Back* (London, 1939), 210–211.

41. F. Edmund Garrett, "The Character of Cecil Rhodes," *Contemporary Review*, LXXXI (1902), 767. See also Sarah Wilson, *South African Memories* (London, 1909), 35.

42. Quoted in Walker, *Schreiner*, 69, 71; Bower to Ommanney, 11 May 1906 (55), Bower Papers, 71; Hamilton to Wright, 27 September 1937, Wright Papers; J.H. Hofmeyr, *The Life of Jan Hendrik Hofmeyr* (Cape Town, 1913), 499; CJR to Garrett, n.d. but Jan. 1896, Mss. Afr. t. 14 (298–299); David Harris, *Pioneer, Soldier and Politician* (London, 1931), 130. (Bower's account says that he was summoned to Groote Schuur on the *"same"* night he had been reassured by Rhodes. Presumably this was a mistake. Or was it?)

43. Hamilton to Wright, 27 September 1937, Wright Papers. See also Bower to CJR, 30 December 1895, Mss. Afr. s. 228 (C28, 238); Albert Grey to Lady Grey, n.d. but 2–3 January 1896, Mss. Afr. s. 424, Rhodes House.

44. Hamilton to Wright, 27 September 1937, in van der Poel, *Raid*, 100–102; Hawksley to CJR, 22 May 1897, Mss. Afr. s. 1647 (234); Chamberlain to Hercules Robinson, 1 January 1896, in Garvin, *Chamberlain*, III, 91.

45. Percy FitzPatrick to his wife, 3 January 1896, in A.H. Duminy and W.R. Guest (eds.), *FitzPatrick: South African Politician: Selected Papers, 1888–1906* (Johannesburg, 1976), 27; Hammond, *Autobiography*, I, 349. See also Florence Phillips, *Some South African Recollections* (London, 1899), 100–101; Lionel Phillips, *Some Reminiscences*, 161.

46. John Xavier Merriman to John Blades Currey, 6 January 1896, in Lewsen, *Selections*, II, 190; Colvin, *Jameson*, II, 134.

47. CJR to Schreiner, 3 July 1896, quoted in Walker, *Schreiner*, 81; Lord Selborne, "Notes of an Interview between Mr. Chamberlain and Mr. Rhodes at Which I Only Was Present . . . ," 26 January 1897, in Garvin, *Chamberlain*, III, 118; Julia Merriman to Agnes Merriman, 11 February 1896, in Lewsen, *Selections*, II, 210; Low, "Recollections," 837; Stead to CJR, 22 September 1900, Stead Papers, Micr. Afr. s. 413, Rhodes House. Wilfrid Scawen Blunt, *My Diaries: Being a Personal Narrative of Events, 1883–1914* (New York, 1921), 218. See also Maurice V. Brett, *Journals and Letters of Reginald Viscount Esher* (London, 1934), I, 193–198. There is a much more favorable account of Brett's role, and how it influenced Rhodes, in James Lees-Milne, *The Enigmatic Edwardian: The Life of Reginald, 2nd Viscount Esher* (London, 1986), 102–103. Hawksley's own crucial commentary on the missing cables is contained in Hawksley to CJR, 22 May 1897, Mss. Afr. s. 1647 (229–234).

48. Quoted in Michell, *Rhodes*, II, 177.

49. Robert A. Yerburgh, interview with Basil Williams, 26 May 1914, Mss. Afr. s. 134 (Box 1, Notebook 1), 173.

50. CJR to Grey, 2 July 1896, Mss. Afr. t. 6, (40–50), Rhodes House; Labouchere, quoted in Charles Boyd to Algar Labouchere Thorold, *The Life of Henry Labouchere* (London, 1913), 394; Harcourt, quoted in entry for 2 November 1899, Blunt, *Diaries*, 334.

51. CJR to Earl Grey, ? July 1897, in Grey to Lord Balfour, 25 May 1904, in Mss. Afr. s. 1279, Rhodes House; Rosebery and Morley, quoted in Marquess of Crewe, *Lord Rosebery* (New York, 1931), 441; Longford, *Raid,* 298–299. Butler convincingly explains Harcourt's handicaps. See Butler, *Raid,* 277–281. CJR to Michell, 26 July 1897, in Michell, *Rhodes,* II, 182; entry of 15 July 1897, Blunt, *Diaries,* 280. The cartoon was entitled "The End of the Game."

52. Longford, *Raid,* 265.

CHAPTER 20

The Risings and Redemption

1. Colin Harding, *Far Bugles* (London, 1933), 45.

2. Reminiscences of M.E. Weale, WE 3/2/5, Zimbabwe archives, quoted in Terence O. Ranger, *Revolt in Southern Rhodesia, 1896–97: A Study in African Resistance* (Evanston, 1967), 75–76.

3. Quoted in Vere Stent, *A Personal Record of Some Incidents in the Life of Cecil Rhodes* (Cape Town, 1925), 45–46.

4. Stent, *Incidents,* 11.

5. CJR to Andrew Duncan, n.d. but 30 March? 1896, quoted in Hugh Marshall Hole, *The Making of Rhodesia* (London, 1926), 351; Maurice Gifford to CJR, 31 March or 1 April 1896, quoted in Michell, *Rhodes,* II, 153.

6. CJR to Hawksley, in Hole, *Making,* 365; CJR to Chamberlain, in Grey to Chamberlain (cable), 13 May 1896, quoted in Michell, *Rhodes,* II, 171; Keppel-Jones, *Rhodes,* 431, 456; Le Sueur, notes and reminiscences, Mss. Afr. s. 229 (III, 394).

7. CJR to D. Tyrie Laing, 25 May 1896, quoted in D. Tyrie Laing, *The Matabele Rebellion, 1896* (London, 1897), 190; Arthur Weston Jarvis to his mother, 17 June 1896, JA 4/1/1, Zimbabwe archives and Micr. A. 1251, Cullen Library, University of the Witwatersrand. For the corpses, see Lockhart and Woodhouse, *Rhodes,* 352. For atrocities, see also Frank W. Sykes, *With Plumer in Matabeleland: An Account of the Operations of the Matabeleland Relief Force during the Rebellion of 1896* (London, 1897), 98–99.

8. CJR to Secretary, Cape Town, 22 May 1896, Lo 5/2/48, Zimbabwe archives, quoted in Ranger, *Revolt,* 181; C.H. Instrap, "Rhodes in Matabeleland, '96," *The Sunrise* (29 March 1902), 24; Michell, *Rhodes,* II, 153.

9. Hervey to his sister, 1 June 1896, in Albert Grey, *Hubert Hervey, Student and Imperialist: A Memoir* (London, 1899), 127. Grey to Charles Grey, 15 June 1896, GR 1/1/1, Zimbabwe archives, quoted in Ranger, *Revolt,* 194.

10. "Wiri" Edwards, reminiscences, ED 6/1/1; Grey to Charles Grey, 3 July 1896, GR 1/1/1, Zimbabwe archives; both quoted in Ranger, *Revolt,* 191–192, 194.

11. Stent, *Incidents,* 13–18; Hans Sauer, *Ex Africa . . .* (London, 1937), 305; Jarvis to his mother, 19 August 1896, JA 4/1/1, Zimbabwe archives, and Micr. A. 1251, Cullen Library, University of the Witwatersrand; Hugh Marshall Hole, "The Courage of Cecil Rhodes: Hitherto Untold Tale of the Matabele Rebellion," *The Morning Post* (London), 1 April 1936. Captain Frederick Courtenay Selous to Colonel William Napier (from the Insiza Hills), 22 May 1896, Mss. Afr. s. 1707, Rhodes House. Herbert Plumer, *An Irregular Corps in Matabeleland* (New York, 1897), 130, 142; Sykes, *With Plumer,* 160. McDonald, *Rhodes,* 208, 210. Plumer (138) says that only three white soldiers lost their lives. Sykes, *With Plumer,* 104, says that only *two* rebels were killed on 16 June. Robert Stephenson Smyth Baden-Powell, *The Matabele Campaign, 1896: Being a Narrative of the*

Campaign in Suppressing the Native Rising in Matabeleland and Mashonaland (London, 1897), 125, says that 10 died, but they need not have been white.

12. CJR to Grey, 13, 16, 17, 24 June, 2, 8 July 1896, Mss. Afr. t. 6, (30–40), Rhodes House.

13. CJR to W.P. Schreiner, 3 July 1896, Jagger Library, University of Cape Town. CJR to Grey, n.d. but 3 July 1896, Mss Afr. t. 6.

14. CJR, speeches of 4 June, August 1896, in Vindex, *Speeches*, 481–492; third speech quoted in Michell, *Rhodes*, II, 155.

15. Lady Grey to children, 27 August 1896, Victoria Grey to Charles Grey, 14? September 1896, GR 1/1/1, Zimbabwe archives, quoted in Ranger, *Revolt*, 236.

16. Stent, *Incidents*, 25. But see Sauer, *Ex Africa*, 308–309. Quoted in Stent, letter to *Cape Times* (15? October 1896), reprinted in Stent, *Incidents*, 96.

17. Stent, *Incidents*, 35–54; Sally and Betty Stent (ed. Paddy Cartwright), *The Forthright Man* (Cape Town, 1972), 52–55; Sauer, *Ex Africa*, 319, 321, 322; CJR to Grey, 21 August 1896, Mss. Afr. t. 6; Hans Sauer, "Cecil Rhodes: As a Man and a Friend," *The Empire Review*, III (1902), 378. Another strong account of the first indaba is in Sykes, *With Plumer*, 217–229. For the matriarch, see also Chapter 15.

18. CJR to Grey, 24, 25 August 1896, Mss. Afr. t. 6.

19. Stent, *Incidents*, 67, 70; Jeannie M. Boggie, "Rhodes' Three Peace Indabas," *The Chronicle* (Bulawayo), (July 1953), 41. There is a circumstantial verbatim account of what Rhodes told the induna at this second indaba in Michell, *Rhodes*, II, 163–164. See also Sykes, *With Plumer*, 229–231; Robert Clermont Witt, "Personal Recollections of Cecil Rhodes: As Peacemaker on the Matoppo Hills," *The Nineteenth Century and After*, LI (1902), 841–848.

20. John Xavier Merriman, letter in *South African Telegraph* (25 August 1896), quoted in Lewsen, *Selections*, II, 238; Grey to Goodenough, 26 August 1896 (telegram; very urgent), Mss. Afr. s. 1707, Rhodes House. Chamberlain to Sir William H. Goodenough, 27 August 1896, quoted in Ranger, *Revolt*, 253. See also London Board of Company to Grey, 28 August 1896 (cable), in Mss. Afr. s. 1707, Rhodes House.

21. CJR to Beit, 3 September 1896, Rand Mines archives; Jarvis to his mother, 27 August 1896, JA 4/1/1, Zimbabwe archives, quoted in Ranger, *Revolt*, 252; CJR, quoted in Keppel-Jones, *Rhodes*, 506.

22. Lady Alice Grey to her aunt, 23 October 1896, Grenfell Papers; Jourdan, quoted in Michell, *Rhodes*, II, 157–158; Jourdan, *Rhodes*, 39–42; CJR to Grey, 21 September 1896, Mss. Afr. s. 1707, Rhodes House; CJR to Grey, 2 October 1896, Mss. Afr. t. 6. For the World's View, see Sauer, *Ex Africa*, 324. For Colenbrander, see Ranger, *Revolt*, 263. For Grootboom, see Sykes, *With Plumer*, 263–269.

23. Quoted in Sykes, *With Plumer*, 237. See also J. W. Mackail and Guy Wyndham, *The Life and Letters of George Wyndham* (London, 1926) I, 304.

24. Quoted in Michell, *Rhodes*, II, 168.

25. CJR to Grey, 10 November 1896, Mss. Afr. s. 1707, Rhodes House; Carrington, in Grey to Secretary, Cape Town, 23 November 1896, LO 5/2/52, Zimbabwe archives, quoted in Ranger, *Revolt*, 285–286. See also Michell, *Rhodes*, II, 169–170.

26. CJR to Beit, 3 September 1896, Rand Mines archives.

27. Jourdan, quoted in Michell, *Rhodes*, II, 159; Milton, quoted in George H. Tanser, *A Scantling of Time: The Story of Salisbury, Rhodesia (1890 to 1900)* (Salisbury, 1965), 178. See also Jourdan, *Rhodes*, 46.

28. Milner to Selborne, 2 June, 15 June 1897, in Cecil Headlam (ed.), *The Milner Papers: South Africa, 1897–1899* (London, 1931), I, 105–106, 110–111.

29. CJR to Sir Arthur Lawley, 9 October; Jameson to Lawley, 20 October, 4 November 1897, in Mss. Afr. s. 227 (telegrams), Rhodes House; CJR to McDonald, 5 November 1897, quoted in McDonald, *Rhodes,* 284; Milner to Basil Williams, 5 September 1920, Mss. Afr. s.134 (7). For the heart attack, see also Chapter 24.

30. See George Pauling (ed. David Buchan), *The Chronicles of a Contractor* (London 1926), 156–157.

31. CJR to John Norris, 24 October 1898, NO 5/1/1, Zimbabwe archives; CJR to McDonald, 5 December 1901, in McDonald, *Rhodes,* 357–358. For Grimmer, see Chapter 15. Rhodes' holdings included 44,000 morgen at Inyanga, 29,120 at Sauerdale, and 10,000 at the Pungwe River source, near Inyanga.

32. *The Chronicle* (26 June 1896), quoted in Keppel-Jones, *Rhodes,* 528. Rhodes' plans are in his private letter book, I, 2 July 1897, Mss. Afr. s. 227 (Box 1), Rhodes House.

33. CJR to McDonald, 8 September 1899; CJR to W.H. Milton, 13 April 1899, 8 August 1900, in Letter Books, II, Mss. Afr. s. 227, Rhodes House.

34. Milner to Selborne, 2 June 1897, in Headlam, *Milner,* I, 106. The full report of Rhodes' Cape Town speech is in *South Africa* (9 January 1897) 99; the account of his departure at 101.

CHAPTER 21

Across the Zambezi and Through Africa

1. See Chapter 13.

2. Johnston to Percy Anderson, 10 October 1893, in FO 2/55, Public Record Office.

3. H. H. Johnston, *British Central Africa* (New York 1897), 100–101.

4. Johnston to Anderson, 23 March 1893, FO 2/54, Public Record Office.

5. Johnston to CJR, 28 January 1893, in CJR to Rosebery, 18 April 1893, Rosebery Papers, Mss. Afr. s. 1826, Rhodes House; Johnston to Anderson, 23 March 1893, FO 2/54.

6. CJR to Johnston, 18 April 1893, in CJR to Rosebery, 18 April 1893; CJR to Rosebery, 16 April 1893, Rosebery Papers. Oliver saw an additional letter from Rhodes in this series to Rosebery. It was never sent. Several of Oliver's dates for crucial letters, however, do not correspond exactly with the dates on the letters themselves. See Roland Oliver, *Sir Harry Johnston and the Scramble for Africa* (London, 1957), 226.

7. CJR to Rosebery, 16 February 1893, Mss. Afr. s. 1826.

8. Johnston to Percy Anderson, 20 June 1893, FO 2/54. See also Johnston to Rosebery, 3 May 1893, FO 2/54; H. H. Johnston, *The Story of My Life* (Indianapolis, 1923), 282–283. See Chapter 15, for Johnston's visit to Cape Town.

9. Harris to CJR , 16 September 1893 (telegram); CJR to Johnston, 16 September 1893; Johnston to CJR, 8 October 1893, all in Johnston to Rosebery, 8 October 1893, FO 2/55. See also Oliver, *Johnston,* 233, 238, 240.

10. Johnston, *Central Africa,* 132.

11. Johnston, *Story,* 459.

12. Sharpe to Johnston, 13 August 1896; Johnston to Thomas Sanderson, 6 October 1896, FO 2/108, Public Record Office; CJR to Milton, 5 August 1897, Mss. Afr. s. 227 (X), Rhodes House.

13. Alfred Sharpe to Clement Hill, 26 May 1896, FO 2/106, Public Record Office;

Johnston to CJR, 31 December 1895, Mss. Afr. s. 228 (26, 14); CJR to Stevens, 14 January 1898, Mss. Afr. s. 227 (XV); Captain Hays Scott Turner to CJR, 5 October 1898, Mss. Afr. s. 228 (C 13, 13); CJR to Milton, 17 March 1898, CJR to William H. Manning, 10 June 1898, Mss. Afr. s. 227 (I), Rhodes House. See also T. William Baxter, "The Angoni Rebellion and Mpeseni," *The Northern Rhodesia Journal,* II (1950), 14–24.

14. Sharpe to the Foreign Office, 29 September 1899, FO 2/210, Foreign Office to Pearce, 4 October 1899 (telegram), FO 2/211; Public Record Office. Codrington to CJR, 13 November 1899 (telegram), Mss. Afr. s. 228, (C 18, 7), Rhodes House; Codrington to Administrator, Southern Rhodesia, 29 October 1899, FO 2/388.

15. CJR to Secretary, London office of the Company, 24 August 1898, Mss. Afr. s. 227 (I); CJR to Grey, 28 August 1897, Mss. Afr. s. 227 (telegrams) X; Coryndon to CJR, 21 July 1898, Mss. Afr. s. 227 (XVIII).

16. Lawley to CJR, 11 June 1900, Mss. Afr. s. 277, Rhodes House; CJR to Grey, 9 February 1898, Mss. Afr. t. 6 (186–188), (Copy in FO 2/147).

17. For conflict between African and whites in Northern Rhodesia, see Robert I. Rotberg, *The Rise of Nationalism in Central Africa: The Making of Malawi and Zambia, 1873–1964* (Cambridge, Mass., 1965).

18. CJR to Sivewright, 31 August 1897, Mss. Afr. s. 227 (XI), Rhodes House.

19. Johnston to CJR, 20 January 1893, in CJR to Rosebery, 18 April 1893, Rosebery Papers. See also Chapter 18.

20. CJR to Kitchener, 6 September 1898, Kitchener to CJR, 26 September 1898 (telegrams) in De Beers archives, and in Michell Papers, A 540/40, Cape archives. See also Chapter 16.

21. CJR to Chamberlain, 23 April 1898, Beit to CJR, 26 November 1898, Mss. Afr. s. 228 (C18, 4M); CJR to Beit, 17 August 1899, Mss. Afr. s. 227 (I), Rhodes House; Assembly, 10th session, *Debates* (1898), 279.

22. CJR to Ewart S. Grogan, 7 September 1900, Mss. Afr. s. 227 (II), Rhodes House. Also printed in Michell, *Rhodes,* II, 287–288.

23. CJR to Chamberlain, 27 April 1899, in Mss. Afr. s. 228, (C18, 8D); Colonial Office to CJR, 1 May 1899; CJR to Colonial Office, 9 May 1899, CO 417/282; CJR to Hawksley, 25 May 1898, Mss. Afr. t. 1 (21). See also Michell Papers (35), A 540/37 Cape archives, Maylam, *Rhodes,* 201.

24. CJR to Grogan, 7 September 1900. Grogan and Arthur W. Sharp wrote *From the Cape to Cairo: The First Traverse of Africa from South to North* (London, 1900) and used Rhodes' letter as a foreword. For Rhodes' impact on the young Grogan—"Give yourself to Africa," he said—see Leda Farrant, *The Legendary Grogan* (London, 1981), 66.

25. Conversation at Madeira or aboard the S.S. *Norman* in April 1900, quoted in Robert Hutchinson and George Martelli, *Robert's People: The Life of Sir Robert Williams* (London, 1971), 115.

26. CJR to Sir Francis Plunkett, H. M. ambassador to Belgium, 23 January 1899; CJR to Francis L. Bertie, undersecretary of State (Foreign Office), 21 March 1899, Mss. Afr. s. 227 (I); Robert Williams, interview with Basil Williams, 9 January 1920; Julia and Rochfort Maguire, interview with Basil Williams, 25 June 1914, Mss. Afr. s. 134 (Box 1, Notebook 1); Lascelles, handwritten account, 11 March 1899, in Mss. Afr. s. 8 (65); also quoted in Henry William Paulet, Marquess of Winchester, *Statesman, Financiers and Felons* (Abbeville, 1935), 238. Hutchinson and Martelli, *Robert's,* 105, 106, 117; William Roger Louis, *Ruanda-Urundi, 1884–1919* (Oxford, 1963), 162–164; Robert O. Collins, *King Leopold, England, and the Upper Nile, 1899–1909* (New Haven, 1968), 275–

277; Edward Hertslet, *The Map of Africa by Treaty* (London, 1909; 3rd ed.), II, 579–580.

27. Lascelles, Mss. Afr. s. 8 (65). Lascelles' original account of what transpired between Rhodes and the kaiser was also collected by Lewis Michell in Berlin on 16 April 1899, in Michell Papers, A 540/37, Cape archives. CJR to Prince of Wales, n.d., March 1899, in George Earle Buckle (ed.), *The Letters of Queen Victoria* (London, 1932), III, 349–351. There is a further record of the meeting in Ambassador Ladislaus von Szogyenyi-Marich to Foreign Minister Agenor von Goluchowski, 15 March 1899, Preussen III, 151, Haupt Hof- und Staätsarchiv, Vienna. (I owe this reference to Lamar Cecil). See also CJR, speeches of 25 October 1898, 18 July 1899, both Cape Town, and 2 May 1899, in London, in Vindex, *Speeches*, 620, 640, 720; Merriman to Abraham Fischer, 16 March 1899, in Lewsen, *Selections*, III, 30; Wilhelm II (trans. Thomas R. Ybarra), *Memoirs* (New York, 1922), 88–89; The original is Wilhelm II, *Ereignisse und Gestalten aus den Jahren, 1878–1918* (Leipzig, 1922), 72–74, thanks to David Brenner; The agreements of 15 March and 27 October 1899 are in Mss. Afr. s. 229, Rhodes House; ? Borel, "Notes of a Conversation betweeen CJR and Gabriel Hanotaux," 11 February 1897 (trans. M. G. L. Jaray), "A Dialogue between Cecil Rhodes and Gabriel Hanotaux," *La Revue* (1 February, 1898).

28. CJR to Beit, 25 November 1900, Mss. Afr. s. 227 (III), Rhodes House.

29. CJR to Robert Williams, 18 October 1901, Rhodes House.

CHAPTER 22

The Last Hurrah and the Guns of October

1. CJR, interview with Edmund Garrett, 9 March 1898, *Cape Times*, in E.T. Cook, *Edmund Garrett: A Memoir* (London, 1909), 223.

2. James Rose Innes to Graham Bower, 29 November 1897, in Wright, *Innes*, 228.

3. CJR, speech in Good Hope Hall, Cape Town, 12 March 1898, quoted in Vindex, *Speeches*, 541, 543.

4. CJR, interview, in Cook, *Garrett*, 223–224. See the report of the same attitude, expressed to others, in Fuller, *Rhodes*, 215.

5. CJR, speech of 12 March 1898, in Vindex, *Speeches*, 545–546; CJR, interview, in Cook, *Garrett*, 227.

6. Innes to Jessie Rose Innes, 2 May 1897, in Wright, *Innes*, 209. Merriman to John Blades Currey, 19 May 1897, in Lewsen, *Selections*, II, 274.

7. For Sigcawu, see Chapter 17. Merriman to James Bryce, 12 July 1897; Merriman to Currey, 14 September 1897, both in Lewsen, *Selections*, II, 275–276, 281; B.A. Tindall (ed.), *James Rose Innes: Chief Justice of South Africa, 1914–27, Autobiography* (London, 1949), 169. Milner, quoted in Eric Walker, *W.P. Schreiner: A South African* (London, 1937), 99.

8. Milner to Chamberlain, 11 May 1897, Chamberlain Papers, Univ. of Birmingham, quoted in J.S. Marais, *The Fall of Kruger's Republic* (Oxford, 1961), 168.

9. The professor was Fray Luis de León, imprisoned from 1571 to 1576 without accusations or trial. "Envy and lies held me in prison," he wrote after his release. For details, see Henry Kamen, *The Spanish Inquisition* (London, 1965), 85. William Watson kindly helped to turn memory into reference.

10. CJR, speech of 12 March 1898, in Vindex, *Speeches*, 521–546. CJR, interview,

in Cook, *Garrett*, 225. Milner to Sir Walter Hely-Hutchinson, n.d.; Milner, speech of 3 March 1898, in Headlam, *Milner*, I, 242, 244–246.

11. CJR, interview, in Cook, *Garrett*, 222; Michell, *Rhodes*, II, 222.

12. Tindall, *Innes*, 167, 168.

13. Merriman to Julia Merriman, 4 June 1898, in Lewsen, *Selections*, II, 306.

14. Walker, *Schreiner*, 108, 110; Innes to John Pooley, 14 April 1898, in Wright, *Innes*, 237; Assembly, 9th Session, *Debates* (1898), 126, 133–134, 169.

15. Innes to Albert Cartwright, 26 June 1898, in Wright, *Innes*, 239; Olive Schreiner to W.P. Schreiner, 13 August 1898, in Schreiner Papers, Jagger Library, University of Cape Town; CJR to Michell, n.d. but June 1898, Mss. Afr. s. 229 (V); CJR to Michell, 30 June 1898 (telegram), Rand Mines archives. The De Beers archives contain a mass of letters and telegrams testifying to Rhodes' methods and expenditures during the 1898 campaign. See especially his Private Letter Book, 4/1/2; Secretarial Correspondence, 5/2/1; contents of Board Room display case.

16. CJR to J.L. Dean, O'Okiep Copper Company, 6 July 1898, registered telegram, copy in Old Board Room collection, De Beers archives.

17. CJR, speech at Longlands, 4 August 1898, at Port Elizabeth, 17 September 1898, in Vindex, *Speeches*, 568, 604, 612; Merriman to Agnes Merriman, 6 August, 21 August 1898, in Lewsen, *Selections*, II, 323.

18. CJR, speech at Klipdam, 26 August 1898; in Vindex, *Speeches*, 572–573, 585–586.

19. CJR, speech at Longlands, 4 August 1898, speech at Vryburg, 5 September 1898, in Vindex, *Speeches*, 568, 569, 603.

20. William Plomer, *Cecil Rhodes* (London, 1933), 132; Tindall, *Innes*, 170–171. Plomer cites an undated issue of the *Eastern Province Herald* (Port Elizabeth) as his source, and he and Innes place the event on the "eve" of the election campaign. A full account of Rhodes' only speech in 1898 at Port Elizabeth (17 September) reveals no trace of any such phrases, but the *Herald* could have reported almost any up-country talk. Innes' autobiography was written after Plomer had published his assessment.

21. CJR, speech of 18 July 1899, Cape Town, in Vindex, *Speeches*, 665.

22. CJR, speeches at Cape Town, 18 July, and Claremont, 20 July 1899, in Vindex, *Speeches*, 643, 645, 668.

23. CJR, speech at Kimberley, 23 February 1900, in Vindex, *Speeches*, 831–832; Michell, *Rhodes*, II, 276; *African Review* (24 March 1900).

24. CJR to Milner, n.d. but August 1898; Milner to Selborne, 14 September 1898; Milner to Sprigg, 15 September 1898, 11 October 1898, in Headlam, *Milner*, I, 270, 273–274; Innes to J.E. Ellis, 27 September 1898, Wright, *Innes*, 249.

25. Innes to Richard W. Rose Innes, 14 October, 25 October 1898, in Wright, *Innes*, 254–256.

26. CJR to Beit, telegram, n.d. but mid-1899, in Michell, *Rhodes*, II, 247; Assembly, 10th Parliament, *Debates* (1898), 48, 164, 239, 271, 372, 430, 449.

27. See Flint, *Rhodes*, 215; David Harris, *Pioneer, Soldier, and Politician* (London, 1931), 140.

28. Assembly, *Debates* (1899) 112–114, 116, 478, 491.

29. *Ibid.*, 176–178, 354–355, 378.

30. *Ibid.*, 389, 473, 478, 570–571.

31. CJR, speech at Claremont, 20 July 1899, in Vindex, *Speeches*, 658–659; Rochfort Maguire to Rothschild, 5 September 1899, RAL B17RH 1899/16, Rothschild archives; CJR to Milner, 13 September 1899, in Headlam, *Milner*, I, 536; Assembly, *De-*

bates (22 August 1899), 284; Harris, *Pioneer*, 144–145; Philip Jourdan, *Cecil Rhodes: His Private Life by His Private Secretary* (London, 1911), 94–95; Leopold S. Amery, *Days of Fresh Air* (London, 1940), 123.

32. Tindall, *Innes*, 184; Jourdan to Stead, 12 September 1899, Mss. Afr. Micr. 413, Rhodes House; George Hough Wilson, *Gone Down the Years* (Cape Town, 1947), 49.

33. Lord Salisbury to Lord Lansdowne, minister of war, 30 August 1899, in Thomas Wodehouse Newton, *Lord Lansdowne: A Biography* (London, 1929), 157.

34. Smuts, "The Military Position of the South African Republic in the Probable Event of War," memorandum, 4 September 1899, Smuts Papers, Transvaal archives, quoted in Marais, *Fall*, 318; W. Keith Hancock, *Smuts: The Sanguine Years, 1870–1919* (Cambridge, 1962), I, 104–106.

35. Milner to Chamberlain, 4 May 1899, in Headlam, *Milner*, I, 349, 351–353.

36. Smuts, memorandum; Chamberlain, quoted in Marais, *Fall*, 318–319; Milner to Chamberlain, 4 September 1899, telegram, in Headlam, *Milner*, I, 525.

37. Hely-Hutchinson to Chamberlain, 29 September 1899; Chamberlain to Hicks Beach, 7 October 1899, Chamberlain Papers, Univ. of Birmingham, quoted in Marais, *Fall*, 320–321; Chamberlain to Hicks Beach, 27 or 29 September 1899, in Ethel Drus, "Select Documents from the Chamberlain Papers Concerning Anglo-Transvaal Relations, 1896–1899," *Bulletin of the Institute of Historical Research*, XXVII (1954), 188.

38. Quoted in Fuller, *Rhodes*, 221. For Jarvis, see Chapter 20.

39. Jourdan, *Rhodes*, 103; Ashe to his mother, 18 November 1899, in E. Oliver Ashe, *Besieged by the Boers: A Diary of Life and Events in Kimberley During the Siege* (London, 1900), 9.

40. CJR to Major Herbert Langton Sapte, 8 August 1899, Mss. Afr. s. 227 (II), Rhodes House.

41. CJR to Sprigg, 2 November 1899, CJR to Milner, 17 October, 5 November 1899 (two messages), Milner to Selborne, 18 October 1899, in Headlam, *Milner*, II, 24.

42. Ashe to his mother, 18 November 1899, in Ashe, *Besieged*, 13–14; Lord Methuen, quoted in Brian Gardner, *The Lion's Cage* (London, 1969), 118. See also Methuen to CJR, 21 February 1900, Mss. Afr. s. 228 (C28, 188); CJR to Baden-Powell, 30 October 1899, Mss. Afr. s. 227, Rhodes House.

43. Jourdan, *Rhodes*, 111–112; Julia Maguire, interview with Basil Williams, 18 May 1914, Mss. Afr. s. 134 (Box 1, Notebook 1), 166.

44. For the details, and for an occasion during the siege when Rhodes, misinformed, criticized unfairly and was told to "go to Hell," see Alpheus F. Williams, *Some Dreams Come True* (Cape Town, 1948), 276–279.

45. CJR, quoted in W.A.J. O'Meara, *Kekewich in Kimberley: Being an Account of the Defence of the Diamond Fields . . .* (London, 1926), 114; Kekewich to Roberts, 9 February 1900, WO 105/14, quoted in Gardner, *Cage*, 168; Harris, *Pioneer*, 172; Ashe to his mother, 18 November 1899 in Ashe, *Besieged*, 15. The "cur" quotation and Kekewich's observations are contained in an extensive set of "strictly confidential" notes by Kekewich (c. 1902–03) on Rhodes' behavior during the siege of Kimberley. That manuscript is in the McGregor Memorial Museum, Kimberley. See also the highly contentious W.A.J. O'Meara, "Notes from the Diary of a Special Service Officer during the Relief of Kimberley," in Rhodes House; George A.L. Green, reminiscences (?1936), in Mss. Afr. s. 69. Green was editor of the *Diamond Fields Advertiser* during the siege. O'Meara was Kekewich's second-in-command. For Green's view of Kekewich, whom he called "blameless," see his *An Editor Looks Back* (Cape Town, 1947), 83. For diseases and death, see Thomas Pakenham, *The Boer War* (London, 1979), 325.

46. O'Meara, *Kekewich*, 118; Kekewich, "Notes," in McGregor Museum; the *Daily Mail* (London), 17 February 1900; CJR quoted in *Daily Mail*, 17 March 1900; the *Morning Leader*, 7 March 1900, all in Gardner, *Cage*, 185–186, 190; Arthur Conan Doyle, *The Great Boer War* (London, 1903; 17th & final ed.), 230–231. Julian Ralph was the *Mail*'s special correspondent with the relief expedition.

47. CJR, speech in Kimberley, 23 February 1900, in Vindex, *Speeches*, 826, 835, 838. Verschoyle ("Vindex") gives the date of the speech as 19 February, but contemporary accounts in the *Cape Times* (26 February 1900) and the *African Review* (24 March 1900) give the date as 23 February.

48. Colvin, *Jameson*, II, 193.

49. Hawksley to Michell, 7 April 1900, Mss. Afr. s. 229 (V, 369); R.A. Young, "Fowler," in *Dictionary of National Biography* (London, 1949), 292–293; G.A. Brown (comp.) *Lives of the Fellows of the Royal College of Physicians* (London, 1955), 313–314.

50. CJR to Edgar Harris Walton, n.d. but January 1900, Walton Papers, Cory Library, Rhodes University; CJR to Milner, 26 May 1900, Ms. Eng. Hist. C687 Milner Papers, XXIX, New Bodleian Library; Milner to Gell, 11 July 1900, Gell Papers, Ms. Eng. Hist. C698, New Bodleian Library. (The Milner Papers are now properly cited as Ms. Milner dep. XYZ.) Jourdan (for CJR) to C.A. Owen Lewis, 19 May 1900, Mss. Afr. s. 227. Sprigg to CJR, 14 June 1900; Smartt and Graham to CJR, 17 June 1900; CJR to Graham, 21 June 1900; all Mss. Afr. s. 229 (V). De Waal to CJR, 5 July 1900; Abrahamson to CJR, 9 July 1900; CJR to Fuller, 11 July 1900, telegram; Smartt, Jameson, and Fuller to CJR, 16 July 1900; all Mss. Afr. s. 228 (C2B, 235, 236, 237); Edward Ridge Syfret to CJR, 19 July 1900, Syfret Trust archives. Walton to CJR, 11 August 1900, Mss. Afr. s. 228 (C28, 112), Rhodes House.

51. Diary of Sir Edward Yewd Brabant, c. 1914, chapter X, 132; in A459, Cape archives. CJR, speech, 10 October 1900, in Cape Town, in Michell, *Rhodes*, II, 288–290.

52. Brocklehurst to CJR, 14 December 1900; Stead to CJR, 22 December 1900, in Lockhart and Woodhouse, *Rhodes*, 471, 477; Milner to CJR, 8 May 1901, Mss. Afr. s. 228 (C27); Milner to Gell, 9 September 1900, Gell Papers, Ms. Eng. Hist. C698; CJR to Milner, 13 May 1900, Milner Papers, New Bodleian Library. CJR to Lewis, 8 June 1901, Mss. Afr. s. 228; Michell to CJR, 4 December 1901, Mss. Afr. s. 229 (V), Rhodes House. Syfret to CJR, 18 December 1901, Syfret archives. For overtures to the Bond, see also Merriman, diary, 12 April 1900, in Lewsen, *Selections*, III, 186.

CHAPTER 23

Of Dreams and Deeds

1. For Southern Rhodesia, see Chapter 20; for Northern Rhodesia and the railways and telegraph, see Chapter 21; for politics, see Chapter 22.

2. See Chapter 14.

3. Quoted in E.P., "A Cape Fruit Nursery, Run on Modern Lines," *Agricultural Journal* (1896), in P.G. Marais, "Fruit Pioneer Harry Ernest Victor Pickstone," (Stellenbosch, 1976), unpub. typescript, 12.

4. CJR to Beit, 25 November 1900; Mss. Afr. s. 227. CJR to Edward Ridge Syfret, 7 October, 17 October, 21 October, 13 December, 18 December 1901, 10 February 1902, Mss. Afr. t. 5 (62–86, 117–118), Rhodes House.

5. Rudyard Kipling to Harry Pickstone, 26 June 1902, from Rottingdean, Sussex, copy in Marais, "Fruit," near 24.

6. CJR to Beit, 25 November 1900, Mss. Afr. s. 227; CJR to E. R. Tymms, secretary of the London board, 23 October 1900, Mss. Afr. s. 227 (II), CJR to Quinan, 30 October 1901, Mss. Afr. s. 227 (III), Rhodes House. See also A.P. Cartwright, *The Dynamite Company: The Story of African Explosives and Chemical Industries Limited* (Johannesburg, 1964), 80–101; no author, *A Short History of Cape Explosives Works, Limited: 1903–1953* (Somerset West, 1953). Quinan himself wrote *High Explosives* (London, 1912), but it is entirely about explosives, with no mention of his time in South Africa.

7. CJR, speech, 23 February 1900; Assembly, first session, 10th parliament, *Debates* (1898), 326, 328, 342, 343, 386.

8. See Chapter 9. CJR to Stow, 14 May 1898, Stow Papers, McGregor Memorial Museum, Kimberley.

9. Newbury calculated that Rhodes' holdings in 1899 amounted only to 13,527 shares, but in addition to that number held in Cape Town, a return for January 1899 shows Rhodes owning 7,036, held for him in London by Beit's firm. See Colin Newbury, "Out of the Pit: The Capital Accumulation of Cecil Rhodes," *Journal of Imperial and Commonwealth History*, X (1981), 37.

10. CJR to Norris, undated but about 1899, "Scraps," Mss. Afr. t. 5 (138), Rhodes House.

11. CJR to Pickering, 4 December, 28 December 1900, telegrams; n.d. but received 4 February 1901; 26 November 1901, Secretarial Correspondence, 5/2/1, De Beers archives. For details of the syndicate, see Colin Newbury, "The Origins and Function of the London Diamond Syndicate, 1880–1914," *Business History*, XXIX (1987), 16–17.

12. The details are contained in a memorandum by James Prinsep, secretary of Consolidated Gold Fields, enclosed in Prinsep to P. Corriden (of Groote Schuur), 19 November 1899, in Rhodes House.

13. CJR to De Beers board, 16 August 1901, Mss. Afr. s. 227 (III), Rhodes House. Rothschild to CJR, 20 August 1901, RAL/B17/RH/XC.

14. CJR to De Beers, 19 April 1899; De Beers' directors to CJR, 26 April 1899, Board correspondence, 4/1/1, De Beers archives; CJR to Rothschild, 21 April 1899; Rothschild to CJR, 19 April, 22 April 1899, 2 November 1900, RAL/B 17/RH/1899–12; B17/RH/XC. CJR, speech in Kimberley, 23 February 1900, in Vindex, *Speeches*, 826.

15. CJR to David Harris, 30 October 1901, Ms. 112, the Brenthurst Library. For details of the negotiated end to the life governorships, see Newbury, "Out of the Pit," 39.

16. Albert Grey, quoted in John Vincent (ed.), *The Crawford Papers* (Manchester, 1984), 48. Mortimer Menpes, *War Impressions: Being a Record in Colour* (London, 1901), 104. Charles W. Furse to his father, November or December 1985, in Katharine Furse, *Hearts and Pomegranates: The Story of Forty-Five Years, 1875 to 1920* (London, 1940), 238–240. Grey to CJR, 11 June 1898, Grey Papers, Mss. Afr. t. 6 (161–163); CJR to Tweed, 1 April 1897, Mss. Afr. t. 11 (238), n.d., February 1899, Mss. Afr. t. 5 (372). Lendal Tweed, *John Tweed, Sculptor: A Memoir* (London, 1936), 86, 92–93; Watts to Grey, quoted in Baker, *Rhodes*, 128; P. Tennyson Cole, *Vanity Varnished: Reminiscences in Many Colours* (London, 1931), 169. 173. Rhodes' comments on profiles and Watts were made in an unpublished interview with Menpes, 22 Feb. 1900, Ms. 66, the Brenthurst Library.

17. For the protest, the citation, and an account of the proceedings at Oxford, see

The Times, 20, 21, 22 June 1899; printed copy of the letter of protest in Mss. Afr. s. 8 (40). The translation is by Harald A.T. Reiche. CJR, speech of 18 July 1899, Cape Town, in Vindex, *Speeches*, 641; CJR, speech, 21 June 1899, Oriel College, Oxford, in Williams, *Rhodes*, 313–314; *Morning Post*, (?) 29 March 1902. For the view of Rhodes as Napoleon, see William Stone, interview with Louis B. Frewer, Librarian of Rhodes House, n.d. but 1955, in Mss. Afr. t. 10, Rhodes House. Stone, b. 1857, met Rhodes through Edward Arthur Maund, and later breakfasted with him at the Burlington Hotel. For Kitchener, see also Chapter 21. For Warren, see Chapter 11.

18. Jourdan, *Rhodes*, 83, 87; Colin Harding, *Far Bugles* (London, 1933), 86–87; George Hough Wilson, *Gone Down the Years* (Cape Town, 1947), 249. Lord Frederic Hamilton, *The Vanished Pomps of Yesterday* (London, 1921), 39, knew Radziwill in Berlin as "the loveliest human being [he had] ever seen." But she also had a "mordant" tongue.

19. McDonald, *Rhodes*, 312; Leopold S. Amery, *Days of Fresh Air* (London, 1940), 149; Violet Milner, *My Picture Gallery, 1886–1901* (London, 1951), 243; Brian Roberts, *Cecil Rhodes and the Princess* (London, 1969), 228–229.

20. Edward Ridge Syfret to CJR, 28 March 1900, Syfret archives.

21. Edward Drew, Metropolitan Police Report, 3 April 1902, in Mss. Afr. t. 22, Rhodes House.

22. Milner to Gell, 11 July, n.d. July (postscript of a letter burnt at Milner's request), 1900, Gell Papers, Mil. 1/565, 1/568, New Bodleian Library.

23. For Schreiner, see above, Chapter 15. For the argument, see Roberts, *Princess*, 246–247.

24. Lewis Michell to CJR, 6 June, 2 September 1901, Michell Papers, Mss. Afr. s. 229 (V). CJR to Michell, 4 September 1901, Mss. Afr. s. 227 (III), Rhodes House.

CHAPTER 24
The End of the Beginning

1. CJR to Beit, 15 January 1901, Mss. Afr. s. 229 (III, 24–26), Rhodes House.

2. For 1883, see above, Chapter 8; for 1892/93, see Chapter 14; for Constantinople, see Chapter 17.

3. See Chapter 5.

4. Olive Schreiner to her sister Het, 31 August 1898, in Schreiner Papers, South African Library.

5. CJR to Jenny Jerome, Lady Randolph Churchill, n.d. but February 1899 (from Vienna), in Beatrice Steller Tanner (Mrs. George Cornwallis-West), *The Reminiscences of Lady Randolph Churchill* (London, 1908), 295. Jourdan, *Rhodes*, 96–97. Modern bridge is contract bridge, and dates from 1918–1929. It was preceded by auction bridge, which may have been invented by Britons in India in 1899 but which became popular only in 1904–1905. In auction bridge the trump suit was determined by competitive bidding; previously it was declared by the dealer or his partner. Bridge whist, although played in France in the 1870s and 1880s (and called simply bridge) became popular in the United States and Britain only in the 1890s. By 1897 nearly all leading whist players had become devotees of bridge. It introduced the exposed dummy and proved an intellectual advance on the older game. The scoring was also much more elaborate than whist.

6. F. Edmund Garrett, "The Character of Cecil Rhodes," *Contemporary Review*, LXXXI (1902), 762. Rhodes apparently was in the habit of showing off his throbbing

pulse. For an identical incident, dated to 1901, see James B. Taylor, *A Pioneer Looks Back* (London, 1939), 202.

7. Will Stuart, "History of the Schreiner Family," unpub. typescript (c. 1946), Appendix 1, South African Library.

8. Le Sueur, *Rhodes*, 152, 170–171; CJR to Grey, 1 January 1897 (should be 1898), Mss. Afr. t. 5 (76); CJR, speeches of 12 March at Cape Town and 26 August 1898 at Klipdam, in Vindex, *Speeches*, 542–544, 580; CJR to Hawksley, 25 May 1898, Mss. Afr. t. 10, Rhodes House. For Schreiner, see Chapter 15. For 1897, see Chapter 20.

9. CJR, speeches of 2 May, London, and 18 July 1899, Cape Town, in Vindex, *Speeches*, 707–708, 639; Wilhelm II (trans. Thomas R. Ybarra), *Memoirs* (New York, 1922), 88.

10. Jourdan, *Rhodes*, 131. For this trip, see also Chapter 20. For the siege and the fall, and Fowler, see Chapter 22.

11. Le Sueur, *Rhodes*, 303; Syfret to Rutherfoord Harris, 21 November 1900, Syfret archives. For Radziwill, see Chapter 23.

12. Rhodes to a "mutual friend," quoted in Harry Currey to Merriman, 27 February 1901, in Lewsen, *Selections*, III, 271–272. Lewsen's editorial note 43 (271) misinterprets Currey's meaning. CJR to William West Jones, Anglican Archbishop of Cape Town, 23 January 1901, Mss. Afr. t. 14 (348).

13. CJR to William Pickering, received 17 March 1898, Ms. 113, the Brenthurst Library. CJR, speech of 2 May 1899, in Vindex, *Speeches*, 733–734. CJR to Jacoba Zirn, n.d., August 1897, property of St. Dominic's Convent, Harare.

14. See Chapters 3, 7, 10. CJR to Stead, Mss. Afr. Micr. 413; CJR, undated holograph, in Mss. Afr. t. 5 (35), Rhodes House.

15. See Chapter 5.

16. J. Astley Cooper, "Many Lands—One People: A Criticism and a Suggestion," *Greater Britain* (15 July 1891), 458–462; "The Proposed Pan-Britannic or Pan-Anglian Contest and Festival," letter in *The Times* (30 October 1891); *idem*, "The Proposed Periodic Britannic Contest and All-English Speaking Festival," *Greater Britain* (15 November 1891), 596–601; Thomas Hudson Beare, "The Proposed Race Festival," ibid. (15 December 1891), 634–635. See "The Genesis of the Rhodes Scholarships," brief notes by Louis B. Frewer, Librarian of Rhodes House; J. Astley Cooper to Leo S. Amery, 7 June 1925, Mss. Afr. t. 10, Rhodes House. See also Colin Newbury, "Cecil Rhodes and the South African Connection: 'A Great Imperial University'?" in Frederick Madden and David K. Fieldhouse (eds.), *Oxford and the Idea of Commonwealth* (London, 1982), 84–85.

17. CJR to Bourchier F. Hawksley, n.d. February 1893, Mss. Afr. t. 1, Rhodes House. The 1892 will was dated 19 December, the next one 8 September 1893.

18. CJR, postscript 8 September 1893, in Mss. Afr. t. 1 (13); Rhodes was quoting Horace's last ode in the third book. The translation is by Harald A.T. Reiche. CJR to Stead, 19 August 1891, Mss. Afr. Micr. 413; Warwick to CJR, 28 September 1898, Mss Afr. s. 228 (C28, 91–93), Rhodes House.

19. CJR to Hawksley, 25 May 1898, Mss. Afr. t. 1 (21), Rhodes House.

20. Copies of the main will and codicils in Mss. Afr. t. 1 (7), also CJR to Hawksley, early July 1899, Mss. Afr. t. 1 (20). See also W. T. Stead, "Mr. Rhodes's Will and Its Genesis," *Review of Reviews*, XXV (June 1902), 479–481. CJR to Grey, 25 August 1901, Mss. Afr. t. 5 (506). John Marlowe, *Milner: Apostle of Empire* (London, 1976), 115, misreads this last letter. CJR to Ernest Bruce Iwan-Müller, 3 December 1901, Mss. Afr. t.

14. Rhodes enclosed two long letters to Milner and Hugh Arnold-Forster about his land settlement schemes. Both were published in *The Telegraph*. W.T. Stead (ed.), *The Last Will and Testament of Cecil John Rhodes, with Elucidatory Notes* (London, 1902), 108–109; Merriman to Goldwin Smith, 17 June 1904, in Lewsen, *Selections*, III, 443–444.

21. CJR to William West Jones, Anglican Archbishop of Cape Town, 23 January 1901, Mss. Afr. t. 14 (348); CJR to West Jones, February 1902, Mss. Afr. t. 5 (531).

22. See Chapter 22; CJR speech of 15 June 1901, in *Bulawayo Chronicle* (17 June 1901).

23. Jourdan, *Rhodes*, 255, 258; Winston S. Churchill, 8 March 1961, quoted in Lockhart and Woodhouse, *Rhodes*, 482; Frances E.M. Greville, Countess of Warwick, *Life's Ebb and Flow* (New York, 1929), 158–159; idem, *Afterthoughts* (London, 1931), 84–85. CJR, quoted in Bramwell Booth, *Echoes and Memories* (New York, 1926), 151–152.

24. Michell, *Rhodes*, II, 302; Edward Dicey, "Cecil Rhodes in Egypt," *Fortnightly Review*, LXXVII (1902), 765.

25. Le Sueur, *Rhodes*, 305; Bernard Rhodes to Ella (Edith? Rhodes), 3 February 1902, Mss. Afr. s. 228 (C28/123–124).

26. Hawksley to CJR, 13 December 1901; Hawksley to Michell (cable), 14 January 1902, Mss. Afr. s. 229 (VI, 213, 307).

27. Innes to Jessie Rose Innes, 9 February 1902, in Wright, *Innes*, 339–340.

28. Innes to Jessie Rose Innes, 9, 16, 23 March 1902, Von Moltke Papers (Norwich, VT), with the kind permission of Freya von Moltke. Harrison Wright shared his copies of these letters with me. They do not appear in Wright, *Innes*. Tindall, *Innes*, 198; Syfret to F. Rutherfoord Harris, 26 March 1902; Syfret to Ludwig Breitmeyer, 12, 26 March 1902, Syfret archives; Michell, *Rhodes*, II, 310–311; George Krieger, memories, n.d., in Mss. Afr s. 69, Rhodes House; Le Sueur to William Pickering, 24 March 1902, in 5/2/1, De Beers archives; Jameson to Hawksley, 10, 14, 17, 21, 22 March 1902 (cables), in Mss. Afr. s. 229 (III, 53–100), Rhodes House.

29. Innes to Jessie Rose Innes, 28 March 1902, Von Moltke Papers; Milner to Lady Edward Cecil, 20 March 1902, in Headlam, *Milner*, II, 411.

30. One version of the autopsy report exists as a telegram from Stevenson to Fowler, 27 March 1902, A540/37, Cape archives; another, attributed to Syfret, is in the Rhodes papers in the Rhodes-Livingstone Museum, Livingstone, Zambia, and in Rhodes House.

31. Wheatcroft, *The Randlords* (New York, 1986) contains the most recent account of Rhodes' atrial septal defect. Like Blake, *Rhodesia*, 33, who lavishly accepted the diagnosis, he draws directly upon J. Charles Shee, "The Ill-Health and Mortal Sickness of Cecil John Rhodes," *Central African Journal of Medicine*, 11 (April, 1965), 93, where this suggestion was first advanced.On syphilis, William Osler, *The Principles and Practice of Medicine* (New York, 1898, 3rd. ed.), 783, 252–255.

32. Assembly, *Debates* (1899) 156; Michell specifically noted that Basil Williams, *Rhodes*, (182) contained "an exaggerated idea" of Rhodes' wealth. Michell, "Half a Century In and Out of South Africa, 1884–1919," unpub. typescript (1920), 196, A540/29, Cape archives and Micr. Afr. 156, Rhodes House. Details of Rhodes' wealth are found in the estate papers, Mss. Afr. t. 1, Rhodes House.

33. N.M. Rothschild, private memorandum, 27 March 1902, RAL B17/RH.

CHAPTER 25

Enigma and Resolution

1. Ian Colvin to Basil Williams, 19 October 1921, Mss. Afr. s. 134 (9).

2. Edmond Sinclair Stevenson, *The Adventures of a Medical Man* (Cape Town, 1925), 39.

3. Bramwell Booth, *Echoes and Memories* (New York, 1926), 147–148.

4. Sidney Low, "Personal Recollections of Cecil Rhodes: Some Conversations in London," *The Nineteenth Century and After*, LI (1902), 830–831, 839–840.

5. F. Edmund Garrett, "The Character of Cecil Rhodes," *Contemporary Review*, LXXXI (1902), 775; Merriman to Basil Williams, 27 August 1919, 6 August 1920, Mss. Afr. s. 134. Rudyard Kipling, "The Burial, 1902," *Rudyard Kipling's Verse: Inclusive Edition, 1885–1926* (Garden City, 1927).

6. Garrett, "Rhodes," 768.

7. Merriman to Williams, 9 July 1919, Mss. Afr. s. 134.

8. Tindall, *Innes*, 84–85. See also Chapter 14.

9. Theodore Levitt, "Management and the 'Post-Industrial' Society," *Public Interest*, XLIV (1976), 73–74; Harry Levinson and Stuart Rosenthal, *CEO: Corporate Leadership in Action* (New York, 1984), 259–284.

10. John H. Plumb, *Men and Centuries* (Boston, 1963), 206; Low, "Recollections," 839.

11. Quoted by Le Sueur, Mss. Afr. s. 229 (III, 400), Rhodes House.

12. Milner to Philip Lyttelton Gell, 28 July 1889, 19 October 1898, Gell Papers, Mil. 1/510, Mil. 1/514, New Bodleian Library, Oxford.

13. See Preface.

Select Bibliography: Rhodes,
His Contemporaries, and His Times

BIOGRAPHIES OF RHODES

Baker, Herbert. *Cecil Rhodes, by His Architect* (London, 1934).

Cloete, Stuart. *African Portraits: A Biography of Paul Kruger, Cecil Rhodes, and Lobengula, Last King of the Ndebele* (London, 1946).

Currey, Ronald. *Rhodes: A Biographical Footnote* (Cape Town, n.d.).

Flint, John. *Cecil Rhodes* (Boston, 1974).

Fuller, Thomas E. *The Right Hon. Cecil John Rhodes: A Monograph and a Reminiscence* (London, 1910).

Green, J.E.S. *Rhodes Goes North* (London, 1936).

Gross, Felix. *Rhodes of Africa* (London, 1956).

Hensman, Howard. *Cecil Rhodes, A Study of a Career* (Edinburgh, 1901).

Hutchinson, G.S. *Cecil Rhodes the Man* (Oxford, 1944).

Imperialist (pseud. John Verschoyle). *Cecil Rhodes: A Biography and an Appreciation* (London, 1897).

Jourdan, Philip. *Cecil Rhodes: His Private Life by His Private Secretary* (London, 1911).

Le Sueur, Gordon. *Cecil Rhodes: The Man and His Work* (London, 1913).

Lockhart, J.G., and C.M. Woodhouse. *Cecil Rhodes: The Colossus of Southern Africa* (New York, 1963).

Marlowe, John. *Cecil Rhodes: The Anatomy of Empire* (New York, 1972).

Maurois, André (trans. Rohan Wadham). *Cecil Rhodes* (London, 1953).

Michell, Lewis. *The Life of the Rt. Hon. Cecil John Rhodes, 1853–1902* (London, 1910), 2 v.

Millin, Sarah Gertrude. *Rhodes* (London, 1933).

Oudard, Georges. *Cecil Rhodes* (Paris, 1939).

Plomer, William. *Cecil Rhodes* (Edinburgh, 1933).

Radziwill, Catherine. *Cecil Rhodes: Man and Empire Maker* (London, 1918).

Roberts, Brian. *Cecil Rhodes and the Princess* (London, 1969).

———. *Cecil Rhodes: Flawed Colossus* (London, 1987).

Williams, Basil. *Cecil Rhodes* (London, 1938).

PRIMARY SOURCES

Alexander, Eleanor (ed.). *Primate Alexander: Archbishop of Armagh* (London, 1913).

An Amateur Cotton Planter. "The Cotton Fields, Upper Umkomanzi," in John Robinson (ed.), *Notes on Natal: An Old Colonists's Book for New Settlers* (Durban, 1872), 143–151.

Amery, Leopold S. *Days of Fresh Air: Being Reminiscences of Outdoor Life* (London, 1940).

Anon. "The Fire at Groote Schuur," *South Africa* (9 January 1897).

Arnot, Frederick Stanley. *The Life and Explorations of Frederick Stanley Arnot* (London, 1921).

Arthur, George. *Not Worth Reading* (London, 1938).

Ashe, E. Oliver. *Besieged by the Boers: A Diary of Life and Events in Kimberley during the Siege* (New York, 1900).

Babe, Jerome L. *South African Diamond Fields* (New York, 1872).

Baden-Powell, Robert Stevenson Smyth. *The Matabele Campaign 1896: Being a Narrative of the Campaign in Suppressing the Native Rising in Matabeleland and Mashonaland* (London, 1897).

Beet, George. *The Grand Old Days of the Diamond Fields: Memories of Past Times with the Diggers of Diamondia* (Cape Town, 1931).

Blennerhasset, Rose, and Lucy Sleeman. *Adventures in Mashonaland* (London, 1893).

Blunt, Wilfred Scawen. *My Diaries: Being a Personal Narrative of Events, 1888–1914* (New York, 1921), 2 v.

Booth, Bramwell. *Echoes and Memories* (New York, 1926).

Boyle, Frederick. *To the Cape for Diamonds: A Story of Digging Experiences in South Africa. With Comments and Criticisms, Political, Social, and Miscellaneous upon the Present State and Future Prospects of the Diamond Fields* (London, 1873).

Brett, Maurice V. (ed.). *Journals and Letters of Reginald Viscount Esher, 1870–1903* (London, 1934), 2 v.

Bryce, James. *Impressions of South Africa* (New York, 1898).

Buchan, David (ed.). *The Chronicles of a Contractor: Being the Autobiography of the Late George Pauling* (London, 1926).

Buckle, George Earle (ed.). *The Letters of Queen Victoria: A Selection from Her Majesty's Correspondence and Journal between the Years 1886 and 1901* (London, 1931, 1932), 3 v.

Burnham, Frederick Russell. *Scouting on Two Continents* (New York, 1927).

Chapman, Charles. *A Voyage from Southampton to Cape Town . . . and Illustrations of the Diamond Fields . . .* (London, 1872).

Churchill, Randolph. *Men, Mines and Animals in South Africa* (London, 1892).

Cohen, Louis. *Reminiscences of Kimberley* (London, 1911).

Cole, P. Tennyson. *Vanity Varnished: Reminiscences in Many Colours* (London, 1931).

Colquhoun, Archibald R. *Dan to Beersheba: Work and Travel in Four Continents* (London, 1908).

Cooper, Diana. *The Rainbow Comes and Goes* (London, 1958).

Cooper-Chadwick, John. *Three Years with Lobengula, and Experiences in South Africa* (London, 1894).

Cornwallis-West, Beatrice Steller Tanner. *The Reminiscences of Lady Randolph Churchill* (London, 1908).

Cronwright-Schreiner, S.C. (ed.). *The Letters of Olive Schreiner, 1876–1920* (London, 1924).

Dachs, Anthony J. (ed.). *Papers of John Mackenzie* (Johannesburg, 1975).

Dixie, Florence. *In the Land of Misfortune* (London, 1882).

Dormer, Frances J. *Vengeance as a Policy in Afrikanderland: A Plea for a New Departure* (London, 1901).

Duminy, A.H., and W.R. Guest (eds). *FitzPatrick: South African Politician: Selected Papers, 1888–1906* (Johannesburg, 1976).

FitzPatrick, J.P. *The Transvaal from Within: A Private Record of Public Affairs* (London, 1899).

Fossor (pseud.). *Twelve Months at the South African Diamond Fields* (London, 1872).

Fraser, Maryna, and Alan Jeeves (eds.). *All That Glittered: The Selected Correspondence of Lionel Phillips, 1890–1924* (Cape Town, 1977).

Fripp, Constance E., and V.W. Hiller (eds.). *Gold and Gospel in the Mashonaland, 1888: Being the Journals of 1) The Mashonaland Mission of Bishop Knight-Bruce; 2) The Concession Journey of Charles Dunell Rudd* (London, 1949).

Furse, Katharine. *Hearts and Pomegranates: The Story of Forty-Five Years, 1875–1920* (London, 1940).

Garrett, Fydell Edmund. *In Afrikanerland and the Land of Ophir* (London, 1890).

———. "The Character of Cecil Rhodes," *Contemporary Review*, LXXXI (1902), 761–779.

Glover, Elisabeth Rosetta Scott. *Memories of Four Continents: Recollections Grave and Gay Events in Social and Diplomatic Life* (Philadelphia, 1923).

Green, George A.L. *An Editor Looks Back: South African and Other Memories, 1883–1946* (Cape Town, 1947).

Greville, Frances Evelyn Maynard. *Life's Ebb and Flow* (New York, 1929).

———. *Afterthoughts* (London, 1931).

Grey of Fallodon (Viscount). *Twenty-Five Years, 1892–1916.* (New York, 1925), 3 v.

Grey, Albert. *Herbert Hervey, Student and Imperialist: A Memoir* (London, 1899).

Haggard, Henry Rider. *The Days of My Life: An Autobiography* (London, 1926).

Haldane, Richard Burdon. *Richard Burdon Haldane (Viscount Haldane): An Autobiography* (Garden City, 1929).

Hamilton, Frederic. *Here, There and Everywhere* (London, 1921).

Hammond, John Hays. *The Autobiography of John Hays Hammond* (New York, 1935), 2 v.

Hammond, Natalie Harris. *A Woman's Part in a Revolution* (London, 1897).

Hardie, J. Keir. *Speeches and Writings* (London, 1928).

Harding, Colin. *Far Bugles* (Croydon, 1933).

Harlow, Vincent. "Sir Frederic Hamilton's Narrative of Events Relative to the Jameson Raid," *English Historical Review*, LXXII (1957), 279–305.

Harris, David. *Pioneer, Soldier and Politician: Summarised Memoirs of Col. Sir David Harris* (London, 1931).

Harris, Frank. *My Life and Loves* (New York, 1979; orig. pub. 1925), 5 v.

Headlam, Cecil (ed.). *The Milner Papers: South Africa, 1899–1905* (London, 1933), 2 v.

Hofmeyr, Adrian. *The Story of My Captivity during the Transvaal War, 1899–1900* (London, 1900).

Holland, A.H. "Personal Memories of Cecil John Rhodes," *The Daily Dispatch* (East London) (10 November 1953).

Hutchinson, G.T. *From the Cape to the Zambesi* (London, 1905).

Instrap, C.H. "Rhodes in Matabeleland, '96," *The Sunrise* (29 March 1902), 24–25.

Iwan-Müller, Ernest Bruce. "Cecil John Rhodes," *Fortnightly Review*, LXXVII (1902), 741–761.

Jameson, Leander Starr. "Personal Reminiscences of Mr. Rhodes," in Imperialist (pseud. John Verschoyle), *Cecil Rhodes: A Biography and Appreciation* (London, 1897), 391–413.

Jarvis, Arthur Weston. "Cecil Rhodes," *United Empire* (1935), 622–624.

———. "Cecil Rhodes as I Knew Him," *African World* (26 October 1935), 44–46.

Jenkins, Stanley John. "The Administration of Cecil John Rhodes as Prime Minister of the Cape Colony (1890–1896)," unpub. M.A. thesis (Univ. of Cape Town, 1951).

Johnson, Frank. *Great Days: The Autobiography of an Empire Pioneer* (London, 1940).

Johnston, Henry Hamilton. *British Central Africa* (New York, 1897).

———. "My Story of the Cape to Cairo Scheme," in Leo Weinthal (ed.), *The Story of the Cape to Cairo Railway and River Route* (London, 1923), I, 65–93.

———. *The Story of My Life* (Indianapolis, 1923).

Johnston, James. *Reality versus Romance in South Central Africa* (New York, 1893).

Kemp, Samuel. *Black Frontiers: Pioneer Adventures with Cecil Rhodes' Mounted Police in Africa* (London, 1932).

Kruger, Paul. *The Memoirs of Paul Kruger* (London, 1902).

Laing, D. Tyrie. *The Matabele Rebellion, 1896: With the Belingwe Field Force* (London, 1897).

Laurence, Perceval Maitland. "A Great Adventurer," *The Examiner* (9 October 1902), 255–261.

———. *On Circuit in Kafirland, and Other Sketches and Studies* (London, 1903).

Leonard, Arthur Glyn. *How We Made Rhodesia* (London, 1894).

Leonard, Charles. *Papers on the Political Situation in South Africa, 1885–1895* (London, 1903).

Lewsen, Phyllis (ed.). *Selections from the Correspondence of J.X. Merriman, 1870–1924* (Cape Town, 1960–1969), 4 v.

Low, Sidney. "Personal Recollections of Cecil Rhodes: Some Conversations in London," *The Nineteenth Century and After*, LI (1902), 828–840.

Lucy, Henry W. *A Diary of the Unionist Parliament, 1895–1900* (Bristol, 1901).

———. "Cecil Rhodes: Some Personal Reminiscences," *Chamber's Journal*, IX (8 February 1919), 145–149.

Mackail, John Williams, and Guy Wyndham (eds.). *Life and Letters of George Wyndham* (London, 1925), 2 v.

Mackenzie, John. *Austral Africa: Losing It or Ruling It* (London, 1887), 2 v.

MacNeill, J.G. Swift. *What I Have Seen and Heard* (Boston, 1925).

March-Phillipps, Lisle, and Bertram Christian (eds.). *Some Hawarden Letters, 1878–1913: Written to Mrs. Drew (Miss Mary Gladstone) before and after Her Marriage* (London, 1917).

Marcosson, Isaac F. *Adventures in Interviewing* (New York, 1920).

———. *An African Adventure* (New York, 1921).

Matthews, Josiah Wright. *Incwadi Yami: Or Twenty Years' Personal Experience in South Africa* (New York, 1887).

Menpes, Mortimer. *War Impressions: Being a Record in Colour* (London, 1901).

Milner, Violet M. *My Picture Gallery, 1886–1901* (London, 1951).

Moffat, Robert Unwin. *John Smith Moffat, C.M.G., Missionary: A Memoir* (London, 1921).

Molteno, James Tennant. *The Dominion of Afrikanderdom: Recollections Pleasant and Otherwise* (London, 1923).

———. *Further South African Recollections* (London, 1926).

O'Meara, W.A.J. *Kekewich in Kimberley: Being an Account of the Defences of the Diamond Fields Oct. 14th, 1899–Feb. 15th, 1900* (London, 1926).

Orpen, Joseph Millerd. *Reminiscences of Life in South Africa from 1846 to the Present Day* (Cape Town, 1964).

Pauling, George (ed. David Buchan). *The Chronicles of a Contractor: Being the Autobiography of the Late George Pauling* (London, 1926).

Payton, Charles Alfred. *The Diamond Diggings of South Africa: A Personal and Practical Account* (London, 1872).

Phillips, Florence. *Some South African Recollections* (London, 1899).

Phillips, Lionel. *Some Reminiscences* (London, 1924).

Pickstone, Harry Ernest Victor. "The Fruit Export Crises: Past and Future of the Industry—Reminiscences of Rhodes," *Cape Times* (5–6 September 1921).

Plumer, Herbert. *An Irregular Corps in Matabeleland* (New York, 1897).

Radziwill, Catherine. *My Recollections* (London, 1904).

Rickson, Charlie. "I Was Rhodes's Valet," *The Outspan*, (9 December 1949), 71.

Roberts, Morley. *A Tramp's Note-Book* (London, 1904).

Robertson, Wilfrid. *The Storm of '96: A Tale of the Mashona Rising* (London, 1951).

Robertson, William. *From Private to Field-Marshall* (London, 1921).

Robinson, John (ed.). *Notes on Natal: An Old Colonist's Book for New Settlers* (Durban, 1872).

Rouillard, Nancy (ed.). *Matabele Thompson: An Autobiography* (London, 1936).

Sauer, Hans. *Ex Africa . . .* (London, 1937).

Scully, William Charles. *Reminiscences of a South African Pioneer* (London, 1913).

———. *Further Reminiscences of a South African Pioneer* (London, 1913).

Selous, Frederick Courtenay. *Travel and Adventure in South Central Africa* (London, 1893).

———. *Sunshine & Storm in Rhodesia: Being a Narrative of Events in Matabeleland Both before and during the Recent Native Insurrection up to the Date of the Disbandment of the Bulawayo Field Force* (London, 1896; 2nd ed).

Shaw, Gerald (ed.). *The Garrett Papers* (Cape Town, 1984).

Simons, Phillida Brooke (ed.). *John Blades Currey, 1850 to 1900: Fifty Years in the Cape Colony* (Johannesburg, 1986).

———. "The Memoirs of Henry Latham (Harry) Currey," (Rondebosch, 1983; written 1942), unpub. typescript.

Simpson, Charles. *A Yankee's Adventures in South Africa* (Chicago, 1897).

Solomon, Vivian (ed.). *Selections from the Correspondence of Percy Alport Molteno, 1892–1914* (Cape Town, 1981).

Stead, Estelle W. *My Father: Personal and Spiritual Reminiscences* (London, 1913).

Stead, William Thomas (ed.). *The Last Will and Testament of Cecil John Rhodes* (London, 1902).

Stent, Vere. *A Personal Record of Some Incidents in the Life of Cecil Rhodes* (Cape Town, 1925).

Stevenson, Edmond Sinclair. *The Adventures of a Medical Man* (Cape Town, 1925).

Steytler, J.G. *The Diamond Fields of South Africa* (Cape Town, 1870).

Sykes, Frank W. *With Plumer in Matabeleland: An Account of the Operations of the Matabeleland Relief Force during the Rebellion of 1896* (London, 1897).

Tallents, Stephen George. *Man and Boy* (London, 1943).

Taylor, James Benjamin. *A Pioneer Looks Back* (London, 1939).

The Times Special Correspondent. *Letters from South Africa* (London, 1893).

Tindall, B.A. (ed.). *James Rose Innes: Chief Justice of South Africa, 1914–17, Autobiography* (London, 1937).

Trevor, Tudor G. *Forty Years in Africa* (London, 1932).

Trollope, Anthony. *South Africa* (Leipzig, 1878).

Twain, Mark (Samuel Clemens). *Following the Equator: A Journey Around the World* (New York, 1897).

Villiers, Frederic. *Peaceful Personalities and Warriors Bold* (London, 1907).

Vincent, John (ed.). *The Crawford Papers* (Manchester, 1984).

Vindex (pseud. John Verschoyle). *Cecil Rhodes: His Political Life and Speeches, 1881–1900* (London, 1900).

Waal, David Christiaan de (trans. Jan H. Hofmeyer de Waal). *With Rhodes in Mashonaland* (Cape Town, 1896).

Wallis, J.P.R. (ed.). *The Southern African Diaries of Thomas Leask, 1865–1870* (London, 1954).

Warner, Pelham. *Long Innings: The Autobiography of Sir Pelham Warner* (London, 1951).

Warren, Charles. "Cecil Rhodes' Early Days in South Africa," *Contemporary Review*, LXXXI (1902), 643–654.

———. *On the Veldt in the Seventies* (London, 1902).

Warwick, Frances Evelyn Maynard Greville, Countess of. *Life's Ebb and Flow* (New York, 1929).

———. *Afterthoughts* (London, 1931).

Weinthal, Leo (comp. and ed.). *Memories, Mines and Millions: Being the Life of Sir Joseph B. Robinson, Bart.* (London, 1929).

Widdicombe, John. *Fourteen Years in Basutoland: A Sketch of African Mission Life* (London, 1891).

Wilhelm II. *Ereignisse und Gestallen aus den Jahren, 1878–1918* (Leipzig, 1922).

Williams, Archibald. *The Romance of Mining* (London, 1905).

Williams, Gardner F. *The Diamond Mines of South Africa: Some Account of Their Rise and Development* (New York, 1902).

Williams, Ralph. *How I Became a Governor* (London, 1913).

Williams, Robert. "My Story of the Schemes," in Leo Weinthal (ed.), *The Story of the Cape to Cairo Railway and River Route* (London, 1923), 104–120.

Wilson, George Hough. *Gone Down the Years* (London, 1947).

Wilson, Sarah. *South African Memories: Social, Warlike & Sporting, from Diaries Written at the Time* (London, 1909).

Winchester, Lord (Henry William Montagu Paulet). *Statesmen, Financiers, and Felons* (Abbeville, France, 1935).

Wirgman, A. Theodore. *Storm and Sunshine in South Africa, with Some Personal and Historical Reminiscences* (London, 1922).

Witt, Robert Clermont. "Personal Recollections of Cecil Rhodes: As Peacemaker on the Matoppo Hills," *The Nineteenth Century and After*, LI (1902), 841–848.

Wright, Harrison M. (ed.). *Sir James Rose Innes: Selected Correspondence (1884–1902)* (Cape Town, 1972).

Ybarra, Thomas R. (trans.). *The Kaiser's Memoirs.* (New York, 1922).

Younghusband, Francis. *South Africa of To-Day* (London, 1898).

SECONDARY SOURCES

Abdullah, Achmed, and T. Compton Pakenham. *Dreamers of Empires* (London, 1930).

Aydelotte, Frank. *The Vision of Cecil Rhodes: A Review of the First Forty Years of the American Scholarships* (London, 1946).

Agar-Hamilton, J.A.I. *The Road to the North: South Africa, 1852–1886* (London, 1937).

Amphlett, George Thomas. *History of the Standard Bank of South Africa Ltd., 1862–1913* (Glasgow, 1914).

Anon. *Groote Schuur: Residence of South Africa's Prime Minister* (Pretoria, 1979).

Anon. "How Mr. Rhodes Went to Oriel," *Westminster Gazette* (9 April 1902).

Anon. *A Short History of Cape Explosive Works, Limited: 1903–1953* (Somerset West, 1953).

Arendt, Hannah. *The Origins of Totalitarianism* (New York, 1958).

Arndt, E.H.D. *Banking and Currency Development in South Africa (1652–1927)* (Cape Town, 1928).

Atmore, Anthony. "The Moorosi Rebellion: Lesotho, 1879," in Robert I. Rotberg and Ali A. Mazrui (eds.), *Protest and Power in Black Africa* (New York, 1970), 3–36.

————, and Shula Marks. "The Imperial Factor in South Africa in the Nineteenth Century: Towards a Reassessment," *Journal of Imperial and Commonwealth History*, III (1974), 105–139.

Bawcombe, Philip. *Kimberley* (Johannesburg, 1976).

Baxter, T. William. "The Angoni Rebellion and Mpeseni," *The Northern Rhodesia Journal*, II (1950), 14–24.

————, and R.W.S. Turner (eds.). *Rhodesian Epic* (Cape Town, 1968).

Baylen, Joseph O. "W.T. Stead and the Boer War: The Irony of Idealism," *Canadian Historical Review*, XL (1959), 304–314.

————. "W.T. Stead's *History of the Mystery* and the Jameson Raid," *Journal of British Studies*, IV (1964), 104–132.

Beare, Thomas Hudson. "The Proposed Race Festival," *Greater Britain* (15 December 1891), 634–635.

Benyon, John. "Cecil John Rhodes and Higher Education," *The American Oxonian*, LVII (1970), 566–569.

Berlyn, Annie. *Bishop's Stortford and Its Story* (Norwich, 1924).

Bett, Walter Reginald. "Cecil John Rhodes (1853–1902), Imperialist and Invalid," *Health Horizon* (Summer, 1953), 21–25.

The Bishop's Stortford and District Local Historical Society. *Bishop's Stortford: A Short History* (Bishop's Stortford, 1969).

Blainey, A. Geoffrey. "Lost Causes of the Jameson Raid," *Economic History Review*, XLVIII (1965), 350–366.

Blake, Robert. *A History of Rhodesia* (London, 1977).

————. "The Jameson Raid and 'The Missing Telegrams,' " in Hugh Lloyd-Jones, Valerie Pearl, and Blair Worden (eds.), *History and Imagination: Essays in Honour of H.R. Trevor-Roper* (London, 1981), 326–339.

Blakeley, Brian L. *The Colonial Office, 1868–1892* (Durham, 1972).

Boggie, Jeannie M. "Rhodes' Three Peace Indabas," *The Chronicle* (Bulawayo), (July 1953).

Bolt, Christine. *Victorian Attitudes to Race* (London, 1971).

Bradlow, Edna. "The Cape Government's Rule of Basutoland, 1871–1883," *Archives Yearbook for South African History* (Pretoria, 1969), 119–217.

————. "General Gordon in Basutoland," *Historia*, XV (1970), 119–217, 223–242.

Brookes, Edgar H. *The History of Native Policy in South Africa from 1830 to the Present Day* (Cape Town, 1924).

Brooks, Henry (ed. R.J. Mann). *Natal: A History and Description of the Colony* (London, 1876).

Brown, Richard. "The Ndebele Succession Crisis," in Terence Ranger (ed.), *Historians in Tropical Africa* (Salisbury, 1962), 159–176.

———. "Aspects of the Scramble for Matabeleland," in Eric Stokes and Richard Brown (eds.), *The Zambesian Past: Studies in Central African History* (Manchester, 1966), 63–93.

Bundy, Colin. "Mr. Rhodes and the Poisoned Goods: Popular Opposition to the Glen Grey Council System, 1894–1906," in William Beinart and Colin Bundy (eds.), *Hidden Struggles in Rural South Africa: Politics and Popular Movements in the Transkei & Eastern Cape* (Johannesburg, 1987), 138–165.

Burrows, Edmund H. *A History of Medicine in South Africa up to the End of the Nineteenth Century* (Cape Town, 1958).

Butler, Jeffrey. *The Liberal Party and the Jameson Raid* (Oxford, 1968).

———. "Cecil Rhodes," *International Journal of African Historical Studies*, X (1977), 259–281.

Campbell, A.A. "Praise Names of CJ Rhodes," *NADA*, 36 (1959), 99–102.

Camplin, Jamie. *The Rise of the Plutocrats: Wealth and Power in Edwardian England* (London, 1978).

Cartwright, A.P. *The Dynamite Company: The Story of African Explosives and Chemical Industries Limited, 1896–1958* (Cape Town, 1964).

———. *The Corner House: The Early History of Johannesburg* (Cape Town, 1965).

———. *Gold Paved the Way: The Story of the Gold Fields Group of Companies* (New York, 1967).

Cary, Robert. *Charter Royal* (Cape Town, 1970).

Cassar, George. *The Tragedy of Sir John French* (Newark, Del., 1985).

Chapman, Stanley D. *The Rise of Merchant Banking* (London, 1984).

———. "Rhodes and the City of London: Another View of Imperialism," *The Historical Journal*, XXVIII (1985), 647–666.

Chesterton, Gilbert K. *A Miscellany of Men* (New York, 1912).

Chilvers, Hedley A. *The Story of De Beers: With Some Notes on the Company's Financial, Farming, Railway and Industrial Activities in Africa, and Some Introductory Chapters on the River Diggings and Early Kimberley* (London, 1939).

Christopher, A.H. "Land Speculation in Colonial Natal, 1843–1910," *Historia*, XVI (1971), 102–111.

Clark, George N. *Cecil Rhodes and His College* (Oxford, 1953).

Clarke, James (ed.). *Like It Was: The Star 100 Years in Johannesburg* (Johannesburg, 1987).

Cobbing, Julian R.D. "The Unknown Fate of the Rudd Concession Rifles," *Rhodesian History*, IV (1972), 77–82.

———. "Lobengula, Jameson, and the Occupation of Mashonaland, 1890," *Rhodesian History*, IV (1973), 39–56.

Collins, Orvis S., and David G. Moore. *The Enterprising Man* (East Lansing, Mich., 1964).

Collins, Robert O. *King Leopold, England and the Upper Nile, 1899–1909* (New Haven, 1968).

Consolidated Gold Fields of South Africa. *The Gold Fields, 1887–1937* (London, 1937).

Cook, Edward T. *The Rights and Wrongs of the Transvaal War* (London, 1901).

Cooper, J. Astley. "Many Lands—One People: A Criticism and Suggestion," *Greater Britain* (15 July 1891), 458–462.

———. "The Proposed Periodic Britannic Contest and All-English Speaking Festival," *Greater Britain* (15 November 1891), 596–601.

Courtney, William Lechand, and J.E. Courtney. *Pillars of Empire: Studies and Impressions* (London, 1918).

Crawford, F. Marion. *An American Politician: A Novel* (New York, 1884).

Currey, Ronald F. *Rhodes University, 1904–1970: A Chronicle* (Grahamstown, 1970).

Curror, W.D. (comp.). *Golden Memories of Barberton* (Barberton, 1965).

Dachs, Anthony J. "Rhodes' Grasp for Bechuanaland, 1889–1896," *Rhodesian History*, II (1971), 1–9.

———. "Missionary Imperialism—The Case of Bechuanaland," *Journal of African History*, XIII (1972), 647–658.

Davenport, T. Rodney H. *The Afrikaner Bond: The History of a South African Political Party, 1880–1911* (Cape Town, 1966).

———. "Cecil Rhodes—His Impact on South Africa," *The American Oxonian*, LVII (1970), 564–566.

Denholm, Anthony F. "Lord Ripon and Liberal Party Policy in Southern Africa, 1892–1902," *Australian Journal of Politics and History*, XXVII (1981), 232–240.

Dennison, C.G., *History of Stellaland* (Vryburg, 1928).

Denoon, D.J.N. " 'Capitalist Influence' and the Transvaal Government During the Crown Colony Period, 1900–1906," *Historical Journal*, XI (1968), 301–331.

Desautels, Paul E. *The Mineral Kingdom* (New York, 1968).

Dicey, Edward. "Cecil Rhodes in Egypt," *Fortnightly Review*, LXXVII (1902), 762–770.

Ditchfield, P.H. "Famous Men of Oriel College," *The Oriel Record*, I (1911), 159–164.

Doyle, Arthur Conan. *The Great Boer War* (London, 1903).

Drus, Ethel. "A Report on the Papers of Joseph Chamberlain Relating to the Jameson Raid and the Inquiry," *Bulletin of the Institute of Historical Research*, XXV (1952), 33–62.

———. "The Question of Imperial Complicity in the Jameson Raid," *English Historical Review*, LXVIII (1953), 582–593.

———. "Select Documents from the Chamberlain Papers Concerning Anglo-Transvaal Relations, 1896–1899," *Bulletin of the Institute of Historical Research*, XXVII (1954), 156–189.

Edgecombe, Ruth. "The Glen Grey Act: Local Origins of an Abortive 'Bill for Africa,' " in J.A. Benyon, C.W. Cook, T.R.H. Davenport, and K.S. Hunt (eds.), *Studies in Local History* (Cape Town, 1976), 89–98.

Eldridge, C.C. *England's Mission: The Imperial Idea in the Age of Gladstone and Disraeli, 1868–1880* (Chapel Hill, 1973).

———. *Victorian Imperialism* (Atlantic Highlands, N.J., 1978).

Emden, Paul H. *Randlords* (London, 1935).

———. *Money Powers of Europe in the Nineteenth and Twentieth Centuries* (New York, 1938).

English, Jane (ed.). *The First Trust Company in the World* (Cape Town, 1984).

Etherington, Norman. "Labour Supply and the Genesis of South African Confederation in the 1870s," *Journal of African History*, XX (1979), 235–254.

———. "Frederic Elton and the South African Factor in the Making of Britain's East African Empire," *Journal of Imperial and Commonwealth History*, IX (1981), 255–274.

Ewbank, W.E.B., et al. *Bishop's Stortford: A Short History* (Bishop's Stortford, 1969).

Ferguson, W.T. "The Native Policy of Cecil John Rhodes in the Eastern Province," unpub. M.A. Thesis (Univ. of Cape Town, 1932).

Frankel, S. Herbert. *Investment and the Return to Equity Capital in the South African Gold Mining Industry, 1887–1965: An International Comparison* (Cambridge, Mass., 1967).

Galbraith, John S. "The British South Africa Company and the Jameson Raid," *British Studies*, X (1970), 145–161.

———. "Engine Without a Governor: The Early Years of the British South Africa Company," *Rhodesian History*, 1 (1970), 9–17.

————. *Mackinnon and East Africa, 1878–1895: A Study in "New Imperialism"* (Cambridge, 1972).

————. "Cecil Rhodes and His Cosmic Dreams: A Reassessment," *Journal of Imperial and Commonwealth History*, I (1973), 173–190.

————. *Crown and Charter: The Early Years of the British South Africa Company* (Berkeley, 1974).

Gale, W.D. *Heritage of Rhodes* (Cape Town, 1950).

Gallagher, John A., and Ronald Robinson. "The Partition of Africa," in F.H. Hinsley (ed.), *The New Cambridge Modern History* (Cambridge, 1962), XI, 593–640.

Gardner, Brian. *The Lion's Cage: The Siege of Kimberley* (London, 1969).

Garrett, F. Edmund, and E.J. Edwards. *The Story of an African Crisis: Being the Truth about the Jameson Raid and Johannesburg Revolt of 1896 Told with the Assistance of the Leading Actors in the Drama* (New York, 1897).

Garson, Noel G. "British Imperialism and the Coming of the Anglo-Boer War," *South African Journal of Economics*, XXX (1962), 140–153.

Giliomee, Hermann. "The Beginnings of Afrikaner Nationalism, 1870–1915," *South African Historical Journal*, XIX (1987), 115–142.

————. "Western Cape Farmers and the Beginnings of Afrikaner Nationalism, 1870–1915," *Journal of Southern African Studies*, XIV (1987), 38–63.

Glass, Stafford. *The Matabele War* (London, 1968).

Goodfellow, C.F. *Great Britain and the South African Confederation, 1870–1881* (Cape Town, 1966).

Gordon, C.T. *The Growth of Boer Opposition to Kruger, 1890–1895* (Cape Town, 1970).

Greville, J.A.S. *Lord Salisbury and Foreign Policy* (London, 1964).

Grundlingh, M.A.S. *The Parliament of the Cape of Good Hope, with Special Reference to Party Politics, 1872–1910* (Pretoria, 1973).

Guy, Jeff. "The Destruction and Reconstruction of Zulu Society," in Shula Marks and Richard Rathbone (eds.), *Industrialisation and Social Change in South Africa: African Class Formation, Culture, and Consciousness, 1870–1930* (New York, 1982), 167–194.

Haggard, Henry Rider. *A History of the Transvaal* (New York, 1899).

Hammond, John Hays, and Alleyne Ireland. *The Truth about the Jameson Raid* (Boston, 1918).

Hanna, Alexander John. *The Beginnings of Nyasaland and North-Eastern Rhodesia, 1859–95* (Oxford, 1956).

Harris, John H. *The Chartered Millions: Rhodesia and the Challenge to the British Commonwealth* (London, 1920).

Harris, José, and Pat Thane. "British and European Bankers, 1880–1914: An 'Aristocratic Bourgeoisie'?," in Pat Thane, Geoffrey Crossick, and Roderick Floud (eds.), *The Power of the Past: Essays for Eric Hobsbawm* (Cambridge, 1984), 215–234.

Hattersley, Alan F. *The British Settlement of Natal: A Study in Imperial Migration* (Cambridge, 1950).

Henry, J.A. (ed. H.A. Siepman). *The First Hundred Years of the Standard Bank* (London, 1963).

Hensman, Howard. *A History of Rhodesia: Compiled from Official Sources* (London, 1900).

Hobson, John A. "Capitalism and Imperialism in South Africa," *Contemporary Review*, LXXVII (1900), 1–17.

Hoernle, R.F. Alfred. *South African Native Policy and the Liberal Spirit* (New York, 1939).

Hole, Hugh Marshall. *The Making of Rhodesia* (London, 1926).

————. *Old Rhodesian Days* (London, 1928).

————. *Lobengula* (London, 1929).

————. *The Jameson Raid* (London, 1930).

————. "The Courage of Cecil Rhodes: Hitherto Untold Tale of the Matabele Rebellion," *The Morning Post* (1 April 1936).

Holland, H.S. "Cecil Rhodes," *The Commonwealth*, (1902), 147–149.

Holmberg, Ake. *African Tribes and European Agencies: Colonialism & Humanitarianism in British South and East Africa, 1870–1895* (Göteberg, 1966).

Huttenback, Robert A. *The British Imperial Experience* (New York, 1966).

Hyde, H. Montgomery. *The Love That Dared Not Speak Its Name: A Candid History of Homosexuality in Britain* (Boston, 1970).

————. *A Tangled Web: Sex Scandals in British Politics and Society* (London, 1986).

Imperialist (pseud. John Verschoyle). "The Position and Policy of Mr. Rhodes," *Fortnightly Review*, CCCLXXVII (1898), 805–815.

Innes, Duncan. *Anglo: Anglo American and the Rise of Modern South Africa* (Johannesburg, 1984).

Irving, Robert Grant. *Indian Summer: Lutyens, Baker, and Imperial Delhi* (New Haven, 1981).

Jeeves, Alan Henry. "The Rand Capitalists and Transvaal Politics, 1892–1899," unpub. Ph.D. thesis (Queen's University, 1971).

————. "The Rand Capitalists and the Coming of the South African War, 1896–1899," *Historical Journal*, XVII (1974), 61–63.

————. *Migrant Labour in South Africa's Mining Economy: The Struggle for the Gold Mines' Labour Supply, 1820–1920* (Kingston, 1985).

Johnson, Paul. *Consolidated Gold Fields: A Centenary Portrait* (London, 1967).

Jones, Charles A. *International Business in the Nineteenth Century: The Rise and Fall of a Cosmopolitan Bourgeoisie* (New York, 1987).

Kaplan, Gerald L. *The Elites of Barotseland, 1878–1969: A Political History of Zambia's Western Province* (Berkeley, 1970).

Kennedy, A.L. *Salisbury, 1830–1903* (London, 1953).

Keppel-Jones, Arthur. *Rhodes and Rhodesia* (Kingston, 1983).

Kiewiet, Cornelis W. de. *The Imperial Factor in South Africa: A Study in Politics and Economics* (Cambridge, 1973).

Kilpin, Ralph. *The Romance of a Colonial Parliament* (London, 1930).

King, James. *Dr. Jameson's Raid: Its Causes and Consequences* (London, 1896).

Kosmin, B.A. "On the Imperial Frontier: The Pioneer Community of Salisbury in November 1897," *Rhodesian History*, II (1971), 25–37.

Kruger, Rayne. *Goodbye Dolly Gray: The Story of the Boer War* (London, 1959).

Kubicek, Robert V. *The Administration of Imperialism: Joseph Chamberlain at the Colonial Office* (Durham, 1969).

————. "Finance Capital and South African Goldmining, 1886–1914," *Journal of Imperial and Commonwealth History*, III (1975), 386–395.

————. *Economic Imperialism in Theory and Practice: The Case of South African Gold Mining Finance, 1886–1914* (Durham, 1979).

Lageman, John Kord. "The Power of an Idea," *Think* (March 1963), 26–29.

Lang, John. *Bullion Johannesburg* (Johannesburg, 1986).

Le May, Geoffrey H.L. *British Supremacy in South Africa, 1899–1907* (Oxford, 1965).

Lenzen, Godehard. *The History of Diamond Production and the Diamond Trade* (Berlin, 1966).

Letcher, Owen. *The Gold Mines of Southern Africa: The History, Technology and Statistics of the Gold Industry* (Johannesburg, 1936).

Leverton, B.J.T. *The Natal Cotton Industry, 1845–1875: A Study in Failure* (Pretoria, 1963).

Lewsen, Phyllis. "The Cape Liberal Tradition—Myth or Reality?" *Race,* XIII (1971), 65–80.

Leyds, Willem Johannes. *The Transvaal Surrounded* (London, 1919).

Lloyd, Trevor. "Africa and Hobson's Imperialism," *Past & Present,* 55 (1972), 130–153.

Longford. *See* Pakenham, Elizabeth.

Ludwig, Emil (trans. Kenneth Burke). *Genius and Character* (New York, 1927).

Lugg, Henry Camp. *Historic Natal and Zululand* (Pietermaritzburg, 1949).

Mabin, Alan, and Barbara Conradie. *The Confidence of the Whole Country: Standard Bank Reports on Economic Conditions in Southern Africa, 1865–1902* (Johannesburg, 1987).

McCracken, J.L. *The Cape Parliament, 1854–1910* (Oxford, 1967).

McDonald, Guy. "Cecil Rhodes in Natal," *Cape Argus* (6 June 1936).

MacKenzie, John M. *Propaganda and Empire: The Manipulation of British Public Opinion, 1880–1960* (Manchester, 1984).

McNish, J.T. *The Road to El Dorado* (Cape Town, 1968).

———. *Graves and Guineas: Kimberley, 1871–1873* (Cape Town, 1969).

———. *The Glittering Road: Kimberley, 1874–1876* (Cape Town, 1970).

Magnus, Philip. *Gladstone* (London, 1954).

Malcolm, Dougal O. *The British South Africa Company Incorporated by Royal Charter, 1899–1939* (London, 1939).

Marais, J.S. *The Fall of Kruger's Republic* (Oxford, 1961).

Marks, Shula, and Anthony Atmore (eds.). *Economy and Society in Pre-industrial South Africa* (London, 1980).

Marks, Shula, and Richard Rathbone (eds.). *Industrialisation and Social Change in South Africa: African Class Formation, Culture, and Consciousness, 1870–1930* (New York, 1982).

Mawby, Arthur Andrew. "Capital, Government and Politics in the Transvaal, 1900–1907: A Revision and a Reversion," *Historical Journal,* XVII (1974), 387–415.

Maylam, Paul. *Rhodes, the Tswana, and the British: Colonialism, Collaboration, and Conflict in the Bechuanaland Protectorate, 1885–1899* (Westport, Conn., 1980).

———. "The Long Arm of Small-Town Enterprise: Wood, Francis and Chapman—Grahamstown Concessionaires in the Interior, 1887–91," in J.A. Benyon, C.W. Cook, T.R.H. Davenport, and K.S. Hunt (eds.), *Studies in Local History* (Cape Town, 1976), 80–88.

Mendelsohn, Richard. "Blainey and the Jameson Raid: The Debate Renewed," *Journal of Southern African Studies,* VI (1980), 157–170.

Moyer, Richard A. "The Mfengu, Self-Defence and the Cape Frontier Wars," in Christopher Saunders and Robin Derricourt (eds.), *Beyond the Cape Frontier: Studies in the History of the Transkei and Ciskei* (London, 1974), 101–126.

Newbury, Colin. "Out of the Pit: The Capital Accumulation of Cecil Rhodes," *Journal of Imperial and Commonwealth History,* X (1981), 25–49.

———. "Cecil Rhodes and the South African Connection: 'A Great Imperial University'?," in Frederick Madden and David K. Fieldhouse (eds.), *Oxford and the Idea of Commonwealth: Essays Presented to Sir Edgar Williams* (London, 1982), 75–96.

———. "Technology, Capital and Consolidation: The Performance of De Beers Mining Company Limited, 1880–1889," *Business History Review,* LXI (1987), 1–42.

————. "The Origins and Functions of the London Diamond Syndicate, 1889–1914," *Business History*, XXIX (1987), 5–26.

Nimrocks, Walter. *Milner's Young Men: The "Kindergarten" in Edwardian Imperial Affairs* (Durham, N.C., 1968).

Nutting, Anthony. *The Scramble for Africa: The Great Trek to the Boer War* (London, 1971).

Odendaal, André. *Vukani Bantu: The Beginnings of Black Protest Politics in South Africa to 1912* (Cape Town, 1984).

O'Rell, Max (pseud. Paul Blouet). *John Bull & Co.: The Great Colonial Branches of the Firm—Canada, Austrialia, New Zealand, and South Africa* (New York, 1894).

Omer-Cooper, John D. *The Zulu Aftermath: A Nineteenth-Century Revolution in Bantu Africa* (London, 1966).

Onselen, Charles Van. *Studies in the Social and Economic History of the Witwatersrand, 1886–1914* (Johannesburg, 1982), 2 v.

Pakenham, Elizabeth. *The Jameson Raid* (London, 1961).

Pakenham, Thomas. *The Boer War* (London, 1979).

Palley, Claire. *The Constitutional History and Law of Southern Rhodesia, 1888–1965, with Special Reference to Imperial Control* (Oxford, 1966).

Perham, Margery. *African Apprenticeship: An Autobiographical Journey* (London, 1974).

Phimister, I.R. "Rhodes, Rhodesia and the Rand," *Journal of Southern African Studies*, I (1974), 74–90.

Platt, D.C.M. (ed.). *Business Imperialism, 1840–1930* (Oxford, 1977).

Plumb, John H. *Men and Centuries* (Boston, 1973).

Porter, Andrew. "Lord Salisbury, Mr. Chamberlain and South Africa," *Journal of Imperial and Commonwealth History*, I (1972), 3–26.

Porter, Bernard. *Critics of Empire: British Radical Attitudes to Colonialism in Africa, 1895–1914* (New York, 1968).

Quinan, William R. *High Explosives* (New York, 1912).

Rademeyer, J.L. *Die land Noord van die Limpopo in die Ekspansie-Beleid van die Suid-Afrikaanse Republiek* (Cape Town, 1949).

Ranger, Terence O. "The Last Word on Rhodes?," *Past & Present*, 28 (1964), 116–127.

————. *Revolt in Southern Rhodesia, 1896–97: A Study in African Resistance* (Evanston, 1967).

Ransford, Oliver. *The Rulers of Rhodesia* (London, 1968).

Raphael, Lois A.C. *The Cape-to-Cairo Dream: A Study in British Imperialism* (New York, 1937).

Reade, William Winwood. *The Martyrdom of Man* (New York, 1874).

Richardson, Peter, and Jean-Jacques van Helten. "Labour in the South African Gold Mining Industry, 1886–1914," in Shula Marks and Richard Rathbone (eds.), *Industrialisation and Social Change in South Africa: African Class Formation, Culture, and Consciousness, 1870–1930* (New York, 1982), 77–98.

————. "The Development of the South African Gold-Mining Industry, 1895–1918," *Economic History Review*, XXXVII (1984), 319–340.

Robert, Rudolph. *Chartered Companies and Their Role in the Development of Overseas Trade* (London, 1969).

Roberts, Brian. *Cecil Rhodes and the Princess* (London, 1969).

————. *Churchills in Africa* (London, 1970).

————. *The Diamond Magnates* (New York, 1972).

————. *Kimberley: Turbulent City* (Cape Town, 1976).

Robertson, Marian. *Diamond Fever: South African Diamond History, 1866–1869 from Primary Sources* (Cape Town, 1974).

Robey, E. M. "Rhodes' Federation Policy," unpub. M.A. thesis (Univ. of Cape Town, 1927).

Robinson, Ronald, and John Gallagher. *Africa and the Victorians: The Climax of Imperialism* (London, 1961).

Rosenthal, Eric. *Gold! Gold! Gold! The Johannesburg Gold Rush* (London, 1970).

Rosenthal, Michael. *The Character Factory: Baden-Powell and the Origins of the Boy Scout Movement* (London, 1986).

Ross, Robert. *Adam Kok's Griquas: A Study in the Development of Stratification in South Africa* (Cambridge, 1976).

Rotberg, Robert I. *Christian Missionaries and the Creation of Northern Rhodesia* (Princeton, 1965).

———. *The Rise of Nationalism in Central Africa: The Making of Malawi and Zambia, 1873–1964* (Cambridge, Mass., 1965).

Ruskin, John. *Lectures in Art* (Oxford, 1870).

Russell, Henry. *The Ruin of the Soudan, Cause, Effect, and Remedy: A Resumé of Events, 1883–1891* (London, 1892).

Samkange, Stanlake. *Origins of Rhodesia* (London, 1968).

———. *What Rhodes Really Said about Africans* (Harare, 1982).

Sampson, Anthony. *Black and Gold: Tycoons, Revolutionaries, and Apartheid* (New York, 1987).

Saunders, Christopher, and Robin Derricourt (eds.). *Beyond the Cape Frontier: Studies in the History of the Transkei and Ciskei* (London, 1974).

Schaefer, D.E. "Diamonds, Diggers, and Dreams," *Optima*, XXXI (1983), 75–90.

Schreuder, Deryck M. *Gladstone and Kruger: Liberal Government and Colonial "Home Rule," 1880–85* (London, 1969).

Shaw, Gerald. *Some Beginnings: The Cape Times,, (1876–1910)* (Cape Town, 1975).

———. *South African Telegraph vs. Cape Times* (Cape Town, 1980).

Shee, J. Charles. "Rhodes and the Doctors," *Central African Journal of Medicine*, IX (1963), 131–134, 183–186, 225–228, 328–331, 401–407, 434–439.

———. "The Ill Health and Mortal Sickness of Cecil John Rhodes," *Central African Journal of Medicine*, XI (1965), 89–93.

Shenton, Robert. "The Chartered Company, 1889–1898: A Financial and Political History of the British South Africa Company," unpub. Ph.D. thesis (Harvard University, 1961).

Sheowring, William (ed.). *British Africa* (London, 1899).

Shepperson, George A. "The Literature of British Central Africa," *The Rhodes-Livingstone Journal*, XXIII (1958), 12–46.

———. "Kipling and the Boer War," in John Gross (ed.), *The Age of Kipling* (New York, 1972).

———. "Cecil Rhodes: Some Documents and Reflections," *Rhodesian History*, IX (1978), 83–89.

———. "Cecil John Rhodes: Some Biographical Problems," *Rhodes [University] Newsletter* (December 1981).

Shillington, Kevin. *The Colonisation of the Southern Tswana, 1870–1900*)Johannesburg, 1985).

Shore, Miles F. "Cecil Rhodes and the Ego Ideal," *Journal of Interdisciplinary History*, X (1979), 249–265.

Sillery, Anthony. *Botswana: A Short Political History* (London, 1974).

Slater, Henry. "Land, Labour and Capital in Natal: The Natal Land and Colonisation Company, 1860–1948," *Journal of African History*, XVI (1975), 257–271.

Smallberger, John M. "I.D.B. and the Mining Compound System in the 1880s," *South African Journal of Economics*, XLII (1974), 398–414.

Smith, Malvern van Wyk, and Don Maclennan (eds.). *Olive Schreiner and After: Essays on Southern African Literature in Honour of Guy Butler* (Cape Town, 1983).

Sparrow, Violet. *Remember Stortford* (Buckingham, 1985).

———. *Yesterday's Stortford* (Buckingham, 1986).

Spender, Dale. *Women of Ideas, and What Men Have Done to Them* (London, 1982).

Stigger, P. "Volunteers and the Profit Motive in the Anglo-Ndebele War, 1893," *Rhodesian History*, II (1971), 11–23

Struben, Charles. *Vein of Gold* (Cape Town, 1957).

Sutton, Inez B. "The Diggers' Revolt in Griqualand West, 1875," *International Journal of African Historical Studies*, XII (1979), 40–61.

Swartz, Marvin. *The Politics of British Foreign Policy in the Era of Disraeli and Gladstone* (New York, 1985).

Tabler, Edward C. *The Far Interior: Chronicles of Pioneering in the Matabele and Mashona Countries, 1847–1879* (Cape Town, 1955).

Tanser, George H. *A Scantling of Time: The Story of Salisbury, Rhodesia (1890 to 1900)* (Salisbury, 1965).

Thompson, Charles Allen. "The Administration of Sir Henry Loch as Governor of the Cape Colony and High Commissioner for Southern Africa, 1889–1895," unpub. Ph.D. thesis (Duke University, 1973).

Trapido, Stanley. "Origins of the Cape Franchise Qualifications of 1853," *Journal of African History*, V (1964), 37–64.

———. "African Divisional Politics in the Cape Colony, 1884–1910," *Journal of African History*, IX (1968), 79–98.

———. " 'The Friends of the Natives': Merchants, Peasants and the Political and Ideological Structure of Liberalism in the Cape, 1854–1910," in Shula Marks and Anthony Atmore (eds.), *Economy and Society in Pre-industrial South Africa* (London, 1980), 247–274.

Troup, Freda. *South Africa: An Historical Introduction* (London, 1972).

Turner, Henry Ashby, Jr. "Bismarck's Imperialist Venture: Anti-British in Origin?," in Prosser Gifford and William Roger Louis (eds.), *Britain and Germany in Africa: Imperial Rivalry and Colonial Rule* (New Haven, 1967), 47–82.

Turrell, Robert Vicat. "The 1875 Black Flag Revolt on the Kimberley Diamond Fields," *Journal of South African Studies*, VIII (1981), 194–235.

———. "Kimberley: Labour and Compounds, 1871–1888," in Shula Marks and Richard Rathbone (eds.), *Industrialisation and Social Change in South Africa: African Class Formation, Culture, and Consciousness, 1870–1930* (London, 1982), 45–76.

———. "Rhodes, De Beers, and Monopoly," *Journal of Imperial and Commonwealth History*, X (1982), 311–343.

———, and Jean-Jacques van Helten. "The Rothschilds, The Exploration Company and Mining Finance," *Business History*, XXVIII (1986), 181–205.

———, *Capital and Labour on the Kimberley Diamond Fields 1871–1890* (Cambridge, 1987).

Uzoigwe, G.N. *Britain and the Conquest of Africa: The Age of Salisbury* (Ann Arbor, 1974).

Vambe, Lawrence. *An Ill-Fated People: Zimbabwe Before and After Rhodes* (London, 1972).

Van der Poel, Jean. *Railway and Customs Policies in South Africa, 1885–1910* (New York, 1933).

———. *The Jameson Raid* (Cape Town, 1951).

Waal, Enid de. "American Technology in South African Gold Mining before 1899," *Optima*, XXXIII (June 1985), 80–85.

Wagner, Percy Albert. *The Diamond Fields of Southern Africa* (Cape Town, 1971).

Warhust, Philip R. *Anglo-Portuguese Relations in South-Central Africa, 1890–1900* (London, 1962).

Warner, Constance. *History of the Kimberley Club* (Tangier, 1966).

Warwick, Peter, and S.B. Spies (eds.). *The South African War: The Anglo-Boer War, 1899–1902* (Harlow, Essex, 1980).

Waterhouse, Nourah. *Private & Official* (London, 1942).

Wheatcroft, Geoffrey. *The Randlords* (New York, 1986).

Wheeler, Douglas L. "Gungunyane the Negotiator: A Study in African Diplomacy," *Journal of African History,* IX (1968), 585–602.

Willan, Brian. "An African in Kimberley: Sol T. Plaatje, 1894–1898," in Shula Marks and Richard Rathbone (eds.), *Industrialisation and Social Change in South Africa: African Class Formation, Culture, and Consciousness, 1870–1930* (New York, 1982), 238–258.

Wilburn, Kenneth E., Jr. "The Climax of Railway Competition in South Africa, 1887–1899," unpub. D. Phil. thesis (Oxford, 1982).

Williams, Alpheus Fuller. *Some Dreams Come True: Being a Sheaf of Stories Leading up to the Discovery of Copper, Diamonds, and Gold in Southern Africa and of the Pioneers Who Took Part in the Excitement of Those Early Days* (Cape Town, 1949).

Worger, William. "Workers as Criminals: The Rule of Law in Early Kimberley, 1870–1885," in Frederick Cooper (ed.), *Struggle for the City: Migrant Labor, Capital, and the State in Urban Africa* (Beverly Hills, 1983), 51–90.

———. *South Africa's City of Diamonds: Mine Workers and Monopoly Capitalism in Kimberley, 1867–1895* (New Haven, 1987).

Worsfold, W. Basil. *Twenty Centuries of England: Being the Annals of Bishop's Stortford* (London, 1926).

———. "The Boyhood of Cecil Rhodes," *The Blue Peter* (July 1934), 326–330.

OTHER BIOGRAPHIES

Abel, Jules. *The Parnell Tragedy* (New York, 1966).

Alex, Wilmot. *The Life and Times of Sir Richard Southey* (London, 1904).

Begbie, Harold. *Albert, Fourth Earl of Grey: A Last Word* (London, 1917).

Bermant, Chaim. *The Cousinhood* (London, 1971).

Blunden, Margaret. *The Countess of Warwick* (London, 1967).

Boulger, Demetrius C. *The Reign of Leopold II: King of the Belgians and Founder of the Congo State, 1865–1909* (London, 1925).

Buchanan-Gould, Vera. *Not Without Honour: The Life and Writings of Olive Schreiner* (London, 1948).

Cecil, Algernon. *A Life of Robert Cecil: First Earl of Salisbury* (London, 1915).

Cecil, Gwendolen. *Life of Robert, Marquis of Salisbury* (London, 1921–1932), 4 v.

Colvin, Ian. *The Life of Jameson* (London, 1922), 2 v.

Cook, E.T. *Edmund Garrett: A Memoir* (London, 1909).

Cowles, Virginia. *The Rothschilds: A Family of Fortune* (New York, 1973).

Creswicke, Louis. *The Life of the Right Honourable Joseph Chamberlain* (London, 1904), 4 v.

Crewe, Marquess of. *Lord Rosebery* (New York, 1931).

Cronwright-Schreiner, S.C. *The Life of Olive Schreiner* (Boston, 1923).

——— (ed.). *The Letters of Olive Schreiner, 1876–1920* (London, 1924).

David, Richard. *The English Rothschilds* (London, 1983).

Denholm, Anthony. *Lord Ripon, 1827–1909: A Political Biography* (London, 1982).

Elton, Lord. *General Gordon* (London, 1954).

Farrant, Leda. *The Legendary Grogan* (London, 1981).

Farwell, Byron. *Eminent Victorian Soldiers: Seekers of Glory* (New York, 1985).

First, Ruth, and Ann Scott. *Olive Schreiner* (New York, 1980).

Fort, George Seymour. *Alfred Beit: A Study of the Man and His Work* (London, 1932).

Foster, R.F. *Lord Randolph Churchill: A Political Life* (Oxford, 1981).

Friedlander, Zelda (ed.). *Until the Heart Changes: A Garland for Olive Schreiner* (Cape Town, 1967).

Gardiner, Alfred George. *The Life of Sir William Harcourt* (London, 1923), 2 v.

Garvin, J.L. *The Life of Joseph Chamberlain: Empire and World Policy* (London, 1934), 3 v.

Gollin, A.M. *Proconsul in Politics: A Study of Lord Milner in Opposition and in Power* (London, 1964).

Gregory, Theodore. *Ernest Oppenheimer and the Economic Development of Southern Africa* (Cape Town, 1962).

Greig, Doreen E. *Herbert Baker in South Africa* (Cape Town, 1970).

Grey, Albert. *Hubert Hervey, Student and Imperialist: A Memoir* (London, 1899).

Gross, John (ed.). *Rudyard Kipling: The Man, His Work, and His World* (London, 1972).

Gwynn, Stephen, and Gertrude M. Tuckwell (completed and ed.). *The Life of the Right Hon. Sir Charles W. Dilke* (New York, 1917), 2 v.

Hancock, W. Keith. *Smuts: The Sanguine Years, 1870–1919* (Cambridge, 1962), I.

Hardinge, Arthur. *The Life of Henry Howard Molyneux Herbert, Fourth Earl of Carnarvon* (London, 1925), 3 v.

Haweis, H.R. *Sir Morell Mackenzie, Physician and Operator: A Memoir* (London, 1893).

Hind, R.J. *Henry Labouchere and the Empire, 1880–1905* (London, 1972).

Hofmeyr, J.H., and F.W. Reitz. *The Life of Jan Hendrik Hofmeyr (Onze Jan)* (Cape Town, 1913).

Hutchinson, G.T. *Frank Rhodes—A Memoir* (London, 1908).

Hutchinson, Robert, and George Martelli. *Robert's People: The Life of Sir Robert Williams* (London, 1971).

Jackson, Stanley. *The Great Barnato* (London, 1970).

James, Robert Rhodes. *Lord Randolph Churchill* (London, 1959).

———. *Rosebery: A Biography of Archibald Philip, Fifth Earl of Rosebery* (London, 1963).

Jay, Richard. *Joseph Chamberlain: A Political Study* (London, 1981).

Kaye, Helga. *The Tycoon & the President: The Life and Times of Alois Hugo Nellmapius, 1847–1893* (Johannesburg, 1978).

Kiernan, R.H. *Baden-Powell* (London, 1939).

Laurence, Perceval. *The Life of John Xavier Merriman* (London, 1930).

Lees-Milne, James. *The Enigmatic Edwardian: The Life of Reginald, 2nd Viscount Esher* (London, 1986).

Lewsen, Phyllis. *John X. Merriman: Paradoxical South African Statesman* (New Haven, 1982).

Loch, Elizabeth, and Christine Stockdale (eds.). *Sister Henrietta: Bloemfontein, Kimberley, 1874–1911* (London, 1914).

Lyons, F.S.L. *Charles Stewart Parnell* (New York, 1977).

Marais, P.G. "Fruit Pioneer Harry Ernest Victor Pickstone" (Stellenbosch, 1976).

Marlowe, John. *Milner: Apostle of Empire* (London, 1976).

Martin, Ralph G. *Jennie: The Life of Lady Randolph Churchill* (Englewood Cliffs, N.J., 1971), 2 v.

Meintjes, Johannes. *Olive Schreiner: Portrait of a South African Woman* (Johannesburg, 1965).

Millais, J.G. *Life of Frederick Courtenay Selous* (London, 1918).

Morton, Frederic. *The Rothschilds: A Family Portrait* (London, 1962).

Newton, Thomas Wodehouse. *Lord Lansdowne: A Biography* (London, 1929).

O'Brien, Conor Cruise. *Parnell and His Party, 1880–1890* (Oxford, 1957).

O'Brien, R. Barry. *The Life of Charles Stewart Parnell, 1846–1891* (London, 1898), 2 v.

Oliver, Roland. *Sir Harry Johnston and the Scramble for Africa* (London, 1951).

Pearson, Corydon, et al. *Some Account of George Grey and His Work in Africa* (London, 1914).

Pearson, Hesketh. *Labby: The Life and Character of Henry Labouchere* (London, 1936).

Porter, Andrew. *Victorian Shipping, Business and Imperial Policy: Donald Currie, the Castle Line and Southern Africa* (New York, 1986).

Raymond, Harry. *B.I. Barnato: A Memoir* (New York, 1897).

Rotberg, Robert I. *Joseph Thomson and the Exploration of Africa* (London, 1971).

Rudd, Alan. *Charles Dunell Rudd, 1844–1916* (Ipswich, 1981).

Schults, Raymond L. *Crusader in Babylon: W.T. Stead and the Pall Mall Gazette* (Lincoln, 1972).

Sillery, Anthony. *John Mackenzie of Bechuanaland: A Study in Humanitarian Imperialism* (Cape Town, 1971).

Smith, Ken. *Alfred Aylward: The Tireless Agitator* (Johannesburg, 1983).

Solomon, W.E. Gladstone. *Saul Solomon: "The Member for Cape Town"* (Cape Town, 1948).

Stead, William Thomas. *Joseph Chamberlain: Conspirator or Statesman?* (London, 1900).

Stent, Sally, and Betty Stent (ed. Paddy Cartwright). *The Forthright Man* (Cape Town, 1972).

Struben, Roy. *Taken at the Flood: The Story of Harry Struben* (Cape Town, 1968).

Thorold, Algar Labouchere. *The Life of Henry Labouchere* (London, 1913).

Turrell, Robert Vicat. "Sir Frederic Philipson Stow: The Unknown Diamond Magnate," *Business History*, XXVIII (1986), 62–79.

Tweed, Lendal. *John Tweed, Sculptor* (London, 1936).

Vanstone, Perry, "Sir Gordon Sprigg: A Political Biography," unpub. Ph.D. thesis (Queens University, 1974).

Wialker, Eric A. *Lord De Villiers and His Times, South Africa, 1892–1914* (London, 1925).

———. *W.P. Schreiner: A South African* (London, 1937).

Wallis, J.P.R. *Fitz: The Story of Sir Percy FitzPatrick* (London, 1955).

Whyte, Frederic. *The Life of W.T. Stead* (London, 1925), 2 v.

Williams, Watkin W. *The Life of General Sir Charles Warren* (Oxford, 1941).

Wilmot, Alexander. *The Life and Times of Sir Richard Southey* (London, 1904).

Wilson, Angus. *The Strange Ride of Rudyard Kipling: His Life and Works* (New York, 1978)

Wolf, Lucien. *Life of the First Marquess of Ripon* (London, 1921), 2 v.

COMPILED BIBLIOGRAPHIES

Botha, Carol (comp.). *Manuscripts and Papers in the Killie Campbell Africana Collection* (Johannesburg, 1967).

Cunningham, Anna M. (ed.). *Guide to the Archives and Papers* (Johannesburg, 1975).

Holli, Melvin G. "Joseph Chamberlain and the Jameson Raid: A Bibliography," *Journal of British Studies*, II (1964), 152–166.

Schioldann-Nielsen, Johan. *Famous and Very Important Persons: Medical, Psychological, Psychiatric Bibliography, 1960–1984* (Odense, 1986).

Stubbings, Elizabeth O., and O.H. Spohr (comps.). *Pictorial Material of Cecil J. Rhodes, His Contemporaries and Later South African Personalities in the C.J. Sibbett Collection of the University of Cape Town Libraries* (Cape Town, 1964).

Thompson, Daphne W. *Cecil John Rhodes: Bibliography* (Cape Town, 1947).

Index

by John O. Gates